**VOLUME ONE**

**FOURTH EDITION**

# Intermediate Accounting

## Thomas H. Beechy
Schulich School of Business
York University

## Joan E. D. Conrod
Faculty of Management
Dalhousie University

**McGraw-Hill Ryerson**

Toronto   Montréal   Boston   Burr Ridge, IL   Dubuque, IA   Madison, WI   New York
San Francisco   St. Louis   Bangkok   Bogotá   Caracas   Kuala Lumpur   Lisbon   London
Madrid   Mexico City   Milan   New Delhi   Santiago   Seoul   Singapore   Sydney   Taipei

Intermediate Accounting
Volume 1
Fourth Edition

ISBN-13: 978-0-07-097885-0
ISBN-10: 0-07-097885-9

1  2  3  4  5  6  7  8  9  10   TCP   0  9  8

Printed and bound in Canada

Care has been taken to trace ownership of copyright material contained in this text; however, the publisher will welcome any information that enables them to rectify any reference or credit for subsequent editions.

Editorial Director: Joanna Cotton
Senior Marketing Manager: Joy Armitage Taylor
Senior Sponsoring Editor: Rhondda McNabb
Developmental Editor: Marcia Luke
Senior Editorial Associate: Christine Lomas
Senior Production Coordinator: Paula Brown
Senior Supervising Editor: Anne Nellis
Copy Editor: Karen Rolfe
Cover Design: ArtPlus Design & Communications
Interior Design: Bookman Typesetting Company/ArtPlus Design & Communications
Cover Image Credits: Canadian Flag © Artplus Ltd.; Handshake © Artplus Ltd.; Canadian Money © Punchstock/Superstock; Handheld © David Chasey/GettyImages; World Map © Cartesia/GettyImages; TSX Sculture © Ingram Publishing/Superstock
Composition: Bookman Typesetting Company
Printer: Transcontinental Printing Group

**Library and Archives Canada Cataloguing in Publication**
Beechy, Thomas H., 1937–
    Intermediate accounting / Thomas H. Beechy, Joan E. D. Conrod. —4th ed.

Includes bibliographical references and index.
ISBN 978-0-07-097885-0 (v. 1)

    1. Accounting—Textbooks.    I. Conrod, Joan E. D. (Joan Elizabeth Davison), 1956–
II.  Title.

HF5635.B466 2008          657'.044          C2007-903274-5

# About the Authors

## Thomas H. Beechy, York University

Thomas H. Beechy is a Professor of Accounting at the Schulich School of Business, York University. For many years, he was also the Associate Dean of the school. He currently holds the additional titles of Executive Director of International Relations and of Assistant Dean—Special Projects. Professor Beechy holds degrees from George Washington University (BA), Northwestern University (MBA), and Washington University (DBA). He has been active in research and publication for almost 40 years, having published six books, including *Canadian Advanced Financial Accounting*, and numerous articles in major accounting journals. Professor Beechy has been a leader in Canadian accounting education, emphasizing the importance of case analysis in developing students' professional judgement and accounting skills. He has been an active researcher and advocate in both business and non-profit financial reporting. He has been particularly active in international accounting circles.

## Joan E. D. Conrod, Dalhousie University

Joan E. D. Conrod is a Professor of Accounting in the Faculty of Management at Dalhousie University. Her teaching excellence has been recognized through awards such as the PWC Leaders in Management Education Award, the Dalhousie University Alumni Award for Teaching Excellence, and the AAU Distinguished Teacher award. She was awarded her FCA from the Nova Scotia Institute of Chartered Accountants in 1999. Joan is an active member of the University community, and has served on the Dalhousie University Senate and the Board of Governors. She is a past president of the Canadian Academic Accounting Association. Joan has a lengthy history of involvement in professional accounting education. She has taught financial and managerial accounting courses to CA students across Canada, but particularly in Atlantic Canada, for 20 years. She has served on CA education committees at the local, regional, and national levels. Her publications include the text *Intermediate Accounting*, with Tom Beechy, *Financial Accounting 3* for CGA-Canada, and a variety of case material and other publications.

# Brief Table of Contents—Volume 1

# Table of Contents—Volume 1

## THE ENVIRONMENT OF FINANCIAL REPORTING    1

**CHAPTER 1**

## CRITERIA FOR ACCOUNTING CHOICES    39

**CHAPTER 2**

## REVENUE AND EXPENSE RECOGNITION   268

**CHAPTER 6**

## CURRENT MONETARY BALANCES   333

**CHAPTER 7**

## INVENTORIES AND COST OF SALES    397

**CHAPTER 8**

## CAPITAL ASSETS, INTANGIBLES, AND GOODWILL    451

**CHAPTER 9**

## AMORTIZATION AND IMPAIRMENT  520

**CHAPTER 10**

## INVESTMENTS IN DEBT AND EQUITY SECURITIES  583

**CHAPTER 11**

## APPENDIX

## FUNDAMENTALS: THE ACCOUNTING INFORMATION PROCESSING SYSTEM          653

# Preface

There is a vast body of knowledge that must be mastered before you can account for the activities of an enterprise. Intermediate accounting is the essential course for gaining the technical skills and judgement you need to succeed. These skills are crucial for anyone who hopes to either use or prepare accounting information.

Accounting in general involves a blend of technical know-how and professional judgement. So that's what *Intermediate Accounting* appropriately dwells on: technical knowledge and professional judgement, covering the range of corporate reporting topics.

In selecting material to include in this book, we have assessed the realities of Canadian business practice. Accounting practices and policies remain in the public eye, with both fraud and judgement issues causing material restatements. This text reviews many critical issues that have been problematic in the past. Our accounting standards will be migrating to international standards in 2011. Many international standards are similar to Canadian standards, but there are important differences. This text describes and explores the alternatives.

*Intermediate Accounting* covers the technical elements of financial reporting, but keeps an eye on the critical judgement issues. After you master the contents of *Intermediate Accounting*, you will be able to account for the wide range of events and transactions found in this unique and challenging business environment.

## TECHNICAL KNOWLEDGE

Accountants have to be able to account for things! There is a base level of expertise that must become part of every accountant's body of knowledge: how to record a receivable, capitalize a lease, account for a pension, or prepare a cash flow statement. Some of the transactions that we must account for are very complex, and their accounting treatment is equally complex. An affinity for numbers is important.

## PROFESSIONAL JUDGEMENT

Judgement, it is often said, is the hallmark of a profession. There are often different ways to account for the same transaction. Professional accountants have to become expert at sizing up the circumstances and establishing the appropriate accounting policy for those circumstances. Once an accounting policy has been established, there are usually estimates that must be made before the numbers can be recorded. Accounting estimates also require the exercise of professional judgement. Professional judgement is not acquired overnight. It is nurtured and slowly grows over a lifetime. In this book, we begin the development process by explicitly examining the variables that companies consider when evaluating their options, and the criteria that accountants use to make choices. Opportunities to practise judgement are provided in the case material.

## A CANADIAN AGENDA

Issues that receive the most attention in this book are those that are relevant in a Canadian context. Many times, the topics covered in other intermediate texts are determined by U.S. standards and priorities because those books are adaptations of U.S. texts. However, there are some significant differences between Canadian and U.S. businesses and business environments that dictate a different emphasis and coverage. In addition, Canadian standards are swiftly being harmonized with international accounting standards. While some U.S. standards are also moving to international accounting standards, their strategic direction remains U.S.–based. We hope you appreciate the Canadian emphasis!

## AN INTERNATIONAL PERSPECTIVE

Following a Canadian agenda means that we all must come up to speed on international standards. Every chapter will explain the differences between current Canadian practice and the policies recommended by the International Accounting Standards Board. If there are differences, the alternatives are reviewed and explained in the chapter material.

## OTHER KEY FEATURES

### Integration of Cash Flow Material throughout the Text

The cash flow statement is covered in Chapter 5, following reviews of the income statement and balance sheet. Students can thus learn how to do the cash flow statement early in the course. Following this chapter, though, the cash flow implications of various complex transactions are reviewed in each relevant chapter. There is cash flow assignment material in most chapters of the book. For those instructors who like to emphasize cash flow material at the end of the course, an appendix has been added to the final chapter that summarizes cash flow statement issues and provides a comprehensive example. This is reinforced with assignment material in the last chapter.

### The Accounting Cycle

The basic debit and credit of the accounting world is not really a topic for an intermediate accounting course. It represents the baby steps; we're trying to learn how to run, or at least jog. For many students, this material was covered in a high school course or an introductory accounting course. Others, who avoided the course in high school and/or who took a conceptually oriented introductory course in college or university, may need a refresher or further grounding in this area. To answer this need, we have included the accounting cycle as an appendix to Volume I. This provides maximum flexibility to instructors. Some courses may formally devote time to this appendix; others may use it as a reference only.

### Accuracy

The text has been extensively reviewed and proofread prior to publication. Chapter material has been reviewed by professional accountants. All assignment materials have been solved independently by multiple individual "assignment checkers" in addition to the authors. Nevertheless, errors may remain, for which we accept full responsibility. If you find errors, please e-mail the authors at **j.conrod@dal.ca** or **tbeechy@schulich.yorku.ca**. There are thousands of calculations in this text—it's a daunting task to bring them to the degree of accuracy we'd like to be famous for. Your help will be greatly appreciated.

# PEDAGOGICAL WALKTHROUGH

## INTRODUCTION

Bombardier Inc., a major transportation manu-facturing company, has operations in Canada, Germany, the United Kingdom, Switzerland, France, Australia, China, and other countries. Bombardier is listed on the Toronto Stock Exchange. As a Canadian public company, the company prepares its financial statements using Canadian generally accepted accounting principles (GAAP).

Many international companies list their securi-ties on the stock exchanges in the foreign countries in which they operate. For example, the giant inter-national automobile company Daimler-Chrysler is listed on all of the world's major stock exchanges including New York, Frankfurt, Tokyo, and London.

In the future, Bombardier may choose to list inter-nationally. However, Canadian GAAP is accepted only in Canada, and Canada is a very small player in the international financial market. Will the company

Fortunately the answer to that question is "no," because almost all other countries permit foreign companies to report their financial results on the basis of *International Financial Reporting Standards* (IFRS).

The CICA's Accounting Standards Board (AcSB) has decided that it is time for Canada's public-company accounting standards to become interna-tional also. Canadian standard setting is changing with the international tide.

But even after Canada adopts IFRS for public companies, a company like Bombardier will need to make many accounting choices. Those choices will be affected by a variety of competing objectives. The company could make choices with an objective of reducing its income taxes, maximizing its reported earnings, or helping investors and creditors to esti-mate the future cash flows of the company.

## Introduction

Each chapter has an introduction that explains the objectives of the chapter in narrative form.

---

In financial reporting, however, there often are multiple users. The various users often have conflicting objectives, and the financial statements must be prepared on a basis that optimizes the trade-offs between the various users' needs. The various (and potentially con-flicting) objectives of financial reporting will be discussed later in this chapter.

### CONCEPT REVIEW

1. What is the essential difference between a bookkeeper and an accountant?

2. What is the general realm of financial reporting? How does financial report-ing differ from management accounting?

3. Describe the difference between point statements and flow statements. Give examples of each.

## Concept Review

Throughout each chapter, there are periodic questions. Students can stop and think through the answers to these basic questions, covering the previously explained material. This helps comprehension and focus! Answers to these questions can be found on the Online Learning Centre.

---

the parent's statements, the subsidiary may use the parent's home country GAAP instead of Canadian GAAP.

Exhibit 1-1 summarizes the reporting requirements for public and private companies.

### EXHIBIT 1-1

#### REPORTING REQUIREMENTS FOR PUBLIC AND PRIVATE COMPANIES

| Reporting Basis | Rationale |
|---|---|
| **Canadian Public Corporations** | |
| Canadian GAAP | Shares traded primarily in Canada |
| U.S. GAAP | Shares traded primarily in U.S. |
| **Canadian Private Corporations** | |
| Canadian GAAP | General purpose statements |
| Canadian GAAP | Subsidiary of Canadian public corporation |
| Canadian GAAP, Differential Reporting | Limited users; shareholders agree |
| DBA | Specialized reporting for specific users |
| Foreign or International GAAP | Subsidiary of non-Canadian parent |

## Figures and Tables

Where appropriate, chapter material is summarized in figures and tables to establish the patterns and help reinforce material.

---

### THE EXERCISE OF ETHICAL PROFESSIONAL JUDGEMENT

Chapter 1 gave examples of the many accounting choices that are affected by the financial reporting objectives *in any particular situation*. Reporting objectives (and motivations) do vary, and choices of accounting policies and accounting estimates are significantly affected by whether the primary reporting objective is, for example, income tax minimization, cash flow prediction, or net income maximization.

### ETHICAL ISSUES

The ability to make appropriate choices in accounting is ethical professional judge-ment. Professional judgement permeates the work of a professional accountant, and it involves an ability to build accounting measurements that take into account:

- The objectives of financial reporting in each particular situation;
- The facts of the business environment and operations; and
- The organization's reporting constraints (if any).

## Ethical Issues

Many chapters discuss accounting issues that raise eth-ical concerns. These concerns are highlighted in the chapter. Where ethics is particularly problematic, we have included a separate "ethical issues" section to help students focus on the ethical aspects of policy choice.

Ethics assignment material has also been incor-porated into the case material. Essentially, when an accountant makes a recommendation on a contentious choice of accounting policy, ethics are tested. Students exercise true-to-life ethical judgement when they have to make a tough judgement call and recommend an accounting policy that is "good" for one group but "bad" for another. These ethical overtones are high-lighted in the case solutions to help instructors draw them out in discussion and evaluation.

### INTERNATIONAL PERSPECTIVE

The IASC accounting principles, or concepts, are set out in a section called a "Framework," which appears essentially as a preface to the IFRS. The Framework is not an IFRS. The Framework has roughly the same structure and content/conclusions as Section 1000 of the *CICA Handbook*, "Financial Statement Concepts," although the terminology is not identical. The Framework has the following (familiar) sections:

- Users of financial statements and their information needs;
- The objective of financial reporting;
- Underlying assumptions;
- Qualitative characteristics of financial statements;
- Elements of financial statements;
- Recognition criteria;
- Measurement of the elements of financial statements; and
- Concepts of capital and capital maintenance.

Refer to Exhibit 2-5 for a listing of the accounting principles identified.

## International Perspective

New to the fourth edition, every chapter includes a review of international accounting policies, highlighting similarities and differences between current Canadian practice and the policies recommended by the International Accounting Standards Board.

### RELEVANT STANDARDS

*CICA Handbook:*
- Section 1000, Financial Statement Concepts

IASB:
- Framework for the Preparation and Presentation of Financial Statements

## Relevant Standards

At the end of each chapter, there is a comprehensive list of the Canadian and international standards that are relevant to the material in the chapter. We have not quoted the standards directly in chapter material and we have not provided paragraph references to either the *CICA Handbook* or to international standards. This omission is intentional—the two sources are harmonized but may use different words. The focus is on the application of standards, not the technicalities.

### SUMMARY OF KEY POINTS

1. Accounting principles consist of three different sets of concepts: (1) underlying assumptions, (2) measurement methods, and (3) qualitative criteria.

2. *Underlying assumptions* include the basic postulates that make accounting measurements possible (such as *separate entity*, *unit of measure*, and *time period*), as well as underlying measurement assumptions that usually, but not always, are true in a given reporting situation. These measurement assumptions include *continuity*, *proprietary approach*, and *nominal dollar financial capital maintenance*.

3. *Qualitative criteria* are the criteria used in conjunction with an enterprise's financial reporting objectives to determine the most appropriate measurement methods to use in that particular reporting situation. Qualitative criteria include relevance, reliability, comparability, objectivity, understandability, materiality, conservatism, and the cost/benefit trade-off.

4. A critical qualitative criterion is that of *relevance*; relevance should be determined with reference to the users of the financial statements and the resulting financial reporting objectives. Relevance is enhanced if information is timely, and has predictive and feedback value.

## Summary of Key Points

A summary of key points concludes each chapter. This provides a list of the key ideas and reinforces the chapter material.

### KEY TERMS

accrual-basis accounting, 44
accruals, 44
commitment, 56
comparability, 51
conservatism, 51
consideration, 59
consistency, 51
constant dollar (capital maintenance), 47
constant dollars, 47
continuity assumption, 45
cost/benefit effectiveness, 52
deferrals, 44
differential reporting, 52
elements, 53
entity concept (assumption), 46
executory contract, 57
freedom from bias, 51
full disclosure, 61
going-concern assumption, 45

nominal dollars, 47
non-arbitrariness, 51
period costs, 60
physical capital maintenance, 47
professional judgement, 42
proprietary assumption, 45
purchasing power parity, 47
qualitative criteria (characteristics), 40
quantifiability, 51
realization, 57
recognition, 55
relevance, 48
reliability, 49
separate-entity assumption, 44
substance over form, 49
time-period assumption, 43
underlying assumptions
    (postulates), 40
uniformity, 51

## Key Terms and the Glossary

Every chapter concludes with a list of key terms used in the chapter. These terms are explained in the chapter, and are also defined in the glossary, which is available on the Online Learning Centre (**www.mcgrawhill. ca/olc/beechy**).

## REVIEW PROBLEM

The following pre-tax amounts are taken from the adjusted trial balance of Killian Corporation at 31 December 20X5, the end of Killian's fiscal year:

| Account | Amount |
|---|---|
| Sales revenue | $1,000,000 |
| Service revenue | 200,000 |
| Interest revenue | 30,000 |
| Gain on sale of capital asset | 100,000 |
| Cost of goods sold | 600,000 |
| Selling, general, and administrative expense | 150,000 |
| Depreciation expense | 50,000 |
| Interest expense | 20,000 |
| Loss on sale of long-term investment | 10,000 |
| Extraordinary item, loss from earthquake damage | 200,000 |
| Cumulative effect of change in accounting policy (gain) | 50,000 |
| Impairment loss on business segment assets | 60,000 |
| Loss on operation of discontinued business segment | 10,000 |

## Review Problem

There is a review problem with a solution in each chapter beginning in Chapter 3. This provides additional reinforcement of chapter content.

### CASE 3-3

#### CASHGO LIMITED

CashGo Ltd. is a food distributor and retailer in eastern Canada. The company also owns both a bakery and a dairy, each of which has significant sales through other market channels in addition to CashGo's stores. CashGo is a private company; all of the shares are owned by the founder's family. The company has not needed external share capital as the company is quite profitable and the banks are eager to provide debt financing as needed. The banks require CashGo to give them annual audited financial statements, prepared in accordance with Canadian GAAP.

The CashGo CFO currently is overseeing the preparation of the company's consolidated financial statements for 20X7. There have been many changes to the recommendations of the *CICA Handbook*, not all of which the CFO is sure that she understands. She has come to you for advice on how to report the results of some of the company's 20X7 transactions and events. She also would appreciate receiving draft statements of income, comprehensive income, and retained earnings. CashGo does not wish to provide any more detail in the statements than is necessary to comply with current reporting requirements.

*Specific concerns:*

1. In the final quarter of 20X7, the Halifax region suffered a major hurricane, which knocked out the electricity in the Halifax region for several days. Hurricanes are extremely uncommon in Nova Scotia. A great quantity of frozen and other perishable foods was spoiled and had to be discarded. The loss amounted to $11 million. The inventory was not insured against this type of loss.

2. CashGo is a private company. In 20X7, the company elected to use the differential reporting option on income taxes, applied retrospectively. The cumulative adjustment for prior years was to eliminate the $46 million credit balance of future income taxes. CashGo has tentatively classified this amount as "Gain on income tax reversals."

## Cases

More than 60 cases are included in *Intermediate Accounting*, and there is at least one new case in every chapter in the fourth edition. The cases are meant to portray circumstances reflective of real life. Students have to put themselves into the situation and grapple with the facts to arrive at appropriate accounting policies for the circumstances. A blend of professional judgement and technical skills is needed to respond to a case. Case coverage is not limited to "one chapter" bites, but often integrates material learned to date. For those trying to build a base of professionalism, the use of cases consistently over the term is highly recommended. Cases can be assigned for class debriefing, class presentations, or written assignments.

## Assignment Material

There is an extensive range of assignment material at the end of each chapter. The assignments give students the opportunity to learn by doing.

 Stars accompanying each assignment indicate length, with one star being the shortest assignment and three stars being the longest assignment.

 Helping students practise on their own, we have selected a few assignments from each chapter and put their solutions on the Online Learning Centre. These selected assignments are highlighted by the icon in the margin.

 Excel® templates for selected assignments provide an introduction to basic spreadsheet applications. These assignments are identified with the icon in the margin and are available on the Online Learning Centre.

## Integrative Problems

From time to time, we include integrative problems that formally deal with accounting topics covered in five or six chapters. These problems are a great pre-test review!

# TOPICAL REVIEW IDENTIFYING KEY CHANGES

## Chapters 1 and 2

The book starts with a review of the GAAP (and non-GAAP) world and establishes the common reporting motivations of companies and financial statement users, as well as the basic concepts of accounting. This is fundamental material that supports professional judgement. Chapter 1 has been extensively revised and rewritten for this edition, with the addition of two new exhibits (Exhibits 1.1 and 1.3) to further clarify the material. Chapter 2 includes a summary of the IASB framework of underlying assumptions, qualitative characteristics, constraints, and concepts of capital.

## Chapters 3 and 4

These chapters review the income statement, retained earnings statement, balance sheet, and disclosure notes. There is a complete explanation of the statement of comprehensive income. Real-life examples show the degree of diversity that exists and how little information some companies provide in their financial statements. The chapters highlight the judgemental issues inherent in the statements and disclosures.

## Chapter 5

The cash flow statement (CFS) is dealt with in sequence, as a primary financial statement. Again, coverage begins with a real-life example, to analyze the nature of information presented and the judgemental issues involved. The chapter deals with the mechanics of statement preparation, using both a format-free approach and the T-account method. T-accounts have been re-emphasized, because they are widely used in the classroom. The journal-entry-based worksheet is included in an appendix. CFS issues are reviewed in every subsequent chapter of the text and include CFS assignment material. We summarize text topics that impact on the CFS in an appendix to Chapter 21, for those who wish to reinforce this topic as a stand-alone topic later in the course.

## Chapter 6

Revenue and expense recognition are surely the most judgemental areas of accounting policy choice in the GAAP world. For the fourth edition of the book, we have extensively revised and reorganized the material for greater clarity and better flow. The increasingly important area of multiple deliverables has been expanded and given more prominence. The emphasis of the text material is on the financial statement impact of these policies on net assets. There is extensive discussion of the criteria to be applied to determine appropriate revenue recognition policy and the numeric implications. Expense recognition is critically reviewed, both from a theoretical and practical perspective.

## Chapter 7

Issues related to monetary balances—cash, receivables, and payables—are gathered and reviewed together. Important topics such as foreign currency translation (a must, in this age of globalization) and the rules governing the transfer of receivables are incorporated. The material on bank reconciliations has been moved to an appendix. Material covering the mathematical basics of present and future value is available on the Online Learning Centre (**www.mcgrawhill.ca/olc/beechy**), as is a more extensive set of compound interest tables.

## Chapter 8

This chapter has been completely revised and reorganized. Introductory accounting texts always cover inventory systems and the cost flow assumptions and so we've moved that basic material into an appendix, available for review if needed. This fourth edition is based on the new Canadian inventory standard, which is harmonized with international standards. The chapter includes a review of policy decisions in this critical area, as well as the mechanics of inventory costing methods, lower of cost or market writedowns, and inventory estimation techniques.

## Chapters 9 and 10

Accounting for capital assets, both tangible and intangible, follows a common pattern. These chapters systematically look at acquisition, amortization, impairment, and disposal. New accounting standards on the international scene will eliminate most instances of costs being reported as long-term deferred assets, such as startup costs, and coverage has been adjusted to reflect this reality. We have also clarified the material on non-monetary exchanges. We explain and illustrate the accounting standards relating to asset retirement obligations, held-for-sale assets, and asset impairments.

## Chapter 11

This chapter reflects the financial instrument rules, a joint project of the AcSB, IASB, and FASB, implemented for publicly accountable enterprises in 2007. Accounting for held-to-maturity, held-for-trading, available-for-sale, significant influence, and control investments is covered. In particular, the fourth edition reflects the new standards for consolidation, to be implemented in 2009. Both policy and numeric issues are thoroughly explored. The chapter includes a number of helpful diagrams and figures, including a comparison of the cost and equity method, to clarify the roadmap through this territory.

## Chapters 12 and 13

These chapters deal with straightforward debt and shareholders' equity issues. The debt chapter looks at the always-challenging long-term debt issues, emphasizing the effective interest method of calculating interest expense. The new approach for accounting for guarantees has been incorporated. The requirement for reporting other comprehensive income, including certain types of unrealized foreign currency gains/losses, is fully explained and assignment material on this topic is included. Summary charts have been incorporated where appropriate.

## Chapter 14

One major topic in this chapter is classification of debt versus equity and appropriate treatment of hybrid financial instruments. Students learn how to determine the substance of a financial instrument, rather than its legal form, and account for it accordingly. Basic patterns for option accounting are established. A major new section on the various forms of incentive contracts (traditional options, SARs, and various kinds of deferred compensation agreements) has been added, with examples and summary charts to help establish the patterns. The material on derivative instruments has been gathered in this chapter and has been clarified with the addition of an example, which traces the impact of derivatives on accumulated other comprehensive income. We think that the revised material is clear and understandable; this is an important topic in financial reporting!

### Chapters 15 and 16

Accounting for income tax remains two separate chapters, to acknowledge that many instructors prefer to spend two blocks of time on this most challenging area. The Chapter 15 material establishes a three-step process for typical situations. The focus of Chapter 16 remains accounting for the tax effect of losses—carrybacks and carryforwards. This is difficult material for students, but the Chapter 16 problems incorporate the prior chapter material and allow solid reinforcement of the steps associated with tax accounting.

### Chapter 17

The main body of this chapter focuses on the lessee. Most companies lease something as a lessee, and thus lessee accounting is very commonly encountered in practice. Both the judgemental issues of lease classification and the complex calculations are extensively reviewed in this chapter, with examples.

Lessors, on the other hand, are rare. They tend to be quite specialized entities—financial intermediaries. Since lessors comprise a specialized industry, accounting by lessors is presented in a chapter appendix. The appendix includes an overview of the major aspects of lessor accounting and how it contrasts with lessee accounting. The appendix may be omitted if the instructor does not wish to address this specialized industry.

### Chapter 18

Pensions and other post-retirement benefits are complex, long-term arrangements with employees. Accounting issues are also complex and have been structured in a worksheet format to improve clarity and comprehension. In addition, this chapter now contains an example of accounting for other post-retirement benefits and enhanced coverage of defined contribution plans, since the latter are gaining in popularity.

### Chapter 19

Earnings per share material includes an explanation of basic and diluted EPS. The procedural steps associated with organizing a complex EPS question are emphasized to provide more comfort and support in this complicated area. Differences between Canadian and international approaches are explained and there are a variety of useful summary figures and tables.

### Chapter 20

Accounting policy changes and error corrections require restatement of one or more prior years' financial statements. Restatement is surely an important topic, given the number of fraud-based restatements reported in the public press in recent years. Also, the ongoing changes in accounting standards means that companies must often restate their accounts. This chapter deals with the theory and mechanics related to such restatement, reflecting current standards.

### Chapter 21

The text concludes with a review of financial statement analysis and emphasizes the importance of accounting policy choice and disclosure in the analysis of published financial statements. There is an extensive case illustration, based on a real Canadian company, which demonstrates the importance of accounting policy choice.

### Appendix

An appendix on the cash flow statement follows as a stand-alone review of Chapter 5. The appendix summarizes the impact on the CFS of many types of transactions that the text has covered since the CFS was first discussed. A comprehensive example is provided. This appendix is meant to reinforce the CFS for instructors who like to deal with the statement as a stand-alone topic that reviews many topics within *Intermediate Accounting*.

## ACKNOWLEDGEMENTS

The text would not have been possible without the contributions of a great many people. We recognize and appreciate all of their efforts.

Our thanks and gratitude are extended to the outstanding faculty reviewers who provided criticism and constructive suggestions on the text material. It hasn't been possible to incorporate all of the (sometimes conflicting!) suggestions, but the quality of this book has improved thanks to the people who reviewed it: Mark Binder, Red River College; Esther Deutsch, Ryerson University; George Fisher, CGA-Canada; Stuart H. Jones, University of Calgary; Michelle Loveland, University of Western Ontario; Marie Madill-Payne, George Brown College; Ron Naraine, Fanshawe College; Joe Nemi, University of Guelph/Humber; Joe Pidutti, Durham College; Carmel Robbins, SAIT Polytechnic; and Douglas Yee, British Columbia Institute of Technology. To numerous other colleagues and users whose constructive comments and suggestions have led to improvements, our thanks.

In this edition, we were also fortunate in having a team of experienced reviewers who were at the cutting edge in technical and judgemental issues. These individuals carefully reviewed our manuscript to ensure that our interpretations and presentations were balanced, correct, and thorough. The quality of this edition owes much to the efforts of Judy Cumby, FCA; Tashia Batstone, FCA; and Tammy Crowell, CA.

We are grateful to our dedicated team of assignment checkers, Jeff Christian, CA; Kimberly Morse; Cheryl Nachtigal, CGA; Duncan Ferguson, CA; and Douglas Cashin, CA, who have exhaustively checked the accuracy of the assignment material.

We also appreciate the permissions granted by the following organizations to use their problem and case material:

- The Canadian Institute of Chartered Accountants
- The Certified General Accountants' Association of Canada
- The Society of Management Accountants
- The Ontario Institute of Chartered Accountants
- The Atlantic School of Chartered Accountancy
- The American Institute of Certified Public Accountants

We are grateful to the people at McGraw-Hill Ryerson who guided this manuscript through its development process. We appreciate the strong support of Rhondda McNabb, our Senior Sponsoring Editor; Marcia Luke, our Developmental Editor; and the production team, led by Kelly Dickson and including Anne Nellis and Erin Moore, who have all contributed in significant ways to this final product. And, of course, Karen Rolfe has been a welcome and active partner in this enterprise, as our copy editor. She has greatly improved the quality of the final manuscript!

On a personal level, we would like to thank our friends and family members for their support and encouragement throughout the lengthy process of bringing this book to fruition, especially, in Halifax—Peter Conrod and Warren and Carmita Fetterly; and in Toronto—Calvin Luong and Brian McBurney.

**Thomas H. Beechy**
Schulich School of Business
York University
Toronto, ON

**Joan E. D. Conrod**
Faculty of Management
Dalhousie University
Halifax, NS

# TECHNOLOGY SOLUTIONS

## Lyryx Assessment for Intermediate Accounting

Lyryx Assessment is a Web-based teaching and learning tool that has captured the attention of post-secondary institutions across the country.

Developed specifically for *Intermediate Accounting*, Fourth Edition by Beechy and Conrod, Lyryx Assessment is a leading-edge online assessment system that delivers significant benefits to both students and instructors.

After registering their course with McGraw-Hill Ryerson, instructors can create labs of their choice by selecting problems from our test bank and setting deadlines. Instructors have access to all the students' marks and can view their best labs. At any time, instructors can download the class grades for their own programs to analyze individual and class performance.

The assessment takes the form of a homework assignment called a "lab," which corresponds to the chapters in the *Intermediate Accounting* text. The labs are algorithmically generated and automatically graded, so students get instant scores and feedback—no need to wait until the next class to get results!

With new labs randomly generated each time, students have unlimited opportunities to try a type of question. Student motivation is high with these labs, because they can be tied to assessment and because students can try as many times as they want prior to the due date, with only their best grade being recorded.

If students are doing their intermediate accounting practice and homework, they will improve their performance in the course. Recent research regarding the use of Lyryx has shown when labs are tied to assessment, even if worth only a small percentage of the total grade for the course, students will do their homework—and more than once. The result is improved student success in intermediate accounting!

Instructors: Please contact your *i*Learning Sales Specialist for additional information on the Lyryx Assessment for *Intermediate Accounting*.

## Lyryx Quick Start

Developed to address the need to quickly "refresh" student learning from their introductory financial accounting course, Lyryx Quick Start is the perfect solution. This product contains the essential material needed to prepare students for *Intermediate Accounting*. There are explorations and labs reviewing:

- The accounting cycle
- Financial statements
- Cash flows.

Like Lyryx for Intermediate Accounting, new labs are generated each time, providing students with unlimited opportunity to practise. The result is students who are well prepared to begin the intermediate accounting course.

Instructors: Please contact your *i*Learning Sales Specialist for additional information on Lyryx Quick Start.

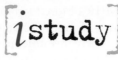

## FOR THE STUDENTS

### *i*Study Intermediate Accounting

Available 24/7: providing instant feedback when you want, how you want, and where you want. This online *i*Study space was developed to help you master concepts and achieve better grades with all the learning tools you've come to expect, including chapter summaries, quiz questions, and additional problems. *i*Study offers the best, most convenient way to learn, interact, and succeed.

iStudy can be purchased through the Online Learning Centre or by purchasing a PIN code card through the campus bookstore.

Instructors: Please contact your *i*Learning Sales Specialist for more information on how to make *i*Study part of your students' success.

### Online Learning Centre (OLC) www.mcgrawhill.ca/olc/beechy

Updated for the fourth edition, the Beechy/Conrod *Intermediate Accounting* OLC provides a wealth of additional content and exercises, including:

- Solutions to Concept Review exercises;
- Solutions to selected text assignments;
- Self-study quizzes;
- A glossary of all key terms in the text;
- Excel assignment downloads to help solve selected in-text assignments;
- Compound interest tables;
- Appendix: Interest—Concepts of Future and Present Value
- Chapter 14 Appendix: Financial Restructuring; and
- Chapter 18 Appendix: Actuarial Cost Methods.

## INSTRUCTOR SUPPLEMENTS

### For the Instructor

- **Instructor's Resource CD-ROM.** A one-stop convenient source of supplemental material.
  - **Instructor's Manual.** There is a brief topical outline for each chapter that indicates the topics to discuss in class and an assignment guide that provides, at a glance, the topical content of each exercise, problem, and case.
  - **Solutions Manual.** This comprehensive manual provides solutions to all cases, questions, assignments, and comprehensive problems.
  - **Computerized Test Bank.** With an abundance of objective questions, multiple-choice questions, and short exercises, this supplement is a valuable resource for instructors when preparing quizzes and examinations.
  - **Microsoft® PowerPoint® Slides.** This PowerPoint® presentation can be used to review chapter concepts.
  - **Excel Template Solutions.** Solutions are provided to all Excel Template assignments.

*Many of these Instructor resources are also available for download from the Instructor Area of the Online Learning Centre.*

# SUPERIOR SERVICE

Service takes on a whole new meaning with McGraw-Hill Ryerson (MHR). More than just bringing you the textbook, MHR has consistently raised the bar in terms of innovation and educational research—both in accounting and in education in general. These investments in learning and the education community have helped MHR understand the needs of students and educators across the country, and allowed MHR to foster the growth of truly innovative, integrated learning.

## Integrated Learning Sales Specialists

- The Integrated Learning Sales Specialists are the McGraw-Hill Ryerson representatives who have the experience, product knowledge, training, and support to help instructors assess and integrate any MHR products, technology, and services into courses for optimum teaching and learning performance. Whether it's using the test bank software, helping students improve their grades, or putting an entire course online, the *i*Learning Sales Specialist is there to help.

Instructors: Contact your local *i*Learning Sales Specialist today to learn how to maximize all of McGraw-Hill Ryerson's resources!

## *i*Services

- McGraw-Hill Ryerson takes pride in developing the tools necessary to ensure a rich teaching and learning experience. MHR can assist in integrating technology, events, conferences, training, and more, into the services surrounding the textbook. MHR calls it *i*Services; for additional information, visit http://www.mcgrawhill.ca/higher education/iservices.

**Teaching, Learning & Technology Conference Series**  The educational environment has changed tremendously in recent years, and McGraw-Hill Ryerson continues to be committed to helping you acquire the skills you need to succeed in this new milieu. Our innovative Teaching, Learning & Technology Conference Series brings faculty together from across Canada with 3M Teaching Excellence award winners to share teaching and learning best practices in a collaborative and stimulating environment.

**Pageout**  Create an individualized course page for free—quickly and easily. The professionally designed website links directly to OLC material, allows instructors to post a class syllabus, offers an online gradebook, and much more! No knowledge of HTML is required. Visit www.pageout.net.

**Course Management**  The *Intermediate Accounting* Online Learning Centre content is available for course management systems, such as Blackboard. Ask your *i*Learning Sales Specialist for details.

## CHAPTER 1

# The Environment of Financial Reporting

## INTRODUCTION

Bombardier Inc., a major transportation manufacturing company, has operations in Canada, Germany, the United Kingdom, Switzerland, France, Australia, China, and other countries. Bombardier is listed on the Toronto Stock Exchange. As a Canadian public company, the company prepares its financial statements using Canadian generally accepted accounting principles (GAAP).

Many international companies list their securities on the stock exchanges in the foreign countries in which they operate. For example, the giant international automobile company Daimler-Chrysler is listed on all of the world's major stock exchanges including New York, Frankfurt, Tokyo, and London.

In the future, Bombardier may choose to list internationally. However, Canadian GAAP is accepted only in Canada, and Canada is a very small player in the international financial market. Will the company have to prepare financial statements using different GAAPs, such as German, British, Australian, and so forth?

Fortunately the answer to that question is "no," because almost all other countries permit foreign companies to report their financial results on the basis of International Financial Reporting Standards (IFRS).

The CICA's Accounting Standards Board (AcSB) has decided that it is time for Canada's public-company accounting standards to become international also. Canadian standard setting is changing with the international tide.

But even after Canada adopts IFRS for public companies, a company like Bombardier will need to make many accounting choices. Those choices will be affected by a variety of competing objectives. The company could make choices with an objective of reducing its income taxes, maximizing its reported earnings, or helping investors and creditors to estimate the future cash flows of the company.

In this chapter, we will look at GAAP, the process of accounting standard setting, and the financial reporting objectives that influence reported results.

## THE DIFFERENCE BETWEEN ACCOUNTING AND BOOKKEEPING

Before proceeding with a discussion of the environment of accounting, it is important to make a distinction between *accounting* and *bookkeeping*. Bookkeeping is a *recording* process. Virtually all bookkeeping is automated through the widespread use of computers, even in very small organizations. The role of the bookkeeper has declined as computers have taken over most of the routine processing of financial data.

In contrast, the accountant is responsible for telling the bookkeeper how to record transactions. In co-operation with management, the accountant decides how to classify and record transactions, how to disclose those transactions in the financial statements, how to measure the value of assets and liabilities and their related revenues and expenses, and what additional disclosures are appropriate.

An accountant must never lose sight of the fact that financial statements are the end product of a large number of accounting policy decisions and measurement estimates by management (often with the advice of accountants). By definition, estimates are based on expectations about future events. Accounting involves many subjective choices. It is not the mechanical task of bookkeeping.

## THE REALM OF FINANCIAL REPORTING

**financial reporting**

methods used to report an organization's financial condition and results of operations to internal and external parties

**Financial reporting** is the communication of financial information about the economic activities of an enterprise to its stakeholders. There are both internal and external stakeholders. The primary internal stakeholder is management, while the primary external stakeholder depends on the nature of the organization. For a large public corporation, the primary external stakeholder group may be the shareholders. For a small private corporation in which the shareholder is also management, the only *external* stakeholder may be the Canada Revenue Agency (CRA), for assessing income taxes.

Financial reporting is concerned primarily with producing financial statements that report on the economic well-being of an organization as a whole and on the flow of its resources. **Financial accounting** applies to all types of organizations, including businesses, non-profit organizations, and governments. In this book, the focus is on business enterprises.

### Financial Statements for Business Enterprises

The basic financial statements for all businesses are:

1. Balance sheet;

2. Income statement (or statement of earnings);

3. Statement of changes in retained earnings; and

4. Cash flow statement.

Many businesses combine the income statement and the statement of changes in retained earnings into a single *statement of income and retained earnings*.

The balance sheet is a *point* statement because it reports on the enterprise at a point in time. The other three statements are *flow* statements because they report on flows during a period of time. Flow statements tie together amounts that are shown on the beginning and ending balance sheets, such as beginning cash and ending cash.

Other flow statements may be required in some circumstances, especially for complex operations. Examples of possible additional flow statements are:

- Statement of other comprehensive income;
- Statement of changes in shareholders' equity; and
- Statement of changes in capital assets.

## Financial versus Managerial Accounting

In this book we focus exclusively on financial reporting for business organizations, primarily for corporations. Indeed, several chapters are applicable *only* to corporations (e.g., the chapters on shareholders' equity, earnings per share, and income taxes). Non-profit and governmental reporting is generally covered in advanced accounting texts, even though both non-business types of organizations are pervasive in our society and economy.

This book does not deal with management accounting. *Management accounting* is concerned with preparing and analyzing information for the exclusive use of management for decision making, planning, employee motivation, and internal performance evaluation. The level of detail is much greater, and the basis of accountability may differ from that presented in the organization's financial statements.

Management accounting deals primarily with segments of an organization and with management's specific internal decision-making needs. The users of management accounting information are known with certainty, and thus the information can be tailored to suit their specific needs.

In *financial reporting*, however, there often are multiple users. The various users often have conflicting objectives, and the financial statements must be prepared on a basis that optimizes the trade-offs between the various users' needs. The various (and potentially conflicting) objectives of financial reporting will be discussed later in this chapter.

## CONCEPT REVIEW

1. What is the essential difference between a bookkeeper and an accountant?
2. What is the general realm of financial reporting? How does financial reporting differ from management accounting?
3. Describe the difference between point statements and flow statements. Give examples of each.

## ACCOUNTABILITY—PUBLIC VERSUS PRIVATE CORPORATIONS

### Public Corporations

A *public corporation* is one that issues securities (either debt or equity, or both) to the public. The securities can then be traded on the open market, usually through an *organized exchange* such as the Toronto Stock Exchange. Public corporations must be *registered* with the securities commissions in each province in which their securities are traded. Registered companies must comply with the reporting requirements of the provincial securities commissions.

**Accountability**   Public corporations must be audited and their reporting must conform to GAAP. In some special industries such as investment funds, chartered banks, and regulated enterprises (e.g., telephone or cable companies), the normal provisions of GAAP may be supplemented by legal requirements. The Canadian chartered banks, for example, are governed by Canada's *Bank Act*.

Although Canadian GAAP is the normal reporting requirement for Canadian public corporations, some Canadian corporations have chosen to follow U.S. GAAP instead. Corporations may prefer to use U.S. GAAP in order to enhance their acceptability in U.S. financial markets. If U.S. GAAP is used, the company must present a reconciliation of net income (and balance sheet items) to Canadian GAAP in the notes to the financial statements.

Conversely, if a Canadian corporation uses Canadian GAAP but its securities are traded in the U.S. financial markets, the company must present a reconciliation from Canadian to U.S. GAAP in its notes.

In other words, a corporation that is listed both in the U.S. and Canada must provide information for earnings and net assets to satisfy both U.S. and Canadian GAAP requirements: (1) the primary financial statements are prepared with one GAAP and (2) significant amounts are converted to the other GAAP in the disclosure notes.

**Reporting Currency** A Canadian company is not required to report in Canadian dollars. If the bulk of the company's operating activities are carried out in U.S. dollars, then it usually makes more sense to convert any non–U.S. currency flows and values into U.S. dollars rather than convert the U.S. dollars into Canadian currency.

The U.S. dollar activities may not necessarily be due to extensive operating activities in the United States. Many commodities (e.g., oil, gold, lumber) are priced worldwide in U.S. dollars. All of the revenue of companies in those industries will be denominated in U.S. dollars regardless of whether they actually do business directly in the U.S. As a result, the U.S. dollar effectively is the company's functional currency and it makes more sense to use U.S. dollar reporting.

**Reporting GAAP versus Reporting Currency** There is no direct relationship between the reporting GAAP (Canadian versus U.S.) and the reporting currency. A company may use Canadian GAAP but U.S. dollars, and vice versa. A quick look at the auditor's report will tell the reader which GAAP is being used.

**Control Blocks** A public corporation may be controlled by a small number of shareholders who hold the majority of the voting shares. The group of voting shares that gives control to a small group of shareholders is called a **control block**.

In the *Financial Post*'s annual listing of Canada's 500 largest corporations, known as the FP500, approximately half of the companies are public. Of the public companies, however, well over half have control blocks. Only about 20% of the companies in the FP500 list are "widely held" public companies.

A control block may exist as the result of a private corporation that has been taken public, but with the original shareholders retaining a majority of the outstanding shares.

A more common Canadian practice is for a public corporation to issue two or more classes of shares, one class with multiple votes and another with few or no voting rights. Shares that have limited voting power are called **restricted shares**. Restricted shares enable a corporation to raise capital from the public without impairing the power of the controlling shareholders.

The implication of the existence of control blocks for Canadian financial reporting is that the accounting approach is unlikely to be dominated by a concern for the public shareholder. Instead, the reporting objectives of the controlling shareholder may well take precedence over those of the public investor.

## Private Corporations

A *private corporation* is one that does not issue securities to the public. All of the company's shares are held privately and cannot be offered for sale on the open market. Usually, all of the shares are owned by the members of a single family and sometimes by senior executives. Some of Canada's largest corporations are private corporations (e.g., McCain Foods Ltd. and Bata Shoes; both companies have multi-billion-dollar annual revenues).

Despite the inability to sell shares to the public, private corporations can obtain capital through **private placements** of debt or equity instruments. The securities that are issued in a private placement cannot be publicly traded, and therefore the company remains outside the jurisdiction of the securities acts and securities regulators. The suppliers of capital to a private corporation are assumed to be either insiders or sophisticated investors who do not need the special protection given to members of the general public who may buy shares on the open market.

**Accountability** A private corporation does not report to the general public and therefore is not governed by the requirements of the securities commissions. Private companies provide information for a limited group of users, including the managers, the shareholders, the taxation authorities, and their lenders and creditors.

---

**control block**

a small number of related or affiliated shareholders collectively having a majority of voting shares of a corporation

**restricted shares**

shares with limited or no voting rights

**private placements (privately placed securities)**

securities that are issued to individuals or organizations (e.g., pension funds, insurance companies) without being listed with a securities commission for public trading

Private companies are not bound by GAAP unless an external user (such as a major lender) requires that GAAP be used. While many private companies do use GAAP, many others deviate from GAAP in one or more respects. The deviation is usually in order to make the statements more useful for specific users or to coincide with the income tax treatment of specific items.

**Differential Reporting** The major concern of standard setters is to develop GAAP that are suitable for public corporations. Some accounting standards are very complex and require a great deal of work to prepare. Additional work means additional cost. In a public company, the cost is borne by the company to better inform the shareholders. In a private company, however, the primary users (e.g., shareholders and creditors) can demand additional information beyond that disclosed in the company's financial statements.

The AcSB has recognized that private companies do not always require the full complexity of reporting that is required for public companies. Indeed, it is quite possible that the shareholders of a private company are better served by simpler information rather than by the more complex information often required by public-company GAAP.

| differential reporting |
| --- |
| financial reporting in which qualifying private companies may use a limited number of simplified accounting options that are not available to publicly traded enterprises; part of Canadian GAAP |

The AcSB has provided a way for private companies to apply somewhat simpler accounting standards in certain situations. The *CICA Handbook* permits *differential reporting* for private corporations. Under the **differential reporting** recommendations, a corporation can choose *not* to apply certain recommendations of the *CICA Handbook* if:

- the company has no shares or other securities that are publicly traded; *and*
- the company is not otherwise publicly accountable, such as a rate-regulated enterprise or a financial institution; *and*
- its shareholders (both voting and non-voting) agree unanimously in writing to use the alternative differential reporting options.

Differential reporting applies only to a limited number of *CICA Handbook* sections. For example, a private corporation can apply a simpler process when testing for goodwill impairment (a subject discussed in Chapter 10).

Differential reporting is a *choice*, not a requirement. Private companies can elect to use some or all of the differential reporting options offered in the *CICA Handbook*.

On the international level, the IASB is working to establish simplified accounting standards for private companies, which the IASB calls SME (Small and Medium Enterprises). Bear in mind, however, that "SME" really is not a particularly accurate designation if it is intended to cover all private companies. A private company can be very large, with billions of dollars of revenue.

**Disclosed Basis of Accounting** Sometimes a private company may prefer to use an accounting policy not included in the *CICA Handbook* recommendations and that is not available under the differential reporting standard. The deviation is usually to make the statements more useful for specific users or to coincide with the income tax treatment of specific items. For example, a company may prepare statements to satisfy contractual requirements, such as compliance with the requirements of a major bank loan. When non-GAAP accounting policies are used, the company is said to be reporting on a **disclosed basis of accounting** (DBA).

| disclosed basis of accounting (DBA) |
| --- |
| a basis of financial reporting that differs in some respects from GAAP. The accounting practices that the organization is using are disclosed in a note to the financial statements |

The description of DBA will normally be included in the accounting policy note to the financial statements, and the auditor's opinion (if any) will refer to the fact that the financial statements have been prepared in accordance with the accounting principles described in the accounting policy note. The auditor's opinion will not include the auditor's usual reference to GAAP.

**Private Corporations Owned by Public Corporations**

Most corporations operate through a series of subsidiaries. Some companies have hundreds of subsidiaries. For example, the big German multinational corporation, Siemens, has over 80 subsidiaries in China alone. The vast majority of any company's subsidiaries are wholly owned by the parent corporation.

A wholly owned subsidiary is a private corporation because there is only one share-holder—the parent corporation. The users of the subsidiary's financial statements normally will be limited to (1) the parent corporation's management, (2) lenders and creditors, and (3) income tax authorities. The subsidiary has no broad public accountability.

However, if the parent company is a public corporation, then the GAAP requirements for public companies will apply to the private subsidiary when the subsidiary is consolidated with the parent.

A special situation arises when a Canadian corporation is the subsidiary of a foreign parent corporation. Examples may include Canadian operating subsidiaries of companies such as Toyota (Japan), IKEA (Sweden), and Philips Electronics (Netherlands). Since the primary user of the statements will be the foreign parent and the statements will be consolidated with the parent's statements, the subsidiary may use the parent's home country GAAP instead of Canadian GAAP.

Exhibit 1-1 summarizes the reporting requirements for public and private companies.

---

### EXHIBIT 1-1

### REPORTING REQUIREMENTS FOR PUBLIC AND PRIVATE COMPANIES

| Reporting Basis | Rationale |
| --- | --- |
| **Canadian Public Corporations** | |
| Canadian GAAP | Shares traded primarily in Canada |
| U.S. GAAP | Shares traded primarily in U.S. |
| **Canadian Private Corporations** | |
| Canadian GAAP | General purpose statements |
| Canadian GAAP | Subsidiary of Canadian public corporation |
| Canadian GAAP, Differential Reporting | Limited users; shareholders agree |
| DBA | Specialized reporting for specific users |
| Foreign or International GAAP | Subsidiary of non-Canadian parent |

---

### CONCEPT REVIEW

1. What is the difference between a public corporation and a private corporation? Which type is dominant in the Canadian economy?

2. How can private corporations obtain capital from outside investors without becoming public companies?

3. What is a control block?

---

## EVOLUTION OF CANADIAN ACCOUNTING STANDARDS

### National Canadian Standards

Canadian accounting standards are set by CICA's AcSB. For most of the late 20th century, the standards were set fairly autonomously without any explicit effort to link Canadian standards with U.S. or international standards. U.S. and international standards were not ignored, but they merely provided reference points for the development of Canadian standards. Indeed, the CICA has been a major contributor to the establishment of international standards since the founding of the International Accounting Standards Committee (IASC) in 1972.

A very important constituency for Canadian standard setting was the Canadian corporate community. A new standard could not be established if major corporations refused to comply—a refusal by major corporations would mean that the proposed standard was not "generally accepted." A corporate revolt would undermine the authoritative nature of the *CICA Handbook*.

As a result of corporate pressure, some Canadian standards become unique in the world, including the ways in which foreign currency gains and losses on long-term debt were accounted for, and the manner in which corporate joint ventures could be recognized on the co-venturers' financial statements. In other instances, Canadian standards simply took a less narrow view of the world than did U.S. standards.

### FASB Harmonization Phase

In the early 1990s, as globalization accelerated, the AcSB realized that Canada could no longer pursue a go-it-alone policy in accounting standard setting. The question then became: whom to follow? The U.S. FASB was widely perceived as the dominant force, but international standards were rapidly gaining acceptance around the world. Should the AcSB harmonize Canadian standards with those of the U.S. or those of the international community?

At that time, there were substantial differences between U.S. and international standards (many of which still remain). In contrast, Canadian standards already were very much in line with international standards as the result of 30 years of co-operative standard-setting effort.

However, there are some large Canadian corporations that are listed on stock exchanges in both Canada and the U.S., and those corporations wished to have a common set of accounting standards in order to simplify their reporting requirements. Although there are fewer than 200 Canadian cross-listed corporations, they do comprise a significant portion of Canadian economic activity.[1] Therefore, the AcSB decided to follow a route of harmonizing with U.S. standards as the first priority, and with international standards second.

As a result, the AcSB issued a flurry of new and revised accounting standards in an attempt both to harmonize with U.S. standards and to keep up with new standards being issued by the FASB.

However, several events occurred at about the same time that caused the AcSB to reconsider its strategic direction:

1. The SEC began to accept international standards for certain specific reporting requirements (e.g., cash flow, business combinations, and goodwill), thereby signalling that the SEC felt that not all was well with U.S. standards.

2. The accounting scandals at Enron, WorldCom, and other major U.S. corporations shook public confidence in the quality of U.S. accounting standards. U.S. standard setters had always considered their standards to be the best in the world, but the scandals undermined their confidence and made the FASB more receptive to international standards.

3. The original IASC was a voluntary organization of representatives from professional accounting bodies. The IASC did not have the active participation of standard setters. In 2002, the IASC was substantially reorganized and became directly linked to the standard-setting organizations of seven major developed countries: Canada, the U.S., the United Kingdom, France, Germany, Australia, and Japan.

4. International accounting standards (IAS) gained much greater acceptability in countries outside North America. Other countries began to view international standards, rather than U.S. standards, as the ones to emulate. Newly independent countries that did not have a domestic set of financial reporting standards (e.g., Hungary) adopted international standards rather than develop their own.

5. International standards became acceptable for foreign registrants on the vast majority of stock exchanges worldwide, including all of the major exchanges.

---

[1] The AcSB estimated that the approximately 200 companies that are cross-listed between U.S. and Canadian stock exchanges account for only 0.02% of Canadian corporations. The implication is that 99.98% of Canada's corporations must follow GAAP that is tailored to the needs of that tiny minority.

6. The European Union began *requiring* international standards for the consolidated financial statements of *all* EU companies in 2005 in an effort to make companies' financial reports more comparable. (Separate-entity non-consolidated financial statements will continue to be prepared in accordance with nation-specific accounting requirements, which are imbedded in national law in many countries.)

7. The U.S. Securities and Exchange Commission (SEC) began seriously considering accepting international standards for financial reporting of *foreign* companies.

After struggling to keep up with increasingly complex U.S. standards for several years, the AcSB decided that the drive to internationalization was inevitable.

## IASB Harmonization—The New Direction

In 2006, the AcSB issued a new strategic policy document in which it announced its plan to change direction. Instead of harmonizing with U.S. standards, the AcSB's new direction will be to harmonize with international standards for *public companies*. The process will take several years, at least through 2011. The AcSB will provide transition guidance for applying IAS that differ significantly from current Canadian standards.

Over the next few years, the AcSB plans will take the following steps:

1. Canadian standards will gradually be harmonized with IFRS. *The harmonized GAAP will apply only to public companies*.

2. The AcSB will establish a separate (and presumably simpler) body of Canadian accounting standards for *private* companies. This is a logical extension of the differential reporting options currently available to private companies.

3. When the transition to IFRS is complete, the AcSB will cease to function as a standard-setting body for public companies; the AcSB will continue to provide accounting standards for private companies.

In this book, we will discuss accounting standards as they exist in Canada. Most Canadian standards already are very similar to IFRS. In fact, quite a few current Canadian standards were developed in partnership with the IASB and are virtually identical, word for word. We will point out similarities as we go along but we generally will not be specific about differences.

At the end of each chapter we will present a separate section, International Perspective. This box explains briefly how international standards differ from existing Canadian standards and what direction we can expect Canadian standards to take in the near future. Over the life of this book, many of those differences will be eliminated as the AcSB's harmonization process moves forward. Updates to new standards will be provided on the book's website: **http://www.mcgrawhill.ca/olc/beechy**. Use the website to watch for new and updated standards.

## WHAT IS GAAP?

**generally accepted accounting principles (GAAP)**

body of accounting practices built up over time for use in preparing external accounting statements

The body of **generally accepted accounting principles (GAAP)** is just what the name implies—accounting principles that have become "generally accepted" in practice. General acceptance can come via two routes:

1. Historical accounting practices that have become widely accepted over time; and

2. Authoritative pronouncements by accounting standard-setting bodies.

## Historical Accounting Practices

**Historical accounting practices** have been developed by businesses and have stood the test of time. Over many decades, preparers (e.g., managers, with advice from professional accountants) have devised measurement and reporting approaches that users accepted as being reasonable and that auditors also accepted. The vast bulk of today's accounting practices evolved this way.

Historical practices also include accounting practices followed by the so-called specialized industries such as real property development, agriculture, and financial services (e.g., insurance, banking, investment funds). Specialized industries account for a majority of the economic activity of Canada.

Many historical practices have found their way into official accounting standards such as the *CICA Handbook* and the body of U.S. standards and **International Accounting Standards**. The standards for many items of measurement and disclosure reflect standard setters' acceptance of past practice. For example, the broad basic practices of historical cost valuation and of expense and revenue recognition owe their origins to historical practice.

### Authoritative Pronouncements

**Authoritative pronouncements** are accounting standards established by accounting standard-setting bodies. As mentioned above, many of those standards are codifications of historically accepted practices. Others, however, may sharply deviate from general practice. Current standards on accounting for derivative instruments, for example, are quite different from historical practice.

Canada's standard-setting body is the CICA's AcSB. In the U.S., the standard setter is the Financial Accounting Standards Board (FASB). Internationally, the accounting standard setter is the International Accounting Standards Board (IASB).

The AcSB is a part of the CICA, which is the national association of chartered accountants. In contrast, the FASB and IASB are independent standard-setting organizations that are not tied directly to professional accounting organizations. We will discuss briefly each of these three standard setting organizations in later sections.

### The Role of Judgement

The term "authoritative standards" sounds very official and precise. However, the application of almost all authoritative standards requires the exercise of professional judgement. Many standards effectively eliminate all but one acceptable accounting policy for a particular event. Thus, a standard may appear to eliminate the need for accounting choices.

However, a choice of accounting policy is not the only type of accounting judgement. Most standards still require accounting estimates and may also require other types of judgement, such as the timing of recognition or the extent of note disclosure. The need for professional judgement is always present in accounting. We cannot rely on "standards" as an excuse to stop thinking.

The remaining chapters in this book will emphasize the judgements that are needed when applying each accounting policy. Judgement is always required, even when only one accounting policy is permitted by the authoritative pronouncements. The ability to apply professional judgement is what differentiates an accountant from a highly competent bookkeeper.

### Development of Accounting Standards

GAAP constantly evolves. The business environment is one of continuous innovation, and accountants must develop ways of accounting for new types of transactions and events.

Accounting standards develop only after a new business practice has developed. For example, the innovations introduced by Enron Corporation for off-balance-sheet financing led to new accounting standards for reporting that type of transaction.

Instead of prescribing a new type of accounting, standard setters usually try to narrow the range of accounting practices for any particular type of transaction or economic event. For example, the standards for inventory valuation restrict the number of methods that can be used and eliminate other alternatives, such as the base-stock method and the last-in, first-out (LIFO) replacement cost method. The standard-setting goal is to improve comparability between different companies that have the same types of transactions or that experience the same types of economic events.

## ACCOUNTING STANDARD SETTING IN CANADA

### Source of AcSB Authority

The AcSB establishes accounting standards in Canada. As we explained above, the AcSB issues accounting recommendations that are incorporated into the *CICA Handbook,* which constitutes the primary authority for Canadian GAAP. The AcSB also occasionally issues Accounting Guidelines, serves as the source of authority for the Emerging Issues Committee, and authorizes other pronouncements that also are primary sources for GAAP.

The AcSB is a creation of the CICA's Board of Directors. There is no direct legal authority for the AcSB to set standards for Canadian companies. However, the federal and provincial corporations acts require that auditors report in accordance with GAAP. "In accordance with GAAP" is defined in the regulations to mean compliance with the recommendations of the *CICA Handbook.*

### Canada's Hierarchy of Standards

In the past, companies sometimes extended a long arm to find standards that they wanted to use. Companies might want to use an obscure practice that has been practised by some companies in other countries, or to invent new accounting methods that twist existing standards into unintended applications. Standard setters do not like that practice. Therefore, the AcSB established a hierarchy of standards to deal with situations in which there appears to be more than one source of "authority." For example, if Canadian standards prescribe one treatment while U.S. standards permit an alternative approach, can a company argue that the U.S. approach is more suitable for its needs? If the company is preparing its statements on the basis of Canadian GAAP, the answer is "no."

Similarly, a Canadian company cannot use a practice that has become common industry practice inside or outside Canada, if the practice is in conflict with Canadian GAAP.

Accounting sources are grouped into two categories:

- Primary sources, consisting of pronouncements of the AcSB; and
- Other sources.

**Primary Sources**   The primary sources of GAAP are the various standards, guidelines, EIC abstracts, and supporting materials issued by the AcSB. Within this group, there is a hierarchy—some sources take precedence over others. In *descending* order of authority, the primary sources are:

1. The accounting sections of the *CICA Handbook,* including the appendices;

2. Accounting Guidelines, including appendices;

3. EIC Abstracts;

4. AcSB documents that describe the background information and basis for conclusions for *CICA Handbook* accounting recommendations and Accounting Guidelines;

5. Illustrative material for the preceding sources, issued separately from the related accounting recommendations, Accounting Guidelines, or EIC abstracts; and

6. *Implementation guides* authorized by the AcSB.

The dominant source is the *CICA Handbook.* When managers of a GAAP–reporting company are selecting accounting policies, they cannot choose a source as being "authoritative" if it conflicts with one or more recommendations in the *CICA Handbook.*

The *CICA Handbook* sections often contain appendices that have been approved by the AcSB and therefore carry the same authority as the recommendations in sections.

The various sections of the *CICA Handbook* contain both italicized and non-italicized paragraphs. The italicized paragraphs are the recommendations themselves, the non-italicized paragraphs provide additional explanation or background. *Italicized and non-italicized paragraphs are of equal importance.*

EXHIBIT 1-2

## HIERARCHY OF GAAP

**Primary sources** (in descending order of authority):

- Accounting sections of the *CICA Handbook*
- *Accounting Guidelines* issued by the AcSB
- Abstracts of Issues Discussed by the Emerging Issues Committee (EIC Abstracts)
- *Background Information and Basis for Conclusions* documents issued by the AcSB in conjunction with *CICA Handbook* recommendations or Accounting Guidelines
- Illustrative material for all of the above sources that is issued by the AcSB
- Implementation guides authorized by the AcSB, but not issued directly by the AcSB

**Other (secondary) sources** (not in order of authority, but as relevant in the particular circumstances):

- FASB accounting standards (U.S.)
- International accounting standards (IAS and IFRS)
- Implementation guides issued independent of the AcSB, particularly those specifically relating to the Canadian environment
- Draft materials for primary sources (above), such as exposure drafts, statements of principles, and discussion documents
- Research reports and research studies issued by the CICA or other groups
- Accounting textbooks, journals, and articles that are relevant to the Canadian environment
- Established practice, whether written or unwritten, that is consistent with the application of professional judgement using the basic financial accounting concepts of *CICA Handbook* Section 1000

---

The second source of GAAP within the primary sources is accounting guidelines issued by the AcSB. **Accounting Guidelines** reflect the Board's opinion on specific accounting issues and are issued very rarely. Guidelines are secondary to the recommendations of the *CICA Handbook* because they have not gone through the full review process required for introducing new recommendations into the *CICA Handbook*.

The third primary source is the **Emerging Issues Committee (EIC)**. The EIC is part of the standard-setting section of the *CICA*. The Committee meets regularly and issues opinions on accounting issues where current practice is unclear and guidance has been requested by accountants and/or managers. The EIC issues brief statements called **Abstracts of Issues Discussed (EIC Abstracts)** that describe the issue, the nature of the EIC's discussion, and the Committee's conclusion. Many of the issues involve interpretation of *CICA Handbook* sections in ambiguous or complex situations.

The fourth primary source is a type of AcSB document called **Background Information and Basis for Conclusions** On occasion, the AcSB issues a background document when the Board introduces a new or significantly revised *CICA Handbook* section. Background documents explain the research that the Board undertook when it examined an issue, including references to standards in other jurisdictions, particularly those of the U.S. FASB and the IASB. The Board explains the reasons for its recommendations. Since these documents explain the reasoning of the Board more fully than the *CICA Handbook* sections, they become a primary source, particularly when there is some doubt about the relevant application of a standard in a specific situation.

The fifth primary source is illustrative material issued by the Board. These illustrations are not part of the *CICA Handbook* section, but are specially issued to provide additional illustrations of how a particular section should be applied. Illustrative material shows how an accounting standard might be applied in particular situations. The material may also summarize certain aspects of the standard, including decision trees and other helpful guidance.

Finally, the sixth primary source consists of *implementation guides* authorized by the Board to help preparers apply complex sections of the *CICA Handbook* such as post-retirement benefits or financial instruments. There is a subtle distinction between the fifth and sixth sources. The fifth source is illustrative material *issued* by the Board. The sixth source is illustrative material that has been *authorized* by the Board, prepared by the CICA accounting standards staff, but *not directly approved* by the Board.

**Other Sources**  Essentially, *other sources* consist of anything that is relevant in a particular situation. These might also be called *secondary* sources, in contrast to AcSB–issued primary sources. Managers may turn to secondary sources when the primary sources of GAAP do not deal with the reporting of a specific transaction or combination of transactions. Whenever secondary sources are used, the accounting policies and disclosures must be:

1. Consistent with the primary sources of GAAP; and

2. Developed through the exercise of professional judgement and the application of financial accounting concepts as described in the *CICA Handbook*.

Secondary sources should be evaluated on the basis of four criteria:

1. *The specificity of the source.* A source that deals with the specific situation confronted by management is more relevant than a more general source.

2. *The authority of the issuer or author.* Other authoritative bodies such as the FASB and the IASB are viewed as better sources than opinions of others in the same jurisdiction.

3. *The continued relevance of the source.* Generally speaking, recent sources are better than possibly outdated sources.

4. *The development process for the source.* A source that is just the opinion of one person or one group is less relevant than a source that has been developed through a process of consultation with other interested individuals and groups.

There is no hierarchy within the secondary sources. Other sources are relevant only if they satisfy the four criteria cited above. If they do not fit the Canadian situation, they are irrelevant, regardless of the apparent "authority" that they carry, such as IASB and FASB standards.

Clearly, an important secondary source is the body of standards (IAS and IFRS) issued by the IASB. As the AcSB brings Canadian standards more closely in line with international standards, the IFRS will become the best reference source for accounting in situations not yet explicitly covered by Canadian standards.

FASB standards are particularly useful when the relevant Canadian standard is more similar to the U.S. standard than to international standards. The FASB provides a lot of implementation guidance that may work well with an existing Canadian standard.

Another secondary source is implementation guidance issued by organizations other than the AcSB. Such guidance may be issued in book form by independent authors or groups, or in loose-leaf form by professional accounting reference services. Since the Board has not authorized these guides, they have less authority than the Board-authorized implementation guides included in the primary sources.

The AcSB issues exposure drafts, research studies, and background studies. Not all of these documents end up being formulated into accounting standards. However, the discussions in these documents may be used as a secondary source, *if* they do not conflict with final standards issued by the Board. The Board does not always follow the proposed recommendations of its research reports and exposure drafts when it issues a final standard, so caution is necessary.

Additional secondary sources include accounting textbooks, accounting journals, independent research studies, and articles that describe specific approaches. Canadian-sourced materials are preferable to non-Canadian publications, which most likely will not consider the Canadian environment.

In all instances where secondary "other" sources are used, the resulting accounting policies must be (1) consistent with the primary sources of GAAP and (2) developed through the exercise of professional judgement and application of basic accounting concepts. The mere fact that an existing practice has been in use in a particular industry does not make it acceptable as GAAP if the practice is inconsistent with primary sources and with basic accounting concepts.

### Summary

GAAP is a historically accepted body of principles that has been developed over a long period of time. Many of the historical principles have been codified into written accounting standards in Canada as recommendations in the *CICA Handbook*. Often, inclusion in the *CICA Handbook* has meant a narrowing of the range of acceptable practices so that different companies report similar transactions and events in a similar manner.

In recent years, the AcSB has significantly altered existing Canadian GAAP by introducing new sections (or modifying existing sections) in accordance with evolving U.S. or international practice. International harmonization is a stated goal of the AcSB.

The hierarchy of GAAP sources goes from the official pronouncements of the AcSB at the highest level to written and unwritten practice and sources at the lowest level. If a company is required to follow GAAP, then a practice that is cited in a lower-level source cannot be used to override a source at a higher level.

## CONCEPT REVIEW

1. Are all Canadian GAAP found in the *CICA Handbook*? Explain.
2. Do the EIC Abstracts of Issues Discussed have the same authority as recommendations in the *CICA Handbook*?
3. What companies are permitted to use differential reporting?
4. Why would a company use DBA instead of GAAP?

### Relationship between Financial Reporting and Income Tax Reporting

Canada Revenue Agency (CRA) is an agency of the federal government established to interpret and enforce the nation's federal tax laws. CRA has adopted procedures and reporting requirements whose primary purpose is to collect money. At times, the government also uses tax law to attain specific social or economic objectives considered important by Parliament, such as encouraging investment in research and development.

The general aim of the *Income Tax Act* is to collect revenue. In general, the act provides for taxation when cash is flowing, so that revenues are usually taxed when they have been substantively realized and costs are deducted from taxable revenue when they are incurred. Taxation principles tend to emphasize cash flows because those flows normally can be measured quite clearly. There are exceptions to the cash flow emphasis in assessing taxable income, of course. For example, the taxation of revenue often is affected by the revenue recognition policy used by the business, which may differ significantly from the revenue cash flow. Nevertheless, tax law and tax regulations generally steer clear of interperiod allocations and subjective estimates.

The general principle of taxing on the basis of cash flows has an impact on the tax treatment of expenses. Expenses may be recognized for tax purposes in a way that is quite different from their accounting treatment. This is particularly true for costs that are subject to a defer-and-amortize approach for accounting purposes, such as development costs, pension costs, and long-term leases.

The Canadian taxation method that is similar in nature to amortization of capital assets is Capital Cost Allowance (CCA). However, CCA is independent of depreciation or amortization expense for financial reporting purposes. CCA follows a basis of allocation that is set by the income tax regulations. Public companies and many private companies use depreciation methods that are unrelated to CCA. Nevertheless, private companies may choose to amortize their capital assets on the same basis as CCA is calculated in order to simplify their financial reporting.

CRA does not require a corporation (or the owners of proprietorships and partnerships) to use the same reporting principles for tax as for accounting, or vice versa. However, corporations must attach their annual financial statements to the tax return. One of the basic parts of the corporate income tax form is a reconciliation of reported pre-tax accounting income to reported taxable income. The corporation must make it clear just what accounting differences caused any discrepancy between the net earnings reported to its shareholders and the taxable income reported to CRA. This is the principle of *exception reporting* as applied to the taxable income calculation.

When corporations adopt the same accounting practices for financial reporting as for tax reporting, this is known as *book-tax conformity*. Many accountants believe that disclosure of variations between tax and book reporting on the tax return acts as a "red flag" for CRA and invites a tax audit. Two tax experts also observe that:

> Firms also adopt book-tax conformity to increase the probability that the courts will uphold the method chosen as appropriate for tax purposes. According to a 1992 decision … the accounting method used in the financial statements will generally prevail unless another method results in a "truer picture of a taxpayer's revenue, which more fairly and accurately portrays income, and which matches revenue and expenditure"[2]

Therefore, although there is no requirement in Canada (unlike some other countries, such as Germany and Japan) that tax reporting be identical to financial reporting, tax treatment of items may have an impact on financial reporting. The impact is most likely to be observed for revenue; CRA generally takes a dim view of a corporation's recognizing revenue in the income statement while deferring revenue recognition for tax purposes.

## INTERNATIONAL FINANCIAL REPORTING STANDARDS (IFRS)

Many multinational companies have securities listed and traded in more than one national market. The shares of Daimler-Chrysler and Siemens, for example, are listed on many stock exchanges around the world. In order to facilitate international capital markets, a substantial body of accounting standards has been developed.

### Early Development

For about 30 years, international standards were developed by the IASC. The IASC was not created by any legal authority but began in 1973 as a volunteer organization to strive for greater consistency in accounting standards among developed nations. Until 2001, IASC members were professional accounting bodies in individual countries, not standard-setting bodies and certainly not the countries' governments. For example, the U.S. member was the American Institute of Certified Public Accountants (AICPA), not the FASB nor the SEC nor the U.S. federal government.

The IASC began with 10 members, dominated by English-speaking countries (the United Kingdom, the U.S., Canada, Australia, and New Zealand), by developed countries, and by western countries, Japan being the only Asian country. The number of member countries grew to 140 member countries by 2000, the last year of the "old" structure.

---

[2] The excerpt from the article entitled "Tax Minimization versus Good Tax Planning," by Alan MacNaughton and Amin Mawani, from the January–February 1997 issue, has beeen reproduced with permission from *CA Magazine*, published by the Canadian Institute of Chartered Accountants, Toronto.

Although the IASC had many member countries, the actual work was carried out by the 13-member IASC Board. Throughout its existence the Board had a core of seven permanent members: the United Kingdom, the U.S., Canada, Australia, Germany, France, and Japan. The same countries have now become permanent liaison members in the new Board structure, as outlined below.

Between 1973 and 2001, the IASC issued 41 IAS. These standards bear a strong similarity to the accounting recommendations of the *CICA Handbook* in style, length, and substance. The similarity is not accidental—the CICA has worked closely with the IASC for 30 years.

## Current IASB Structure

In 2002, the IASC was significantly restructured. The purpose of the restructuring was to tie international standard setting more directly into national standard setting, and to give international standards more stature and more rigour. The current structure is as follows:

- The IASC Foundation, incorporated in Delaware (U.S.A.), is responsible for the overall strategy and effectiveness of the IASC. The Foundation has 19 trustees, of whom six are from North America (including five from the U.S.), seven from Europe, four from the Asia-Pacific region, one from South America, and one from Africa. The trustees appoint the members of the IASB.

- The International Accounting Standard Board, located in London, England, is solely responsible for issuing IFRS. The Board has 14 members, seven of whom are direct liaisons with seven national standard-setting bodies (the United Kingdom, the U.S., Canada, Australia, Germany, France, and Japan).

- The Standards Advisory Council (SAC) has approximately 40 members who are knowledgeable about the problems and impact of financial reporting or possess an expertise of value to IASB. The SAC meets with the IASB at least three times a year to advise the Board on agenda decisions, priorities, and other matters.

- The Standing Interpretations Committee provides technical updates for interpreting IAS.

The structure is illustrated graphically in Exhibit 1-3.

The name for the overall organization continues to be the IASC. However, the standard-setting unit is now designated specifically as the International Accounting Standards Board (IASB). Essentially, this name change recognizes the pre-existing reality—it always was the Board that made the decisions and issued the standards.

**International Financial Reporting Standards (IFRS):**

accounting standards developed and issued by the International Accounting Standards Board (IASB) for use by companies with securities traded in international financial markets. IAS were issued prior to 2001; standards issued in later years are designated as IFRS

The IASB issues **International Financial Reporting Standards (IFRS)** to differentiate them from the earlier IAS. However, the IASB will assume jurisdiction over the preceding IAS. By definition, IFRS will include the earlier IAS. As needed, the IASB issues revisions to existing IAS. Both identifiers, IAS and IFRS, will continue to be used.

The IASB has no authority to require companies to use international standards; financial reporting requirements are the jurisdiction of the securities exchanges and securities regulators in each country. Nevertheless, international standards already are in widespread use:

- The vast majority of stock exchanges around the world accept financial statements based on international standards for foreign-listed companies—that is, from companies based in a country other than the exchange's home country. These exchanges include most of the world's major exchanges: Tokyo, London, Frankfurt, Hong Kong, Buenos Aries, and Paris. Some exchanges require a reconciliation of IASB–based GAAP to local domestic GAAP, but most do not.

- Companies based in the European Community have been required to use international standards for their consolidated financial statements since 2005. Separate-entity statements (that is, unconsolidated) will continue to be prepared using the home country's GAAP in order to comply with national tax and corporations laws.

The few major exchanges that do not yet accept financial statements based on international standards are those of the U.S., Canada, and Chile. However, the Ontario Securities Commission and the U.S. Securities and Exchange Commission (SEC) currently are considering accepting international standards for foreign registrants. The New York Stock

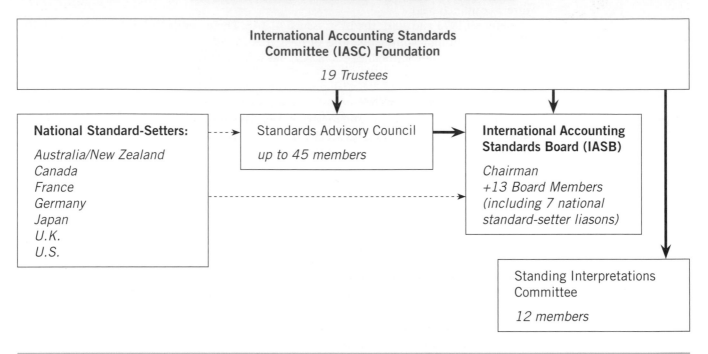

**EXHIBIT 1-3**

**INTERNATIONAL STANDARD-SETTING STRUCTURE**

Exchange already accepts international reporting for foreign companies, provided that the company's statements provide a reconciliation to U.S. GAAP.

## USER OBJECTIVES FOR FINANCIAL REPORTING

Managers and accountants must make many judgements. They must (1) choose appropriate accounting policies, (2) make suitable accounting estimates, and (3) decide what information to disclose in both the statements and the notes. To exercise judgement, the accountant must have *criteria* against which to measure the suitability of alternatives. The most fundamental criteria for deciding on policies, estimates, and disclosures are the **objectives of financial reporting** for the specific reporting enterprise or organization.

> **objectives of financial reporting**
>
> the various users' needs and managers' motivations that are the basic criteria for choices from among different possible accounting policies, accounting estimates, and note disclosures

The purpose of financial statements is to communicate information to one or more groups or types of users. To be useful to the users, the financial statements must convey information that is useful for their decision purposes. These decision purposes may vary widely, and the information that is suitable for one purpose may not be suitable for another purpose.

Financial statements often have direct economic impacts for either the enterprise or its stakeholders, or both. For example,

- Reported earnings may be used as the basis for employee profit sharing and/or management bonuses.
- Accounting methods may increase or decrease a corporation's income tax liability.
- The reported level of accounts receivable and inventories affects the level of financing provided by a bank through an operating line of credit.
- Reported earnings and reported net asset value affect the permitted return in regulated industries, such as cable companies and pipelines.
- Various reported numbers in the financial statements may trigger a default on loan requirements, known as covenants.
- In partnerships, co-operatives, and mutual insurance companies, the reported financial results affect the financial rewards of the partners, members, and policyholders.

In addition, many of the decisions that users must make are *evaluative* decisions that may not have immediate economic impacts, but that do affect the users' perceptions of the reporting enterprise and affect their relations with (or stake in) the enterprise:

- Lenders evaluate the cash flow potential of a borrower in order to assess the ability of the borrower to service the loan (that is, to pay the interest and principal as they come due).
- Income tax authorities evaluate the financial statements to see whether the information that a corporation is reporting to its owners is compatible with (but not necessarily the same as) the information it is reporting to CRA.
- Employees evaluate an employer's ability to pay higher compensation (or the validity of employer requests for reductions in compensation).
- Shareholders assess management's ability to conduct the affairs of the enterprise.
- Security analysts evaluate public companies' performance and issue recommendations to buy, hold, or sell shares.
- Regulators evaluate a regulated enterprise to see if the enterprise's earnings are reasonable.

The *CICA Handbook* asserts that the objective of financial statements is to communicate information that is useful to investors, members, contributors, creditors, and other users in making their resource allocation decisions and/or assessing management stewardship.

The problem with this general view of reporting objectives is that it puts all users together into a single group and all decisions into a single category. The statement provides no guidance for accountants to use in exercising professional judgement. Therefore, we must look beyond this very general definition. The following sections discuss some of the more common objectives of financial reporting.

Bear in mind that, as we discussed in previous sections, relatively few Canadian enterprises are widely held public companies. To be able to recommend suitable accounting policies, a professional accountant must be able to discern the financial reporting objectives that affect each individual enterprise. Otherwise, there is no basis for choosing one accounting policy instead of another.

## Assessing and Predicting Cash Flows

A financial reporting objective that has received much attention in both the professional and academic accounting literature is that of *cash flow prediction*—investors and creditors are interested in predicting the ability of the company to earn sufficient income and generate sufficient cash flows in the future to be able to pay the company's obligations and to provide a return to shareholders.

Bankers and creditors need to assess a business's ability to generate enough cash through its normal operations to be able to pay interest and to repay debt principal. The shareholders of public companies may also be interested in cash flow prediction because, in theory, share value is derived from the present value of the perpetual stream of future dividend payments. To the extent that earnings are retained (instead of being paid out as dividends), the reinvested earnings increase the asset base and should generate increased cash flow (and increased dividends) in the future.

There is a subtle difference between the assessment of *current* cash flows and the prediction of *future* cash flows. To assess current cash flows, the financial statement user wants to know the cash inflows and outflows of the enterprise in the current period. Normally, the user places particular emphasis on the cash flow *from operating activities* to assess the entity's ability to generate cash. The availability of other sources of financing is also important, as is the disposition of those funds: *How much cash is the company generating or raising externally, and what is the company doing with that money?*

Improvements in the presentation of the cash flow statement have helped this objective in recent years, although much remains hidden from view. In particular, details of cash flow from operations are buried in very broad summary figures, and it is not easy to discern anything beyond gross cash flow from operations. As we will see in later chapters, accounting policy decisions can affect the amount reported as cash flow from operations. As well, companies sometimes select accounting policies that have the effect of increasing the *apparent* cash flow from operations.

Cash flow *prediction* requires extrapolating the current cash flow into future years. Assumptions must be made in order to do this, and accounting can help this process by measuring and/or disclosing the company's commitments to future cash flows (e.g., forthcoming lease and loan payments).

As all accountants are fully aware, a company's operating cash flow for a year is very different from its earnings for that year. In the long run, however, earnings are the result of cash flows. Revenues and expenses arise from cash flows, but differ from the actual cash flows to the extent that accountants engage in the processes of *accrual accounting* and *interperiod allocation* in order to estimate earnings. Financial analysts and bankers, too, are aware of the difference.

**Earnings Quality** Creditors and analysts who attempt to assess and predict future cash flows tend to prefer earnings measures that are supported by operating cash flows. For this reason, analysts often use the reported *cash flow from operating activities* to calculate *cash flow per share* for public companies. They compare the operating cash flow per share with the earnings per share.

If there is a high degree of correlation between the two measures, the company has *high-quality earnings*. If the two measures fluctuate widely from year to year, then the company is said to have *low-quality earnings*. The perceived quality of earnings is good when the relationship between operating cash flow and net income is fairly stable.

Sometimes a company will report positive earnings but negative cash flow from operations; this situation is not viewed kindly by analysts because it suggests that management may be manipulating earnings through accruals and interperiod allocations.

**Effect on Financial Reporting Choices** What impact does an objective of cash flow prediction have on financial reporting? The consequences of adopting cash flow prediction as a primary reporting objective include the following:

- Accounting policies are chosen that tend to reduce interperiod allocations. For example, revenue is recognized when cash is received. Similarly, costs that could be deferred and amortized (e.g., patent costs) will be expensed instead, so that the impact on earnings (as an expense) will coincide with the cash flow.
- Full disclosure of future cash flow commitments is given in the notes. There is a great deal of leeway permitted in disclosing future commitments of various kinds. Under a cash flow reporting objective:, the choice is to provide liberal disclosure of future cash flows, and particularly to signal forthcoming changes in cash flows (positive or negative).

When cash flow assessment and prediction is the primary objective, financial reporting policies are chosen that provide the clearest indication of the cash flows underlying reported earnings. Accrual accounting and interperiod allocation are still used, but their use is restricted to those instances in which there is little or no choice, such as amortization of capital assets for profit-oriented enterprises.

### Income Tax Minimization

A very common objective, particularly for private companies, is that of *income tax minimization*. Since there is a time value of money, why pay taxes this year if they can be delayed until next year? The cash saved by reducing the income tax bill can be invested to earn a return, or can be used to service debt or pay dividends. A company has a lot of better things to do with its money than pay income taxes, if the payment is unnecessary.

**Tax Minimization versus Tax Evasion** When we discuss tax minimization, we are not talking about *cheating* on the income tax. There is some flexibility in the timing of reporting certain revenues and expenses on the corporate tax return. To a limited extent, a company can affect the amount of tax that it pays through its selection of accounting policies. The use of legitimate options for reducing a company's current taxable income is known as *tax minimization or tax deferral*. In contrast, deliberate misstatement on the tax return is *tax evasion*, which is fraud.

**Effect on Financial Reporting Choices** If a company wishes to minimize the amount of taxes that it pays, it will adopt accounting policies that tend to:

- Delay the recognition of revenue to the extent permitted by the *Income Tax Act*, particularly for long earnings cycles; and
- Speed the payment of expenses that can legitimately be deducted for tax purposes.

A common example of legitimate minimization of *personal* income taxes is the rush of Canadians at the end of February each year to invest in RRSPs. By investing up to the permitted level within 60 days following the taxation year, individuals reduce their income tax bill. The motivation is so strong that customers borrow from their banks in order to make the investment. The same principle applies to businesses' motivation to speed expense payments to reduce their income tax.

Why wouldn't every company attempt to reduce its income tax bill? The reason is that if the company adopts accounting policies that reduce taxable income, those policies may also reduce reported net income.

This might be a problem for managers whose compensation is tied to book income. A lower book income may also lead to a poorer performance evaluation and hence reduced promotion possibilities for managers. Furthermore, many executive compensation packages include significant amounts of stock options. Anything that lowers the firm's stock price will lower the value of those options. Many managers believe that a firm's stock price is determined more by its net income than by its cash flows.[3]

As a result of the impact on reported earnings, income tax minimization is more likely to be an objective for private corporations and, to a lesser extent, for public corporations that have a strong family control block. The owner-managers of these types of corporations have independent sources of information about the company, and their bankers usually are kept closely informed about the activities of the corporation. A tax-minimization objective is in the best interests of bankers and creditors, but they must recognize that reported earnings under a tax minimization objective will *look* poorer, but the cash flow will actually be better. In contrast, public corporations are likely to place less emphasis on tax minimization because their managers are more concerned about external stakeholder perceptions of the company's earnings ability.

Some aspects of taxation are independent of their accounting treatment. For example, the *Income Tax Act* provides for CCA for capital assets; accounting depreciation is irrelevant to determining taxable income. Similarly, the tax deduction for an employer's liability for an employee pension plan is linked to the cash flow, and does not depend on the accounting treatment. For these types of expenses, adopting an *income tax minimization* objective will have no accounting choice implications.

### Contract Compliance

External users often use financial statements as the basis for assessing whether an enterprise has complied with contract provisions. The most common type of financial statement contracting is for debt, particularly with bank loans and with issues of bonds (both publicly issued and privately placed). Debt contracts or agreements usually have provisions that require companies to maintain a certain level of performance, such as:

- Maximum debt-to-equity ratio;
- Maximum percentage of dividend payout;

---

[3] The excerpt from the article entitled "Tax Minimization versus Good Tax Planning," by Alan MacNaughton and Amin Mawani, from the January–February 1997 issue of *CA Magazine*, has been reproduced with permission of the Canadian Institute of Chartered Accountants, Toronto.

- Minimum times-interest-earned ratio; and
- Minimum level of shareholders' equity.

**covenants or maintenance tests**

contract requirements that specify a minimum level of organization performance, usually in debt contracts

**shareholders' agreements**

a contract signed by shareholders that stipulates the rights and restrictions that govern shareholder behaviour. Shareholders' agreements are normal in a private corporation

These provisions are known as **covenants** or **maintenance tests**. If a company fails to meet the covenants, the lender (or trustee, in the case of publicly issued bonds) has the right to call the loan and force immediate repayment. Since the debtor seldom will be able to satisfy the call for repayment, the company is forced into reorganization or receivership.

**Shareholders' agreements** in private corporations also usually contain provisions that affect the valuation of shares if a shareholder decides to sell her or his shares. Sales of shares in a private corporation can be made only through private contracting with a third party or by selling the shares back to the corporation. Often shareholders' agreements include a requirement that shares offered for sale must first be offered to the other existing shareholders, who have the *right of first refusal*. If existing shareholders do not agree to buy the shares, then the selling shareholder can approach other interested investors.

Since there is no public market for the shares of private corporations, there is no easily identifiable market price. The market price is normally determined on the basis of the financial statements. In theory, the value of shares is a function of future earnings (and cash flow) and of the fair value of the corporation's net assets. In practice, most shareholders' agreements stipulate that the price is based on historical earnings and on net asset book values.[4]

**Effect on Financial Reporting Choices** Accounting policy choices and accounting estimates can have a significant effect on the ratios used in debt agreements and for share valuation in shareholders' agreements. GAAP provides quite a bit of flexibility in accounting policy choice, and accounting policy choices can have a substantial impact on financial statement ratios.

For example, electing to use straight-line amortization instead of accelerated amortization for buildings and equipment will result in relatively higher earnings, higher shareholders' equity, lower debt-equity ratio, and higher times-interest-earned.

Therefore, some debt agreements (particularly in private placements) specify what accounting policies must be used for calculating the ratios. When specific policies are stipulated in the debt agreement, management's ability to select policies that will enhance the ratios is restricted.

Similarly, the share valuation components of private company shareholders' agreements often contain specific provisions concerning the valuation of net assets. These provisions are not constrained by GAAP, and therefore may be more suitable to the needs of the shareholders for a fair valuation of their shares than would a GAAP-based valuation.

## Stewardship

A question commonly asked by lenders and investors is, "What did they do with my money?" A *steward* is a person who is responsible for managing an enterprise on behalf of someone else. The word originally applied to the person who managed large household estates on behalf of the owners. Stewardship reporting, therefore, focuses on showing the financial statement reader just how the resources entrusted to management's care were managed. Transparency is important; full disclosure should exist and the financial affairs should be transparent. Financial reporting should not be complicated by a large number of allocations that obscure the operating results for the year.

**Effect on Financial Reporting Choices** The objective of stewardship is reflected in two ways: (1) minimization of interperiod allocations and (2) full disclosure.

Interperiod allocations make it difficult for financial statement readers to see how management is managing the funds entrusted to its care. For example, some types of expenditure either can be expensed immediately or can be capitalized (as an asset) and amortized. A stewardship objective would lead to expensing rather than capitalization.

---

[4] See: Jeffrey Kantor, *Valuation of Unlisted Shares* (Toronto: CCH Canadian Limited, 1988), p. 224.

In the notes to the financial statements, the company should reveal much useful information on the company's financial position. Disclosure may be well in excess of the mandatory requirements of GAAP. The role of stewardship is especially clear in the case of mutual fund reporting, where the investment activity of the organization is fully documented in order to satisfy investors' natural inquisitiveness about the nature of the fund's investments and the level of investment activity during the year.

### Performance Evaluation

Financial statement readers often use the statements to evaluate management performance. The common use of bonus schemes based on reported earnings as means of compensating managers attests to the widespread use of financial statements for this purpose.

Performance evaluation is a concern not only of external users, but also of managers themselves. Managers are users of financial statements in order to (1) evaluate their own performance and (2) evaluate the performance of the managers of subsidiaries and other related companies in a corporate family of companies.

**Effect on Financial Reporting Choices** In order to be useful for performance evaluation, financial statements should reflect the basis on which management decisions are made, at least to the extent possible. For example, suppose that a cruise line builds and introduces a new ship. There are substantial costs involved in set-up costs for a new ship. These costs are essential to successful operation of the ship. If performance evaluation is a reporting objective, these costs are deferred and amortized in order to be matched against the revenue that they are intended to enhance. If, instead, cash flow prediction were the dominant objective, then the costs would be expensed when incurred.

Managers are fully aware of the performance evaluation objective of financial statements, and the managers of widely held public companies are apt to be quite sensitive to the earnings impacts of accounting policy choices. Therefore, managers have strong motivations to select accounting policies that will enhance their apparent performance. The issue of management motivations in financial accounting policy selection is important and is the subject of the next section.

## MANAGEMENT MOTIVATIONS

The needs of external financial statement users are vital to developing appropriate financial reporting objectives for each specific enterprise. However, managers have their own motivations that influence their selection of accounting policies and their accounting estimates. These motivations often conflict with users' objectives and may dominate the accounting choice process if the users lack the power to enforce the dominance of their objectives. This section will briefly discuss the most common management motivations.

### Income Maximization or Minimization

*Maximization of net income* is one of the most common motivations of managers, particularly in public companies. This motive stems from three powerful concerns:

1. To make it easier to comply with debt covenants, and to provide a margin of safety between the covenant requirements and the reported numbers (to keep lenders from getting edgy);

2. To positively influence users' judgement in evaluating the performance of management (to help them keep their jobs and to enhance their public standing); and

3. To enhance managers' compensation in the many corporations wherein management compensation is tied either to net income or to stock price performance (or both).

These concerns are particularly relevant for the managers of public companies because ownership is dispersed and there is a general concern on the part of the shareholders and the Board of Directors about the share price. Managers believe, with good reason, that share prices are affected by reported earnings.

There is ample evidence to show that investors in an efficient public market are able to "see through" accounting manipulations that are intended to maximize earnings. However, this ability may be effective only in the short run. In the long run, the information that is necessary to make adjustments for accounting policy differences often disappears from view, and there is no evidence that shareholders are able to "see through" complex earnings maximization objectives. Enron is a prime example of complex earnings maximization devices gone wild.

As well, the wide distribution of shares of a widely held public company makes it infeasible for the managers to point out that their "true" performance may be better than that indicated by earnings numbers that are prepared with the objective (for example) of minimizing income taxes.

**Big Bath**  Sometimes, a corporation will elect to *maximize a loss* in one year as part of an ongoing strategy to *maximize earnings*. The philosophy is that if there will be an operating loss anyway, they might as well take advantage of the opportunity to load as many losses into that year as possible (known as "taking a big bath" or a "big hit").

It is not at all unusual to see a corporation (in a bad year) announcing changes to accounting estimates that increase the total loss, including substantial writedowns of investments and capital assets. If a company writes down its capital assets, less amortization will be charged to expense in future years, thereby enhancing *future* earnings.

Another ploy is to make a substantial provision (charged to expense) for restructuring costs. If these costs turn out to have been overestimated (justified by the principle of *conservatism*), the company will be able to recognize a *gain* in future periods.

**Minimizing Earnings**  Instead of *maximizing* reported earnings, management may wish to *minimize* reported earnings as an ongoing endeavour. In addition to the possible objective of minimizing income taxes, management may strive to reduce earnings for any of the following reasons:

- To avoid public criticism of earnings that may be viewed by the public as "excessive"
- To avoid attracting competitors into a very profitable business
- To discourage hostile takeover bids
- To avoid the scrutiny of regulators or politicians
- To discourage large wage claims by employees, or to justify management initiatives for wage reductions and cutbacks

Accounting policies that *maximize* earnings include early revenue recognition and delayed expense recognition (including a defer-and-amortize approach to the widest possible array of costs). Accounting policies for *minimizing* earnings are just the opposite: delay revenue recognition and expense every cost as soon as possible.

### Income Smoothing

Managers often like to show a smooth record of earnings, free of disturbing peaks and valleys. Widely fluctuating earnings are an indication of business risk, and managers often do not want investors or creditors to perceive the company as being risky.

Income can be smoothed by taking advantage of the many opportunities available (within GAAP) for spreading both revenues and costs over several periods. The defer-and-amortize approach beloved by many managers and by some recommendations of the *CICA Handbook* is a reflection of wide acceptance of the income-smoothing motivation.

Accounting estimates also provide a great opportunity for income smoothing. By edging various accounting estimates up or down within the feasible range, management often can significantly affect the net income amount. Remember that net income is a residual that is only a small proportion of the overall level of activity of the business. It doesn't take much change in the amount of accruals, the estimate of bad debts, or the writedown of inventory to smooth this residual. The impact of accounting estimates is invisible to the external user. There is no need for management to disclose the vast majority of accounting estimates; their impact is simply impounded in the numbers to which they relate.

## Minimum Compliance

**Minimum compliance** refers to the motivation of managers to reveal the least amount of information that is possible while still complying with GAAP.

Minimum compliance may be a motivation for managers in a public company because management does not wish to give outsiders any more information about the company than is absolutely necessary. Managers may wish to maintain confidentiality about their business activities in order to keep competitors in the dark.

*Minimum compliance* is usually equated with *minimum cost* of providing accounting information. However, the buyers and sellers of public companies' shares may value a company's shares at a lower level if they feel that the company is being less than forthcoming about its operations and financial position. Minimum compliance may save accounting and auditing costs, but may bear a cost in reduced share prices.

In a private company, management and the shareholders have access to whatever information they need, and the general financial statements may be used only to accompany the tax return. The information needs of bankers and other lenders may be served by special-purpose reports. In these circumstances, the company is likely also to use accounting policies that coincide (to the extent possible) with the policies used for income tax purposes. Amortization on capital assets, for example, will be calculated on the same basis as for CCA for tax purposes; inventory costs will be calculated on the same basis for accounting and tax purposes; costs that are deductible immediately for income tax purposes will be expensed immediately on the income statement; and so forth.

## Expanded Disclosure

The opposite to minimum compliance may be called **expanded disclosure**. Management may wish to disclose a great deal of information that is not required by GAAP. The motivation for expanded disclosure may simply be to indicate that the company and its management are "good citizens" that have nothing to hide and wish to provide the most informative financial statements possible. Sometimes expanded disclosure is motivated by the expected concerns of specific stakeholders.

For example, a company that might be accused of polluting the environment may choose to disclose its environmental record and its efforts to curb pollution and/or clean up an already-polluted environment. By providing additional disclosure, management may hope to forestall criticism of the company's pollution-control efforts.

In other situations, the company may be complying voluntarily with the disclosure expectations of current or expected future stakeholders outside Canada. For instance, a company that expects to do significant business (or raise significant capital) in Europe may provide supplemental disclosure on its employment record and employment benefits, as well as on environmental and ethical aspects of its business. Such disclosure is expected of responsible companies in Europe, even though these types of disclosures are not a normal part of Canadian (or American) reporting practice.

Finally, a company may provide expanded voluntary disclosures in order to reassure the capital markets that the company is a good investment. For example, management may include information on product demand in the financial statement notes or in management's discussion and analysis, such as (1) the value of current contracts for a service company or (2) the order backlog for a manufacturer.

## ETHICAL ISSUES

Users' objectives and managers' motivations often conflict. Managers are aware of users' objectives, and therefore managers may attempt to present the best picture of the corporation's operations and financial position. The resolution of this conflict depends on general concepts of fair presentation and often presents an ethical dilemma for management, the company's accountants, and auditors.

The WorldCom saga provides an example of an accountant who held her ground in the face of senior management pressure to make an unethical "estimate":

> In an early 2001 effort to reduce costs, Sullivan [CFO] directed General Accounting to reduce the Wireless division's expense for line costs by $150 million. When General Accounting called Delores DiCicco, Vice President of Wireless Finance, requesting her to reduce her line costs, she was surprised because there was no support for the entry. Even after Yates [Director, General Accounting] made several follow-up calls, asking her to make the journal entry following Sullivan's instructions, DiCicco firmly refused. In response, Sullivan told DiCicco that she should make the entry because she would eventually find $150 million in savings from disputed billings ... Still refusing, she argued that she would not book the entry until she found the savings. As a consequence, the requested journal entry was prepared in General Accounting.[5]

## CONCEPT REVIEW

1. Why is it important to establish the financial reporting objectives for a company?

2. Give an example of how the reporting objectives of a public company may differ from those of a private corporation.

3. How might a shareholders' agreement influence a company's financial reporting objectives?

4. Why might the objectives of financial statement users conflict with the motivations of managers?

## INTERNATIONAL PERSPECTIVE

### Format

International standards (both IAS and IFRS) are very similar to Canadian standards in format. They are "principles-based" standards that state the objectives of each standard and then provide guidance for application. Also similar to the AcSB approach, each standard applies to a specific accounting issue or problem. For example, when the standards applying to inventory accounting are revised, the original standard is revised and replaced. This process is similar to the AcSB practice of issuing periodic revisions to sections of the *CICA Handbook*.

In contrast, the U.S. FASB issues a new standard every time accounting for an item is revised. As a result, there are several standards that apply to the same accounting issue, necessitating a thorough search to identify all relevant standards before deciding on the appropriate U.S. accounting treatment.

---

[5] "Behind Closed Doors at WorldCom: 2001," *Issues in Accounting Education,* (February 2004). Copyright © 2004 American Accounting Association. Full text of American Accounting Association articles available at http://aaahq.org/pubs.cfm. See also the *Report of Investigation by the Special Investigative Committee of the Board of Directors of WorldCom Inc.* by Beresford et al., March 31, 2003, available at http://fl1.findlaw.com/news.findlaw.com/hdocs/docs/worldcom/bdspcomm60903rpt.pdf (accessed April 18, 2007).

## Hierarchy of Standards

The IASB identifies a hierarchy for applying accounting sources for resolving reporting issues, although the IASB does not explicitly call it a hierarchy. The hierarchy is similar to the AcSB's:

- All IASB statements, interpretations, and published guidance must be used if they fit the circumstances.

- Other sources may be used if IAS and IFRS do not fit the circumstances, including standards of other jurisdictions when those standards are based on a conceptual framework that is similar to the IASB's.

The IASB conceptual framework is similar to that used by the AcSB and the FASB; Canadian or U.S. standards therefore can be used if they fit the circumstances. We will discuss the conceptual framework in Chapter 2.

## Financial Reporting Objectives

International standards are designed for use in general-purpose financial statements. The IASB specifically states that "general purpose financial statements are those intended to meet the needs of users who are not in a position to demand reports tailored to meet their particular information needs" (IAS 1, para 3). The IASB Framework cites seven different types of financial statement users, but then asserts that meeting the needs of shareholders will "also meet most of the needs of other users" (*Framework for the Preparation and Presentation of Financial Statements,* para 10).

To meet the needs of private companies, the IASB is developing a separate set of standards that will apply to non-public companies that don't need general-purpose statements that are circulated publicly.

Canadian, U.S., and U.K. accounting standards are known as "common law" standards; they emerged over time without statutory authority or explicit legal sanction. In contrast, the accounting standards in many countries (e.g., France, Germany, and China) are set by law. These are known as "code law" countries. Code law is more difficult to change than common law. Therefore, companies in code law countries prepare their separate-entity financial statements in accordance with the legally required national standards and then prepare their consolidated financial statements on the basis of international GAAP.

In the U.S. and Canada, the principle focus of general-purpose statements is on residual earnings for the shareholder. Other countries may place greater emphasis on other stakeholder groups or have different cultural practices. For example,

- Corporations in Sweden are expected to provide information about social responsibility and environmental protection in their annual reports. Accounting information relating to these issues is highlighted in financial reporting.

- German financial reporting places a strong emphasis on creditor protection. The tendency is to understate earnings and to provide for income reserves that have no correspondence in Canadian or international GAAP.

- Many countries emphasize employee protection. Information on employee compensation and benefits must be disclosed in the financial statements, in contrast to Canadian and U.S. practice where it is usually impossible to find out how much operating expense goes to employees.

- Companies that follow Muslim practice do not enter into lending relationships. Instead, banks and other sources of financing enter into equity-based arrangements. Therefore, amounts that would be reported as interest expense in Canada will be dividends in those companies.

- Many countries base income tax on reported earnings; taxable income is equal to accounting income. Income tax minimization therefore becomes a dominant financial reporting objective.

It may seem that these nation-specific reporting objectives for separate-entity statements would have no impact on the consolidated statements prepared under international standards. However, the policy, estimate, and disclosure choices made for the separate-entity statements will flow through to the consolidated statements.

International comparisons of financial statements are fraught with hazard because of these differences. For example, a very high debt load is usually viewed in North America as a bad sign, while low debt is usually a sign of good management. In Germany and Japan, however, low debt indicates that the banks have no confidence in the company—banks will support only strong companies, and thus strong companies have high debt.

## RELEVANT STANDARDS

*CICA Handbook:*
- Introduction to Accounting Standards
- Section 1000, Financial Accounting Concepts
- Section 1100, Generally Accepted Accounting Principles
- Section 1300, Differential Reporting
- Section 1400, General Standards of Financial Statement Presentation

IASB:
- Framework for the Preparation and Presentation of Financial Statements
- *IAS* 1, Presentation of Financial Statements
- *IAS* 8, Accounting Policies, Changes in Accounting Estimates and Errors

## SUMMARY OF KEY POINTS

1. Financial accounting is concerned with the preparation of financial statements that report on the financial position and results of operations for an entity as a whole.

2. A corporation that issues securities (debt or equity) to the general public is a *public corporation* that must abide by the regulations of the securities commissions in the jurisdiction(s) in which its securities are traded.

3. Public corporations generally must comply with GAAP in their financial reporting.

4. The vast majority of corporations in Canada are private corporations. About half of the corporations listed in the FP500 are private. Many large private corporations are wholly owned subsidiaries of non-Canadian parents; many others are family owned. Of large public Canadian corporations, most have a control block that is in individual or family hands.

5. If all of the shareholders agree, a private corporation that does not have public accountability may use *differential reporting*. Differential reporting is permitted by the *CICA Handbook* for a few specific topics. Differential reporting is intended to improve the cost/benefit relationship for corporations with few financial statement users.

6. Private corporations that use other than GAAP and do not use differential reporting may prepare their financial statements on a disclosed basis of accounting (DBA).

7. The AcSB is the standard-setting organization for Canada. The AcSB is part of the CICA.

8. Over the past half century, the AcSB has established Canada-specific accounting standards. In the 1990s, the AcSB decided to harmonize Canadian standards with U.S. standards. In 2006, however, the AcSB decided to go along with the widespread internationalization of accounting standards. Canadian standards for public companies will be replaced by international standards over a transition period expected to last until at least 2011.

9. Once the conversion to international standards is complete, the AcSB will no longer establish standards for public companies. However, the AcSB will continue to establish and maintain standards for private companies.

10. The *CICA Handbook* identifies two levels of authority for GAAP: (1) *primary* sources, which consist of AcSB–issued recommendations, guidelines, EIC abstracts, and related background and illustrative material; and (2) *other* (or secondary) sources, including standards issued by the FASB and the IASB, implementation guides issued by groups other than the AcSB, research studies, and other materials that reflect the Canadian reporting environment. Secondary sources are appropriate only if their application is based on the accounting concepts in *CICA Handbook* Section 1000 and reflect the exercise of professional judgement.

11. The *Income Tax Act* and the regulations and policies of the CRA are *not* a part of GAAP. However, income taxation does have an impact on the accounting policies used by corporations because the accounting policies may affect the amount of tax paid. A copy of a corporation's financial statements (unconsolidated) must be appended to its tax return, and all differences between taxable income and accounting income must be reconciled in a supporting schedule to the tax return, the T2(S1).

12. International standards are developed by the IASB, the successor to the IASC that was founded in 1973.

13. IAS are widely accepted on international stock exchanges for the financial reporting of foreign companies. European companies are required to use international standards for consolidated statements. Developing countries usually adopt international standards instead of attempting to establish their own accounting standards.

14. It is impossible to impose a single, dominant objective on financial reporting. The objectives of financial reporting must be determined with reference to the organization's environment and its stakeholders, and with regard to the users' decisions that the financial statements are intended to facilitate.

15. *Cash flow prediction* is a financial reporting objective that is often appropriate for lenders, creditors, and shareholders. Financial stakeholders need to predict a corporation's ability to generate cash flow from operations and to service debt or to pay dividends. Under a cash flow objective, revenues and expenses are recognized in a way that corresponds (on an accrual basis) with cash flow.

16. *Income tax minimization* is another very common objective, especially for private corporations. Public corporations are less likely to have this as a primary objective because they may be more concerned about the perceptions of other users of the statements than about saving taxes in the short run. An income tax minimization objective leads to delayed revenue recognition and faster expense recognition.

17. Financial statement readers often use the statements to assess the corporation's adherence to contract requirements, such as those in loan agreements and shareholders' agreements.

18. A major objective is that of performance evaluation. Statements that are prepared to facilitate the evaluation of management's performance will use reporting policies that coincide as closely as possible to the basis for management's operating decisions.

19. Managers are the preparers of financial statements. Managers often have motivations that stem from their desire to influence the decisions of external users, particularly those of public companies. Managers may be tempted to adopt accounting policies and make accounting estimates that tend to maximize reported earnings, minimize earnings, smooth earnings, or show compliance with contract provisions such as loan covenants.

20. The motivations of preparers often conflict with the financial reporting objectives that are appropriate for external users in a particular situation. Accountants must use their professional judgement to try to reconcile such conflicts ethically and to avoid issuing financial statements that contain biased measurements.

## KEY TERMS

Accounting Guidelines, 11
authoritative pronouncements, 9
control block, 4
covenants, 20
differential reporting, 5
disclosed basis of accounting, 5
expanded disclosure, 23
financial accounting, 2
financial reporting, 2
generally accepted accounting principles
  (GAAP), 8

historical accounting practices, 8
International Accounting Standards
  (IAS), 9
International Financial Reporting Standards
  (IFRS), 15
maintenance tests, 20
minimum compliance, 23
objectives of financial reporting, 16
private placements, 4
restricted shares, 4
shareholders' agreements, 20

## QUESTIONS

Q1-1    What is the difference between public and private companies? What are the accounting implications of this difference?

Q1-2    What is a control block? What are the accounting policy implications?

Q1-3    Define GAAP, including their sources.

Q1-4    What body sets standards in Canada? What organizations have given authority to these standards?

Q1-5    What are the primary sources of GAAP? Explain.

Q1-6    What is differential reporting?

Q1-7    What is a disclosed basis of accounting? Explain.

Q1-8    Explain the evolution of Canadian accounting standards. What is the policy that the AcSB is now following?

Q1-9    What is the IASB? Describe the status of IASB standards.

Q1-10   Explain the importance of IASB standards around the world.

Q1-11   What are the objectives of general purpose financial statements? What common specific objectives may a set of financial statements be tailored to serve?

Q1-12   If a set of financial statements were meant to portray the cash flows of an organization, what kinds of accounting policies would likely be chosen?

Q1-13   What accounting policies would best serve the reporting objective of tax minimization?

Q1-14   What is a covenant? What kinds of accounting policies would be common among companies with severe restrictive covenants?

Q1-15   Describe how the motivations of managers are different than those of shareholders. What accounting policies might be commonly found if managers receive bonuses based on net income?

Q1-16   What is income-smoothing? What is a "big bath"?

Q1-17   What would characterize a set of financial statements designed to provide minimum compliance?

## CASE 1-1

## INTERNATIONAL FASHIONS INC.

You are an accounting student who has obtained a summer internship with the national public accounting firm of Nash & Crosby. Your manager has been giving you various tasks to test your abilities and your perceptions.

The firm has recently acquired a new corporate audit client, International Fashions Inc. (IFI). Your manager has given you the previous year's financial statements (unaudited) and has asked you to conduct some research into the client's operations. You are to prepare a memo in which you describe the objectives that you believe should shape the financial reporting of the company.

After viewing the company's website and searching other information sources, you learn the following information:

- The company is an Ontario corporation founded in 1976. The corporate headquarters and executive offices are near Toronto.
- The shareholders are two brothers who immigrated to Canada from Hong Kong in 1972. The brothers are both active managers of the company and its affiliates. The directors are all members of the brothers' families.
- The company operates a chain of 126 women's fashion clothing stores. There is one store in each of Toronto, Montreal, and New York City. All of the other stores are located in Hong Kong, Taiwan, Singapore, and mainland China (P.R.C.).
- Most of the company's clothing is produced by factories in Xiamen, China, by a separate company that is also owned by the two brothers. Two designers work full-time in the company's headquarters near Toronto to design the clothing that is manufactured in Xiamen.
- The stores in North America are owned and operated by IFI directly. Those three stores are the "flagship" stores, intended to give an upscale North American flavour to the company's products. To further enhance the Canadian "origin" of the company, all models used in IFI's advertising, in all markets, are western rather than Asian. The company prefers to use high-profile international public figures and entertainers as its fashion models.
- The stores in Hong Kong, Taiwan, and Singapore are operated by three separate wholly owned IFI subsidiaries, one for each area. Some of the profits from these subsidiaries are returned to the parent company through management fees, while the rest remain in the subsidiary to finance expansion and store renewal.
- The stores in mainland China are operated through an IFI subsidiary that has a local partner. As a foreign corporation, the company is entitled to special tax advantages that are not available to Chinese companies. The China subsidiary must pay 35% of the subsidiary's net income to the partner.
- IFI, as a separate entity, currently has no long-term debt. IFI has relied almost exclusively on retained earnings to finance its growth for the past 20 years. In its early stages, the company narrowly averted bankruptcy caused by high debt and various supply problems. Since then, management has been reluctant to use debt financing. However, the company does stretch payment periods for its accounts payable and effectively forces the suppliers to bear the cost of the inventory until the product is sold. The accounts payable debt is on the books of whichever company (i.e., the IFI parent or each of the Asian subsidiaries) received the inventory. About two-thirds of the total company-wide accounts payable is owed to the brothers' Xiamen company.
- IFI is eager to rapidly expand the number of stores that it operates in cities in eastern China. Rapid expansion will require external sources of funds.

**Required:**

Prepare the memo for your manager.

**CASE 1-2**

## METROPOLITAN TRANSIT INCORPORATED

Metropolitan Transit Inc. (MTI) is a privately owned corporation that runs a bus service between the city of Metropolis and the suburb of Sprawl. The company is owned by Mr. Victor Li and his father. Victor is the CEO and president of the company.

The company has long-term mortgages on most of its bus fleet. The mortgages are held by the Royal Dominion Bank of Nova Scotia.

The bus service is run under a franchise granted by the town council of Sprawl. The franchise is for 10 years and is renewable by mutual agreement of MTI and Sprawl town council at the end of the 10-year period.

MTI is eligible for subsidies from Sprawl if the company is unable to achieve a rate of return on total assets of at least 12% per year. The subsidy is equal to the difference between MTI's reported net income and the 12% target.

As a private for-profit corporation, MTI is subject to federal and provincial taxation.

### Required:

Explain the probable financial reporting objectives for Metropolitan Transit Inc. Rank the probable objectives from most important to least important, and explain the reasons for your ranking.

**CASE 1-3**

## CHAN & BAAZ

Sandy Chan and Philip Baaz have operated an import and sales partnership for 15 years. They import a variety of food products into Canada and distribute them through small grocery stores and some chains in southern Ontario. At times, they have made up to $150,000 per year (profits and losses are split evenly); however, a recession has hurt their business, and profits were $80,000 last year. Philip Baaz, in his late 50s and financially secure, has decided to retire. Tired of Canadian winters, he has retired to Mexico and left the partnership in Sandy Chan's hands.

Sandy Chan is in his mid-40s, and through a series of personal tribulations, is nowhere near as financially secure as his partner. He does not have the resources to buy out Baaz personally, and there is no cash in the partnership at the moment. Assets consist of receivables and inventory. A significant downsizing would be required to buy out Baaz with a payment from the partnership right now. Baaz, however, is in no hurry for his money. The partners have agreed that for the rest of this year, Chan will operate the business alone, and profits will be split evenly. At year-end, Baaz will leave the partnership and take back a five-year note payable for the book value of the balance in his partnership account, which would include his share of current-year profits. While Baaz would not have helped generate this year's profits, this allocation was agreed to be fair due to his past contributions.

At the end of the year, you have arrived to prepare the financial statements for the year. You are a professional accountant. The partnership has been your client for 15 years (since the partnership was formed), and you are on excellent terms with the partners and their staff. You have met with the bookkeeper and obtained the following information:

- The partnership has always established an allowance for doubtful accounts based on specific identification of problem accounts, since Chan and Baaz had personal contact with their customers. This year, the allowance has been based on a percentage of sales—at a rate that is double the historical trend. The bookkeeper has assured you that most receivables are current, but "there's a recession on and we expect some problems to crop up."

- During the year, a sizable amount of inventory acquired during the last two years was written off. The bookkeeper explained that the product was not perishable, and it was still in the warehouse. The product was very slow moving, and Chan had given up trying to sell it.

- A personal computer and laser printer were acquired for office use late in the year. Consistent with prior policy, a full year's amortization was booked in the year of acquisition. Previous office equipment has been amortized using the straight-line method, but the computer is being amortized on a 40% declining-balance scheme "because of the risk of technological obsolescence."

You have a meeting scheduled with Chan this afternoon to discuss accounting policies and operating results; Baaz is still in Mexico.

### Required:

Write a brief report on which to base your discussion with Chan. Describe how Chan and Baaz have different reporting objectives. Outline the issues and alternatives, then write an analysis of each issue and your recommendation.

(CGA-Canada, adapted) Extracts from *Financial Accounting* 1 and 2, published by the Certified General Accountants Association of Canada, © CGA-Canada, reproduced with permission. Because of *Tax Act* updates and/or changes to the *CICA Handbook*, the contents of examinations published before 2005 may be out of date; therefore, the currency of the contents is the sole responsibility of the user.

# ASSIGNMENTS

★ **A1-1 Chapter Overview:** Indicate whether each of the following statements is true or false.

1. All GAAP are the result of a designated rule-making body.
2. Canada's accounting standards are completely harmonized with international standards.
3. Canadian GAAP must be used for the financial statements of every Canadian corporation.
4. GAAP includes practices that have evolved and gained acceptance over time, even when not codified in writing.
5. The primary objective of financial accounting is for appraising the performance of management.
6. The presence of restrictive bond covenants, specifying minimum times-interest-earned ratios, means that an organization will have a tendency to pick discretionary accounting policies that minimize income. (Note: Times-interest-earned is calculated as income before interest and taxes, divided by interest.)
7. External decision makers have direct access to the information generated by the internal operations of a company.
8. Income tax law has no impact on the accounting choices made by management.
9. The presence of a control block can have an impact on a company's choice of accounting policies.
10. IFRS are developed by an international association of exchange commissions in order to facilitate international capital markets.
11. The EIC provides technical guidance to the AcSB on matters of broad importance and scope.

★ **A1-2 Chapter Overview:** Indicate whether each statement is true or false.

1. Financial accounting focuses primarily on the needs of creditors.
2. The standard-setting process followed by the AcSB allows for due process input by the user and preparer communities before a standard is promulgated.

3. Under the *CICA Handbook* recommendations, there can be no difference in financial reporting between public and private companies.
4. The debt and equity securities of a private company cannot be traded on public exchanges. Therefore, private companies have no external sources of financing.
5. IFRS and the *CICA Handbook* have equal stature in Canada for public company financial reporting.
6. A company that wishes to report smooth earnings is attempting to appear less risky to financial statement users.
7. Entities whose financial reports are meant to address cash flow objectives are primarily concerned with maximizing cash flows from operating activities.
8. The AcSB plans to shut down and let all Canadian companies use international standards.
9. The IASB can require transnational companies to use IASB standards.
10. A public company may not use DBA for external public financial reporting.

★★ **A1-3 Neutrality and Standard Setting:** You have recently attended a conference on behalf of your manager. One speaker stated:

> Accounting standards must be precise in order to prevent manipulation by unethical managers and professional accountants. We must tighten the restrictions on all types of transaction reporting in order to prevent the sort of flagrant misstatement that occurred in Enron, WorldCom, Nortel, and others. Rule-based U.S. standards are far superior to principles-based standards such as those of the CICA and IASB, even though U.S. standards also need strengthening.

**Required:**
Write a memo to your manager that discusses the issues raised by this speaker.

★ **A1-4 Acronyms:** The language of accounting is littered with acronyms, abbreviations for common organizations or phrases. Match the phrase or organization on the left with its abbreviation.

| Phrase or Organization | Abbreviation |
| --- | --- |
| 1. International Accounting Standards Board | A. AcSB |
| 2. Emerging Issues Committee | B. GAAP |
| 3. Ontario Securities Commission | C. IFRS |
| 4. Accounting Standards Board | D. CICA |
| 5. Financial Accounting Standards Board | E. SEC |
| 6. Canadian Institute of Chartered Accountants | F. CBCA |
| 7. Securities and Exchange Commission | G. DBA |
| 8. *Canada Business Corporations Act* | H. OSC |
| 9. Disclosed Basis of Accounting | I. IASB |
| 10. Generally Accepted Accounting Principles | J. FASB |
| 11. International Financial Reporting Standards | K. EIC |

★ **A1-5 Accounting Choices:** The practice of accounting requires many choices. Making informed and reasonable choices is the exercise of *professional judgement.* Professional judgement must be used for

a. accounting policies
b. accounting estimates

For each of the accounting decisions listed below, indicate whether the required choice is one of policy, measurement, or estimate:

1. The useful life of a newly acquired building;
2. The types of overhead cost to include in the cost of manufactured inventory;

3. The amount of bad-debt expense for the year;

4. Depreciation method to use for trucks (e.g., straight line or declining balance);

5. The future costs to be incurred in a planned restructuring of an operating division (e.g., employee severance payments, relocation costs, the costs of rearranging a factory's physical layout);

6. The costs to be capitalized as part of the total cost of buying and installing new equipment;

7. Inventory cost flow assumption (e.g., FIFO or average cost); and

8. The Canadian dollar equivalent of funds held in a Mexican bank account in Mexican pesos.

---

★ **A1-6 Accounting Choices:** For each of the situations listed below, state what judgements are necessary when preparing financial statements:

1. Due to slow sales volume during December, a toy store has an unexpectedly large inventory at the end of its fiscal year, 31 January.

2. IMF Inc. has been sued by another company for trademark infringement. The other company has won a judgement against IMF for $1.5 million. IMF is appealing the decision to a higher court. IMF's lawyers are confident that IMF will win the appeal.

3. One of Sukkor Corporation's major clients has gone into creditor protection. The client accounts for 40% of Sukkor's outstanding accounts receivable. Sukkor has filed a court claim against the client (along with other unsecured creditors), but a loss of somewhere between 20% and 35% of the receivable is likely.

4. Pacific Alliance has just finished producing a new computer-animated motion picture intended for DVD distribution for children. The total accumulated production cost is $3.4 million. Pacific Alliance has signed a distribution agreement with a major supplier of educational materials, including DVDs. Normally, Pacific Alliance's earlier movies of the same general type have a sales life of about 3 years—slow to start, then increasing acceptance, followed by market saturation and obsolescence.

5. CanBuild Ltd. signed a fixed-price contract for construction of a 45-storey condominium apartment building in downtown Calgary. Construction has been underway for almost a full year, and about 40% of the estimated total costs have been incurred so far. Construction costs are rising rapidly in Calgary due to the Alberta oil boom.

---

★★ **A1-7 Effect of Accounting Policies:** A company has two debt covenants in place:

a. Maximum debt-to-equity ratio
   • Current and long-term liabilities, excluding future income taxes, are divided by total shareholders' equity

b. Minimum times-interest-earned ratio
   • Income before interest and taxes is divided by total interest expense

For each of the accounting policy choices listed below, indicate which ratio(s), if any, would be affected, and whether the policy would increase or decrease the ratio.

1. Depreciation method is straight line, rather than declining balance.

2. Costs that could either be deferred and written off or expensed immediately are expensed immediately.

3. Interest expense could be measured using straight-line amortization for the debt discount; alternatively, the effective interest rate method could be used. The straight-line method results in lower interest expense in the early years, and is the chosen policy.

4. An issue of preferred shares that has the characteristics of debt (guaranteed cash flows to the investor), is reclassified as debt, from the equity section.

5. Warranty expense is accrued as sales are made, rather than expensing it as warranty claims are paid.

6. Revenue is recorded as goods are delivered, rather than when cash is later collected.

★ **A1-8 Differential Reporting:** For each of the situations below, explain whether or not the company can use the differential reporting provisions of the *CICA Handbook*:

1. The owner-manager of Bon Nuit Limited wishes to use the "taxes payable" method of reporting income tax expense. In all other respects, Bon Nuit will follow the recommendations of the *CICA Handbook*. The owner-manager is the only shareholder.

2. Both shareholders of Gute Nacht Corporation have agreed with management's intent to report the company's land and buildings on the balance sheet at appraised market value instead of cost, although this valuation is not specifically included in the differential reporting section of the *CICA Handbook*.

3. The management of Wahn-Ahn Inc., a private B.C. corporation, wishes to issue unconsolidated financial statements, as permitted by the differential reporting provisions. The owners of 90% of Wahn-Ahn's shares have agreed.

4. Buouno Notte Financial Corporation is a private corporation wholly owned by a public holding company based in Winnipeg. The company wishes to avail itself of all the differential reporting provisions specified by the *CICA Handbook*. The shareholder (i.e., the holding company) approves.

★ **A1-9 Reporting Alternatives:** For each of the situations below, explain whether the company can use its preferred basis of accounting instead of Canadian GAAP:

1. A Great Lakes shipping company based in Thunder Bay, Ontario, wishes to use U.S. dollars as its reporting currency. Shipping on the Great Lakes is always priced in U.S. dollars. The company prefers to use Canadian GAAP rather than U.S. GAAP.

2. The Canadian subsidiary of a U.K. carpet manufacturer wishes to use U.K. GAAP instead of Canadian GAAP. The subsidiary is wholly owned by the U.K. parent.

3. A privately owned rapidly expanding auto parts manufacturer based in Ontario has rapidly expanding operations in the U.S., China, and Korea. The company is in the early planning stages for an initial public offering of restricted shares. The company's new shares will be listed on the Toronto Stock Exchange. Because of the increasing globalization of the company, management wants to use IASB standards to facilitate possible future listings on European and Asian stock exchanges.

4. An expanding publicly owned airline corporation is soliciting substantial new investment from private Canadian investors. One potential investor has requested that the corporation submit to him special private financial statements that do not follow certain recommendations of the *CICA Handbook*.

5. Eighty-five percent of the shares of Oreluxe Corporation, a Canadian mining company, have been acquired by an Australian mining company. In prior years, Oreluxe reported on the basis of Canadian GAAP and Canadian dollars. The new parent corporation proposes to change to Australian GAAP, which is completely harmonized with international GAAP. Oreluxe's shares are traded on the Toronto Stock Exchange.

★ **A1-10 GAAP Hierarchy:** Listed below are several sources of GAAP:

1. Accounting textbooks
2. Statements of Financial Accounting Standards issued by the FASB (U.S.)
3. Research reports issued by the Certified General Accountants Association of Canada
4. Implementation guides issued by authority of the AcSB
5. IAS and IFRS issued by the IASB
6. Non-italicized paragraphs in the *CICA Handbook*
7. Accounting guides published by industry trade associations
8. EIC Abstracts
9. Accounting law in China, as applied to a wholly owned subsidiary of a Canadian company that will be consolidated with the parent
10. Illustrative examples accompanying the appendices in accounting guidelines

**Required:**

Using the item number, rearrange the list in order of authority, from the highest authority to the lowest. For each item in the list, indicate whether it is a primary source or another source.

---

 **A1-11 Authoritative Sources of GAAP:** The Thistle Whistle Corporation is a private company incorporated in Alberta. The company's banker insists that the company submit audited financial statements "in accordance with GAAP" in order to maintain a line of credit that is essential to the company's financial health. The company has recently developed a new method of selling its products that involves the Internet, brokers, out-of-country warehouses, and various intermediary offshore bankers. Management has been recognizing revenue as soon as possible, but the company's auditors have indicated that they are not pleased with the revenue recognition method Thistle is using.

The *CICA Handbook* recommendations are silent on Thistle's particular type of transaction, but Thistle's desired accounting policy does not seem to fit the *CICA Handbook's* general requirements for revenue recognition. However, the company's controller has gone to other sources of GAAP and has found the following:

a. An Internet industry guide published by an Internet trade association that encourages early revenue recognition and indirectly supports Thistle's position.
b. An exposure draft in another country that suggests Thistle's method as one possible option.
c. A private report from a Canadian accounting consultant that states that Thistle's proposed methodology "recognizes the full earnings potential of Thistle's innovative ways of doing business."
d. An article in a U.S. financial analysis magazine that cites Thistle's revenue recognition policy as a particularly innovative method of accounting.

There is no EIC Abstract that deals with this issue, nor has the AcSB issued an Accounting Guideline on the subject.

**Required:**

Write a report to the controller of Thistle to explain whether the authoritative support for Thistle's revenue recognition policy is adequate.

---

 **A1-12 Non-GAAP Situations:** A manager of a medium-sized, private company recently complained, "I'm confused! I always thought that companies had to comply with GAAP. Now I hear that there are many companies that don't use GAAP, and other circumstances where GAAP is not really appropriate."

**Required:**

Explain the status of GAAP to this manager. Be sure to distinguish between general-purpose and special-purpose financial statements.

---

 **A1-13 Impact of Differing Objectives:** BlueScreen Corporation is primarily a retailer of computer equipment for individuals and small business. The effective cost of computer equipment and peripherals, both at retail and at the manufacturing level, has been declining rapidly for many years and shows every sign of continuing that decline.

The company also develops software intended for small business applications—that is, for companies with up to 500 employees. The software is sold in BlueScreen's own stores as well as through the company website. However, most sales come through general software distributors (e.g., download.com).

For sales through the distributors, purchasers can obtain a 30-day limited-feature trial by paying an initial fee equal to 10% of the retail price of the software. If the customer decides to buy after 30 days, the trial fee is credited to the total cost of the purchase. On average, about 2/3 of the trials result in final purchase. Software development is a continuous process, including updates of existing software.

Some of BlueScreen's accounting issues are as follows:

1. What inventory methods should be used for retail merchandise in its stores and warehouses?
2. How should the software development cost be accounted for?
3. How should the company account for tangible capital assets such as the warehouse building (which it owns), stores (which are leased), and store fixtures.
4. All of the company's personnel—retail, managerial, and software development—are sent annually to professional development programs to keep their skills at the cutting edge of performance. The company spends many millions of dollars on these programs each year.
5. The company opens an average of 20 new stores each year. About five stores are closed each year.

**Required:**

Using the chart below, indicate the accounting policies that the company should choose for each of these issues under each of three *different* primary financial reporting objectives:

1. Earnings maximization
2. Cash flow prediction
3. Earnings minimization

| Issue | Earnings Maximization | Cash Flow Prediction | Earnings Minimization |
|-------|----------------------|---------------------|----------------------|
| 1 | | | |
| 2 | | | |
| 3 | | | |
| 4 | | | |
| 5 | | | |

 **A1-14 Canadian versus IASB Standards:** There are many similarities, but also some significant differences, between most national GAAP and IASB standards. Explain the factors that support common standards, and the factors that cause differences between accounting standards of countries.

**A1-15 International Harmonization of Accounting Standards:** What will Canada gain from achieving a greater harmonization (less diversity) in worldwide accounting standards? Write a brief essay to support your opinion. Include a description of the IASB and the status of IASB standards in your response.

 **A1-16 Standard-Setting Process:** The accounting profession has a long history of developing accounting standards that are part of GAAP. Listed below are some stages in the due process that creates accounting standards.

| Order Description | Step | Activity |
|-------------------|------|----------|
| | 1. Re-exposure Draft | A. Circulated to accountants and interested users |
| | 2. Analyze public comments | B. Identify accounting problems and issues |
| | 3. Revisions | C. Modifications recirculated for feedback |
| | 4. Project proposal | D. Comments from specific individuals on the ED |
| | 5. Exposure draft | E. Final product |
| | 6. *CICA Handbook* section | F. Changes based on written feedback |

**Required:**
Consult the CICA website (www.cica.ca; home>standards>accounting>about ACSB). Indicate the order of the steps above, and match each step with a description of the activity.

---

★ **A1-17 Accounting Policy Disagreement:** You have been hired as the assistant in the finance department of a medium-sized publicly traded firm. Realizing the importance of accounting to your new duties, you have recently completed an introductory course in financial accounting. In this course, you learned that research costs are expensed during the period they are incurred. You also recall, however, that accountants believe in matching the costs of a given activity with the revenues resulting from that activity.

Recently your firm has developed an important breakthrough in electronic copying equipment. The research cost has been considerable. If this cost were capitalized this year and written off against expected future revenues from the new machine that will eventually be developed, this year's earnings per share would increase by 10% rather than show a modest decline.

Your superior clearly favours capitalization because the firm's CEO wants to continue a 20-quarter record of increasing earnings per share figures. She has asked your opinion based on your recent exposure to accounting standards. A meeting with your superior is set for tomorrow morning.

In the meantime, you have researched your firm's past practice in this area and you have reread the relevant accounting standard. Although your firm has not previously experienced the level of research expenses associated with the present project, past practice in your firm has been to expense these costs. Your reading of the accounting standard confirms what you recall from class—namely, that these expenditures should be expensed.

Unfortunately, your superior is anxious to take the alternative position and has been known to be intolerant of views differing from her own. How would you handle the meeting the next day?

**Required:**
Explain the status of GAAP to this manager. Be sure to distinguish between general purpose and special purpose financial statements.

---

★ **A1-18 Accounting Policies and Reporting Objectives:** Entities may have a variety of corporate reporting objectives specific to their circumstances, such as

a. Assessing and predicting cash flows;
b. Income tax minimization;
c. Contract compliance (in this case, debt covenants that specify minimum levels of shareholders' equity); and
d. Performance evaluation of managers.

For each of the accounting policies listed below, indicate which of the objectives of corporate reporting is best served. Each policy may serve more than one objective.

1. Capitalize and amortize costs.
2. Provide full disclosure of five-year cash flow for loan repayments.
3. Defer expenses to match them against revenue generated from the activity.
4. Recognize revenue as cash is collected.
5. Defer revenue as long as possible.
6. Recognize revenues as effort is spent.
7. Recognize expenses close to the time that they are paid for.

---

★★ **A1-19 Objectives of Financial Reporting:** The *CICA Handbook* sets out the objectives of general purpose financial statements, but companies and their managers have objectives that relate to their specific circumstances. Explain how these objectives impact on the choice of accounting policy and when differential reporting may be appropriate.

 **A1-20 Policy Choice:** Marcon Properties Ltd. is a diversified company that owns approximately 60 retail properties, which the company has operated as discount department stores. These stores are small, stand-alone properties that Marcon owns outright, although most properties are heavily mortgaged. In 20X1, the company decided, due to increasing losses from retail operations, that all discount department stores should be closed and properties converted to rental units. This process was successfully started in 20X1, with 22 of 60 properties signed to long-term rental agreements with tenants. It is now the end of 20X1, and all retail operations have ceased. There are 38 properties currently sitting vacant. Marcon believes that it can successfully lease the remaining properties over the next 9 to 23 months.

An accounting policy issue has come up, in relation to the vacant properties, for the 20X1 fiscal year; namely, whether the properties should be amortized during the period that they sit vacant prior to rental. Those in favour of recording amortization point out that the properties continue to deteriorate during the period in which they are idle, and that amortization is meant to allow for obsolescence, not just wear and tear. Those who favour suspension of amortization point out that amortization should be matched with the rental revenue that the properties will generate in the future.

Marcon is reporting a positive net income in 20X1, generated from a variety of other activities.

### Required:

Explain which accounting policy you would expect to be adopted in the following independent circumstances. Note that in some circumstances, the company will be indifferent as to the policy chosen.

1. Marcon has a team of senior managers who are compensated with a cash bonus based on a percentage of annual net income. Senior managers will pick the policy.
2. Marcon is financed 60% through debt and 40% through equity, and has debt covenants that specify minimum debt-to-equity and return on assets (net income divided by total assets.)
3. Marcon is managed by its major shareholders, who wish to minimize income tax payments.
4. Marcon is a public company and wants to show a smooth earnings trend.
5. Marcon has a team of senior managers who are compensated with a cash bonus based on a percentage of annual income. Assume for this part only that the company will report a loss in 20X1 from other sources, and managers will not receive any bonus this year.
6. Marcon's controlling shareholders are not directly involved in the business and they wish to use the financial statements as a method to evaluate the stewardship and performance of managers.

## CHAPTER 2

# Criteria for Accounting Choices

## INTRODUCTION

This chapter lays out the common criteria that accountants use to develop financial statements that can be relied on by external decision makers. Accounting policy choice is often a matter of professional judgement, and there is reasonable evidence to indicate that choice is difficult and contentious.

For example, Nortel announced in October 2003 that it intended to restate approximately $900 million of liabilities, along with net income and retained earnings, following an internal review of these liabilities. This first restatement was followed by an announcement of a second planned restatement regarding revenue recognition, this time involving billions of dollars. Twelve senior executives returned bonuses of $8.6 million that were based on erroneous information, and 10 senior executives were ousted in 2004. However, restated 2003 financial statements were not issued until April 2006, following several delays, while the appropriate accounting treatment for revenue issues haunted the company. Nortel, of course, demonstrated the burst of the "tech bubble" on financial markets—

the Nortel share price hit a high of $124 in 2000 and plunged to $0.69 at its lowest point.

The root cause of the incorrect financial reporting at Nortel, and the delays in restatement, is hotly debated—and the subject of ongoing investigation. However, some of the uncertainty surely reflects basic disagreements about how a given set of economic circumstances should be reflected in the financial statements. Why do such disagreements occur?

There are underlying concepts and principles of accounting to help to guide standard setters, and all accountants using professional judgement to deal with policy issues. This chapter lays out the underlying assumptions of our accounting model, and discusses the qualitative criteria needed to provide useful information. The chapter reviews recognition and measurement criteria. The elements of the financial statements are established in theoretical terms. We emphasize the critical role of professional judgement, based on set criteria rather than uninformed opinion or bias.

## SORTING OUT ACCOUNTING "PRINCIPLES"

The general body of accounting principles can be sorted into three different types of concepts: *underlying assumptions, measurement methods,* and *qualitative criteria.* They may be distinguished as follows:

- **Underlying assumptions** (or **postulates**) are the basic foundation upon which generally accepted accounting rests. For example, the accounting principle (or *concept*) of continuity (also called going concern) is an *underlying assumption.*
- **Measurement methods** (or **measurement conventions**) are the various ways in which financial position and the results of operations can be reported. These are the *accounting choices* that must be made. The accounting principles of historical cost and matching are examples of measurement conventions, both of which are based on the underlying assumption of continuity.
- **Qualitative criteria** (or **qualitative characteristics**) are the criteria that, *in conjunction with the organization's reporting objectives,* are used to evaluate the possible measurement options and choose the most appropriate accounting policies *for the given situation.* The principles of comparability and understandability are examples of *qualitative criteria.*

Measurement methods are *how* transactions and events are measured and reported; qualitative criteria are *why* they are measured that way, provided that the underlying assumptions are valid in the particular situation.

For example, historical cost is a widely used measurement method in which assets are reported at their acquisition cost. Historical cost (a *measurement method*) is commonly used because it is perceived as being more objective (a *qualitative criterion*) than possible alternative measurement methods. But the use of historical cost depends on the reporting enterprise's continuity as a continuing entity (an *underlying assumption*).

To set standards and to understand the accounting choice process, it is necessary to clearly differentiate between underlying assumptions, measurement methods, and qualitative characteristics. Otherwise one becomes hopelessly entangled in fuzzy conceptualization that fails to recognize implicit assumptions.

For example, *historical cost* is not a fundamental concept of financial accounting, but *objectivity* is. Without a high degree of objectivity provided by historical cost, accounting reports would have less credibility and accounting would not serve its most basic societal mission of conveying information. But there are many situations in which historical cost is not the appropriate measurement method, situations in which market value is both highly objective and more *relevant* (which is another qualitative criterion).

### Structure of Policy Choice

To construct financial statements for a particular enterprise, it is necessary to first establish the facts of the business and its operating and economic environment, then determine the objectives of financial reporting, and finally develop the statements by using situation-appropriate accounting policies to measure the elements of the financial statements.

This process can be illustrated by the pyramid shown in Exhibit 2-1. The financial statements themselves are the apex of the process; the foundation is provided by the objectives, facts, and constraints for the reporting enterprise. The objectives, facts, and constraints were introduced in Chapter 1; this chapter will focus on the three levels of principles that build upon the objectives, facts, and constraints. Exhibit 2-1 can be used to organize a very complex structure for both standard setting and application.

## THE FINANCIAL STATEMENT CONCEPTS

The *CICA Handbook* establishes certain "Financial Statement Concepts" (FSC) in Section 1000. The IASC covers this material in a segment called a "Framework," although this framework is not a standard per se. The purpose and scope of this material is to set out the concepts that underlie the preparation and presentation of financial statements for external users.

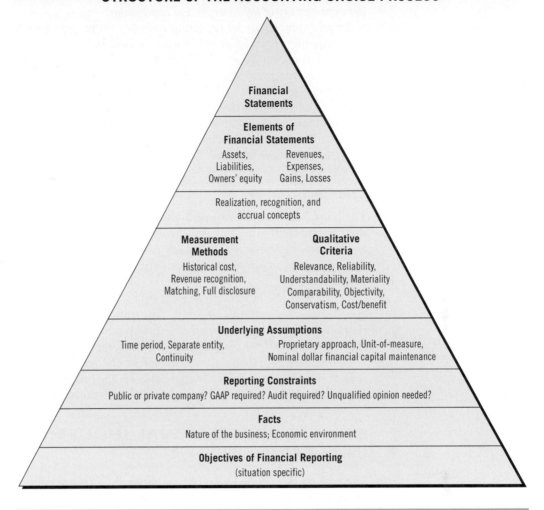

**EXHIBIT 2-1**

## STRUCTURE OF THE ACCOUNTING CHOICE PROCESS

**Financial Statements**

**Elements of Financial Statements**
Assets, Liabilities, Owners' equity
Revenues, Expenses, Gains, Losses

Realization, recognition, and accrual concepts

**Measurement Methods**
Historical cost, Revenue recognition, Matching, Full disclosure

**Qualitative Criteria**
Relevance, Reliability, Understandability, Materiality Comparability, Objectivity, Conservatism, Cost/benefit

**Underlying Assumptions**
Time period, Separate entity, Continuity
Proprietary approach, Unit-of-measure, Nominal dollar financial capital maintenance

**Reporting Constraints**
Public or private company? GAAP required? Audit required? Unqualified opinion needed?

**Facts**
Nature of the business; Economic environment

**Objectives of Financial Reporting**
(situation specific)

---

This material is sometimes characterized as a *conceptual framework*, or *theory*, but these words are not used by the standard setters. The material constitutes an attempt to codify the theoretical basis that the standard setters have used and will use to support solutions to financial reporting problems. In general, the intended users of this material include

- Standard setters, whether setting new standards or evaluating existing standards;
- Those working to understand the rationale for standards;
- Accountants seeking to establish appropriate accounting policy in areas where there are no standards, using ethical professional judgement; and
- Financial statement users who are interpreting information prepared in conformity with the concepts.

The material defines the elements of financial statements (e.g., assets, liabilities, revenues, expenses) and describes basic recognition and measurement criteria. Only some of the underlying assumptions (e.g., nominal dollar financial capital maintenance and understandability) and a few qualitative criteria are discussed. Therefore, this material is not comprehensive.

## Limitations of the Concepts

The financial statement concepts established by the standard setters pertain to general-purpose financial statements. *General-purpose* statements are those prepared for distribution to a wide, undefined public. Thus, statements prepared for a *specific* use may well have attributes different than those described in the concepts. Since one of the primary purposes of the material is to help standard setters determine appropriate policies for wide application, their focus on generalities is appropriate. *But it also means that there are exceptions to the applicability of the concepts and conclusions!*

In addition, financial reporting includes more than just financial statements; for public companies, it includes other information in the annual report as well as information included in prospectuses. The concepts relate only to the statements themselves. Remember, too, that an enterprise can communicate financial results through various media. For example, press releases and statements made in interviews result in fast, widespread dissemination of information as does information posted on a company's website.

The financial statements themselves are limited to financial information about transactions and events. The information is based on past transactions, not future events, although many estimates are required about future transactions and events.

### The Environment

The basic business environment affects financial reporting. In Canada, much of the economy is represented by investor-owned business enterprises, although many activities, like health care, are carried out through government-owned enterprises. Financing of business comes from equity investors and lenders, and these are the external users that financial statements serve.

If the business environment were different, the choices made in the FSC would not be appropriate. For example, in some countries, the norm is that *all* economic activity is carried out by government-owned enterprises, and there is no public stock exchange or private share ownership. In these countries, financial reporting has a much different flavour.

Remember, too, that if the environment changes, we must expect the FSCs to change as well, and that what is generally applicable for the business community as a whole may not be appropriate for one firm in its own unique environment.

## ETHICAL PROFESSIONAL JUDGEMENT IN ACCOUNTING

**professional judgement**

the ability of a professional to make appropriate choices based on established criteria, recognizing facts and circumstances surrounding the specific choices to be made

The process of making (or recommending) choices in accounting is the process of exercising **professional judgement**. Professional judgement is pervasive in accounting, and accounting standards make frequent references to the exercise of professional judgement. Indeed, one of the differentiating characteristics of many Canadian accounting standards, in contrast to their FASB cousins south of the border, is that they place a great deal of reliance on professional judgement in preference to stipulating rigid rules. As well, the need for judgement is pervasive in many aspects of accounting that are not dealt with specifically in accounting standards. As we examine various specific accounting topics throughout this text, we will emphasize their judgemental aspects.

Accountants must act ethically, and exercise judgement to be fair to all stakeholders. In any specific situation, an accountant exercises ethical professional judgement by taking into account many factors:

- The users of the financial statements, and their *specific* information needs;
- The motivations of managers;
- The organization's operations (e.g., the type of ownership, the sources of financing, the nature of its operating or earnings cycle, etc.); and
- The organization's reporting constraints, if any (e.g., audit requirements, reporting to securities regulators, constraints imposed by foreign owners, etc).

Alternative measurement methods, both accounting *policies* and accounting *estimates*, are considered in light of the foregoing factors, and a selection of appropriate policies is made with reference to the qualitative criteria, after ensuring that the underlying assumptions are valid.

At the end of this chapter, we will return to a discussion of ethical professional judgement and the way that accounting policy choices are made. But first, we must examine the three types of accounting principles: (1) underlying assumptions, (2) qualitative criteria, and (3) measurement conventions.

## CONCEPT REVIEW

1. Who uses financial statement concepts?
2. What are general-purpose financial statements?
3. What factors must a professional accountant take into account in order to exercise ethical professional judgement?

## UNDERLYING ASSUMPTIONS

Underlying assumptions provide a foundation for accounting policy choice, as shown in Exhibit 2-1. Six basic assumptions significantly affect the recording, measuring, and reporting of accounting information.[1] They are

1. *Time period*—meaningful information can be assembled and reported for a time period that is less than the enterprise's life span.

2. *Separate entity* —the enterprise can be accounted for and reported independent of its owners and other stakeholders.

3. *Continuity* —the enterprise will continue in operation for a reasonable future period; also known as the *going-concern assumption.*

4. *Proprietary approach*—the results of the enterprise's operations should be reported from the viewpoint of its owners.

5. *Unit of measure* —the results of the enterprise's operations can meaningfully be measured in monetary terms.

6. *Nominal dollar financial capital maintenance* —the enterprise has generated a profit if its revenues are higher than the historical cost of the resources used.

These six assumptions underlie GAAP. There are times when one or more of the assumptions is not valid, in which case GAAP is not appropriate. GAAP might be useless or highly misleading if used when the assumptions are not valid.

### Time-Period Assumption

The operating results of any business enterprise cannot be known with certainty until the company has completed its life span and ceased doing business. In the meantime, external decision makers require timely accounting information to satisfy their analytical needs. To meet their needs, the **time-period assumption** requires that changes in a business's financial position be reported over a series of shorter time periods.

Although the reporting period varies, one year is the standard. Some companies use a calendar year, and others use a fiscal year-end that coincides with the low point in business activity over a 12-month period. Some businesses (e.g., retail, movie chains) report on a 52-week basis (53 weeks every few years) because their activity cycle is weekly. In addition,

---

[1] An early, and still very relevant, study of the underlying assumptions of accounting was published by the American Institute of Certified Public Accountants as its *Research Study No. 1*: Maurice Moonitz, *The Basic Postulates of Accounting* (New York: AICPA, 1961).

companies also report summarized financial information on an interim basis, usually quarterly for public reporting or monthly for internal purposes.

The time-period assumption recognizes that decision makers need timely financial information. However, recognition of accruals and deferrals is necessary for reporting information that reasonably represents the operations of the enterprise. *Accruals* and *deferrals* are associated with **accrual-basis accounting**.

**accrual-basis accounting**

a basis of accounting that reflects transactions as they occur rather than when cash flows occur

**Accruals and Deferrals** **Accruals** are the accounting recognition of assets and liabilities that have not yet been *realized* as a cash flow; **deferrals** refer to the delayed recognition of costs and receipts that have been *realized* through cash flows but have not yet contributed to the earnings process as expenses and revenues. For example,

| Terminology Used | Cash Timing | Results In |
| --- | --- | --- |
| Accrued revenue | Cash received after revenue recognition is appropriate | Accrued revenue (asset) (perhaps a receivable) |
| Deferred revenue | Cash received before revenue recognition is appropriate | Deferred revenue (liability) (perhaps an unearned revenue) |

**Fiscal Period** The traditional one-year time-period assumption may not be appropriate for limited-life enterprises that will last longer than one year. While financial statements may be prepared at the end of a year (for income tax purposes, for example), the statements will be meaningless if both the revenue-generating and expense-incurring activities are in midstream, with no obvious basis for estimation. For example, the statements of junior mining companies that are still in the process of exploring or developing their sites do little more than convey the amount expended to date. The attempted measurement of annual operating results in the income statement is of little predictive or evaluative use; the value of the company and its earnings ability will not be known until the exploration and development process is completed.

## Separate-Entity Assumption

**separate-entity assumption**

accounting information that reflects the assumption that a business and its owners are separate economic entities

The **separate-entity assumption** means each specific, identifiable business entity is considered an accounting unit separate and apart from its owners and from other entities. This may be quite artificial. For example, an enterprise carried out as a corporation may be inseparable from its owner if it has a single shareholder who is the owner-manager. The same is true for partnerships and sole proprietorships. The separate-entity assumption lets accounting, in essence, draw a line around the business unit and account only for its activities.

**Legal and Tax Status** This separate-entity "line" is independent of the legal and tax status of an entity. For a corporation, there is no difference. A corporation is an entity that is legally quite distinct from its owners. For taxation purposes as well, a corporation is considered to be different from its owners, and files its own tax return. On the other hand, partnerships and sole proprietorships do not share the legal or tax status of separate entities; in law and in taxation, they are viewed as an extension of their owners. Partners and proprietors are fully liable for the debts of the business, and the personal assets of the owners cannot legally be isolated from the business. Only one tax return is filed, by the individual, and there is no separate tax return for the partnership or sole proprietorship.

For accounting purposes, however, the separate-entity assumption establishes that every business is distinct from its owners; otherwise, accounting for the business would be impossible. Under the separate-entity assumption, all accounting records and reports are developed from the viewpoint of a single entity, whether it is a proprietorship, a partnership, or a corporation. The assumption is that an individual's transactions are distinguishable from those of the business he or she might own. For example, the personal residence of a business owner is not considered an asset of the business even though the residence and the business are owned by the same person.

The accountant must be aware of the relationship between the corporation and its owner(s), and must take care to portray this relationship realistically. For example, loans by a controlling shareholder to the corporation are usually, in substance, equity infusions. These have the legal form of debt, and are classified as such in the financial statements. However, lenders routinely insist that such loans be subordinated (or made secondary) to their own loans and reclassify the shareholder loan as equity when performing any analysis of the company. The accountant must strive to disclose the nature of the shareholder loan so that any external user is able to understand that there is a special relationship between the creditor and the debtor.

## Continuity Assumption

The **continuity assumption** is also known as the **going-concern assumption**. Under the continuity assumption, the business entity is expected to continue operations for a reasonable future period. The business is not expected to liquidate. That is, the entity will stay in business for a period of time sufficient to carry out contemplated operations, contracts, and commitments. This is not an assumption of perpetual life, but rather an assumption that the business will continue in operation long enough to recover (or use up) its assets and repay its outstanding liabilities. Management must assess the entity's ability to continue as a going concern, considering all available information.

This going-concern assumption provides a conceptual basis for many of the measurement methods used in accounting. For example, the historical cost concept assumes that the business's capital assets will be used up over their lifetime, which gives rise to the process of amortization. If the entity is to be wound up, then financial statements cannot be prepared on a going-concern basis, and assets and liabilities would be valued at their realizable values, not amortized historical cost.

The continuity assumption also justifies the classifications used in accounting. Assets and liabilities, for example, are classified as either current or long term on the basis of this assumption. If continuity is not assumed, the distinction between current and long term loses its significance; all assets and liabilities become current.

**Exceptions to the Continuity Assumption**   Two instances in which the continuity assumption is not valid are (1) when a business is a limited-life venture, and (2) when a business is in financial difficulty and is expected to be shut down or liquidated. In these circumstances, many commonly used measurement methods are not appropriate.

As an example of the first instance, consider a summer carnival or fair that is organized by an entrepreneur in a resort area. The fair is a one-time event, even if it may be repeated in future years. The future repetition is a separate business decision and a separate venture, and not a continuation of a going concern. In such a situation, the principle of interperiod allocation is rendered nonsensical. There will not necessarily be more than one period, and therefore the practice of interperiod allocation of revenues and expenses becomes irrelevant; what matters is the short-term cash flows from revenue and expenditure.

In the second instance, the business may be intended to continue but is unable to do so due to continuing losses. Some combination of the owners, creditors, and the courts decide that the only remedy is to terminate the business. In a liquidation scenario, the historical cost of the assets is irrelevant and useless; conventional accounting, based on the continuity assumption, is not appropriate. Such circumstances call instead for the use of *liquidation accounting*, where assets and liabilities are valued at estimated net realizable amounts, or liquidation values.

## Proprietary Assumption

One of the fundamental assumptions of North American business accounting is the proprietary assumption. This is one of two possible approaches that can be used in accounting:

- **Proprietary assumption**: An organization's financial condition and results of operations are reported from the point of view of the owners, or proprietors. All other claims on the assets are liabilities and all payments other than those to the owners are expenses. Returns to owners are returns on capital and are not expenses. This is our view of a business enterprise—all outsiders are paid off, and the owners keep the residual wealth.

**entity concept (assumption)**

the assumption that the owners are just one of many stakeholders in an entity; others have a claim to value added and are equally important

- **Entity concept (assumption)**: The owners are just one of many participants, or stakeholders, in the enterprise. A **value added** by the enterprise (that is, revenue minus purchases of goods and services from third parties) is distributed to the various *factors of production*, consisting of providers of capital (both interest on debt and dividends on equity), labour (i.e., wages, salaries, and benefits), and government (taxes and fees for services), with any residual representing reinvestment in the enterprise. Under the entity view, the owners are just another group to be paid off, and the corporation itself is the entity that benefits if there is residual wealth. Another perspective on this is that if the enterprise is healthy, all stakeholders benefit, not just the people who own shares.

In North America, the proprietary assumption dominates our reporting practices. In some other countries, however, the entity concept is either permitted or required for business reporting. For example, some developing countries require corporations to report on the entity basis because this permits public policy-makers to discern whether a foreign-owned corporation is contributing to the national economy or might be "milking" the economy for the benefit of non-domestic shareholders. The information conveyed in a value-added report is not visible in a traditional, North American–style income statement.

## Unit-of-Measure Assumption

The **unit-of-measure assumption** means that the results of a business's economic activities can be reported in terms of a standard monetary unit throughout the financial statements. Simply stated, the assumption is that it is possible to meaningfully prepare financial statements for an enterprise because everything of relevance can be measured using the dollar as the unit of measure. Money amounts are thus the language of accounting: the common unit of measure enables dissimilar items such as the cost of a ton of coal and the amount of an account payable to be aggregated into a single total.

Unfortunately, the use of a standard monetary unit for measurement purposes poses a dilemma. If financial statements are to be meaningful, they must include complete relevant information to enable a user to make informed decisions. The unit-of-measure assumption implies that *if it can't be measured, it can't be reported.* And, by extension, that *if it can't be reported, it can't be used for decision making by external users.* Because of the unit-of-measure assumption, many important aspects of a modern business's operations are a challenge to include in the financial statements, such as:

- The value of customer goodwill;
- The impact of operations on the environment; and
- The value of intellectual and human capital.

Many companies attempt to fill this information void with non-financial information, but its quality and consistency are often questionable.

## Nominal Dollar Financial Capital Maintenance Assumption

The monetary unit of measure is often compared to a ruler, by which the dimensions of a business and its operations are measured. But unlike a ruler, which is always the same length, the relative value of a currency changes over time. The relative value of a currency can be measured in two ways:

1. In relation to the value of other currencies (its *exchange rate*), or

2. In relation to the amount of goods and services that it will buy (its *purchasing power*).

These two relative values are themselves related. As the general purchasing power of a currency declines, its value in relation to currencies that have constant purchasing power also declines. A decline in the general level of purchasing power is a condition of *inflation*. Over time, the relative values of currencies of different nations will adjust to maintain their relative purchasing powers; this is known as maintaining **purchasing power parity**.

**Stable Dollar** Accounting is performed under the assumption that every dollar of revenue and expense has the same stable value, regardless of whether the dollar was a 1935 dollar, a 1970 dollar, or a 2018 dollar. Dollars of different vintages are accounted for without regard to the fact that some have greater purchasing power than others. We call these **nominal dollars**, unadjusted for their purchasing power (inflation). The assumption of an absolutely stable dollar is not correct, but it is used because North American inflation has been relatively modest. Unfortunately, over time, even modest annual rates of inflation can cause large cumulative changes in purchasing power. For example, the purchasing power of the 2008 Canadian dollar was only about one-fifth of the purchasing power of the 1970 dollar.

**Capital Maintenance** Capital maintenance refers to our protocols for determining the amount of profit that has been earned. The North American norm is **nominal dollar financial capital maintenance**. First, financial measurements are in *nominal dollars* (not inflation-adjusted *constant dollars*). Second, financial capital must be maintained, and then profits are recognized. Other alternative capital maintenance concepts include maintenance of financial capital in **constant dollars** (inflation adjusted) or **physical capital maintenance**, which can be measured in nominal dollars or constant dollars.

**Example** For example, assume that $1,000 of inventory is held for one year and then sold for $1,500. Inflation during the period was 10%. It would cost $1,350 to replace the item in inventory at the end of the period because of supplier price increases. Here are three different measure of profit that could be reported:

| Capital Maintenance | Measure of Profit | Commentary |
|---|---|---|
| Nominal dollar financial capital maintenance | $1,500 − $1,000 = $500 | Profits are reported after original costs in nominal dollars are recovered |
| Constant dollar financial capital maintenance | $1,500 − ($1,000 × 1.10) = $1,500 − $1,100 = $400 | Profits are reported after inflation, ensuring that the purchasing power of the original investment is maintained |
| Nominal dollar physical capital maintenance | $1,500 − $1,350 = $150 | Profits are reported only after the entity keeps enough capital to replace assets used |

Although nominal dollar financial capital maintenance is normal in North America, it is not the only alternative found in practice around the world. For example, countries with high levels of inflation (sometimes at a rate of 100% per year or more), use constant dollar financial capital maintenance, and account for business transactions in constant dollars, not nominal dollars. Countries that have used this basis include Mexico, Brazil, Argentina, and Israel. This way of looking at profit performance seems very different. However, the accounting model can adapt very quickly to an inflation-adjusted model. Such a change would be necessary if our Canadian economic environment shifted to higher inflation and nominal dollars were no longer stable.

---

**purchasing power parity**

over time, different relative values of currencies will adjust in the currency markets to reflect relative purchasing power; reflects level of country's inflation

**physical capital maintenance**

the concept that income is recognized only after preserving physical capital or capacity

## CONCEPT REVIEW

1. Why may the separate-entity assumption be artificial for a small corporation with a single shareholder?

2. When might the continuity assumption not be valid?

3. What is the alternative to the proprietary concept?

4. Which underlying assumption is not appropriate in a country that suffers triple-digit annual inflation?

## QUALITATIVE CRITERIA

Qualitative criteria are needed to establish accounting policies, as demonstrated in Exhibit 2-1. Many attempts to develop, clarify, and/or codify these criteria have been made, beginning in 1966.[2] Those presented here are an amalgamation of these publications, plus the material published as part of the FSCs and the IASC Framework. We will examine the following qualitative criteria:

- Relevance (including timeliness, predictive value, and feedback value);
- Reliability (including representational faithfulness, verifiability, and freedom from bias);
- Understandability;
- Materiality;
- Comparability (including consistency);
- Objectivity;
- Conservatism; and
- Cost/benefit.

### Relevance

**relevance**

information that is useful or influential for decision makers; such information is timely, and has predictive and feedback value

**Relevance** may be the most important qualitative characteristic because it means that accounting information must be useful for decisions. Relevance refers to the capacity of accounting information to make a difference to the external decision makers who use financial reports. Relevance relates to the objectives of financial reporting. Chapter 1 pointed out that the accounting choices that are made when cash flow prediction is the primary reporting objective are not necessarily the same choices that are made when performance evaluation is the primary objective.

Qualities that contribute to relevance are

1. *Timeliness.* Accounting information should be reported soon enough for it to be useful for decision making. Like the daily news, stale financial information has less impact than fresh information. Lack of timeliness reduces relevance.

2. *Predictive value.* Accounting information should be helpful to external decision makers by increasing their ability to make predictions about the outcome of future events. Decision makers working from accounting information that has little or no predictive value are merely speculating intuitively.

---

[2] See *A Statement of Basic Accounting Theory* (American Accounting Association, 1966); *Statement of Financial Accounting Concepts No. 2: Qualitative Characteristics of Accounting Information* (Financial Accounting Standards Board, May 1980); and *Corporate Reporting: Its Future Evolution* (Canadian Institute of Chartered Accountants, 1980).

3. *Feedback value.* Accounting information should be helpful to external decision makers who are confirming past predictions or making updates, adjustments, or corrections to predictions.

## Reliability

reliability

Another key component of decision usefulness is **reliability**. Information is reliable if users can depend on it as a sufficiently accurate measure of what it is intended to measure. Reliability is closely related to the general concept of usefulness, but has additional subcomponents.

**reliability**

information that can be depended upon as accurate; reliable information is representationally faithful, verifiable, and free from bias

To ensure reliability, accounting information must be free from error and bias and faithfully represent what it claims to represent. It must not mislead or deceive. There are three components to reliability:

1. Representational faithfulness (including substance over form);

2. Verifiability; and

3. Freedom from bias (or neutrality).

**validity**

information reported accurately reflects actual events and transactions

**Representational Faithfulness** This attribute is also sometimes called **validity**.[3] Information must give a faithful picture of the facts and circumstances involved, as a city map should accurately represent the layout of a city.

In accounting, the balance sheet is considered to be a "statement of financial position," but it represents the financial position of the organization faithfully only if it really does portray all of the assets and liabilities of the business. If the accounting conventions and measurement models do not show all of the assets or liabilities, then the balance sheet does not represent faithfully the financial position of the business.

An important aspect of representational faithfulness is **substance over form**. Accounting information should represent what it purports to represent and should report the economic substance of transactions, not just their form or surface appearance.

As an example of accountants' efforts to portray substance over form, consider a company that rents, or leases, a computer system. The form of the contract is a rental agreement, which would seem to suggest that payments made by the company should simply be reported as rent expense with no other financial statement impact. However, suppose that the accountant discovers that this company decided to lease the computer instead of buying one outright with money borrowed from a bank. The lease term covers the full expected useful life of the computer, cannot be cancelled by the company, and provides a full return of the cost of the computer, plus a profit margin (in the form of interest) to the lessor. Now it appears as though, *in substance*, the company has acquired property rights over the computer, far more than a simple rental contract would imply. In substance, the company owns full rights to the use of the asset and is financing it with a lease agreement. Thus, to reflect *substance over form*, and be representationally faithful, the asset and the obligation should be shown on the balance sheet of the lessee, and the income statement should reflect both depreciation of the computer and interest on the liability.

**Verifiability** If knowledgeable and independent observers can apply an accounting measurement and obtain essentially the same result, the measurement is said to be *verifiable*. This is often suggested as a component of reliability, but many would suggest that verifiability is the essence of *objectivity*. Verification implies that independent measures *using the same measurement methods* would reach substantially the same conclusion. Verifiability of a measurement does not, however, mean that the measurement was necessarily objective or non-arbitrary, but only that its computation can be reproduced or replicated.

**Freedom from Bias** Accounting information is biased if the measurements result in consistent overstatements or understatements of the items being measured. If statements are prepared with freedom from bias, such overstatements and understatements do not exist.

---

[3] In the CICA's 1980 *Corporate Reporting* study, this characteristic is known as isomorphism. *Isomorphism* is a well-established concept in science that indicates a similarity between two different forms or constructs.

Sometimes, "neutrality" is the term used to indicate the characteristic of freedom from bias. However, the concept of neutrality is sometimes taken to mean that reported accounting information should be neutral in its impact and should not influence economic decisions one way or the other. This seems curious, since information that has no impact on economic decisions is essentially useless or lacks relevance.

**Another Alternative: True and Fair View/Fair Presentation** Financial statements are normally expected to present fairly the financial position, changes in financial position, and performance of an entity. This would appear to be consistent with representational faithfulness. One would expect that application of the qualitative characteristics would naturally result in a true and fair view of an entity. For this reason, the IASC's Framework includes the expectation that financial statements reflect a *true and fair view* or *fair presentation*.

North American accounting concepts do not refer to this expectation as a separate qualitative criterion. This may be because it is not clear whether there is a separate test for "fair presentation" over and above selection of appropriate accounting principles for a given situation. If there was such a test, there might be some legal consequences. For example, say that a company applies a standard as approved by standard setters, but then feels that the result does not result in fair presentation. Is management justified in following a different accounting policy? Which accounting policy would be deemed "GAAP" if things went wrong and an investor came before the courts claiming that the financial statements were not in accordance with GAAP? Perhaps for this reason, the North American approach to concepts rests solely on representational faithfulness.

### Conflict between Relevance and Reliability

*Reliability* often conflicts with *relevance*. While both relevance and reliability are needed to established decision usefulness, some of the potentially most useful or relevant information may be very unreliable. This conflict is illustrated in Exhibit 2-2. For example, relevant information such as the value of intellectual capital or market values for intangible capital assets may not be recorded because of its lack of reliability.

### EXHIBIT 2-2

## TRADE-OFF BETWEEN RELEVANCE AND RELIABILITY

*Source:* A portion of FASB Concepts Statement No. 2 Qualitative Characteristics of Accounting Information, Copyright © by the Financial Accounting Standards Board, 410 Merritt 7, PO Box 5116, Norwalk, CT 06856-5116, is reprinted with permission. Complete copies of this document are available from the FASB.

## Understandability

Information must be understandable to be useful to users in their decision-making process. Understandability does not mean that all information has to be reduced to the lowest common level or simplified so that the least sophisticated investor should understand it. Investors and creditors should have a reasonable understanding of business and economic activities, as well as some understanding of accounting. These users are expected to study the information with reasonable diligence. User groups include those who provide advice to investors and creditors; users who lack expertise are assumed to be properly advised.

## Materiality

The term **materiality** is used to describe the significance of an item. Something is said to be material if its omission or misstatement would probably influence or change a decision. Essentially, it doesn't matter how an immaterial item is accounted for, because errors or omissions would not cause different behaviour. Materiality may be caused by the size of an item or its nature.

Size-wise, an arbitrary limit of 5% of income from continuing operations is often used to measure materiality. If an operation is not profitable, then materiality could be based on revenues or assets. Materiality might be determined by the nature of an item, not its size. For example, assume that a large company with a $500,000 materiality limit, based on sales, discovered that a $10,000 payment that might have been a bribe had been paid. This item, which is immaterial dollar-wise, would have to be brought to the attention of audit committee of the Board of Directors, for further action because of its questionable legality.

## Comparability

**comparability**

the relationship between two pieces of information; data that has been prepared using the same accounting policies for a corporation over time, or for different corporations in order that they can be logically compared

**Comparability** is a factor when considering the relationship between two pieces of information. There are two aspects of comparability—**consistency**, which entails using the same accounting policies from year to year within a firm, and **uniformity**, which means that companies with similar transactions and similar circumstances use the same accounting treatments.

Consistency involves applying accounting concepts and principles from period to period in the same manner. There is a presumption that an accounting principle once used should not be changed. However, if consistency is carried too far, it adversely affects relevance. A change to a preferred accounting principle is permitted, even though this would impair consistency. This apparent conflict is usually resolved by retrospective restatement of financial statements to reflect the new policy, and appropriate note disclosure.

## Objectivity

Objectivity is a frequently cited concept in accounting, comprising one or a combination of the following characteristics:

- **Quantifiability**, the ability to attach a number to an event or transaction. For example, the impact of some events, like some contingent losses, cannot be measured with any degree of reliability, and any attempt to measure them is said not to be objective.

**verifiability**

independent persons using a specific measurement method would reach substantially the same results

- **Verifiability**, or the ability of independent accountants to replicate the results of an accounting measurement, discussed previously as a component of *reliability*.
- **Freedom from bias**, the absence of intentional or unintentional misstatement or skewing of an accounting measurement. This also is a component of *reliability*.
- **Non-arbitrariness**, the requirement to base accounting measurements on observable values.

Because of the wide variety of possible interpretations of *objectivity*, many discussions of qualitative criteria avoid using the word completely.

## Conservatism

**conservatism**

when two accounting methods are acceptable, the one having the less favourable effect on net income and net assets is preferable

**Conservatism** is sometimes called *prudence*, and is needed because uncertainty underscores many measurements in accounting. Such uncertainties must be dealt with in an appropriate manner, and accountants try to include all relevant information in as reliable a fashion as possible. To protect users in the face of uncertainty, accountants are encouraged to use caution, and fully consider uncertainties and risks. Generally, the conservative decision is one that understates assets and income, and/or overstates liabilities and expenses. Excessive overstatement or understatement must be avoided, however: bias is not acceptable and deliberate understatement of net assets cannot be justified with conservatism.

Conservative measurements in one period almost inevitably have offsetting effects in one or more later periods. If assets are "conservatively" measured by understating assets, then expenses are accordingly reduced when those assets are transferred to the income statement when the assets are used (or amortized). Reducing expenses has the effect of increasing net income, which is not conservative. For example, management has been known to use conservatism to justify excessive asset writedowns, even though the obvious result of the writedowns would be to enhance future earnings. Auditors, required to use skepticism, would often be uncomfortable arguing against the "conservative" writedown. Conservatism is a tricky animal.

## The Cost/Benefit Tradeoff

The concept of **cost/benefit effectiveness** holds that any accounting measurement or disclosure should result in greater benefits to the users than it costs to prepare and present. Benefits should exceed costs.

In standard setting, this is a very difficult concept to implement, since the benefits of an accounting standard are very vague while the costs of compliance are very real. Furthermore, the costs are borne by the companies while the benefits are usually enjoyed by the external users. The cost/benefit perceptions of standard setters and of the preparers of financial statements do not always coincide, with the result that some standards enjoy less than full compliance, even by public companies.

For private companies that are not bound by the GAAP constraint for public companies, the cost/benefit trade-off is very pragmatic. In particular, if there are no external users of a private company's financial statements (other than the CRA), then there is no benefit to be derived from incurring higher accounting costs. Commonly, such companies will use accounting methods that coincide with their tax treatment even though they are not GAAP. Examples include calculating depreciation/amortization expense on the same basis as capital cost allowance (tax depreciation), and recognizing revenue on the same basis for accounting as for tax purposes.

Canadian accounting standards acknowledge this cost/benefit threshold in the GAAP model by formally allowing **differential reporting** for certain companies. Companies that do not have public accountability (no public debt or publicly traded shares), and that can establish unanimous shareholder approval for the use of differential accounting are eligible. Differential reporting allows these companies to follow simpler accounting policies, which typically follow cash flow, in a few key areas. For example, these companies can simply expense income tax as paid, instead of using the more complex accrual method. This would be considered GAAP for the company.

## Other Trade-Offs

As discussed at the beginning of this section, there is often a trade-off between qualitative characteristics, but especially between relevance and reliability. For example, timeliness may have to be reduced to increase the degree of verifiability, or vice versa. If financial statements were delayed until all the future events that affect them were to come to pass, measurements would be far more verifiable. Uncollectible accounts, warranty reserves, and useful lives of depreciable assets would not have to be estimated and reliability would increase. On the other hand, the timeliness of the financial statements would suffer, and thus the statements would lack relevance. Thus, a degree of reliability is sacrificed to gain relevance. The relative importance of the characteristics changes from situation to situation and calls for the exercise of professional judgement.

The extent of trade-offs is, in itself, subjective. This is particularly apparent in the standard-setting process, where there often is a vigorous debate amongst the participants about what is relevant and what is measurable. The concerns of the auditing profession often show up in the presence of standards that seem to emphasize verifiability. The historical cost measurement convention often seems to override what many observers perceive to be the relevance of other highly objective measurements.

## CONCEPT REVIEW

1. How does relevance relate to financial reporting objectives?

2. Does the criterion of understandability mean that anyone should be able to understand the financial statements?

3. What are the three components of reliability?

4. What are the four characteristics of objectivity?

5. Why must there often be trade-offs between different qualitative criteria?

## ELEMENTS OF FINANCIAL STATEMENTS AND RECOGNITION

Periodic financial statements are the primary medium used to communicate accounting information about a business enterprise. The building blocks of financial statements are called **elements**. Elements are the classes of items that financial statements should contain and they are affected by accounting policy choice, as indicated in Exhibit 2-1. There are seven elements, as shown in Exhibit 2-3. The first three elements (assets, liabilities, and owners' equity/net assets) relate directly to the balance sheet; the next four elements (revenues, expenses, gains, and losses) relate directly to the income statement. The definitions of these seven elements are particularly important because they provide the basis for deciding whether or not to recognize the results of a transaction or event in the financial statements.

**Assets and Liabilities** Assets and liabilities are central to the definitions, since all other definitions are *derived from* asset and liability definitions. That is, owners' equity equals assets less liabilities. Revenues are defined as increases in assets or decreases in liabilities; expenses are decreases in assets or increases in liabilities. Obviously, the definitions place emphasis on the balance sheet and the assets and liabilities that comprise it.

So, what are assets? Assets have three essential characteristics:

1. They embody a future benefit, involving a capacity to contribute to future net cash flows;

2. The entity must be able to control access to the benefit; and

3. The asset must be the result of a past transaction or event.

Similarly, consider the three characteristics of liabilities:

1. They embody a duty or a responsibility to others that will involve a future transfer or use of assets, or other economic benefits, or rendering service, at a specific time or after a specific event;

2. The entity has little or no discretion to avoid the obligation; and

3. The liability must be the result of a past transaction or event.

**Necessary Conditions** The definitions of assets and liabilities include three components and embody three time frames:

1. An asset must involve a *future benefit* (e.g., through a direct future cash flow or through its use in generating a future cash flow), and a liability must entail a future sacrifice (either a payment of cash or performance of service).

### elements

the building blocks of financial statements, i.e., assets, liabilities, revenues, expenses, etc.

**EXHIBIT 2-3**

## ELEMENTS OF FINANCIAL STATEMENTS

| Elements | Transaction Characteristics |
|---|---|
| **Balance Sheet [discussed in Chapter 4]** | |
| 1. **Assets** are economic resources controlled by an entity as a result of past transactions or events from which future economic benefits may be obtained. | 1. To qualify as assets, the resources involved must<br>a. Have future economic benefits;<br>b. Be under the entity's current control; and<br>c. Result from past transactions. |
| 2. **Liabilities** are obligations of an entity arising from past transactions or events, the settlement of which will result in the transfer or use of assets, provision of services, or other yielding of economic benefits in the future. | 2. To qualify as liabilities, obligations must<br>a. Require future transfer of assets or economic benefits;<br>b. Be an unavoidable current obligation; and<br>c. Result from past transactions. |
| 3. **Owners' equity/net assets** is the ownership interest in the assets of an entity after deducting its liabilities. While equity in total is a residual, it includes specific categories of items, for example, types of share capital, other contributed capital, and retained earnings. | 3. The dollar amounts reported represent the residual interest in the assets after deducting liabilities. In addition, the equity element is used to report capital transactions. |
| **Income Statement [discussed in Chapter 3]** | |
| 4. **Revenues** are increases in economic resources, either by way of **(a)** inflows or enhancements of assets or **(b)** reductions of liabilities, resulting from the ordinary activities of an entity. Normally from the sale of goods, the rendering of services, or the use by others of entity resources yielding rent, interest, royalties, or dividends. | 4. An essential characteristic of a revenue transaction is that it arises from the company's ordinary earning activities, and not from **(a)** capital transactions, **(b)** the settlement of monetary liabilities, or **(c)** the sale of capital assets or investment assets. |
| 5. **Expenses** are decreases in economic resources, either by way of **(a)** outflows or reductions of assets or **(b)** incurrences of liabilities, resulting from the ordinary revenue-earning activities of an entity. | 5. The essential characteristic of an expense is that it must be incurred in conjunction with the company's revenue-generating process. Expenditures that do not qualify as expenses are treated either as assets (future economic benefit to be derived), as losses (no economic benefit), or as distributions to owners. |
| 6. **Gains** are increases in net assets from peripheral or incidental transactions and events affecting an entity and from all other transactions, events, and circumstances affecting an entity that are given accounting recognition except those that result from revenues or equity contributions. | 6. The transaction must not be one that meets the characteristics of **(a)** a revenue-producing transaction or **(b)** a capital transaction (e.g., capital infusion by the owners). |
| 7. **Losses** are decreases in equity from peripheral or incidental transactions and events affecting an entity and from all other transactions, events, and circumstances affecting an entity that are given accounting recognition except those that result from expenses or distributions of equity. | 7. The transaction must not be one that meets the characteristics of **(a)** an expense transaction or **(b)** a capital transaction (e.g., dividends or other distributions to owners). |

*Source: CICA Handbook*, Section 1000, "Financial Statement Concepts."

2. The reporting enterprise has a clear *present right* to the asset or obligation for the liability.

3. The asset or liability arose as the result of a *past transaction* or event.

**Income Statement Elements**  The definitions of the income statement elements—revenues, expenses, gains, and losses—are related to changes in net assets (i.e., total assets minus total liabilities):

- Revenues are increases in net assets, either by way of inflows or enhancements of assets or reductions of liabilities, resulting from the ordinary activities of the enterprise.
- Expenses are decreases in net assets, either by way of outflows or reductions of assets or incurrences of liabilities, resulting from an enterprise's ordinary revenue-generating or service-delivery activities.
- Gains are increases in net assets from peripheral or incidental transactions.
- Losses are decreases in net assets from peripheral or incidental transactions.

The only difference between revenues and gains and between expenses and losses is the nature of the activity that gave rise to them. Revenues and expenses relate to the ordinary operating activities of the enterprise; gains and losses relate to non-operating activities.

The "ordinary" versus "peripheral" criterion is rather vague. For example, some movie theatre chains regularly report "gains" from the sale of theatre properties in their income statements. But if an enterprise operates hundreds of movie screens, then isn't the purchase and sale of theatre properties an ordinary business activity rather than a peripheral activity? The key is that the business of a theatre chain is not that of buying and selling theatres; such an activity is essential to the health of the company, but it is *incidental* to the primary business activity of exhibiting movies. Revenue should include only the proceeds from the sale of tickets and popcorn and the delivery of other routine services and products, and not from the sale of the capital assets.

## Recognition

**Recognition** is the process of measuring and including an item in the financial statements. A recognized item is given a title and numerical value. Recognition applies to all financial statement elements in all accounting entities. *Disclosure* (information in the notes to the financial statements) is not the same as recognition; when a financial statement element is recognized, it is reported on the face of the financial statements. To be recognized, three criteria must be met, as shown in Exhibit 2-4.

Recognition is appropriate if:

- The item meets the definition of an element.
- The item has an appropriate basis of measurement, and a reasonable estimate can be made of the amount.
- For assets and liabilities, it is probable that the economic benefits will be received or given up, i.e., realized.

It seems obvious that financial statement elements are the things measured in financial statements—this is the first criteria. Next comes measurability. If an item cannot be measured, it cannot be recognized, even if it has a high probability of being realized. To be measurable, there must be both a basis of measurement (such as historical cost or replacement cost), and a reasonable estimate of the amount. Probability is the final criteria. It is entirely possible that an item that meets the first two recognition criteria will not be recognized because of failure of the last criterion—probability of realization.

Suppose a company was suing a supplier for $125,000 for damages incurred because faulty materials provided by the supplier were used in a production process. The future economic benefit, or asset, can be measured at $125,000 or a lower amount if the parties are likely to settle. The difficulty arises when assessing the probability of the receipt of the economic benefit, because the lawsuit may not be successful. It may be proven that the company ordered the wrong materials or used them incorrectly. For this reason, such items are

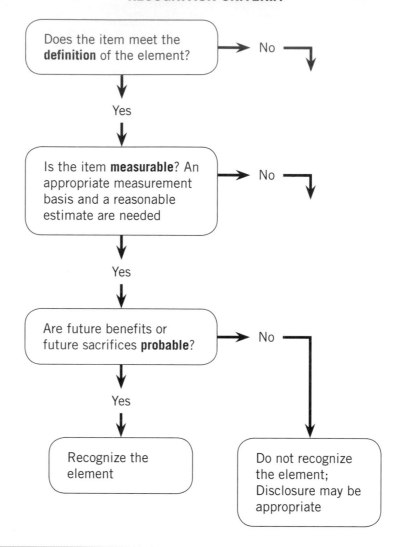

**EXHIBIT 2-4**

**RECOGNITION CRITERIA**

Does the item meet the **definition** of the element? → No

Yes ↓

Is the item **measurable**? An appropriate measurement basis and a reasonable estimate are needed → No

Yes ↓

Are future benefits or future sacrifices **probable**? → No

Yes ↓

Recognize the element

Do not recognize the element; Disclosure may be appropriate

included in the disclosure notes as contingencies and are not recognized until the result of the court decision is known and the probability of collection assessed.

**Commitments**  As another example, suppose that a company signs a three-year contract to hire a special consultant; the contract is non-cancellable. Should the company recognize a liability? The definition of an element might seem to be satisfied: (1) the contract will require a cash outflow over the next three years; (2) there is a present obligation that is unavoidable; and (3) the transaction has already occurred. However, such a contract is *not* recognized in business accounting because the consultant has not yet rendered the services for which she was hired. The element definition is not met for a contract that is a **commitment**.

**commitment**

a promise, either written or oral, that obligates an entity to provide a future service or deliver an asset at some future time

From a practical standpoint, a useful way of approaching the question of whether a transaction or event has given rise to a recognizable asset or liability is to ask: "What do I do with the offset?" If the commitment to the consultant were recognized as a liability, there would have to be an offsetting debit. There are only two choices for the debit: an asset or an expense. Clearly, the expense has not been incurred yet, because the service has not yet been rendered nor has the contract time passed. Therefore, the only choice for an offset is an asset. But what is the asset? It would have to be the future benefit to be derived from the costs that have not yet been incurred. The prospect of recognizing an asset for costs to be incurred in the future for services not yet rendered is a prospect that most accountants would find objectionable. Therefore, the commitment would be viewed as an **executory contract**—a contract wherein neither party has yet fulfilled the requirements of the contract—and would not be recognized because the first recognition criterion is failed.

### Recognition versus Realization

Recognition means that an item is recorded in the accounts. **Realization** is the process of converting an asset, liability, or commitment into a cash flow. A receivable is said to be *realized* when it is collected, revenues are *realized* when received, expenses and liabilities are *realized* when the cash payment occurs.

Once realization has occurred, recognition *must* occur because there has been a cash flow impact that cannot be ignored in the accounts. For example,

- A customer makes a deposit (or pays in advance) for goods yet to be produced and delivered; since the cash has been received (realized), it must be recognized. Since revenue will not yet have been earned, the offsetting credit is to recognize unearned revenue.
- A company pays a retainer to a lawyer who will be acting on the company's behalf in the next fiscal year; the cash outflow triggers recognition of a prepaid expense.

However, recognition often occurs prior to realization. For example,

- An accounts receivable is recognized when a service has been performed for a client; realization occurs when the client pays the account. The offset is to recognize revenue.
- A liability for a purchase of inventory is recognized when the goods are received; realization occurs when the creditor is paid. The offset is to recognize inventory as an asset.
- A change in the value of cash held in a U.S.–dollar bank account is recognized at the balance sheet date; realization occurs only when the U.S. dollars are converted to Canadian dollars. The offset is to a gain or loss account, depending on the direction of the change in value.

**The Accrual Concept** When we recognize the effects of transactions and events prior to their realization, we are using the *accrual concept*. The accrual concept says that we recognize transactions when they occur. Cash flow may well happen in this period, or in a different period. For example:

- Inventory is purchased on account. The liability is *accrued* as an account payable, and the asset is recorded as inventory. Both an asset and a related liability are recognized. This is an application of the accrual concept because the transaction is recorded prior to its cash flow impact. When the inventory is sold, its cost is transferred to cost of goods sold, which is recognition of an expense. However, this subsequent expense recognition is not an application of the accrual concept; the liability had already been accrued. The temporary classification of the cost of the inventory as an asset, which then is transferred to an expense, is the result of *matching*, not of accrual.
- Equipment is purchased by giving a 20% cash down payment and giving a promissory note for the remaining 80%. The full cost of the equipment is *recognized* as an asset, including the 80% portion of the cost represented by the liability that is *accrued*. The equipment is recorded as an asset; it is expected to have a four-year useful life. For each of the next four years, 25% of the cost is transferred to the income statement as depreciation, thereby recognizing depreciation expense in each year. The recognition of depreciation is *not* an accrual; it is an *interperiod allocation* (which also is a function of *matching*).

In matching and interperiod allocation, amounts originally recognized as assets are transferred to (or *recognized* as) expense, and amounts recorded as liabilities are transferred to the income statement as revenue (or as reduction of expense).

**Cash Flow Is Central** Before leaving the concepts of realization and recognition, we must stress that accounting recognition always relates to realized cash flows—past, present, and future. The recognition issue is always one of fitting the actual (or predicted) cash flows into time periods through a complex system of accruals and interperiod allocations. If actual cash flows deviate from those that we presumed in recognizing revenues and expenses, then we must adjust our accounts. *At no time can accounting recognize financial statement elements that are not based on actual or predicted cash flows!*

## CONCEPT REVIEW

1. What are the seven elements of financial statements?

2. What are the three criteria that must be met to justify recognition of an item in the financial statements?

3. What is the difference between realization and accounting recognition?

4. What is the difference between accrual and interperiod allocation?

## MEASUREMENT METHODS

Measurement is the process of determining the amount at which an item is recognized in the financial statements. It is integral to accounting choice, as illustrated in Exhibit 2-1. Although measurement underlies the financial statement elements, this chapter described the elements first, to make the measurement discussion more meaningful. If there is no appropriate basis of measurement, a transaction fails the second recognition criterion, as previously defined.

Measurement methods encompass not only the process of attaching a number to a construct such as a specific asset or a liability, but also the process of income measurement as it is conventionally practised in Canadian accounting. The process of income measurement involves the initial measurement and the disposition of that measurement as it moves through the financial statements. There are four pervasive measurement conventions:

1. Historical cost;

2. Revenue recognition;

3. Matching; and

4. Full disclosure.

### Historical Cost Method

There are many alternative measurement bases. Common alternatives include historical cost, replacement cost, current sales value (or *market value*), net realizable value, and discounted cash flow, which is the sum of the cash flows an item will generate over its life, discounted at an appropriate rate. In our accounting model, *generally*, historical cost is used as a measurement base.

Our GAAP model is described as an historical cost model, yet there are many examples in it of other valuation bases— investments carried at market value, obsolete inventory carried at net realizable value when this amount is less than cost, asset retirement obligations carried at discounted cash flow, and so on. Different measurement bases seem appropriate for different elements and circumstances. Therefore, this ad hoc measurement approach will likely continue and we will continue to see a variety of measurement bases, although historical cost will dominate.

**historical cost convention**

economic transactions are recorded using the cost (historical cost) of the transaction

Normally applied in conjunction with asset acquisitions, the **historical cost convention** specifies that the actual acquisition cost be used for initial accounting recognition purposes. The cost principle assumes that assets are acquired in business transactions conducted at arm's length—that is, transactions between a buyer and a seller are at a fair market value prevailing at the time of the transaction.

If an asset is acquired via some means other than cash, the cost of the asset is based on the *value of the consideration given up*. **Consideration** is whatever the buyer gives the seller. For non-cash transactions conducted at arm's length, the cost principle assumes that the fair value of the resources *given up* in a transaction provides reliable evidence for the valuation of the item acquired. This may be the amount of money paid, market value of common shares issued, or the present value of debt assumed in the transaction. Sometimes, though, it is hard to value the consideration given up, and then the fair market value of the assets received is referred to as a more reliable indicator. For example, if a company gives up common shares valued at $50,000 for land appraised at $60,000, what value should be assigned to the transaction? Both measures have some degree of subjectivity, especially if the shares are thinly traded. One of these values, or a mid-point, must be used for valuation.

The cost principle provides guidance primarily at the initial acquisition date. Once acquired, the original cost basis of long-lived assets is then subject to amortization, depletion, depreciation, or writedown.

## Revenue Recognition

**General Recogniton Criteria**  Revenue recognition requires the recognition of revenues when all three of the recognition criteria—definition, measurability, and probability—are met.

Revenue has been *defined* as inflows of cash or other enhancements of a business's assets, settlements of its liabilities, or a combination of the two. Such inflows must be derived from delivering or producing goods, rendering service, or performing other activities that constitute a company's ongoing business operations over a specific period of time. Revenue is *measured* as the transaction amount, set by contract. If there is a non-cash (or barter) transaction, then revenue is measured at the market value of the resources received or the fair value of the product or service given, whichever is the more reliably determinable. Revenue is *probable* when collection is assured.

**Explicit Recognition Criteria**  Revenue recognition is often a problematic policy choice, because it affects net income in a substantial way. Therefore, explicit revenue recognition criteria have been established to bolster the general recognition criteria. Three explicit conditions have to be met to recognize revenue:

1. All significant acts required of the seller have been performed, and the risks and rewards of ownership have passed to the buyer.

2. Consideration is measurable.

3. Collection is reasonably assured.

These conditions are easily applied to traditional trading activities, wherein a company buys and sells inventory or manufactures items for sale. Many sectors of the Canadian economy do not fit into these traditional modes of business, and multiperiod earnings cycles are common. Transactions that do not quite fit into the three conditions above include instalment sales, long-term construction contracts, sales of land with minimal down payments, software development contracts, long-term leases, and sales of franchises that require a certain level of performance on the part of the franchisor as a condition of sale. In these transactions and others, there are significant uncertainties concerning one or more of the listed criteria.

When the earnings cycle is long, the first condition is particularly troublesome. If *all* significant acts must be performed before revenue can be recognized, there would be no such thing as percentage-of-completion accounting, instalment-basis revenue recognition, loan interest revenue, and so forth. Instead, revenue would be recognized only when all of the effort has been expended and the earnings process is complete. There are obviously conditions under which revenue is recognized before all significant acts have been performed.

**Accrual**  The revenue recognition convention pertains only to accrual-basis accounting. Completed transactions for the sale of goods or services on credit usually are recognized as revenue for the period in which the product is delivered or service occurs. Furthermore, related expenses are accrued and matched to these revenues. (On the other hand, if the cash basis is used, revenue is recognized when cash is collected, *not* according to the three recognition criteria.)

The issue of revenue recognition is one of the most pervasive and most difficult in the practice of accounting. Chapter 6 is devoted exclusively to a discussion of this important issue.

## Matching

**matching**

the recognition of expenses in the same time period that the revenues (generated by incurring the expenses) are recognized

**Matching** refers to the timing of expense recognition in the income statement. Under this concept, all expenses incurred in earning revenue should be recognized in the same period that the revenue is recognized. For example,

- If revenue is carried over (deferred) for recognition in a future period, any related expenses should also be carried over or deferred, since they are incurred in earning that revenue.
- If revenue is recognized in the current period but there are expenditures yet to be incurred in future periods, the expenses are accrued and a liability is created (e.g., the estimated provision for warranty costs).
- If costs are incurred to enhance the revenue-generating ability of the company in future periods and the future benefits are measurable, the costs are capitalized and amortized.

Matching is useful for evaluating the ability of a company to generate net income and thus for performance evaluation. After all, if revenue is recognized, then surely all of the expenses related to earning that revenue should also be recognized in the same period.

The problem is that most costs are not *directly* related to revenue. For many types of cost, expenses are only indirectly related to specific revenue-generating activity. These indirect costs are often called *overhead*, and they constitute a majority of the costs of most companies.

As a result, most matching is not directly to revenue, but is instead to *time periods*. Examples are the expenditures for administration and for promotional activities. These items are **period costs**—they are recognized as expenses during the period in which they are incurred. Another example is amortization of capital assets. Amortization seldom is allocated on the basis of revenues but instead is usually allocated over an estimated useful life or, in the case of intangible assets, often over an arbitrary number of years.

**Illustration**  To illustrate the matching principle, assume a home appliance is sold for cash with a 100% warranty on parts and labour in effect for the first 12 months from date of sale. The revenue from the sale is recognized immediately, and the immediate costs are recognized and therefore matched to revenue. These expenses include the costs of manufacturing and assembling the unit and the shipping and direct selling expenses incurred. In order to fully achieve matching, though, the expenses involved in honouring the warranty should also be recognized in the same period as the sales revenue, even though the actual warranty cost may not be known until the next year. At the end of the year in which the sale occurs, the warranty expense should be estimated and recorded, and thus recognized. In this way, the warranty expense is matched with the revenue to which it is related even though the cash may be expended at a later time.

**Matching Summary**  A simple table is helpful in summarizing the accounting disposition of costs and expenses in accordance with the matching principle and the definitions of elements:

| Time Frame of Benefit | Expenditure Should Be |
|---|---|
| Future verifiable economic benefits | Recorded as an asset |
| Current economic benefits | Recorded as an expense |
| No economic benefits | Recorded as a loss |

The timing of expense recognition and the measurement of the cost is another matter for professional judgement. There is hardly an expense item in the income statement that is not the subject of several interrelated judgements and estimates. Chapter 6 discusses the issue of expense recognition at some length, and most of the other chapters in this book deal with expense recognition in the context of specific accounting issues, such as inventories, capital assets, leases, pensions, income tax, and so forth.

## Full Disclosure

**Full disclosure** means that the financial statements should report all *relevant* information bearing on the economic affairs of a business enterprise. The aim of full disclosure is to provide external users with the accounting information they need to make informed investment and credit decisions. Full disclosure requires, among other things, that the chosen accounting policies be explained in the disclosure notes.

Although the common expression is "full disclosure," perhaps a more realistic expression is "adequate disclosure." Obviously, not all information that may be relevant to a financial statement user can be disclosed. Instead, the objective is to disclose enough supplemental information to keep from misleading the users of the statements who are likely to be using the statements to predict cash flows or to evaluate the earnings ability of the company.

A useful guide to deciding what to disclose is as follows:[4]

- Disclose accounting policy choice information.
- Disclose further detail about recognized items that have been summarized or are unusual.
- Disclose items that have not been recognized because they have failed one of the recognition criteria but are still potentially relevant.
- Disclose information about future cash flow.
- Disclose alternate measurement bases.
- Disclose information to assist investors in calculating return on investment.

Chapter 4 contains more analysis of the content of disclosure notes.

## THE EXERCISE OF ETHICAL PROFESSIONAL JUDGEMENT

Chapter 1 gave examples of the many accounting choices that are affected by the financial reporting objectives *in any particular situation*. Reporting objectives (and motivations) do vary, and choices of accounting policies and accounting estimates are significantly affected by whether the primary reporting objective is, for example, income tax minimization, cash flow prediction, or net income maximization.

### ETHICAL ISSUES

The ability to make appropriate choices in accounting is ethical professional judgement. Professional judgement permeates the work of a professional accountant, and it involves an ability to build accounting measurements that take into account:

- The objectives of financial reporting in each particular situation;
- The facts of the business environment and operations; and
- The organization's reporting constraints (if any).

---

[4] Based on Mary Barth and Christine Murphy, "Required Financial Statement Disclosures: Purposes, Subject, Number and Trends," *Accounting Horizons*, (December, 1994) pp. 1–22. See also Maurice Moonitz, *The Basic Postulates of Accounting* (AICPA, 1961), pp. 48–49.

The result of properly applied ethical professional judgement is fair financial information. Failure of ethical professional judgement may result in false or misleading information. Think about the steps required to apply professional judgement in an ethical fashion. The building blocks for accounting choice were illustrated in Exhibit 2-1 in the form of a pyramid.

1. At the base of the pyramid, on which all else is built, are the objectives of financial reporting. There usually are multiple objectives, and the objectives must be ethically and appropriately prioritized in order to be able to resolve conflicts between them when decisions about specific accounting policies or estimates must be made.

2. The facts of the organization's operations and its economic environment must be determined in order to understand just what is to be measured. Fraud may interfere with fact finding and an accountant must be very careful.

3. Next, the reporting constraints must be determined. Is the reporting enterprise a public company, bound by the reporting constraints of the securities commissions? Is it a private company that uses the financial statements only for its owner(s) and for income tax purposes? Is an audit required? If an audit is required (or desired by management), is a "clean" audit opinion necessarily needed? Does the company qualify for *differential reporting*? Can the enterprise report on the basis of disclosed (or tailored) accounting policies rather than GAAP?

4. The underlying assumptions must be tested. In preparing the financial statements for the vast majority of Canadian business organizations, the normal underlying assumptions of continuity, nominal dollar financial capital maintenance, proprietary approach, etc., are quite valid. But they cannot be taken for granted, and their appropriateness in the specific reporting situation must be evaluated.

5. Once the objectives have been discerned and prioritized, the facts and constraints determined, and the underlying assumptions evaluated, only then should the measurement choices or accounting policies be considered.

6. The measurement choices must be consistent with the objectives, facts, and constraints. The measurement choices are further tempered by the qualitative criteria, especially in the realm of recognition. When should revenues be recognized? When should costs incurred or committed be recognized? When costs are recognized, should they be recognized as assets or as expenses? If they are recognized as assets, when should they be transferred to expense? There are many ethical decisions to be made.

7. The measurement and recognition criteria lead to the financial statement elements, which then are classified in a manner that is appropriate to the industry and consistent with the operational activities of the enterprise. The result is, finally, the financial statements themselves. To be appropriate for the specific reporting situation, the final financial statements must satisfy the specific reporting objectives that are at the foundation of the whole pyramid.

8. The ethical requirements are met if the financial statements are a fair representation of the underlying business activity.

## CONCEPT REVIEW

1. List three different possible measurement bases for inventory.
2. What are the three explicit revenue recognition criteria?
3. How is the concept of matching usually applied to period costs?
4. Does full disclosure mean that all available information is provided in the disclosure notes?

## INTERNATIONAL PERSPECTIVE

The IASC accounting principles, or concepts, are set out in a section called a "Framework," which appears essentially as a preface to the IFRS. The Framework is not an IFRS. The Framework has roughly the same structure and content/conclusions as Section 1000 of the *CICA Handbook*, "Financial Statement Concepts," although the terminology is not identical. The Framework has the following (familiar) sections:

- Users of financial statements and their information needs;
- The objective of financial reporting;
- Underlying assumptions;
- Qualitative characteristics of financial statements;
- Elements of financial statements;
- Recognition criteria;
- Measurement of the elements of financial statements; and
- Concepts of capital and capital maintenance.

Refer to Exhibit 2-5 for a listing of the accounting principles identified.

## EXHIBIT 2-5

### IASB FRAMEWORK

| Underlying Assumptions | Qualitative Characteristics | Constraints | Concepts of Capital |
|---|---|---|---|
| Accrual basis<br>Going concern | Understandability<br>Relevance<br>Materiality<br>Reliability<br>Faithful<br>    representation<br>Substance over<br>    form<br>Neutrality<br>Prudence<br>Completeness<br>Comparability | Timeliness<br>Balance between<br>    benefits and<br>    cost<br>Balance between<br>    qualitative<br>    characteristics<br>True and fair<br>    view/fair<br>    presentation | Financial capital<br>    maintenance<br>Physical capital<br>    maintenance |

As compared to its Canadian counterpart, the Framework uses some different language to describe the concepts, and includes some concepts in different categories. From the perspective of business entities, the major differences are

1. The IASB Framework describes the concepts of physical and financial capital maintenance without choosing either capital maintenance concept. Canadian standards adopt nominal dollar financial capital maintenance.

2. The IASB Framework includes "true and fair view/fair presentation" as a constraint. This constraint is not mentioned in the Canadian "Financial Statement Concepts."

3. The IASB Framework does not explicitly mention the separate-entity assumption, the proprietary approach, or the unit-of-measure assumption.

The implications of such differences are difficult to assess because they are indirect. Since the concepts are used to guide standard setters, they would be expected to affect the direction of standards and choices, where appropriate.

## RELEVANT STANDARDS

*CICA Handbook:*
- Section 1000, Financial Statement Concepts

IASB:
- Framework for the Preparation and Presentation of Financial Statements

## SUMMARY OF KEY POINTS

1. Accounting principles consist of three different sets of concepts: (1) underlying assumptions, (2) measurement methods, and (3) qualitative criteria.

2. *Underlying assumptions* include the basic postulates that make accounting measurements possible (such as *separate entity, unit of measure,* and *time period*), as well as underlying measurement assumptions that usually, but not always, are true in a given reporting situation. These measurement assumptions include *continuity, proprietary approach,* and *nominal dollar financial capital maintenance.*

3. *Qualitative criteria* are the criteria used in conjunction with an enterprise's financial reporting objectives to determine the most appropriate measurement methods to use in that particular reporting situation. Qualitative criteria include relevance, reliability, comparability, objectivity, understandability, materiality, conservatism, and the cost/benefit trade-off.

4. A critical qualitative criterion is that of *relevance*; relevance should be determined with reference to the users of the financial statements and the resulting financial reporting objectives. Relevance is enhanced if information is timely, and has predictive and feedback value.

5. *Reliability* is a qualitative criterion that has several components, including verifiability, freedom from bias, and representational faithfulness.

6. Some qualitative criteria conflict with each other. For example, the most *relevant* measurement in a particular situation may not be sufficiently *reliable* to permit its use.

7. The role of *conservatism* in accounting is to ensure that the uncertainties and risks inherent in measuring the effects of any given business situation are given adequate consideration. Conservatism may not be used as a justification for overstating liabilities or understating assets.

8. The *elements of financial statements* are the seven types of accounts that appear on the balance sheet and income statement: assets, liabilities, owners' equity, revenues, expenses, gains, and losses.

9. The asset and liability definitions require that three time references be present: a *future* benefit or sacrifice and a *present* right or obligation, arising from a *past* transaction or event.

10. Initial accounting *recognition* occurs when the effects or results of a transaction or event are first measured and assigned to an account or *element.* To be recognized, or recorded, an item must meet the element definition, be measurable, and be probable.

11. *Realization* occurs when a cash flow occurs. Realization often occurs after recognition, but can never occur prior to recognition because the cash flow forces recognition if it has not occurred previously.

12. The accrual concept relates to the recognition of receivables when the right to receive cash arises, and to the recognition of liabilities when the obligation is created. Accrual does not refer to subsequent matching and interperiod allocations.

13. *Measurement methods* are the various ways that the results of transactions and events can be reported in the financial statements. Measurement conventions include historical cost, the revenue recognition convention, matching, and full disclosure.

14. Accounting is full of choices. Financial statements are constructed from the financial statement elements that have been recognized using measurement methods that optimize the qualitative characteristics and that are based on the appropriate underlying assumptions. The organization's reporting constraints as well as the facts of its business and environment all impact on the choice of accounting policy. The result is information that best satisfies the objectives of financial reporting in any given situation. This series of related decisions constitutes *ethical professional judgement in accounting.*

## KEY TERMS

accrual-basis accounting, 44
accruals, 44
commitment, 56
comparability, 51
conservatism, 51
consideration, 59
consistency, 51
constant dollar (capital maintenance), 47
constant dollars, 47
continuity assumption, 45
cost/benefit effectiveness, 52
deferrals, 44
differential reporting, 52
elements, 53
entity concept (assumption), 46
executory contract, 57
freedom from bias, 51
full disclosure, 61
going-concern assumption, 45
historical cost convention, 58
matching, 60
materiality, 51
measurement methods (conventions), 40
nominal dollar financial capital
    maintenance, 47

nominal dollars, 47
non-arbitrariness, 51
period costs, 60
physical capital maintenance, 47
professional judgement, 42
proprietary assumption, 45
purchasing power parity, 47
qualitative criteria (characteristics), 40
quantifiability, 51
realization, 57
recognition, 55
relevance, 48
reliability, 49
separate-entity assumption, 44
substance over form, 49
time-period assumption, 43
underlying assumptions
    (postulates), 40
uniformity, 51
unit-of-measure assumption, 46
validity, 49
value added, 46
verifiability, 51

## QUESTIONS

Q2-1    Identify the three different building blocks that comprise accounting principles.

Q2-2    What is the importance of establishing a document such as the *CICA Handbook's* Section 1000, Financial Statement Concepts, or the IASB's Framework?

Q2-3    Why is ethical professional judgement important in accounting?

Q2-4    Identify and describe the six underlying assumptions included in accounting principles.

Q2-5    Explain why the time-period assumption causes accruals and deferrals in accounting.

Q2-6    Does the separate-entity assumption follow the tax and legal status of a corporation? A sole proprietorship?

Q2-7    Relate the continuity assumption to use of historical cost in financial statement measurements of assets.

Q2-8    How are owners viewed under the proprietary assumption as compared to the entity assumption?

Q2-9    Financial statements record goodwill only when it has been purchased in a business combination. How does this relate to the unit-of-measure assumption and the historical cost convention?

Q2-10    Which assumption or principle discussed in this chapter is most affected by the phenomenon of inflation? Give reasons for your choice.

Q2-11    Define both financial and physical capital maintenance and explain the difference between them.

Q2-12    An item in inventory is sold for $1,200. It cost $800, and could be replaced from the supplier for $895. Inflation for the period is 5%. Give three different measures of income, and explain each.

Q2-13    List and describe the significant qualitative criteria that are part of accounting principles.

Q2-14    Describe the characteristics that make information (1) relevant and (2) reliable.

Q2-15    Explain the trade-off that occurs between relevance and reliability.

Q2-16    "If the financial statements are to be understandable to users, they must be reduced to a very simple level for the benefit of those who are less sophisticated." Is this true? Explain.

Q2-17    Describe how consistency and uniformity promote comparability.

Q2-18    When a company evaluates an accounting policy with reference to its cost/benefit effectiveness, what benefits are under consideration? What are the costs?

Q2-19    The definitions of assets and liabilities involve a consideration of the past, present, and future. Explain.

Q2-20    Why is it said that the definitions of assets and liabilities are central to the financial statement element definitions?

Q2-21    What is the difference between a revenue and a gain?

Q2-22    Explain why commitments are not recognized in the financial statements.

Q2-23    What are the general recognition criteria?

Q2-24    Contrast recognition and realization. Why can realization not precede recognition?

Q2-25    Explain the historical cost convention. Why is it used in the basic financial statements instead of current replacement value?

Q2-26    What criteria must be met before revenue can be recognized?

Q2-27    What is the purpose of full, or at least adequate, disclosure?

Q2-28    Describe the role of ethical professional judgement in the choice of accounting policies. What are the influencing factors?

## CASE 2-1

# XBL CONTAINER SHIPPING LIMITED

XBL Container Shipping Ltd. is a Canadian public company, having issued 42% of its common shares in public markets in 20X2. The remainder of XBL shares are privately held, primarily by four family trusts. In general, the company has been profitable (see Exhibit 1) although results in 20X5, the most recent fiscal year, did not meet market expectations and share price has declined from $20 to $14. The company owns or leases 32 container vessels, and has containers with total capacity of 170,000 teu (a measurement of size used in the industry; the equivalent of a 20-foot container), primarily dry-van containers (92%) but also more lucrative temperature-controlled units (6%).

The container shipping industry has facilitated world trade because of its simplicity, efficiency and low cost, and is now an integral part of global sourcing strategies for many of the world's major manufacturers and retailers. The industry has experienced compound growth in volume of about 9% over the last 20 years, several times higher than the increase in global gross domestic product. However, the industry is highly price competitive and cyclical. There are over 500 carriers operating worldwide.

You have been contacted by a friend, who views the lower market price of XBL shares as a potential growth opportunity. Your friend knows that you're studying accounting, and has asked you to consider two accounting policies of XBL that she finds curious.

First, for revenue recognition, XBL reports that

> Revenue and costs directly attributable to loaded container movements are recognized when delivery of the container is completed. A substantial element of the cost of delivery of each container to its ultimate destination is estimated and accrued because there can be delays in determining the final charges from agents and suppliers throughout the world. Consequently, significant accruals are outstanding at each financial period-end. XBL has considerable experience in estimating costs of transporting containers.

However, your friend also notes that in the past year, XBL was forced to restate 20X4 and prior years' earnings by $41 million ($29 million related to 20X4) primarily because costs were understated. According to the company's annual report,

> The errors came to light during the implementation of a new financial accounting system and resulted from deficiencies in certain accounting and related business processes during a period of unprecedented increases in container shipping costs and adverse exchange rates.

In the period after these deficiencies were brought to light, the newly hired CEO left the company, and was replaced.

Your friend wonders whether the company really has the experience to estimate the costs related to a shipment, when the restatement implies otherwise. Accordingly, she has asked you to evaluate the two alternatives, of recording revenue when the container is delivered, versus revenue recognition at a later time at which the costs are known with certainty. Your evaluation should include a review of the appropriate accounting concepts and the impact on financial statement users. Data relating to the volume of shipments is found in Exhibit 2.

Second, for dry-dock costs, XBL reports that

> Dry-docking costs are deferred and amortized over the dry-docking cycle, typically between two and five years.

In dry-dock, a vessel is subject to repairs and repainting, and refit for general use. Normally, repairs are expensed as operating costs. You have been asked to evaluate the two alternatives for your friend, that is, deferral and amortization versus immediate expensing. Your evaluation should again include a review of the appropriate accounting concepts and the impact on financial statement users. Data relating to dry-docking expenditures is found in Exhibit 2.

You decide that it would be helpful to recalculate revenue, and after-tax net income, for 20X2 to 20X5 to show what reported results would have been if revenue were recognized when all costs were known, and if dry-dock expenditures were expensed as incurred.

**Required:**
Prepare the appropriate analysis.

### EXHIBIT 1

## XBL CONTAINER SHIPPING LTD.

(amounts in millions)

| Year | 20X5 | 20X4* | 20X3* | 20X2* | 20X1** |
|------|------|-------|-------|-------|--------|
| Revenue | $1,100 | $939 | $807 | $795 | $564 |
| Net income | $27.2 | $30.6 | $22.8 | $41.7 | $22.4 |

### EXHIBIT 2

## XBL CONTAINER SHIPPING LTD.

(amounts in millions)

| Year | 20X5 | 20X4* | 20X3* | 20X2* | 20X1** |
|------|------|-------|-------|-------|--------|
| Revenue accrued at year-end | $316 | $148 | $244 | $95 | $152 |
| Costs associated with accrued revenue—as corrected in 20X4 restatement | $95 | $60 | $86 | $36 | $53 |
| Dry-docking expenditures | $30 | $10 | $2 | $24 | $12 |
| Amortization of dry-docking expenditures | $14 | $18 | $16 | $17 | $15 |

*As restated
**As restated; prior to public offering when company was private.
Note: The overall corporate tax rate is 40%. Any increase or decrease in income tax expense would increase or decrease recorded future income tax.

## CASE 2-2

### FUTURELINK CABLE INCORPORATED

FutureLink Cable Inc. (FutureLink) is a communications provider offering data transmission and data services to businesses and consumers. Brian MacInnis has been head accountant for three years, and is more than satisfied with the salary and stock option package that lured him away from a competitor. Stock options, awarded at each year-end, are especially attractive, as the share price has increased significantly each year up to this year.

This year, the financial picture has been of considerable concern. Share price has been depressed, largely because of a slowdown in the economy that has affected FutureLink's revenue stream. Internal projections indicate that customer volume is down between 15% and 20%. The FutureLink management team is focusing efforts on cost containment for the remainder of the year, hoping that reduced costs will allow the company to almost make its publicly announced projected income levels. This might avoid further erosion of share price. Costs are being cut to the bone, and layoffs have been announced. FutureLink has had cash flow challenges, which are about to be addressed through a new $50 million credit facility with a chartered bank.

Brian is examining the budget, and accounting policies, for line costs. FutureLink rents capacity on data transmission lines owned by other companies at an annual cost of approximately $48 million. This rent is paid regardless of the actual use of the line. The payment has been expensed as time passes, but Brian is no longer sure that this accounting policy is appropriate. In the past, most of the daily capacity rented was used by FutureLink customers. In the current year, usage is closer to 75%. FutureLink cannot reduce the level of capacity rented, as the company would then not be assured of additional capacity once volumes recover. It would not be possible to replace this capacity in a cost-effective manner, and thus FutureLink is committed to the existing level of payment.

Brian is considering whether it would be appropriate to defer the line costs in proportion to the unused capacity in the current period (i.e., 25%). Deferred line costs would be a capital asset, amortized over a relatively short period of five years, commencing when volumes returned to normal. Brian believes this treatment is justified because future periods will benefit from access to the full rented capacity, and this capacity would be necessary to handle the larger number of customers. Brian, along with other members of top management, is convinced that the reduction in volume is temporary, although there has been additional competition in the past year.

Deferral of approximately $12 million in line costs will go a long way toward eliminating the current shortfall in earnings. Brian knows this will be a huge relief to the senior management team, and it might help expedite the $50 million loan and improve the share price.

**Required:**

Write a report evaluating the proposed change in policy. Include your recommendations to Brian.

---

## CASE 2-3

### SPACESAT LIMITED

SpaceSat Limited (SSL), a Canadian public company established in 1972, is involved in global telecommunication transmissions. SSL has over $1.4 billion in assets, financed by $900 million in liabilities and $500 million in equity. As a federally regulated monopoly in the public spotlight, the company adheres to high standards of disclosure and accountability. SSL owns satellite and underground (and under-ocean) cable communication networks. Access to these facilities is rented to North American customers, including broadcasters, telephone companies, and banking institutions. SSL also has extensive computer facilities, specializing in the development of technology associated with data transmission. Operating revenue for the most recent fiscal year was $420 million. Net income of $26 million provided a reasonable (but not spectacular) return on equity. Income has been stable.

Recently, concern has arisen regarding SSL's abandoned satellites. When satellites reach the end of their technologically useful life, state-of-the-art replacement satellites are launched; the old satellites are either shot out of orbit and into deep space or shut down and "abandoned" in orbit, where they remain indefinitely. There is a risk of the orbit becoming unstable and the satellite crashing to earth. Because of this risk, and the increasing volume of "space junk," there is talk internationally, and within the Canadian government, of requiring owners to properly dispose of abandoned space equipment. No one is quite sure how this could be accomplished. Alternatives include destruction by explosion, retrieval by a shuttle, creation of a "junkyard" on the moon, and so on. All of these alternatives seem far-fetched and extremely expensive. Technology does not exist to achieve many of these alternatives, and the ultimate method of disposal would necessitate extensive research.

SSL is uncertain as to whether it should record, or even disclose, a liability for its abandoned satellites. Legal liability is not established, and at present there is no feasible disposal method. Satellite abandonment is current industry practice; everyone does it. Furthermore, estimates of disposal cost would be based on significant assumptions. It seems clear that any solution will require large initial expenditures.

SSL's CFO has asked the controller's office to prepare a brief report that examines SSL's reporting alternatives for this situation and provides a recommendation. As assistant controller, you have been assigned the task. You have decided to structure your report around a discussion of the recognition criteria, and whether this item meets these criteria.

**Required:**

Prepare the report.                                                    (CGA-Canada, adapted)

## ASSIGNMENTS

★ **A2-1 Underlying Assumptions:** Indicate whether each of the following statements is true or false:

1. The time-period assumption justifies assuming a stable dollar.
2. The continuity assumption justifies the use of historical cost in the financial statements.
3. The separate-entity assumption means that the tax, legal, and accounting status of sole proprietorships are identical.
4. Consistency entails different companies using the same methods for similar transactions.
5. The continuity assumption states that a business entity will last forever.
6. Nominal dollar financial capital maintenance takes inflation into account before profits are recognized.
7. Objectivity includes the characteristics of quantifiability, verifiability, freedom from bias, and non-arbitrariness.
8. Owners are viewed as one of many stakeholders in the proprietary assumption.
9. Matching involves matching revenue to expenses incurred.
10. Quantification is a key element of the unit-of-measure assumption.

★ **A2-2 Explanation of Underlying Assumptions:** Explain each of the following statements:

1. Land is acquired in exchange for shares, but the shares are thinly traded and cannot be easily valued. If two appraisals are received for the land, the lower of the two values would normally be used to recognize the transaction because of conservatism.
2. Since the balance sheet of a partnership excludes the personal assets of the partners, it reflects the separate-entity assumption but not the assets that a creditor could demand to meet partner obligations.
3. Inventory, purchased for $50 per unit, is sold for $75 per unit and a $25 per unit profit is recorded, following nominal dollar financial capital maintenance, even though it will cost $60 to replace the inventory units.
4. Many important assets are excluded from the balance sheet of biotechnology companies because of the unit-of-measure assumption.
5. Long-term rental contracts are shown on the balance sheet as though the assets were bought and a liability taken on, because of the need to show substance over form.

★ **A2-3 Concepts Identification:** In the blanks provided to the left below, enter the letters of the underlying assumption, measurement method, qualitative criteria, or constraint most closely associated with the statements. Some letters may be used more than once and some may not be used at all.

A. Separate entity
B. Continuity
C. Unit of measure
D. Time period
E. Historical cost
F. Revenue recognition

G. Matching
H. Full disclosure
I. Materiality
J. Reliability
K. Conservatism
L. Cost/benefit

_____ 1. Provides that a complicated accounting method that will not improve decisions of financial statement users will not be required in the financial statements.

_____ 2. Assets that increase in value are not written up in the financial statements.

_____ 3. Distinguishes personal transactions of the owners from transactions of the business.

_____ 4. Any accounting method is acceptable for small items that will not change users' decisions.

_____ 5. Warranty expense that takes place two years after a sale is accrued in the (earlier) period of the sale.

_____ 6. Information must be verifiable.

_____ 7. Determines the timing of recognition of revenues.

_____ 8. Means consciously understating assets and income.

_____ 9. Allows historical cost, rather than liquidation values, to be used.

_____ 10. Requires recognized and many non-recognized items to be fully described in the notes to the financial statements.

_____ 11. Requires measurement of the income and financial position of entities at regular intervals.

_____ 12. Assumes that all financial statement elements can be meaningfully described in dollar terms.

★ **A2-4 Capital Maintenance:** Bertha Corp. recently sold inventory for $65,000. The goods had originally cost $46,500. Inflation during the period was 6%. The goods could be replaced from their long-time supplier for $53,300. For simplicity, assume that there are no other costs of doing business.

**Required:**

1. Calculate a measure of accounting income, consistent with
    a. Nominal dollar financial capital maintenance
    b. Constant dollar financial capital maintenance
    c. Physical capital maintenance, in nominal dollars

2. Assume in each case in requirement 1, that the company collected revenue in cash and paid out 100% of net income in dividends to owners. Calculate the remaining cash balance.

3. If the company were planning to replace the inventory, which capital maintenance concept allows it to keep enough money to accomplish this with no further investment or borrowing?

4. Which capital maintenance concept is dominant in North America?

★ **A2-5 Relevance versus Reliability:** Tannino Limited is a private investment company that manages investments for a group of about 30 wealthy individuals. The company is owned and managed by two experienced investment managers, each of whom owns 50% of the shares. The company merges all of its clients' money into a single investment fund. A majority of the investments are in publicly traded companies, but a significant portion is invested in real estate and in private companies as (quite speculative) venture capital. The company is preparing its financial statements for its first fiscal year ended 31 December 20X4. GAAP is not a constraint. The two owner-managers are discussing the proper method of reporting the company's investment portfolio. On the one hand, they wish to present the most useful and relevant information to their investors, as well as to the bank that provides some debt financing. On the other hand, they are concerned about the reliability of the reported asset values for various parts of the investment portfolio.

**Required:**
Discuss the trade-off between relevance and reliability for reporting the asset value of the various types of investments: publicly traded securities, real estate, and venture capital. Your discussion must be relevant to Tannino Limited's specific situation.

---

★ **A2-6 Relevance and Reliability:** Relevance is characterized by the presence of the qualities of timeliness, predictive value, and feedback value. Reliability is characterized by the presence of the qualities of representational faithfulness, verifiability, and freedom from bias. For each of the following, indicate the quality demonstrated:

1  The value assigned to equipment is checked by referring to the original invoice.
2. Predictions concerning this year's income, issued 12 months ago, are compared to the actual results to assess the accuracy of the prediction.
3. Past trends are used to forecast this year's sales.
4. An outside expert is retained to review estimates of warranty liability.
5. Adjustments are made to financial statements that both increase and decrease net income, despite the manager's preference to report lower net income.
6. Financial statements are issued four weeks after the year-end, even though this requires the use of estimates for some elements.
7. Preferred shares that have to be repaid on a given date are classified as a liability despite their legal status as equity.
8. The company releases estimates of operating results for the coming year, based on their budgets.
9. Cash received in advance of work done is recorded as a liability, unearned revenue.

---

★ **A2-7 Questions on Principles:** For each of the following situations, indicate whether you agree or disagree with the practice described, list *one* accounting concept/assumption/qualitative criteria/measurement method that is related to the situation (either followed or violated), and indicate how it is related.

1. Inventory that the company paid $450 for is carried on the balance sheet at $620 because it can be easily sold for $620.
2. The Book Printer Ltd. has an operating cycle of three years. It takes three years to have a book written, published, and sold. The company, therefore, produces financial statements every three years.
3. WLZ Co. must estimate and record a warranty liability and has obtained three estimates—one for $75,000, one for $92,000, and one for $106,000. The company records $75,000.
4. Cambria Corporation has purchased a rare manuscript that the major shareholder, whose passion is antiquities, has wanted. The manuscript is kept at the shareholder's house for his sole use but is carried on the company's books as a long-term investment.
5. Elocom Ltd. has an account receivable *from* Maddox Ltd. for $40,000, and an account payable *to* Maddox Ltd. for $37,000. Elocom shows a net account receivable of $3,000, and no accounts payable, on its balance sheet.
6. Darlington Designs Ltd. has not fixed a $5,000 error in inventory accounting because it would have a trivial effect on cost of goods sold and net income.

---

★ **A2-8 Questions on Principles:** If the following statements are true, write "True" after the statement. However, most are false. For a false statement, write "False" and *briefly* indicate why the statement is false.

1. Full disclosure involves telling financial statement users everything about the company's transactions.
2. Matching means that revenue is matched to the time period in which the enterprise does the work.
3. The continuity assumption means that a manufacturing company will stay in business long enough to use or sell its inventory.
4. The proprietary approach is the reason that dividends declared are classified on the retained earnings statement rather than on the income statement.
5. An asset is something owned by a company.
6. Relevance suffers when market values are included in the financial statements.
7. In order to preserve comparability, accounting policies may never be changed.
8. Many intangible assets are not recorded because of the nominal dollar capital assumption.
9. Materiality is based only on size.

---

★ **A2-9 Application of Principles:** The following list of statements poses conceptual issues:

1. The business entity is considered to be separate and apart from its owners for accounting purposes.
2. A transaction is always recorded in such a way as to reflect its legal form.
3. It is permissible for a company to use straight-line depreciation, even though the rest of the industry uses declining balance, because the company believes that straight-line better reflects the pattern of benefits received from these assets.
4. All details of transactions must be disclosed in the notes to the financial statements.
5. The lower of cost or market method must be used in valuing inventories.
6. The cost principle relates only to the income statement.
7. Revenue should be recognized only when the cash is received.
8. Accruals and deferrals are necessary because of the separate-entity assumption.
9. Revenue should be recognized as late as possible and expenses as early as possible.

**Required:**
1. Indicate whether each statement is correct or incorrect.
2. Identify the principle(s) posed.
3. Provide a brief discussion of its (their) implications.

---

★ **A2-10 Realization versus Recognition:** For each of the following transactions, indicate the point at which (1) the transaction is recognized and (2) the financial statement element is realized.

1. Expected warranty claims on products sold are accrued as the sales are made. Cash payments for warranty claims are made in the subsequent fiscal year.
2. Inventory is bought on 1 August, on credit. It is paid for on 12 September.
3. A customer orders a custom-built machine, and pays when the order is placed on 20 February. The machine is delivered on 10 March.
4. A customer buys a product as a cash sale, on 1 July.
5. Interest is accrued daily, and collected at the end of six months.
6. A sale on credit is completed, and the product delivered, on 1 February. Payment is received on 1 March.

---

★ **A2-11 Recognition of Elements:** In each of the following situations, identify the element or elements, if any, that would appear in financial statements. If no element is recognized, give the reason.

1. Unpaid electricity bill
2. A reputation for quality products

3. A patent on a new invention developed by a firm

4. Unissued common shares of a company that will likely be issued for cash next year

5. A good credit rating

6. The reputation for not paying accounts payable on time

7. University degrees held by employees

8. Cash received from a customer for work to be done next year

★ **A2-12 Elements of Financial Statements:** Financial statement elements have specific definitions. To the right, some important aspects of the definitions are listed. Match the aspects with the elements by entering appropriate letters in the blanks. More than one letter can be placed in a blank.

| Elements of Financial Statements | Important Aspect of the Definition of the Element |
|---|---|
| A. Assets | ____ 1. Using up of assets or incurrence of liabilities |
| B. Liabilities | |
| C. Owners' equity/net assets | ____ 2. Probable future economic benefits obtained by an entity |
| D. Revenues | |
| E. Expenses | ____ 3. Enhancement of assets or settlements of liabilities |
| F. Gains | |
| G. Losses | ____ 4. Residual interest in assets after deducting liabilities |
| H. None of the above | |
| | ____ 5. Increases in net assets from peripheral or incidental activities |
| | ____ 6. From peripheral or incidental transactions of the entity |
| | ____ 7. Future sacrifices arising from past transactions |
| | ____ 8. Results from the entity's ongoing major or central operation |

★ **A2-13 Accrual Accounting:** Under accrual accounting, the effects of transactions and events are reflected in the financial statements relatively independently of the underlying cash flow. Accruals and deferrals are created as a result. Give an example of a transaction that illustrates each of the following:

1. An accrued account receivable is recognized.

2. An accrued liability is recorded.

3. Prepaid expenses are increased.

4. Unearned revenue is recorded.

5. Unearned revenue is decreased.

★ **A2-14 Questions on Principles:** For each of the following circumstances, give the letter item(s) indicating the accounting principle involved:

A. Comparability

B. Conservatism

C. Continuity

D. Cost/benefit effectiveness

E. Full disclosure

F. Historical cost

G. Matching

H. Nominal dollar financial capital maintenance

I. Proprietary

J. Relevance

K. Reliability

L. Revenue recognition

M. Separate entity

N. Time period

O. Unit of measure

1. Goodwill is recorded in the accounts only when it arises from the purchase of another entity.

2. A note describing the company's possible liability in a lawsuit is included with the financial statements even though no formal liability exists at the balance sheet date.

3. Owners are considered the primary focus of the financial statements; others who have a significant stake in the profitability of the company, such as lenders or employees, are not given equal status.

4. The personal assets of partners are excluded from the partnership balance sheet, even though pledged as security for partnership loans.

5. A retail store uses estimates rather than a complete physical count of its inventory for purposes of preparing monthly financial statements.

6. Marketable securities are valued at market value.

7. An entity reports a $50 profit after buying a unit of inventory for $100 and selling it for $150, even though the cost to replace the unit has escalated to $112, due to inflation.

8. An advance deposit on a sale contract is reported as unearned revenue.

9. Accounting policies chosen for revenue recognition are the same as those of the entity's major competitors.

10. Capital assets are amortized over their useful lives.

---

★ **A2-15 Identification of Accounting Principles:** In the following cases, indicate the principle that applies to each case and state whether it was followed or violated.

*Case A* Loran Company used FIFO in 20X2; LIFO in 20X3; and FIFO in 20X4.

*Case B* A tract of land was acquired on credit by signing a $55,000, one-year, non-interest-bearing note. The asset account was debited for $55,000. The going rate of interest was 10%.

*Case C* Loran Company always issues its annual financial report nine months after the end of the annual reporting period.

*Case D* Loran Company recognizes all sales revenues on the cash basis.

*Case E* Loran Company records interest expense only on the payment dates.

*Case F* Loran Company includes among its financial statement elements an apartment building owned and operated by the owner of the company.

*Case G* Loran Company never uses notes or supplemental schedules as a part of its financial reports.

---

★ **A2-16 Recognition and Elements:** Indicate if each of the following items would be recognized in a company's financial statements for 20X3, and what elements would be recognized. For any items that would not be recognized, explain the reason for non-recognition.

1. A purchase order to buy inventory early in the following year.

2. The company's share price has increased from $42 to $65 on the stock exchange. Therefore, unissued shares are worth more.

3. The month of December has passed, and tenants have occupied space in the company's building but have not yet paid, although payment is assured.

4. The right to use an international industrial trademark over the next five years, purchased from a Taiwanese computer manufacturer.

5. Increases in the value of cash deposits held in U.S. dollars because of improving exchange rates.

6. Recording employee morale as an asset.

7. The company's major competitor has gone out of business, resulting in a flood of new customers.
8. The estimated future cost of restoring a mining site to its original condition.

---

★ **A2-17 Revenue Recognition:** Which of the following events would normally involve revenue recognition, assuming use of accrual accounting and revenue recognition on delivery:

1. Collection of cash from a customer 30 days after the product is delivered.
2. Collection of cash from a customer 30 days before the product is delivered.
3. Delivery of a magazine as part of a 12-month subscription.
4. Land that cost $40,000 is known to have a value of $67,000.
5. A financial institution loans $100,000 to a client; interest is due after 12 months; the financial institution is preparing financial statements two months after the loan was granted.
6. Goods are delivered to a customer with an invoice price of $26,000; the customer is notoriously slow in paying.

---

★ **A2-18 Application of Principles:** During an audit of LRT Company, the following situations were found to exist:

a. The company uses the straight-line method of measuring depreciation on manufacturing machinery, even though it knows that a method based on actual usage would provide better matching, more accurate income determination, and thus better information for financial statement users. The straight-line method is significantly cheaper to calculate, because of the level of data needed to implement a usage method.
b. For inventory purposes, LRT switched from FIFO to average cost to FIFO for the same items during a five-year period.
c. LRT does not provide information about future contracts, called the "order backlog" in its financial statements, even though this disclosure is quite common in the industry.
d. LRT follows a policy of depreciating plant and equipment on the straight-line basis over a period of time that is 50% longer than the most reliable useful life estimate.
e. Rent expense is reported at the end of each fiscal year as the net amount of rent expense less rent revenue but the amounts are so small, on a gross basis, that no one's overall perception of the company would be changed.

**Required:**

1. Identify and briefly explain the accounting principle that is directly involved in each situation.
2. Indicate what, if anything, the company should do in the future by way of any change in accounting policy.

---

★ **A2-19 Application of Principles:** An inspection of the annual financial statements and the accounting records revealed that the George L. Massey Hardware Company had violated some aspect of accounting principles. The following transactions were involved:

a. Merchandise purchased for resale was recorded as a debit to inventory for the invoice price of $80,000 (accounts payable was credited for the same amount); terms were 2/10, n/30. Ten days later, the account was paid at the net amount due, $78,400 ($80,000 less the 2% discount for paying within 10 days). The $1,600 discount was credited to a revenue account. The goods purchased were still in inventory at $80,000 at year-end.
b. Depreciation expense of $227,000 was recorded as a debit to retained earnings and was deducted directly from retained earnings on the balance sheet.
c. Usual and ordinary repairs on operational assets were recorded as follows: debit operational assets, $500; credit cash, $500.

d. The company sustained a $96,000 storm damage loss during the current year (no insurance). The loss was recorded and reported as follows:

| | |
|---|---|
| Income statement: Extraordinary item—storm loss | $24,000 |
| Balance sheet (assets): Deferred charge—storm loss | $72,000 |

e. Accounts receivable of $95,000 were reported on the balance sheet; this amount included a $42,000 three-year loan to the company president. The maturity date of the loan was not specified.

**Required:**

1. For each transaction, identify the inappropriate treatment and the principle(s) violated, if any.
2. Give the original entry that should have been made or the appropriate reporting.

★★ **A2-20 Implementation of Principles:** The following summarized transactions were recorded as indicated for Carleton Builders Limited during the current year.

a. The company originally sold and issued 100,000 common shares. During the current year, 94,000 of these shares were outstanding and 6,000 were repurchased from the shareholders and retired. Near the end of the current year, the Board of Directors declared and paid a cash dividend of $8 per share. The dividend was recorded as follows:

| | | |
|---|---|---|
| Retained earnings | 800,000 | |
| Cash | | 752,000 |
| Dividend income ($8 × 6,000) | | 48,000 |

b. Carleton Builders Limited purchased a machine that had a fair value of $90,000, although there were few comparable transactions to support this. The company paid for the machine in full by issuing 10,000 common shares (market price $8.50). The purchase was recorded as follows:

| | | |
|---|---|---|
| Machine | 90,000 | |
| Share capital | | 85,000 |
| Gain on acquisition | | 5,000 |

c. Carleton needed a small structure for temporary storage. A contractor quoted a price of $769,000. The company decided to build the structure itself. The cost was $542,000, and construction required three months. The following entry was made:

| | | |
|---|---|---|
| Buildings—warehouse | 769,000 | |
| Cash | | 542,000 |
| Revenue—self-construction | | 227,000 |

d. Carleton owns a plant located on a river that floods every few years. As a result, the company suffers a flood loss regularly. During the current year, the flood was severe, causing an uninsured loss of $97,000, which was the amount spent to repair the flood damage. The following entry was made:

| | | |
|---|---|---|
| Retained earnings, flood loss | 97,000 | |
| Cash | | 97,000 |

e. On 28 December, the company collected $76,000 cash in advance for merchandise to be available and shipped during February of the next accounting year (the accounting period ends 31 December). This transaction was recorded on 28 December as follows:

| | | |
|---|---|---|
| Cash | 76,000 | |
| Sales revenue | | 76,000 |

**Required:**

1. For each transaction, determine which accounting principle (if any) was violated.
2. Explain the nature of the violation.
3. In each instance, indicate how the transaction should have been originally recorded.

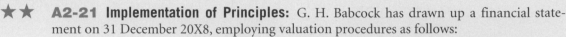

★★    **A2-21 Implementation of Principles:** G. H. Babcock has drawn up a financial statement on 31 December 20X8, employing valuation procedures as follows:

| | | |
|---|---|---|
| Cash | $40,000 | Includes cash in the bank, $35,000, plus $5,000 of American money; the exchange rate today is US$1 = Cdn$1.15 |
| Marketable securities | $90,000 | Represents the cost of common shares held in another company. At 31 December 20X8, the market value was $140,200 |
| Accounts receivable | $50,000 | Recorded in 20X8 when an order was received from a customer for $50,000. The goods have not been manufactured or shipped, but revenue and an account receivable were recognized |
| Sundry payables | $     1 | Recorded as a result of a timber property owned by Babcock. Trees are currently being harvested, and the property will have to be replanted when harvesting ends in 20X9. Replanting will likely cost $30,000. |

**Required:**

1. Indicate what change, if any, you would make in reporting each of the preceding items.
2. In each case, discuss the accounting principle involved.

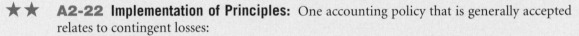

★★    **A2-22 Implementation of Principles:** One accounting policy that is generally accepted relates to contingent losses:

> If the loss is measurable, and likely to be paid, then the amount is accrued in the financial statements. If the amount is not measurable, and/or is not likely to be paid out, then it is not recorded. Also, if the probability of payment cannot be determined (is not estimable) the loss is not recorded.

For example, this policy can be directly applied to lawsuits. If a company is being sued by a disgruntled ex-customer, and the matter is before the courts, there can be a long delay in dispute resolution. A company will record a loss from the lawsuit prior to the court decision only if an amount, if any, of the court-ordered award can be predicted, *and* it appears likely that the company will lose the lawsuit or agree to a settlement. If an amount is not recorded, the existence of the lawsuit is typically disclosed in the disclosure notes.

**Required:**

1. List the recognition criteria.
2. Explain the accounting policy for contingent losses with reference to the recognition criteria.

★★    **A2-23 Policy Choice and Recognition; Comprehensive:** YHK Ltd. recently spent $350,000 on staff training regarding new business processes. This is far in excess of regular annual training programs. YHK expects these business processes to quickly decrease operating costs.

YHK has two alternatives for accounting for the $350,000 of staff training costs:

a. Expense all costs in the current year, when they were incurred.
b. Defer the $350,000 as an asset, and amortize it straight line over five years.

**Required:**

1. If YHK Ltd. were trying to establish GAAP in this area, what sources would it consult?
2. Why might it be unable to determine GAAP for this issue?

3. What policy choice would you expect YHK to adopt in each of the following scenarios (policy a, policy b, or indifferent). The scenarios are independent. *Briefly* explain your choice.
   a. YHK is in a loss position before considering this issue. Management makes the choice and is compensated with a bonus based on 10% of net income.
   b. YHK will report a profit this year (before considering the issue) and has a loan covenant that specifies a minimum current ratio.
   c. YHK will show a profit this year (before considering the issue) and had a loan covenant that specifies a maximum debt-to-equity ratio.
4. How would you justify the deferral of costs using the definition of an asset? Explain your reasoning.

**A2-24 Implementation of Principles:** Analyze each of the following situations and indicate which accounting principle or principles, as described in the chapter, is in evidence.

*Case A*  The financial statements of Raychem Corporation included the following note:

> During the current year, plant assets were written down by $8,000,000. This writedown will reduce future expenses. Depreciation and other expenses in future years will be lower, and as a result this will benefit profits of future years.

*Case B*  During an audit of the Silvona Company, certain liabilities such as taxes appear to be overstated. Also, some quasi-obsolete inventory items seem to be undervalued, and the tendency is to expense rather than capitalize as many items as possible. Management states that "the company has always taken a very conservative view of the business and its future prospects." Management suggests that it does not wish to weaken the company by reporting any more earnings or paying any more dividends than are absolutely necessary because it does not expect business to continue to be good. Management points out that the lower valuations for assets and so on do not lose anything for the company but do create reserves for "hard times."

*Case C*  There was no comment or explanation of the fact that ABC Company changed its inventory method from FIFO to average cost at the beginning of the current reporting period. A large changeover difference was involved, and there was no retrospective restatement.

*Case D*  Current assets amounted to $314,000 and current liabilities, $205,000; the balance sheet of Nelta Corp. reported a single amount "Working capital, $109,000."

*Case E*  In 20X1, the Tryler Corporation switched its inventory method for financial reporting from LIFO to FIFO. Tryler publicly explained, "Our major competitors have consistently used the FIFO method. Therefore, the reported loss for 20X1 and the restated profit for 20X0 are on a comparable basis as to inventory valuation with competitors." The impact on opening balances is not material.

**A2-25 Recognition Criteria:** In each case below, discuss issues surrounding recognition of the element in the financial statements.

*Case A*  Airlines offer frequent-flyer mileage credits to customers. Currently there exists a huge resource of potential trips the public could sign up for at the airlines' expense. Most airlines allow passengers to use mileage credits only for unused capacity—otherwise empty seats. Industry experts estimate that the incremental cost of putting a passenger on a plane is around only $15—the cost of the meal and extra fuel for the additional weight. If the passenger were to use mileage credits to "bump" a full-fare passenger, then there is obviously a significant opportunity cost associated with the trip. The element to be recognized is the liability to frequent flyers but airlines grapple with alternative values for the liability.

*Case B*  The value of Coca-Cola's trademark has been estimated in excess of $1 billion. Yet even though Coca-Cola reports over $4 billion of goodwill and other intangible assets, none of this reported value is due to the Coca-Cola trademark, which is unrecognized despite its considerable commercial value.

*Case C*  Waste Disposal Limited is being sued to force it to clean up contamination at over 60 sites; this information is reported in the notes to the company's annual report, but no amount is accrued in the financial statements. The extent of the future cleanup costs is reported to be "substantial."

## CHAPTER 3

# The Income Statement and the Retained Earnings Statement

## INTRODUCTION

CHC Helicopter operates helicopter services in 35 countries. The company provides air ambulance, search and rescue, and offshore oil and gas platform services. The company's head office is in Vancouver.

CHC's 2006 income statement shows several different earnings amounts—operating income; earnings from continuing operations; net earnings; and comprehensive income. As well, there is net earnings according to Canadian GAAP ($90.7 million) and net earnings according to US GAAP ($130.6).

This chapter explains the various aspects of earnings and how they are displayed on the face of the income statement. The chapter also explains what is *not* necessarily shown on the income statement, such as major categories of expense. Not all components of a company's earnings are equal—some are continuing revenues and costs while others are occasional or rare. Current income can be affected by one-time events and by changes in accounting standards.

Our purpose in this chapter is to help you understand the information contained in the income statement. Measurement and recognition issues are critical, but those issues will be discussed in the following chapters. This chapter focuses on the display of revenues, expenses, gains, and losses after they have been recorded. Accounting standards require that certain items of information be reported on the income statement. In general, however, the level of information provided on the income statement is left to the discretion of management.

In this chapter, we will begin by discussing the alternative presentation formats. We then will discuss extraordinary items, discontinued operations, and other required disclosures that are specifically mandated by accounting standards. We then turn our attention to *other comprehensive income*, a very recent addition to the accounting vocabulary. The chapter will end with a discussion of the retained earnings statement.

## NATURE OF INCOME

A company's *net earnings* or *income* is defined as follows:

> Increases in economic benefits during the accounting period in the form of inflows or enhancements of assets or decreases of liabilities that result in increases in equity, other than those relating to contributions from equity participants.[1]

Three aspects of this definition deserve special attention:

1. "Increases in economic benefits" means all transactions with outside parties, plus changes in value that are recognized in accounting. "Increases" means *net* increases, or net income. Obviously, there are both increases and decreases, and if decreases exceed increases, then the company has a net loss.

2. Implicit in this definition is that the only increases (and decreases) that enter net income are those that are *recognized* under existing accounting standards. There will be other value changes that affect the company that are not recognized in accounting. We will discuss that aspect in the next section.

3. Transactions with *owners* are excluded from this definition. Income is measured only as the result of interactions (transactions or value changed) with *non-owners*.

The income statement links a company's beginning and ending balance sheets for a given accounting period. The income statement explains changes in owners' equity caused by operations and certain other activities during the period. When there is no new investment or disinvestment by owners (or other minor technical changes), the change in owners' equity from the beginning to the end of the period equals net income. Exhibit 3-1 illustrates this point.

### Economic Income versus Accounting Income

The term "income" means different things to different people. For example, an economist defines income as a *change in wealth*, whether or not that change in wealth has been realized. Suppose that a company owns a parcel of land for which it paid $10,000 several years ago. A new highway has just been built next to the property, and several individuals have offered to pay $125,000 to $150,000 for the land. The firm has not yet agreed to sell. The economist would say that an increase in wealth has occurred because the land is worth more than historical cost. The wealth increase is called economic income, and it is based on an *events approach* rather than on completed transactions.

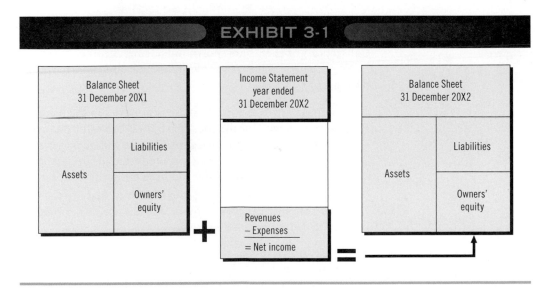

**EXHIBIT 3-1**

---

[1] Extracted from Glossary of Terms. © IASC Foundation.

Using the historical cost measurement principle, an accountant would not recognize such an increase in wealth as income. Only if the land is sold to another party in an arm's-length transaction would the accountant recognize the increase in wealth as income. This is **accounting income**, based on the *transactions approach*.

Historically, accounting had been based strictly on the transactions approach and the historical cost measurement principle. Changes in value were recognized only when there was a transaction that *realized* the change in value. The only exceptions to the transaction approach occurred in the writedown or downward valuation of items such as obsolete inventory and accounts receivable.

Now, however, accounting recognizes not only value changes realized through transactions, but also certain types of value changes that have not been realized. A prime example is the reporting of financial assets and liabilities, many of which are reported on the balance sheet at market values. The reporting of market values leads to accounting recognition of value changes as either realized or unrealized income.

But only some value changes are recognized and reported. Many other value changes, such as increases in the value of capital assets, are not recognized in accounting. Therefore, accounting income is still very different from economic income.

Revenue and expense recognition are key concepts in accounting. The concepts determine when and how revenues, gains, expenses, and losses are recorded. Determining the proper treatment for a particular transaction or event is often difficult. Indeed, a large part of the study of accounting addresses measurement and recognition issues as they apply to assets and liabilities, as well as to revenues, gains, expenses, and losses. Chapter 2 discussed the general nature of recognition criteria. Because revenue and expense recognition is such a significant aspect of accounting, Chapter 6 is devoted exclusively to revenue and expense recognition.

## Inclusiveness of the Income Statement

Which items affecting shareholders' equity should be included in the computation of net income and reported in the income statement? That is, what items, if any, should be excluded from net income and recorded elsewhere in the financial statements?

There are three possible places to record recognized changes in assets and liabilities from non-owner sources:

- Income statement;
- Statement of comprehensive income; and
- Statement of retained earnings.

The vast majority of items (other than transactions with owners) are included in net income. In accounting terminology, this is the *all-inclusive* approach to income reporting—very few transactions or events are shown outside net income.

Nevertheless, there are some items that are reported elsewhere. In general, the exceptions are

- Some changes in value that are recognized in the balance sheet, but which have not yet been realized. For the most part, these are value changes (1) that will be recognized in income only when realized, or (2) that will be matched by an offsetting gain or loss in a future period. These items are reported in the *statement of comprehensive income*. We will discuss *comprehensive income* later in this chapter.
- Cumulative changes to retained earnings that are the result of (1) changes in accounting policy or (2) correction of errors in prior periods. These items are reported in the *statement of retained earnings*.

Otherwise, the results of all transactions and all *recognized* value changes are reported in the income statement.

Before we turn to these excluded types of items, let's take a close look at the content and composition of the income statement.

---

**accounting income**

an increase in the reported wealth of a corporation based only on transactions completed and value changes recognized; a measure of income based on the accounting model

## CONCEPT REVIEW

1. Explain the relationship between the income statement and the balance sheet.

2. Explain the difference between accounting income and economic income.

3. What general types of changes in assets and liabilities are *not* reported on the income statement? In which statement(s) are the excluded items reported?

## GENERAL PRESENTATION FORMAT

Accounting standards do not prescribe the format of the income statement in much detail. Companies are quite free to use various presentation formats, as long as they do report certain types of items that are required by accounting standards.[2]

Within this general presentation flexibility, however, a company is required to show three specific totals (or subtotals) on its income statement, when applicable:

- Income before discontinued operations and extraordinary items (often referred to as *income from continuing operations*);
- Income before extraordinary items (that is, after adding or subtracting the results of discontinued operations); and
- Net income (that is, after adding and subtracting gains and losses from extraordinary items).

Of course, if the company has no discontinued operations and/or extraordinary items, then the first and/or second subtotal will not be applicable.

### Continuing Operations

There is no specific positive definition of *continuing operations*. Continuing operations are defined by what they exclude—continuing operations are activities of a company for which the company has no formal short-term plan of sale or divesture. The accounting classification of discontinued operations and extraordinary items will be explained later in this chapter. Every segment of the business that does *not* fit the definition of a discontinued operation is included in the catch-all phrase of continuing operations.

Accounting standards have very few prescribed formats for the income statement (also known as the *statement of earnings* or *statement of operations*). Instead, accounting standards enumerate some specific items that should be disclosed. The major mandatory disclosures are:

- Revenues recognized
- The amount of inventories recognized as expense (that is, cost of goods sold)
- Investment income
- Government assistance (when credited directly to income)
- Amortization expense, separately for tangible and intangible assets
- Research and development expense
- Interest expense (separately for short-term debt, long-term debt, and leases)
- Unusual items
- Income tax expense
- Earnings per share

---

[2] This situation may change. The IASB has been working on a framework for financial reporting that would also become effective in Canada.

Although *disclosure* of these items of revenue and expense is required, the *format* of presentation usually is not prescribed. Earnings per share (EPS) must be shown on the face of the income statement, but the other amounts can be disclosed either on the face of the income statement or in the disclosure notes.

The list above is notable for the narrow range of required disclosures. Accounting standards do not require disclosure of many major categories of expense.

To present the components of income from continuing operations, companies may use a variety of formats ranging from *single step* to extensive *multiple step*. The following two sections describe these two ends of the continuum of income statement presentation. Most companies use presentations that fall between these two extremes.

### Single-Step Format

The single-step format uses only two broad classifications for presenting income from continuing operations: (1) a section showing revenues and gains and (2) a section showing expenses and losses. Income from continuing operations is computed in one step, without intermediate subtotals.

Petro-Canada (Exhibit 3-2) uses a modified version of the single-step method. The company groups all of the revenues together and all of the expenses together, except income tax. The company then shows a subtotal for *earnings from continuing operations before income taxes*. In a "pure" single-step statement, income tax expense would be listed as just another expense, with no subtotal for earnings before income taxes.

The company discloses the required items of income and expense on the face of its income statement, including operating revenue, investment income, amortization (i.e., "depreciation, depletion, and amortization"), interest expense, and income tax expense. The company reports major categories of expense, but shows no amount labelled as cost of goods sold. Earnings per share also are shown on the face of the statement, following net earnings.

Notice that the word "income" does not appear in either the statement heading or the body of the statement. Instead, the company's preferred term is "earnings." *Financial Reporting in Canada* reports that there is an almost equal split between the use of "earnings" and "income" by Canadian companies, with a slight edge in favour of "earnings."

Petro-Canada reports three years' earnings rather than the two years normally required in Canada because the company also reports to the Securities and Exchange Commission (SEC) in the U.S. The SEC requires a three-year presentation on the income statement.

Petro-Canada's retained earnings statement is shown at the bottom of Exhibit 3-2. It is easy to see the transfer of annual net earnings into the retained earnings (e.g., $1,740 million for 2006), as described by the diagram in Exhibit 3-1.

### Multiple-Step Format

Exhibit 3-3 presents the income statement for Gennum Corporation, a large Canadian producer of semiconductors and semiconductor-based products. Gennum uses a classified income statement. This format is known as *multiple-step*, to differentiate it from the *single-step* format.

A multiple-step income statement shows several subtotals before arriving at operating income. The most common characteristic of multiple-step statements is that they usually have separate categories for (1) operating revenues and expenses and (2) non-operating revenues and expenses.

For example, Gennum shows investment income and other income/loss following the subtotal for *Earnings from operations*. In comparison, Petro-Canada shows investment income along with operating revenue, and lists interest expense along with operating expenses.

Gennum shows four subtotals:

- Gross margin (also known as *gross income* or *gross profit*)
- Earnings from operations
- Earnings before income taxes
- Net earnings for the year

Only the last total is required by accounting standards.

EXHIBIT 3-2

## PETRO-CANADA
## Consolidated Statement of Earnings

[stated in millions of Canadian dollars, except per share amounts]

| For the years ended December 31, | 2006 | 2005 | 2004 |
|---|---|---|---|
| **Revenue** | | | |
| Operating | $18,911 | $17,585 | $14,270 |
| Investment and other income (expense) | (242) | (806) | (312) |
| | 18,669 | 16,779 | 13,958 |
| **Expenses** | | | |
| Crude oil and product purchases | 9,649 | 8,846 | 6,740 |
| Operating, marketing and general | 3,180 | 2,962 | 2,572 |
| Exploration | 399 | 271 | 235 |
| Depreciation, depletion and amortization | 1,365 | 1,222 | 1,256 |
| Unrealized gain on translation of foreign currency denominated long-term debt | (1) | (88) | (77) |
| Interest | 165 | 164 | 142 |
| | 14,697 | 13,377 | 10,868 |
| **Earnings from continuing operations before income taxes** | 3,972 | 3,402 | 3,090 |
| **Provision for income taxes** | | | |
| Current | 2,073 | 1,794 | 1,365 |
| Future | 311 | (85) | 27 |
| | 2,384 | 1,709 | 1,392 |
| **Net earnings from continuing operations** | 1,588 | 1,693 | 1,698 |
| **Net earnings from discontinued operations** | 152 | 98 | 59 |
| **Net earnings** | $ 1,740 | $ 1,791 | $ 1,757 |
| **Earnings per share from continuing operations** | | | |
| Basic | $ 3.15 | $ 3.27 | $ 3.21 |
| Diluted | $ 3.11 | $ 3.22 | $ 3.17 |
| **Earnings per share** | | | |
| Basic | $ 3.45 | $ 3.45 | $ 3.32 |
| Diluted | $ 3.41 | $ 3.41 | $ 3.28 |

## Consolidated Statement of Retained Earnings

[stated in millions of Canadian dollars]

| For the years ended December 31, | 2006 | 2005 | 2004 |
|---|---|---|---|
| **Retained earnings at beginning of year** | $ 7,018 | $ 5,408 | $ 3,810 |
| Net earnings | 1,740 | 1,791 | 1,757 |
| Dividends on common shares | (201) | (181) | (159) |
| **Retained earnings at end of year** | $ 8,557 | $ 7,018 | $ 5,408 |

*Source:* www.sedar.com, Petro-Canada 2006 Annual Report released March 29, 2007, page 48.

**EXHIBIT 3-3**

## GENNUM CORPORATION

### Consolidated Statements of Earnings and Retained Earnings

Years ended November 30 (Canadian dollars, amounts in thousands except per share data)

|  | 2006 | 2005 |
|---|---|---|
| **Revenue** | 147,336 | 142,766 |
| Cost of goods sold | 48,238 | 44,049 |
| Gross margin | 99,098 | 98,717 |
| Sales, marketing and administration expense | 37,943 | 35,398 |
| Research and development expense | 44,918 | 44,666 |
| Less government assistance | (8,890) | (8,489) |
| Operating expenses before restructuring charge | 73,971 | 71,575 |
| Restructuring charge | 1,964 | — |
| Earnings from operations | 23,163 | 27,142 |
| Investment income | 1,486 | 697 |
| Other income | 1,872 | 2,407 |
| Share of loss in equity investment | — | (310) |
| Earnings before income taxes | 26,521 | 29,936 |
| Provision for income taxes | 9,256 | 9,548 |
| **Net earnings for the year** | 17,265 | 20,388 |
| Retained earnings, beginning of year | 132,765 | 116,666 |
| Dividends | (4,848) | (4,289) |
| Repurchase of common shares | (2,114) | — |
| **Retained earnings, end of year** | 143,068 | 132,765 |
| **Earnings per share** | | |
| Basic | $0.48 | $0.57 |
| Diluted | $0.48 | $0.57 |

*Source:* www.sedar.com, Gennum Corporation 2006 Annual Report released February 16, 2007, page 39.

Notice that Gennum uses a continuous format for income and retained earnings. This is common form of presentation. A combined statement of earnings and retained earnings is used by about 25% of the sample companies in *Financial Reporting in Canada*.

The various categories of revenue and expense that often appear on a multiple-step statement are as follows. Not every multiple-step income statement will include all of these sections. Remember that the only prescribed format for the income statement is that there must be an earnings subtotal both before discontinued operations and before extraordinary items, if either of those types of items exist.

**Operating Revenues** Multiple-step statements begin by showing revenue from operations. Investment and other income, such as investment income or miscellaneous gains, are shown later in the statement. Gennum's statement of earnings starts with just one line for operating revenue. A disclosure note shows the revenue by type (i.e., from video, audio, datacom, and other), which is common practice.

**Cost of Sales** The second step of a multiple-step income statement shows the cost of the goods sold or of services provided. Subtracting cost of sales from operating revenues gives gross margin. Gross margin also is called "gross profit." As well, it sometimes is called "net revenue" because gross margin indicates how much of the revenue is left over after the product (or service) costs are paid. Some analysts like to see a high gross margin as a percentage of revenue because a company with a high margin may have more flexibility in dealing with economic downturns.

However, some costs can be allocated either to cost of sales or to operating expenses, which is the next section of the statement. An outside reader has no way of knowing what specific costs the company includes in cost of sales. Does cost of sales represent mainly variable costs, or is there a large component of allocated fixed overhead? Inventory costs should include some overhead costs (discussed in Chapter 8), but much is left to the discretion of management.

**Operating Expenses** The next section shows the operating expenses that are not included in cost of sales. Gennum shows only two expense items in this category: (1) sales, marketing and administrative expense, and (2) research and development expense. These expenses are reduced by an amount received for government assistance. The company provides no additional information about the composition of these expenses (nor of cost of goods sold). Companies very seldom disclose any of the components of these major expense categories, such as labour costs, materials costs, selling commissions, and so forth.

**Operating Income from Continuing Operations** This subtotal gives an indication of the ability of the company to generate earnings from its continuing operations excluding (1) income and expense from investing and financing activities, (2) income taxes, and (3) the results of discontinued operations. Gennum labels this total as *earnings from operations*.

**Other Income and Expense** The next section on Gennum's income statement shows non-operating income and expense. This section normally shows investment income and interest expense, as well as foreign exchange gains and losses. *Unusual items* may be shown in this section as well.

**Unusual Items** Some companies experience events or transactions that have a significant impact on earnings but which are not a part of normal operations. Most often, these unusual events are losses, but they can also be gains. Although the gains and losses are rare or unusual, they are the result of a normal business risk. These gains or losses should be disclosed separately on the income statement to emphasize their nature as unusual or infrequent. However, even though they are large and unusual, they still are part of net income before tax. Unusual items should *not* be shown net of income tax or be labelled as extraordinary items.

For example, assume a timber company has a large writedown of its pulp and paper inventory and timber resources (a capital asset) due to prevailing low prices in the timber industry. The writedown, an impairment of value, has been determined by management but caused by outside events—low market prices. It is certainly infrequent, since the company reports that it is the first time in the company's 40-year history that such a writedown has been necessary. However, risks associated with price fluctuations in a natural resource market are a *typical business risk* in the timber industry. The item is part of the company's operations.

Classification of an item as "unusual" is quite open to management discretion: Any item deemed "unusual" may be reported in this fashion. Common examples of losses or expenses given separate disclosure include restructuring costs, writedowns of capital assets and investments, and severance payments. Common types of gains that are given separate disclosure are gains on debt restructuring, gains on disposal of an investment, and gains on sale of capital assets.

**Income Tax** The contents of this section are rather obvious—both current and future income tax expense (or recovery) are recognized. Gennum shows those two components as a single amount; detail is given in a disclosure note.

**Discontinued Operations** This section includes the results for any parts of the business that either were discontinued during the year or that the Board of Directors has decided to discontinue, either by sale or by shutting them down. The discontinued operations section includes the revenues and expenses for the operation for the year, as well as any asset writedowns. Petro-Canada (Exhibit 3-2) shows earnings of $152 million from discontinued operations.

The objective of reporting discontinued operations separately is to make it clear to users that the revenues and expenses relating to these operations will not contribute to earnings in future periods.

We will discuss discontinued operations more fully later in this chapter.

**Extraordinary Items** Neither Petro-Canada nor Gennum shows extraordinary items. It is very rare to report an extraordinary item under Canadian GAAP. We will discuss extraordinary items more fully later in the chapter.

## Which Format?

The single-step format has the advantage of simplicity. A single-step statement contains the same information as a multiple-step income statement, and users can rearrange components of the statement to suit their needs.

The multiple-step format is potentially more informative to decision makers because it highlights important relationships and intermediate subtotals in the report. Advocates of the multiple-step format believe that there are important relationships in revenue and expense data and that the income statement is more useful when these relationships are explicitly shown.

In practice, very few Canadian companies use a pure single-step statement. About 50% provide one intermediate subtotal, similar to the almost-single-step statement of Petro-Canada (Exhibit 3-2). Only about 10% of surveyed public companies in *Financial Reporting in Canada* show all three subtotals of gross margin, operating income, and pre-tax income. Therefore, the vast majority of companies use a format that falls between the extremes of pure single-step (2%) and fully classified multiple-step (10%) statements.

Finally, remember that a subtotal for gross margin can be reported only if the company discloses its cost of sales. About 40% of companies report cost of sales, and only a minority of those companies deducts cost of sales from revenues. When a company does disclose cost of sales, it most likely will show cost of sales as a separate item within other expenses—an approach consistent with single-step format.

## Minimum Disclosure

Exhibits 3-2 and 3-3 show income statements that contain some detail in the expense and revenue categories, but also involve a lot of grouping. For example, in Exhibit 3-3 Gennum reports three expense categories that account for 87% of sales. The company discloses no additional quantitative detail about the components of those three substantial items. Would you like to know how much of Gennum's expenses comprise labour costs? You won't find out from the financial statements.

Gennum is not unusual in this respect. Income statements seldom disclose much useful information about the operating revenues and expenses of a company.

Management has a lot of flexibility in presenting revenue, expense, gain, and loss items in the income statement. Grouping reduces the length and complexity of the statement, but it may also reduce its predictive value and the information content of the statement. Grouping also hides sensitive information from competitors.

Since there is no requirement that major items of expense be reported, it is not even necessary for an income statement to show major components of expense. An income statement can be prepared by showing only those few items specifically mandated by accounting standards. We will illustrate this type of income statement a little later in this chapter, in Exhibit 3-6.

## CONCEPT REVIEW

1. What income statement sections are *required* by accounting standards?

2. How might interest expense on long-term debt be presented differently in a single-step versus a multiple-step income statement?

3. What distinguishes expense items that are reported as operating expense from those that are reported as other expense?

## OTHER FORMAT CHOICES

There is a lot of flexibility in format issues for the income statement, leaving companies leeway to pick reporting policies that suit their individual circumstances and that best serve their user groups and themselves.

**Title** The income statement is also known as the *earnings statement* or *statement of operations*. In this text, we will most often use the term *income statement*. When a parent company and its subsidiaries are combined for the report, the statement is identified as a *consolidated income statement*.

International standards refer to this statement as the *Statement of Recognized Income and Expense*, a title that is not yet used in North America.

**Fiscal Year-End** A company must choose a fiscal year-end. Normally, companies try to pick a point that represents the low point in their seasonal pattern. This is to ensure that year-end adjustments and the annual report do not have to be prepared during their busy season. However, there are other factors to consider. For example, having the same year-end as other companies in the industry facilitates comparisons. Companies that are part of a corporate group prefer to have the same year-end as their parent to allow consolidation. Some industries are governed by legislation that mandates a certain year-end. For example, the federal *Bank Act* requires banks to use a 31 October year-end. Most businesses pick the calendar year as a fiscal year.

**Reporting Period Length and Composition** Another basic issue to decide is the length of the reporting period. Annual reports are the norm, as companies are expected to use a 12-month period. The 12-month period facilitates preparation of required annual reports to shareholders and securities commissions.

The operating cycle of some companies leads them to end their fiscal period at the end of a *week* instead of the end of a month. Such companies are usually in the retail trade or are suppliers to retail companies. For example, the Hudson Bay Company's fiscal year-ends on January 31 each year. This puts the year-end after (1) the busy holiday retailing season, (2) the January merchandise returns period and (3) the post-holiday accounts receivable collection period. In late January, it is much easier to make the necessary accounting adjustments for uncollectible accounts, inventory writedowns, and purchase returns. As well, the accounting and managerial staff are less overwhelmed by the holiday season's business activities.

Companies often also issue financial statements for shorter periods, most often quarterly. Public companies are required by securities commissions to issue quarterly statements to their shareholders.

**Reporting Currency** Companies must also determine the reporting currency used to report to shareholders. Normally, one might assume that a Canadian company, reporting with Canadian GAAP, would report in Canadian dollars. This is the norm, but it is not required. Although a Canadian company usually will follow Canadian GAAP, any reporting currency can be used.

Why would a Canadian company choose to report in, say, U.S. dollars? The primary reason is that most of the company's business is conducted in U.S. dollars. U.S. dollars may be used by companies that have the bulk of their operations in the U.S. or whose product is priced worldwide in U.S. dollars (e.g., gold mining companies, paper products companies).

Bear in mind, though, that reporting in U.S. dollars doesn't mean reporting in U.S. GAAP. Canadian-based public companies that report in U.S. dollars normally still use Canadian GAAP.

**Selection of GAAP** The vast majority of Canadian companies report in accordance with Canadian GAAP. This is true even for many companies that report in U.S. dollars. One such company is Stratos Global Corporation. Note 2 to Stratos Global Corporation's financial statements explains that

> The Corporation and each of its subsidiaries use the U.S. dollar as its currency of measurement and reporting as a substantial portion of the Corporation's ongoing business is conducted in U.S. dollars.

There are a few large Canadian companies that report in U.S. GAAP. Such companies inevitably also report in U.S. dollars. A company may choose to use U.S. accounting standards because the vast majority of its share trading takes place on U.S. exchanges. For example, Canadian beverage giant Cott Corporation says in its financial statements that

> These consolidated financial statements have been prepared in accordance with United States generally accepted accounting principles using the U.S. dollar as the reporting currency, as the majority of our business and the majority of our shareowners are in the U.S.

Similarly, software company Corel Corporation (known for WordPerfect, CorelDRAW, and WinZip) reports in U.S. dollars using U.S. GAAP.

A mutual recognition agreement between the Ontario Securities Commission and the SEC enables Canadian companies to report in U.S. GAAP, although they must then provide a reconciliation to Canadian GAAP in the disclosure notes.

**Rounding** Unrounded figures give an illusion of precision that is not appropriate, since so many estimates are used in accounting. Reported accounting numbers are the result of many accounting policy decisions and estimates, and the numbers would be quite different under different policies and different, equally valid, estimates and assumptions. Rounding helps to emphasize the approximate nature of the numbers.

The extent of rounding depends on the size of the company. A company with revenues and assets in the billions will round to the nearest million dollars at least, but many round to the nearest billion. Smaller companies will round to the nearest thousand.

**Language** What is the language of the user group? Obviously, financial statements are written for that group, in their language. Companies that are incorporated in Quebec must publish their statements in French, but many other Canadian public companies publish French versions of their annual reports (and Quebec companies publish English versions). Some present the English and French version together in the same report, but the majority provide a separate French version on request.

Of course, there's no reason for limiting financial statements to English and French—the financial statements can be prepared in any language. Some companies, seeking investment from Germany or Japan, prepare reports that are in the appropriate languages for their target audiences.

The fact that a company translates its financial statements into other languages does not mean that the statements have been adjusted to reflect GAAP in that language's home country. For example, some Canadian companies translate their financial statements into Japanese for the convenience of Japanese investors and business partners, but the statements still reflect Canadian GAAP and not Japanese GAAP. On the other hand, many Japanese companies translate their financial statements into English. Here one must be careful; some of the Japanese companies report in U.S. GAAP (even in Japan), while others use Japanese GAAP in their English-language statements. Users must be careful to ascertain the GAAP choices made by the company.

**Comparative Data** Accounting numbers are meaningless unless they can be compared to some other numbers. The most obvious comparison for a company is to look at how it did this year compared to the preceding year. Trends in financial information are much more revealing than information for only one period. In recognition of this fact, accounting standards recommend that comparative figures be presented *when they are meaningful*. In most situations, comparative statements are meaningful. Presentation of one year's comparative information is the norm, although some companies present two years' comparative results on the income statement to comply with the U.S. SEC regulation requiring this expanded disclosure.

Public companies also often provide a longer-term comparison of selected numbers, usually on a five-year basis. Five-year comparative numbers usually include operating earnings, net income, earnings per share, and total assets, among others.

**Detail** As we have explained above, accounting standards specify certain items that have to be separately disclosed on the income statement. Other items may be grouped, or separately disclosed. The extent of this grouping is a major policy decision for the company. How much detail should be included on the income statement? Typically, disclosures meet little more than the minimum standards. We'll come back to discuss this policy decision in a few pages, when we review the minimum recommended income statement disclosures.

---

## CONCEPT REVIEW

1. Why might a company have a year-end other than December 31?

2. When might a Canadian company choose to prepare its financial statements in U.S. dollars?

3. Why are comparative statements usually presented, instead of just the current year's amounts?

---

## SPECIAL ASPECTS OF THE INCOME STATEMENT

In the preceding sections we have discussed the general format of the income statement. We also have described relevant reporting requirements for GAAP–constrained financial statements, including the GAAP requirements for disclosing certain items of revenue and expense.

However, some aspects still need further explanation, especially:

- Intraperiod income tax allocation;
- Discontinued operations; and
- Extraordinary items.

The following sections will discuss these special aspects of income reporting.

### Intraperiod Tax Allocation

**intraperiod tax allocation**

allocating the income tax expense within the period to various subclassifications on the income statement and retained earnings statements

If an item is shown net of *related tax*, it means that the tax consequences of the item have been determined and the reported amount is shown after these tax effects have been adjusted for. Determining this amount is the process of **intraperiod tax allocation**. *Intra* means that the allocation is within the period and within the income statement and retained earnings statement. **Interperiod tax allocation** is the allocation of tax expense to different reporting periods, which is covered in depth in Chapter 15.

**interperiod tax allocation**

allocating the tax paid to appropriate reporting periods based on accounting recognition of individual revenue and expense items

To demonstrate *intraperiod* tax allocation, consider the following situation for the Calgary Storage Company. Sales for 20X1 total $1 million, and expenses before income taxes total $700,000. During 20X1, the company experiences an extraordinary loss of $200,000 when an earthquake destroys several of the company's uninsured warehouses. Assume that the income tax rate is 40% and that the $200,000 earthquake loss is deductible for income tax purposes. Calgary Storage Company's income statement with and without intraperiod tax allocation is as shown in Exhibit 3-4.

In the column without intraperiod tax allocation, the tax expense is shown at the actual amount that will be paid, or 40% of the $100,000 taxable income (revenues of $1 million less expenses of $700,000 and less the loss of $200,000). In the column with intraperiod tax allocation, the tax effects of the two activities (operations and the earthquake loss) are

## EXHIBIT 3-4

### Calgary Storage Company Income Statement

| For the year ended December 31, 20X1 | Without Intraperiod Tax Allocation | With Intraperiod Tax Allocation |
|---|---|---|
| Sales | $1,000,000 | $1,000,000 |
| Expenses | 700,000 | 700,000 |
| Income from operations | 300,000 | 300,000 |
| Income tax expense: | | |
| On operations ($300,000 × 40%) | — | 120,000 |
| On taxable income ($100,000 × 40%) | 40,000 | — |
| Income before extraordinary loss | 260,000 | 180,000 |
| Extraordinary item: | | |
| Loss from earthquake damage: | | |
| Gross amount | (200,000) | (200,000) |
| Tax reduction | — | 80,000 |
| Net extraordinary item | (200,000) | (120,000) |
| Net income | $   60,000 | $   60,000 |

shown separately. Thus, the income tax expense that would be paid if there were no loss from the earthquake would be 40% of $300,000, or $120,000. The tax effect of the earthquake loss reduces income tax for the period by 40% of the loss, or $80,000. The $80,000 tax savings resulting from the loss is subtracted from the gross loss of $200,000 to arrive at the after-tax amount of $120,000.

In Exhibit 3-4, the tax impact of the extraordinary item is shown directly on the face of the statement for illustrative purposes, but usually only the net amount of $120,000 would be shown. The tax effect is usually disclosed in a note rather than on the face of the income statement, if it is disclosed at all.

Canadian, U.S., and international accounting standards all require intraperiod tax allocation, as illustrated, for discontinued operations and extraordinary items. Intraperiod tax allocation also applies to the *cumulative effect of a retrospective change in accounting policy*, shown on the retained earnings statement. Accounting policy changes are discussed later in the chapter.

## Discontinued Operations

Sometimes a company decides to discontinue part of its operations. Often, the decision is due to insufficient profitability for that operation. At other times, the operation is successful, but the company wishes to sell it either to gain cash or because management is narrowing the range of businesses that the company is engaged in.

There are two broad alternative approaches to discontinuance. The company can dispose of an operation by either:

- Shutting down the operation, laying off the employees, and selling any salvageable assets; or
- Selling the operation as an operating unit (i.e., as a going concern) to the highest bidder, thereby transferring the operation to the buyer intact and as a functioning unit.

In the year that a company decides to dispose of an operation, the revenues, expenses, losses, and gains relating to that unit are removed from the general operations on the income statement and reclassified separately as *discontinued operations*. One of the functions of the income statement is to provide a basis for investors and others to predict future earnings. Investors need to be told if a significant part of the company's revenues and earnings will not continue into the future. Therefore, operating results of a discontinued operation are segregated so that financial statement users will not expect the revenues and earnings relating to this unit to continue into the future. The segregation happens not only in the year that the discontinuance decision is made, but also for the prior year's comparative income statement.

Similarly, the assets and liabilities of the discontinued operation are segregated on the balance sheet. The assets of a discontinued operation become *held-for-sale* assets. Amortization is discontinued, and the assets are revalued at their fair value.

**Definition of a Discontinued Operation** Many corporations restructure their business operations by shutting down factories or distribution centres, or by dropping products or eliminating product lines. When a company decides to exit from some part of its operations, the first financial reporting issue is whether termination of that part of the business fits the definition of a "discontinued operation."

Canadian and international accounting standards define a **discontinued operation** as a part of an enterprise that is clearly distinguishable from the rest of the enterprise. The operation must have its own operational activities and must be a financial reporting unit within the company. A discontinued operation can be a subsidiary or an operating division; it can either comprise an asset group or an operation that does not have any long-lived assets.

The important aspect of a discontinued operation is that the operation must be *separable* from the rest of the enterprise. That is, the operation must not be so well integrated with the other (continuing) operations that its revenues and assets cannot be separately identified.

For example, suppose that a U.S. automobile manufacturer decides to shut down a Canadian factory. Certainly, for the people working in that plant, shutting down appears to be the discontinuance of an operation. However, for financial reporting purposes, the Canadian factory is just one of a larger group of factories producing the same or similar products. The individual factory does not have its own revenue stream from outsiders. Therefore, shutting down one factory in the group does not fit the definition of *discontinued operations* for financial reporting.

Instead, however, suppose that the automobile manufacturer also manufactures buses. The manufacturer decides to shut down its entire bus-manufacturing operation. The bus business is a separate division of the larger company, with separate responsibility and reporting lines within the company and with separately measurable revenues and expenses. In that case, the bus operation is a *discontinued operation* for accounting purposes.

**Effective Date of Discontinuance** An operation is reported as *discontinued* when management has moved decisively to cease operations by either selling the operation or shutting it down. It is not necessary that the operation actually be discontinued during the reporting period. Six criteria must be satisfied before an operation (or an asset) can be categorized as a discontinued operation:

1. Management commits itself (usually by action of the Board of Directors) to a plan to sell.

2. The operation is available for immediate sale.

3. A buyer is actively being sought, or a plan to shut down the operation has begun.

4. A sale or shutdown is probable and is expected to be completed within one year.

5. The price being solicited for a sale is reasonable.

6. It is unlikely that significant changes to the plan will occur or that the plan will be withdrawn.

The objective of the criteria is to ensure that management really is serious about discontinuing the operation, and not acting on a whim that might be reversed in the next year. Management must take clear action for discontinuance.

There are two additional requirements for reporting a *discontinued operation*:

1. The operations and cash flows of the operations will be eliminated from the future reported results of the company after the disposal transaction.

2. The selling company will not have any significant continuing involvement in the future operations of the discontinued operations.

These two additional requirements prevent management from "discontinuing" an operation in a legal sense but still benefiting from the operation. This is an example of applying substance over form.

An operation is reported as discontinued when management has made the decision and has begun the process of selling it or shutting it down. It is quite likely that a plan of discontinuance will be begun in one fiscal year and finished in the next. Almost certainly, any discontinuance plan will extend over more than one quarterly reporting period. Therefore, an operation that is reported as discontinued may, in fact, still be in operation at the end of the fiscal period.

*Discontinued* should not be taken too literally. Remember that there is a one-year future time horizon. An operation that can feasibly be sold or shut down within the next year can still be reported as discontinued.

**Reporting Discontinued Operations** As discussed earlier in this chapter, the results of discontinued operations, less applicable income taxes, should be reported as a separate element of income or loss *after* earnings from continuing operations but *before* extraordinary items. There are three broad components of the amount reported as gain or loss on discontinued operations:

- The net profit or loss from operating the discontinued operation to the date of disposal or the end of the reporting period, if the disposal is not complete by year-end;
- Writedowns of asset carrying value to *fair value less cost to sell*; and
- For completed sales or shutdowns of an operation, the realized gain or loss on disposal to the extent not previously recognized.

All amounts are *net of related income taxes*, as we explained under *intraperiod tax allocation* earlier in this chapter.

We will discuss the measurement of writedowns when we get to Chapter 10. The measurement criteria for disposing of a discontinued operation are the same as for disposing of an asset or a group of assets. For now, just bear in mind that the gain or loss on disposal is a combination of the current year's operating revenues and expenses plus the gains and losses on disposal, including any appropriate reduction of assets' book value to their net realizable value. A reduction to net realizable value is known as an *impairment loss*.

There is an important restriction on the amount of gain or loss that can be reported. Losses that might occur between the reporting date and the final date of discontinuance (sale or shutdown) cannot be accrued and reported prior to the loss actually happening. Forecasts of *future* operating results must not be included.

On the balance sheet, the accounting basis of the assets is changed. The assets change their status to become *held-for-sale* assets. This is a significant change in status. When a long-lived asset is reclassified as "held for sale," its carrying value must be reduced to its net realizable value—the fair value in sale minus the costs to sell. Of course, if the cost-basis carrying value of the asset is below net realizable value, there will be no writedown. Also, once long-lived assets are reclassified as held for sale, amortization stops. The balance sheet reporting effects are:

- Amortization ceases, effective on the date of the discontinuance decision.
- Current assets are carried on the balance sheet at fair value.
- Capital assets (tangible and intangible) are carried at lower of amortized cost or net realizable value.
- Liabilities continue to accrue.

**Disclosure** Several aspects of the circumstances and amounts relating to discontinued operations should be disclosed. The recommended disclosures are:

- A description of the facts and circumstances leading to the disposal or expected disposal, along with the expected manner and timing of the disposal
- The carrying amount of the major classes of assets and liabilities included in the discontinued operations

- The impairment loss that is included in the net gain or loss for discontinued operations
- The amounts of revenue and of pre-tax profit (loss) reported in discontinued operations

The last two items are amounts that may be reported on the face of the income statement. If they are reported on the face of the income statement, they don't also have to be disclosed in the notes.

If the disposal is not finalized during the current fiscal year, there will be additional revenues, expenses, gains, and losses between the beginning of the following year and the date that the disposal is completed. Those amounts will be recognized in that following period, when they are realized, and must not be anticipated by any accruals in the year that the decision to discontinue was made. Subsequent-year adjustments must be reported separately as *discontinued operations* and not "hidden" in other revenues and expenses.

**Illustration**   The Board of Directors of Pacific & Eastern Corporation (PEC), a large consumer products company, approved a plan to sell its Automatic Transmission Diagnostic Centres division at a Board meeting on 30 August 20X1. The company engaged professional business valuators to appraise the fair value of the division's assets and solicited competitive bids from prospective buyers for the division. PEC engaged the consultancy firm of KMPG to assist with the bidding and selling process. At 31 December 20X1, the following information is available:

- From 1 January 20X1 through 30 August 20X1, the division earned $7 million before tax.
- From 1 September through 31 December 20X1, the division earned an additional $2 million before tax.
- The evaluators estimate that the net realizable value of the division's net assets is $40 million; this is $5 million less than the $45 million carrying value on PEC's books.
- The bidding process closes on 31 January 20X2. Final negotiations and preparation for sale are expected to extend to at least the end of April, after which date PEC expects to have no continued interest in the division.
- PEC managers estimate that due to uncertainty surrounding the fate of the division, the division will probably lose $4 million between 1 January 20X2 and the closing date of the sale.
- PEC managers expect to receive a total purchase price of at least $50 million when the deal is finalized.
- PEC will have to pay a 5% commission to KMPG on any sale.
- PEC's marginal income tax rate is 30%.

The disposal of this division qualifies for reporting as a *discontinued operation* in 20X1 because the sale has been properly authorized, the division is a separate and separable division of the company, a plan is in place to actively sell the division, PEC will have no interest in the cash flows or operations after the sale, and the other criteria cited above appear to have been met.

The next issue is what amount should be reported in the discontinued operations section of PEC's 20X1 income statement. The total reported amount will be $1,400,000, consisting of the following components:

| | |
|---|---:|
| Earnings from operations for 20X1, before income tax ($7 m + $2 m) | $9,000,000 |
| Reduction in carrying value of the assets to estimated net realizable value | (5,000,000) |
| 5% commission to be paid on the estimated asset net realizable value of $40 million (that is, the estimated *cost to sell*) | (2,000,000) |
| Income tax expense related to all of the above [($9 m − $5 m − $2 m) × 30%] | (600,000) |
| Total gain (loss) on discontinued operations, net of tax, 20X1 | $1,400,000 |

The gain of $1,400,000 is the division's profit, adjusted for the asset impairment and the cost to sell the division. The anticipated operating loss for 20X2 is not included, nor is the estimated gain or loss arising from the final sale.

Suppose that in 20X2, the division is finally and irrevocably sold to an Australian company for $53 million, minus the 5% commission and minus estimated additional income tax expense of $3 million. The net amount to be shown in PEC's 20X2 income statement is:

| | |
|---|---:|
| Sales price, gross | $53,000,000 |
| Less carrying value of assets sold (net of cost to sell, recognized in 20X1) | (40,000,000) |
| Sales commission not previously recognized [($53 m − $40 m) × 5%] | (650,000) |
| Income tax expense not previously recognized | (3,000,000) |
| Gain on discontinued operation, 20X2 | $ 9,350,000 |

**Disclosure Example** Exhibit 3-5 shows the lower portion of La Senza Corporation (a Quebec-based chain of clothing stores), as well as part of the note relating to the discontinued operation. Continuing operations earned $30,855 (thousand) before income tax. Income tax expense of $11,171 is deducted, including both current taxes and future (i.e., deferred) taxes, obtaining a subtotal for "earnings from continuing operations" of $19,684. From that subtotal, the company deducts a loss of $1,947 from continuing operations, *net of income tax*, to yield a final "net earnings" (or net income) figure of $17,737.

The disclosure note explains that the decision to close the U.S. division was made in fiscal year 2005. Therefore the fiscal 2005 operating loss and an asset writedown were recorded in fiscal 2005. The actual sale occurred in fiscal 2006, leading to recognition of a 2006 loss of $1,947 net of taxes.

## Extraordinary Items

**Criteria for Extraordinary Items** In Canadian standards, an extraordinary item arises from a transaction or event that has *all* of the following three characteristics:[3]

1. They are not expected to occur frequently over several years.

2. They do not typify the normal business activities of the entity.

3. They do not depend primarily on decisions or determinations by management or owners.

Gains or losses resulting from the risks inherent in an entity's *normal business activities* are not extraordinary, no matter how large the gain or loss. For example, the following events should *not* be considered extraordinary because they are expected during the customary and continuing business activities of a firm:

- Losses and provisions for losses with respect to bad debts and inventories;
- Gains and losses from fluctuations in foreign exchange rates;
- Adjustments in major contract prices; and
- Gains and losses from writedown or sale of property, plant, equipment, or other investments.

A very important criterion for classifying a gain or loss as an extraordinary item is that the gain or loss *does not depend primarily on the decisions of managers or owners*. A transaction is considered to be outside the control of managers or owners if their decisions would

---

[3] International standards are even stricter. No item of revenue or expense can ever be reported as an *extraordinary item*, either on the face of the income statement or in the notes.

## EXHIBIT 3-5

## LA SENZA CORPORATION
## Discontinued Operation

| Income Statement (partial) (in thousands) | January 28, 2006 | January 29, 2005 |
|---|---|---|
| Earnings from continuing operations before income taxes | $30,855 | $9,583 |
| Income taxes: | | |
| Current | 2,480 | 1,134 |
| Future | 8,691 | 821 |
| | 11,171 | 1,955 |
| Earnings from continuing operations | 19,684 | 7,628 |
| Discontinued operations, net of income taxes (note 5) | (1,947) | (7,547) |
| Net earnings | $17,737 | $   81 |

*Note 5: Discontinued operations:*

*In January 2005, the Company approved a plan to discontinue the U.S. operations of La Senza and, accordingly, the results and cash flows of the U.S. operations for the current and prior periods have been presented as discontinued operations. The net assets of these operations were presented as assets and liabilities of discontinued operations in the periods in which they qualified as held for sale. In fiscal 2006, all of the U.S. stores were closed.*

*The results of the discontinued operations are as follows:*

| | January 28, 2006 | January 29, 2005 |
|---|---|---|
| Sales | $3,507 | $10,774 |
| Operating losses | (3,198) | (5,574) |
| Write-down of net assets | — | (5,605) |
| Discontinued operations before income taxes | (3,198) | (11,179) |
| Income taxes: | | |
| Current | (1,251) | 80 |
| Future | — | (3,712) |
| | (1,251) | (3,632) |
| Discontinued operations, net of income taxes | $(1,947) | $ (7,547) |

---

not influence the transaction. This third criterion has virtually eliminated extraordinary items on Canadian income statements.

As illustrated in our Calgary Storage Company example (Exhibit 3-4), extraordinary items are reported in the income statement under a separate classification and are net of any income tax effect. If an extraordinary item is taxable, a *gain* increases income tax and a *loss* reduces income tax. In both cases, the extraordinary gain or loss is adjusted for its tax effects and reported net of tax. Extraordinary items are explained in disclosure notes.

**Disclosure Example of Unusual and Extraordinary Items**  Exhibit 3-6 illustrates an income statement that includes disclosure of an extraordinary item as well as several unusual items. Notice how concise the statement is. Very little detail is given, with no information other than those few items that are required for minimum disclosure under Canadian accounting standards.

## EXHIBIT 3-6

### PREMIER TECH LTD.

### Consolidated Statements of Earnings

for the fiscal years ended June 3, 2006, and May 28, 2005

| (in thousands of dollars) | 2006 | 2005 |
|---|---|---|
| Sales | $267,367 | $296,299 |
| Earnings before the following items, net of investment tax credits and government assistance of $2,645 ($3,940 in 2005) (note 3) | 23,971 | 16,410 |
| Depreciation and amortization (note 4) | 9,078 | 10,736 |
| Scientific research expenses, net of investment tax credits and government assistance of $1,442 ($1,734 in 2005) | 1,127 | 1,657 |
| Interest on long-term debt | 3,734 | 4,679 |
| Interest and bank charges | 2,441 | 2,655 |
| | 16,380 | 19,727 |
| Special items | (2,233) | 1,267 |
| | 14,147 | 20,994 |
| Earnings (loss) before taxes and extraordinary item | 9,824 | (4,584) |
| Income taxes (note 7) | | |
| Current | 5,410 | 2,021 |
| Future | (1,651) | 243 |
| | 3,759 | 2,264 |
| Net earnings (loss) before extraordinary item | 6,065 | (6,848) |
| Extraordinary item (note 5) | 286 | 0 |
| Net earnings (loss) | 6,351 | (6,848) |
| Earnings (loss) per share before extraordinary item (note 8) | | |
| Basic | 0.37 | (0.42) |
| Diluted | 0.37 | (0.42) |
| Earnings (loss) per share (note 8) | | |
| Basic | 0.39 | (0.42) |
| Diluted | 0.39 | (0.42) |

*Source:* www.sedar.com, Premier Tech Ltd. 2005/2006 Annual Report released July 27, 2006, page 44.

Quebec-based Premier Tech Ltd.'s income statement is non-continuous. That is, the statement starts with a total for Sales. No major expense categories are shown below the sales figure. The next line is "Earnings before the following items ..." The items listed below that amount are items that the *CICA Handbook* specifically requires to be disclosed. After drawing an expense subtotal for those specific items of $16,380 (thousands) for fiscal year 2006, the company reduces expenses by a credit of $2,233 for "Special items." The special items are listed in a disclosure note (in thousands):

| SPECIAL ITEMS: | 2006 | 2005 |
|---|---|---|
| Gain upon renegotiation of a long-term debt | $(2,833) | $   0 |
| Write-off of goodwill | 0 | 535 |
| Severance pay and other involuntary costs | 650 | 450 |
| Write-off of other assets | 0 | 282 |
| | $(2,233) | $1,267 |

The extraordinary item is a gain, added to earnings as the final item. The gain is the result of a fire, explained in the disclosure notes as follows:

> On September 17, 2005, a plant owned by the Company, including building and equipment, was completely destroyed by fire. As a result, and given the terms of the Company's insurance coverage, the Company posted an extraordinary gain of $424,000, which corresponds to the difference between the net carrying value of the property destroyed by the fire and its depreciated replacement value, net of payment by the Company of the deductible and excess operating costs resulting from the incident until the new plant is operational. Future income taxes for this extraordinary gain amount to $138,000.

The gain qualifies as extraordinary because it is not recurring, is not a part of operations, and was not the result of decisions or actions of management.

## EARNINGS PER SHARE

**basic earnings per share**

net income for a period minus dividend entitlements of senior shares, divided by the weighted average of common shares outstanding during that same period; see also diluted earnings per share

Public companies are required to report earnings per share. Earnings per share (EPS) is a summary figure that is often quoted by analysts and investors as the primary (and sometimes only) indication of a company's earnings record. Investors find EPS useful because it relates the income of the company to a single common share and automatically adjusts for changes in the number of shares outstanding from year to year. EPS numbers are very widely quoted in the financial press. Financial analysts and investment services often present EPS graphs.

Public companies must show EPS on the face of the income statement. EPS should be reported for both (1) income before discontinued operations and extraordinary items, and (2) net income. The Premier Tech Ltd. income statement (Exhibit 3-6) shows EPS both before and after the extraordinary gain. In this case the relative amount of the extraordinary item is too small to cause a perceptible difference between the two amounts, but both must nevertheless be shown.

**diluted earnings per share**

similar to basic earnings per share, but the weighted average number of shares is adjusted to reflect all of the shares that would be outstanding if the common share entitlements of dilutive convertible senior securities and stock options were issued. The numerator also is adjusted to reflect the potential impact of conversions.

**Basic earnings per share** is computed by dividing reported income available to the holders of common shares by the weighted average number of common shares outstanding during the year. For computation of EPS on common shares, income must be reduced by any preferred share dividend claims since such dividends are not available to common share owners and have not been subtracted in computing income.

**Diluted earnings per share** shows how earnings per share would change in the event that all common shares promised under the terms of existing option agreements, conversion privileges on bonds or preferred shares, etc., were actually issued. We'll study earnings per share in depth in Chapter 19.

## CONCEPT REVIEW

1. What are the three required basic subsections of an income statement?
2. Explain what intraperiod income tax allocation is.
3. Why is separate disclosure of discontinued operations important to users?
4. What are the three criteria that a gain or loss must satisfy before it can be classified as extraordinary?
5. Why have extraordinary items become rare in Canadian financial statements while unusual items have become quite common?

## COMPREHENSIVE INCOME

In 2006, Canadian GAAP began requiring companies to report *comprehensive income*. Comprehensive income has two components:

1. Net income, and
2. Other comprehensive income.

A company should present a separate statement of comprehensive income that shows (1) *net income* and (2) the components of *other comprehensive income*. "Other comprehensive income" is not a mandatory title. Some companies call it "other changes in shareholders' equity."[4]

Net income is determined via the income statement. *The concept of comprehensive income makes no change in the measurement of net income and the presentation of the income statement.*

However, changes in the reporting of financial instruments and of available-for-sale assets have led to a need for the new classification of other comprehensive income. Other comprehensive income (OCI) includes only those items specifically identified by the *CICA Handbook*. Generally speaking, OCI includes unrealized gains and losses and a few other minor items. At the time of writing this book, OCI consists of these items:[5]

**other comprehensive income**

amounts that are not included in determining net income but that also do not represent investment or disinvestment by owners; examples include unrealized gains and losses on held-for sale assets

- Unrealized gains and losses on available-for-sale financial assets;
- Unrealized gains and losses from translating the financial statements of foreign subsidiaries;
- Unrealized gains and losses on cash flow hedges relating to anticipated transactions; and
- Unfunded pension liabilities that have not been recognized as an expense, or over-funded pension liabilities that have not yet been recognized as a gain.[6]

Obviously, all three components involve unrealized gains/losses. We will briefly discuss each of these items.

## Available-for-Sale Financial Assets[7]

A *financial asset* is any contractual asset that gives the holder the right to receive cash. It includes debt and shares of other corporations, as well as short-term money market instruments.

As we discuss more fully in later chapters, accounting standards distinguish between three types of financial assets, each of which is given a different accounting treatment:

1. Financial assets that the holder intends to hold to maturity, such as long-term bonds;

2. Strategic investments, usually shares, that give the holder control or significant influence over the issuer; and

3. Financial assets that are available for sale if the holder needs cash.

Basically, available-for-sale financial assets include any financial asset that is not included in the first two categories.

Available-for-sale financial assets are valued at market value on each balance sheet date. When these financial assets are revalued to market value, the company writes the asset's carrying value up or down, with the gain/loss credited/debited to OCI. This gain or loss is *recognized* in the financial statements, but it is not included in income because it has not yet been *realized*.

The cumulative unrealized gains and losses are carried in a separate component of shareholders' equity—*Accumulated Other Comprehensive Income* (*AcOIC*). When investments are sold, the gain or loss is *realized*. The realized gain or loss is removed from the separate component of shareholders' equity and is transferred to the income statement, a process that is known as "recycling." We will demonstrate this process in Chapter 11.

---

[4] "Other changes in shareholder's equity" is the term used in international standards.

[5] Two other items are (1) appraisal increases on property, plant, and equipment recorded at appraised value, and (2) donations from non-owners. These types of events are rare in Canadian accounting practice and will not be discussed further.

[6] This item will be explained in Chapter 18.

[7] It is important to distinguish between *held-for-sale* assets relating to discontinued operations and *available-for-sale* financial assets. The valuation rules are different.

Unrealized gains and losses must be kept separate from realized gains and losses, and the concept of other comprehensive income is designed to deal with this problem as the accounting world moves toward fair value accounting.

### Translation Gain/Loss

Many corporations have foreign operations. When these foreign subsidiaries operate reasonably autonomously, they are called "self-sustaining foreign operations." Foreign operations are almost always subsidiaries of the parent company. Foreign subsidiaries normally keep their accounting records in a foreign currency. To consolidate the subsidiary in the Canadian parent's financial statements, the subsidiary's financial statements must be translated into Canadian dollars. The conversion process inevitably leads to an imbalance, which is "plugged" by an amount called the "translation gain or loss." This amount is an accounting phenomenon. It has no economic significance, but it must be included in the consolidated financial statements or the balance sheet won't balance. Prior to 2007, the solution to this problem had been to put the cumulative translation gain or loss into a separate component of shareholders' equity. Now, instead, the translation gain/loss will be reported as a component of other comprehensive income.

Intensive study of foreign operations is reserved for advanced accounting courses.

### Cash Flow Hedges

Often a company will make a commitment that is denominated in a foreign currency. The commitment might be to acquire an asset at a price that is expressed in a foreign currency, such as U.S. dollars, euros, or Japanese yen. Alternately, the commitment may be to deliver goods or services in the future at a price fixed in a foreign currency. Either way, the Canadian company is subject to foreign exchange risk.

For example, suppose that a company signs a contract to buy advanced electronic equipment from Japan. The price of the equipment is ¥8.5 million. If the exchange rate is Cdn$1.00 = ¥85 at the time of the commitment, the commitment is worth Cdn$100,000. But suppose that the exchange changes before the equipment is delivered and paid for. If the exchange rate drops to Cdn$1.00 = ¥77, the company will have to pay Cdn$110,390, a 10% cost increase.

To protect against foreign exchange risk, most companies will use a derivative instrument, usually a "forward contract," which is an agreement with a bank that has the effect of offsetting the risk. If the value of the commitment goes up, then the value of the forward contract goes down, and vice versa. The gain on one offsets the loss on the other.

Changes in the value of the commitment will be *realized* only when the contract is complete and payment has been made. Therefore, the *unrealized* gain or loss on the derivative instrument must be deferred and matched against the realized gain/loss on the transaction.

As we will discuss in Chapter 14, all derivative instruments are reported at fair value on the balance sheet. However, because the cash flow for commitment has not yet occurred, the unrealized gains/losses on the cash flow hedge are not included in net income, but instead are reported as a part of other comprehensive income.

Accounting for hedges is definitely a topic for advanced accounting! We will not go into hedging further in this book. But you should have a general understanding of the nature of cash flow hedges for anticipated transactions, and why the gains and losses are included in other comprehensive income.

### Reporting Example

Since the comprehensive income concept is new to Canada, we cannot provide a Canadian example. Instead, we will turn to a well-known U.S. company to illustrate the general approach. Exhibit 3-7 presents the income statement, the statement of comprehensive income, and part of the statement of shareholders' equity for Nike Inc. Nike is a well-known manufacturer of athletic shoes and other sports equipment, clothing, and accessories. We have modified the presentation slightly in order to avoid confusion about the differences between Canadian and U.S. GAAP.

**EXHIBIT 3-7**

## NIKE INC.
### Consolidated Statement of Income

[In millions of U.S. dollars; presentation modified slightly from the original]

Year ended May 31, 2006

| | |
|---|---:|
| Revenues | $14,954.9 |
| Cost of sales | 8,367.9 |
| Gross margin | 6,587.0 |
| Selling and administrative | 4,477.8 |
| Interest expense | (36.8) |
| Other expense, net | 4.4 |
| Operating and other income/expense | 4,445.4 |
| Income before income taxes | 2,141.6 |
| Income taxes | 749.6 |
| Net income | $  1,392.0 |

### Statement of Comprehensive Income

| | |
|---|---:|
| Net income | $  1,392.0 |
| Other comprehensive income (loss): | |
| Change in cumulative translation adjustment (net of tax) | 87.1 |
| Net unrealized gain (loss) on hedge derivatives (net of tax) | (5.6) |
| Reclassification to net income of previously unrealized gains (losses) on hedge derivatives (net of tax) | (33.2) |
| Other comprehensive income (loss) | 48.3 |
| Total comprehensive income | $  1,440.3 |

### Consolidated Statement of Shareholders' Equity [Partial]

| | Accumulated Other Comprehensive Income (Loss) | Retained Earnings | Total |
|---|---:|---:|---:|
| Balance at May 31, 2005 | $  73.4 | $4,396.5 | $4,469.9 |
| Repurchase of Class B Common Stock | | (769.9) | (769.9) |
| Dividends on Common Stock ($1.18 per share) | | (304.9) | (304.9) |
| Forfeiture of shares from employees | | (0.3) | (0.3) |
| Changes from transactions with shareholders | | (1,075.1) | (1,075.1) |
| Net income | | 1,392.0 | 1,392.0 |
| Foreign currency translation | 87.1 | | 87.1 |
| Adjustment for fair value of hedge derivatives (net) | (38.8) | | (38.8) |
| Comprehensive income | 48.3 | 1,392.0 | 1,440.3 |
| Balance at May 31, 2006 | $121.7 | $4,713.4 | $4,835.1 |

*Source:* www.nike.com, Nike Inc. 2006 Annual Report, page 46.

The income statement, at the top of the Exhibit, is perfectly straightforward.[8] It shows a final net income figure of $1,392 million. The middle section of the Exhibit shows Nike's statement of comprehensive income. The company has two components in this category:

1. Unrealized changes in foreign currency translation, relating to foreign subsidiaries; and

2. Changes in the market value of derivative instruments.

The statement has two entries relating to the second component. The first (a loss of $5.6 million) is the unrealized loss that arose in 2006. The second (a $33.2 million loss) is the net amount of previously unrealized gains and losses that were realized in 2006 and therefore moved (*recycled*) to the income statement.

The bottom section of the Exhibit shows the shareholders' equity reconciliation for retained earnings and for accumulated other comprehensive income. Notice that the only part of OCI that goes into retained earnings is the net income of $1,392 million. Retained earnings also includes some other items that were transactions with shareholders—share repurchases, dividends, and forfeitures of shares by employee-shareholders.

The components of OCI are placed in the separate column for AcOCI. In that column, the adjustment for fair value of hedge derivatives is the combination of two separate lines on the statement of comprehensive income: $(5.6) + (33.2) = $(38.8).

The items in the two columns are combined only in the final column. (In Nike's original presentation, the amounts of paid-in capital also are added into the total column.)

## CONCEPT REVIEW

1. What are the components of other comprehensive income?

2. What is an alternative title for "other comprehensive income"?

3. Explain an available-for-sale financial asset.

4. How should comprehensive income be reported in a company's financial statements?

## RETAINED EARNINGS STATEMENT

A statement of retained earnings is one of the four basic financial statements. The retained earnings statement ties together the income statement and the balance sheet by showing the changes that occurred in retained earnings for the year. The purpose of the retained earnings statement is to report all changes in retained earnings during the accounting period, to reconcile the beginning and ending balances of retained earnings, and to provide a connecting link between the income statement and the balance sheet. The ending balance of retained earnings is reported on the balance sheet as one element of shareholders' equity.

For many companies, the only changes in retained earnings are (1) net income for the year and (2) dividends declared. Because of the simplicity of the retained earnings statement, it often is appended to the income statement. When a company does combine the retained earnings statement with the income statement, the combined statement's title must reveal that fact, such as by titling it the *Statement of Income and Retained Earnings*. Gennum Corporation uses a combined statement, as shown in Exhibit 3-3.

Instead of a retained earnings statement, some companies present a *statement of shareholders' equity*, which shows changes in all shareholders' equity accounts, using a column for each shareholders' equity account. The columns will be for (1) common shares, (2) other paid-in capital (if any), (3) accumulated other comprehensive income, and (4) retained

---

[8] As an aside, referring to the discussion earlier in this chapter, it is worth noting just how brief the Nike income statement is for a company that has revenues of almost US$15 *billion*.

earnings, plus a column for *total*. Nike uses this type of format, two columns of which are shown in Exhibit 3-7.

The five major components of a statement of retained earnings are:

1. Net income or loss for the period

2. Dividends

3. Prior-period error corrections

4. Cumulative effect of retrospective changes in accounting policy

5. Other changes, such as capital transactions, appropriations, and restrictions

Exhibit 3-8 shows the retained earnings statement for Shoppers Drug Mart. This example shows four of the five possible components of a retained earnings statement—everything except error corrections:

- Adjustment as the result of changed accounting standards;
- Net earnings of $364,494,000 for the year;
- Dividends of $85,246,000; and
- Premium on shares purchased for redemption.

## Retrospective Effect of a Change in Accounting Policy

When an accounting policy is changed, the comparability of the financial statements is reduced unless all comparative numbers, including prior years' net incomes, are restated using the newly adopted principle. This change in prior years' income also changes opening retained earnings as previously reported.

Consider the following example. A company's management decides to change from accelerated to straight-line amortization for its capital assets and has made the change to comply with industry practice. The difference between the accumulated amortization under the accelerated method previously used and the amortization that would have accumulated if the straight-line method had been used in all previous periods is $60,000. That is, amortization expense has been $60,000 more using the accelerated method than would have been recorded using straight-line amortization. Assume an income tax rate of 30%. The cumulative effect

---

### EXHIBIT 3-8

### SHOPPERS DRUG MART CORPORATION

### Consolidated Statement of Retained Earnings

52 weeks ended December 31, 2005 and January 1, 2005 (fiscal year 2004)

| (in thousands of dollars) | 2005 | 2004 |
|---|---|---|
| **Retained earnings, beginning of period as reported** | $733,682 | $417,940 |
| Impact of the adoption of new accounting standard, Accounting Guideline 15, "Consolidation of Variable Interest Entities" | (71,245) | (62,697) |
| Retained earnings, as restated | 662,437 | 355,243 |
| Net earnings | 364,494 | 307,322 |
| Premium on share capital purchased for cancellation | (13) | (128) |
| Dividends | (85,246) | — |
| **Retained earnings, end of period** | $941,672 | $662,437 |

*Source:* www.sedar.com, Shoppers Drug Mart Corporation 2005 Annual Report released March 30, 2006, page 40.

of the change in accounting policy, net of applicable income taxes, is $60,000 × 70%, or $42,000. The entry to record the effect of the change in accounting policy is as follows:

| | | |
|---|---|---|
| Accumulated amortization—machinery | 60,000 | |
|     Retained earnings—cumulative effect of change<br>       in accounting principle | | 42,000 |
|     Future income tax liability | | 18,000 |

The tax amount is deferred because the change is made for accounting purposes only —the tax return (and taxes payable) is not changed. We discuss this type of tax effect in Chapter 15.

The effect of a retrospective change in accounting policy is shown on the retained earnings statement as follows:

| | |
|---|---|
| Opening retained earnings, as previously reported (assumed) | $400,000 |
| Effect of change in accounting policy (net of tax) | 42,000 |
| Opening retained earnings, as restated | $442,000 |

Prior financial statements are changed so that only straight-line amortization is shown on the income statements, which obviously would change prior years' net income for all comparative years shown. Appropriate note disclosure would also be prepared.

Accounting policy changes are not always applied with full retrospective restatement. They may also be applied prospectively. Prospective treatment means that the new policy is used for current periods and future periods, but past periods are left as is, with a resulting loss of consistency. This is allowable when specific new accounting standards specifically permit prospective treatment. Prospective treatment is also used as a practical matter when it is simply not feasible to reconstruct data for prior periods.

For example, the current recommendations for reporting available-for-sale financial assets came into effect for years ending after 30 September 2007. The shift from cost basis to market value is a significant change in accounting policy, but there was no need to go back and restate prior years. Application of the new recommendations was *prospective* rather than retrospective.

In other circumstances, the company can determine the impact of the change in accounting policy on opening balances in total, but cannot reconstruct the detail needed to restate individual prior years. This will result in an adjustment to opening retained earnings, as illustrated, but no restatement of previous income statements. Again, practicalities force the use of less desirable disclosure of the effect of the new policy on prior years.

It's worth pointing out that changes in accounting *estimates* are never applied retrospectively; the new estimate is used for this year, and future years, but previous income statements are not changed and retained earnings is not touched.

## Prior-Period Error Corrections

Errors happen. They usually arise from classifying amounts and transactions incorrectly. Error corrections are not the same as changes in accounting estimates. For example, we may discover in 20X6 that our estimate of net realizable value of year-end 20X4 inventory was far too optimistic; much more should have been written down as obsolete. When we discover that fact, we are not finding an error. Accounting estimates are almost always wrong, because they are estimates about the future, not facts. Subsequent adjustments for past accounting estimates are included in revenues and expenses for the current period; they are not errors.

Usually, errors are accidental. However, some "errors" can be viewed as intentional; management may have been trying to affect reported results by intentionally misclassifying some transactions. Prosecutors allege that major public companies (such as WorldCom, Enron, Live Entertainment, Philip Services, and Tyco) deliberately misstated their financial results. In accounting terms the cause of the errors is irrelevant. All errors are corrected in the same manner, whether they occurred innocently or not so innocently.

When errors are discovered, they must be corrected. This sometimes involves restating the financial statements of prior years, and thus changing prior income, which is summarized in retained earnings. Proper disclosure of these changes is accomplished by making an adjustment to opening retained earnings for the cumulative impact of the change to prior income, net of tax. Opening retained earnings *as restated* are presented. Then, the comparative financial statements are adjusted to give effect to the error correction. In effect, the transaction is backed out of the current income statement and into the appropriate prior year. A description of the error and its effect on the financial statements must be included in the disclosure notes.

To illustrate the recording of a retrospective adjustment for an error correction, assume that a machine that cost the Bailey Retail Company $10,000 (with a 10-year estimated useful life and no residual value) was purchased on 1 January 20X2. Further, assume that the total cost was erroneously debited to an expense account in 20X2. The error was discovered 29 December 20X5. A correcting entry would be required in 20X5. Assuming that any income tax effects are recorded separately, the entry is as follows:

| *29 December 20X5:* | | |
|---|---|---|
| Machinery | 10,000 | |
| Amortization expense, straight line (for 20X5) | 1,000 | |
|     Accumulated amortization (20X2 through 20X5) | | 4,000 |
|     Retained earnings, error correction | | 7,000 |

The $7,000 retrospective adjustment corrects the 1 January 20X5 retained earnings balance on a pre-tax basis. The balance is understated $7,000 before tax:

| | |
|---|---|
| *Understatement* of 20X2 income ($10,000 − $1,000) | $9,000 |
| Overstatement of 20X3 and 20X4 income ($1,000 × 2) | (2,000) |
| Net pre-tax understatement | $7,000 |

Assuming that the same error was also made on the income tax return, the entry to record the income tax effect of the error, assuming a 30% income tax rate, would be as follows:

| Retained earnings, error correction | | |
|---|---|---|
|     ($7,000 × 30%) | 2,100 | |
|     Income tax payable | | 2,100 |

Appropriate reporting on the retained earnings statement is illustrated in Exhibit 3-9. Amounts other than the error correction are assumed.

> ===== EXHIBIT 3-9 =====

## BAILEY RETAIL COMPANY RETAINED EARNINGS STATEMENT

### (stated in thousands of Canadian dollars)

For the year ended December 31, 20X5

| | |
|---|---:|
| Retained earnings, 1 January 20X5, as previously reported | $378,800 |
| Correction of error (net of income tax of $2,100) (Note 6) | 4,900 |
| Retained earnings, 1 January 20X5, as restated | 383,700 |
| Net income | 81,200 |
| Cash dividends declared and paid during 20X5 | (30,000) |
| Retained earnings, 31 December 20X5 (Note 7) | $434,900 |

*Note 6. Error correction—During the year, the company discovered that a capital expenditure made in 20X2 was incorrectly expensed. This error caused net income of that period to be understated and that of subsequent periods to be overstated. The adjustment of $4,900 (a $7,000 credit less income tax of $2,100) corrects the error.*

*Note 7. Restrictions—Of the $434,900 ending balance in retained earnings, $280,000 is restricted from dividend availability under the terms of the bond indenture. When the bonds are retired, the restriction will be removed.*

## Capital Transactions

The retained earnings statement contains other increases and decreases in equity caused by capital transactions. Most capital transactions are share transactions. Since a corporation is dealing with itself (its owners) in share transactions, gains and losses caused by these transactions are not shown on the income statement because they are not arm's-length transactions. Gains normally create contributed capital—separate shareholders' equity accounts—and losses reduce retained earnings. We'll study these more carefully in Chapter 13.

Other charges to retained earnings result from share issue expenses incurred on the issuance of new shares, taxes resulting from a change in control or triggered by dividend payments to shareholders, and adjustments to retained earnings caused by a reorganization.

**Appropriations of and Restrictions on Retained Earnings** Retained earnings can be subject to either (1) appropriations or (2) restrictions, or both. Appropriations and restrictions have the effect of limiting the ability of management to declare dividends.

**Restrictions** result from legal requirements, such as a statutory requirement that retained earnings be restricted for dividend purposes by the cost of any treasury stock held, or contractual agreements, such as a bond agreement (i.e., indenture) requiring that retained earnings of a specified amount be withheld from dividend purposes until the bonds are retired.

**Restrictions on retained earnings** are especially common in non-profit organizations, such as social service agencies, hospitals, universities, etc. Restrictions indicate that some of the funds shown on the asset side of the balance sheet are available only for special purposes, such as for specific research activities or for constructing new buildings.

**Appropriations of retained earnings** result from formal decisions by the corporation to set aside, or to *appropriate*, a specific amount of retained earnings (temporarily or permanently). The effect of an appropriation is to remove the specified amount of retained earnings from dividend availability. For example, corporations often set up appropriations such as "retained earnings appropriated for future plant expansion." Appropriations are created by the Board of Directors, and they also can be reduced or eliminated by the Board.

The primary purpose of restrictions and appropriations is to inform statement users that a portion of retained earnings is set aside for a specific purpose (usually long term) and that these amounts are therefore not available for dividend declarations.

Exhibit 3-9 illustrates a restriction of $280,000 on the retained earnings of Bailey Retail Company. The unrestricted balance of retained earnings is $154,900 ($434,900 − $280,000 = $154,900). Details regarding restrictions and appropriations are usually reported in a note, as illustrated in Exhibit 3-9.

## CONCEPT REVIEW

1. What types of items will appear on the retained earnings statement?

2. Explain the difference between a restriction and an appropriation of retained earnings.

3. What is the normal approach to accounting for a change in accounting policy?

4. How are errors in prior years corrected? How does this differ from the way we correct the results of accounting estimates made in prior years?

5. Why aren't gains and losses from capital transactions reported on the income statement?

## INTERNATIONAL PERSPECTIVE

The financial reporting requirements in virtually every country include an income statement of one form or another. The measurement basis and specific measurement rules vary, but there is always some attempt to measure the results of operations.

The International Accounting Standards Board recommends a list of income statement disclosures that looks a lot like the AcSB recommendations. But the IAS recommends "an analysis of expenses" either by type of expense or by function within the enterprise. The AcSB makes no such recommendation, as we have seen.

Income statements in some countries' reporting environments may be even less revealing than those in Canada. Some statements are terse, with very few accounts being reported. In the extreme, an income statement consists of the single net earnings line or of the three lines: earnings before taxes, tax expense, and net earnings. Until Australia converted to IASB standards, that country's earnings statements usually started with "operating profit before interest, tax, depreciation, and amortization," and then proceeded to deduct each of interest, tax, depreciation, and amortization step by step. However, total revenue usually was disclosed in a note.

The biggest difficulty a reader has with international financial income statements is understanding what an item means and how it was measured. Although Australia, Canada, the U.S., and the United Kingdom identify items as "unusual or infrequent" (these items are called "exceptional" in the United Kingdom, and "abnormal" in Australia) and "extraordinary," the reporting requirements in most countries do not make these distinctions. Moreover, very few countries other than Canada and the United States require separate reporting of discontinued operations, although the practice is beginning to spread, thanks largely to efforts by the IASB.

Some countries have higher disclosure standards, or require disclosure of a longer list of specific items. France, for example, has a fairly detailed list of income statement items, including wages and salaries. Germany also requires disclosure of employment costs and materials costs.

However, the income statements of many European countries may include a wide variety of provisions and reserves that have no counterpart in Canada or the U.S. Germany and Austria have a number of profit reserves that are required by law—an officially sanctioned smoothing technique!

In many countries, the accounting measurement rules are greatly influenced by tax law. For example, an item that is deducted for tax reporting may be required to be expensed in the financial statements. A firm might take a large tax deduction for an item such as bad debt expense, for example, and this same amount would have to be reported on the income statement even though it is an overestimate of the actual expense. Such reporting could mislead the reader who assumes that bad debt expense means the same thing in the foreign financial statement as in a Canadian financial statement.

When reading an income statement generated outside Canada, it is important to remember that even though it may appear very much like a statement prepared under Canadian GAAP, the terms and labels may have quite different meanings. It is important to understand how revenues, expenses, gains, and losses are defined in the environment in which the statement was prepared before trying to interpret the information in the statement.

## Retained Earnings

Most other countries are more permissive about charging items directly to retained earnings. When looking at a non-Canadian set of financial statements, the reader should not ignore the retained earnings statement; sometimes it contains interesting expenses or losses that don't appear on the income statement!

## Comprehensive Income

Comprehensive income in Canada is partially the result of convergence efforts between U.S. GAAP, Canadian GAAP, and IASB GAAP. The FASB was the first to establish the concept of comprehensive income. The goal was to find a place to put items that did not seem to fit into net income but that the FASB was reluctant to allow into retained earnings. Historically, the FASB has refused to let companies "hide" things by burying them in retained earnings. These items included the correction of errors and other adjustments. For example, the cumulative impact of changes in accounting standards was included in net income in the U.S. but in retained earnings in other countries (including Canada). The FASB did not permit restatement of prior years' financial statements.

On the international scene, the IASB has been moving steadily toward market values for a wide variety of assets and liabilities, especially financial instruments. The trend clearly is to "mark-to-market," in which assets and liabilities are revalued at every balance sheet date. As well, the IASB was concerned that writedowns (and, in some countries, write-ups) of assets for "impairment" were not really realized and should be reported separately from the primary measurement of transaction-based net income. Therefore, the IASB also moved toward a separate reporting of value changes. The IASB calls them "other changes in equity" rather than "comprehensive income," but the result is the same.

In Canada, the AcSB has an explicit objective of harmonizing Canadian GAAP with U.S. and international GAAP as much as possible. For example, the CICA standard on comprehensive income is not identical to either the U.S. or the IASB standards, but it is harmonized with both. A company that reports into the U.S. but uses Canadian GAAP will not have to restate for comprehensive income for U.S. purposes. A company can report the same comprehensive income numbers in the U.S. and Canada and be in compliance with both countries' accounting standards.

## Resolving Accounting Differences

In the chapter introduction, we mentioned that CHC Helicopter reported 2006 net income of $90.7 million under Canadian GAAP but $130.6 using U.S. GAAP. Why the large difference?

Bear in mind is that net income is a residual. Relatively small differences in revenue or expense recognition can have quite a large impact on net income. CHC had 2006 revenue of $1,011.5 million, or over a billion dollars. The Canada–U.S. difference in net income is $39.9 million (that is, $130.6 − $90.7), which seems large but actually is only 3.9% of total revenue or 4.1% of total expenses and other deductions.

The basic reason for the difference is that there are some items that accountants haven't quite figured out how to handle. Changes in certain types of foreign currency translations, for example, must be reported somewhere in order to make the accounts balance. However, these changes will never be realized in any meaningful sense, and accounting standard setters in different countries have reached different conclusions about where to put these items—essentially an arbitrary choice.

One underlying rationale for creating international standards is to harmonize the treatment of many stray items. One might say that the goal of international standards is to be consistently arbitrary about the reporting of unrealized or difficult-to-classify amounts. By being consistent although somewhat arbitrary, national standard setters avoid the embarrassing question: So which income number is "right," the U.S. or Canada or IASB one? In truth, there is no "right" answer—only different ways of perceiving the same set of circumstances and accounting anomalies.

## RELEVANT STANDARDS

*CICA Handbook:*
- Section 1506, Accounting Changes
- Section 1520, Income Statement
- Section 1530, Comprehensive Income
- Section 3251, Equity
- Section 3475, Disposal of Long-lived Assets and Discontinued Operations
- Section 3480, Extraordinary Items

IASB:
- *IAS* 1, Presentation of Financial Statements
- *IAS* 8, Accounting Policies, Changes in Accounting Estimates and Errors
- *IFRS* 5, Non-current Assets Held for Sale and Discontinued Operations

## SUMMARY OF KEY POINTS

1. Accounting income is the result of recording transactions in accordance with established measurement rules. Accounting income suffers from its reliance on *transactions*, which ignore economic events that indicate wealth increases. Accounting income may also be affected by the nature of accounting policies chosen, which determines the quality of earnings.

2. Companies must report *comprehensive income*, which has two components: (1) net income, and (2) *other comprehensive income*. Other comprehensive income (which can be called by other names, such as "other changes in shareholders' equity") includes unrealized gains and losses on available-for-sale assets, translation gains/losses on foreign operations, unrealized gains/losses on cash flow hedges of anticipated future transactions, and unfunded or overfunded pension obligations.

3. Many format issues are not governed by accounting pronouncements, and the company must make choices to create an income statement that is useful to financial statement users. Minimum disclosures are recommended by the *CICA Handbook*; additional note disclosures and format decisions are important for full disclosure.

4. Two general formats for presenting income statement information not specifically regulated by accounting pronouncements are the single-step and the multiple-step formats.

5. The single-step format uses only two broad classifications in its presentation: (1) a revenues and gains section and (2) an expenses and losses section. Total expenses and losses are deducted from total revenues and gains in a single computation to determine the net income (earnings) amount.

6. A multiple-step income statement presents several intermediate subtotals, designed to emphasize important relationships in the various revenue and expense categories. Most companies use a format that is between single step and full multiple step.

7. The gains or losses resulting from the sale or abandonment of a business segment, whose activities represent a separate major line of business or class of customer, must be reported, net of income tax effects, as a separate component of income, positioned after income from continuing operations and before extraordinary items.

8. Extraordinary items result from transactions or events that are infrequent, not normal business activities, and do not result from the decisions or actions of management. They are required to be reported, net of income tax effects, as a separate component of income, positioned after income from continuing operations. Extraordinary items are very rare in Canadian practice.

9. Large unusual or infrequent items should be shown separately on the income statement, before tax.

10. Earnings per share amounts relate earnings to common shares outstanding.

11. The statement of retained earnings reports all changes in retained earnings during the period, including net income or loss, dividends declared, capital transactions, and adjustments for changes in accounting policies.

12. Error corrections that affect the financial statements of prior periods are recorded (net of tax) as a change to opening retained earnings, and comparative statements are restated.

13. A change in accounting principle is normally applied retrospectively, with the cumulative effect of the change shown as an adjustment to opening retained earnings. Comparative financial statements should be restated. If this treatment is not feasible, only the cumulative effect is shown on the retained earnings statement. In certain circumstances, the change in principle is reflected prospectively. An accounting estimate is always changed prospectively.

## KEY TERMS

accounting income, 82
appropriations of retained earnings, 107
basic earnings per share, 99
diluted earnings per share, 99
discontinued operations, 93

interperiod tax allocation, 91
intraperiod tax allocation, 91
other comprehensive income, 100
restrictions, 107
restrictions on retained earnings, 107

## REVIEW PROBLEM

The following pre-tax amounts are taken from the adjusted trial balance of Killian Corporation at 31 December 20X5, the end of Killian's fiscal year:

| Account | Amount |
| --- | --- |
| Sales revenue | $1,000,000 |
| Service revenue | 200,000 |
| Interest revenue | 30,000 |
| Gain on sale of capital asset | 100,000 |
| Cost of goods sold | 600,000 |
| Selling, general, and administrative expense | 150,000 |
| Depreciation expense | 50,000 |
| Interest expense | 20,000 |
| Loss on sale of long-term investment | 10,000 |
| Extraordinary item, loss from earthquake damage | 200,000 |
| Cumulative effect of change in accounting policy (gain) | 50,000 |
| Impairment loss on business segment assets | 60,000 |
| Loss on operation of discontinued business segment | 10,000 |

*Other information:*

a. The income tax rate is 40% on all items.

b. There were 100,000 common shares outstanding throughout the year. No preferred shares are outstanding.

c. Assume that the capital cost allowance deductible for tax purposes is equal to the depreciation expense shown on the income statement.

**Required:**

1. Prepare a single-step income statement in good form.
2. Prepare a multiple-step income statement in good form.

# REVIEW PROBLEM—SOLUTION

1. Single-step income statement:

### KILLIAN CORPORATION
### Income Statement

for the year ended 31 December 20X5

| | |
|---|---:|
| Revenues and gains: | |
| Sales revenue | $1,000,000 |
| Service revenue | 200,000 |
| Interest revenue | 30,000 |
| Gain on sale of operational asset | 100,000 |
| Total revenue and gains | 1,330,000 |
| | |
| Expenses and losses: | |
| Cost of goods sold | 600,000 |
| Selling, general, and administrative expenses | 150,000 |
| Depreciation | 50,000 |
| Interest expense | 20,000 |
| Loss on sale of long-term investment | 10,000 |
| Income tax expense [see computations below] | 200,000 |
| Total expenses and losses | 1,030,000 |
| | |
| Income from continuing operations | 300,000 |
| Discontinued operations: | |
| Loss from discontinued operations, net of tax | |
| of $28,000 | (42,000) |
| Income before extraordinary item | 258,000 |
| Extraordinary item: | |
| Loss from earthquake damage, net of tax | |
| benefit of $80,000 | (120,000) |
| Net income | $ 138,000 |
| | |
| Earnings per share: | |
| Income from continuing operations | $      3.00 |
| Net income | $      1.38 |
| *Computation of income tax expense:* | |
| Total revenues | $1,330,000 |

Expenses before income taxes:

| | | |
|---|---:|---:|
| Cost of goods sold | $600,000 | |
| Selling, general, and administrative expenses | 150,000 | |
| Capital cost allowance (equal to depreciation) | 50,000 | |
| Interest expense | 20,000 | |
| Loss on sale of long-term investment | 10,000 | 830,000 |
| Taxable income | | 500,000 |
| Tax rate | | 40% |
| Income tax expense | | $200,000 |

The discontinued operations and extraordinary item are reported net of tax, reflecting intraperiod allocation, and therefore are not included in the computation of income tax expense. The cumulative effect of a change in accounting policy is shown on the retained earnings statement.

2. Multiple-step income statement:

## KILLIAN CORPORATION
### Income Statement

for the year ended 31 December 20X5

| | | |
|---|---:|---:|
| Sales revenue | | $1,000,000 |
| Cost of goods sold | | 600,000 |
| Gross margin | | 400,000 |
| Operating expenses: | | |
| Selling, general, and administrative expenses | $150,000 | |
| Depreciation expense | 50,000 | 200,000 |
| Income from operations | | 200,000 |
| Other revenues and gains: | | |
| Service revenue | 200,000 | |
| Interest revenue | 30,000 | |
| Gain on sale of operational asset | 100,000 | 330,000 |
| Other expenses and losses: | | |
| Interest expense | 20,000 | |
| Loss on sale of long-term investment | 10,000 | 30,000 |
| Net other items | | 300,000 |
| Income from continuing operations before income tax | | 500,000 |
| Income tax expense | | 200,000 |
| Income from continuing operations | | 300,000 |
| Discontinued operations: | | |
| Loss from discontinued operations, net of tax of $28,000 | | (42,000) |
| Income before extraordinary item | | 258,000 |
| Extraordinary item: | | |
| Loss from earthquake damage, net of tax effects of $80,000 | | (120,000) |
| Net income | | $ 138,000 |
| Earnings per share: | | |
| Income from continuing operations | | $ 3.00 |
| Net income | | $ 1.38 |

Alternative arrangements of the information above the income from continuing operations line are allowed for both single- and multiple-step formats. In particular, the other revenues and other expenses are commonly combined into a single category of other revenues and expenses instead of being shown in two categories.

The presentation of the items below income from continuing operations should be the same for both single-step and multiple-step statements.

## QUESTIONS

**Q3-1** Briefly explain how the income statement is a connecting link between the beginning and ending balance sheets.

**Q3-2** What is the difference between economic income and accounting income?

**Q3-3** How does comprehensive income differ from net income?

**Q3-4** Unrealized gains and losses on available-for-sale financial assets are *recycled* when the asset is sold. Explain the meaning of "recycled."

**Q3-5** Where does accumulated other comprehensive income appear on the balance sheet?

**Q3-6** What factors determine the choice of a fiscal year-end?

**Q3-7** Why might a Canadian company prepare its financial statements in U.S. dollars?

**Q3-8** Briefly define intraperiod tax allocation.

**Q3-9** Regis Publishing Corporation computed total income tax expense for 20X5 of $16,640. The following pre-tax amounts were used: (a) income before extraordinary loss, $60,000; (b) extraordinary loss, $12,000; and (c) correction of a prior year's error, $4,000 (a credit on the retained earnings statement). The average income tax rate on all items was 32%. Compute the intraperiod income tax allocation amounts.

**Q3-10** What totals or subtotals do accounting standards *require* in arriving at net income on the income statement?

**Q3-11** A company has a segment that it decides to sell, effective 1 September, after incurring operating losses of $45,000 to date in the fiscal year. The segment, with net assets of $310,000, was sold for $240,000 on 1 November, after incurring further operating losses of $30,000. Assume a tax rate of 40%. What amounts would be disclosed in the income statement?

**Q3-12** Define an extraordinary item. How should extraordinary items be reported on (a) a single-step and (b) a multiple-step income statement?

**Q3-13** How are items that are unusual or infrequent reported on the income statement?

**Q3-14** Why are extraordinary items so seldom reported on the statements of Canadian companies?

**Q3-15** Define earnings per share (EPS). Why is it required as an integral part of the income statement?

**Q3-16** What types of items are reported on a statement of retained earnings?

**Q3-17** A company has a machine that cost $21,000 when acquired at the beginning of year 1. It had a 10-year useful life and a $1,000 residual value. Toward the end of year 5, the company discovered that, in error, the machine had been expensed when acquired. Straight-line depreciation is appropriate. What adjustment to opening retained earnings is appropriate in year 5?

Q3-18　Describe how a change in accounting policy is reflected in the financial statements. Describe two alternative, less desirable approaches and state when each can be used.

Q3-19　What is meant by appropriations or restrictions on retained earnings? How are such items usually reported?

Q3-20　What are capital transactions and why are they reported on the retained earnings statement?

## CASE 3-1

## STARBURST INVESTMENTS LIMITED

Starburst Investments Ltd. is a private investment fund formed in early 20X5 to sell shares to wealthy economics professors and then invest the money in other company's securities. Since the company is private, Starburst shareholders cannot sell their shares to other investors; instead, Starburst will redeem shares at their net book value (that is, the net assets of the company divided by the number of shares outstanding) at the end of any fiscal year, provided that the investor has given at least 60 days notice of her or his intent to redeem.

One of your professors is considering joining this investment fund and investing all of the royalties that he receives from his best-selling university economics textbook. He has come to you for advice on the historical cost accounting methods that are being used by the fund manager. The fund manager believes that a strict historical cost accounting system is preferable to one based on market values because both reinvestment and cash distributions can be made only from realized earnings, not from changes in market value of the investment portfolio. As a private investment fund, the fund is constrained neither by public mutual fund legislation nor by public-company GAAP.

The economics professor believes that the manager's methodology does not properly reflect the underlying value of the shares, and he would like to see a comparison of capital growth under historical cost as compared to other methods of measurement that better reflect market values.

By the end of 20X4, the fund manager had attracted $140,000 from interested investors. He then conducted the following transactions (in chronological order):

**20X5:**
a. Purchased 1,000 shares of Kieso Ltd. for $50 per share.
b. Purchased 2,000 shares of Lemon Inc. for $30 per share.
c. Sold 200 shares of Kieso Ltd. for $65 per share.
d. Invested $20,000 in 100 shares of Nepotist Corp., a new venture being established by the manager's uncle.

**20X6:**
e. Purchased 500 shares of Hilton Ltd. for $60 per share.
f. Sold 700 shares of Lemon Inc. for $45 per share.

**20X7:**
g. Purchased another 400 shares of Hilton Ltd. for $40 per share.
h. Sold 800 shares of Kieso Ltd. for $70 per share.

The market values of these shares at the end of each year were as follows:

|      | Hilton | Kieso | Lemon | Nepotist* |
|------|--------|-------|-------|-----------|
| 20X5 | $62    | $70   | $60   | $180      |
| 20X6 | $50    | $90   | $40   | 195       |
| 20X7 | $45    | $50   | $65   | 210       |

*Book values per share. Nepotist is a private company, and thus no market values are available.

**Required:**
Prepare a memo to your economics professor in which you comment on the methods being used by the fund manager. Explain any alternatives that might be used instead, including the asset values and capital growth of the fund under each alternative.

## CASE 3-2

### TRAVEL INCORPORATED

Travel Inc. (TI) is a holding company that has wholly owned interests in the travel and entertainment industry. The company has four separate operating divisions—(1) a scheduled airline, operating mainly in Western Canada and the U.S.; (2) a hotel management company that manages hotels throughout North America; (3) a real estate division that owns and operates many commercial developments in Canada, including some of the hotels; and (4) a travel services company that sells vacation packages at both retail and wholesale.

Each division operates through one or more separate corporations and is subject to federal and provincial income tax. TI is the sole shareholder in all of its subsidiaries. The senior executives of each of the operating divisions report directly to the senior executives of TI.

TI is listed on the Toronto Stock Exchange and is subject to the reporting requirements of the exchange and of the Ontario Securities Commission. TI prepares consolidated financial statements. TI's income tax rate is 25%.

In 20X5, TI had major transactions affecting two of its four divisions:

*Sale of the real estate division*
On 15 June 20X5, TI's Board of Directors decided that the company's shares were undervalued in relation to the underlying value of the various divisions. The low valuation was largely attributable to continuing losses in the airline division. Therefore, the Board decided to sell the real estate development company in order to capture the "true" value of that division for the benefit of TI shareholders.

On 23 November 20X5, after conclusion of a 60-day open bidding period, the Board accepted a purchase proposal from Lincoln Goodview Ltd. (LGL). LGL agreed to acquire all of TI's shares in the real estate division for cash consideration of $450 million. LGL will acquire all of the division's assets and assume all debt related to the division's real estate properties. The purchase price is $450 million, based on the fair value of the division's assets less the present value of the related debt that LGL will assume. The transaction is contingent upon the completion of LGL's due diligence review of the division's books. LGL's due diligence is expected to be completed in February 20X6. In the meantime, TI will continue to operate the division and will receive all profits until the sale is finalized, which is expected to occur in February 20X6.

The net book value of the division's real estate asset portfolio was $1,670 million on 23 November 20X5. The appraised fair value on 23 November was $2,240 million. At 31 December 20X5, the fair value of the portfolio is $2,450. The fair value of the related debt was $1,430 on 23 November and $1,420 on 31 December.

In 20X5, the division had total revenues of $300 million and net income of $50 million. Of those amounts, $130 million of revenue and $28 million of net income were earned prior to 15 June.

*Forced sale of bus operations*
In 20X2, the TI airline division established a long-distance bus operation, BlueSky, to complement its air service. The intent was to provide a seamless transportation experience for airline passengers who were travelling to smaller cities and towns in Alberta. Because TI sold tickets that included both the airline and BlueSky segments of each passenger's voyage, the bus operation was organized as part of the airlines operations. The company did not allocate revenue to airline and bus; BlueSky was operated as a cost centre.

A competing bus company complained that the air-bus combination was in restraint of trade. The regulator agreed. In early January 20X5, TI was ordered by transportation regulators to divest itself of its bus operation within 12 months.

Therefore, TI's airline division sold the bus operations to Trillium Express, an Ontario bus company. The transaction was completed on 17 July 20X5. Trillium Express paid $25 million for the net assets of BlueSky. At the time of the sale, the net book value of BlueSky's net assets was $33 million.

### Required:

What are the reporting implications of these two transactions? Explain how each would be shown on TI's consolidated statements for the year ending 31 December 20X5. Be specific.

## CASE 3-3

## CASHGO LIMITED

CashGo Ltd. is a food distributor and retailer in eastern Canada. The company also owns both a bakery and a dairy, each of which has significant sales through other market channels in addition to CashGo's stores. CashGo is a private company; all of the shares are owned by the founder's family. The company has not needed external share capital as the company is quite profitable and the banks are eager to provide debt financing as needed. The banks require CashGo to give them annual audited financial statements, prepared in accordance with Canadian GAAP.

The CashGo CFO currently is overseeing the preparation of the company's consolidated financial statements for 20X7. There have been many changes to the recommendations of the *CICA Handbook,* not all of which the CFO is sure that she understands. She has come to you for advice on how to report the results of some of the company's 20X7 transactions and events. She also would appreciate receiving draft statements of income, comprehensive income, and retained earnings. CashGo does not wish to provide any more detail in the statements than is necessary to comply with current reporting requirements.

*Specific concerns:*

1. In the final quarter of 20X7, the Halifax region suffered a major hurricane, which knocked out the electricity in the Halifax region for several days. Hurricanes are extremely uncommon in Nova Scotia. A great quantity of frozen and other perishable foods was spoiled and had to be discarded. The loss amounted to $11 million. The inventory was not insured against this type of loss.

2. CashGo is a private company. In 20X7, the company elected to use the differential reporting option on income taxes, applied retrospectively. The cumulative adjustment for prior years was to eliminate the $46 million credit balance of future income taxes. CashGo has tentatively classified this amount as "Gain on income tax reversals."

3. Early in 20X7, the company invested $24 million of excess cash in a portfolio of marketable securities that are available for sale. The company sold some of these securities in November for $14 million; the original cost was $9 million. The remaining securities have a market value of $18 million at year-end 20X7.

4. A major customer of the dairy division went bankrupt in 20X7. The customer owed CashGo $6 million. As an unsecured creditor, CashGo is unlikely to receive any payment on this receivable; therefore, the receivable was written off. CashGo has never before experienced a bad debt of this magnitude.

5. As part of a structuring of retail operations, the company closed a significant number of smaller stores during the year and sold the buildings and land for a gain of $12 million. This was partially offset by $8.5 million in severance costs paid to the employees. The company will continue its restructuring in 20X8 at an estimated net cost of $7 million.

6. CashGo has a U.S. subsidiary that operates a food distribution centre in New England. The subsidiary operates autonomously. CashGo translates the subsidiary's U.S.-dollar

financial statements into Canadian dollars in order to consolidate the subsidiary. The mechanical result of the translation is an annual gain or loss. A 20X7 translation loss of $6 million arose when the subsidiary's statements were converted to Canadian dollars.

*Additional information:*

The CashGo year-end 20X7 trial balance shows the following amounts, not including amounts explained above:

| millions of Canadian dollars | Debit | Credit |
|---|---|---|
| Sales revenue—Retail | | $390 |
| Sales revenue—Wholesale | | 251 |
| Sales revenue—Dairy division | | 45 |
| Sales revenue—Bakery division | | 65 |
| Sales revenue—U.S. | | 67 |
| Bank interest paid | $ 12 | |
| Amortization expense | 96 | |
| General advertising expense | 21 | |
| Investment income | | 3 |
| Operating expenses—Retail | 194 | |
| Operating expenses—Wholesale | 256 | |
| Operating expenses—Dairy | 20 | |
| Operating expenses—Bakery | 23 | |
| Operating expenses—U.S. subsidiary | 46 | |
| General corporate administrative expense | 33 | |
| Income tax expense | 44 | |
| Retained earnings, 31 December 20X6 | | 359 |
| Dividends paid, 20X7 | 48 | |

**Required:**

1. Advise the CFO on the proper treatment of each of her six specific concerns, with explanation.
2. Prepare the draft statements as requested.

**CASE 3-4**

## KIDSAWARE

KIDSaWARE (KW) is a retailer of children's clothing that has been in operation for over 30 years. The stores are located in central Canada—Ontario and Quebec.

Four years ago, KW bought all of the shares of Prairie Kids (PK), an existing chain of retail children's clothing stores that operated throughout western Canada. PK was suffering from severe competition, particularly from Wal-Mart. KW had just had a successful initial public offering and believed that it could return PK to profitability by injecting fresh capital to modernize the stores, coordinating PK's marketing with KW's, and introducing KW merchandise into PK stores.

PK was maintained as a separate corporate entity. The PK store managers reported to the PK district managers, as before, and the district managers reported to the sales manager of KW. All corporate affairs were conducted through KW's head office in Brampton, Ontario.

On 17 September 20X1, however, the KW Board of Directors decided that the PK venture was not successful, and the Board decided to put PK up for sale. KW paid a broker $100,000 to find a buyer for PK. If an acquiror could not be found, PK would be shut down.

In January 20X2, the broker did find a potential buyer. The buyer would agree to acquire PK on 15 March, paying $0.15 per share for 100% of PK shares, plus assuming the outstanding debt and all future lease commitments (see Exhibit 1). Because the potential buyer has no direct experience with children's wear, a condition of the sale is that KW management continues to be involved in managing PK until the end of the next fiscal year—that is, through the Christmas 20X2 selling season.

Meanwhile, the audit committee has been presented with a draft of the KW income statement (Exhibit 2) that treats the PK disposal as a discontinued operation. KW's fiscal year ends on 31 January 20X2.

## Required:

1. Assume that the disposal of PK qualifies as a discontinued operation. Is the draft KW presentation correct? If not, how should it be reported?
2. Assume instead that the disposal does not qualify as a discontinued operation, but that PK has become a held-for-sale asset as the result of the Board meeting on 17 September 2001. How would the potential disposal of PK be reported?
3. Does PK qualify for reporting as a discontinued operation, under the requirements of Section 3470 of the *CICA Handbook*? Explain.                                     (CICA, adapted)

---

## EXHIBIT 1

### Prairie Kids Incorporated Balance Sheet (Unaudited)
### (stated in thousands of Canadian dollars)

| January 31, 20X2 | Book Values | Estimated Liquidation Values |
|---|---|---|
| **Assets** | | |
| Accounts receivable | $    584 | $    584 |
| Inventory | 10,846 | 3,841 |
| Prepaid expenses | 2,870 | NIL |
| Capital assets | 22,869 | 5,717 |
| Total assets | $37,169 | |
| **Liabilities** | | |
| Bank indebtedness | $ 8,051 | $ 8,051 |
| Accounts payable and accrued liabilities | 18,389 | 18,389 |
| Long-term debt | 4,936 | 4,936 |
| Deferred lease inducements | 854 | |
| | 32,230 | |
| **Shareholders' equity** | | |
| Common shares (8,342,000 shares issued and outstanding) | 17,573 | |
| Deficit | (12,634) | |
| | 4,939 | |
| **Total liabilities and shareholders' equity** | $37,169 | |

*Note 1.* The rent expense for the year is $7,147. The minimum rental payments for the leases of the premises are as follows:

| | |
|---|---|
| 20X3 | $ 7,253 |
| 20X4 | $ 7,012 |
| 20X5 | $ 6,889 |
| 20X6 | $ 6,599 |
| 20X7 | $ 6,156 |
| 20X8–2012 | $32,035 |

The rental payments for the store premises are guaranteed by KW. The rent guarantee is limited to three years of minimum rental payments.

## EXHIBIT 2

### Income Statements (Unaudited)
### (stated in thousands of Canadian dollars)

| For the year ended January 31, 20X2 | KW Consolidated | PK |
|---|---|---|
| Sales | $258,420 | $48,421 |
| Cost of sales and store, warehouse, and administrative expenses | (233,122) | (51,209) |
| Other expenses | (11,859) | (3,088) |
| Earnings before income taxes and discontinued operations | 13,439 | (5,876) |
| Income taxes (current and future) | (4,829) | |
| Earnings (loss) from continuing operations | 8,610 | (5,876) |
| Loss from discontinued operations* | (9,664) | |
| Net loss | $ (1,054) | $ (5,876) |

*The loss from discontinued operations was calculated, in thousands of dollars, as:*

| | | |
|---|---|---|
| Loss from PKI's operations | | $ (5,876) |
| Sale of 8,342,000 shares at $0.15 per share | $ 1,251 | |
| Broker's fee | (100) | |
| Book value of PKI's net assets | (4,939) | |
| Loss on disposal at $0.15 per share | $ (3,788) | (3,788) |
| Loss from discontinued operations | | $ (9,664) |

## ASSIGNMENTS

★ **A3-1 Accounting Income versus Economic Income:** On 1 January 20X1, Tyler Trading Company was incorporated by Jim Tyler, who owned all the common shares. His original investment was $100,000. Transactions over the subsequent three years were as follows:

| 2 | January 20X1 | Purchased 10 cars for resale at $10,000 each. |
|---|---|---|
| 30 | June 20X1 | Sold six cars for total proceeds of $90,000. |
| 31 | December 20X1 | Remaining four cars have an estimated sales value of $48,000. |
| 15 | July 20X2 | Bought three cars for resale at $20,000 each. |
| 3 | October 20X2 | Sold four cars from 20X1 purchase for total proceeds of $50,000. |
| 31 | December 20X2 | Cars from 20X2 purchase have an estimated sales value of $84,000. |
| 30 | November 20X3 | Sold all three cars bought in 20X2 for total proceeds of $106,000. |

**Required:**

1. Calculate accounting income, based on transactions, for 20X1, 20X2, and 20X3.
2. Calculate economic income, based on events or changes in value, for 20X1, 20X2, and 20X3.
3. Compare total accounting income with total economic income and explain your findings.
4. In what ways is accounting income superior to economic income? In what ways is economic income superior? Use the accounting principles from Chapter 2 to explain.

★ **A3-2 Accounting Income versus Economic Income:** Hoskins & Sells is a partnership that was established in March 20X6. If a partner decides to leave the partnership, the value of her or his partnership share will be determined by the net book value of the partnership's net assets at the end of the last-preceding fiscal year.

The following transactions and events occurred during 20X6, in thousands of dollars:

- Acquired land for $200 and constructed a building at a cost of $800. Hoskins expects to use the building productively for about 20 years, after which the company will sell the building and move to new premises. Hoskins will amortize the building at a declining balance rate of 10% per year.
- Purchased furniture for $60. The useful life for the furniture is expected to be 10 years; it will be amortized on a straight-line basis, assuming no residual value.
- Had sales of $900 and operating and other expenses (excluding amortization) of $560.
- At the end of the year, net realizable value for the assets were as follows:
  - Land, $220
  - Building, $775
  - Furniture, $45

**Required:**

1. How much is Hoskins & Sells's accounting income?
2. Calculate the economic income.
3. If you were a partner in Hoskins & Sells, would you prefer for the partnership to report its earnings and value its net assets in accordance with accounting income or economic income? Explain.
4. Many managers resist the concept of reporting investments at fair value or market value. What are the advantages for managers of reporting investments on an historical cost basis?

★★ **A3-3 Interpreting the Components of Income:** Excerpts from the Stanley Produce Company comparative income statements for the years 20X2 through 20X4 are as follows:

| (stated in millions of Canadian dollars) | 20X2 | 20X3 | 20X4 |
|---|---|---|---|
| Income from continuing operations, after tax | $20 | $25 | $30 |
| Discontinued operations: | | | |
|   Income from operations of discontinued | | | |
|     segment, net of tax | 15 | 10 | 0 |
|   Gain on disposal of discontinued | | | |
|     segment, net of tax | 0 | 0 | 50 |
| Extraordinary items: | | | |
|   Loss from earthquake damage, net of tax | 0 | (40) | 0 |
|   Gain on expropriation of property | 35 | 0 | 0 |
| Net income (loss) | $70 | $ (5) | $80 |

**Required:**

1. Stanley Produce has experienced volatile earnings over the three-year period shown. Do you expect this to continue? Why or why not?
2. Net income increased from a loss of $5 million in 20X3 to a profit of $80 million in 20X4. Suppose the company's common share price increased only approximately 20% during the same period. Why might this be the case? Relate the 20% increase in share price to the components of net income.
3. Would you expect net income in 20X5 to be more or less than the amount reported in 20X4? More specifically, assuming no new unusual, non-recurring items, what amount would you estimate net income to be in 20X5?

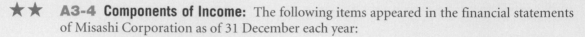

**A3-4 Components of Income:** The following items appeared in the financial statements of Misashi Corporation as of 31 December each year:

| (millions of Canadian dollars Dr./(Cr.) | 20X7 | 20X8 | 20X9 |
|---|---|---|---|
| Sales revenue | $(350) | $(410) | $(505) |
| Gross margin | (80) | (90) | (110) |
| Operating expenses | 30 | 40 | 55 |
| Restructuring charges | — | 15 | 40 |
| Loss (gain) on disposal of operating segments* | 10 | (20) | (25) |
| Loss on nationalization of foreign property* | — | 13 | 12 |
| Income tax expense on continuing operations | 12 | 6 | (1) |
| Interest on long-term debt | 10 | 12 | 18 |
| Dividends declared and paid | 7 | 10 | 14 |

*net of income taxes

**Required:**

1. Construct an income statement for each of the three years, in good form.
2. What trends can you see in this data? Comment on the relative trends in sales, gross margins, earnings from continuing operations, net income, and so forth.

**A3-5 Income Statement Format:** The following selected items were taken from the adjusted trial balance of Amick Manufacturing Corporation at 31 December 20X5. All amounts are before income tax.

| | |
|---|---|
| Sales revenue | $600,000 |
| Cost of goods sold (including amortization, $43,000) | 300,000 |
| Dividends received on investment in shares | 6,500 |
| Distribution expenses | 65,000 |
| Interest expense | 4,200 |
| Extraordinary item: tornado damage (pre-tax) | 60,000 |
| Dividends declared and paid | 70,000 |
| General and administrative expenses | 48,000 |
| Loss on discontinued operation | 50,000 |
| Restructuring expense | 27,000 |
| Accounts receivable | 136,500 |
| Allowance for doubtful accounts | 3,500 |
| Interest revenue | 2,500 |
| Income tax, assuming an average 30% tax rate | ? |

**Required:**

1. Prepare a single-step income statement.
2. Prepare a multiple-step income statement.

**A3-6 Income Statement Format:** The Sandvik Cement Company's records provided the following information at 31 December 20X5 (the end of the accounting period). All amounts are before income tax.

| | |
|---|---|
| Sales revenue | $95,000 |
| Rental revenue | 35,000 |
| Gain on disposal of pre-cast division | 40,000 |
| Gain on sale of short-term investments | 14,000 |
| Distribution expense | 18,000 |
| Cost of goods sold | 45,000 |
| General and administrative expense | 12,000 |
| Depreciation expense | 9,000 |

| | |
|---|---|
| Interest expense | 4,000 |
| Income tax expense (25% rate on all items) | ? |
| Earthquake loss on building | 25,000 |
| Gain on sale of equipment | 15,000 |
| Loss on flood damage | 20,000 |
| Loss on sale of warehouse | 3,000 |

**Required:**

1. Prepare a single-step income statement. State any assumptions that you make.
2. Prepare a multiple-step income statement.

---

★ ★ **A3-7 Income Statement Format:** The following items were taken from the adjusted trial balance of the Biggler Manufacturing Corporation on 31 December 20X5. Assume an average 30% income tax on all items (including the divestiture loss). The accounting period ends 31 December. All amounts given are pre-tax.

| | |
|---|---|
| Sales revenue | $745,200 |
| Rent revenue | 2,400 |
| Interest revenue | 900 |
| Gain on sale of capital assets | 2,000 |
| Distribution expenses | 136,000 |
| General and administrative expenses | 110,000 |
| Interest expense | 1,500 |
| Depreciation for the period | 6,000 |
| Court-ordered divestiture loss | 22,000 |
| Cost of goods sold | 330,000 |
| Operating loss of discontinued operation to disposal date | 28,000 |
| Loss on sale of assets of discontinued operation | 10,000 |

**Required:**

1. Prepare a single-step income statement.
2. Prepare a multiple-step income statement.

---

★ **A3-8 Minimum Disclosure:** MLP Ltd. wishes to present an income statement that complies with minimum required disclosure requirements. Data related to the 20X2 income statement is presented below.

| | |
|---|---|
| Sales revenue | $2,600,000 |
| Investment revenue | 12,300 |
| Rent revenue | 7,000 |
| Royalty revenue | 102,000 |
| Cost of goods sold | 860,000 |
| Selling expenses | 235,000 |
| General and administrative expenses | 210,000 |
| Salaries and wages, sales | 420,000 |
| Salaries and wages, administration | 236,000 |
| Personnel and placement expense | 55,000 |
| Travel expenses | 86,000 |
| Amortization expense | 120,000 |
| Impairment of capital assets | 300,000 |
| Interest expense | 13,000 |
| Income tax expense (tax rate = 25%) | ? |
| Gain on discontinued operation (before income tax) | 30,000 |

**Required:**

Using the above information, prepare an income statement that discloses only the minimum information required by accounting standards.

**A3-9 Income Statement Formats, Extraordinary Item:** The following pre-tax information was taken from the adjusted trial balance of Turkey Hill Foods Corporation at 31 December 20X5, the end of the accounting period:

| | |
|---|---|
| Sales revenue | $957,000 |
| Sales returns | 7,000 |
| Gain on sale of equipment | 8,000 |
| Depreciation expense | 25,000 |
| Distribution expense | 140,000 |
| General and administrative expense | 92,300 |
| Rent revenue | 18,000 |
| Investment revenue | 7,000 |
| Gain on sale of land | 6,000 |
| Interest expense | 9,000 |
| Gain on expropriation of property | 80,000 |
| Loss on sale of long-term investments | 10,000 |
| Cost of goods sold | 550,000 |
| Loss due to leaky roof | 4,000 |
| Earthquake damage loss | 30,000 |

All items listed above are before tax; the tax rate is 30% on all items. There are 40,000 common shares outstanding.

**Required:**

1. Prepare a single-step income statement. State any assumptions you make.
2. Prepare a multiple-step income statement.
3. Calculate the EPS disclosures that would be included on the income statement. Include one EPS figure for net income, and one for income before extraordinary items.

★★ **A3-10 Income Statement Format, Tax Allocation:** Listed below, in alphabetical order, are selected account balances at 31 December 20X3 for Irving Limited, a Nova Scotia public company. All amounts are before income taxes.

| | |
|---|---|
| Accounts receivable | $ 47,000 |
| Accumulated amortization | 82,000 |
| Administrative expenses | 113,000 |
| Advances from customers | 17,000 |
| Amortization expense | 18,000 |
| Common shares, 10,000 issued and outstanding | 50,000 |
| Cost of goods sold | 186,000 |
| Dividends declared | 14,000 |
| Dividends payable | 5,000 |
| Extraordinary gain | 18,000 |
| Gain on disposal of equipment | 4,000 |
| Goodwill impairment | 6,000 |
| Interest expense | 3,000 |
| Investment revenue | 5,000 |
| Loss from discontinued operations | 20,000 |
| Premium paid on redemption of preferred shares | 10,000 |
| Restructuring costs and accrued severance costs | 22,000 |
| Sales discounts and allowances | 14,000 |
| Sales, gross | 543,000 |
| Selling expenses | 51,000 |

The income tax rate on all types of income is 40%.

**Required:**
Prepare a multiple-step income statement in good form for the year ended 31 December 20X3.

(CGA-Canada, adapted)

---

★★★

**A3-11 Income Statement Formats, Extraordinary Item:** The following information was taken from the adjusted trial balance of Montreal Retail Corporation at 31 December 20X6, the end of the accounting period:

| | |
|---|---|
| Cost of goods sold | $102,000 |
| Accounts payable | 121,400 |
| Sales revenue | 405,000 |
| Accumulated depreciation | 139,500 |
| Sales returns | 5,000 |
| Unearned revenue | 2,000 |
| Depreciation expense (70% administrative expense, 30% distribution expense) | 50,000 |
| Rent revenue | 4,000 |
| Interest expense | 6,000 |
| Investment revenue | 2,500 |
| Distribution expenses (exclusive of depreciation) | 105,500 |
| General and administrative expenses (exclusive of depreciation) | 46,000 |
| Royalty revenue | 6,000 |
| Loss on sale of long-term investments | 3,600 |
| Income tax expense | ? |
| Flood loss (extraordinary) | 10,000 |

Assume an average 35% income tax rate on all items, including gains and losses on assets sold and extraordinary items.

**Required:**
1. Prepare a single-step income statement.
2. Prepare a multiple-step income statement.

---

★★

**A3-12 Minimum Disclosure:** Review the data given for A3-11, above. Assume that the company wished to publish an income statement that provides only the minimum disclosures required by accounting standards.

**Required:**
1. Draft a single-step income statement that provides only the minimum required disclosures. Lump all revenues and expenses that need not be shown separately into "other revenues" and "operating expenses," respectively.
2. Explain why the company might prefer minimal disclosures, referring to material explained in Chapters 1 and 2.

---

★

**A3-13 Classification of Elements on the Income Statement:** Fifteen items are listed to the left below that may or may not affect the income statement. Income statement classifications are listed by letter to the right. Match each transaction with the appropriate letter to indicate the usual classification that should be used.

| Answer Selected Transactions | Income Statement Element Classifications |
|---|---|
| _____ 1. Sales of goods and services | A. Revenues |
| _____ 2. Prepaid insurance premium | B. Extraordinary loss |
| _____ 3. Loss on disposal of service trucks | C. Extraordinary gain |
| _____ 4. Cost of goods sold | D. Expenses |
| _____ 5. Value of services rendered | E. Unusual loss |
| _____ 6. Gain (unusual but not infrequent) | F. Loss (ordinary) |
| _____ 7. Rent collected in advance | G. Unusual gain |
| _____ 8. Cash dividends received on an investment in African diamond mine | H. Gains (ordinary) |
| _____ 9. Wages liability (unpaid but recorded) | I. None of the above |
| _____ 10. Cost of successful oil wells in a foreign country that are taken over (expropriated) by that country's government without compensation | |
| _____ 11. Fire loss (infrequent) | |
| _____ 12. Loss due to a very rare freeze that destroys the fruit trees in the Okanagan Valley | |
| _____ 13. Gain on sale of long-term investments not held for resale | |
| _____ 14. Cash dividend declared and paid | |
| _____ 15. Loss due to explosion that completely destroys the factory | |

★ **A3-14 Comprehensive Income:** Quebecor World Inc. is one of the world's largest commercial print media services company. The company is listed on both the Toronto Stock Exchange and the New York Stock Exchange. The company reported the following items in its 2005 financial statements (in millions of U.S. dollars, except per-share amounts—Dr/(Cr)):

| | |
|---|---|
| a. Revenues | $(6,283.3) |
| b. Cost of sales | 5,201.0 |
| c. Minority interest in earnings | (0.3) |
| d. Restructuring charges | 44.2 |
| e. Depreciation and amortization | 304.2 |
| f. Income tax expense—continuing operations | 50.4 |
| g. Income tax expense—discontinued operations | 14.3 |
| h. Goodwill impairment | 243.0 |
| i. Impairment of assets | 53.9 |
| j. Income (loss) from discontinued operations (pre-tax) | 0.5 |
| k. Translation adjustment for self-sustaining foreign operation (loss) | (96.4) |
| l. Premium over book value paid on repurchased shares | 9.8 |
| m. Earnings per share | (1.53) |

**Required:**

Identify whether each of the items above would be included in (1) the income statement, (2) statement of changes in other comprehensive income, or (3) statement of retained earnings.

★ **A3-15 Comprehensive Income:** Shaw Communications Inc. reported the following items in its comparative consolidated financial statements for 2006:

| | Dr./(Cr.) |
|---|---|
| a. Amortization of property, plant and equipment | 385,607 |
| b. Foreign exchange gains on hedged long-term debt | (66,802) |
| c. Foreign exchange gains on unhedged long-term debt | (5,369) |
| d. Gain on sale of investments | (50,315) |
| e. Unrealized gain on available-for-sale securities, net of tax | (30,045) |

|  | Dr./(Cr.) |
|---|---|
| f. Debt retirement costs | 12,248 |
| g. Adjustment for change in accounting policy | (42,633) |
| h. Adjustment to fair value of cash flow hedge derivative instruments | (51,033) |
| i. Equity income on investees | (44) |
| j. Unrealized foreign exchange gain on translation of self-sustaining foreign operations | (35) |
| k. Writedown of investments | 519 |

**Required:**

For each item, identify whether Shaw should include the item in determining net income or report it as a component of other comprehensive income.

 **A3-16 Comprehensive Income** Acrimony Limited has the following balances in its general ledger on 31 December 20X8 (in thousands of Canadian dollars):

|  | Debit | Credit |
|---|---|---|
| Retained earnings, 31 December 20X7 |  | $40,000 |
| Sales revenue |  | 18,000 |
| Interest expense | $ 780 |  |
| Cost of sales | 8,000 |  |
| Accumulated other comprehensive income, 31 December 20X7 |  | 1,350 |
| Dividends paid | 2,000 |  |
| Foreign currency gains and losses on 20X8 transactions |  | 3,000 |
| Income tax expense | 1,070 |  |
| Selling and administrative expense | 3,400 |  |
| Amortization on furniture and fixtures for 20X8 | 1,050 |  |
| Write-off of obsolete inventory | 530 |  |
| Impairment of tangible capital assets | 970 |  |
| Unrealized gain on available-for-sale investments |  | 42 |
| Additional contributed capital |  | 18,000 |
| Loss on redemption of long-term debt | 670 |  |
| Unrealized foreign currency translation loss on self-sustaining U.S. subsidiary for 20X8 | 495 |  |

**Required:**

1. Prepare, in good form, a single-step statement of income and comprehensive income. Use a continuous format.

2. Prepare a statement of accumulated other comprehensive income.

3. Prepare a statement of retained earnings.

 **A3-17 Comprehensive Income, Intraperiod Tax Allocation:** Decolite Corporation is based in Halifax. For 20X4, the company's accounting records show the following items:

a. A $400,000 loss from hurricane damage. Hurricanes are very rare in Nova Scotia.

b. Total sales revenue of $2,600,000, including $400,000 in the Decolite division, which the company is in the process of selling.

c. Interest expense on long-term debt of $65,000.

d. Gain on sale of marketable securities of $55,000.

e. Operating expenses of $2,100,000, including depreciation and amortization of $500,000. Of this total, $390,000 of expenses (including $75,000 in depreciation and amortization) was incurred in the Decolite division.

f. The company wrote down tangible capital assets by $35,000 during the year, to reduce the Decolite division's assets to their estimated recoverable value.

g. The company has long-term debt that is denominated in U.S. dollars. Due to the weakening of the U.S. dollar during 20X4, the company has an unrealized gain of $20,000.

h. The company has a subsidiary in France. The euro strengthened during the year, with the result that Recolite has an unrealized gain of $15,000 on its net investment in the subsidiary.

i. Decolite's income tax expense for 20X4 is $110,000. This amount is net of a tax recovery of $30,000 on the Decolite division and a $120,000 tax benefit from the hurricane damage.

**Required:**

Prepare a statement of comprehensive income, including both net income and other comprehensive income, if any.

---

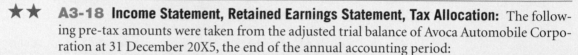

**A3-18 Income Statement, Retained Earnings Statement, Tax Allocation:** The following pre-tax amounts were taken from the adjusted trial balance of Avoca Automobile Corporation at 31 December 20X5, the end of the annual accounting period:

| | |
|---|---:|
| Sales revenue | $ 520,000 |
| Cost of goods sold | 160,000 |
| Operating expenses | 172,000 |
| Gain on expropriation of property | 40,000 |
| Writedown of capital assets to reflect impairment of value | 44,000 |
| Retained earnings, balance 1 January 20X5 | 1,060,000 |
| Effect of a change in accounting principles, applied retrospectively (a credit) | 100,000 |
| Dividends declared and paid | 60,000 |
| Dividends declared and not paid | 50,000 |
| Restriction of retained earnings due to loan covenant (Amount is included in opening balance of $1,160,000) | 100,000 |
| Common shares, no-par, shares outstanding, 20,500 shares | |

**Required:**

1. Prepare a single-step income statement. Assume an average 30% tax rate on all items. Include EPS disclosures.

2. Prepare a statement of retained earnings. Disclose the restriction in a note.

---

**A3-19 Income and Retained Earnings Statements:** The 31 December 20X2 year-end trial balance for Unlimited Dynamics Ltd. showed the following account balances:

| | Dr./(Cr.) |
|---|---:|
| Retained earnings, 31 December 20X1 | $(7,450,000) |
| Sales revenue | (9,450,000) |
| Dividend income from investments | (75,000) |
| Cost of sales | 4,560,000 |
| Loss on discontinued plant assets, held for sale (before tax) | 750,000 |
| General, selling, and administrative expenses | 1,400,000 |
| Interest expense | 80,000 |
| Reduction in prior years' earnings due to change in accounting policy, cumulative to 31 December 20X1 (before tax) | 410,000 |
| Dividends declared, to be paid 15 January 20X3 | 600,000 |
| Loss due to bankruptcy of major client | 135,000 |

The company pays income tax at a rate of 30%.

**Required:**

Prepare a single-step income statement and a statement of retained earnings for the year ended 31 December 20X2.

★★ **A3-20 Combined Income and Retained Earnings Statement:** The following amounts were taken from the accounting records of Curtis Recyclers Corporation at 31 December  20X5, the end of the annual accounting period:

| | |
|---|---|
| Sales revenue | $340,000 |
| Service revenue | 64,000 |
| Cost of goods sold | 170,000 |
| Distribution and administrative expenses | 67,000 |
| Depreciation expense | 19,000 |
| Investment revenue | 6,000 |
| Interest expense | 4,000 |
| Loss on sale of long-term investment (pre-tax) | 10,000 |
| Earthquake damage loss | 14,000 |
| Cash dividends declared | 8,000 |
| Correction of error from prior period, pre-tax (a debit) | 12,000 |
| Balance, retained earnings, 1 January 20X5 | 80,300 |

a. Common shares, 30,000 shares outstanding.
b. Restriction on retained earnings, $50,000 regarding a bond payable indenture.
c. Assume an average 35% income tax rate on all items.

**Required:**

Prepare a combined single-step income and retained earnings statement, including tax allocation and EPS for income before extraordinary items and net income. Show computations. Restrictions to retained earnings should be disclosed in a note. State any necessary assumptions.

★★ **A3-21 Statements of Income, Comprehensive Income, and Retained Earnings; Tax Allocation:** The following information pertains to Green Girl Limited (GGL) for the year ended 31 December 20X7. GGL's income tax rate is 30%.

| | Dr./(Cr.) |
|---|---|
| Accumulated other comprehensive income, 31 December 20X6 | $ (36,000) |
| Amortization expense | 295,000 |
| Common shares (40,000 weighted average shares outstanding) | (4,200,000) |
| Cost of goods sold | 5,000,000 |
| Cumulative effect to 1 January 20X7 of a change in accounting policy (net of tax) | 165,000 |
| Dividends declared | 30,000 |
| Translation loss for 20X7 on self-sustaining Jamaican subsidiary* | 23,000 |
| Excess above book value for GGL preferred shares purchased and retired* | 17,000 |
| Foreign currency gain for 20X7 on notes receivable (hedged) | (15,000) |
| Gain on debt restructuring | (102,000) |
| Interest expense on long-term debt | 6,000 |
| Loss from discontinued operation | 250,000 |
| Operating expenses | 1,190,000 |
| Restructuring costs | 65,000 |
| Retained earnings, 31 December 20X6 | (3,979,000) |
| Sales | (9,124,000) |

*Not included in taxable income

**Required:**

For the year ended 31 December 20X7, prepare in good form:

1. Income statement (single-step)
2. Statement of comprehensive income
3. Statement of changes in accumulated other comprehensive income
4. Statement of retained earnings

---

 **A3-22 Error Correction:** In 20X5, the newly appointed controller of Butch Baking Corporation conducted a thorough review of past accounting, particularly of transactions that exceeded the company's normal level of materiality. As the result of his review, he instructed the company's chief accountant to correct two errors:

a. In 20X2, the company made extensive improvements to the baking process and installed a substantial amount of new equipment. The entire cost of the process improvements and equipment was accidentally charged to income as restructuring expense in 20X2. However, the equipment should have been capitalized and added to the factory equipment account. The cost of the equipment was $1,200,000. Butch depreciates its factory equipment on the straight-line basis over 10 years. A full year's depreciation is charged in the year that equipment is acquired.

b. A year-end cut-off error occurred in 20X3. A large shipment of non-perishable supplies arrived from China on the last day of 20X3 and had been left in the shipping containers outside the main plant. As a result, the supplies were recorded as received in 20X4 and had not been included in the year-end 20X3 inventory count. The account payable also had not been recorded in 20X3. The supplies cost $160,000.

Like most companies, Butch Baking presents a five-year financial summary in its annual report. The 20X4 summary contained the following information (in thousands of dollars, except EPS):

|  | 20X0 | 20X1 | 20X2 | 20X3 | 20X4 |
|---|---|---|---|---|---|
| Gross revenue | $ 15,000 | $ 16,000 | $ 17,500 | $ 17,000 | $ 18,000 |
| Net income | 1,980 | 2,100 | 850 | 2,300 | 2,100 |
| Total assets | 140,000 | 155,000 | 148,000 | 147,000 | 152,000 |
| Total liabilities | 50,000 | 65,000 | 70,000 | 69,000 | 73,000 |
| Net assets | 90,000 | 90,000 | 78,000 | 78,000 | 79,000 |
| Earnings per share* | $19.80 | $21.00 | $8.50 | $23.00 | $21.00 |

*100,000 shares outstanding

**Required:**

1. Explain the impact of these two errors on the summary financial information.
2. Revise the financial summary.
3. Prepare the journal entry or entries that are necessary to correct the accounts at 31 December 20X5.

---

 **A3-23 Error Correction:** On 23 November 20X7, when engaged in preparing for the 20X7 fiscal year-end, the chief accountant of Harper Limited discovered two accounting errors in the 20X5 statements:

a. Inventory purchases of $2.1 million had inadvertently been charged to equipment, a capital asset account, and had been amortized by 10% for 20X5. The accounting amortization rate is the same as the CCA rate for tax purposes. The ending and beginning inventories had been properly stated. Therefore, the mistake caused cost of sales to be understated by $2.1 million and pre-tax earnings to be overstated by the same amount.

b. A government ministry had paid $3.2 million in partial settlement of an amount due for a large contract. The contract revenue had already been recognized. However, the payment was accidentally credited to contract revenue instead of to accounts receivable, and was included in taxable income.

Harper's income tax rate is 32%.

**Required:**

1. Calculate the earnings correction that Harper must show in the 20X7 financial statements. Where will these amounts be disclosed?
2. Prepare a general journal entry to record the correction of each error.

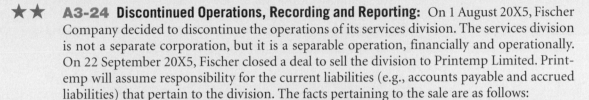

**A3-24 Discontinued Operations, Recording and Reporting:** On 1 August 20X5, Fischer Company decided to discontinue the operations of its services division. The services division is not a separate corporation, but it is a separable operation, financially and operationally. On 22 September 20X5, Fischer closed a deal to sell the division to Printemp Limited. Printemp will assume responsibility for the current liabilities (e.g., accounts payable and accrued liabilities) that pertain to the division. The facts pertaining to the sale are as follows:

| | |
|---|---|
| Divisional assets, book values at 1 August 20X5 (cost of $950,000, less accumulated depreciation of $335,000) | $615,000 |
| Division assets, estimated fair values at 1 August 20X5 | 550,000 |
| Liabilities assumed by purchaser; fair value = book value | 270,000 |
| Purchase price paid by Printemp Ltd. | 470,000 |
| Division revenue to 22 September 20X5 | 690,000 |
| Division profit (before taxes) to 22 September 20X5 | 55,000 |
| Commission fee paid to the business brokerage that facilitated the sale | 80,000 |
| Fischer Corp. marginal income tax rate | 30% |

On 31 December 20X5, the after-tax income from all income from all operations, including the services division, was $400,000.

**Required:**

1. Give the entry or entries to record the sale of the services division.
2. Complete the 20X5 income statement, starting with income from continuing operations, after tax.
3. Explain what other disclosures and/or reclassifications are necessary in the 20X5 comparative financial statements and notes.

**A3-25 Discontinued Operations:** Salmonese Inc. is a food processing company that operates divisions in several types of food, such as cereals, frozen fish, chocolate candy, jams and jellies, and dessert mixes. However, on 13 September 20X1, the Board of Directors voted to put the candy division up for sale. The division's operating results had been declining for the past several years due to intense competition from large international players such as Nestlé and Cadbury.

The Board hired the consulting firm Atelier LLP to conduct a search for potential buyers. The consulting fee was to be 4% of the value of any sale transaction.

By 31 December 20X1, Atelier had found a highly interested buyer for the candy division, and serious negotiations were underway. The potential buyer was a food conglomerate based in Brazil; the company offered to buy the division for $3.6 million cash.

On 25 February 20X2, after further negotiations with the potential buyer, the Salmonese Board accepted an enhanced Brazilian offer to buy the division for $3.8 million. The Salmonese shareholders approved the sale on 5 March 20X2. The transfer of ownership took place on 31 March 20X2.

Salmonese's income tax rate is 30%. Other information is as follows (before tax, in millions of dollars):

| | 13 September 20X1 | | 31 December 20X1 |
|---|---|---|---|
| | Book Value | Fair Value | Fair Value |
| Candy division's net assets: | | | |
| Current assets | $ 610 | $ 510 | $ 440 |
| Property, plant, and equipment (net) | 4,400 | 3,200 | 3,400 |
| Current liabilities | 900 | 900 | 1,100 |
| Net earnings (loss) of the candy division, 1 January to 31 December 20X1 | | | 350 |
| Net earnings (loss) of the candy division, 1 January to 31 March 20X2 | | | (550) |

**Required:**

Prepare the journal entries that are appropriate at 13 September 20X1, 31 December 20X1, 25 February 20X2, 5 March 20X2, and 31 March 20X2.

---

 **A3-26 Disposal of Business Segment:** NSC Ltd. has a 31 May fiscal year-end. NSC disposed of its Information Systems Group (ISG) on 31 January 20X3. ISG had a net loss (after taxes) of $37,700,000 in 20X3, to the date of disposal. The division was sold for $475,600,000 in cash plus future royalties through 31 May 20X4, which were guaranteed to be $30,000,000. The minimum guaranteed royalties were included in the computation of the 20X3 gain on the sale of the division. Actual royalties received in 20X4 were $35,500,000. Excerpts from comparative income statements found in the 31 May 20X4 financial statements are as follows:

($ millions)

| Year ended 31 May | 20X4 | 20X3 |
|---|---|---|
| Earnings (loss) from continuing operations | $(29.3) | $(205.5) |
| Discontinued operations: | | |
| Gain on sale of discontinued operation (net of income taxes of $1.2 in 20X4 and $34.0 in 20X3) | 4.3 | 182.3 |
| Net income (loss) | $(25.0) | $ (23.2) |

**Required:**

1. Determine the net book value of ISG at the date of disposal.
2. Why does NSC report a gain on the sale of the discontinued operation of $4,300,000 in the year ending 31 May 20X4?
3. NSC reports an after-tax loss from discontinued operations of $37,700,000 for the year ending 31 May 20X3. Over what period was the loss accrued?

---

**A3-27 Discontinued Operations, Unusual Item:** In December 20X4, the Board of Directors of Mead Corporation approved a plan to curtail the development of the company's imaging products division. As a result, the company recognized an asset impairment loss before tax totalling $77,000,000. The imaging products division had incurred before-tax losses of $50,000,000 in 20X3 and $41,700,000 in 20X4.

In addition, during 20X4, the company retired an issue of bonds early. These bonds had a carrying value of $200,000,000 and were retired at a cost of $185,000,000, resulting in a pre-tax gain of $15,000,000. The company had never had such a transaction before.

The tax rate on all the above items is Mead Corporation's average income tax rate of 34%. Assume that earnings from other sources, before income taxes, were $392,500,000 in 20X3 and $168,900,000 in 20X4. This does not include the bond retirement transaction. The average number of common shares outstanding was 65,100,000 shares in 20X3 and 62,200,000 shares in 20X4. Mead Corporation has no preferred shares outstanding.

**Required:**
Prepare the income statements for Mead Corporation for 20X3 and 20X4, beginning with income from continuing operations. Include appropriate earnings per share computations.

---

★ **A3-28 Change in Policy, Retained Earnings Statement:** The Hannam Company decided to change from the declining-balance method of depreciation to the straight-line method effective 1 January 20X7. The following information was provided:

| Year | Net Income as Reported | Excess of Declining-Balance Depreciation over Straight-Line Depreciation |
|------|------------------------|--------------------------------------------------------------------------|
| 20X3* | $ (60,000) | $10,000 |
| 20X4 | 70,000 | 30,000 |
| 20X5 | 45,000 | 25,000 |
| 20X6 | 105,000 | 14,000 |

*First year of operations.

The company has a 31 December year-end. The tax rate is 40%. No dividends were declared until 20X7; $35,000 of dividends were declared and paid in December 20X7. Income for 20X7, calculated using the new accounting policy, was $210,000.

**Required:**
Assuming that the change in policy was implemented retrospectively, present the 20X7 retained earnings statement.

---

★★ **A3-29 Change in Accounting Policy, Retained Earnings Statement:** Moncton Developments Limited was formed in 20X2. During the year ended 31 December 20X4, the company changed its method of accounting for product development expenses from expensing such items to capitalizing them and amortizing them over the period of expected benefit. The 20X4 statements have been prepared using the old policy. Preliminary statements appear as follows:

**Moncton Developments Limited**
**Statement of Income and Retained Earnings**

For the year ended 31 December 20X4

| | |
|---|---|
| Sales | $2,400,000 |
| Costs and expenses (including product development) | 1,482,000 |
| Amortization | 70,000 |
| Income before tax | 848,000 |
| Tax expense | 339,200 |
| Net income | 508,800 |
| Retained earnings, opening | 690,000 |
| | 1,198,800 |
| Dividends ($1 per share) | 50,000 |
| Retained earnings, closing | $1,148,800 |
| EPS | $10.18 |

The following pre-tax information was gathered:

|  | 20X4 | 20X3 | 20X2 |
| --- | --- | --- | --- |
| Net income, old policy | $508,800 | $540,000 | $210,000 |
| Product development costs | 200,000 | 150,000 | 250,000 |
| Amortization, prior to change | 70,000 | 70,000 | 60,000 |
| Amortization, after change* | 118,000 | 110,000 | 90,000 |

*Using new policy.

**Required:**

1. Prepare a revised 20X4 income and retained earnings statement, giving appropriate treatment to the change in accounting policy. All amounts are taxable at 40%. Include note disclosure.

2. If insufficient information is available to treat the accounting policy change as in (1), what other options does the company have? Describe the impact of the alternatives on the financial statements.

 **A3-30 Financial Statement Classification:** Listed below are some financial statement classifications coded with letters and, below them, selected transactions and account titles. For each transaction or account title, enter in the space provided a code letter to indicate the usual classification. Comment on doubtful items.

| Code | Financial Statement Classification |
| --- | --- |
| | **Income Statement** |
| A | Revenue, or ordinary gain |
| B | Expense, or ordinary loss |
| C | Unusual gain or loss |
| D | Extraordinary item |
| | **Statement of Other Comprehensive Income** |
| E | Changes during the year |
| | **Statement of Retained Earnings** |
| F | An addition to or deduction from beginning balance |
| G | Addition to retained earnings |
| H | Deduction from retained earnings |
| | **Disclosure Notes** |
| I | Note to the financial statements |
| | **Balance Sheet** |
| J | Appropriately classified balance sheet account |

| Response | Transaction or Account Title |
| --- | --- |
| _____ | 1. Estimated warranties payable |
| _____ | 2. Allowance for doubtful accounts |
| _____ | 3. Gain on sale of equipment |
| _____ | 4. Translation gain on self-sustaining foreign subsidiary |
| _____ | 5. Total amount of cash and credit sales for the period |
| _____ | 6. Payment of $30,000 additional income tax assessment on prior year's income |
| _____ | 7. Cash dividends declared and paid |
| _____ | 8. Earthquake damages in Saskatoon |
| _____ | 9. Distribution expenses |
| _____ | 10. Foreign currency loss on current year transactions |
| _____ | 11. Gain on disposal of long-term investments in shares (non-recurring) |

| Response | Transaction or Account Title |
|---|---|
| _____ | 12. Net income for the period |
| _____ | 13. Insurance gain on fire—insurance proceeds exceed the book value of the assets destroyed |
| _____ | 14. Loss due to expropriation of a plant in a foreign country |
| _____ | 15. Rent collected on office space temporarily leased |
| _____ | 16. Interest paid during the year plus interest accrued on liabilities |
| _____ | 17. Dividends received on shares held as an investment |
| _____ | 18. Damages paid as a result of a lawsuit by an individual injured while shopping in the company's store; the litigation lasted three years |
| _____ | 19. Cumulative effect of a change in accounting policy |
| _____ | 20. A $100,000 bad debt is to be written off—the receivable had been outstanding for five years. The company estimates bad debts each year and has an allowance for bad debts |
| _____ | 21. Adjustment due to correction of an error during current year; the error was made two years earlier |
| _____ | 22. On 31 December of the current year, paid rent expense in advance for the next year |
| _____ | 23. Cost of goods sold |
| _____ | 24. Interest collected on 30 November of the current year from a customer on a 90-day note receivable, dated 1 September of the current year |
| _____ | 25. Year-end bonus of $50,000 paid to employees for performance during the year |
| _____ | 26. A meteor destroys manufacturing facilities ($5 million book value, no insurance) |

★★ **A3-31 Analytical—Discuss Statement Classification:** The following transactions have been encountered in practice. Assume that all amounts are material.

a. A company discovered that, in error, a payment to the employee's pension fund was all that was expensed last year; the appropriate calculation of expense was $20,000 higher than the payment.

b. A company suffered a casualty loss (a fire) amounting to $500,000. The company has had three fires in the last 10 years, but this was significantly more than any such loss experienced before by the company.

c. A company paid $175,000 damages assessed by the courts as a result of an injury to a customer on the company premises three years earlier.

d. A company sold a significant capital asset and reported a gain of $70,000.

e. A major supplier of raw materials to a company experienced a prolonged strike. As a result, the company reported a loss of $150,000. This is the first such loss; however, the company has three major suppliers, and strikes are not unusual in the industry.

f. A company owns several large blocks of common shares of other corporations. The shares have been held for a number of years and are viewed as long-term investments. During the past year, 20% of the shares were sold to meet an unusual cash demand. Additional disposals are not anticipated.

g. A timber company wrote down inventory and natural resources (a capital asset) after five years of low pulp and paper prices on world markets. The amount was material, it was the first such writedown in the company's history, and it is not expected to recur.

**Required:**

1. Classify each of the above transactions. Explain the basis for your decision in each situation.

2. Without reference to the above transactions, define the following: unusual gains and losses, extraordinary gains and losses, and error corrections. Explain how the effects of each should be reported.

★★★ **A3-32 Correction of Income and Retained Earnings Statements:** The following statements were prepared for Nepal Corporation by the company's new bookkeeper:

## Nepal Corporation Profit Sheet
### (stated in thousands of Canadian dollars)

31 December 20X8

| | |
|---|---|
| Revenues: | |
| Sales income | $1,010 |
| Gain on expropriation of land | 130 |
| | 1,140 |
| Expenses: | |
| Amortization | 70 |
| Cost of goods sold | 600 |
| Income tax | 67 |
| Other | 270 |
| | 1,007 |
| Profit | $ 133 |

## Nepal Corporation Retained Earnings
### (stated in thousands of Canadian dollars)

31 December 20X8

| | | |
|---|---|---|
| Balance, beginning of year | | $500 |
| Add: | Profit | 133 |
| Deduct: | Severance pay | (200) |
| | Dividends | (30) |
| Balance, end of year | | $403 |

*Additional information (all amounts are in thousands of dollars):*

a. In December 20X8, the local government expropriated some land (original cost of $70) from Nepal Corporation. The land was needed to provide thoroughfare for a major road bypass around the city. Under the terms of the expropriation, the government paid $130 to Nepal and took possession of the land.

b. Goods costing $42 that were purchased from Finland Company and paid for in November 20X8 were sold in the last week of 20X8 and appropriately recorded as sales of $50. The goods were included in the physical count of goods in Nepal's warehouse on 31 December 20X8, because the goods were on the loading dock waiting to be picked up by the customer.

c. Nepal pays income tax at a rate of 40% on all income except for the gain on the expropriation of the land that is taxed at a rate of 30%. Assume that all revenues, expenses, gains, and losses, are taxable or deductible for income tax purposes.

d. Details of amounts recorded in "other expenses" were as follows:

| | |
|---|---|
| Loss on closure of transportation division | $300 |
| Miscellaneous | 10 |
| Outstanding cheques | (40) |
| | $270 |

The transportation division had been losing money for the last three years. Management decided to shut down the division to avoid future losses.

The bank reconciliation at the end of December showed outstanding cheques of $40. The new bookkeeper thought that these amounts should not be reported as expenses since these cheques had not yet cleared the bank. Therefore, he processed an entry to debit cash and credit other expenses. On 1 January 20X9, he recorded another entry to debit other expenses and credit cash.

e. In 20X8, Nepal laid off five employees who no longer had the skills required to work for the company. In order to avoid a wrongful dismissal lawsuit, the company paid the employees $40 each as severance pay. In turn, the employees agreed not to take any legal action against the company.

f. The company paid $30 to a major shareholder for management services rendered. Since the payment was made to a shareholder, the bookkeeper recorded it as dividends paid.

**Required:**

1. Briefly explain whether the gain on land expropriation should be shown as an extraordinary item.

2. Prepare, in good form, a multiple-step income statement for Nepal for 20X8. Correct any deficiencies and/or errors contained in the draft statements prepared by the new bookkeeper.

(CGA-Canada, adapted)

---

 **A3-33 Income Statement, Choice of Accounting Policies:** You have been asked to prepare the financial statements for Ali Corporation for the year ended 31 December 20X4. The company began operations in early 20X4. The following information is available about its business activities during the year:

a. On January 2, Ali issued no par common shares for $600,000.

b. On January 3, machinery was purchased for $510,000 cash. It was estimated to have a useful life of 10 years and a residual value of $80,000. Management is considering using either the straight-line amortization method or the declining-balance method at twice the straight-line rate.

c. On January 4, Ali purchased 20% ownership in a long-term investment, ABC Company, for $90,000. During the year, ABC paid dividends of $7,000 and earned net income of $16,000. Ali can use either the cost method or the equity method of accounting for its investment in ABC.

d. Inventory purchases for the year were, in order of acquisition:

| Units | Unit Cost | Total Cost |
|---|---|---|
| 100,000 | $4.20 | $  420,000 |
| 160,000 | 4.25 | 680,000 |
| 60,000 | 4.30 | 258,000 |
| 35,000 | 4.40 | 154,000 |
| 355,000 | | $1,512,000 |

Ali uses a periodic inventory system. There were 50,000 units in ending inventory on 31 December. Management is considering using LIFO, FIFO, or weighted average as the inventory accounting method.

e. Sales during the year were $3,000,000, of which 90% were on account and 10% for cash.

f. Management has estimated that approximately 1% of sales on account will be uncollectible. During the year, $2,070,000 was collected on accounts receivable. When management scrutinizes the year-end outstanding accounts, it estimates that approximately 6% of the accounts will prove to be uncollectible.

g. Additional operating expenses for the year were $1,100,000.

h. On 31 December, the company paid a $10,000 cash dividend on common shares.

i. On 31 December, accounts payable pertaining to operating expenses and inventory purchases totalled $307,000.

j. The cash balance on 31 December was $205,000.

**Required:**

1. Choosing from the alternative accounting policies described above, prepare a single-step income statement for the year ended 31 December 20X4 that will produce the lowest net income.

2. What are the ethical implications to be considered when selecting from among alternative accounting policies?

(CGA-Canada, adapted)

---

 **A3-34 Comprehensive:** The following trial balance of the Puget Petroleum Corporation at 31 December 20X5 has been prepared and is correct, except that income tax expense has not been allocated.

## Puget Petroleum Corporation Trial Balance

| 31 December 20X5 | Debit | Credit |
|---|---|---|
| Cash | $ 636,000 | |
| Accounts receivable (net) | 1,695,000 | |
| Inventory | 2,185,000 | |
| Property, plant, and equipment (net) | 8,660,000 | |
| Accounts payable and accrued liabilities | | $ 1,856,000 |
| Income tax payable | | 399,000 |
| Future income tax | | 285,000 |
| Common shares, 215,000 shares outstanding | | 5,975,000 |
| Retained earnings, 1 January 20X5 | | 3,350,000 |
| Net sales, regular* | | 10,750,000 |
| Net sales, plastics division | | 2,200,000 |
| Cost of sales, regular | 5,920,000 | |
| Cost of sales, plastics division | 1,650,000 | |
| Selling and administrative expenses, regular | 2,600,000 | |
| Selling and administrative expense, plastics division | 660,000 | |
| Interest income, regular | | 65,000 |
| Error correction | | 200,000 |
| Depreciation adjustment from accounting change | 350,000 | |
| Gain on disposal of plastics division | | 150,000 |
| Income tax expense | 874,000 | |
| Totals | $25,230,000 | $25,230,000 |

*Accounts identified as regular include all but plastics division for that account.*

*Other financial data for the year ended 31 December 20X5:*

a. Income tax expense:

| | |
|---|---|
| Tax payments | $475,000 |
| Accrued | 399,000 |
| Total charged to income tax expense | $874,000 |

Tax rate on all types of income: 40%. The $874,000 does not reflect intraperiod income tax allocation, which is required for financial statement purposes.

b. The *error correction* involves a revenue item not recorded in 20X3, the year in which it was earned.

c. *Discontinued operations.* On 31 October 20X5, Puget sold its plastics division for $2,950,000, when the carrying amount was $2,800,000. For financial statement reporting, this sale was considered a disposal of a segment of a business. The disposal date was 31 October 20X5.

d. *Change in depreciation method.* On 1 January 20X5, Puget changed to the declining-balance method from the straight-line method of depreciation to conform to industry practice. The pre-tax cumulative effect of this accounting change was determined to be a charge of $350,000. There was no change in depreciation method for income tax purposes.

**Required:**

Using the multiple-step format, prepare an income statement for Puget for the year ended 31 December 20X5 (separate disclosure of depreciation and interest expense is not required). Also, prepare a retained earnings statement. All components of income tax expense should be appropriately shown.

Copyright © 1990–2006 by the American Institute of Certified Public Accountants, Inc. All rights reserved. Reprinted with permission.

**A3-35 Comprehensive:** In its 20X3 annual report, MBL Limited identified the following accounts and amounts in thousands of Canadian dollars—Dr./(Cr.):

| | 52 weeks ended: | |
| --- | --- | --- |
| | 25 Jan. 20X3 | 26 Jan. 20X2 |
| Sales | $(132,742) | $(178,318) |
| Selling and promotion expenses | 39,089 | 51,653 |
| Opening balance of retained earnings | ? | (11,560) |
| Opening balance of other contributed capital | ? | (3,200) |
| Opening balance of accumulated other comprehensive income | ? | (9,500) |
| Discontinued operations—loss on disposal of real estate division* | 2,250 | — |
| Franchise revenue | (3,000) | (3,817) |
| Settlement with ex-senior executive | 1,959 | — |
| Loss on closure of selected retail operations | — | 1,384 |
| Provision for income taxes (recovery) | (443) | (4,400) |
| Foreign currency gain on US-dollar long-term notes payable (hedged) | (1,600) | — |
| Purchase of common shares—excess of redemption price over original proceeds | — | 15 |
| General and administration expenses | 15,491 | 17,246 |
| Discontinued operations—loss from operations of real estate division* | 196 | 13 |
| Cost of goods sold | 85,959 | 122,593 |

*net of relevant taxes
Common shares outstanding: 10,000,000

**Required:**

Prepare a multiple-step format income statement, a statement of comprehensive income, and a retained earnings statement in good form.

## CHAPTER 4

# The Balance Sheet and Disclosure Notes

## INTRODUCTION

The balance sheet of Bell Canada Enterprises (BCE) shows total assets of $37 billion. Assets include current assets; assets of discontinued operations, buildings, and equipment; assets under capital lease; finite-life intangible assets; infinite-life intangible assets; and goodwill. All $37 billion is captured by only eight lines on the balance sheet. Yet these assets are reported on a variety of different measurement bases and give only a general overview of the company's asset position.

On the equities side, BCE reports a variety of short-term and long-term liabilities, including derivative instruments. The company has shareholders' equity of $13 billion, including a *deficit* of over $4 billion in the retained earnings account.

When assets and liabilities are shown in such a summarized manner, how can a financial statement reader know what underlies a large summary number such as the $22 billion that BCE reports for capital assets? That is where the disclosure notes come in. BCE provides 36 pages of notes to the consolidated financial statements. The notes contain much of the detail that a user may seek.

This chapter gives a general introduction to the balance sheet—its format and content as well as the nature and content of the disclosure notes. The various types of assets, liabilities, and shareholders' equity accounts will be discussed extensively in the chapters that follow.

## SAMPLE BALANCE SHEETS

The **balance sheet** is a summary statement of the assets and liabilities of an organization at a single point in time. It is like a financial photograph. But every photograph is *static*—it may yield a detailed and seemingly precise portrait, yet a photograph taken a little later may appear quite different.

"Balance sheet" may seem to be a rather meaningless title for an important financial statement. Some people prefer to call this statement a "statement of financial position," which is perfectly acceptable. However, "balance sheet" is the most common name simply because it emphasizes a very important aspect of this statement—it balances!

The amounts shown on the balance sheet are a combination of historical costs, partially amortized historical costs, discounted present values, fair values, and residuals. Many of a company's most important assets (and liabilities, to a lesser extent) are not shown on the balance sheet at all. Some examples of "missing" assets are the values of trademarks, customer goodwill, and intellectual capital. Liabilities shown on the balance sheet do not include items such as loan guarantees and potential legal liabilities.

Essentially, the balance sheet is a combination of three types of accounts:

1. Accounts that show the amounts of cash, and amounts owed *to* the company or owed *by* the company (known as **monetary items** or *financial assets and liabilities*).

2. Accounts that represent costs that are being held for recognition in income in future periods (known as **non-monetary items**).

3. Residual accounts that indicate the extent to which the recorded assets exceed the recorded liabilities.

Exhibits 4-1 through 4-4 show the balance sheets for four quite different Canadian corporations. We did not choose these companies at random; each balance sheet was chosen to emphasize particular reporting aspects. Read through them now and reflect on their similarities and differences. We will comment on certain aspects of these sample balance sheets as we go through the chapter.

The first example, Exhibit 4-1, is the balance sheet of the Saskatchewan Wheat Pool. This company was created by special legislation of the Saskatchewan government. The company has two types of shareholders: (1) farmer members who hold the voting shares but receive no dividends and (2) public shareholders who hold non-voting shares but may receive dividends if declared.

The components of the Saskatchewan Wheat Pool's balance sheet are common. Assets consist of current assets, capital assets, and other long-term assets. Other long-term assets includes intangible assets such as goodwill, and deferred charges such as capitalized start-up costs.

The company lists its current assets and current liabilities in some detail, but long-term assets and liabilities are highly condensed into a few lines. To find out what is included in these highly summarized balances, one must look at the accompanying *notes to financial statements*. All but two items on the balance sheet have explanatory disclosure notes, where more detail can be found.

Observe that Saskatchewan Wheat Pool has a *deficit*—a debit balance in the retained earnings account. A deficit indicates that the company's accumulated net income is less than the dividends paid over the years. If the company has not paid any dividends, then the negative retained earnings balance indicates that, cumulatively, the company has had more losses than profits over its history.

Bombardier Inc., Exhibit 4-2, is active in a number of different industry sectors. The company is involved in transportation, aerospace, defence, financial services, and real estate. Notice that there are no subtotals on this balance sheet. This presentation is uncommon but is acceptable under accounting standards. The company believes that because the company operates in such a wide range of businesses, subtotals would be meaningless. It is not practical for Bombardier to classify its assets and liabilities into *current* and *long term* because of the long operating cycles for some of its business segments.[1]

---

[1] Remember that the definition of a *current* item is one that will be used or come due within one year or one operating cycle, *whichever is longer*.

---

### monetary items

assets or liabilities whose face value is fixed or determinable in terms of dollars; for example, accounts receivable, accounts payable, and bonds payable

### non-monetary items

account balances that are not fixed in terms of currency. Non-monetary accounts usually reflect costs incurred in the past (e.g., inventories, buildings, and equipment) or obligations to deliver services in the future (e.g., deferred revenue)

## EXHIBIT 4-1

### SASKATCHEWAN WHEAT POOL INC.

### Consolidated Balance Sheets

(in thousands)

| As at | July 31, 2006 | July 31, 2005 |
|---|---|---|
| **Assets** | | |
| Current assets | | |
| Cash | $    5,071 | $    2,074 |
| Cash in trust (Note 15b) | 508 | 771 |
| Short-term investments (Note 4) | 104,892 | 79,264 |
| Accounts receivable (Note 5) | 123,176 | 127,102 |
| Inventories (Note 6) | 142,925 | 117,416 |
| Prepaid expenses and deposits | 13,074 | 20,737 |
| Future income taxes (Note 22c) | 772 | 78 |
| | 390,418 | 347,442 |
| | | |
| Investments (Note 7) | 4,904 | 5,437 |
| Property, plant and equipment (Note 8) | 255,552 | 251,489 |
| Other long-term assets (Note 9) | 20,605 | 14,822 |
| Future income taxes (Note 22c) | 102,551 | 102,670 |
| | $774,030 | $721,860 |
| | | |
| **Liabilities and shareholders; equity** | | |
| Current liabilities | | |
| Bank indebtedness (Note 10) | $  13,238 | $    8,060 |
| Short-term borrowings (Note 11) | — | 392 |
| Members' demand loans (Note 12) | 18,965 | 21,476 |
| Accounts payable and accrued liabilities (Note 13) | 129,940 | 115,319 |
| Long-term debt due within one year (Note 14) | 8,890 | 5,461 |
| | 171,033 | 150,708 |
| | | |
| Long-term debt (Note 14) | 101,917 | 148,928 |
| Other long-term liabilities (Note 15) | 37,616 | 37,424 |
| Future income taxes (Note 22c) | 2,034 | 3,559 |
| | 312,600 | 340,619 |
| | | |
| Shareholders' equity | | |
| Share capital (Note 16) | 502,760 | 439,485 |
| Contributed surplus | 308 | 243 |
| Retained earnings (deficit) | (41,638) | (58,487) |
| | 461,430 | 381,241 |
| | $774,030 | $721,860 |

*Commitments, contingencies and guarantees (Note 27).*

*Source:* www.sedar.com, Saskatchewan Wheat Pool Inc. 2005/2006 Annual Report released on November 14, 2006, page 70.

Bombardier reports in U.S. dollars because most of its business is carried out in U.S. dollars. However, the company uses Canadian GAAP, not U.S. GAAP, because it is a Canadian company (based in Montreal).

As with the Saskatchewan Wheat Pool, Bombardier directs the reader to disclosure notes for almost every item on the balance sheet. There is no note specified for shareholders'

---

**EXHIBIT 4-2**

## BOMBARDIER INC.

## Consolidated Balance Sheets

as at January 31
(in millions of U.S. dollars)

| | Notes | 2007 | 2006 |
|---|---|---|---|
| **Assets** | | | |
| Cash and cash equivalents | | $ 2,648 | $ 2,917 |
| Invested collateral | 8 | 1,129 | — |
| Receivables | 1 | 1,789 | 1,684 |
| Aircraft financing | 2 | 1,042 | 1,457 |
| Inventories | 3 | 3,961 | 3,805 |
| Property, plant and equipment | 4 | 2,936 | 3,090 |
| Goodwill | 5 | 2,286 | 2,142 |
| Fractional ownership deferred costs | | 390 | 270 |
| Deferred income taxes | 16 | 813 | 653 |
| Accrued benefit assets | 20 | 461 | 384 |
| Assets held for sale | 6 | — | 237 |
| Other assets | 7 | 1,122 | 843 |
| | | $18,577 | $17,482 |
| **Liabilities** | | | |
| Accounts payable and accrued liabilities | 9 | $ 6,839 | $ 6,866 |
| Advances and progress billings in excess of related costs | 3 | 2,443 | 2,191 |
| Fractional ownership deferred revenues | | 487 | 325 |
| Deferred income taxes | 16 | — | 9 |
| Long-term debt | 10 | 5,080 | 4,747 |
| Accrued benefit liabilities | 20 | 995 | 877 |
| Liabilities related to assets held for sale | 6 | — | 42 |
| | | 15,844 | 15,057 |
| Shareholders' equity | | 2,733 | 2,425 |
| | | $18,577 | $17,482 |

*Source:* www.sedar.com, Bombardier Inc. 2006 Annual Report released March 28, 2007, page 123.

equity, but in fact there are several notes (and an additional financial statement) that explain the changes in and components of shareholders' equity.

The Royal Bank of Canada is one of Canada's largest financial institutions. The balance sheet in Exhibit 4-3 is peppered with subtotals, and some fairly exotic assets and liabilities. For the most part, however, its assets are cash, investments, and loans to clients. Liabilities are customer deposits.

Notice that this $536.8 billion company has just $22.1 billion in shareholders' equity—only 4% of total assets. Banks are highly levered, which means they have lots of debt in their financial structures.

The financial statements of banks must be prepared in accordance with the accounting requirements of the Superintendent of Financial Institutions for Canada. Banks have to prepare a fairly rigidly defined set of financial statements so that regulators can be effective; GAAP is defined by these specific accounting requirements in this industry.

Finally, Exhibit 4-4 shows the balance sheet of Shaw Communications Incorporated, active in cable TV, Internet access, and satellite services. Notice that capital assets are a major

**EXHIBIT 4-3**

## ROYAL BANK OF CANADA
## Consolidated Balance Sheets

| As at October 31 (C$ millions) | 2006 | 2005 |
|---|---|---|
| **Assets** | | |
| Cash and due from banks | $ 4,401 | $ 5,001 |
| Interest-bearing deposits with banks | 10,502 | 5,237 |
| Securities (Note 3) | | |
|   Trading account | 147,237 | 125,760 |
|   Investment account | 36,976 | 34,060 |
|   Loan substitute | 656 | 675 |
| | 184,869 | 160,495 |
| Assets purchased under reverse repurchase agreements and securities borrowed | 59,378 | 42,973 |
| Loans (Notes 4 and 5) | | |
|   Residential mortgage | 96,675 | 91,043 |
|   Personal | 44,902 | 41,045 |
|   Credit cards | 7,155 | 6,200 |
|   Business and government | 61,207 | 53,626 |
| | 209,939 | 191,914 |
| Allowance for loan losses | (1,409) | (1,498) |
| | 208,530 | 190,416 |
| **Other** | | |
|   Customers' liability under acceptances | 9,108 | 7,074 |
|   Derivative-related amounts (Note 7) | 37,729 | 38,834 |
|   Premises and equipment, net (Note 8) | 1,818 | 1,708 |
|   Goodwill (Note 10) | 4,304 | 4,203 |
|   Other intangibles (Note 10) | 642 | 409 |
|   Assets of operations held for sale | 82 | 263 |
|   Other assets (Note 12) | 15,417 | 12,908 |
| | 69,100 | 65,399 |
| | $536,780 | $469,521 |
| **Liabilities and shareholders' equity** | | |
| Deposits (Note 13) | | |
|   Personal | $114,040 | $111,618 |
|   Business and government | 189,140 | 160,593 |
|   Bank | 40,343 | 34,649 |
| | 343,523 | 306,860 |
| **Other** | | |
|   Acceptances | 9,108 | 7,074 |
|   Obligations related to securities sold short | 38,252 | 32,391 |
|   Obligations related to assets sold under repurchase agreements and securities loaned | 41,103 | 23,381 |
|   Derivative-related amounts (Note 7) | 42,094 | 42,592 |
|   Insurance claims and policy benefit liabilities (Note 14) | 7,337 | 7,117 |
|   Liabilities of operations held for sale | 32 | 40 |
|   Other liabilities (Note 15) | 22,649 | 18,408 |
| | 160,575 | 131,003 |

continued on next page

EXHIBIT 4-3 *(cont'd)*

## ROYAL BANK OF CANADA
### Consolidated Balance Sheets

| As at October 31 (C$ millions) | 2006 | 2005 |
|---|---|---|
| Subordinated debentures (Note 16) | 7,103 | 8,167 |
| Trust capital securities (Note 17) | 1,383 | 1,400 |
| Preferred share liabilities (Note 18) | 298 | 300 |
| Non-controlling interest in subsidiaries (Note 19) | 1,775 | 1,944 |
| Shareholders' equity (Note 18) | | |
| Preferred shares | 1,050 | 700 |
| Common shares (1) (shares issued – 1,280,889,745 and 1,293,501,544) | 7,196 | 7,170 |
| Contributed surplus | 292 | 265 |
| Retained earnings | 15,771 | 13,704 |
| Treasury shares – preferred (shares held – 93,700 and 90,600) | (2) | (2) |
| – common (1) (shares held – 5,486,072 and 7,052,552) | (180) | (216) |
| Net foreign currency translation adjustments | (2,004) | (1,774) |
| | 22,123 | 19,847 |
| | $536,780 | $469,521 |

*Source:* www.sedar.com, Royal Bank of Canada 2006 Annual Report released February 9, 2007, page 102.

part of the company's asset structure—it's all those cable installations! But Shaw's largest single asset is *intangible*—broadcast licenses, representing 62% of assets ($4,691,484 ÷ $7,522,543). This balance sheet is more conventional than Bombardier's in that it provides subtotals for current assets and liabilities.

What policy choices do these very different companies face when preparing a balance sheet? We saw in the previous chapter that income statement preparation is quite judgemental—now it's time to take a more detailed look at the balance sheet.

## PURPOSE AND LIMITATIONS

### The Purpose of the Balance Sheet

The balance sheet will reflect (1) the fair value of most monetary assets, plus (2) the unamortized cost of the company's major groups of assets, and (3) the sources used to finance those assets. If you want to know how Shaw's capital structure is organized, the balance sheet provides this information: long-term debt is 40% of total assets ($2,995,936 ÷ $7,552,543), down slightly from 42% ($3,148,162 ÷ $7,430,185) in the prior year.

The balance sheet can also provide some insight into the *risk profile* of a business and its *financial flexibility*. Are the company's assets old and fully amortized or relatively new? Is the organization in a position to finance new activities with relative ease without incurring excessive debt? These are important questions that the balance sheet helps address.

For example, the Saskatchewan Wheat Pool reports higher total assets in 2006, with a significant improvement in the balance of its cash and short-term investments. Accounts receivable has decreased somewhat, reducing risk of customer default. At the same time, long-term debt has been reduced substantially (offset somewhat by an increase in current liabilities), indicating a healthier financial picture with less risk. Clearly, the financial position of this company has improved; even the deficit has decreased during the year.

While the balance sheet provides some information about actions and strategy over the year, the cash flow statement contains more information about the investing and financing activities of the company; we'll take a look at that statement in Chapter 5.

EXHIBIT 4-4

# SHAW COMMUNICATIONS INC.
## Consolidated Balance Sheets

As at August 31

| [thousands of Canadian dollars] | 2006 $ | 2005 $ |
|---|---|---|
| | | **(Restated – note 1)** |
| **Assets** [note 9] | | |
| Current | | |
| Cash | — | 1,713 |
| Accounts receivable [note 3] | 138,142 | 114,664 |
| Inventories [note 4] | 53,994 | 45,224 |
| Prepaids and other | 20,870 | 19,116 |
| | 213,006 | 180,717 |
| Investments and other assets [notes 5 and 11] | 17,978 | 36,229 |
| Property, plant and equipment [note 6] | 2,250,056 | 2,189,235 |
| Deferred charges [note 7] | 261,908 | 251,246 |
| Intangibles [note 8] | | |
| Broadcast licenses | 4,691,484 | 4,684,647 |
| Goodwill | 88,111 | 88,111 |
| | 7,522,543 | 7,430,185 |
| | | |
| **Liabilities and Shareholders' Equity** | | |
| Current | | |
| Bank indebtedness [note 9] | 20,362 | — |
| Accounts payable and accrued liabilities [note 13] | 461,119 | 408,033 |
| Income taxes payable | 4,918 | 6,263 |
| Unearned revenue | 106,497 | 98,420 |
| Current portion of long-term debt [note 9] | 449 | 51,380 |
| | 593,345 | 564,096 |
| Long-term debt [note 9] | 2,995,936 | 3,148,162 |
| Other long-term liabilities [notes 17 and 19] | 37,724 | 40,806 |
| Deferred credits [note 10] | 1,100,895 | 1,010,723 |
| Future income taxes [note 14] | 984,938 | 1,068,849 |
| | 5,712,838 | 5,832,636 |
| | | |
| Commitments and contingencies [notes 9, 16 and 17] | | |
| Shareholders' equity | | |
| Share capital [note 11] | | |
| Class A Shares | 2,475 | 2,487 |
| Class B Non-Voting Shares | 1,974,491 | 2,021,686 |
| Contributed surplus [note 11] | 5,110 | 1,866 |
| Deficit | (172,701) | (428,855) |
| Cumulative translation adjustment [note 12] | 330 | 365 |
| | 1,809,705 | 1,597,549 |
| | 7,522,543 | 7,430,185 |

*Source:* www.sedar.com, Shaw Communications Inc. 2005/2006 Annual Report released November 29, 2006, page 49.

The balance sheet also reflects *liquidity*, often evaluated with reference to **working capital** (current assets minus current liabilities). Working capital may also be evaluated by using more restrictive measures that exclude non-monetary current assets such as inventories.

**Liquidity** is evidence of a company's ability to pay short-term debts from its current assets as well as to meet short-term and long-term obligations. Creditors are obviously interested in assessing liquidity. Beyond this, equity investors are interested in liquidity because it affects dividend payments. Unions examine liquidity to establish bargaining positions. Employees are concerned with the company's continuing ability to pay wages. Liquidity is a major concern to many financial statement users.

The balance sheet also provides data needed to determine *rates of return*, including **return on equity (ROE)**, **return on assets (ROA)**, and a variety of other ratios. Of course, the income statement has to provide the earnings information used to calculate these ratios. Return figures are very important to financial statement users, both lenders and equity investors, as they help determine the company's credit rating and share price. The figures used in ratio calculations will depend on the accounting policies chosen by the company, however, and therefore must be interpreted with caution.

**return on equity ratio**

measure of the historical after-tax return to shareholders for the period; focus is on the common equity; income available to common shareholders is compared to common equity

**return on assets ratio**

the measure of income before interest expense earned in relation to the assets employed by an entity

## Limitations of the Balance Sheet

A balance sheet based on GAAP has limitations as a result of several aspects of applying GAAP:

### Amounts Shown on the Balance Sheet Are the Result of the Company's Reporting Policies

Even within the constraints of GAAP, alternative accounting policies are acceptable. Virtually every amount shown on the balance sheet is the result of a company's chosen accounting policies; different policies will result in different balance sheet amounts. For example, a company's choice of amortization policy (e.g., *straight line* or *declining balance*) will significantly affect the amounts shown for net capital assets, and thereby the amounts shown for total assets and for net assets (i.e., owners' equity). Ratios such as return on assets and debt equity will be affected.

### The Typical Balance Sheet Includes Many Estimated Amounts

The amounts reported on the balance sheet are affected not only by accounting *policies*, but also by accounting *estimates*. For example, the amounts shown for capital assets will be affected not only by the application of a given amortization policy (such as straight line), but also by the estimates used in applying the policy, such as each asset's useful life and estimated salvage value. Other examples of estimates include the estimated loss from uncollectible receivables and the estimated liability arising from warranties.

The impacts of estimates are difficult, sometimes impossible, to figure out. As we will see, companies must disclose the nature of measurement uncertainty that could affect financial statement elements. Although the *nature* of measurement uncertainty is disclosed, the potential variation that could be caused by using different estimates (from within a range of feasible estimates) is *not* disclosed in the notes to financial statements. A public company may disclose sensitivity to estimation error in the MD&A (Management's Discussion and Analysis), however.

### Very Few Balance Sheet Values Are Current Values and Are Not Intended for Valuation Purposes

Most major items on many companies' balance sheet are reported at historical cost, which is not always a relevant attribute. Investors and creditors may be far more interested in market values. Market value (or fair value) reporting is not a generally accepted practice in Canada or internationally, except for certain types of financial instruments and some types of non-monetary assets held for sale.

In a set of GAAP statements, market values may be disclosed for non-monetary assets, but generally are not. Companies may choose to prepare non-GAAP statements when market value is significantly different than cost and important decisions have to be based on market value, not cost.

The amounts reported for major asset categories such as plant and equipment may be significantly different than fair value or current replacement cost, given even a modest level of price changes. Individual companies are affected by this problem differently, depending on the date and rate of capital acquisitions and the level of specific price changes for the types of capital assets they use. Uncritical comparisons between companies can therefore be very misleading.

The historical cost–based balance sheet can have especially little relationship to market values when a company's assets are primarily intangible. At least tangible capital assets are valued at their fair value on the date of acquisition; the often negligible *cost* of many *internally generated* intangible assets is not even close to their fair value. For example, a patent is often recorded only at the legal cost involved in registration. Rate-of-return percentages and ratio comparisons are questionable in these circumstances.

**Certain Assets and Liabilities Simply Do Not Appear on the Balance Sheet** Remember the recognition criteria that must be met for an element to be recognized: an item must be an element and be measurable, and cash flows must be probable. If recognition criteria are not met, elements are not recognized. Assets that do not appear on the balance sheet include intangible assets acquired at no ascertainable cost, such as the abilities and morale of the workforce, customer loyalty, or brand names. These assets have future benefit—usually future revenue cash flows—but cannot be recognized either because the future cash flows are not measurable or because the future cash flows are not probable. As another example, research costs fail recognition criteria at acquisition and must be expensed.

Significant tangible assets may not appear on the balance sheet because they are rented or leased rather than owned. Only certain types of lease arrangements are recognized on the balance sheet; most are not. An airline, for example, may lease most or all of its aircraft, with the result that the planes do not appear on its balance sheet. Clearly, however, the airline has to have the aircraft in order to operate—they are necessary capital assets, but are not recorded. Again, these financial statement elements are excluded from the financial statements because they do not meet the recognition criteria.

On the liability side, omitted items include some types of lease commitments, hazardous waste cleanups whose cost cannot be estimated, and unrecorded commitments, such as purchase commitments. Again, these financial statement elements are excluded from the financial statements because they do not meet the recognition criteria. Measurement is usually the problem—things that cannot be reliably quantified are not recorded.

**Numbers are Consolidated** A company can be in a single business or can be diversified. The Saskatchewan Wheat Pool, for example, operates in one industry. On the other hand, Bombardier operates in four major sectors, each quite different from the others. If users are relying on balance sheet information to portray relationships, those relationships may be different for each individual sector.

Adding the data from the four different segments is problematic, as the aggregated amounts may mask important information. Bombardier, for example, presents two additional balance sheets (not reproduced here) in addition to its consolidated balance sheet—one for its manufacturing operations, and one for the real estate and financial services sector. Many companies rely on disaggregated, or segmented, information to get around this dilemma; we'll talk about these disclosures later in this chapter.

Consolidated statements also do not tell creditors what assets are available to satisfy their claims. A creditor, whether a trade supplier or a lender, has recourse only to the assets owned by the legal entity to which credit has been extended. Assets held by other corporations within the consolidated accounting entity cannot be claimed. It is not unusual for one corporation in a consolidated group to go bankrupt while other corporations in the group remain solvent. The creditors of the bankrupt corporation would be out of luck, if they based their lending decisions only on consolidated statements!

## FORMATTING CHOICES

Many presentation issues are open to choice by the company. We reviewed some choice issues in the last chapter, such as choice of year-end, reporting currency, language, etc. Some additional issues are unique to the balance sheet.

### Form of Presentation

The **financing form** follows the classic accounting identity, A = L + OE. This format emphasizes the means used to finance the organization's assets. Funds must be raised from creditors (liabilities) or from owners (owners' equity), often by retaining the organization's earnings. Alternatively, the basic accounting identity can be rearranged to reflect the owners' viewpoint, in the **net assets form**. Thus, A − L = OE. That is, net assets, or assets less liabilities, are totalled on the balance sheet to a number that is equal to owners' equity.

According to *Financial Reporting in Canada*, the financing form is the dominant choice, used by virtually all of the 200 surveyed public companies. The Saskatchewan Wheat Pool balance sheet in Exhibit 4-1 has a total for assets and another for liabilities plus equities, so it is in the financing form.

## Classification and Aggregation

To make accounting information as understandable and usable by decision makers as possible, items are grouped and arranged in the balance sheet according to certain guidelines. Some of these groupings are non-judgemental, as companies have little choice but to comply with generally accepted practice—users have certain expectations, after all. Other display decisions are very subjective.

In Canadian and U.S. practice, assets typically are classified and presented in *decreasing order of liquidity*, or convertibility into cash. Those items nearest to cash, that is, those that can be readily converted to cash at any time without restriction, are ranked first. Assets with the least liquidity, or least likely to be converted to cash, are listed last.

Liabilities are generally classified and presented based on *time to maturity*. Thus, obligations currently due are listed first, and those carrying the most distant maturity dates are listed last.[2]

Owners' equity items are classified and presented in *order of permanence*. Thus, paid-in capital accounts, which typically change the least, should be listed first. Equity accounts that are used to report accumulated earnings and profit distributions are listed last.

**Current Assets and Liabilities**  The most common groupings on the balance sheet are current assets and current liabilities; the net amount of current assets minus current liabilities is called working capital. Minimum working capital ratios (e.g., a minimum **current ratio**) are often stipulated in loan agreements. It's easier for financial statement users to look at working capital when the company provides the current asset and current liability subtotals.

While most companies group current assets and liabilities, not all follow this practice. As we saw, Bombardier uses an unclassified balance sheet, claiming that each of its major sectors of activity has its own operating cycle and therefore that the aggregated totals lack meaning. Banks are not required to segregate assets as current or non-current according to the accounting requirements of the Superintendent of Financial Institutions Canada.

**Current assets** includes cash and other assets that are reasonably expected to be realized in cash or to be sold or consumed during the normal operating cycle of the business or within one year from the balance sheet date, whichever is longer. The normal **operating cycle** of a business is the average length of time from the expenditure of cash for inventory, to sale, to accounts receivable, and finally back to cash. This is sometimes called the *cash-to-cash cycle*. Almost all companies use one year as the time period for classifying items as current or long term because either the operating cycle is less than one year or the length of the operating cycle may be difficult to measure reliably.

Judgement is required in defining the "normal operating cycle" and elements "reasonably expected to be realized in cash." When there is uncertainty, management may be inclined to classify certain items as current assets in order to produce a positive effect on working capital. For example, an investment in debt or equity securities of another company could be

**current ratio**

current assets divided by current liabilities; one measure of short-term solvency

---

[2] In other parts of the world, the order is reversed, showing the long-term items first and the most liquid at the end. See "International Perspective" at the end of this chapter for more information.

classified as a current or non-current asset, depending on the intended holding period and on the likely saleability of the securities. The placement of this asset on a company's balance sheet could be based on the actual intent of management or, alternatively and inappropriately, on management's desire to show its accounts in a better light; this is a problem both for the auditors and for external decision makers.

**Current liabilities** are those obligations that are due within one year or one operating cycle, whichever is longer. The current liability classification includes the typical range of short-term liabilities such as accounts payable, accrued liabilities, payroll and tax liabilities, and short-term loans (including loans payable "on demand"). Also included is unearned revenue, which is an obligation to provide service, not cash. The current portion of long-term debt is an important element of current liabilities. As well, current liabilities will include any long-term loans for which the company has not met all of its loan covenants.

**Other Classifications** Other classifications on the balance sheet are basically the major asset, liability, and equity items—investments, tangible and intangible capital assets, long-term debt, and so on. Classifications are strongly influenced by the unique characteristics of each industry and each business enterprise. You can readily see by comparing Exhibit 4-2 and Exhibit 4-3 that the balance sheet of a manufacturing company has classifications that are very different from those of a bank.

In these classifications, there is some choice, while some accounting policies are established by standards and industry norms. "Typical" balance sheet categories are listed in Exhibit 4-5. Next, we'll investigate each of these categories individually, looking at their presentation on the balance sheet and disclosure notes.

## CONCEPT REVIEW

1. Why may major "assets" not appear on the balance sheet?
2. What interpretive problems arise from the fact that the financial statements of public companies are consolidated?
3. What is the definition of "current" for current assets and current liabilities?

## SPECIFIC BALANCE SHEET ITEMS

Most of this book is devoted to examining financial statement elements; their recognition, valuation, and required disclosures. This overview of balance sheet items can't replace the detailed study that lies ahead of you. Instead, try to gain an appreciation for the overall nature of balance sheet accounts and disclosures.

### Assets

In most industries, assets are classified into a minimum of two categories: (1) current assets, and (2) other assets, including capital assets, both tangible and intangible. Other categories are used if there are enough items to warrant a separate category instead of including them under the "other assets" classification. The major categories and the items included therein are described below. Later chapters discuss each type of asset in more detail.

### Current Assets

**Cash** Cash available for operating activities is a current asset. Accounts held for designated purposes (e.g., bond sinking funds) are long term. Short-term, highly liquid investments are known as **cash equivalents** and usually are combined with the cash figure (see the Bombardier balance sheet, Exhibit 4-2). Cash equivalents are specifically defined as short-term (usually no longer than three months), interest-bearing investments, providing little risk of market value fluctuations.

> **EXHIBIT 4-5**

## TYPICAL BALANCE SHEET CLASSIFICATIONS

The classification and presentation order below are
representative of current reporting practice and terminology.

**A. ASSETS**

  **1. Current assets**
  - **a.** Cash
  - **b.** Short-term investments
  - **c.** Receivables
  - **d.** Inventories
  - **e.** Prepayments (also called prepaid expenses)
  - **f.** Other current assets

  **2. Non-current assets**
  - **a.** Investments and funds
  - **b.** Tangible capital assets (also called property, plant, and equipment, or fixed assets)
  - **c.** Intangible capital assets
  - **d.** Held-for-sale assets
  - **e.** Other assets

**B. LIABILITIES**

  **1. Current liabilities** (including the current portion of long-term liabilities)

  **2. Long-term liabilities** (including share equity elements that have the characteristics of debt)

  **3. Future income tax liability***

  **4. Long-term deferred credits**

**C. NON-CONTROLLING INTEREST IN SUBSIDIARIES**

**D. SHAREHOLDERS' EQUITY**

  **1. Contributed (or paid-in) capital**
  - **a.** Share capital
  - **b.** Equity components of debt instruments
  - **c.** Other contributed (or paid-in) capital

  **2. Retained earnings**

  **3. Accumulated other comprehensive income** (also can be titled *other changes in shareholders' equity*)

---

*\*Future income tax may also appear as a current asset, non-current asset, and/or current liability. (This is explained in Chapter 15.)*

**Short-Term Investments** Short-term investments must be *both* readily marketable *and* intended to be held only for the short term. Examples include investments in both debt and equity securities. As noted, some short-term debt investments are cash equivalents that companies group with the cash account. Others are shown separately as short-term investments and are known as *available-for-sale* investments.

    Cash equivalents and other short-term investments are reported at their current market value. Unrealized changes in market value of available-for-sale investments are reported in *other comprehensive income*, as explained in the previous chapter. These investments are **financial instruments**, and, as such, information concerning their terms and conditions, interest rates, credit risk, and market values should be disclosed. Financial instruments and related disclosures are discussed later in this chapter.

**financial instrument**

any contract that gives rise to both a financial asset of one party and a financial liability or equity instrument to the other party

<table>
<tr><td>

**accounts receivable**

cash due to a corporation from customers because of purchases of goods or services on credit

**inventories**

goods held for resale (finished goods) or use in operations (supplies)

</td><td>

**Receivables** Accounts receivable, and notes receivable, should be reported net of estimated uncollectible amounts. Any receivables pledged as security for an obligation of the firm should be disclosed. Receivables are also financial instruments, and appropriate disclosures are required.

**Inventories** Inventories usually are reported at the lower of cost or market (LCM). "Market" normally is defined as net realizable value for raw materials, work in process, and finished goods. In some sectors of the economy, inventories are valued at net realizable value (NRV), whether NRV is higher or lower than cost. An example is financial instruments held by investment companies (e.g., mutual funds or investment bankers) which are reported at market values. Also, inventories of some minerals and agricultural products may be reported at net realizable value even if NRV is higher than cost. For long-term projects, inventories may be reported at cost plus profits recognized when revenue is recognized throughout the earnings process.

**Prepayments** Prepayments, or prepaid expenses, are cash outlays made in advance of receipt of service. Rent paid in May for the month of June is an example. A short-term prepayment should be classified as a current asset, whereas a long-term prepayment should be classified as a non-current asset. Prepaid expenses are current assets because an investment is made by paying cash in advance, thereby reducing cash outlays for the coming reporting period.

**Other Current Assets** Any other assets that are expected to produce cash in the next fiscal year should be reported as a current asset. Loans receivable within the next year, including those to shareholders, will be reported as current assets. Current assets that are part of a designated discontinued operation should be segregated from the aggregate assets and reported separately as *other current assets*.

</td></tr>
</table>

## Non-Current Assets

Assets are non-current if:

1. Assets will not be used up in the next operating cycle or in one year, whichever is longer, *or*

2. Management plans to retain the assets beyond the next year or operating cycle, whichever is longer.

**Investments and Funds** The principal classifications for investments are as follows:

- *Available-for-sale financial assets.* These are investments in share capital or debt instruments that the company is holding for eventual sale. This classification is for investments that are *intended* to be held for the long term; if they are intended as a short-term investment, they are classified as a current asset. Such investments are reported at fair market value at each balance sheet date.

- *Held-to-maturity investments.* A company may invest in the long-term debt instruments of another company with the intent to hold the debt to maturity. This is common in Canada, as most corporate debt is privately placed and therefore is not available for trading. Held-to-maturity investments are reported at amortized cost. Amortization is calculated on the effective interest method, which will be discussed in Chapter 12. Any unamortized premium is added to the investment, and any unamortized discount is subtracted.

- *Long-term loans and receivables.* These are reported at amortized cost using the effective interest method, as with held-to-maturity investments.

- *Financial assets held for trading.* This classification applies only to companies that engage in the trading of financial securities, such as banks, insurance companies, investment trusts, and securities dealers. Trading assets are reported at their fair values.

- *Strategic investments.* These are investments in the shares of related companies. Share investments in subsidiaries are carried at cost in the parent's separate-entity balance sheet and disappear when consolidated statements are prepared. Another type of strategic investment is in the shares of another company where significant influence is present. Such investments are carried at cost plus unremitted earnings, using the equity method.

- *Special funds.* Sometimes a company will set aside funds for long-term future use, either as required by contractual arrangements (e.g., bond sinking funds and compensating bank balances) or as directed by the company's Board of Directors (e.g., expansion funds, share retirement funds, and long-term savings deposits). Special funds are segregated from funds available for current operations. Funds may include cash, but usually the cash is invested in interest-bearing securities. Special funds are shown at the accumulated amount in the fund—contributions plus interest earned to date.

- *Investments in tangible capital assets, such as land and buildings, that represent excess capacity and that are not being used in operations.* These assets are sometimes left in the tangible asset section, but segregated. Although capital investments are usually shown at their original cost less amortization, they may be recorded at market value if market value is lower than cost and the impairment of value is judged (by management) to be permanent.

The basis of valuation being used for long-term investments should be disclosed. Major classifications of long-term investments should be disclosed separately. Extensive disclosure is required for many kinds of investments.

**Tangible Capital Assets** Tangible capital assets include all property, plant, equipment, and resources that are used in the company's production or service process, either directly or indirectly. The category does not include property that is held for resale. Historically, tangible capital assets have been called **fixed assets** because of their relative permanence, or by the more descriptive term *property, plant, and equipment* (PP&E). A wide variety of terminology is found in practice.

Tangible capital assets include both (1) items that are amortized, such as buildings, machinery, fixtures, mineral deposits, and timber stands; and (2) items that are not subject to amortization, such as land. Tangible capital assets also include certain leased assets if the lease arrangement is deemed to be a method of financing a permanent acquisition of the facilities.

The balance sheet or the related notes should report additional information on capital assets, including the following:

- Balances of major classes of capital assets
- Accumulated amortization, by major class of capital assets
- Description of the methods used in computing amortization for the major classes of capital assets

Tangible capital assets are usually shown on the balance sheet at their historical cost or cash-equivalent cost (for assets acquired by any means other than a direct cash purchase) minus any accumulated amortization (or depreciation) to date.

**Intangible Capital Assets** Intangible capital assets are long-lived assets that lack physical substance. Examples of intangible assets include brand names, copyrights, franchises, licences, patents, software, subscription lists, and trademarks. Intangible assets usually are reported as a separate element in the balance sheet, although sometimes companies will combine tangible and intangible capital assets in a single line on the balance sheet and then provide a breakdown in the notes.

By convention, amortization sometimes is deducted directly from the intangible asset account instead of being recorded in a contra account (i.e., *accumulated amortization*) as is done with tangible capital assets. Intangible assets are shown net of accumulated amortization on the balance sheet and in the notes. The accumulated amount of amortization usually is disclosed in the notes or elsewhere in the financial statements.

Some intangible assets are not amortized because they don't have a finite life span. Goodwill acquired by buying another business is one example.

Whether amortizable or not, all intangible assets are subjected to regular *impairment tests* to ensure that they still have a value that is at least equal to their carrying value.

Some important intangible assets are not on company balance sheets at all. This is because intangibles are usually capitalized *only* when they are purchased as part of the acquisition of another firm or when expenditures such as legal fees are made in regard to them. Internally developed intangible assets also are capitalized if they meet certain criteria.

**Held-for-Sale Assets** These are long-term assets of discontinued operations, as explained in the previous chapter. They must be segregated from the assets of continuing operations and carried at the lower of (1) amortized cost or (2) estimated net realizable value.

*Held-for-sale* assets must not be confused with *available-for-sale* financial assets, since the valuation method is different.

**Other Assets** The *other assets* classification is used for assets that are not easily included under alternative asset classifications. An example is long-term receivables from company officers.

Long-term investments, special funds, and long-term deferred charges often are lumped together (though separately listed) under the category of other assets. Companies should not use the classification of "other" to hide or disguise certain assets. The nature of, and valuation basis for, these assets should be disclosed. If a reported asset has no future economic benefit, it must be written off and reported in the income statement as a loss.

Canadian companies sometimes include long-term deferred charges in the category of "other assets." These items are the result of the prepayment of long-term expenses. An example is payments that a company has made into a pension fund that are greater than the amount recorded as pension expense. Costs should be reported in this category only if they have reliably determinable future economic benefits. The only conceptual difference between a prepaid expense (classified as a current asset) and a deferred charge is the length of time over which the amount is amortized. The nature of these items, their valuation base, and the method and future accounting should be disclosed.

Some companies also report items such as restructuring costs, start-up costs, and training costs as deferred charges because they are expected to benefit future periods. However, these costs don't fit the definition of an asset because their future benefit is not measurable. Therefore, the AcSB has proposed that such costs not be reported as assets in the future. Once this change is made, Canadian standards will be consistent with both international and U.S. standards.

## Liabilities

Most companies classify liabilities into two categories: (1) current liabilities and (2) other liabilities. Within other liabilities, the most common are (a) long-term financial liabilities and (b) the long-term future income tax liability. Occasionally, a company also will report long-term deferred credits. The major categories and the items included therein are described below. Later chapters discuss each type of asset in more detail.

**Current Liabilities** The current liabilities section of the balance sheet includes all obligations of the company that are due within one year or one operating cycle, whichever period is longer. Commonly found elements include:

- Accounts payable for goods and services that enter into the operating cycle of the business (sometimes called "trade payables");
- Special short-term liabilities (i.e., payables) for non-operating items and services;
- Short-term notes payable;
- Short-term bank debt, including loans due on demand (even if they have been outstanding for a long time);
- Current maturities of long-term liabilities (including the current portion of capital lease obligations);
- Unearned revenue (such as rent collected in advance) that will be earned within the next year or operating cycle, whichever is longer;
- Accrued expenses for payroll, interest, and taxes; and
- Future income taxes relating to current assets and current liabilities.

**Long-Term Liabilities** A long-term (non-current) liability is an obligation that is due beyond the next operating cycle or during the next reporting year, whichever is longer. All liabilities not appropriately classified as current liabilities are reported as long term. Typical long-term liabilities are bonds payable, long-term notes payable, pension liabilities, deferred long-term revenues (advances from customers), and long-term capital lease obligations. Most long-term liabilities are recorded at the exchange value of the assets or services received.

Long-term liabilities also will include any financial instrument (or the portion of a complex instrument) that has the legal characteristics of debt, even though the instrument may be described by the company as share equity. Financial instruments are discussed a little later in the chapter under "Specific Significant Disclosures."

Note disclosures for long-term debt can be extensive, especially if the debt issue contains unusual features. Disclosure of terms and conditions includes the interest rate, maturity date, sinking fund requirements, redemption and conversion provisions, security, and loan covenants, if applicable. Effective interest rates and fair values should be disclosed. Finally, the aggregate payments (cash flow) required over each of the next five years should be disclosed.

**Future Income Tax Liabilities** Income tax is paid on the basis of revenues and expenses that comprise taxable income. Revenue and expenses on the income statement may be different, due to differences in the tax and accounting bases of assets and liabilities. Income tax expense is based on those revenues and expenses that will be included in taxable income, even if they will be included in future years. Therefore, income tax expense consists of two components:

1. Tax payable to the government for the current year, known as *current income tax*; and

2. Tax that pertains to revenues and expenses that were recognized on the income statement in the current period but have a future tax impact, known as *future income tax*.

Future income tax is segregated into current and long-term portions. Future income tax relates to current assets or liabilities that are classified as current, such as prepaid expense or inventories. The remainder is classified as long term.

The future income tax accounts can have either a debit or credit balance. A debit balance in the long-term account is shown under other assets. A credit balance is shown as a long-term liability.

Future income tax is measured as the future cash flow through increased taxes (or reduction in cash flow due to tax benefits). The amounts are *not* discounted. If future income tax has a credit balance, it is a liability. However, it is qualitatively different from other liabilities in that (1) there is no creditor, (2) there is no current obligation actually owing at the balance sheet date, and (3) long-term balances are not discounted. Therefore, many companies show it as a separate item following long-term debt. For example, Shaw Communications (Exhibit 4-4) shows future income taxes as the last item in the liabilities section, just before shareholders' equity. Notice that the balance of Shaw's future income taxes is quite large—13% of total assets.

A company may show as many as four future income tax balances on its balance sheet. Multiple balances are the result of (1) segregation between current and long term, and (2) obligations in different taxing jurisdictions, which cannot be offset against each other. The issues of future income tax are discussed extensively in chapters 15 and 16.

**Long-Term Deferred Credits** Deferred credits can arise from several sources. One example occurs in pension accounting, when the expense recorded is greater than the payments made to date. Another example is revenue that has been received (i.e., as a deposit) but that will not become earned revenue within the next year.

## Non-controlling Interest in Subsidiaries

Financial statements of public companies are almost always *consolidated statements*. Consolidated statements include all of the assets and liabilities of the parent and its subsidiaries. However, sometimes the parent does not own 100% of the subsidiary. The amount not owned by the parent is called the *non-controlling interest*.

In order to make the parent's consolidated balance sheet actually balance, it is necessary to include an amount on the right side of the balance sheet to recognize the proportionate part of the subsidiary's net assets that are *not* owned by the parent. For example, suppose one company controls 80% of the shares of another company. The parent will combine 100% of the subsidiary's assets with the parent's assets even though the parent holds only an 80% equity interest. The 20% equity of the outside shareholders must be reported on the right side of the balance sheet to make it balance.

Non-controlling interest (sometimes called *minority interest*) is not usually shown as a liability because the parent company doesn't owe anything to the outside investors. Non-controlling interests are not shown as shareholder's equity because they represent outsiders' direct share interest in a subsidiary, and do not represent the equity of the parent's owners. Therefore, this amount traditionally has been shown *between* liabilities and shareholders' equity.

Royal Bank (Exhibit 4-3) shows non-controlling interest after liabilities and before shareholders' equity. In contrast, the Saskatchewan Wheat Pool (Exhibit 4-1) adds non-controlling interest into the total liabilities.

A new standard on consolidated financial statements is expected to take effect in 2009. Thereafter, minority interest will be classified as a separate part of shareholders' equity. This change will bring Canadian practice into line with international standards.

## Shareholders' Equity

Shareholders' equity is a residual interest. It has three basic components:

**1.** Contributed (or paid-in) capital

**2.** Retained earnings

**3.** Accumulated other comprehensive income (or other shareholders' equity)

**Contributed (or Paid-in) Capital** Because of legal requirements, contributed capital is subclassified to reflect detailed sources. For Canadian corporations, the most commonly reported subclassifications are:

**a.** Share capital

**b.** Contributed surplus

The breakdown between these two subclassifications generally has little significance; they tend to be defined more by legal specifications than by substantive accounting measurement. In some jurisdictions, the amount of share capital is designated as legal capital or stated capital, but also with little real significance.

**Share Capital** Share capital is the paid-in value or par value of the issued or outstanding preferred and common shares of the corporation. This amount is not available for dividend declarations.

Each share class should be reported at its paid-in amount, or, in the case of par value shares, at par value. Par value shares are found only in a very few provincial jurisdictions in Canada, but may be found in other jurisdictions (e.g., in the U.S., United Kingdom, and Hong Kong).

Details of the terms and conditions of each class of share capital must be reported separately, including the number of shares authorized, issued, outstanding, and subscribed; also disclosed are conversion features, callability, preferences, dividend rates, and any other special features. Changes in share capital accounts during the period must be disclosed, along with outstanding options.

Share capital also will include any financial instrument (or the portion of a complex instrument) that might be described by the company as debt but that lacks the legal characteristics of debt. Financial instruments are discussed a little later in the chapter under "Specific Significant Disclosures."

**Equity Components of Debt Instruments** Corporations sometimes issue debt securities that have some characteristics of debt and other characteristics of equity. For example, a company may issue debt securities that require the company to pay interest in cash each year, but that are convertible into common shares at maturity, at the holder's option. The interest obligation is legally binding and must be treated as a debt obligation, while the holder's conversion option has some characteristics of share equity. As a result, the proceeds of the debt issue are shown partially as debt and partially as equity. Accounting for these "complex instruments" is explained in Chapter 14.

**Other Contributed Capital** Other contributed capital arises from such transactions as (1) the retirement of shares for less than the original amount paid in for the shares and (2) capital arising from recapitalizations or donations from shareholders. Details and changes during the period should be disclosed. Other contributed capital is also known as contributed surplus.

For corporations that issue par-value shares, other contributed capital also includes an account called "contributed capital in excess of par." If shares are issued for an amount in excess of par value, additional contributed capital is created. Details and changes during the period should be disclosed.

**Retained Earnings** Retained earnings is essentially a corporation's accumulated net earnings since the company's inception minus dividends paid out. In many corporations, retained earnings is the largest amount in the owners' equity section. A negative balance in retained earnings is called a **deficit** and usually arises when a company experiences continuing operating losses.

Retained earnings may be subdivided into two or more accounts through an appropriation or restriction. The additional accounts are shown on the balance sheet, or the total can be included on the balance sheet and the appropriation disclosed.

**Accumulated Other Comprehensive Income** There are some changes in the reported value of net assets that standard setters don't want to appear in net income. If value changes are not recognized in net income, their effect must be included elsewhere in shareholders' equity in order to make the balance sheet balance. A direct entry to retained earnings is not permitted because retained earnings should be affected by only two things: (1) net income and (2) other transactions with shareholders.

Generally speaking, these value changes are unrealized gains and losses. They are of two main types:

1. Certain types of value changes due to fluctuating foreign exchange rates; and

2. Unrealized changes in the value of certain types of assets and/or liabilities that are reported on the balance sheet at fair value (also known as *mark-to-market*) but which won't be realized until later periods.

Each year, these unrealized gains and losses are reported as "other comprehensive income" in the statement of comprehensive income. The *cumulative* amount is reported in shareholders' equity as **accumulated other comprehensive income** (AcOCI).

For example, assume that a company has a subsidiary in Mexico that operates in pesos and that prepares its financial statements in pesos. At year-end, the financial statements of the subsidiary are translated from the peso to the Canadian dollar so that the subsidiary's accounts can be consolidated. Since different exchange rates are used for different financial statement elements according to the accounting rules, an overall exchange gain or loss arises. For independent *self-sustaining* subsidiaries, the cumulative amount of the gain or loss is included in AcOCI as a component of equity.

In Exhibit 4-4, Shaw Communications reports a credit balance of $330,000 for *cumulative translation adjustment* in its shareholders' equity at fiscal year-end 2006. In contrast, Royal Bank (Exhibit 4-3) shows a *debit* balance of $2.0 billion for *net foreign currency translation adjustments* for 2006.

Certain types of investments (e.g., available-for-sale financial assets) are reported at fair market value, but gains and losses enter net income only when the investment is sold and the gain or loss is *realized*. The unrealized difference between cost and market value is reported in accumulated other comprehensive income until realization. We will explore these issues in Chapter 11.

## Offsetting Assets and Liabilities

**offset (netting)**

showing one account less another at their net balance in the financial statements; allowed only if the legal right to offset exists and the entity plans to settle on a net basis

Normally, assets and liabilities should not be **offset** against one another. Offsetting or netting is a procedure by which a liability is subtracted from an asset or vice versa, and the resulting net amount is disclosed. Such practice circumvents full disclosure and could permit a business to show more favourable ratios. Offsetting is permissible only when:

- A legal right to offset exists, *and*
- The entity plans to settle the items on a net basis or at least simultaneously.

For instance, it would be permissible to offset a $5,000 overdraft in one bank account against another account reflecting $8,000 on deposit in that same bank, since the bank can legally offset the two deposit accounts. In contrast, it is not acceptable to offset a sinking-fund investment account against its related long-term loan, as the company does not have the legal right to offset without creditor acceptance.

## CONCEPT REVIEW

1. What is the difference between tangible and intangible capital assets?
2. In what order are assets normally presented on a Canadian company's balance sheet?
3. What are the major classifications within shareholders' equity?

## DISCLOSURE NOTES

You've probably noticed that almost every item on our four illustrative balance sheets refers to a disclosure note. **Disclosure notes** are an integral part of the financial statements and must be presented if the statements are to be complete. If the financial statements are audited, so are the notes.

**disclosure notes**

explanatory notes to the financial statements that include information on accounting policy and description of financial statement elements, recognized and unrecognized

Disclosure notes can adhere to minimal disclosure requirements or be far more extensive; this is management's decision based on corporate reporting objectives and the needs of user groups. Unlike the purely quantitative financial statements, information in disclosure notes can be provided in qualitative terms. Readers can then make their own assessment of the potential quantitative ramifications of the information presented. Notes are sometimes complex and highly technical.

### General Classification of Disclosure Notes

In general, notes can fulfill many functions:

1. Provide accounting policy information that allows users to evaluate data, including the ability to compare data to other companies and between years. Accounting standards require a company to disclose the company's choice of accounting policies. The information may be presented as the first note to the financial statements, or in a separate summary of significant accounting policies. Accounting policies include specific accounting principles and the methods of applying these principles. Disclosure should explain important judgements that involve:

    - A selection from acceptable alternatives; and
    - Principles and methods specific to the industry in which the company operates.

Changes in policy and significant changes in estimate must also be described in disclosure notes, along with the impact on earnings and net assets, if ascertainable.

2. *Explain items that have been recognized in the statements.* Some items that have been recognized in the financial statements should be described, especially those that are unusual in nature or that are not expected to continue. The notes in this regard contribute to the predictive power of the financial statements. Sometimes, though, even the *nature* of a recognized item is mysterious and must be described.

For example, the Royal Bank balance sheet shows *Assets purchased under reverse repurchase agreements.* This is not a common type of item, and therefore the notes explain that "we purchase securities under agreements to resell." That is, the Royal Bank has purchased, or invested in, notes or other securities from a company and the company (or a third party) has agreed to repurchase, or redeem, the investment at a particular time at a particular price. This is another form of lending.

Another type of note that describes a recognized item provides *disaggregation.* Some items are added together on the balance sheet to reduce clutter, but more detail has to be provided to comply with accounting standards or to convey important information to users. For example, the Saskatchewan Wheat Pool reports the following breakdown of its 2006 aggregated inventory balance sheet amounts (in thousands of dollars) in the notes:

|  | **2006** | **2005** |
|---|---|---|
| Grain | $ 55,872 | $ 58,485 |
| Agri-products | 74,974 | 47,591 |
| Agri-food processing | 12,079 | 11,340 |
|  | $142,925 | $117,416 |

3. *Explain unrecognized items.* Liabilities such as contingent liabilities that are not probable, or are probable but not measurable, do not qualify for recognition. If a contingent liability is probable but not measurable, the situation giving rise to the contingent liability is described in the notes. It is then up to the users to assess risks for themselves. For example, in its note on guarantees and commitments, Bombardier discloses the following information about one type of credit guarantees:

In connection with the sale of aircraft, Bombardier provides credit guarantees in the form of lease and loan payments guarantees, as well as services related to the remarketing of aircraft. These guarantees, which are mainly issued for the benefit of providers of financing to customers, mature in different periods up to 2025. Substantially all financial support involving potential credit risk lies with commercial airline customers. The credit risk relating to three commercial airline customers accounted for 61% of the total maximum credit risk at January 31, 2006. In most circumstances, a claim under a credit guarantee may be made only upon sale of the underlying aircraft to a third party.

Other examples of unrecognized items include dividends in arrears, liabilities for environmental cleanups, and so on.

4. *Provide information regarding future cash flows.* Financial statements are often used to predict future cash flows; often specific information regarding future cash flows is required by accounting standards, or the company deems such disclosure desirable. Companies must disclose principal payments due for the next five years for long-term debt, minimum lease payments for a five-year period, and so on. Bombardier reports, in $ millions:

The repayment requirements on the long-term debt during the next five fiscal years and thereafter are as follows:

| | |
|---|---|
| 2008 | $    44 |
| 2009 | 388 |
| 2010 | 609 |
| 2011 | 21 |
| 2012 | 25 |
| Thereafter | 3,993 |
| | $5,080 |

5. *Provide alternate measurement bases for recognized and unrecognized amounts.* Does the company think that historical costs are irrelevant and market values important? Is the company constrained to GAAP for some reason and thus is reporting cost? Not to worry—market value can be disclosed. In fact, companies are required to disclose market values, however defined, for many items. For example, Shaw Communications's balance sheet includes investments in publicly traded companies at a cost of $9,392 million. The notes, however, disclose that the market value of those investments is $9,645 million.

6. *Provide measures to help investors assess return on investment.* Preferred share dividend rates and effective yields on debt all help investors assess their return on investment.

## Specific Significant Disclosures

There are several disclosure requirements that are significant enough to warrant separate discussion, either because they are new or are relatively complex.

**Financial Instruments** Financial instruments have special disclosure and presentation requirements. Financial instruments include the following:

- *Financial assets:* basically *cash* or *contractual rights to receive cash*, or *equity investments* in other firms. Thus, in addition to cash, all types of receivables, loans, and investments in shares are financial assets.
- *Financial liabilities:* those that establish a contractual obligation to *deliver cash*, and encompass most liabilities as we know them, except obligations to provide services, such as warranty liabilities and unearned revenues. (Financial assets and liabilities also include more complicated risk management tools, including swap and option agreements.)
- *Equity instruments:* those that confer a residual interest in net assets of an entity.

The thrust of accounting standards is to classify each financial instrument in accordance with its substance. For example, suppose that a company issues preferred shares that carry a legal obligation both to pay the annual dividend and to redeem the share at the investor's request. *Legal obligation to pay* is the defining characteristic of a liability. Therefore, the preferred shares should be reported in the balance sheet as a liability (its substance) instead of as equity (its nominal form).

Some financial instruments have features that reflect characteristics of both debt and equity. In that case, the instrument may need to be broken apart (for financial reporting purposes) into its component parts. For example, suppose that a company has convertible bonds with a legal obligation for the issuer to pay the annual interest, but the investors can request common shares to "repay" the principal at maturity if they wish. The interest flow is a legal obligation, and therefore constitutes debt. The principal amount is debt, but has an option on equity, however. For financial reporting purposes, the two components of the instrument will be segregated on the balance sheet—the debt portion is clearly long-term debt, while the value of the option is owners' equity.

A company must present three types of information about its financial instruments:

1. The *accounting policy* used for reporting each type of financial asset and financial liability;

2. The *fair value* for each class of financial asset or financial liability, presented in a way that enables the user to compare the fair value with the reported carrying value. The methods used to measure fair values should be disclosed; and

3. The *nature and extent of risks* arising from financial instruments, including, as appropriate, credit risk, liquidity risk, and market risk.

The financial instruments disclosures are interesting in that they extend fair-value disclosures to broad classes of balance sheet items. The financial instrument disclosures also apply to items that are currently unrecognized on the financial statements, such as options and swap agreements. The Royal Bank includes four pages of densely packed notes outlining specifics related to derivative financial instruments including the estimated fair value of financial instruments.

**Segment Disclosures** Consolidated financial information may mask important trends, risks, and opportunities for a diversified company. Therefore, *public companies* are required to disaggregate their reported results by geographical region and by business segment.

Every public company must identify its various operating segments—enough segments to explain 75% of its total revenue. Sometimes this is easier said than done. Is an integrated oil company in exploration, refining, and distribution industries, or just in the oil industry? The company must report selected information such as revenues, profits, and assets for each segment. In addition, information about the geographic spread of its operations and customer base must be disclosed.

The company must reconcile the disaggregated data back to the numbers reported on the primary financial statements, to avoid confusion. The segment disclosures can be quite long and complex if the company is involved in a large number of segments.

Bombardier discloses two business segments—aerospace and transportation. The segmented disclosures indicate, for example, that aerospace accounted for 56% of revenues, 83% of assets, 77% of capital expenditures, and 58% of operating earnings (before tax) in 2007.

Bombardier also discloses its revenue and assets for seven specific countries and five regional groups. Canada accounted for only 4% of consolidated revenue but 34% of the company's total assets.

**Related Party Transactions** When a firm engages in a transaction where one of the parties has the ability to influence the actions and policies of the other, the transaction is termed a *related party transaction*. Such transactions cannot be assumed to be at arm's length because the conditions necessary for a competitive, free-market interaction are not likely to be present. Related parties include management, individuals, and/or corporations with significant shareholdings; other corporations with common major shareholders; family members of related parties; etc. There can be a large number of related parties!

Accounting standards require that related party transactions be recorded at *carrying value*, which is the *book value of the transferor*. Cost would be carrying value for inventory, net book value for capital assets, and so on. Carrying value is considered appropriate because no transaction of substance has taken place—a different related party simply owns the asset in question. However, related party transactions must be recorded at the *exchange value* (usually *fair market value*) if the transaction is made in the normal course of business. That is, a regular sale of inventory that happened to be to a sister company would be recorded at the exchange value, not carrying value. The exchange amount is also used to value the transaction if the transaction is monetary (that is, if money changes hands), the change of ownership interest is substantive, and the exchange amount can be verified with reference to independent evidence.

Unfortunately, financial statement users tend to assume that all transactions are recorded at fair market value, and the presence of related party transactions may make the financial statements difficult to interpret. Accordingly, the following disclosures are recommended for these transactions:

- The nature of the relationship(s) involved
- A description of the nature of the transactions, including the dollar amounts, and the measurement basis used
- Any amounts due to or from related parties as of the balance sheet date, and the terms and conditions
- Any contingencies or contractual obligations with related parties

The disclosure of related party transactions is intended to alert financial statement readers to the existence of these relationships, either individual or corporate. The disclosures do not include any measurement of the fair value of transactions (as opposed to the recorded value of the transactions), and therefore there is little opportunity for readers to judge the impact of the non–arm's length transactions on the reporting enterprise's financial statements.

**Economic Dependence** Sometimes a company depends on the business of one large customer or a small group of major customers. An auto parts manufacturer may sell all of its output to a single large automobile manufacturer such as General Motors or Toyota. A medical research lab may perform all of its work under contract to a government health ministry. The company's continuance may depend on this customer's continued business. If the customer switches supplier or goes bankrupt, the company may fail if it can't replace that business quickly with new customers.

Financial statement readers need to know whether the company is highly dependent on one or a small group of customers. When a company is heavily dependent on one or a few customers, this fact, and the volume of business involved, should be disclosed in the notes. It is not necessary to disclose who the customer is, although knowledgeable readers may well know from other sources or from their knowledge of the industry.

For example, the financial statements of Pan American Silver Corp. contain the following disclosure:

> In 2005, the Company's ten customers (2004 and 2003—six customers) accounted for 100 percent of concentrate and ore sales revenue. The loss of certain of these customers or curtailment of purchases by such customers could have a material adverse affect on the Company's results of operations and financial condition.

**contingency**

an event that will occur only if another event occurs; as a liability, may be recorded or disclosed depending on its nature

**Contingencies** A **contingency** is an event or transaction that will occur only if some other event happens. For example, a civil lawsuit poses a contingent gain for the plaintiff and a contingent loss for the defendant. However, the parties will not know whether they have a gain or a loss until the court reaches a decision. Generally speaking, a contingent loss should be accrued in the financial statements when both of the following conditions are met:

1. It is likely that a future event will confirm that an asset has been impaired or a liability incurred at the date of the financial statements; *and*

2. The amount of the loss can be reasonably estimated.

Few situations meet both conditions and therefore few contingent losses are recognized in the financial statements. If a loss is probable or estimable but not both, or if there is at least a reasonable possibility that a liability may have been incurred, the nature of the contingency must be disclosed in a note along with an estimate of the possible loss or the range of the possible loss if an estimate can be made. Most companies refrain from estimating any expected loss, arguing that:

- The situation does not meet the required reasonable probability level; *and*
- It is not possible to estimate the loss.

Companies are particularly reluctant to disclose potential losses arising from litigation because such disclosure might provide the appearance of wrongdoing. The desire not to release information that might be unfavourable to the company coupled with the vagueness of such words as "it is likely that a future event will confirm" allows many contingencies to go unreported. Shaw Communications, for example, mentions that the company and its subsidiaries are involved in litigation arising from the normal course and conduct of business. The company then states that "such matters cannot be predicted with certainty" and that "management does not consider the Company's exposure litigation to be material to these financial statements."

Although contingent *gains* are also possible, the accounting profession has adopted a conservative position of non-recognition. Contingent gains may be disclosed in notes, but only if there is a high probability of realization. Many instances of this take-the-loss-but-defer-the-gain approach are found throughout accounting standards.

**Guarantees** We are all familiar with a *guarantee* that relates to a product or services provided by the reporting enterprise. However, the concept of a guarantee goes beyond these simple (and usually estimable) warranty arrangements. More broadly, a **guarantee** is an agreement by the reporting enterprise to pay compensation, to undertake to perform services, or to assume the obligation of another entity under certain conditions. Guarantees are really a type of *contingency*, but they are given special attention because they are so common in business affairs and because they can be the hidden elephant in a company's otherwise undisclosed contingent obligations. Examples of guarantees are:

- A promise to pay the debts or obligations of another party, such as the line of credit or long-term loans of an affiliated corporation;
- A promise to make good on non-performance, such as when a subcontractor is unable to carry out the contracted services. This is known as a *performance guarantee*; or
- A promise to remedy any deficiency or shortfall of assets held by another entity. For example, a company may issue shares in payment for services received from another company, and guarantee that the value of the shares won't fall below a certain level. This is also known as *indemnification*.

When a company has given any guarantees beyond normal product warranties, the nature and potential maximum amount of these guarantees should be disclosed in a separate disclosure note.

### Measurement Uncertainty

Estimates are required for many financial statement elements. Examples of estimated values include such things as warranty liabilities, the likelihood of contingencies, environmental cleanup obligations, and the extent of possible asset impairment based on future cash flows. The list is long.

Financial statement readers are generally aware of the pervasive nature of estimates. Nevertheless, it is appropriate to call attention to **measurement uncertainty**—the extent to which errors in significant estimates can affect the financial statements. Disclosing the nature and extent of measurement uncertainty requires a description of the estimated amount, the amount recorded, and an indication of possible dollar change that is possible. Disclosure might also include key assumptions, ranges, and the sensitivity of the range to changes in assumptions.

For example, assume that a company had guaranteed a $100,000 loan of an associated company that was now in financial distress. The associated company will likely be able to partially repay the loan, and the guarantor believes that it will have to pay $45,000 under the guarantee. This $45,000 amount is recorded on the guarantor's books. To disclose measurement uncertainty, the notes would indicate the amount recorded, and the maximum liability under the guarantee.

But what if the amount estimated is a lawsuit? Assume that a company is being sued for $100,000 but is willing to settle for $45,000, and thus records this amount. Negotiations surrounding a possible settlement are ongoing; the settlement might be less or more than $45,000, or the case might still go to court. To avoid disclosure of the company's position to the plaintiff, the $45,000 accrual is grouped with other liabilities on the balance sheet. However, if the amount accrued is then specifically disclosed in a measurement uncertainty note, the plaintiff would be privy to information that would hurt the company's bargaining position in negotiations, and thus jeopardize the legitimate interests of the company's other stakeholders. In these circumstances, the standard allows that the amount recorded need not be specifically identified.

**Going Concern** The financial statements are prepared using the continuity assumption, as we discussed in Chapter 2. This assumption establishes that the business is expected to continue in operation for a reasonable period of time, and is not expected to liquidate.

However, there are situations in which this assumption is not valid. Canadian and international accounting standards require managers to explicitly assess the ability of the company to continue as a going concern.

For example, a company may have operated at a loss for several years in a row, eroding its equity base. Management may be unable to arrange operating financing with a financial institution, or new long-term debt with institutional lenders. Financing may not be available to allow continued operations. Alternatively, an adverse outcome from a contingency may suddenly call the viability of the company into question. If the operation is not a going concern, then historical costs are not appropriate for valuation, and all assets and liabilities have to be valued and classified based on immediate liquidation.

But what about the times when a company appears *perhaps* headed for financial distress, but is not quite ready to, or forced to, liquidate? Companies do not usually go directly from financial health to liquidation. There are often years of an intermediate level of poor financial position. This deteriorating financial position is, of course, obvious from analysis of the financial statements. At some stage, these companies "cross the line" and the situation becomes urgent.

In the later intermediate stages, clear disclosure of the seriousness of the situation is important. If clear and adequate disclosure is present, then the financial statements can still be produced on a going-concern basis. These financial statements will comply with GAAP. Such a disclosure note is usually the first (or perhaps second) disclosure note, given a prominent position so it cannot be missed.

Of course, inclusion of this note is a difficult decision, as disclosure of this nature can be self-fulfilling. Some creditors will take this as a cue to further tighten up on credit terms, which may hasten financial distress. Careful management of stakeholders is critical.

**subsequent events**

events that occur after the year-end but before the financial statements are issued; may be recorded or disclosed depending on nature

**Subsequent Events** What happens if the company unexpectedly sells a division soon after the end of the fiscal year? It's not an event of the past fiscal year, but shouldn't it be part of the report? Users have probably learned about this significant event through the financial press or other sources, as news travels fast. The financial statements must retain their credibility and relevance by reflecting up-to-date information.

Therefore, disclosure is required for significant events that take place *after the end of the fiscal year*, but *before the date that the statements are completed*. The date of the auditor's report is usually used as a cut-off date.

Examples of subsequent events that have been disclosed are:

- A decline in the market value of an investment after the balance sheet date;
- An event that results in a loss, such as fire or flood;
- Issuance of debt or equity instruments that changed the common shares, or potential common shares, outstanding; and
- Announcing or commencing a restructuring.

Some events that take place *after* the year-end actually reflect economic conditions existing at the year-end; *these events are recognized in the accounts*. For example, if a customer unexpectedly announces bankruptcy after the year-end, the accounts receivable relating to that customer at the year-end would be written down under the reasoning that the customer was actually insolvent at the end of the fiscal year, but this fact did not become known to the company until after the year-end.

Other examples of information to be recorded include the settlement of a court case related to events that took place before the balance sheet date, and evidence uncovered of asset impairment existing at the balance sheet date. Such events can be taken into account *in retrospect*, as part of the accounting estimation process that occurs at every financial reporting date.

## THE AUDITOR'S REPORT

When financial statements are audited (e.g., for public companies), the auditor's report is presented along with the financial statements. The audit report expresses the auditor's professional opinion on the company's financial statement presentation.

The auditors have sole responsibility for all opinions expressed in the auditor's report, while company management has the primary responsibility for the financial statements, including the supporting notes. Compilation and presentation of the accounting information and all supporting text contained in a company's financial statements is company management's concern and responsibility; the auditors, in rendering their opinion, affirm or disaffirm what management has compiled and presented.

Seven required elements in the auditor's report have special significance. They are identified by number in Exhibit 4-6, the auditor's report for Maple Leaf Reforestation Inc.

1. Salutation (the auditor is hired by, and reports to, the shareholders)

2. Identification of the statements examined

3. Statement of scope of the examination

4. Opinion

5. Reference to fair presentation in conformity with generally accepted accounting principles

6. Signature of the independent auditor

7. Date

---

### EXHIBIT 4-6

## AUDITORS' REPORT

*To the Shareholders of Maple Leaf Reforestation Inc.* **[1]**

**[2]** We have audited the balance sheets of Maple Leaf Reforestation Inc. as at January 31, 2006 and 2005 and the statements of operations and deficit, and cash flows for the years then ended. These financial statements are the responsibility of the Company's management. Our responsibility is to express an opinion on these financial statements based on our audits.

**[3]** We conducted our audits in accordance with Canadian generally accepted auditing standards. Those standards require that we plan and perform an audit to obtain reasonable assurance whether the financial statements are free of material misstatement. An audit includes examining, on a test basis, evidence supporting the amounts and disclosures in the financial statements. An audit also includes assessing the accounting principles used and significant estimates made by management, as well as evaluating the overall financial statement presentation.

**[4]** In our opinion, these consolidated financial statements present fairly, in all material respects, the financial position of the Company as at January 31, 2006 and 2005 and the results of its operations and its cash flows for the years then ended **[5]** in accordance with Canadian generally accepted accounting principles.

(signed)
Morgan & Company **[6]**
Vancouver, Canada
May 9, 2006 **[7]**

---

*Source:* www.sedar.com, Maple Leaf Reforestation Inc. Audited Annual Financial Statements released May 30, 2006.

When an audit is finished, the auditors are required to draft an opinion paragraph that communicates their professional opinion about the company's financial statements. The auditors can render one of four opinions, although an unqualified opinion is most common.

1. *Unqualified opinion.* An unqualified opinion is given when the auditor concludes that the statements fairly present the results of operations, financial position, and cash flows in compliance with GAAP and provide reasonable assurance that the financial statements are free of material misstatement. Maple Leaf Reforestation Inc.'s audit report is unqualified, as is necessary for any company listed on the TSX.

2. *Qualified opinion.* A qualified opinion is given when the auditor takes limited exception to the client's financial statements in a way that does not invalidate the statements as a whole. A qualified opinion must explain the reasons for the exception and its effect on the financial statements.

3. *Adverse opinion.* An adverse opinion is given when the financial statements do not fairly present the results of operations, financial position, and changes in financial position. An adverse opinion means that the statements, taken as a whole, are not presented in accordance with GAAP. Adverse opinions are rare.

4. *Disclaimer of opinion.* When the auditors have not been able to obtain sufficient evidence, they must state that they are unable to express an opinion (i.e., they issue a disclaimer). The disclaimer must provide the reasons the auditor did not give an opinion.

A major purpose of the auditor's report is to give reasonable assurance to the reader that the financial statements conform to GAAP. However, an audit report does not assure the reader that the numbers in the financial statements are the "right" numbers for the reader's purpose. As the preceding chapters have emphasized (and the following chapters will illustrate), management's selection of "acceptable" accounting practices and estimates will strongly colour the resultant financial statements. The auditor's report states only that the accounting policies chosen by the company are within the set deemed generally acceptable. Different choices would have given different reported results while still being generally acceptable.

## MANAGEMENT DISCUSSION AND ANALYSIS

As part of their annual report, public companies in Canada and the U.S. are required to provide a Management Discussion and Analysis (MD&A). The MD&A accompanies the annual financial statements, but it is not actually a part of the financial statements and therefore it is not audited. The MD&A is meant to give investors insight into management's interpretation of current financial results and plans for the future. An effective MD&A will present an analysis of both past results and future prospects, so that the investor can assess the company's operations and prospects. According to the securities commission rules, information must be presented in the following areas:

1. A general review of the financial statements, as well as areas of risk and uncertainty;

2. Quarterly information—usually the past eight quarters are presented to allow analysis of trends;

3. Liquidity and capital resources, analyzed by management, including a forward look at capital expenditures commitments, requirements for operations, and resources to meet these requirements; and

4. Results of operations, analyzed by management to identify trends.

The CICA, in support of MD&A reporting, issued extensive general guidance on the preparation and disclosure of the MD&A. General disclosure principles are established as follows:

1. The MD&A should enable readers to view the company through the eyes of management.

2. The MD&A should complement as well as supplement financial statements.

3. The MD&A should be reliable, complete, and fairly balanced, providing material relevant information for decision making.

4. The MD&A should have a forward-looking orientation.

5. The MD&A should focus on management's strategy for generating value for investors over time.

6. The MD&A should be written in plain language, with candour and without exaggeration, and embody the qualities of understandability, relevance, comparability and consistency over reporting periods.[3]

The CICA provides guidance as to appropriate disclosures, establishing an extensive disclosure framework. These pronouncements also include guidelines for continuous disclosure and outline the responsibilities of management, the Board of Directors, and the Audit Committee with respect to the MD&A.

It is clear that the MD&A must be prepared with a view to relevant information. In the past, MD&A disclosures relating to future plans have been criticized for being quite vague and therefore of limited use to investors. Companies have been reluctant to divulge future plans because positive expectations may not be fulfilled and negative projections may cause an overreaction in the stock market. Nonetheless, companies must begin to meet reporting expectations in this area.

## CONCEPT REVIEW

1. In general, what functions are served by disclosure notes?

2. Why might financial statement users want to see segmented information? What companies are required to disclose segmented information?

3. Define a related party transaction.

4. What two conditions must be fulfilled in order for a contingent liability to be recognized on the balance sheet instead of just being disclosed in a note?

5. What is measurement uncertainty?

6. What disclosure is needed if a firm's ability to continue as a going concern is questionable?

7. What is the purpose of the management discussion and analysis (MD&A)? Which companies are required to present an MD&A?

## INTERNATIONAL PERSPECTIVE

In Canada and the U.S., we show the assets first, followed by the liabilities and owners' equity. This is the practice in some other countries, such as Japan, Australia, Sweden, and Switzerland. In most other industrialized counties, however, the order is reversed.

Germany, the United Kingdom, France, Austria, Spain, and the Netherlands all begin the listing of assets with fixed assets; within fixed assets, intangibles are listed first. Liquid short-term assets are at the bottom of the listing. This approach is also the one prescribed by *The Fourth Directive*, the European Union regulation concerning the reporting of individual company financial statements. On the right side, shareholders' equity is the usual starting point, although some countries permit liabilities to be shown first.

---

[3] *Management's Discussion and Analysis*, The Canadian Institute of Chartered Accountants, Toronto, Canada, 2002, Part 2.

The widespread acceptance of international standards for consolidated statements has helped to harmonize the recognition and measurement of financial statement elements, although not the order of presentation on the balance sheet. However, international standards are not usually applied to financial statements for individual corporate entities, and especially not for private companies. For individual entities, national accounting prevails!

The U.S. and Canada permit public reporting only with consolidated statements. In contrast, European countries require disclosure of both consolidated statements (using international GAAP) and parent company separate-entity statements (using national GAAP). Accounting standards in many countries are set by law and measurement principles often do not conform to international standards.

## RELEVANT STANDARDS

*CICA Handbook:*
- Section 1400, General Standards of Financial Statement Presentation
- Section 1505, Disclosure of Accounting Policies
- Section 1508, Measurement Uncertainty
- Section 3290, Contingencies
- Section 3820, Subsequent Events
- Section 3841, Economic Dependence
- Accounting Guideline AcG-14, Disclosure of Guarantees

IASB:
- *IAS* 1, Presentation of Financial Statements

## SUMMARY OF KEY POINTS

1. The balance sheet provides information about an entity's assets, liabilities, and equities. The balance sheet, taken together with other financial statements, allows financial statement users to assess financial position, risk profile, financial flexibility, liquidity, and rates of return.

2. Most of the amounts on the balance sheet are reporting historical costs, not fair value, which may reduce its relevance for certain decisions. The specific amounts reported are the result of the company's reporting policies. The balance sheet also contains many estimates, excludes assets and liabilities that GAAP deems unrecognizable, and often consolidates financial data from very different types of industry segments. Financial statement users must proceed with caution.

3. Classification of balance sheet items is governed by accounting standards and industry norms and characteristics, but has much room for judgement. Most, but not all, balance sheets classify current assets and current liabilities to facilitate evaluation of short-term liquidity. Other classifications follow the major asset, liability, and equity groups. Elements are often highly condensed and summarized on the balance sheet.

4. Various balance sheet categories have specific display and disclosure requirements in order to meet accounting standards and users' expectations.

5. Disclosure notes provide information regarding accounting policies, describe recognized and unrecognized items, and provide supplemental information regarding future cash flows and fair values.

6. For financial instruments, a company should make appropriate disclosures of accounting policies, fair values, and risk exposure.

7. Important disclosures include segment disclosures, related party transaction data, economic dependence, subsequent events, contingencies and guarantees, and measurement uncertainty. If a company's future is in doubt such that the continuity assumption might not apply, going-concern disclosures are needed.

## KEY TERMS

## REVIEW PROBLEM

The post-closing balance sheet accounts of Ibsen Icons Incorporated at 31 December 20X3 are as follows:

| Account | Debit | Credit |
|---|---|---|
| Cash (overdraft) | | $  3,500 |
| Accounts payable | | 15,000 |
| Future income tax liability—long term | | 30,000 |
| Common shares | | 40,000 |
| Preferred shares | | 24,000 |
| Long-term investment in common shares of Grieg Graphics Inc. | $ 14,000 | |
| Accounts receivable | 19,000 | |
| Loan from shareholder, due 1 July 20X9 | | 40,000 |
| Land | 120,000 | |
| Leasehold improvements (net of amortization) | 30,000 | |
| Furniture and equipment (at cost) | 90,000 | |
| Accumulated amortization, furniture and equipment | | 30,000 |
| Retained earnings—unappropriated | | 75,000 |
| Accumulated other comprehensive income, 1 January 20X3 | 500 | |
| Deferred revenue | | 7,000 |
| Unrealized gain on marketable securities for 20X3 | | 1,500 |
| Instalment notes receivable | 7,500 | |
| Goodwill | 9,000 | |
| Appropriation for restructuring costs | | 20,000 |
| Prepaid expenses | 3,500 | |
| Marketable securities (available for sale) | 5,000 | |
| Note payable to bank, due 15 October 20X4 | | 25,000 |
| Allowance for doubtful accounts | | 2,000 |
| Supplies inventory | 14,500 | |
| | $313,000 | $313,000 |

**Required:**
Prepare a classified balance sheet in good form, using the financing form and the report format.

## REVIEW PROBLEM—SOLUTION

### IBSEN Icons Incorporated Balance Sheet

31 December 20x3

**Assets**

Current assets:

| | | | |
|---|---|---|---|
| Marketable securities | | $ 5,000 | |
| Instalment notes receivable | | 7,500 | |
| Accounts receivable | $19,000 | | |
| Less: allowance for doubtful accounts | 2,000 | 17,000 | |
| Supplies inventory | | 14,500 | |
| Prepaid expenses | | 3,500 | $ 47,500 |

Investments:

| | | | |
|---|---|---|---|
| Investment in Grieg Graphics Inc. | | | 14,000 |

Capital assets:

| | | | |
|---|---|---|---|
| Land | | 120,000 | |
| Furniture and equipment | 90,000 | | |
| Less: accumulated amortization | 30,000 | 60,000 | |
| Leasehold improvements (net) | | 30,000 | |
| Goodwill | | 9,000 | 219,000 |
| Total assets | | | $280,500 |

**Liabilities and shareholders' equity**

Liabilities:

Current liabilities:

| | | |
|---|---|---|
| Bank overdraft | $ 3,500 | |
| Note payable to bank, due 15 October 20X4 | 25,000 | |
| Accounts payable | 15,000 | |
| Deferred revenue | 7,000 | $ 50,500 |

Long-term liabilities:

| | | |
|---|---|---|
| Loan from shareholder, due 1 July 20X9 | 40,000 | |
| Future income tax liability | 30,000 | 70,000 |
| Total liabilities | | 120,500 |

Shareholders' equity:

Contributed capital:

| | | |
|---|---|---|
| Common shares | 40,000 | |
| Preferred shares | 24,000 | 64,000 |

Retained earnings:

| | | |
|---|---|---|
| Appropriated for restructuring costs | 20,000 | |
| Unappropriated | 75,000 | |
| Accumulated other comprehensive income* | 1,000 | 96,000 |
| Total shareholders' equity | | 160,000 |
| Total liabilities and shareholders' equity | | $280,500 |

*$500 Dr. beginning balance combined with $1,500 Cr. gain for 20X3.

Capital assets could be separated into tangible and intangible categories. Deferred revenue and instalment notes receivable are assumed to be within normal business practice for this company and therefore are classified as current.

## QUESTIONS

Q4-1    What is the primary purpose of a balance sheet?

Q4-2    What valuations are reported on the balance sheet?

Q4-3    Describe the limitations of the balance sheet.

Q4-4    Define current assets, current liabilities, and working capital. Must these subtotals be disclosed on the balance sheet?

Q4-5    What items are included in the balance sheet category of cash?

Q4-6    Describe the usual order of current asset accounts in North American balance sheets.

Q4-7    When is an asset non-current?

Q4-8    What does the "investments and funds" caption cover in a balance sheet?

Q4-9    What are capital assets? Distinguish between tangible and intangible capital assets.

Q4-10   Comment on the difficulties associated with evaluating the balance sheet of an entity whose primary assets are intangible.

Q4-11   Why is the caption "other assets" sometimes necessary? Name two items that might be reported under this classification.

Q4-12   Explain the term "deferred charge."

Q4-13   Under what conditions would an amount previously classified as a long-term liability be reclassified as a current liability?

Q4-14   What disclosure should accompany a long-term liability? Why is this disclosure important?

Q4-15   Why is "future income tax" classified as a liability? Why is the account classification subject to question?

Q4-16   Explain the term "non-controlling interest."

Q4-17   When is it proper to offset current liabilities against current assets?

Q4-18   What is owners' equity? What are the main components of owners' equity?

Q4-19   When is debt reclassified as owners' equity?

Q4-20   List the primary types of disclosure notes. Give two examples of each type.

Q4-21   Define financial instruments and identify the three areas of disclosure that are required for financial instruments.

Q4-22   When is a contingency *recognized* versus *disclosed*?

Q4-23   When is a subsequent event *recognized* versus *disclosed*?

Q4-24   What is the purpose of segment disclosures?

Q4-25   Why might the presence of large volumes of related party transactions make it difficult to evaluate a company based on its financial statements?

Q4-26   What is measurement uncertainty? Why must it be disclosed?

Q4-27   Identify some of the differences between balance sheets around the world.

Q4-28   What is the auditors' report? What are its basic components? Why is it especially important to the statement user?

**CASE 4-1**

## WPB LIMITED

The management of WPB Ltd. has spent the past year reorganizing the company's business activities. The company has been a service provider to hospitals, in not only Canada, but also parts of Africa. Originally the company had operated only in Canada, where hospital care is provided at government expense through public health care systems. After demonstrating successful operations, the company subsequently was invited by several African governments to extend its expertise to providing services on that continent, particularly as a result of the intense need for external support that arose from the AIDS crisis. The African operations were supported by the various nations' governments, with additional aid provided through the Stephan Louis Foundation. The Foundation requires WPB to provide audited financial statements each year as a condition for continuing its support.

WPB had been under pressure to decrease the cost of its services to hospitals as a result of severe budget pressure on the governments that bear the ultimate cost of hospital care. The company has consolidated some services, reduced its workforce, and sold some parts of its operations.

It now is 31 December 20X7, the end of the fiscal year. The vice-president—Finance has requested your advice on how certain items should be reflected in the company's financial statements. She has provided you with a description of the items about which she is uncertain (below) and she has requested that you prepare a report in which you recommend appropriate financial statement presentation and note disclosure for each item, in accordance with Canadian and international GAAP.

### Items of Concern

1. In the last quarter of the year, we struck a deal with LaidLow Corporation to take over the ambulance service division that we had acquired in 20X4 from Asper Inc. for $12 million. The deal won't be finalized until 15 March 20X8, dependent on the results of Asper's due diligence inspection. We have operated the division as a separate unit, reporting directly to senior management. We struck the deal on 17 August 20X7. At that time, we estimated that the fair value of the division's assets was $24 million, of which $7 million is current assets, mainly billings receivable from the hospitals and other agencies for which we provided service. We estimated that the fair value of the $17 million non-current assets was $14 million at the end of the third quarter, 30 September 20X7, and we wrote the non-current assets down to that amount. Now, at 31 December, we have good reason to believe that the non-current assets are worth $16 million.

2. We also sold off some of our laboratory facilities to HealthCom Limited. HealthCom paid the purchase price of $5 million in its shares. The value of the HealthCom shares at the end of 20X7 was $5.5 million. We don't intend to hold these shares over the long term.

3. Our facilities in the nation of Albageria were confiscated by the government after a coup and we had to terminate our operations in that country. The facilities cost us $3 million to establish and were carried on our books at $2.7 million at the time of the confiscation. We estimated that the value of the facilities at the date of the confiscation was $4.3 million. We received compensation of $4.0 million from the Canadian federal government's Export Development Corporation (EDC), which had provided us with "political risk" insurance.

4. We have billings receivable of US$13.0 from African countries (not including Albageria). The billings are in U.S. dollars. We have arranged hedges for 90% of that amount. The Canadian dollar equivalent of the receivables at the time of billing was Cdn$14.4 million. At 31 December 20X7, the receivables were the equivalent of $15.3 million.

5. As the result of our restructuring activities during this past year, we estimate that we will have to make severance payments and give resettlement allowances of approximately $2.5 million during 20X8. The amount may vary up or down by $0.6 millon, depending on whether our estimate of voluntary early retirements is correct.

6. We have guaranteed the operating lines of credit of several international agencies that cooperate with us in providing services abroad. The total amount of the guarantees varies, of course, because the draw on the credit lines fluctuates. At year-end 20X7, I'd estimate that our total guarantees come to about $4.2 million. We don't expect any of these agencies to default on their credit obligations, however.

**Required:**
Prepare the report requested by the vice president. Be sure to consider the impacts on all of the year-end 20X7 financial statements.

## CASE 4-2

## BROWN LIMITED

Brown Ltd. is an integrated oilfield service company involved in drilling activities in the Calgary area. The company rents drilling equipment to oil exploration companies; provides crews to staff drill sites; and offers a wide range of testing, maintenance, and well-site services. Brown also manufactures polycrystalline diamond drill bits and various other specialty drilling components.

Brown has been identified as a possible acquisition target by Orion Investments Inc., a multinational public holding company. Orion specializes in acquisitions of undercapitalized companies and those in financial distress. After suitable reorganization and/or capital investment, these investees may be retained as long-term investments, or resold if market conditions appear appropriate.

For the fiscal year ended 31 December 20X2, Brown reported total assets of $2,380 (million), consisting primarily of tangible capital assets (55%), intangible capital assets (goodwill from acquisitions, 18%) and accounts receivable (18%). Net assets (shareholders' equity) in 20X2 was $1,210 (million), increased from the $1,105 reported in 20X1. Financing is through current payables to suppliers, operating lines of credit from the bank, and a modest amount of long-term debt.

You have recently joined Orion as a financial analyst in the mergers and acquisitions group. You are working on the file of Brown Limited. Your current task is to evaluate several disclosure notes provided by Brown, and potentially recalculate net assets. In doing so, you may also comment on the quality and usefulness of note disclosures, and how they reflect on the management team of Brown Company.

**Required:**
Prepare a report to complete the assigned analysis. Brown has a 40% tax rate.

## EXHIBIT 1

### Brown Limited Selected Disclosure Notes

*Measurement uncertainty*
The preparation of financial statement in conformity with Canadian GAAP requires the Company's management to make estimates and assumptions about future events that affect the amounts reported in the financial statements and related notes. Actual results may differ from those estimates.

*Contingencies*
In 20X2, the company received Notices of Reassessment from the income tax officials reconfirming a 20X0 reassessment that required the Company to report, as 20X0 taxable revenue, work done in December 20X0 but not billed until January 20X1. The Company's practice, which is consistent and is in accordance with U.S. industry norms, is to record revenue on a billed basis.

The Company believes it has reported its tax position appropriately, and has filed a Notice of Objection with the Canada Revenue Agency (CRA). No provision has been made in the accounts for additional income tax, if any, which may be determined to be payable.

The amounts in dispute are as follows (in millions):

| | Net Revenue | Income tax Interest and Penalties |
|---|---|---|
| 20X0 and prior | $20.6 | $ 9.9 |
| 20X1 | 1.2 | 0.6 |
| 20X2 | 2.3 | 1.1 |
| | $24.1 | $11.6 |

The provisions of the *Income Tax Act* require the Company to deposit one-half of the amounts in dispute with the CRA. The amount on deposit with the CRA amounts to $5.5 million and is reported as a long-term deferred charge.

*Subsequent event*
On January 21, 20X3, an ice storm of unprecedented proportions damaged certain of the Company's drilling equipment, at risk because of an exposed field location. Equipment with a net book value of $389 (million) as of 31 December 20X2 was destroyed. The Company self-insures for such risks.

*Related party transactions*
The Company has agreements with a company controlled by Brown's CEO for the provision of business development and consulting services. The Company has a marketing agreement with a company controlled by a family member of the chairman of Brown's Board that covers certain products manufactured by the Company. All products in three specific lines are sold to this related company, which then assumes the risks and rewards of resale to third parties. All the above-mentioned transactions are measured at the exchange values, which are amounts established and agreed to by the related parties.

Transaction volumes are as follows (millions):

| | 20X2 | 20X1 |
|---|---|---|
| Sales | $566 | $459 |
| Consulting services | 2.2 | 1.8 |
| Accounts receivable | $239 | $176 |
| Accounts payable | 0.8 | 0.5 |

During the year ended 31 December 20X2, the Company purchased land and improvements for a proposed plant facility from a company controlled by the executive vice-president for $175 million.

## CASE 4-3

## AUTOPART MANUFACTURING LIMITED

Autopart Manufacturing Ltd., incorporated 15 years ago, has grown to be a successful competitor in the cost- and quality-conscious auto parts manufacturing market. Autopart specializes in relatively standard replacement parts sold under store brand labels in hardware stores. Since people are owning cars longer than ever before (now an average of 8.5 years), the auto repair business is a growth sector of the economy.

You've obtained the balance sheet of Autopart Manufacturing Limited, and have analyzed the basic financial structure of the company. You're thinking of investing in Autopart's common shares, but looking at the balance sheet, you are reminded of the definitions of financial statement elements. You've decided to see how well the balance sheet items conform to the definitions. In particular, it's important to explain to yourself exactly why each item is an asset, liability, or equity item. The balance sheet is shown in Exhibit 1, and the notes to the financial statements in Exhibit 2.

### EXHIBIT 1

## Autopart Manufacturing Limited Consolidated Balance Sheet
### (Stated in Thousands of Canadian Dollars)

| 31 December | 20X1 | 20X0 |
|---|---|---|
| **Assets** | | |
| Current assets | | |
| Cash and short-term investments | $ 9,800 | $ 4,390 |
| Accounts receivable | 12,464 | 12,570 |
| Inventories (Note 1) | 15,730 | 14,400 |
| Capital assets | | |
| Property, plant, and equipment (net) (Note 2) | 21,529 | 19,200 |
| Goodwill (Note 3) | 5,100 | 4,750 |
| Licences (Note 4) | 1,640 | 1,490 |
| Other assets | | |
| Future contract costs (Note 5) | 1,950 | 2,300 |
| | $68,213 | $59,100 |
| | | |
| **Liabilities and shareholders' equity** | | |
| Current liabilities: | | |
| Accounts payable and accrued liabilities | $11,384 | $15,875 |
| Current portion of long-term debt | 450 | 475 |
| Other | 615 | 655 |
| Long-term liabilities (Note 6) | 27,190 | 10,580 |
| Commitments payable (Note 7) | — | 1,900 |
| Prepaid contract (Note 8) | 1,650 | 2,900 |
| Future income tax (Note 9) | 950 | 890 |
| Shareholders' equity (Note 10) | 25,974 | 25,825 |
| | $68,213 | $59,100 |

### EXHIBIT 2

## Notes to the Financial Statements ($ thousands)

As of 31 December

*Note 1. Inventories*

| | 20X1 | 20X0 |
|---|---|---|
| Raw materials | $ 6,700 | $ 6,300 |
| Finished goods | 7,700 | 7,200 |
| Supplies | 400 | 380 |
| Returnable containers | 930 | 520 |
| | $15,730 | $14,400 |

*Note 2. Property, Plant, and Equipment (Net)*

| | Cost | Accumulated Amortization | Net Balance, 31 Dec. 20X1 |
|---|---|---|---|
| Land | $    990 | $    — | $    990 |
| Buildings | 5,910 | 696 | 5,214 |
| Machinery and equipment | | | |
| Owned | 11,480 | 2,600 | 8,880 |
| Leased | 3,720 | 200 | 3,520 |
| Furniture and fixtures | 2,600 | 310 | 2,290 |
| Transportation equipment | 1,120 | 485 | 635 |
| | $25,820 | $4,291 | $21,529 |

*Note 3. Goodwill*
During the year ended 31 December 20X1, the company acquired 100% of the shares of Benn Mufflers Limited for $1,240 in cash. Benn Mufflers Limited had tangible assets, at fair value, of $890 on the acquisition date, and goodwill of $350 arose. The opening balance in the goodwill account is from a series of similar acquisitions over the past 12 years.

*Note 4. Licences*
The company manufactures certain autoparts under licence. Licences are acquired for cash at the beginning of the licence period, usually five years.

*Note 5. Future Contract Costs*
The company enters into three-year contracts with retailers, guaranteeing the company a market and specific shelf space for its goods. Payments are made to the retailers to secure these multiyear contracts. The payments are amortized against sales over the term of the related contracts.

*Note 6. Long-Term Liabilities*

| | **20X1** |
|---|---|
| Term bank loans, 8%, maturing in 20X9 | $17,830 |
| Mortgages, 7–10%, maturing 20X3–20X6 | 6,910 |
| Capital leases, 8.5%–14.3%, maturing 20X3–20X9 | 2,900 |
| | $27,640 |
| Less: current portion | 450 |
| | $27,190 |

*Note 7. Commitments Payable*
In 20X0, the company set up a provision of $1,900 for potential losses relating to a guarantee provided for Carburetor King Limited, an associated company. Autoparts had guaranteed a bank loan of Carburetor King, and it appeared in 20X0 that financial difficulties within that company would trigger a payment by Autoparts under the guarantee. In 20X1, Carburetor King was sold and reorganized, and Autoparts was released from its guarantee after a payment of $400,000.

*Note 8. Prepaid Contract*
Certain customers in long-term contracts with the company prepay a portion of the estimated total contract value. This prepayment is taken into income over the life of the contract, in proportion to deliveries.

*Note 9. Future Income Tax*
Certain expenses, primarily depreciation, are reported in different periods for income tax and financial statement reporting purposes. The result is a future tax liability.

*Note 10. Shareholders' Equity*

|  | **20X1** |
| --- | --- |
| Common shares, unlimited shares authorized, 26,837 shares issued | $14,499 |
| Contributed capital from share retirement | 49 |
| Retained earnings | 11,426 |
|  | $25,974 |

## ASSIGNMENTS

★ **A4-1 Balance Sheet Formats:** Hobbit Enterprises Inc. had the following post-closing trial balance on 31 December 20X4:

|  | Debit | Credit |
| --- | --- | --- |
| Cash | $    35,000 |  |
| Accounts receivable | 52,000 |  |
| Notes receivable (long term) | 120,000 |  |
| Inventories | 110,000 |  |
| Equipment | 500,000 |  |
| Accumulated amortization |  | $  300,000 |
| Trademarks | 80,000 |  |
| Long-term investments | 130,000 |  |
| Accounts payable |  | 90,000 |
| Long-term notes payable |  | 200,000 |
| Common shares |  | 250,000 |
| Retained earnings |  | 187,000 |
|  | $1,027,000 | $1,027,000 |

**Required:**

1. Prepare the balance sheet for Hobbit Enterprises by using the report format.
2. Prepare the balance sheet using the net assets form instead.

★ **A4-2 Balance Sheet Classification:** Imposing Ltd. has the following accounts in its year-end 20X7 trial balance:

a. Advances from customers for goods to be shipped in 20X8
b. Accounts payable
c. Security deposit on building lease (refundable at the end of the five-year lease)
d. Cash held in foreign banks (in foreign currencies)
e. Note payable to a supplier, payable in equal instalments over three years (not a usual arrangement)
f. Inventory held in bonded warehouse. The product needs to be aged for five years before being finished and released for sale.
g. Prepaid insurance (covers three years of catastrophe losses, such as earthquakes and tornados)
h. Investment—the marketable securities of another company in which Imposing has significant influence
i. Estimated liability on product warranty (the warranty lasts four years)
j. Income tax payable; the amount is being contested by Imposing

k. Liability under bank operating credit line—the credit line has no maturity as long as impos-ing does not violate any of the bank's requirements, but can be called if there is a violation

l. Investment in short-term money-market instruments

**Required:**

Explain how each item would be reported on Imposing Ltd.'s 20X7 balance sheet.

---

 **A4-3 Balance Sheet Classification:** Consider each of the following separate situations that arose in 20X1:

a. Corporation A has the equivalent of Cdn$200,000 cash in a bank in Elbonia. Elbonia's laws prohibit transferring the cash to the Canadian parent company. Corporation A has ongoing operations in Elbonia.

b. Corporation B has $300,000 in notes receivable from customers. The notes mature over a three-year period. The company normally sells its products on an instalment basis that requires payments over three years.

c. Corporation C has a major customer that recently went into receivership. As a result of an agreement among all creditors, Corporation C will receive payment on the customer's $240,000 outstanding account over a four-year period.

d. Corporation D has negotiated a $600,000 loan from its bank to finance equipment. The loan will be repaid in a lump sum in two years. The bank will charge 6% interest, com-pounded, which is the market rate of interest.

e. Corporation E invested $55,000 in corporate bonds as a short-term investment. The year-end 20X1 market value of the bonds is $58,000.

f. Corporation F paid $330,000 into the employees' pension plan. The company will recog-nize the pension expense over future years.

g. Corporation G received $72,000 from a customer as advance payment for special-order goods to be delivered in 20X2.

h. Corporation H holds 10,000 shares in Theo Limited; the shares cost $14 each. At year-end 20X1, the market value is $20 per share. Corporation H intends to hold the shares for a long time.

**Required:**

For each item indicate the amount(s) that will shown as current and the amount(s) that will shown as non-current in each company's 20X1 balance sheet.

---

 **A4-4 Balance Sheet Formats:** The following list of accounts and balances pertains to Mon-ish Corporation on 31 December 20X3, the end of the company's annual accounting period:

| | |
|---|---:|
| Accounts payable | $ 56,000 |
| Accounts receivable | 74,000 |
| Accumulated amortization—furniture and fixtures | 20,000 |
| Advances from customers (pertaining to goods that Monish will supply in 20X4) | 12,000 |
| Allowance for doubtful accounts | 3,600 |
| Bank loan payable, payable 10 July 20X4 | 50,000 |
| Bond sinking fund | 180,000 |
| Bonds payable (8%, due 1 January 20X16) | 300,000 |
| Cash | 52,000 |
| Common shares | 80,000 |
| Contributed capital, gain on redemption of preferred shares | 70,000 |
| Franchise (net) | 172,000 |
| Furniture and fixtures | 190,000 |
| Merchandise inventory | 96,400 |
| Preferred shares | 30,000 |
| Premium on bonds payable | 8,000 |
| Prepaid insurance | 16,800 |
| Retained earnings (to be determined) | ? |

**Required:**
Prepare a balance sheet using the following formats:

1. Financing form, report form
2. Net assets form

---

★ **A4-5 Balance Sheet Classification:** A typical balance sheet has the following classifications:

A. Current assets
B. Investments and funds
C. Tangible capital assets (property, plant, and equipment)
D. Intangible capital assets
E. Other assets
F. Deferred charges
G. Current liabilities
H. Long-term liabilities
I. Share capital (common or preferred)
J. Accumulated other comprehensive income
K. Additional contributed capital
L. Debt elements that have the characteristics of equity
M. Retained earnings

___–C___   1. Accumulated depreciation

_____   2. Bonds payable (due in 10 years)

_____   3. Accounts payable (trade)

_____   4. Prepaid insurance

_____   5. Land (in use)

_____   6. Restriction or appropriation of retained earnings

_____   7. Office supplies inventory

_____   8. Investment in marketable securities (held as temporary use of cash)

_____   9. Loan to company president (collection not expected for two years)

_____  10. Accumulated income less accumulated dividends

_____  11. Investment in shares of X Company (long term)

_____  12. Unamortized bond discount (on bonds payable; a debit balance)

_____  13. Bond sinking fund (to retire long-term bonds)

_____  14. Trademarks

_____  15. Accounts receivable (trade)

_____  16. Allowance for doubtful accounts

_____  17. Building (held for sale)

_____  18. Cumulative effect (gain) due to change in accounting policy

_____  19. Bonds payable (principal payments may be made by issuing common shares at the investor's request)

_____  20. Interest accrued on long-term debt but not yet paid

_____  21. Translation gain on foreign subsidiary

_____  22. Land, held for investment

**Required:**
Use the code letters above to indicate the usual classification for each balance sheet item listed. If an item is a contra amount (i.e., a deduction) under a caption, place a minus sign before the lettered response. The first item is completed for you as an example.

★ **A4-6 Balance Sheet Classification:** Serious Corp. is a magazine publisher. The company has the following categories on its 31 December 20X5 balance sheet:

A. Current assets
B. Investments
C. Property, plant, and equipment
D. Intangible assets
E. Other assets
F. Current liabilities
G. Long-term liabilities
H. Share capital
I. Accumulated other comprehensive income
J. Other contributed capital
K. Retained earnings

_____  1. Unearned magazine subscriptions received
_____  2. Discount on bonds payable, due in 20X6
_____  3. Unrealized gain on securities held for resale
_____  4. Bonds payable due in 20X9; Serious intends to redeem the bonds early in 20X6
_____  5. Advances to suppliers
_____  6. Subscription lists purchased
_____  7. Preferred shares issued
_____  8. Rare coins
_____  9. Gain on redemption of preferred shares
_____  10. Future income tax liability relating to capital assets
_____  11. Cumulative effect of a change in accounting policy
_____  12. Loss on discontinued operation
_____  13. Allowance for decline in market value of inventory
_____  14. Operating expenses for the current year
_____  15. Machinery retired and held for resale
_____  16. Dividends declared, to be paid 31 January 20X6
_____  17. Account receivable from company president; to be repaid in two years' time

**Required:**
Indicate where each of the following items would be classified. If the item is not on the balance sheet, enter an X.

★★ **A4-7 Balance Sheet Classification:** Typical balance sheet items are as follows:

A. Current assets
B. Investments and funds
C. Tangible capital assets (property, plant, and equipment)
D. Intangible assets
E. Other assets
F. Deferred charges
G. Current liabilities
H. Long-term liabilities
I. Debt elements that are equity
J. Contributed capital, share capital, and other
K. Retained earnings

Typical balance sheet items are as follows:

_____  1. Cash

_____  2. Cash set aside to meet long-term purchase commitment

_____  3. Land (used as plant site)

_____  4. Accrued salaries

_____  5. Investment in the common shares of another company (long term; not a controlling interest)

_____  6. Inventory of damaged goods

_____  7. Idle plant

_____  8. Assets of discontinued operations held for resale

_____  9. Preferred shares that have guaranteed redemption for cash

_____ 10. Goodwill

_____ 11. Natural resource (e.g., a timber tract)

_____ 12. Allowance for doubtful accounts

_____ 13. Investment in bonds of another company

_____ 14. Lump sum prepayment of office lease for next three years

_____ 15. Discount on bonds payable

_____ 16. Service revenue collected in advance

_____ 17. Accrued interest payable

_____ 18. Accumulated amortization on patent

_____ 19. Prepaid rent

_____ 20. Short-term investment (common shares)

_____ 21. Rent revenue collected but not earned

_____ 22. Net amount of accumulated revenues, gains, expenses, losses, and dividends

_____ 23. Trade accounts payable

_____ 24. Current maturity of long-term debt

_____ 25. Long-term debt that may be convertible to common shares

_____ 26. Bond issue costs

_____ 27. Special cash fund accumulated to build plant five years hence

_____ 28. Bonds issued—to be repaid within six months out of bond sinking fund

_____ 29. Long-term investment in rental building

_____ 30. Copyright

_____ 31. Accumulated amortization

_____ 32. Advance payment on special-order equipment to be delivered in two years

_____ 33. Franchise

_____ 34. Revenue earned but not collected

_____ 35. Premium on bonds payable (unamortized)

_____ 36. Common shares (no par)

_____ 37. Petty cash fund

_____ 38. Deficit

_____ 39. Contributed capital on share retirement

_____ 40. Earnings retained in the business

**Required:**

Enter the appropriate letter for each item to indicate its usual classification on the balance sheet. When it is a contra item (i.e., a deduction), place a minus sign before the lettered response.

(AICPA, adapted)

★★     **A4-8 Setting up the Balance Sheet:** Below is a typical chart of accounts (in alphabetical order) for Altar Paving Corporation for 20X5.

Accounts payable
Accounts receivable
Accrued expenses
Accumulated amortization, all intangible assets
Accumulated depreciation, all tangible assets
Allowance for decline in value of marketable securities
Allowance for doubtful accounts
Amortization expense
Bad debt expense
Bonds payable
Bond sinking fund
Buildings
Cash
Common shares
Contributed capital from share retirement
Cost of goods sold
Depreciation expense
Discount on bonds payable
Dividends payable
Equipment
Finished goods
Future income tax liability
Gain on sale of marketable securities
General and administrative expense
Goodwill
Income tax expense
Income tax payable
Interest payable
Investment in common shares, not intended for resale
Land
Licences
Loss on sale of land
Marketable securities
Miscellaneous expense
Overhead
Patents
Prepaid expense
Purchases
Raw materials
Restricted cash for long-term debt retirement
Retained earnings
Sales revenue
Travel and entertainment expense
Wages expense
Wages payable
Work in process

**Required:**

Prepare a blank, classified balance sheet in proper form using the financing format. Include all balance sheet accounts—do not summarize.

★★     **A4-9 Determining Values in the Balance Sheet:** The consolidated balance sheet of Mutron Lock Incorporated, is shown below.

## Mutron Lock Incorporated Consolidated Balance Sheet

As of 31 December 20X5

**Assets**

Current assets

| | | |
|---|---|---|
| Cash and cash equivalents | | $ 10,195 |
| Marketable securities | | a |
| Accounts receivable | $153,682 | |
| Allowance for doubtful accounts | b | 147,421 |
| Inventories | | 201,753 |
| Prepaid expenses | | 8,902 |
| Total current assets | | c |

Capital assets

| | | |
|---|---|---|
| Land | | 12,482 |
| Building (net) | | d |
| Equipment and machinery | 195,467 | |
| Accumulated depreciation | (103,675) | 91,792 |
| Total capital assets | | 261,056 |
| Investments | | 14,873 |
| Other assets | | 7,926 |
| Total assets | | $661,774 |

**Liabilities and Shareholders' Equity**

Current liabilities

| | |
|---|---|
| Accounts payable | $ 85,476 |
| Notes payable | e |
| Income taxes payable | 6,421 |
| Current portion of long-term debt | 4,893 |
| Accrued expenses | 5,654 |
| Total current liabilities | 110,763 |
| Long-term debt | 122,004 |
| Future income taxes | f |
| Non-controlling interest | 35,136 |
| Total liabilities | g |

Shareholders' equity

| | |
|---|---|
| Preferred shares, no-par value (authorized 10,000 shares, issued 2,400 shares for $14,281) | h |
| Common shares, no-par value (authorized 400,000 shares, issued 20,000 shares) | i |
| Total contributed capital | j |
| Retained earnings | 206,471 |
| Total shareholders' equity | 347,668 |
| Total liabilities and shareholders' equity | $          k |

**Required:**

1. For each of the items (a) through (k) in the balance sheet above, calculate the amount that should appear for that item.

2. What kinds of notes would be commonly found for each balance sheet item? Select from the following list:
    i. Financial instruments: disclosure of terms and conditions
    ii. Financial instruments: disclosure of interest rates, including effective rates
    iii. Financial instruments: disclosure of credit risk
    iv. Financial instruments: disclosure of fair value, by class
    v. Breakdown of accounts aggregated to arrive at a balance sheet total
    vi. Disclosure of accounting policy
    vii. Details of changes during the period

★ **A4-10 Financial Statement Classification:** The first list below shows the financial statements normally included in a company's annual financial statements. The second list shows some amounts that often appear in those financial statements.

A. Balance sheet
B. Income statement
C. Cash flow statement
D. Statement of changes in retained earnings
E. Statement of comprehensive income
F. Statement of changes in accumulated other comprehensive income

| B, C, D, E | 1. Net income |
| :---: | :--- |
| _____ | 2. Retained earnings (opening) |
| _____ | 3. Bond premium |
| _____ | 4. Factory reorganization costs |
| _____ | 5. Cumulative translation gain or loss |
| _____ | 6. Dividends declared and paid |
| _____ | 7. Appropriation for bond sinking fund |
| _____ | 8. Loss on discontinued operation |
| _____ | 9. Bond sinking fund |
| _____ | 10. Accrued pension liability |
| _____ | 11. Unrealized gains/losses on hedge derivatives |
| _____ | 12. Cumulative effect of change in accounting policy |
| _____ | 13. Proceeds from issuance of common shares |
| _____ | 14. Factory building held for sale |
| _____ | 15. Deferred pension cost |

**Required:**
Use the letters given in the first list to indicate the financial statement on which each item in the second list will appear. Comment on any doubtful items. Some letters may be used more than once or not at all. The first item is completed for you as an example.

★★ **A4-11 Financial Statement Classification:** A company's financial statements normally include the following:

A. Balance sheet
B. Statement of earnings
C. Statement of changes in retained earnings
D. Statement of comprehensive income
E. Statement of changes in accumulated other comprehensive income

The following account balances appear on Sirus Limited's adjusted trial balance at 31 December 20X3:

a. Common shares
b. Adjustment for cumulative effect to 1 January 20X3 of a change in accounting policy
c. Unrealized gain for 20X3 on available-for-sale investments
d. Dividends declared on 20 December 20X3, payable on 20 January 20X4
e. Loss on operations of discontinued operation
f. Capital assets held for sale
g. Gain on retirement of long-term debt
h. Appropriation for plant expansion
i. Change in translation gain/loss on French subsidiary
j. Current income tax payable
k. Future income taxes relating to plant, property, and equipment

  l. Non-controlling interest in subsidiaries
 m. Goodwill
  n. Net income
  o. Correction of understatement made in counting inventory at year-end 20X2
  p. Allowance to reduce inventory to net realizable value
  q. Gain on government expropriation of land
  r. Reclassification to net income of previously unrealized gains on available-for-sale investments purchased in 20X1 and sold in 20X3

**Required:**

For each account, indicate the financial statement(s) on which it will appear. Use the letter keys (A, B, etc.) in the first list to indicate the correct financial statement. If an item appears on more than one financial statement, use more than one letter.

---

★  **A4-12 Valuation on the Balance Sheet:** The first list below shows the measurement or valuation approaches commonly used for reporting individual items on the balance sheet. The second list indicates some items from a typical balance sheet of a corporation.

 A. Amount payable or receivable when due (usually no interest is involved because of the short term)
 B. Lower of cost or NRV
 C. Original cost when acquired
 D. Fair market value at date of the balance sheet
 E. Original cost less accumulated amortization
 F. Amount received on sale or issuance
 G. Face amount of the obligation adjusted for unamortized premium or discount
 H. Accumulated income less accumulated losses and dividends
 I. None of the above (when this response is used, explain the valuation approach usually used)

| Valuation | Balance Sheet Items |
|---|---|
| __B__ | 1. Land (held as an investment) |
| _____ | 2. Merchandise inventory, FIFO |
| _____ | 3. Short-term investments |
| _____ | 4. Accounts receivable (trade) |
| _____ | 5. Long-term investment in bonds of another company held to maturity (purchased at a discount; the discount is a credit balance) |
| _____ | 6. Land used as a plant site (in use) |
| _____ | 7. Plant and equipment (in use) |
| _____ | 8. Patent (in use) |
| _____ | 9. Accounts payable (trade) |
| _____ | 10. Bonds payable (sold at a premium; the premium is a credit balance) |
| _____ | 11. Common shares, no par |
| _____ | 12. Prepaid expenses |
| _____ | 13. Retained earnings |
| _____ | 14. Land (future plant site; not in use) |
| _____ | 15. Idle plant (awaiting disposal) |
| _____ | 16. Natural resource (in use) |

**Required:**

Use the letters given in the first list to indicate the usual measurement method (or valuation method) commonly used in the balance sheet for each item in the second list. Comment on any doubtful items. Some letters may be used more than once or not at all. The first item is completed for you as an example.

★★    **A4-13 Prepare a Balance Sheet:** The following trial balance was prepared by Vantage Electronics Corporation as of 31 December 20X5. The adjusting entries for 20X5 have been made, except for any specifically noted in the information below.

### Vantage Electronics Trial Balance

31 December 20X5

| | | |
|---|---:|---:|
| Cash | $15,000 | |
| Accounts receivable | 15,000 | |
| Inventories | 17,000 | |
| Equipment | 22,400 | |
| Land | 6,400 | |
| Building | 7,600 | |
| Deferred charges | 1,100 | |
| Accounts payable | | $ 5,500 |
| Note payable, 10% | | 8,000 |
| Share capital, no par, 2,500 shares outstanding | | 38,500 |
| Retained earnings | | 32,500 |
| Totals | $84,500 | $84,500 |

*Other information:*
You find that certain errors and omissions are reflected in the trial balance below:

a. The $15,000 balance in accounts receivable represents the entire amount owed to the company; of this amount, $12,400 is from trade customers and 5% of that amount is estimated to be uncollectible. The remaining amount owed to the company represents a long-term advance to its president.

b. Inventories include $1,000 of goods incorrectly valued at double their cost (i.e., reported at $2,000). No correction has been recorded. Office supplies on hand of $500 are also included in the balance of inventories.

c. When the equipment and building were purchased new on 1 January 20X0 (i.e., six years earlier), they had estimated lives of 10 and 25 years, respectively. They have been amortized using the straight-line method on the assumption of zero residual value, and depreciation has been credited directly to the asset accounts. Amortization has been recorded for 20X5.

d. The balance in the land account includes a $1,000 payment made as a deposit on the purchase of an adjoining tract. The option to buy it has not yet been exercised and probably will not be exercised during the coming year.

e. The interest-bearing note dated 1 April 20X5 matures 31 March 20X6. Interest on it has not been recorded for 20X5.

**Required:**

1. Prepare a balance sheet with appropriate captions and subcaptions. Use preferred terminology and the financing report form format. Show the computation of the ending balance in retained earnings.

2. How would your balance sheet be different if the net assets form were used? The account format? Explain, do not illustrate.

---

★★    **A4-14 Prepare Balance Sheet, Analytical Questions:** The data on the following page is from the accounts of Fleury Corporation on 31 December 20X5, the end of the current reporting year.

**Required:**

1. Prepare a complete balance sheet. Assume that all amounts are correct, and round to the nearest thousand dollars. Use the account titles as given.

2. Refer to your response to requirement (1) and respond to the following:
   a. Give the amount of working capital.
   b. By what percent was the building amortized?
   c. How much of the company is financed by debt, and how much by equity?
   d. What are the more important assets of the company?

|  | Dr. | Cr. |
|---|---|---|
| Cash | $    116,000 | |
| Accounts receivable, trade | 337,000 | |
| Short-term investment in marketable securities | 440,000 | |
| Inventory of merchandise, FIFO | 1,295,000 | |
| Prepaid expense (short term) | 11,000 | |
| Bond sinking fund (to pay bonds at maturity) | 147,000 | |
| Advances to suppliers (short term) | 24,000 | |
| Dividends (cash) declared during 20X5 | 120,000 | |
| Rent receivable | 34,000 | |
| Investment in shares of Life Systems Corporation | | |
| (long term, at market) | 322,000 | |
| Unamortized discount on bonds payable | 42,000 | |
| Loans to employees (company president; | | |
| payment date uncertain) | 225,000 | |
| Land (building site in use) | 3,300,000 | |
| Building | 7,450,000 | |
| Equipment | 3,236,000 | |
| Franchise (used in operations) (net) | 610,000 | |
| Deferred equipment rearrangement cost | | |
| (long term) | 74,000 | |
| Total debits | $17,783,000 | |
| Mortgage payable (due 20X9 14%) | | $ 6,500,000 |
| Accounts payable, trade | | 426,000 |
| Dividends (cash) payable (payable 1 March 20X6) | | 10,000 |
| Deferred rent revenue | | 63,000 |
| Future income tax | | 544,000 |
| Accumulated amortization, building | | 4,210,000 |
| Accumulated amortization, equipment | | 420,000 |
| Allowance for doubtful accounts | | 32,000 |
| Bonds payable (12.5%, maturity 20X13) | | 2,200,000 |
| Common shares (50,000 shares outstanding) | | 1,400,000 |
| Preferred shares (8,000 shares outstanding) | | 400,000 |
| Retained earnings, 1 January 20X5 | | 1,190,000 |
| Net income for 20X5 | | 388,000 |
| Total credits | | $17,783,000 |

---

★ **A4-15 Analyzing Data and Reporting on the Balance Sheet:** Akeman Seed Corporation is preparing its balance sheet at 31 December 20X5. The following items are under consideration:

a. Note payable, long term, $80,000. This note was issued on 1 August 20X5 and will be paid in eight equal instalments. The first instalment, $10,000, will be paid 1 January 20X6.
b. Bonds payable, 10%, $200,000, maturing 31 December 20X9. Unamortized premium amounted to $6,000 at the end of 20X5.
c. Bond sinking fund, $40,000; this fund is being accumulated to retire the bonds at maturity.
d. Rent paid in advance for the first quarter of 20X6, $16,000.
e. After the balance sheet date, but prior to issuance of the 20X5 balance sheet, 40% of the merchandise inventory was destroyed by flood (13 January 20X6); the loss is estimated at $125,000.

f. Long-term note payable, $500,000, maturing 30 June 20X6. At maturity, the investor may choose to receive cash or the equivalent amount in market value of common shares. Interest at 8% must be paid 30 June each year.

g. Redeemable preferred shares, $300,000. At maturity, the company has to repay investors the stated value of the shares plus dividends in arrears, if any.

**Required:**

Show by illustration, with appropriate captions, how each of these items should be reported on the 31 December 20X5 balance sheet. If amounts are not quantifiable, describe the appropriate reporting that would be followed when numbers are available.

 **A4-16 Redraft a Deficient Balance Sheet:** Rutgers e-Terminal Limited is a private corporation that is wholly owned by Mr. Adonis Rutgers. Mr. Rutgers also personally owns 40% of the common shares of a company named Princeton Corporation. A further 20% of the Princeton common shares are held by Rutgers e-Terminal Limited. The bookkeeper for Rutgers e-Terminal prepared the following balance sheet:

## RUTGERS E-TERMINAL LIMITED

### Financial Situation

For the year ending 31 December 20X3

| | | |
|---|---:|---:|
| *Short-term assets* | | |
| Cash on hand | $    600 | |
| Cash in the Royal Dominion chequing account | 15,200 | |
| Overdraft in the ScotiaTrust chequing account | −3,800 | |
| Accounts receivable (includes credit balances of $22,000) | 52,600 | |
| Automobile held for resale, fully depreciated (estimated market value, $10,000) | 10,000 | |
| Supplies on hand, at cost | 1,800 | |
| Inventory, at cost (estimated market value, $35,000) | 37,900 | |
| Final month's rent on office space (lease expires in 20X7) | 3,000 | |
| Investment in shares of subsidiary (market value, $150,000) | 130,000 | |
| | | $247,300 |
| *Long-term assets* | | |
| Furniture | 40,000 | |
| Warehouse | 500,000 | |
| Prepaid expenses | 4,500 | |
| Note receivable from customer (issued 5 March 20X1, due on Mr. Rutger's demand) | 30,000 | |
| Loan receivable from shareholder | 120,000 | 694,500 |
| *Total financial assets* | | $941,800 |
| *Liabilities* | | |
| Payable to suppliers | $175,300 | |
| Amounts on purchase orders issued | 50,000 | |
| Reserve for depreciation on furniture | 10,000 | |
| Reserve for depreciation on warehouse | 75,000 | |
| Mortgage due to the Montreal National Bank | 380,000 | |
| Common shares of Rutgers e-Terminal held by Mr. Rutgers | 150,000 | |
| Accumulated surplus | 101,500 | |
| *Total financial liabilities* | | $941,800 |

**Required:**
Prepare a corrected classified balance sheet, using appropriate terminology.

★★★ **A4-17 Criticize and Redraft a Deficient Balance Sheet:** The most recent balance sheet of Blackstone Tire Corporation appears below:

### Blackstone Tire Corporation Balance Sheet

For the year ended 31 December 20X5

*Assets*

| | | | |
|---|---|---|---|
| Current | | | |
| Cash | | | $ 23,000 |
| Short-term investments | | | 10,000 |
| Accounts receivable | | | 15,000 |
| Merchandise | | | 31,000 |
| Supplies | | | 5,000 |
| Shares of Wilmont Co. (not a controlling interest) | | | 17,000 |
| | | | $101,000 |
| Investments | | | |
| Loan to shareholder | | | 82,500 |
| Tangible: | | | |
| Building and land ($10,000) | $86,000 | | |
| Less: reserve for depreciation | 40,000 | 46,000 | |
| Equipment | $20,000 | | |
| Less: reserve for depreciation | 15,000 | 5,000 | 51,000 |
| Deferred | | | |
| Prepaid expenses | | | 5,000 |
| Total | | | $239,500 |

*Debt and Capital*

| | | | |
|---|---|---|---|
| Current | | | |
| Accounts payable | | $16,000 | |
| Reserve for future, deferred income tax | | 17,000 | |
| Customers' accounts receivable with credit balance | | 100 | $ 33,100 |
| Fixed (interest paid at year-end): | | | |
| Bonds payable, 8.5%, due 20X9 | | 45,000 | |
| Mortgage, 11% | | 12,000 | 57,000 |
| Reserve for bad debts | | | 900 |
| Capital | | | |
| Preferred shares, authorized and outstanding, 6,000 redeemable shares. Must be repaid in 20X9 | | 50,000 | |
| Common shares, authorized 10,000 shares, no par | | 67,000 | |
| Earned surplus | | 22,500 | |
| Donated capital | | 9,000 | 148,500 |
| Total | | | $239,500 |

**Required:**

1. List and explain in writing your criticisms of the above statement.
2. Prepare a complete balance sheet as far as possible; use appropriate format, captions, and terminology.

★★ **A4-18 Redraft a Balance Sheet:** Prime Essentials Limited is a small private corporation. The owner plans to approach the bank for an additional loan or a line of credit to facilitate expansion. The company bookkeeper, after discussion with the owner of the company, has prepared the following draft balance sheet for the fiscal year ended 30 September 20X3, the company's first full year of operations:

## PRIME ESSENTIALS LIMITED

### Balance Sheet

Year Ended 30 September 20X3

| | |
|---|---:|
| **Assets** | |
| Cash in the bank | $   9,000 |
| Patent | 25,000 |
| Goodwill | 50,000 |
| Equipment | 100,000 |
| Amounts owed by customers | 27,000 |
| Stocks and bonds owned by the company | 8,000 |
| Total | $219,000 |
| | |
| **Financing Sources for Assets** | |
| Amounts owed to suppliers | 34,000 |
| Amount owed to owner for automobile expenses | 4,000 |
| Amount owed to owner's brother-in-law | 14,000 |
| Amount owed to bank | 16,000 |
| Earnings accumulated in the business | 19,000 |
| Shares paid for by owner | 50,000 |
| Cash flow from used-up portion of equipment | 20,000 |
| Increases in value | 62,000 |
| Total | $219,000 |

The bookkeeper has provided some notes on the amounts included in the draft balance sheet:

a. The owner invested $50,000 of his own money to start the business.

b. The patent was purchased from the owner's brother-in-law for $13,000. The owner believes that the patent could easily be sold for $25,000, and probably more.

c. The equipment is being depreciated at the same rate as allowed for income tax. Depreciation represents a source of financing for the company because it is added back to net income and increases the operating cash flow.

d. The owner uses his personal automobile for occasional business errands. He estimates that the company owes him $4,000 for his use of his personal car.

e. Because the business has been profitable from the very first, the owner estimates that he could sell the company at a $50,000 premium, thereby doubling the return on his initial investment after only one year.

f. The bank gave a five-year loan to the company, with the proviso that the company had to maintain a 25% "compensating balance" in its cash account until the loan is repaid.

g. The company holds some shares in other companies. These shares are traded on the New York Stock Exchange. The value of these securities was US$8,000 when they were given to the company on 1 April 20X3 by the owner's brother-in-law as a loan. The securities originally cost the brother-in-law US$5,000, for which he paid Cdn$6,000. On 30 September 20X3, their market value was US$10,000. The brother-in-law also lent $6,000 cash to the company, repayable on demand. The company is free to sell the securities, but all of the profit must be returned to the brother-in-law.

h. One of the customers is a bit unsteady, financially. That customer owes $2,000.

**Required:**

Redraft the balance sheet. Provide an explanation for each change that you make. Explain any note disclosures that you think are needed.

**A4-19 Full Set of Statements—Comprehensive Income:** Amana Cement Corporation is a private corporation controlled by Amin Amana. The company's adjusted trial balance and other related data at 31 December 20X5 are given below. Although the company uses some obsolete terminology, the amounts are correct. As is permitted under differential reporting, Amana does not prepare consolidated statements by written consent of all of the shareholders.

## AMANA CEMENT CORPORATION

## Adjusted Trial Balance

31 December 20X5

| Debit Balance Accounts | |
|---|---:|
| Cash | $ 38,600 |
| Land (used for building site) | 129,000 |
| Cost of goods sold | 150,000 |
| Short-term securities, at market (cost, $32,000) | 42,000 |
| Investment in U.S. subsidiary | 100,000 |
| Goodwill | 120,000 |
| Merchandise inventory | 29,000 |
| Office supplies inventory | 2,000 |
| Patent | 7,000 |
| Operating expenses | 55,000 |
| Income tax expense | 17,500 |
| Bond discount (unamortized) | 7,500 |
| Prepaid insurance | 900 |
| Building (at cost) | 150,000 |
| Land (held for speculation) | 75,000 |
| Translation loss on U.S. subsidiary, 31 December 20X4 | 12,000 |
| Accrued interest receivable | 300 |
| Accounts receivable (trade) | 22,700 |
| Note receivable, 10% (long-term investment) | 30,000 |
| Subscriber lists (net) | 22,000 |
| Prepayments to pension fund in advance of expensing (long-term) | 26,000 |
| Dividends declared in 20X5, payable in 20X6 | 15,000 |
| Correction of error from prior year—no income tax effect | 15,000 |
| | $1,066,500 |

| Credit Balance Accounts | |
|---|---:|
| Reserve for bad debts | $ 1,100 |
| Accounts payable (trade) | 15,000 |
| Revenues | 275,000 |
| 20X5 translation gain on U.S. subsidiary | 15,000 |
| Deferred income tax | 47,500 |
| Note payable (short term) | 12,000 |
| Common shares, no par, 10,000 shares outstanding | 160,000 |
| Reserve for depreciation, building | 90,000 |
| Retained earnings, 1 January 20X5 | 188,500 |
| Unrealized gain on short-term securities | 10,000 |
| Gain on new accounting policy | 40,000 |
| Accrued wages | 2,100 |
| Non-controlling interest (balance sheet account) | 10,000 |
| Reserve for patent amortization | 4,000 |
| Cash advance from customer | 3,000 |
| Accrued property taxes | 800 |
| Note payable (long term) | 16,000 |
| Rent revenue collected in advance | 1,500 |
| Bonds payable, 11% ($25,000 due 1 June 20X6) | 175,000 |
| | $1,066,500 |

*Additional information* (no accounting errors are involved):

a. Merchandise inventory is based on FIFO, lower of cost or market.
b. The patent is being amortized (written off) over a 10-year period. The amortization for 20X5 has already been recorded.
c. Operating expenses as given include amortization and interest expense, and revenues include interest and investment revenues.
d. The "cash advance from customer" was for a special order that will not be completed and shipped until March 20X6; the sales price has not been definitely established because it is to be based on cost (no revenue should be recognized for 20X5).

**Required:**
Prepare a (1) single-step income statement, (2) statement of comprehensive income, (3) statement of accumulated other comprehensive income, (4) retained earnings statement and (5) balance sheet (not consolidated). Include EPS disclosures.

---

 **A4-20 Income Statement and Balance Sheet—Disclosure:** The adjusted trial balance for Decca Industries Corporation at 31 December 20X5 is given below in no particular order. Debits and credits are not indicated; however, debits equal credits. All amounts are correct.

| | |
|---|---:|
| Work-in-process inventory | $ 87,000 |
| Accrued interest on notes payable | 3,000 |
| Accrued interest receivable | 3,600 |
| Accrued interest on short-term investments | 3,000 |
| Common shares, no par, 120,000 shares issued | 450,000 |
| Cash in bank | 90,000 |
| Trademarks (amortized cost) | 4,200 |
| Land held for speculation | 81,000 |
| Supplies inventory | 1,800 |
| Goodwill | 54,000 |
| Raw materials inventory | 39,000 |
| Bond sinking fund | 30,000 |
| Accrued property taxes | 4,200 |
| Accounts receivable (trade) | 87,000 |
| Accrued wages | 6,300 |
| Mortgage payable (due in three years) | 30,000 |
| Building | 390,000 |
| Cash equivalent short-term investments, at market value | 5,700 |
| Deposits (cash collected from customers on sales orders to be delivered next quarter: no revenue yet recognized) | 3,000 |
| Long-term investment in bonds of Royal Corp. (at amortized cost) | 150,000 |
| Patents (amortized cost) | 42,000 |
| Reserve for depreciation, office equipment | 11,400 |
| Reserve for depreciation, building | 15,000 |
| Cash on hand for change | 1,200 |
| Preferred shares, $1, no par, authorized 40,000 shares, issued 18,000 shares, non-cumulative, non-convertible | 204,000 |
| Pre-collected rent income | 2,700 |
| Finished goods inventory | 129,000 |
| Notes receivable (short term) | 12,000 |
| Bonds payable, 12% (due in six years) | 105,000 |
| Future income tax liability | 45,000 |
| Accounts payable (trade) | 51,000 |
| Reserve for bad credits | 4,200 |

| Notes payable (short term) | 21,600 |
| Office equipment | 105,000 |
| Land (used as building site) | 24,000 |
| Short-term investments (at market) | 46,500 |
| Retained earnings (1 January 20X5) | 69,600 |
| Cash dividends, declared and paid during 20X5 | 60,000 |
| Revenues during 20X5 | 1,500,000 |
| Cost of goods sold for 20X5 | 900,000 |
| Expenses for 20X5 (including interest, amortization, and income tax) | 300,000 |
| Income taxes payable | 120,000 |

**Required:**

1. Prepare a single-step income statement; use preferred terminology. Include EPS disclosure; to compute EPS, deduct $18,000 from net income as an allocation to non-convertible preferred shares and then divide by the common shares outstanding.

2. Prepare a complete balance sheet; use preferred terminology, format, captions, and subcaptions. Indicate likely note disclosure.

3. Assume that between 31 December 20X5, and issuance of the financial statements, a flood damaged the finished goods inventory in an amount estimated to be $60,000. How should this event be reflected in the 20X5 financial statements?

★ **A4-21 Note Disclosures:** Note disclosures provide the following information:

1. Provide accounting policy information (information to evaluate data and make comparisons).
2. Provide information regarding future cash flows.
3. Provide alternative measurement information.
4. Help assess return on investment.
5. Describe recognized items.
6. Describe unrecognized items.

   Typical notes include:

   __5__ a. Description of income statement item, discontinued operations
   _____ b. Consolidation policy
   _____ c. Revenue recognition policy
   _____ d. Breakdown of balance sheet total for other assets.
   _____ e. Preferred share dividend rate
   _____ f. Description of contingent loss that is not measurable
   _____ g. Amortization policy and amounts of accumulated amortization by asset class
   _____ h. Details of outstanding stock options (not recorded in the financial statements)
   _____ i. Inventory note—breakdown of inventory into component parts and description of valuation method
   _____ j. Description of related party transactions
   _____ k. Information on key operating segments of the business
   _____ l. Description of subsequent event not relating to conditions before balance sheet date
   _____ m. Long-term debt note—interest rates, terms to maturity, five-year cash flow, market value
   _____ n. Fair value of debt

**Required:**
For each note (a) to (n) above, indicate the type(s) of disclosure (numbers (1) to (6)) provided. A note may provide more than one type of disclosure. The first one is done for you as an example.

**A4-22 Contingencies:** Unlimited Possibilities Limited (UPL) is finalizing the financial statements for 20X5. The company's managers are uncertain how each of the following events and situations should be reported:

a. The company introduced a major new product in the last quarter of the year. Initial sales were $5 million in 20X5. The product carries a two-year replacement guarantee. By the end of 20X5, 0.5% of the units sold had been returned for replacement, at a total cost to UPL of $10,000. Management estimates that return will continue at that rate for the next two quarters, and then taper off over the remainder of the guarantee period.

b. The company owns a lot adjacent to its building that once was the site of a gasoline station. UPL bought the land from the prior owners three years ago, and uses the lot for employee parking. The company has applied to the city for permission to use the lot for expanding its current building, but the city will not issue a building permit until the land is decontaminated. The estimated cost of cleaning the soil ranges from $500,000 to $1,500,000—the exact cost will not be known until the pavement has been removed and full soil testing is possible, which will not occur for at least four months.

c. UPL is the guarantor on a $10 million bank loan that was obtained by another company controlled by the same shareholders who control UPL. The other company has more liabilities than assets, and its cash flow from operations is declining rather alarmingly.

d. UPL has a subsidiary in Japan. UPL has reached agreement to sell the Japanese subsidiary to a Taiwanese company, subject to approval by regulators in Japan. Approval is expected, but it will be at least six months before the outcome will be known for sure. When the sale closes, UPL will realize a profit of $20 million as the purchase price is $20 million higher than the subsidiary's net book value.

e. A minority shareholder alleges that UPL's controlling shareholders entered into transactions that had the effect of reducing the minority shareholder's equity in the company. (In securities legislation this type of action is known as "shareholder oppression.") The minority shareholder filed a complaint with the provincial securities commission, claiming damages of $50 million. The securities commission ruled in favour of the minority shareholder. UPL is appealing the case and UPL's lawyers are confident that the court will overturn the ruling in approximately one year.

**Required:**

Discuss the appropriate reporting for each of these items on UPL's 20X5 financial statements.

 **A4-23 Subsequent Events:** The auditor has completed her work on the financial statements of Leslie Kwok Incorporated (LKI) for the year ended 31 December 20X7, but the statements have not yet been issued. The auditor signed the audit opinion on 23 March 20X8. The following transactions and events occurred after 31 December 20X7:

a. On 27 January, LKI entered into a long-term lease for a private airplane for the company president and CEO. The lease requires payments of US$75,000 per month for 60 months.

b. On 28 January, LKI acquired all of the shares of Phan Limited by issuing LKI shares in exchange. The acquisition more than doubled the size of LKI, and the former shareholders of Phan now have a majority of the votes in LKI.

c. On 15 February, the Board of Directors of LKI decided to discontinue a major segment of the company's business due to continuing losses and a change of strategy.

d. The Royal Toronto Bank of Montreal extended a $50 million line of credit to LKI on 5 March.

e. One of the company's major customers declared bankruptcy on 22 March. The customer accounted for 27% of LKI's revenue in 20X7.

f. On 31 March, LKI reached an agreement with a major institutional investor to issue $500 million in secured debentures through a private placement.

g. A new Board of Directors was elected on 7 April.

h. On 10 April, the new directors cancelled the lease on the private airplane. The contract calls for a cancellation penalty of US$1 million.

**Required:**

Discuss how each item should be reported in LKI's 20X7 financial statements as a *subsequent event*, if at all.

---

★ ★ **A4-24 Subsequent Events:** Northern Switching Ltd. (NSL) is a manufacturer of digital switching equipment and systems. The company has total assets of approximately $784 million. Each of the following events occurred after the end of Northern Switching Ltd.'s 20X8 fiscal year, but before the statements had been finalized:

a. Northern Switching Ltd. (NSL) finalized an agreement to sell a major production facility to Cascade Cable Corporation for approximately $84 million cash. The sale includes buildings of approximately one million square feet, fixtures, equipment, and 63 acres of land. The property has an amortized cost of $56 million on NSL's draft 20X8 balance sheet.
b. NSL reached agreement with an international banking corporation for credit support for up to $46 million of new sales to customers abroad.
c. The company has a U.S. subsidiary. NSL (i.e., the parent company) signed a repayment guarantee on a $100 million line of credit that Citibank issued to the subsidiary.
d. Marketable securities held by NSL at 20X8 year-end, reported on the year-end draft balance sheet at their market value of $27 million, were sold for $23 million.
e. The CEO of Crisco Corporation, NSL's major competitor, accused a senior NSL executive of improperly accessing confidential information via an employee-only portal on Crisco's website and using that information for competitive advantage. Crisco said that the company will file a lawsuit to recover $76 million in damages. NSL vehemently denies the allegation.

**Required:**

Discuss what disclosure, if any, NSL should give to each of these events in its 20X8 financial statements.

---

★ **A4-25 Contingencies, Subsequent Events:** Zero Growth Limited has completed financial statements for the year ended 31 December 20X6. The financial statements have yet to be finalized or issued. The following events and transactions have occurred:

a. The office building housing administrative staff burned to the ground on 15 January 20X7.
b. On 15 November 20X6, a customer sued the company for $1,000,000 based on a claim of negligence leading to personal injury; Zero Growth is actively defending the suit and claims it is unfounded. Nothing has yet been recorded in the 20X6 financial statements in relation to this event.
c. On 1 February 20X7, Zero Growth received a $49,700 income tax reassessment for 20X5.
d. On 20 December 20X6, Zero Growth applied for a bank loan to replace an existing line of credit. The loan was granted on 2 January 20X7. Nothing was recorded in the 20X6 financial statements in relation to this event.
e. Zero Growth has reinterpreted a legal agreement entitling it to commission revenue for the sale of a client's products. Zero Growth's interpretation would entitle it to an extra $60,000 over and above amounts recognized in 20X6. The amount has not been recorded in the accounts. The client was billed for this amount in 20X6 but has disagreed with Zero Growth on the contract interpretation. Both parties have consulted their lawyers; resolution of the issue is not expected soon.
f. On 1 March 20X7, Zero Growth issued common shares for cash.

**Required:**

Discuss the appropriate accounting treatment for the contingencies and subsequent events described.

★ **A4-26 Financial Instruments:** Financial instruments may require disclosure of

1. Terms and conditions
2. Credit risk
3. Interest rates
4. Fair value

Consider the following balance sheet elements:

A. Accounts receivable
B. Inventory
C. Customers' advance deposits
D. Unearned revenue
E. Current income tax payable
F. Bank loan payable
G. Preferred shares issued
H. Instalment notes receivable (from customers)
I. Land
J. Dividends payable
K. Investment in common shares
L. Bonds payable

### Required:

1. Which of the above items are financial instruments? Specify whether the item is a financial asset, financial liability, or equity instrument.
2. For the items designated as financial instruments in requirement 1, specify which of the listed disclosures, above, are required.

★ **A4-27 Financial Instruments:** The AcSB recommends that financial instruments be classified by their nature, as debt (with required cash payment) or equity (a residual interest). When a financial instrument has characteristics of both debt and equity, the carrying value of the instrument should be separated into its debt and equity components for reporting in the financial statements. Kreiz Corporation issued the following financial instruments in the current year, 20X3:

a. Preferred shares that carry a dividend of $100 per share. On 1 January 20X9, the holder can require Kreiz to redeem the shares at a price of $750. There are 100,000 shares issued and outstanding.
b. Bonds payable with a term of 10 years, with required annual interest payments. At maturity, the investor may elect to receive cash or a specified number of common shares of Kreiz.

### Required:
Discuss how each of these financial instruments should be reported on Kreitz's balance sheet at the end of 20X3.

★ **A4-28 Special Disclosures:** Respond to the specific questions in each of the two cases, below.

*Case A* The following disclosure note is from the 31 October 20X2 financial statements of GreenWorld Limited, a mining company:

> The preparation of the financial statements, in conformity with generally accepted accounting principles, requires management to make estimates and assumptions that affect the reported amounts of assets and liabilities and disclosure of contingent assets and liabilities at the date of the financial statements and the reported amounts of revenues and expenses during the reporting period. The most significant estimates are related to the physical and economic lives and the recoverability of mining assets, mineral reserves, site restoration and related

obligations, commodity contracts and financial instruments, and income taxes. Actual results could differ from those estimates.

**Required:**

1.  What is the purpose of this disclosure note?
2.  How could this note be made more meaningful to the financial statement user?
3.  List four other financial statement elements (not listed above) that are affected by estimates.

*Case B*  The following disclosure note is from the 31 December 20X2 financial statements of UMM Limited, a software company:

> UMM has entered into an agreement with Vitech Ltd., a shareholder, with respect to acquiring certain rights to Vitech's software, technology, services, and other benefits. In the current year, UMM acquired $200 (million) of specific software products from Vitech. These assets were recorded at the transaction price, which represents fair market value as determined by an independent appraisal. UMM has expensed $68 (million) in services received from Vitech in 20X2. Sales in 20X2 to Vitech amounted to $151 (million). These transactions were conducted in the normal course of business at prices established and agreed to by both parties.

**Required:**

1.  What is the purpose of this disclosure note?
2.  In general, what makes two parties related?
3.  What measurement attribute has been used to record software assets, and revenues and expenses between these related parties? Comment.
4.  What evidence has UMM gathered to support the value for software purchased?

★ **A4-29 Special Disclosures:** Respond to the specific questions in each of the two cases, below.

*Case A*  The following disclosure note appeared in the 31 December 20X5 financial statements of Dridell Corporation, a manufacturer of electronic equipment:

> Dridell is exposed to liabilities and compliance costs arising from its past and current generation, management, and disposal of hazardous substances and wastes. As of 30 December 20X5, the accruals on the consolidated balance sheet for environmental matters were $27 million. Based on information available as of 31 December 200X5, management believes that the existing accruals are sufficient to satisfy probable and reasonably estimable environmental liabilities related to known environmental matters. Any additional liabilities that may result from these matters, and any additional liabilities that may result in connection with other locations currently under investigation, are not expected to have a material adverse effect on the business, results of operations, financial condition, and liquidity of Dridell.

**Required:**

1.  What is the purpose of this disclosure note?
2.  What types of management estimates are implied by this disclosure?
3.  What implications might this note have for the financial reporting in future years?

*Case B*  The following disclosure note is from the 31 December 20X2 financial statements of Zing Limited, a property developer:

> On 7 January 20X3, the Corporation contracted to acquire 60 residential housing units from a third party for a purchase price of $2.8 million, cash. On 24 January 20X3, the Company issued 240,000 stock options to senior officers of the company. These options have a three-year vesting period, with one-third vesting on each anniversary date.

**Required:**

1. What is the purpose of this disclosure note?
2. Why are these events disclosed rather than recorded in the financial statements?

 **A4-30 Special Disclosures:** Respond to the specific questions in each of the three cases, below.

*Case A* The following disclosure note is from the 30 April 20X2 financial statements of Miller Mining Limited:

> The Company has negative working capital and significant obligations with respect to long-term debt in the first quarter of 20X3. This serious financial position has been caused by consistently low commodity prices for the base metals mined by the Company. These financial statements have been prepared in accordance with Canadian generally accepted accounting principles applicable to a going concern, which assumes that the company will continue in operations for the foreseeable future and will be able to realize its assets and discharge its liabilities in the normal course of business. The Company must complete negotiations with major creditors and potential new investors in the immediate future to ensure its viability.

**Required:**

1. What is the purpose of this disclosure note?
2. What will be the outcome if the company is unsuccessful in negotiations with creditors and investors?
3. What items on the financial statement will change, and how will they change, if negotiations are not successful?

*Case B* The following disclosure note is from the 31 December 20X4 financial statements of Riconda Limited:

> The Company operates one operating segment, that being the design, manufacture, and sale of graphics and multimedia products for personal computers and consumer electronic devices.

|  | 20X2 | 20X1 | 20X0 |
|---|---|---|---|
| **Sales** | | | |
| Canada | $ 23,104 | 31,119 | $ 41,175 |
| U.S. | 325,464 | 424,472 | 425,000 |
| Europe | 247,795 | 396,805 | 412,855 |
| Asia-Pacific | 441,446 | 430,669 | 307,320 |
| Consolidated sales | $1,037,809 | $1,283,065 | $1,186,350 |
| **Product Sales** | | | |
| Components | $ 481,083 | $ 499,859 | $ 390,238 |
| Boards | 548,053 | 778,015 | 796,112 |
| Other | 8,673 | 5,191 | — |
| Consolidated sales | $1,037,809 | $1,283,065 | $1,186,350 |
| **Capital and Intangible Assets** | | | |
| Canada | $ 54,162 | $ 42,494 | $ 36,590 |
| U.S. | 297,417 | 421,955 | 31,341 |
| Europe | 5,071 | 5,364 | 5,410 |
| Asia-Pacific | 706 | 919 | 1,051 |
| Consolidated capital and intangible assets | $ 357,356 | $ 470,732 | $ 74,392 |

**Required:**

1. What is the purpose of this disclosure note?
2. Evaluate the information presented. What does it tell you about the company's operations?

3. Review the requirements for segmented disclosures. What information is lacking in the note presented above? Why?

***Case C*** The following disclosure note is from the 31 December 20X3 financial statements of Limpid Limited:

> All of the Company's sales take place with the parent company, Limpid U.S. Limited. Sales are recorded at the exchange value, which is negotiated by and agreed to by both parties. At year-end, Limpid U.S. owed the Company $540 million with respect to these sales. This amount is in the normal course of business and subject to payment in 60 days.

**Required:**

1. What is the purpose of this disclosure note?
2. What value is used to record the sale transactions? What conclusions would you draw about the company's income statement as a result of this information?
3. How could fair market value be determined in these circumstances?

★★ **A4-31 Balance Sheet Interpretation:** The balance sheet of Karmax Ltd. discloses the following assets:

### Karmax Limited Extracts from the Balance Sheet
### (stated in thousands of Canadian dollars)

At year ended 31 December 20X6

| Assets | | |
|---|---:|---:|
| Current assets | | |
| Cash | $ 710 | |
| Short-term investments | 416 | |
| Accounts receivable | 1,011 | |
| Inventory | 2,600 | |
| Prepaid expenses | 410 | |
| Total current assets | | $ 5,147 |
| Tangible capital assets, net | | 14,755 |
| Intangible capital assets, net | | 984 |
| Long-term investments | | 1,077 |
| Total assets | | $21,963 |

The following information has been established in relation to market values (amounts in $ thousands):

| | Market Value | Source |
|---|---|---|
| Short-term investments | $416 | Quoted stock market price |
| Inventory | $4,190 | Karmax price list |
| Tangible capital assets | $20,000–$25,000 | Real estate appraisal |
| Long-term investment | $3,000 | (Note 1) |
| Intangible capital assets | $10,000 | (Note 2) |

*Note 1*
The long-term investment is an investment in the common shares of a company owned and operated by the two sons of Karmax's major shareholder. The Karmax investment is 25% of the outstanding shares. The long-term investment is accounted for using the equity method. The sons' company has never sold shares to a non-family investor, and the Karmax shareholder provided this estimate of value.

*Note 2*
Karmax holds patents on a successful consumer product, licensed to various manufacturers. Significant annual royalties are earned; the recorded balance sheet value consists of legal fees paid during patent infringement cases. The $10 million estimate of market value is based on discounted future cash flow.

**Required:**

Prepare a brief report that contains:

1. An analysis of the reliability of the various market value estimates as a good predictor of future cash flows
2. An assessment of the usefulness of the (primarily historical cost) balance sheet to
   a. A banker making a lending decision
   b. An investor evaluating return on investment

---

★★    **A4-32  Balance Sheet Interpretation:** The following balance sheet reports the financial position of a junior Canadian gold-mining company (amounts in $ thousands):

**Assets**

Current assets

| | | |
|---|---:|---:|
| Cash and cash equivalents | $   8,260 | |
| Accounts receivable, less allowance for doubtful accounts | 20,338 | |
| Taxes recoverable | 200 | |
| Inventories | 20,800 | |
| Prepaid expenses | 500 | |
| Investments (cost is equal to market value) | 1,830 | $  51,928 |
| Plant, equipment, and mine development costs, net | | 95,000 |
| Goodwill | | 2,000 |
| Total assets | | $148,928 |

**Liabilities and shareholders' equity**

Current liabilities

| | | |
|---|---:|---:|
| Accounts payable and accrued liabilities | $   6,550 | |
| Royalties payable | 560 | $   7,110 |
| Future liability for site restoration costs | | 2,280 |
| Convertible bonds | | 12,000 |
| Future income taxes payable | | 1,830 |
| Non-controlling interest | | 1,080 |
| Shareholders' equity | | |
| Convertible bonds | 1,128 | |
| Share capital | 100,000 | |
| Retained earnings | 23,000 | |
| Cumulative exchange adjustment | 500 | |
| | | 124,628 |
| Total liabilities and shareholders' equity | | $148,928 |

**Required:**

1. Explain the meaning of the following accounts:
   a. Mine development costs
   b. Goodwill
   c. Future liability for site restoration costs
   d. Future income tax
   e. Non-controlling interest
   f. Convertible bonds
   g. Cumulative exchange adjustment
2. What items on the above balance sheet would most likely be estimated? Explain.
3. For what assets would you expect the market value and book value to be the most different? Explain.
4. As a potential shareholder, what additional information would be relevant to any decision to acquire shares in this company? Why is this information not presented with the audited financial statements?

## CHAPTER 5

# The Cash Flow Statement

## INTRODUCTION

The income statement provides information about the results of operations. The balance sheet includes information about the financial position of the company. What additional information can a cash flow statement provide?

Consider the 2006 financial statements of Royal Standard Minerals Limited, a public company engaged in the business of gold and silver resource properties. Its shares are traded on the TSX Venture Exchange. The statement of operations shows that the company has no revenues and a 2006 net loss of $1.6 million (all dollar figures in U.S. dollars). The balance sheet shows a cumulative deficit of $9.5 million, and total assets of only $6.6 million. Several balance sheet accounts show large changes in the year. Is this a story of doom and gloom? An analyst could piece the changes together. Or the cash flow statement (CFS) could be consulted. The CFS shows the cash effect of significant operating, investing, and financing decisions.

The CFS for Royal Standard Minerals shows that the $1.6 million operating loss was really "only" a net *cash* outflow of $0.2 million. Much of the reported income statement loss was the result of non-cash expenses such as amortization and compensation to employees in the form of stock options. Neither of

these items used cash during the period. The company raised $4 million in cash through issuing new shares—surely a vote of confidence from shareholders. The company spent $1.5 million on exploration properties, and $1.5 million on exploration equipment. This major investment in exploration equipment was the first such investment in several years, implying increased activity and/or use of new technology.

Thus, the *strategic activity* during the year—modest cash outflow for operations, major new equity financing, significant investment in exploration properties and equipment—is *most obvious* from the CFS. (Any investor or creditor interested in this company would want to investigate the geological prospects of the properties under exploration, and gather information about gold and silver prices. The historical cost financial statements have well-established limits.) But the CFS is the statement that provides the best insights into the actions of the company and their cash impact. It unravels the accruals and deferrals needed in the other statements.

This chapter discusses the preparation and interpretation of the CFS. As individual categories of assets, liabilities, and shareholders' equity are covered in following chapters, the cash flow impact of that topic will be reviewed at the same time.

## PURPOSE OF THE CASH FLOW STATEMENT

Standard setters have identified cash flow prediction as a principal objective of financial reporting. The starting point of cash flow prediction is the analysis of historical cash flows. Therefore, the objective of the CFS is to disclose the historical cash flows of the enterprise during the reporting period.

Most users of financial statements are interested in cash flows because, in the long run, users base their own projections of cash flow on those of the company. For example, investors are interested in the amount that is available to pay out in dividends, bankers need to know how a company expects to generate cash to pay its loans, employees need to know the company's "ability to pay" when negotiating wages, salaries, and fringe benefits, and so forth.

The **cash flow statement** (CFS) (**or statement of changes in financial position**) will reveal the various types of cash flows within the company. Cash flows relate to (1) operating activities, (2) investing in (or selling) assets, and (3) financing decisions, such as issuing or redeeming debt and equity. The CFS discloses the amount of cash (as distinct from income) that flows from operations, and also the reasons for the difference between net income and cash flow from operations. Users can see more than the net change on balance sheet accounts—users can see where the cash came from and where it went.

**cash flow statement**

an accounting statement describing the uses and sources of cash for a specific period of time

## EVOLUTION OF THE CASH FLOW STATEMENT

The cash flow statement has changed more over the past 20 years than any other financial statement. Even the title of CFS is fairly recent. Previously, the generic name for the statement was the *statement of changes in financial position*. Earlier names included the *statement of source and application of funds*, and the more general *funds flow statement*.

The original focus of the statement was on changes in non-current assets, non-current liabilities, and owners' equity. Instead of cash from operating activities, *working capital* from operating activities was calculated. Unfortunately, there were several very public cases of companies going bankrupt despite a positive working capital from operations. It turned out that working capital was increasing because inventories were increasing and receivable collection periods were lengthening, but actual cash flow was down. This led to the focus on the CFS of cash flows only, not working capital. In addition, the CFS used to include non-cash transactions, like land exchanged for common shares. This obviously blurred the line of cash flow, and was potentially misleading. Such transactions are now excluded from the statement.

## CASH FLOW REPORTING

### Reporting Requirement

Companies are required to include a CFS with their financial statements. Companies may choose to not disclose a CFS if:

1. The company is not a public company.

2. Cash flow information is readily apparent from other financial statements or is adequately disclosed in the notes.

The norm is that the CFS is included with the financial statements.

### Definition of "Cash"

On the CFS, cash is defined as cash, plus cash equivalents, less any temporary bank overdrafts.

**cash**

an asset; the amount of money on hand and in the bank

**CASH** Cash includes currency, which would include cash held for daily operating purposes in cash registers or petty cash funds. Cash also includes the amount that is held in the company's **current account**(s) with the bank. The current account is the chequing account, except that, unlike personal chequing accounts, deposited cheques are not held for collection and the company's cheques are less likely to be returned NSF ("not sufficient funds") if the account is temporarily overdrawn. Cash excludes cash held in restricted accounts if the money is not available for general purposes.

**CASH EQUIVALENTS**  Cash is a non-productive asset, and therefore companies strive to keep their immediately accessible cash balance at a minimum. Companies place their cash in term deposits, guaranteed investment certificates, certificates of deposit, or other money market instruments to earn interest. If these investments are highly liquid short-term investments, they are known as **cash equivalents**, and are included with cash on the CFS. The standard requires that, to be a cash equivalent, an investment has to be readily convertible to a known amount of cash, and be subject to an insignificant risk of change in value. Three months is suggested as the maximum maturity period. Investments in shares are explicitly excluded.

**OVERDRAFTS**  Corporations often are authorized by their banks to have an **overdraft**, which is a negative balance in their chequing account. For example, suppose that a company begins the year with a balance of $10,000 in its current account. By the end of the year, the cash balance is completely used up and the company has written $15,000 more in cheques than it has cash. The current account will have a negative balance, or an overdraft, of $15,000. The change in cash for the year is not simply the decline in cash from $10,000 to zero, but is the change from a $10,000 asset to a $15,000 liability—a decrease of $25,000.

Bank overdrafts may form an integral part of an enterprise's cash management plan. Bank overdrafts are included as a component of cash and cash equivalents when the bank balance fluctuates from positive to negative on a regular basis. That is, if the current account is always overdrawn, it is in substance a bank loan and not a cash equivalent. The current account must be regularly positive and then be overdrawn to qualify as "cash." Furthermore, the overdrafts have to be repayable at any time that the bank demands payment.

In addition, many companies rely on a **line of credit**, which is a pre-approved short-term bank loan. The borrowing limit has been negotiated with the lender in advance. Lines of credit often are used to cover seasonal fluctuations in cash flows. However, lines of credit and other types of short-term bank loans normally are viewed as financing activities and are not part of the cash definition.

**RECONCILIATION**  The components of cash and cash equivalents (including overdrafts) must be disclosed, and the net change that is reported in the CFS should be reconciled to the equivalent items in the balance sheet. An example of this is shown later in the chapter in Exhibit 5-9.

## Classification of Cash Flows

The CFS is classified on the basis of the type of cash flow:

- **Operating activities** are the principal revenue-producing activities of the enterprise and the related expenditures. The cash inflow from operations is measured as the cash received from customers or clients, plus other revenue-generating activities such as cash received from finance revenue. The cash outflows are those **disbursements** that are incurred to earn the inflow, such as cash paid for inventories, wages and salaries, and overhead costs. Cash flow is not accrual accounting, and cash from customers is different than **revenue** recognized, just as cash paid for **expenses** is different than expenses recognized on the income statement.
- **Investing activities** are those activities that relate to resources used to generate future revenue—essentially capital assets and investments. The acquisition and disposal of tangible capital assets, intangible capital assets, other assets and investments are included in this section. Transactions involving investments that are classified as cash equivalents are excluded, as are current operating assets such as inventory and accounts receivable.
- **Financing activities** relate to liabilities and owners' equity. Cash flows that increase or decrease the size or composition of the non-operating accounts on the right side of the balance sheet are reported in this section. Changes in operating liabilities, such as accounts payable, are excluded from this section and included in operating activities.

Exhibit 5-1 lists some of the transactions that fall into each category.

---

**cash equivalents**

one of the components of cash on the cash flow statement; highly liquid, short-term (e.g., three-month term) investments

**overdraft**

a negative bank balance reported as a current liability; usually part of cash on the cash flow statement

EXHIBIT 5-1

## Examples of Cash Flows by Category

### OPERATING CASH FLOWS

| **Inflows** | **Outflows** |
|---|---|
| Receipts from customers | Payments to suppliers |
| Advance deposits from customers | Wages and salaries to employees |
| Income tax refunds | Income tax payments, related to |
| Interest received on customers' |   any year |
|   notes or accounts | Other tax payments |
| Dividends and interest received | Interest paid on liabilities |
|   from investments | |

### INVESTING CASH FLOWS

| **Inflows** | **Outflows** |
|---|---|
| Cash received from sale of capital | Payments for purchase of capital |
|   assets |   assets |
| Cash from sale of debt or equity | Cash flows capitalized as intangible |
|   investments |   assets, such as: |
| Collection of principal on loans |   &bull; capitalized interest |
|   to others |   &bull; exploration costs |
| | Purchase of debt or equity securities |
| |   of others |
| | Loans extended to others |

### FINANCING CASH FLOWS

| **Inflows** | **Outflows** |
|---|---|
| Net proceeds of issuing debt or | Payment of principal on bonds or |
|   equity securities |   bank loans |
| Cash proceeds received from | Repurchase of the entity's own |
|   bank loans |   shares |
| | Dividends paid to shareholders |

## Sample Cash Flow Statement

Exhibit 5-2 shows the 2006 CFS for Research in Motion (RIM). A few important formatting aspects of this statement:

1. For all three categories, the cash flows can be either positive or negative. For example, financing activities include both cash outflows for buyback of common shares and the proceeds from issuing new share capital.

2. Positive and negative flows are *not* netted. For example, as shown, RIM had a cash inflow of $514,431 thousand in 2006 from sale or maturity of short-term investments, and also had a cash outflow of $199,194 thousand to acquire short-term investments.

3. The cash provided by operations is calculated indirectly, by starting with net income and then taking out all of the things that did *not* require cash. This is the most common approach—we will discuss an alternative later in the chapter.

Notice also that RIM provides two years of comparative data, and reports in U.S. dollars. Both of these reporting choices serve the U.S. stock markets, because RIM is listed on the New York Stock Exchange.

EXHIBIT 5-2

### RESEARCH IN MOTION LIMITED
### CONSOLIDATED STATEMENTS OF CASH FLOWS
#### (United States dollars, in thousands)

| For the Year Ended | March 4, 2006 | February 26, 2005 | February 28, 2004 |
|---|---|---|---|
| **Cash flows from operating activities** | | | |
| Net income | $382,078 | $ 213,387 | $ 51,829 |
| Items not requiring an outlay of cash: | | | |
| Amortization | 85,873 | 66,760 | 54,529 |
| Deferred income taxes | 77,938 | (143,651) | — |
| Issuance of restricted share units | 159 | — | — |
| Loss (gain) on disposal of capital assets | (147) | (69) | 223 |
| Loss on foreign currency translation of long-term debt | 597 | 12 | 859 |
| Unrealized foreign exchange loss (gain) | 57 | (80) | — |
| Net changes in working capital items | (396,464) | 141,623 | (43,605) |
| | 150,091 | 277,982 | 63,835 |
| | | | |
| **Cash flows from financing activities** | | | |
| Issuance of share capital | 23,269 | 54,151 | 994,640 |
| Financing costs | — | — | (39,629) |
| Common shares repurchased pursuant to Common Share Repurchase Program | (391,212) | — | — |
| Repayment of long-term debt | (229) | (199) | (6,130) |
| | (368,172) | 53,952 | 948,881 |
| | | | |
| **Cash flows from investing activities** | | | |
| Acquisition of investments | (103,179) | (615,098) | (186,989) |
| Proceeds on sale or maturity of investments | 61,495 | 18,385 | 43,746 |
| Acquisition of capital assets | (178,732) | (109,363) | (21,815) |
| Acquisition of intangible assets | (23,702) | (17,061) | (32,252) |
| Business acquisitions | (3,795) | (3,888) | 478 |
| Acquisition of short-term investments | (199,194) | (227,072) | (24,071) |
| Proceeds on sale or maturity of short-term investments | 514,431 | 76,022 | 24,071 |
| | 67,324 | (878,075) | (196,832) |
| | | | |
| **Effect of foreign exchange loss (gain) on cash and cash equivalents** | ( 57) | 76 | (146) |
| **Net increase (decrease) in cash and cash equivalents for the year** | (150,814) | (546,065) | 815,738 |
| **Cash and cash equivalents, beginning of year** | 610,354 | 1,156,419 | 340,681 |
| **Cash and cash equivalents, end of year** | $459,540 | $ 610,354 | $1,156,419 |

*References to disclosure notes deleted.*

*Source:* www.sedar.com. Research in Motion, May 10, 2006.

## Interpreting the Cash Flow Statement

Interpretation involves examining the CFS for the major sources and uses of cash. The following questions must be considered, with professional judgement:

- Has operations provided cash or used cash?

- Why is net income different than cash from operating activities? What are the major adjustments?
- What are the major investing activities?
- What are the major financing activities?
- How are these activities interrelated?
- How do the company's cash activities compare to prior years? To competitors?
- What accounting policy choice might affect classification of cash flows?

Refer to the RIM CFS. RIM reported net income of $382,078 (all amounts are in thousands of U.S. dollars) in 2006, but cash flow from operating activities is a much more modest $150,091. There are two large non-cash items *added back*— amortization and deferred taxes. These items were expenses on the income statement but did not require cash this period. Overwhelming these addbacks, though, was the large negative adjustment for "net changes to working capital." Reference to the explanatory notes shows that there was a massive reduction in the short-term liability called accrued litigation expenses. This reflects the $612.5 million settlement of the patent infringement lawsuit that RIM had been engaged in since 2001 with U.S.–based NTP Ltd. Much of the cost had been accrued and expensed in prior years. This litigation accrual was added back in prior years. However, actual payment of most of the settlement is reflected in cash flow from operations in 2006 because most of the cash was moved to escrow (restricted, court-controlled) accounts during the 2006 fiscal year.

In financing activities, RIM spent $391,212 to buy back shares, while shares were issued for $23,269. In investing activities, there was a $514,431 sale of short-term investments, and a stream of acquisitions: long-term investments, capital assets, intangible assets, businesses, and so on.

Overall, the cash balances decreased by $150,814 this year. The company ended the year with a still-significant $459,540 in cash. The level of cash balances is largely dictated by the nature of the business: RIM operates in a relatively risky business and needs cash reserves to finance future operations.

## CONCEPT REVIEW

1. What are the three categories of cash flows that should be reported on a company's CFS?
2. What is the definition of *cash* for purposes of the CFS?
3. How does *cash from operations* differ from *net income*?

## PREPARING THE CASH FLOW STATEMENT

### Basic Approach to Preparation

The balance sheet, income statement, and retained earnings statement are all prepared from the trial balance. Preparation of these statements can be manual or, more commonly, by computerized systems. The classification of the balance of each account is unambiguously pre-specified in the programming, and these statements emerge more or less automatically from the system.

**Analyzing Cash Flow** The CFS is not a statement that is an automatic output from account balances. Instead, it is a statement that is prepared by analyzing account balances and changes in balances. It is not enough, for example, to know by how much the equipment balance has changed over the course of an accounting period; one must analyze the sources of the accounting entries in the account. Standard computerized accounting systems normally cannot do that, and therefore the CFS is usually a hand-prepared statement.

If the statement explains all of the cash flows, it seems logical to start by analyzing the sources of the flows in and out of the cash account(s). The entries to the general ledger cash account are usually summary entries from subsidiary records such as specialized journals or cumulative transaction records. For example, it should be possible to see how much cash was received from customers by summarizing the debits to the cash account from the accounts receivable department and/or from the summary posting of the daily cash **receipts**; cash paid to employees for wages and salaries can be obtained by looking at the payroll accounts, etc.

Unfortunately, direct analysis of the cash accounts is difficult and time consuming. Therefore, the normal approach is to describe the cash activities by analyzing the changes in all of the *non-cash* accounts. Since the basic, indisputable characteristic of the balance sheet is that it *balances*, cash flows can be determined by looking at the causes of the changes in all of the other accounts *except* cash (and cash equivalents.) For example, it is possible to quickly determine how much cash was received from customers by looking at the total sales revenue figure (on the income statement) and adjusting that accrual-basis amount by the change in trade accounts receivable for the period. If the balance in accounts receivable went up, then the company received less cash than was recognized in sales for the period; if the accounts receivable balance went down, then the company received more cash than was recognized in sales.

## A Simple Example

The data for preparing the CFS for Simple Limited is shown in Exhibit 5-3. The cash account shows a change from $20 at the beginning of the year to $35 at the end, for a net increase of $15. However, there is a short-term investment account. Assuming that this account is a *cash equivalent*, it must be included with cash. In that case the net change in the balance of cash and cash equivalents from the end of 20X4 to the end of 20X5 is a *decrease* of $35:

| | Ending | Beginning | Change | |
|---|---|---|---|---|
| Cash balance | $35 | $20 | $ 15 | increase |
| Short-term investments | 20 | 70 | (50) | decrease |
| Total | $55 | $90 | | |
| Net increase (decrease) in cash and cash equivalents | | | $(35) | decrease |

The CFS that can be derived from the information in Exhibit 5-3 is shown in Exhibit 5-4. (The letters in the "key" column in Exhibit 5-4 refer to the explanations below.) In order to explain the flows that resulted in the net decrease of $35, all of the changes in the *non-cash* accounts are analyzed, starting with information from the statement of income and retained earnings and with the *additional information*, as follows:

a. Net income of $330 is the basis for determining cash flow from operations. Therefore, the amount of net income is placed first in the operating activities section of the CFS. Net income, of course, includes all revenues and expenses, so using net income on the CFS places all revenues in operating activities as inflows, and all expenses in operating activities as outflows. It is then reconciled to the real cash inflow and outflow for revenue and expenses.

b. Dividends of $225 were declared (and paid) during the year. This amount is placed in the financing section. Note that net income and dividends completely explain the change in retained earnings during the year.

c. *Additional information* reveals that operating expenses includes $200 in amortization. Since amortization is an interperiod allocation of previous years' investment cash flows, its impact must be removed from net income. The $200 amortization is *added back* to net income to eliminate the effect of this interperiod allocation.

## EXHIBIT 5-3

### Simple Limited
### Balance Sheets

| (in thousands) 31 December | 20X5 | 20X4 |
|---|---|---|
| Current assets: | | |
| Cash | $    35 | $    20 |
| Short-term investments | 20 | 70 |
| Accounts receivable | 110 | 125 |
| Inventory | 100 | 135 |
| | $  265 | $  350 |
| Fixed assets: | | |
| Plant and equipment | 1,100 | 1,000 |
| Accumulated amortization | (250) | (300) |
| | 850 | 700 |
| Total assets | $1,115 | $1,050 |
| Current liabilities: | | |
| Bank loan | $    65 | $    50 |
| Accounts payable | 100 | 125 |
| | 165 | 175 |
| Long-term note payable | 300 | 330 |
| Shareholders' equity: | | |
| Common shares | 100 | 100 |
| Retained earnings | 550 | 445 |
| | 650 | 545 |
| Total liabilities and shareholders' equity | $1,115 | $1,050 |

### Simple Limited
### Statement of Income and Retained Earnings

Year ended 31 December 20X5

| | |
|---|---|
| Revenue: | |
| Sales revenue | $2,000 |
| Gain on sale of equipment | 70 |
| | 2,070 |
| Operating expenses: | |
| Cost of goods sold | 1,100 |
| Other expenses | 640 |
| | 1,740 |
| Net income | 330 |
| Retained earnings, 1 January | 445 |
| Dividends paid on common shares | (225) |
| Retained earnings, 31 December | $  550 |

*Additional information:*
i.  Other operating expenses includes $200 of amortization expense.
ii. During the year, Simple sold equipment originally costing $310 for net
    proceeds of $130.

**d.** *Additional information* reveals that equipment that originally cost $310 was sold for $130. The income statement also shows a gain from the sale of equipment amounting to $70. The following entry must have been made when the equipment was sold:

| | | |
|---|---|---|
| Cash | 130 | |
| Accumulated amortization | 250 | |
|     Plant and equipment | | 310 |
|     Gain on sale of equipment | | 70 |

On the CFS, the $130 cash received is an investing activity, the $70 gain is eliminated (subtracted) from operating cash flow. The gain is eliminated for two reasons:

1. The sale of assets is not an operating activity but reflects a change in asset structure; the disposal of assets must be reported as an investing activity.

2. The gain does not measure the actual cash flow during the period, but instead it is the difference between the proceeds of the sale and net book value of the asset. The net book value is the original expenditure for the asset, reduced by amortization to date.

**e.** Accounts receivable decreased by $15 during the year. This means that customers paid more than the amount reported as sales. The $15 is added to net income in the operations section, in order to restate the sales from an accrual to a cash basis.

**f.** Inventory decreased by $35. The change in inventory is a component of cost of goods sold (COGS). By definition, the beginning-of-year inventory was acquired in a previous period and not the current period. Therefore, a decrease in inventory indicates that less cash was paid for the goods than were sold during the year.

**g.** Accounts payable decreased by $25. This indicates that suppliers were paid more cash for goods and services than the company accrued during the period. The $25 decrease reduces the amount of cash from operations. The accounts payable adjustment is related to the inventory adjustment, since trade accounts payable relate largely to inventory purchases. This will be further explained later in the chapter.

**h.** Plant and equipment increased by $100 during the year. However, this amount is the net result of both new investment and retirement of old equipment. From (d) (above), the disposal was $310. The amount of the 20X5 acquisition is as follows:

| | |
|---|---|
| Beginning balance | $1,000 |
| Cost of equipment sold during the year | − 310 |
| Amount invested in equipment during the year | + ??? |
| Ending balance | $1,100 |

The amount that makes the account balance is $410.

**i.** Accumulated amortization decreased by $50. Amortization expense of $200 for 20X5 was added to this account, and accumulated amortization on the equipment sold was $250. These two transactions combine to verify the $50 reduction and no additional entry to the CFS is needed.

**j.** The current bank loan increased by $15. This is a loan, and not an overdraft; therefore, the loan will *not* be included as a component of cash and cash equivalents. The increase in the loan is a source of financing, and will go into the financing section of the CFS.

### EXHIBIT 5-4

**Simple Limited**
**Cash Flow Statement**

| Year ended 31 December 20X5 | Key | | | |
|---|---|---|---|---|
| Operating activities: | | | | |
| Net income (from income statement) | (a) | $330 | | |
| Add (deduct) to reconcile net income to net operating cash flows: | | | | |
| Amortization expense | (c) | 200 | | |
| Gain on sale of equipment | (d) | (70) | | |
| Decrease in accounts receivable | (e) | 15 | | |
| Decrease in inventory | (f) | 35 | | |
| Decrease in accounts payable | (g) | (25) | $485 | |
| Investing activities: | | | | |
| Proceeds from sale of equipment | (d) | 130 | | |
| Purchase of new equipment | (h) | (410) | (280) | |
| Financing activities: | | | | |
| Increase in current bank loan | (j) | 15 | | |
| Dividends paid | (b) | (225) | | |
| Reduction of long-term notes payable | (k) | (30) | (240) | |
| Increase (decrease) in cash and cash equivalents | | | (35) | |
| Cash and cash equivalents, 1 January | | | 90 | |
| Cash and cash equivalents, 31 December | | | $ 55 | |

**k.** Long-term note payable decreased by $30. This represents a financing activity.

**l.** Common shares did not change during the period. Therefore, in the absence of any information that shares were purchased and new shares were issued (that is, in offsetting amounts), there will be no impact on the CFS relating to common shares.

The net result of entering all of these amounts in the CFS is that net decrease in cash of $35 is explained.

## Presentation of Operating Activities

There are two approaches for presenting the operating activities section:

- *Indirect presentation:* Operations begins with net income, and all interperiod allocations and accruals are reversed out of net income to derive the cash from operations.
- *Direct presentation:* The revenues and expenses are adjusted to a cash basis of reporting and shown directly in deriving cash provided by (or used by) operations on the cash flow section.

In Exhibit 5-4, the indirect method of presentation was used. Operating activities began with net income of $330 and was then adjusted for amortization, the accounting gain on sale of equipment, and changes in the balances of the other current assets and current liabilities *except* for those included in the definition of "cash."

Exhibit 5-5 shows the operating activities section of Simple Limited's CFS, using the direct approach of presentation. The amounts are obtained as follows:

**1.** To convert from accrual-basis sales to cash received from customers, start with sales and add the decrease in accounts receivable during the year ($15). This converts sales ($2,000) to cash received from customers ($2,015). This $15 adjustment is the same as adding the amount that customers owed at the beginning of the year ($125 opening balance) and subtracting the amount owing at the end of the year ($110 ending balance):

| | |
|---|---:|
| Sales, accrual basis (per income statement) | $2,000 |
| Plus cash collected on opening accounts receivable | + 125 |
| Minus cash *not* collected at year-end | − 110 |
| Cash received from sales during 20X5 | $2,015 |

2. COGS requires two adjustments. The first adjustment is for the decrease in inventory of $35 during the year. Since inventory purchased in the previous year was used this year, the cash flow requirements for buying inventory were $35 less than the expense shown for COGS. Therefore, subtract the $35 decrease from the $1,100 expense to arrive at cash flow. Partially offsetting the decline in inventory is the decrease in accounts payable. The decrease in accounts payable of $25 indicates that more cash was expended to pay creditors (presumably, for inventory purchases and other expense components that comprise COGS). Therefore, increase the expense by $25 to arrive at cash flow. The $1,090 cash flow for COGS is lower than the expense by $10.

3. Other operating expenses are decreased by the $200 amortization.

Other items, such as amortization and the gain on sale of equipment are not cash flows and have no place in the statement under the direct presentation approach.

**Direct or Indirect?** The standards permit either the direct or indirect method of reporting cash flows from operations, but enterprises are "encouraged" to report cash flows from operating activities using the direct method. Regardless of any possible advantages in clarity of using the direct approach, the indirect method of presentation has been by far the more popular approach. *Financial Reporting in Canada 2006* reports that only one, sometimes two, of the surveyed companies used the direct method of reporting in the years 2002–05. There is certainly no trend toward the direct method of presentation.

It can be argued that the direct approach is clearer to financial statement users, because they do not have to untangle the adjustments that are made under the indirect approach. In particular, there is the concern that the indirect method encourages the idea that amortization is a source of funds. The addback of amortization is usually a large positive element in the operations section, and business people have often been heard to remark that they will be using their "amortization funds" for certain projects. Of course, this is a mistaken impression, but the indirect presentation method certainly strengthens the myth.

---

### EXHIBIT 5-5

### Simple Limited
### Cash Flow Statement
### Sample of Direct Presentation of Operations

Year ended 31 December 20X5

| | | |
|---|:---:|---:|
| Operating activities: | | |
| Cash received from customers ($2,000 + $15) | **(1)** | $2,015 |
| Operating expenses: | | |
| Cash paid to suppliers ($1,100 − $35 + $25) | **(2)** | (1,090) |
| Cash paid for other operating expenses ($640 − $200) | **(3)** | (440) |
| Cash provided by operations | | $ 485 |

**Two-Step Indirect Presentation**  A common refinement of the indirect method of presentation is a two-step approach. First, net income is adjusted for interperiod allocations, and then it is adjusted for changes in other working capital accounts (often as a single, summary amount rather than in detail). The operations section of Simple Limited's CFS is illustrated in Exhibit 5-6, using the two-step approach.

Notice the subtotal after "items not affecting cash." This subtotal may pose a problem by implying that there is some special significance to that amount, which does *not* equal cash flow from operating activities.

The RIM CFS uses the indirect method in operating activities. Operating activities begins with net income, and first adjusts for "items not requiring an outlay of cash." Second, there is an adjustment for the net changes in working capital items. (The detail of these changes is shown in the disclosure notes to streamline the CFS.) However, RIM does not include a subtotal after the non-cash items, so its operating activities section presentation is yet another version of the two-step method.

## Offsetting Transactions

Accounting standards emphasize that offsetting should not occur in the CFS. That is, gross cash receipts and gross cash payments must be reported separately for investing and financing activities.

A basic objective of the CFS is to explain the investing and financing activities of the enterprise. Within each of those two categories, there often are transactions that, overall, have the effect of offsetting or partially offsetting each other. For example, if a company refinances its debt by retiring an outstanding bond issue and issuing new bonds, the *net* impact on the balance sheet may be relatively minor. However, these activities do demonstrate the company's ability to renew its capital structure. The flows associated with the refinancing should be disclosed separately and not offset, or netted.

**Conditions for Offsetting**  There are some exceptions to the general rule against offsetting, but they are narrowly defined and relate more to specialized entities such as financial institutions, investment companies, and rental agents. In essence, offsetting (or netting) is permitted for:

- Cash receipts and payments that are on behalf of customers rather than for the reporting enterprise itself. An example is the cash flows of a rental agent that collects rents

---

### EXHIBIT 5-6

### Simple Limited CFS
### Operating Activities
### Two-Step Indirect Presentation

Year ended 31 December 20X5

| | |
|---|---:|
| Operating activities: | |
| Net income | $330 |
| Plus (less) items not affecting cash: | |
| Amortization | 200 |
| Gain on sale of equipment | (70) |
| | 460 |
| Changes in other working capital items: | |
| Decrease in accounts receivable | 15 |
| Decrease in inventory | 35 |
| Decrease in accounts payable | (25) |
| Cash provided by operations | $485 |

for landlords and passes those rents on to the property owners. The agent will keep a commission, which is the reported *net* cash flow to the agent.

- Cash receipts and payments for items where the volume of activity is high, the holding period is short (i.e., the *turnover* is quick), and the maturities are short. An example is the investing and liquidating of investments by an investment dealer. As another example, a cereal manufacturer may routinely buy and sell a large volume of grain futures on the commodity market. Cash flow for this activity would be shown net.

Accounting standards also contain recommendations that allow financial institutions to net cash flows relating to additional specific types of specialized activities, which fit the two general guidelines above.

## Non-Cash Transactions

Some transactions have a significant effect on the asset or equity structure of an entity without involving any direct cash flow at all. These non-cash transactions are economically similar to cash transactions. For example, settling a debt by issuing shares directly to the debt holder has the same effect as issuing the shares for cash and using the proceeds to settle the debt. Or, an asset may be acquired without cash by entering into a mortgage or a long-term capital lease; the effect is the same as borrowing money to buy the asset. Common types of non-cash transactions include:

- Retiring bonds through share issuance;
- Converting bonds to common shares;
- Converting preferred shares to common shares;
- Settling debt by transferring non-cash assets;
- Bond refinancing;
- Incurring capital lease obligations in exchange for leased assets;
- Acquiring shares in another company in exchange for shares of the reporting enterprise; and
- Distributing assets other than cash as dividends.

At one point, non-cash transactions such as those listed above were required to be included in the CFS as both an inflow and an outflow. However, current reporting standards specifically *exclude non-cash transactions* from the CFS on the grounds that such transactions are not cash flows. For example, the acquisition of a building (an investing activity) that is financed through a capital lease (a financing activity) would not be shown on the face of the CFS because there was no cash involved.

**Partial Cash Transactions**    Sometimes, an acquisition will take place where part of the consideration is in cash and the remainder is in another asset (or a debt instrument or shares). In this case, *the cash portion of the transaction* would be reported in the CFS while the non-cash portion would be omitted. For example, suppose that a building costing $4,000,000 is acquired by paying $1,000,000 cash and issuing a $3,000,000 long-term note. The CFS would disclose only the $1,000,000 cash paid (as an investing activity), although the entry on the CFS should be referenced to the note that contains the details of the entire transaction.

**Evaluation**    In one sense, the exclusion of non-cash transactions is an appropriate focus on cash flows. On the other hand, the total exclusion of non-cash transactions from the CFS seems to give precedence to form over substance. For example, the purchase of another company (i.e., a business combination) through an issue of shares would not be reported in the CFS, while the issuance of shares for cash and the use of the proceeds to buy the company *would be* reported in the cash flow statement.

## Extraordinary Items

The CFS begins with net income in the operating activities section, and gains and losses from such things as the sale of capital assets are added back as non-cash items. Proceeds from the sale of these assets are included in investing activities. The same treatment applies to gains and losses classified as extraordinary items. That is, the operating activities section begins with bottom-line net income, and any extraordinary gain or loss, to the extent it does not reflect cash flow, is adjusted as a non-cash item. The cash inflows or outflows are then classified according to their nature. In addition, cash flows are shown on a before-tax basis. *The tax related to the extraordinary item remains in the operating activities section.*

For example, assume that a company reported $3.5 million as net income, after a (gross) extraordinary gain of $210,000, reported on the income statement as $180,000 after a tax provision of $30,000. The extraordinary item was the gain on the expropriation of a piece of land, with a cost of $50,000 and expropriation proceeds of $260,000. The CFS would reflect the following:

| | |
|---|---|
| Operating activities: | |
| Net income | $3,500,000 |
| Less: items not affecting cash: | |
| Extraordinary item (pre-tax) | (210,000) |
| Cash from operating activities | $3,290,000 |
| Investing activities | |
| Cash proceeds on expropriation of land | $ 260,000 |

### Income Tax

In general, income tax should be shown in the operating activities section. This presents no problem if income tax is reported on the income statement. Occasionally, however, income tax is reported on other statements. For example, if an error correction, reported on the retained earnings statement, were to be shown net of $20,000 of tax currently payable, this $20,000 should be reported on the CFS as a reduction to the cash provided by operations.

There are times when tax is specifically related to investing or financing activities. In these cases, tax may be classified as investing or financing. The standards provide no examples of these situations, and this requirement seems to contradict the requirement that cash flows from extraordinary items be shown on a before-tax basis in the appropriate section. However, there are times when capital transactions, such as dividend distributions, attract specific taxes. It seems logical that the related tax be shown with the cash flow.

### Interest and Dividends

Interest income and expense, and other investment income as well, offer a particular classification challenge. Current Canadian standards are clear that interest income and interest expense that have been included in determining net income should remain as part of operating cash flow. That is, interest expense and/or interest income is part of net income and stays there in the CFS, adjusted for changes in related accounts such as interest receivable or payable, if needed. Sometimes, interest payments are not included in net income; this interest would be classified according to its nature. For example, interest that has been capitalized would be reported as part of the investing category as an outflow to acquire the asset.

Dividend revenue from investments is subject to the same rule. Because the revenue is part of net income, cash from dividends is classified as an operating cash flow. If the accrual amount is different than cash received, an adjustment reflecting the change in dividends receivable is necessary.

Dividends paid, on the other hand, are usually on the retained earnings statement and would appear as a financing outflow. Occasionally, though, preferred shares are reclassified as debt if they have to be repaid at a certain point in time and at a set amount. If this happens, dividends paid are in substance an interest expense and are placed on the income statement. Then, the cash flow is an operating item.

**Other Alternatives** This classification of interest and dividends rests on whether or not the element gave rise to an *income statement* item—if so, then the cash flow goes in operating activities. The alternative view is that these are investing or financing cash flows. The choices, and their rationale, can be summarized:

| Cash Flow | Canadian Standards— CFS Classification | Alternative CFS Classification |
|---|---|---|
| Interest received | *Operating activities*—as long as related to income statement interest revenue | *Investing activities*—caused by an investment that is an investing decision |
| Interest paid | *Operating activities*—as long as related to income statement interest expense | *Financing activities*—caused by a loan that is a financing decision |
| Dividends received | *Operating activities*—as long as related to income statement investment revenue | *Investing activities*—caused by an investment that is an investing decision |
| Dividends paid | *Financing activities*—a return to shareholders *not* reported as an operating expense | *Operating activities*—a return to a provider of capital, analogous to interest paid on long-term debt |

**Disclosure of Cash Flow for/from Interest, Dividends, and Income Tax**  Perhaps because of the controversy over classification, or because the cash flows provide critical insights into important decisions of the company, Canadian companies are required to separately disclose cash flows from or for the following items, *if they are included on the income statement:*

- Interest received;
- Interest paid;
- Dividends received;
- Dividends paid; and
- Income tax paid.

Separate classification of these cash flows can be accomplished through supplementary disclosure, or the information can be included on the bottom of the CFS. For example, assume that Gerard Company reported $123,400 of interest expense and $21,600 of interest revenue. There were no dividends paid or received on the income statement. Interest payable increased by $5,700 during the year, and interest expense included $3,500 of bond discount amortization. Finally, interest receivable decreased by $2,300 during the year. Supplementary disclosure would appear as follows:

| | |
|---|---|
| Cash paid for interest ($123,400 − $5,700 − $3,500) | ($114,200) |
| Cash received for interest ($21,600 + $2,300) | $23,900 |

RIM includes the following in a disclosure note:

*Note 18 Supplemental information*

| | March 4 2006 | Feb. 26 2005 | Feb. 28 2004 |
|---|---|---|---|
| Interest paid during the year | $ 483 | $460 | $ 770 |
| Income taxes paid (refunded) during the year | 2,449 | 879 | (196) |

Note that if the direct method of presentation is used, then these cash flows are included on the face of the CFS, and no supplementary disclosure is required.

## SUMMARY OF REPORTING RECOMMENDATIONS

Canadian reporting standards require the following reporting with respect to the CFS:

- The CFS reports the changes in cash, cash equivalents (highly liquid investments with no more than a three-month term), net of bank overdrafts (if the overdraft account fluctuates regularly). The various components of cash must be reconciled to the balance sheet accounts.
- The statement should include only cash flows; non-cash transactions should not be reported on the CFS, but should be disclosed elsewhere in the financial statements as appropriate.
- Cash flows during the period should be classified as *operating*, *investing*, and *financing* activities.
- Reporting enterprises are *encouraged* to report cash flows from operations by the direct method, but are allowed to use the indirect method of presentation.
- Cash flows from various activities should not be netted or offset; the *gross* amount of inflows and outflows should be reported.
- Cash flows relating to extraordinary items should be classified according to their nature as operating, investing, or financing activities, and should be separately disclosed on a before-tax basis.
- Cash paid for dividends is a financing outflow.
- The amount of cash from/for interest and from dividends (and occasionally *for* dividends) that has been included in net income should be disclosed separately. This may be accomplished in a disclosure note.
- Cash flows arising from income tax on operating income should be separately disclosed as an operating activity. *If* income tax cash flows can be specifically identified with investing or financing activities, they should be classified as investing or financing activities.
- The cash flows arising from acquisitions and disposals of subsidiaries or other business units should be presented separately and classified as investing activities. Non-cash exchanges involving such acquisitions or disposals would *not* be reported on the CFS (but would be disclosed in a note). Disposals are not netted against acquisitions.

## CONCEPT REVIEW

1. When the operating activities section starts with net operating income, why is amortization added to derive cash flow from operating activities? Is amortization a source of cash?

2. Explain why a gain on the sale of equipment is subtracted in the reconciliation of income and operating cash flows.

3. Why are changes in the balance of accounts receivable included in the CFS under the indirect presentation approach, but not disclosed under the direct presentation approach?

4. If salaries payable increases during the year, why does this imply that salary expense exceeds salary payments?

5. How are extraordinary items shown on the CFS?

6. What special disclosure is needed for cash paid for interest?

# INTERPRETATION ISSUES

## Quality of Earnings

Investment analysts sometimes refer to the **earnings quality** of a company that they are analyzing. This concept relates the amount of net income to the amount of cash flow from operations. A company is said to have high earnings quality when there is a close correspondence between *net income* and *cash flow from operations*, especially if the close relationship between earnings and cash flow persists over several years.

In contrast, a company that reports earnings that are not closely related to cash flows is said to have low earnings quality. In some companies, cash flows and earnings are actually counter-indicative. That is, a company can have high earnings but a negative cash flow from operations because of soaring receivables or expanding inventories; this situation often makes analysts a bit nervous, especially if it continues for more than one year.

On the other hand, a company can have low earnings (or even a loss) and still have positive cash flows from operations. This commonly happens when net income includes a large amount of amortization of capitalized costs. Lenders may be quite willing to lend to such a company on the strength of the cash flow, despite the existence of losses, because they are convinced that there is adequate cash flow to service the loan (that is, to pay the interest and repay the principal).

## Effect of Accounting Policy Choices on the Cash Flow Statement

One of the reasons that users like to see the CFS is that "cash doesn't lie." A perception exists among many users that while managers and accountants can adopt accounting policies that can have a significant and substantial effect on the measurement of net income, they have little room to manipulate cash flows.

To a considerable extent, this perception is correct. For example, management of almost every type of enterprise makes policy decisions about revenue recognition, operating expense recognition, and amortization policy (i.e., method, life, and salvage value).

In addition, there are many accounting estimates made by management regarding almost every asset on the balance sheet (such as year-end accruals, bad-debt provisions, inventory obsolescence writedowns, and investment write-offs). These estimates are influenced by external events and are not entirely under the control of management, but management is responsible for making those estimates and certainly can influence their amount and timing of recognition.

Accounting policy decisions and management's measurement estimates can significantly affect net income, but they will have no impact on the underlying cash flow. It is true, therefore, that the overall net cash flow for an accounting period is unaffected by accounting policy choices and estimates.

**Policy and Cash Flow**   However, there is a certain type of accounting policy decision that affects the CFS by changing the classification of items on the CFS, and that is whether to expense or **capitalize** one or more types of cost. If expenditures of a certain category (i.e., development costs) are charged to expense, they will be included as a deduction in net income and be included in operating cash flow.

On the other hand, if those expenditures are capitalized, they will appear on the CFS as an *investing* activity. In subsequent years, amortization of capitalized costs is deducted in determining net income, but is then added back to net income to derive cash flow from operations.

The result is that capitalized costs *never* enter into operating cash flow but will appear only as an investing activity. For example, an organization that capitalizes and amortizes its development costs will show a consistently higher cash flow from operations than one that charges such costs to expense, all other things being equal.

## ETHICAL ISSUES

Choice of accounting policy must be based on the facts, the user environment and the competitive situation. Policies that are chosen to manipulate certain measurements, or foster erroneous conclusions by financial statement users, are not acceptable. However, accountants must be aware of the implication of picking a certain policy. A decision to defer costs, and amortize them over the period of use instead of immediate expensing, will definitely change the presentation of cash flows in the various categories of the CFS.

## CONCEPT REVIEW

1. If cash from operating activities increases as net income increases, and declines when net income declines, what does this imply about the quality of earnings?

2. If development costs are deferred and amortized, how will they be reflected on the CFS? If they are expensed?

## ANALYZING MORE COMPLEX SITUATIONS

### T-Account Method

When preparing the CFS for Simple Limited, we used an informal, ad hoc approach. We went down the balance sheet and filled in the appropriate amounts in the CFS. In the process, we explained all of the changes in the non-cash accounts, and thus indirectly explained all of the changes in the cash accounts.

While the informal approach is completely acceptable, in complex situations it is easy to lose track. Therefore, it is common to use some form of T-account approach, or a spreadsheet (see chapter appendix), to force some discipline on the process and to help ensure that relevant transactions are not overlooked. The method used to organize information does not affect the final CFS. A more formal approach is useful because it:

- Provides an organized format for documenting the preparation process;
- Facilitates review and evaluation by others;
- Provides proofs of accuracy; and
- Formally keeps track of the changes in balance sheet accounts and ensures that all accounts are explained.

The T-accounts used in this approach are not actual ledger accounts. Rather, they are workspaces in account format used to accumulate the information necessary to prepare the CFS and to explain all account balance changes. The cash T-account accumulates all changes in cash (and cash equivalents) and is divided into three sections, corresponding to the three CFS categories.

### Example

The comparative balance sheet and the income statement for Ling Corporation are shown in Exhibit 5-7, along with some important supplementary information. From the balance sheet, we can see that cash increased by $14,000 during the year. (The most recent year is shown in the first numerical column, as is standard practice in Canadian financial statements.) Short-term liquid investments, however, decreased by $24,000. Short-term liquid investments are *cash equivalents*, and thus the actual change in cash is really a decrease of $10,000.

| | Ending | Beginning | Change | |
|---|---|---|---|---|
| Cash balance | $50,000 | $36,000 | $ 14,000 | increase |
| Short-term investments | 10,000 | 34,000 | (24,000) | decrease |
| Total | $60,000 | $70,000 | | |
| Net increase (decrease) in cash | | | $(10,000) | decrease |

The task of the CFS is to explain the transactions that caused this decrease of $10,000 in cash and cash equivalents. As cash flows are identified by reconciling the individual balance sheet accounts, the offsetting cash effect is entered into the cash T-account.

## EXHIBIT 5-7

## Ling Corporation
## Balance Sheet

| 31 December | 20X5 | 20X4 |
|---|---|---|
| **Assets** | | |
| Current assets: | | |
| Cash | $ 50,000 | $ 36,000 |
| Short-term liquid investments | 10,000 | 34,000 |
| Accounts receivable | 84,000 | 70,000 |
| Inventories | 42,000 | 30,000 |
| Prepaid expenses | 15,000 | 11,000 |
| | 201,000 | 181,000 |
| Fixed assets: | | |
| Land | 50,000 | 50,000 |
| Plant and equipment | 740,000 | 615,000 |
| Accumulated amortization | (260,000) | (215,000) |
| | 530,000 | 450,000 |
| Deferred development costs | 82,000 | 76,000 |
| Long-term investments | 92,000 | 70,000 |
| Total assets | $905,000 | $777,000 |
| **Liabilities and shareholders' equity** | | |
| Current liabilities: | | |
| Bank loan | $ 20,000 | $ 5,000 |
| Accounts payable | 36,000 | 45,000 |
| Dividends payable | 10,000 | 5,000 |
| | 66,000 | 55,000 |
| Long-term liabilities: | | |
| Bonds payable | 146,000 | 133,000 |
| Future income tax | 27,000 | 24,000 |
| Total liabilities | 239,000 | 212,000 |
| Shareholders' equity: | | |
| Preferred shares | 142,000 | 120,000 |
| Common shares | 230,000 | 180,000 |
| Retained earnings | 294,000 | 265,000 |
| | 666,000 | 565,000 |
| Total liabilities and shareholders' equity | $905,000 | $777,000 |

continued on next page

| EXHIBIT 5-7 | | (cont'd) |

## Ling Corporation
## Statement of Income and Retained Earnings

Year ended 31 December 20X5

| | | |
|---|---:|---:|
| Sales revenue | $960,000 | |
| Gain on sale of equipment | 4,000 | |
| | | $964,000 |
| Operating expenses | | |
| Cost of goods sold | 597,000 | |
| Interest expense | 18,000 | |
| Provision for income taxes | 54,000 | |
| Wages expense | 100,000 | |
| Other operating expenses | 131,000 | 900,000 |
| Net income | | 64,000 |
| Dividends declared | | (35,000) |
| Retained earnings, 1 January | | 265,000 |
| Retained earnings, 31 December | | $294,000 |

*Additional information:*
1. Cost of goods sold includes amortization of $65,000.
2. Other operating expenses includes amortization of deferred development costs of $5,000.
3. During 20X5, the corporation issued preferred shares with a market value of $22,000 for 1,000 common shares of THB Corporation. The THB shares are being held as a long-term investment. Market value and cost are identical for long-term investments.
4. Old equipment was sold for $9,000; the original cost was $25,000.
5. Bonds with a face value of $20,000 were repurchased at par and retired.
6. Other operating expenses includes a loss of $2,000 from liquidating the short-term investments (for net proceeds of $22,000).

## T-Account Procedures

The starting point is to sketch a simple T-account for each balance sheet account, including a single T-account for *cash and cash equivalents*. See Exhibit 5-8. The cash T-account has to be physically large; it is where all the information necessary for preparing the CFS will be accumulated. Within the cash T-account, three subsections are set up, one for each type of cash activity: operating, investing, and financing.

The second step is to insert the beginning balance of each account at the top, and the ending balance at the bottom of each T-account. Accuracy is critical. Alternatively, only the net *change* in the account may be used. This is a matter of personal preference.

The third step is to make reconciliation entries directly in the T-accounts that duplicate the entries that were made during the year, including those made to cash. It is essential to cross-reference the entries, so that it is straightforward to relate the different elements of a particular transaction. Generally speaking, the place to start is with the reconciliation of retained earnings, because it is where the net income for the year has been transferred. Net income is the top line in the operating activities section. Starting with net income also focuses attention on the income statement and on the adjustments that are necessary to remove the effects of interperiod allocations.

Ling Corporation's statement of income and retained earnings reveals that the change in retained earnings consists of two items: (1) net income, and (2) dividends declared. The net

$29,000 increase in the retained earnings balance came about as the result of $64,000 in net income and $35,000 in dividends declared. Therefore, the first reconciling entry is to disaggregate the net income into its separately reported components:

a.

| | | |
|---|---|---|
| *Cash: operating activities*, net income | 64,000 | |
|     Retained earnings | | 64,000 |

The second reconciling entry is to record the dividends declared:

b.

| | | |
|---|---|---|
| Retained earnings | 35,000 | |
|     *Cash: financing activities*, dividends declared | | 35,000 |

Observe that these entries are recreations of the original entries to (a) transfer net income into the retained earnings account and (b) to record the declaration of dividends. Dividends, for example, are debited to the retained earnings balance sheet account in the T-accounts and credited to cash. The actual cash paid for dividends will be later calculated after including the change in the dividends payable account.

The rest of the reconciliation entries are as follows, considering first the list of items of additional information in Exhibit 5-7:

c. Amortization of $65,000 was expensed during the period. The entry is as follows:

| | | |
|---|---|---|
| Amortization expense (*Cash: operating*) | 65,000 | |
|     Accumulated amortization | | 65,000 |

This entry is reproduced in the T-accounts, with the debit placed in cash, under *operating activities*.

d. Amortization of deferred development costs amounting to $5,000 was recorded during the year. The entry is entered in the T-accounts:

| | | |
|---|---|---|
| Amortization of development costs (*Cash: operating*) | 5,000 | |
|     Deferred development costs | | 5,000 |

e. The company entered into an exchange of shares that was worth $22,000. That is, it acquired a long-term investment in another company's shares in exchange for Ling's own preferred shares. No cash changed hands, so this is an example of a non-cash transaction. Even though the transaction resulted in a material change in the asset and equity structure of the company, it will be disclosed in a note to the financial statements and will not be reported on the CFS. Therefore, the effects of the increase of $22,000 on long-term investments and on preferred shares are offset against each other in the balance sheet T-accounts, with no corresponding entry to cash:

| | | |
|---|---|---|
| Long-term investments | 22,000 | |
|     Preferred shares | | 22,000 |

f. Old equipment was sold for $9,000; the original cost was $25,000. Since the income statement shows a gain of $4,000, the net book value at the time of sale must have been $5,000. (The gain is the amount by which the proceeds exceed the net book value; since the gain was $4,000 and the proceeds were $9,000, the net book value must have been

$5,000.) Accumulated amortization on the asset sold must therefore have been $20,000. That is,

| | | |
|---|---|---|
| Proceeds from sale | | $9,000 |
| Net book value of the asset sold: | | |
| Historical cost | $25,000 | |
| Accumulated amortization | ? | 5,000 |
| Gain on sale | | $4,000 |

The "?" must be $20,000. The entry for the sale is as follows:

| | | |
|---|---|---|
| *Cash: investing activities*, sale of equipment | 9,000 | |
| Accumulated amortization | 20,000 | |
| Plant and equipment | | 25,000 |
| Gain on sale (*Operating*) | | 4,000 |

**g.** Bonds with a face value of $20,000 were repurchased and retired (at par, since there is no gain or loss on the income statement).

| | | |
|---|---|---|
| Bonds payable | 20,000 | |
| *Cash: financing activities*, bonds retired | | 20,000 |

The only other piece of additional information in Exhibit 5-7 is that other operating expenses includes a loss of $2,000 on liquidation of short-term investments. The initial reaction may be to eliminate this by adding it back to operating and to record $22,000 as an investing activity inflow. However, the catch here is that the loss relates to a component of cash. Since short-term liquid investments are a cash equivalent and included within our definition of cash, the loss really did cause cash and cash equivalents to decrease by $2,000. This amount is appropriately included in net income. Therefore, *there is no adjustment for gains and losses that are incurred within the cash and cash equivalent accounts*, including foreign currency exchange gains and losses.

**h.** The reconciliation entries that have been described above are those that result from the information provided in Exhibit 5-7. However, there obviously have been other transactions during the year that caused as-yet unexplained changes in the asset and equity accounts. An example is that of bonds payable. The bonds payable account grew from $133,000 to $146,000 during the year, a net increase of $13,000. However, to have a net increase of $13,000 after the $20,000 retirement, the company must have issued $33,000 in new bonds during the year:

| | | |
|---|---|---|
| *Cash: financing activities*, bonds issued | 33,000 | |
| Bonds payable | | 33,000 |

Reconciliations such as this one for the bond issuance sometimes are referred to as *hidden entries*, because they become apparent only as the result of reconciling those changes that are known beforehand. Once the known elements are entered, as above, the remaining reconciliation entries are all balancing entries that simply record the change in each account that is required to explain the net change, *after* taking into consideration the reconciliation entries already made. Starting with the first non-cash account, accounts receivable, they are as follows:

i.

| Accounts receivable | 14,000 | |
| Cash: operating | | 14,000 |

j.

| Inventories | 12,000 | |
| Cash: operating | | 12,000 |

k.

| Prepaid expenses | 4,000 | |
| Cash: operating | | 4,000 |

l.

| Plant and equipment | 150,000 | |
| Cash: investing activities, purchase of equipment | | 150,000 |

The *net* increase of $125,000 in plant and equipment is due to acquisitions of $150,000 and the retirement of equipment that originally cost $25,000.

m.

| Deferred development costs | 11,000 | |
| Cash: investing activities, investment in development costs | | 11,000 |

Since the net account increase was $6,000 *after* amortization, $11,000 must have been capitalized during the year.

n.

| Cash: financing activities, increase in bank loan | 15,000 | |
| Bank loan | | 15,000 |

o.

| Accounts payable | 9,000 | |
| Cash: operating | | 9,000 |

p.

| Cash: financing (dividends) | 5,000 | |
| Dividends payable | | 5,000 |

The change in dividends payable does not affect operating cash flows, because dividends are a financing cash flow. The change in dividends payable is posted to the financing portion of the cash T-account, and reduces the cash outflow for dividends. This is logical—dividends payable increased, and therefore comparatively less of the dividends declared were actually paid. Dividends paid is shown as one number on the CFS, calculated as dividends declared combined with the change in the payable account.

q.

| Cash: operating | 3,000 | |
| Future income tax | | 3,000 |

The $3,000 increase in the balance sheet account for future income tax represents the part of income tax expense that was not paid in cash.

r.

| Cash: financing activities, common shares issued | 50,000 | |
| Common shares | | 50,000 |

Once all of the reconciliation entries are in the T-accounts, check for completeness by adding each balance sheet T-account to make sure that the beginning balance plus the reconciliation entries equals the ending balance. Then, total the inflows and outflows in the cash account to ensure that it adds correctly.

The cash account in Exhibit 5-8 now contains all of the information that is necessary for preparing a CFS. It is important to remember that Exhibit 5-8 is *not* a CFS in itself; it is only the data analysis that supports the CFS.

## EXHIBIT 5-8

### Ling Corporation
### T-Account Analysis

#### Cash and cash equivalents

| Opening | 70,000* | | |
|---|---|---|---|
| **Operating activities** | | | |
| a) net income | 64,000 | f) gain on sale | 4,000 |
| c) amortization | 65,000 | i) accounts receivable | 14,000 |
| d) amortization | 5,000 | j) inventory | 12,000 |
| q) future income tax | 3,000 | k) prepaid expenses | 4,000 |
| | | o) accounts payable | 9,000 |
| **Investing activities** | | | |
| f) sale of equipment | 9,000 | l) purchased plant and equipment | 150,000 |
| | | m) purchased deferred development costs | 11,000 |
| **Financing activities** | | | |
| h) issued bond | 33,000 | b) dividends | 35,000 |
| n) increased loan | 15,000 | g) repaid bond | 20,000 |
| p) reduced dividends payable | 5,000 | | |
| r) issued common shares | 50,000 | | |
| Closing | 60,000* | | |

*Cash plus short-term liquid investments

| Accounts receivable | | | | Inventories | | | | Prepaid expenses | | | | Land | | |
|---|---|---|---|---|---|---|---|---|---|---|---|---|---|---|
| Op. | 70,000 | | | Op. | 30,000 | | | Op. | 11,000 | | | Op. | 50,000 | |
| i) | 14,000 | | | j) | 12,000 | | | k) | 4,000 | | | | | |
| Cl. | 84,000 | | | Cl. | 42,000 | | | Cl. | 15,000 | | | Cl. | 50,000 | |

| Plant and equipment | | | | Accumulated amortization | | | | Deferred development costs | | | | Long-term investments | | |
|---|---|---|---|---|---|---|---|---|---|---|---|---|---|---|
| Op. | 615,000 | | | | | Op. | 215,000 | Op. | 76,000 | | | Op. | 70,000 | |
| l) | 150,000 | f) | 25,000 | f) | 20,000 | c) | 65,000 | m) | 11,000 | d) | 5,000 | e) | 22,000 | |
| Cl. | 740,000 | | | | | Cl. | 260,000 | Cl. | 82,000 | | | Cl. | 92,000 | |

| Bank loan | | | | Accounts payable | | | | Dividends payable | | | | Bonds payable | | |
|---|---|---|---|---|---|---|---|---|---|---|---|---|---|---|
| | | Op. | 5,000 | | | Op. | 45,000 | | | Op. | 5,000 | | | Op. | 133,000 |
| | | n) | 15,000 | o) | 9,000 | | | | | p) | 5,000 | g) | 20,000 | h) | 33,000 |
| | | Cl. | 20,000 | | | Cl. | 36,000 | | | Cl. | 10,000 | | | Cl. | 146,000 |

| Future income tax | | | | Preferred shares | | | | Common shares | | | | Retained earnings | | |
|---|---|---|---|---|---|---|---|---|---|---|---|---|---|---|
| | | Op. | 24,000 | | | Op. | 120,000 | | | Op. | 180,000 | | | Op. | 265,000 |
| | | q) | 3,000 | | | e) | 22,000 | | | r) | 50,000 | b) | 35,000 | a) | 64,000 |
| | | Cl. | 27,000 | | | Cl. | 142,000 | | | Cl. | 230,000 | | | Cl. | 294,000 |

## Cash Flow Statement—Indirect Method

The CFS using the indirect approach for operating activities is shown in Exhibit 5-9. The indirect approach starts with net income, and makes all of the adjustments that are necessary to convert from the accrual basis to the cash basis. The two-step approach shown in Exhibit 5-9 is the most common format.

---

### EXHIBIT 5-9

### Ling Corporation Cash Flow Statement (Indirect Approach)

Year ended 31 December 20X5

| | | |
|---|---:|---:|
| Operating activities: | | |
| Net income | $ 64,000 | |
| Adjustments for items not affecting cash: | | |
| Amortization of plant and equipment | 65,000 | |
| Amortization of development costs | 5,000 | |
| Gain on sale of equipment | (4,000) | |
| Future income tax | 3,000 | |
| | 133,000 | |
| Changes in working capital amounts: | | |
| Increase in accounts receivable | (14,000) | |
| Increase in inventory | (12,000) | |
| Increase in prepaid expenses | (4,000) | |
| Decrease in accounts payable | (9,000) | |
| Cash provided (used) by operating activities | | $ 94,000 |
| Investing activities: | | |
| Acquisition of plant and equipment | (150,000) | |
| Investment in development costs | (11,000) | |
| Proceeds from sale of equipment | 9,000 | |
| Cash provided (used) by investing activities | | (152,000) |
| Financing activities: | | |
| Increase in short-term bank loan | 15,000 | |
| Issuance of bonds | 33,000 | |
| Retirement of bonds | (20,000) | |
| Common shares issued | 50,000 | |
| Dividends paid ($35,000 − $5,000) | (30,000) | |
| Cash provided (used) by financing activities | | 48,000 |
| Increase (decrease) in cash and cash equivalents during 20X5 | | $ (10,000) |
| Opening cash and cash equivalents | | $ 70,000 |
| Closing cash and cash equivalents | | $ 60,000 |
| Reconciliation of cash and cash equivalents: | | |
| Increase in cash | | $ 14,000 |
| Decrease in short-term investments | | (24,000) |
| Increase (decrease) in cash and cash equivalents | | $ (10,000) |
| Supplemental disclosures: | | |
| Cash payment for interest | | $ 18,000 |
| Cash payments for income tax ($54,000 − $3,000) | | $ 51,000 |

*Other disclosure note:*
Preferred shares were issued for 1,000 shares of THB Company, held as a long-term investment. The transaction was valued at $22,000.

The "non-cash" items are usually shown first. The "non-cash" adjustments represent the expenses and/or revenues that result from interperiod allocations, such as capital asset amortization, future income tax, deferred revenues, and also gains and losses. The second set of adjustments reflects the changes in the working capital balances.

The cash flow for income tax, investment revenue, and interest expense may be shown at the bottom of the CFS or in a disclosure note. In Exhibit 5-9, the disclosures are at the bottom of the statement. Cash paid for income tax is the $54,000 expense, less the $3,000 increase in the long-term liability, income tax. Interest expense of $18,000 has no related balance sheet accounts and therefore is assumed to be equal to cash paid.

## Cash Flow Statement—Direct Method

The operating activities section of the CFS can be presented using the direct method. The direct method may be prepared through the following steps:

1. Begin with the analysis of operating activities under the indirect method. Specifically, refer to the journal entry analysis (or the summary of adjustments to operating activities in the T-accounts in Exhibit 5-8.)

2. Prepare a schedule to support the calculations for the direct method. This schedule should have three columns. In the first column, copy the income statement amounts,

---

### EXHIBIT 5-10

#### Ling Corporation
#### Cash Flow Statement (Direct Method)

| Year ended 31 December 20X5 | Income Statement | | Adjustments (refer to journal entries) | Cash Flow |
|---|---|---|---|---|
| Sales revenue | $960,000 | i. | (14,000) | $946,000 |
| Gain on sale of equipment | 4,000 | f. | (4,000) | 0 |
| Cost of goods sold | (597,000) | c. | 65,000 | (553,000) |
| | | j. | (12,000) | |
| | | o. | (9,000) | |
| Interest expense | (18,000) | | | (18,000) |
| Provision for income tax | (54,000) | q. | 3,000 | (51,000) |
| Wages expense | (100,000) | | | (100,000) |
| Other operating expenses | (131,000) | d. | 5,000 | (130,000) |
| | | k. | (4,000) | |
| Net income and cash flow from operations | $ 64,000 | | | $ 94,000 |

#### Ling Corporation
#### Partial Cash Flow Statement

Year ended 31 December 20X5

| | |
|---|---|
| Operating activities | |
| Cash received from customers | $946,000 |
| Cash paid to suppliers ($553,000 + $130,000) | (683,000) |
| Cash paid to employees | (100,000) |
| Cash paid for interest | (18,000) |
| Cash paid for income tax | (51,000) |
| Cash from operating activities | $ 94,000 |

with all expenses in brackets. This column should add to net income (See Exhibit 5-10, first column.)

3. Copy all the adjustments collected in Step 1 into the second column. Make sure the credit adjustments are in brackets. (See second column, Exhibit 5-10.) Sort the adjustments to the line of the income statement to which they pertain. For example, accounts receivable is copied onto the revenue line, the adjustment for amortization on the COGS line, since the question states that amortization is part of COGS, and so on.

4. Cross-add the schedule, entering cash flows in the third column (See Exhibit 5-10.) Notice that non-cash items, such as amortization and gains and losses, disappear as they are adjusted to zero.

5. Prepare the operating activities section of the CFS, using the numeric data from the schedule, but changing the captions to appropriate cash flow descriptions, and group cash flows as is considered desirable.

The final product is shown at the bottom of Exhibit 5-10. The $94,000 total cash from operating activities is the same as in Exhibit 5-9, but the presentation is different. The investing and financing sections of the CFS are not dependent on the format chosen for the operating section, and are not repeated here because they would be identical to those shown in Exhibit 5-9.

## SUMMARY OF ADJUSTMENTS IN OPERATING ACTIVITIES

To prepare the CFS, it is necessary to convert accrual-basis earnings to the cash basis. Basically, there are three types of adjustments that must be made to the accrual-basis income number:

| Type of Adjustment | Reason for Adjustment | Examples |
|---|---|---|
| The effects of cost/revenue allocations must be reversed | • Income statement item has no related cash flow this period<br>• Intent is to arrive at net income as if the item were not included | • Add back amortization of all kinds<br>• Add back increase in future income tax, deduct decrease in future income tax<br>• Add back bond discount amortization, deduct bond premium amortization<br>• Add back writedown of assets<br>• Add back non-cash compensation expense from stock options<br>• Deduct investment revenue under the equity method unless it was received in the form of dividends |
| Certain transactions, the net effects of which are included in net income, must be reclassified as investing or financing activities. | Net effect in net income does not equal cash flow | • Add back losses<br>• Deduct gains |

continued on next page

| Type of Adjustment | Reason for Adjustment | Examples |
|---|---|---|
| Accruals must be "backed out" of various asset and liability accounts to determine cash inflows and outflows for operations. | • Income statement item has caused balance sheet account because cash flow is before or after income statement recognition<br>• Balance sheet accounts must be directly related to an income statement account (e.g., sales is related to accounts receivable) | • Change in accounts receivable, accounts payable, prepaid expenses, inventory, income tax payable, etc.<br>• See chart below for direction of change |

When adjustments must be made for changes in working capital accounts related to operations, the protocol is:

| Change in Account Balance During the Year | | |
|---|---|---|
| | **Increase** | **Decrease** |
| Asset (e.g., accounts receivable) | *Subtract* increase from net income | *Add* decrease to net income |
| Liability (e.g., accounts payable) | *Add* increase to net income | *Subtract* decrease from net income |

## INTERNATIONAL PERSPECTIVE

The IASB CFS reporting requirements are found in IAS 7. The standard is compatible with the Canadian standard, and indeed is identical to the Canadian standard in many respects. IAS 7 requires a CFS to be included as an integral part of the financial statements. Cash flows are categorized in operating, investing, and financing sections, reconciled to the change in cash. Cash is defined as cash plus cash equivalents, less bank overdrafts. The description of operating, investing, and financing cash flows is familiar. Either the direct or indirect method of operating activities is permitted. Netting is not permitted, except as described in the Canadian standards. Non-cash transactions are excluded. Classification of income tax, and supplementary disclosures for cash flow for interest, dividends, and tax, are again familiar.

However, while the Canadian classification system for interest and dividends is *allowed* under IAS rules, the IAS permits a different classification at the company's option, as illustrated in the table below.

| Financial Statement Element | Canadian Classification Requirement | IAS Classification Requirement |
|---|---|---|
| Interest paid, included in net income | Operating activities | Operating activities *or* financing activities |
| Interest received, included in net income | Operating activities | Operating activities *or* investing activities |

| Financial Statement Element | Canadian Classification Requirement | IAS Classification Requirement |
|---|---|---|
| Dividends paid | Financing activities | Operating activities *or* financing activities |
| Dividends received, included in net income | Operating activities | Operating activities *or* investing activities |

These classification differences might make comparisons of cash flows difficult unless differences were adjusted.

## CONCEPT REVIEW

1. What is the effect on the CFS of selling a short-term investment, classified as a cash equivalent, at a $3,000 loss?

2. A company acquires a substantial amount of capital assets by issuing its own common shares to the seller. What is the impact of this transaction on the CFS?

3. What section(s) of the CFS will be identical if the direct or indirect methods are chosen?

4. How are Canadian and IAS standards different?

## RELEVANT STANDARDS

*CICA Handbook:*
- Section 1540, Cash Flow Statements

IASB:
- *IAS 7,* Cash Flow Statements

## SUMMARY OF KEY POINTS

1. The CFS is one of the three major financial statements. It is structured to report cash flows in meaningful categories.

2. The basic objective of the CFS is to reveal the cash inflows and outflows of the reporting period, segregated between cash flows from operating activities, cash flows relating to investing activities, and cash flows relating to financing activities. In each category, *cash flow* includes both inflows and outflows.

3. Cash flow information is used to predict future cash flows and to assess liquidity, the ability of a firm to pay dividends and obligations, the ability of a firm to adapt to changes in the business environment, the quality of earnings, and for other purposes.

4. The reporting basis for the CFS is the net cash position. The net cash position includes cash and cash equivalents, less bank overdrafts.

5. Cash equivalents include all short-term liquid investments that are readily convertible into cash and that bear little risk of change in value (maximum three-month term).

6. The components of cash plus cash equivalents should be disclosed and should be reconciled to the balance sheet.

7. Operating cash flows are related to the main activities of the business and are connected to the earnings process.

8. Investing cash flows describe long-term asset acquisitions and the proceeds from sale of long-term assets.

9. Financing cash flows describe the sources of debt and equity financing and repayments of liabilities and equities, excluding liabilities directly relating to operations such as accounts payable.

10. Dividend payments to shareholders are reported as a financing outflow.

11. There are two allowable methods of reporting cash from operations—the direct and the indirect presentation methods. The indirect method reports operating activities by showing a reconciliation of net income with net cash flow from operating activities. The direct method reports the cash inflows from the main classifications of revenues and cash outflows from the main classifications of expenses. Standard setters encourage companies to use the direct method but few Canadian companies use this formatting option.

12. The operating activities sections of both the direct and indirect CFSs convert accrual income to cash-basis income, the net cash flow from operations. The indirect method uses a series of addbacks to negate the effects of accruals and interperiod allocations. Examples of adjustments are adding back amortization and adjusting for changes in operating working capital accounts.

13. In the investing and financing sections, gross cash flows are reported. Transactions are not netted against other flows in the same category.

14. Non-cash transactions (e.g., acquiring plant assets by issuing a long-term note) are not shown as outflows and inflows on the CFS. These transactions should be disclosed elsewhere in the financial statements, normally in a note.

15. Extraordinary items are an addback in the operating activities section. Cash generated or used by/for extraordinary items is disclosed in the investing or financing section as appropriate. Addbacks and cash flows are disclosed at the pre-tax amount.

16. Interest paid and interest received, included in net income, are included in the operating activities section, as are dividends received. There are other classifications available internationally. Income tax is generally included in the operating activities section.

17. The amount of cash from/for interest and from dividends (and occasionally *for* dividends) that have been included in net income should be disclosed separately. This may be accomplished in a disclosure note.

18. Net cash flow is not affected by accounting policy choices or by management's accounting estimates. However, the reported cash flow from operations can be increased by capitalizing certain types of costs (e.g., development costs), because the costs are reclassified as investing activities and amortization has no effect on operating cash flows in future periods.

19. There are many approaches to preparing the CFS. The same objectives apply to all—analyze transactions to identify all cash flows, reconciling items, and non-cash transactions.

20. The format-free approach to preparing the CFS emphasizes transaction analysis and uses no particular format. Search for transactions in the following order: income statement, additional information, and comparative balance sheets.

21. The T-account method is an alternative way to analyze information prior to preparing the CFS. The T-account method is an analytical approach; it is not a method of presentation.

22. In the T-account method, a T-account for cash (and cash equivalents) is used to accumulate all of the information needed to prepare the CFS. All changes in balance sheet accounts are traced through the accounts to isolate their cash effects.

23. IAS 7 is compatible with Canadian reporting standards, but allows additional reporting alternatives for interest paid and received, and dividends paid and received.

## KEY TERMS

## REVIEW PROBLEM

The Phillies Corporation assembled the following information relevant when preparing its 20X7 CFS:

| Balance sheet accounts 31 December | 20X7 | 20X6 |
|---|---|---|
| Cash | $ 62,000 | $ 50,000 |
| Temporary investments; two-month term | — | 150,000 |
| Accounts receivable, net | 80,000 | 60,000 |
| Inventory | 30,000 | 18,000 |
| Equipment, net of accumulated amortization | 500,000 | 300,000 |
| Goodwill | 70,000 | 90,000 |
| Total assets | $742,000 | $668,000 |
| Accounts payable | $ 60,000 | $ 40,000 |
| Salaries payable | 50,000 | 60,000 |
| Interest payable | 9,000 | 6,000 |
| Income tax payable | 22,000 | 12,000 |
| Mortgage payable | 110,000 | 120,000 |
| Bonds payable | 100,000 | 200,000 |
| Premium on bonds payable | 3,000 | 8,000 |
| Common shares | 170,000 | 150,000 |
| Retained earnings | 218,000 | 72,000 |
| Total liabilities and shareholders' equity | $742,000 | $668,000 |

| Income statement accounts, year ended 31 December 20X7 | |
|---|---|
| Sales | $820,000 |
| Cost of goods sold | (380,000) |
| Amortization expense | (100,000) |
| Write-off of goodwill | (20,000) |
| Other expenses | (46,000) |
| Loss on bond retirement | (3,000) |
| Interest expense | (22,000) |
| Income tax expense | (73,000) |
| Unusual gain | 10,000 |
| Net income | $186,000 |

*Additional information:*

1. Phillies declared $40,000 in dividends in 20X7.

2. Equipment (cost $100,000, accumulated amortization, $60,000) was destroyed by fire. Proceeds from insurance, $50,000.

3. Bonds were retired on 1 January 20X7 for $107,000. The net book value of the bonds was $104,000: $100,000 at par value plus $4,000 premium.

4. The temporary investments are short-term money-market certificates.

5. Goodwill was written down by $20,000 because of impairment.

**Required:**

Prepare the 20X7 CFS for Phillies Corporation. Use the indirect method of presentation for the operating activities section. Use whichever method of preparation you feel most comfortable with (i.e., choose from among the format-free, T-account, or spreadsheet [see the Appendix to this chapter] methods). The suggested solution uses T-accounts.

## REVIEW PROBLEM—SOLUTION

*The T-account analysis appears on the following page.* Other approaches are equally valid—it's the result that matters. The actual CFS is shown at the end of this solution. Explanations for T-account entries are as follows:

a. Net income is $186,000. The T-account entry records net income.

b. Increase in accounts receivable; less cash was received from customers than was recognized as revenue.

c. Increase in inventories; more cash paid for inventories than recognized as COGS.

d. Increase in accounts payable; less paid to trade creditors than recognized as expenses.

e. Amortization expense removed from operating expenses—a non-cash expense.

f. Goodwill write-off removed from operating expenses—another non-cash expense.

g. Salaries payable decreased, requiring more cash.

h. Adjustment to write off destroyed equipment and to record the insurance proceeds; $10,000 gain removed from operating earnings, and proceeds recorded as an inflow in the investing activities section. Proceeds of $50,000 are shown on the CFS.

i. Increase in interest payable, indicating that less cash was paid for interest than the amount of interest expense accrued.

j. Entry to record the bond retirement on 1 January 20X7:

| | | |
|---|---:|---:|
| Bonds payable | 100,000 | |
| Bond premium (1/2 of $8,000 beginning balance) | 4,000 | |
| Loss on bond retirement | 3,000 | |
|     *Cash: financing activities*, bond repayment (given) | | 107,000 |

k. Amortization of bond premium on those bonds not retired in 20X7: total reduction in bond premium account was from $8,000 to $3,000; bond retirement accounted for $4,000 of the reduction; remaining $1,000 must be due to amortization, which would have been charged to interest expense.

l. Increase in income taxes payable; less tax paid than accrued.

m. Dividends declared *and paid* (i.e., there is no dividends payable account, so all must have been paid).

n. "Plug" entry to account for the otherwise unexplained change in the balance of the equipment account; the increase must have been due to the purchase of new equipment.

o. Decrease in mortgage payable implies repayment of mortgage, in the absence of other information.

p. Increase in common shares implies issuance of additional shares, in the absence of evidence to the contrary.

## T-Account Analysis

### Cash and cash equivalents

| | | | | |
|---|---|---|---|---|
| Opening | 200,000 | | | |
| *Operating activities* | | | | |
| a) net income | 186,000 | b) accounts receivable | | 20,000 |
| d) accounts payable | 20,000 | c) inventory | | 12,000 |
| e) amortization expense | 100,000 | g) accrued salaries | | 10,000 |
| f) goodwill write-off | 20,000 | h) unusual gain | | 10,000 |
| i) interest payable | 3,000 | k) premium amortization | | 1,000 |
| j) loss on bond retirement | 3,000 | | | |
| l) income tax payable | 10,000 | | | |
| *Investing activities* | | | | |
| h) insurance proceeds | 50,000 | n) equipment bought | | 340,000 |
| *Financing activities* | | | | |
| p) issued common shares | 20,000 | j) bond retirement | | 107,000 |
| | | m) dividends paid | | 40,000 |
| | | o) mortgage repayment | | 10,000 |
| Closing | 62,000 | | | |

| Accounts receivable, net | | | | | Inventory | | | | | Equipment, net | | | | | Goodwill | | | |
|---|---|---|---|---|---|---|---|---|---|---|---|---|---|---|---|---|---|---|
| Op. | 60,000 | | | | Op. | 18,000 | | | | Op. | 300,000 | | | | Op. | 90,000 | | |
| b) | 20,000 | | | | c) | 12,000 | | | | h) | 60,000 | e) | 100,000 | | | | f) | 20,000 |
| | | | | | | | | | | n) | 340,000 | h) | 100,000 | | | | | |
| Cl. | 80,000 | | | | Cl. | 30,000 | | | | | | | | | Cl. | 70,000 | | |
| | | | | | | | | | | Cl. | 500,000 | | | | | | | |

| Accounts payable | | | | Salaries payable | | | | Interest payable | | | | Income tax payable | | | |
|---|---|---|---|---|---|---|---|---|---|---|---|---|---|---|---|
| | | Op. | 40,000 | | | Op. | 60,000 | | | Op. | 6,000 | | | Op. | 12,000 |
| | | d) | 20,000 | g) | 10,000 | | | | | i) | 3,000 | | | l) | 10,000 |
| | | Cl. | 60,000 | | | Cl. | 50,000 | | | Cl. | 9,000 | | | Cl. | 22,000 |

| Mortgage payable | | | | Bonds payable | | | | Premium on bonds | | | | Common shares | | | |
|---|---|---|---|---|---|---|---|---|---|---|---|---|---|---|---|
| | | Op. | 120,000 | | | Op. | 200,000 | | | Op. | 8,000 | | | Op. | 150,000 |
| o) | 10,000 | | | j) | 100,000 | | | j) | 4,000 | | | | | p) | 20,000 |
| | | | | | | | | k) | 1,000 | | | | | | |
| | | Cl. | 110,000 | | | Cl. | 100,000 | | | | | | | Cl. | 170,000 |
| | | | | | | | | | | Cl. | 3,000 | | | | |

| Retained earnings | | | |
|---|---|---|---|
| | | Op. | 72,000 |
| m) | 40,000 | a) | 186,000 |
| | | Cl. | 218,000 |

## Phillies Corporation
## Cash Flow Statement

Year ended 31 December 20X7

**Operating activities:**

| | | |
|---|---:|---:|
| Net income | | $ 186,000 |
| | | |
| Plus (less) items not affecting cash: | | |
| Amortization expense | 100,000 | |
| Write-off of goodwill | 20,000 | |
| Loss on bond retirement | 3,000 | |
| Premium amortization | (1,000) | |
| Unusual gain | (10,000) | 112,000 |
| | | 298,000 |
| | | |
| Plus (less) changes in non-cash working capital | | |
| Increase in accounts receivable | (20,000) | |
| Increase in accounts payable | 20,000 | |
| Increase in inventories | (12,000) | |
| Decrease in accrued salaries | (10,000) | |
| Interest accrued, but not paid | 3,000 | |
| Increase in income tax payable | 10,000 | (9,000) |
| | | 289,000 |
| | | |
| **Investing activities:** | | |
| Insurance proceeds from equipment | | |
| destroyed by fire | 50,000 | |
| New equipment purchased | (340,000) | (290,000) |
| | | |
| **Financing activities:** | | |
| Retirement of bonds | (107,000) | |
| Dividends paid | (40,000) | |
| Reduction of mortgage principal | (10,000) | |
| Issuance of common shares | 20,000 | (137,000) |
| | | |
| **Net increase (decrease) in cash** | | $(138,000) |
| Opening cash and cash equivalents | | $ 200,000 |
| Closing cash and cash equivalents | | $  62,000 |
| | | |
| **Reconciliation of cash and cash equivalents:** | | |
| Cash | | $  12,000 |
| Temporary investments | | (150,000) |
| Net change | | $(138,000) |

# APPENDIX

## SPREADSHEET METHOD

The main body of the chapter pointed out that the analytical method used to derive the CFS is not important; what matters is the result. This chapter has illustrated two approaches—the ad hoc approach and the T-account approach. Another method that is popular, especially when complete documentation is important, is the spreadsheet approach. In essence, the spreadsheet approach puts the T-account data into columnar form.

## SPREADSHEET PROCEDURES

To set up the spreadsheet, transfer the accounts and account balances from the balance sheet to a four-column spreadsheet. Exhibit 5-A1 demonstrates the set-up for Ling Corporation, based on the chapter example and data in Exhibit 5-7. The 20X4 account balances are entered into the first column, and the 20X5 balances are entered into the last column. Reconciling entries are entered in the two middle columns.

The reconciling entries are exactly the same for the spreadsheet and the T-accounts. Refer to the chapter for an explanation of the cross-referenced entries. One additional entry is needed on the spreadsheet to record the change in cash.

**s.** The final reconciling entry transfers the change in cash and cash equivalents to the lower spreadsheet section. The $14,000 increase in cash and the $24,000 decrease in short-term investments are reconciled as follows:

| | | |
|---|---|---|
| Cash | 14,000 | |
| Change in cash and cash equivalents | 10,000 | |
| Short-term liquid investments | | 24,000 |

Entering the net change into the lower part of the statement balances the inflows and outflows. Totalling the debit and credit columns in the upper part of the worksheet reveals that they are in balance (at $311,000). The total of the debit and credit columns is meaningless *except* for the important fact that they balance. Any imbalance would indicate a debit-credit imbalance in the reconciliation entries.

The lower section of Exhibit 5-A1 now contains all of the information that is necessary for preparing a CFS.

## EXHIBIT 5-A1

### Ling Corporation
### Cash Flow Statement Worksheet

| | 31 December 20X4 | Key | Reconciliation Debit | Reconciliation Credit | Key | 31 December 20X5 |
|---|---|---|---|---|---|---|
| **Assets:** | | | | | | |
| Cash | $ 36,000 | (s) | $ 14,000 | | | $ 50,000 |
| Short-term liquid investments | 34,000 | | | $ 24,000 | (s) | 10,000 |
| Accounts receivable | 70,000 | (i) | 14,000 | | | 84,000 |
| Inventories | 30,000 | (j) | 12,000 | | | 42,000 |
| Prepaid expenses | 11,000 | (k) | 4,000 | | | 15,000 |
| Land | 50,000 | | | | | 50,000 |
| Plant and equipment | 615,000 | (l) | 150,000 | 25,000 | (f) | 740,000 |
| Accumulated amortization | (215,000) | (f) | 20,000 | 65,000 | (c) | (260,000) |
| Deferred development costs | 76,000 | (m) | 11,000 | 5,000 | (d) | 82,000 |
| Long-term investments | 70,000 | (e) | 22,000 | | | 92,000 |
| Total assets | $777,000 | | | | | $905,000 |

continued on next page

EXHIBIT 5-A1                                                    (cont'd)

## Ling Corporation
## Cash Flow Statement Worksheet

| | 31 December 20X4 | Key | Reconciliation Debit | Reconciliation Credit | Key | 31 December 20X5 |
|---|---|---|---|---|---|---|
| **Liabilities and shareholders' equity:** | | | | | | |
| Bank loan | $ 5,000 | | | $ 15,000 | (n) | $ 20,000 |
| Accounts payable | 45,000 | (o) | $ 9,000 | | | 36,000 |
| Dividends payable | 5,000 | | | 5,000 | (p) | 10,000 |
| Bonds payable | 133,000 | (g) | 20,000 | 33,000 | (h) | 146,000 |
| Future income tax | 24,000 | | | 3,000 | (q) | 27,000 |
| Preferred shares | 120,000 | | | 22,000 | (e) | 142,000 |
| Common shares | 180,000 | | | 50,000 | (r) | 230,000 |
| Retained earnings | 265,000 | (b) | 35,000 | 64,000 | (a) | 294,000 |
| Total equities | $777,000 | | $311,000 | $311,000 | | $905,000 |

## Components of the Cash Flow Statement

| | | Key | Debit | Credit | Key | |
|---|---|---|---|---|---|---|
| **Operating activities:** | | | | | | |
| *Net Income* | | (a) | $ 64,000 | | | |
| *Non-cash items* | | | | | | |
| Amortization expense | | (c) | 65,000 | | | |
| Amortization of development costs | | (d) | 5,000 | | | |
| Gain on sale of equipment | | | | 4,000 | (f) | |
| *Working capital changes* | | | | | | |
| Increase in accounts receivable | | | | 14,000 | (i) | |
| Increase in inventory | | | | 12,000 | (j) | |
| Increase in prepaid expenses | | | | 4,000 | (k) | |
| Decrease in accounts payable | | | | 9,000 | (o) | |
| Increase in future income tax | | (q) | 3,000 | | | 94,000 |
| **Investing activities:** | | | | | | |
| Proceeds from equipment sold | | (f) | 9,000 | | | |
| Purchase of plant and equipment | | | | 150,000 | (l) | |
| Development costs | | | | 11,000 | (m) | (152,000) |
| **Financing activities:** | | | | | | |
| Dividends paid | | | | 35,000 | (b) | |
| Increase in dividends payable | | (p) | 5,000 | | | |
| Bonds retired | | | | 20,000 | (g) | |
| Increase in short-term bank loan | | (n) | 15,000 | | | |
| Bonds issued | | (h) | 33,000 | | | |
| Common shares issued | | (r) | 50,000 | | | 48,000 |
| Subtotal | | | 249,000 | 259,000 | | |
| Change in cash and cash equivalents: | | (s) | 10,000 | | | $(10,000) |
| | | | $259,000 | $259,000 | | |

Once all of the accounts have been reconciled, the CFS can be prepared by using the information that has been summarized at the bottom of the spreadsheet. This CFS is shown in Exhibit 5-9 in the chapter.

The disadvantage of spreadsheets is the time it takes to format and to do all the adding and balancing. Some of this challenge can be eliminated with the use of computer programs. Spreadsheets are commonly used in very complex situations, or where work has to be carefully documented so it can be reviewed.

## SUMMARY OF KEY POINTS

1. The spreadsheet method is an alternative way to analyze information prior to preparing the CFS. The spreadsheet method is an analytical approach; it is *not* a method of presentation.

2. In setting up a spreadsheet, opening balances are entered in the first column of a four-column spreadsheet, and closing balances in the final column. Reconciling entries are entered in the middle two columns. Items that involve cash flow are collected at the bottom of the spreadsheet.

## QUESTIONS

Q5-1    Compare the purposes of the balance sheet, income statement, and CFS.

Q5-2    During the year, a company records $100,000 in cash sales and $160,000 in credit sales, of which $40,000 was collected from customers. Also during the year, $80,000 was collected from last year's credit sales. Use this data to explain the difference between the accrual and cash basis. Which is reflected on the CFS?

Q5-3    A company pays $80,000 cash for a piece of machinery. On the date of acquisition, is the expenditure an expense? A cash disbursement? Will it become an expense?

Q5-4    How is cash defined for CFS purposes? Why is disclosure of the definition important?

Q5-5    Explain the basic difference between the three activities reported on the CFS: operating, investing, and financing.

Q5-6    List three major cash inflows and three major cash outflows properly classified on the CFS under (a) operating activities, (b) investing activities, and (c) financing activities.

Q5-7    Assume that a company reported net income of $5,000, which included sales revenue of $100,000; the balance sheet shows an increase in accounts receivable of $10,000. What will the operations section of the CFS include, assuming that the indirect presentation approach is used?

Q5-8    During the year, a capital asset with an original cost of $750,000 and accumulated amortization on the date of sale of $560,000 was sold for $216,000. What will appear on the CFS as a result of this transaction? Assume the indirect presentation approach.

Q5-9    Explain why an adjustment must be made for amortization to compute cash flow from operating activities if the indirect presentation approach is used.

Q5-10   Foley Corporation's records showed the following: Net income, $60,000; increase in accounts payable, $15,000; decrease in inventory, $20,000. What items would appear in the operating activities section of the CFS if the indirect presentation approach is used?

Q5-11   Explain the difference between the direct and indirect presentation approaches to the operating activities section of the CFS. Use the following data to illustrate the difference: a company reports $116,000 of net income, which includes sales of $750,000. During the year, accounts receivable increased by $47,000.

Q5-12   Why might the direct method of disclosing cash flows from operations be preferable to the indirect method? Which one dominates current practice?

Q5-13   Describe the two-step method to disclose cash flow from operations using the indirect method.

Q5-14  Explain offsetting. Is it ever allowable to offset cash flows in the CFS?

Q5-15  Give three examples of significant non-cash transactions. Are these items included in the CFS?

Q5-16  Barnum Company reported net income of $40,000, after a net extraordinary loss of $140,000 on the destruction of capital assets. The assets had a book value of $80,000 and insurance proceeds were $240,000. There was $20,000 income tax on the gain. What would appear on the CFS?

Q5-17  What is the classification issue in classifying interest paid on the CFS?

Q5-18  Where are dividends paid classified on the CFS?

Q5-19  What special disclosure is required for investment income, interest, and tax? Explain.

Q5-20  Why would the gain on sale of temporary investments (classified as a cash equivalent) not be reflected on a CFS?

Q5-21  Explain three types of reconciling items used to adjust from net income to cash flow from operating activities using the indirect method.

Q5-22  Forward Co. reports a net loss of ($100,000). Is its earnings quality higher if cash flow from operating activities is $75,000 or ($75,000)?

Q5-23  Developing Ltd. spends $46,700 on development. Under what circumstances will this cash outflow be reported in operating activities in the year of the expenditure, and in what circumstances will it be shown as a cash outflow for investing activities?

Q5-24  Beattie Ltd. has a $75,000 cash payment for dividends to common shareholders. What are its reporting alternatives if the provisions of IAS 7 are followed? Why are these alternatives present?

## CASE 5-1

### WOMEN'S HOCKEY POWER

On 14 February 20X6 Dana Samuels e-mailed you, Chris Morgan, a public accountant. Samuels is a famous female Canadian hockey player. In anticipation of retirement from competitive ice hockey following the current season, Samuels incorporated Women's Hockey Power (WHP). WHP has established an excellent reputation for its coaching clinics aimed toward women's hockey and the quality of the Deek line of women's hockey equipment and accessories that it manufactures. In fact, the company has been so successful that it hopes to go public when volumes are higher.

Another firm will audit WHP's financial statements, but Samuels would like you to analyze the attached information. She really doesn't have much time to discuss financial information at the moment, as hockey season is in full swing. She has, however, attached the partial 31 January unaudited financial statements (Exhibit 1) and some supporting explanations (Exhibit 2). Samuels' request:

You need to look at this financial information and correct anything that might be misstated. If there are things you can't correct, or I'll need to deal with later, let me know what will have to be done. Please provide corrected GAAP-compliant financial statements and the necessary information. If you adjust any of the numbers in these financial statements, I would like you to provide me with the supporting journal entries. I did take a little accounting once, and it will help me understand what you've done. And if there are any other issues I need to deal with before taking WHP public, please provide an explanation and your advice.

**Required:**
Prepare a report and revised financial statements for Samuels.

(Judy Cumby, adapted)

---

## EXHIBIT 1

### WOMEN'S HOCKEY POWER LTD.
### Balance Sheet (draft)

31 January 20X6

| | |
|---|---:|
| Accounts receivable | $226,300 |
| Inventory | 150,020 |
| Investment in Deek Inc. | 100,000 |
| Equipment | 480,000 |
| Accumulated amortization | (106,700) |
| Total assets | $849,620 |
| | |
| Bank overdraft | $ 7,000 |
| Accounts payable | 12,000 |
| Wages and bonus payable | — |
| Interest payable | — |
| Income taxes payable | 36,500 |
| Unearned revenue | 35,000 |
| Note payable, 9% | 100,000 |
| Note payable, 7%, four payments of $120,000 due starting 31 May 20X6. Interest payable annually on 31 May. | 480,000 |
| Loan payable, 8% to Regal Bank | 75,000 |
| Common shares | 5,000 |
| Retained earnings | 99,120 |
| Total liabilities and shareholders' equity | $849,620 |

### WOMEN'S HOCKEY POWER LTD.
### Selected Income Statement Information (draft)

For the Year Ended 31 January 20X6

| | |
|---|---:|
| Selected accounts and balances include: Interest expense (all sources) | $ 12,700 |
| | |
| Income before income tax | $141,600 |
| Income tax expense (30%) | 42,480 |
| Net income | $ 99,120 |

---

## EXHIBIT 2

### INFORMATION RELATED TO WOMEN'S HOCKEY POWER
### For the year ended 31 January 20X6

1. WHP was incorporated on 1 February 20X5 and has a 31 January year-end. The company was formed by issuing common shares for cash. Samuels owns 60% of the common shares of WHP and the remaining shares are owned by three teammates.

2. In anticipation of WHP becoming fully operational, WHP secured a loan of $75,000 from the Regal Bank on 1 May 20X5. The loan bears interest at 8% and is payable on demand. Principal payments of $5,000 are due each April 30. Interest is payable monthly. The loan covenants stipulate that the company's financial statements must comply with GAAP, and WHP's debt-to-equity ratio cannot exceed 6:1.

> **EXHIBIT 2**    *(cont'd)*

3. There is no CFS, and one must be prepared in proper format. All balance sheet numbers as of 31 January 20X5 would be zero as WHP did not exist on that date.

4. On 1 September 20X5, WHP acquired all of the common shares of Deek Inc. (Deek), a women's sporting apparel company by issuing a $100,000, 9% note payable to the former shareholder. This was felt to be a very clever strategic choice as Deek Inc. manufactures and distributes a line that enjoys popular brand recognition in the marketplace. In fact, Deek recorded net income of $40,000 in the period from 1 September 20X5 to 31 January 20X6.

5. On June 1, 20X5, WHP acquired equipment from Super Shot Inc., a company wholly owned by one of the WHP minority shareholders. As payment for the equipment, WHP signed a 7% note payable. The principal will be paid in four equal instalments of $120,000 with the first payment due on 31 May 20X6.

6. During the year, WHP conducted a number of successful hockey clinics. The amount in unearned revenue relates to clinics conducted through December 20X5.

7. The WHP accountant is entitled to a bonus of 10% of before-tax net income over $50,000 but no accrual has been made.

8. Point Shot, a hockey school company wholly owned by another minority shareholder, placed an order for $40,000 worth of hockey sticks in November 20X5. Point Shot, which has an excellent credit rating and history with WHP, e-mailed WHP and asked that it not ship the sticks until early March 20X6. Accordingly, WHP has not made any journal entries related to this transaction. The hockey sticks were fully manufactured by 31 January 20X6 at a cost of $15,000 and are in inventory. Point Shot will pay the full $40,000 during the first week of March.

---

### CASE 5-2

### BARNARD DEVELOPMENTS LIMITED

Barnard Developments Ltd (BDL) is a public company that operates as a diversified Canadian communications company. Its core business is providing cable television services, high-speed Internet access, Internet infrastructure services, and, recently, telephone service. The company has a large investment in capital assets, and a high debt load. It has a history of operating losses, but positive cash flow from operations after material amortization charges are added back. Cash flows for investing activities, representing the purchase of capital assets, are negative. BDL is gradually building the volume that it needs to break even in this high fixed-cost business.

BDL reports the following in the 20X2 financial statements:

*Note 1 Significant Accounting Policies*
Customer lists represent equipment subsidies granted to customers. These amounts are deferred and amortized straight-line over a 24-month period. These costs are incurred in order to expand the Company's customer base, and represent the cost of equipment provided to subscription cable customers.

*Note 7 Customer Lists*

| | 20X2 | | 20X1 | |
| --- | --- | --- | --- | --- |
| (amounts in thousands) | Cost | Accumulated Amortization | Cost | Accumulated Amortization |
| Customer lists | $418,742 | $270,908 | $291,600 | $117,277 |

There were no disposals or write-offs of these assets during the year.

*Cash flow statement (excerpts) (amounts in thousands)*

| | 20X2 | 20X1 |
|---|---|---|
| **Operating activities** | | |
| Cash flow from operations | $335,400 | $289,100 |
| **Investing activities** | | |
| Cash flow for investing | ($825,100) | ($1,107,200) |

You have been asked to prepare a report that evaluates BDL's accounting policy for customer lists. This should include an analysis of the impact of the policy on the CFS.

In talking with the senior management of BDL, you understand that management feels that the customer base for a particular service product is critical. Once a customer is signed on, there is little turnover. The equipment subsidies are the result of BDL's policy, common in the industry, of providing needed hardware to a customer far below cost. Once a customer is established, there is very low turnover, and the future revenue stream from the customer is secure. In fact, BDL's management is convinced that the 24-month amortization stream is very conservative, since the average customer stays for at least 10 years.

**Required:**

Prepare the report.

## CASE 5-3

## COMPUCO LIMITED

You have just started work with a firm of public accountants. You've been given a partially completed set of financial statements for a client, Compuco Limited. You have been asked to prepare a CFS for Compuco Limited, using the balance sheet provided in Exhibit 1, the statement of income and retained earnings provided in Exhibit 2, and the selected notes provided in Exhibit 3. Use indirect disclosure for the operating activities section. (Include separate disclosure of cash paid/received in regards to interest and tax in the disclosure notes.) Based on your CFS, you've also been asked to draft an analysis of the strategic operating, financing, and investing strategies of the company that are apparent from the CFS.

### EXHIBIT 1

### COMPUCO LIMITED
### Extracts from Consolidated Balance Sheet
(in $ thousands)

| As at 31 December | 20X5 | 20X4 |
|---|---|---|
| **Assets** | | |
| Current | | |
| Cash and term deposits | $ 3,265 | $ 3,739 |
| Accounts receivable | 23,744 | 18,399 |
| Inventories | 26,083 | 21,561 |
| Income taxes recoverable | 145 | — |
| Prepaid expenses | 1,402 | 1,613 |
| | 54,639 | 45,312 |

continued on next page

**EXHIBIT 1** *(cont'd)*

## COMPUCO LIMITED
### Extracts from Consolidated Balance Sheet

(in $ thousands)

| As at 31 December | 20X5 | 20X4 |
|---|---|---|
| Loans receivable (Note 1) | 5,960 | 6,962 |
| Capital assets (Note 2) | 37,332 | 45,700 |
| Future income taxes | 4,875 | 2,245 |
| Goodwill | — | 12,737 |
| Development costs (Note 3) | 4,391 | 1,911 |
| | $107,197 | $114,867 |
| **Liabilities** | | |
| Current | | |
| Bank overdraft | $ 6,844 | $ 6,280 |
| Accounts payable | 3,243 | 4,712 |
| Current portion of long-term debt | 1,800 | 1,200 |
| | 11,887 | 12,192 |
| Long-term debt (Note 4) | 14,900 | 14,500 |
| **Shareholders' equity** | | |
| Share capital (Note 5) | 79,257 | 62,965 |
| Retained earnings | 1,153 | 25,210 |
| | 80,410 | 88,175 |
| | $107,197 | $114,867 |

**EXHIBIT 2**

## COMPUCO LIMITED
### Extracts from Consolidated Statement of Income and Retained Earnings

(in $ thousands)

| For the years ended 31 December | 20X5 | 20X4 |
|---|---|---|
| Revenue | | |
| Operating | $ 89,821 | $ 68,820 |
| Interest and other | 1,310 | 446 |
| | 91,131 | 69,266 |
| Expenses | | |
| Operating | 76,766 | 62,355 |
| General and administrative | 13,039 | 12,482 |
| Amortization | 10,220 | 11,709 |
| Goodwill write-off | 12,737 | — |
| Interest | 1,289 | 1,521 |
| Loss on sale of capital assets | 394 | — |
| | 114,445 | 88,067 |
| Loss before writedown and income taxes | (23,314) | (18,801) |

continued on next page

| For the years ended 31 December | **20X5** | **20X4** |
|---|---|---|
| Writedown of loans receivable to recoverable amounts (Note 1) | (2,518) | — |
| Loss before income taxes | (25,832) | (18,801) |
| Income taxes | 2,775 | 5,161 |
| Net loss | (23,057) | (13,640) |
| Retained earnings, beginning of year | 25,210 | 38,850 |
| | 2,153 | 25,210 |
| Stock dividend | (1,000) | — |
| Retained earnings, end of year | $ 1,153 | $ 25,210 |

## EXHIBIT 3

## COMPUCO LIMITED

## Extracts from Selected Notes to Financial Statements

For the year ended 31 December

1. Loans receivable

    The company's loans receivable at 31 December are due from related parties. Amounts as follows:

    (in $ thousands)

| | **20X5** | **20X4** |
|---|---|---|
| XYZ Inc. | $5,962 | $5,962 |
| Writedown to recoverable amount | (2,518) | — |
| | 3,444 | 5,962 |
| Other investments | 2,516 | 1,000 |
| | $5,960 | $6,962 |

2. Capital assets

    Additions to capital assets for the current year amounted to $2,290 and proceeds from the disposal of capital assets amounted to $250.

3. Development costs

    Development costs for a product are amortized once the product is ready for market. The rate depends on the expected life of the product. In 20X5, $206 of amortization was expensed.

4. Long-term debt

    (in $ thousands)

| | **20X5** | **20X4** |
|---|---|---|
| Debentures | $12,500 | $12,500 |
| Bank term loans, due 31 December 20X2; Principal repayable $150 a month (20X4, $100 a month) | 4,200 | 3,200 |
| | 16,700 | 15,700 |
| Current maturities | (1,800) | (1,200) |
| | $14,900 | $14,500 |

    Debentures bear interest at 12% per annum and are due in 20X8. Bank term loans bear interest at 8% and the bank advanced $2.2 million during the year.

> **EXHIBIT 3**    *(cont'd)*
>
> 5. Share capital
>    On 14 May 20X5, Compuco Limited issued 3.8 million shares. Net proceeds amounted to $15.292 million. On 31 December 20X5, a stock dividend of $1 million was issued.
>
> **Required:**
> Respond to the request.                                (CICA, adapted)

## ASSIGNMENTS

★ **A5-1 Cash and Cash Equivalents:** The following amounts appear on Vanier Corporation's trial balance at 31 December 20X9:

| Account | Dr (Cr) |
|---|---|
| Cash on hand | $ 1,400 |
| Cash held in trust for bond retirement—bank #1 | 50,000 |
| Current account—bank #1 | 50,600 |
| Current account—bank #2 (overdraft) | (14,000) |
| Short-term money market certificates | 300,000 |
| Investment in Morton Limited shares | 150,000 |
| Short-term bank borrowings (line of credit) | (500,000) |

**Required:**
Determine the amount of cash and cash equivalents held by Vanier Corporation at the end of 20X9, for use in the CFS.

★ **A5-2 Cash Flow Analysis of Sales:** The records of JMV Company showed sales revenue of $800,000 on the income statement and a change in the balance of accounts receivable and unearned revenue. To demonstrate the effect of changes on cash, five independent cases are used. Complete the following tabulation for each independent case:

| Case | Sales Revenue | Accounts Receivable Increase (Decrease) | Unearned Revenue* Increase (Decrease) | Cash Flow Amount** |
|---|---|---|---|---|
| A | $800,000 | $ 80,000 | $ 0 | |
| B | 800,000 | (80,000) | 0 | |
| C | 800,000 | 72,000 | 40,000 | |
| D | 800,000 | (72,000) | (40,000) | |
| E | 800,000 | 80,000 | (40,000) | |

*Cash received but unearned
**Amount of cash collected from customers

★ **A5-3 Cash Flow Analysis of Cost of Goods Sold:** The records of Van Company showed COGS on the income statement of $480,000 and a change in the inventory and accounts payable balances. To demonstrate the effect of these changes on cash outflow for COGS (i.e., payments to suppliers), five independent cases are used. Complete the following tabulation for each case:

| Case | Cost of Goods Sold | Inventory Increase (Decrease) | Accounts Payable Increase (Decrease) | Cash Outflow Amount* |
|------|-------------------|------------------------------|--------------------------------------|----------------------|
| A | $480,000 | $ (8,000) | $ 0 | |
| B | 480,000 | 8,000 | 16,000 | |
| C | 480,000 | (48,000) | (16,000) | |
| D | 480,000 | 48,000 | (32,000) | |
| E | 480,000 | 32,000 | 32,000 | |

*This is the amount of cash paid during the current period for past and current purchases.

★ **A5-4 Cash Flow Statement—Item Analysis:** The records of Borden Company provided the following data:

a. Sales revenue, $290,000; accounts receivable decreased, $10,000.
b. Paid a cash dividend, $8,000; dividends payable increased by $2,000.
c. Amortization expense, $8,000.
d. Sold a capital asset for $16,000 cash; original cost, $40,000, accumulated amortization, $28,000.
e. Purchased capital asset for $46,000; paid $10,000 down and gave a two-year, interest-bearing note for the balance.
f. Borrowed $40,000 cash from the bank.
g. Converted long-term bonds into common shares, $50,000.
h. Paid a note payable, $10,000 principal plus $700 interest.
i. Wages expense, $86,000; wages payable decreased, $4,000.

**Required:**
For each of the above items give:

1. The CFS category (operating, investing, financing).
2. The item that would appear on the CFS (indirect presentation method for operating activities).
3. The item that would appear on the CFS (direct presentation method for operating activities).

★ **A5-5 Transaction Analysis, Indirect Method:** You are requested by the controller of a large company to determine the appropriate disclosure of the following transactions in the CFS. Assume all adjusting entries have been recorded.

a. Accounts receivable increased $50,000 during the year.
b. Pension expense is $50,000; the balance of the long-term accrued pension liability increased $12,000.
c. Future income tax (long term, credit balance) increased $40,000; income tax payable decreased $10,000.
d. Interest of $10,000 was capitalized to a building under construction, now completed and in use. There is no change in interest payable.
e. The company sold short-term investments (cash equivalents) at a $2,000 gain; cash proceeds, $8,000.
f. The company sold short-term investments (not cash equivalents) at a $4,000 loss; cash proceeds, $6,000.

**Required:**
Indicate the complete disclosure of each item in the CFS under the indirect method of presentation for operating activities.

★ **A5-6 Cash Flow Statement Classification:** The main parts of a CFS are shown below with letter identification. Next, several transactions are given. Match the transactions with the CFS statement parts by entering a letter in each blank space. Assume loans and notes receivable are long-term investments not related to operating activities. State other assumptions or explanations if needed.

**CASH FLOW STATEMENT:**

A. Cash inflows (outflows) from operating activities (indirect method of presentation)
B. Cash inflows (outflows) from investing activities
C. Cash inflows (outflows) from financing activities
D. Not a cash flow

**TRANSACTIONS:**

_____ 1. Issuance of the company's common shares, for cash
_____ 2. Net loss
_____ 3. Proceeds from bond payable
_____ 4. Sale of operational assets at a gain
_____ 5. Purchase long-term investment
_____ 6. Purchase of a 30-day treasury bill with excess cash
_____ 7. Acquisition of operational assets; paid cash
_____ 8. Change in prepaid expenses
_____ 9. Amortization expense
_____ 10. Payment of debt, 60% cash and 40% common shares issued
_____ 11. Sale of land at a loss
_____ 12. Cash dividends declared but not paid
_____ 13. Repurchase and retirement of preferred shares
_____ 14. Payment on notes payable
_____ 15. Change in interest payable

★ **A5-7 Cash Flow Statement, Operating Section:** The data given below were provided from the accounting records of Trent Company. Prepare the operations section of the CFS using the indirect method. Also calculate cash paid for interest and cash paid for income tax, which is supplementary note disclosure.

a. Net income (accrual basis) $400,000, including interest expense of $70,000 and income tax expense of $270,000
b. Amortization expense, buildings and equipment, $80,000
c. Increase in interest payable, $12,000
d. Increase in trade accounts receivable, $18,000
e. Decrease in merchandise inventory, $40,000
f. Amortization of patent, $10,000
g. Purchase of equipment, $410,000
h. Increase in long-term liabilities, $10,000
i. Sale of common shares for cash, $25,000
j. Accounts payable decrease, $50,000
k. Increase in future income tax liability, $20,000

★ **A5-8 Cash Flow Statement, Indirect Method—Individual Transactions:** For each of the following independent transactions for LeClerc Limited, indicate how the transaction would appear and be classified in the 20X8 CFS, using the indirect method.

a. On March 15, 20X8, LeClerc spent $98,500 purchasing a bond as a long-term investment
b. On 31 October 20X8, the company paid a $70,000 income tax reassessment relating to the 20X4 fiscal period.

c. On 31 December 20X8, LeClerc Limited had accounts payable levels that were $20,000 higher than the previous year.

d. On 30 June 20X8, LeClerc sold land with a book value of $56,000, for $82,000. The resulting gain was recorded on the income statement.

e. On 31 July 20X8, the corporation issued 1,000 common shares when a $400,000 bond issued by LeClerc Limited five years ago converted into common shares.

f. On 31 December 20X8, the company sold a piece of machinery with an original cost of $139,000, and accumulated amortization of $104,000, for $14,000. The resulting loss of $21,000 was recorded on the income statement.

---

★★

**A5-9 Cash Flow Statement: Analysis of Cash Flows and Reporting:** Selected transactions from the records of Dover Company are given below. The annual reporting period ends 31 December 20X2. The company uses the indirect method to present cash flows in the operating activities section. Analyze each transaction and give the following:

1. Classification of the transaction on the CFS (operating, investing, financing, or none of these).

2. How the amount would be reported on the CFS.

*Example:*
Declared and paid a cash dividend, $10,000.

*Response:*
Financing activity. Cash outflow, dividends paid, $10,000.

a. Purchased operational asset (machine) for $40,000; gave a one-year interest-bearing note for $25,000 and paid cash for the difference.

b. Sold long-term investment, at book value. Received cash of $12,000 and a three-year interest-bearing note for $13,000.

c. Net income, $60,000.

d. Inventory increased $20,000 during the year.

e. Declared a cash dividend of $8,000 and set up a short-term dividends payable account for $6,000 (to be paid in 20X3).

f. Repurchased and retired common shares for $17,000.

g. Amortization expense, $12,000.

h. Paid a loan payable in full, $5,000.

i. Sold an old capital asset for $5,000 cash; original recorded cost, $20,000; accumulated amortization to date, $16,000.

j. Issued a stock dividend that was debited to retained earnings and credited to common shares, $12,000.

k. Sold an investment in land for $35,000; received $10,000 cash and a one-year interest-bearing note for the remainder. The land was originally recorded in the accounts at $13,000; therefore, a $22,000 gain on sale of land was recorded.

l. Received a cash dividend of $6,000 on a long-term investment in the common shares of Harken Corporation.

m. Interest payable decreased $3,000.

n. Income tax payable increased $6,000.

---

★★

**A5-10 Prepare a Cash Flow Statement:** The records of Rangler Paper Company provided the selected data given below for the reporting period ended 31 December 20X5.

| Balance sheet data | |
|---|---|
| Paid cash dividend | $ 10,000 |
| Established restricted construction cash fund (a long-term investment) to build a new building, at 8% interest | 60,000 |
| Increased inventory of merchandise | 14,000 |
| Borrowed on a long-term note | 25,000 |

| | |
|---|---:|
| Acquired five acres of land for a future site for the company; paid in full by issuing 3,000 shares of Rangler common shares, no par, when the quoted market price per share was $15 | 45,000 |
| Increase in prepaid expenses | 3,000 |
| Decrease in accounts receivable | 7,000 |
| Payment of bonds payable in full at book value | 97,000 |
| Increase in accounts payable | 5,000 |
| Cash from disposal of old operational assets (sold at book value) | 12,000 |
| Decrease in rent receivable | 2,000 |

**Income statement**

| | |
|---|---:|
| Sales revenue | $400,000 |
| Rent revenue | 10,000 |
| Cost of goods sold | (190,000) |
| Amortization expense | (20,000) |
| Remaining expenses | (97,000) |
| Net income | $103,000 |

**Required:**

Prepare a CFS. Use the indirect method for operations. Group all changes in non-cash working capital in operations as one amount. Assume a beginning cash balance of $62,000.

---

★★    **A5-11 Cash Flow Categories—Transaction Analysis:** Denton Corporation's balance sheet accounts as of 31 December 20X4 and 20X5, and information relating to 20X5 activities, are presented below.

| 31 December | 20X5 | 20X4 |
|---|---:|---:|
| **Assets** | | |
| Cash | $ 230,000 | $ 100,000 |
| Short-term investments | 300,000 | — |
| Accounts receivable | 510,000 | 510,000 |
| Inventory | 680,000 | 600,000 |
| Long-term investments | 200,000 | 300,000 |
| Plant assets | 1,700,000 | 1,000,000 |
| Accumulated depreciation | (450,000) | (450,000) |
| Patent | 90,000 | 100,000 |
| Total assets | $3,260,000 | $2,160,000 |
| **Liabilities and shareholders' equity** | | |
| Accounts payable and accrued liabilities | $ 825,000 | $ 720,000 |
| Short-term bank debt | 325,000 | — |
| Common shares | 1,170,000 | 950,000 |
| Retained earnings | 940,000 | 490,000 |
| Total liabilities and shareholders' equity | $3,260,000 | $2,160,000 |

**INFORMATION RELATING TO 20X5 ACTIVITIES:**

- Net income for 20X5 was $690,000.
- Cash dividends were declared and paid in 20X5.
- Equipment costing $400,000 and having a net book value of $150,000 was sold for $150,000.
- A long-term investment was sold for $135,000. There were no other transactions affecting long-term investments in the year.
- Short-term investments consist of treasury bills maturing on 15 February 20X6.

**Required:**

Determine the following amounts for Denton for the year 20X5:

1. Net cash from operating activities (indirect method)
2. Net cash from investing activities
3. Net cash from financing activities                    (AICPA, adapted)

 **A5-12 Cash Flow Statement, Indirect Method:** The records of HKL Company provided the following information for the year ended 31 December 20X8:

## Income Statement

For the year ended 31 December 20X8

| | |
|---|---:|
| Sales revenue | $180,000 |
| Cost of goods sold | (136,000) |
| Depreciation expense | (10,000) |
| Insurance expense | (1,000) |
| Interest expense | (2,000) |
| Salaries and wages expense | (12,000) |
| Remaining expenses | (13,000) |
| Loss on sale of capital assets | (2,000) |
| Income tax expense | (3,000) |
| Net income | $    1,000 |

## Balance Sheet

| At 31 December | 20X8 | 20X7 |
|---|---:|---:|
| Cash | $ 61,000 | $ 35,000 |
| Accounts receivable | 31,500 | 28,500 |
| Inventory | 15,000 | 10,000 |
| Prepaid insurance | 1,400 | 2,400 |
| Buildings and equipment | 81,000 | 80,000 |
| Accumulated depreciation | (21,000) | (20,000) |
| Land | 81,100 | 40,100 |
| Total | $250,000 | $176,000 |
| Accounts payable | $ 21,000 | $ 18,000 |
| Wages payable | 1,000 | 4,000 |
| Rent payable | 6,000 | — |
| Notes payable, long-term | 56,000 | 30,000 |
| Common shares | 143,000 | 100,000 |
| Retained earnings | 23,000 | 24,000 |
| Total | $250,000 | $176,000 |

**ADDITIONAL INFORMATION:**

a. Sold equipment for cash (cost, $15,000; accumulated depreciation, $9,000).
b. Purchased land, $20,000 cash.
c. Acquired land for $21,000 and issued common shares as payment in full.
d. Acquired equipment, cost $16,000; issued a $16,000, three-year, interest-bearing note payable.

**Required:**

Prepare the CFS, using the two-step indirect method. Analyze all accounts to ensure all changes are included. Assume unexplained changes are from logical sources. Also prepare supplementary disclosure of cash paid for interest and taxes.

**A5-13 Prepare a Cash Flow Statement:** The following financial information is available for Buffalo Incorporated for the 20X3 fiscal year:

## BUFFALO INCORPORATED
### Balance Sheet

| As at 31 December | 20X3 | 20X2 |
|---|---:|---:|
| Cash | $ 5,000 | $ 20,000 |
| Receivables | 220,000 | 180,000 |
| Marketable securities | 190,000 | 230,000 |
| Inventory | 731,000 | 632,000 |
| Land | 330,000 | 410,000 |
| Building | 1,040,000 | 1,120,000 |
| Accumulated amortization, building | (470,000) | (380,000) |
| Machinery | 1,080,000 | 875,000 |
| Accumulated amortization, machinery | (219,000) | (212,000) |
| Goodwill | 110,000 | 110,000 |
| | $3,017,000 | $2,985,000 |
| | | |
| Current liabilities | $ 76,000 | $ 146,000 |
| Bonds payable | 1,000,000 | 1,000,000 |
| Premium on bonds | 180,000 | 185,000 |
| Preferred shares | 1,048,000 | 843,000 |
| Common shares | 565,000 | 500,000 |
| Retained earnings | 148,000 | 311,000 |
| | $3,017,000 | $2,985,000 |

## BUFFALO INCORPORATED
### Income Statement

| For the year ended 31 December 20X3 | |
|---|---:|
| Sales | $1,684,000 |
| Cost of goods sold | 1,103,000 |
| Gross profit | 581,000 |
| Amortization | |
|   Building | 110,000 |
|   Machinery | 75,000 |
| Interest | 115,000 |
| Operating expenses | 361,000 |
| Selling expenses | 40,000 |
| Gain on sale of land | (22,000) |
| Loss on sale of machine | 27,000 |
| | 706,000 |
| Net income (loss) before income tax | (125,000) |
| Income tax | 54,000 |
| Net income (loss) | $ (71,000) |

**ADDITIONAL INFORMATION:**

1. Marketable securities were sold at their carrying value. The marketable securities are not cash equivalents.
2. A partially amortized building was sold for an amount equal to its net book value.
3. Cash of $40,000 was received on the sale of a machine.
4. Preferred shares were issued for cash on 1 March 20X3. Dividends of $50,000 were paid on the non-cumulative preferred shares.
5. On 1 September 20X3, 25,000 common shares were purchased and retired for $55,000, their original issuance price. On 1 November 20X3, 65,000 common shares were issued in exchange for machinery.
6. Because of its loss, the company received a refund of taxes paid in prior years of $54,000.

The company has a 31 December year-end.

**Required:**
Prepare a CFS, in good form. Use the indirect method for cash flows from operations.

---

★★  **A5-14  Prepare a Cash Flow Statement:** Norton Corp's 20X2 financial statements showed the following:

| | | |
|---|---:|---:|
| Sales | | $1,642,700 |
| Cost of goods sold | $ 720,000 | |
| Amortization | 168,000 | |
| Other cash expenses | 525,600 | |
| Income tax | 93,600 | |
| Gain on sale of equipment | (7,200) | |
| Loss on sale of investment | 2,000 | 1,502,000 |
| Net income | | $ 140,700 |

| December 31 | 20X2 | 20X1 |
|---|---:|---:|
| Cash | $ 273,800 | $ 30,600 |
| Accounts receivable | 99,000 | 142,200 |
| Inventory | 408,000 | 384,000 |
| Equipment | 960,000 | 888,000 |
| Less accumulated amortization | (432,000) | (384,000) |
| Investment | 80,000 | 142,000 |
| Total | $1,388,800 | $1,202,800 |
| Accounts payable | $ 98,400 | $ 79,200 |
| Income tax payable | 9,600 | 21,600 |
| Bonds payable | 100,000 | 0 |
| Common shares | 504,000 | 504,000 |
| Retained earnings | 676,800 | 598,000 |
| Total | $1,388,800 | $1,202,800 |

**ADDITIONAL INFORMATION:**
During the year, equipment with an original cost of $187,000 was sold for cash.

**Required:**
Prepare a CFS in good form. Make logical assumptions regarding the nature of change in balance sheet accounts.

★★ **A5-15 Prepare a Cash Flow Statement:** The following trial balance is available for Billard Ltd for the year ended 31 December 20X5:

| | 20X5 | 20X4 |
|---|---|---|
| **Assets:** | | |
| Cash | $   45,600 | $ 21,200 |
| Accounts receivable, net | 345,700 | 322,800 |
| Prepaid rent | 16,100 | 33,200 |
| Investment in common shares of Matthew Corp. | 345,000 | 165,000 |
| Machinery | 562,800 | 551,300 |
| Accumulated amortization, machinery | (130,900) | (120,800) |
| | $1,184,300 | $972,700 |
| | | |
| **Liabilities:** | | |
| Bank overdraft | $        — | $ 24,000 |
| Bank loan payable | 384,900 | 52,900 |
| Accounts payable | 56,200 | 134,800 |
| Unearned revenue | 54,200 | 34,500 |
| Bonds payable | — | 50,000 |
| Premium on bonds payable | — | 4,500 |
| | | |
| **Equity:** | | |
| Common shares | 187,000 | 106,000 |
| Retained earnings | 502,000 | 566,000 |
| | $1,184,300 | $972,700 |

**OTHER INFORMATION:**

1. Net income for the year was $41,000; depreciation expense on the machinery was $56,000.

2. There were stock dividends of $20,000, which decreased retained earnings and increased common shares

3. Machinery with an original cost of $60,000 was sold at a loss of $4,000

4. The bond payable was repaid for $56,000. Premium amortization of $2,000 was recorded prior to the repayment.

5. Assume that the (remaining) unexplained change in accounts is from logical sources.

**Required:**
Prepare a CFS, in good form.
   Make logical assumptions regarding the nature of change in balance sheet accounts.

★★★ **A5-16 Prepare a Cash Flow Statement:** The trial balance for March Ltd, for the year ended 31 December, 20X4:

| | 20X4 | 20X3 |
|---|---|---|
| **Debits:** | | |
| Cash | $   77,600 | $   54,400 |
| Accounts receivable (net) | 160,000 | 89,000 |
| Inventory | 364,400 | 322,800 |
| Capital assets | 975,500 | 626,800 |
| Discount on bonds payable | 3,000 | 4,000 |
| | $1,580,500 | $1,097,000 |

**Credits:**

| | | |
|---|---|---|
| Accumulated amortization | $  276,500 | $  241,000 |
| Accounts payable | 187,000 | 204,000 |
| Loan payable | 32,000 | 10,000 |
| Bonds payable | 405,000 | 175,000 |
| Preferred shares | 60,000 | 50,000 |
| Common shares | 275,000 | 200,000 |
| Retained earnings | 345,000 | 217,000 |
| | $1,580,500 | $1,097,000 |

**OTHER INFORMATION:**

1. There were $100,000 of cash dividends and $20,000 of stock dividends.
2. The loan payable is a bank overdraft.
3. Capital assets were acquired for $200,000 of bonds.
4. Preferred shares of $30,000 were converted to bonds payable.
5. Capital assets with an original cost of $80,000 and a book value of $30,000 were sold for a gain of $16,000.
6. Bad debt expense was $18,000. The opening allowance for doubtful accounts was $21,000 and the closing allowance was $24,000.

**Required:**

Prepare the CFS for 20X4, in good form.

Make logical assumptions regarding the nature of change in balance sheet accounts.

---

★★★  **A5-17 Partial Cash Flow Statement; Missing Data:** The following selected information is available for Smith & Co. Ltd., for the year ended 31 December 31 20X8:

### Income Statement

| | | |
|---|---|---|
| Sales | $600,000 | |
| Gain of sale of equipment | 4,500 | $604,500 |
| Cost of goods sold | | 375,000 |
| Operating expenses, including | | |
| $45,000 of depreciation | | 60,000 |
| Interest expense | | 6,000 |
| Loss on sale of land | | 15,000 |
| Net income | | $148,500 |

### Selected Balance Sheet Accounts as of 31 December:

| | 20X8 | 20X7 |
|---|---|---|
| Inventory | $  56,000 | $  42,000 |
| Equipment | 550,000 | 460,000 |
| Accumulated depreciation, equipment | (322,000) | (316,000) |
| Land | 200,000 | 250,000 |
| Notes payable (long term) | (60,000) | (80,000) |
| Common stock | (490,000) | (415,000) |
| Retained earnings | (352,000) | (306,000) |

**OTHER INFORMATION:**

1. Equipment with an original cost of $50,000 was sold for cash.
2. Other equipment was bought for cash.
3. Cash dividends were paid during the year as well as a $25,000 stock dividend that reduced retained earnings and increased common stock.

**Required:**

Present, in good form, the operating, investing, and financing section of the CFS for the year ended 31 December 20X8. **Note:** You have not been provided with enough information (cash, other balance sheet accounts) to balance the CFS to the change in cash.

 **A5-18 Partial Cash Flow Statement; Missing Data:** Sternhill Limited reported the following selected balances:

| Account Title | 20X4 | 20X3 |
|---|---|---|
| Machinery | $567,800 | $344,900 |
| Accumulated amortization, machinery | (214,800) | (123,600) |
| Bonds payable | (300,000) | (200,000) |
| Common shares | (780,000) | (500,000) |
| Preferred shares | (50,000) | (300,000) |
| Retained earnings | (467,500) | (356,900) |

**OTHER INFORMATION:**

1. There was a common stock dividend of $50,000 and a cash dividend of $70,000.
2. Of the preferred shares, $100,000 were retired for cash, and $150,000 were converted into bonds payable.
3. Some common shares were issued for cash during the period.
4. Machinery with a net book value of $56,200 and an original cost of $97,300 was sold during the year at a loss of $2,100. Other machinery was purchased for cash.
5. Any unexplained change in the accounts should be assumed to be because of logical transactions. Be sure to clear *all* accounts.

**Required:**

List the items that would appear on the CFS for 20X4, considering the changes in the accounts above, and the other information. Organize your CFS appropriately (operating, investing, financing) and indicate whether each item is added or subtracted.

 **A5-19 Partial Cash Flow Statement; Missing Data:** A partial trial balance for Wellco:

| | 20X2 | 20X1 |
|---|---|---|
| **Debits:** | | |
| Accounts receivable | $140,000 | $ 99,000 |
| Inventory | 244,600 | 302,900 |
| Capital assets | 988,500 | 326,800 |
| **Credits:** | | |
| Accumulated amortization | $487,600 | $371,000 |
| Accounts payable | 187,000 | 104,000 |
| Bank overdraft | 45,800 | — |
| Bonds payable | 400,000 | 200,000 |
| Preferred shares | 10,000 | 50,000 |
| Common shares | 275,000 | 200,000 |
| Retained earnings | 345,000 | 217,000 |

**OTHER INFORMATION:**

1. Cash dividends were $100,000.
2. Capital assets were acquired for $200,000 of bonds.
3. Preferred shares of $40,000 were converted to common shares.

4. Capital assets with an original cost of $80,000 and a book value of $30,000 were sold for a gain of $7,000.

**Required:**

Prepare the CFS for 20X2, in good form, as far as possible. Note that only a partial trial balance is provided. It is not possible to do a complete CFS, or have the CFS balance, with the information given. Use the indirect method for operating activities. Assume that unexplained differences in balance sheet accounts flow from logical sources.

---

★★ **A5-20 Partial Cash Flow Statement; Missing Data:** A *partial* trial balance for Rankin Limited:

| As of 31 December | 20X4 | 20X3 |
|---|---|---|
| **Debits:** | | |
| Temporary investments, 2-month term | $ 20,000 | $ — |
| Accounts receivable | 17,000 | 27,000 |
| Inventory | 138,500 | 123,200 |
| Capital assets | 614,000 | 455,000 |
| **Credits:** | | |
| Accumulated amortization | 312,400 | 266,000 |
| Accounts payable | 116,000 | 84,000 |
| Income tax payable | 10,600 | 19,500 |
| Bonds payable | 400,000 | — |
| Preferred shares | 95,000 | 95,000 |
| Common shares | 113,000 | 84,000 |
| Retained earnings | 23,100 | 31,000 |

## Income Statement

For the year ended 31 December 20X4

| | | |
|---|---|---|
| Sales | | $592,000 |
| Cost of goods sold | $266,000 | |
| Selling expenses | 40,000 | |
| Amortization expense | 111,600 | |
| Loss on sale of capital asset | 4,300 | |
| Interest expense | 10,500 | |
| Income tax expense | 16,000 | |
| | | 448,400 |
| Net income | | $143,600 |

**OTHER INFORMATION:**

1. Stock dividends of $29,000 were declared and distributed, reducing retained earnings and increasing common shares.
2. Capital assets were acquired for $100,000 of bonds.
3. Capital assets with an original cost of $80,000 were sold for cash during the period.

**Required:**

1. Prepare the operating and investing sections (only) of the CFS for 20X4, in good form. Use the indirect method for operating activities. Assume that unexplained differences in balance sheet accounts flow from logical sources.
2. Calculate cash dividends paid.

★★ **A5-21 Partial Cash Flow Statement; Missing Data:** Shukla Corporation has the following balances:

|  | 20X3 | 20X2 |
|---|---|---|
| Inventory | $125,000 | $ 136,200 |
| Prepaid expenses | 12,700 | 9,500 |
| Buildings | 998,000 | 1,206,000 |
| Accumulated amortization, buildings | (545,000) | (654,200) |
| Dividends payable | (21,000) | (15,000) |
| Accounts payable | (78,700) | (35,300) |
| Bonds payable | — | (300,000) |
| Premium on bonds payable | — | (44,200) |
| Common shares | (600,000) | (400,000) |
| Retained earnings | (870,600) | (637,900) |

### ADDITIONAL INFORMATION:

1. Net income was $376,500. This included a $2,000 loss on the bond retirement, $1,000 of premium amortization, and a gain on sale of building for $51,000. Amortization expense was $74,200 on the building.

2. There was a $500,000 addition to the building account, financed through the issuance of common shares in the amount of $100,000; the balance was paid in cash.

3. Any other unexplained change in the above accounts should be assumed to be from the most logical underlying transaction.

### Required:

Prepare the *investing* and *financing* (only) sections of the CFS.

---

★★ **A5-22 Cash Flow Statement; Indirect Method:** The following data were provided by the accounting records of Breca Company at year-end, 31 December 20X9:

## Income Statement

Year ended 31 December 20X9

| Sales | $640,000 |
|---|---|
| Cost of goods sold | (360,000) |
| Amortization expense | (48,000) |
| Remaining expenses | (160,000) |
| Loss on sale of operational assets | (8,000) |
| Gain on sale of investments | 24,000 |
| Net income | $ 88,000 |

## Balance Sheet

| 31 December | 20X9 | 20X8 |
|---|---|---|
| **Debits** | | |
| Cash | $ 360,000 | $ 232,000 |
| Accounts receivable | 136,000 | 96,000 |
| Inventory | 112,000 | 128,000 |
| Long-term investments | — | 48,000 |
| Operational assets | 784,000 | 640,000 |
| Total debits | $1,392,000 | $1,144,000 |

**Credits**

| | | |
|---|---:|---:|
| Accumulated amortization | $  320,000 | $  384,000 |
| Accounts payable | 96,000 | 152,000 |
| Bonds payable | 240,000 | 80,000 |
| Common shares | 520,000 | 400,000 |
| Retained earnings | 216,000 | 128,000 |
| Total credits | $1,392,000 | $1,144,000 |

**ANALYSIS OF SELECTED ACCOUNTS AND TRANSACTIONS:**

a. Sold operational assets for cash; cost, $168,000; two-thirds depreciated.
b. Purchased operational assets for cash.
c. Purchased operational assets and exchanged unissued bonds payable of $120,000 in payment.
d. Sold the long-term investments for cash.
e. Retired bonds payable at maturity date by issuing common shares, $40,000.

**Required:**

Prepare the CFS. Use the two-step indirect method to present the operations section. Assume that unexplained differences in balance sheet accounts flow from logical sources.

---

★ **A5-23 Cash Flow Statement; Direct Method:** Repeat A5-22, operating activities section, using the direct method to disclose the operations section.

---

★★ **A5-24 Prepare a Cash Flow Statement:** The accounting records of Laurent Company provided the following data:

## Income Statement

For year ended 31 December 20X8

| | |
|---|---:|
| Sales | $900,000 |
| Cost of goods sold | (540,000) |
| Depreciation expense | (12,000) |
| Operating expenses | (192,000) |
| Net income | $156,000 |

## Balance Sheet

| At 31 December | 20X8 | 20X7 |
|---|---:|---:|
| **Debits** | | |
| Cash | $102,000 | $     — |
| Accounts receivable | 54,000 | 57,000 |
| Inventory | 75,000 | 60,000 |
| Investment, long term | — | 9,000 |
| Capital assets | 279,000 | 180,000 |
| Total debits | $510,000 | $306,000 |
| **Credits** | | |
| Bank overdraft | $     — | $ 15,000 |
| Accumulated depreciation | 42,000 | 30,000 |
| Accounts payable | 36,000 | 18,000 |
| Short-term bank loan | 12,000 | 9,000 |
| Notes payable, long term | 108,000 | 60,000 |
| Common shares | 240,000 | 150,000 |
| Retained earnings | 72,000 | 24,000 |
| Total credits | $510,000 | $306,000 |

**ANALYSIS OF SELECTED ACCOUNTS AND TRANSACTIONS:**

a. Paid a $24,000 long-term note payable by issuing common shares.

b. Purchased capital assets that cost $99,000; gave a $72,000 long-term note payable and paid $27,000 cash.

c. Sold the long-term investment at cost, for cash.

**Required:**

Prepare the CFS, using the two-step indirect method of presentation for the operations section. Assume that unexplained differences in balance sheet accounts flow from logical sources.

★ **A5-25 Prepare a Cash Flow Statement; Direct Method:** Repeat A5-24, using the direct method to disclose the operating activities section.

★★★ **A5-26 Cash Flow Statement, Indirect and Direct Method (Optional Spreadsheet):** Todd Corporation reported the following on its 20X4 income statement:

## TODD CORPORATION

## Income Statement

| For the year ended 31 December 20X4 | |
| --- | --- |
| Sales | $624,000 |
| Cost of goods sold | (330,000) |
| Depreciation expense | (48,000) |
| Patent amortization | (1,800) |
| Remaining expenses | (106,200) |
| Net income | $138,000 |

## TODD CORPORATION

## Balance Sheet

| As of 31 December | 20X4 | 20X3 |
| --- | --- | --- |
| Cash | $129,000 | $ 90,000 |
| Investments, short term | 18,000 | — |
| Accounts receivable | 126,000 | 102,000 |
| Inventory | 90,000 | 60,000 |
| Investments, long term | 60,000 | — |
| Property, plant, and equipment (net) | 354,000 | 360,000 |
| Patent (net) | 16,200 | 18,000 |
| Other assets | 42,000 | 42,000 |
| Total | $835,200 | $672,000 |
| | | |
| Accounts payable | $132,000 | $ 72,000 |
| Accrued expenses payable | 52,200 | — |
| Bonds payable | 120,000 | 240,000 |
| Common shares | 267,000 | 210,000 |
| Retained earnings | 264,000 | 150,000 |
| Total | $835,200 | $672,000 |

**ANALYSIS OF ACCOUNTS:**

a. Retired bonds, paid $120,000 cash.

b. Bought long-term investment in common shares, $60,000 cash.

c. Purchased equipment, $42,000 cash.

**Required:**
1. Prepare the CFS, using the indirect method. The solution to this assignment features an optional spreadsheet.
2. Prepare the operations section of the CFS using the direct method.

---

★★★ **A5-27 Cash Flow Statement, Indirect Method (Optional Spreadsheet):** Shown below are the income statement, comparative balance sheets, and additional information useful in preparing the 20X5 CFS for Sells Company.

## Income Statement

For the year ended 31 December 20X5

| | |
|---|---|
| Net sales | $300,000 |
| Cost of goods sold | 80,000 |
| Gross margin | 220,000 |
| Depreciation expense | 45,000 |
| Amortization of intangibles | 2,000 |
| Other expenses | 44,000 |
| Interest expense | 3,000 |
| Income tax expense | 65,000 |
| Net income | $ 61,000 |

## Balance Sheets

| As of 31 December | 20X5 | 20X4 |
|---|---|---|
| Cash | $ 32,000 | $ 16,000 |
| Accounts receivable | 47,000 | 50,000 |
| Other receivables | 2,000 | 3,000 |
| Inventory | 32,000 | 30,000 |
| Equipment | 77,000 | 80,000 |
| Accumulated depreciation | (5,000) | (6,000) |
| Intangibles, net | 53,000 | 55,000 |
| Total assets | $238,000 | $228,000 |
| Accounts payable | $ 60,000 | $ 50,000 |
| Income taxes payable | 50,000 | 70,000 |
| Interest payable | 1,000 | 2,000 |
| Bonds payable | — | 32,000 |
| Discount on bonds payable | — | (2,000) |
| Common shares | 80,000 | 70,000 |
| Retained earnings | 47,000 | 6,000 |
| Total liabilities and owners' equity | $238,000 | $228,000 |

**ADDITIONAL INFORMATION:**
a. Equipment costing $66,000 with a book value of $20,000 was sold at book value. New equipment was also purchased; common shares were issued in partial payment.
b. The bonds were retired at net book value; $500 of bond discount had been amortized in 20X5.

**Required:**
Prepare the 20X5 CFS, indirect method, for Sells Company. The solution to this assignment features an optional spreadsheet.

★★★  **A5-28 Cash Flow Statement (Optional Spreadsheet):** The records of Alberta Company provided the following data for the fiscal year ended 31 December 20X5:

## Balance Sheet

| At 31 December | 20X5 | 20X4 |
|---|---|---|
| **Debits** | | |
| Cash | $ 75,000 | $ 30,000 |
| Investment, short term (cash equivalent) | 8,000 | 10,000 |
| Accounts receivable | 86,000 | 56,000 |
| Inventory | 30,000 | 20,000 |
| Prepaid interest | 2,000 | — |
| Land | 25,000 | 60,000 |
| Machinery | 90,000 | 80,000 |
| Other assets | 39,000 | 29,000 |
| Discount on bonds payable | 900 | 1,000 |
| Total debits | $355,900 | $286,000 |
| **Credits** | | |
| Accumulated depreciation | $ 26,900 | $ 20,000 |
| Accounts payable | 54,000 | 39,000 |
| Salaries payable | 2,000 | 5,000 |
| Income taxes payable | 8,000 | 2,000 |
| Bonds payable | 55,000 | 70,000 |
| Common shares | 130,000 | 100,000 |
| Preferred shares | 30,000 | 20,000 |
| Retained earnings | 50,000 | 30,000 |
| Total credits | $355,900 | $286,000 |

## Income Statement

For the year ended 31 December 20X5

| | |
|---|---|
| Sales revenue | $180,000 |
| Cost of goods sold | (90,000) |
| Depreciation expense | (6,900) |
| Salaries | (33,900) |
| Interest expense | (6,100) |
| Remaining expenses | (4,000) |
| Gain on sale of land | 18,000 |
| Income tax expense | (12,100) |
| Net income | $ 45,000 |

### ANALYSIS OF SELECTED ACCOUNTS AND TRANSACTIONS:

a. Retired $20,000 bonds payable by issuing common shares; the common shares had a market value of $20,000.

b. Acquired other assets by issuing preferred shares with a market value of $10,000.

c. Statement of retained earnings:

| | |
|---|---|
| Balance, 1 January 20X5 | $30,000 |
| Net income for 20X5 | 45,000 |
| Cash dividends | (15,000) |
| Stock dividend issued | (10,000) |
| Balance, 31 December 20X5 | $50,000 |

**Required:**

1. Prepare the CFS, using the two-step indirect method. (The solution to this assignment features an optional spreadsheet.)

2. Prepare the operations section of the CFS using the direct method of presentation.

---

★★  **A5-29 Derive Balance Sheet from Cash Flow Data:** Bewards Limited's balance sheet for 1 January 20X8, its income statement for the year ended 31 December 20X8, and the CFS for the year ended 31 December 20X8 are presented below.

## BEWARDS LIMITED
### Balance Sheet

1 January 20X8

| | |
|---|---:|
| **Assets** | |
| Cash | $   24,000 |
| Accounts receivable | 200,000 |
| Inventory | 160,000 |
| Prepaid insurance | 4,000 |
| Capital assets (net) | 620,000 |
| Total assets | $1,008,000 |
| | |
| **Liabilities and shareholders' equity** | |
| Salaries payable | 8,000 |
| Notes payable | 100,000 |
| Common shares | 150,000 |
| Retained earnings | 750,000 |
| Total liabilities and shareholders' equity | $1,008,000 |

## BEWARDS LIMITED
### Income Statement

Year ended 31 December 20X8

| | | |
|---|---:|---:|
| Sales revenue | | $2,300,000 |
| Expenses: | | |
| Cost of goods sold | $1,600,000 | |
| Salaries expense | 200,000 | |
| Amortization expense | 40,000 | |
| Insurance expense | 24,000 | |
| Other expenses | 336,000 | 2,200,000 |
| Net income | | $   100,000 |

## BEWARDS LIMITED
### Cash Flow Statement

Year ended 31 December 20X8

| | | |
|---|---:|---:|
| *Cash flows from operating activities:* | | |
| Cash receipts from customers | $2,200,000 | |
| Cash paid to suppliers | (1,700,000) | |
| Cash paid to employees | (202,000) | |
| Cash paid to insurers | (22,000) | |
| Cash paid for other expenses | (336,000) | |
| Net cash used in operating activities | | $   (60,000) |

*Cash flows from financing activities:*

| | | |
|---|---|---|
| Proceeds from increase in note payable | $    46,000 | |
| Proceeds from issue of common shares | 50,000 | |
| Net cash provided by financing activities | | 96,000 |
| Net increase in cash | | 36,000 |
| Cash, 1 January 20X8 | | 24,000 |
| Cash, 31 December 20X8 | | $    60,000 |

**ADDITIONAL INFORMATION:**

a. All inventory was purchased for cash.

b. The company did not purchase or sell any capital assets during the period.

c. During the year, all transactions related to notes payable and common shares were conducted for cash.

**Required:**

Based on the financial statements and other information, prepare the balance sheet at 31 December 20X8. Show all supporting calculations.

(CGA-Canada)

---

 **A5-30 Prepare Cash Flow Statement, Indirect Method:** Linda Ray, the president of Zabron Electric Corporation, has asked the company controller for a CFS for the reporting year ended 31 December 20X1. The following balance sheet data has been obtained from the accounting records:

a. Cash account balances: 1 January 20X1, $43,000; 31 December 20X1, $18,000.

b. The balance in accounts receivable decreased by $10,000 during the year. Wages payable decreased by $5,000.

c. Inventory increased $9,000, and accounts payable increased $3,000 during the year.

d. Income tax payable increased $4,000 during the year.

e. During December 20X1, the company settled a $10,000 note payable by issuing its own common shares with equivalent value.

f. Cash expenditures during 20X1 included (1) payment of long-term debts, $64,000; (2) purchase of new capital assets, $74,000; (3) payment of a cash dividend, $16,000; and (4) purchase of land as an investment, $25,000.

g. In 20X1, shares were issued for $20,000 cash.

h. In 20X1, Zabron issued a long-term mortgage note, $30,000.

i. Some capital assets were sold; the following entry was made:

| | | |
|---|---|---|
| Cash | 5,000 | |
| Accumulated amortization | 12,000 | |
| Capital assets | | 15,000 |
| Gain on sale of capital assets | | 2,000 |

**Income statement data:**

| | |
|---|---|
| Sales revenue | $295,000 |
| Cost of goods sold | (140,000) |
| Amortization expense, capital assets | (14,000) |
| Patent amortization | (1,000) |
| Income tax expense | (17,000) |
| Remaining expenses | (42,000) |
| Gain on sale of capital assets | 2,000 |
| Net income | $ 83,000 |

**Required:**

Prepare a CFS using the indirect method.

★★ **A5-31 Cash Flow Statement:** The items from the 31 December 20X2 CFS for Moon Limited are given below, in no particular order.

| | |
|---|---:|
| Closing cash | ? |
| Repayment of long-term debt | $594,800 |
| Amortization expense | 372,000 |
| Decrease in inventories | 196,000 |
| Capital expenditures | 573,600 |
| Proceeds from issuance of common shares | 42,400 |
| Decrease in accounts payable | 180,000 |
| Net income | 76,600 |
| Dividends paid | 96,500 |
| Proceeds from sale of land (a $17,500 extraordinary gain was recorded) | 181,000 |
| Opening cash | 233,000 |
| Decrease in prepaid expenses | 1,000 |
| Increase in future income tax liability | 64,800 |
| Proceeds from the sale of a long-term investment (no gain or loss) | 560,000 |
| Increase in long-term borrowings | 61,300 |
| Depletion | 120,100 |
| Increase in accounts receivable | 134,000 |

**Required:**

1. Using the above information, prepare a CFS in good form, using the two-step indirect method.

2. Based on this statement, what would you conclude about the company's cash flows for 20X2?

---

★★ **A5-32 Cash Flow Statement, Direct Method:** The balance sheet, income statement, and additional information are given below for Supreme Company.

### Balance Sheet

| 31 December | 20X5 | 20X4 |
|---|---:|---:|
| **Debits** | | |
| Cash | $ 44,900 | $ 40,000 |
| Accounts receivable | 52,500 | 60,000 |
| Merchandise inventory | 141,600 | 180,000 |
| Prepaid insurance | 1,200 | 2,400 |
| Investments, long term | — | 30,000 |
| Land | 38,400 | 10,000 |
| Capital assets | 259,000 | 250,000 |
| Patent (net) | 1,400 | 1,600 |
| | $539,000 | $574,000 |
| | | |
| **Credits** | | |
| Accumulated depreciation | $ 79,000 | $ 65,000 |
| Accounts payable | 53,000 | 50,000 |
| Wages payable | 1,500 | 2,000 |
| Income taxes payable | 13,400 | 9,000 |
| Bonds payable | 50,000 | 100,000 |
| Premium on bonds payable | 1,700 | 5,000 |
| Common shares | 324,000 | 315,000 |
| Retained earnings | 16,400 | 28,000 |
| | $539,000 | $574,000 |

## Income Statement

| For the year ended 31 December 20X5 | **20X5** |
|---|---|
| Sales revenue | $399,100 |
| Cost of goods sold | (224,400) |
| Depreciation expense | (14,000) |
| Patent amortization | (200) |
| Salary expense | (80,000) |
| Interest expense | (4,400) |
| Other expenses | (44,000) |
| Investment revenue | 900 |
| Gain on sale of investments | 10,000 |
| Income tax expense | (24,600) |
| Net income | $ 18,400 |

**ANALYSIS OF SELECTED ACCOUNTS AND TRANSACTIONS:**

a. Purchased capital asset, $9,000; payment by issuing 600 common shares.
b. Payment at maturity date to retire bonds payable, $50,000.
c. Sold the long-term investments for $40,000.
d. Reassessment for prior years' income taxes; paid during 20X5 and added to 20X5 tax expense, $6,600.
e. Purchased land, $28,400; paid cash.
f. Cash dividends declared and paid, $30,000.

**Required:**
Prepare the CFS, using the direct method.

---

 **A5-33 Cash Flow Statement, Direct and Indirect Method:** The income statement and balance sheet of Kenwood Company and related analysis are given below.

## KENWOOD COMPANY

### Income Statement

| For the year ended 31 December 20X4 | | |
|---|---|---|
| Sales revenue | | $1,000,000 |
| Less expenses: | | |
| Cost of goods sold | 560,000 | |
| Salaries and wages | 190,000 | |
| Depreciation | 20,000 | |
| Patent amortization | 3,000 | |
| Interest expense | 16,000 | |
| Miscellaneous expenses | 8,000 | |
| Total expenses | | 797,000 |
| Plus other: | | |
| Loss on sale of equipment | (4,000) | |
| Gain on bond retirement | 12,000 | 8,000 |
| Income before income tax | | 211,000 |
| Income tax expense | | 82,000 |
| Net income | | $ 129,000 |

## KENWOOD COMPANY
## Balance Sheet

| As of 31 December | 20X4 | 20X3 |
|---|---|---|
| **Assets** | | |
| *Current assets:* | | |
| Cash | $ 100,000 | $ 90,000 |
| Accounts receivable | 210,000 | 140,000 |
| Inventory | 260,000 | 220,000 |
| Total current assets | 570,000 | 450,000 |
| Land | 325,000 | 200,000 |
| Plant and equipment | 580,000 | 633,000 |
| Less: Accumulated depreciation | (90,000) | (100,000) |
| Patents | 30,000 | 33,000 |
| Total assets | $1,415,000 | $1,216,000 |
| **Liabilities and shareholders' equity** | | |
| *Liabilities:* | | |
| Current liabilities: | | |
| Accounts payable | $ 260,000 | $ 200,000 |
| Salaries and wages payable | 200,000 | 210,000 |
| Income tax payable | 140,000 | 100,000 |
| Total current liabilities | 600,000 | 510,000 |
| Bonds payable (due 15 December 20X14) | 130,000 | 180,000 |
| Total liabilities | 730,000 | 690,000 |
| *Shareholders' equity:* | | |
| Common shares, no par; authorized | | |
| 100,000 shares, issued and outstanding | | |
| 50,000 and 42,000 shares, respectively | 483,000 | 380,000 |
| Retained earnings | 202,000 | 146,000 |
| Total shareholders' equity | 685,000 | 526,000 |
| Total liabilities and shareholders' equity | $1,415,000 | $1,216,000 |

### ANALYSIS OF SELECTED ACCOUNTS AND TRANSACTIONS:

a. On 2 February 20X4, Kenwood issued a 10% stock dividend to shareholders of record on 15 January 20X4. This increased common shares, and decreased retained earnings, by $63,000.

b. On 1 March 20X4, Kenwood issued 3,800 common shares for land. The common shares had a current market value of approximately $40,000.

c. On 15 April 20X4, Kenwood repurchased long-term bonds payable with a face value of $50,000 for cash. The gain of $12,000 was correctly reported on the income statement.

d. On 30 June 20X4, Kenwood sold equipment that cost $53,000, with a book value of $23,000, for cash.

e. On 30 September 20X4, Kenwood declared and paid a cash dividend.

f. On 10 October 20X4, Kenwood purchased land for cash.

### Required:

1. Prepare the CFS, using the indirect method. Use the two-step method for operations. Prepare supplementary disclosure for the cash flows for interest and income tax.

2. Prepare the CFS, using the direct method, to disclose cash flows in the operating activities section.

(AICPA, adapted)

★★ **A5-34 Cash Flow Statement, Indirect Method:** The differences between the Boole Incorporated balance sheet accounts of 31 December 20X4 and 20X5 are presented below:

| | Increase (decrease) |
|---|---|
| **Assets** | |
| Cash | $ 120,000 |
| Short-term investments (cash equivalents) | 300,000 |
| Accounts receivable | — |
| Inventory | 80,000 |
| Long-term investments | (100,000) |
| Capital assets | 700,000 |
| Accumulated amortization | — |
| | $1,100,000 |
| | |
| **Liabilities and shareholders' equity** | |
| Accounts payable and accrued liabilities | $ (5,000) |
| Dividends payable | 160,000 |
| Bank overdraft (part of net cash position on CFS) | 325,000 |
| Long-term debt | 110,000 |
| Common shares, no par, an additional 10,000 shares | 220,000 |
| Retained earnings | 290,000 |
| | $1,100,000 |

**ADDITIONAL INFORMATION FOR 20X5:**

1. A building costing $600,000 and having a carrying amount of $350,000 was sold for $350,000.

2. Equipment costing $110,000 was acquired through issuance of long-term debt.

3. A long-term investment was sold for $135,000. There were no other transactions affecting long-term investments.

4. Common shares were issued for $22 a share.

5. Net income was $790,000.

**Required:**
Prepare Boole's CFS in as much detail as possible, using the indirect method for the operating activities section. (AICPA, adapted)

★★★ **A5-35 Integrative Problem, Chapters 1–5:** Account balances, taken from the ledger of Argot Flooring Limited as of 31 December 20X5, appear below.

| | | | |
|---|---|---|---|
| Accounts payable | $280,000 | Inventory, 1 Jan. 20X5** | $ 344,000 |
| Accounts receivable | 632,000 | Land | 398,000 |
| Accumulated amortization, | | General operating expenses | 338,000 |
|   building equipment | 42,000 | Notes payable | 232,000 |
| Allowance for doubtful | | Notes receivable | 120,000 |
|   accounts | 3,000 | Property tax expense | 3,200 |
| Building and equipment | 198,000 | Purchases | 1,218,000 |
| Cash | ? | Purchase discounts | 8,000 |
| Common shares | 204,100 | Purchase returns and | |
| Discontinued operation loss | 71,000 |   allowances | 32,000 |
| Dividends declared | 80,000 | Retained earnings, | |
| Error correction (credit) | 29,400 |   1 Jan. 20X5 | 806,400 |
| Future income taxes | | Revenue | 2,632,000 |
|   (credit) | 116,700 | Salaries expense | 232,000 |
| Income tax expense* | 334,600 | Store supplies inventory | 12,400 |
| Interest revenue | 5,000 | Unearned revenue | 32,000 |

*Assume this amount is properly stated after all subsequent adjustments are considered. Tax expense includes $28,400 of tax reduction caused by the discontinued operation loss, and a $12,000 expense related to the error correction.

**Inventory at 31 December is $480,000.

## ADDITIONAL INFORMATION:

1. Store supplies were counted at 31 December and found to be valued at $5,600.

2. Amortization of building and equipment is over eight years with an expected salvage value of $10,000.

3. Property taxes of $3,200 were paid on 1 October 20X5, and relate to the year 1 October 20X5 to 30 September 20X6.

4. The note payable was issued on 1 November 20X5 and has an annual interest rate of 12%. Interest must be paid each 30 October along with $30,000 of principal.

5. The note receivable has been outstanding all year. Interest at 10% is collected each 1 June. The note is due 1 June 20X11.

6. The allowance for doubtful accounts now has a $3,000 credit balance. Aging of accounts receivable indicates that $76,000 of the accounts are doubtful.

7. Unearned revenue represents an advance payment from a customer; 75% was still unearned at year-end.

8. At year-end, $10,000 (at retail value) of goods were shipped to customers but the sale was not yet recorded. Correctly, the goods were not included in closing inventory. Only the revenue must be recorded.

## Required:

1. Explain the meaning of GAAP.

2. Identify common objectives of financial reporting.

3. Prepare adjusting journal entries to reflect the additional information provided above.

4. Explain the following (a) through (e) and give an example of an adjusting journal entry in requirement (3) caused by each.
   a. time-period assumption
   b. continuity assumption
   c. accrual concept
   d. revenue recognition convention
   e. matching convention

5. Prepare a multiple-step classified income statement, retained earnings statement, and a classified balance sheet based on the adjusted accounts.

6. Assume that accounts have changed (after the entries made in requirement (3)) as follows over the period:

| | | |
|---|---|---|
| Accounts receivable (net) | $41,900 | decrease |
| Interest receivable | no change | |
| Inventory | 136,000 | increase |
| Store supplies inventory | 8,000 | decrease |
| Prepaid property tax | no change | |
| Buildings and equipment | 40,000 | increase |
| Accounts payable | 75,000 | increase |
| Interest payable | 4,640 | increase |
| Notes payable | 232,000 | increase |
| Future (deferred) income tax | 26,400 | increase |
| Unearned revenue | 24,000 | increase |

Prepare the operating activities section of the CFS using the indirect method of presentation. Assume that there is no adjustment needed for the discontinued operation for this part. Begin the CFS with net income.

7. List the major areas of choice that are present in the format of the income statement and balance sheet.

8. List six functions of disclosure notes and give an example of each.

## CHAPTER 6

# Revenue and Expense Recognition

## INTRODUCTION

Nortel Networks Corporation has had problems with its revenue recognition policies. The company restated its revenues in each of four successive fiscal years, 2003 through 2006. Nortel engages in many complex contracts for its products and services, and a large part of the problem has been to disaggregate contract revenue between hardware sales, software sales, and continuing services.

Revenue recognition is probably the most difficult single issue in accounting, largely because modern business activities can be very complex. Much economic activity involves long-term earnings processes. In complex and long-term earnings processes, it is not at all obvious just when revenue should be recognized. As well, many "sales" actually involve the delivery of more than one product and/or service. How should revenue for each component be measured, and when should the revenue be recognized?

To enhance comparability and reliability, accounting standard setters have attempted to narrow revenue recognition choices by providing more explicit criteria. Measurability is a crucial aspect of revenue recognition—the ability not only to measure revenue reliably, but also to measure expenses reliably. This chapter will examine the nature of the earnings process and the various points at which revenue could be recognized, depending on the nature of the revenue-earning process.

Then we will discuss the basic concepts of expense recognition. A cost can be either an asset or an expense. If a cost is recorded as an asset (that is, if the cost is capitalized), then at some point the cost must be transferred from asset to expense. This chapter examines the general area of expense policy—the standards, practices, and policies that govern this crucial area of accounting policy choice and accounting estimates. Later chapters will discuss detailed expense recognition policies that are appropriate for specific types of expenditures.

All of the issues in revenue and expense recognition have a direct impact on net income measurement—a relatively small change in revenue or expense recognition can have a major impact on net income. Therefore, there are many ethical implications to the choice of revenue recognition policies.

## DEFINITIONS

**Revenue and Expenses** What is revenue? It's not defined on its own as, for example "the value of goods and services delivered during the period." Instead, revenue is defined by its increase in net assets (i.e., assets minus liabilities). An expense also is defined by its decrease in net assets. Revenues and expenses are reported on the income statement, but their recognition really is the result of changes that occur on the balance sheet.

For example, suppose that a company sells merchandise on credit:

- Revenue is the result of an increase in an account receivable. Creation of the account receivable increases assets.
- Cost of goods sold (COGS) is the result of a reduction in inventory. Reduction in inventory decreases net assets.

Thus, *revenue and expenses are defined by changes in net assets.* This is the asset-liability definitional approach to measuring net income.

In earlier years, the sequence was reversed—first came the decision on when to recognize revenue, and then net assets were increased as the result. Now, the increase in net assets is paramount; only then can revenue be recognized.

**Assets and Liabilities** The definitions of revenue and expense are derivative definitions in that they are based on the terms "assets" and "liabilities." Therefore, clear understanding of assets and liabilities is needed in order to understand revenues and expenses. As we pointed out in Chapter 2:

- *Assets* are economic resources controlled by an entity as a result of past transactions or events and from which future economic benefits can be obtained.
- *Liabilities* are present obligations of an entity arising from past transactions or events, the settlement of which may result in the transfer or use of assets, provision of services, or other yielding of economic benefits in the future.

Although our attention in this chapter is focused on recognition and measurement of revenue and expense, this discussion cannot be separated from the issues of asset and liability recognition and measurement.

**Gross or Net Revenue?** To recognize and report revenue on its income statement, a company must be entitled to the full benefits of the increase in net assets. For example, what should the on-line auction website eBay Inc. report as revenue—the total amount of sales that are transacted through its website? To do so would imply that the total sales value will increase eBay's net assets. But eBay has no control over the transaction prices. The company sets the commission and other fees that it charges, but the price of the goods is set between the buyer and the seller. eBay is not entitled to the full benefits of the negotiated price—only to the commission—even if the company collects the purchase price from the buyer and then passes on the proceeds, net of commission, to the seller.

Similarly, Company A may be holding goods on consignment—goods that belong to Company B. When A sells the goods, A can report as revenue only the fee or commission that it has earned. Company A cannot report the full sales price of the goods as revenue because it is not entitled to that revenue. On the other hand, Company B must recognize the full sales price as revenue and not just the net amount received from Company A (that is, net of A's commission and fees).

In general, then, a seller reports its gross revenues if the company bears the risks and rewards of ownership of whatever it is selling. The *risk* is the possible loss of inventory or credit risk for cash collection; the *reward* is the revenue—the increase in net assets. In contrast, if the seller acts as an agent or broker in the transaction, the seller can report only the fees and commissions that it earns on the transaction.

# THE REVENUE RECOGNITION PROCESS

## Economic Value Added

At a conceptual level, a firm earns revenue as it engages in activities that increase the value of an item or service. A company buys raw materials and supplies, and then employees perform services that change the raw materials into a product of higher value. The final product becomes worth more than the cost of its inputs in materials and labour. The difference between the input cost and the eventual value of the product (or service) is known as the **economic value added** (EVA).

For example, an automobile parts manufacturer increases the value of sheet metal when it undertakes activities to cut, shape, and weld the sheet metal into automobile fenders. Transporting completed fenders to a regional warehouse also adds value because it makes the fenders readily available for purchase and use by automobile repair shops. The earnings process is fully completed when the fenders are sold and delivered to a customer in return for cash or a promise to pay cash: finally, assets actually increase. All of these activities, and many more, are part of the earnings process.

Although added value is created throughout the earnings process, the impact on net assets is difficult to measure. Accountants cannot recognize revenue and expenses until they become measurable. Thus, the ability to measure impacts on net assets is essential. Relevance and reliability depend on reasonably accurate measurement of changes in assets and liabilities.

# GENERAL REVENUE RECOGNITION PRINCIPLE

The general **revenue recognition principle** is that changes in net assets (as a result of the earnings process) should be recognized in the financial statements when (1) performance is complete and has been accepted by the customer, and (2) the consideration and any future costs can be measured with reasonable assurance.

This broad principle sounds simple. Indeed, in many businesses, revenue recognition is not a major challenge. In other business, however, the challenge can be quite significant. There are two general issues:

1. *When* to recognize; and

2. *How much* to recognize.

In most businesses, *when* to recognize revenue is more of an issue than *how much* to recognize. The revenue amount is part of the contract between the buyer and the seller and only the timing of recognition is subject to interpretation.

However, measuring *how much* can also be problematic. There are two potential problems:

- Assigning revenue to different parts of a complex contract, known as *multiple deliverables*; and

- Measuring the amount of revenue when part of it will be received in future years, an issue of recording *present value.*

An example of a multiple deliverable would be an agreement to sell computer software that includes staff training and free upgrades. How much of the price is really for the initial software and how much is for future services?

An example of discounting is a sale agreement that sets a price but allows the purchaser to pay over two or more fiscal periods with no interest charges. Since money is never interest free, part of the agreement's contract price really is hidden interest.

In really interesting situations, both of these problems arise in the same transaction—multiple deliverables with a long time frame. This is the type of situation that caused Nortel's difficulties (cited at the beginning of this chapter) in measuring revenue.

# APPROACHES TO REVENUE RECOGNITION

To recognize revenue, the changes in net assets must be measurable with reasonable reliability. Measurability includes not only the revenues, but also the expenses. In the past, many companies recognized revenue too aggressively. *Aggressively* means premature recognition—too early in the earnings process. Sometimes the premature recognition was done innocently; the companies thought that they could measure future costs and revenue yet to be received, but discovered that their estimates were not reliable.

Other companies were not so innocent, however. Some deliberately recognized revenue prematurely in order to increase earnings per share, attract investors, or meet debt covenants.

In order to prevent abuses, standard setters developed criteria that must be satisfied before revenue can be recognized. We will discuss these criteria in greater detail in the following sections. In general, however, the criteria expand on the general concept outlined above: *performance* and *measurability*.

## Recognition at a Single Point—The Critical Event

**critical event**

the latest point in an earnings process that satisfies the criteria for revenue recognition

Accounting standard setters have developed criteria for recognizing revenue, depending on the type of revenue-generating activity. Revenue should be recognized only when *all* of the criteria have been satisfied. The last criterion to be satisfied is known as the **critical event**— the event that triggers revenue recognition.

For most product sales and many services, revenue is recognized at one point in the chain of revenue-generating activities. The most common recognition point is when the sale is made and the product or service is transferred to and accepted by the customer. In some cases, however, revenue is recognized only when *cash is collected*.

Until the critical point is reached, all costs must be deferred and recorded either as *inventory* or as a *deferred cost* (or prepaid expense), and any cash received from the customer must be recorded as *unearned revenue*. When the recognition point has been reached:

1. Unearned revenue is transferred from the balance sheet to the income statement as revenue;

2. Additional cash to be received in the future is recorded as an account receivable and added to revenue; and

3. Accumulated inventory and deferred costs are transferred to cost of sales; and estimated future costs (e.g., warranty costs) are recorded as a liability and added to expenses.

Exhibit 6-1 illustrates these interrelations.

Expense recognition must coincide with revenue recognition. Recognition of revenues and expenses is the result of changes in net asset value—if revenue is recognized, it must be the result of changes in net assets.

## Recognition over Time

For some earnings processes, revenue can be recognized gradually over time if:

1. Cash receipt is the critical event and the buyer is paying by instalments; or

2. The earnings process spans more than one accounting period and the nature of the earnings process makes it possible for a portion of the total revenue to be recognized in each period.

The first situation arises when the creditworthiness of the customer is in doubt. This can happen if the seller's policy is to sell to people who have poor credit records. The seller expects that, on average, enough people will pay to make overall sales profitable. However, the risk of non-payment is sufficiently unpredictable that revenue cannot be estimated reliably. Accounting practice has developed two recognition methods to deal with this situation. We will review these methods a little later in this chapter.

Sometimes the earnings process spans more than one accounting period, such as in a long-term construction project. Revenue may be recognized in each period even though the earnings process is not completed. This is acceptable when both (1) the total potential revenue and (2) the costs required to complete the earnings process can be reliably estimated. Multiperiod recognition is known as the *percentage-of-completion* method, which is discussed later in this chapter.

---

**EXHIBIT 6-1**

## THE REVENUE RECOGNITION PROCESS

### Pre-Recognition Balance Sheet

**Assets:**
Costs incurred before recognition—
Inventoried product costs; deferred
costs

**Liabilities:**
Cash received in advance—
unearned revenue

---

### Period-of-Recognition Income Statement

Sales revenue, consisting of:
Cash received in advance—unearned revenue
Additional cash or other assets received at time of sale
Cash to be received in the future

Cost of sales and related expenses, consisting of:
Costs incurred before recognition—inventoried product costs; deferred costs
Additional product costs incurred during the period
After-sale expenses yet to be incurred (e.g., warranty costs)

Net income

---

### Post-Recognition Balance Sheet

**Assets:**
Cash or other assets received from
the sale, minus cash paid for sale-
related costs
Cash to be received in the future—
accounts or notes receivable

**Liabilities:**
After-sale expenses yet to be incurred
(e.g., warranty costs)

**Owners' Equity:**
Increase in net assets—net income

---

Recognizing revenue from a long-term contract over several accounting periods poses some challenging measurement problems. However, the problems (and potential estimation errors) that are inherent in multiperiod recognition are offset by the relevance and timeliness of the information that is provided to financial statement readers. Thus, there is a trade-off between the qualitative characteristics of *relevance* on the one hand, and *reliability* on the other.

## CONCEPT REVIEW

1. What is the general revenue recognition principle?
2. What effect does revenue recognition have on the balance sheet?
3. What is meant by the *critical event* in revenue recognition?
4. When might revenue be recognized at more than one point in time?

## SALE OF GOODS AND SERVICES

### Sale of Goods

A seller can recognize revenue only when the seller's performance is complete. Completion means:[1]

- The seller's performance is complete and the seller has transferred the significant risks and rewards of ownership to the buyer.
- The buyer has *accepted* the significant risks and rewards of ownership.
- The seller can reliably measure all costs relating to the transaction, past and future.
- The amount of revenue can be measured reliably.
- The seller retains no continuing managerial involvement or control over the goods sold.

These criteria are described more fully in the following paragraphs and are summarized in Exhibit 6-2.

**Seller's Completion and Transfer of Risks and Rewards.** A crucial aspect of a sale is that the seller has no remaining significant responsibilities regarding the item sold. After the transfer, the risk is borne by the buyer instead of the seller. Of course, this doesn't rule out the provision of after-sale support or warranties, as long as the cost of future support can be estimated reliably. But if these costs cannot be estimated reliably, performance is not really complete because a significant aspect of risk has been retained by the seller.

Often, after-sale costs can be measured reliably for the company's sales as a whole, even if the follow-up costs of individual sales maybe be substantial. For example, automobile manufacturers recognize revenue when they sell cars, even though they may have to issue a *product recall* to fix design problems detected later. Recalls can be very expensive for the manufacturer. This situation is analogous to the risk of accounts receivable—a company makes an annual estimate for bad debts that may be quite measurable on average, even though an individual customer may go bankrupt and cause significant loss. But if potentially significant costs *cannot* be reliably estimated for the class of buyers as a whole, performance is not really complete and a significant aspect of risk has been retained by the seller.

The seller must also transfer all of the product's *benefits*. If one company "sells" a product to another company but continues to collect royalties or a portion of the product's revenue stream, a sale cannot be recognized as such.

For example, suppose that a doughnut chain "sells" one of its stores to an entrepreneur for $500,000, but the chain will continue to hold title to the store and will receive 5% of the store's gross revenue. In such a case, the chain has not transferred substantially all of the rewards to the buyer; no sale has taken place and revenue cannot be recognized.

In summary, an important aspect of performance completion is that the seller has no more significant responsibilities and receives no future benefits regarding the item sold. "No significant responsibility" implies that all of the costs have been incurred or can be measured reliably.

**Buyer Acceptance.** It is not enough for the seller to *claim* that the risks and rewards have been transferred. The buyer also must *accept* the risks and rewards. A company may sell a complex product and consider the sale as final, but the buyer may not accept the product until it has been fully tested.

For example, suppose that a software development company completes a large-scale custom software project for a large insurance company. The software company may believe that it has completed the project according to the contract. The insurance company, however, must install the software and make sure that it is functioning properly. From the buyer's point of view, the software's risks and returns have not been transferred until the buyer is satisfied with the product.

---

[1] These criteria capture the substance of the standards of both the CICA and the IASB, although not in exactly the same words.

**EXHIBIT 6-2**

## REVENUE RECOGNITION CRITERIA FOR SALE OF GOODS AND SERVICES

a. **Seller's performance is complete; seller has transferred the significant risks and rewards of ownership to the buyer.**

The seller has delivered the goods or services and has no more significant risks; the seller also will not benefit from the goods or services in the future.

b. **Buyer accepts the significant risks and rewards of ownership.**

Transfer is not complete until the buyer is satisfied that the product functions as expected, or that the service has been performed according to contract.

c. **The seller can reliably measure all costs relating to the transaction, past and future.**

There are no significant uncertainties about measuring the costs incurred in the past or any after-sale costs yet to be incurred in the future.

d. **The amount of revenue can be measured reliably.**

There is no significant uncertainty about the amount of revenue to be received; there should be no revenue that is contingent on future events or performance, and the collectibility of amounts owing is reasonably assured.

e. **The seller retains no continuing managerial involvement or control over the goods sold.**

The seller cannot retain the right to affect the buyer's use of the product or service, and can retain no continuing interest in future benefits that are derived from the product.

**The last one of these criteria to be satisfied is the *critical event*. Revenue is recognized at the critical event.**

---

As another example, consider Bombardier Inc.'s delivery of high-speed rail cars. Bombardier may believe that the cars meet specifications and record the sale. But buyers have been known to refuse delivery if the cars don't perform as expected.

If the buyer delays or refuses acceptance, the sale is not complete and revenue should not be recognized.

**Measurable Costs** All costs, both past and future, must be measurable. Measuring past costs is not usually a problem, but it can be a problem if the final contract price for a subcontractor's work is unknown or is under dispute.

Measuring *future* costs can be more of a challenge. If the product is not unusual and the seller has ample experience with it, the estimation of after-sale costs is not difficult. If the product is more unusual, then estimation may be more difficult. If the seller has no basis for reliable measurement of after-sale costs, then revenue recognition must be delayed until the costs are known or measurable, whichever comes first.

**Measurable Revenue** The amount of revenue may be quite obvious in many situations. If you go to an appliance dealer and buy a washing machine, you pay a fixed price and either pay cash or charge it to a credit card. The dealer's revenue is the amount of cash received (or the net amount credited to the dealer's bank account by the bank, for a credit card purchase). In other situations, however, the amount may not be quite so clear. Situations in which the amount of revenue is not reliably determinable include the following:

- Total revenue from the sale depends on future performance of the asset sold.
- The credit status of the buyer is unstable, and the risk of default is high.

- Future costs of guarantees may be substantial and cannot be estimated reliably.
- There is a possibility that a large proportion of the products will be returned to the seller, and the quantity cannot be estimated reliably.

Some revenue may not be received until future years. This situation does not mean that revenue cannot be measured reliably. It simply becomes necessary to discount the future payments to find the present value of the cash flow stream. The amount of revenue is the present value of the discounted cash flows. The discount rate will normally be the incremental borrowing rate of the seller, because effectively the seller will be financing the buyer's obligation. Some companies transfer their long-term receivables to a third company, a process that in one form is known as securitization. If receivables are transferred, the proceeds from the transfer determine the value of the revenue. The transfer of receivables is discussed in Chapter 7.

**No Future Involvement or Control** Some managers have used questionable revenue recognition policies in the past. For example, a producer of farm equipment forced its dealers to accept excess inventory at the end of the year so that the manufacturer could show high sales revenue. However, there was an implicit promise that the manufacturer would take back the excess inventory in the following year and dispose of it elsewhere, such as in foreign markets at a lower price. Similarly, some automobile manufacturers have been known to require dealers to accept the manufacturers' excess inventories at the end of the fiscal year.

This criterion is intended to prevent such practices. Indeed, it overlaps with the first criterion because performance has not really been completed or achieved if the seller can control the behaviour of the buyer even when the buyer is at arm's length.

No revenue should be recognized if the buyer's obligation to pay the seller is contingent on the resale of the product. If payment is contingent, this is a **consignment**, a marketing arrangement in which the owner of the product (the *consignor*) ships the product to another party (the *consignee*), which acts as a sales agent. The consignee does not purchase the goods, but assumes responsibility only for their care and resale. Upon sale, the consignee remits the proceeds (less specified expenses and commission) to the consignor. Goods on consignment are part of the inventory of the consignor until sold by the consignee. They are not a sale of the consignor when shipped to the consignee, but only when they are sold by the consignee.

*Product-financing arrangements* include agreements in which a sponsoring company sells a product to another company and in a related transaction agrees to repurchase the product at some future point in time if the customer has been unable to resell the product. This is consignment selling in a different legal form, and it is clear that the risks and rewards of ownership have not passed to the customer.

In these kinds of product-financing agreements, the sponsoring company must record a liability at the time the proceeds are received. It can neither record a sale nor remove the product from its inventory account. Only when the product is sold to an outside party without a related repurchase agreement can the sponsoring company record a sale.

## Rendering of Services

The criteria for recognizing service revenue is similar to those for product sales. For short-term services, the transaction must be complete and the revenue and expense of service must be recognized at the same time. Short-term services include things like income tax services, banking services, hair styling, and so forth.

Most short-term services are delivered continuously, and expenses incurred in delivering those services are not inventoried—they are treated as period costs, expensed immediately. There is no great challenge to accounting for these services. More of a challenge arises when service is provided over a long period of time.

Some long-term services are really a series of short-term performances. An example is sale of a service contract on heating and air conditioning systems. The contract states that the service company will perform routine servicing of the system on a monthly basis as needed, providing whatever labour and materials are necessary without additional charge. Ordinarily, the costs are recorded as expense when incurred, and a proportionate part of the revenue is recorded month by month, assuming there is no significant doubt about its collectibility.

Suppose that the customer pays a large lump sum at the beginning of the contract. This type of payment is commonly referred to as a *retainer.* The amount would be recorded as unearned revenue when received, and then transferred to revenue month by month, as the revenue is earned through the contract term. It doesn't matter whether the customer actually required any service in a particular month. The supplier stood ready to supply the service on demand as the contract requires.

## CONCEPT REVIEW

1. What criteria must be satisfied before revenue from a sale can be recognized?

2. Why is it important that the buyer *accept* the risks and rewards?

3. What measurement issues may arise when revenue is recognized?

4. Give an example in which the seller might control the product even after the sale.

## REVENUE RECOGNITION AT A CRITICAL EVENT

### Recognition at Delivery

The conditions for revenue recognition are usually met at the time goods or services are delivered. Revenue from the sale of products is usually recognized at the date of sale. *Date of sale* means when (1) the product is *delivered* to the customer and (2) the customer *accepts* delivery and responsibility for the product. Revenue from services rendered is likewise recognized when the services have been completed and accepted by the client.

Exhibit 6-3 illustrates a situation in which a company buys inventory, customizes it, and then holds it until sale. It is sold, on account, subject to a four-month warranty. Subsequently, the customer pays, some warranty costs are incurred, and, finally, the warranty expires.

The first column of Exhibit 6-3 traces the entries appropriate if delivery is considered to be the critical event. Customization costs are added to the inventory account and not recognized as an expense when incurred. When the item is delivered, the sales price is accrued, inventory (including the customization cost) is expensed to COGS, and warranty costs are estimated. In this simplified example, collection is assumed to be certain, and no bad-debt accrual is required. Subsequent cash transactions—cash collection and payment of warranty costs—reduce receivables and estimated liabilities that had been established at the critical event. *Net assets (i.e., assets minus liabilities) are increased only at the critical event. Other transactions change the composition but not the total of net assets.*

### Revenue Recognition After Delivery

In certain circumstances, revenue recognition must be delayed until after delivery. Typically, this is appropriate when there are uncertainties over the costs associated with the remaining activities in the earnings process, revenue collection, or measurement.

Revenue from the sale of goods should be recognized only when the risks and rewards of ownership pass from the vendor to the customer. This condition is met only when substantially all of the elements of the earnings process are complete. If there is a major warranty and the potential future cost cannot be estimated reliably, revenue recognition cannot occur until the warranty—and the risk—is over.

**Unpredictable Future Costs** Refer to the second column of entries in Exhibit 6-3. This alternative is appropriate if the cost of the warranty may be significant but cannot be estimated at the point of sale, or at any point up to its expiration. In this case, even delivery does not cause a change in net assets. An account receivable is recognized, inventory (including

**EXHIBIT 6-3**

## CRITICAL EVENTS AND IMPACT ON NET ASSETS

**Data**

| | |
|---|---|
| January 15 | Inventory purchased, $14,500 |
| January 17 | Inventory repackaged and customized— labour and materials cost $2,250. Now ready for sale. |
| March 6 | Inventory delivered to customer on account. Agree-upon price, $28,000. Collection is assured |
| | Case (a): there is a 4-month warranty; future cost of warranty estimated as $3,900. |
| | Case (b): there is a 4-month warranty; potential cost cannot be measured reliably. |
| April 30 | Customer pays 100% of sales price. |
| June 14 | Warranty work done, at a cost of $3,900. |
| July 6 | Warranty expired. |

| Date | (a) Revenue Recognized on Delivery | | | (b) Post-Delivery: Revenue Recognized on Warranty Expiration | | |
|---|---|---|---|---|---|---|
| Jan. 15 | Inventory | 14,500 | | Inventory | 14,500 | |
| | Cash, A/P, etc. | | 14,500 | Cash, A/P, etc. | | 14,500 |
| Effect on net assets | None | | | None | | |
| Jan. 17 | Inventory | 2,250 | | Inventory | 2,250 | |
| | Cash, A/P, etc. | | 2,250 | Cash, A/P, etc. | | 2,250 |
| Effect on net assets | None | | | None | | |
| March 6 | Accounts receivable | 28,000 | | Accounts receivable | 28,000 | |
| | Revenue | | 28,000 | Deferred gross margin | | 11,250 |
| | Cost of goods sold | 16,750 | | Inventory | | 16,750 |
| | Inventory | | 16,750 | | | |
| | Warranty expense | 3,900 | | | | |
| | Estimated warranty liability | | 3,900 | | | |
| Effect on net assets | Increase $7,350 | | | None | | |
| April 30 | Cash | 28,000 | | Cash | 28,000 | |
| | Accounts receivable | | 28,000 | Accounts receivable | | 28,000 |
| Effect on net assets | None | | | None | | |
| June 14 | Estimated warranty liability | 3,900 | | Deferred warranty cost | 3,900 | |
| | Cash | | 3,900 | Cash, A/P, etc. | | 3,900 |
| Effect on net assets | None | | | None | | |
| July 6 | No entry | | | Cost of goods sold | 16,750 | |
| | | | | Deferred gross margin | 11,250 | |
| | | | | Revenue | | 28,000 |
| | | | | Warranty expense | 3,900 | |
| | | | | Deferred warranty cost | | 3,900 |
| Effect on net assets | None | | | Increase $7,350 | | |

customization cost) is reduced, but the gross margin is deferred. The deferred gross margin account is shown as deferred revenue in the liabilities section of the balance sheet.

Warranty costs actually incurred (on 14 June) also are carried forward as deferred cost on the balance sheet. *None of the transactions prior to the critical event—the expiration of the warranty period—triggers a change in net asset value.*

When the warranty expires on 6 July, then and only then can the sale transaction pass through to the income statement. Note that the revenue recognition is recorded by disaggregating the realized gross margin of $11,250 into its two components of sales ($28,000) and COGS ($16,750). Both Canadian and international standards require sellers to disclose both (1) the gross amount of revenue and (2) COGS on the income statement.

**High and Unpredictable Returns.** In several industries, such as book publishing and equipment manufacturing, the sales terms allow customers the right to return goods under certain circumstances and over long periods of time. If the quantity of returns is reasonably predictable, the company can recognize revenue at delivery for the estimated volume of goods that will not be returned.

If, on the other hand, there is little or no history about product returns, or if returns have been volatile over the recent past, it will not be possible to predict the level of returns. If no reasonably reliable estimates are possible, revenue recognition must be delayed until the return period is over.

These points deserve special emphasis:

- If the risk and the future cost can be quantified reliably, the sale can be recorded on delivery and the future costs accrued as an estimated liability.
- If risk cannot be quantified reliably, the sale can be recognized as revenue only after expiry of the return privilege.

## Recognition at Cash Collection

In some situations, the critical event is the *cash collection*. Suppose, for example, that we alter the situation in Exhibit 6-3 slightly:

- The product is purchased for $14,500 on 15 January, and customized at a cost of $2,250 on 17 January—the same facts as in Exhibit 6-3.
- On 13 February, the customer's financial situation becomes doubtful and the customer is hovering on the edge of bankruptcy or receivership. At that point, it becomes clear that the critical event will be collection of cash.
- The product has already been customized and is now unsuitable for sale to another customer, and so delivery occurs on 6 March, as in Exhibit 6-3.
- Estimated warranty cost of $3,900 is recorded at the time of delivery, 6 March.
- Warranty cost of $3,900 is incurred on 14 July.
- The customer pays nothing on 30 April, but pays in full on 5 August.

Exhibit 6-4 illustrates this series of transactions. As in the second situation in Exhibit 6-3, revenue recognition is delayed. But in Exhibit 6-4, recognition is delayed until the cash is actually received instead of when the warranty expires. In this example, *both* warranty expiration and cash collection are required. *The critical event is the last one to occur.*

We could have recognized a substantial allowance for doubtful accounts when the sale was recorded on 6 March, but we have left out that step for simplicity.

Now, what happens if a sale is complete and the seller has no future involvement, but the amount of realizable revenue cannot be estimated reliably due to substantial credit risk? Often, the buyer is given a deferred payment plan (e.g., "no payments for 18 months!" as the TV ads cry out), or the buyer is paying by instalments. This situation is not uncommon in certain types of retail operations, where a dealer sells to people who have shaky credit history or no credit history at all (i.e., first-time users of credit). The dealer knows that a significant proportion of buyers will not be able to finish their payments, but the predictability depends on future economic conditions that cannot be predicted reliably.

## EXHIBIT 6-4

### REVENUE RECOGNITION WHEN CASH COLLECTION IS THE CRITICAL EVENT

| | | | |
|---|---|---|---|
| January 15 | Inventory | 14,500 | |
| | Cash, A/P, etc. | | 14,500 |
| January 17 | Inventory | 2,250 | |
| | Cash, A/P, etc. | | 2,250 |
| March 6 | Accounts receivable | 28,000 | |
| | Deferred gross margin | | 11,250 |
| | Inventory | | 16,750 |
| June 14 | Deferred warranty cost | 3,900 | |
| | Cash, A/P, etc. | | 3,900 |
| August 5 | Cash | 28,000 | |
| | Accounts receivable | | 28,000 |
| | Cost of goods sold | 16,750 | |
| | Deferred gross margin | 11,250 | |
| | Sales revenue | | 28,000 |
| | Warranty expense | 3,900 | |
| | Deferred warranty cost | | 3,900 |

Accounting practice has developed two approaches to dealing with this problem: the *instalment* method and the *cost recovery* method.

**Instalment Sales Method** If future customer defaults cannot be predicted reliably, a company that sells its products on an instalment plan may choose to use the **instalment sales method** of accounting. Revenue under the instalment sales method is recognized when cash is collected rather than at the time of sale. Under this method, revenue (and the related COGS) is recognized only when realized. For example, the instalment method may be used to account for sales of real estate when the down payment is relatively small and ultimate collection of the sales price is not reasonably assured.

Suppose that Truro Limited makes $80,000 of instalment sales in 20X2. The COGS is $60,000, and thus the gross margin is $20,000, or 25% of sales. The sale is recorded with a *deferred* gross margin. The deferred gross margin is reported as unearned revenue in the liabilities section of the balance sheet because it represents net revenue that has not yet been recognized. The entry at the date of sale is as follows:

**instalment sales method**

a system that recognizes proportionate revenue at each cash instalment payment date rather than at the time of delivery

| | | |
|---|---|---|
| Instalment accounts receivable | 80,000 | |
| Inventory | | 60,000 |
| Deferred gross margin | | 20,000 |

Recording the sale does not result in an increase in the company's net assets, because the increase of $20,000 in assets (that is, the increase from $60,000 inventory to $80,000 accounts receivable) is completely offset by the $20,000 increase in the unearned revenue account—deferred gross margin. The deferred gross margin represents the *net* amount of unearned revenue—revenue that has not yet been recognized in income.

If $10,000 is subsequently collected, the entries to record the collection and to recognize a proportionate part of the deferred revenue are as follows:

| | | |
|---|---|---|
| Cash | 10,000 | |
|     Instalment accounts receivable | | 10,000 |
| Deferred gross margin ($10,000 × 25%) | 2,500 | |
| Cost of goods sold | 7,500 | |
|     Sales revenue | | 10,000 |

It is the second entry that records the increase to net assets that is the sign of revenue recognition. The increase in net assets is accomplished by reducing the amount of the deferred gross margin.

**The Cost Recovery Method** On occasion, the collectibility of a receivable is so questionable that a company will use the *cost recovery method*. This method usually is used when a customer gets into financial difficulty at about the time that the product is being delivered.

The cost recovery method is most appropriate when substantial costs have been invested in a contract or product, and the seller is trying to make the best of a bad situation. Since the eventual recovery of the full contract price is in doubt, the seller recognizes no profit until the seller has received enough of the revenue to completely offset all the related costs incurred. Profit is recognized only after all of the costs have been recovered. Because past costs are known as *sunk costs*, this method is sometimes known as the *sunk-cost method*.

**cost recovery method**

used normally in high-risk transactions; revenue offsets all costs incurred before any profit is recognized

To contrast cost recovery method with the instalment method, suppose that Truro Limited sells $80,000 of product to a customer whose financial stability is uncertain. Truro decides to use the cost recovery method because the likelihood of receiving full payment is unpredictable. The cost of the goods sold is $60,000. Suppose that the customer makes one payment of $45,000, followed by another payment of $35,000. If Truro uses the cost recovery method, the entry at the time of sale will be exactly the same as under the instalment sales method:

| | | |
|---|---|---|
| Accounts receivable | 80,000 | |
|     Inventory | | 60,000 |
|     Deferred gross margin | | 20,000 |

When the first cash payment is received, the receivable is reduced and the entire amount is recognized as revenue, but the offset is entirely to COGS. None of the gross margin is recognized yet:

| | | |
|---|---|---|
| Cash | 45,000 | |
|     Accounts receivable | | 45,000 |
| Cost of goods sold | 45,000 | |
|     Revenue | | 45,000 |

When the second payment is received, the remaining revenue of $35,000 is recognized, as is the remaining $15,000 of COGS. The residual $20,000 reflects recognition of the deferred gross margin:

| | | |
|---|---|---|
| Cash | 35,000 | |
|     Accounts receivable | | 35,000 |
| Cost of goods sold | 15,000 | |
| Deferred gross margin | 20,000 | |
|     Revenue | | 35,000 |

This revenue recognition method is highly skewed toward later profit recognition and does a poor job of reflecting performance and cash flows. Its use is justified *only* in the face of significant uncertainties.

## Recognition at Production

Sometimes, the critical event could be viewed not as sale or delivery, but *production*. Historically, production has been viewed as the key activity for refined minerals and for agricultural produce. The reason is that these products have an active, open market. Products such as wheat or gold or oil can be sold by a simple phone call to a trader or broker, or by a click of a computer mouse. Selling requires no significant effort, and cash collection is assured.

Canadian practice sometimes has been to recognize revenue when certain types of mineral resources were produced, such as gold and silver. However, the revenue recognition guidelines clearly specify that a product must be *delivered* to the buyer before revenue can be recognized. Therefore, the use of production as the critical event for revenue recognition has sharply declined.[2]

Nevertheless, recent changes in Canadian accounting standards have protected the ability to recognize revenue from minerals at the point of production, but only if production is the critical point, which can happen under either of two circumstances:

- The minerals have been extracted and sale is assured because the company has a firm contract to sell; or
- There is an active public market for the mineral.

Under either of these circumstances, the sale is assured with virtually no risk, and therefore recognition is permitted even though delivery and acceptance have not occurred.

International standards don't give any special treatment to minerals and mineral products. However, there is an international standard devoted specifically to agriculture (including livestock production). The standard *requires* the producers of "biological assets" to recognize revenue on the basis of fair value less costs to sell—net realizable value (NRV)—at the time of production. Biological assets include harvested plant products (e.g., wheat and soybeans) and animals. The birth of a calf, for example, increases the net assets of the entity and therefore triggers revenue recognition under the international standard.

Canadian standards *permit* inventories of agricultural produce (and of minerals and mineral products) to be carried at NRV if it is common in the industry. This provision seems more intended for the use of intermediate holders of those products rather than the producer. Examples of intermediate holders for grain, for example, would be (1) a grain elevator operator that will resell the grain or (2) a company that converts grain into flour. Such users are very vulnerable to changes in the price of grain. If an intermediate holder uses hedges to protect against price changes, the changes in the fair value of the product can be offset against changes in the value of the hedge (which must be reported at fair value). If

---

[2] Indeed, a review of the SEDAR listings for every publicly listed Canadian gold producer revealed none that recognized revenue at production or that carried their finished product inventories at market value.

this sounds mysterious, just remember for now that a Canadian company that holds inventories of agricultural and mineral products may be permitted to value its inventories at NRV. Hedging is a topic covered much later in the book, in Chapter 14.

These differences between Canadian and international GAAP will have to be resolved in the future.

### Revenue Earned with the Passage of Time

Some types of revenue are earned by permitting others to use our resources. If a landlord owns an office building and leases space to tenants, the landlord earns revenue simply by letting the tenants use the space. Similarly, when a bank permits others to use its cash resources by lending money, the bank earns revenue over time, through interest. Or, a company may license others to use its brand name or trademarks and collect a licence fee.

There is no great challenge to accounting for revenue earned this way. The passage of time is the critical event. Therefore, we must not be fooled by irregular payment schemes.

For example, suppose that a company licenses a manufacturer in a foreign market to use a trademark for 10 years. The licensee makes an initial payment of $6 million and promises to pay an additional $1 million for each of the following four years. Effectively, the licensee is paying $10 million for using the trademark for five years, which is $2 million per year. The company should recognize only $2 million as revenue for the first year, not $6 million. It has received the cash and delivered the license, but the critical event is the passage of time.

As another example, suppose that WestJet pays $20 million to the developer of a new sports centre. The payment is for "naming rights" to call the sports centre the WestJet Centre for the next 10 years. Although the cash has been received, the developer still would recognize only $2 million per year as revenue.

When such revenue is not a normal revenue-producing activity of a company, it often is labelled "other *income*" in the income statement rather than as *revenue*, as we pointed out in Chapter 3—dividend income, interest income, rental income, etc. Whether called revenue or income, the accounting is the same. The critical event is *time*.

## NON-MONETARY TRANSACTIONS

**barter transaction**

an exchange of non-cash assets, usually with no cash consideration involved

Measurement issues also are significant if the sale transaction is a **barter transaction;** a barter transaction is one in which no money changes hands. Instead, two companies exchange assets.

For example, an accountant may prepare a tax return for an innkeeper in exchange for a three-day weekend vacation at the innkeeper's facility. At what amount should this transaction be valued? The accountant could keep track of her time, multiply by her hourly rate, and determine the amount she would have billed the client. Alternatively, she could ascertain the value of the weekend vacation to which she is entitled.

Accounting standards indicate that the transaction should be valued at the fair value of the asset or service given up. The *value* of the asset given up is the *cost* of the asset acquired. However, if the value of the asset or service received is more reliable, it should be used to value the transaction.

For our accountant, this means that she'll look at the value of her time, then look at the value of the weekend trip, and ask which value she's more confident about. Likely she'll use the value of her time, but a comparison of the two values is always informative. If they're close, there's a high degree of comfort with the decision. It's not as easy as it seems: she may have been using otherwise-idle time to do this job, which implies that her time may not have been "worth" the full rate. She may be able to use the vacation weekend only in shoulder periods, when the room would otherwise have been vacant at the inn—implying that it may not be "worth" the advertised price. Judgement is pivotal to the measurement process.

Accounting standards contain some specific rules on accounting for non-monetary transactions. Basically, revenue is recognized only if there is real economic substance, called "commercial substance," to the transaction. Otherwise, no gains or losses can be recognized on the transaction. Non-monetary transactions are discussed more fully in Chapter 9.

## CONCEPT REVIEW

1. When would revenue recognition be delayed to a point later than production and delivery?

2. Suppose that a company has significant possible future after-sale costs that cannot be measured reliably. At what point does the net asset value of the company change as the result of the sale?

3. In what basic way does the cost recovery method differ from the instalment method?

4. What is a non-monetary transaction?

## LONG-TERM CONTRACTS

In some instances the earnings process extends over several accounting periods. Delivery of the final product may occur years after the initiation of the project. Examples are construction of large ships and office buildings, development of space-exploration equipment, and development of large-scale custom software. Contracts for these projects often provide for progress billings at various points in the earnings process.

If the seller waits until the project or contract is completed to recognize revenue, the information on revenue and expense included in the financial statements will be reliable, but it may not be relevant for decision making because the information is not timely.

For example, the financial reporting objective of performance evaluation is reasonably well served only if the financial statements report on the results of the enterprise's economic activity during the period. Delaying revenue recognition on long-term projects until the project is complete tells the financial statement reader nothing about economic activity (i.e., performance) during the period.

The cash flow reporting objective also is not well served by delaying revenue recognition, because the cash is flowing out (and usually in, as well) as the project is performed, not at the end. Therefore, it often is worthwhile to trade off reliability in order to provide more timely and relevant earnings information. There are two general methods of accounting for revenue on long-term contracts:

1. *Completed-contract method.* Revenues, expenses, and resulting gross profit are recognized only when the contract is completed. As costs are incurred, they are accumulated in an inventory account called "projects in progress," "work in progress," or some similar title. Progress billings are not recorded as revenues, but are accumulated in a "billings on contracts" or "progress billings" account that is deducted from the inventory account (i.e., a *contra* account to inventory). At the completion of the contract, all the accounts are closed, and the entire gross profit from the project is recognized.

2. *Percentage-of-completion method.* The percentage-of-completion method recognizes revenue on a long-term project as work progresses so that timely information is reported on the income statement. Revenues, expenses, and gross profit are recognized each accounting period based on an estimate of the percentage of completion of the project. Project costs and gross profit to date are accumulated in the inventory account ("projects in progress"). Progress billings are accumulated in a contra inventory account ("billings on projects in progress").

The percentage-of-completion and completed-contract methods are not intended to be free choice alternatives for the same circumstances. Is there a contract that establishes the contract price with a high degree of reliability? Is collection reasonably assured? These conditions would be met by the standard provisions of a long-term contract that involves a creditworthy customer expected to make regular progress payments.

The critical criteria are whether the seller can estimate with reasonable assurance:

- The progress toward completion of the contractual obligation;
- The costs to complete the project; and
- The total revenue.

If these criteria are met, percentage of completion is the method that very clearly *relates the revenue to the work performed*. If the criteria are not met, the completed-contract method should be used. Of course, judgement plays a role in determining whether the criteria are met, and company-specific reporting objectives usually influence the selection of method.

There can be dramatic differences between the revenue and income effects of the completed-contract and percentage-of-completion methods. The completed-contract method is the simplest and most straightforward and it is discussed first.

### Example—Completed-Contract Method

Under the completed-contract method, there is no recognition of the project *in the income statement* until the project is completed and has been legally accepted by the customer.

Assume that the Ace Construction Corporation has contracted to erect a building for $1.5 million, starting construction on 1 February 20X1, with a planned completion date of 1 August 20X3. Total costs to complete the contract are estimated at $1.35 million, so the estimated gross profit is expected to be $150,000. Progress billings payable within 10 days after billing will be made on a predetermined schedule.

The data shown in the upper portion of Exhibit 6-5 pertain to the three-year construction period. The facts for each of the three years will be revealed as each year goes by. That is, in 20X1, the contractor does not know the information that is shown in the columns for 20X2 and 20X3.

---

### EXHIBIT 6-5

## ACE CONSTRUCTION CORPORATION
## EXAMPLE OF COMPLETED CONTRACT ACCOUNTING

### Construction Project Fact Sheet, Three-Year Summary Schedule

| Contract Price: $1,500,000 | 20X1 | 20X2 | 20X3 |
|---|---|---|---|
| 1. Estimated total costs for project | $1,350,000 | $1,360,000 | $1,365,000 |
| 2. Costs incurred during current year | 350,000 | 550,000 | 465,000 |
| 3. Cumulative costs incurred to date | 350,000 | 900,000 | 1,365,000 |
| 4. Estimated costs to complete at year-end | 1,000,000 | 460,000 | — |
| 5. Progress billings during year | 300,000 | 575,000 | 625,000 |
| 6. Cumulative billings to date | 300,000 | 875,000 | 1,500,000 |
| 7. Collections on billings during year | 270,000 | 555,000 | 675,000 |
| 8. Cumulative collections to date | 270,000 | 825,000 | 1,500,000 |

### Journal Entries to Record Construction in Progress:

| | 20X1 | | 20X2 | | 20X3 | |
|---|---|---|---|---|---|---|
| Construction-in-progress inventory | 350,000 | | 550,000 | | 465,000 | |
|   Cash, payables, etc. | | 350,000 | | 550,000 | | 465,000 |
| Accounts receivable | 300,000 | | 575,000 | | 625,000 | |
|   Billings on contracts | | 300,000 | | 575,000 | | 625,000 |
| Cash | 270,000 | | 555,000 | | 675,000 | |
|   Accounts receivable | | 270,000 | | 555,000 | | 675,000 |

The total construction costs were originally estimated at $1,350,000, of which $350,000 were incurred in 20X1. In 20X2, another $550,000 in costs were incurred, but the estimated total costs rose by $10,000 in 20X2, to $1,360,000. In 20X3, the total costs rose by another $5,000, and the total cost to complete the project turns out to be $1,365,000. Contract profit therefore drops from the original estimate of $150,000 to an actual amount of $135,000.

As costs are incurred, they are debited to an inventory account called "construction in progress." This inventory account is a current asset even for a multiyear project because the operating cycle of the contractor is the length of the longest project (rather than one year).

**progress billings**

*in a long-term project, the amounts that are invoiced to the client or customer for work accomplished to date on the project*

Construction companies do not wait until the end of the project to collect their money. Instead, **progress billings** are made throughout the duration of the project. The amount of progress billings is based on the amount of work accomplished to the date of the billing, as verified by an independent facilitator.

Progress billings are debited to *accounts receivable* and credited to *billings on contracts*, which is subtracted from the construction-in-progress inventory on the balance sheet. If the net construction-in-progress inventory (inventory less billings on contract) is a debit balance, it is reported as a current asset. This account balance represents the contractor's net ownership interest in the construction project; it is sometimes referred to as the *contractor's draw*.

If the net amount in the construction-in-progress inventory is a credit balance, it represents the developer's (buyer's) interest in the project and is referred to as the *developer's draw*. A credit balance is reported as a current liability in the contractor's financial statements.

The journal entries to record the construction-in-progress inventory, progress billings, and cash collections (of progress billings) for each year for Ace Construction are shown in the lower portion of Exhibit 6-5.

At the completion of the contact, income is recognized as the difference between the accumulated credit balance in the billings on contracts account and the debit balance in the construction-in-progress inventory account, assuming that the total price of the contract has been billed. The accumulated amount of billings on contracts is recognized as sales revenue, and the accumulated amount of construction-in-progress inventory on completion of the contract is recognized as COGS. It is this series of entries that increases net assets:

| | | |
|---|---|---|
| Billings on contracts | 1,500,000 | |
|     Revenue from long-term contracts | | 1,500,000 |
| Costs of construction | 1,365,000 | |
|     Construction-in-progress inventory | | 1,365,000 |

On balance sheets during the construction period, the construction-in-progress inventory is reported as total accumulated costs to date less the total progress billings to date.

**Advantages of Completed-Contract Method** The completed-contract method has the advantage of delaying profit measurement until substantially all of the costs and revenues are known. There may be some remaining costs that are roughly similar to warranty costs; these can be estimated and accrued.

Although the costs and revenues are known with a high degree of assurance, the *timing* of their recognition in the income statement is a matter for some manipulation. Contractors have been known to informally suggest to customers that they may want to delay formal acceptance of the project until after the contractor's year-end, usually in order to delay taxation. Taxation officials are aware of this practice, however, and often reach into the next year and claim tax on the profits generated on projects "closed" during the first two months of the contractor's next fiscal year.

The completed-contract method ranks high on the qualitative characteristic of reliability because there is so little estimation involved. On the other hand, the method is perceived as lacking in the qualitative attributes of relevance and timeliness because the benefit of the contractor's economic activity during the year is not reflected on the income statement as long as the project is underway. Therefore, the completed-contract method is not very helpful if the dominant reporting objective is performance evaluation.

The completed-contract method may potentially appear to be quite useful for income tax minimization since there may be no taxation until the project is complete. This advantage is severely limited in Canada, however, because Canada Revenue Agency permits use of the completed-contract method only for contracts lasting two years or less. Percentage-of-completion *must* be used for tax purposes for all longer contracts.

### Example—Percentage-of-Completion Method

The objective of the percentage-of-completion method is to provide an estimate of the earnings of the company that will arise as the result of its economic activity (i.e., working on construction projects) during the year. Since the contractor spent a lot of time, effort, and money working on projects in progress, performance evaluation is better served if periodic profit (or loss) is measured on the basis of *effort expended* rather than contracts completed.

Under the percentage-of-completion method, a portion of revenue and expense (and thus income) is recognized as it is earned in each accounting period. The amount of income that is recognized is added to the "construction-in-progress" inventory. By adding the income earned to the inventory, the inventory is being increased to its net realizable value. Total actual income on the contract will not be known until the project is completed; what is recognized each period is an estimate of income that is based on many other estimates, as we discuss shortly.

**Measuring Progress toward Completion**   Measuring progress toward completion of a long-term project can be accomplished by using either input measures or output measures:

1. *Input measures.* The effort devoted to a project to date is compared with the total effort expected to be required in order to complete the project. Examples are (1) costs incurred to date compared with total estimated costs for the project and (2) labour hours worked compared with total estimated labour hours required to complete the project.

2. *Output measures.* Results to date are compared with expected total results when the project is completed. Examples are the number of kilometres of highway completed compared with total kilometres to be completed, or progress milestones established in a software development contract.

An expert, such as an engineer or architect, is often hired to assess percentage of completion or achievement of milestones. This is an art as much as a science.

The goal is to have a realistic measure of progress made toward completion of the project. Neither input nor output measures are ideal. Input measures are often used when it is difficult to measure progress using output measures. However, input measures can be misleading when a constant relationship between the input measure and productivity does not exist. Cost overruns on projects would cause erroneous levels of completion to be estimated. Costs incurred also may be misleading as a measure of progress if costs include one-time, upfront expenditures for quantities of materials and supplies to be used during the construction period.

Despite their shortcomings, input measures are most frequently used because they are the most readily available. Among input measures, the cost-to-cost method is the most common. The cost-to-cost method measures the percentage completed by the ratio of costs incurred to date to the current estimate of the total costs required to complete the project:

$$\text{Percentage complete} = \frac{\text{Total costs incurred to date}}{\text{Most recent estimate of total costs of project (past and future)}}$$

The estimate of costs incurred to date should include only those costs pertaining to the work done to date. Sometimes materials are brought on-site that will be used in later stages of construction. In that case, the materials for future use should be classified as raw materials and not included in the numerator of the cost ratio. They would be included in the denominator, of course, because they will be used later in the project.

The most recent estimate of total project costs is the sum of the total costs incurred to date plus the estimated costs yet to be incurred to complete the project. Once the percentage completed has been computed, the amount of revenue to recognize in the current period is determined as:

Current period's revenue = (Percentage complete × Total contract revenue) − Revenue previously recognized

**Applying the Method** Using the data shown in the upper portion of Exhibit 6-5, the relative proportion of the total costs that have been incurred to date can be used to determine percentage completed:

|  | 20X1 | 20X2 | 20X3 |
|---|---|---|---|
| Costs incurred to date | $ 350,000 | $ 900,000 | $1,365,000 |
| Estimated total costs | 1,350,000 | 1,360,000 | 1,365,000 |
| Percent completed | 26% | 66% | 100% |

The percentage completed is computed by dividing the estimate of *costs incurred to date* by the *estimated total costs.* For example, estimated total costs at the end of 20X1 ($1,350,000) equals costs incurred to date ($350,000) plus estimated costs to complete at the end of 20X1 ($1,000,000). The percentages shown above have been rounded to the nearest full percentage point. The "exact" percentage for 20X2, to be precise, is 66.17647 ... %. But there is no point in calculating the percentage of completion to more than two digits (or, at the most, three). We are working with estimates here, and it is silly to be "precise" in calculating percentages that are based on approximations.

The next step is to compute the total amount of revenue recognizable up to each year-end by multiplying the total contract revenue by the percentage completed for each year. Then, revenue previously recognized is subtracted. The result is the revenue that is recognized in each specific year.

|  | 20X1 | 20X2 | 20X3 |
|---|---|---|---|
| *20X1*: $1.5 million × 26% | $390,000 | — | — |
| *20X2*: $1.5 million × 66% | — | $990,000 | — |
| *20X3*: $1.5 million × 100% | — | — | $1,500,000 |
| *Less:* revenue previously recognized | — | (390,000) | (990,000) |
| Recognized revenue for the year | $390,000 | $600,000 | $ 510,000 |

The gross profit to be recognized is the difference between revenue and costs incurred in the period:

| | 20X1 | 20X2 | 20X3 | Total |
|---|---|---|---|---|
| Revenue for the current year | $390,000 | $600,000 | $510,000 | $1,500,000 |
| Costs incurred in the current year | 350,000 | 550,000 | 465,000 | 1,365,000 |
| Gross profit for the year | $ 40,000 | $ 50,000 | $ 45,000 | $ 135,000 |

The journal entries to record the costs incurred on the construction, the progress billings, and the collections of progress billings are the same as those for the completed-contract method. An additional entry is needed to record the recognition of revenue and expense each year. The gross profit is debited to the construction-in-progress inventory:

| | 20X1 | | 20X2 | | 20X3 | |
|---|---|---|---|---|---|---|
| Construction-in-progress inventory (B/S) | 40,000 | | 50,000 | | 45,000 | |
| Costs of construction (I/S) | 350,000 | | 550,000 | | 465,000 | |
| Revenue from long-term contracts (I/S) | | 390,000 | | 600,000 | | 510,000 |

The construction-in-progress inventory account is greater under the percentage-of-completion method than under the completed-contract method by the amount of gross margin recognized to date. *This is the increase in net assets that always accompanies revenue recognition.*

Notice that the balance of the construction-in-progress inventory account is *not* reduced each year as the revenue and related costs are recognized in the income statement. On the income statement, the recognized gross profit is disaggregated into revenue less costs of construction. The offset to the inventory account is the billings on contracts account, just as for the completed-contract method.

When the project is completed, the billings on contracts will completely offset the construction-in-progress inventory. A journal entry is needed to remove both accounts:

| | | |
|---|---|---|
| Billings on contracts | 1,500,000 | |
| Construction-in-progress inventory | | 1,500,000 |

## Comparison of Results

Exhibit 6-6 shows the impact of the two methods on net assets.

Exhibit 6-7 shows the financial statement presentations for the two methods. Under the completed-contract method, inventory is carried at cost. Under the percentage-of-completion method, inventory is carried at cost plus recognized gross profit.

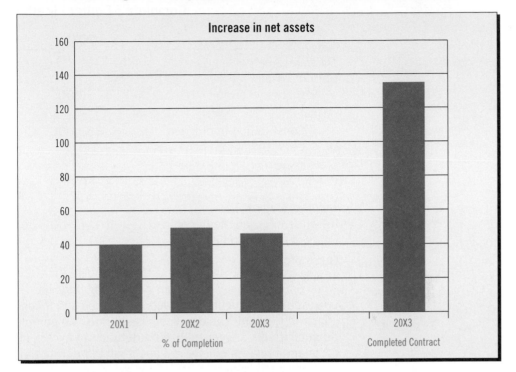

EXHIBIT 6-6

# CHANGE IN NET ASSETS
## Percentage of Completion Compared to Completed Contract

The difference between year-end inventory amounts under the two methods is the amount of accumulated gross margin recognized under the percentage-of-completion method. Exhibit 6-7 also shows the dramatic difference in gross profit between the two methods on a year-to-year basis. However, *total gross profit over the three years is the same for each method*. This is another of the allocation games of which accountants are so fond.

## Percentage-of-Completion Measurement Issues

It is important to understand the extent of the estimates and approximations that underlie the percentage-of-completion method. Virtually every cost, revenue, and percentage-of-completion figure reflects not just one, but multiple, estimates.

**Estimating Costs**  Obviously, the cost to complete is an estimate. It may be wildly off the mark, because large-scale projects are often begun before the final design is even completed. Complications often arise during construction, and costs mount up. In home renovation projects, for example, it is common for total costs to be 50% above the contract price, even when the contractor is being as realistic as possible in making the initial cost estimate.

"Costs incurred to date" may seem like a definite figure. After all, the contractor must know how much has been spent on the project so far. But it really is an estimate. How much of the contractor's overhead is to be included in the costs assigned to the project, and how much is charged as a period cost? What proportion of purchased and/or contracted materials should be included in cost to date? If the contractor has ordered and delivered 5,000 tonnes of bricks for exterior sheathing, should the cost of those bricks be included in the

```
                    EXHIBIT 6-7
```

## FINANCIAL STATEMENT PRESENTATION OF ACCOUNTING FOR LONG-TERM CONSTRUCTION CONTRACTS

### Completed-Contact Method

|  | 20X1 | 20X2 | 20X3 |
|---|---|---|---|
| *Balance sheet:* | | | |
| Current assets: | | | |
| Accounts receivable | $ 30,000 | $ 50,000 | |
| Inventory: | | | |
| Construction in progress | 350,000 | 900,000 | |
| Less: Billings on contracts | 300,000 | 875,000 | |
| Construction in progress in excess of billings | $ 50,000 | $ 25,000 | |
| *Income Statement:* | | | |
| Revenue from long-term contracts | $        0 | $        0 | $1,500,000 |
| Costs of construction | 0 | 0 | 1,365,000 |
| Gross profit | 0 | 0 | $   135,000 |

*Note 1: Summary of significant accounting policies.*
Long-term construction contracts: Revenues and income from long-term construction contracts are recognized under the completed-contract method. Such contracts are generally for a duration in excess of one year. Construction costs and progress billings are accumulated during the periods of construction. Only when the project is completed are revenue, expense, and income recognized on the project.

### Percentage-of-Completion Method

|  | 20X1 | 20X2 | 20X3 |
|---|---|---|---|
| *Balance sheet:* | | | |
| Current assets: | | | |
| Accounts receivable | $ 30,000 | $ 50,000 | |
| Inventory: | | | |
| Construction in progress | 390,000 | 990,000 | |
| Less: Billings on contracts | 300,000 | 875,000 | |
| Construction in progress in excess of billings | $ 90,000 | $115,000 | |
| *Income Statement:* | | | |
| Revenue from long-term contracts | $390,000 | $600,000 | $   510,000 |
| Costs of construction | 350,000 | 550,000 | 465,000 |
| Gross Profit | $ 40,000 | $ 50,000 | $     45,000 |

*Note 1: Summary of significant accounting policies.*
Long-term construction contracts: Revenues and income from long-term construction contracts are recognized under the percentage-of-completion method. Such contracts are generally for a duration in excess of one year. Construction costs and progress billings are accumulated during the periods of construction. The amount of revenue recognized each year is based on the ratio of the costs incurred to the estimated total costs of completion of the construction contract.

cost to date when the bricks are purchased or should the cost be excluded until the bricks are actually used in construction of the building?

**Estimating Revenue** Most people assume that the amount of revenue is known at the outset and is not an estimate. True, any long-term construction contract starts out with a contract price, but that initial contract price hardly ever ends up being the real revenue figure. As was mentioned above, unexpected costs will raise the contract price. For example, construction of a building foundation may encounter unstable ground or water conditions and require extensive extra work. The client must accept the additional cost (plus, usually, an additional amount for the contractor's overhead and profit) or work on the project will stop.

As well, contractors often bid on jobs at zero profit or even at a loss in order to get the job. The reason is that every construction job involves *change orders*, which is a change in the original design of the building (or of whatever is being constructed). Change orders require additional revenue, and the contractor often bids low on the original contract because she knows that she will make her money on the change orders (which can hardly be submitted to a competitive bidding process!). So, in the course of a construction project:

- Estimated cost to complete will change each period;
- Cost incurred in the current period (to be used in the percentage calculation) is an estimate; and
- Estimated total revenue will change from period to period.

It is safe to say that the percentage-of-completion method is an approximation! It represents a trade-off between conflicting qualitative criteria; reliability is sacrificed for timeliness and relevance.

## Accounting for Losses on Long-Term Contracts

When the costs necessary to complete a contract result in losses, two situations are possible:

1. *The loss results in an unprofitable contract.* In this situation, the loss is recognized in full in the year it becomes estimable. For example, assume that, at the end of 20X2, Ace's costs incurred are as shown ($350,000 in 20X1 and $550,000 in 20X2), but the estimate of the costs to complete the contract in 20X3 increases to $625,000 from $465,000, an increase of $160,000.

   Since costs incurred through 20X2 total $900,000, the total estimated cost of the contract becomes $1,525,000 (instead of $1,365,000), and there is now an expected loss on the contract of $25,000.

The $25,000 loss would be recognized in 20X2 under both methods of accounting for long-term construction contracts. A simple accrual entry is made for the completed contract method, and the percentage-of-completion would record a gross loss of $65,000 ($25,000 + $40,000), which records the loss and reverses the profit recorded in prior years:

| | 20X1 | 20X2 |
|---|---|---|
| Total estimated revenue | $1,500,000 | $1,500,000 |
| Cumulative costs to date | 350,000 | 900,000 |
| Estimated costs to complete | 1,000,000 | 625,000 |
| Estimated total costs | 1,350,000 | 1,525,000 |
| Estimated total profit (loss) | $  150,000 | $  (25,000) |
| Profit previously recognized | — | 40,000 |
| Profit (loss) recognized in current year | $   40,000 | $  (65,000) |

The journal entry for 20X2, using the percentage-of-completion method, will be as follows:

| | | |
|---|---|---|
| Costs of construction (I/S) | 550,000 | |
|     Construction-in-progress inventory (B/S) | | 65,000 |
|     Revenue from long-term contracts (I/S) | | 485,000 |

The loss is credited to the inventory account, which reduces the inventory to lower-of-cost-or market—not all of the costs can now be recovered.

2. *The contract remains profitable, but there is a current-year loss.* Suppose Ace's costs incurred to the end of 20X2 are as shown, but the estimate to complete the contract has increased to $550,000. Total costs of $900,000 have already been incurred; thus, the total estimated cost of completing the contract has risen to $1,450,000. The contract will still generate a gross margin of $50,000.

Under the completed-contract method, all items are deferred until 20X3, and no entry is needed in 20X2. For the percentage-of-completion method, the 20X2 completion percentage is reworked (now 62%; $900,000 ÷ $1,450,000). This decreases the amount of revenue that will be reported, and results in a reported gross loss in 20X2.

## Proportional-Performance Method for Service Companies

The proportional-performance method is used to recognize service revenue that is earned by more than a single act, when the service extends beyond one accounting period. In fact, recording interest revenue or rental revenue as time passes is really application of proportional-performance methods. Revenue is recognized based on the proportional performance of each act.

The proportional-performance method of accounting for service revenue is similar to the percentage-of-completion method and has to meet the same criteria as a long-term construction contract:

- A fixed or estimable amount of revenue with reasonable assurance of collection;
- A way to measure extent of performance; and
- An ability to estimate the remaining costs to completion.

Many service contracts are subject to at least as many uncertainties as are construction contracts. In particular, it is not unusual for the revenue to change as the client changes the scope of the assignment or the specifications of the task. Software contracts, for example, can double or triple in price if the client keeps changing his mind about what he wants the software to do.

Proportional measurement takes different forms depending on the type of service transaction:

1. *Similar performance acts.* An equal amount of service revenue is recognized for each such act (for example, processing of monthly mortgage payments by a mortgage banker).

2. *Dissimilar performance acts.* Service revenue is recognized in proportion to the seller's direct costs to perform each act (for example, providing examinations, and grading by a correspondence or Internet-based school). If the direct cost of each act cannot be measured reliably, the total service sales revenue should be prorated to the various acts in proportion to the relative sales value of each act. If sales values cannot be identified with each act, the straight-line method to measure proportional performance can be used.

3. *Similar acts with a fixed period for performance.* Service revenue is allocated and recognized by the straight-line method over the fixed period, unless another allocation method is more appropriate (for example, providing maintenance services on equipment for a fixed periodic fee).

### "Bill-and-Hold" Arrangements

A *bill-and-hold* arrangement is a contract between a buyer and seller wherein the buyer promises to accept a specified quantity of the seller's product over a specific period of time at a predetermined price. Delivery is at the buyer's request, but the buyer takes title and accepts billing for the product either as it is produced or on a regular schedule (e.g., monthly).

For example, an electronics dealer may agree to accept (and pay for) 10,000 units of a new cell phone over the next six months. The dealer benefits from the transaction if demand for the new phone is expected to exceed the manufacturer's production capacity. The dealer then has a guaranteed source of supply, although no price flexibility. If the dealer cannot sell as many as she contracted for, she still will have to pay for the phones. This is also known as a *take-or-pay* arrangement.

As the manufacturer produces the phones, he may wish to recognize the revenue at completion of production rather than when the dealer asks for shipment of the product. This arrangement implies that the critical event is *production* rather than delivery or cash receipt.

Revenue recognition at production is rather aggressive accounting. If revenue recognition prior to delivery is generally acceptable, then companies could ask friendly customers to enter into bill-and-hold agreements so that the seller could recognize revenue on existing inventory earlier. The agreements could provide various escape clauses for the buyer so that the buyer could avoid the purchase requirements. Examples of such clauses might give the buyer cancellation clauses, generous return rights, and the right to renegotiate the price.

To guard against revenue manipulation, both the AcSB and the IASB have developed guidelines for revenue recognition under bill-and-hold arrangements. The two sets of guidelines differ in detail, but in general, the broad requirements are as follows:

- The buyer initiated the agreement and specifically acknowledges the deferred delivery provisions.
- The buyer must agree to accept the risks of ownership prior to delivery.
- The buyer's inventory (being held by the seller) must be segregated from the seller's inventory.
- The arrangement must be for the buyer's genuine business purposes.
- The agreement must be in writing or verifiable electronic form.

## CONCEPT REVIEW

1. What qualitative characteristics are better served by completed-contract reporting than by percentage-of-completion reporting?
2. Which financial reporting objectives are satisfied more by percentage-of-completion accounting than by completed-contract accounting?
3. What estimates are required in order to use the percentage-of-completion method?
4. How does the construction-in-progress inventory balance differ between the completed-contract method and the percentage-of-completion method?

## MULTIPLE-DELIVERABLE CONTRACTS

A **multiple-deliverable contract** is a sales contract that includes several different components, or *deliverables*. For example, a software company may sell an advanced processing system to a client. The sales contract includes three years of free service, as well as periodic software updates at a reduced rate. There are three identifiable components to this contract: (1) the processing system, (2) the updates, and (3) the service agreement. Each of these three components is a separate *deliverable*, and thus this is a multiple-deliverable agreement.

Under current standards, a sales or performance contract has multiple deliverables only if it meets *both* of two criteria:[3]

1. Each component of the contract has value to the customer *on a stand-alone basis*, and

2. There is objective and reliable evidence of the fair value of each component.

If these two criteria are met, each of the three components is accounted for separately as a distinct revenue-generating activity. The overall revenue stream must be allocated to the stand-alone components on the basis of the relative fair values of the components.

For example, suppose that on 20 December 20X4 Crease Computers Ltd. enters into a $900,000 contract with a customer to supply a sophisticated mainframe computer plus three years of regular service. Both the computer and the service could be negotiated separately, either with Crease Computers or with another supplier. The fair value of the computer is $800,000 and the fair value of the service contract is $200,000. The total revenue will be allocated as follows (in thousands):

| | | |
|---|---|---|
| Revenue from sale of computer | $900 × [$800 ÷ ($800 + $200)] | = $720 |
| Revenue from service contract | $900 × [$200 ÷ ($800 + $200)] | = $\underline{180}$ |
| Total revenue | | $\underline{\underline{\$900}}$ |

If the customer is paying for the entire contract at the outset and the computer is shipped, the journal entry to record the sale will appear as follows:

| *20 December 20X4:* | | |
|---|---|---|
| Accounts receivable | 900,000 | |
|    Revenue—sales of equipment | | 720,000 |
|    Deferred revenue | | 180,000 |

The revenue from the service contract normally will be recognized evenly over each of the following three years:

| *31 December 20X5, 20X6, and 20X7:* | | |
|---|---|---|
| Deferred revenue | 60,000 | |
|    Revenue—service contracts | | 60,000 |

The term "each component" in the first criterion should not be taken too literally. If a contract seems to have four different components but one of them does not have a value on a stand-alone basis, then that component can be combined with another one to form a single unit for accounting purposes.

### An Example: Franchise-Fee Revenue

Accounting for franchise-fee revenue provides an example of the problems that can arise in revenue recognition. For revenue recognition purposes, it often is difficult to determine when performance is achieved and the franchisor's service has been delivered.

---

[3] There is a third criterion involving the vendor's control over the right of return (EIC-142), which we will not include in this discussion.

Franchisees usually agree to pay a substantial fee to the franchisor. In return for the fee, the franchisee usually receives a series of benefits. For a food service franchise, the benefits may include:

- Location vetting and selection
- Legal assistance in obtaining the site and appropriate licenses
- Facility design
- Initial equipment and other tangible assets
- Intangible right to use the franchisor's brand name;
- Recipes and continuing menu development
- Access to the franchisor's bulk ordering system and/or favoured status with suppliers
- Troubleshooting, inspection, and quality-monitoring services.

Clearly, a franchise fee is a multiple deliverable. The franchisor is delivering many services over a potentially extended period of time. The problem is to determine which of those components has a stand-alone value. Can the franchisee purchase each of those components independently, either with the franchisor or from other sources? If the services are available from other sources, are they really comparable to the services that the franchisor will provide? These are not easy questions to answer. However, the initial design and set-up of the franchise may be one deliverable, provision of the tangible assets may be a second deliverable, and ongoing services may be a third.

An additional problem with franchise fee revenue recognition is estimating the collectibility of the initial franchise fee. If the franchisee pays the fee upfront, this is less of a concern; if the franchisee plans to pay it over time with profits from the franchise operation, then collection is contingent on profitable operations, and careful assessment of business risk is necessary. A franchisor that has little or no historical experience may have to delay revenue recognition because it has no credit history on which to base its provision for doubtful accounts.

Canadian accounting standards include a guideline[4] that suggests that "substantial performance" has occurred only when:

**a.** The franchisor has performed substantially all of the initial services required by the franchise agreement or volunteered by the franchisor as a result of normal business practice.

**b.** The franchisor has no remaining obligation or intent to refund amounts received or forgive unpaid amounts owing.

**c.** There are no other material unfulfilled conditions affecting completion of the sale.

Thus, "delivery" has occurred only when the franchisor has done what is expected and gets to keep the money. This still doesn't address the issue of multiple deliveries. These guidelines need to be applied to each of the franchisor's services that (1) have a stand-alone value and (2) for which there is objective and reliable evidence of its fair value. Not an easy task!

Accounting for multiple-deliverable agreements can become very complex. The issue is under discussion among standard-setting bodies. We will not discuss it further in this book.

## CHOOSING A REVENUE RECOGNITION POLICY

This chapter has illustrated many different ways in which revenue can be recognized. Revenue recognition is the most pervasive and most difficult single accounting policy choice that many companies must face.

Although there may seem to be many alternatives, revenue recognition policy is not really a free choice. The policy is, first and foremost, a function of the revenue activity of the enterprise. When there is more than one revenue-generating activity, then there *may* be a different policy for each. For example, a retail company that engages in straightforward sales

---

[4] "Franchise Fee Revenue," Accounting Guideline 2, *CICA Handbook*, July 1984.

activity for cash or credit will probably recognize sales revenue at the point of delivery, while for interest revenue on its outstanding credit card balances the company will likely recognize interest revenue as time elapses.

A chosen revenue recognition policy must satisfy the general recognition criteria of *performance*, *measurability*, and *probability of collection*. The products or services must be delivered to and accepted by the customer. Revenue and any future costs must be measurable with reasonable assurance. The eventual collection (in cash) must be highly probable. It is important to bear in mind that the act of revenue (and expense) recognition *increases the net assets of the company*. The increase may be through an increase in cash, accounts receivable, or the value of inventories, but ultimately the amount must be realizable in cash.

## ETHICAL ISSUES

Companies bring a variety of motives to the revenue recognition policy decision. Firms that are anxious to show increasing sales and profits sometimes have followed questionable and possibly even improper accounting procedures. A relatively innocent-looking example occurs when a firm records revenue for goods that have been ordered for a later delivery. For example, suppose a firm receives an order in December for goods that the customer desires to receive in mid-January, and agrees to pay for the goods by the end of December. Should the sale be recorded in December or January?

Even more problematic is a "sale" recorded for goods shipped to a customer that regularly purchases such goods in approximately the amounts shipped, but which has not yet ordered the goods! There have also been cases where the invoices for goods shipped after the fiscal year-end are backdated to the current fiscal year in order to record them as sales in the earlier period. Yes, this really happens, but it's not acceptable, either ethically or under GAAP. Such actions are deliberate attempts to mislead users, and are tantamount to fraud.

Accounting standard setters have developed criteria in an attempt to discourage the most egregious revenue recognition practices. However, bear in mind that revenue recognition often involves a lot of estimates—revenue collectibility, future costs, management intent, and customer acceptance (and returns). There still is a lot of flexibility for unscrupulous managers to manipulate revenue recognition. All accountants must be on guard!

## CONCEPT REVIEW

1. When should a contract be accounted for as a multiple-deliverable contract?
2. What is the basis of valuation for the several parts of a multiple-deliverable contract?
3. Why does revenue recognition pose an ethical challenge for accountants?

## RECOGNITION OF GAINS AND LOSSES

Gains and losses are distinguished from revenues and expenses in that they usually result from peripheral or incidental transactions, events, or circumstances. Whether an item is a gain or loss or an ordinary revenue or expense depends in part on the reporting company's primary activities or businesses.

For example, when a company that is primarily involved in manufacturing and marketing products sells some of its land, the transaction is accounted for as a net gain or loss because this is not the primary business of the company. When a real estate sales company sells land, however, the transaction gives rise to revenues and expenses.

Most gains and losses are recognized when the transaction is completed. Thus, gains and losses from disposal of capital assets, sale of investments, and early extinguishment of debt are recognized only when the final transaction is recorded.

A gain or loss may result from purely internal transactions, such as a writedown related to a plant closing. Such gains and losses are recognized in the period when the transaction occurs. However, estimated losses are recognized before their ultimate realization if a future event is likely to confirm that assets were impaired and a loss thereby created as of the end of the current year. Examples include losses from pending litigation, expropriation of assets, and construction-in-progress inventories when estimated revenue is less than the total of (1) costs incurred to date plus (2) costs to complete.

In contrast, gains are almost never recognized before the completion of a transaction that establishes the existence and amount of the gain. The exception is for assets that are reported at market value instead of cost. The primary types of market-valued assets are:

- *Inventories that are carried at market value.* If a company produces commodities that are readily saleable on an open public market or to a marketing board, as described above for *recognition prior to delivery,* the act of revenue recognition means that the inventories are revalued from the cost of production to their market price. If the company holds the inventory from one period to another, changes in market value are recognized as gains or losses for the period. Examples include farm products (e.g., hogs, cattle, wheat, eggs) and many mineral resources (e.g., gold, silver, copper, oil). Market-valued inventories are discussed further in Chapter 8.

- *Available-for-sale financial assets.* Companies often hold assets that are intended for sale. The most common available-for-sale assets are financial assets—temporary investments in debt or equity instruments that the company does not intend to hold to maturity. Available-for-sale financial assets are reported at fair value at the balance sheet date. Unrealized gains and losses are reported as a component of *other comprehensive income* (OCI) until realized; then they are moved from OCI and included as a gain in net income. Available-for-sale financial assets are discussed in Chapter 11.

- *Held-for-sale long-lived assets.* Capital assets, both tangible and intangible, may be declared surplus to a company's operations and put up for sale. If the fair value of the assets is less than the carrying value, the loss is recognized in net income. If the fair value recovers subsequent to the writedown a gain is recognized, but the asset cannot be written up above the original carrying value at the time it was declared held for sale. Held-for-sale assets are discussed in Chapter 3 (discontinued operations).

It should be noted that changes in the market value of these types of items are referred to as gains and losses even though they are a part of the normal business activities of the enterprise.

## REVENUE ON THE CASH FLOW STATEMENT

This chapter discussed the concept that economic revenue grows or is earned over time—sometimes in a brief time span, but often over quite a long period of time. Accounting, on the other hand, tends to recognize revenue at a particular *point* in a more continuous earning cycle. On occasion, revenue recognition also coincides with the cash inflow, but that circumstance is quite rare. Usually, a company recognizes revenue prior to receiving the cash.

In order to report cash flow from operations, the accruals relating to revenue recognition must be removed. Assuming that the *indirect* method is used for reporting cash from operations, the primary adjustments are:

- Any increase in accounts receivable or notes receivable from customers must be deducted from net income (or from revenue); a decrease in receivables would be added.

- Expenses that have been accrued (but not expended) must similarly be added back to net income (or deducted from total operating expenses, if the direct method is used); examples include warranty provisions and bad-debt expense.

- Unearned revenue must be added to revenue; the cash has been received but revenue has not yet been recognized.

Revenue can be recognized only if the cash flow is highly probable. The reporting problem is that revenue recognition and cash flow often do not occur in the same accounting period.

## DISCLOSURE

The choice of revenue recognition method can have enormous impact on a company's reported earnings. As we have seen, most methods require some accounting estimates, and some methods require a great deal of estimation.

Because of the high level of choice, accounting standards require a company to disclose its policies when there is a choice of policy. In practice, a substantial majority of public companies make some disclosure of their revenue recognition policies.

Exhibit 6-8 shows a few excerpts from Bombardier's note on the company's revenue recognition policy. The company devotes a paragraph to each major business activity and explains how revenue is recognized. We've selected several passages from Bombardier's full note because they illustrate application of many of the revenue recognition principles that we've discussed throughout this chapter:

- Revenue from narrow-bodied aircraft are recognized upon final delivery of the product—the basic approach to revenue recognition.
- For wide-body business aircraft, the company emphasizes "final acceptance ... by customers," an important aspect of revenue recognition.
- Percentage of completion is used for long-term contracts, but excluding some costs that are tangential to contract performance.
- Revenue from long-term service contracts is recognized proportionate to the costs incurred.
- Percentage of completion is used for maintenance contracts.
- Application of the percentage-of-completion method includes estimates of future revenues from change orders, which emphasizes the fact that revenue is not always a clear and definite amount in a long-term contract.

Bombardier's revenue recognition policies are disclosed quite extensively. The revenue recognition disclosures of other companies often are less informative. For example, Gateway Technologies Corporation states only that "Revenue is recognized when the product is sold or the service is provided." Indeed, 15 percent of the public companies surveyed for *Financial Reporting in Canada* had no disclosure note for revenue recognition.

## CONCEPT REVIEW

1. When might a company recognize a gain due to an event rather than a transaction?
2. What adjustments must be made to revenue when the cash flow statement is prepared?
3. Why is it important for a company to disclose its revenue recognition policies in some detail?

## EXPENSE RECOGNITION

The principles of revenue recognition have been discussed quite extensively in the preceding sections. In order to keep the discussion within reasonable length, we have intentionally omitted many details and complicating factors.

Now, what about expense recognition? When revenue is recognized, we must also recognize the expenses that relate to that revenue. But how are expenses measured?

**EXHIBIT 6-8**

### BOMBARDIER INC.

## Accounting Policies for Revenue Recognition [excerpts]

*Aerospace programs*—Revenues from the sale of regional aircraft and narrow-body business aircraft (*Learjet* Series) are recognized upon final delivery of products and presented in manufacturing revenues.

Wide-body business aircraft (*Challenger 300, Challenger 604, Challenger 605, Global Express* and *Bombardier Global 5000*) contracts are segmented between green aircraft (i.e., before interiors and optional avionics are installed) and completion of interiors. Revenues are recognized based on green aircraft deliveries (when certain conditions are met), and upon final acceptance of interiors and optional avionics by customers.

*Long-term contracts*—Revenues from long-term contracts related to designing, engineering or manufacturing of products, including vehicle and component overhaul, are recognized using the percentage-of-completion method of accounting ... The percentage of completion is generally determined by comparing the actual costs incurred to the total costs anticipated for the entire contract, excluding costs that are not representative of the measure of performance.

Revenues from maintenance service contracts entered into on or after December 17, 2003 are recognized in proportion to the total costs originally anticipated to be incurred at the beginning of the contract ... Maintenance service contracts entered into before this date are recognized using the percentage-of-completion method of accounting.

Revenues from other long-term service contracts are generally recognized as services are rendered and are presented in Services revenues in the consolidated statements of income.

Estimated revenues from long-term contracts include revenues from change orders and claims when probable that they will result in additional revenues in an amount that can be reliably estimated.

---

*Source:* www.sedar.com, Bombardier Inc. 2006 Annual Report released March 28, 2007, pages 26–137.

Much of the remainder of this book is devoted to many individual types of expenses and the timing of their recognition; we address cost of sales, amortization of capital assets, lease expense, pension expense, income tax expense, and so forth. However, some broad principles underlie all of the expense recognition principles that are discussed in the following chapters. To set the stage, we will conclude this chapter with an overview of the basic principles of expense recognition.

## Cost, Expenditure, and Expense

Before embarking on an extended discussion of expense recognition, we should firmly establish the terminology:

**cost**

the amount, measured in money, to obtain goods or services

**expenditure**

payment of cash (or other asset) to acquire a good or service

- A **cost** is incurred when we agree to pay out cash (or other assets) for goods or services received.
- An **expenditure** is the result of actually *paying* cash.
- If the measurable benefits of that cost will be realized in future periods, the cost is recognized on the balance sheet as an **asset**.
- An **expense** is recognized when the benefits of the cost (or a portion of the benefits) have been used, or whenever the future benefits can't be measured.

Usually, three of the four occur in the same accounting period. For example, when a company pays salaries to administrative employees, the company incurs a *cost* for labour, makes an *expenditure*, and recognizes the full amount on the income statement as an *expense*. This sort of simultaneous occurrence is common for many routine transactions.

**Expense or Not?** There are many expenditures that result in a cost that is *not* recognized immediately as an expense. A purchase of equipment is an obvious example. Equipment is recorded as an asset, and is gradually amortized to expense as the equipment is used.

Furthermore, the cost assigned to the equipment may comprise several expenditures rather than just one; expenditures for shipping, installation, set-up, and testing may be included in the cost of the equipment (or they may be expensed separately—this accounting policy choice is discussed in Chapter 9). Even expenditures for labour may not be an expense; for example, factory labour is added to the cost of manufactured inventory.

An expenditure may *follow* recognition of an expense. For example, think of a common year-end adjustment:

| | | |
|---|---|---|
| Income tax expense | 176,000 | |
| Income tax payable | | 176,000 |

This adjustment is made in order to recognize the income tax expense for the period, even if the company has not yet made the *expenditure* to pay the tax.

Thus, we must be very careful not to use the word "expense" when we really mean "cost" or "expenditure"—terminology does matter, especially when it comes to other people's understanding of what we are doing.

## General Recognition Criteria

In order for an item to be recorded in the financial statements, it must meet the general recognition criteria that were outlined in Chapter 2. Recognized items must:

- Meet the definition of a financial statement element; and
- Have a valid measurement basis and amount.

Financial statement elements are based on future economic benefits or sacrifices; these must be *probable* for recognition to be appropriate.

**Expenses** How do the recognition criteria apply to expenses? Like revenues, expenses are not defined on their own. Their definition rests on reduction of assets or increases in liabilities. Expenses are decreases in economic resources, either as reductions of assets or incurrences of liabilities, which result from an entity's ordinary revenue-generating or service delivery activities.

Expenses are costs that are charged against revenue and that are related to the entity's ordinary or core business. The business may be the sale of a consumer or industrial product, design or management services, natural resource exploration, or any one of hundreds of other activities that represent core activities. The enterprise must incur expenses in order to generate revenue from these normal business activities. The expense is matched to the revenue, but never netted against the revenue.

For example, suppose that a land developer sells a parcel of land for $250,000. The developer originally paid $300,000 for the land. Since land sales are a normal part of the business, the developer will report revenue of $250,000 and will report cost of sales of $300,000, for a gross margin of $−50,000.

**Losses** Activities that are not a part of normal business operations are treated somewhat differently. Losses are defined as decreases in net assets from peripheral or incidental transactions and events. The costs of peripheral activities are netted against the related revenue to report a net gain or loss, which is reported as a single amount in the income statement. For example, suppose that a manufacturer of auto parts has idle land costing $300,000.

The company decides that it will never use the land and sells it for $250,000. On its income statement, the manufacturer will report only a net loss of $−50,000 rather than separately reporting revenue and expense for that transaction.

The distinction between an expense and a loss depends only on whether the decrease in net assets is the result of normal business activities or of peripheral transactions and events. In either case, the cost results in a decrease in net assets. The basic recognition criteria are identical.

## Approaches to Expense Recognition

What have you learned about expense recognition?

1. The debit to offset an outflow of cash (i.e., the credit) is either an expense or an asset. Criteria must be met to justify recognizing an asset.

2. The activity must be central to the core operations of the entity in order to classify the item as an expense. Otherwise, it is reported as a *loss*.

Given these two initial requirements, we can identify two general approaches to deciding whether an expenditure results in an asset or an expense.

**Definitional Approach** In this approach, expenses are determined in relation to the definition of assets and liabilities. Expenses are created either through the reduction of an asset or the increase in a liability. This is a *definitional approach* to expense recognition. The definitional approach is oriented toward the balance sheet.

**Matching Approach** In this approach, expense recognition policy is justified using the doctrine of *matching*. Matching requires that once revenues are determined in conformity with the revenue principle for any reporting period, the expenses incurred in generating the revenue should be recognized in that same period.

The essence of the matching principle is that as revenues are earned, expenses are incurred to generate those revenues. These expenses must be recognized and reported as expenses of the period during which the related revenue is recognized. Matching typically involves the primacy of revenue and expense recognition and accurate net income measurement, not an analysis of changes in asset and liability balances.

To illustrate how expense recognition is explained by each of these two approaches, consider the following two examples of accounting policy and how they are justified under the definitional approach versus the matching approach:

> **Policy 1.** Defer expenditures related to revenue generation activities incurred prior to the revenue recognition point. Expense these items when revenue is recognized.
>
> **Definitional:** Up to the revenue recognition point, these items have probable future benefit arising from the revenue transaction: the cash flow, etc., that will be provided by the customer. As long as the revenue transaction is probable, the expenditure meets the recognition criteria for an asset. After revenue recognition, the asset becomes an expense.
>
> **Matching:** The expenses must be deferred prior to the revenue recognition point so that they can be matched with the associated revenue.
>
> **Policy 2.** Accrue future expenses if they relate to revenue recognized on the income statement.
>
> **Definitional:** The entity has incurred an obligation for the expenditures by virtue of the revenue transaction. The element (the liability) exists and must now be recognized.
>
> **Matching:** The expenses must be accrued at the revenue recognition point to properly match revenues and all expenses.

Both lines of reasoning appear to support the same types of policies. So what's the big deal?

**Historical Perspective** Matching has been with us for a long time. It dominated accounting thought for decades. Matching involves deferring expenditures as assets on the balance sheet if projected revenues are still on the horizon. Criteria for such deferral were never well developed, and there were problematic cases of assets—cost deferrals—that had, in the end, no associated cash flow. Application of matching sometimes led to recording an expense even though no real liability was created.

Accountants feel that the balance sheet must have integrity. That is, only "real" assets and liabilities should be included on the balance sheet. Thus, revenues and expenses are recognized only when balance sheet accounts, with real integrity, are created. This is the basis of the definitional approach. However, the continued devotion of accounting standards to interperiod allocations calls into question the real impact of the definitional approach.

Where does that leave us? The habit of talking about matching is firmly entrenched, but it takes a different perspective than the definitional approach. The safest thing to say is that the accounting profession is in transition! Many traditional customs and established accounting policies are justified with reference to matching. But new rules are increasingly based on the definitional approach. It is considered theoretically superior by those who subscribe to the balance sheet view of the financial statements. Given the evolution of accounting concepts and standards, it will be useful for you to orient your thinking about accounting policy toward the definitional approach.

## Measurement

Recognition is not possible unless there is a reliable amount to record. When is measurement an issue for expenses? Obviously, if the item is one where the cost transaction precedes the revenue recognition point, there's likely an invoice sitting around and measurement isn't much of an issue. A more complicated problem arises when the expense has to be accrued at the revenue recognition point, prior to settlement. Accurate measurement of the liability, and, by inference, the expense, is a major concern.

Revenue may need to be estimated as well, if there is some uncertainty about the exact amount of revenue or its collectibility. This is an issue particularly with long-term contracts, as the Bombardier percentage-of-completion disclosure note reveals (at the end of Exhibit 6-8).

Clearly, reporting entities must make an effort to measure costs. Companies are expected to make their best efforts in cost measurement. Companies are generally required to disclose the nature and extent of a measurement uncertainty in a disclosure note to the financial statements. This encourages firms to record items despite any lack of precision in the numbers. It should also help financial statement users understand the "soft spots" in the financial statements themselves.

Another major issue in expense measurement deals with the issue of *interperiod allocation*: what amortization policies are appropriate? How much amortization should be booked in a given period? Amortization clearly is based on the matching concept, because amortization is explicitly disconnected from asset value. We will return frequently to this issue in subsequent chapters.

## Asset or Expense?

An entity spends cash (or incurs a liability) to acquire a good or a service. The offset to that expenditure or liability will be a debit. Is the debit an *expense* or an *asset*? The definitions tell us that an entity has an asset if there is future economic benefit (that is, a cash flow, either direct or indirect) that will come from the item. If there is no such benefit, then the entry involves a debit to an expense because the item has no intrinsic value or future cash flow. If there is no future benefit that is both probable and measurable, then the item is treated as an expense.

Historically, companies often treated some major expenditures as assets because they were assumed to benefit future periods. For example, the costs of starting up a major new operation—a hotel, a factory, a shopping mall—often were treated as a *deferred charge*, recorded as an asset, and then amortized over the period during which the benefits would be received. Similarly, corporate restructuring costs often were treated as assets and amortized over future years. The concept was based squarely on *matching*. Future periods will benefit from these costs—after all, that was the point of spending the money in the first place—and therefore the costs should be matched to the future benefits.

There are two difficulties with this approach:

1. It is virtually impossible to reliably estimate the impact of these expenditures on future earnings. Therefore, it is not clear whether any actual future earnings increase is the result of these expenditures or is due to other factors.

2. The "asset" created by these expenditures has no value, except for the unmeasurable future benefit that is attributed to them by management.

In essence, these deferred charges were treated as internally generated intangible assets. But as we discussed previously, an asset must contribute a measurable future cash flow benefit. Since any future benefit of these deferred charges cannot be measured, they do not fit the definition of an asset.

Neither U.S. standards nor international standards permit recognizing these types of cost as an asset. Immediate expensing is required. Therefore, the AcSB issued an exposure draft on internally generated intangible assets in 2005, followed by a re-exposure draft in 2007, to harmonize Canadian standards with international standards.

In the future, expenditures that are expected to have future benefit will be required to meet criteria that are essentially the same as those for capitalizing development costs. We will discuss development costs in Chapter 9, but the result of harmonization with international standards is that companies can no longer record start-up and restructuring costs as assets to be amortized in future periods.

**Impact on Financial Statements** Exhibit 6-9 identifies the impact that the alternatives of expense versus asset recognition will have on the financial statements. In one, the *distribution of assets* is changed; in the other, *net assets and shareholder wealth goes down*. The decision about what to debit is not a free choice: if the asset recognition criteria are met, an asset is recorded. If not, an expense is recorded.

Think about a transaction that involves buying goods for resale in a cash exchange. Cash goes down; what goes up? The goods are for resale, so they can be sold to a customer for at least their cost; the goods clearly represent a future cash flow to the entity and are an asset,

## EXHIBIT 6-9

### IMPACT OF AN EXPENDITURE: ASSET VERSUS EXPENSE

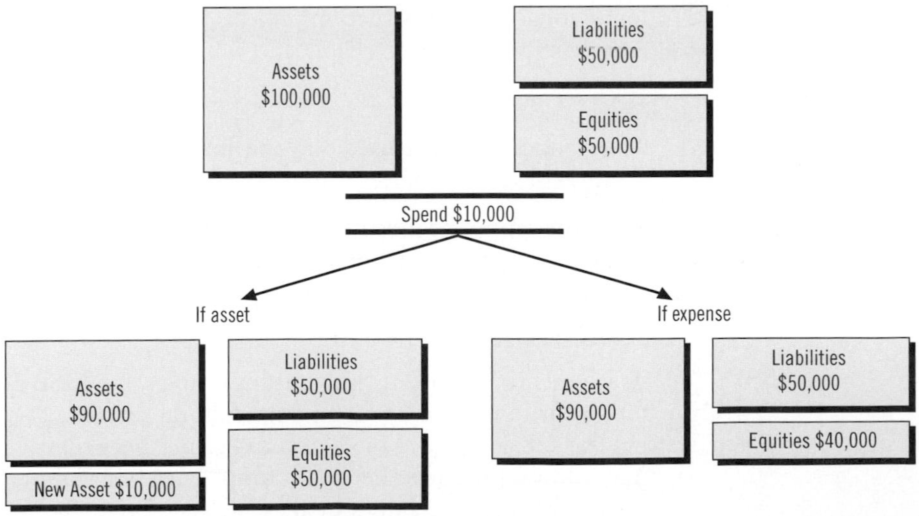

*inventory*. Inventory becomes an expense, called "COGS," when it's sold. At this point, inventory is converted into cash, a financial instrument, or some other benefit to the entity.

When might goods bought for resale *not* be an asset? If the goods were bought and became unsaleable due to their physical condition or because they were obsolete, then the entity has no future cash flowing from the ownership of the items and the purchase would be reported as an expense. Inventory is an asset only if it can be resold for at least its carrying value. Unsaleable inventory must be written down, a common occurrence.

Earlier in this chapter, we emphasized that revenue recognition is accompanied by an increase in net assets. When expenses are recognized, net assets go down. When revenues and expenses are recognized simultaneously, one expects that revenues will exceed expenses and the combined impact on net assets will be positive.

Expense recognition is highly dependent on the revenue recognition point chosen by a company. If a company buys an item that will later be sold, its cost is deferred. If the revenue recognition point comes and goes but not all costs are yet incurred, then they must be accrued. Remember that deferred costs are assets, and the future sale transaction is the future cash flow that backs up the asset value.

## CONCEPT REVIEW

1. What is the difference between an expenditure, an expense, and a cost?

2. What are the general recognition criteria for financial statement elements?

3. How do we decide whether a cost should be reported as an asset or as an expense?

## INTERNATIONAL PERSPECTIVE

### Construction Contracts

Under Canadian standards, companies can choose whether to use completed-contract or percentage-of-completion accounting for long-term contracts. In practice, however, Canadian tax regulations *require* the percentage-of-completion method for all contracts lasting more than two years. Although there is no requirement that the same method be used for tax and book purposes, the tax restriction has a strong influence on financial reporting.

In contrast, international standards require use of the percentage-of-completion method for all long-term construction projects, provided that the current and future costs and revenues can be measured reliably. If reliable measurement is not possible:

1. Costs are recognized as expenses (on the income statement) when incurred, and

2. Revenues are recognized only for the amount that the customer is legally required to pay up to the balance sheet date.

The costs cannot be inventoried if the outcome of the contract cannot be reliably estimated. The completed-contract method cannot be used.

### Agriculture

As we mentioned in the body of this chapter, the IASB specifically requires revenue recognition for biological assets and agricultural produce at their fair value less estimated selling costs. Examples of biological assets are sheep, dairy cattle, grape vines, and fruit trees. Agricultural products that result from "harvesting" these assets are wool, milk, grapes, and picked fruit. As the values of these assets change, the change is recognized in the income statement as a gain or loss.

The conditions necessary for recognizing these assets at net realizable value are:

- The entity controls the asset;
- The future economic benefits will flow to the entity; and
- The fair value of the asset can be measured reliably.

The standard presumes that fair values can be measured reliably; why would an entity engage in producing an asset that has no estimable fair value? However, if the fair value cannot be measured reliably, then historical cost is used until it becomes possible to estimate the fair value.

## Joint IASB-FASB Project on Revenue Recognition

The IASB and the U.S. FASB have had a wide-ranging convergence project since 2002 to harmonize IASB and FASB standards. One of the major issues has been revenue recognition.

Revenue recognition issues are complex, as this chapter has pointed out. In general, the approach taken in this joint project has been to define revenue recognition on the basis of legal liability. For example, in 2006, the two Boards agreed on this tentative basis for recognizing revenue:

> Revenue shall be recognized if the customer must accept performance to date. That is, the contract's legal remedy for breach is, or is like, specific performance or in the event of customer cancellation, the customer is obligated to pay damages reflecting performance to date.[5]

This really is not too different from the current IASB position on construction contracts, as described in the preceding section.

In addition, the FASB has been considering fair value methods in which the value of a sales or performance contract would be determined as the amount for which a company could sell its performance obligation to another company.

This discussion has been going on for quite a while and has been subject to much controversy in both North America and Europe. It seems clear that no resolution will be reached in the near future. Once the two Boards do agree on a recommended approach, it will take some time for a detailed exposure draft to be prepared. Then the fun starts, with much argument and lobbying swirling around the Boards as they struggle to gain acceptance for the proposals. Whatever happens internationally clearly will affect Canadian reporting as well. But significant change is not likely to come soon.

## RELEVANT STANDARDS

*CICA Handbook:*
- Section 1000, Financial Statement Concepts
- Section 1508, Measurement Uncertainty
- Section 1520, Income Statement
- Section 3400, Revenue
- EIC-141, Revenue Recognition
- EIC-142, Revenue Arrangements with Multiple Deliverables
- Accounting Guideline AcG-2, Franchise Fee Revenue

IASB:
- *IAS* 11, Construction Contracts
- *IAS* 18, Revenue
- SIC 31, Barter Transactions Involving Advertising Services

---

[5] *IASB Update*, April 2006, p. 3.

## SUMMARY OF KEY POINTS

1.  For most companies, the earnings process is continuous. That is, the profit-directed activities of the company continually generate inflows or enhancements of the assets of the company.

2.  Revenue recognition policies must be chosen carefully because of their profound effect on key financial results.

3.  Before the results of the earnings process are recognized in the accounting records, revenue must meet the recognition criteria of *delivery to* and *acceptance by* the customer, *measurability*, and *collectibility*.

4.  A sale transaction is usually measured at the sales invoice price. When there are long-term, interest-free payment terms, discounting may be appropriate.

5.  The critical event that triggers revenue recognition is the last transaction or event that satisfies all of the revenue recognition criteria. The primary critical events are at delivery, after delivery (if there are significant uncertainties about measurement, collection, or remaining costs), or at cash collection. *Delivery* is the most common critical event.

6.  The recognition of revenue results in an increase in net assets, which is recognized at the critical event. Costs incurred prior to the critical event are deferred. When revenue is recognized, deferred costs are expensed, and future costs are accrued.

7.  Barter transactions are typically recognized at the value of the asset or service given in the exchange.

8.  The instalment sales method of revenue recognition delays recognition of gross profit until cash is collected.

9.  The cost recovery method is a conservative method in which no profit is recognized until all costs associated with the sale item have been recovered in cash. All subsequent cash collections are profit.

10. Long-term contracts can be accounted for using the percentage-of-completion method or the completed-contract method. If a long-term, fixed-price contract with a creditworthy customer is accompanied by reasonably reliable estimates of (a) total revenue, (b) cost to complete, and (c) percentage of completion, based either on output or input, then percentage of completion is appropriate.

11. Under the completed-contract method, revenues and expenses are recognized when the contract obligations are completed. Costs incurred in completing the contract are accrued in an inventory account, and any progress billings are accrued in a contra-inventory account.

12. Long-term contracts are often accounted for on the basis of effort expended. Under the percentage-of-completion method, revenues and expenses are recognized each accounting period based on an estimate of the percentage of completion. Costs incurred in completing the contract and recognized gross profit are accrued in an inventory account.

13. Cash flow from operations must be computed by adjusting revenue (or net income) for changes in accounts and notes receivable, for changes in unearned revenue, and for accrued expenses that do not represent cash expenditures during the period.

14. An expenditure may be either an asset or an expense. Items that meet the recognition criteria for assets are capitalized as assets; other expenditures are expensed. Of key importance in establishing an asset is the presence of future economic benefits, essentially cash flow. This is the definitional approach to expense recognition.

15. An expenditure that results in asset recognition simply reorganizes the asset section of the balance sheet but does not affect net assets, assets less liabilities. In contrast, expense recognition reduces net assets.

16. Expense policy has traditionally been described as a matching process, where expenses are matched to revenues recognized on the income statement. Matching may result in questionable deferred asset and liability items recognized on the balance sheet; the definitional approach avoids this, which many accountants regard as preferable.

17. Measurement of an expense is usually an issue only when the expense is to be incurred at some future point in time, but must be accrued in the current period. Expenses may be estimated, and the presence of measurement uncertainty should be disclosed.

## KEY TERMS

asset, 299
barter transaction, 282
consignment, 275
cost, 299
cost recovery method, 280
critical event, 271
economic value added, 270

expenditure, 299
expense, 299
instalment sales method, 279
multiple-deliverable contract, 293
progress billings, 285
revenue recognition principle, 270

## REVIEW PROBLEM 1

Precision Punctual Construction Company (PPCC) has agreed to build a 10-storey office building for Mountain Bank Limited. The contract calls for a contract price of $15,000,000 for the building, with progress payments being made by Mountain as the construction proceeds. The period of construction is estimated to be 30 months. The contract is signed on 1 February 20X5, and construction begins immediately. The building is completed and turned over to Mountain Bank on 1 December 20X7.

Data on cost incurred, estimated costs to complete, progress billings, and progress payments over the period of construction are as follows:

($ thousands)

|  | 20X5 | 20X6 | 20X7 |
|---|---|---|---|
| Costs incurred this period | $ 1,500 | $ 7,875 | $ 3,825 |
| Costs incurred to date | 1,500 | 9,375 | 13,200 |
| Estimated costs to complete at year-end | 10,500 | 3,125 | 0 |
| Estimated total costs of project | 12,000 | 12,500 | 13,200 |
| Progress billings this period | 1,200 | 6,000 | 7,800 |
| Progress payments received this period | 825 | 6,300 | 7,875 |

**Required:**

1. Show the entries to account for this project over the period of construction, assuming that PPCC uses:

   a. the completed-contract method of recognizing revenue

   b. the percentage-of-completion method of recognizing revenue

2. Show the relevant balance sheet and income statement items for 20X5, 20X6, and 20X7 for PPCC, assuming that the company uses:

   a. the completed-contract method

   b. the percentage-of-completion method

## REVIEW PROBLEM 1—SOLUTION

1. The entries to record the construction of the building for both the completed-contract method and the percentage-of-completion method are as follows (in $ thousands):

| Entries for 20X5: | Completed-Contract Method | | Percentage-of-Completion Method | |
|---|---|---|---|---|
| a. To record incurrence of construction costs: | | | | |
|    Construction-in-progress inventory | 1,500 | | 1,500 | |
|      Cash, payables, etc. | | 1,500 | | 1,500 |
| b. To record progress billings: | | | | |
|    Accounts receivable | 1,200 | | 1,200 | |
|      Billings on contract | | 1,200 | | 1,200 |
| c. To record billing collections: | | | | |
|    Cash | 825 | | 825 | |
|      Accounts receivable | | 825 | | 825 |
| d. To recognize revenue for percentage of completion:* | | | | |
|    Construction-in-progress inventory | | | 375 | |
|    Cost of construction | | | 1,500 | |
|      Revenue from long-term contract | | | | 1,875 |

*The percentage of completion is the cost incurred to date divided by total estimated project costs, or $1,500 \div $12,000 = 12.5\%$. The total amount of revenue recognizable to this point is $15,000 \times 12.5\% = $1,875$.

| Entries for 20X6: | Completed-Contract Method | | Percentage-of-Completion Method | |
|---|---|---|---|---|
| a. To record incurrence of construction costs: | | | | |
|    Construction-in-progress inventory | 7,875 | | 7,875 | |
|      Cash, payables, etc. | | 7,875 | | 7,875 |
| b. To record progress billings: | | | | |
|    Accounts receivable | 6,000 | | 6,000 | |
|      Billings on contract | | 6,000 | | 6,000 |
| c. To record billing collections: | | | | |
|    Cash | 6,300 | | 6,300 | |
|      Accounts receivable | | 6,300 | | 6,300 |
| d. To recognize revenue for percentage of completion:* | | | | |
|    Construction-in-progress inventory | | | 1,500 | |
|    Cost of construction | | | 7,875 | |
|      Revenue from long-term contract | | | | 9,375 |

*The percentage of completion is the cost incurred to date divided by total estimated project costs, or $9,375 \div $12,500 = 75\%$. The total amount of revenue recognizable to this point is $15,000 \times 75\% = $11,250$. Since $1,875 was recognized in 20X5, the amount recognizable in 20X6 is $11,250 - $1,875 = $9,375$.

| Entries for 20X7: | Completed-Contract Method | | Percentage-of-Completion Method | |
|---|---|---|---|---|
| a. To record incurrence of construction costs: | | | | |
|    Construction-in-progress inventory | 3,825 | | 3,825 | |
|      Cash, payables, etc. | | 3,825 | | 3,825 |

b. To record progress billings:

| | | | |
|---|---|---|---|
| Accounts receivable | 7,800 | | 7,800 |
| Billings on contract | | 7,800 | 7,800 |

c. To record billing collections:

| | | | |
|---|---|---|---|
| Cash | 7,875 | | 7,875 |
| Accounts receivable | | 7,875 | 7,875 |

d. To recognize revenue for percentage of completion:*

| | | |
|---|---|---|
| Cost of construction | 3,825 | |
| Revenue from long-term contract | | 3,750 |
| Construction-in-progress inventory | | 75 |

e. To record elimination of contract costs from inventory:

| | | |
|---|---|---|
| Billings on contract | 15,000 | |
| Construction-in-progress inventory | | 15,000 |

f. To recognize revenue for completed contract:

| | | |
|---|---|---|
| Billings on contract | 15,000 | |
| Cost of earned construction revenue | 13,200 | |
| Revenue from long-term contracts | | 15,000 |
| Construction-in-progress inventory | | 13,200 |

*The project is completed; any remaining portion of the contract price not previously recognized as revenue should be recognized this period. In prior years, $1,875 + $9,375 = $11,250 was recognized, thus $3,750 (i.e., $15,000 − $11,250) is recognized in 20X7.

2. Financial statement items:

| | 31 Dec. 20X5 | | 31 Dec. 20X6 | | 31 Dec. 20X7 | |
|---|---|---|---|---|---|---|
| | Completed Contract | Percentage of Completion | Completed Contract | Percentage of Completion | Completed Contract | Percentage of Completion |
| **Balance sheet:** | | | | | | |
| Accounts receivable | $ 375 | $ 375 | $ 75 | $ 75 | 0 | 0 |
| Inventory: | | | | | | |
| Construction in progress | $1,500 | $1,875 | $9,375 | $11,250 | 0 | 0 |
| Less: Billings on contract | (1,200) | (1,200) | (7,200) | (7,200) | 0 | 0 |
| Construction in progress In excess of billings | $ 300 | $ 675 | $2,175 | $ 4,050 | 0 | 0 |
| **Income statement:** | | | | | | |
| Revenue from long-term contracts | $ | $1,875 | $ | $ 9,375 | $15,000 | $3,750 |
| Cost of construction | $ | (1,500) | $ | (7,875) | (13,200) | (3,825) |
| Gross profit | $ | $ 375 | $ | $ 1,500 | $ 1,800 | $ (75)* |

*This is an example of a current-year loss on a contract that is profitable overall.

## REVIEW PROBLEM 2

Cromax Corporation is a Canadian public company whose shares are listed on the TSE. The following transactions and events occurred in 20X5. For each item, indicate the preferred accounting treatment. Assume all amounts are material.

1. Cromax paid $700,000 to a firm of engineers who undertook a study to determine more energy-efficient practices in Cromax's production facilities.

2. Cromax diverted workers and equipment to help prepare for government-sponsored public celebrations revolving around the Tall Ships festival in Halifax; the out-of-pocket cost was approximately $127,000; depreciation on equipment was $40,000. Cromax does a great deal of business with governments at all levels, and regards the expenditures as relationship building that will have future benefit.

3. Cromax has recently signed a four-year contract with a new customer. As part of the terms of the contract, Cromax paid $500,000 upfront to the customer to defray expenses the customer will incur as a result of changing suppliers. The contract involves substantial volumes of sales over the next four years between Cromax and the customer.

4. Cromax spent $4.2 million defending itself against an unfair-competition lawsuit launched by six smaller firms. The lawsuit has been settled out of court. Of the $4.2 million, $3 million is the settlement, $800,000 is legal fees, and $400,000 is public relations spending to counteract the negative publicity surrounding the dispute. Cromax's future markets are secure as a result of the terms of the settlement.

5. Cromax has just set up a $20 million line of credit with its bank, which allows Cromax to borrow these funds on 24-hours' notice at any time over the next five years. The interest rate will be prime plus 1%. By year-end, Cromax had not borrowed any money under the lending arrangement, but expects to do so in the next fiscal year as a result of some planned capital expansion. Cromax paid an upfront fee of $125,000 to the bank in order to obtain the agreement.

(ASCA, adapted)

## REVIEW PROBLEM—SOLUTION 2

1. Items are recognized if they meet the recognition criteria. This $700,000 payment may be an asset, if it has future benefits that are probable. Can the energy savings be documented? (That is, are they probable?) If sufficient appropriate evidence exists, the expenditure may be deferred, to be amortized on a basis consistent with the projected savings. Otherwise, the item is an expense.

2. An amount of $167,000 can be directly attributed to the activities, which may be an "asset" if it has future benefit. While demonstrating that Cromax is a good corporate citizen may help solidify relationships with governments that are major customers, is there *probable* future cash flow that will validate the asset? It would be difficult to quantify the benefits, and this is most likely an expense of the period.

3. Cromax has future economic benefit associated with the long-term contract with the customer, and, as long as the contract is firm, it is acceptable to defer this payment and amortize it in some fashion over the life of the contract.

4. Should the $4.2 million be recognized as an expense or as an asset, amortized to earnings over some future period of (now secure) profitable operations? All the items are incremental expenditures related to one event and should be accounted for the same way.

   Expenditures can be viewed as an asset if they have future benefits that are probable. In this situation, asset treatment would be inappropriate. Future operations are not enhanced by the expenditures; the status quo has been only preserved. Patents have finite legal lives, but operations in this case might be weakened by the precedent of the lawsuit settlement. Are they better off because of this payment? Would they be even "more" better off (i.e., have higher assets) if the settlement were higher? Under the definitions, in Section 1000, assets are *not* expenses deferred, but rather items with associated future cash flow. An appropriate analogy might be repairing a machine damaged in transportation, or fixing fire damage: the status quo is preserved by subsequent repairs, but no asset is created.

   The arguments for expensing appear strong; the amount should not be capitalized.

5. Cromax has incurred a cost that is analogous to prepaid interest expense. It can be deferred but should be amortized over the life of the agreement, five years. It does not

simply relate to the period of time in which funds are actually borrowed under the facility, as Cromax is benefiting from the flexibility and locked-in interest rate for the entire five years. Deferred financing charges are common in Canada.

## QUESTIONS

**Q6-1**   Explain the relationship between the definition of revenue and the definitions of assets and liabilities.

**Q6-2**   When is revenue earned in economic terms? How does this relate to typical accounting revenue recognition?

**Q6-3**   What are the fundamental criteria for recognizing any element in the financial statements? Explain the additional criteria that revenue must meet before being recognized.

**Q6-4**   Under the revenue recognition principle, when is performance achieved?

**Q6-5**   How is revenue measured in a barter transaction?

**Q6-6**   What is meant by revenue recognition at a critical event? Give examples of three critical events.

**Q6-7**   Why is revenue typically recognized on delivery?

**Q6-8**   Under what circumstances is revenue recognized at a critical event after delivery?

**Q6-9**   What conditions must be met in order for revenue to be recognized when a customer has the right to return purchased products? What accounting procedures are used until all conditions are met?

**Q6-10**   Describe the instalment sales method of recognizing revenue and when it is appropriately used.

**Q6-11**   Describe the cost recovery method of recognizing revenue. When is it appropriate?

**Q6-12**   Identify and explain two different approaches for determining the extent of progress toward completion of a construction project.

**Q6-13**   Why is the ending inventory of construction in progress different in amount when the percentage-of-completion method is used compared with the completed-contract method? Explain the amount of the difference.

**Q6-14**   When a loss is projected on an unprofitable long-term construction contract, in what period(s) is the loss recognized under (a) percentage-of-completion and (b) completed-contract methods?

**Q6-15**   Under what circumstances do gains and losses reflect changes in value, rather than realized transactions?

**Q6-16**   When does a cash expenditure result in recognition of an asset? An expense?

**Q6-17**   At what point in time will the purchase of a capital asset for cash result in a decline in net assets?

**Q6-18**   Contrast the definitional and matching approaches to explaining expense recognition policies.

**Q6-19**   Assume that a company has an expense recognition policy for bad debts that requires bad debt expense to be recognized, and an allowance for doubtful accounts established, as sales occur. The amount is measured as a percentage of sales. This accrual is to take place even though the actual amount of bad debt expense will not be known until specific customers actually default over the following 12 to 24 months. Justify this policy using the definitional approach, and then using the matching approach.

**Q6-20**    Give two examples of expenses for which measurement is an issue.

## CASE 6-1

### THOMAS TECHNOLOGIES CORPORATION

Thomas Technologies Corporation (TTC) is an engineering services company based in Calgary. The company's Class B common shares are listed on the Toronto Stock Exchange. The Class A common shares are all owned by Theodore Thomas, the company founder, and his immediate family. The Class A shares are multiple voting shares that assure that the Thomas family retains voting control over the company.

The company's shares have risen sharply in price over the past two years, driven mainly by the strength of the Alberta economy and the need for engineering services by the many resource and exploration companies based in Calgary. Stock analysts have been very enthusiastic about TTC shares, and the analysts have issued very favourable earnings forecasts for TTC's 20X4 year-end results.

In 20X4, TTC entered into special long-term contracts with two of its largest clients. The company's accounting staff recorded the transactions as directed by the TTC chief financial officer. The two transactions were as follows:

1. TTC entered into a three-year contract with Howard Limited to provide engineering services. The services will be rendered on an as-needed basis over the three years. The contract stated that Howard would pay $3 million to TTC during 20X4, $2 million during 20X5, and $1.6 million during 20X6. Howard paid for the first year's service as agreed. TTC recorded the payment as revenue for 20X4. The cost of services rendered by TTC to Howard is not separately tracked, but is part of the regular service provided by TTC to many clients.

2. TTC and Porter Inc. signed an agreement on 14 October 20X4. As one part of the agreement, TTC designed and built a special-purpose piece of equipment for Porter. Porter did not solicit bids from other manufacturers due to the close working relationship that has been established between Porter and TTC over the years. It is possible, however, that similar equipment could have been obtained for about 20% less from a heavy equipment manufacturer in Japan. The agreement provided that Porter would pay $5.6 million for the equipment. The equipment was delivered to Porter on 22 December 20X4. Porter paid 40% of the purchase price on 30 December, with a promise to pay the remaining 60% within the first 90 days of 20X5. The equipment cost TTC $3.4 million to construct. The agreement provided that Porter cannot sell or otherwise convey the equipment to any other user.

In addition to the equipment sale, the agreement stipulated that Porter would pay $1.5 million per year for the next four years as a service contract. The price is about 25% less than TTC would normally charge a client for that type of service.

TTC recorded revenue of $5.6 for the equipment, and included $3.4 million in cost of services. The company also recorded the first year's service revenue by crediting $1.5 million to revenue and debiting accounts receivable—long term. This revenue was matched by charging $1.0 million to cost of services (for the estimated cost of providing the service) and crediting an equal amount to estimated service liability.

It now is January 20X5. You are working for the audit firm of Andrew, Athens, and Argoyle on the annual audit of TTC. The audit manager is preparing to meet with the TTC CFO tomorrow morning. She has asked you to prepare a memorandum in which you set out your views on the accounting used by TTC for these two contracts, with a recommendation on whether or not to accept TTC accounting, and any alternative that you propose.

**Required:**
Prepare the memorandum for your audit manager.

---

**CASE 6-2**

## TEMPUS FUGIT INC.

Tempus Fugit Inc. is a large conglomerate of 30 subsidiary companies with plants and branches throughout the world. The company has been in the business of manufacturing and distributing clocks, watches, and other timepieces for over 50 years. Recently, the company experienced a change in management when the original founder retired and sold his controlling interest.

On 1 May 20X5, Smith & Smith, a publicly traded international consulting firm, was awarded the contract to design and install a computerized management information system in each of Tempus Fugit's subsidiaries. The project was projected to take four years to complete. Michael Smith, the founder and managing partner of Smith & Smith, and his staff, worked exclusively on this project from May to October. Currently, one-half of the company's workforce is working on the job. Smith & Smith obtained this project after submitting a bid on 1 March 20X5, which took most of February to prepare; the bid price was $45,000,000.

It is January 20X6, and annual financial statements for Smith & Smith are being prepared. Michael Smith has come to you, the controller of the company, to discuss how the contract will be reported. He is anxious to present the contract as favourably as possible under the limitations of GAAP. His comments to you are:

> I know this is the first long-term contract that we have entered into, and I have heard that we can recognize revenue based on the percentage of the project that is complete. That percentage should be based on management's best estimates, as are so many things under GAAP. In my opinion, even though we are behind in the installation, we should recognize revenue according to the percentage that we estimated would be done in our contract bid. If we don't, Tempus Fugit's management will be on our backs, wondering what is going on and slowing us down even more. I sure don't need that with all of the problems we are experiencing on this project!

You ask Smith about the problems that are being experienced on the project. He responds that they are of a highly technical nature. He urges you to complete the financial statements as soon as possible, since Smith & Smith is experiencing a cash flow shortage and Tempus Fugit will not release the first payment on the contract until the year-end statements have been received.

You are aware of the following facts about Smith & Smith and Tempus Fugit:

- Smith & Smith has been in business for five years. This is the first time the company has landed a contract of this magnitude. Previous contracts have all been completed within a one-year time frame.

- The contract provides for Tempus Fugit to pay in four equal annual instalments on receipt of audited statements from Smith & Smith. One-quarter of the project should be completed each year.

- Much of the contract involves design and testing of computer programs, and it is difficult to determine the degree of completion of the project at any time. Few external experts in the area exist, since Smith & Smith is in a new industry and a specialized field. The company has never been too concerned about estimating completion before because all of its contracts have been short term.

- The auditor has no way of determining the percentage of completion of the project, since the work is so subjective. Because the same audit firm has been engaged by Smith & Smith for the past five years and has found the partners to be reputable, the auditor is generally able to rely on management's best estimates.

After your conversation with Michael Smith, you find yourself in the coffee room with Rachel Harris, the chief programmer on the Tempus Fugit project. You have always had a good relationship with Rachel. Out of curiosity, you ask her how much of the project she believes is done and about the problems the company is experiencing. Her response is:

> You know, the partners bid on this one to get us into the big leagues, and let me tell you, the big leagues are tough! We have never handled a project this large, and it is taking us a lot longer to get some of the basic systems developed than we ever imagined. Although it's hard to tell, I would say we are only about 10% done at this time. We are in the process of hiring more staff and establishing supplier relationships, and all of this takes time. I am still confident that we will complete the project in four years, but I don't think we will catch up to our original estimates until the third year. By then, the staff will be trained and we will be much more effective.

After coffee, you run into Michael Smith again. He asks that you meet him in his office Monday morning, ready to discuss the accounting options available for the project and your recommended accounting treatment. He is rushing out the door to a meeting with the banker, who called with some concerns about the company's cash flow problems.

### Required:

Identify and analyze the alternative treatments available to account for the timing of the revenues and expenses that will be recognized in the contract with Tempus Fugit. What are the ethical issues you must consider before making your recommendation to Michael Smith? What should you say during the Monday morning meeting with Smith?

(CGA-Canada, adapted)

## CASE 6-3

## CERAMIC PROTECTION COMPANY LIMITED

Ceramic Protection Company Limited (CP) is experiencing financial difficulties. Earnings have never been strong in the six-year history of the company and CP will record operating losses in 20X6. A tax loss will also be reported. A group of key executives, primarily in the production and technology areas, is compensated by cash bonuses based on operating income before financing charges and income tax. This group will earn no bonuses in 20X6.

CP manufactures ceramic ballistic armour products that are used in personal, vehicular, and structural armour systems (e.g., bulletproof vests, armour on tanks, etc.). While its ceramic production methods were well recognized for quality, CP experienced significant technical difficulties in the early stages of a 70-unit order for tank armour from NATO for use in Kosovo. The order was produced on time, and 24 additional units were ordered and delivered. However, cost overruns in the initial stages were a major driving force behind 20X6 operating losses.

To make matters worse, CP discovered in 20X6 that a procurement manager had been involved in unauthorized speculation in a commodity used in ceramic production. Significant losses were incurred in 20X4, 20X5, and 20X6, and were hidden in fictitious inventory records. Inventory and other accounts turned out to be overstated by $1,500,000.

In mid-year, one of the shareholders of CP took advantage of the weak financial position of the company and purchased all of the other shares from the remaining shareholders. Mark Fortin, a multimillionaire from investments in the technology industry, was convinced of the long-term potential for the company. Thus, the company ended 20X6 with only one shareholder. Mr. Fortin is managing the company with an eye on cash flow, his major concern. Lenders, fully secured with company assets and Fortin's guarantees, are interested primarily in cash flow reporting and performance evaluation. Although GAAP is not a constraint, all users of the financial statements are concerned with the representational faithfulness of the financial information.

In order to stem losses, Mr. Fortin is streamlining several areas of the company. He has made, or is about to make, several decisions that will reduce the level of management personnel and reduce the diversity of manufacturing operations to specialize in certain lines of ceramics. The area of chosen emphasis will be tank armour. Certain ceramic manufacturing facilities are understood to be for sale, although no offers have yet been received.

Employee labour groups have agreed to layoffs where necessary, with the following terms:

- Severance pay equal to one month's salary for each year worked, paid monthly after severance until the entitlement is extinguished.
- In addition to the above item, bonus payment of 6 months' salary paid monthly over 12 months after severance.
- Pension benefits automatically vest for any severed employee, even if vesting had not legally taken place.

CP has received orders for tank armour from Australia and Israel, and production is in full gear for these orders. These orders, started in 20X6, will not be completed until 20X7, as they will take 9 to 14 months to complete. The orders are paid for 50% on receipt of the signed contract for the order, 40% on delivery, and 10% one month after delivery. This latter 10% is in the nature of a holdback to ensure completion of minor fitting adjustments by CP. Management anticipates no cost overruns on these projects as the technology used is identical to that used for the NATO project.

Significantly more speculative, however, is the contract entered into with the Egyptian army. Thirty sets of armour will be produced, again over 9 to 14 months of production. Each unit will cost CP approximately $95,000 to manufacture. The revenue generated will be in the range of $100,000 to $220,000 per unit, based on the customer's experience with the armour over the first 12 months of operation. Egyptian officials will run tests on the armour at the 6- and 12-month milestones, with CP's help. The better the armour performs, the higher the price paid (in essence, a bonus of up to $120,000 per unit). CP will receive the minimum price per unit ($100,000) when the order is placed, with the "bonus" paid after entitlement is established (on testing) after 12 months. CP is extremely confident that it will be entitled to the maximum price, although new production operations will have to be established to meet the specifications. This will involve investing at least $200,000 to $300,000 in activities to research and develop improved production methodologies.

It is now one month before the fiscal 20X6 year-end. You are the recently hired manager of accounting. The vice-president, Finance has asked you to draft a memo to her discussing the accounting issues that CP is facing, including an analysis of alternative accounting treatments and your supported recommendations.

**Required:**

Prepare the memo.                                                    (ASCA, adapted)

---

**CASE 6-4**

## OTTAWA ORIOLES LIMITED

The Ottawa Orioles Limited (OOL) operates a professional baseball club, which won the Canadian Baseball League title in October 20X4.

The club's owners are two brothers, wealthy financiers who live in Vancouver. The club is financed about 50/50 through debt and equity. The brothers' financial goal for the club is to have it break even with its total cash flows (that is, not require infusions of operating capital from the brothers). They also wish to be associated with the glamour and excitement of major league baseball.

The following accounting issues must be addressed for the year ended 30 November 20X4.

1. OOL moved into Big Top, a newly built stadium with a retractable roof, on 1 August 20X4. Seating capacity is 70,000. The new stadium is a great improvement over the 30,000-seat NoWay Park stadium used for the preceding seven years. On 24 July 20X4, OOL signed a 10-year lease with the new stadium's owners. However, OOL's lease on the old premises was not due to expire until 1 January 20X8. OOL therefore paid $3.6 million to terminate its lease.

2. Immediately before the start of the 20X4 baseball season in April, three of the club's top players were signed to long-term contracts. Amounts of the contracts are as follows:

|  | Term | Salary |
|---|---|---|
| Frank Ferter | 3 years | $1,500,000 per year |
| Hugh G. Blast | 5 years | 900,000 per year |
| Bill Board | 4 years | 1,200,000 per year |

The contracts of Ferter and Blast specify that if they suffer a career-ending injury, their contracts will become null and void. Board's contract is guaranteed for the full term.

On 27 April 20X4, Board was injured, forcing him to retire from playing baseball. As required by his contract, he has since been moved to the front office and is performing public relations and administrative services. Other equivalent PR staff are paid $50,000–$60,000 per annum.

Ferter has a bonus clause in his contract under which he will be paid $50,000 if he is selected to play for the All Star Team. Although he is favoured to capture this honour in 20X4, the selections will not be announced until after the financial statements will have been issued.

Because of Ferter's exceptional ability and the fact that he is considered a "player who will increase the popularity of the sport in this city for many years to come," management proposes to amortize the total cost of his contract ($4,500,000) over a 10-year period.

3. On 3 October 20X4, the day before the last playoff game, a wind storm caused the roof at Big Top to collapse, resulting in structural damage of $4,500,000 to the stadium. This damage will be paid for by OOL, under the terms of its lease agreement. This unforeseen event forced OOL's last playoff game to be played at NoWay Park. Hence, the club announced that some of the 70,000 tickets sold for Big Top could be used at NoWay Park and that the $35 cost of the remaining tickets could either be refunded or applied toward the cost of tickets for any of OOL's pre-season games next year. Also, the 40,000 fans who could not attend the game at NoWay were given $10 gift certificates that could be used toward purchasing tickets for any future OOL game. The rate and the extent to which these gift certificates will be redeemed is uncertain at 30 November 20X4. What is certain is that the fans who were left seatless were very upset, and talked about a boycott of the 20X5 season.

**Required:**

Write a report that evaluates the accounting issues raised and includes your recommendations.

(CICA, adapted)

# ASSIGNMENTS

★★ **A6-1 Revenue Recognition:** For each of the following independent items, indicate when revenue should be recognized.

a. Interest on loans made by a financial institution, receivable in annual payments.
b. Interest on loans made by a financial institution, receivable in three years when the customer, who has an excellent credit rating, will make payment.
c. Interest on loans made by a financial institution, where the loans are in default and payment of principal and interest is highly uncertain.
d. Recognition of revenue from the cash sale of airline tickets, where the travel purchased will occur in the next fiscal period.
e. Transportation of freight by a trucking company for a customer; the customer is expected to make payment in accordance with the terms of the invoice in 60 days.
f. Growing, harvesting, and marketing of Christmas trees; the production cycle is 10 years.
g. Building houses in a subdivision, where the project will take two years to complete and each house must be individually sold by the contractor.
h. Building houses in a subdivision, where the project will take two years to complete and the contractor is building the houses under a contract from the local government.
i. Selling undeveloped lots for future retirement homes in a western province, with very low down payment and long-term contracts.
j. Sale of a two-year parking permit by a parking garage, with one-half the sale price received on the sale, and the remainder to be received in equal monthly payments over the period of the permit.
k. A fixed-price contract with the government to design and build a prototype of a space arm; the costs to complete the project cannot be reliably estimated.
l. A silver-mining company produces one million ounces of silver but stores the silver in a vault and waits for silver prices to increase.

★ **A6-2 Revenue Recognition—Gross or Net:** Each of the following situations is independent:

a. A company sells books through the Internet. The company obtains the books from the publishers and carries them in inventory for immediate shipment. Customer payment is by credit card.
b. An interior design company operates a showroom. Furniture manufacturers send samples of their products to the showroom for display. When a customer orders furniture, the company transmits the order to the manufacturer, and the manufacturer ships the products directly to the customer. Customers pay a deposit by cash or credit card, with the balance due (cash or credit card) when the product is delivered.
c. CanLight Ltd. is a company that sells electrical lighting fixtures. The fixtures are produced in China and shipped to CanLight by container ship. The producer pays shipping costs and retains title to the fixtures both while in transit and while they are in CanLight's inventory. CanLight markets and sells the fixtures to builders for inclusion in new construction. When a sale is made, CanLight delivers the fixtures to the building site and invoices the builder. When the builder pays the invoice, CanLight sends 70% of the cash to the producer by international bank transfer.

**Required:**
For each of the preceding situations, explain:

1. Whether the seller should report the gross amount of the sales transactions as revenue; and
2. Your basis for deciding whether to recognize gross or net revenue.

**A6-3 Revenue Recognition—Four Cases:** Three independent cases are given below for 20X5. The accounting period ends 31 December.

*Case A* On 31 December 20X5, Zulu Sales Company sold a machine for $100,000 and collected $40,000 cash. The remainder plus 10% interest is payable 31 December 20X6. Zulu will deliver the machine on 5 January 20X6. The buyer has an excellent credit rating.

*Case B* On 17 October 20X5, the law firm of Pearlstein and Wolf received $30,000 from a client. The payment was a retainer for legal services to be provided, as needed, from 1 November 20X5 though 31 October 20X6.

*Case C* On 15 November 20X5, Victor Cement Company sold a tonne of its product for $500. The cement was delivered on that date. The buyer will pay for the product with two units of its own merchandise that are commonly sold for $250 each. The buyer promised to deliver the merchandise around 31 January 20X6.

*Case D* On 2 January 20X5, Remer Publishing Company collected $900 cash for a three-year subscription to a monthly magazine, *Investor's Stock and Bond Advisory*. The first issue will be mailed to subscribers in March 20X5.

### Required:
Write a brief report covering the following:

1. When revenue should be recognized.
2. Any entry that should be made on the transaction date.
3. An explanation of the reasoning for your responses to requirements (1) and (2).

 **A6-4 Revenue Recognition—Accounting Estimates:** As we perform a specific task, we get better and more efficient at that task (even at solving accounting problems!). This basic principle was quantified in the aircraft industry many decades ago, and is known as a learning curve. Learning curves also have been applied extensively in other industries such as automobile manufacturing.

A learning curve is a downward-sloping curve that is based on a prediction of constantly increasing efficiency. (For those students who are mathematically inclined, a learning curve is a logarithmic straight line.) Learning curves are used to predict the costs of aircraft production for planning and cost control purposes.

In the financial statements of HayJet, a manufacturer of private jets, a note discloses the following information regarding accounting policies for revenue and expense recognition:

> The Company determines an average unit cost (AUC) for the entire predicted production run of an aircraft model. The AUC is based on the estimated total production costs for a total probable number of aircraft to be produced plus the substantial total deferred cost of developing that aircraft model. Target production quantities are based on Management's assessment of market conditions and on the foreseeable demand at the beginning of the production stage. Management takes into consideration, among other factors, existing firm orders and options.
>
> Using the target production quantity, your Company calculates the AUC of that model's production, recognizing that production costs go down as more and more aircraft are produced. The Company uses the learning curve concept, which anticipates a predictable decrease in unit costs as tasks and production techniques become more efficient through repetition.
>
> As each aircraft is sold and delivered, cost of sales is recorded at the AUC. In the early stages of production, actual production costs are in excess of AUC. The excess is recorded as deferred cost. In the later stages of production, when actual production costs are less than AUC, the excess of average unit cost (charged to cost of sales) and the actual lower-than-average costs reduces the accumulated deferred cost.

**Required:**

1. Explain what estimates management must make in order to use the accounting policies described in HayJet's notes.

2. What is the consequence for profit if actual sales are far in excess of management's estimated total production quantity?

3. What will be the impact on the company's profit if fewer aircraft are sold than management estimated?

★ **A6-5 Revenue Recognition—Accounting Estimates:** TaCheng Building Systems Incorporated is a construction contractor that specializes in high-tech building projects, that is, buildings that must incorporate a high level of technology such as hospitals, interactive learning centres, and chemical processing plants. The company has considerable experience in constructing buildings that must incorporate cutting-edge technology. The contracts usually are turn-key applications, in which the building and its technology must be ready for use the day that the tenant moves in. TaCheng works closely with the client throughout design and the construction process. The contract provides for incorporating changes during construction due to technological improvements that arise while construction is underway. Any changes in specifications or updating normally will require a change in the value of the contract. TaCheng uses the percentage-of-completion method of accounting.

**Required:**

Explain what accounting estimates TaCheng managers must make at the end of each reporting period in order to apply the percentage-of-completion method.

★★ **A6-6 Revenue Recognition—Critical Event:** Each of the following situations is independent of the others:

a. Carnegie Corporation commissions, produces, and sells books through faith-based non-profit organizations. The books are sold on the basis that a maximum of 50% of the quantity purchased can be returned within six months. Payment is due within 30 days of the end of the return period. Carnegie has a good historical record of the proportion of books returned, on average.

b. Maxwell Limited is a gatherer and distributor of coffee beans. The beans are purchased from harvesters in Brazil and Columbia, roasted, and packaged in large burlap bags. Maxwell then resells the bagged beans to food processors, coffee houses, and grocery chains in North America. Collectibility of receivables is not a problem. Coffee beans have an open trading market and are traded on several major commodity exchanges in the United States. Raw beans can be purchased and/or sold in the open market at any time.

c. Heckinger Inc. customized a substantial quantity of its product for sale by a large retail chain. The product was to be sold under the chain's "Director's Choice" in-house label. Just prior to shipping the customized product, the chain voluntarily entered creditor protection. Under creditor protection, creditors cannot force payment of their claims until a judge approves a comprehensive plan for settling the claims of all creditors, a process that can take several years. Since the product had already been customized, Heckinger did deliver the product, believing that it would be better off in the long run to receive some payment instead of scrapping the product.

d. Nevo Corporation develops large-scale custom software. Nevo's main area of expertise is in designing complex systems for managing health care. It takes the company an average of three years to complete a project, from concept and specifications through programming, debugging and testing. The client makes interim payments as Nevo accomplishes "milestones" that are specified in the contract. Nevo offers "turn-key" service, in which Nevo is responsible for installation in the client's facilities (including additional hardware, if necessary), on-site testing, and training for the client's staff. Nevo has never failed to deliver a contract on time and on budget, provided that the client does not change the system specifications while the system is being designed.

**Required:**

For each situation, explain what the critical point is for revenue recognition, and how costs and payments should be accounted for both before and after the critical point.

---

 **A6-7 Revenue Recognition—Critical Event:** Luke Windows Limited manufactures custom-made windows for homes. The company deals directly with some individual customers, but mainly does business with contractors that are building tract housing under contract with a developer—that is, a real property development company that is constructing a large number of houses in a single new development.

For tract housing, Luke bids on the contract according to specifications given by the developer. The costs of preparing the bid are not substantial, but they are not insignificant either. If Luke wins the contract, the company then sets up a production line in the factory to manufacture the windows according to specification. As the windows are finished, they are stored in Luke's factory temporarily, until the contractor is ready to receive them. When they are delivered to the building site (usually in batches, not all together), the contractor is responsible for any damage or breakage that occurs. Also, the contractor is responsible for proper installation.

The houses are built (and sold) in batches. The sales from one batch help the developer to finance the next batch. After each batch of houses is finished and has been standing empty through a few rain or snow storms, the developer inspects for any failure in design, construction, or installation. If all is satisfactory, the developer authorizes payment for that part of the development. Payment is made to the contractor, which then is responsible for paying Luke. In the unlikely event that the contractor does not pay Luke, Luke can establish a "lien" on the houses that requires the developer (or the new owners who have purchased the houses) to satisfy Luke's claim.

Depending on the size of the housing development, the entire project, from bid preparation to final collection, can take anywhere from two to five years. Each batch of houses usually is completed within about 18 months. However, Luke's construction and delivery of the windows for a batch seldom takes more than two months.

**Required:**

1. From the information given, identify the critical point at which Luke should recognize revenue from windows for tract housing. Explain your reasoning.

2. Using the critical point identified in requirement (1), explain how Luke should account for costs and revenues related to this project over time.

---

 **A6-8 Revenue Recognition:** Shawinegan Development Company (SDC) conducts research and development on specific projects under contract for clients; SDC also conducts basic research and attempts to market any new products or technologies it develops.

In January 20X4, scientists at SDC began research to develop a new industrial cleaner. During 20X4, $2,340,000 of costs were incurred in this effort. Late in July 20X5, potentially promising results emerged in the form of a substance the company called Scourge. Costs incurred through the end of July 20X5 were $1,260,000. At this point, SDC attempted to sell the formula of and rights to Scourge to Pride and Glory Industries Limited (P&G), for $15,000,000. P&G, however, was reluctant to sign before further testing was done. It did wish, though, to have the first option to acquire the rights and formulas to Scourge if future testing showed the product to be profitable. SDC was very confident that Scourge would pass further testing with flying colours. Accordingly, the two companies signed an option agreement that allowed P&G to acquire the formulas and rights to Scourge any time before 31 December 20X6. Testing costs on the product incurred by SDC for the remainder of 20X5 amounted to $1,620,000.

In early 20X6, P&G exercised its option and agreed to purchase the formulas and rights to Scourge for $15,000,000. P&G paid $750,000 immediately with the balance payable in five equal annual instalments on 31 December 20X6 to 20X10. The formula was to be completed and delivered within 18 months.

In April 20X7, SDC delivered the formulas and samples of Scourge to P&G Industries. Additional costs incurred by SDC during 20X6 amounted to $540,000; in 20X7, $180,000.

**Required:**

1. When should revenue be recognized by SDC from its work on Scourge? Why?
2. Assume that the total costs of $5,940,000 actually incurred by SDC over the years 20X4 to 20X6 were accurately estimated in 20X4. Determine the amount of revenue and expense that should be recognized each year from 20X4 to 20X10, assuming revenue is to be recognized:
   a. At the time the option is signed.
   b. At the time the option is exercised.
   c. At the time the formulas are delivered.

Note that the $1,560,000 of research costs must be expensed in all alternatives to comply with accounting standards for research costs. Other costs may be deferred if appropriate. Do not attempt journal entries; your solution should focus on income statement presentation.

---

**A6-9 Entries for Critical Events:** Maypole Industries imports goods from Taiwan and resells them to domestic Canadian markets. Maypole uses a perpetual inventory system. A typical transaction stream follows:

| | | |
|---|---|---|
| 18 | July | Purchased goods for Cdn$456,000 |
| 24 | August | Goods repackaged and ready for sale. Cost incurred, $60,000 |
| 10 | September | Goods delivered to customer. Agreed-on price, $712,000 |
| 22 | November | Customer paid |

**Required:**

1. Prepare journal entries assuming the following critical events:
   a. Delivery to customer.
   b. Cash receipt.
   c. Preparation of goods for resale.
2. Explain the circumstances under which each of these methods would be appropriate.

---

**A6-10 Entries for Critical Events:** Dominum Corporation is a mining company that mines, produces, and markets teledine, a common mineral substance. The mineral is mined and produced in one large batch per year, as the mine is accessible only for a brief period in the summer due to severe weather conditions at the mine site. Dominum has an advance purchase contract with a group of regular customers that takes all of Dominum's output each year. Transactions in 20X6:

| | | |
|---|---|---|
| 30 | August | 186,000 tonnes of teledine ore removed from mine, at a cost of $4,300,000. |
| 30 | September | All of the ore refined to 115,000 tonnes of teledine, at a cost of $640,000. |
| 15 | October | All of the teledine delivered to 25 customers, total contract price, $13,500,000. |
| 25 | October | Five percent of the teledine returned for full credit; ore had been improperly refined and the teledine was unusable; customer given full credit for $675,000 and the unusable teledine scrapped. No other returns are anticipated. |
| 30 | November | Customers all paid except one that went bankrupt still owing $155,000. |

**Required:**

1. Prepare all journal entries to record these events, assuming three different revenue recognition points:
   a. 30 September

  b. 15 October

  c. 25 October

  Assume that at each of these dates, the company can make reasonable estimates of accruals for future events such as sales returns and bad debts, if needed.

2. Explain the point at which net assets change for each alternative in requirement (1).

3. Explain the circumstances under which revenue recognition at each of these dates would be appropriate.

---

  **A6-11 Unconditional Right of Return:** In 20X5, Balla Shoe Corporation developed a new product, an electric shoe tree. To increase acceptance by retailers, Balla sold the product to retailers with an unconditional right of return, which expires on 1 February 20X6. Balla has no basis for estimating returns on the new product. The following information is available regarding the product:

| | | |
|---|---|---|
| Sales—20X5 | $360,000 | |
| Cost of goods sold—20X5 | 240,000 | |
| Returns—20X5 | 24,000 | (cost, $16,000) |
| Returns—January 20X6 | 30,000 | (cost, $20,000) |

All sales are on credit. Cash collections related to the sales were $80,000 in 20X5 and $226,000 in 20X6. Balla uses a perpetual inventory system.

**Required:**

Give journal entries for sales, returns, and collections related to the new product. Include the entry made on 1 February 20X6 when the right of return expires. How much sales revenue should Balla recognize in 20X5?

---

  **A6-12 Unconditional Right of Return:** McLaughlin Novelty Corporation developed an unusual product, electric clip-on eyeglass wipers. McLaughlin felt the product would appeal to hikers, joggers, and cyclists who engaged in their sports in rainy climates. Because retail establishments were skeptical about the market appeal of the product, McLaughlin sold the product with a declining unconditional right of return for up to 10 months, with 10% of the right-of-return amount of the purchase expiring each month for 10 months. Thus, after the retailer had the product for one month, only 90% could be returned. After two months, only 80% could be returned, and after 10 months, the right of return was fully expired.

  McLaughlin had no basis for estimating the amount of returns. Consistent with the terms McLaughlin offered its customers, all retailers paid cash when purchasing the clip-on eyeglass wipers but received cash refunds if goods were returned. McLaughlin had its first sales of the product in September 20X5. Sales for the remainder of the year, and returns prior to 31 December 20X5, were as follows:

| Month of Sale | Units Sold | Sales Price | Monthly Sales | Units Returned |
|---|---|---|---|---|
| September | 10,000 | $10 | $100,000 | 2,500 |
| October | 12,000 | 10 | 120,000 | 1,000 |
| November | 15,000 | 12 | 180,000 | 1,000 |
| December | 11,000 | 12 | 132,000 | 0 |
| Totals | 48,000 | | $532,000 | 4,500 |

Each unit of product costs McLaughlin $6 to produce.

**Required:**

1. Show the journal entries to record the four months of sales transactions, including the deferral of gross margin. Prepare one summary entry.

2. Show a summary entry to record the returns in 20X5.

3. Compute the amount that McLaughlin can record as (realized) sales for 20X5. How much is gross margin? Record the revenue recognition entry.

4. For the above transactions, total returns in all of 20X6 were as follows:

| Month of Sale | Units Returned |
|---|---|
| September | 1,000 |
| October | 2,000 |
| November | 2,500 |
| December | 4,000 |

Show the entries to record the returns in 20X6 and to record sales revenue and cost of sales from the 20X5 shipments of this product.

---

★★ **A6-13 Revenue Recognition:** Fly and Mattox, a professional corporation, contracted to provide, as required, all legal services for Brown Company until the end of 20X5. The contract specified a lump-sum payment of $60,000 on 15 November 20X4. Assume that Fly and Mattox can reliably estimate future direct costs associated with the contract. The following services were performed based on the estimate by Fly and Mattox:

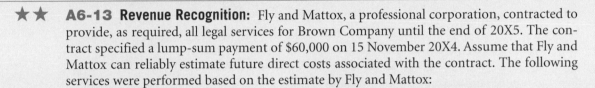

| | Direct Costs | Date Completed |
|---|---|---|
| Research potential lawsuit | $ 5,000 | 15 December 20X4 |
| Prepare and file documents | 15,000 | 1 March 20X5 |
| Serve as Brown's counsel during legal proceedings | 15,000 | 15 October 20X5 |

**Required:**

1. When should Fly and Mattox recognize revenue in this situation? Explain.

2. Give entries to recognize revenues related to this contract for Fly and Mattox.

---

★★ **A6-14 Critical Event:** BC Corporation sells large items of construction equipment. The company had the following three customers in 20X5:

a. Byron Landscaping. The contract sales price was $345,700; cost of the equipment sold was $210,000. Byron was given unlimited right of return until 30 June 20X6. BC has no basis for reliably estimating the likelihood of the equipment's being returned.

b. Addison Road. This is a new type of equipment that Addison Road has no experience with. The contract provides that the price will be determined on the basis of revenue generated and costs saved by Addison over the first six months of operation, with a minimum base price of $180,000. BC believes that the sales price will likely be in the range of $230,000 to $260,000, but has no previous experience with this kind of contract. The equipment cost BC $176,000 to produce.

c. Carson Construction. The sales price was $576,000; BC's cost of production was $401,000. BC delivered the equipment just as Carson was entering bankruptcy, and therefore BC retained title to the equipment so that it doesn't become lost in the bankruptcy proceedings. Carson paid $60,000 in advance as a security deposit. The remainder was to have been paid within 12 months, but collection will be contingent upon Carson's survival and continuing operations.

**Required:**

1. At what point should BC recognize revenue for each of the above sales transactions?

2. Show how the transactions would be reflected in the 20X5 balance sheet and income statement.

★★ **A6-15 Critical Event:** Manzer Manufacturing had transactions in 20X6 as follows:

| | |
|---|---|
| 30 June | Purchased inventory, $378,000. |
| 17 July | Sale to customer, $271,000, on account. Cost of goods sold, $164,500. |
| 15 September | Warranty work of $20,000 was performed. |
| 30 November | Customer returns $29,000 of goods for full credit; goods were spoiled and worthless. |
| 15 December | Customer paid all outstanding amounts. |

All goods were sold with unlimited right of return for 60 days and a one-year warranty. Manzer's year-end is 31 December.

**Required:**

1. Prepare 20X6 entries to record the above transactions assuming that the critical event is deemed to be
   a. The date of delivery.
   b. The date that the warranty expires.
   c. The date that the return privilege expires.
   
   If necessary, assume that total warranty cost can be estimated to be $41,000, and returns, $29,000.

2. Show how the income statement and balance sheet would reflect each of the alternatives in requirement (1).

3. Comment on the relative timing of the increase in net assets.

---

★★ **A6-16 Instalment Sales:** Baxter Land Corporation made a number of sales in 20X4 and 20X5 that required use of the instalment method. The following information regarding the
 sales is available:

| | 20X4 | 20X5 | 20X6 |
|---|---|---|---|
| Instalment sales | $200,000 | $150,000 | $     0 |
| Cost of instalment sales | 160,000 | 112,500 | 0 |
| Collections on 20X4 sales | 40,000 | 50,000 | 60,000 |
| Collections on 20X5 sales | | 30,000 | 75,000 |

Baxter uses a perpetual inventory system.

**Required:**

1. Give journal entries relating to instalment sales for the years 20X4 to 20X6.

2. What is the year-end balance in instalment accounts receivable (net of any deferred gross margin) for 20X4, 20X5, and 20X6?

3. If the sales qualified for revenue recognition on the date of sale (i.e., delivery), what amounts of gross margin would Baxter report in 20X4, 20X5, and 20X6?

---

★★★ **A6-17 Instalment Sales Method:** Ontario Retail Company sells goods for cash, and on normal credit terms of 30 days. However, on 1 July 20X4, the company sold a used computer for $2,200; the inventory carrying value was $440. The company collected $200 cash and agreed to let the customer make payments on the $2,000 whenever possible during the next 12 months. The company management stated that it had no reliable basis for estimating the probability of default. The following additional data are available: (a) collections on the instalment receivable during 20X4 were $300 and during 20X5 were $200, and (b) on 1 December 20X5, Ontario Retail repossessed the computer (estimated net realizable value, $700).

**Required:**

1. Give the required entries for 20X4 and 20X5; assume that the instalment method is used.

2. Give the balances in the following accounts that would be reported on the 20X4 and 20X5 income statements and balance sheets: instalment sales revenue and cost of sales, instalment accounts receivable, and inventory of used computers.

3. How much profit would be recognized in 20X4 and 20X5 if the cost recovery method is used?

★★ **A6-18 Cost Recovery Method:** Slatt Department Store has accumulated a stock of obsolete merchandise. Routine efforts have been made to dispose of it at a low price. This merchandise originally cost $84,000 and was marked to sell for $184,000. Management decided to set up a special location in the basement to display and (it was hoped) sell this stock starting in January 20X5. All items will be marked to sell at a cash price that is 30% of the original marked selling price. On 31 December 20X4, the company accountant transferred the purchase cost to a perpetual inventory account called "inventory, obsolete merchandise," at 30% of its purchase cost, which approximates estimated net realizable value. Management knows that a reliable estimate of the probable sales cannot be made. Therefore, the cost recovery method will be used. Subsequent sales were $15,000 in 20X5 and $8,000 in 20X6. In early 20X7 the entire remaining stock of merchandise was sold for $7,000.

**Required:**
Give the entries that Slatt should make for 20X4 through 20X7.

★★ **A6-19 Cost Recovery Method:** The Trusett Merchandising Company has an inventory of obsolete products that it formerly stocked for sale. Efforts to dispose of this inventory by selling the products at low prices have not been successful. At the end of the prior year (20X4), the company reduced the value to a conservative estimate of net realizable value of $22,000. On 1 March 20X6, Watson Trading Company purchased this entire inventory for $10,000 cash as a speculative investment. Watson hopes to be able to dispose of it in some foreign markets for approximately $30,000. However, prior to purchase, Watson concluded that there was no reliable way to estimate the probable profitability of the venture. Therefore, Watson decided to use the cost recovery method. Subsequent cash sales have been as follows: 20X6, $4,000; 20X7, $5,000; and 20X8, $8,000. Approximately 12% of the inventory remains on hand at the start of 20X9.

**Required:**
Give the 20X6, 20X7, and 20X8 entries for Watson Trading Company to record revenues and cost of sales.

★★ **A6-20 Instalment and Cost Recovery Methods:** Beaver Limited is a retail company that sells goods for cash and on normal credit terms of 30 days. On 1 March 20X0, the company sold merchandise for $1,500 that cost $900. Management has stated it has no reliable basis on which to determine the collectibility of the account. The company collected $500 when the sale was made and agreed to allow the customer to make payments whenever possible over the next 12 months. On 14 September 20X0, the customer made a payment of $300.

**Required:**
1. Prepare the entries for the above transactions assuming the instalment sales method is used.

2. If the sale qualified for revenue recognition on the date of delivery, what amount of gross profit would be recognized in the year 20X0?

3. If the sale is accounted for by the cost recovery method, what amount of gross profit would be recognized in the year 20X0?

(CGA-Canada)

**A6-21 Instalment, Delivery, and Cost Recovery Methods:** Purple Limited uses the instalment sales method to recognize revenue on its sales to its customers. During August, instalment sales of $160,000 were recorded. The gross profit margin on instalment sales is 20%. During the month of September, $45,000 is collected on the previous month's instalment sales.

**Required:**

1. Prepare the entries to record the transactions for the instalment sales of $160,000 and the subsequent collection of $45,000.

2. Explain the impact on Purple's financial statements for the two months ending 30 September, assuming revenue is earned at delivery instead of on an instalment basis.

3. Explain the impact on Purple's financial statements for the two months ending 30 September, assuming revenue is reported by the cost recovery method instead of on an instalment basis.

(CGA-Canada, adapted)

 **A6-22 Percentage-of-Completion Method:** Star Construction Corporation has a contract to construct a building for $7,300,000. Total costs to complete the building were originally estimated at $5,900,000. Construction commenced on 4 February 20X5. Total construction costs incurred in each year were as follows:

| 20X5 | $1,700,000 |
|------|------------|
| 20X6 | $3,100,000 |
| 20X7 | $1,200,000 |

Actual costs were in line with estimated costs until 20X7, when actual costs exceeded estimated costs by $100,000. The additional costs reduced the total gross profit on the project from an estimated $1,400,000 to $1,300,000. Progress billings based on the amount of work completed were collected each year. Star Construction uses the percentage-of-completion method. The percentage of completion is based on costs incurred compared to estimated total costs of the project.

**Required:**

1. Calculate the revenues and gross profit for the construction project for each of the three years

2. Prepare the journal entries for revenue recognition for each year and for contract completion in 20X7.

(CGA-Canada adapted)

 **A6-23 Percentage-of-Completion Method:** Thrasher Construction Company contracted to construct a building for $975,000. The contract provided for progress payments. Thrasher's accounting year ends 31 December. Work began under the contract on 1 July 20X5, and was completed on 30 September 20X7. Construction activities are summarized below by year:

20X5    Construction costs incurred during the year, $180,000; estimated costs to complete, $630,000; progress billings during the year, $153,000; and collections, $140,000.

20X6    Construction costs incurred during the year, $450,000; estimated costs to complete, $190,000; progress billing during the year, $382,500; and collections, $380,000.

20X7    Construction costs incurred during the year, $195,000. Because the contract was completed, the remaining balance was billed and later collected in full per the contract.

**Required:**

1. Give Thrasher's entries assuming that the percentage-of-completion method is used. Assume that percentage of completion is measured by the ratio of costs incurred to date divided by total estimated construction costs.

2. Prepare income statement and balance sheet presentation for this contract by year; assume that the percentage-of-completion method is used.

3. Prepare income statement and balance sheet presentation by year; assume that the completed-contract method is used. For each amount that is different from the corresponding amount in (2), explain why it is different.

4. Which method would you recommend to this contractor? Why?

---

 **A6-24 Completed-Contract and Percentage-of-Completion Methods Compared:** Watson Construction Company contracted to build a plant for $600,000. Construction started in January 20X4 and was completed in November 20X5. Data relating to the contract are summarized below:

|                                        | 20X4      | 20X5      |
|----------------------------------------|-----------|-----------|
| Costs incurred during year             | $350,000  | $144,000  |
| Estimated additional costs to complete | 150,000   | —         |
| Billings during year                   | 320,000   | 280,000   |
| Cash collections during year           | 300,000   | 300,000   |

**Required:**

1. Give the journal entries for Watson in parallel columns, assuming (a) the completed-contract method and (b) the percentage-of-completion method. Use costs incurred to date divided by total estimated construction costs to measure percentage completed.

2. Complete the following table:

|                                                     | Completed-Contract Method | Percentage-of-Completion Method |
|-----------------------------------------------------|:-------------------------:|:-------------------------------:|
| **Income statement:**                               |                           |                                 |
| Income:                                             |                           |                                 |
| 20X4                                                | $                         | $                               |
| 20X5                                                | $                         | $                               |
| **Balance sheet:**                                  |                           |                                 |
| Receivables:                                        |                           |                                 |
| 20X4                                                | $                         | $                               |
| 20X5                                                | $                         | $                               |
| Inventory—construction in progress, net of billings: |                           |                                 |
| 20X4                                                | $                         | $                               |
| 20X5                                                | $                         | $                               |

---

 **A6-25 Percentage-of-Completion—Revenue Change:** Catalina Construction Corporation signed a contract to build an apartment building for $2,800,000. Construction began in October 20X4 and was scheduled to be completed in May 20X6. Catalina has a 31 December year-end. Data for the first two years of the contract were as follows:

| ($ thousands)                          | 20X4    | 20X5    |
|----------------------------------------|---------|---------|
| Costs incurred during year             | $  400  | $1,500  |
| Estimated additional costs to complete | 2,200   | 400     |
| Billings during year                   | 350     | 1,450   |
| Cash collections during year           | 325     | 1,300   |

Late in 20X5, the client made some design changes to the apartment layouts in the upper floors. After negotiations, Catalina agreed to a contract amendment that increased the total price to $3,200,000 and delayed the completion date until 31 October 20X6. Catalina estimated that the contract change would increase total costs by $300,000 (not included in the $400,000 "costs to complete" for 20X5 above).

Actual costs incurred during 20X6 were $850,000. The full remaining contract price was billed during 20X6. By the end of 20X6, the client had paid the full contract price except for the 10% holdback permitted by law for 90 days.

**Required:**

Prepare the journal entries for Catalina, assuming the percentage-of-completion method. Use costs incurred to date divided by total estimated construction costs to measure percentage complete. Round your estimate of revenue to the nearest thousand.

★★  **A6-26 Completed-Contract and Percentage-of-Completion Methods Compared:** Mullen Construction Company contracted to build a municipal warehouse for the city of Moncton for $750,000. The contract specified that the city would pay Mullen each month the progress billings, less 10%, which was to be held as a retention reserve. At the end of the construction, the final payment would include the reserve. Each billing, less the 10% reserve, must be paid 10 days after submission of a billing to the city. Transactions relating to the contract are summarized below:

20X4    Construction costs incurred during the year, $210,000; estimated costs to complete, $390,000; progress billing, $190,000; and collections per the contract.

20X5    Construction costs incurred during the year, $342,000; estimated costs to complete, $138,000; progress billings, $280,000; and collections per the contract. A contract change during 20X5 increased the total contract revenue to $800,000.

20X6    Construction costs incurred during the year, $148,000. The remaining billings were submitted by 1 October and final collections completed on 30 November.

**Required:**

1. Complete the following table:

| Year | Method | Net Income Recognized | Contract Receivables, Ending Balance | Construction-in-Progress Inventory, Ending Balance |
|---|---|---|---|---|
| 20X4 | Completed contact | $ | $ | $ |
|  | Percentage of completion* |  |  |  |
| 20X5 | Completed contract |  |  |  |
|  | Percentage of completion* |  |  |  |
| 20X6 | Completed contract |  |  |  |
|  | Percentage of completion* |  |  |  |

*Use costs incurred to date divided by total estimated construction costs to measure percentage of completion.

2. Explain what causes the ending balance in construction-in-progress to be different for the two methods.

3. Which method would you recommend for this contractor? Why?

★★★ **A6-27 Long-Term Construction: Methods Compared:** Wallen Corporation contracted to construct an office building for Ragee Company for $1,000,000. Construction began on

15 January 20X4, and was completed on 1 December 20X5. Wallen's accounting year ends 31 December. Transactions by Wallen relating to the contract are summarized below:

| | 20X4 | 20X5 |
|---|---|---|
| Costs incurred to date | $400,000 | $ 850,000 |
| Estimated costs to complete | 420,000 | — |
| Progress billings to date | 410,000 | 1,000,000 |
| Progress collections to date | 375,000 | 1,000,000 |

**Required:**

1. In parallel columns, give the entries on the contractor's books. Assume:
   a. The completed contract method
   b. The percentage-of-completion method

   Assume that percentage of completion is measured by the ratio of costs incurred to date divided by total estimated construction costs.

2. For each method, prepare the income statement and balance sheet presentation for this contract by year.

3. What is the nature of the item "costs in excess of billings" that would appear on the balance sheet?

4. Which method would you recommend that the contractor use? Why?

---

★★★ **A6-28 Percentage-of-Completion and Completed-Contract Methods:** Banks Construction Company contracted to build an office block for $3,200,000. Construction began
 in September 20X4 and was scheduled to be completed in May 20X6. Banks has a 31 December year-end. Data related to the contract are summarized below:

| ($ thousands) | 20X4 | 20X5 | 20X6 |
|---|---|---|---|
| Costs incurred during year | $ 500 | $1,800 | $ 850 |
| Estimated additional costs to complete | 2,500 | 800 | 0 |
| Billings during year | 450 | 1,300 | 1,450 |
| Cash collections during year | 400 | 1,100 | 1,700 |

**Required:**

1. Prepare the journal entries for Banks, assuming the completed-contract method.

2. Prepare the balance sheet and income presentation for this contract by year, assuming the completed-contract method is used.

3. Prepare the journal entries for Banks, assuming the percentage-of-completion method. Use costs incurred to date divided by total estimated construction costs to measure percentage complete.

4. Prepare the balance sheet and income presentation for this contract by year, assuming the percentage-of-completion method is used.

---

★ **A6-29 Multiple Deliverables:** BigBoy Equipment Inc. sells heavy-duty forklift trucks. Model 217A has a price of $120,000. BigBoy offers to sell the 217A inclusive of a three-year service contract for $150,000. A comparable service contract would sell for $60,000.

**Required:**

Prepare a journal entry to record the sale of one Model 217A forklift truck for $150,000, including the service contract.

---

★ **A6-30 Multiple Deliverables:** Dominion Mobile Incorporated provides cellular phone services. The company conducts a special sales campaign in which new subscribers will get a high-end cell phone for only $400 if he signs a 24-month contract that has a service fee of $100 per month. Thus, the total price of the cell phone plus 12 months of service is $2,800.

The company normally sells the phone for $1,000. Current subscribers pay $75 per month for comparable service; they are not permitted to take advantage of the $400 cell phone offer.

**Required:**

How should Dominion recognize the revenue earned from each new customer under this offer?

 **A6-31 Multiple Deliverables:** Milbank Appliance Corporation (MAC) sells major appliances (such as refrigerators, stoves, etc.) at retail. MAC sells its top-line home refrigerator, the Zero-Line, for $6,000. The refrigerator comes with a one-year unconditional warranty on all parts and labour except for the electronic control panel, which is limited to a 90-day warranty.

For an additional $400 at time of the refrigerator purchase, the warranty on the control panel can be extended to one year. This warranty can be purchased only when the refrigerator is purchased from MAC. It is not offered as a separate item by any other company.

As well, MAC offers a three-year extension to the basic one-year warranty. The cost is $1,000 if it is purchased along with the refrigerator. The extended warranty can also be purchased later (but prior to expiry of the basic warranty) for $1,600. The extended warranty can be purchased by owners of Zero-Line refrigerators purchased from other dealers, as long as the customer provides dated proof of purchase.

**Required:**

Explain how revenue should be recognized in each of the following situations (be specific, with calculations):

a. MAC sells a refrigerator with a three-year extended warranty for $7,000.
b. For a total price of $7,200, MAC sells a refrigerator together with the control panel one-year extended warranty and a three-year extended warranty.

 **A6-32 Expense Recognition:** XYZ Company recorded a series of recent transactions, in chronological order, as follows:

| Date | Entry # | | | |
|------|---------|--|--|--|
| 2 June | 1 | Inventory | 165,000 | |
| | | Accounts payable | | 165,000 |
| | 2 | Prepaid insurance | 3,600 | |
| | | Cash | | 3,600 |
| | 3 | Inventory | 56,000 | |
| | | Cost of goods sold | 60,000 | |
| | | Sales | | 116,000 |
| | 4 | Warranty expense | 9,000 | |
| | | Estimated liability for warranty | | 9,000 |
| 2 June | 5 | Commissions expense | 11,600 | |
| | | Commissions payable | | 11,600 |
| 20 June | 6 | Accounts receivable | 116,000 | |
| | | Inventory | | 116,000 |
| 30 June | 7 | Cash | 116,000 | |
| | | Accounts receivable | | 116,000 |
| | 8 | Insurance expense | 400 | |
| | | Prepaid insurance | | 400 |
| | 9 | Accounts payable | 165,000 | |
| | | Cash | | 165,000 |
| | 10 | Estimated liability for warranty | 3,000 | |
| | | Cash | | 3,000 |

**Required:**

1. Explain the effect that each entry has on net assets. What is the revenue recognition point?
2. For each asset recognized above, explain how the asset meets the definition of an asset.
3. For each expense recognized above, explain whether the expense is a direct or indirect expense, and how the expense meets the expense definition.

---

★★ **A6-33 Expense Recognition:** Pacific Alliance Corporation (PAC) experienced the following transactions and events during 20X0:

a. Paid $2,000,000 for the right to use the trademark of a European company for PAC's products in Canada and Mexico for the next eight years, starting in 20X1. The agreement is renewable by mutual agreement, at a price to be negotiated as the current agreement nears expiration.
b. Incurred one-time costs of $365,000 to convert the company's product labelling and packaging to correspond with the requirements of the European company.
c. Paid an advertising company $250,000 to design a publicity campaign to familiarize customers with the change in product identity. The campaign will be launched at the beginning of 20X1.
d. Purchased new production equipment for $1,230,000 for use with the newly rebranded product line.
e. Discontinued use of some production equipment as part of the conversion to the new product identity. The equipment cost $760,000 and is 40% depreciated. PAC is attempting to sell the equipment through a broker, as it is still fully functional. The broker estimates that it can be sold for approximately $300,000, although PAC may have to agree to pay shipping costs. The broker's fee is 15% of the sales price. PAC will have to incur costs of about $80,000 to dismantle the equipment.
f. Existing inventory, which bears the old product identity, will be sold to discount clearance brokers early in 20X1. The inventory cost $160,000. PAC managers expect that they can recover about 20% of that through the sale.
g. Internal manuals and training materials have been revised at a cost of $74,000 for the English version. The new materials currently are being used in training at PAC's home office in Vancouver and in Calgary, and will be used in other offices once the ongoing translations into Spanish (for Mexico) and French have been completed and tested for accuracy.

**Required:**

Explain how PAC should account for each item above. Justify your recommendation in terms of changes in PAC's net assets.

(AICPA, adapted)

---

★★★ **A6-34 Revenue and Expense Recognition:** Pewter Publishing Company (PPC) prepares and publishes a monthly newsletter for an industry in which potential circulation is limited. Because information provided by the newsletter is available only piecemeal from other sources and because no advertising is carried, the subscription price for the newsletter is relatively high. To increase circulation, PPC recently purchased a contact list from the industry's trade association for $110,000. PPC then engaged in a campaign to increase circulation. The campaign involved extensive use of long-distance telephone calls to industry members on the list who were not current subscribers. The telephone cost of the campaign was $38,000, plus salary payments to individuals who made the calls amounting to $51,000.

As a direct result of the campaign, new one-year subscriptions at $175 each generated revenue of $294,100. New three-year subscriptions at $450 each generated revenue of $224,700, and new five-year subscriptions at $625 each generated $187,500. Cancellations are rare, but when they occur, refunds are made on a half-rate basis (e.g., if a subscriber has yet to receive $100 worth of newsletters, $50 is refunded).

Aside from the direct costs of the campaign cited above, indirect costs, consisting of such items as allocated office space, fringe benefit costs for employees making telephone calls, and supervision, amounted to $21,000.

The subscription campaign was conducted during November 20X0. New subscriptions began with the January 20X1 issue of the monthly newsletter. The company's accounting year ends 31 December.

**Required:**

Identify the specific accounting issues involved in recognizing revenue and costs for PPC. Explicitly consider each of the following cost items:

1. The subscription list.
2. Direct costs of the subscription campaign.
3. Indirect costs of the subscription campaign.
4. Newsletter production costs incurred in 20X0 for 20X1 issues.

(AICPA, adapted)

 **A6-35 Expense Policy:** Computer Training Limited (CTL) is owned by a small group of investors, but plans to go public in five years' time. The company delivers an eight-month computer training program. While CTL is a new operation, the president has a successful history in the business, and has been successful in other training ventures over the last 10 years. He is paid a substantial salary, and will also receive common stock options based on his performance.

Management has prepared an operating cash flow forecast for the first six years of operation. These show an excess of cash disbursements for operating costs over cash receipts from tuition revenue for the first three years. In Years 4 and 5, the combination of additional student enrolment and projected tuition fee increases is expected to turn the tide: cash receipts and cash disbursements are expected to be equal. In Year 6, it is expected that cash receipts will exceed cash disbursements. The major costs fall into three categories: (1) costs for marketing and administration; (2) direct operating costs, primarily instructor salaries and occupancy costs; and (3) expenditures for capital assets (computer equipment), leasehold improvements, and similar long-lived assets.

The president has told you, the controller, that he wishes to use the following accounting policies:

a. Marketing and administration costs are to be capitalized and, commencing in Year 6, amortized over five years.
b. Direct operating costs in excess of tuition revenue in years 1 to 3 are to be capitalized and amortized in years 6 and 7.
c. Capital assets are to be capitalized and amortized on a sinking-fund basis.

**Required:**

Are the proposed accounting policies acceptable? Your answer must use the definitional approach (as distinct from the matching approach) to analyze policy.

## CHAPTER 7

# Current Monetary Balances

## INTRODUCTION

One objective of financial reporting is to help users assess the amounts, timing, and uncertainty of future cash flows. Their accurate treatment in the financial statements will help financial statement readers understand the business cycle of the operation, and the results of past transactions and decisions.

Levels of current monetary items are critical when assessing the liquidity and viability of an operation. For example, consider Comet Industries, a Canadian public company that has various development projects and also resource properties in B.C., exploring for copper, gold, silver and other minerals. For the 2006 fiscal year, the balance sheet reports $22,700 of cash and $5,600 of accounts receivable, out of assets of $1.27 million. Current liabilities are over $861,000, including accounts payable of approximately $132,000 and a current term loan of approximately $728,000. Comet is obviously in a position where its current monetary assets fall far short of current monetary obligations. This is potentially a high-risk situation, and the disclosure notes state that the continued operation of the company is dependent on its ability to obtain new sources of financing and operate profitably in the future. Current liquidity is a major issue for this company.

This chapter develops accounting principles for the recognition, measurement, and reporting of the primary categories of liquid resources: cash, accounts receivable, and notes receivable, and the primary short-term claims to cash—the various types of payables. These financial statement elements are all monetary items: cash, or claims to cash. The emphasis in this chapter is on short-term monetary balances. Long-term balances are discussed in Chapter 12.

This chapter deals with presentation issues and valuation. Allowances that reduce the book value of various receivables for such issues as bad debts, cash discounts, and sales allowances are reviewed. Various ways to speed cash flow from receivables are covered, including transfer of accounts receivable. Such transfers can be accounted for as a sale or a loan, depending on the circumstances. Finally, when receivables are low interest or no interest, application of present value techniques to the related cash flows is needed to reflect the substance of the transactions.

Most students will already be familiar with present value calculations. If practice is needed, the Online Learning Centre for this text contains a review of compound interest situations. All readers should consult the present value tables, found at the back of each volume, to acquaint themselves with the notation that is used throughout this book.

# DEFINITION OF MONETARY ITEMS

**Monetary items** include money, as well as claims to or for money if the amount is fixed by contract or agreement. Note the two key aspects:

1. Cash must be involved; and

2. The amount of cash must be fixed (or determinable) by contract or agreement.

Cash and cash equivalents are obviously *monetary*. Accounts and notes receivable and payable also are monetary items; their amount has been fixed or predetermined through a transaction, such as the sale of goods or services, the purchase of goods or services, or the borrowing of a fixed sum of money. In contrast, balances such as inventories and equity investments are not monetary items, even though they eventually will be converted into cash, because their cash value is not fixed in advance. The amount of cash to be obtained from such items will depend on future market conditions.

Monetary items include balances that represent assets and obligations to be received or paid in a *determinable* amount of cash. An example of a *determinable* amount is a cash deposit held in foreign currency. The foreign currency cash deposit (or a foreign current account receivable or payable) represents a claim to a fixed amount of cash, but its value in Canadian dollars is determinable from the exchange rate in effect at the balance sheet date. These balances are monetary items.

# ACCOUNTING FOR CASH

## Cash and Cash Equivalents

**Components of Cash** The cash account includes only those items immediately available to pay obligations. Cash includes balances on deposit with financial institutions, coins and currency, petty cash, and certain negotiable instruments accepted by financial institutions for immediate deposit and withdrawal, like cashier's cheques, certified cheques, and money orders. Technically, recently deposited cheques from customers on account are not cash until the company is sure that they are "good," but few companies make any adjustment in this area and classify outstanding deposits and recent deposits as cash.

**Restricted Cash Accounts** Cash may be held in a separate account because of a legal agreement or legislation requirement. This segregated cash can be used only for a specific purpose. Examples include a bond sinking fund, which can be used only to repay bonds, and asset reclamation funds, which can be used only for environmental restoration. Such cash amounts are shown separately, and classified as long term or short term in conjunction with the related liability. That is, if the environmental liability is short term, the restricted cash is short term as well.

| | |
|---|---|
| **T-bill** | **Cash Equivalents** Cash equivalents are items that can readily be converted to cash. In Chapter 5, cash on the cash flow statement was defined as cash plus cash equivalents (and less bank overdrafts). On the balance sheet, cash and cash equivalents are often lumped together, appropriately described. |
| treasury bill; a short-term government security issued at a discount in lieu of interest | |

**Cash Equivalents** Cash equivalents are items that can readily be converted to cash. In Chapter 5, cash on the cash flow statement was defined as cash plus cash equivalents (and less bank overdrafts). On the balance sheet, cash and cash equivalents are often lumped together, appropriately described.

Cash equivalents are limited to temporary investments that are highly liquid and have little risk of price fluctuation—**money market instruments**—but not investments in common or preferred shares. The most common examples of cash equivalents are treasury bills (**T-bills**), guaranteed investment certificates (**GICs**), commercial paper (short-term notes receivable from other companies), and money market funds. To be classified as a *cash equivalent*, the term of these investments must be short—three months is suggested—to minimize possible price fluctuations caused by interest rate changes.

**Overdrafts** An **overdraft** is a negative bank account balance. Overdrafts occur when the dollar amount of cheques honoured by the bank exceeds the account balance. An overdraft is reported as a separate current liability on the balance sheet, despite the fact that it may be included as cash on the cash flow statement. Netting is not allowed on the balance sheet.

---

**guaranteed investment certificate (GIC)**

a certificate showing that a deposit of a specified amount has been made at a financial institution for a specific period of time, at a specified interest rate

However, if a depositor overdraws an account but has positive balances in other accounts *with that bank*, it is appropriate to offset the negative and positive balances on the balance sheet as long as:

- The bank has the legal right to offset, which is usual; *and*
- The company plans to settle the overdraft in this way—by a transfer from one of the other accounts.

Accounts with different financial institutions may not be offset against each other, since they fail the first condition, above. For example, Loblaw indicates that it complies with the criteria listed above, in the disclosure notes to the financial statements:

> Cash balances which the company has the ability and intent to offset are used to reduce reported bank indebtedness.

**Compensating Balances**  A **compensating balance** is a minimum balance that must be maintained in a depositor's account as support for funds borrowed by the depositor. Technically, compensating balances are long term, and should not be included in the current cash account because they are not currently available for use. Many companies include these balances in cash and disclose the restrictions in notes to the financial statements. Either disclosure option avoids overstating the firm's liquidity position.

**Foreign Currency**  The Canadian dollar value of cash holdings in foreign currency fluctuates with changes in the relevant exchange rate. To get the Canadian dollar equivalent, it is necessary to multiply the amount of foreign currency by the *current exchange rate.*

For example, assume that DGF Group Limited has a U.S. bank account, with US$4,500 on deposit at year-end. The money was received as a result of a cash sale that took place when the exchange rate was US$1.00 = C$1.17, and was recorded at a Canadian dollar amount of $5,265:

| | | |
|---|---|---|
| Cash, U.S. dollars [$4,500 × $1.17] | 5,265 | |
| Sales | | 5,265 |

At the end of the year, the exchange rate is US$1.00 = Cdn$1.14. The current Canadian dollar equivalency must be established:

| | | |
|---|---|---|
| Exchange loss | 135 | |
| Cash, U.S. dollars [$4,500 × ($1.14 − $1.17)] | | 135 |

The cash is included on the balance sheet at the 31 December exchange rate, $1.14, or $5,130. Of course, foreign cash holdings can be converted to the current exchange rate every time the rate changes, but this is a lot of extra work, and valuation is usually important only at reporting dates.

Only foreign currencies convertible to Canadian dollars without restriction are included in cash. Restricted currency balances (e.g., foreign currency in a bank account in a foreign country that cannot be converted to another currency and/or spent anywhere except locally) are reported as other assets because they cannot be readily accessed.

## Internal Control over Cash

The need to safeguard cash is crucial. Cash can be stolen in a lot of creative ways in addition to simply being physically picked up; for example, cheques can be issued to fictitious suppliers. The risk of theft is directly related to the ability of individuals to access the accounting system

**internal control system**

system of organizational design meant to safeguard assets and the integrity of the accounting system

and obtain custody of cash. Firms address this problem through an **internal control system**, designed to protect all assets and the integrity of the information system. A sound internal control system for cash increases the likelihood that the reported values for cash and cash equivalents are accurate and may be relied on by financial statement users.

A fundamental principle of internal control is *division of duties*—the person who handles cash must not keep the books. This is also called "segregation of duties." The functions of cash handling and record keeping must be separated, so it will be difficult to embezzle cash unless two people agree together (or *collude*) to take the money. Internal control is built largely on the principle that dishonest collusion is significantly less likely than individual action.

## ETHICAL ISSUES

If the bookkeeper handles cash, it is both possible and occasionally tempting for him or her to set cash aside for personal use and cover up the cash shortage by making a fictitious entry in the books. In a large enterprise, quite a large amount of cash (in personal terms) can go missing before anyone starts to notice. Modest embezzlement may unfortunately go undetected for years.

**bank reconciliation**

a schedule that analyzes the firm's cash account versus the bank's reported cash amount to ensure that transaction recording is complete and accurate; one means of internal control

**Bank Reconciliation as Internal Control**  By comparing the bank account to the cash general ledger account, the company can ensure that the books are being kept accurately. The **bank reconciliation** provides the correct cash balance for the balance sheet and information for adjusting entries. Since cash forms a part of so many transactions, the accuracy of the cash account is often a good surrogate for the accuracy of other accounts. Thus, the bank reconciliation is an important internal control. Of course, it is crucial that the individual who is in charge of cheques and/or deposits is not also in charge of the bank reconciliation—it would be too easy to cover up something. It is not appropriate for individuals to check their own work; there is no segregation of duties.

**Bank Reconciliation Adjustments**  A bank reconciliation begins with the two cash balances (bank and book), lists the specific items that are different between those balances, and ends with the true cash balance, as follows:

| Adjustments to the Bank Balance | Adjustments to the Book Balance (Adjustments to be Journalized) |
|---|---|
| *Starting point:* Cash balance per the bank statement | *Starting point:* Balance per the books |
| *Add:* Outstanding deposits | *Add:* Deposits recorded by the bank but not yet recorded by the company (e.g., customers that paid by direct deposit) |
| *Deduct:* Outstanding cheques | *Deduct:* Charges recorded by the bank but not yet recorded by the company (e.g., service charges, customers' cheques returned NSF) |
| *Add or deduct:* Bank errors in recording transactions | *Add or deduct:* Company errors in recording transactions |
| *Ending point:* Adjusted cash balance | *Ending point:* Adjusted cash balance |

The adjustments to the book balance usually represent transactions processed by the bank that the company has not yet recorded, or that the company has improperly recorded.

These items are journalized to retain the accuracy of the accounting records. Bank reconciliations are illustrated in the Appendix to this chapter.

**Reporting**  Cash and cash equivalents are reported as the first asset on the balance sheet. Companies are required to show the components of cash, which they often do in conjunction with the cash flow statement. Others provide a breakdown in the disclosure notes. For instance, Petro-Canada, in its 31 December 2006 financial statements, provides disclosure of the components of its cash account, including a separate deduction for the cash held by a discontinued operation, since the assets of discontinued operations are classified as "other assets":

| Note 13 Cash and Cash Equivalents | | |
| --- | --- | --- |
| | **2006** | **2005** |
| Cash | $ 42 | $ 48 |
| Short-term investments | 457 | 741 |
| | 499 | 789 |
| Less: discontinued operations | — | 68 |
| | $499 | $721 |

## CONCEPT REVIEW

1. What is the definition of monetary items?
2. What is the valuation problem for cash that is in a foreign currency?
3. What is a basic principle of internal control?
4. Why is it necessary to perform a regular bank reconciliation?

## ACCOUNTING FOR RECEIVABLES

Receivables represent claims for money, goods, services, and other non-cash assets from other firms. Receivables may be current or non-current, depending on the expected collection date. Accounts receivable, also called **trade accounts receivable**, are amounts owed by customers for goods and services sold in the firm's normal course of business. These receivables are supported by sales invoices or other documents rather than by formal written promises to pay, and they include amounts expected to be collected either during the year following the balance sheet date or within the firm's operating cycle.

**non-trade receivable**

cash due to a corporation from transactions other than the sale of goods and services

**Notes receivable** are also amounts receivable but are usually supported by formal promissory notes. **Non-trade receivables** arise from many other sources, such as tax refunds, contracts, investments, finance receivables, instalment notes, sale of assets, and advances to employees. The main accounting issues pertaining to receivables are *recognition* and *measurement*. Both are affected by collectibility.

### Recognition and Measurement of Accounts Receivable

Accounts receivable are recorded only when the recognition criteria are met. That is, the amounts have to be probable, measurable, and collectible. Accounts receivable are valued at the original exchange price between the firm and an outside party. Generally, a 30- to 60-day period is allowed for payment, beyond which the account is considered past due.

Individual accounts receivable for customers with *credit balances* (from prepayments or overpayments) are reclassified and reported as *liabilities* on the balance sheet if they are material. Credit balances should not be netted against other accounts receivable, but netting is a common practice if the amounts are small (i.e., immaterial).

The receivable balance is meant to be an approximation of the cash that will be collected. Say a company has $2,000,000 in accounts receivable at the end of 20X8. This may not be the amount of money it will actually collect. Usually adjustments have to be made at year-end to reduce receivables to net realizable value, for things like:

- Cash discounts;
- Sales returns and allowances; and
- Allowance for uncollectible accounts.

**Cash Discounts**  Companies frequently offer a cash discount, or sales discount, for payment received within a designated period. Cash discounts are used to increase sales, encourage early payment by the customer, and increase the likelihood of collection. Sales terms might be 2/10, n/30, which means that the customer is given a 2% cash discount if payment is made within 10 days from sale; otherwise, the full amount net of any returns or allowances is due in 30 days. Theoretically, the sale and the receivable should be recorded at the lowest cash price, or the net amount after deducting the discount. This would be $980 for a $1,000 sale, if the discount for prompt payment is 2%. In practice, though, sales are usually recorded gross, because it is easier to relate the account receivable to the (gross) invoice if they are the same amount.

Under the gross method, if material cash discounts are expected to be taken on outstanding accounts receivable at year-end, an adjusting entry is required to decrease net sales and to reduce accounts receivable to the estimated amount collectible. To illustrate, assume that the $2 million of accounts receivable mentioned above all have terms of 2/10, n/30, and are recorded gross. Management expects 60% of these accounts to be collected within the discount period. There is no balance in an allowance account. The adjusting entry on 31 December 20X8:

| | | |
|---|---|---|
| Sales discounts [$2,000,000 × 2% × 60%] | 24,000 | |
|     Allowance for sales discounts | | 24,000 |

The sales discounts account is a contra account to sales. The allowance account is a contra account to accounts receivable, and reduces accounts receivable to the net cash value. If there had been a $3,000 credit balance in the allowance account prior to this entry, the entry would have been made for $21,000 ($24,000 − $3,000).

During 20X9, assuming that the estimates were correct, a summary entry reflects the receipts.

| | | |
|---|---|---|
| Allowance for sales discounts | 24,000 | |
| Cash | 1,176,000 | |
|     Accounts receivable [$2,000,000 × 60%] | | 1,200,000 |

Alternatively, and more commonly, the sales discounts account can be directly debited when customers use discounts during the year, and the allowance can be adjusted at the end of each reporting period.

**Sales Returns and Allowances**  Return privileges are frequently part of a comprehensive marketing program required to maintain competitiveness. Sales returns occur when merchandise is returned by the customer; sales *allowances* occur when a company gives a price reduction to a customer who is not completely satisfied with purchased merchandise but does not actually return it.

Sales returns and allowances are significant amounts in some industries, including retailing and book publishing. Of course, if returns are material and unestimable, sales revenue cannot be recorded until after the uncertainty is resolved. This issue was discussed in Chapter 6. This chapter deals with the more likely case, *estimable returns*, and the problem again is to reduce receivables to their probable cash flow or *net realizable value*, which is net of returns. Sales returns and allowances reduce both net accounts receivable and net sales.

The company must estimate and recognize the returns and allowances expected for the accounts receivable outstanding at the end of 20X8. Assume that total estimated sales returns and allowances relating to the closing receivables balance is $9,000, and there is no balance in the allowance for sales returns account. The company records an adjusting entry on 31 December 20X8:

| | | |
|---|---|---|
| Sales returns and allowances | 9,000 | |
|     Allowance for sales returns and allowances | | 9,000 |

If there had been a $5,000 credit balance in the allowance account prior to this entry, the entry would have been made for $4,000 ($9,000 − $5,000). Note that the sales returns and allowances account is a contra account to sales and the allowance is a contra account to accounts receivable.

As accounts receivable that arose in 20X8 are reduced in 20X9 because of returns, the reduction in accounts receivable can be charged to the allowance account. It is usually easier, though, to charge the reduction directly to the sales returns and allowances account and adjust the balance in the allowance account at the end of each reporting period.

**Allowance for Doubtful Accounts**  When credit is extended, some amount of uncollectible receivables is generally inevitable. Firms attempt to develop a credit policy that is neither too conservative (leading to excessive lost sales) nor too liberal (leading to excessive uncollectible accounts). Past records of payment and the financial position of customers are key factors to consider.

If uncollectible receivables are both likely and estimable, an amount of uncollectible accounts must be recognized, so that accounts receivable and net income are not overstated. This is a form of asset valuation that is a common theme in accounting for assets: at the end of the accounting period, you must ensure that assets are not overvalued.

Because accounting recognition criteria require companies to anticipate a writedown before actually giving up on a particular account, the writedown is made to an allowance account, called the **allowance for doubtful accounts**. That is, individual accounts are not credited at this point because the company doesn't know which accounts will turn out to be uncollectible—if the company knew which accounts would go bad, it wouldn't have sold to those customers in the first place! Estimated uncollectibles are recorded in *bad debt expense*, an operating expense usually classified as a selling expense.

If uncollectible accounts are likely to arise and are estimable, an adjusting entry is needed at the end of an accounting period. For example, if our company estimates that $120,000 of the $2,000,000 in receivables will not be collected, and the existing credit balance in the allowance account is $12,000, the adjusting entry is as follows:

**allowance for doubtful accounts**

a contra account to accounts receivable that represents the portion of outstanding receivables whose collection is doubtful

| | | |
|---|---|---|
| Bad debt expense | 108,000 | |
|     Allowance for doubtful accounts | | 108,000 |

Notice that both net income and net assets decline on this entry: this is expense recognition, after all.

This estimate of uncollectible amounts is made at the end of the year, but takes into consideration all facts known at the date of the review. For example, if a customer went into bankruptcy in January, the allowance established for the 31 December accounts receivable, estimated in January as the financial statements are finalized, would include the customer's likely uncollectible balance. This is an example of a subsequent event that must be recorded in the current year.

**Write-Offs** Two other events must be considered:

1. The write-off of a specific receivable; and

2. The collection of an account previously written off.

The adjusting entry for bad debt expense creates the allowance for doubtful accounts for future uncollectible accounts. When specific accounts are determined to be uncollectible, they are removed from the accounts receivable and that part of the allowance is no longer needed. The bad debt estimation entry had previously recognized the estimated economic effect of future uncollectible accounts. Thus, write-offs of specific accounts do not further reduce net assets unless they exceed the estimate.

For example, the following entry is recorded by a company deciding not to pursue collection of R. Knox's $1,000 account:

| | | |
|---|---|---|
| Allowance for doubtful accounts | 1,000 | |
| Accounts receivable, R. Knox | | 1,000 |

This write-off entry affects neither income nor the net amount of accounts receivable outstanding. Instead, it is the culmination of the process that began with the adjusting entry to estimate bad debt expense. The write-off entry changes only the components of net accounts receivable, not the net amount itself (amounts assumed):

| | Before Knox Write-Off | After Knox Write-Off |
|---|---|---|
| Accounts receivable | 2,000,000 | $1,999,000 |
| Allowance for doubtful accounts | (120,000) | (119,000) |
| Net accounts receivable | $1,880,000 | $1,880,000 |

When amounts are received on account after a write-off, the write-off entry is reversed to reinstate the receivable and cash collection is recorded. Assume that R. Knox is able to pay $600 on account some time after the above write-off entry was recorded. These entries are required:

| | | |
|---|---|---|
| Accounts receivable, R. Knox | 600 | |
| Allowance for doubtful accounts | | 600 |
| Cash | 600 | |
| Accounts receivable, R. Knox | | 600 |

The net effect of these two entries is to increase cash and *reinstate* the allowance for doubtful accounts to the extent of the cash recovery. The reason for reinstating the allowance is that, since $600 cash was collected, the writedown of $1,000 was excessive; the writedown should have been for only $400. The adjustment of $600 to the allowance will have a direct (or indirect) effect on the amount of bad debt expense later recorded.

**Reporting** The balance sheet presentation of net accounts receivable provides focus on the realizable cash amount.

| Accounts receivable, net | $1,847,000 |
|---|---|

The net balance is $2,000,000 less the $24,000 allowance for cash discounts, less the $9,000 allowance for sales returns, and less the $120,000 allowance for doubtful accounts.

Accounting standards do not require the amount of any allowances to be disclosed. Disclosure is required concerning:

- Amounts of ordinary trade accounts;
- Amounts owing by related parties;
- Other unusual items of substantial amount; and
- Amounts and maturity dates of instalment receivables.

Accounts receivable are financial instruments, and therefore the following information must be presented:

1. The *accounting policies used;*

2. The *fair value,* which would be carrying value after deducting allowances;

3. The *nature and extent of risks* arising from things such as credit risk and currency risk.

In some cases, concentration of credit risk in certain geographic locations or with certain customers might be appropriate. For instance, the following breakdown according to type of currency is provided in the 2007 Bombardier Incorporated financial statements:

## 1. Receivables

| Receivables were as follows as at January 31: | 2007 | 2006 |
|---|---|---|
| Trade receivables[1] | | |
|   Aerospace | | |
|     U.S. dollar | $ 660 | $ 603 |
|     Other currencies | 45 | 26 |
|   Transportation | | |
|     Euro | 322 | 384 |
|     U.S. dollar | 291 | 171 |
|     Sterling pound | 86 | 145 |
|     Various Western European currencies | 105 | 67 |
|     Other currencies | 121 | 123 |
| | 1,630 | 1,519 |
| Sales tax | 49 | 57 |
| Other | 189 | 209 |
| | 1,868 | 1,785 |
| Allowance for doubtful accounts | (79) | (101) |
| | $1,789 | $1,684 |

[1] Trade receivables are presented based on the invoicing currency.

*Source:* www.sedar.com, Bombardier Inc. 2006 Annual Report released March 28, 2007, pages 26–137.

## Calculation of the Allowance for Doubtful Accounts

The previous section illustrated that when an allowance for doubtful accounts is established, the entry increases bad debt expense and increases the allowance. There are two approaches to determining how to get the amount of the entry: the "TO" and the "BY" methods.

**aging method**

a method of estimating uncollectible accounts receivable and bad debt expense by applying probability estimates of non-collection to specific balances that have been classified by age; the allowance for doubtful accounts is increased to the desired balance

**credit sales method**

a method of estimating uncollectible accounts receivable by establishing the percentage of sales that are historically uncollectible; the allowance for doubtful accounts is increased by this amount

*Aging method* (*TO a calculated balance*): Accounts receivables can be examined item by item, or aged, or analyzed statistically, category by category, to determine net realizable value and the size of an appropriate allowance. The allowance is then increased TO this amount, which involves a consideration of the opening balance. This is formally called the **aging method**.

*Credit sales method* (*BY a calculated amount*): Bad debt experience over time can be correlated to credit sales, to establish a percentage of sales that is normally uncollectible. The allowance is then increased BY this amount, irrespective of the opening balance. This is formally called the **credit sales method**.

Exhibit 7-1 presents background information for several examples. The $500 debit balance in Rally's allowance account does not necessarily indicate that past estimates of bad debt losses were too low, although this is one explanation. Alternatively, it is possible that some receivables originating in 20X2 were written off and the debit balance does not yet reflect the estimate for bad debts based on 20X2 sales.

**Aging Method** This method emphasizes the net realizable value of net accounts receivable and uses historical data to estimate the percentage of accounts receivable expected to become uncollectible. Exhibit 7-2 illustrates Rally's aging schedule and the application of the collection loss percentages. The $177,500 receivable balance is divided into four age classifications with a collection loss percentage applied to each age category. This percentage is usually based on past experience. Rally's collection loss percentages (logically) increase with the age of the accounts, because when accounts are collected, good accounts are removed from each category, and what is left is more likely to be uncollectible.

The computation in Exhibit 7-2 indicates that the allowance account should be increased TO $5,690 (credit). Because the allowance balance is $500 (debit) before adjustment, the entry is for $6,190, yielding an ending $5,690 balance.

---

## EXHIBIT 7-1

### RALLY COMPANY

### Information for Bad Debt Estimation Examples

| | |
|---|---:|
| 1 January 20X2 balances: | |
| Accounts receivable (debit) | $101,300 |
| Allowance for doubtful accounts (credit) | 3,300 |
| Transactions during 20X2: | |
| Credit sales | 500,000 |
| Cash sales | 700,000 |
| Collections on accounts receivable | 420,000 |
| Accounts written off as uncollectible during 20X2 | 3,800 |

After posting of sales, collections, and write-offs, accounts receivable and the allowance for doubtful accounts appear as follows:

#### Accounts Receivable

| | | | |
|---|---:|---|---:|
| 1 Jan. 20X2 balance | 101,300 | Collections | 420,000 |
| Credit sales | 500,000 | Write-offs | 3,800 |
| 31 Dec. 20X2 balance | 177,500 | | |

#### Allowance for Doubtful Accounts

| | | | |
|---|---:|---|---:|
| Write-offs | 3,800 | 1 Jan. 20X2 balance | 3,300 |
| 31 Dec. 20X2 balance *before* adjustments | 500 | | |

> ━━━━━━━━━━━ **EXHIBIT 7-2** ━━━━━━━━━━━

## RALLY COMPANY
## Accounts Receivable Aging Schedule

31 December 20X2

| Customer account | Balance 31 Dec. 20X2 | Age of account balance | | | |
| --- | --- | --- | --- | --- | --- |
| | | Current | 31–60 days | 61–90 days | Over 90 days |
| Denk | $       500 | $       400 | $       100 | | |
| Evans | 900 | 900 | | | |
| Field | 1,650 | | 1,350 | $       300 | |
| Harris | 90 | | | 30 | $       60 |
| King | 800 | 700 | 60 | 40 | |
| Zabot | 250 | 250 | | | |
| Total | $177,500 | $110,000 | $31,000 | $29,500 | $7,000 |
| Percent estimated uncollectible | | 0.2% | 1.0% | 8.0% | 40.0% |
| Amount estimated uncollectible | | $       220 | $       310 | $   2,360 | $2,800 |

**Total amount to include in allowance: $220 + $310 + $2,360 + $2,800 = $5,690**

---

| | | |
| --- | --- | --- |
| Bad debt expense [$5,690 + $500] | 6,190 | |
| Allowance for doubtful accounts | | 6,190 |

Had the allowance balance been a $500 credit before adjustment, bad debt expense would have been $5,190 ($5,690 − $500). Since the allowance is $5,690, net accounts receivable will be shown on the balance sheet at $171,810 ($177,500 − $5,690).

Aging may be more cumbersome than is warranted, and a composite rate, based on the accounts receivable total, may be used. Assume that experience leads Rally Company (Exhibit 7-1) to use a single 3% composite rate. Therefore, the required ending allowance credit balance is $5,325 (3% × $177,500). The allowance account currently has a $500 debit balance, so the adjusting entry increases the allowance account TO $5,325 through an entry for $5,825 ($5,325 + $500).

| | | |
| --- | --- | --- |
| Bad debt expense [$5,325 + $500] | 5,825 | |
| Allowance for doubtful accounts | | 5,825 |

The estimated net realizable value of accounts receivable is $172,175 in this case, a reasonable approximation.

**Credit Sales Method**  This method emphasizes the matching principle and the income statement. The average percentage relationship between actual bad debt losses and net credit sales is estimated on the basis of experience. The percentage must be updated periodically to approximate the rate of actual write-offs. Once established, the percentage is applied to a period's net credit sales to determine bad debt expense.

Assume that in the past, 1.2% of Rally's credit sales have not been collected. Barring changes in Rally's credit policies or major changes in the economy, Rally expects this rate to continue. Under this method, the following is the required 20X2 adjusting entry, which increases the allowance BY a percentage of credit sales.

| | | |
|---|---|---|
| Bad debt expense [$500,000 × 1.2%] | 6,000 | |
|    Allowance for doubtful accounts | | 6,000 |

After this entry is posted, the balance in the allowance account is $5,500 ($6,000 from the adjusting entry less the prior $500 debit balance). This method directly computes bad debt expense *without regard to the prior balance in the allowance account*. Rally would disclose $172,000 ($177,500 − $5,500) of net accounts receivable in the 20X2 balance sheet.

**Evaluation of Methods** Either method of estimation is acceptable for financial reporting as long as the resulting allowance is reasonable. Statistical support for the rates used to establish the allowance under either method helps establish this reasonableness.

The credit sales and aging methods may be used together. Each is used to validate the other, although only one may be used in the accounts. For interim financial statements, many companies base monthly or quarterly adjusting entries on the credit sales method because of its low cost. At the end of the year, they may age their accounts receivable to check the reasonableness of the allowance balance. It is also fairly standard to evaluate the allowance with reference to major accounts receivable in various categories, in conjunction with the year-end audit or review. This evaluation uses all known facts at the date of the review including subsequent payments and defaults.

The general condition of the economy, the economic health of specific customers, and the seller's credit policy and collection effort affect the rate of account write-offs. Over time, this rate changes, necessitating adjustment to the percentages applied to credit sales or receivables. If the balance in allowance for doubtful accounts is found to increase each year, the estimate of uncollectibles is decreased to reflect actual experience. Alternatively, if the allowance is inadequate, future estimates will increase.

## Direct Write-off of Uncollectible Accounts

In some circumstances, receivables are written off directly, with no allowance used. No adjusting entry is made at the end of an accounting period under the direct write-off method. Instead, bad debt expense is recognized only when an account is eventually acknowledged to be finally uncollectible. The entry for the direct write-off of a $2,000 account receivable from M. Lynx is as follows:

| | | |
|---|---|---|
| Bad debt expense | 2,000 | |
|    Accounts receivable, M. Lynx | | 2,000 |

The inability to estimate uncollectible accounts creates several unavoidable problems:

- Receivables are reported on the balance sheet at a value higher than their net realizable value, because it is virtually certain that not all receivables are collectible.
- The write-off is often recorded in a different year than the original sale that created the account receivable, violating the matching principle. At the extreme, if bad debts are material and inestimable, revenue cannot be recognized until the uncertainty is cleared up—usually on collection.
- Direct write-off opens the potential for income manipulation by arbitrary selection of the year in which to record the write-off.

For these reasons, only *new operations with no basis to estimate bad debts*, or those with *immaterial bad debts*, may use the direct write-off method.

# SPEEDING CASH FLOW FROM RECEIVABLES

## Credit Card Transactions

At one point in time, many retail stores offered credit to customers—in fact, some built a business primarily on offering credit. (For example, consider People's Credit Jewellers, now usually just called People's.) Now, most retailers prefer to get their money up front, and let the customers owe the credit card company. Retailers are charged a fee for the privilege, a percentage of the total sale, but prefer this charge because they avoid bad debts, there is no delay in receiving cash, and they hope that customers will spend more when they can charge their purchases. Except for the corner variety store and some coffee shops, there aren't many cash-only businesses these days. Retail customers expect to be able to use credit cards.

Other retailers have gone to the other extreme, and expanded their credit-granting operations into separate credit card companies. These operations make money by charging interest on overdue accounts. Their largest expenses are the cost of money and bad debts.

Visa and Mastercard are the two primary independent credit card companies. Merchants enter into contracts with these companies, agreeing on fees and payment arrangements. When automated point-of-sale systems are used, the merchant receives money the same day, through direct deposit to the company's bank account.

Assume that a merchant has $2,000 in credit card sales. The credit card company deducts a commission of a contracted amount for its services and the money is electronically transferred. Assuming that the fee is 2% in this example, the appropriate entry is as follows:

| | | |
|---|---:|---:|
| Cash | 1,960 | |
| Credit card fees expense [$2,000 × 2%] | 40 | |
|     Sales | | 2,000 |

Alternatively, a merchant will accumulate credit card sales in batches, for low-volume credit cards. Credit card vouchers are submitted by mail or deposited with a bank acting as agent for the credit card company. The company receives its money by cheque or direct deposit, after the request is reviewed and processed.

## Debit Card Transactions

Most merchants also accept debit cards. The primary difference between a debit card and a credit card is from the point of view of the customer: a debit card will remove the transaction amount immediately from the customer's bank account. The merchant has to go through the same motions as with credit cards: an agreement must be negotiated with the sponsoring financial institution for a fee (again a percentage of the transaction amount) and payment terms. All transactions are authorized through automated point-of-sale systems, and the merchant receives the cash immediately through direct deposit. No receivables are created; this is like a cash sale with a fee for the merchant attached.

## Loans Secured by Accounts Receivable

If a company has a $100,000 account receivable from a creditworthy customer that will not pay for 45 days, how can the company get cash sooner? First, it would be nice if the customer would pay sooner, and a variety of policies are usually explored to speed collection. Then what? One common course of action is to go to a bank and borrow money using the account receivable as collateral.

This isn't very complicated on the books: a loan is recorded, and interest expense will be accrued as time passes. When the account is collected, the bank is repaid. Assets pledged as collateral are disclosed in the financial statements. Of course, it is less common to make credit arrangements for one receivable at a time: the overall balance of accounts receivable, and usually inventory, too, are used to secure working capital loans. These loans are a relatively permanent part of most companies' financial structure.

## Transfer of Accounts Receivable

Accounts receivable can also be *transferred* to a financial institution to speed cash flow. This is sometimes called *factoring*. A transfer of accounts receivable can be recorded as a sale or a borrowing. These two arrangements are described as follows:

1. *A sale.* The accounts receivable come off the books of the selling company, and a financing fee is recognized.

2. *A borrowing.* The accounts receivable are left on the books of the selling company, and the amount received from the finance company is recorded as a loan until the customer actually pays.

To illustrate a transfer recorded as a sale, consider the following case. Largo Incorporated sells $200,000 of accounts receivable on 15 August 20X2. The buyer is a finance company. The finance company charges a 12% financing fee. The entry to record the *sale* is:

| Largo Incorporated | | | Finance Company | | |
|---|---|---|---|---|---|
| Cash | 176,000* | | Accounts receivable | 200,000 | |
| Financing expense | 24,000** | | Deferred financing revenue*** | | 24,000 |
| Accounts receivable | | 200,000 | Cash | | 176,000 |

*$200,000 − (12% × $200,000)
**12% × $200,000; expensed immediately
***Deferred and recognized over the collection period.

This looks relatively straightforward. Accounts receivable can be sold, like any other asset![1]

Now, what if an identical transaction was recorded as a *borrowing*?

| Largo Incorporated | | | Finance Company | | |
|---|---|---|---|---|---|
| Cash | 176,000 | | Note receivable | 200,000 | |
| Discount on note payable | 24,000 | | Discount on note receivable | | 24,000 |
| Note payable | | 200,000 | Cash | | 176,000 |

*Notice that both the accounts receivable and the loan are reported on Largo's books.* The discount is amortized to finance/interest expense and revenue over the life of the note. When the receivables are collected, the money is remitted to the finance company, and the note is repaid:

---

[1] To simplify this, and the following examples, no consideration is given to the likely sales discounts or returns that are inherent in the receivables balance. In a real situation, the finance company would hold back an allowance for this cause, and settle up with the company at the end of the arrangement. Such refinements do not change the substance of the transaction.

| Largo Incorporated | | | Finance Company | | |
|---|---|---|---|---|---|
| Cash | 200,000 | | | | |
|    Accounts receivable | | 200,000 | | | |
| Notes payable | 200,000 | | Cash | 200,000 | |
|    Cash | | 200,000 |    Notes receivable | | 200,000 |
| Financing expense* | 24,000 | | Discount on notes receivable | 24,000 | |
|    Discount on notes payable | | 24,000 |    Finance revenue* | | 24,000 |
| *recognized as time passes | | | | | |

**notification basis**

in the transfer of accounts receivable to a third party, the original customer is informed of the transfer and makes payment to the third party

**Terms** Agreements to sell receivables are made either on a **notification basis** (customers are directed to remit to the new party holding the receivables, the finance company) or a **non-notification basis** (customers continue to remit to the original seller, which then, in turn, remits to the finance company). The Largo example above was an example of a non-notification arrangement since the customer paid Largo.

Receivables can be transferred with recourse, or without recourse. **Recourse** means that the finance company can come back to the company that sold the account receivable for payment if the account turns out to be uncollectible. Recourse arrangements often allow the company to replace defaulted receivables with "good ones" in the event of default. This may be part of a *removal of accounts provision* (ROAP).

**recourse**

in the assignment of accounts receivable, the right of a third-party financer to demand reimbursement from the transferor of receivables if they prove uncollectible

**Criteria for Classification** Sale versus borrowing accounting represent radically different views of the substance of the transaction, and will significantly change financial statement relationships, such as the current ratio. Current Canadian standards require that a transfer of receivables will be accounted for as a sale as long as:

1. The transferred receivables have been *legally isolated*, or put beyond the legal reach of the company (deemed the **transferor**), even in the event of bankruptcy;

2. The finance company (the **transferee**) has the unrestricted right to *pledge the assets* in other loan transactions, or even resell them, without conditions attached by the transferor; and

**transferee**

in the transfer of accounts receivable to a third party, the third-party entity that receives the accounts receivable; the finance company

3. The transferor does not *maintain effective control* over the transferred receivables, which means that there is *no repurchase arrangement* that allows or permits the transferor to repurchase the receivables.

If control has irrevocably passed, it seems obvious that the amount of consideration (the proceeds) must be set. Measurable consideration is not on the above list, but it is a natural part of any recognition decision.

You should understand that the complexity of these arrangements, with their extensive call and put options, makes accounting in this area very specialized. This discussion only scratches the surface. Several examples follow.

**transferor**

in the transfer of accounts receivable to a third party, the entity that delivers the accounts receivable; the company that has the account receivable

*Case 1 Transfer recorded as a sale.* Assume that Largo sells $200,000 of accounts receivable to a finance company with recourse on 15 August 20X2. A ROAP clause is included in the agreement. The parties agree that uncollectible accounts will amount to $3,000; that is, Largo will replace any account over the first $3,000 that proves uncollectible. This $3,000 amount is already in the allowance for doubtful accounts. The financing fee is 6%. (The prior example had a rate of 12%; note that financing costs are lower when there is recourse).

Assume that conditions are met to record this transfer as a sale. The difference between the book value of receivables transferred and assets received from the finance company is recognized immediately as an expense.

| | | |
|---|---:|---:|
| Cash {$200,000 − $3,000 − [6% × ($200,000 − $3,000)]} | 185,180 | |
| Allowance for doubtful accounts* | 3,000 | |
| Financing expense** [6% × ($200,000 − $3,000)] | 11,820 | |
| Accounts receivable | | 200,000 |

*Or, bad debt expense if not already part of allowance estimate.
**Also perhaps called "a loss on sale of receivables."

Largo receives $197,000, the net "good" receivables balance, less the $11,820 financing fee on $197,000. The allowance for doubtful accounts is reduced.

When there is recourse, *there will be a final reckoning with the finance company.* If the finance company collects exactly $197,000, the transaction is over. If the finance company collects less, Largo will have to provide new receivables for the deficit, because there is recourse and a ROAP clause is in effect. If the finance company collects more than $197,000, Largo will get a cheque. If arrangements met the criteria for a sale, collection estimates should have been accurate enough so that the final reckoning is immaterial.

*Case 2* *Transfer recorded as a borrowing.* In a transfer recorded as a borrowing, receivables stay on the books, and a loan is recorded. The transferor recognizes the difference between the assets received from the finance company and the book value of the receivables as interest *over the term of the loan.* This is in contrast to the sale example, in which the financing fee was immediately recognized as an expense. Assume the same facts as Case 1, except that Largo retains the option to repurchase the receivables. This means that the transaction is recorded as a borrowing. Entries to record the borrowing and estimated uncollectible accounts are:

| | | |
|---|---:|---:|
| Cash {$200,000 − $3,000 − [6% × ($200,000 − $3,000)]} | 185,180 | |
| Discount on payable to finance company [6% × ($200,000 − $3,000)] | 11,820 | |
| Payable to finance company | | 197,000 |

The discount account is a contra account to the payable to finance company account and represents the total interest to Largo. This contra account is amortized as interest expense over the loan term. Largo records sales adjustments, such as sales discounts and returns, as they occur and reduces the receivable from the customer and payable to the finance company as customers remit cash. At the end of the arrangement, Largo must pay any outstanding balance on the payable, whether or not customers have remitted on time.

It is worth noting that the payable to the finance company must be shown as a current liability on the balance sheet, and may *not* be netted with the related accounts receivable. Netting is appropriate only when there is a legal right to net, *and* intent to net; while intent is present in this case, there is no legal right to net and the balances must be shown as the separate elements they really are.

**Allowance for Bad Debts**  Review the entry for case 1 again, and note that the allowance for bad debts was debited, because of the $3,000 of problematic accounts transferred. *If the allowance were inadequate, or did not include any provision for these accounts, bad debt expense might be debited.* Similarly, when the transaction is recorded as a loan, there might be an additional allowance of $3,000 set up, with a corresponding debit to bad debt expense, if the allowance were deemed inadequate at this time. However, this decision to acknowledge additional bad debt expense need not be part of the sale or transfer transaction. The adequacy of the allowance is reviewed regularly in the reporting cycle, based on aging or credits sales, and transfer of accounts receivable does not have to disturb this routine. Some companies may choose to record some bad debt expense as needed when accounts are transferred.

**Disclosure** Companies are required to disclose the details of any transfer of accounts receivable, and the extent of their obligations under recourse arrangements. An example of disclosure of sale of accounts receivable in 2007 for Bombardier Inc. is shown in Exhibit 7-3. These transfers are accounted for as a sale.

---

### EXHIBIT 7-3

### Sale of Accounts Receivable Disclosure
### Bombardier Inc.

The Corporation has access to factoring facilities in Europe, under which it can sell without recourse trade receivables in the normal course of business. Under these facilities, the Corporation received proceeds of $298 million during fiscal year 2007 ($408 million during fiscal year 2006). As at January 31, 2007, the outstanding balance of receivables transferred under these facilities amounted to $113 million ($2 million as at January 31, 2006).

---

*Source:* www.sedar.com, Bombardier Inc. 2006 Annual Report released March 28, 2007, pages 26–137.

### Transfer of Accounts Receivable to a VIE

A final alternative for speeding cash flow from accounts receivable is to transfer accounts receivable to a **variable-interest entity** (**VIE**), also called a *special-purpose entity* (SPE). A variable-interest entity is a separate entity that carries out a specific part of a company's business, but is not owned by the company; the VIE has a separate shareholder group. After buying the accounts receivable from the company, the VIE then raises money from investors using the accounts receivable as security. This is referred to as **securitization.** The company gets money for the accounts receivable when they are transferred to the VIE, and records the transaction as a sale.

The use of VIEs may be a legitimate way to segregate a particular kind of asset, and raise money using these assets as collateral at low cost. They may also be used to manipulate financial reporting and keep assets and liabilities off the company's balance sheet. As a result, there are accounting standards that require that a VIE be **consolidated**, in certain circumstances. This topic is covered in depth in advanced accounting courses. However, note that most VIEs established to securitize accounts receivable do not have to be consolidated.

**consolidation**

combining the financial statements of a parent company and its subsidiary/ subsidiaries; fair value on acquisition is established and intercompany transactions are eliminated

---

### CONCEPT REVIEW

1. Why is it necessary to establish an allowance for doubtful accounts?
2. What is the purpose of an aging schedule?
3. Explain the difference between recording the transfer of accounts receivable as a sale versus a borrowing.

## NOTES RECEIVABLE AND PAYABLE

A note receivable is a written promise to pay a specified amount at a specified future date (or a series of amounts over a series of payment dates). Notes receivable are a current asset if the term is a year or an operating cycle; notes payable are a current liability and are the mirror image of receivables. Notes payable are also called "short-term commercial paper," notes issued by large companies with excellent credit ratings, and bought by other companies as temporary investments. Some notes formalize **collateral security** for the lender.

Compared to accounts payable, notes payable usually provide:

- Extended payment terms;
- More security than sales invoices and other commercial trade documents;
- A formal basis for charging interest; and
- Negotiability.

Notes may be non-current assets or liabilities if their term exceeds the cut-off for current classification. Accounting for non-current notes is no different than that explained here; only the classification changes. Remember that classification is as much a function of intent as of term—how long does management mean to hang on to the note?

We'll look at notes receivable and payable together in the material that follows.

**Terminology** Most notes represent loans from financial institutions. Notes also arise from normal sales, extension of the payment period of accounts receivable, exchanges of long-term assets, and advances to employees. The borrower is the *maker* of the note and the lender is the *payee*.

The **face value**, or **maturity value**, is the dollar amount stated on the note. The face value is the amount, excluding interest, payable at the end of the note term, unless the note requires that principal repayments be made according to an instalment schedule. The principal value equals the maturity value if the stated interest rate equals the market interest rate. The total interest over the life of the note equals the total cash receipts less the principal amount.

Notes may be categorized as **interest-bearing** or **non-interest-bearing** notes. Interest-bearing notes specify the interest rate to be applied to the face amount in computing interest payments. Non-interest-bearing notes do not state an interest rate but command interest through the difference between cash lent and (higher) cash repaid.

Interest-bearing notes in turn can be divided into two categories according to the type of cash payment required: (1) notes whose cash payments are interest only, except for final maturity payment and (2) notes whose cash payments are *blended*, and include both interest and principal. Actually, there are an unlimited number of principal and repayment options. Payment schedules are not limited to those used in the examples.

The **stated interest rate** in a note may not equal the market rate prevailing on obligations involving similar credit rating or risk. The **market interest rate** is the rate accepted by two parties for loans of equal profile. If the rate is not given, but the value of the transaction is known, the rate can be determined by equating the present value of the cash flows called for in the note to the market value of the transaction. The rate can be determined with a computer program or calculator that determines the correct rate iteratively—that is, by trial and error.

If notes are for less than a year, low interest rates are ignored, because the effect of interest is immaterial. However, for terms beyond one year, the *market rate is used to value the note and the transaction. The market rate is also used to measure interest revenue or expense.* The stated rate is used to determine the cash interest payments.

## Examples

Notes with stated interest rates below market may be used by companies to increase sales. Accounting for these arrangements involves appropriate recognition of the principal as the proceeds on sale, and interest as time passes.

*Example 1: Interest-bearing note.* On 1 April 20X2, Lionel Company sold merchandise for $12,000 to Baylor Company and received a two-year, 4% note. Interest is payable each 31 March, and the principal is payable at the end of the second year. *The stated and market interest rates are equal.* The entry to record the sale is as follows:

### collateral security

assets of the borrower that the secured lender can seize if the note goes into default

### market interest rate

the prevailing or last quoted interest rate for borrowing or lending identical amounts, with identical credit risk, terms, and conditions

| **Lionel** | | | **Baylor** | | |
|---|---|---|---|---|---|
| 1 April 20X2 | | | 1 April 20X2 | | |
| Note receivable | 12,000 | | Inventory (1) | 12,000 | |
|    Sales (1) | | 12,000 |    Note payable | | 12,000 |
| (1) If this were a loan transaction instead of a sale, Lionel and Baylor would pay or receive cash | | | | | |

Accounting for this note is very simple because the 4% interest rate charged is also the market rate. Cash interest received equals interest revenue recognized over the terms of the note, as indicated in the remaining entries. The computation for interest assumes months of equal length; in real life, interest is accrued by days if it is material.

| **Lionel** | | | **Baylor** | | |
|---|---|---|---|---|---|
| *31 December 20X2 and 20X3—Adjusting entries* | | | | | |
| Interest receivable | 360* | | Interest expense | 360 | |
|    Interest revenue | | 360 |    Interest payable | | 360 |
| *$12,000 × 4% × 9/12 | | | | | |
| | | | | | |
| *31 March 20X3 and 20X4—Interest payments* | | | | | |
| Cash | 480 | | Interest payable | 360 | |
|    Interest receivable | | 360 | Interest expense | 120 | |
|    Interest revenue | | 120* |    Cash | | 480 |
| *$12,000 × 4% × 3/12 | | | | | |

| **Lionel** | | | **Baylor** | | |
|---|---|---|---|---|---|
| *31 March 20X4—Payment at maturity* | | | | | |
| Cash | 12,000 | | Note payable | 12,000 | |
|    Note receivable | | 12,000 |    Cash | | 12,000 |

*Example 2: Different market and stated rates.* Assume the same facts for the Lionel and Baylor $12,000 sale as illustrated in Example 1. This time, though, assume that the market interest rate is 10%. That is, the stated rate on the note is 4%, and the market rate is 10%. Assume also that the inventory sold does not have a readily determinable market value. To value the transaction, it is necessary to calculate the present value of the note, including both principal and interest:

| | |
|---|---|
| Present value of maturity amount: | |
|    $12,000(P/F, 10%, 2) = $12,000(.82645) = | $ 9,917 |
| Present value of the nominal interest payments: | |
|    $480(P/A, 10%, 2) = $480(1.73554) = | 833 |
| Present value of the note at 10% | $10,750 |

Notes are recorded at gross (face) value plus a premium or minus a discount amount (the gross method), or at the net present value (the net method). The two methods are illustrated below.

| 1 April 20X2: | Gross | Net |
|---|---|---|
| For Lionel Company | | |
| Note receivable | 12,000 | 10,750 |
| Discount on note receivable | 1,250 | — |
| Sales (1) | 10,750 | 10,750 |
| For Baylor Company | | |
| Inventory (1) | 10,750 | 10,750 |
| Discount on note payable | 1,250 | — |
| Note payable | 12,000 | 10,750 |

(1) If this were a loan transaction instead of a sale, Lionel and Baylor would pay or receive cash

**effective-interest method**

a measure of interest expense or revenue over the life of a financial instrument not issued at par; measures expense or revenue as a constant rate over the term of the financial instrument

Under either method, the *net book value* of the note is $10,750, the present value. The discount account is a contra account to notes receivable or payable. Since the note is disclosed net of its discount on the balance sheet, the two methods are identical in presentation. In the remaining parts of the example, only the gross method will be illustrated, as it is more comparable with accounting for bonds payable, which you will see in Chapter 12.

In each year of the note, the market rate of interest is applied to the beginning balance of the net note receivable to compute interest. This approach, called the **effective-interest method**, results in a constant rate of interest throughout the life of the note. The calculations may be organized in a table:

| (1)<br><br>Opening Net Liability/Receivable | (2)<br>Interest Expense/ Revenue<br>10% Market Rate<br>(1) × 10% | (3)<br>Interest Paid/ Received<br>4% Stated Rate<br>$12,000 × 4% | (4)<br><br>Discount Amortization<br>(2) − (3) | (5)<br><br>Closing Net Liability/Receivable<br>(1) + (4) |
|---|---|---|---|---|
| $10,750 | $1,075 | $480 | $595 | $11,345 |
| $11,345 | 1,135 | 480 | 655 | 12,000 |

The net notes receivable and payable balance is always the present value of remaining payments. For example, the $11,345 balance is the present value on 31 March 20X3, of the remaining payment (principal plus interest), a payment that is due on 31 March 20X4.

$12,480(P/F, 10%, 1) = $12,480(.90909) = $11,345

If the fiscal year corresponded with the dates of the note, the interest and payment information from this table would correspond directly to the interest entry, that is:

Hypothetical full year entry—31 March 20X3:

| Lionel | | | Baylor | | |
|---|---|---|---|---|---|
| Cash | 480 | | Interest expense | 1,075 | |
| Discount on note receivable | 595 | | Discount on note payable | | 595 |
| Interest revenue | | 1,075 | Cash | | 480 |

Since the fiscal year is different than the dates of the note, accruals must be made that also include discount amortization. In this case, the year-end is 31 December, or 9/12 of the year. The entries at the end of the fiscal year are as follows:

31 December 20X2:

| Lionel | | | Baylor | | |
|---|---|---|---|---|---|
| Interest receivable ($12,000 × 4% × 9/12 ) | 360 | | Interest expense | 806 | |
| Discount on note receivable | 446 | | Discount on note payable | | 446 |
| Interest revenue ($10,750 × 10% × 9/12 ) | | 806 | Interest payable | | 360 |

Entries on cash payment:

31 March 20X3:

| Lionel | | | Baylor | | |
|---|---|---|---|---|---|
| Cash ($12,000 × 4%) | 480 | | Interest expense | 269 | |
| Discount on note receivable | 149 | | Interest payable | 360 | |
| Interest receivable | | 360 | Discount on note payable | | 149 |
| Interest revenue ($10,750 × 10% × 3/12 ) | | 269 | Cash | | 480 |

In the second year of the note:

31 December 20X3:

| Lionel | | | Baylor | | |
|---|---|---|---|---|---|
| Interest receivable | 360 | | Interest expense | 851 | |
| Discount on note receivable | 491 | | Discount on note payable | | 491 |
| Interest revenue ($11,345 × 10% × 9/12 ) | | 851 | Interest payable | | 360 |

Entries on cash payment:

**31 March 20X4:**

| **Lionel** | | | | **Baylor** | | |
|---|---|---|---|---|---|---|
| Cash ($12,000 × 4%) | 480 | | | Interest expense | 284 | |
| Discount on note receivable | 164 | | | Interest payable | 360 | |
|    Interest receivable | | 360 | |    Discount on note payable | | 164 |
|    Interest revenue ($11,345 × | | | |    Cash | | 480 |
|      10% × 3/12 ) | | 284 | | | | |

After the 31 March 20X5 entry, the net notes receivable and payable balance is $12,000, the face value. The discount account balance is zero, and the note is paid.

**31 March 20X4:**

| **Lionel** | | | | **Baylor** | | |
|---|---|---|---|---|---|---|
| Cash | 12,000 | | | Note payable | 12,000 | |
|    Note receivable | | 12,000 | |    Cash | | 12,000 |

*Straight-line measurement of interest expense/revenue.* Another approach to measuring interest, the straight-line method, amortizes an equal amount of discount each period. The straight-line method produces the same interest amount each period, but shows a varying *rate* of interest period by period (that is, "interest ÷ note" will vary). It is less accurate for this reason. However, it is much simpler and may yield results that are not materially different from the effective interest method. In this example, the straight-line method results in discount amortization of $625 ($1,250 ÷ 2 years) and interest revenue or expense of $1,105 ($625 + $480) in both years.

*Example 3: Blended payments.* Consider a 10%, $4,000, two-year note issued by Vancouver Sea Lines that requires interest to be paid on its face value. This is an interest-bearing note, since the annual interest of $400 ($4,000 × 10%) is payable at the end of each year of the note term. The $4,000 face amount is paid at the end of the second year. In total, $800 of interest is required over the term of the note. In notes of this type, the original principal is not decreased by the yearly payment.

Now assume instead that Vancouver's note requires blended payments, involving *two equal* annual amounts payable at the end of each year. These payments each contain some interest and some principal in the amount necessary to discharge the debt at 10% in two payments. The payment is computed as follows:

$4,000 = Present value of an annuity = Payment × (P/A, 10%, 2)
$4,000 ÷ (P/A, 10%, 2) = Payment
$4,000 ÷ 1.73554 = $2,305 = Payment (rounded)

| Payment | Interest Component | Principal Component |
|---|---|---|
| 1 | $400 ($4,000 × 10%) | $1,905 ($2,305 − $400) |
| 2 | 210 ($4,000 − $1,905) × 10% | 2,095 ($2,305 − $210) |
| | $610 | $4,000 |

Total interest for the second type of note ($610) is less than for the first note ($800) because part of the first payment of $2,305 is a principal payment, which reduces the principal on which interest is paid in the second period. Vancouver would record the note and its payments as follows:

| | | |
|---|---|---|
| Initial entry: | | |
| Cash (etc) | 4,000 | |
| Note payable | | 4,000 |
| | | |
| First payment: | | |
| Interest expense | 400 | |
| Note payable | 1,905 | |
| Cash | | 2,305 |
| | | |
| Second payment: | | |
| Interest expense | 210 | |
| Note payable | 2,095 | |
| Cash | | 2,305 |

Sometimes, blended payment notes may not include an explicit disclosure of the interest rate. The implicit interest rate must be calculated before the transaction can be recorded. For example, assume that on 30 June 20X5, a firm sells equipment with a cash price of $10,000 and receives in exchange a note that requires a payment of $6,000 on 30 June 20X6, and another $6,000 on 30 June 20X7. The note does not explicitly mention interest, but $2,000 of interest is implicit in the note ($6,000 × 2) − $10,000. The interest rate is computed using the present value of an annuity as follows:

$$\$10,000 = \$6,000 \times (P/A, \; i, \; 2)$$
$$\$10,000 \div \$6,000 = 1.66667 = (P/A, \; i, \; 2)$$

The value 1.66667 does not appear in the table for the present value of an ordinary annuity, but is almost halfway between the 12% and 14% values; a calculator equipped for present value tells us that $i = 13.066\%$. This rate should be comparable to the rate incurred by the debtor on similar financing.

## Impairment

Notes receivable will be an asset only if the maker of the note pays—both the principal and interest are to be considered in this regard. Revenue cannot be recognized, i.e., interest cannot be accrued, unless it is collected or collectible. An allowance for doubtful notes receivable must be established if the value is impaired.

In calculating the extent of such an allowance, the following information may be considered and compared to the book value of the loan receivable:

1. *The present value of the cash flows expected from the maker of the note over its remaining life.* While some customers will pay nothing, it is quite common to get partial payment, or even complete payment, several months or years late. To assess the fair value of this cash flow, the present value is calculated using the interest rate set for the original loan. If this information is too uncertain to be measured, then the lender also assesses items (2) and (3).

2. *The fair value of any collateral security (assets)* that the lender can legally repossess; this collateral has to be valued at its fair market value.

3. *Observable market prices for the loan;* this information may be available if there is a market for distressed loans.

For example, assume that a note receivable was on the books for $4,800, including both principal and interest, and the customer has encountered financial difficulties. As a result, the cash flows associated with the note are expected to have a present value of $1,200. Some of this will come from a cash payment from the customer, and some from selling repossessed collateral assets. A $3,600 loan loss or bad debt expense is recognized, and an allowance for doubtful accounts is established.

Accounting standards are very technical in this area, because impairment is hard to estimate. It is extremely challenging to make accurate predictions of cash flows to be received from a party in financial difficulty, and to assess appropriate interest revenue recognition on balances as time passes. There is some room to be pessimistic, take large loan losses, and then watch income bounce back with loan loss recoveries.

## Discounting Notes Receivable

**discounting notes receivable**

- the transfer of notes receivable, usually to a financial institution; the purchasing institution reduces the face value of the note plus required interest payments by the interest fee charged to arrive at proceeds

Rather than hold a note receivable to maturity, payees may **discount notes receivable** with a bank or financial institution. Notes can be discounted by any holder, as well as by the original payee, at any time before the note's maturity date. Discounting notes receivable may be done with or without recourse, and the area is similar to the transfer of accounts receivable. The criteria for accounting treatment are the same: the transaction can be recorded as a sale or a borrowing.

The more common outcome for transfer of notes receivable is that the transaction is recorded as a sale—the company records a gain or loss equal to the difference between the proceeds and book value of the note, including accrued interest, and has a contingent liability until the note is paid by the maker.

**Other Arrangements** A common version of this is an arrangement whereby a retail store's sales are immediately financed by a consumer loan company. It's like discounting a note, but skipping a step—the customer directly deals with the finance company. Here's how it works: the customer goes to a store and decides on a purchase. The customer fills in a finance company loan application right in the retail store, and credit is granted by the finance company or not, usually on the spot. The payment scheme may start immediately, or may be deferred for some time (e.g., "Don't Pay a Cent!"). The store receives the present value of the loan agreement from the finance company, less some kind of financing fee, which is usually built into the discount rate. Since the finance company has approved the credit application, it has no recourse to the retail store, whose relationship with the customer is over as soon as the goods are delivered.

## Disclosure

Notes receivable and payable are financial instruments. Information about due dates, payments, and interest rates must be disclosed, as well as:

1. The *accounting policy* used for reporting.

2. The *fair value* for each class, if different from book value. Fair value would be different than book value if interest rates had shifted from the time that the notes were issued, since fair value would be established through present value techniques using current market interest rates.

3. The *nature and extent of risks* arising from financial instruments, including concentration of credit risk.

## CONCEPT REVIEW

1. What is a low-interest loan? How is it valued?

2. What happens to the discount on a note payable over time?

3. What is a blended payment?

## MONETARY LIABILITIES

Current (short-term) liabilities are amounts payable within one year from the date of the balance sheet or within the normal operating cycle, where this is longer than a year. The time dimension (*year* versus *operating cycle*) that applies to current assets also generally applies to current liabilities. Liabilities that are not due within this current time frame are called long-term, or non-current, liabilities. Long-term liabilities are discussed in Chapter 12.

Most current liabilities are monetary items; they obligate the reporting enterprise to pay a fixed sum of cash in the future, sometimes with interest added. Common monetary current liabilities are reviewed in the sections that follow.

### Accounts Payable

**trade accounts payable**

amounts owed to suppliers for goods and services purchased on credit

Accounts payable—more descriptively, **trade accounts payable**—are obligations arising from the firm's ongoing operations, including the acquisition of merchandise, materials, supplies, and services used in the production and sale of goods or services. Current payables that are not trade accounts (such as income tax and the current portion of long-term debt) should be reported separately from accounts payable. In determining the amount of the liability, the accountant must adjust for purchase discounts, allowances, and returns, exactly as discussed for accounts receivable. Of course, a company never accrues an allowance for non-payment, since it is the payer!

### Cash Dividends Payable

Cash dividends declared but not yet paid are reported as a current liability if they are to be paid within the coming year or operating cycle. Declared dividends are reported as a liability between the date of declaration and payment because declaration gives rise to an enforceable contract.

Liabilities are not recognized for undeclared dividends in arrears on preferred shares or for any other dividends not formally declared by the Board of Directors. Dividends in arrears on cumulative preferred shares should be disclosed in the notes to the financial statements. These dividends must be paid before any common dividends can be paid.

### Monetary Accrued Liabilities

Examples of monetary accrued liabilities include wages and benefits earned by employees, interest earned by creditors but not yet paid, and the costs of goods and services received but not yet invoiced by the supplier. Monetary accrued liabilities are recorded in the accounts by making adjusting entries at the end of the accounting period.

### Advances and Returnable Deposits

A company may receive advances or cash deposits from customers as guarantees for payment of future obligations or to guarantee performance on a contract or service. Deposits may also be made as guarantees in case of non-collection or for possible damage to property. For example, deposits required from customers by gas, water, electricity, and other public utilities are liabilities of such companies to their customers. Employees may also make returnable deposits to ensure the return of keys and other company property, for locker privileges, and for club memberships.

Advances from customers and deposits should be reported as current or long-term liabilities depending on the time involved between date of deposit and expected termination of the relationship. If the advances or deposits are interest bearing, an annual adjusting entry is required to accrue interest expense and to increase the related liability.

### Taxes

Provincial and federal laws require businesses to collect certain taxes from customers and employees for remittance to governmental agencies. These taxes include sales taxes, income tax withheld from employee paycheques, property taxes, and payroll taxes. Similar collections are made on behalf of unions, insurance companies, and employee-sponsored activities. Collections made for third parties increase both cash and current liabilities. The collections represent liabilities that are settled when the funds are remitted to the designated parties. Common examples of such taxes follow.

**Sales Taxes** Retail businesses are required to collect sales taxes from customers and remit them to the appropriate government agency. Taxes include the goods and services tax (GST) and, in most provinces, provincial sales taxes (PST), or both together, the harmonized sales tax (HST). Revenues are recorded net of GST collected, and purchases of goods and services should be recorded net of any GST recoverable. Any GST that is not recoverable should be accounted for as a component of the cost of the goods or services to which it relates. (On the other hand, PST is never refundable and PST paid is part of the cost of whatever was bought: capital assets or inventory, for example.)

GST is remitted periodically, net of GST paid on purchases. The *net amount* of GST payable or receivable should be carried as a liability or asset, as appropriate. Typical entries, with 6% GST and assuming 9% provincial sales tax and $500,000 of sales, are as follows:

| | | |
|---|---|---|
| 1. At date the tax is assessed (point of sale): | | |
| Cash and accounts receivable | 575,000 | |
| Sales revenue | | 500,000 |
| GST payable ($500,000 × 6%) | | 30,000 |
| PST payable ($500,000 × 9%) | | 45,000 |

Assume that $300,000 of inventory was purchased, subject to GST and PST:

| | | |
|---|---|---|
| 2. At inventory purchase: | | |
| Inventory ($300,000 × 1.09) | 327,000 | |
| GST payable ($300,000 × .06) | 18,000 | |
| Cash or accounts payable ($300,000 × 1.15) | | 345,000 |

Taxes are remitted:

| | | |
|---|---|---|
| 3. At date of remittance to taxing authority: | | |
| GST payable ($30,000 − $18,000)* | 12,000 | |
| Cash | | 12,000 |
| PST payable | 45,000 | |
| Cash | | 45,000 |

*GST remitted is reduced by GST paid on purchased goods and services.

**Payroll Taxes** Employers act as a collection agent for certain taxes and payments. They withhold appropriate amounts from their employees and send the money off to the appropriate party shortly thereafter; a liability exists in the meantime. Common withholdings include:

- *Personal income tax.* An employee's personal federal and provincial tax are deducted at source and remitted regularly (at least monthly) to the federal government. At the end of the year, the employee receives a record of deductions, and determines, on his or her annual tax return, who owes whom and how much.
- *Canada pension plan (CPP)*. Employees have to pay a percentage of their salary to the CPP; employers have to match this amount dollar for dollar.

- *Employment insurance (EI).* Employees have to pay a percentage of their salary to secure EI benefits; the employer must pay 1.4 times the employees' contributions as its share.

- *Insurance premiums, pension plan payments, union dues etc.* A variety of employee benefits, such as group insurance, medical insurance, and pension plans, require that employees pay all or a portion of the premiums; these are deducted at source. If stipulated in labour agreements, union dues are also deducted at source. Other deductions may include charitable donations and parking fees. All of these are remitted to the appropriate party after deduction.

Payroll deduction accounting is illustrated in Exhibit 7-4.

**Property Taxes.** Property taxes paid directly by a company are based on the assessed value of real property. Unpaid taxes constitute a lien on the assessed property. Property taxes are based on the assessed value of the property, which may or may not correspond to market value, and the mill rate (tax rate per thousand dollars of assessed value).

Estimates are needed for monthly property tax accruals because tax rates are usually set by the taxing authority partway through the fiscal year. When corrections are needed, prior years are NOT restated—changes in these estimates are lumped into the current year.

---

## EXHIBIT 7-4

### ILLUSTRATION OF PAYROLL DEDUCTIONS

*Thor Company reported the following information relating to payroll for January 20X5:*

| | | |
|---|---:|---:|
| Gross wages | | $100,000 |
| Deductions: | | |
| Income tax | $ 20,000 | |
| Canada Pension Plan | 2,250 | |
| Employment insurance | 2,100 | |
| Union dues | 1,400 | |
| Charitable contributions | 1,600 | 27,350 |
| Net pay | | $ 72,650 |

*To record salaries and employee deductions:*

| | | |
|---|---:|---:|
| Salary expense | 100,000 | |
| Employee income tax payable | | 20,000 |
| CPP payable | | 2,250 |
| EI payable | | 2,100 |
| Union dues payable | | 1,400 |
| Charitable contributions payable | | 1,600 |
| Cash | | 72,650 |

*To record payroll expenses payable by the employer:*

| | | |
|---|---:|---:|
| Salary expense | 5,190 | |
| CPP payable (matching payment) | | 2,250 |
| EI payable ($2,100 × 1.4) | | 2,940 |

*To record remittance of payroll deductions (composite entry):*

| | | |
|---|---:|---:|
| Employee income tax payable | 20,000 | |
| CPP payable | 4,500 | |
| EI payable | 5,040 | |
| Union dues payable | 1,400 | |
| Charitable contributions payable | 1,600 | |
| Cash | | 32,540 |

## Conditional Payments

Some liabilities are established on the basis of a firm's periodic income. These items can be established at year-end, but a liability must be estimated whenever interim statements are prepared throughout the year—monthly or quarterly. Until paid, they represent current liabilities of the organization.

**Income Tax Payable** Interim reports require a provision for both federal and provincial tax liabilities, so estimates are required. The estimated liability should be reported as a current liability based on the firm's best estimates. After year-end, the tax return is prepared and the estimate is adjusted for the year-end financial statements before the books are finally closed. Periodic instalment payments are required. Accounting for corporate income tax is reviewed in Chapters 15 and 16.

**Bonuses** Many companies pay cash bonuses, which depend on earnings. These are estimated at interim periods, but calculated "for real" at the end of the fiscal year. Calculations must be made in accordance with established formula or the authorization of the Board of Directors. Bonuses can be material—both to the company and to the employee, so it's important that they're properly approved.

## Compensated-Absence Liabilities

The Canada Labour Code requires that employees receive paid vacations and holidays. The expense for salaries and wages paid during these absences from work is recognized in the current year. When employees can carry over unused time to future years, any expense due to compensated absences must be recognized (accrued) in the year in which it is earned, provided that certain criteria are met. Compensated absence liabilities may also be recorded if there are sick days or parental leaves that are earned but not used in a given year (that is, carry over) or if employees have sabbatical entitlements. The criteria are:

- The absence from work relates to services already rendered.
- The benefits accumulate (carry over) or *vest*.
- The payment is probable (the absence will occur).
- The amount (i.e., cost) can be reliably estimated.

These should look like fairly standard recognition criteria by now!

Implementing the accrual of compensated absences requires an adjusting entry at the end of each fiscal year to accrue all of the compensation cost for the vacation and medical leave time that is carried over. An expense and a current liability are recorded. When the time is taken, the liability account may be debited at the time the employee is paid. Alternatively, the liability may be adjusted only at year-end. Either approach will recognize the cost of the compensated absences as an expense in the period earned rather than when taken.

For example, consider the carryover of vacation time of the Conway Company, which has 500 employees. Each employee is granted three weeks paid vacation time each year. Vacation time, up to a maximum accumulation of four weeks, may be carried over to subsequent years prior to termination of employment. At the end of 20X5, the end of the annual accounting period, personnel records revealed the following information concerning carryover vacation amounts:

| **Carryovers from 20X5\*** | | | | |
|---|---|---|---|---|
| Number of Employees | Weeks per Employee | Total Weeks | Salary per Week | Total Accrual |
| 10 | 2 | 20 | $1,500 | $30,000 |
| 3 | 1 | 3 | 2,000 | 6,000 |
| | | | | $36,000 |

\*These are carryovers from 20X5 to future years.

Disregarding payroll taxes, which are excluded here to simplify the analysis, the indicated entries are as follows:

| 31 December 20X5—adjusting entry to accrue vacation salaries not yet taken or paid | | |
|---|---|---|
| Salary expense | 36,000 | |
|    Liability for compensated absences | | 36,000 |

| During 20X6—vacation time carryover taken and salaries paid (all employees took their carried-over vacation time, except for one person who still carried over two weeks, valued at $1,500 per week) | | |
|---|---|---|
| Liability for compensated absences | 33,000 | |
|    Cash ($36,000 − $3,000) | | 33,000 |

The balance remaining in the liability account is $3,000: 2 weeks @ $1,500 per week.

This illustration assumes that there was no change in the rate of pay from 20X5 to 20X6 (when the carryover was used) for those employees who had the carryover. If there were rate changes, the pay difference would be debited (if an increase) or credited (if a decrease) to salary expense during 20X6. The change is considered a change in estimate.

This item is a liability only if a company allows employees to *carry over vacation entitlements:* many do not, and no liability exists. Most financial institutions, for example, require employees to take all their vacation entitlements before the end of each calendar year; it's important to their internal control systems to have someone else go in and do the employee's job regularly, so that the employee can't hide suspicious activities indefinitely.

### Loans as Current Liabilities

Loans may be long-term liabilities or current liabilities. These amounts are material, and must be carefully classified. Loans are current liabilities if:

1. *Loans are due on demand.* Demand loans are payable on demand, or after a short delay of 7 to 30 business days to arrange alternate financing. These loans are legally current liabilities, and must be classified as such, even if a demand for payment within the current year is not expected.

2. *Loans are due within the next year.* If the loan has a due date within the next year, it is a current liability, even if the company expects to renegotiate the loan. If debt is partially due within the next year, the current portion must be reclassified. For example, consider the classification of this $500,000 liability:

| Current liabilities: | |
|---|---|
|    Current portion of bonds payable | $100,000 |
| Long-term liabilities: | |
|    Bonds payable ($500,000 less current portion: | |
|     $100,000) | $400,000 |

3. *Long-term debt is in violation of covenants and thus can be called by the lender at any time.* For example, a company might be in arrears on interest payments, or has exceeded the maximum debt-to-equity ratio on the balance sheet date. The company may not yet have had the opportunity to negotiate with the lender. Often all that happens in these circumstances is that the lender increases the interest rate. But the lender could demand repayment, and thus the current classification is required.

**Short-Term Obligations Expected to be Refinanced** A company may want to reclassify liabilities from current to long term to improve the reported working capital position. This reclassification is not to be taken lightly—a large reclassification has a material impact on the financial statements.

*Intention* to restructure a short-term loan as a long-term loan is not enough to justify reclassification. However, it is common to enter into an agreement to restructure debt, prior to actually doing it. A *contractual arrangement* may be relied on to support classification of short-term obligations as long-term debt, as long as it is indeed a legal contract with a reputable party. If a short-term obligation is to be excluded from current liabilities under a future financing agreement, note disclosure of the details would be appropriate.

### Disclosure of Monetary Current Liabilities

Again, current liabilities are *financial instruments*, and must satisfy disclosure requirements for accounting policy, fair value, and the nature and extent of risks. This disclosure includes interest rate risk, collateral pledged, and fair value. Disclosure primarily relates to loans and notes payable, and would include interest rates, payments, and due date.

### Foreign Currency Receivables and Payables

If a company has a bank account in a currency other than Canadian dollars, the cash account on the balance sheet must include the Canadian dollar equivalent of that foreign currency. The same principle applies to receivables and payables. If a company has accounts or notes that are receivable or payable in foreign currencies, they must be *restated to Canadian dollars* at the current exchange rate at the balance sheet date.

Monetary items that are denominated in a foreign currency always arise from a transaction, of course. The transaction may be sales to a foreign customer, purchases from a foreign supplier, investments in foreign currency financial instruments, or foreign currency loans from a foreign bank (or from a Canadian bank but in a foreign currency). When the transaction occurs, it is recorded at the exchange rate in effect at the date of the transaction. For example, suppose that Talud Limited has a sale to a customer in England for 10,000 euros when the exchange rate was 1 euro = $2.20. The sale would be recorded as follows:

| | | |
|---|---|---|
| Accounts receivable (10,000 euros) | 22,000 | |
| Sales (10,000 euros × $2.20) | | 22,000 |

The receivable is stated (or *denominated*) in euros, not in dollars. The sale is recorded at the Canadian dollar equivalent of the British sales price. However, when the British company pays the account, it will pay 10,000 euros, not $22,000. The cash receipt must be recorded at the current exchange rate. Suppose that the customer pays the 10,000 euros when the exchange rate is 1 euro = $2.10. Talud will receive only $21,000 in Canadian currency when it converts the cash. The loss is recognized in the current period's income statement.

| | | |
|---|---|---|
| Cash (10,000 euros × $2.10) | 21,000 | |
| Foreign exchange gains and losses | 1,000 | |
| Accounts receivable | | 22,000 |

**Exchange Gain or Loss** The difference between the Canadian equivalent of the receivable and of the cash receipt is charged to an *exchange gain or loss* account. Gains and losses are netted in this account, and the net balance is reported in the income statement. It is important to understand that changes in the exchange rate following the initial transaction *do not affect the amount initially charged or credited to the nonmonetary account*. In the Talud Limited example above, the sales account is not affected by the subsequent exchange rate change.

Similarly, if inventory or capital assets (such as equipment) are purchased in a foreign currency, changes in the exchange rate between the date of purchase and the date of payment will not affect the originally recorded value of the asset. *Historical cost is determined by the exchange rate at the date of the purchase transaction.* Subsequent gains and losses on the outstanding monetary balance are recognized directly and immediately in the income statement, provided that the balance is classified as current.

**Year-End** Assume instead that at Talud's balance sheet date, the receivable (recorded at $22,000) is still outstanding. The receivable must be translated to the then-current exchange rate. If the exchange rate at the balance sheet date is 1 euro = $2.25, the value of the account receivable will be $22,500 (10,000 euros × $2.25). The increase of $500 in the Canadian equivalent of the 10,000 euros balance would be recorded as follows:

| | | |
|---|---|---|
| Accounts receivable ($22,500 − $22,000) | 500 | |
|     Foreign exchange gains and losses | | 500 |

## INTERNATIONAL PERSPECTIVE

In IAS 1, *Presentation of Financial Statements*, general balance sheet presentation requirements for current monetary assets and liabilities are established. Canadian presentation and disclosure requirements are converged with IAS 1. The *CICA Handbook* has specific sections on cash and accounts receivables, while standards for these elements fall under the more general financial instruments rules of the IASB. However, the accounting approach is consistent.

In more technical topics, there are more technical differences. For example, in the Canadian rules that govern transfer of accounts receivable classification as a sale or a loan, the approach focuses on legal isolation and surrender of control. The IAS requirements, in IAS 39, have a broader scope. IAS 39 uses more general criteria that cover more general circumstances. A transfer is treated as a sale if:

- The contractual rights to the assets' cash flows expire for the transferor;
- The asset, and substantially all the risks and rewards of ownership, have been transferred; and
- The transferee may sell the asset, even if the transferor has some risks and rewards of ownership.

These different criteria may be significant for companies who undertake securitizations.

Another difference is in IAS 39, which has more guidance on the assessment of impairment in a portfolio of loans, which may again be significant if an entity has a large loan portfolio. In particular, it has been suggested that it is almost impossible to structure a transfer so that it is a sale under *both* Canadian and IAS standards. This will be a major issue on initial adoption of the IASB standards.

## CONCEPT REVIEW

1. What are the major categories of current liabilities?

2. Does a company remit all GST collected during a period?

3. How should monetary items that are denominated in a foreign currency be reported at each balance sheet date?

## RELEVANT STANDARDS

*CICA Handbook:*
- Section 1510, Current Assets and Current Liabilities
- Section 1650, Foreign Currency Translation
- Section 3000, Cash
- Section 3020, Accounts and Notes Receivable
- Section 3025, Impaired Loans
- Section 3855, Financial Instruments—Recognition and Measurement
- Section 3861, Financial Instruments—Disclosure and Presentation
- Section 3862, Financial Instruments—Disclosures
- Section 3863, Financial Instruments—Presentation
- AcG-12, Transfers of Receivables

IASB:
- *IAS* 1, Presentation of Financial Statements
- *IAS* 21, The Effects of Changes in Foreign Exchange Rates
- *IAS* 39, Financial Instruments: Recognition and Measurement
- *IFRS* 7, Financial Instruments: Disclosure

## SUMMARY OF KEY POINTS

1. Monetary items are those that will be paid or received in fixed or determinable amounts of money.

2. The current asset, cash, includes only those items immediately available to pay current obligations.

3. A bank reconciliation is an internal control mechanism. Reconciliation of the book balance to the correct cash balance provides the data for end-of-month adjusting entries for cash.

4. In a bank reconciliation, adjustments to the bank are made for outstanding cheques and deposits, and bank errors. The book balance is adjusted for unrecorded items and errors.

5. Doubtful accounts, cash discounts, and sales returns and allowances represent adjustments to the recorded value of receivables, which are necessary to provide an estimate of net realizable value.

6. The allowance for doubtful accounts can be estimated through aging or a percentage-of-sales method.

7. Accounts receivable can be used as collateral for a loan to speed the cash cycle. Alternatively, accounts receivable can be transferred to a finance company to obtain immediate cash. The key accounting issue is whether the transfer of accounts receivable is treated as a sale or borrowing. When there is legal isolation, the transferee has the power to pledge the receivables as collateral, and there is no repurchase arrangement, the transfer is accounted for as a sale. Otherwise, it is treated as a borrowing.

8. Long-term notes are recorded at the present value of all cash payments to be received using the appropriate market rate of interest. Interest is based on the market interest rate and the outstanding principal balance at the beginning of the period. Impaired notes are reduced to the present value of future cash flows.

9. Current liabilities are obligations that are payable within one year or within the normal operating cycle, whichever is longer.

10. Current liabilities commonly include accounts, notes, accruals, property taxes, cash dividends, taxes, bonuses, and other payables.

11. Loans are a current liability if due on demand. Current liabilities are the current portion of long-term debt and long-term debt in default. Current debt that is to be refinanced as long term may be reclassified as long term only if contractual arrangements are in place.

12. Transactions that are denominated in a foreign currency are recorded at the exchange rate that exists at the transaction date. Monetary balances (i.e., cash, receivables, and payables) are restated to the exchange rate that exists on the balance sheet date. Gains and losses are recognized in income.

## KEY TERMS

aging method, 342
allowance for doubtful accounts, 339
bank reconciliation, 336
cash equivalents, 334
collateral security, 350
compensating balance, 335
consolidation, 349
credit memo, 372
credit sales method, 342
debit memo, 372
discounting notes receivable, 356
effective-interest method, 352
face value, 350
guaranteed investment certificate
   (GIC), 334
interest-bearing, 350
internal control system, 336
market interest rate, 350

maturity value, 350
monetary items, 334
money market instruments, 334
non-interest-bearing, 350
non-notification basis, 347
non-trade receivable, 337
notes receivable, 337
notification basis, 347
overdraft, 334
recourse, 347
securitization, 349
stated interest rate, 350
T-bill, 334
trade accounts payable, 357
trade accounts receivable, 337
transferee, 347
transferor, 347
variable-interest entity, 349

## REVIEW PROBLEM

At the end of 20X5, three companies ask you to record journal entries in three different areas associated with receivables. The fiscal year of each company ends on 31 December.

1. *Mandalay Company—uncollectible accounts receivable.* Mandalay Company requests that you record journal entries for its bad debt expense and uncollectible accounts receivable in 20X5. Mandalay's 1 January 20X5 balances relevant to accounts receivable are as follows:

| | |
|---|---|
| Accounts receivable | $400,000 (dr.) |
| Allowance for doubtful accounts | 20,000 (cr.) |

During 20X5, $45,000 of accounts receivable are judged to be uncollectible, and no more effort to collect these accounts will be made. Total sales for 20X5 are $1,200,000, of which $200,000 are cash sales; $900,000 was collected on account during 20X5.

a. Assuming that Mandalay uses the credit sales method to estimate bad debt expense and uses 4% of credit sales as its estimate of bad debts, provide the journal entries to record write-offs and bad debt expense for 20X5. Also, provide the 31 December 20X5 balance sheet amount for net accounts receivable.

b. Assuming that Mandalay uses the aging method to estimate net accounts receivable and uses 9% of accounts receivable as its estimate of uncollectibles, provide the journal entries to record write-offs and bad debt expense for 20X5. Also, provide the 31 December 20X5 balance sheet amount for net accounts receivable.

2. *Berkshire Company—transfer of accounts receivable.* Berkshire Company requests that you record journal entries for accounts receivable transferred in 20X5:

> On 1 January 20X5, Berkshire transferred $45,000 of accounts receivable with recourse to a finance company, on a notification basis. Bad debts are estimated to be $2,500, an amount which is already part of the allowance for doubtful accounts. The financing fee is 10%. Criteria for sale are met.

3. *White Mountain Company—accounting for long-term notes*: White Mountain Company requests that you record journal entries for a note it received in 20X5. On 1 January 20X5, White Mountain Company sold merchandise for $12,000 and received a $12,000, three-year, 6% note; 12% was the current market rate of interest at that time. Interest is paid annually at the end of each year and the principal is due at the end of the third year. Provide journal entries from inception to final payment. Use the gross method to record the note.

# REVIEW PROBLEM—SOLUTION

1. Mandalay Company

   a. Summary entry for write-offs during 20X5:

   | | | |
   |---|---:|---:|
   | Allowance for doubtful accounts | 45,000 | |
   |     Accounts receivable | | 45,000 |

   *Adjustment on 31 December 20X5:*

   | | | |
   |---|---:|---:|
   | Bad debt expense ($1,000,000 × 4%) | 40,000 | |
   |     Allowance for doubtful accounts | | 40,000 |

   *Balance sheet amounts at 31 December 20X5:*

   | | |
   |---|---:|
   | Accounts receivable | $455,000* |
   | Allowance for doubtful accounts | (15,000)** |
   | Net accounts receivable | $440,000 |

   *$400,000 + $1,000,000 − $900,000 − $45,000
   **$20,000 − $45,000 + $40,000

   b. Summary entry for write-offs during 20X5:

   | | | |
   |---|---:|---:|
   | Allowance for doubtful accounts | 45,000 | |
   |     Accounts receivable | | 45,000 |

   *Adjustment on 31 December 20X5:*

   | | | |
   |---|---:|---:|
   | Bad debt expense | 65,950* | |
   |     Allowance for doubtful accounts | | 65,950 |

   *Calculation of adjustment:*

   | | | |
   |---|---:|---:|
   | Ending gross accounts receivable | | $455,000 |
   | | | |
   | Required allowance balance ($455,000 × 9%) | | $ 40,950 |
   | Allowance balance before adjustment for 20X5: | | |
   |     Beginning balance, 1 January 20X5 | $ (20,000) | |
   |     Write-offs during 20X5 | 45,000 | 25,000 |
   | Increase necessary to adjust balance | | $ 65,950 |

   *Balance sheet amounts at 31 December 20X5:*

   | | |
   |---|---:|
   | Accounts receivable | $455,000 |
   | Allowance for doubtful accounts | (40,950) |
   | Net accounts receivable | $414,050 |

2. Berkshire Company

| | | |
|---|---:|---:|
| Cash ($45,000 − $2,500 − (10% × $42,500)) | 38,250 | |
| Allowance for doubtful accounts | 2,500 | |
| Financing fee (10% × $42,500) | 4,250 | |
| Accounts receivable | | 45,000 |

3. White Mountain Company

Present value of note

| | |
|---|---:|
| $12,000 (P/F, 12%, 3) = $12,000 (.71178) | $ 8,541 |
| $720 (P/A, 12%, 3) = $720 (2.40183) | 1,729 |
| | $10,270 |

a. 1 January 20X5:

| | | |
|---|---:|---:|
| Note receivable | 12,000 | |
| Sales revenue | | 10,270 |
| Discount on note receivable | | 1,730 |

b. 31 December 20X5:

| | | |
|---|---:|---:|
| Cash | 720 | |
| Discount on note receivable ($1,232 − $720) | 512 | |
| Interest revenue ($10,270 × .12) | | 1,232 |

c. 31 December 20X6:

| | | |
|---|---:|---:|
| Cash | 720 | |
| Discount on note receivable ($1,294 − $720) | 574 | |
| Interest revenue ($10,270 + $512) × .12 | | 1,294 |

d. 31 December 20X7:

| | | |
|---|---:|---:|
| Cash | 720 | |
| Discount on note receivable | 644 | |
| Interest revenue ($10,270 + $512 + $574) × .12 | | 1,364 |

e. 31 December 20X7:

| | | |
|---|---:|---:|
| Cash | 12,000 | |
| Note receivable | | 12,000 |

# APPENDIX

## BANK RECONCILIATION

The purpose of a bank reconciliation is to ensure that transactions in both the company's cash account and the bank's cash account have been recorded accurately. This involves comparing every deposit and cheque/charge in both accounts. Items that are different are reconciling amounts, which may lead to adjusting entries.

Review the information in Exhibit 7A-1 for North Company. The bank statement reported an ending $23,760 balance, and the cash account reflects an ending $22,980 cash balance. Of course, if they were the same amount, the reconciliation would be over before it even began! These figures are reconciled to $23,160, as shown in Exhibit 7A-2. Here are the steps to follow:

**Step 1** Compare all deposits made in the bank account with those in the books. If there are differences, determine why. If the bank has processed something that should be on the books, adjust the book balance. If the bank has made errors, or if deposits are in transit, adjust the bank balance. If the company has made errors, adjust the balance per the books. A careful bank reconciliation includes a comparison of the dates of deposits—there should be no delays in getting money to the bank. Deposits in transit from the prior month should clear in the first few days of the next month, and this month's deposits in transit should relate only to the last day or two.

**Step 2** Compare all cheques and charges that went through the bank account to the cash disbursements journal. All cheques that the bank paid should be in the cash disbursements journal this month, or have been outstanding last month. If the bank has made errors, or cheques are still outstanding, adjust the bank balance. If the bank has processed something that should be on the books, adjust the book balance. If the company has made errors, adjust the balance per the books. Again, watch for irregularities; cheques are usually cashed after only a short delay.

**Step 3** Make journal entries for all adjustments *to the book balance*, and inform the bank of any errors made by the bank, so they can be corrected before the end of next month.

Review the bank reconciliation in Exhibit 7A-2 in detail:

**Adjustments** Look at deposits, and then the cheques/charges. When they are not identical, either the bank balance or the book balance has to be adjusted.

**A. *Deposits.*** For North Company, compare (cross off) the list of deposits in the bank versus those on the books (or last month's reconciliation.) Each item should be in both places. Circle the items that are in one place *or* the other, but not both, *or* if the items are for different amounts. These are the reconciling items.

The first deposit in the bank was the outstanding deposit from last month (see last month's bank reconciliation at the bottom of Exhibit 7A-1.) It was recorded in the books last month, and now has cleared so needs no adjustment. There is a $1,000 deposit made by a customer directly to the bank account. This should be recorded by the company and is added to the balance per the books.

All other deposits are identical until the end of the month, when there is a deposit of $2,700 in the books that is not in the bank. This is an outstanding deposit, made too late to be reflected in the bank statement. It is added to the bank balance in Exhibit 7A-2.

Note also that if there were any cash on hand such as a petty cash fund or change fund, cash on hand is also added to the bank balance. It could be deposited if desired.

**B. *Cheques and charges.*** Compare cheques cleared through the bank account with cheques recorded in the books, and the cheques that were outstanding last month. For North Company, compare (cross off) the two lists. Circle the items that are in one place or the other, or are for different amounts. These are the reconciling items.

Outstanding cheques at the end of June are, first, the outstanding cheques from last month that have not yet been cashed, and, second, any cheques written this month that

---

**EXHIBIT 7A-1**

## North Company Information for Bank Reconciliation

30 June 20X8

**Bank Statement Summary:**

| | |
|---|---|
| Opening balance, 1 June | $23,000 |
| Deposits (see below) | 12,600 |
| Cheques and charges (see below) | (11,740) |
| Service fees | (100) |
| Ending balance, 30 June | $23,760 |

| Deposits | | | | Cheques and charges | | | |
|---|---|---|---|---|---|---|---|
| 1 June | $ 2,000 | 2 June #61 | $1,000 | 17 June #65 | $ 400 | | |
| 8 June | 3,000 | 7 June #63 | 2,000 | 23 June #60 | 1,100 | | |
| 17 June | 4,500 | 9 June #66 | 3,000 | 27 June #67 | 2,300 | | |
| 18 June | 1,000* | | | | | | |
| 22 June | 2,100 | 14 June #64 | 1,420 | | | | |
| | | 15 June NSF** | 520 | | | | |
| Total | $12,600 | | | | $11,740 | | |

*Customer Franklin paid his outstanding account receivable through a direct deposit to North's bank account.

**NSF: Customer Treetoe's $500 cheque, deposited on 1 June, was returned NSF; there was a $20 bank fee.

**Balance per Books:** transactions recorded in the cash account in the general ledger:

| | |
|---|---|
| Opening balance, 1 June | $23,900 |
| Cheques (see below) | (13,220) |
| Deposits (see below) | 12,300 |
| Closing balance, 30 June | $22,980 |

Deposits and cheques:

| Deposits | | Cheques | | | |
|---|---|---|---|---|---|
| | | #60 | $1,100 | #65 | $ 400 |
| June 8 | $ 3,000 | #61 | 1,000 | #66 | 3,000 |
| June 17 | 4,500 | #62 | 900 | #67 | 2,100* |
| June 22 | 2,100 | #63 | 2,000 | #68 | 1,300 |
| June 30 | 2,700 | #64 | 1,420 | | |
| | $12,300 | | | | $13,220 |

This cheque was actually for $2,300 and was to a supplier, on account.

The bank reconciliation at 31 May showed the following items:
  Bank balance, $23,000, add deposit outstanding, $2,000,
  Deduct cheque #59 outstanding, $1,100,
  Book balance, $23,900.

---

**EXHIBIT 7A-2**

## North Company Bank Reconciliation

30 June 20X8

| | | |
|---|---:|---:|
| *Bank statement* | | |
| Ending bank balance, 30 June | | $23,760 |
| Additions: | | |
| Deposits in transit, 30 June | 2,700 | |
| Deductions: | | |
| Cheques outstanding 30 June | | |
| (#59, $1,100; #62, $900; #68, $1,300) | (3,300) | (600) |
| Adjusted balance | | $23,160 |
| | | |
| *Book balance* | | |
| Ending book balance, 30 June | | $22,980 |
| Additions: | | |
| Accounts receivable collected by bank | | 1,000 |
| Deductions: | | |
| NSF cheque, Treetoe, $500, plus $20 NSF fee | (520) | |
| Bank service charges | (100) | |
| Error in recording cheque | (200) | (820) |
| Adjusted balance | | $23,160 |

---

haven't been cashed. There are three such cheques, and they are subtracted from the bank balance in the reconciliation.

There was an NSF cheque returned from a deposit; this amount has reduced North's bank balance and has to be recorded on the books. It is recorded as a reconciliation deduction on the book side. There was a bank service charge that reduced North's bank balance. It also has to be recorded on the books and is recorded as a reconciliation deduction on the book side.

Finally, one cheque was recorded correctly by that bank and incorrectly by North. Since this was the company's error, it affects the book balance. There must be an additional $200 reduction on the book side.

There were no bank errors in this example, but if there were, the adjustment would be made to the bank side of the reconciliation. For example, if the bank charged a cheque of a different company to this account, or charged too much service fees, the bank balance would be adjusted and the bank notified to correct its error.

Book and bank balances are now reconciled to the same value, $23,160.

**Balancing** But what if the two amounts are *not* equal? What if it didn't work? Then, the reconciler gets to do it again … and again … until it does work! The nightmare is that a $10 difference is really a $10,000 error in one direction, and a $10,010 error in the other direction! So the bank reconciliation really is expected to "work." Here are a couple of "tricks" to help find the most common errors:

1. If a reconciling item is deducted when it should have been added (or vice versa), the amount will be *double* the item. Therefore, try dividing the unreconciled amount by 2, then look for an item of that amount. That, if $170 is the unreconciled amount, look for an $85 item that is added when it should be subtracted, or vice versa.

2. Transposition errors are *always* divisible by 9. For example, if $5,012 was written as $5,102, the unreconciled amount will be $90. If $5,012 was written as $5,210, the error will be $198, which also is divisible by 9.

Of course, if there are multiple errors, these tricks won't help much. In practice, after things have been very carefully reviewed a few times to make sure there is no possibility of large counterbalancing errors, small differences are written off to miscellaneous expense.

**Adjusting Entries** Each of the reconciliation items on the book side requires an adjusting journal entry to correct the cash balance. *Notice that there are no entries in North's books for anything that is a reconciling item to the bank balance.*

**A.** *Account receivable collected by bank.* An account receivable for $1,000 was collected by the bank but was not recorded by North. Usually, the bank informs the company immediately, but if the item has not been recorded by month-end, it shows up as a reconciling item and is recorded at that time.

| | | |
|---|---|---|
| Cash | 1,000 | |
|     Accounts receivable | | 1,000 |

**B.** *Not sufficient funds (NSF) cheque.* The $500 cheque from customer Treetoe, which was not supported by sufficient funds in Treetoe's chequing account, was returned to North by the bank. North had deposited the cheque, increased cash, and decreased accounts receivable, but the bank was unable to get any money from Treetoe's account. Again, the company is usually informed immediately, so it can pursue its delinquent customer. However, if there are delays, or the NSF cheque occurs late in the month, it is a reconciling item, and will be recorded at that time. Note that the company will try to recover the bank fee charged as well as the original receivable.

| | | |
|---|---|---|
| Accounts receivable, Treetoe | 520 | |
|     Cash | | 520 |

Is this really a bad debt? Treetoe might be delinquent, but no company will give up after only one try—it will create a receivable when an NSF cheque is received. The receivable may end up as part of the amount included in the allowance for doubtful accounts.

**C.** *Bank service charges.* The bank debited North's account for $100 of bank charges in June for cheque printing, chequing account privileges, and so on. North deducts this amount from the cash account as a reconciling item and records an entry:

| | | |
|---|---|---|
| Miscellaneous expense (or Bank service charge expense) | 100 | |
|     Cash | | 100 |

**D.** *Error in recording.* North recorded a $2,300 cheque in the cash disbursements journal as $2,100, debiting accounts payable and crediting cash for *too little*. The book balance of cash and accounts payable is now overstated by $200 ($2,300 − $2,100). North corrects the recording error as a reconciling item, and makes an entry.

| | | |
|---|---|---|
| Accounts payable | 200 | |
|     Cash | | 200 |

This entry corrects the cash disbursement amount and reduces the payable. Correction entries of this kind always either debit or credit the cash account, and the other side of the entry is made to whatever the first cheque was charged to: in this case, accounts payable. It helps to reconstruct the original (incorrect) entry.

**Bank Debit and Credit Memos** Deposits and withdrawals may take place that are initiated by the bank or others, rather than the company. These show up on the bank statement as debit and credit memos, and include items such as interest earned, cash collected by the bank from customers, and service charges. For a bank, a depositor's cash balance is a liability, the amount the bank owes to the company. A bank **debit memo** describes a transaction from the bank's point of view—a decrease in liability to the account holder. Therefore, a debit memo reports the amount and nature of a *decrease* in the company's cash account. A **credit memo** indicates an *increase* in the cash account. Since this debit-credit memo terminology is derived from the bank's point of view, it seems backward to the debit and credit convention in the company's cash account. This tends to create a little confusion.

## SUMMARY OF KEY POINTS

1. To prepare a bank reconciliation, deposits and cheques/charges are compared between the bank account and the cash account in the general ledger. Where there are differences, there are reconciliation items.

2. Common adjustments to the bank balance in a bank reconciliation are outstanding cheques, outstanding deposits, and bank errors.

3. Common adjustments to the books in a bank reconciliation are deposits recorded by the bank but not yet in the books, charges recorded by the bank but not yet in the books, and recording errors made in the books.

4. Adjusting journal entries are prepared for the adjustments in a bank reconciliation that affect the books.

## QUESTIONS

**Q7-1**    Define cash as it is used for accounting purposes. What is a cash equivalent?

**Q7-2**    ABC Company has US$160,000 in a U.S. bank account. It received the money from a customer, for a cash sale, when the exchange rate was US$1 = Cdn$1.10. At year-end, the exchange rate is US$1 = Cdn$1.15. At what amount is the sale recorded? What amount of cash is reported on the end-of-year balance sheet?

**Q7-3**    Why is internal control over cash so important? What is a major component of internal control?

**Q7-4**    Briefly explain the basic purposes of a bank reconciliation. Who should perform the reconciliation?

**Q7-5**    A company allows 10% of gross sales to be returned within a month, and estimates that this amounts to $25,000 at year-end. The allowance for sales returns is now $10,000 (credit). What entry should be made?

**Q7-6**    At the end of an accounting period, a company has $4,000,000 recorded in accounts receivable, all from sales. It is not likely that the company will collect all of the $4,000,000, even though all the sales really took place. Give three reasons why collections might not equal $4,000,000.

**Q7-7**    Briefly describe the different methods of estimating bad debt expense and the allowance for doubtful accounts for trade accounts receivable.

**Q7-8**    It sometimes happens that a receivable that has been written off as uncollectible is subsequently collected. Describe the accounting entries in such an event.

**Q7-9** Under what circumstances should the direct write-off method for bad debts be used?

**Q7-10** A company has a credit balance of $700 in its allowance for doubtful accounts. The amount of credit sales for the period is $80,000, and the balance in accounts receivable is $15,000. Assume that the bad debt estimates are as follows: (a) related to accounts receivable, 8%, or (b) related to credit sales, 0.4%. What would be the balance of the allowance for doubtful accounts and the bad debt expense, if (a) the credit sales method and (b) the aging method were used?

**Q7-11** Describe several different ways a company could speed cash flow associated with accounts receivable.

**Q7-12** A company with $200,000 in receivables could sell them for $169,000 without recourse, or for $195,000 with recourse. What do the terms "with recourse" and "without recourse" mean? Why is the "without recourse" alternative more expensive? How could the transfer be recognized?

**Q7-13** Under what conditions will a transfer of receivables be recognized as a sale? As a borrowing?

**Q7-14** A company transferred accounts receivable of $10,000 for $8,500, with recourse. Uncollectible accounts are estimated at $700, and this amount is already in the allowance for doubtful accounts. Give the required entry, assuming that the transaction is recorded as (a) a borrowing and (b) a sale. What conditions attached to the transfer arrangement would make it likely that the transaction would be recorded as a sale? As a borrowing?

**Q7-15** Why is a note receivable sometimes preferred to an account receivable?

**Q7-16** How is a note receivable valued if it is (a) a no-interest note and (b) a low-interest note? Assume in all cases that the note had a term of two years. How would your answer change if the note had a term of two months?

**Q7-17** Compute the present value of a $20,000, one-year note payable that specifies no interest, although 10% would be a realistic rate. What is the true amount of the principal and interest?

**Q7-18** Distinguish between the stated rate of interest and the market rate of interest (yield).

**Q7-19** Assume that $6,000 cash is borrowed on a $6,000, 10%, one-year note payable that is interest bearing and that another $6,000 cash is borrowed on a $6,600 one-year note that is non–interest bearing. For each note, give the following: (a) face amount of the note, (b) principal amount, (c) maturity amount, and (d) total interest paid. The market interest rate is 10%.

**Q7-20** Define a current liability.

**Q7-21** Are undeclared dividends on cumulative preferred shares a liability? Explain.

**Q7-22** What is a compensated absence? When should the expense related to compensated absences be recognized?

**Q7-23** A company has a short-term bank loan outstanding, due on demand. The loan has been outstanding for several years, and will not be repaid in the coming year. Can it be classified as a long-term loan?

**Q7-24** A company has an account receivable from a U.S. customer, for US$100,000. It also is payable to another U.S. company, a supplier, in the amount of US$75,000. The payable was incurred when the exchange rate was US$1 = Cdn$1.12; the receivable, when the rate was $1.08. At year-end, the rate is $1.13. What amount of total exchange gain or loss will the company report for the year? Can the receivable and payable be offset in the financial statements?

**CASE 7-1**

## MITRIUM CORP.

Mitrium Corp. is a large privately held company, manufacturing frozen ice cream products, which are sold to large and small retailers across North America. The shares of this company are held by 12 individuals, some of them related, some of them not. Four of these shareholders are actively involved in the management of the company and are compensated with bonuses based on net income. There are annual dividend payouts to provide some return to the remaining shareholders. The company has been prosperous in the past but the current retail grocery market, slowly being taken over by private label goods, is proving a challenge for Mitrium. However, the company is actively engaged in manufacturing private-label goods, and enjoys healthy sales and profit margins in several of its flagship products, which have strong brand recognition with the end consumer.

The VP, Finance has come to you has come to you, a staff member, for commentary on two key financial ratios (Exhibit 1) based on the draft balance sheet (Exhibit 2) for the most recent fiscal year. She has isolated these ratios because they are the subject of loan covenants. In specific, one chartered bank provides the $6 million financing that appears as long-term debt on the balance sheet. As part of this lending agreement, the current ratio on audited financial statements must not go below 2:1, and the debt-to-equity ratio must not go above 12:1. If either of these ratio requirements is violated, or if interest is not paid annually, the debt becomes payable on demand. The current ratio condition is not met in the financial statements, although it is very close. The VP, Finance suspects that the draft financial statements will change based on the additional information she has provided to you. Your task is to analyze this additional information and restate the ratios, providing any commentary or advice you feel is appropriate.

### Required:
Prepare a report to the VP, Finance that responds to her concerns. The tax rate is 40%.

## EXHIBIT 1

### MITRIUM CORP.
### Debt Covenant Ratios

| Ratio | Definition | Calculation (Based on Draft Statements) |
|---|---|---|
| Current ratio | $\dfrac{\text{Current assets}}{\text{Current liabilities}}$ | $\dfrac{\$2,360}{\$1,211} = 1.95$ |
| Debt/equity | $\dfrac{\text{Total debt}}{\text{Total shareholders' equity}}$ | $\dfrac{8,808}{867} = 10.2$ |

```
                          EXHIBIT 2
```

## MITRIUM CORP.
## Draft Balance Sheet 31 December 20X8 (in thousands)

*Assets*
*Current assets:*

| | | | |
|---|---|---|---|
| Cash | | $ 300 | |
| Accounts receivable | $1,443 | | |
| Allowance for doubtful accounts | (12) | 1,431 | |
| Inventory | | 533 | |
| Prepaid expenses | | 96 | $2,360 |

*Capital assets:*

| | | |
|---|---|---|
| Property, plant and equipment | | 7,293 |
| *Other assets* | | 22 |
| Total assets | | $9,675 |

*Liabilities*
*Current liabilities:*

| | | |
|---|---|---|
| Bank indebtedness | $ 405 | |
| Accounts payable and accrued liabilities | 576 | |
| Current portion of long-term debt | 230 | |
| Total current liabilities | | $1,211 |

*Long-term liabilities:*

| | |
|---|---|
| Secured bank debt, 6% | 1,442 |
| Secured bank debt, floating interest rate | 6,000 |
| Future income tax | 155 |
| Total liabilities | 8,808 |

*Owner's Equity*

| | | |
|---|---|---|
| Common share capital | 583 | |
| Retained earnings | 284 | |
| Total owners' equity | | 867 |
| Total liabilities and owners' equity | | $9,675 |

*Additional information* (all amounts in thousands):

At year-end, there was a balance of $22 in the cash account in the general ledger, a $300 bank balance less $278 in outstanding cheques. Cash is shown as the balance before outstanding cheques, which have been reclassified as accounts payable.

In 20X8, certain accounts receivable were transferred to a financial institution on a non-recourse basis. The transfer was accounted for as a sale of accounts receivable. An undivided percentage interest in the designated pool of receivables was transferred, with Mitrium retaining the right to repurchase the receivables and use them as collateral against the 6% bank loan. Servicing of the accounts receivable is done by Mitrium on a fee-for-service basis. At the end of the year, $210 of accounts receivable were outstanding on such a transfer. This transaction took place on December 20, and is expected to be of a 45-day duration. Mitrium recognized financing expense of $1.9, and reduced the allowance for doubtful accounts by $4 when the transfer was recorded. This was felt to be an accurate representation of the doubtful accounts in this account receivable population.

Of the accounts receivable, $412 is receivable from one grocery chain, which is wholly owned by a shareholder of Mitrium. This account has been outstanding for some time, but Mitrium has had the shareholder personally pledge his share investment in Mitrium as security in the event of non-payment. Activity in the account this fiscal year:

| | |
|---|---|
| Opening balance | $256 |
| Sales | 455 |
| Payments on account | (341) |
| Interest accrued | 42 |
| Closing balance | $412 |

Of this amount, the interest ($42) and $106 of sales are current, and the remainder is over 90 days past due.

Mitrium instituted a sales discount program for all customers this year, with the intent of speeding collections of accounts receivable. The discount program allows 1% of the invoice to be deducted if payment for the invoice is received by Mitrium within 10 business days of the invoice date. This program has been quite successful, and Mitrium feels that its accounts receivable balances are lower this year as a result. However, since many of the company's highest credit rating customers use these discounts, Mitrium feels that the traditional non-collection percentage for current accounts receivable should likely triple this year. Other categories (30 days past due, etc.) are expected to be stable.

Sales data for the latter portion of December 20X8:

| Date: December 20X8 | Business Day | Sales on Account (thousands) | Percentage Using Sales Discount as of December 31 |
|---|---|---|---|
| 11 | Yes | $53.4 | 54%* |
| 12 | Yes | 71.2 | 53%* |
| 13 | Yes | 68.9 | 61%* |
| 14 | Yes | 56.7 | 45%* |
| 15 | Yes | 48.1 | 24% |
| 16–17 | No | | |
| 18 | Yes | 81.6 | 12% |
| 19 | Yes | 41.3 | 14% |
| 20 | Yes | 24.4 | 9% |
| 21 | Yes | 22.2 | 12% |
| 22 | Yes | 51.4 | 5% |
| 23–26 | No | | |
| 27 | Yes | 10.4 | 4% |
| 28 | Yes | 78.4 | 2% |
| 29 | Yes | 46.4 | 0% |
| 30–31 | No | | |

*discount period now expired.

The allowance for doubtful accounts has not yet been addressed in the year-end financial statements. An aging of accounts receivable shows the following:

| Status | Amount | Percentage Uncollectible* |
|---|---|---|
| Current | $ 424 | 3% |
| 30 days past due | 208 | 8% |
| 60 days past due | 231 | 10% |
| 90+ days past due | 580 | 40% |
|  | $1,443 |  |

*Based on prior experience. These percentages exclude the receivable from the grocery chain described above, which has not been included in the allowance in any prior year.

## CASE 7-2

## NETWORK TOOLS INCORPORATED

Network Tools Incorporated (NTI) is a public company with revenues of over $40 million. The company is a leading producer of network testing and measurement products, and also network storage and application servers. The company has a strategy to design, market, and sell network server appliance products that provide users with easy-to-operate, scalable, reliable, and cost-effective solutions. Its products are characterized by rapidly changing technology, short product life cycles, and evolving industry standards. NTI has a current stable of approximately 24 products, but recent sales have been concentrated in seven products.

NTI has experienced considerable volatility in its stock price. This volatility has been fuelled by fluctuations in quarterly financial results, conditions in the computer network markets, technological change that has made some NTI products obsolete, and business conditions in general.

NTI depends on third-party distributors for product sales. These distributors support sales teams across North America and internationally. Sales teams must develop long-term relationships with customers, and have an in-depth understanding of customers' information network and needs. That is, effective distributors must devote considerable technical and sales resources to an often-long sales cycle. The distributors carry a variety of competitors' products, and help make decisions on the best fit. NTI's success depends on being that best fit within its primary markets.

NTI is occasionally vulnerable to changes in distributors' inventory strategies. Distributors will usually carry a certain level of inventory, but other times will place an order with NTI only when a customer order has been confirmed.

NTI has particularly close relationships with five dealers, one of which accounted for 12% of 20X2 sales; all five together accounted for 28% of worldwide 20X2 sales.

Selected data from NTI's draft 20X2 financial statements are shown in Exhibit 1. NTI management is pleased with the draft 20X2 financial statements, which show a return to profitability after several challenging years. The improved results reflect increased sales to the five critical dealers. In the fourth quarter, when it was clear that revenue targets would not be met, senior executives met individually with these five dealers, and learned that all were carrying what they considered to be adequate inventory of NTI products. To encourage sales, special terms were offered:

1. Payment terms were changed from the current 45 days to 110 or 150 days, depending on the distributor. Two distributors were also allowed an additional 90 days to pay for inventory not sold at the end of the 110-day or 150-day period.

2. Return rights, normally any goods to a total of 10% of the yearly sales value with a distributor, were increased. Three distributors received (in addition to 10% returns) the right to return up to 100% of the initial orders in exchange for other products within 180 days of delivery. NTI referred to this as "stock rotation rights"—that is, alternate stock would replace unsalable items at the distributor's warehouse. One distributor was permitted, with no restrictions on time, to return all products made obsolete by new NTI products.

Total sales to these five distributors under this program in the fourth quarter totalled $4,104,000. No allowance for doubtful accounts was set up for the resulting receivables, as the five distributors all have excellent payment histories with NTI. Sales returns were accrued at the 10% rate, normal on prior sales.

Another initiative undertaken in the fourth quarter was a special direct marketing program, which used a telephone sales team. The terms listed on the sales order form indicated that the sales were made "at absolutely no risk with a 30-day money-back guarantee." The customer was usually permitted to try the product with no money down for 30 days, and pay for it only after the 30 days were up and the customer had decided to buy the product. Direct marketing sales were $1,316,000 in the fourth quarter, primarily in the last two months. These sales were recognized on delivery, with a 10% allowance for doubtful accounts and a 10% allowance for sales returns accrued on the balance still owing at year-end.

These revenue recognition policies are under discussion as part of the annual audit. You, an analyst in NTI's accounting group, have been asked to quantify the impact of three alternatives:

1. The current policy, as reflected in the financial statements;

2. Recognition of sales only upon payment; and

3. Recognition of sales on delivery with allowances for return of 25% established for distributor sales, and allowances of 20% for return and 25% for non-payment for direct marketing sales.

Your analysis must include the likely impact of these alternatives on accounts receivable, current assets, net income, and the components of net income. Various estimates, assumptions, and approximations will be needed to quantify the alternatives. Your report should also analyze the original policies with respect to appropriate revenue recognition criteria.

**Required:**
Prepare the report.

### EXHIBIT 1

**Network Tools Incorporated**
**Selected Financial Data**
**Consolidated Balance Sheet**

| Year ended 31 December (in thousands) | 20X2 | 20X1 |
|---|---|---|
| Assets | | |
| Current Assets | | |
| Cash and cash equivalents | $10,431 | $ 9,618 |
| Restricted investments | 293 | 1,124 |
| Accounts receivable (net) (Note 1) | 7,828 | 8,171 |
| Inventories | 4,289 | 6,572 |
| Prepaid expenses | 864 | 1,148 |
| Income tax receivable | 2,777 | 2,897 |
| Future income tax | 1,030 | 1,556 |
| | $27,512 | $31,086 |

Note 1: Accounts receivable are net of allowances for doubtful accounts of $871 (20X2) and $637 (20X1), and allowances for sales returns of $422 (20X2) and $392 (20X1).

| EXHIBIT 1 | | *(cont'd)* |
| --- | --- | --- |

**Consolidated Income Statement**

| Year ended 31 December (in thousands) | 20X2 | 20X1 |
| --- | --- | --- |
| Net revenue | $45,759 | $41,650 |
| Cost of revenue | 20,020 | 17,903 |
| Gross profit | 25,739 | 23,747 |
| Operating expenses | | |
| Sales and marketing (including bad debt expense) | 12,791 | 12,720 |
| Research and development | 5,432 | 7,912 |
| General and administrative | 5,829 | 5,605 |
| Total | 24,052 | 26,237 |
| Income (loss) before income tax | 1,687 | (2,490) |
| Income tax (recovery) | 32 | (522) |
| Net income | $ 1,655 | $ (1,968) |

---

**CASE 7-3**

## NEW DESIGN LIMITED

New Design Limited (NDL) is a jewellery wholesaler that plans to sign an agreement with Canadian Financial Company, in which Canadian will commit to purchase up to $10 million of NDL foreign customer accounts receivable. Under the terms of the agreement, Canadian receives the rights to all collections on the accounts sold, directly from the customer. All these customer accounts are for export sales, and all receivables are denominated in Canadian dollars. Two options are being considered:

### Option 1

1. Canadian purchases accounts from NDL within six days of the transaction. Only transactions that are EDC-guaranteed are eligible. EDC is the Canadian federal government's Export Development Corporation, which guarantees collection of accounts receivable with specific foreign countries or companies, as long as there are no legal deficiencies in them. For example, if the customer claimed that it did not receive all the goods, or that the goods received were not those ordered, EDC insurance would not be effective. However, if the buyer could simply not pay, EDC insurance would be effective. EDC insurance has to be purchased by NDL and is based on country and company risk.

2. NDL receives, from Canadian, cash equal to the face value of the receivable, less a financing charge, based on the term of the receivable. There is no bad debt allowance because of the EDC guarantee. NDL cannot be forced, and does not have the right, to repurchase the receivables, nor can NDL pledge the accounts receivable as collateral for any other financing arrangement.

This agreement would cover approximately $6 million of the total $10 million foreign receivables of NDL; the remainder is not EDC-insured (due to country of origin or identity of specific customer) and would not be eligible.

### Option 2

All foreign receivables are eligible for this option, which has the following key features:

- NDL is responsible for all bad debts. NDL has been in business for more than 20 years and is able to accurately forecast bad debt losses. Thus, its liability under this recourse provision can be reasonably estimated.

- Accounts are transferred to Canadian at the beginning of each month. This date is called the "settlement date."

- Interest on the outstanding loan is determined monthly. The interest rate charged will change regularly based on prime interest rates and risk of the portfolio.
- NDL can be required to repurchase or replace receivables if there are legal deficiencies in them. See the above discussion for an explanation of legal deficiencies.
- NDL may repurchase the receivables on the first settlement date subsequent to transfer of the receivables (i.e., monthly) if NDL and Canadian cannot agree on an interest rate for purposes of calculating the monthly payment (principal less interest) that Canadian pays to NDL. This repurchase option must be exercised within one week of the settlement date.
- NDL does not have the right to pledge the accounts receivable as collateral for any other financing arrangement.
- NDL has the right to repurchase the receivables when the balances fall to a low level. The repurchase price will be the total forecasted collections less the actual collections to date.

Joe Basinger, the VP, Finance for NDL, has asked you, the company's independent auditor, how each option would be accounted for. He's aware that some transfers of accounts receivable are treated as borrowings, while others are treated as sales, and he needs to know which treatment is appropriate.

The first option is more expensive for the company (because of the requirement to arrange EDC insurance) and involves a lower dollar value of receivables than the second option. Joe knows that another alternative is to arrange a loan secured by accounts receivable, and he's wondering if this arrangement would be any different on the balance sheet. He's particularly concerned about the key debt-to-total-assets ratio that is the subject of a loan covenant.

**Required:**
Respond to the request.

## ASSIGNMENTS

★ **A7-1 Define Cash:** Lu Ltd. is preparing its 20X8 financial statements; the accounting period ends 31 December. The following items, related to cash, are under consideration. You have been asked to indicate how each item should be reported on the balance sheet and to explain the basis for your responses.

a. Lu Ltd. has two chequing accounts: one with a balance of $66,000, and another with a different bank that has an overdraft of $4,000. The company plans to show the two balances net, since it could easily pay off the overdraft with available cash.

b. In addition, Lu Ltd. has $50,900 is a third separate bank account. This money is held separately according to provincial legislation, because Lu is engaged in mining operations in the province and must have a certain amount of money segregated for environmental restoration. The money may be used only for this purpose.

c. A customer's $6,000 cheque was included in the 22 December deposit. It was returned by the bank stamped NSF. No entry has yet been made by Lu Ltd. to reflect the return.

d. Lu Ltd. has a $60,000 three-month GIC. Interest accrued to 31 December of $700 has just been recorded by debiting interest receivable and crediting interest revenue. The chief accountant proposes to report the $60,700 as part of cash on the balance sheet.

e. Lu Ltd. has a $500 petty cash fund. This is cash held in a safe for miscellaneous disbursements. Postage stamps that cost $260 are also in the safe.

f. A $1,600 cheque received from a customer, dated 1 February 20X9, is in the safe, as is a cheque for of $575 payable to Lu Ltd. dated 29 December.

g. Three cheques, dated 31 December 20X8, totalling $9,065, payable to vendors that have sold merchandise to Lu Ltd. on account, were not mailed by 31 December 20X8. They have not been entered as payments in the cheque register and ledger.

---

★ **A7-2 Classification of Balances:** For each of the items listed below, identify the correct balance sheet classification by using one of the following classifications:

Cash
Short-term cash equivalent
Investments (specify long term or short term)
Accounts receivable, trade
Contra account to accounts receivable
Other accounts receivable
Accounts payable, trade
Other accounts payable
Other (identify)

The first item is completed for you.

| Item | Classification |
|---|---|
| 1. Chequing account | Cash |
| 2. Expense advances to salespersons | |
| 3. Interest-bearing GIC; two months remain in term | |
| 4. Compensating cash balance for a short-term loan | |
| 5. Debit balances in supplier accounts payable | |
| 6. Unpaid wages | |
| 7. Credit balances in customer accounts | |
| 8. Separate cash account containing money that must be used for environmental cleanup according to law | |
| 9. Rare coins kept for long-term speculation | |
| 10. Allowance for sales returns | |
| 11. Accounts receivable—officers (current collection expected) | |
| 12. Accounts payable for merchandise | |
| 13. Short-term loan payable | |
| 14. Cash held in a separate bank account called a sinking fund; cash must be used to retire a bond in five years | |
| 15. Canada Savings Bond (10-year term; immediately liquid) | |
| 16. Short-term investment in marketable equity securities | |
| 17. Accounts receivable—customers | |
| 18. Rent receivable | |
| 19. Allowance for doubtful accounts | |

**Required:**
Classify the above accounts, as indicated.

---

★ **A7-3 Net Accounts Receivable:** At 31 December 20X8, LGC Company reported gross accounts receivable of $3,241,700. Investigation showed the following:

a. Customers are permitted to return 5% of annual sales for full credit, as long as goods are returned in good condition within 60 days of delivery. Based on past years experience, $18,100 of goods might be returned. As returns are received during the year, the sales returns account, a contra account to sales, is increased. An allowance for sales returns exists, at $22,600, unchanged from the previous year-end.

b. The credit balance in the allowance for doubtful accounts was $164,100 after write-offs for the year but before any bad debt adjustment. Bad debt expense is based on a percentage of recorded credit sales. Sales revenue for 20X8 amounted to $54 million, of which three-quarters was on credit. Based on the latest available facts, one-quarter of 1% of recorded credit sales will not be collected.

c. Terms of 1/10, n/30 were granted to all customers. Accounts receivable were recorded gross, and the discounts taken were recorded when taken by the customers in a discounts account, reported contra to the sales account. Estimated discounts inherent in the closing accounts receivable balance were $24,140. The allowance for sales discounts account was established at $20,970 last year, and has not been adjusted since.

**Required:**

1. Prepare year-end adjusting entries with respect to accounts receivable.
2. Show how the net accounts receivable appear on the balance sheet on 31 December 20X8.

---

★ **A7-4 Recognizing Cash Discounts:** The annual reports of the following two companies provided information about cash discounts:

1. K&V Manufacturing: *Income statement*

| *Income statement* | |
|---|---|
| Sales | $ 65,438,800 |
| Less: Sales discounts | 865,432 |
| *Balance sheet* | |
| Current assets: | |
| Accounts receivable, less allowance of $297,000 | |
| for doubtful accounts and sales discounts | $ 16,938,624 |

2. GenCo, Inc.: *Income statement*

| *Income statement* | |
|---|---|
| Sales | $167,435,890 |
| Finance revenue; discounts lost | 1,576,320 |
| *Balance sheet* | |
| Accounts receivable | $ 61,781,000 |
| Allowance for bad debts | (3,173,000) |
| Net receivables | $ 58,608,000 |

**Required:**

1. Briefly comment on which method (gross versus net) you believe was used to account for cash discounts by these two companies. Assume they offered similar credit and payment terms.
2. How would an allowance for cash discounts be measured?

---

★ **A7-5 Accounts Receivable and Bad Debts:** Given below is the history of a sale on credit by Airport Company to J. Doe.

a. 24 December 20X1—Sold merchandise to J. Doe, $2,000, terms 2/10, n/30.
b. 2 January 20X2—Doe paid half of the receivable and was allowed the discount.
c. 31 December 20X4—Because of the disappearance of Doe, Airport Company wrote Doe's account off as uncollectible.
d. 31 December 20X6—Doe reappeared and paid the debt in full, plus 6% annual interest (not compounded, compute annually for five years).

**Required:**
Give the entry/entries that Airport Company should make at each of the above dates. Record the receivable initially at its gross amount.

★★ **A7-6 Estimating Bad Debt Expense:** The accounts of Long Company provided the following 20X5 information at 31 December 20X5 (end of the annual period):

| | |
|---|---|
| Accounts receivable balance, 1 January 20X5 | $ 51,000 |
| Allowance for doubtful accounts balance, 1 January 20X5 | 3,000 |
| Total sales revenue during 20X5 (on credit) | 160,000 |
| Uncollectible account to be written off during 20X5 (ex-customer Slo) | 1,000 |
| Cash collected on accounts receivable during 20X5 | 170,000 |

**ESTIMATES OF BAD DEBT LOSSES**

a. Based on credit sales, 1%.
b. Based on ending balance of accounts receivable, 8%.
c. Based on aging schedule (excludes Slo's account):

| Age | Accounts Receivable | Probability of Non-Collection |
|---|---|---|
| Less than 30 days | $28,000 | 2% |
| 31–90 days | 7,000 | 10 |
| 91–120 days | 3,000 | 30 |
| More than 120 days | 2,000 | 60 |

**Required:**

1. Give the entry to write off customer Slo's long-overdue account.
2. Give all entries related to accounts receivable and the allowance account for the following three cases:

   Case A—Bad debt expense is based on credit sales.
   Case B—Bad debt expense is based on the ending balance of accounts receivable.
   Case C—Bad debt expense is based on aging.

3. Show how the results of applying each case above should be reported on the 20X5 income statement and balance sheet.
4. Briefly explain and evaluate each of the three methods used in Cases A, B, and C.
5. On 1 August 20X6, customer Slo paid his long-overdue account in full. Give the required entries.

---

★★ **A7-7 Alternatives for Estimation—Allowance for Doubtful Accounts:** At 31 December 20X9, the end of the annual reporting period, the accounts of Geometric Company showed the following:

a. Sales revenue for 20X9, $2,850,000, of which one-sixth was on credit.
b. Allowance for doubtful accounts, balance 1 January 20X9, $16,200 credit.
c. Accounts receivable, balance 31 December 20X9 (prior to any write-offs of uncollectible accounts during 20X9), $273,900.
d. Uncollectible accounts to be written off, 31 December 20X9, $14,100. These accounts are all in the "past due over 90 days" category.
e. Aging schedule at 31 December 20X9, showing the following breakdown of accounts receivable:

| Status | Amount |
|---|---|
| Not past due | $150,600 |
| Past due 1–60 days | 42,900 |
| Past due over 60 days | 63,600 |
| Past due over 90 days | 16,800 |

**Required:**

1. Give the 20X9 entry to write off the uncollectible accounts.

2. Give the 20X9 adjusting entry to record bad debt expense for each of the following independent assumptions concerning bad debt loss rates:
   a. On credit sales, 2.1%.
   b. On total receivables at year-end (after write-off), 3.9%.
   c. On aging schedule: not past due, 0.9%; past due 1–60 days, 1.9%; past due over 60 days, 10%, and past due over 90 days, 75%.

3. Show what would be reported on the 20X9 balance sheet relating to accounts receivable for each assumption.

★★  **A7-8 Allowance for Doubtful Accounts:**  In 20X9, the following transactions took place by Time Ltd:

| | |
|---|---:|
| Sales on account | $426,582 |
| Cash collected on account | 408,970 |
| Sales returns and allowances | 2,320 |
| Accounts written off | 1,950 |
| Accounts previously written off but recovered | 430 |

Accounts receivable for the Time Ltd. were reported on the balance sheet prepared at the end of the prior year, 20X8, as follows:

| | | | |
|---|---:|---:|---:|
| Accounts receivable | | $62,400 | |
| Less:   Allowance for doubtful accounts | $2,630 | | |
| Allowance for sales returns | 870 | 3,500 | $58,900 |

**ADDITIONAL INFORMATION:**

The company sells goods on account. At the end of the year, accounts receivable are aged and the following percentages are applied in arriving at an estimate of the charge for doubtful accounts.

| | Estimated Loss |
|---|---:|
| Current accounts | 0% |
| Accounts 1–2 months overdue | 8% |
| Accounts 3–6 months overdue | 25% |
| Accounts 7–12 months overdue | 60% |
| Accounts more than 1 year overdue | 100% |

At the end of the year, most of the accounts receivable are current. However, the aging schedule (after write-offs and recoveries) shows the following:

| | |
|---|---:|
| Accounts 1–2 months overdue | $6,500 |
| Accounts 3–6 months overdue | 3,100 |
| Accounts 7–12 months overdue | 1,200 |
| Accounts more than 1 year overdue | 1,380 |

An analysis shows that the allowance for sales returns should have a balance of $1,050 at the end of the year.

**Required:**

1. Give the entries required to record the transactions listed above and also to adjust the accounts.

2. Calculate the balance for accounts receivable and the related allowances as at 31 December 20X9, and show these accounts as they will appear on the balance sheet.

**A7-9 Allowance for Doubtful Accounts:** The accounting records of Sine.Com Limited provided the following for 20X9:

| | |
|---|---|
| Balance in accounts receivable, 1 January 20X9 | $ 90,000 |
| Balance in accounts receivable, 31 December 20X9 | 120,000 |
| Balance in allowance for doubtful accounts, 1 January 20X9 | 3,000 (cr) |
| Accounts written off as uncollectible during 20X9 | 5,500 |

Cash sales were $900,000, while credit sales were $650,000. Recently, Sine.Com's management has become concerned about various estimates used in its accounting system, including those relating to receivables and uncollectible accounts. The company is considering various alternatives with a view to selecting the most appropriate approach and related estimates.

For analytical purposes, the following 20X9 alternative estimates have been developed for consideration:

a. Bad debts approximate 0.75% of credit sales.
b. Bad debts approximate 0.4% of total sales.
c. Six percent of the uncollected accounts receivable at year-end will be uncollectible.
d. Aging of the accounts receivable at the end of the period indicated that 80% would incur a 2% loss, while the remaining 20% would incur a 10% loss.

**Required:**

1. For each of the four alternatives listed above, give the following:
   a. 20X9 adjusting entry
   b. Ending 20X9 balance in the allowance account
   c. An evaluation of the alternative.
2. Explain which of the four alternatives you would recommend.     (ASCA, adapted)

---

 **A7-10 Allowance for Doubtful Accounts:** Technical Armour Company has $5,471,100 of accounts receivable at 30 September 20X7. Sales for the year have been $29,461,400. These accounts are categorized as follows:

| Age | Percentage of Total | Probability of Collection |
|---|---|---|
| 0–30 days | 60* | 98 |
| 30–45 days | 14 | 90** |
| 45–60 days | 8 | 80 |
| 60–90 days | 6 | 60 |
| over 90 days | 12 | 55** |

*round receivable to the nearest hundred
**percentage applies to remainder after write-off

**ADDITIONAL INFORMATION:**

a. Before any adjustments, the allowance for doubtful accounts has a credit balance of $67,900.
b. Write-offs are required for $138,700 of existing accounts receivable in the 30–45-day category, and $291,700 in the over-90-day category. The probability of collection provided above relates to the remaining accounts receivable in these categories.

**Required:**

1. Calculate bad debt expense, and the net balance of accounts receivable, as shown on the balance sheet, for the period ended 30 September 20X7.
2. Repeat requirement (1) assuming that the company uses the percentage-of-sales method and that 2.95% of sales are expected to be uncollectible. All other information is unchanged.

★ **A7-11 Transfer of Accounts Receivable:** On 1 April 20X5, XCourt Company transferred $75,000 of accounts receivable to Prima Finance Company to obtain immediate cash. Consider the two following independent circumstances.

**Required:**

1. The transfer agreement specified a price of $64,200 on a without-recourse, notification basis that effectively transferred legal control to Prima. Give the entry/entries that XCourt Company should make. The $10,800 reduction from face value represents a $6,800 financing fee and $4,000 of expected bad debts that are already in the allowance for doubtful accounts. Explain the basis for your response.

2. The transfer agreement specified a price of $70,000 on a with-recourse, notification basis. The $5,000 reduction from face value is related to expected bad debts, $2,000, and a $3,000 financing fee. The bad debt amount is already in the allowance for doubtful accounts. XCourt retained the right to repurchase the receivables. Give the entry/entries that XCourt should make.

3. Explain the difference to the balance sheet between (1) and (2).

★ **A7-12 Transfer of Accounts Receivable:** The following two cases are independent.

*Case A* Appa Apparel manufactures fine sportswear for many national retailers and frequently sells its receivables to financing companies as a means of accelerating cash collections. Appa transferred $600,000 of receivables from retailers to a financing company and has no control over, or continuing interest in, the accounts receivable. The receivables were transferred without recourse on a notification basis. The financing company charged 12% of the receivables total.

**Required:**

1. Should Appa record the transfer of receivables as a sale or as a borrowing? Why?
2. Record all entries related to the transfer for Appa.

*Case B* Bappa Apparel manufactures fine sportswear for many national retailers and frequently sells its receivables to financing companies as a means of accelerating cash collections. Bappa transferred $600,000 of receivables from retailers to a financing company. The receivables were transferred with recourse on a notification basis. The financing company charged 8%. Bappa has no obligation to the financing company other than to pay the account of a retailer in the event of a default. However, Bappa retains legal control over the receivables, and the financing company may not use the receivables as collateral in any other financing arrangement.

**Required:**

1. Should Bappa record the transfer of receivables as a sale or as a borrowing? Why?
2. Record Bappa's entries related to the transfer.

★★ **A7-13 Transfer of Accounts Receivable:** The following situations involve transactions that should be classified as either a sale or a borrowing:

a. Sherman Company pledges $400,000 of accounts receivable as collateral for a loan (notification basis). Interest is charged on the monthly outstanding loan balance, and a 2% finance fee is charged immediately on the accounts assigned.

b. Hopper Company transfers $50,000 of accounts receivable on a non-recourse basis. The finance company charges an 8% fee and withholds 10% to cover sales adjustments. The finance company obtains full legal title to the receivables and assumes collection responsibilities.

c. Pineapple Company transfers $40,000 of accounts receivable on a recourse basis. Pineapple assumes the cost of all sales adjustments. The receivables are part of a much larger group of receivables. Pineapple's business is stable, and sales adjustments are readily estimable. Pineapple is compelled under the ROAP clause of the transfer agreement to replace any defaulting receivables with others from its portfolio. If Pineapple were to go bankrupt, the bankruptcy trustee would obtain control over the receivables, and the financing obligation would rank as a general secured creditor.

d. Helms Company transfers $80,000 of accounts receivable on a recourse basis. At the finance company's option, Helms must repurchase the receivables.

e. Franklin Company transfers a $10,000 note received in a sale, on a recourse basis. Franklin has no legal access to the receivable after the transfer. Franklin must reimburse the bank in the event of default by the original maker of the note. The risk of default is negligible.

f. Puget Company transfers on a recourse basis a $30,000 note received in a sale. Puget may repurchase the discounted notes at face value for a small fee if it desires.

g. Pobedy Company pledges all of its accounts receivable as collateral for a loan. Pobedy must use the proceeds from the accounts receivable to service the loan. Pobedy retains title to the receivables. In the event of default by Pobedy on the loan, the finance company has a claim against any of these receivables for payment of the loan.

**Required:**

1. For each of the preceding situations, explain whether the financing of the receivables should most likely be recorded as a sale or a borrowing.

2. Explain, in general, the impact that the sale versus borrowing policy decision will have on the financial statements.

---

★ **A7-14 Note Receivable:** The following cases are independent. For each case:

1. Give all entries related to the transactions through to maturity. The company uses the gross method to account for accounts and notes receivable.

2. Show the items that will be reported on the 20X8 income statement and balance sheet.

*Case A* On 1 May 20X8, Archibald Company sold merchandise to Customer Morrison and received a $150,000 (face amount), one-year, non-interest-bearing note. The going (i.e., market) rate of interest is 6%. The annual reporting period for Archibald Company ends on 31 December. Customer Morrison paid the note in full on its maturity date.

*Case B* On 15 April 20X8, O'Malley Company sold merchandise to Customer MacLean for $780,000, terms 2/10, n/EOM (i.e., end of month). The sale is recorded gross, at $780,000. Because of non-payment by MacLean, O'Malley received a $780,000, 8%, 12-month note on 1 May 20X8. The annual reporting period ends 30 September. Customer MacLean paid the note in full on its maturity date.

---

★★ **A7-15 Note Receivable:** MacDonald Company sells large construction equipment. On 1 January 20X5, the company sold Chowdury Company a machine at a quoted price of $60,000. MacDonald collected $20,000 cash and received a two-year note payable for the balance.

**Required:**

1. Give MacDonald's required entries for the two years, assuming an interest-bearing note, face value $40,000. (8% interest, simple interest, payable each 31 December.)

2. Assume that the market interest rate is still 8%. Give MacDonald's required entries for the two years, assuming a 2% interest-bearing note, face value $40,000. Prepare the entries based on the gross basis.

3. Compare the interest revenue and sales revenue under requirements (1) and (2).

---

★★ **A7-16 Note Receivable:** MacDiarmid Limited sold a $20,000 car to a customer on 1 January 20X6, and granted the customer a three-year, 2% loan. The customer has to pay interest every 31 December, but the $20,000 principal is due only after three years. Market interest rates are in the range of 8%.

**Required:**

1. What is the present value of the loan?
2. Record the sale/loan on January 1, 20X6, the interest each December 31 (three times) and the loan repayment on December 31, 20X8. Use the gross method to record the note.
3. Assume that MacDiarmid had a fiscal year-end of September 30. What adjusting entry would the company make on September 30, 20X6?

---

★ **A7-17 Non-Interest-Bearing and Low-Interest Notes:**

a. On 1 January 20X8, a heavy-duty forklift was purchased with a list price of $17,750. Payment included $2,750 cash and a two-year, non-interest-bearing note of $15,000 (maturity date, 31 December 20X9). A realistic interest rate for this level of risk is 8%.
b. On 1 January 20X8, earth-moving equipment was purchased and payment was made as follows: cash, $20,000, and a two-year, 2%, interest-bearing note of $60,000, maturity date 31 December 20X9. A realistic interest rate for this level of risk is 8%.

**Required:**
Give all entries for each case from purchase date through maturity date of each note. Disregard depreciation. Round to the nearest dollar. Use the gross method to record the note. The accounting period ends on 31 December.

---

★ **A7-18 Notes Payable:** Sable Corporation signed a $125,000 four-year note payable. The note required annual blended payments, to be paid at the end of each year. The market interest rate is 6%.

**Required:**

1. Calculate the required blended payment. Round to the nearest dollar.
2. Prepare a schedule that shows the annual interest and principal portion of the four payments.
3. Prepare journal entries to record the initial loan and each payment.

---

★★ **A7-19 Notes Payable:** Mercury Limited reports the following transactions in 20X3:

1. Mercury bought goods from NTY Limited, signing a note payable in return. The note was a $65,000, three-year note that required annual end-of-period payments in the amount of $24,768. The interest charged was the market interest rate at the time.
2. Mercury borrowed money from the Bank of Toronto, signing a $50,000, four-year, 8% note payable.
3. Mercury bought a piece of equipment, paying $5,000 in cash and signing a $50,000, two-year 2% note. Interest is paid at the end of each year. Market interest rates are in the range of 8%.

**Required:**

1. What interest rate is implicit in the $65,000 note?
2. Record each note at its inception. Use the gross method, where appropriate.
3. How much interest expense will be recorded on the income statement with respect to the three notes in year 1? Year 2? Assume that these notes were issued at the beginning of the fiscal year.
4. What is the balance in each note payable (net) at the end of the first fiscal year? Again, assume that these notes were issued at the beginning of the fiscal year.

---

★ **A7-20 Analysis and Comparison of Notes:** On 1 September 20X5, Dyer Company borrowed an amount of cash on a $100,000 note payable due in one year. That is, Dyer agreed to repay $100,000 in one year, plus interest if specified in the loan contract. Assume the going rate of interest was 12% per year for this particular level of risk. The accounting period ends 31 December.

**Required:**
Complete the following tabulation; round to the nearest dollar:

| | Assuming the Note Was | |
| --- | --- | --- |
| | Interest Bearing | Non Interest Bearing |
| 1. Cash received | $ | $ |
| 2. Cash paid at maturity date | $ | $ |
| 3. Total interest paid (cash) | $ | $ |
| 4. Interest expense in 20X5 | $ | $ |
| 5. Interest expense in 20X6 | $ | $ |
| 6. Amount of liabilities reported on 20X5 balance sheet: | | |
|     Note payable (net) | $ | $ |
|     Interest payable | $ | $ |
| 7. Principal amount | $ | $ |
| 8. Face amount | $ | $ |
| 9. Maturity value | $ | $ |
| 10. Stated interest rate | % | % |
| 11. Yield or effective interest rate | % | % |

---

★ **A7-21 Cash Flow and Doubtful Accounts:** Excerpts from Marston's income statement, balance sheet, and statement of cash flows follow:

| | ($ millions) | |
| --- | --- | --- |
| | 20X1 | 20X0 |
| *Income statement:* | | |
| Revenues | $29,600 | $29,300 |
| Bad debt expense | 344 | 280 |
| *Balance sheet:* | | |
| Current assets: | | |
|   Receivables, less allowance for uncollectibles | | |
|     of $220 and $270, respectively | $ 3,700 | $ 3,440 |
| *Statement of cash flows:* | | |
| Cash flows from operating activities: | | |
|   Net income | $ 2,580 | $ 2,740 |
|   Add back non-cash expenses: bad debts | 344 | 280 |

**Required:**
Answer the following questions assuming that (a) Marston uses the allowance method to estimate bad debts (provision for uncollectibles) and (b) all revenues are credit sales.

1. Are estimated uncollectible accounts increasing or decreasing as a percentage of revenues?
2. How much were net write-offs of accounts receivable during 20X1?
3. How much cash was collected on receivables during 20X1?

---

★★ **A7-22 Impairment; Change in Present Value:** On 1 January 20X5, Robertson Inc. sold merchandise (cost, $8,000; sales value, $14,000) to Russell, Inc., and received a non-interest-bearing note in return. The note requires $17,636 to be paid in a lump sum on 31 December 20X7.

On 1 January 20X6, Russell requested that the terms of the loan be modified as follows: $7,000 to be paid in five years (at the end of 20X10), $10,636 due in six years (at the end of 20X11). Robertson refused Russell's request.

During 20X6, however, news of Russell's deteriorating financial condition prompted Robertson to reevaluate the collectibility of the note. Consequently, the modified terms requested by Russell were accepted and used to estimate the future cash flows to be received, as of 31 December 20X6.

**Required:**

1. Prepare the entry to record the sale by Robertson, assuming a perpetual inventory system. Also prepare the 31 December 20X5 adjusting entry. Use the net method. You will need to establish the interest rate implicit in the original note.

2. Prepare the entry to record the impairment on 31 December 20X6. (Compare the book value of the note at 31 December to the present value of the newly acknowledged cash flow stream. Assume that no interest revenue is accrued in 20X6.)

3. Prepare the entry to record interest revenue at 31 December 20X7.

★ **A7-23 Compensated Absences:** Tunacliff Mowers allows each employee to earn 15 fully paid vacation days each year. Unused vacation time can be carried over to the next year; if not taken during the next year, it is lost. By the end of 20X5, all but 3 of the 30 employees had taken their earned vacation time; these 3 carried over to 20X6 a total of 20 vacation days, which represented 20X5 salary of $6,000. During 20X6, each of these three used their 20X5 vacation carryover; none of them had received a pay rate change from 20X5 to the time they used their carryover. Total cash wages paid: 20X5, $700,000; 20X6, $740,000.

**Required:**

1. Give the entries for Tunacliff related to vacations during 20X5 and 20X6. Disregard payroll taxes.

2. Compute the total amount of wage expense for 20X5 and 20X6. How would the vacation time carried over from 20X5 affect the 20X5 balance sheet?

★★ **A7-24 Entries to Record Sales Taxes, Payroll, and Related Entries:** Chernin Limited had the following transactions in February 20X8:

a. Recorded sales of $2,600,000, plus GST of 6%.
b. Recorded sales of $13,400,000, plus GST of 6%.
c. Bought capital assets of $1,350,000, plus GST of 6%.
d. Recorded the bimonthly payroll of $171,800. CPP deductions were $2,400, EI deductions were $3,000, and income tax withheld amounted to $14,400. (Employer portions are recorded only at the end of the month.)
e. Recorded sales of $3,000,000, plus GST of 6%.
f. Bought inventory for $15,600,000, plus GST of 6%.
g. Recorded the bimonthly payroll. The amounts were identical to the prior bimonthly payroll.
h. Recorded the employer portion of payroll expenses for the entire month.
i. Remitted payroll taxes for the month.
j. Remitted net GST for the month.

**Required:**
Provide journal entries to record all transactions. Assume all transactions were for cash.

★ **A7-25 Balances for Sales Taxes, Payroll Taxes:** Hoffman reported opening balances as at 1 June 20X8:

| | |
|---|---|
| GST payable | $21,500 cr. |
| Income tax deductions payable | 1,300 cr. |
| CPP payable | 950 cr. |
| EI payable | 400 cr. |

The company had the following transactions in June 20X8:

a. Collected $354,000 of GST on sales to customers.
b. Recorded the bimonthly payroll, which included CPP deductions of $1,400, EI deductions of $1,200, and income tax withheld of $10,700.
c. Recorded the second bimonthly payroll. The payroll included CPP deductions of $1,500, EI deductions of $1,400, and income tax withheld of $11,700.
d. Bought capital assets of $800,000, plus GST of 6%.
e. Recorded the employer portion of payroll expenses for the entire month.
f. Paid $266,500 GST on inventory purchases.

**Required:**
Calculate the balances in the four accounts listed above as at 30 June 20X8. No payments on account were paid during the month.

---

★★ **A7-26 Recording and Reporting Transactions:** The following selected transactions of Mattingly Company were completed during the accounting year just ended, 31 December 20X5:

a. Merchandise was purchased on account; a $10,000, one-year, 16% interest-bearing note, dated 1 April 20X5, was given to the creditor. Assume a perpetual inventory system.
b. A customer paid for merchandise on 1 February 20X5, with a two-year, $16,000, 3% note. The going interest rate for this term and risk was 15%. Cost of goods sold was $8,320.
c. A supplier delivered goods costing US$13,580. The Canadian dollar was worth US$0.925 on this day.
d. On July 1, the company borrowed $25,000 in cash from the bank on a demand basis. The interest rate was 15%, to be paid on the anniversary date of the loan.
e. Payroll records showed the following:

| | Employee | | | | Employer | |
| --- | --- | --- | --- | --- | --- | --- |
| Gross Wages | Income Tax | EI | CPP | Union Dues | EI | CPP |
| $50,000 | $15,000 | $3,100 | $2,900 | $500 | $4,340 | $2,900 |

f. Remittances were income tax, $14,350; EI, $7,250; CPP, $5,720; union dues, $480.
g. The company sold goods to a foreign customer and charged US$23,790. On this day, the Canadian dollar was worth US$0.914. Cost of goods sold was $11,110.
h. Cash dividends declared but not yet paid were $14,000.
i. Accrued appropriate interest at 31 December, and adjusted foreign-denominated receivables and payables to the year-end rate, Cdn$1 = US$0.913.

**Required:**
1. Give the entry or entries for each of the above transactions and events.
2. Prepare a list (title and amount) of the balance sheet receivables and payables at 31 December 20X5.

---

★ **A7-27 Foreign Exchange:** Golden Limited had the following transactions in 20X5:

a. Sold goods on 1 June to a British company for 70,000 euros with payment to be in four month's time.
b. Bought goods from a U.S. supplier on 15 June for US$150,000; payment was due in one month's time.
c. Bought goods from a British supplier on 15 July for 20,000 euros; settlement was to be in two month's time.
d. Paid the U.S. supplier on 15 July.
e. Paid the British supplier on 15 September.
f. Received payment from the British customer on 1 October.

**EXCHANGE RATES:**

| Canadian Equivalencies | Euros | US$ |
|---|---|---|
| 1    June | 2.11 | 1.07 |
| 15  June | 2.19 | 1.11 |
| 15  July | 2.13 | 1.17 |
| 15  September | 2.20 | 1.03 |
| 1    October | 2.17 | 1.06 |

**Required:**
Prepare journal entries for the above transactions.

---

★★★  **A7-28 Comprehensive:** Data regarding Fortunay Corp. in March 20X9:

| Selected opening balances: | GST payable | $64,400 cr. |
|---|---|---|
| | CPP payable | 2,950 cr. |
| | EI payable | 4,600 cr. |
| | Income tax deductions payable | 16,360 cr. |

a. Inventory purchases on account, $1,580,000 plus 6% GST.
b. Credit card sales for the period, $2,300,000, plus 6% GST. The credit card fee is 2%, and is taken from the gross amount, including GST.
c. Cash sales for the period, $690,000 plus 6% GST.
d. Monthly payroll, $118,000; less EI, $3,800; CPP, $2,200; income tax, $12,400. The employer portion of payroll taxes was also recorded.
e. Sales to U.S. customer on account, US$107,000. There was no GST on the sale. The U.S. dollar was worth Cdn$1.17 on this date.
f. The U.S. customer paid US$50,000 on account, when the U.S. dollar was worth $1.20. The remaining amount will be paid in June.
g. A sale was made on account at the end of the month. The customer gave a $75,000, three-year, 4% note in exchange for the goods. Interest will be paid annually. The market interest rate was 9% on this date. For the sake of simplicity, assume that this sale is not subject to GST. Record the note using the gross method.
h. GST owing was remitted.
i. 75% of the amount owing to suppliers was paid.
j. At the end of the month, the U.S. exchange rate was Cdn$1.19

**Required:**

1. Journalize all transactions listed above.
2. List the accounts and amounts that would appear on the 31 March balance sheet. Exclude cash and inventory.

---

★★  **A7-29 Comprehensive:** The following situations are independent:

1. YST Company sold goods to a U.S. company, for US$125,000. The goods were carried in inventory at Cdn$97,600. On the date of sale, the exchange rate was US$1 = Cdn$1.05. Thirty days later, when the exchange rate was $1.08, the customer paid. YST uses a perpetual system to account for inventory. Record all entries associated with the sale and the collection of cash.
2. Mirabella Company uses an allowance system for bad debts. At the beginning of the year, the allowance had a balance of $45,000 credit. The following transactions and events took place during the year:
   a. Accounts receivable of $34,000 were written off.

b. GTT Company, which owed $1,000, was one of the accounts written off in (a). GTT subsequently paid $300. The balance of this account is now expected to be paid in the next six months.

c. Aging of outstanding accounts receivable at the end of the year showed that an allowance of $60,000 is needed.

Record all entries for (a), (b), and (c).

3. RRR Limited has $350,000 of accounts receivable. These are transferred to a financial institution at a discount rate of 8%. Of the total, $12,250 of the accounts are expected to be bad and are already represented in the allowance for doubtful accounts. The 8% financing fee relates to the net balance. The transaction is to be recorded as a sale of receivables.

a. Record the transaction.

b. Why is recording the transaction as a sale sometimes criticized?

**Required:**
Answer the questions as indicated in each of the above situations.

---

 **A7-30 Comprehensive:** April Ltd. reported various selected balances in its 31 December 20X7 unadjusted trial balance:

| | |
|---|---:|
| Accounts receivable | $1,800,000 dr. |
| Special accounts receivable | 225,000 dr. |
| Accounts receivable—U.S. | 116,000 dr. |
| Allowance for doubtful accounts | 158,050 cr. |
| Allowance for sales discounts | 45,000 cr. |
| Compensated absence liability | 221,600 cr. |

The following transactions and events are noted:

1. An analysis of accounts receivable indicates that $800,000 are still in the discount period. Approximately 10% may be returned.

2. An analysis of accounts receivable indicated that $198,000 of accounts receivable should be written off. Of the remaining balance, 80% was current, and, after the allowance for sales discounts, approximately 5% was deemed doubtful. Of the 20% non-current, 75% was doubtful.

3. The U.S. account receivable was recorded when the exchange rate was $1.16. The exchange rate at year-end was $1.12.

4. The special account receivable was a single account receivable from a customer with an excellent credit rating that was transferred to a financial institution at a discount rate of 4% during the period. The cash collected from the financial institution was credited to an account called "Miscellaneous credits." Management has determined that this transaction was to be recorded as a sale, but has not yet made the necessary entry.

5. The company has a note receivable that has not yet been recorded. The note is a $70,000, three-year note that bears an interest rate of 4%. Interest is paid annually. The note was issued on 1 November 20X7 because of a sale. The market interest rate for accounts of this risk is 8%.

6. The compensated absence liability is unadjusted from last year. All employees from last year's accrual have taken their vacation, as per company policy. At the end of this year, 45 employees have vacation entitlements; 30 for 1.5 weeks, and 15 for 2 weeks. Salary per week is an average of $2,200 for all employees. In addition, four executives have three weeks' vacation entitlement at $3,500 per week.

**Required:**
Provide journal entries to reflect the above items.

★ **A7-31 Cash Flow Statement:** Selected accounts from the Finch Company balance sheet at 31 December:

| 31 December | 20X5 | 20X4 |
|---|---|---|
| Cash | $172,000 | $110,000 |
| Receivables, net | 150,000 | 170,000 |
| Marketable securities | 140,000 | 190,000 |
| Inventory | 575,000 | 498,000 |
| Current liabilities | 193,000 | 186,000 |
| Bank overdraft | 130,000 | 168,000 |

a. Net income for the year was $59,100.
b. There was a bad debt expense of $27,500 for the year. The allowance of doubtful accounts was $34,500 at the end of 20X5, and had been $24,600 at the end of 20X4.
c. Marketable securities were short-term interest-bearing securities, considered to be cash equivalents.

**Required:**

1. Calculate the opening and closing cash figure that would appear on the cash flow statement.
2. Calculate cash from operations for the year based on the information given, using the indirect method of presentation.

(CGA-Canada, adapted)

★★ **A7-32 Bank Reconciliation (Appendix):** The following information is available concerning the cash accounts of Scholastic Ltd:

a. **Balances:**

| | Balance per Bank | Balance per Books |
|---|---|---|
| 30 November 20X9 | $18,570 | $12,368 |
| 31 December 20X9 | 19,362 | 18,808 |

b. There were $6,352 of outstanding deposits at the end of November and $7,504 of outstanding cheques at the end of December. There were no outstanding deposits in November, but $3,210 was outstanding in December.
c. In December, there were $930 of NSF cheques charged to Scholastic's bank account. These have not yet been recorded by Scholastic.
d. Scholastic received $1,342 in a bank loan during December, an increase to the current loan outstanding. This has not been recorded by Scholastic.
e. Interest on the bank loans for the month of December charged by the bank against the bank account was $1,829. This has not been recorded by Scholastic.
f. On 31 December 20X9, a $2,323 cheque of Scholar Corp was charged to the company's account in error.

**Required:**

1. Prepare a bank reconciliation for 31 December 20X9.
2. Give the adjusting entries relating to the bank reconciliation.

★★ **A7-33 Bank Reconciliation (Appendix):** The August bank reconciliation for Sour Patch Limited:

| | |
|---|---|
| Balance per bank | $31,570 |
| Plus: outstanding deposits | 6,900 |
| Less: Outstanding cheques ($1,245, $650, $570, $890, $120) | (3,475) |
| Cash, per general ledger | $34,995 |

September information, per books:

| Cash Receipts Journal Deposits: | | Cash Disbursements Journal Cheques: | |
|---|---|---|---|
| 7 Sept. | $ 4,600 | 1030 | $ 9,000 |
| 11 Sept. | 22,500 | 1031 | 4,650 |
| 14 Sept. | 7,800 | 1032 | 4,780 |
| 22 Sept. | 3,400 | 1033 | 75 |
| 25 Sept. | 11,600 | 1034 | 165 |
| 30 Sept. | 3,210 | 1035 | 15,700 |
| 30 Sept. | 1,750 | 1036 | 10,420 |
| | $54,860 | | $44,790 |

September information, per bank:

Opening balance: $31,570

| Deposits: | Cheques: |
|---|---|
| $ 6,900 | $   570 |
| 4,600 | 890 |
| 22,500 | 175 (Cheque of Patch Co.)* |
| 7,800 | 90 (service charges) |
| 1,750 (direct deposit by customer on account) | 9,000 |
| | 4,780 |
| 3,400 | 120 |
| 11,600 | 9,700** |
| $58,550 | 4,650 |
| | $29,975 |

*Charged to this account in error
**For automobile; incorrectly recorded as $15,700 by company.

**Required:**

1. Prepare a bank reconciliation in good form at the end of September.
2. Prepare any adjusting journal entries required as a result of the reconciliation.

**A7-34 Bank Reconciliation (Appendix):** Ample Company carries its chequing account with Commerce Bank. The company is ready to prepare its 31 December bank reconciliation. The following information is available:

a. The 30 November bank reconciliation showed the following:
   (i) Cash on hand (held back each day by Ample Company for change), $400 (included in Ample's Cash account);
   (ii) Deposit in transit, #51, $2,000; and
   (iii) Cheques outstanding, #121, $1,000; #130, $2,000; and #142, $3,000.

b. Ample Company cash account for December

| | |
|---|---|
| Balance, 1 December | $ 64,000 |
| Deposits: #52—#55, $186,500; #56, $3,500 | 190,000 |
| Cheques: #143—#176, $191,000; #177, $2,500; #178, $3,000; and #179, $1,500 | (198,000) |
| Balance, 31 December (includes $400 cash held for change) | $ 56,000 |

c. Bank statement, 31 December

| | |
|---|---:|
| Balance, 1 December | $ 67,600 |
| Deposits: #51—#55 | 188,500 |
| Cheques: #130, $2,000; #142, $3,000; #143—#176, $191,000 | (196,000) |
| Account receivable collected for Ample Co. | 6,720 |
| Cash received from foreign customer: | |
| prepayment on order; not yet recorded by Ample Co. | 10,000 |
| NSF cheque, Customer Belinda | (200) |
| United Fund (automatic charitable donation per transfer | |
| authorization signed by Ample Co.) | (50) |
| Bank service charges | (20) |
| Balance, 31 December | $ 76,550 |

**Required:**

1. Identify by number and dollars the 31 December deposits in transit and cheques outstanding.

2. Prepare the 31 December bank reconciliation.

3. Give all journal entries that should be made at 31 December, based on your bank reconciliation.

---

★★ **A7-35 Comprehensive; Bank Reconciliation (Appendix), Allowance, Recourse:** The following questions are unrelated. Answer each question independently.

1. Barr Limited had a balance in its general ledger cash account of $45,645 and a balance in its bank statement of $56,000 at the end of February. You also learn that there was $1,990 of outstanding cheques from last month, of which $420 has cleared this month. Most of this month's cheques have been cashed by the bank, except for one for $560 and one for $740. In comparing the cheques as cashed by the bank to the cash disbursements journal, you notice that one cheque, to a supplier on account, was recorded as $3,500 but was actually for $350. Another cheque for $120 was cashed by the bank but was a cheque of another company. The bank took service charges of $45 out of the accounting during the period, and one customer paid its $4,500 account by making a deposit directly into Barr's bank account. Barr has not yet recorded this. There are no outstanding deposits. What is the adjusted balance per the books?

2. Savoy Limited uses an allowance for doubtful accounts, which has a credit balance of $45,000 at the beginning of the year. During the year, $56,000 of accounts were written off, and $12,000 of accounts that had been written off last year paid unexpectedly. At the end of the year, the allowance should be adjusted to $29,500 according to an aging schedule prepared by your staff. How much is bad debt expense?

3. McFadden Limited was short of cash and decided to use $450,000 of accounts receivable to raise immediate cash. Accordingly, it transferred these accounts receivable to a financial institution and received $413,000. The $450,000 includes $12,000 of accounts that are doubtful but are already in the allowance for doubtful accounts. Present journal entries for two different ways that this transfer could be recorded if the circumstances warranted.

## CHAPTER 8

# Inventories and Cost of Sales

## INTRODUCTION

In late 2003, Parmalat—a huge international dairy company that is well known in Canada for the Lactantia, Beatrice, and Astro brands—was found to have overstated assets and net income by as much as $20 billion over several years. A large part of the misstatement was in the inventory accounts. Parmalat executives allegedly recorded fictitious purchases of inventory, followed by fictitious sales to customers.[1]

In another incident, bookstore chain Chapters Incorporated reported a $14.7 million loss from "inventory shrinkage" at its troubled distribution centre in July 2001. The company said this represented the difference between what the new management (Indigo Books) thought it had in stock and what it actually found when it did an inventory count.

Inventory is a high-risk asset. Inventories typically represent the largest current asset of manufacturing, wholesale, and retail companies. In today's competitive economic climate, inventory accounting methods and management practices have become profit-enhancing tools. Better inventory systems can increase profitability; poorly conceived systems can drain profits and put businesses at a competitive disadvantage. The success of Wal-Mart is largely the result of finely tuned inventory and supply chain systems.

This chapter covers the various accounting methods used to value and report inventories on the balance sheet. Inventory valuation simultaneously affects measurement of the cost of sales required to determine income.

Inventories usually are carried at historical cost, but will be reported at net realizable value (NRV) if NRV is less than historical cost (this is the lower of cost or market valuation principle). However, certain types of inventory may be valued at market value, such as some agricultural and mineral inventories.

It often is necessary to estimate inventory amounts, particularly for interim statements and as a check on the reasonableness of physical inventory counts—to test for possible "missing" inventory, for example. The main body of this chapter concludes with an overview of inventory estimation methods.

Good inventory control depends on up-to-date, efficient, and reliable inventory accounting systems. The basic concepts of cost flow and of perpetual inventory are discussed in introductory accounting textbooks. We have included these two basic concepts in the Appendix to this chapter, in case you need to refresh your memory.

---

[1] You may wonder why auditors did not detect the fraud earlier. One of the basic postulates of auditing is that top management is not lying to the auditors. If top management is deliberately misleading auditors or hiding parts of the business, it is not easy for an auditor to uncover these systemic frauds.

# TYPES OF INVENTORY

Inventories consist of costs that have been incurred in an earnings process that are held as assets until the earnings process is complete. We typically think of inventories as tangible goods and materials such as raw materials, work in process, finished goods, or merchandise held by retailers. But, depending on the nature of the company's business, inventory may include a wider range of costs incurred and held in an inventory account for matching against revenue that will be recognized later.

For example, a professional services firm such as a software development company or a law firm may accumulate the costs of fulfilling a particular contract as "inventory" until the contract has been substantially completed and the criteria for revenue recognition have been met.

Even in companies that deal with physical goods, "inventory" is likely to consist mostly of costs such as labour and overhead. Tangible raw materials and purchased parts are likely to be a relatively small part of the total cost.

The term "inventory," therefore, must be viewed more broadly than simply the cost of goods purchased for resale. The mercantile business (i.e., retailing and wholesaling) accounts for only about 15% of the Canadian economy. Most other types of companies also have inventories of some type.

Items that may be capital assets for one company may be inventory for another. Machinery and equipment, for example, is inventory for the company that manufactures it. It becomes a capital asset for the company that buys and uses the assets. Even a building, during its construction period, is an inventory item for the builder.

**Classification of Inventory** The major classifications of inventories depend on the operations of the business. A wholesale or retail trading entity acquires merchandise for resale. A manufacturing entity acquires raw materials and component parts, manufactures finished products, and then sells them. A service company has no raw materials or finished goods but does have work in progress. Inventories are classified as follows:

1. *Merchandise inventory.* Goods on hand purchased by a retailer, wholesaler, or a trading company, such as an importer or exporter, for resale. Generally, goods acquired for resale are not physically altered by the purchasing company; the goods are in finished form when they leave the supplier's plant. In some instances, however, parts are acquired and then further assembled into finished products. A bicycle dealer may assemble bicycles from frames, wheels, gears, and so on, prior to selling them at retail, for example.

2. *Production inventory.* The combined inventories of a manufacturing or resource entity, consisting of:
   a. *Raw materials inventory.* Tangible goods purchased or obtained in other ways (e.g., by mining) and on hand for direct use in the manufacture or further processing of goods for resale. Parts or subassemblies manufactured before use are sometimes classified as *component parts inventory.*
   b. *Work-in-process inventory.* Goods or natural resources requiring further processing before completion and sale. Work-in-process inventory includes the cost of direct material and direct labour incurred to date, and normally an allocation of overhead costs.
   c. *Finished goods inventory.* Manufactured or fully processed items completed and held for sale. Finished goods inventory cost includes the cost of direct material, direct labour, and allocated manufacturing overhead related to its manufacture.
   d. *Production supplies inventory.* Items on hand, such as lubrication oils for the machinery, cleaning materials, and small items, such as bolts or glue, that make up an insignificant part of the finished product.

3. *Contracts in progress.* The accumulated costs of performing services required under contract. The costs of performing contract services are charged to a work-in-progress or contracts-in-progress account. The inventory will include the *direct* costs (mostly allocated salaries and wages) of working on the contract, and may include an allocation of overhead or *indirect* costs as well, including amortization of production facilities and depletion of

natural resources. Construction companies will also include the costs of raw materials and of equipment leased or purchased for use exclusively on a particular contract.

4. *Supplies inventories*. Items such as office, janitorial, and shipping supplies. Inventories of this type are typically used in the near future and may be recorded as selling or general expense when purchased instead of being accounted for as inventory.

## INVENTORY POLICY ISSUES

Since cost of sales is often the largest single expense category on the income statement, and since inventory is an integral part of current and total assets, it makes sense that accounting policies in this area can cause income and net assets to change significantly. In what areas can policies be set? There are four basic policy decisions:

1. Items and costs to include in inventory

2. Choice of accounting procedure: periodic versus perpetual systems

3. Cost flow assumptions for measuring cost of sales (COGS)

4. Application of lower of cost or market (LCM) valuations.

Strictly speaking, the choice of periodic or perpetual systems is a *procedural* choice rather than a *policy* choice, but the choice can affect financial reporting and thus should be viewed as an accounting policy choice.

Since (1) periodic versus perpetual and (2) cost flow assumptions are normally covered extensively in introductory accounting textbooks, these two topics have been placed in the Appendix to this chapter. If you need to refresh your knowledge, please read the Appendix.

## ITEMS AND COSTS INCLUDED IN INVENTORY

### Items Included in Inventory

All goods for resale or use owned by the company on the balance sheet date should be included in inventory, regardless of their location. At any time, a business may hold goods that it does not own or own goods that it does not hold. Therefore, care must be taken to identify the goods that should be included in inventory.

Goods *purchased and in transit* should be included in the purchaser's inventory provided ownership has passed to the purchaser. Passage of title for goods in transit depends on the terms of the shipping contract. In some cases, title transfers to the buyer when the goods are passed to the carrier (e.g., a trucking company or railroad). This is sometimes described as FOB (free on board) shipping point. In other cases, the seller has title until the carrier delivers the goods to the final customer. This is sometimes described as FOB destination. There are at least a dozen common shipping arrangements, so contracts must be carefully scrutinized to establish ownership of goods in transit.

Goods that are owned by a company but are out on *consignment* (that is, held by agents) should be included in inventory. Goods should be *excluded* from inventory if they (1) are held for sale on commission or on consignment but owned by someone else or (2) have been received from a supplier but rejected and are awaiting return to the supplier for credit.

**Repurchase Agreements** Some suppliers enter into repurchase agreements to sell and buy back inventory items at prearranged prices if they are not resold by a certain date. This practice has several advantages. Inventory is, in effect, "parked" outside the company, so the supplier may be able to avoid finance and storage expenses that would be incurred if the inventory stayed in-house.

The buyer usually pays all or most of the retail value of the inventory covered in the repurchase agreement until the goods are reacquired by the seller, again at a prearranged price. However, when a repurchase agreement exists, the inventory must remain on the seller's books. In effect, repurchase agreements may be loans from customers rather than sales because the vendor has an obligation to pay back the customer if the goods are not resold.

Special sales agreements exist in some industries, including those selling items to retailers; sporting goods manufacturers and book publishers provide examples. These agreements permit goods to be returned if not sold. Should such goods be considered sold when delivered to the retailer? Revenue recognition rules suggest that these goods should be considered as sales only if returns can be reasonably estimated or if the return privilege has expired. Otherwise, the items remain in the seller's inventory account.

Although legal ownership is a useful starting point to identify items that should be included in inventory, a strict legal determination is often impractical. In such cases, the sales agreement, industry practices, and other evidence of intent should be considered.

## Elements of Inventory Cost

The basic principle for measuring inventory cost is that the cost of inventories should include *all costs incurred to bring the inventories to their present location and condition.*

**Goods Purchased for Resale**   In general, inventory cost is measured by the total cash equivalent outlay made to acquire the goods and to prepare them for sale. These costs include materials purchase cost and incidental costs incurred until the goods are ready for sale to the customer. Cost also includes customs and excise duties. The total of these costs is known as the **laid-down** cost.

Freight charges and other incidental costs incurred in connection with the purchase of tangible inventory are additions to inventory cost. When these costs can be attributed to specific goods, they should be added to the cost of such goods. However, specific identification often is impractical. Therefore, freight costs are commonly recorded in a special account, such as freight-in, which is reported as an addition to the cost of goods available for sale.

Certain incidental costs often are not included in inventory valuation but are reported as separate expenses, even though they theoretically are a cost of goods purchased. Examples include insurance costs on goods in transit, material handling expenses, and import brokerage fees. These expenditures are usually not included in determining inventory costs because the cost of allocating them to specific purchased goods is not worth the benefit.

Companies in some industries regularly offer *cash discounts* on purchases to encourage timely payment from buyers (which speeds cash flow and may save on borrowing costs). Terms of 2/10, n/30, for example, mean that if the invoice is paid within 10 days, a discount of 2% can be taken. Alternatively, the full balance, *n*, is due in 30 days. Most buyers make timely payments and take advantage of cash discounts because the savings are normally quite substantial.[2] In fact, some companies borrow money in order to take advantage of cash discounts. Inventory should be recorded at the lowest available cash price, which is 98% of the invoice price in this case. *Lost discounts are a cost of financing and should not be included in inventory amounts.*

General and administrative (G&A) expenses should not be included as part of the cost of inventory. G&A costs are not directly related to purchase or manufacture of inventory. Distribution and selling costs also are operating expenses and are not allocated to inventories. These costs are treated as period costs and charged to expense when incurred.

**Service Contracts**   When a company enters into a contract to deliver services, there are two elements of cost:

- *Direct costs.* These are the costs of fulfilling the service obligations for each specific contract, such as direct labour and any material or equipment (e.g., special computer equipment or software) that is necessary to complete a particular service contract.

---

[2] Discounts for prompt payment are very expensive for the vendor. If a 2% discount speeds customers' payments by 20 days, on average, then the annual interest rate is equivalent to 37%. The vendor is better off to not give a discount and to borrow from the bank to finance the receivables (or sell the receivables). An annoying aspect of discounts is that some large customers will blithely deduct the discount from their payment even if they pay late; the customer views the discount as a price reduction rather than a reward for quick payment.

Direct labour normally includes the costs of the service company's employees, such as the staff of an accounting or law firm who are working directly on an assignment for a particular client.

- *Overhead costs.* Overhead consists of costs that are necessary to complete service contracts but that cannot be attributed specifically to individual contracts. Overhead includes general items such as office rental, amortization of general office and computer equipment, and supervision. It also includes supplies and other small costs that are theoretically assignable to specific contracts, but are not worth the effort to assign.

For a service company, inventory consists of the accumulated costs of contract work performed to date for which the company has not yet recognized the revenue. This inventory is called *work in progress* or *work in process*, and is shown on the balance sheet as a current asset.

The cost of inventory includes the direct costs of staff who are working on the contract, as well as an allocation of the costs of supervisory personnel and overheads. As with other types of inventory, general administrative and sales expenses are not included in inventory cost.

As a practical matter, when service contracts are short-term contracts, only the direct costs are normally inventoried; overhead costs usually are treated as period costs. When the contract is complete and the revenue is recognized, the inventoried costs are transferred from *work in process* on the balance sheet to *cost of services* provided (or some similar title) on the income statement.

The two approaches for recognizing revenue from long-term contracts were explained in Chapter 6.

**Manufactured Goods** In a retail or wholesale business, there is just one type of inventory—the laid-down cost of goods available for sale. In a service company, we also will see just one inventory type—work in progress. In contrast, a manufacturing or producing company will normally have three types of inventory:

- *Raw materials*—the laid-down cost of raw materials and purchased parts that will be used in production.
- *Work in progress*—the costs incurred on goods that are in production, but not yet finished; work in progress comprises raw materials, direct labour, and an allocation of production overhead.
- *Finished goods*—the cost of goods manufactured and ready for sale, including raw materials, direct labour, and an allocation of production overhead.

Costs move through the different levels of inventory and finally into cost of sales:

- The cost of purchased raw materials and parts starts out in raw materials inventory.
- When raw materials enter production, their cost is transferred to work in progress, with direct labour and overhead costs added to work in progress.
- When production is complete, the accumulated costs are transferred to finished goods.
- When the goods are sold, the cost is transferred from finished-goods inventory to cost of sales.

Overhead should be allocated on the basis of *normal capacity*. **Normal capacity** is the operating level at which the factory is expected to operate most of the time, not full capacity or maximum capacity. You will study cost allocation systems in management accounting courses, but the significant point for financial accounting is that the cost of inventory should *not* absorb all of the manufacturing costs if the manufacturing plant is operating below normal capacity. The costs of idle capacity are expensed as a period cost.

Standard costs may be used for inventory costing purposes, provided that the standards are based on normal capacity.

**Supplies Inventory** In addition to the inventory types described above, most companies also will have an inventory of supplies. *Supplies* are items that are used in the productive activities of the company but that are either (1) used during production (such as lubricant for machinery) or (2) too small to try to keep track of individually, even though they may enter the product directly (such as adhesives, bolts, and rivets). Supplies inventories seldom are disclosed on a balance sheet or in the notes. Instead, they usually are combined with raw materials inventory.

## CONCEPT REVIEW

1. Identify four policy issues to be considered when accounting for inventory.

2. What categories of inventory does a manufacturer have?

3. What are the three elements of cost that should be included in a manufacturer's finished-goods inventory cost?

## PERIODIC OR PERPETUAL RECORDING METHOD

Inventory cost may be measured by either a periodic inventory system or a perpetual inventory system. The essential difference between these two systems from an accounting point of view is the *frequency with which the cost flows are calculated.*

In a *periodic* system, the inventory is physically counted at least once each year and then the total inventory cost is calculated from cost records using the chosen cost flow policy (e.g., FIFO or average cost).

In a full accounting *perpetual* system, the inventory is continuously updated for each purchase and sale. After each change in inventory quantities, the total cost of inventory is recalculated, using the chosen cost flow policy.

For accounting purposes, a perpetual system exists only when the total inventory cost is continually updated. It is possible to use a perpetual system for quantities only, and then to calculate the dollar cost only at the end of each accounting period. In this case, the accounting is based on periodic method; it is not a perpetual system as far as accounting is concerned.

The Appendix contains a more extensive discussion of this topic.

## COST FLOW ASSUMPTIONS

There are only three basic cost flow assumptions acceptable in Canadian and international GAAP:[3]

1. Specific identification

2. First-in, first-out (FIFO)

3. Average cost.

Specific identification and FIFO are unaffected by the decision to use periodic or perpetual inventory systems—under each method, the cost allocated to inventory and cost of sales will be the same under both periodic and perpetual. Average cost *is* affected by the inventory system, however. The Appendix illustrates the details.

Specific identification is used only when inventory items are not ordinarily interchangeable. Specific identification is applied to special-order inventory items that are significantly unlike other items. Most often these are very large items, such as ships or custom-designed yachts. However, the sheer size of the item is not really a factor. Large airplanes cost hundreds of millions of dollars, but they come off a production line and can be costed by FIFO or average cost, despite the fact that there is some relatively minor adaptation of specific models for specific airline customers. Essentially, every Boeing 777 or Airbus A350 is the same and is not accounted for by specific identification.

---

[3] LIFO (last-in, first-out) is not acceptable within Canadian or international GAAP. It remains acceptable in the U.S. and Japan, but even in those countries it is very seldom used.

The "workhorses" of inventory cost flow assumptions are (1) FIFO and (2) average cost. In hand-kept bookkeeping systems, FIFO was more popular, especially for perpetual systems, because there was no need to continuously recalculate the average cost. With the almost universal adoption of computer-based accounting systems, however, the average cost method has increased dramatically in popularity, especially as it works well with point-of-sale bar code scanners to continuously track quantities.[4]

## APPLYING LCM VALUATION

### Estimating Net Realizable Value

GAAP requires that most inventories be valued either at *laid-down cost* or at **net realizable value (NRV)**, whichever is lower. The NRV is the estimated selling price in the normal course of business, minus estimated costs of completion (if any) and the estimated amount of any costs that are necessary in order to make the sale. For finished goods, there will be no costs of completion but there may be sales commissions or brokerage fees, and there may be special concessions (such as free shipping) that are necessary to close the sale. These costs must be subtracted from the year-end selling price in order to find NRV.

For example, suppose a retailer has an inventory consisting of a single line of office electronics products, all purchased during 20X2 at a cost of $150 per unit. The retail price was $200 at the time of acquisition. Late in the year, stiff competition in the electronics and office products market causes retail prices to drop significantly. At year-end, the retailer's remaining inventory can be sold in the normal course of business for no more than $160 per unit.

The year-end retail price is above the original unit cost, but what is the NRV of the unit? To determine the NRV, the retailer must subtract any direct costs of making the sale. If the retailer pays a 15% commission to the salesperson, the $24 sales commission must be subtracted from the $160 sales price. The NRV is $160 − $24 = $136. The carrying value of the inventory must be written down from its historical cost of $150 to its NRV of $136, a loss of $14 per unit. This $14-per-unit loss must be reported in the retailer's 20X2 financial statements, the period during which the market price decline took place.

For work in process, the costs of completing the product or project must be estimated and then subtracted, as well as any further costs to sell (e.g., commissions), to find NRV.

The determination of NRV is fairly straightforward in concept, but its application requires a lot of estimation of both sales value (which can be difficult in a rapidly changing market) and costs of completion and sale.

One important point to note: the sales price is the estimated selling price in the normal course of business. In this context, the sales price is not the amount that could be obtained by selling the inventory to another party to dispose of, such as to a clearance house. Such a transaction is outside the normal course of business, and any loss would be recognized at the time of the sale, not through an inventory writedown preceding the sale.

### Reversing Writedowns

Inventory is written down to NRV on the basis of the best information available at the balance sheet date. However, the NRV may go up after inventory has already been written down. For example, prices may rise significantly due to the failure of a major competitor, the discovery of major defects or dangers in a competitor's product, or a shortage of supply. It also is possible that a change in economic environment may cause a recovery of selling price to a higher level than anticipated.

Suppose that the inventory in the example above is written down from $150 historical cost to $136 NRV in 20X2. In 20X3 the estimated $160 sales price recovers to $180. Sales commission remains at 15%, or $27 on a sales price of $180. NRV has increased to $153: $180 − $27. The increase in NRV is $17 per unit (i.e., $153 − $136). The writedown should be reversed for those items still in inventory, thereby restoring the unit inventory carrying

---

[4] The use of bar code scanners does not necessarily mean that a company is accounting for *costs* on a perpetual basis. Often, the bar code system is used only to keep track of inventory *quantities*, not costs.

value to $150. On the income statement, the increase in NRV is recognized as a *reduction in the cost of sales*, not as a separately recognized gain.

The upper limit for recognizing an increase in NRV is the originally recorded historical cost of the asset. Inventory cannot be written up above its historical cost except for those few types of inventory described later, in the "Market Valuation Bases" section.

As a practical matter, reversals seldom occur. The normal expectation is that inventory will turn over within a year, and usually several times during a year. It is unlikely that written-down inventory will still be on the books a year later. If the inventory still is in stock, it almost certainly will merit an additional writedown rather than a reversal. Reversals are more likely to occur for shorter reporting periods, such as monthly or quarterly reporting.

## Extent of Aggregation

An important aspect of LCM inventory valuation is the basis on which the measurement basis is applied. LCM can be applied either (1) item by item or (2) by groupings of related or similar items.

Exhibit 8-1 shows the application of each approach. Inventory is valued at $67,500, a loss of $3,500, if the individual approach is used. If valued in groups, inventory is reported at $69,000, a loss of $2,000.

Consistency in application over time is essential. The item-by-item basis produces the most conservative inventory value because units whose market value exceeds cost are not allowed to offset items whose market value is less than cost. This offsetting occurs to some extent when inventory is valued in groups. The more you aggregate, the less you write down. The less you aggregate, the more you write down.

What level of aggregation is appropriate? There is no easy answer to this question. In general, there should be a relationship between the items that are grouped together. The groupings should not be arbitrary, and they should reflect the sales reality of the organization. Inventories should be not evaluated by general classification of such raw materials or finished products, nor by geographic region. However, the products in a single product line can be grouped together because they represent a "product" in the broad sense of a range of related products. For competitive reasons, some products may be sold at a loss in order to support the sales of products that are highly profitable.

Therefore, some degree of offsetting within categories seems appropriate given the nature of sales efforts in general and the fact that LCM requires a lot of estimation.

## EXHIBIT 8-1

### APPLICATION OF LCM TO INVENTORY GROUPS

| Inventory Types | Cost | NRV | LCM Applied to Individual Items | Groupings |
|---|---|---|---|---|
| Group A: | | | | |
| Item 1 | $10,000 | $ 9,500 | $ 9,500 | |
| Item 2 | 8,000 | 9,000 | 8,000 | |
| | 18,000 | 18,500 | | $18,000 |
| Group B: | | | | |
| Item 3 | 21,000 | 22,000 | 21,000 | |
| Item 4 | 32,000 | 29,000 | 29,000 | |
| | 53,000 | 51,000 | | 51,000 |
| Total | $71,000 | $69,500 | | |
| Inventory valuation under different approaches | | | $67,500 | $69,000 |

### Using a Valuation Allowance

Two methods of recording and reporting the effects of the application of LCM are used in practice:

1. *Direct inventory reduction method.* The inventory holding loss is not separately recorded and reported. Instead, the LCM amount, if it is less than the original cost of the inventory, is recorded and reported each period. Thus, the inventory holding loss is automatically included in cost of sales, and ending inventory is reported at LCM. This method is feasible only when LCM is applied to each item of inventory separately.

2. *Inventory allowance method.* The inventory holding loss is separately recorded using a contra inventory account, *allowance to reduce inventory to LCM.* The inventory remains at historical cost on the books but is reported on the balance sheet net of the valuation account. Assume that the company illustrated in Exhibit 8-1 had an existing allowance of $2,500, and decided to apply LCM by individual items. The entry would be as follows:

| | | |
|---|---|---|
| Holding loss on inventory | 1,000 | |
|   Allowance to reduce inventory to LCM | | |
|     ($2,500 − $3,500) | | 1,000 |

Bear in mind that the balance sheet inventory account is a *control account*—it must be possible to reconcile the control account balance to the detailed subsidiary inventory records by classes and items. The direct reduction method is practical only if LCM has been applied item by item. Only then can individual inventory items be written down in the subsidiary records. If LCM has been applied to inventory groups, it is impossible to record the writedown to specific inventory items.

Therefore, the valuation allowance method is inevitably used when LCM is applied through groupings so that the detailed subsidiary records will correspond with the balance in the balance sheet control account. The valuation allowance method is not limited to group writedowns; it may also be used for when item-by-item LCM is applied.

Another significant advantage of the valuation allowance method is that reversals can also be handled easily. If NRV rises after an initial writedown, only the allowance need be adjusted; the inventory accounts themselves are not touched.

### ETHICAL ISSUES

LCM valuations require estimations. Both the current selling price and the costs to complete and sell must be determined. In a stable market, these estimates may be not too difficult. In a volatile market, both estimates may require quite a lot of judgement.

The difficulty of estimating NRV allows some room for income manipulation, especially if inventories are substantial. Inventory can be written down in one year, and sold at a substantial profit in a later year. Sometimes this happens with no intent to mislead if weak market conditions and poor selling prices dictate writedowns. A recovery in later years may be unexpected.

In other cases, unethical decisions may drive high write-offs in a big bath scenario. Managers who receive bonuses based on net income may be particularly motivated if tentative net income in the first year, or writedown year, is below the level needed to trigger a bonus. In thin-margin businesses, estimation errors can have a significant impact on reported net income.

## MARKET VALUATION BASES

Certain types of inventory are excluded from the measurement rules explained above. Canadian and international accounting standards provide for different treatments for the types of inventories described below. Basically, the exclusions all use NRV as the measurement base without historical cost as the upper limit. That is, the concept of LCM is not used—the inventories are valued at NRV, with gains and losses recognized in income in the year that they occur.

**Financial Instruments Held for Trading** The accounting standards for inventory do not apply to financial instruments. Securities dealers and financial institutions trade in financial instruments—that is the inventory for these types of organizations. Financial instruments held for trading are reported at market value. The inventory of trading securities held by a broker or an investment banker must be recorded at fair value. Similarly, the investments of a mutual fund are required by law to be reported at market value so that the holders of mutual fund shares can see the underlying asset value of their holdings.

**Commodities** A significant exclusion from LCM applies to agricultural and mineral inventories held by producers or by traders such as grain elevator operators. The exclusion includes:

- Agricultural inventories
- Agricultural and forest products
- Minerals and mineral products
- Commodity inventories held by broker-traders.

These inventories often are measured at NRV or at fair value less cost to sell, as we discussed in Chapter 6. Using the NRV as the measurement basis is acceptable when crops have been harvested or minerals extracted, *provided that there is an active market for the commodity and the risk of not selling the product is negligible.* An **active market** is one that has *all* of the following characteristics:

- The items traded in the market are homogeneous (i.e., indistinguishable and interchangeable).
- Willing buyers and sellers can normally be found at any time.
- The prices are available to the public.

This definition fits all major securities exchanges, such as the Toronto and Tokyo and New York Stock Exchanges, as well as NASDAQ. It also fits commodity exchanges such as the Chicago Board of Trade and the Chicago Mercantile Exchange.

When inventories are measured at NRV, all increases and decreases in NRV are routinely recognized in net income in the period in which the changes occur.

Companies that deal in commodities or financial instruments often try to offset the risk of price change by hedging. If a company holds 1,000 tonnes of wheat, the company is vulnerable to a fall in the market price of wheat. To protect its investment, the company usually will enter into a contract to deliver the grain in the future at a fixed price. That contact is a hedge. Hedging contracts can be sold at any time prior to maturity; it is not necessary to actually deliver the wheat.

The value of the hedge contract fluctuates along with changes in the price of wheat. Canadian, U.S., and international accounting standards all require that gains or losses on a hedge contract be reported in net income. Therefore, to offset the gain or loss from the hedge, the company is likely to value the wheat at market value (NRV) as well.

Hedging issues are discussed a little more fully later in the book, in Chapter 14, so don't worry about them now. Just remember that since financial instruments must be reported at market value, any hedged assets should also be reported at market value even though GAAP does not *require* market value for commodities. For example, the 2006 annual report of Agricore United explains the carrying value of its inventories as follows:

---

**Inventories**

Grain inventories include both hedged and non-hedged commodities. Hedgeable grain inventories are valued based on the closing market quotations less execution costs. Non-hedgeable grains are valued at the lower of cost or market. Crop inputs, feed and livestock, and other merchandise inventories are valued at the lower of cost or NRV.

Notice that the company values "hedgeable" inventories at market value, not just "hedged" inventories. If hedges are available for a type of inventory, the inventory is reported at market value (NRV) regardless of whether or not it actually is hedged. The key is that if a commodity is *hedgeable*, then there is an active market for that commodity and the inventory can be sold with negligible effort.

## ETHICAL ISSUES

Companies that deal in commodities are not *required* to report their inventories by NRV; market valuation is a choice, not a requirement. However, it is an available choice only if market valuation is a well-established practice in that industry. If market valuation is not a well-established practice, then LCM valuation must be used.

Some managers may prefer to use historical cost (or LCM) to value commodity inventories even if they are not bound by fixed price contracts and have not hedged the inventory. While we might be tempted to praise their choice of a "conservative" accounting policy, we must bear in mind that historical cost inventory valuation gives the manager an opportunity to manipulate reported earnings by deciding when to engage in transactions that trigger an accounting gain or loss. Commodity prices (and real economic value) change regardless of whether or not the changes are recognized in the books.

**Construction Contracts** Work in progress inventories for construction contracts (and for directly related service contracts) are measured on the percentage-of-completion basis, as we explained in Chapter 6. The percentage-of-completion method gives an inventory value that is similar to NRV but limited by LCM as the upper bound:

- Work in progress comprises costs incurred to date plus the proportionate share of estimated gross profit that has been earned to date.
- NRV is the anticipated sales price minus cost of completion.
- The difference between these two amounts is the amount of profit not yet recognized through construction.
- If NRV is less than the accumulated inventory balance of cost plus recognized profit, it means that the total final profit will be less than the amount of profit already recognized. Therefore, a loss will be recognized in the current period to reduce the inventory to LCM.

## CONCEPT REVIEW

1. What is the definition of NRV?
2. What are the reasons for using a valuation allowance for inventory write-downs rather than using the direct inventory reduction method?
3. When may inventories be valued at NRV, even if it is higher than historical cost?
4. What conditions are necessary for using NRV as the inventory measurement method for commodities?

## OTHER ISSUES

### Damaged and Obsolete Inventory

Special inventory categories are created for items that are damaged, shopworn, obsolete, defective, or are trade-ins or repossessions. These inventory items are valued at NRV.

To illustrate accounting for inventory at NRV, assume that Allied suffers fire damage to 100 units of its regular inventory. The items, which originally cost $10 per unit (as reflected in the perpetual inventory records), were marked to sell before the fire for $18 per unit. No established used market exists. The company should value the item for inventory purposes at its NRV. Allied estimates that after cleaning and making repairs, the items would sell for $7 per unit; the estimated cost of the repairs for all the units is $150, and the estimated selling cost is 20% of the new selling price. Given this data, the total inventory valuation for the items is as follows:

| | | |
|---|---:|---:|
| Estimated sale price (100 × $7) | | $700 |
| Less: Estimated cost to repair | $150 | |
| Estimated selling costs ($700 × 20%) | 140 | (290) |
| NRV for inventory | | $410 |

Damaged inventory is segregated in a separate account as part of the writedown entry:

| | | |
|---|---:|---:|
| Inventory, damaged goods | 410 | |
| Loss from fire damage | 590 | |
| Inventory (100 × $10) | | 1,000 |

## Losses on Purchase Commitments

To lock in prices and ensure sufficient quantities, companies often contract with suppliers to purchase a specified quantity of materials during a future period at an agreed unit cost. Some purchase commitments (contracts) are subject to revision or cancellation before the end of the contract period; others are not. Each case requires different accounting and reporting procedures. A loss must be accrued on a purchase contract when:

- The purchase contract is not subject to revision or cancellation, *and*
- A loss is likely and material, *and*
- The loss can be reasonably estimated.

Assume that the Bayshore Company enters into a noncancellable purchase contract during October 20X2 that states, "During 20X3, 50,000 tanks of compressed chlorine will be purchased at $5 each," a total commitment of $250,000. Suppose that the current replacement cost of the chlorine is $240,000 by year-end. Thus, a $10,000 loss is likely.[5] The loss on the purchase commitment should be recorded at the end of 20X2 as follows:

| | | |
|---|---:|---:|
| Estimated loss on purchase commitment | | |
| ($250,000 − $240,000) | 10,000 | |
| Estimated liability on noncancellable | | |
| purchase commitment | | 10,000 |

The estimated loss is reported on the 20X2 income statement, and the liability is reported on the balance sheet. When the goods are acquired in 20X3, merchandise inventory (or purchases) is debited at the current replacement cost, and the estimated liability account is debited. Assume that the above materials have a replacement cost at date of delivery of $235,000. The purchase entry would be as follows:

---

[5] This is known as an *opportunity cost*, because the company missed the opportunity to buy the chlorine at a lower price.

| | | |
|---|---|---|
| Materials inventory (or purchases) | 235,000 | |
| Estimated liability on non-cancellable | | |
|     purchase commitment | 10,000 | |
| Loss on purchase commitment | 5,000 | |
|     Cash | | 250,000 |

This treatment records the loss in the period when it became likely. Note that inventory is never recorded for more than its replacement cost—so, if the actual historical cost is higher than the replacement cost, historical cost is not used.

If there were a full or partial recovery of the purchase price, the recovery would be recognized (only as a loss recovery; gains are not recognized) in the period during which the recovery took place. Thus, if in 20X3 the materials had a replacement cost at date of delivery of $255,000, the purchase entry would be as follows:

| | | |
|---|---|---|
| Materials inventory (or purchases) | 250,000 | |
| Estimated liability on non-cancellable | | |
|     purchase commitment | 10,000 | |
|     Recovery of loss on purchase commitment | | 10,000 |
|     Cash | | 250,000 |

Review the three criteria for accounting recognition of a loss listed above. What if the contract were cancellable? Then the loss is no longer likely, and the amount would not be accrued. What if the loss were not estimable? Recognition criteria are not met, and again no entry can be made. What if commodity prices are going up, not down? Then a loss is not likely and no entry is appropriate. Gains are not recognized. Disclosure of the contracts and terms is appropriate when the contracts are significant, or out of the ordinary, or when an inestimable loss is present.

### Inventory Errors

In our discussion so far, we have focused mainly on the relationship between inventory and cost of sales. Obviously, we won't get the correct cost of sales if we have problems with our inventory calculations.

But inventory interacts with more than just cost of sales. Incoming inventory relates directly to accounts payable and purchases, while outgoing inventory relates directly to accounts receivable and to revenue. Because of the sheer volume of transactions involving inventory, it takes special vigilance to ensure that there are no errors.

There may be some estimation errors in inventory, especially in lower-of-cost-or-market estimates, in work-in-process inventories relating to long-term contracts, and in estimation techniques such as the retail inventory method (which we will discuss shortly). However, estimates are a fact of life in accounting. They may turn out to be wrong, but they are not errors—we just do the best we can with the information that we have at the time we exercise our professional judgement.

The errors that we are primarily concerned about are *cut-off errors*. "Cut-off" refers to the closing of the books. When we reach the end of a fiscal period, we must draw a line between transactions at (1) the period just ending and (2) the start of the next period. In theory, this is a simple exercise. But in practice, accurate cut-offs are both difficult and crucial.

Think of an ongoing factory. New inventory is delivered almost continuously during every day, and finished goods are shipped to customers all day long. If the factory operates 24 hours a day, when do we stop counting for last year and start counting for next year? Consistency is crucial. If we say that the year-end inventory is the amount in our factories, warehouses, and offices at midnight on 31 December, we must use that same cut-off time each year. The physical count of inventory must be taken as of that specific time, even though inventory is flowing in and out of our factory while the physical count is taking place over the following days.

Counting inventory is only part of the problem. We must be sure that goods shipped on the closing days of the year have also been invoiced to the customers—revenue and accounts receivable must include last-minute shipments. Goods and raw materials flowing into the factory in the final days must be included in purchases and accounts payable. Similarly, we must ensure that revenue has not been recorded for shipments that won't be made until the early days of the next year.

Assuring proper cut-off is a major accounting (and auditing) control issue due to the sheer volume of activity and the need to coordinate all of the accounting activities that involve inventory. As well, unethical managers may be tempted to delay or accelerate shipments around year-end in order to manipulate income. As a result, one of the most common types of accounting error is inventory cut-off error.

Suppose that a company discovers in 20X7 that its 20X6 year-end inventory was overstated by $750,000. The error is discovered after its 20X6 financial statements were issued. An overstatement of ending inventory leads to an (1) understatement of cost of sales, (2) overstatement of income, and (3) overstatement of retained earnings. Therefore, the correction in 20X7 will be recorded as follows:

| | | |
|---|---|---|
| Retained earnings | 750,000 | |
| Inventory (1 January 20X7) | | 750,000 |

When the 20X7 financial statements are prepared, the comparative 20X6 financial statements will be restated to show the correct inventory and income amounts. Errors are always corrected by restatement, and never by showing special charges or credits in the income statement.

Later in the book, we devote a full chapter (Chapter 20) to accounting changes, including error correction. Therefore, we will not elaborate further at this point in the text.

## INVENTORY ESTIMATION METHODS

Many large companies rely on the periodic inventory method. Does this mean that they can't prepare monthly or quarterly statements without also taking a physical inventory? Generally, it is very expensive to conduct inventory counts and therefore physical counts may be done only once each fiscal year. So what can be done when interim statements must be prepared?

The answer is quite simple: inventory can be *estimated*. In a small business, the owner or inventory manager might be able to provide an accurate estimate. Alternatively, a more formal calculation can be made, using methods such as the gross margin method or the retail inventory method. It's important to understand that these are estimation methods. They necessarily introduce some level of unreliability to the financial results, while increasing their timeliness.

Estimation methods are also useful for providing a cross-check on the results of accounting inventory systems. It should be possible to reconcile the estimated inventory (or, more importantly, cost of sales) to a physical inventory count or to the accounting records of perpetual inventory. Obviously the reconciliation will not be exact, but there should be a rough similarity between the results of the accounting inventory system (periodic or perpetual) and the estimated inventory. Large discrepancies raise questions of the accuracy of the accounting system, the effectiveness of the system of internal control, or the possibility of theft.

For example, a local manufacturer of fruit juices and soft drinks also distributed Coca-Cola syrup to restaurants and bars. The Coca-Cola syrup was, in fact, the company's biggest single seller and was also the most profitable product. Despite high sales, the company was only marginally profitable. A gross profit analysis revealed that the recorded cost of sales was much too high, given the level of sales. A closer examination revealed that the inventory of syrup was too low for the amount that was actually recorded as being sold. It finally was discovered that, due to a supervisory lack of vigilance in reconciling each driver's sales with the inventory loaded onto the truck, it was possible for unethical truck drivers to sell jugs of syrup "on their own account," pocketing the money.

Estimation methods are used primarily in mercantile firms: retailing and wholesaling. They are of more limited usefulness in manufacturing but still are useful for finished goods inventories.

Estimates of inventory cannot be used for audited annual financial statements—a physical count is required.

## Gross Margin Method

**gross margin method**

a method of estimating inventories based on historical gross profit margins

The **gross margin method** (also known as the *gross profit method*) uses a constant gross margin to estimate inventory values from current sales. The gross margin rate (that is, gross margin ÷ sales) is estimated on the basis of recent past performance and is assumed to be reasonably constant in the short run. The gross margin method has two basic characteristics:

1. It requires the development of an *estimated gross margin rate* for different lines or products.

2. It applies the rate to *relevant groups of items*.

Is the method accurate? Well, it depends on whether or not gross margins really are reasonably constant in the short run. If retail prices are slashed this year to spur consumer demand, or theft has increased, the gross margin method will overstate earnings and inventory, perhaps significantly. Similarly, if the product mix changes a lot in the current period, the results will not be accurate.

For example, if a company has traditionally sold about half its volume in a high-profit category, and half in a low-profit category, the historical gross profit margin will reflect this mix. In the current year, if volumes fall off in the high-profit side, the estimation method will produce inaccurate results. It's better to do separate estimates for each different product line. Mis-estimates will be uncovered at the end of the year, when inventory is actually counted—which may be an unpleasant surprise for those who relied on the interim statements.

**Estimating by Gross Margin Method** Estimating the ending inventory by the gross margin method requires five steps, as illustrated in Exhibit 8-2:

**Step 1** Estimate the gross margin rate on the basis of prior years' sales: gross margin rate = (sales − cost of sales) ÷ sales.

**Step 2** Compute total cost of goods available for sale in the usual manner (beginning inventory plus purchases), based on actual data provided by the accounts.

**Step 3** Compute the estimated gross margin amount by multiplying sales by the estimated gross margin rate.

**Step 4** Compute cost of sales by subtracting the computed gross margin amount from sales.

**Step 5** Compute ending inventory by subtracting the computed cost of sales from the cost of goods available for sale.

**Uses of the Gross Margin Method** The gross margin method is used to:

- Test the reasonableness of an inventory valuation determined by some other means such as a physical inventory count or from perpetual inventory records. For example, assume the company in Exhibit 8-2 counted inventory, and got a figure of $10,000. The gross margin method provides an approximation of $7,000, which suggests that the physical count may be overvalued and should be examined.

- Estimate the ending inventory for interim financial reports prepared during the year when it is impractical to count the inventory physically and a perpetual inventory system is not used.

- Estimate the cost of inventory destroyed by an accident such as fire or storm. Valuation of inventory lost is necessary to account for the accident and to establish a basis for insurance claims and income taxes. This is an example of a case where it would be

## EXHIBIT 8-2

### GROSS MARGIN METHOD

|  | Known Data | Following Computations:*<br>Estimated Results |
| --- | --- | --- |
| Net sales revenue (base amount) | $10,000 | $10,000 |
| Cost of goods sold: |  |  |
|    Beginning inventory | $ 5,000 | $ 5,000 |
|    Add: Purchases | 8,000 | 8,000 |
|    Goods available for sale | 13,000 | 13,000 |
|    Less: Ending inventory |  | 7,000 |
|    Cost of sales |  | 6,000 |
| Gross margin |  | $ 4,000 |

***Steps:**

1. Gross margin rate (estimated as percent of sales based on last year's results) = 40%
2. Goods available for sale, above: $13,000
3. Gross margin: $4,000 (i.e., $10,000 × 40%)
4. Cost of sales: $6,000 ($10,000 − $4,000)
5. Ending inventory $7,000 ($13,000 − $6,000)

helpful to know the markup on cost (i.e., gross profit ÷ cost of sales) since cost is used for the insurance claim and to establish the loss.

- Develop budget estimates of cost of sales, gross margin, and inventory for budgets.

## Retail Inventory Method

The **retail inventory method** is often used by retail stores, especially stores that sell a wide variety of items. In such situations, perpetual inventory procedures may be impractical, and a complete physical inventory count is usually taken only once, annually. The retail inventory method is appropriate when items sold within a department have essentially the same markup rate and articles purchased for resale are priced immediately. Two major advantages of the retail inventory method are its ease of use and reduced record-keeping requirements, compared to perpetual inventory systems.

The retail inventory method uses both retail value and actual cost data to:

1. Compute a ratio of cost to retail (referred to as the **cost ratio**);

2. Calculate the ending inventory at *retail value*, and

3. Convert that retail value to an LCM value by applying the computed cost ratio to the ending retail value.

Application of the retail inventory method requires that internal records be kept to provide data on:

- Sales revenue
- Beginning inventory valued at both cost and retail
- Purchases during the period valued at both cost and retail
- Adjustments to the original retail price, such as additional markups, markup cancellations, markdowns, markdown cancellations, and employee discounts
- Other adjustments, such as interdepartmental transfers, returns, breakage, and damaged goods.

The retail inventory method differs from the gross margin method in that it uses a computed cost ratio based on the actual relationship between cost and retail for the current period, rather than an historical ratio. The computed cost ratio is often an average across several different kinds of goods sold.

**Estimating by Retail Inventory Method** The retail inventory method is illustrated in Exhibit 8-3. The steps are as follows:

**Step 1** *Determine cost of goods available for sale at cost and retail.*

The total cost of goods available for sale during January 20X2 is determined to be $210,000 at cost and $300,000 at retail, as shown in Exhibit 8-3.

**Step 2** *Compute the cost ratio (ratio of cost to sales).*

This is done by dividing the total cost of goods available for sale at cost ($210,000) by the same items at retail ($300,000). In this instance, the cost ratio is ($210,000 ÷ $300,000) = .70, or 70%, as shown in Exhibit 8-3. This is an *average cost* application of the retail method, because both beginning inventory and purchases are included in determining the cost ratio.

**Step 3** *Compute closing inventory at retail (goods available for sale at retail, less sales).*

This is done by taking the total cost of goods available for sale at retail ($300,000) less the goods that were sold in January ($260,000), resulting in the value of the ending inventory at retail ($40,000), as shown in Exhibit 8-3.

**Step 4** *Compute ending inventory at cost.*

This is done by applying the cost ratio (70%), derived in (2), to the ending inventory at retail ($40,000), derived in (3). The result is an ending inventory of $28,000 at cost ($40,000 × 70%).

**Markups and Markdowns** The data used for Exhibit 8-3 assumed no changes in the sales price of the merchandise as originally set. Frequently, however, the original sales price on merchandise is changed, particularly at the end of the selling season or when replacement costs are changing. The retail inventory method requires that a careful record be kept of all changes to the original sales price because these changes affect the inventory cost computation. To apply the retail inventory method, it is important to distinguish among the following terms:

- **Original sales price.** Sale price first marked on the merchandise.
- **Markup.** The original or initial amount that the merchandise is marked up above cost. It is the difference between the purchase cost and the original sales price, and it may be

---

**EXHIBIT 8-3**

### RETAIL INVENTORY METHOD, AVERAGE COST

|  | At Cost | At Retail |
|---|---|---|
| Goods available for sale: |  |  |
| Beginning inventory | $ 15,000 | $ 25,000 |
| Purchases | 195,000 | 275,000 |
| Total goods available for sale | $210,000 | 300,000 |
| Cost ratio: |  |  |
| $210,000 ÷ $300,000 = 70%; average, January 20X2 |  |  |
| Deduct January sales at retail |  | 260,000 |
| Ending inventory: |  |  |
| At retail |  | $ 40,000 |
| At cost ($40,000 × 70%) | $ 28,000 |  |

expressed either as a dollar amount or a percentage of either cost or sales price. Sometimes this markup is called "initial markup" or "markon."

- **Additional markup.** Any increase in the sales price above the original sales price. The original sales price is the base from which additional markup is measured.
- **Additional markup cancellation.** Cancellation of all, or some, of an additional markup. Additional markup less additional markup cancellations is usually called *net additional markup*.
- **Markdown.** A reduction in the original sales price.
- **Markdown cancellation.** An increase in the sales price (that does not exceed the original sales price) after a reduction in the original sales price markdown.

The definitions are illustrated in Exhibit 8-4. An item that cost $8 is originally marked to sell at $10. This item is subsequently marked up $1 to sell at $11, then marked down to a sales price of $7.

In the application of the retail method, additional markups, markup cancellations, markdowns, and markdown cancellations are all included in the early calculations that determine goods available for sale at cost and at retail. However, in order to provide a conservative cost ratio that will approximate LCM, the denominator of the cost ratio *excludes net markdowns*.

See the example in Exhibit 8-5. If all of the markups and markdowns had been included in the cost ratio, the cost ratio would have been 72.0% (i.e., $6,840 ÷ $9,500). Applying that ratio to the estimated inventory at retail would have given an estimated ending inventory of $720 at cost. However, when the $500 net markdowns (that is, $600 markdowns minus $100 markdown cancellations) are *excluded* from the cost ratio, the cost ratio becomes 68.4% (i.e., $6,840 ÷ $9,500), thereby yielding a lower estimated ending inventory of $684. This lower value approximates the LCM.

**Uses of the Retail Inventory Method**    Like the gross margin method, the retail inventory method is used only to estimate the amount of the ending inventory and cost of goods sold. A physical inventory count must be taken at least annually as a check on the accuracy of the estimated inventory amounts. This method provides a test of the overall reasonableness of a physical inventory.

The retail inventory method is also useful if the entity counts its inventory and then extends the inventory sheets *at retail*. Remember, retail prices are much easier to determine on the selling floor than cost! The retail value then is converted to cost by applying the retail inventory method without reference to the costs of individual items. This value may be used for external reporting if sufficient evidence is accumulated to support the accuracy of the cost percentages.

Perhaps even more than the gross margin method, though, the retail inventory method is subject to estimation errors. A lot of its accuracy depends on how carefully the company keeps track of markups and markdowns and other data needed to develop an accurate cost ratio.

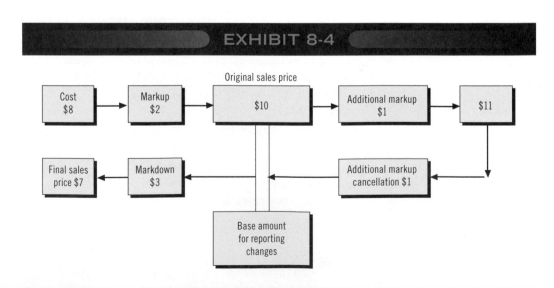

EXHIBIT 8-4

**EXHIBIT 8-5**

## RETAIL INVENTORY METHOD, LCM

|  | At Cost | At Retail |
|---|---|---|
| Goods available for sale: | | |
| Beginning inventory | $  550 | $    900 |
| Purchases during period | 6,290 | 8,900 |
| Plus: additional markups during period | | 225 |
| Less: additional markup cancellations | | (25) |
| | | $10,000 |
| Less: markdowns | | (600) |
| Plus: markdown cancellations | | 100 |
| Total goods available for sale | $6,840 | $ 9,500 |
| Cost ratio (excluding net markdowns): | | |
| $6,840 ÷ $10,000 = 68.4% | | |
| Deduct: | | |
| Sales | | (8,500) |
| Ending inventory: | | |
| At retail | | $ 1,000 |
| At cost, approximating LCM ($1,000 × 68.4%) | $   684 | |

## CONCEPT REVIEW

1. Why would a company use an inventory estimation method?

2. What is the basic difference between the gross profit method and the retail inventory method?

3. Why are markdowns excluded from the cost ratio when the retail inventory method is used?

## REPORTING ISSUES

### Cash Flow Statement

Inventory costs represent expenditures. However, the expenditures do not make their way to the income statement until the inventory is sold. Therefore, the amount of inventory expenditures that are included in cost of goods sold in any accounting period will be different from the amount that was spent to acquire inventory. The cash flow statement must show the amount of inventory *paid for*, not the amount *sold*.

To determine the amount of cash provided by operations using the indirect method, net income must be adjusted by the change in inventory during the period:

- An *increase* in inventory means that the cash flow to purchase inventory was higher than the amount of expense reported as cost of goods sold—the increase must be subtracted from net income in order to reflect higher cash outflow.

- A *decrease* in inventory means that the cash flow to acquire inventory was less than the amount of expense reported as cost of goods sold—the decrease must be added to net income.

A further adjustment must be made for a manufacturing, resource, or service company. The cost of sales (or cost of services provided) of such companies almost always includes amortization (e.g., depreciation on facilities or depletion on resources). Any depreciation or amortization that has been charged to inventory, whether to work in process or finished goods, must be added back to net income when determining the cash flow from operations.

Finally, there must be an adjustment for accounts payable, since accounts payable primarily relates to inventory purchases.

### Disclosure

The prescribed disclosures for inventories include the following:

- Cost of goods sold (expressed in Canadian and international standards as *the amount of inventories recognized as expense during the period*)
- The basis for valuation (e.g., FIFO, average cost, LCM, NRV)
- Major categories of inventory
- Amount of any writedown
- The amount of any reversal of writedowns, and the reasons for the reversal
- The amount of inventories carried at NRV (i.e., based on market value) as permitted for commodity inventories.

An example of inventory disclosure is that of Le Château Incorporated, a Montreal-based manufacturer and retailer of women's and men's fashions. Le Château's accounting policy note contains the following statement about inventory valuation:

> Raw materials and work-in-process are valued at the lower of average cost and net realizable value. Finished goods are valued, using the retail inventory method, at the lower of average cost and net realizable value less normal profit margin.

The company uses LCM, with NRV as the measure of "market" for raw materials and work in process. For finished-goods inventory, the company uses the retail inventory method for estimating the NRV.

In Note 5 to Le Château's financial statements, the company shows the breakdown of the total inventory amounts that are shown on the balance sheet:

|  | **January 27, 2007** | **January 28, 2006** |
|---|---|---|
| Raw materials | $ 4,029 | $ 5,620 |
| Work-in-process | 2,113 | 1,094 |
| Finished goods | 34,825 | 28,730 |
|  | $40,967 | $35,444 |

*Source:* www.sedar.com, Le Chateau Inc. Consolidated Financial Statements, January 27, 2007.

### ETHICAL ISSUES

As we stated in the Introduction to this chapter, inventory accounting has often been abused. By its nature, inventory accounting requires many judgements and estimates.

Accounting policies, once chosen, are not easily changed. The challenge is in enforcing the policies. The accounting policy issues are relatively straightforward:

- Costs and items to include in inventory rather than as period expenses or as capital assets;
- Cost flow assumption; and
- Measurement of NRV in lower-of-cost-or-market calculations.

These issues are particularly challenging in manufacturing, where more decisions must be made about whether a cost should be a part of inventory or an expense of the period.

### Assigning Costs to Inventory

Applying costs to the physical count, whether periodic or perpetual, requires careful tie-in. This is especially important when input costs change significantly during the period, such as for natural resources like oil, copper, and gold. Management may be tempted to be less than completely accurate in allocating overall purchase cost to inventory versus cost of sales.

### Accurate Cut-Off

It is essential to maintain a consistent and effective cut-off at the end of each reporting period. Cut-off errors, either accidental or deliberate, can have a significant impact on net income. Inventory shipments and sales recording must be carefully coordinated. Estimates such as damaged goods, missing inventory, probable returns, and cash discounts offer additional opportunities for misstatement.

Major financial reporting software, such as SAS, has internal control safeguards that can guarantee that sales records and inventory records are in harmony. Cut-off is more easily controlled through the use of these systems. Accounting software for smaller companies (or for those that have designed their own systems) is less likely to have effective built-in cut-off safeguards.

### False Transactions

As past frauds have illustrated, inventories can be used by senior managers to generate apparent earnings by creating complex fake transactions through nonexistent purchases and sales. It is very difficult for external audit procedures to detect fraud by senior executives; a basic assumption of external auditing is that senior managers are not lying to the auditors. However, internal auditors and accountants often become aware of suspicious transactions. Most wrongdoing by senior management has been uncovered by internal accountants, not by external auditors. It is the company accountant's responsibility to watch for suspicious account activity and to alert the Board of Directors' Audit Committee that something improper might be going on.

### Writedowns

One very difficult ethical area is the use of inventory writedowns (that is, LCM). The need for a writedown is a matter of judgement. Management may refuse to write down inventory, even in the face of slow-moving inventory and strong competitive pressures. Conversely, management may write down inventory prematurely. Management's decisions can be the result of an unintentionally inaccurate assessment of NRV or of a temporarily prevailing business mood. In either case, the writedown is legitimately motivated.

In other cases, however, management has used inventory writedowns as a way of manipulating profit. This is a problem not only with inventory, but also with capital assets, as we shall discuss in Chapter 10. There have been many instances of management opposing demands by auditors to write down obviously obsolete inventory so as not to reduce net income. There have been many other instances of management writing down inventories excessively in order to shift profits from the current year to a future year.

We have seen that LCM requires many judgements. A primary issue is just how to measure NRV. How should the potential selling price be estimated—as a year-end spot rate or as a prediction for the expected inventory turnover period? How can *costs to complete and sell* be estimated? What level of aggregation should be used in applying LCM? All of these questions are subject to significant estimation errors. The task of the accountant is to assure that these questions are answered reasonably.

When the allowance method is used for LCM, an additional concern arises (especially for public companies) because the methodology and the reasonableness of the estimates are subject to audit review only at year-end. Interim results are not audited; management may be tempted to use inventory valuation allowances to "adjust" quarterly earnings to meet analysts' quarterly earnings projects or management's own earnings targets. The allowance method permits earnings to be shifted from one quarter to another within a fiscal year.

### Conclusion

Inventory accounting raises many opportunities for improper accounting. Company accountants can get drawn into significant ethical dilemmas if they are not careful.

## INTERNATIONAL PERSPECTIVE

Canadian standards have been harmonized with international standards, effective in 2008. The major changes in Canadian standards as a result were:

- Dropping LIFO as an acceptable measurement method
- Narrowing the definition of "market" in LCM to mean NRV
- Accepting reversals of writedowns (which previously had been prohibited)
- Giving explicit recognition to NRV as the basis for measuring agricultural and mineral inventories if an active market exists.

Although LIFO has been prohibited in international standards for quite some time, it previously was permitted under Canadian standards largely to accommodate any U.S.–based enterprises that use LIFO. The U.S. still accepts LIFO for reporting purposes, but only if that method is also used for income tax purposes. In contrast, LIFO was never acceptable for tax purposes in Canada. LIFO is also acceptable under Japanese GAAP, which is based largely on U.S. GAAP.

International standards have a separate standard for Agriculture (IAS 41), but Canada had and still has no comparable standard. Therefore, the general nature of IAS 41 was incorporated into the new Canadian standard on inventories, based on current practice (and international practice) of using market value–based measurement for these types of inventories.

## RELEVANT STANDARDS

*CICA Handbook:*
- Section 3031, Inventories

IASB:
- *IAS* 2, Inventories
- *IAS* 41, Agriculture

## SUMMARY OF KEY POINTS

1. Inventories are assets consisting of goods owned by the business and held either for future sale or for consumption in manufacturing or service provision.

2. The cost of inventories includes all costs that were required to bring the inventories to their present location and condition.

3. Work in process and finished-goods inventories of manufacturers should include raw materials, direct labour, and an allocation of manufacturing overhead determined on the basis of normal capacity.

4. All goods owned at the inventory date, including those out on consignment, should be counted and valued.

5. Either a periodic or a perpetual inventory system may be used to track inventory. Computer technology now makes it easier and less costly to use a perpetual system, which also provides up-to-date inventory records, at least of quantities if not costs.

6. The only cost flow assumptions that are acceptable in Canada and most countries are (1) specific identification, (2) average cost, and (3) FIFO. LIFO is not permitted under Canadian or international standards.

7. The LCM method of estimating inventory recognizes declines in sales value in the period of the decline. LCM values inventories at NRV if NRV is below cost.

8. Market value may be used as the inventory valuation basis if the inventories are commodities, such as traded securities, minerals, and agricultural commodities if there is an active market for that commodity. Changes in value are reported in income in the period in which they occur.

9. Inventories of financial instruments held for trading are measured at fair value; gains and losses are recognized immediately in income.

10. The cash flow from operations is affected by (1) changes in inventory levels and (2) amortization and other interperiod allocations that have been included in the inventory. Cash flow must be adjusted to reflect the amount of inventory *purchased* rather than sold, and must be adjusted by adding back any amortization.

11. The gross margin method is used to estimate inventory values when it is difficult or impractical to take a physical count of the goods. The method is most accurate when profit margins are stable.

12. The retail inventory method of estimating inventory applies the ratio of actual cost to sales value to the ending inventory at sales value to estimate the inventory value. When net markdowns are excluded when calculating the cost ratio, the resulting valuation is an estimate of LCM.

## KEY TERMS

active market, 406
additional markup, 414
additional markup cancellation, 414
cost ratio, 412
first-in, first-out (FIFO), 426
gross margin method, 411
laid-down cost, 400
last-in, first out (LIFO), 426
markdown, 414
markdown cancellation, 414

markup, 413
moving average, 424
net realizable value (NRV), 403
normal capacity, 401
original sales price, 413
perpetual inventory system, 420
retail inventory method, 412
specific identification, 424
weighted average system, 424

# APPENDIX

## PERIODIC VERSUS PERPETUAL SYSTEMS

### Periodic Inventory

In a periodic inventory system, the quantity of the ending inventory is established at the end of the accounting period. The unit costs are then applied to derive the ending inventory valuation by using a particular cost flow assumption (e.g., FIFO or average cost). Cost of goods sold (or cost used in production or in a service contract) is determined by subtracting the ending inventory value from the cost of goods available for sale.

In a periodic system, purchases are debited to a purchases account, and end-of-period entries are made to close the purchases account, to close out beginning inventory, and to record the ending inventory as an asset (i.e., the ending inventory replaces the beginning inventory in the accounts). Additional accounts, for costs tracked separately (e.g., freight-in or customs duties) are also closed at this time. Finally, any contra accounts to purchases, such as accounts for purchase returns and allowances or purchase discounts, must also be closed.

Under a periodic system, cost of sales is computed as a residual amount (beginning inventory plus net purchases less ending inventory) and for all practical purposes cannot be verified independently from an inventory count. The lack of verifiability is one reason that estimation methods may be used as a check.

### Perpetual Inventory

**perpetual inventory system**

an inventory record-keeping system that continuously updates the quantity of inventory on hand and cost of goods sold on the basis of transaction records that report units acquired and sold

In a **perpetual inventory system**, each receipt and each issue of an inventory item is recorded in the inventory records to maintain an up-to-date perpetual inventory balance at all times. The result of the perpetual system is verified at least once a year by physically counting the inventory and matching the count to the accounting records. Thus, the perpetual inventory records provide the units and costs of inventory and cost of goods sold at any time. The unit costs applied to each issue or sale are determined by the cost flow assumption used.

It is important to make a distinction between tracking the *physical flow* of goods and the *costing* of the goods. Many companies maintain an ongoing record of physical flows as quantity information only. A continuous tracking of physical flows does not constitute a perpetual inventory system (from an accounting standpoint) unless the costs associated with those flows are simultaneously tracked. A good example is provided by supermarkets that use automated scanners at checkout stations to keep track of physical inventory levels but place accounting values on the physical flows only periodically.

### Periodic versus Perpetual—Illustration

To illustrate the periodic versus the perpetual systems, consider the following data for the Lea Company:

|  | Units | Unit Cost | Total |
|---|---|---|---|
| Beginning inventory | 500 | $4.00 | $2,000 |
| Purchases | 1,000 | 4.00 | 4,000 |
| Goods available for sale | 1,500 |  | $6,000 |
| Less: Sales | 900 |  |  |
| Ending inventory, as calculated | 600 |  |  |
| Ending inventory, based on physical count | 580 |  |  |

Note that there should have been 600 units on hand, not 580; 20 must have been damaged and discarded or stolen. The amount by which the physical count falls short of the expected level of inventory is generally (and euphemistically) referred to as "shrinkage." However, it also is possible that the sales records are not completely accurate.

Based on the prior data, the computation of the cost of sales yields the following amounts:

| | |
|---|---:|
| Beginning inventory (carried forward from the prior period): 500 × $4 | $2,000 |
| Merchandise purchases (accumulated in the purchases account): | |
|    1,000 × $4 | 4,000 |
|   Total goods available for sale during the period | 6,000 |
| Less: Ending inventory (quantity determined by a physical count): | |
|    580 × $4 | 2,320 |
| Equals: Cost of sales (a residual amount) | $3,680 |

**Periodic Recording**   At the beginning of the year, the balance of the inventory account will be the $2,000 cost of the 500 units that were on hand. The entries to record the purchases and cost of sales under a periodic inventory system are as follows:

| | | |
|---|---:|---:|
| *To record the purchases* | | |
|   Purchases | 4,000 | |
|     Accounts payable | | 4,000 |
| *To re-allocate the cost of opening inventory and purchases* | | |
|   Cost of sales | 3,680 | |
|   Inventory (closing, per count) | 2,320 | |
|     Inventory (opening) | | 2,000 |
|     Purchases | | 4,000 |

A slight variation on the second entry above is to explicitly recognize the shrinkage of 20 units as an expense, instead of lumping it in with cost of goods sold:

| | | |
|---|---:|---:|
| Cost of sales (900 × $4) | 3,600 | |
| Inventory shrinkage expense (20 × $4) | 80 | |
| Inventory (closing, per count: 580 × $4) | 2,320 | |
|   Inventory (opening) | | 2,000 |
|   Purchases | | 4,000 |

The inventory shrinkage expense will appear as an expense on the income statement.[6]

Under a periodic inventory system, the inventory is counted at least once a year. For interim financial statements, however, the amount of inventory may be estimated. If a perpetual record of only the *physical units* of inventory is maintained, then only the cost of that inventory needs to be estimated. If the company maintains no perpetual inventory count, then both the quantity and unit cost must be estimated.

---

[6] It may be shown as a separate expense line on an income statement prepared for management use. It will not be found on published income statements, however. In public financial statements, the amount is included in cost of sales.

**Perpetual Recording** When a perpetual inventory system is used, detailed perpetual inventory records, in addition to the usual ledger accounts, are maintained for each inventory item, and an inventory control account is maintained in the general ledger. The perpetual inventory record for each item must provide information for recording receipts, issues, and balances on hand, both in units and in dollar amounts. With this information, the physical quantity and the valuation of goods on hand at any time are available from the accounting records. Therefore, a physical inventory count is still necessary but only to verify the accuracy of the perpetual inventory records. A physical count is made annually to compare the inventory on hand with the perpetual record and to provide data for any adjusting entries needed (errors and losses, for example).

When a difference is found between the perpetual inventory records and the physical count, the perpetual inventory records are adjusted to the physical count. In such cases, the inventory account is debited or credited as necessary for the correction, and cost of sales is increased or decreased. The loss may be accumulated in a separate account such as inventory shortages, to keep track of inventory shrinkage for internal purposes.

In the Lea Company example above, the company began the year with 500 units in inventory, at a cost of $4 per unit. The purchase of 1,000 additional units is recorded as a debit to the inventory account (not to a purchases account):

| | | |
|---|---|---|
| Inventory (1,000 × $4) | 4,000 | |
| Accounts payable | | 4,000 |

When goods are sold, two entries are made; one to record the sale and the other to transfer their cost to COS. Assuming that Lea sells 900 units at a price of $10:

| | | |
|---|---|---|
| Accounts receivable (900 × $10) | 9,000 | |
| Sales revenue | | 9,000 |
| Cost of sales (900 × $4) | 3,600 | |
| Inventory | | 3,600 |

The company will end the accounting period with an inventory balance of $2,400 (600 × $4). At the end of the year, a physical count would reveal only 580 units, and the additional expense would be recorded (it may also be recorded in a separate expense account):

| | | |
|---|---|---|
| Cost of sales | 80 | |
| Inventory ($2,320 − $2,400) | | 80 |

Thus at the end of the period, both the perpetual and periodic systems report identical inventory ($2,320) and cost of sales ($3,680) amounts.

## Choosing a Recording Method

The choice of a periodic or perpetual system is one of practicality—which method gives the best cost-benefit relationship?

A perpetual inventory system is especially useful when inventory consists of items with high unit values or when it is important to have adequate but not excessive inventory levels. Perpetual inventory systems require detailed accounting records and therefore tend to be more costly to implement and maintain than periodic systems. Computer technology has made perpetual inventory systems more popular today than ever before. Thanks to robotics and computer technology, automated inventory systems can not only account for the inventory but also manage the stocking and handling of inventory goods and materials. For example, a store may have a point-of-sale perpetual inventory system (using bar codes) to keep track of its merchandise and to facilitate prompt reordering of popular items. This is information that a periodic system could not possibly provide on a timely basis.

The choice of method depends on whether the company really needs to have *both* quantity information and cost information at its fingertips for control purposes:

- Does the company need to know exactly how many units it has at any point in time? If so, then it needs a perpetual system *for quantities* but not necessarily for costs. Point-of-sale computer terminals that read bar codes are very useful for maintaining quantity flow information, but need not necessarily be tied to the accounting records.

- Does the company need to know exactly how many units it has on hand, how old they are, *and how much they cost* on a regular basis (such as weekly or monthly)? The need for frequent interim financial statements will make perpetual tracking of costs more useful.

Bank operating lines of credit are often tied to the carrying value of receivables and inventory. If, for example, a company's bank is willing to lend up to 60% of the carrying value of the inventory, it is necessary to know at least monthly (and to report to the bank) the value of the inventory. In this case, a perpetual system makes sense. Also, full information on quantities and costs may be needed for insurance purposes.

The basic question is whether the additional cost of a perpetual accounting inventory system is worth the cost. If a company doesn't need the full capabilities of a perpetual system, it's likely that the company will use the cheaper, less complicated, periodic system.

Even with the most sophisticated perpetual system, it still is necessary to take a physical inventory at the end of each fiscal year. A physical inventory is necessary not only to satisfy the auditors, but also to verify the integrity of the perpetual system. If there is a significant difference between the count revealed by the physical inventory and the quantity of inventory that the perpetual system says should be there, there can be only two reasons: (1) there is a problem with the perpetual system or (2) someone is stealing the merchandise. Prompt investigation and remedial action is required in either case.

## COST FLOW METHODS

At date of acquisition, inventory items are recorded at their cash equivalent laid-down cost. Subsequently, when an item is sold, net assets decline and expenses increase as a result of the transfer of the item's cost from inventory to cost of sales. The cost value assigned to the end-of-period inventory of merchandise and finished goods is an allocation of the total cost of goods available for sale between that portion sold (cost of sales) and that portion held as an asset for subsequent sale (ending inventory).

Each cost flow assumption changes the income statement and the balance sheet, since both cost of sales and inventory change. There is no difference in reporting the cash flow from operating activities, however.

The major cost flow methods are:

- Specific cost identification;
- Average cost;
- First-in, first-out (FIFO); and
- Last-in, first-out (LIFO).

LIFO is no longer permitted under either Canadian or international GAAP. Its use was always very rare, even in those jurisdictions in which it is permitted for income tax purposes, such as the U.S.

The example that follows is a numeric example of the methods applied to both a perpetual and periodic system. We will not develop the perpetual system application of LIFO, however, because of its complexity and because LIFO is so seldom used anywhere in the world.

## Specific Identification

This method is, in theory, the most straightforward of all the methods. At the end of the year (periodic method) or on each sale (perpetual method) the specific units sold, and their specific cost, are identified to determine inventory and cost of sales. In the example in Exhibit 8A-1, there are 300 units left in closing inventory. **Specific identification** under a periodic system reveals that, at the end of January, there are 100 units from the 9 January purchase, 100 units from the 15 January purchase, and 100 units from the 24 January purchase. Ending inventory is then valued at $352, and cost of sales at $768 ($1,120 − $352).

In practice, specific identification may not be so simple for most businesses because it is inconvenient and difficult to establish just which items were sold and what their specific initial cost was. However, it is the method used when each product or service is unique (and substantial), such as for shipbuilding, special-order heavy equipment, custom software, construction contracts, consulting operations, and so forth.

## Average Cost

When the average cost method is used in a periodic system, it is called a **weighted average system**. A weighted average unit cost is computed by dividing the sum of the beginning inventory cost plus total current-period purchase costs by the number of units in the beginning inventory plus units purchased during the period. That is,

$$\text{Average cost} = \frac{\text{Opening inventory} + \text{Purchases}}{\text{Units in opening inventory} + \text{Units purchased}}$$

Exhibit 8A-2 illustrates application of the weighted average method under a periodic system using the data given in Exhibit 8A-1 for the Chase Container Corporation.

When the average cost method is used in a perpetual inventory system, a **moving average** unit cost is used. *The moving average provides a new unit cost after each purchase.* When goods are sold or issued, the moving average unit cost at the time is used. Application of the moving average concept in a perpetual inventory system is shown in Exhibit 8A-3, based on Exhibit 8A-2.

---

### EXHIBIT 8A-1

### Chase Container Corporation Inventory Data

| Transaction Date | Purchased | Units Sold | On Hand |
|---|---|---|---|
| 1 January—Inventory @ $1.00 | | | 200 |
| 9 January—Purchase @ $1.10 | 300 | | 500 |
| 10 January—Sales | | 400 | 100 |
| 15 January—Purchase @ $1.16 | 400 | | 500 |
| 18 January—Sale | | 300 | 200 |
| 24 January—Purchase @ $1.26 | 100 | | **300** |

The costs to be allocated; goods available for sale:

| | | | |
|---|---|---|---|
| Beginning inventory | 200 × $1.00 = | | $ 200 |
| Purchases | 300 × $1.10 = | $330 | |
| | 400 × $1.16 = | 464 | |
| | 100 × $1.26 = | 126 | 920 |
| Cost of goods available for sale | | | $1,120 |

The $1,120 is allocated between ending inventory and cost of sales, using one of the cost flow assumptions described.

## EXHIBIT 8A-2

### CHASE CONTAINER CORPORATION

### Weighted Average Inventory Cost Method, Periodic Inventory System

| Goods Available | Units | Unit Price | Total Cost |
|---|---|---|---|
| 1 January—Beginning inventory | 200 | $1.00 | $   200 |
| 9 January—Purchase | 300 | 1.10 | 330 |
| 15 January—Purchase | 400 | 1.16 | 464 |
| 24 January—Purchase | 100 | 1.26 | 126 |
| January—Total available | 1,000 | | $1,120 |
| Weighted average unit cost ($1,120 ÷ 1,000) | | 1.12 | |
| Ending inventory at weighted average cost:<br>    31 January | 300 | 1.12 | 336 |
| Cost of sales at weighted average cost:<br>Sales during January | 700* | 1.12 | 784 |
| Total cost allocated | | | $1,120 |

*400 units on 10 January plus 300 units on 18 January.

## EXHIBIT 8A-3

### CHASE CONTAINER CORPORATION

### Moving Average Inventory Cost, Perpetual Inventory System

| | Purchases | | | Sales | | | Inventory Balance | | |
|---|---|---|---|---|---|---|---|---|---|
| Dates | Units | Unit Cost | Total Cost | Units | Unit Cost | Total Cost | Units | Unit Cost | Total Cost |
| 1 January | | | | | | | 200 | $1.00 | $   200 |
| 9 January | 300 | $1.10 | $330 | | | | 500 | 1.06(a) | 530 |
| 10 January | | | | 400 | $1.06 | $424 | 100 | 1.06 | 106 |
| 15 January | 400 | 1.16 | 464 | | | | 500 | 1.14(b) | 570 |
| 18 January | | | | 300 | 1.14 | 342 | 200 | 1.14 | 228 |
| 24 January | 100 | 1.26 | 126 | | | | 300 | 1.18(c) | 354 |
| Ending inventory | | | | | | | | | $   354 |
| Cost of sales | | | | | | $766 | | | 766 |
| Total cost allocated | | | | | | | | | $1,120 |

(a) $530 ÷ 500 = $1.06
(b) $570 ÷ 500 = $1.14
(c) $354 ÷ 300 = $1.18

For example, on 9 January, the $1.06 moving average cost is derived by dividing the total cost ($530) by the total units (500). The January ending inventory of 300 units is costed at the latest moving average unit cost of $1.18 ($354 ÷ 300). The cost of sales for the period is the sum of the sales in the total cost column, $766.

Moving average requires a lot of calculating if it's done by hand, but it's no big deal if the inventory system is computerized. Indeed, on a computerized system, moving average cost is probably the easiest method to use.

### First-In, First-Out

The **first-in, first-out (FIFO)** method treats the first goods purchased or manufactured as the first units costed out on sale or issuance. *Goods sold (or issued) are valued at the oldest unit costs, and goods remaining in inventory are valued at the most recent unit cost amounts.* Exhibit 8A-4 demonstrates FIFO for the periodic system.

Exhibit 8A-5 demonstrates the perpetual system. Using the perpetual system, a sale is costed out either currently throughout the period or each time there is a withdrawal. In Exhibit 8A-5, issues from inventory on 10 January and 18 January (FIFO basis) are costed out as they occur. FIFO always produces the same numeric results whether a periodic or perpetual system is used.

### Last-In, First-Out

The **last-in, first-out (LIFO)** method of inventory costing matches inventory valued at the most recent unit acquisition cost with current sales revenue. It is a method that places emphasis on income measurement rather than balance sheet valuation. When the cost of inventory is rising, LIFO attempts to give an approximation of *economic income* by recognizing that replacement inventory must be purchased at a cost closer to the most recent purchases rather than the oldest purchases, as under FIFO.

The units remaining in ending inventory are costed at the oldest unit costs incurred, and the units included in cost of sales are costed at the newest unit costs incurred, the exact opposite of the FIFO cost assumption. Like FIFO, application of LIFO requires the use of inventory cost layers for different unit costs.

When LIFO is used, the ending inventory is costed at the oldest unit costs. Cost of sales is determined by deducting ending inventory from the cost of goods available for sale. The periodic LIFO system permits the cost of purchases occurring after the last sale to be included in cost of sales, which cannot occur in the perpetual system. This method is

---

### EXHIBIT 8A-4

## CHASE CONTAINER CORPORATION

### FIFO Inventory Costing, Periodic Inventory System

| | | |
|---|---:|---:|
| Beginning inventory (200 units at $1) | | $ 200 |
| Add purchases during period (computed as in Exhibit 8A-1) | | 920 |
| Cost of goods available for sale | | 1,120 |
| Deduct ending inventory (300 units per physical inventory count): | | |
| 100 units at $1.26 (most recent purchase—24 January) | $126 | |
| 200 units at $1.16 (next most recent purchase—15 January) | 232 | |
| Total ending inventory cost | | 358 |
| Cost of sales | | $ 762* |

*Can also be calculated as 200 units on hand 1 January at $1 plus 300 units purchased 9 January at $1.10, plus 200 units purchased 15 January at $1.16.*

EXHIBIT 8A-5

## CHASE CONTAINER CORPORATION

### FIFO Inventory Costing, Perpetual Inventory System

| Dates | Purchases | | | Sales | | | Inventory Balance | | |
|---|---|---|---|---|---|---|---|---|---|
| | Units | Unit Cost | Total Cost | Units | Unit Cost | Total Cost | Units | Unit Cost | Total Cost |
| 1 January | 200 | $1.00 | $200 | | | | | | |
| 9 January | 300 | $1.10 | $330 | | | | 200 | 1.00 | 200 |
| | | | | | | | 300 | 1.10 | 330 |
| 10 January | | | | 200 | $1.00 | $200 | | | |
| | | | | 200 | 1.10 | 220 | 100 | 1.10 | 110 |
| 15 January | 400 | 1.16 | 464 | | | | 100 | 1.10 | 110 |
| | | | | | | | 400 | 1.16 | 464 |
| 18 January | | | | 100 | 1.10 | 110 | | | |
| | | | | 200 | 1.16 | 232 | 200 | 1.16 | 232 |
| 24 January | 100 | 1.26 | 126 | | | | 200 | 1.16 | 232 |
| | | | | | | | 100 | 1.26 | 126 |
| Ending inventory ($232 + $126) | | | | | | | | | $  358 |
| Cost of sales | | | | | | $762 | | | 762 |
| Total cost allocated | | | | | | | | | $1,120 |

illustrated in Exhibit 8A-6. For the current example, the LIFO cost of the 18 January sale includes the cost of the 24 January purchase! The ending inventory therefore consists of two layers, one at $1.00 and one at $1.10.

## SUMMARY—COST FLOW METHODS

Let's review the basics of the cost flow assumption again. This is an accounting policy choice. When prices are rising, as they often are, FIFO will produce higher inventory, lower cost of sales, and higher income. It's popular with firms that would like to see higher income and net assets

EXHIBIT 8A-6

## CHASE CONTAINER CORPORATION

### LIFO Inventory Costing, Periodic Inventory System

| | | |
|---|---|---|
| Cost of goods available (see Exhibit 8A-1) | | $1,120 |
| Deduct ending inventory (300 units per physical inventory count): | | |
| 200 units at $1.00 (oldest costs available, from 1 January inventory) | $200 | |
| 100 units at $1.10 (next oldest costs available; from 9 January purchase) | 110 | |
| Ending inventory | | 310 |
| Cost of sales | | $  810* |

*Can also be calculated as 100 units at $1.26 plus 400 units at $1.16 plus 200 units at $1.10

in their financial statements. LIFO has the opposite effect: lower inventories, higher cost of sales, and lower incomes. Average cost methods provide inventory and cost of sales amounts between the LIFO and FIFO extremes, and are better for income and tax minimization when inventory costs are rising. Canadian practice is about evenly divided between FIFO and average cost.

## CONCEPT REVIEW

1. Explain the essential differences in accounting for inventories under the periodic and perpetual inventory systems.

2. If the price to acquire inventory is rising, and the company is pursuing an income maximization reporting strategy over the long term, which inventory cost flow assumption is management most likely to choose?

3. Why is LIFO unlikely to be used by Canadian companies?

## REVIEW PROBLEM

The inventory data for the Black Eagle Lounge for the beginning of June is shown below. Compute the inventory value at 30 June, using both perpetual inventory and periodic inventory approaches, under each of the following methods:

1. Specific cost identification
2. Average cost
3. FIFO

    1 June—no inventory on hand
    2 June—bought one case of Red Hook Ale @ $10
    13 June—bought one case of Red Hook Ale @ $16
    24 June—sold one case of Red Hook Ale @ $20*
    28 June—bought one case of Red Hook Ale @ $18

*This case of Red Hook Ale was purchased on 13 June.

## REVIEW PROBLEM—SOLUTION

At 30 June, there are two cases of ale on hand. The carrying value of the 30 June inventory is shown below under each method:

1. Specific cost identification:
    Periodic    $(1 \times \$10) + (1 \times \$18) = \$28$
    Perpetual   $(1 \times \$10) + (1 \times \$18) = \$28$

2. Average cost:
    Periodic    $[[(1 \times \$10) + (1 \times \$16) + (1 \times \$18)] \div 3] \times 2$ remaining
              $= \$14.67 \times 2 = \$29.34$

    Perpetual (moving average):

| Average Bought (Sold) | Units @ Cost | Units Cost | Total Inventory Units | Total Inventory Cost |
|---|---|---|---|---|
| 1 | $10 | $10 | 1 | $10.00 |
| 1 | 16 | 26 | 2 | 13.00 |
| (1) | (13) | 13 | 1 | 13.00 |
| 1 | 18 | 31 | 2 | 15.50 |

3. FIFO:

Periodic   $(1 \times \$16) + (1 \times \$18) = \$34$
Perpetual  $(1 \times \$16) + (1 \times \$18) = \$34$

**Comments:**

- Under specific identification, *periodic* and *perpetual* always give the same result, because the cost of each specific item sold is identified. Therefore, the same inventory amount is shown for both.
- Average cost yields different results under the periodic and perpetual methods, because the numbers of items and their costs are averaged together differently under a moving average (perpetual) than under a historical tabulation of purchases (periodic).
- FIFO always yields the same result under both periodic and perpetual methods.

## QUESTIONS

**Q8-1** In general, why should financial statement users and preparers be especially concerned with inventories?

**Q8-2** List and briefly explain the usual inventory classifications for a trading entity and a manufacturing entity.

**Q8-3** Which of the following items should be included in inventory?

a. Goods held by our agents for us.
b. Goods held by us for sale on commission.
c. Goods held by us but awaiting return to vendor because of damaged condition.
d. Goods returned to us from buyer, reason unknown to date.
e. Goods out on consignment.
f. Goods sold under conditional resale agreements, where we have agreed to repurchase the items that our customer does not resell, and reimburse the customer for carrying costs incurred.
g. Merchandise at our branch for sale.
h. Merchandise at a convention for display purposes.

**Q8-4** What types of inventory are most frequently measured at selling price or NRV in excess of cost?

**Q8-5** Why is the LCM rule applied to inventory valuation?

**Q8-6** What is the holding loss (gain) recognized using the LCM, inventory allowance method, for each of the years 20X4 through 20X8?

|  | Cost | Net Realizable Value |
|---|---|---|
| 20X3 Ending inventory | $     0 | $     0 |
| 20X4 Ending inventory | 12,000 | 14,000 |
| 20X5 Ending inventory | 15,000 | 13,000 |
| 20X6 Ending inventory | 18,000 | 17,000 |
| 20X7 Ending inventory | 20,000 | 16,000 |
| 20X8 Ending inventory | 22,000 | 23,000 |

**Q8-7** Explain why it is important to decide whether to apply the LCM test by individual inventory items versus by categories.

Q8-8    List the required financial statement disclosures for inventory.

Q8-9    Approximate the value of ending inventory, assuming the following data:

| | |
|---|---|
| Cost of goods available for sale | $170,000 |
| Sales | 150,000 |
| Gross margin (on sales) | 25% |

Q8-10    Explain the gross margin method. What basic assumption is implicit in the gross margin method?

Q8-11    Explain the approach of the retail method for estimating inventories. What data must be accumulated in order to apply the retail method?

Q8-12    Why is the year-end inventory cut-off so important? What are the complexities inherent in assuring that the year-end inventory cut-off is correct?

Q8-13    Briefly explain the differences between periodic and perpetual inventory systems. Under what circumstances is each generally used?

Q8-14    Does the adoption of a perpetual inventory system eliminate the need for a physical count or measurement of inventories? Explain.

Q8-15    Explain four different cost flow assumptions that can be used to measure cost of sales. Which alternative will always result in the highest net income when prices are rising? Which ones are acceptable for financial reporting under Canadian and international GAAP?

Q8-16    Distinguish between a *weighted average* and a *moving average* in determining inventory unit cost. When is each generally used? Explain.

## CASE 8-1

### SIEGFRIED AIR CONTROL

Siegfried Air Control Ltd. (SAC) manufactures and installs air conditioning and ventilation systems, mainly for businesses but also for home use. The company was founded 18 years ago by a group of 5 professional engineers who had previously worked for a multinational air conditioning company based in Germany. The five engineers are the only shareholders. Additional financing is provided through bank loans and a bank line of credit. The line of credit is limited to 70% of SAC's accounts and notes receivable plus 50% of the book value of inventory.

Over the years, SAC developed a sophisticated air conditioning system that could be installed in older buildings without the need for extensive reconstruction. The AirRing System, as it was called, was very popular for old residences and commercial buildings.

AirRing evolved through several designs over the years. In 20X4, due to severe energy shortages, SAC developed a new energy-efficient model (Sigmund) that reduced energy consumption by 40% and also substituted a new type of refrigerant that was safe for the environment, unlike refrigerants in prior years that caused damage to the ozone layer if they leaked into the atmosphere.

The only difficulty with Sigmund was that both the condenser and the air-handler (the fan unit that circulates the air) were appreciably larger than the older, less efficient, models. The larger size meant that customers that had to replace their old air conditioning units would need to provide larger spaces for both units—not always an easy task in older buildings.

SAC began manufacturing, selling, and installing Sigmund in 20X5. Most of the components were subcontracted to other manufacturers in the region and in Europe. Subcontractors were intentionally scattered so that the exact design of the new system would not be immediately obvious to competitors. Of course, SAC knew that other companies would successfully copy its design through reverse-engineering. Therefore, SAC set a high price on the new systems at the beginning to recover the development costs before similar systems became available from other manufacturers.

The total cost to manufacture Sigmund was $6,000 for a medium-sized unit suitable for homes. Commercial systems were designed to custom-designed specifications and could run up to a million dollars to manufacture and install.

It is now the end of 20X5. The VP, Finance, who is one of the founding engineers and shareholders, is pondering the proper presentation of some transactions and events. Because it is a private company, SAC has never been audited. Nevertheless, SAC's shareholders want the company's financial statements prepared on the basis of GAAP so that the bank does not ask any awkward questions and perhaps force an expensive audit in future years.

You have been hired as an accounting expert to advise the company on the proper treatment of the following matters:

1. The company has been charging all direct manufacturing costs to inventory—raw materials, direct labour, and the full cost (including taxes, foreign exchange gains and losses, and shipping costs) of subcontracted components. All other costs are charged to expense in the year incurred.

2. Accounts payable includes several million dollars worth of unpaid subcomponent costs that were invoiced to SAC in euros. On advice from the bank, SAC hedged the euro commitment when the company signed the subcontracting agreement and established the euro price of the subcontracted components. Due to the strength of the Canadian dollar (compared to the euro), the Canadian dollar value of the accounts payable has decreased by $156,000.

3. Historically, SAC has incurred very little cost in honouring its warranties on its equipment and installations. These costs have been charged to expense when incurred. Call-backs for service on newly installed Sigmunds have been largely the result of their having been installed in small spaces with inadequate ventilation, which has caused the overall cost of honouring warranties on Sigmund to be higher than usual in the short run.

4. SAC has an inventory of older units (the Erda model) that are about to become obsolete in Ontario due to pending new regulations on energy and refrigerant. Some customers are hurrying to purchase the Erdas in advance of the effective date of the new regulations. Unsold units can be shipped into the U.S. and sold through another company, but would have to be discounted by at least 50% below Erda's usual selling price, which is about 10% below the recorded inventory cost. SAC would have to pay shipping costs to get the units to the U.S.

5. In October 20X6, SAC signed a contract to retrofit an old factory building that is being converted into condominiums. The contract price is $1,200,000; SAC's estimated cost is $1,000,000. By the end of the year, SAC had spent $600,000 on the project, including the $250,000 cost of the compression and air-handling equipment that had not yet been installed. Just before the end of the year, the SAC project supervisor advised SAC that due to more difficult conversion problems than expected, an additional $150,000 would probably have to be spent. The project supervisor estimated that about 40% of the physical work had been finished.

### Required:

Prepare a memorandum to the VP, Finance, in which you discuss alternative accounting treatments for these five issues and recommend which treatment SAC should adopt.

**CASE 8-2**

## HIGHQ BOOKS

HighQ Books Limited (HighQ) is a small book publishing company located in Kingston, Ontario. HighQ specializes in history and biography titles, and currently has 76 titles in print. Each year, 10 to 15 titles are added.

On 2 September, there was a fire in the company premises, which destroyed a large quantity of inventory and printing equipment. Smoke and water damaged the physical premises.

The company has prepared an insurance claim (Exhibit 1), and has asked you, the external accounting advisor, to review the claim for reasonableness. HighQ expects the claim to be paid 30 days from the submission date, and needs the cash flow as the cleanup expenses and loss of revenue have created a cash flow crunch. Fortunately, HighQ has had an excellent relationship with its banker, who has provided interim funding. However, the insurance money is sorely needed, and HighQ is aware that a contested claim would be delayed. Thus, your review is considered advisable to ensure that the claim is appropriate.

Based on your prior experience with this company, you know that its internal cost system has proven reliable. Perpetual inventory records are kept, but are not relied on for external reporting, since a physical count is always taken. For external reporting, HighQ establishes an allowance for inventory obsolescence based on the age of the books in inventory. Titles printed in the current year are written down 5% at year-end; one-year-old books, 10%; two-year-old books, 15%; and books three or more years old, 25%.

Approximately 75% of HighQ's sales occur in the fall season, as retailers deal with the Christmas rush. HighQ has and is struggling to meet its delivery requirements this year, largely successfully, although some sales have been lost due to inventory shortages.

HighQ's insurance policy specifies that capital assets will be covered based on replacement cost, but limited to the amount that would be needed to repair the damaged asset (if repairs are possible). Replacement cost is based on replacement with an asset of like kind. Inventory is insured for replacement cost or net realizable value (NRV), whichever is lower. All cleanup work is covered; cleanup work done by outsiders is covered with no limit, but cleanup/repair work performed internally may not include any allocation for overhead or profit. Furthermore, only 50% of internal labour for cleanup is covered. Business interruption insurance covers lost profits caused by the insured event. Your notes on the various elements of the insurance claim are in Exhibit II.

**Required:**

Prepare a report evaluating the statement of claim, including a revised claim and additional information needed, as appropriate.

(CICA, adapted)

**EXHIBIT 1**

### HighQ Statement of Claim

| | |
|---|---:|
| Building repairs and cleaning | $    53,067 |
| Printing equipment | 485,000 |
| Inventory—books | 512,850 |
| Inventory—materials | 115,985 |
| Display books | 15,000 |
| Promotion costs | 7,500 |
| Profit on lost sales | 512,850 |
| | $1,702,252 |

## EXHIBIT 2

### Notes on Statement of Claim

- Display books are signed first editions of all company books. The 150-book collection is displayed in glass cabinets in the HighQ administrative office. Smoke damage was repaired by Restorers'R'Us at a cost of $15,000.
- The normal markup on books is 100% of cost. Profit on lost sales is calculated as equal to the cost of inventory lost. HighQ had expected to operate at capacity all fall.
- Building repairs and cleaning included $23,500 of labour, done internally to save time and money. All other costs in this category were for external services.
- Damaged equipment, which was approximately one-third depreciated, was not repairable. The equipment lost in the fire, an XT100 printing press, is no longer available. One alternative was an XP550, at a cost of $475,000. This machine has enhanced features as compared to the XT100 that allows a wider range of print styles. The other alternative was an XP750, also with a broader range of print styles, but faster and with higher capacity, lowering operating costs by 10%. The XP750 costs $485,000. HighQ purchased the XP750, reasoning that the operating efficiencies and capacity improvements were well worth the additional cost.
- Inventory of materials included paper of $72,700, inks of $34,040, and other items of $9,245. This represents cost, although the replacement cost of paper was approximately 5% less than cost, and the replacement cost of ink was approximately 10% above cost on 2 September.
- Estimates of books and materials lost have been based on the quantities recorded in the perpetual inventory system, less the quantity of inventory salvaged after the fire and counted at that time.

The claim for book inventory is summarized as follows:

| Year Printed | Number of Books | Average Cost | Total Cost |
|---|---|---|---|
| Current year | 26,827 | $7.50 | $201,200 |
| 1 year prior | 5,329 | 7.60 | 40,500 |
| 2 years prior | 16,350 | 7.75 | 126,710 |
| 3 or more years prior | 18,284 | 7.90 | 144,440 |
| | 66,790 | | $512,850 |

HighQ spent $15,000 promoting books for the new season. Because of the fire, HighQ anticipates not being able to produce enough copies to meet demand and has included 50% of this cost in the statement of claim.

## CASE 8-3

### AGRICULTURAL MARKETING BOARD

The Agricultural Marketing Board (AMB) has recently been awarded a monopoly to export four different agricultural products grown on a Caribbean island. That is, AMB is the only enterprise allowed to buy the goods from local farming enterprises and market the products on the international market. AMB is incorporated in the Caribbean island, which has no tax on corporate earnings. The Board hopes to be able to expand its operations to nearby islands, thereby increasing its market power and providing a better return for farmers in the Caribbean. If and when AMB is able to expand, management would like to attract debt or equity investment on international markets in the future.

AMB deals in four agricultural products; the products can be stored for lengths of time ranging from nine months to several years. AMB acquires the inventory from local farmers for "current market value less 10%." Market value is quite volatile. AMB is expected to earn profits by timing the sale of these products, and selling during periods of high prices. The Board uses government equity and private bank loans to finance inventory. AMB is permitted to hedge its inventory, if the company so chooses. Profits of AMB, after bonuses and interest, are distributed to the government, as a owner, and to the farmers, in relation to their volume with AMB.

It is now the end of the first fiscal year, and you, the accountant, have been asked to comment on issues surrounding the choice of an inventory costing method: FIFO, average cost, or market value.

The president has reminded you that managers' bonuses are a function of reported net income. There continues to be some pressure to create a competitor to AMB, in the hopes that competition would inspire best operating results.

**Required:**

Write a report to the president in which you evaluate the alternative inventory valuation methods and recommend the most appropriate one for AMB.

(CGA-Canada, adapted)

## ASSIGNMENTS

★ **A8-1 Inventory Cost—Items to Include in Inventory:** The bookkeeper for Interior Advances Ltd. is uncertain which of the following items he should include when he calculates the inventory balance for the year-end financial statements:

a. Goods counted in the physical inventory, including $4,500 in sales taxes and $1,500 in import brokerage fees $30,000

b. Goods received and included in inventory count but not yet paid for; the cost includes a potential 2% cash discount if the invoice is paid within 30 days of year-end 6,000

c. Cost of general insurance coverage on inventory 2,000

d. Goods shipped to a wholesale distributor; the distributor has the right to return up to 50% of the goods if they are not sold within 6 months; not included in inventory count 8,000

e. Items included in inventory count that have been returned by customers for repair (counted at original sales price, which was 50% above cost) 3,000

f. Cost of goods on consignment at Big Box Inc. (including 25% commission that will be paid to Big Box when it sells the goods) 10,000

g. Total expected cost of goods in inventory that are being modified by the company for private-branding for Canada Designs Limited; 60% of the cost has been incurred by year-end 12,000

**Required:**

Determine the amount of ending inventory that should be reported on Interior Advances' balance sheet.

★ **A8-2 Inventory Cost—Items to Include in Inventory:** On 31 December 20X5, Patco computed an ending inventory valuation of $490,000 based on a periodic inventory system. The accounts for 20X5 have been adjusted and closed. Subsequently, the accountant prepared a schedule that showed that the inventory should be $563,000, not $490,000.

| | |
|---|---:|
| a. Merchandise in store (at 40% above cost) | $490,000 |
| b. Goods purchased, in transit (shipped FOB destination, estimated freight, not included, $800), invoice price | 9,000 |
| c. Goods held for later shipment to Davis Electronics at sales price, 40% above cost (already billed to Davis Electronics) | 14,000 |
| d. Merchandise out on consignment at sales price (including markup of 60% on selling price) | 25,000 |
| e. Goods (office equipment) removed from the warehouse and now used in company marketing office (at cost) | 20,000 |
| f. Goods out on approval, sales price, $5,000, cost, $2,000 | 5,000 |
| Total inventory as corrected | $563,000 |

Average income tax rate 40%

**Required:**

1. Review the items making up the list of inventory. Compute the correct ending inventory amount.

2. The income statement and balance sheet now reflect a closing inventory of $490,000. List the items on the income statement and balance sheet for 20X5 that should be corrected for the above errors; give the amount of the error for each item affected, if possible.

★ **A8-3 Inventory Cost:** Majestic Stores Incorporated, a dealer in radio and television sets, buys large quantities of a television model that costs $500. The contract reads that if 200 or more sets are purchased during the year, a rebate of $20 per set will be made. On 15 December, the records showed that 150 sets had been purchased; purchases are recorded at $75,000 (150 × $500). All these units were sold. Fifty more sets were ordered FOB destination. The sets were received on 22 December, and a request for the rebate was made. The rebate cheque was received on 20 January, after Majestic's books were closed. Furthermore, the supplier provides terms of 2/10, n/30. Majestic has a policy of always paying invoices within the discount period. Discounts are recorded as a credit to an interest income account. Further investigation reveals that a total of $1,760 of freight was paid to acquire the sets purchased this year, including $375 on the last order of 50 sets.

**Required:**

1. Calculate the ending inventory value at 31 December.
2. What entry should be made relative to the rebate on 31 December? Why?
3. What entry would be made on 20 January?

★★ **A8-4 Inventory Cost—Items to Include in Inventory:** Gerard Limited reported inventory of $689,600 and accounts payable to suppliers of $456,300 for the year ended 31 December 20X6. The company has a periodic inventory system, and the inventory value given is the result of the physical count.

a. The inventory count took place on 31 December. Late in the day on 31 December, goods with a cost of $54,300 and a retail price of $98,500 were delivered to a customer. These goods had been counted earlier in the day, and were included in the inventory count. The company did not record the sale until 3 January, due to the New Year's break.

b. Goods from a supplier, in transit on 31 December, were neither counted nor recorded as a purchase and account payable as of 31 December. The goods, with a cost of $37,500, legally belonged to Gerard while they were in transit over the year-end.

c. Goods received from a supplier on 30 December were counted and included in inventory, but the invoice had not been recorded as a purchase or accounts payable by the end of December. The invoice was for $51,100.

d. On 4 January 20X7, a $5,000 bill for freight for the month of December was received. The freight was for goods bought from a supplier and delivered to the Gerard warehouse. None of these goods has been resold.

e. The inventory count was subsequently determined to include $21,900 of goods on consignment from a supplier; the goods have to be paid for only if they are sold to Gerard's customers.

f. Gerard had goods with a recorded cost of $12,700 that were properly recorded as a purchase and account payable, and counted in inventory. However, the goods were damaged and Gerard entered into negotiations with the supplier that resulted in a discount of $4,000 off the price. The negotiations were completed in early January 20X7.

g. Market value of remaining inventory *after* any adjustments appropriate for items (a)–(f), at NRV, was determined to be $605,000. The allowance to reduce inventory to LCM, unchanged for the end of the last fiscal period, was $32,200.

**Required:**

1. Calculate the correct balances for inventory (net) and accounts payable, as of 31 December 20X6.

2. Calculate the holding loss on inventory that will appear on the income statement for the year ended 31 December 20X6.

3. Assume that cost of goods sold had been calculated to be $2,211,400 based on the original physical count. What is the new cost of goods sold? Assume that the holding loss on inventory is reported as part of cost of goods sold.

---

 **A8-5 Inventory Issues:** Consider each of the following independent situations. In each, describe the accounting policy decision. Describe the impact that the chosen policy has had on the income statement and balance sheet. If the company's policy is not correct, or if there is an alternate policy that should be considered, explain the alternative.

*Case A* Inventory was bought for $675,000 in 20X6 and was recorded at cost. The inventory was bought under the terms of a purchase agreement signed in 20X4; the market value of these goods had been $695,000 at the end of 20X4, $640,000 at the end of 20X5, and $660,000 on the date of acquisition.

*Case B* Inventory was received and recorded at the invoice price of $56,000. The goods had not been sold at year-end. Subsequently, a discount of $5,000 was received on the goods. This discount was recorded as other revenue.

*Case C* In the lower-of-cost-or-market valuation at year-end, replacement cost was used as the definition of "market." The evaluation resulted in a writedown of $135,500. The company reports that, although its supplier's prices were lower for certain products at year-end, thus causing the writedown, both its prices to its own customers and its direct selling costs had remained at constant levels.

*Case D* Inventories, costing $56,000, with a sales price of $79,000, were with a customer on consignment. These goods were excluded from the physical inventory count, and the $79,000 sale was recorded in the current fiscal year, because in the past this customer has always been able to sell all the goods sent on consignment.

---

 **A8-6 Accounting Policies:** The president of Aggressive Limited has come to you for advice. Aggressive is a newly established company with prospects for high growth. Decisions must soon be made concerning accounting policies for external financial reporting. The following information pertains to the company's first year of operations (in $ thousands):

| | |
|---|---:|
| Revenue | $48,000 |
| Purchases | 18,000 |
| Closing inventory—FIFO | 6,000 |
| Closing inventory—average cost | 4,800 |
| Depreciation—straight line | 2,400 |
| Depreciation—declining balance | 4,800 |
| Advertising and promotion expense | 2,400 |
| Amortization of advertising and promotion over five years | 480 |
| Other expenses | 5,000 |
| Common shares outstanding (in thousands) | 1,200 |
| Income tax rate | 30% |

**Note:** The choice of depreciation method will have no effect on income taxes; maximum CCA on capital assets will be claimed for tax purposes. For tax purposes, advertising and promotion expenses may be expensed as incurred, again, regardless of accounting policy.

**Required:**

1. Prepare a columnar income statement. In column 1, show net income assuming the use of FIFO, declining-balance depreciation, and expensing of advertising and promotion. Also calculate earnings per share. In successive columns, show the separate effects of the following on net income and earnings per share: in column 2, average cost; in column 3, straight-line depreciation; and column 4, amortization of advertising and promotion. In column 5, show all effects of choosing the alternatives presented separately in columns 2 through 4.

2. As president, which accounting policies would you choose? Explain.

---

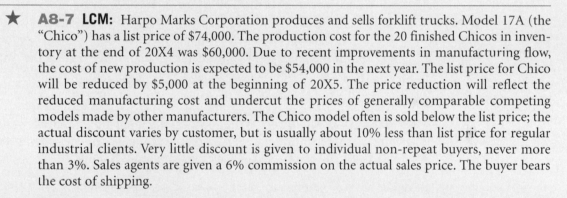

★ **A8-7 LCM:** Harpo Marks Corporation produces and sells forklift trucks. Model 17A (the "Chico") has a list price of $74,000. The production cost for the 20 finished Chicos in inventory at the end of 20X4 was $60,000. Due to recent improvements in manufacturing flow, the cost of new production is expected to be $54,000 in the next year. The list price for Chico will be reduced by $5,000 at the beginning of 20X5. The price reduction will reflect the reduced manufacturing cost and undercut the prices of generally comparable competing models made by other manufacturers. The Chico model often is sold below the list price; the actual discount varies by customer, but is usually about 10% less than list price for regular industrial clients. Very little discount is given to individual non-repeat buyers, never more than 3%. Sales agents are given a 6% commission on the actual sales price. The buyer bears the cost of shipping.

**Required:**

1. What value should be used for the LCM test? What amount of writedown is required?

2. Assume that early in 20X5 the company sells five Chicos to a shipping company for $63,000 each. How much gross profit will be recorded, assuming that the company uses FIFO?

---

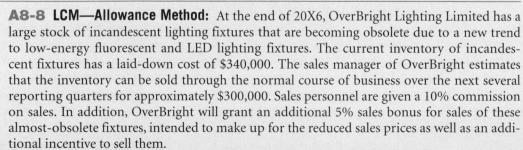

★★ **A8-8 LCM—Allowance Method:** At the end of 20X6, OverBright Lighting Limited has a large stock of incandescent lighting fixtures that are becoming obsolete due to a new trend to low-energy fluorescent and LED lighting fixtures. The current inventory of incandescent fixtures has a laid-down cost of $340,000. The sales manager of OverBright estimates that the inventory can be sold through the normal course of business over the next several reporting quarters for approximately $300,000. Sales personnel are given a 10% commission on sales. In addition, OverBright will grant an additional 5% sales bonus for sales of these almost-obsolete fixtures, intended to make up for the reduced sales prices as well as an additional incentive to sell them.

In early 20X7, OverBright's production manager decided that the fixtures can be adapted to not only accept the new LED lighting but also compete quite effectively with new products coming on the market. During 2007, the fixtures are converted at a cost of $50,000. The sales manager estimates that after the conversion, the newly adapted inventory can be repriced to fetch $370,000 (before 10% sales commission) in the market.

**Required:**

Using the valuation allowance method, prepare the appropriate journal entries to record inventory adjustments at the end of each of 20X6 and 20X7.

---

**A8-9 LCM—Allowance Method:** The records of Loren Moving Company showed the following inventory data:

| | | 20X1 Cost | NRV | 20X2 Cost | NRV |
|---|---|---|---|---|---|
| *Category 1* | | | | | |
| | Item A | $10,000 | $ 9,000 | $ 5,000 | $ 3,000 |
| | Item B | 40,000 | 35,000 | 10,000 | 9,000 |
| | Item C | 25,000 | 33,000 | 45,000 | 52,000 |
| *Category 2* | | | | | |
| | Item D | $18,000 | $16,500 | 12,000 | 10,500 |
| | Item E | 20,000 | 4,000 | 4,000 | 1,000 |
| | Item F | 42,000 | 42,000 | 56,000 | 54,000 |

**Required:**

1. Calculate two different amounts that could justifiably be recorded as the allowance to reduce inventory to the LCM at the end of 20X1.

2. Record the 20X1 LCM adjustments (if any) for each of the two amounts from requirement (1), using the valuation allowance method.

3. Record the 20X2 LCM adjustments (if any) under each of the two LCM methods, using the valuation allowance.

---

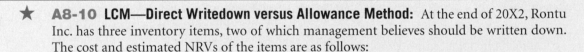

**A8-10 LCM—Direct Writedown versus Allowance Method:** At the end of 20X2, Rontu Inc. has three inventory items, two of which management believes should be written down. The cost and estimated NRVs of the items are as follows:

| | | Per Unit | |
|---|---|---|---|
| | Quantity | Cost | Market |
| Item A | 100 | $90 | $80 |
| Item B | 150 | 70 | 50 |
| Item C | 200 | 50 | 60 |

**Required:**

1. Determine the amount by which the inventory should be written down if the carrying value of each type of item is calculated separately. Prepare the journal entry to record the writedown.

2. Determine the inventory writedown if market value is compared with market value for all inventory items taken together. Prepare the journal entry to establish an inventory allowance.

3. Suppose that in 20X3, the market value of Item A recovers to an amount higher than its cost, and stays higher throughout the year. Prepare journal entries to record the recovery in value, if feasible, under each of the two methods.

4. Explain the advantages and disadvantages of using an allowance instead of direct writedown.

★★ **A8-11 LCM—Three Ways to Apply:** The information shown below relating to the ending inventory was taken from the records of Components Company.

| Inventory Classification | Quantity | Per Unit Cost | Per Unit NRV |
|---|---|---|---|
| Keyboards | | | |
|   Stock A | 9 | $ 75 | $ 70 |
|   Stock B | 5 | 95 | 80 |
|   Stock C | 8 | 100 | 110 |
| Zip drives | | | |
|   Stock X | 400 | 100 | 115 |
|   Stock Y | 120 | 75 | 65 |
| CD burners | | | |
|   Stock D | 30 | 160 | 180 |
|   Stock E | 15 | 180 | 170 |

**Required:**

1. Determine the valuation of the above inventory at cost and at LCM, assuming application of LCM by (a) individual items, and (b) classifications.

2. Give the entry to record the writedown, if any, to reduce ending inventory to LCM. Assume periodic inventory and the allowance method.

3. Of the two applications described in (2) above, which one appears preferable in this situation? Explain.

★ **A8-12 LCM—Income Effects:** Hessian Limited has been suffering the effects of strong price competition on a particular inventory item from an overseas company that has moved into Hessian's Canadian market. At the end of 20X6, Hessian management decided that the carrying cost (at historical value) of its year-end inventory was not recoverable, and that Hussein would have to reduce its prices drastically in order to meet the competitor's prices. Management estimated that inventory currently carried at $20,000 (at historical cost) will have a NRV of $16,000. Hessian normally priced its products at 50% above historical cost.

Early in 20X7, Hessian's competitor unexpectedly withdrew from the Canadian market because of financial difficulties in its home country. Consequently, Hessian restored the prices of its goods to full pre-markdown selling price. By the end of 20X7, 60% of the inventory had been sold.

**Required:**

1. Prepare the journal entry for 31 December 20X6 to write down the inventory to NRV. Use the direct writedown method.

2. Prepare a summary journal entry to record the sale of the goods (and the cost of sales) in 20X7 and the writeup of remaining inventory.

3. Suppose that Hussain Limited's net income (after the writedown) was $50,000 in 20X6 and $60,000 in 20X7. What would each year's net income have been if Hussain Limited had not written down the inventory?

★★ **A8-13 LCM and Foreign Currency—Income Effects:** StarCross Resources Ltd. is a public company incorporated in Alberta and traded on the Toronto Stock Exchange. As a public company, StarCross is required to submit quarterly financial statements (unaudited) to the provincial securities commissions and to its shareholders.

At the end of the second quarter of 20X8, StarCross management decided that cost exceeded NRV for a significant portion of the inventory. Consequently, the company wrote the inventory down from $700,000 to $300,000 just before the end of the quarter.

Toward the end of the fiscal year, management realized that prices had recovered to earlier levels due to a world-wide shortage of that type of item. In the first quarter of 20X9, the inventory was sold in bulk for a price of €1,200,000. At the time of the sale, €1 = Cdn\$1.50. The buyer paid StarCross's invoice one month later, when €1 = Cdn\$1.40.

**Required:**

1. Prepare all entries related to the above series of events for 20X8 and 20X9, assuming that the direct writedown method is used for LCM.

2. Prepare all entries related to the above series of events for 20X8 and 20X9, assuming that the allowance method is used for LCM.

★★ **A8-14 Net Realizable Value of Damaged Goods:** A fire damaged some of the merchandise held for sale by Adams Appliance Company. Six flat-screen LCD television sets and 14 combo VHS/DVD player sets were damaged. They were not covered by insurance. The appliances will be repaired and sold "as is." Data follows:

| | Per Appliance | |
| --- | --- | --- |
| | Television | DVD |
| Inventory (at cost) | $1,200 | $300 |
| Estimated cost to repair | 105 | 90 |
| Estimated cost to sell | 45 | 30 |
| Estimated sales price | 675 | 160 |

**Required:**

1. Compute NRV for each appliance and for the inventory in total.

2. Give the separate entries to record the damaged merchandise inventory for the televisions and VHS/DVD players. Assume a perpetual inventory system.

3. Give the entries to record the subsequent repair of the televisions and the VHS/DVD players (credit cash).

4. Give the entries to record sale for cash of two televisions and one VHS/DVD player. It will be necessary to record payment of the sales costs in a separate entry. Credit sales costs in the entry to record the sale. Assume that actual sales prices equalled the estimated sales prices.

★★ **A8-15 Net Realizable Value:** During shipping, merchandise purchased by the Atlantic Trading Company was damaged. The original total invoice price of this material was $50,000. Atlantic, which was responsible for shipping, has no insurance covering this type of damage. The company has decided to repair and resell the damaged items.

| Item | 1 | 2 | 3 |
| --- | --- | --- | --- |
| Volume | 500 units | 300 units | 100 units |
| Cost (per unit) | $55 | $17 | $250 |
| Estimated cost to rebuild (per unit) | 15 | 6 | 110 |
| Estimated sales price (per unit) | 45 | 19 | 180 |
| Estimated cost to sell (per unit) | 5 | 2 | 18 |

**Required:**

1. Calculate the NRV for each item and for the inventory as a whole. Also calculate total cost and the required writedown.

2. Prepare the entry to write down the inventory to NRV. The inventory account should be reduced directly; an allowance should not be used. The damaged inventory should be transferred to a separate damaged-inventory account.

3. Prepare entries to record rebuilding, sales, and selling expenses. Assume all estimates are accurate. Prepare summary entries for the three products together. A perpetual inventory is kept. Assume all units are sold.

4. Explain which of the entries recorded in requirements (2) and (3) have an impact on net income.

★ **A8-16 Loss on Purchase Commitment:** During 20X5, Mossback Company signed a contract with Alpha Corporation to "purchase 15,000 subassemblies at $30 each during 20X6."

**Required:**

1. On 31 December 20X5, the end of the annual accounting period, the financial statements are to be prepared. Assume that the cost of the subassemblies is dropping and the total estimated current replacement cost is $425,000. Under what additional contractual and economic conditions would note disclosure only be required? Prepare an appropriate note.

2. What contractual and economic conditions would require accrual of a loss? Give the accrual entry.

3. Assume that the subassemblies are received in 20X5 when their replacement cost was $410,000. The contract was paid in full. Give the required entry, assuming the entry in (2) was made, and a periodic inventory system is used.

★ **A8-17 Inventory Error:** When the accounting staff of Nicodemus Limited was preparing the first-quarter 20X5 interim financial statements, they discovered an error in the 31 December 20X4 financial statements. Inventory costing $225,000 had been in transit and was not received until 4 January 20X5. The accounts payable department had recorded the purchase as an account payable on 28 December 20X4. Title to the inventory had passed to Nicodemus on 27 December, the date that the supplier had loaded the shipment onto the shipping company's trucks.

Nicodemus uses a periodic inventory method.

**Required:**

1. What impact did the error have on Nicodemus's 20X4 financial statements?

2. When the error is discovered in the first quarter of 20X5, what correcting entry should Nicodemus make?

★★ **A8-18 Inventory-Related Errors:** McGoo-Person Publishers Inc. prepared its draft 20X4 financial statements in February 20X5. The draft income statement showed a tentative net income of $550,000. After the draft statements were prepared, but prior to their approval and release, the auditors discovered several errors:

a. The company had made a calculation error in the worksheets used for the year-end 20X5 physical inventory. Inventory actually should have been $50,000 greater than recorded.

b. Books costing $80,000 were shipped to a large chain of bookstores in the final week of the fiscal year; a sale (and receivable) of $120,000 had correspondingly been recorded. However, the bookstore chain had accepted the books only on consignment.

c. Inventory of $40,000 that was received from an offshore publisher on 29 December 20X4 (and included in the 31 December 20X4 physical inventory count) had not been recorded as an account payable until well into January 20X5.

d. The company had shipped books worth $150,000 to a distant customer on 28 December 20X4. The revenue (and account receivable) was recorded by Nicodemus on 4 January 20X5.

**Required:**

1. What effect will correction of these errors have on the tentative net income of $550,000? What will the revised net income be?

2. Suppose that these errors were not discovered until *after* the 20X4 statements were released. What adjustment(s), if any, should the company make on its books in 20X5?

★  **A8-19 Gross Margin Method:** You are auditing the records of Yu Sun Coldridge Corporation. The company took a physical inventory under your observation. However, the valuations have not been completed. The records of the company provide the following data: sales, $756,000 (gross); returned sales, $40,000 (returned to stock); purchases (gross), $372,000; beginning inventory, $240,000; freight-in, $16,800; and purchase returns and allowances, $4,400. The gross margin last period was 40% of net sales; you anticipate that it will be 35% for the year under audit.

**Required:**
Estimate the cost of the ending inventory using the gross margin method. Show computations.

★★  **A8-20 Gross Margin Method:** The manager of Seton Book Company, a book retailer, requires an estimate of the inventory cost for a quarterly financial report to the owner on 31 March 20X5. In the past, the gross margin method was used because of the difficulty and expense of taking a physical inventory at interim dates. The company sells both fiction and non-fiction books. Due to their lower turnover rate, non-fiction books are typically marked up to produce a gross profit of 37.5%. Fiction, on the other hand, generates a 28.6% gross profit. The manager has used the average gross profit of 33.333% to estimate interim inventories.

You have been asked by the manager to estimate the book inventory cost as of 31 March 20X5. The following data are available from Seton's accounting records:

|  | Fiction | Non-Fiction | Total |
|---|---|---|---|
| Inventory, 1 January 20X5 | $100,000 | $ 40,000 | $140,000 |
| Purchases | 600,000 | 200,000 | 800,000 |
| Freight-in | 5,000 | 2,000 | 7,000 |
| Sales | 590,000 | 160,000 | 750,000 |

**Required:**
*(Round gross margin ratios to three decimal places.)*

1. Using the average gross profit margin of 33.333%, compute the estimate of inventory as of 31 March 20X5, based on the method applied to combined fiction and non-fiction books.
2. Compute the estimate of ending inventory as of 31 March 20X5, based on the gross margin method applied separately to fiction and non-fiction books.
3. Which method is preferable in this situation? Explain.

★★  **A8-21 Retail Inventory Method:** Dan's Clothing Store values its inventory using the retail inventory method at the lower of average cost or market. The following data are available for the month of September 20X7:

|  | Cost | Selling Price |
|---|---|---|
| Inventory, 1 June | $161,400 | $240,000 |
| Markdowns |  | 63,000 |
| Markups |  | 87,000 |
| Markdown cancellations |  | 30,000 |
| Markup cancellations |  | 27,000 |
| Purchases | 519,600 | 670,800 |
| Sales |  | 750,000 |
| Purchase returns and allowances | 9,000 | 10,800 |
| Sales returns and allowances |  | 30,000 |

**Required:**
Prepare a schedule to compute the estimated inventory at 30 September, using the retail inventory method to approximate LCM.

(AICPA, adapted)

★★   **A8-22 Retail Inventory Method:** Auditors are examining the accounts of Acton Retail Corporation. They were present when Acton's personnel physically counted the Acton inventory; however, the auditors made their own tests. Acton's records provided the following data for the current year:

| | At Retail | At Cost |
|---|---|---|
| Inventory, 1 January | $ 300,000 | $180,500 |
| Net purchases | 1,453,000 | 955,000 |
| Freight-in | | 15,000 |
| Additional markups | 31,000 | |
| Additional markup cancellations | 14,000 | |
| Markdowns | 8,000 | |
| Employee discounts | 2,000 | |
| Sales | 1,300,000 | |

Inventory at 31 December (per physical count valued at retail) = $475,000

**Required:**

1. Compute the ending inventory at LCM as an audit test of the overall reasonableness of the physical inventory count.

2. Note any discrepancies indicated. What factors should the auditors consider in reconciling any difference in results from the analysis?

3. What accounting treatment (if any) should be accorded the discrepancy?

★★★   **A8-23 Gross Margin and Retail Inventory Methods:** The records of Diskount Department Store provided the following data for 20X5:

| | |
|---|---|
| Sales (gross) | $800,000 |
| Sales returns | 2,000 |
| Additional markups | 9,000 |
| Additional markup cancellations | 5,000 |
| Markdowns | 7,000 |
| Purchases: | |
|   At retail | 850,000 |
|   At cost | 459,500 |
| Purchase returns: | |
|   At retail | 4,000 |
|   At cost | 2,200 |
| Freight on purchases | 7,000 |
| Beginning inventory: | |
|   At retail | 80,000 |
|   At cost | 45,000 |
| Markdown cancellations | 3,000 |

**Required:**

1. Estimate the valuation of the ending inventory and cost of goods sold using the gross margin method. Last year's gross margin percentage was 51%.

2. Estimate the valuation of the ending inventory and cost of goods sold using the retail sales method, which approximates LCM.

3. Which method is likely to be more accurate? Comment.

★★   **A8-24 Inventory Estimation:** Banff Mountain Equipment Limited (Banff) sells skiing and hiking equipment to retailers. After a very successful ski season and just as it was about to commence shipping its hiking equipment for the upcoming season, Banff lost all of its hiking equipment in a fire in March 20X8. Fortunately, the company's insurance policy will cover 80% of the loss suffered in this fire. The loss is to be determined based on the cost of the inventory. Corporate records disclose the following:

| | |
|---|---:|
| Inventory—1 January 20X8 | $150,000 |
| Purchases (all on credit) during 20X8 | 480,000 |
| Purchase returns | 30,000 |
| Payments to suppliers for purchases | 440,000 |
| Customs and duty on purchases | 8,000 |
| Sales (all on credit) at retail price | 615,000 |
| Sales returns at retail price | 15,000 |
| Cash collected from accounts receivable | 580,000 |

Banff normally realizes a gross profit of 30% on its sales. It accounts for its inventory using a periodic inventory system. The net loss from the fire is deductible for income tax purposes. Banff's tax rate is 40%.

**Required:**

1. Calculate the net loss from the fire.
2. Should the loss from the fire be reported as an extraordinary item? Why or why not?

(CGA-Canada, adapted)

 **A8-25  Inventory Concepts—Recording, Adjusting, Closing, Reporting:** Gamit Company completed the following selected (and summarized) transactions during 20X5:

a. Merchandise inventory on hand 1 January 20X5, $105,000 (at cost, which was the same as LCM).
b. During the year, purchased merchandise for resale at cost of $200,000 on credit, terms 2/10, n/30. Immediately paid 85% of the cash cost.
c. Paid freight on merchandise purchased, $10,000 cash.
d. Paid 40% of the accounts payable within the discount period. The remaining payables were unpaid at the end of 20X5 and were still within the discount period.
e. Merchandise that had a quoted price of $3,000 (terms 2/10, n/30) was returned to a supplier. A cash refund of $2,940 was received because the items were unsatisfactory.
f. During the year, sold merchandise for $370,000, of which 10% was on credit.
g. A television set caught fire and was damaged internally; it was returned by the customer. The set was originally sold for $600, of which $400 cash was refunded. The set originally cost the company $420. Estimates are that the set, when repaired, can be sold for $240. Estimated repair costs are $50, and selling costs are estimated to be $10.
h. Operating expenses (administrative and distribution) paid in cash, $120,000; includes the $10 in (k).
i. Excluded from the purchase given in (b) and from the ending inventory was a shipment for $7,000 (net of discount). This shipment was in transit, FOB shipping point at 31 December 20X5. The invoice had arrived.
j. Paid $50 cash to repair the damaged television set; see (g) above.
k. Sold the damaged television set for $245; selling costs allocated, $10.
l. The ending inventory (as counted) was $110,000 at cost, and $107,000 at NRV. Assume an average income tax rate of 40%.

Accounting policies followed by the company are:

(1)  The annual accounting period ends 31 December.
(2)  A periodic inventory system is used.
(3)  Purchases and accounts payable are recorded net of cash discounts.
(4)  Freight charges are allocated to merchandise when purchased.
(5)  All cash discounts are taken.
(6)  Used and damaged merchandise is carried in a separate inventory account.
(7)  Inventories are reported at LCM and the allowance method is used.

**Required:**

1. Give the entries for transactions (b) through (k).
2. Give the end-of-period adjusting entries.
3. Prepare a multiple-step income statement for 20X5. Assume that 20,000 common shares are outstanding.
4. Show how the ending inventory should be reported on the balance sheet at 31 December 20X5.

---

 **A8-26 Inventory Issues—Overview and Explanation:** HHL Limited has significant investment in inventory of retail goods. It has a periodic inventory system, but uses the gross profit method to estimate inventory for its monthly statements. At the end of the current fiscal period, 31 December 20X5, the following issues have arisen:

a. In October 20X5, HHL bought goods for $355,600. This amount was recorded as the cost of purchases. The goods were purchased under a contract that had guaranteed the price for 12 months; prices have been volatile. When the goods were delivered, their replacement cost was $321,000. Replacement cost had rebounded to the price paid by the end of the year. All of the goods were still in inventory at the end of the period. If any adjustment is needed, prepare the entry.

b. The gross profit method, by category, is used to estimate inventory amounts and cost of goods sold during the period. The gross profit method produced an estimate of $2,456,000 of inventory that should have been present on 31 December. The actual count showed that $2,009,100 of goods was present. Explain at least three reasons this discrepancy could occur. What impact will the discrepancy have on the balance sheet and the income statement as compared to the preliminary numbers, based on the actual count?

c. The company is wondering whether the retail method would produce more accurate numbers for inventory. In the past year, opening inventory was $1,788,900 at cost and $2,500,000 at retail. Freight-in was $66,800. Purchases were $11,300,000 at cost and $19,710,000 at retail. There were no additional markups, but there were $544,200 of markdowns. Sales were $17,750,000. What estimated inventory value would the retail sales method have produced?

d. In light of the discrepancies discovered this year, the company is considering switching to a perpetual inventory system. Explain what would be required and how the company's information would change or not change as compared to its existing information system.

e. The actual physical count was $2,009,100. This inventory was categorized as follows:

|        | Cost      | NRV       |
|--------|-----------|-----------|
| Type A | $322,000  | $260,000  |
| Type B | 540,000   | 575,000   |
| Type C | 675,900   | 650,000   |
| Type D | 471,200   | 475,000   |

The allowance to reduce inventory to LCM has a balance of $45,000, unchanged from the last fiscal year-end. Prepare any needed entry to adjust the allowance, and justify your decision.

f. All inventories are now carried at weighted average cost. Management would like to know how inventory, cost of sales, and net income would be affected if the FIFO inventory method were to be used.

**Required:**
Respond to each request, (a)–(f), above.

---

 **A8-27 Cash Flow Statement:** Therot Corporation reported the following items in its 20X5 financial statements:

|  | 20X5 | 20X4 |
|---|---|---|
| *From the balance sheet:* | | |
| Inventories (net) | | |
| Finished goods | $ 477,226 | $ 404,477 |
| Work in progress | 197,368 | 166,193 |
| Materials and supplies | 269,974 | 271,374 |
|  | 944,568 | 842,044 |
| | | |
| Accounts payable | 615,904 | 597,211 |
| Estimated liability on non-cancellable | | |
| purchase commitments | 7,943 | — |
| | | |
| *From the income statement:* | | |
| Cost of goods sold* | $4,919,316 | $4,101,564 |
| Loss on purchase commitment | 7,943 | — |

*Includes loss due to decline in market value

### FROM THE NOTES:

Inventories are carried at FIFO cost, net of an allowance to reduce finished goods inventory to the LCM of $64,816 (20X4, $45,719). Market value is defined as NRV.

At year-end, the company has outstanding purchase commitments in the amount of $13,299 (20X4, $6,587). The market value of these goods is equal to, or exceeds, the purchase commitment cost except as accrued in the financial statements.

### Required:

1. What items would appear on the cash flow statement as a result of the inventory transactions of the year? Assume the use of the indirect method of presentation in the operating activities section.

2. How much did the company pay for inventory during the period?

3. Assume that inventory values as reflected above were standard cost. The income statement reflected unfavourable price variances of $43,110, and favourable usage variances of $19,850. These variances were considered immaterial, so inventory could be reported at standard cost for external reporting. Other facts are unchanged. How much money did the company pay for inventory during the period?

4. Would the LCM writedown have been the same, greater than, or less than that recorded if the company had used (a) average cost or (b) LIFO as a cost flow assumption? Assume that prices have generally been rising in these markets over the last several years.

★★ **A8-28 Perpetual Inventory—FIFO:** Berzo Company maintains perpetual inventory records on a FIFO basis for the three main products distributed by the company. A physical inventory is taken at the end of each year in order to check the perpetual inventory records. The following information relating to one of the products, blenders, for the year 20X5, was taken from the records of the company:

|  | Units | Unit Cost |
|---|---|---|
| Beginning inventory | 7,200 | $6.60 |
| Purchases and sales (in order given): | | |
| Purchase 1 | 4,000 | 6.65 |
| Sale 1 | 8,000 | |
| Purchase 2 | 12,800 | 6.70 |
| Sale 2 | 8,800 | |
| Purchase 3 | 3,200 | 7.00 |
| Purchase 4 | 5,600 | 6.75 |

|  | Units | Unit Cost |
|---|---|---|
| Sale 3 | 11,200 | |
| Purchase 5 | 4,000 | 6.60 |

Ending inventory (per count), 8,300
Replacement cost (per unit) at year-end, $6.60; sales price was constant all year at $19.00. Replacement cost is used for LCM valuation.

**Required:**

1. Reconstruct the perpetual inventory record for blenders.
2. Give all entries indicated by the above data. Similar transactions can be summarized into one entry.
3. Prepare the income statement through gross margin for this product.
4. Comment on the possible need for a LCM writedown of the inventory.

★ **A8-29 Inventory Cost Flow:** FIFO has been used as a cost flow assumption by the Hwan Company since it was first organized in 20X0. Hwan is a private company. An audit is not required by the company's bank. Results for the past four years have been as follows (in $ thousands):

|  | 20X0 | 20X1 | 20X2 | 20X3 |
|---|---|---|---|---|
| Reported net income (FIFO) | $26,250 | $ 45,000 | $ 48,750 | $ 67,500 |
| Reported ending inventories—FIFO | 82,250 | 142,000 | 164,000 | 173,000 |
| Ending inventory— average cost | 78,500 | 101,650 | 117,500 | 135,500 |

**Required:**

1. Restate net income assuming use of the average cost method.
2. What inventory cost flow policy would you expect this company to adopt if it was trying to:
   a. Match the most recent cost of acquisition with sales revenue
   b. Minimize income tax payments
   c. Report maximum inventory values on the balance sheet

★ **A8-30 Cost Flow Assumptions:** The records of Cairo Company showed the following data relating to one of the major items held in inventory. The transactions occurred in the order given.

|  | Units | Unit Cost |
|---|---|---|
| Beginning inventory | 9,000 | $8.45 |
| Purchase No. 1 | +10,500 | 8.90 |
| Sale No. 1 (at $25) | − 9,750 | |
| Purchase No. 2 | +12,000 | 9.50 |
| Sale No. 2 (at $27) | − 8,250 | |
| Ending inventory | 13,500 | |

**Required:**
For each independent assumption given, calculate the total dollar amount for ending inventory and cost of goods sold.

a. Weighted average cost, periodic inventory system
b. FIFO, perpetual inventory system                    (CGA-Canada, adapted)

★★ **A8-31 Inventory Cost Methods:** The inventory records of Acme Appliances showed the following data relative to a food processor in inventory (the transactions occurred in the order given):

| Transaction | Units | Unit Cost |
|---|---|---|
| 1. Inventory | 30 | $19.00 |
| 2. Purchase | 45 | 20.00 |
| 3. Sale | 50 | |
| 4. Purchase | 50 | 20.80 |
| 5. Sale | 50 | |
| 6. Purchase | 50 | 21.60 |

**Required:**
Compute the cost of goods sold for the period and the ending inventory, assuming the following (round unit costs to nearest cent):

a. Weighted average (periodic inventory system)
b. Moving average (perpetual inventory system)
c. FIFO
d. LIFO (periodic inventory system)

★★★ **A8-32 Inventory Cost Methods:** The College Store inventory records showed the following data relative to a particular item sold regularly (transactions occurred in the order given):

| Transaction | Units | Unit Cost |
|---|---|---|
| 1. Inventory | 2,000 | $5.00 |
| 2. Purchase | 18,000 | 5.20 |
| 3. Sales (at $13 per unit) | 7,000 | |
| 4. Purchase | 6,000 | 5.50 |
| 5. Sales (at $13.50 per unit) | 16,000 | |
| 6. Purchase | 3,000 | 6.00 |

**Required:**

1. Complete the following schedule (round unit costs to nearest cent and total costs of inventory to the nearest $10):

| | Ending Inventory | Cost of Goods Sold | Gross Margin |
|---|---|---|---|
| a. FIFO | | | |
| b. Weighted average | | | |
| c. Moving average | | | |

2. Prepare journal entries, including year-end adjusting entries to establish ending inventory, if needed, for the two average calculations (b) and (c) above. Assume that the weighted average method is used with a periodic system and the moving average method with a perpetual system.

3. Explain how your entries in (2) would be different if a standard cost system were used, with the standard cost established at $5.50 at normal capacity.

★★★ **A8-33 Inventory Policy Comparison:** Carlyon and Dennis are North American manufacturers of auto parts. The two firms use different inventory cost flow accounting policies. This question asks you to determine some of the differences due to the reporting. The two firms report the following selected information for 20X1:

| | ($ thousands) | |
| --- | --- | --- |
| | **Carlyon** | **Dennis** |
| Earnings from continuing operations | $ (538) | $ (3,432) |
| Cost of sales | 24,803 | 71,826 |
| Net earnings per share (continuing operations) | (2.22) | (7.21) |
| Assets (total) | 43,076 | 174,429 |
| Inventories | 3,571 | 6,215 |
| Total shareholders' equity | 6,109 | 22,690 |
| Comparative units sold: U.S. and Canada (millions) | 1.661 units | 3.114 units |
| Comparative units sold: Worldwide (millions) | 1.866 units | 5.346 units |

## CARLYON CORPORATION

**Note 1:** *Summary of Significant Accounting Policies*
Inventories are valued at the LCM. The cost of approximately 41% and 49% of inventories at 31 December 20X1 and 20X0, respectively, is determined on an average cost basis. The balance of inventory cost is determined on a first-in, first-out (FIFO) basis.

**Note 2:** *Inventories and Cost of Sales*
Inventories are summarized by major classification as follows (in $ thousands):

| | 31 December | |
| --- | --- | --- |
| | **20X1** | **20X0** |
| Finished products, including service parts | $1,192 | $1,114 |
| Raw materials, finished, production parts, and supplies | 873 | 1,100 |
| Work-in-process | 1,476 | 911 |
| Other | 30 | 25 |
| Total | $3,571 | $3,150 |

If inventories valued by FIFO had instead been valued on an average cost basis, inventory would have been $239 million and $208 million lower at 31 December 20X1 and 20X0, respectively (see Note 1). Total manufacturing cost of sales aggregated $24.81 million, and $24.13 million for 20X1 and 20X0, respectively.

## DENNIS MOTOR COMPANY

**Note 1:** *Accounting Policies (Inventory Valuation)*
Inventories are stated at the lower of cost or market. The cost of substantially all North American inventories is determined by the average cost method. The cost of the remaining inventories is determined substantially by the first-in, first-out (FIFO) method.

If FIFO were the only method of inventory accounting used by the company, inventories would have been $1,323 and $1,331 higher than reported at 31 December 20X1 and 20X0, respectively. The major classes of inventory at 31 December were as follows (in $ thousands):

| | **20X1** | **20X0** |
| --- | --- | --- |
| Finished products | $2,979.2 | $3,628.2 |
| Raw materials and work-in-process | 2,800.9 | 3,025.7 |
| Supplies | 435.2 | 461.5 |
| Total | $6,215.3 | $7,115.4 |

## Required:

1. Are prices rising or falling in the 20X1 supplier markets in which Dennis (and Carlyon) buys? How do you know?

2. Compare Dennis's and Carlyon's inventory levels and comment on the comparison.

3. Is it desirable to have similar companies using different inventory cost flow policies? If not, why do accounting standard setters not require uniformity?

**A8-34 Inventory Cost and Cost of Sales—Two Methods:** The following data relates to Sirshi Corporation for the month of March:

| | Units | Cost per Unit |
|---|---|---|
| Opening inventory | 180 | $14.00 |
| Sale 3 March | 75 | |
| Purchase, 5 March | 2,700 | 14.40 |
| Purchase, 13 March | 1,050 | 15.20 |
| Sale, 15 March | 2,000 | |
| Sale, 18 March | 500 | |
| Purchase, 21 March | 4,700 | 15.80 |
| Purchase, 25 March | 2,800 | 16.00 |
| Sale, 26 March | 5,000 | |

**Required:**

1. Calculate the inventory cost and cost of goods sold under the following cost flow assumptions:
   a. FIFO
   b. Weighted average, periodic inventory system

2. Give all entries to record purchases and sales using a FIFO cost system and perpetual inventory costing. Assume all sales were for $22 per unit, and were on credit. All inventory purchases were also on credit.

3. Repeat (2) using a weighted average cost system and periodic inventory. The inventory was counted on 31 March, and cost of sales was recorded on that date.

4. Prepare the entry that would be made if FIFO was used and the actual physical count revealed that 3,800 units were on hand.

---

 **A8-35 Inventory Cost Methods:** The records of Clayton Company showed the following transactions, in the order given, relating to the major inventory item:

| | Units | Unit Cost |
|---|---|---|
| 1. Inventory | 3,000 | $6.90 |
| 2. Purchase | 6,000 | 7.20 |
| 3. Sale (at $15) | 4,000 | |
| 4. Purchase | 5,000 | 7.50 |
| 5. Sale (at $15) | 9,000 | |
| 6. Purchase | 11,000 | 7.66 |
| 7. Sale (at $18) | 9,000 | |
| 8. Purchase | 6,000 | 7.80 |

**Required:**

Complete the following schedule for each independent assumption (round unit costs to the nearest cent; show computations):

| | Units and Amounts | | |
|---|---|---|---|
| **Independent Assumptions** | **Ending Inventory** | **Cost of Goods Sold** | **Gross Margin** |
| a. FIFO | | | |
| b. LIFO, periodic inventory system | | | |
| c. Weighted average, periodic inventory system | | | |
| d. Moving average, perpetual inventory system | | | |

## CHAPTER 9

# Capital Assets, Intangibles, and Goodwill

## INTRODUCTION

The main focus of this chapter is on the very broad category of long-lived assets known generally as capital assets—both tangible and intangible. Capital assets of many descriptions have future benefit to companies because they contribute to the revenue stream. For example, IMAX Corporation, the large-screen movie operation, reports film assets (the company makes its own movies), projection equipment, motion simulation equipment, and camera equipment, in addition to the more classic tangible capital assets such as land, buildings, office equipment, production equipment, and leasehold improvements. Intangible assets include patents, trademarks, and capitalized computer software. IMAX also reports goodwill from acquired businesses. Quite a collection, but all necessary to operate in this industry!

This chapter will examine the issues surrounding the measurement and recording of capital assets, both tangible and intangible, and goodwill. A major topic in this chapter is acquisition cost. The determination of acquisition cost may be complex because decisions must be made about what expenditures to include and exclude from capital cost. In addition, there are many ways to acquire an asset that do not involve a clear and unambiguous payment of cash in return for a capital asset. Chapter 10 deals with accounting following acquisition, including amortization, impairment, and revaluation.

## CATEGORIES OF LONG-LIVED ASSETS

Long-lived assets may be separated into three categories:

1. Tangible capital assets;

2. Intangible capital assets; and

3. Goodwill.

**Capital Assets** A **capital asset** can be defined as an *identifiable long-lived asset, acquired for use in the revenue-producing activities of the enterprise.* There are several important aspects of this definition:

1. Capital assets are held for use in the production or supply of goods and services or for rental to others. Capital assets may also be used for administrative purposes or for maintenance of other capital assets.

2. Capital assets must be separately identifiable.

3. Capital assets are acquired to be used on a continued basis.

4. Capital assets are not intended for sale in the ordinary course of business.

It is important to distinguish between capital assets and inventory. A computer is a *capital asset* to the company that buys and uses it, but it was *inventory* to the manufacturer that made it and to the dealer that sold it. It is not the asset itself that governs classification as a capital asset; it is the intended *use* of the asset that matters. If an asset is held for sale, it is not a capital asset.

*Goodwill* is excluded from the general term "capital assets." It is not a *separately identifiable* asset; goodwill arises as a residual in the purchase of other assets acquired in a business combination. The superior earning potential of the purchased entity is assumed be the reason that goodwill exists.

Long-lived assets that were originally acquired for use in generating revenue but that no longer are intended for that purpose cease to be capital assets. Instead, they become investment assets or assets held for sale, and are reported in the long-term other assets classification on the balance sheet.

**Tangible versus Intangible Capital Assets** Capital assets can be described as *tangible* or *intangible*. Tangible capital assets are items of property, plant, and equipment. These assets have a physical presence; the word "tangible" means, literally, that the asset can be touched. Tangible assets include land, buildings, equipment, furniture, leasehold improvements, and other such physical assets. Tangible assets also include long-lived property held to generate revenue through rental, such as office buildings, apartments, cars and trucks, industrial property, furniture, computers, airplanes, etc.

**Intangible capital assets** are long-lived assets that do *not* have a physical substance. They often arise from legal or contractual rights. These assets are held to generate revenue, and are not intended for sale in the ordinary course of business. Intangible assets are separately identifiable and are thus capital assets. Examples include customer lists, copyrights, patents, subscription lists, mineral rights, franchises, computer software, licences, and trademarks.

## VALUATION OF CAPITAL ASSETS

### Historical Cost

Capital assets are normally recorded at *historical cost,* which is normally acquisition price. It includes all costs directly attributable to the acquisition, construction, development, or betterment of the asset including installing it in the location and in the condition necessary for its intended use.

## Fair Value

Historical cost is usually the *fair value* at the date of purchase. That is, the asset is bought for its fair value as of the date of acquisition. As time passes, the fair value of the asset will change as the price for a comparable asset changes in the market, due to changes in technology and supply and demand forces. Since capital assets are held for lengthy periods of time, (amortized) historical cost and fair value may be quite different. Historical cost financial statements do not attempt to reflect the current value of capital assets, just the sacrifice made to acquire them.

In North America, the accounting model retains historical cost as a valuation rule for capital assets. It is not permissible to adjust historical cost to fair value. However, recording fair value is allowed under international standards and in various countries around the world. The argument is that when these assets are pledged as collateral for loans, or in a number of other circumstances, the fair value of capital assets may be highly relevant to financial statement readers.

Assume that land is on the books for $235,000, but its fair value is established to be $460,000. The following entry would revalue land under international standards:

| | | |
|---|---|---|
| Land ($460,000 – $235,000) | 225,000 | |
|     Other comprehensive income: revaluation surplus | | 225,000 |

Note that the credit in this entry is not a gain that would appear on the income statement; it is recorded in other comprehensive income, a component of shareholders' equity on the balance sheet.

## Determination of Cost

**Constructed or Developed Assets** Many capital assets are not purchased, per se, but are constructed (tangible assets) or developed (for intangible assets) by the enterprise. The cost of a constructed or developed asset is the sum of the expenditures relating to its construction or development. These costs may not reflect the fair value of the asset, even at the time of its creation. A tangible asset may be constructed at a lower cost than its purchase price, and an intangible asset may be developed for far less than it would cost to buy it fully developed from someone else.

Indeed, developed assets may not be available for purchase at any price; they often are unique, which is what gives them their revenue-generating value. Examples include computer software and natural resource deposits. The capitalized value for these assets is not, was not, and was never intended to be, fair value at acquisition. It is undeniably difficult to interpret the earnings potential of companies with significant assets of this nature, without detailed knowledge of the assets beyond that provided in the financial statements.

Constructed and developed assets may not be recorded at costs that *exceed* fair value. Fair value may be determined with reference to future benefits: future cash flow. This can be hard to establish! Sometimes, especially for tangible assets, it is feasible to compare the capitalized cost with a hypothetical purchase price (for example, what it would have cost to pay a commercial contractor to construct a building). For other capital assets, however, such a comparison may not be feasible. It may be impossible to determine whether an intangible asset is worth what was spent to develop it, until its development is complete. For example, the costs of developing a mining site are capitalized until it is known whether the value of the mineral resources is worth continued development of the mine site.

## Capitalization Norms

Accounting practice has developed steadily in this area, and there is normal practice surrounding the typical kinds of costs that should be capitalized versus expensed in each category. Common practices for capital expenditures are summarized in Exhibit 9-1. Careful analysis will show that each capitalized item creates some sort of future enhancement of cash flows. Often, it is because the expenditure is inescapable in order to get the capital asset into operation.

Exhibit 9-1 is fairly comprehensive. No such list can really be complete, but this list includes a wide range of tangible capital assets, intangible capital assets, and goodwill.

---

## EXHIBIT 9-1

### COMMON CAPITALIZATION PRACTICES

| Capital Asset | Capitalize |
|---|---|
| Buildings, purchased | • purchase price<br>• cost of modifications |
| Buildings, constructed | • architectural fees<br>• payments to contractors<br>• cost of permits<br>• excavation costs<br>• legal fees, closing costs |
| Buildings, self-constructed | • direct construction costs<br>• excavation costs<br>• reasonable apportionment of overhead<br>• legal costs, permits, etc.<br>• interest on *specific* construction loans |
| Machinery and equipment | • invoice cost, net of discounts, whether taken or not<br>• taxes, freight, and duty<br>• special platforms, foundations, other required installation costs<br>• costs of building modifications necessary for installation<br>• cost of preparing asset for use, including testing |
| Land | • purchase price<br>• back taxes on acquisition, paid in order to release title<br>• legal fees, closing costs<br>• general land preparation costs, including grading, filling, draining, and surveying<br>• cost of removing structures and other obstructions, if land is acquired for development (proceeds from salvaged materials reduce the cost capitalized)<br>• special assessments for local government-maintained improvements, including streets, sidewalks, sewers, and streetlights<br>• property taxes, insurance, and other holding costs incurred on land not in current productive use (may be expensed on grounds of expedience and conservatism)<br>• landscaping and other property enhancements, if permanent<br>• present value of asset retirement obligations |
| Land improvements | • driveways, parking lots, fencing<br>• streets and sidewalks that the company must maintain<br>• landscaping, if not permanent |
| Patents | • purchase price, transfer and legal fees if bought from another entity<br>• if internally developed, criteria must be met to justify capitalization<br>• development costs to internally develop a patented item; research costs are expensed |

EXHIBIT 9-1    (cont'd)

## COMMON CAPITALIZATION PRACTICES

| Capital Asset | Capitalize |
|---|---|
| Patents, continued | • legal and other necessary documentation costs to register the patent, if self-developed<br>• costs of a successful court defence (unsuccessful defences are expensed, along with the now-worthless patent) |
| Industrial design registrations (e.g., a five-year renewable registration of the shape, pattern, or ornamentation of a manufactured item) | • acquisition and registration cost, as per patents<br>• if internally developed, criteria must be met to justify capitalization<br>• successful defence costs, as per patents |
| Copyrights | • acquisition and registration cost, as per patents<br>• if internally developed, criteria must be met to justify capitalization<br>• successful defence costs, as per patents |
| Trademarks and trade names | • acquisition cost, as per patents<br>• if internally developed, criteria must be met to justify capitalization<br>• legal and other necessary documentation costs to register the trademark, if self-developed<br>• successful defence costs, as per patents |
| Franchise rights | • initial franchise fees, not related to annual volumes<br>• legal fees, closing costs |
| Development costs | • costs involved in translation of research findings into new products, etc., prior to commercial production<br>• specific criteria must be met to justify capitalization |
| Internally developed intangibles | • specific criteria must be met to justify capitalization |
| Leasehold improvements (alterations, improvements, or refurbishing of leased space) | • invoice cost, installation costs |
| Resource exploration and development costs | • resource exploration and development costs incurred<br>• present value of asset retirement obligations<br>• under full costing, all sites deferred<br>• under successful efforts, only productive sites deferred |
| Computer software costs | • if internally developed, criteria must be met to justify capitalization<br>• for software for resale, capitalize costs after technical feasibility is established, if markets ensure recoverability |
| Website development costs | • if internally developed, criteria must be met to justify capitalization<br>• application and infrastructure costs capitalized<br>• graphics costs capitalized<br>• some content development capitalized, depending on longevity and nature |

**Impact of Policy Choice** Expenditures might be capitalized and amortized, or immediately expensed. If you don't expense now, you will expense later. That is, capitalized costs, in almost all cases, are carried to income through amortization. The two approaches will provide different income and asset values throughout the life of the asset.

## ETHICAL ISSUES

Is there any room for choice or manipulation? Some firms are quick to disclaim any future benefit associated with a variety of expenditures related to capital assets. They expense these amounts immediately. For whatever reason, these companies seem to be attempting to minimize current net income and net assets, and enjoy lower future amortization expenses. A company may also prefer to expense rather than capitalize if it has cash flow prediction as a primary reporting objective. By including the expenditures in current expenses, a company achieves a net income figure that is closer to the actual cash flow.

At the other end of the spectrum, some companies are very aggressive in their capitalization policies, seeking higher current income and capital assets, and accepting higher future amortization. For example, a regulated public utility will generally capitalize as many costs as possible because the enterprise's permitted (i.e., regulated) profit is based on its regulated rate of return multiplied by the asset base. The higher the asset base, the larger the profit it is entitled to earn.

Materiality plays a role in this area, as well. Small capital expenditures are often expensed on the basis that the more correct capitalization and amortization would not produce results different enough to cause investors to make different decisions.

## CONCEPT REVIEW

1. What is the difference between tangible and intangible capital assets?

2. What are the characteristics of an intangible capital asset?

3. If fair value of capital assets were to be recorded, what other financial statement element is recognized?

4. What difference does it make to a company's reported financial results if the company is highly aggressive in its capitalization policies?

## DETERMINING THE COST OF CAPITAL ASSETS

### Tangible Capital Assets

Carefully analyze Exhibit 9-1 for common practices for tangible capital assets such as buildings, machinery and equipment, land, and land improvements. Note in particular the conventions surrounding land. Since land does not amortize, but other capital assets do, a decision to capitalize an amount in the land account means that there is no impact on net income until the land is sold. In particular, note that land cost includes costs specifically related to obtaining clear title to the land, such as legal fees and back property taxes. Any costs associated with preparing the land for its intended use, such as clearing existing structures and excavation, are also capitalized to the land account. Other expenditures, for things that will wear out over time, are put in a separate land improvements account, which is amortized. These expenditures include non-permanent landscaping, as well as fences and paving.

## Basket Purchase of Several Assets

Occasionally, several assets are acquired for a single lump-sum price that may be lower than the sum of the individual asset prices, to encourage the sale. In other cases, the assets are attached, for example, land and building. This type of acquisition is called a **basket purchase**, **group purchase**, or lump-sum purchase. A portion of the single lump-sum price must be allocated to each asset acquired.

Any portions of the lump-sum price directly attributable to particular assets in the group are assigned in full to those assets. For example, land survey costs and back property taxes applicable to land are assigned only to the land account. Allocation of the remaining lump-sum price to each asset is necessary. Under the cost principle, the sum of the individual asset account balances at acquisition is limited to the lump-sum price.

Allocation is based on the relative fair values of the several assets involved. Possible indicators include:

1. Market prices for similar assets;

2. Current appraised value;

3. Assessed value for property tax purposes; and

4. The present value of estimated future net cash flows, including manufacturing cost savings.

The seller's book values are not relevant because they do not reflect the current value of the assets.

Each asset is valued according to the ratio of its value to the total value of the group; this valuation is called the *proportional method*. If the value of only the first asset(s) in a group is determinable, the second (or remaining) asset is valued at the cost remaining to be allocated. This less desirable procedure is called the *incremental method*.

**Proportional Method** To illustrate the proportional method, assume that $90,000 is the negotiated acquisition price paid for land, a building, and machinery. These assets are appraised individually, as the best available indication of value in this case: land, $30,000; building, $50,000; and machinery, $20,000. The cost apportionment of the single lump-sum price and the entry to record the transaction are as follows:

|  | Appraised Asset Value | Apportionment of Cost | Apportioned Cost |
|---|---|---|---|
| Land | $ 30,000 | 30%* × $90,000 | $27,000 |
| Building | 50,000 | 50%  × $90,000 | 45,000 |
| Machinery | 20,000 | 20%  × $90,000 | 18,000 |
| Total | $100,000 |  | $90,000 |

*30% = $30,000 ÷ $100,000

To record the basket purchase:

| | | |
|---|---|---|
| Land | 27,000 | |
| Building | 45,000 | |
| Machinery | 18,000 | |
| Cash | | 90,000 |

**Incremental Method** Assume, instead, that the building was worth $48,000, and the machinery, $17,000, but it was not possible to determine an objective value for the land. In this case, land would be assigned the residual $25,000, using the incremental method.

## Capital Assets Financed with Low-Interest Debt

Sometimes, payment terms for an asset stretch out over a long period. This presents no special accounting problems, unless the debt bears a reduced interest rate, perhaps offered by the vendor to encourage purchase. In such a case, the asset is recorded at the most objective amount, considering:

1. The cash equivalent price, or fair value of the capital asset, versus

2. The present value of the future cash payments required by the debt agreement discounted at the prevailing (market) interest rate for that type of debt.

When a low-interest debt instrument is issued, the normal procedure is to record its face value as a liability. The difference between the face value and the (lower) fair value of the asset is debited to a contra-liability account as *discount on note payable*. The discount is amortized over the term of the debt, thereby increasing interest expense each period. The fair value of the asset may be calculated as the present value of the loan plus any cash paid.

**Example** To illustrate the purchase of a capital asset on credit, assume that Cobb Corporation purchases equipment on 1 January 20X2, with a $600 cash down payment and a $1,000, one-year 12% note payable due on 31 December 20X2. The stated interest rate is equal to the current market rate, so the present value of the note equals its face value. That is,

$$P = (\$1,000 + \$120) \times (\text{P/F, 12\%, 1})$$
$$= \$1,120 \times .89286$$
$$= \$1,000$$

The asset is recorded at the sum of the cash down payment plus the present value of the note because the cash equivalent price of the asset is not available. The recorded amount is:

$$\text{Equipment value} = \text{Cash down payment} + \text{Present value of note}$$
$$= \$600 + \$1,000 = \$1,600$$

Cobb's entries to record the asset and the note are as follows:

**1 January 20X2**

| | | |
|---|---|---|
| Equipment | 1,600 | |
|     Cash | | 600 |
|     Note payable | | 1,000 |

Assume instead that Feller Company acquires a machine on 1 January 20X2, with a non-interest-bearing note that requires $8,615 to be paid on 31 December 20X2, 20X3, and 20X4. The note has no explicit interest, but the prevailing interest rate is 14% on liabilities of similar risk and duration. The face amount of the note is $25,845 ($8,615 × 3). The cash equivalent cost of the machine is unknown, so the asset is recorded at the present value of the three payments discounted at 14%.

$$
\begin{aligned}
\text{Recorded cost} &= \$8,615 \times (\text{P/A, 14\%, 3}) \\
&= \$8,615 \times 2.32163 \\
&= \$20,000 \text{ (rounded)}
\end{aligned}
$$

Feller's entries to record the asset and the note are as follows:

| 1 January 20X2 | Gross Method | | Net Method | |
| --- | --- | --- | --- | --- |
| Equipment | 20,000 | | 20,000 | |
| Discount on note payable | 5,845 | | — | |
| Note payable | | 25,845* | | 20,000 |

*$8,615 \times 3$

The discount on note payable is a contra note payable account. It reduces the net note payable balance to the present value of the future cash flows ($20,000). The discount is amortized to interest expense over the life of the liability.

## Capital Assets Acquired in Exchange for Equity Securities

When equity securities (e.g., common shares) are issued to acquire capital assets, the assets are recorded at the fair market value of the securities issued, or, if more objectively determinable, at the fair market value of the asset.

The market value of the shares issued provides a reliable fair market value for publicly traded securities if the number of shares in the exchange is below the typical daily trading volume. Assume that Medford Corporation purchases used equipment in 20X5. The equipment is in reasonable condition but is not normally sold before the end of its useful life. Thus, it has no reliable market value. In payment for this equipment, Medford issues 2,000 common shares. Medford's common shares are listed on the Toronto Stock Exchange and currently trade at $10 per share. Medford has 10 million common shares outstanding. The proper value for the equipment is 2,000 × $10, or $20,000.

**Complicating Factors**  Several factors can complicate the situation, however. The effect of a substantial share offering on the market price of the shares is often not known until after issuance. Also, the shares of many companies are not traded with sufficient frequency to establish a daily market price. In other cases, organizers of a newly formed corporation may issue a substantial number of shares for capital assets when there is no established fair value for the shares.

If the market value of the securities (in the volume exchanged) cannot be determined reliably, the market value of the assets acquired is used if it can be reliably determined. In the absence of recent cash sale evidence, an independent appraisal can be used to value the assets. This may be easier said than done: unexplored or unproven mineral deposits, manufacturing rights, patents, chemical formulas, and mining claims are all difficult to value.

If no reliable market value can be determined for either the securities issued or the assets acquired, the Board of Directors of the corporation must establish a reasonable valuation. The directors have considerable discretion in establishing values, and firms experiencing financial difficulty may be tempted to overstate asset values, overstating owners' equity as well. A disincentive to overvaluation, however, is the increased amortization expense in future years.

## Donated Assets

Shareholders and other parties occasionally donate assets and services to corporations. For example, shareholders may donate valuable paintings to adorn the corporate boardroom.

The assets cost the company nothing; that is, they are obtained in a *non-reciprocal transfer*, meaning that the company gives nothing in return. Does that mean that the assets need not be recognized? If the balance sheet is to provide a record of assets controlled by the entity, and the income statement is to record the costs of doing business, then it seems logical to include these assets at fair value. But the entity sacrificed no resources to obtain the assets. If the assets are depreciable, recorded assets will create an expense in future years, as they are used. Should future years' income be reduced because of a charge created in such a way? Is the return on shareholders' investment understated in such circumstances? It's a thorny issue.

Current practice in Canada is often to record the asset at its fair value, and increase a shareholders' equity contributed capital account. Depreciation based on the market value of the donated asset is matched against future revenue presumably generated by the assets.

However, an additional procedure that sometimes is used is to also amortize the balance of the contributed capital account using the same pattern as the depreciation of the related asset. The credit may be either directly to a revenue or expense account. The net effect is to remove the impact of the depreciation from net income. There is no Canadian standard on this issue, but such amortization is suggested for donations of capital assets to not-for-profit enterprises.

**Example** To illustrate accounting for a donated asset, assume a building (fair market value $400,000), and the land on which it is located (fair market value $100,000) are donated to Sui Limited. A $5,000 legal and deed transfer cost for the land is borne by Sui, which records the donation as follows:

| | | |
|---|---|---|
| Building | 400,000 | |
| Land | 105,000 | |
|   Cash | | 5,000 |
|   Contributed capital—donated assets | | 500,000 |

## Self-Constructed Assets

Companies sometimes construct plant assets for their own use. For example, a utility employs its personnel to extend transmission lines and construct pipelines. All costs directly associated with the construction are capitalized to the constructed asset. These costs include incremental material, labour, and overhead costs. Overhead includes general costs not directly related to production, such as utility costs, maintenance on equipment, and supervision.

**Overhead Cost** Overhead incurred during construction, *if it is directly attributable to the construction or development activity*, is included in the cost of self-constructed or self-developed assets. Application of this principle can require careful judgement.

Many accountants contend that failure to allocate some portion of the general overhead to self-construction projects causes an undervaluation of self-constructed assets. On the other hand, others argue that assets are often self-constructed during slack periods when the production facility and workers would otherwise be idle. Using this line of reasoning, no general overhead should be capitalized because of the income-manipulation potential associated with this "make-work" project. Companies that want to show high asset values will tend to interpret "overhead" quite broadly and will allocate significant amounts of overhead cost to the project.

If overhead is allocated, it should be done on a pro-rata basis. That is, if general overhead is allocated on the basis of labour-hours, and 8% of labour-hours are associated with self-construction, then at most, 8% of total general overhead should be included as a cost of the self-constructed asset.

**Interest Cost** The period required for construction of capital assets can be lengthy. There is general agreement that time-related costs, including interest, property taxes, and insurance during construction, should be capitalized to the asset under construction. (And also, interest can be capitalized to *any asset* where a substantial time period is needed to get the item ready for use or sale.) After all, if the asset were purchased rather than self-constructed, the purchase price would normally include a cost component to cover the seller's financing expenses during construction. Also, many firms would be unable to construct assets without debt financing.

Interest is usually a period cost, not eligible for capitalization. Current practice in Canada is to allow cash paid for interest costs on loans related to a long-term construction project to be capitalized, if the company wishes. A company can set its own policy in this regard; it is not forced to capitalize interest. Imputed interest on equity is *not eligible* for capitalization unless the company is a regulated utility and the regulator allows such a practice. Furthermore, Canadian standards allow for interest capitalization but do not contain detailed guidelines to implement the policy. As a result, variety in practice is to be expected. Other standard-setting bodies, including international and U.S. standards, have far more detailed rules that determine the maximum amount of interest eligible for capitalization.

The Canadian standards require disclosure of interest capitalized, allowing financial statement users to determine the effect of capitalized interest on earnings and assets.

**Fair Market Value Cap** The actual cost of a self-constructed asset does not necessarily equal fair market value at the point of acquisition, as is also the case for natural resources and intangible assets. Using the higher market value would result in recording a gain on construction. A company cannot record a gain as the result of expenditures! The lower construction cost is ultimately reflected in higher net income through lower depreciation expense in future years.

Consistent with the valuation of other assets, the maximum valuation allowed for self-constructed assets is fair market value. If total capitalized cost exceeds the market value of a similar asset of equal capacity and quality, the excess is recognized as a loss. Failure to do so carries forward cost elements that have no future benefit and causes overstated depreciation in future years.

**Example** To illustrate the accounting for a self-constructed asset, assume that Kelvin Corporation completes a project with total construction costs as follows:

| | |
|---|---|
| Material | $200,000 |
| Labour | 500,000 |
| Incremental overhead | 60,000 |
| Applied general overhead | 40,000 |
| Capitalized interest | 100,000 |
| Total | $900,000 |

Kelvin has recorded costs in an account called equipment under construction. If the asset's market value at completion equals or exceeds $900,000, the summary entry to record the completion of the project is:

| | | |
|---|---|---|
| Equipment | 900,000 | |
|     Equipment under construction | | 900,000 |

If the asset's market value is only $880,000, the entry is:

| | | |
|---|---:|---:|
| Equipment | 880,000 | |
| Loss on construction of equipment | 20,000 | |
|    Equipment under construction | | 900,000 |

It is important to watch capitalization practices very carefully—many firms, with a desire to maximize earnings or assets by deferring costs, seize on self-construction as an opportunity to try to defer lots of interesting things! Others wish to capitalize as little as possible. Remember, though, that the higher asset value generated is a base for future depreciation.

## Asset Retirement Obligations

Some companies may have a legal requirement, either through legal statute or contract, to incur costs when an asset (or group of assets) is retired. For example,

- Companies often are required by law to restore mine sites to their original condition.
- Land fills must be covered, capped (e.g., with concrete), and perhaps landscaped when they are full.
- Companies that use rooftops for billboard advertising or for relay antennas usually are required by contract to physically remove billboards or antennas at the end of the contract, and to repair the roofs as well.

These **asset retirement obligations** are recognized *only* when there is a legal commitment. Costs undertaken voluntarily are expensed when paid.

**Initial Recognition** When a legal retirement obligation exists, the cost of fulfilling that obligation must be recognized when the asset is acquired. The process is as follows:

- Estimate the amount required;
- Discount the cash flow at the company's *credit-adjusted* risk-free interest rate;
- Credit a liability account for the present value of the estimated liability; and
- Capitalize the amount: that is, increase the acquisition cost of the asset by the amount of the liability.

For example, suppose that on 2 January 20X0 Firkin Limited purchased equipment for $500,000 to install in a leased building. The company is legally required by the building lease to remove the equipment at the end of 10 years. The estimated cost of removal is $70,000.

To recognize the liability, the $70,000 must be discounted at an appropriate interest rate. Suppose that the risk-free rate is 3.5%, and that Firkin pays a premium of 1.5% above the risk-free rate. The future obligation must be discounted at 5.0% for 10 years:

$$P = \$70,000 \times (P/F, 5\%, 10) = \$70,000 \times 0.61391 = \$42,974$$

The asset purchase and the retirement obligation are recorded as follows:

| | | |
|---|---:|---:|
| Equipment | 500,000 | |
|    Account payable (to equipment vendor) | | 500,000 |
| [To record the purchase of equipment] | | |
| Equipment | 42,974 | |
|    Asset retirement obligation | | 42,974 |
| [To record the legal obligation to remove the equipment in the future] | | |

The asset's beginning book value will be $542,974.

**Subsequent Amortization and Accrual**  Once the asset and the retirement obligation have been recorded, the combined book value must be amortized. Assuming that Firkin uses straight-line amortization with zero residual value, the initial book value will be amortized at $54,297 per year. The amortization is recorded exactly the same way as any other amortization expense. For 20X0, the entry will be:

| | | |
|---|---|---|
| Amortization expense—equipment | 54,297 | |
| Accumulated amortization—equipment | | 54,297 |

**Accretion**  In addition to amortization expense, an expense must also be recorded to reflect the increase to the liability because of the passage of time. The retirement obligation was recorded at its present value. By the end of 10 years, the obligation must be $70,000 on Firkin's books, not $42,974. Therefore, Firkin must accrue an expense each year in order to build up the total obligation to $70,000. The increase is calculated using the same interest rate as was used in the initial measurement, which was 5%. The expense is akin to interest expense, but Canadian standards are emphatic that the expense is an operating expense, not a financing expense, and therefore should not be called interest expense. Another word for increasing a liability over time is accretion, and thus the expense has been labelled **accretion expense**. For 20X0, the accrual will be:

**accretion expense**

an increase in the carrying amount of an asset retirement obligation because of the passage of time.

| | | |
|---|---|---|
| Accretion expense [$42,974 × 5%] | 2,149 | |
| Asset retirement obligation | | 2,149 |

At the end of 20X0, the book value of the obligation will be $42,974 + $2,149 = $45,123. For 20X1, the interest accrual will be $45,123 × 5% = $2,256. Each year's accrual is based on the accumulated obligation at the end of the preceding year.

**Remeasurement**  In addition to amortizing the cost and accruing interest on the obligation, Firkin must also adjust the amount of the obligation if there is a change in the amount or timing of the expected retirement obligation cash flows. In Firkin's case, the timing could change if the lease term is extended, or if the estimated amount changes. The current cost is quite likely to change from year to year as legislation changes, technology changes, and cost components change due to increasing or decreasing prices.

Suppose that at the end of 20X1, Firkin decides that the cost of fulfilling the retirement obligation has gone up to $80,000, but that the timing has not changed (that is, the asset still must be retired at the end of 20X9). The increase of $10,000 must be recognized, again by using the company's *current* credit-adjusted risk-free borrowing rate. At the beginning of 20X2, the risk-free rate has gone down to 2.5% but Firkin still pays 1.5% above the risk-free rate. The discount rate for the *additional* obligation is 4.0%. The increment to the retirement obligation is:

$$\$10,000 × (P/F, 4\%, 8) = \$10,000 × 0.73069 = \$7,307$$

The additional obligation will be recorded as follows:

| | | |
|---|---|---|
| Equipment | 7,307 | |
| Asset retirement obligation | | 7,307 |

At the end of 20X1, Firkin's balance sheet will show the following amount for the obligation:

| | |
|---|---:|
| Initial recognition, 2 January 20X0 | $42,974 |
| Accretion, 31 December 20X0 | 2,149 |
| Accretion, 31 December 20X1 | 2,256 |
| Balance of original estimated obligation | 47,379 |
| Additional obligation estimate, 31 December 20X1 | 7,307 |
| Balance, 31 December 20X1 | $54,686 |

Notice that the interest is computed first, and then any increase (or decrease) in the expected future retirement cost is recognized.

On 31 December 20X2, the revised amount in the asset account will be amortized over the remaining eight years before retirement. The amortization for 20X2 will be ($542,974 ÷ 10) + ($7,307 ÷ 8) = $55,210 (rounded):

| | | |
|---|---:|---:|
| Amortization expense—equipment | 55,210 | |
|    Accumulated amortization—equipment | | 55,210 |

The 20X2 accretion expense on the retirement obligation will have two layers: (1) the original estimate, accrued at 5%, and (2) the additional amount from the 20X1 remeasurement, accrued at 4%:

| | |
|---|---:|
| Accretion re: initial 2 January 20X0 estimate: $47,379 × 5% | $2,369 |
| Accretion re: 31 December 20X1 remeasurement: $7,307 × 4% | 292 |
| Total accretion expense for 20X2 | $2,661 |

Exhibit 9-2 shows the derivation of the balances in both the asset account and the liability account through 31 December 20X2.

## CONCEPT REVIEW

1. Why is it necessary to allocate the overall cost of a basket purchase of assets to the individual assets in the basket?

2. What amount would be recorded for a capital asset purchased for common shares, if the asset does not have a ready market value?

3. Under what circumstances can a company capitalize interest cost?

4. When must a company record the present value of the costs of future asset retirement? How is the present value calculated?

---

### EXHIBIT 9-2

## EQUIPMENT AND RELATED ASSET RETIREMENT OBLIGATION

**Equipment account:**

| | |
|---|---:|
| Acquisition cost, 2 January 20X0 | $500,000 |
| Present value of expected asset retirement cost, 2 Jan. 20X0 | 42,974 |
| | 542,974 |
| Increase in expected asset retirement cost, 31 Dec. 20X1 | 7,307 |
| Balance, 31 December 20X2 | $550,281 |

**Accumulated amortization, equipment account:**

| | |
|---|---:|
| Amortization for 20X0 ($542,974 ÷ 10) | 54,297 |
| Amortization for 20X1 ($542,974 ÷ 10) | 54,297 |
| Amortization for 20X2: initial cost ($542,974 ÷ 10) | 54,297 |
| : additional cost ($7,307 ÷ 8) | 913 |
| Balance, 31 December 20X2 | $163,804 |

**Asset retirement obligation account:**

| | |
|---|---:|
| Present value of expected asset retirement cost, 2 January 20X0 | $ 42,974 |
| Accretion at 5% ($42,974 × 5%) | 2,149 |
| Balance, 31 December 20X0 | 45,123 |
| Accretion at 5% ($45,123 × 5%) | 2,256 |
| Subtotal | 47,379 |
| Present value of increase in expected asset retirement cost, 31 December 20X1 | 7,307 |
| Balance, 31 December 20X1 | 54,686 |
| Accretion on initial estimate ($47,379 × 5%) | 2,369 |
| Accretion on 20X1 increase ($7,307 × 4%) | 292 |
| Balance, 31 December 20X2 | $ 57,347 |

---

## INTANGIBLE ASSETS

### Specific Intangible Assets

Intangible assets are similar to tangible capital assets in that their cost is capitalized, and they are later subject to systematic and rational amortization. (Note, though, that intangible assets with an indefinite life are not amortized.) Refer to Exhibit 9-1, and reread the capitalizable costs for specific intangibles such as copyrights, trademarks, franchise fees, and the like. Note that if the intangible asset is internally developed, certain criteria will have to be met to qualify for capitalization; these will be reviewed in a later section. If the intangible asset is purchased, then the purchase price is capitalized. Legal costs are a major part of the recorded cost of intangible assets. This includes the legal costs to register these assets, and also legal costs for successful defence of the restricted use of these assets.

Specific intangibles can be quite significant. For example, the 2006 financial statements for Shaw Communications Incorporated show an intangible asset of $4.7 billion for "broadcast licenses." This one intangible asset is 63% of Shaw's total assets of $7.5 billion. Shaw does not amortize the broadcast licenses because they are assumed to have an indefinite life.

### Research and Development Costs

Broadly defined, research and development (R&D) includes the activities undertaken by firms to create new products and processes, or to improve old ones, and to discover new knowledge that may be of value in the future. For many firms, R&D is a very important part of ongoing activities and can be a significant expenditure. These expenditures are undertaken because the R&D effort is expected to more than pay for itself in the future by providing the firm with competitive, profitable products and processes.

**Research versus Development** *Research* is defined as original and planned investigation undertaken with the hope of gaining new scientific or technical knowledge and understanding. Such investigation may or may not be directed toward a specific practical aim or application. *Development*, on the other hand, is the application of research findings or other knowledge into a plan or design for the production of new or substantially improved products and such before commercial production begins. The distinction matters because the accounting treatment is different for research costs and development costs.

**R&D Accounting Requirements** Essentially, the accounting standards require that all research costs be expensed. Development costs may be capitalized *after* certain specific criteria are met, but otherwise must be expensed as well. The following criteria must *all* be met for a development asset to be capitalized:

1. The asset must be proven to be technologically feasible so it will be available for sale or use;

2. Management must have the intent to complete and then produce and market, or use, the asset;

3. The entity must be *able to* use or sell the asset;

4. The probable future economic benefits for (or external market or internal usefulness) of the product or process is clearly established.

5. Adequate resources exist, or are expected to be available, to complete the project; and

6. Costs must be identifiable.

These criteria are subject to some potential for manipulation. Management plays a large role in assessing technological feasibility, future markets, and available resources. If management wishes to capitalize identifiable development costs for products or processes that the company is undertaking, it will be a brave auditor who tries a challenge. Note that expenditures initially recognized as an expense may not subsequently be restated and capitalized if the criteria are met at a later date.

**The Definitional Approach to Development** Nevertheless, these criteria do represent an effort by standard setters to recognize that some development efforts do have future benefit, and that they qualify as assets. Thus, this standard is an example of the definitional approach to asset recognition.

Research and development programs are undertaken by entities with a clear expectation of future profitable results. Their future benefits establish them as assets. Why do accounting standards recommend that all research and many development costs be expensed? Typically, research costs fail the recognition criteria of "probability." That is, one cannot be certain that future cash flows will accrue. Unfortunately, for some firms, expensing research costs means that the firm's most valuable asset is not shown at all on its balance sheet and that current-period expenses are overstated.

**Alternatives** In the U.S., the uncertainty over future benefits has led to the requirement that *all* research and *all* development costs be expensed. There are no judgemental criteria that can be applied to justify capitalizing any development. This is an area where Canadian and U.S. standards are very different. Fortunately, Canadian and IAS standards are in line, and it is the U.S. that is the outlier.

## Internally Developed Intangibles

A proposed Canadian standard would establish criteria that must be met for any internally developed intangible asset. These criteria are:

1. First, the asset must be an *identifiable* intangible, which means that the intangible asset must be separable or able to be divided from an entity, or the asset must derive from contractual or legal rights;

2. Second, the recognition criteria must be met:
   a. The intangible asset must be controlled by the entity as a result of past transactions or events;
   b. Future economic benefits must flow from the intangible asset, for example, markets for the related product or the internal usefulness of the intangible asset must be clearly established; and
   c. The cost must be reliably measurable.

These criteria are an attempt to provide some rigor over the cost-deferral practices of some companies.

## Deferred Charges

Canadian practice has included deferring certain costs, usually justified on the basis that deferring and later expensing some items provides better matching with later revenues. However, the deferred charge, or long-term prepaid, was an "iffy" asset, and the practice was generally open to abuse. Standard setters have indicted that the established criteria for internally developed intangibles, listed above, will prevent such capitalization practice. To be specific, the following items have been identified by standard setters as costs that would *not* meet the criteria and therefore would be expensed as incurred:

1. The costs of starting up a business (start-up costs);

2. Training;

3. Advertising and promotion; and

4. Costs of relocating or reorganizing all or part of an entity.

In the past, some companies have been quite aggressive in the capitalization of these costs, and this has been acceptable. Policies will change when the revised standard comes into effect, and will eliminate many things previously termed "deferred charges."

## Computer Software Costs

Computer software is often internally generated. Accounting issues concerning the costs of developing computer software arise in two different contexts:

1. Many companies develop computer software systems for their own use, either by developing the software with their own staff or by contracting with an outside developer.

2. Other companies develop software as a product, to be sold to outsiders.

**Software Developed for Internal Use** The first category of companies, those that develop software for their own use, are typically involved in expensive, large-scale systems and program development. *The capitalization criteria as outlined* for *internally developed intangibles would apply.* Companies that develop large-scale systems will usually meet the deferral criteria, and will accordingly capitalize their software development costs. A common amortization period is three to five years.

However, many different measures of cost can be used and there is significant variation in practice. For example:

1. Should all costs be capitalized, from the very beginning of the project, or should early feasibility and systems development studies be expensed?

2. Should only direct costs be capitalized, or should indirect and overhead costs also be capitalized?

**Software Developed as a Product** Companies that develop software as a product may have a somewhat different approach. Software product development, like most other types of product development activities, has an initial period of feasibility testing to determine whether a proposed product is technically and financially feasible. Costs incurred during this period are viewed as research costs rather than as development costs and are written off. Technological feasibility (and a defined product) is usually considered to be present only when a *working model* exists. Of course, other criteria must also be met (a market must exist, and there must be management intent and adequate resources to take the product to market) before development can be deferred.

This approach is generally consistent with the U.S. standard, which allows capitalization of costs once the technological feasibility of the software product is established.

**Reporting Practice** The following accounting policy statement from the 2006 annual report of Absolute Software Corporation is typical:

---

(e) Research and development costs:

Research costs are charged to expense in the year in which they are incurred. Development costs are deferred if they meet specific criteria, otherwise they are expensed as incurred. At June 30, 2006 and 2005 no development costs have been deferred.

---

Remember that there is a lot of judgement involved in deciding whether the capitalization criteria have been met. Financial reporting objectives play a big role in the selection *and application* of accounting policies. The financial analyst community has tended to look unfavourably on software companies that capitalize a lot of their development costs. Therefore, to please the investment community, software companies tend to be conservative when applying capitalization policies.

## Website Development Costs

Another type of software development cost is the sometimes material amount that companies spend to create websites. The companies may be traditional enterprises with more traditional marketing channels, or they may base their business model on electronic transactions or a blend of both strategies. That is, websites may be used to promote or advertise products or services, replace traditional products or services, and/or sell things.

How should the costs of website development be accounted for? *Again, the listed criteria* for *internally developed intangible assets must be satisfied in order to support capitalization.* There is some advice from the Canadian Emerging Issues Committee, which breaks down website development costs into five areas:

| Type of Website Expenditure | Accounting Policy Suggested; Deferral Criteria Must Also Be Reviewed |
|---|---|
| Costs incurred in the planning stage | *Expense as incurred* |
| Costs incurred for website application and infrastructure | *Capitalize and amortize* |
| Costs incurred to develop graphics | *Capitalize and amortize* |
| Costs incurred to develop content | *Either expense or capitalize/amortize* There are many case-specific factors involved in this area |
| Operating costs | *Expense as incurred* |

So, what's the overall theme? If costs are very early in the process, (planning) then there is nothing tangible to pin the asset flag on, and the costs must be expensed. After that, the question is always whether there is a long-term benefit from the expenditure. Future benefits support asset treatment, otherwise, the expense category wins.

## Exploration and Development Costs

Exploration and development (ED) costs are the costs that oil and gas companies and mining companies incur in exploring and developing their resource properties. *Exploration* is the process of seeking mineral deposits, while *development* is the process of turning a found deposit into a productive mine site or oil field. Much exploration is fruitless; that is the nature of the business. Most development does work out, since development is not undertaken unless there is reasonable assurance of generating enough revenue from the site to recover the development costs. However, it can take years to develop a mine site or an oil field. How should the costs of exploration and development be accounted for?

**full cost method**

the costs associated with exploration for and development of a natural resource, whether successful or not, are capitalized to the natural resources account on the balance sheet, to be subsequently amortized

**Alternatives for ED Costs** The accounting for exploration and development costs varies widely but there are two major approaches. These approaches are:

1. The **full cost method**, in which ED costs for the company's entire sphere of operations are accumulated as a deferred charge and amortized on the basis of global production; or

2. The **successful efforts method**, in which the ED costs are accumulated by site. If a site has been determined to be unproductive, ED costs are expensed. The ED costs of successful sites are segregated as a deferred charge and amortized.

In the *full cost method*, the assumption is that unsuccessful efforts are a part of doing business; not every attempt to find mineral deposits or oil and gas reserves will be successful. A resource company not will hit "pay dirt" every time it tries to find natural resources, and the cost of a productive resource includes unproductive efforts.

**successful efforts method**

the costs associated with successful exploration and development activities of a natural resource are capitalized to a balance sheet natural resource account to be subsequently amortized; the costs of unsuccessful exploration activities are expensed

Under the *successful efforts method*, unsuccessful efforts are written off *once they are determined to be unsuccessful*. The costs are initially capitalized, since the effort may last more than one reporting period and the results are not known, but the accumulated costs relating to that site are charged to the income statement when management gives up the effort. Note that this is a management decision; timing of that decision will determine which accounting period's earnings bear the cost.

These methods require management to segregate ED costs by geographic area. There is a great deal of flexibility in this regard. One company may decide to segregate its successful sites on the basis of geological formation, while another may choose to use national boundaries as the definition of area. Some may view the U.S. and Canada as a single area, while others may view Oklahoma as one area, Alberta as another, and the Atlantic Provinces' offshore fields as yet another. Management choice is at the core of the successful efforts method.

The choice of accounting policy does not change the cash flow patterns of the company. The monies are spent when they are spent, usually up front. The question is, will they be *expensed* upfront, with low subsequent amortization (successful efforts) or will they be *deferred*, with higher subsequent amortization (full cost). Allocation methods are inherently arbitrary; there are good arguments that support both full cost and successful efforts.

*There are no accounting standards in North America on this topic, and companies have free choice between the two alternatives.* Since the choice of policy will make a big difference to income patterns, there is clearly an urgent need to check the disclosure notes.

**Policy in Practice** In practice, large integrated companies tend to use the successful efforts method. Large companies engage in a more or less constant search for new assets, and there is no undue strain on profitability as a result of immediately expensing this regular cost. Obviously, expensing is also the least complicated accounting method.

Junior resource companies typically have only a few sites under exploration. They do not engage in perpetual, worldwide exploration. Junior resource companies in Canada tend to use the full cost method. They have no revenue when their sites are under development, and expensing would result in a huge deficit in retained earnings, perhaps increasing the anxiety of investors and the cost of capital. Capitalization looks pretty good under these circumstances.

Review Exhibit 9-3 for disclosure notes that describe the two policies. Bonavista Energy Trust uses full cost, and Petro-Canada uses successful efforts.

---

**EXHIBIT 9-3**

## EXAMPLES OF ACCOUNTING POLICY DISCLOSURE FOR ED COSTS

### Bonavista Energy Trust

For the year ended 31 December 2006

*(b) Oil and natural gas operations*
The Trust follows the full cost method of accounting, whereby all costs associated with the exploration for and development of oil and natural gas reserves are capitalized in cost centres on a country-by-country basis. Such costs include land and property acquisitions, geological and geophysical activities, drilling, well equipment, and facilities.

### Petro-Canada

For the year ended 31 December 2006

**Property, plant and equipment**
Investments in exploration and development activities are accounted for on the successful efforts method. Under this method, the acquisition cost of unproven acreage is capitalized. Costs of exploratory wells are initially capitalized pending determination of proved reserves. Costs of wells which are assigned proved reserves remain capitalized while costs of unsuccessful wells are charged to earnings. All other exploration costs, including geological and geophysical costs, are charged to earnings as incurred. Development costs, including the cost of all wells, are capitalized.

---

## CONCEPT REVIEW

1. What is the difference between research and development?

2. In general, when is it appropriate to capitalize development costs?

3. What circumstances support the capitalization of costs associated with internally developed software?

4. Explain the two general methods for accounting for exploration and development costs.

## DISPOSALS OF CAPITAL ASSETS

The disposal of capital assets may be *voluntary*, as a result of a sale, exchange, or abandonment, or *involuntary*, as a result of a *casualty* such as a fire, or storm, or by government action, such as expropriation.

If the asset to be disposed of is subject to depreciation, it is depreciated up to the date of disposal in order to update the recorded book value. Applicable property taxes, insurance premium costs, and similar costs are also accrued up to the date of disposal. At the date of disposal, the original cost of the asset and its related accumulated depreciation are removed from the accounts.

The difference between the book value of a capital asset and the amount received on disposal is recorded as a *gain or loss*. Ideally, the gain or loss is segregated from ordinary income and reported in the income statement separately as part of income from continuing operations.

**involuntary conversions (disposition)**

conversion (loss or sale) of an asset that takes place unintentionally; for example, as the result of a casualty or government action

Disposals that are not the choice of the company are called **involuntary conversions.** This may happen in a natural disaster or as the result of a government expropriation. Involuntary conversions are unusual items. They might be extraordinary items, although very few circumstances are outside normal business risk.

To illustrate the disposal of a capital asset, assume that on 1 February 20X1, Brown Company paid $32,000 for office equipment with an estimated service life of five years and an estimated residual value of $2,000. Brown uses straight-line depreciation and sells the asset on 1 July 20X5, for $8,000. The entries for Brown, a calendar-year company, at date of disposal are as follows:

| | | |
|---|---|---|
| Depreciation expense | 3,000* | |
|     Accumulated depreciation—equipment | | 3,000 |
| *($32,000 − $2,000) × (1/5) × (6/12) | | |
| | | |
| Cash | 8,000 | |
| Accumulated depreciation—equipment | 26,500** | |
|     Equipment | | 32,000 |
|     Gain from disposal of equipment | | 2,500 |
| **($32,000 − $2,000) × (53 months used) ÷ (60 months total useful life) | | |

However, the economic value of Brown Company is unaffected by the disposal. Brown received an asset worth $8,000 (cash) for an asset worth $8,000. Why is a gain recognized? Brown depreciated the equipment faster than it declined in value. The book value ($5,500) is less than market value ($8,000) at date of disposal. If depreciation exactly reflected all changes in value, there would be no gain or loss from disposal. *The accounting gain in this example is a correction for excessive depreciation charges recognized before disposal.* In effect, the gain records a change in estimate.

If the asset is destroyed in an accident, and was insured, then the entry will mirror the one recorded above. That is, the insurance proceeds will produce a certain amount of cash, and the difference between cash and net book value will determine the gain or loss.

This approach is also used when an asset is abandoned or destroyed without insurance, when there are no proceeds. The loss recognized equals the book value of the asset at disposal. For the Brown Company example, the loss recognized would be $5,500.

The costs of dismantling, removing, and disposing of plant assets are treated as reductions of any proceeds obtained from disposal. Therefore, the resulting gain is reduced, or the resulting loss is increased by these costs. If Brown Company incurs $500 in disposal costs, the net cash debit is $8,000 − $500, or $7,500, reducing the gain to $2,000 in the original example.

When the decision to sell or abandon plant assets is made near the end of a fiscal year, an estimated loss from disposal is recognized in that year if the loss is estimable. Gains are not recognized before disposal, however.

## CONCEPT REVIEW

1. What is an involuntary conversion?
2. Why would a company dispose of a capital asset at a loss? Is the company necessarily in a worse position economically after doing so?
3. How would you interpret the gain on the disposal of a capital asset?

# EXCHANGES OF NON-MONETARY ASSETS

Capital assets are often exchanged for other non-monetary assets. Remember that monetary assets are those whose value is fixed in terms of dollars, like cash and receivables. Non-monetary assets, such as inventory and capital assets, *do not have a value fixed in terms of dollars.*

**Non-monetary transactions** are any exchange of non-monetary assets, liabilities, or services for other non-monetary assets, liabilities, or services, or any exchange that has little or no monetary consideration involved. Valuation of the acquired asset is the substantive issue in non-monetary asset exchanges. This valuation determines whether a gain or loss is recognized.

## Valuation Alternatives

When a capital asset is given in exchange for another asset, how should the transaction be valued? There are two general approaches to valuation:

- Measure the acquired asset at the *fair value,* or
- Record the acquired asset at the *book value* of the asset given up *(also called carrying value.)*

To illustrate a non-monetary exchange, assume that Company 1 and Company 2 are to exchange assets. Since Company 1's asset is worth $40,000 versus the $45,000 for Company 2's asset, Company 1 will pay $5,000 to make the exchange even. This monetary amount is low in relation to the value of the transaction, so the transaction is still classified as non-monetary. The facts:

|  | Co. 1 | Co. 2 |
|---|---|---|
| Asset original cost | $76,400 | $91,600 |
| Accumulated depreciation | 58,000 | 61,900 |
| Net book value | $18,400 | $29,700 |
| Fair value of asset | $40,000 | $45,000 |
| Cash to change hands: $5,000, paid by Co. 1 to Co. 2 | | |

Here are the two alternative ways to record the transaction on Company 1's books:

| At Fair Value | | | At Book Value | | |
|---|---|---|---|---|---|
| New asset | 45,000 | | New asset** | 23,400 | |
| Accumulated depreciation, old | 58,000 | | Accumulated depreciation, old | 58,000 | |
| Gain on exchange* | | 21,600 | Cash | | 5,000 |
| Cash | | 5,000 | Old asset | | 76,400 |
| Old asset | | 76,400 | | | |

*$40,000 − $18,400
**$5,000 + $18,400

Both entries record the disposal of the old asset, removing original cost and accumulated depreciation from the books. Both record the $5,000 cash paid. But they differ significantly in the valuation of the new asset and recognition of a gain or loss. Under fair value treatment, the new asset is recorded at its $45,000 fair value, and a gain is recorded as the difference between the $18,400 book value of the old asset and its fair value, or trade-in value—$40,000. Under the book value alternative, the new asset is recorded at a deflated value—the book value of the old asset, $18,400, plus $5,000 cash paid. Quite a difference!

**Valuation Rule** To determine whether to use the fair value method or the book method, the valuation rule is applied. That is:

| Use the Fair Value Method | Use the Book Value Method |
|---|---|
| 1. Normally, exchanges involve *commercial substance*. The configuration of cash flows changes as a result of the exchange. | 1. The transaction has no *commercial substance*. The configuration of cash flows has not changed. |
| | 2. The exchange has been in the ordinary course of business to facilitate a sale to a third party. |
| | 3. Fair values cannot be determined. |
| | 4. The exchange is a distribution to shareholders (part of a restructuring, spin-off, or liquidation). |

**Commercial Substance** If there is commercial substance, the fair value method is usually used. Essentially, commercial substance exists if there is a significant change in the company's cash flows after the exchange. A transaction has commercial substance when:

1. The configuration (that is, the risk, timing, or amount) of the cash flows of the asset received differs significantly from the configuration of the cash flows of the asset given up; or

2. The present value of the after-tax cash flow from use of new asset is significantly different from that of the old asset. (The present value of the cash flows is called the "entity-specific value" of the asset.)

Significance is measured relative to the fair value of the assets exchanged, not to the overall operations of the company, and is a matter for professional judgement.

When commercial substance does not exist, the carrying value method must be used and no gain or loss is recognized. This seems logical if there is no real difference in cash flows to the company "before" versus "after." Indeed, the two assets may be substantially similar and may perform the same function. By trading assets and using the fair value method, the two companies could create a gain or loss that has little economic substance. In such a situation, accounting standards require that the acquired asset be recorded at the carrying value of the asset being given up.

**Exchange to Facilitate a Sale** It will sometimes happen that a company will have to assemble a group of goods to be sold to an external customer. For example, Customer Hu wants products A, B, and C shipped together. If the vendor produces A and C, the vendor needs to acquire B to complete the sale. If the vendor buys B for cash, there is no particular difficulty. However, if the vendor swaps some of the existing product A for the needed product B with another supplier, this is a non-monetary exchange.

Say that $10,000 of A, with a cost of $2,500, is exchanged with the other supplier, for B that is also worth $10,000. Can a gain of $7,500 be recognized? The standard states that *if inventory is swapped in the normal course of business to facilitate a sale*, then no gain or loss on the exchange can be recognized. Product B is valued in the non-monetary exchange at $2,500. Profit will be recognized only when the sale to Customer Hu is completed.

**Determining Fair Value** If the exchange does cause a significant change in cash flows or present value, then the fair value method must be used. This presents obvious challenges if neither fair value can be reliably measured, and book value is the fallback.

The standard also requires that the *more reliable* fair value must be used, regardless of whether it is the asset being given up or the asset being received. Two arm's-length companies would not trade assets unless the fair value of each was similar. In all instances, the fair value of the new asset must be based on the more reliable estimate. For example, if an asset with a fair value of $25,000 were exchanged for an asset with a fair value of $32,000, and no cash changed hands, *a determination must be made as to which value is more reliable, and the valuation flows from there.*

Sometimes, one fair value is known but not the other. In this case, the exchange is valued at the known fair value, adjusted for cash paid. Consider the following cases:

|                                        | Case 1   | Case 2    | Case 3   |
|----------------------------------------|----------|-----------|----------|
| Fair value of (old) asset given up     | $14,000  | $100,000  | $73,000  |
| Fair value of (new) asset received     | 50,000   | ?         | ?        |
| Cash paid                              | 34,000   | 4,000     | —        |
| Cash received                          | —        | —         | 50,000   |

In Case 1, the values indicate some measurement uncertainty. The cash paid of $34,000 plus the fair value of the old asset of $14,000 equals $48,000, but the new asset is reportedly worth $50,000. In this situation, *either* the $50,000 is used as the reliable value, and is used to record the new asset, and therefore the "real" fair value of the old asset would be treated as $16,000, *or* the new asset is valued at $48,000, relying on the $14,000 fair value of the old asset. It depends on which value is considered more reliable. An average could also be considered.

In Case 2, the fair value of the new asset is unknown and its fair value must be implied by the value of the old asset, $100,000. However, the company also had to pay $4,000 to get the new asset, so the new one must have been worth $104,000. In Case 3, the fair value of the new asset is again unknown. The old asset was worth $73,000, but the company received $50,000 in the exchange. Therefore, the new asset must have been worth $23,000.

**Sources of Fair Values** Where do fair value numbers come from? Sometimes they are quoted cash prices from suppliers of new and used assets. When a quoted cash price is unavailable, a company can invite bids for the asset to be exchanged. The highest reasonable bid for the asset in question is used as the market value. However, this approach is not always appreciated by the companies that invest time and energy submitting quotes, only to discover that the asset wasn't really to be sold! A less reliable but commonly used alternative is published information on the average price of specific used assets, such as the *Kelley Blue Book Auto Market Report* for automobiles. Appraisal is another commonly used approach, but appraisals are notoriously subjective. List prices are often unreliable, as they do not represent the lowest cash price the vendor will accept.

**Distribution to Shareholders** When the non-monetary transaction is a distribution to shareholders, the company receives nothing in return. These distributions should not trigger a gain and are recorded at book value.

## Fair Market Value Cap

When non-monetary assets are exchanged, the highest value that can be recorded is the fair value of the acquired asset, regardless of other valuation rules. For example, consider the following exchange (facts assumed), recorded at book value because the transaction lacked commercial substance.

| | | |
|---|---|---|
| New asset | 97,000 | |
| Accumulated amortization, old asset | 56,000 | |
|    Old asset | | 153,000 |

The new asset is valued at the $97,000 book value of the old asset. Now, assume that there was reliable information available that indicated that the fair value of the new asset was $80,000. This is the *maximum value* that can be used for the new asset, and the entry becomes:

| | | |
|---|---|---|
| New asset | 80,000 | |
| Accumulated amortization, old asset | 56,000 | |
| Loss on asset exchange ($97,000 – $80,000) | 17,000 | |
|    Old asset | | 153,000 |

Of course, what is really implied in this situation is that the old asset was underdepreciated at the time of exchange, and was worth only $80,000, not its $97,000 book value. Since depreciation is not meant to track fair value of the life of an asset, this is not surprising. However, a thorough review of depreciation methods and rates, coupled with an impairment review, should minimize this risk.

## Examples of Non-Monetary Asset Exchanges

The following information for Regina Corporation is used in the examples that follow:

| **Asset Transferred—Crane** | |
|---|---|
| Original cost | $90,000 |
| Accumulated depreciation, updated to date of exchange | $60,000 |

1. Transaction has commercial substance
   a. *Fair values are determinable; no cash payment.* Assume that the crane has a fair value of $47,000 and is exchanged for a truck whose value is not more clearly measurable; no cash is paid or received. The book value of the crane is $30,000; therefore, a $17,000 gain is recognized. The entry is:

| | | |
|---|---|---|
| Equipment—truck | 47,000 | |
| Accumulated depreciation—crane | 60,000 | |
|    Equipment—crane | | 90,000 |
|    Gain on capital asset disposal | | 17,000 |

   b. *Fair values are determinable; with cash payment.* Assume that the crane's fair value is not easily determinable, but that the truck has a fair value of $33,000. In addition, Regina receives $12,000 cash. The acquired truck is recorded at its fair value. The entry is:

| | | |
|---|---|---|
| Equipment—truck | 33,000 | |
| Cash | 12,000 | |
| Accumulated depreciation—crane | 60,000 | |
|    Equipment—crane | | 90,000 |
|    Gain on capital asset disposal | | 15,000 |

c. *Fair values are not determinable; no cash payment.* Assume that neither fair value is reliably measurable. The acquired truck is recorded at the book or carrying value of the crane. There can be no gain or loss recognized on the transaction:

| | | |
|---|---|---|
| Equipment—truck | 30,000 | |
| Accumulated depreciation—crane | 60,000 | |
|     Equipment—crane | | 90,000 |

2. Transaction does not have commercial substance
   a. *Fair values are determinable; no cash payment.* Assume that the crane has a fair value of $47,000 and is exchanged for another crane whose fair value is not more reliably measurable. There is no cash payment. Because the transaction does not significantly affect Regina's cash flows, the acquired crane is recorded at the book value of the crane being given up. There can be no gain or loss recognized on the transaction:

| | | |
|---|---|---|
| Equipment—crane 2 | 30,000 | |
| Accumulated depreciation—crane 1 | 60,000 | |
|     Equipment—crane 1 | | 90,000 |

   b. *Fair values are determinable; with cash payment.* Assume that the old crane's fair value is not easily determinable, but that the new crane has a fair value of $33,000. In addition, Regina receives $12,000 cash. Since there is no commercial substance to the transaction, the acquired crane is recorded at the old crane's book value minus the cash received. The entry is:

| | | |
|---|---|---|
| Equipment—crane 2 | 18,000 | |
| Cash | 12,000 | |
| Accumulated depreciation—crane 1 | 60,000 | |
|     Equipment—crane 1 | | 90,000 |

    Whenever cash is involved in a transaction without commercial substance, the new asset always is recorded at the book value of the old asset, *minus any cash received or plus any cash paid.* Fair values are irrelevant. No gain or loss may be recognized.

   c. *Fair values are determinable; with cash payment and fair value cap.* Assume that the old crane's fair value is not easily determinable, but that the new crane has a fair value of $14,000. In addition, Regina receives $12,000 cash. Since there is no commercial substance to the transaction, the acquired crane is recorded at the old crane's book value minus the cash received ($18,000 = $30,000 book value less $12,000) to a maximum of $14,000. A loss of $4,000 is recorded. The entry is:

| | | |
|---|---|---|
| Equipment—crane 2 | 14,000 | |
| Cash | 12,000 | |
| Accumulated depreciation—crane 1 | 60,000 | |
| Loss on exchange of assets | 4,000 | |
|     Equipment—crane 1 | | 90,000 |

## POST-ACQUISITION EXPENDITURES

After acquisition, many costs related to capital assets are incurred. Examples include repairs, maintenance, betterments, and replacements.

Expenditures that increase service potential are capitalized. Such expenditures are called **capital expenditures**. Service potential is enhanced when the useful life of the asset is extended, operating costs are decreased, or quality or quantity of output is increased. A capitalized post-acquisition expenditure is depreciated over the number of periods benefited, which can be less than the remaining useful life of the original asset.

The service potential of assets and their estimated useful life at acquisition assume a certain minimum level of maintenance and repair. Costs for maintenance are expensed in the period incurred. Some companies expense all post-acquisition expenditures less than a certain dollar amount (for example, $1,000). This policy is acceptable because the amounts are not material.

Expenditures that result from accident, neglect, intentional abuse, or theft are recognized as losses. For example, if a computer workstation is damaged during installation, the repair cost is recognized as a loss. After repair, the asset is no more valuable than it was before the mishap. Outlays made to restore uninsured assets damaged through *casualty*, or accident, are also recorded as losses. They do not enhance the utility of the asset beyond the value before the casualty.

Significant post-acquisition expenditures fall into four major categories:

1. Maintenance and ordinary repairs;

2. Betterments, and

3. Additions.

## Maintenance and Ordinary Repairs

Maintenance expenditures include lubrication, cleaning, adjustment, and painting incurred on a continuous basis to keep plant assets in usable condition. Ordinary repair costs include outlays for parts, labour, and related supplies that are necessary to keep assets in operating condition but neither add materially to the use of assets nor prolong their useful life significantly. Ordinary repairs usually involve relatively small expenditures. *Most expenditures made on capital assets are repairs, and expensing is the norm.* Keep this in mind as a rule of thumb—capitalization may look too tempting at times!

Many firms accrue repairs each month, and charge actual repairs to the accrued repair liability account, in order to report smooth monthly expenses. This makes some sense, especially in a business where regular repairs and maintenance are all done in a regular slack season. At the end of the year, any remaining balance in the liability account is reversed, so that repair expense represents the amount actually spent during the year.

## Betterments

A **betterment** is the cost incurred to enhance the service potential of a capital asset. It often involves the replacement of a major component of a capital asset with a significantly improved component. Examples include the replacement of an old shingle roof with a modern fireproof tile roof, installation of a more powerful engine in a ship, and significant improvement of the electrical system in a building.

But, as the name implies, the result should be *better* than the old—not just more attractive, but *better* from an asset sense. That is, the asset should be able to deliver enhanced cash flows to the firm, either through more revenue (higher quality or quantity of output, more service hours per day, or a longer life) or through reduced operating costs. Then, the betterment has status as an asset and capitalization is warranted. Otherwise, the expenditure is a repair. Repairs and maintenance are the norm, betterments are the exception.

Betterments may be replacements or renewals. A *replacement* is the substitution of a major component of a plant asset with one of comparable quality. *Renewals* involve large expenditures, are not recurring in nature, and usually increase the utility or the service life of the asset beyond the original estimate. Major overhauls of equipment, rearrangements, and strengthening of a building foundation are examples.

Two different approaches have evolved to account for these expenditures: substitution and an increase to the asset account.

1. *Substitution.* This approach removes the cost of the old component and related accumulated depreciation, recognizes a loss equal to the remaining book value, and increases the

original asset account in the amount of the expenditure. To illustrate, assume that a shingle roof with an original cost of $20,000 and now 80% depreciated is replaced by a fireproof tile roof costing $60,000. The two entries to record the betterment are as follows:

| | | |
|---|---|---|
| To remove old component accounts | | |
| Accumulated depreciation (old roof, $20,000 × 80%) | 16,000 | |
| Loss on asset improvement | 4,000 | |
| Building (old roof) | | 20,000 |
| To record cost of new component | | |
| Building (new roof) | 60,000 | |
| Cash | | 60,000 |

This approach works well in theory. The only problem is that, by the time the building needs a new roof, the portion of the cost of the building that relates to the old roof is virtually impossible to figure out.

2. *Increase asset account.* This approach is used when the costs and depreciation amounts of the old component are not known and when the primary effect is to increase efficiency rather than the economic life of the basic asset. The cost of the betterment is simply debited to the original asset account. It may also be used when economic life is lengthened, if substitution is not practical.

One result of this treatment is an overstatement of the basic asset's book value and subsequent depreciation, although this value is usually relatively minor at time of replacement. For example, simply capitalizing the new roof in the previous example means that the building would have two roofs in its capital cost. The net effect is to *overstate* net book value by $4,000 (the net book value of the old roof).

Sometimes replacements are required by law to ensure public safety or to meet environmental standards. For example, many localities require removal of asbestos insulation for health reasons. Is asbestos removal and replacement capitalizable, or should it be expensed? A case can be made either way. The useful life of the building is likely to remain unchanged as will the overall productivity of the building. On the other hand, employee safety is increased, and the firm has less exposure to health-related lawsuits. Capitalization is quite justified.

### Additions

Additions are extensions, enlargements, or expansions of an existing asset. An extra wing or room added to a building is an example. Additions represent capital expenditures and are recorded in the capital asset accounts at cost. Related work on the existing structure, such as shoring up the foundation for the addition or cutting an entranceway through an existing wall, is a part of the cost of the addition and is capitalized. If the addition is an integral part of the older asset, its cost (less any estimated residual value) is normally depreciated over the shorter of its own service life or the remaining life of the original asset. If the addition is not an integral part, it is depreciated over its own useful life.

## CONCEPT REVIEW

1. If an asset is acquired in an exchange transaction, when is the transaction valued at book value? Fair value?

2. When should expenditures made on a capital asset after its acquisition be capitalized instead of expensed?

3. What is the difference between maintenance and betterment? What accounting treatment is given to expenditures for each?

# GOODWILL

Goodwill is a common intangible asset. It represents the value associated with favourable characteristics of a firm that result in earnings in excess of those expected from identifiable assets of the firm. Goodwill is *internally generated*, but is recorded only when *purchased*, along with identifiable tangible and intangible assets that constitute an operating unit. Goodwill typically cannot be separated from those identifiable assets. In the absence of an arm's-length transaction, it is difficult to measure the value of goodwill that a firm creates as it engages in business activities.

A few examples of factors that cause enhanced financial performance are:

- A superior management team;
- An outstanding sales organization;
- Especially effective advertising;
- Exceptionally good labour relations;
- An unusually good reputation for total quality; and
- A highly advantageous strategic location.

For accounting purposes, **goodwill** is the difference between the actual purchase price of an acquired firm or operation and the estimated fair market value of the identifiable net assets acquired (assets less liabilities, valued at fair value).

**Measuring Goodwill**  The value of goodwill is calculated indirectly in an acquisition of a business unit. The steps are:

1. *Establish the cost of the acquisition.* This is the value of whatever the purchaser gives up to acquire the business unit. The cost is measured as the cash payment plus the fair value of shares or assets given to the seller.

2. *Establish the fair value of all identifiable assets and liabilities assumed.* The fair value of the *net* assets acquired is the total fair value of the assets minus the total fair values of the liabilities:

> Fair value of tangible and identifiable intangible assets − Fair value of liabilities
> = Fair value of net assets acquired

3. *The cost less fair value of net identifiable assets is goodwill.* Goodwill is the excess purchase cost that cannot otherwise be assigned to specific assets or liabilities:

> Cost of acquisition (#1) − Fair value of net assets acquired (#2) = Goodwill

**Example**  Assume that Hotel Company is considering the acquisition of the net assets of Cafe Corporation. Hotel Company obtains financial statements and other financial data on Cafe and estimates the fair value of Cafe's identifiable assets at $530,000 and the fair value of the liabilities at $400,000. See Exhibit 9-4.

The fair value column in Exhibit 9-4 shows that several assets have an estimated fair value different from their book value as reported in the published historical cost financial statements. Fair values include specific identifiable intangibles, such as customer lists.

The total fair value of Cafe's identifiable net assets is determined to be $130,000 ($530,000 total assets less liabilities of $400,000). Assume that Hotel negotiates a purchase price with the owners to acquire Cafe as of 31 December 20X4, for $202,000. Goodwill inherent in this price is $72,000; that is, the purchase price of $202,000, less current market value of the

---

**EXHIBIT 9-4**

## Cafe Corporation
## Balance Sheet Book Value and Fair Value

| As of 31 December 20X4 | Book Value | Fair Value |
|---|---|---|
| **Assets** | | |
| Cash | $ 30,000 | $ 30,000 |
| Receivables | 90,000 | 85,000 |
| Inventory | 60,000 | 60,000 |
| Other current assets | 33,000 | 30,000 |
| Plant and equipment (net) | 220,000 | 235,000 |
| Other assets | 85,000 | 90,000 |
| Total assets | $518,000 | $530,000 |
| **Liabilities** | | |
| Short-term notes payable | $ 85,000 | $ 85,000 |
| Accounts payable | 45,000 | 45,000 |
| Other current liabilities | 30,000 | 30,000 |
| Long-term debt | 250,000 | 240,000 |
| Total liabilities | 410,000 | 400,000 |
| **Shareholders' equity** | 108,000 | |
| Total liabilities and equities | $518,000 | |
| Net assets at fair market value | | $130,000 |

---

identifiable net assets of $130,000. The entry Hotel Company makes to reflect the acquisition of Cafe's operations, at their *fair values*, is as follows:

| | | |
|---|---|---|
| Cash | 30,000 | |
| Receivables | 85,000 | |
| Inventory | 60,000 | |
| Other current assets | 30,000 | |
| Plant and equipment | 235,000 | |
| Other assets | 90,000 | |
| Goodwill | 72,000 | |
|     Short-term notes payable | | 85,000 |
|     Accounts payable | | 45,000 |
|     Other current liabilities | | 30,000 |
|     Long-term debt | | 240,000 |
|     Cash | | 202,000 |

Recording this $72,000 goodwill asset implicitly means that Hotel was willing to pay for anticipated superior earnings/cash flow from Cafe's operations. These superior results could be caused by a superior location, reputation for service or quality, and so on.

Do you *know* that goodwill is present, just because Hotel paid more than the fair value of the net assets? After all, Hotel may have been outbargained by the old owners of Cafe. The $72,000 could be the result of an inflated price. Just because the price is arm's length doesn't mean it can't be stupid. Accountants, however, don't account for stupidity (think of the arguments with clients!) and always make the comfortable assumption that goodwill explains excess purchase price. But beware—the assets acquired are supposed to provide a return consistent with the existence of goodwill, or the goodwill does not, in substance, exist.

In the 1990s, many companies purchased Internet-based developing enterprises (the so-called "dot-com" companies) at prices that turned out to be exorbitant. There were very few identifiable assets in the acquired businesses, and therefore almost all of the purchase price was accounted for as goodwill. When the stock market for dot-coms collapsed, any prospect of future earnings collapsed as well.

If it becomes apparent that superior earnings ability doesn't really exist, the goodwill does not meet the definition of an asset, and its carrying value must be written down as an impairment loss. The moral of this story is that goodwill must be regularly reviewed with reference to profit performance to ensure continued recognition of goodwill is appropriate. This issue will be reviewed in Chapter 10.

### Negative Goodwill

**negative goodwill**

in a purchase of a business unit, when the purchase price is less than fair value of acquired net assets

When the fair market value of the identifiable net assets acquired is *higher* than the purchase price, the acquiring firm has made what is sometimes called a bargain purchase. Goodwill is negative, that is, **negative goodwill** has been created. Even though it would seem that the seller could benefit from selling the assets individually rather than selling the firm as a whole, such situations do occasionally occur. For example, the seller may be in financial difficulty and have an immediate cash need. Alternatively, the seller may not have the time or resources to take on the risks of selling the assets separately.

Any negative goodwill should be allocated to reduce the values assigned *proportionately* to *identifiable non-monetary assets* to the extent that the negative amount is eliminated.

Assume now that Hotel Company purchases Cafe Corp. for $91,500, which is $38,500 less than the fair value of the net assets acquired. The negative goodwill of $38,500 must be allocated *proportionally* to reduce the recorded values for plant, equipment, inventory, and most other non-monetary assets. In the rather unlikely case that negative goodwill is larger than identifiable non-monetary assets, the non-monetary assets would be reduced to zero and the excess recorded as an extraordinary gain.

### Form of Acquisition

In the previous example, one company bought the net assets of another company, and goodwill was directly recorded on the purchaser's books. In many acquisition transactions, the acquiring company buys the shares of the target company, which is then left to operate as before, only with new shareholders.

At *reporting dates*, the two sets of financial statements are combined, or *consolidated*, to produce a report of the economic activity of the combined entity. In consolidation, the assets of the target company are recorded at fair value at the date of acquisition, and the goodwill inherent in the purchase price is recorded. The nature of goodwill is identical, but the form of the transaction is different. We'll take a brief look at consolidation in Chapter 11.

## CAPITAL ASSETS ON THE CASH FLOW STATEMENT

Investments in capital assets are shown as *investing activities* on the cash flow statement, provided that the acquisition is for cash. If a capital asset is acquired in a non-cash transaction, the transaction will be described in the notes to the financial statements, but it would not be reported as part of the cash flow statement because no cash was involved. If cash was only part of the consideration to acquire a capital asset, then only the cash portion will be shown.

### Gains and Losses

Gains and losses on the sale of capital assets are non-cash items, from the viewpoint of operating activities. These are excluded from cash flow operations either through adjustment (indirect presentation) or omission (direct presentation). When an asset is sold for cash, what appears on the cash flow statement is the amount of the proceeds (i.e., the cash actually received) for the asset. The proceeds are shown in the investing activities section as a cash *inflow*.

If a capital asset is disposed of through a non-cash transaction or exchange, the transaction will not appear on the cash flow statement.

## Cash Flow Reporting of Capitalized Costs

*An interesting wrinkle to the issue of capitalizing instead of expensing certain costs is the impact that the capitalization policy has on the reporting of cash flows.*

It is obvious that the accounting policy decision to capitalize or expense a cost will not affect actual cash flows. The cost has been incurred and either has been or will be paid in cash. The accounting policy choice is only of whether to put the cost on the balance sheet (as an asset) or on the income statement (as an expense). Consider these differences in *cash flow reporting*, however:

- Costs that are accounted for as expenses are included in the cash flow from *operations*.
- Costs that are capitalized as assets are included in the *investing activities* section of the cash flow statement.
- Amortization on capitalized assets is deducted in determining net income but is removed from cash flow from operations either by adding it back in the indirect approach, or leaving it out in the direct approach.

For example, assume that Lorimer Limited spends $100,000 on development costs during 20X2, and that net income before deducting the development costs is $300,000. If the development costs are capitalized, they will be amortized straight line over the five years *following* their incurrence (that is, from 20X3 through 20X7).

If Lorimer's management decides to expense the development costs (that is, decides that not all of the deferral criteria have been met), the net income for 20X2 is $200,000, and that amount is shown in the cash flow statement as the cash flow from operations (ignoring the many other adjustments that may be made to net income to convert it to cash flow).

If the 20X2 costs are capitalized and amortized, however, an interesting thing occurs. Because the costs are not charged as an expense, that $100,000 is shown as an investing activity outflow rather than being included in operations. Cash flow from operations therefore is reported as $300,000. In 20X3, $20,000 of the development costs (i.e., one-fifth) are amortized and charged against net income. In the operations section, however, amortization is added back to net income, and therefore the effect of the amortization is removed. The result is that *if costs are capitalized, they will never affect reported cash flow from operations.*

---

### ETHICAL ISSUES

A company that follows a policy of capitalizing as many expenditures as possible will, over time, show a consistently higher cash flow from operations than one that expenses those costs. While this may not fool a sophisticated user of the financial statements, management may choose to follow the capitalize-and-amortize approach consistently in an attempt to increase the company's apparent operating cash flow used to evaluate some debt covenants.

---

## PRESENTATION AND DISCLOSURE

Companies are required to disclose the cost of each major category of property, plant, and equipment, and the related accumulated amortization. Goodwill is presented as a separate line item on the balance sheet. Other intangible assets may be aggregated and then presented as a separate line item.

Segregation by major asset category is important, as the various categories of capital assets are associated with different levels of business risk and may have dissimilar useful lives and amortization policies. Typically, tangible capital assets are shown as one net amount on the balance sheet, with the required detailed breakdown shown in the disclosure notes.

For example, the 2006 balance sheet of Mediagrif Interactive Technologies Incorporated shows several separate amounts for capital assets—e.g., tangible assets, intangible assets, acquired intangible assets, and goodwill, Exhibit 9-5 contains excerpts from Mediagrif's accounting policy note. Exhibit 9-6 shows the asset breakdown that is included in other notes relating to long-lived assets. Notice that the company refers to "impairment" in the accounting policy notes. Public companies are now required to conduct an annual impairment test for these types of assets. We will discuss impairment tests in the next chapter.

---

### EXHIBIT 9-5

## MEDIAGRIF INTERACTIVE TECHNOLOGIES INCORPORATED
## ACCOUNTING POLICIES FOR CAPITAL ASSETS

### PREMISES AND EQUIPMENT
Premises and equipment are recorded at cost less accumulated amortization. Amortization is provided for based on the estimated useful lives of the related assets using the following methods and periods or annual rate:

|  | Method | Period/Rate |
|---|---|---|
| Office furniture | Declining balance | 20% |
| Computer and other equipment | Straight-line | 3 years |
| Leasehold improvements | Straight-line | Maximum of 5 years |

### IMPAIRMENT OF LONG-LIVED ASSETS
Long-lived assets are reviewed for impairment upon the occurrence of events or changes in circumstances indicating that the carrying value of the assets may not be recoverable, as measured by comparing their net book value to the estimated undiscounted future cash flows generated by their use. Impaired assets are recorded at fair value, determined principally by using discounted future cash flows expected from their use and eventual disposal.

### INTANGIBLE ASSETS
Intangible assets comprise the following:

*Software*
Software assets are purchased to fulfill the Company's technological needs and are recorded at cost. They also include internally developed software and web sites, which comprise capitalized personnel costs of the Company's research and development group meeting accepted criteria for deferral. These costs are amortized on a straight-line basis over their estimated useful lives ranging from three to five years.

*Acquired intangible assets*
Acquired intangible assets, which consist of exclusive contracts, customer base and other items, derive from business acquisitions and are recorded at cost less accumulated amortization. Acquired intangible assets are amortized on a straight-line basis over the estimated useful lives of the related assets, generally ranging from five to ten years.

### GOODWILL
Goodwill is not amortized but instead the Company assesses periodically whether a provision for impairment in the value of goodwill should be recorded to earnings. This is accomplished mainly by determining whether projected discounted future cash flows exceed the net book value of the respective business units. Goodwill is tested for impairment annually on March 31, or when an event or circumstance occurs that could potentially result in a permanent decline in value.

The Company has performed impairment tests on the carrying amount of goodwill as at March 31, 2006 and has concluded that no impairment loss should be recognized.

---

*Source:* www.sedar.com, Mediagrif, Annual Report, June 29, 2006.

EXHIBIT 9-6

## MEDIAGRIF INTERACTIVE TECHNOLOGIES INCORPORATED SELECTED NOTE DISCLOSURES FOR CAPITAL ASSETS (ALL AMOUNTS FOR 31 MARCH 2006)

### 6. Premises and Equipment

Premises and equipment comprise the following:

**2006**

|  | Cost $ | Accumulated Amortization $ | Net $ |
|---|---|---|---|
| Office furniture | 965,616 | 642,913 | 322,703 |
| Computer and other equipment | 10,411,062 | 8,440,642 | 1,970,420 |
| Leasehold improvements | 1,266,165 | 1,045,741 | 220,424 |
|  | 12,642,843 | 10,129,296 | 2,513,547 |

**2005**

|  | Cost $ | Accumulated Amortization $ | Net $ |
|---|---|---|---|
| Office furniture | 1,009,681 | 613,741 | 395,940 |
| Computer and other equipment | 9,043,369 | 7,258,441 | 1,784,928 |
| Leasehold improvements | 1,129,368 | 945,063 | 184,305 |
|  | 11,182,418 | 8,817,245 | 2,365,173 |

### 7. Intangible Assets and Acquired Intangible Assets

| a)  Intangible assets comprise the following: | 2006 $ | 2005 $ |
|---|---|---|
| Software, net of accumulated amortization of $3,402,426 (2005 − $3,287,061) | 1,043,936 | 1,274,185 |
| Internally developed software and web sites, net of accumulated amortization of $4,928,825 (2005 − $3,717,612) | 4,451,706 | 4,174,031 |
|  | 5,495,642 | 5,448,216 |

| b)  Acquired intangible assets comprise the following: | 2006 $ | 2005 $ |
|---|---|---|
| Customer base, net of accumulated amortization of $1,688,277 (2005 − $877,326) | 4,305,819 | 4,874,281 |
| Other items, net of accumulated amortization of $877,033 (2005 − $489,454) | 1,016,975 | 1,344,650 |
|  | 5,322,794 | 6,218,931 |

### 8. Goodwill

| a)  Goodwill | 2006 $ | 2005 $ |
|---|---|---|
| Beginning of year | 20,048,536 | 4,223,021 |
| Acquisition of businesses | 553,673 | 16,167,146 |
| Adjustment for acquisition | 451,978 | 111,982 |
| Reclassification of goodwill | (468,978) | (453,613) |
| End of year | 20,585,209 | 20,048,536 |

All goodwill relates to the E-business Networks segment except for an amount of $201,694 for the year ended March 31, 2006 (2005 − $201,694) which relates to the Software and Services segment.

*Source:* www.sedar.com, Mediagrif, Annual Report, June 29, 2006.

## CONCEPT REVIEW

1. Do all companies with goodwill have the asset listed on the balance sheet? Why is it often not recorded?

2. How is goodwill calculated when net assets are bought?

3. When there is a non-monetary exchange of assets, what will be recorded on the cash flow statement?

4. Suppose that a company is very aggressive at capitalizing expenditures related to intangible assets. How will the capitalization of large amounts of expenditures affect the cash flow statement, compared to a company that expenses many of the same types of expenditures?

5. What long-lived asset has to be shown separately on the balance sheet?

## INTERNATIONAL PERSPECTIVE

There are many aspects to accounting for capital assets, and many different standards that govern accounting policy in this area. Overall, Canadian and international standards are similar, but there are also many specific differences. Exhibit 9-7 summarizes some of the obvious areas where Canadian and international standards are different.

## EXHIBIT 9-7

### COMPARISON OF CANADIAN VERSUS INTERNATIONAL STANDARDS FOR LONG-LIVED ASSETS

| Accounting Policy | Canadian Standard | International Standard |
|---|---|---|
| Valuation rule for capital assets | Historical cost is normally used | Historical cost is permitted, but companies may also revalue many long-lived assets, by class, to fair value. This applies to property, plant, and equipment, and many specific intangibles. |
| Interest capitalization | No guidance on calculation of interest eligible for capitalization | Guidance provided on how to calculate interest eligible for capitalization |
| Asset retirement obligations | Recognition of legal obligations on asset acquisition; regular remeasurement is required | Requirements are broadly similar but specific measurement guidance is slightly different |
| Negative goodwill | Assigned pro-rata to most non-monetary assets; when non-monetary assets are exhausted, remainder is an extraordinary item | Negative goodwill is recognized immediately in net income |

In addition to these differences, the guidance given for exploration and development in the mineral exploration industry contains many subtle and no-so-subtle differences. However, companies are free to choose between full cost and successful efforts under both sets of standards.

Some of the differences outlined above are the subject of convergence projects. Others, such as the option to revalue major classes of capital assets at fair value rather than historical cost, are more problematic.

## RELEVANT STANDARDS

*CICA Handbook:*
- Section 1581, Business Combinations
- Section 3061, Property, Plant and Equipment
- Section 3062, Goodwill and Other Intangible Assets
- Section 3110, Asset Retirement Obligations
- Section 3450, Research and Development Costs
- Section 3831, Non-monetary Transactions
- Section 3850, Interest Capitalized—Disclosure Considerations
- AcG–11, Enterprises in the Development Stage
- AcG–16, Oil and Gas Accounting—Full Cost
- EIC 118, Accounting for Costs Incurred to Develop a Web Site
- Re-exposure Draft, Intangible Assets

IASB:
- *IAS* 16, Property, Plant and Equipment
- *IAS* 23, Borrowing Costs
- *IAS* 37, Provisions, Contingent Liabilities and Contingent Assets
- *IAS* 38, Intangible Assets
- *IFRS* 6, Exploration for and Evaluation of Mineral Resources

## SUMMARY OF KEY POINTS

1. Capital assets are identifiable long-lived assets, acquired for use in the revenue-producing activities of the enterprise. Capital assets may be tangible property, like plant and equipment. Identifiable intangible properties are also capital assets.

2. Capital assets are recorded at cost, including cost to install assets and prepare them for use. Specific guidelines exist to aid in classification of expenditure for various asset categories including buildings, self-constructed assets, machinery and equipment, land, land improvements, resource exploration and development costs, patents, industrial design registrations, copyrights, trademarks, franchise rights, research and development costs, software costs, website development costs, and other intangibles.

3. Cost less accumulated amortization equals net book value, which is not meant to reflect fair value after acquisition.

4. Assets acquired in a basket purchase must be individually valued using the proportional method, although the incremental method is used when information is not complete.

5. Capital assets purchased with low-interest debt are valued at the cash equivalent price, or at the present value of the cash payments required.

6. Assets acquired for share capital are valued at the fair value of the shares issued, unless that value is less reliable than the fair value of the asset received. Donated assets are valued at fair value, and give rise to contributed capital.

7. Self-constructed assets are recorded at cost, which includes reasonable amounts of overhead and may include interest on specific construction loans. Self-constructed assets may not be valued at an amount higher than fair value.

8. If there is a legal requirement to incur costs when an asset is retired, the present value of this is recorded as an asset and liability when the asset is acquired. Estimates are adjusted as time passes, the asset is amortized, and the liability is increased though accretion.

9. Specific intangible assets are recorded at cost, if purchased externally, or the cost to develop the asset, if internally generated. Legal costs are a major component of the cost of most intangible assets.

10. All research and many development costs must be expensed as incurred. Development costs may be deferred if specific criteria, including marketability or economic value, are met. Since the criteria are based on management estimates; substantial variation in practice can arise.

11. Internally developed intangible assets will have to meet certain capitalization criteria before they can be capitalized; the proposed criteria in this area include that the asset is severable or the result of contractual or legal rights, and the asset must meet the recognition criteria, be controlled, have future benefits, and have a measurable cost.

12. The practice of deferring some operating costs, such as training, promotion, and other start-up costs, has been common in the past but will not meet capitalizaion criteria for internally developed intangible assets as they come into effect.

13. Computer software costs for internally developed software will often be capitalized as capital costs, although there is significant variation in practice.

14. Website development costs are subject to either capitalization or expensing, depending on the nature of the cost. Planning, some content costs, and all operating costs are expensed. Website application, infrastructure costs, and some content costs are deferred.

15. Resource companies may use either the full cost method or the successful efforts method of accounting for exploration and development costs. The full cost method combines the costs of all exploration and development activities for purposes of amortization; the successful efforts method capitalizes the costs of successful wells and writes off the costs of exploration in unsuccessful wells. Costs are segregated by geographic region for amortization purposes.

16. When assets are sold or otherwise retired or disposed, the difference between proceeds, if any, and book value is the gain or loss on disposal. The gain or loss is, in substance, a correction of the recorded amortization over the period that the asset was used.

17. When non-monetary assets are exchanged, the transaction is valued at fair market value and a gain or loss on the exchange is recorded. The transaction is valued at book value with no gain or loss if there is no commercial substance, the exchange is to facilitate a sale to a third party, when fair values are not available, or if the exchange is a distribution to owners. Regardless, an asset cannot be recorded at a value higher than fair value.

18. Post-acquisition expenditures are typically repairs, which are expensed. If the expenditure results in enhanced cash flows for the asset, it is classified as a betterment and is capitalized and amortized over the asset's remaining useful life.

19. Goodwill is recognized on the purchase of another business unit. It is measured as the excess of purchase price over the fair value of identifiable net assets acquired.

20. On the cash flow statement, cash expenditures to acquire capital assets and cash received on sale are reported as investing activities. Capital assets acquired in a non-cash exchange are not included on the cash flow statement. Some expenditures will be operating outflows if the item is expensed and investing outflows if the item is capitalized.

21. Required disclosure for long-lived assets includes capital assets by major category, and the accumulated amortization for each category. Identifiable intangibles may be grouped on the balance sheet. Goodwill must be disclosed as a separate line item.

## KEY TERMS

accretion expense, 463

asset retirement obligation, 462

basket purchase, 457

betterment, 477

capital assets, 452

capital expenditures, 477

commercial substance, 473

forgivable loans, 491

full cost method, 469

goodwill, 479

group purchase, 457

intangible capital assets, 452

involuntary conversions, 471

negative goodwill, 481

non-monetary transactions, 472

successful efforts method, 469

## REVIEW PROBLEM

The following four questions are independent.

1. *Plant asset cost classification.* Maldive Company completed the construction of a building. The following independent items are the costs and other aspects relevant to the purchase of the lot and construction:

| | |
|---|---:|
| Cash payments to contractor | $100,000 |
| Total provincial non-refundable sales tax on materials used in construction in addition to payments made to contractor | 3,000 |
| Cost of land (building site) | 50,000 |
| Gross cost to demolish old building on land | 20,000 |
| Proceeds from old building salvage | 5,000 |
| Power bill for electricity used in construction | 2,000 |
| Interest on loans to finance construction | 3,000 |

   What is the final recorded cost (i.e., carrying value) for *each* of the land and building?

2. *Accounting for debt incurred on acquisition.* The Round Wheel Barn Company purchases a tractor by making a down payment of $10,000. In addition, Round Wheel Barn signs a note requiring monthly payments of $2,000, starting one month after purchase and continuing for a total of 20 months. The contract calls for no interest, yet the prevailing interest rate is 24% per annum on similar debts. What is the cost (and initial carrying value) of the asset? What is the interest expense that should be recognized for the month following purchase?

3. *Accounting for exchange of plant asset.* Ocular Company trades an electron microscope for new optical equipment and receives $30,000 cash as well. The old microscope had an original cost of $200,000 and has accumulated depreciation of $80,000 at the time of the trade. The old microscope has a fair market value of $160,000 at trade in time. The exchange does not have commercial substance. What entry should be made to record the exchange?

4. *Post-acquisition costs.* After one-quarter of the useful life had expired on equipment with an original cost of $100,000 and no salvage value, a major component of the equipment is unexpectedly replaced. The old component was expected to last as long as the equipment itself. Company records indicate that the component originally cost $20,000 and had no expected salvage value. The replacement component cost $30,000 and has no usefulness beyond that of the equipment. What is the entry to record the replacement? Assume straight-line depreciation.

## REVIEW PROBLEM—SOLUTION

1. Cost components of the land and building:

| Land | | Building | |
|---|---|---|---|
| Land cost | $50,000 | Cash payments to | |
| Demolition | 20,000 | contractor | $100,000 |
| Salvage proceeds | (5,000) | Sales tax on materials | 3,000 |
| | | Power bill | 2,000 |
| | | Capitalized loan interest | 3,000 |
| Total land cost | $65,000 | Total building cost | $108,000 |

2. The cost of the tractor is the present value of the monthly payment annuity:

$$P = \$10,000 + \$2,000(P/A, 2\%, 20) = \$42,703$$

Interest cost for the first month is the present value times the monthly interest rate:

$$\$32,703 \times 2\% = \$654$$

3. Since there is no commercial substance to the transaction, the new equipment is recorded at the book value of the old equipment, minus the cash received:

| | | |
|---|---|---|
| Equipment ($120,000 − $30,000) | 90,000 | |
| Accumulated depreciation | 80,000 | |
| Cash | 30,000 | |
|     Equipment | | 200,000 |

4. The new component is a replacement of an old component, and such is a *substitution*. It is not a betterment, because it does not improve or extend the functioning of the asset. The entries to remove the old component and substitute the new are as follows:

| | | |
|---|---|---|
| Loss on asset replacement | 15,000 | |
| Accumulated depreciation ($20,000 ÷ 4) | 5,000 | |
|     Equipment | | 20,000 |
| Equipment | 30,000 | |
|     Cash | | 30,000 |

# APPENDIX

## GOVERNMENT ASSISTANCE

Assets sometimes are acquired with monetary assistance from various levels of governments. This may be in the form of a *cash* grant. The terms of the grant may require the firm to maintain certain employment levels or pollution-control levels. If the conditions are not met, the firm may be required to refund the amounts received.

Another common program is in the form of an investment tax credit, which reduces the amount of *income tax payable* based on a set percentage of eligible capital expenditures for a period. For example, assume that a company had a tax bill of $675,000. During the year, it spent $750,000 on new manufacturing machinery, which qualifies for a 10% investment tax credit. The company can reduce its tax bill by $75,000, to $600,000. Taxes payable go down, and are debited, for $75,000. What account is credited?

This question has been very controversial. There are three alternatives.

1. An account in shareholders' equity could be credited.

2. Tax expense, or another current income statement account, could be credited, reflecting cash flow and the impact on current taxes.

3. The capital asset could be credited, or a related deferred credit established. This would reduce the amount of future depreciation charged: that is, only depreciation on the *firm-financed* portion of the capital asset would be expensed over time. Thus, the income statement will reflect the benefit of the government assistance, but only over the useful life of the asset.

Through lobbying behaviour, some firms have demonstrated their clear preference for the second alternative, which has the happy effect of increasing current earnings. The first alternative is consistent with the treatment given to donated assets. However, the third alternative is very firmly entrenched in Canadian practice.

Basically, Canadian accounting standards require that government assistance toward the acquisition of fixed assets in any form should be either:

a. Deducted from the related fixed assets with any depreciation calculated on the net amount; or

b. Deferred and amortized to income on the same basis as the related depreciable fixed assets are depreciated.

The choice allowed—really a presentation issue—is relatively insignificant. The major decision is that the government assistance is deferred with capital assets, and recognized on the income statement with depreciation.

**Example**  To illustrate accounting for a government grant, assume that machinery costing $100,000 was eligible for assistance of 30%. The machinery has a 10-year life with no salvage value. Because both the *net method* and *deferral method* of accounting are acceptable, both sets of journal entries are provided.

|  | Net Method | | Deferral Method | |
|---|---|---|---|---|
| Record purchase: | | | | |
| Machinery | 100,000 | | 100,000 | |
| Cash | | 100,000 | | 100,000 |
| Record receipt of government assistance: | | | | |
| Cash* | 30,000 | | | 30,000 |
| Machinery | | 30,000 | | — |
| Deferred government grant | | — | | 30,000 |

*Cash is debited if government assistance is in the form of money. If assistance was investment tax credit, taxes payable would be debited.

| | Net Method | | Deferral Method | |
|---|---|---|---|---|
| Record straight-line depreciation expense at the end of years 1 to 10: | | | | |
| Depreciation expense | 7,000 | | 10,000 | |
| Accumulated depreciation | | 7,000 | | 10,000 |
| Deferred government grant | — | | 3,000 | |
| Depreciation expense | | — | | 3,000 |

The effect on income is the same under either method. The difference is on the balance sheet where with the deferral method, the gross amount of the capital asset would appear. The credit may be a contra account to the asset, or shown on the opposite side of the balance sheet. Which method would you choose if you were trying to maximize assets to reassure creditors? Companies often prefer higher asset values.

**Other Government Assistance** Before we leave government assistance, perhaps it's worth mentioning that government assistance can be obtained for a wide variety of purposes, not just capital asset acquisition. The purpose of the government assistance governs its accounting. For example, if the assistance is to offset current expenses, then accounting for government assistance must reflect that fact, and recognize government assistance on the income statement when the related expenses appear. If assistance is for future expenses, then assistance should be deferred and recognized when the expenses are recognized.

Finally, government assistance is sometimes in the form of **forgivable loans**. The loans are forgiven when certain conditions are met, such as maintenance of a stated level of employment or volume levels for specific periods of time. In these circumstances, management must assess the conditions that are attached to the "loan." If the conditions are deemed likely to be met, the "loan" is recorded as a grant, and the conditions and unforgiven balance are disclosed in the notes. Should management's expectations prove wrong and the loan becomes repayable in the future, this event should be accounted for in the period that conditions change.

## INTERNATIONAL PERSPECTIVE

There are no differences between Canadian and international standards on the subject of government grants for capital assets. However, this is an area where Canadian and U.S. accounting practices are different. In the U.S., practice allows government assistance received in the form of investment tax credits to be included in income in the year in which they arise—that is, alternative (2), above. U.S. standard setters have tried to switch to alternative (3) a few times. Political action by firms, that obviously prefer the potential to increase income by the use of this accounting policy, has prevented any change to accounting standards.

## RELEVANT STANDARDS

*CICA Handbook:*
- Section 3800, Government Assistance
- Section 3805, Investment Tax Credits

IASB:
- *IAS* 20, Accounting for Government Grants and Disclosure of Government Assistance

## SUMMARY OF KEY POINTS

1. Government assistance for capital assets, in the form of grants or tax credits, is amortized to net income over the life of the related capital asset. On the balance sheet, the grant amount is credited directly to the capital asset account or is shown in a separate deferred credit account.

2. Other government assistance is recognized on the income statement when the related expenses, meant to be supported by the assistance, are also recognized.

## QUESTIONS

Q9-1 To determine the cost of a capital asset, how should the following items be treated: (a) invoice price, (b) freight, (c) discounts, (d) title verification costs, (e) installation costs, (f) testing costs, and (g) cost of a major overhaul before operational use?

Q9-2 Why might a company prefer to value capital assets at fair value rather than historical cost? Is this allowable under Canadian accounting standards?

Q9-3 When several capital assets are purchased for a single lump-sum consideration, cost apportionment is usually employed. Explain the alternatives. Why is apportionment necessary?

Q9-4 A machine was purchased on the following terms: cash, $100,000, plus five annual payments of $5,000 each. How should the acquisition cost of the machine be determined? Explain.

Q9-5 How is an asset's acquisition cost determined when the consideration given consists of equity securities?

Q9-6 Some businesses construct capital assets for their own use. What costs should be capitalized for these assets? Explain what policy to follow for (a) general company overhead, (b) costs of construction in excess of the purchase price of an equivalent asset from an outsider, and (c) interest on construction loans.

Q9-7 Does cost necessarily equal fair value on the date of acquisition for self-constructed assets, and intangibles? Explain.

Q9-8 Under what circumstances must a company record a liability for future costs of retiring an asset? What judgements are necessary to record a retirement obligation? What is the offsetting debit?

Q9-9 Suppose that an asset retirement liability is recorded, and that the original estimates are not changed in subsequent years. Is any accounting treatment required for the liability in the intervening years until retirement? Explain.

Q9-10 What outlays are properly considered part of the cost of an intangible asset?

Q9-11 What is the difference between research and development? How must a company account for research? For development?

Q9-12 What criteria have been suggested to determine whether an internally generated intangible asset can be capitalized?

Q9-13 Why would advertising and promotional expense, which might have a long-term positive effect on a company's reputation, not qualify for capitalization?

Q9-14 Computer software development costs present a particular challenge for policy makers. What is the basic problem?

Q9-15   At what point is it normal to begin to defer costs incurred for a software program that will be sold to external customers?

Q9-16   What is the most appropriate treatment for costs incurred in planning features of a company's website?

Q9-17   Describe two different policies to account for exploration and development costs incurred by oil and gas companies.

Q9-18   If a company wished to pick accounting policies that are closer to actual cash flows, would you expect the company to use full cost or successful efforts for exploration and development costs?

Q9-19   An asset is purchased for $10,000 and has a net book value of $2,000 after three years, at which time it is sold for $4,500. Explain the meaning of the $2,500 gain.

Q9-20   How are assets recorded when they are acquired by exchanging another asset? Explain when fair value versus book value recording would be appropriate.

Q9-21   An asset with a book value of $12,000 and a fair value of $25,000 is exchanged for another asset with a net book value of $17,000. No cash is exchanged. There is no commercial substance to the transaction. What is the value assigned to the new asset?

Q9-22   Return to the facts of question 9-21. Assume that $5,000 cash is also included with the old asset, in order to obtain the second asset. This time, there is commercial substance to the transaction. What is the value assigned to the second asset?

Q9-23   When are post-acquisition costs capitalized rather than expensed?

Q9-24   Explain two approaches used when recording a betterment. Which is preferable?

Q9-25   Explain the impact on income, net assets, and cash flow, over an asset's life, of a decision to capitalize or write off certain expenditures made at the time of the purchase of a capital asset.

Q9-26   What items commonly are reported on the cash flow statement in relation to capital assets?

Q9-27   Under what circumstances will cash flow for development expenses appear in the investing activities section of the cash flow statement? Explain.

Q9-28   Define goodwill and describe how it is calculated.

Q9-29   What is negative goodwill? How does it arise? How is it treated for accounting purposes?

---

## CASE 9-1

### THOR LIMITED

Thor Ltd. (TL) is a Canadian private company that produces, sources, and supplies agriculture products, including farm equipment, fertilizer, and seed. These products are sold to large and small distributors across Canada. TL deals with some large farm accounts directly. Sales volumes are healthy and stable, but profit margins are thin and have been squeezed by rising fuel prices. Transportation is a major cost item.

James Watkins manages a project for TL. He is paid a salary of $60,000 and has been promised a bonus of 100,000 performance units if this project breaks even in the current period. Performance units are the bonus system used by TL. Units must be held for three years, and are then assigned a value based on a formula that considers the overall profit performance of the company, along with key customer and employee satisfaction data. In the last valuation round, one unit was worth $3.15.

The project is a no-tillage agricultural precision planting system called Land-Plant. It is a patented process over which TL owns the world patent rights. This system minimizes moisture loss, makes rich topsoil less likely to be blown or washed away after planting, and reduces the release of carbon dioxide (a greenhouse gas) into the environment. Since the latter is a major goal of the Kyoto accord, the federal government has announced that Canadian farmers could get funding of up to $1 billion for adopting such zero-plowing systems and adopting other energy-saving practices. For farmers, the system also allows lower operating costs, precision planting, decreased soil compaction and more precise application of needed fertilizers. While there are several no-till or low-till technologies on the market, TL's product line is of high quality and is being very well received at agricultural shows. Land-Plant is capable of placing seed and fertilizer in optimum relative positions while leaving 90% of the surface undisturbed.

Costs of the project to date (in thousands):

| | | Current Year | | | |
| Description | Prior Year | 1st Quarter | 2nd Quarter | 3rd Quarter | 4th Quarter |
|---|---|---|---|---|---|
| Development costs | $1,698 | | | | |
| Legal costs re: patent | 134 | $60 | $ 10 | | |
| Independent product testing | | 82 | | | |
| Production planning | | | 156 | $ 18 | |
| Market research | 20 | 47 | 12 | | |
| Sales and marketing support | | | | 56 | $ 76 |
| Production set-up | | | | 41 | |
| Production training | | | | 29 | |
| Production equipment (1), (2) | | | | 3,423 | |
| Production cost over-runs (3) | | | | 225 | |
| Administrative costs (4) | 35 | 35 | 35 | 35 | 35 |
| Production costs (5) | | | | 366 | 1,914 |

(1) The production equipment is expected to have a service life of eight years, or approximately 18,000 manufacturing hours. It was used in the third and fourth quarter of the current year, for 570 hours.
(2) The expenditure on manufacturing equipment will entitle TL to an investment tax credit (income tax relief) equal to 20% of the cost of the equipment.
(3) Quality concerns with the initial units produced led them to be scrapped.
(4) Watkins' salary of $15 per quarter, plus an administrative fee of $20 for overall supervision and accounting/systems support.
(5) In the third and fourth quarter, a total of 48 good units of the 3300T Land-Plant system were produced. These costs exclude amortization on related assets.

Financing of this project was uncertain until the third quarter of the current year. While TL's Board of Directors has been very enthusiastic about the project, and has funded the development work, TL had no deep well of financing as would be needed to finance the project. Then, late in the second quarter, TL was approved as an Eligible Business Corporation under the provincial *Small Business Venture Capital Act.* This allowed the company to issue 50,000 preferred shares in a private placement at $100 per share. The individual shareholders are entitled to a 30% investment tax credit on their investment. These shares were successfully issued in the third quarter. This funding, plus a lending arrangement, secured the project and production was geared up.

Production was limited to the latter part of the third quarter and all the fourth quarter. Manufacturing operations were increased to full capacity to meet demand. Fortunately for Watkins, he had a backlog of orders from marketing efforts, especially trade shows. He sold 42 units of model 3300T before the end of the fourth quarter at an average price of $67,400. TL, in all other divisions, ships essentially the same day as the order is received and thus recognizes revenue when orders are received. Because of the size and complexity of the Land-Plant equipment, it can take up to a week to have the unit shipped. Investigation showed that four units of model 3300T were not yet shipped at the end of the fourth quarter, although they were completed and ready for shipment.

In addition, invoices show that 12 units of model 3300T were to dealers who were told that if the units did not sell in six months, they could be returned to TL with no penalty or charge. Watkins views this as a clever marketing strategy, because he is confident that if the units are shown to agriculture producers, they will be very impressed with the operation and ingenuity of the system. He plans more volume under this plan in the coming year.

Overall market demand for the system is hard to predict, because much depends on continued federal government support for the system, and the development of rival systems by competitors. Watkins feels that he likely has three to five years before competition is much of a factor, but he acknowledges that this is largely a guess.

Watkins has requested a preliminary income statement, along with a discussion of the accounting issues. He knows that any income statement used for performance evaluation will have to be in accordance with GAAP, as it will be based on the information that is used for external reporting and TL's lenders require GAAP financial statements. The tax rate is 40%.

### Required:

Prepare the information requested by Watkins.

## CASE 9-2

### MULTI-COMMUNICATIONS LIMITED

Multi-Communications Ltd. (MCL) is a Canadian-owned public company operating throughout North America. Its core business is communications media, including newspapers, radio, television, and cable. The company's year-end is 31 December.

You have recently joined MCL's corporate office as a finance director, reporting to the chief financial officer, Robert Allen. It is October 20X2. Mr. Allen has asked you to prepare a report that discusses the accounting issues that might arise when the auditors visit in November.

MCL's growth in 20X2 was achieved through expansion into the U.S. MCL acquired a conglomerate, Peters Holdings (PH), which had substantial assets in the communications business, including a number of newspapers, and television and cable operations. Since the U.S. side of MCL's operations is now significant, management will begin reporting its financial statements in U.S. dollars in 20X2.

Over the past three months, MCL has sold off 80% of PH's non-communication-related businesses. The remaining 20% are also for sale, and are reported as long-term investments in the MCL statements.

To date, the sale of these non-communications assets has generated proceeds of $175 million, while their cost on the date of acquisition was $153 million. The proceeds have been treated as a reduction of the cost of acquiring PH, and no gain on sale has been reported on income statements prepared to date.

Overall, the cost of PH was $498 million, which MCL has reduced by $175 million, to $323 million. The retained tangible assets acquired have a value in the range of $240–$280 million, depending on the appraiser's report used (three were obtained). The major variation between the appraiser's reports is the interest rate used in the valuation; interest rates have been volatile.

In MCL's major newspaper markets, newspaper readership has peaked and there is little or no room for expansion. To increase its readership in one major urban market, MCL bought all the assets of a competing newspaper for $10 million in 20X2, which represented $4 million for tangible assets and $6 million for customer lists and goodwill. Later in the year, MCL ceased publication of the competing paper—publicly billed as a merger of the two papers—and liquidated the tangible assets for $3.2 million. MCL has classified the $0.8 million loss on sale of these capital assets as an increase in goodwill, bringing the total goodwill from the acquisition to $6.8 million. This is based on the underlying rationale for acquiring the newspaper: to increase MCL's own readership by restricting choice in this particular urban market. While MCL has not kept the entire customer group, readership in MCL's "merged" newspaper is higher than the single paper circulation before. MCL feels that this enhanced readership clearly justifies the capitalization of goodwill.

MCL estimates the value of its entire intangibles at $250 million. Included as intangibles are newspaper and magazine publication lists, cable subscriber lists, and broadcast licences. Some of these have been acquired through the purchase of existing businesses; others have been generated internally by operations that have been part of MCL for some time.

Amounts paid for acquired intangibles are not hard to determine, but the cost of internally generated intangibles is much more difficult to ascertain. Subscription lists are built through advertising campaigns, cold calls, and product giveaways. MCL estimates that it has expensed $35 million because of such activities over the last 10 years. Independent appraisers have determined the fair value of these internally generated assets to be in the range of $60 to $80 million. Because management feels that accurate portrayal of these assets is crucial to fairly present MCL's financial position, management has included these assets at $60 million on the balance sheet.

**Required:**

Prepare the report for Mr. Allen. (CICA, adapted)

## CASE 9-3

# BIOTECH WONDERS INCORPORATED

Biotech Wonders Inc. (BWI) was founded by Dr. Sam Hickey six years ago. Hickey has a PhD in organic chemistry and is guiding his team of scientists as they develop all-natural products to help deal with the damage caused by repetitive stress injuries. The demand for this type of product is expected to grow as baby boomers age and continue their active lifestyles.

Initially, all the capital came from Hickey and government grants. Several venture capital funds became investors two years ago. As a result, 40% of the common shares are held by three venture capital funds and Hickey owns 60%. The venture capital investors are looking forward to a public offering of BWI shares, likely when the company has at least one more product in commercial development.

Biotechnology companies have significant hurdles to clear before a product can be commercially marketed. These products are subject to significant government regulation, in three phases. Phase I testing must establish product safety with animals. Phase II testing must establish product safety with humans, and Phase III clinical trials, the most expensive and risky, must establish that the product is effective for treating the condition for which it is designed. Fewer than 3% of Phase I compounds reach commercial production. The major risks are that the product will not be safe or effective, or that another treatment, a competitor product, will be developed that is more effective. However, once product approval is received, profit margins are very high—80 to 90%.

BWI has two products in commercial production, one in Phase III testing, and two in Phase II testing. A number of other compounds are "in the lab" and are being considered for Phase I testing. The two products in commercial production have been modest successes, but not blockbusters.

BWI hired a reputable marketing research company, which reported that there is significant demand for BWI's proposed products, that is, those still being developed. There is significant interest in the product now in Phase III testing, as the condition that it will treat is widespread.

You have been approached by one of the venture capital companies with a common share investment in BWI. The BWI balance sheet and some additional information has been provided to you (Exhibit 1). However, the income statement, cash flow statement, and disclosure notes have not been completed. You understand that BWI will report a loss of about $2,300,000 this year, which is largely the result of expenditures of $2,100,000 for the product in Phase III testing. Hickey has described the loss as "a good thing, because it demonstrates our commitment to Phase III testing of a product with significant commercial potential." Hickey is unhappy that these costs have not been deferred, as they represent a major investment in a future revenue-producing product.

The venture capital investor is interested in any financial statement adjustments that you feel are necessary. You must provide the dollar amount, where possible, and rationale for any suggested changes to BWI's financial information. Furthermore, you have been asked to suggest any qualitative factors or other performance measures that the venture capital investor should consider as part of its evaluation of BWI.

**Required:**

Prepare the report.　　　　　　　　　　　　　　　　　　　　　　(ASCA, adapted)

### EXHIBIT 1

## BIOTECH WONDERS INCORPORATED
## BALANCE SHEET (UNAUDITED)

31 March 20X1

**Assets**

Current assets:

| | | |
|---|---|---|
| Cash | | $   549,059 |
| Inventory | | 11,651 |
| Total current assets | | 560,710 |

**Long-term assets:**

| | | |
|---|---|---|
| Investment in Ocean Growers (Note 1) | | 60,000 |
| Deferred development costs (Note 2) | | 112,250 |
| Leasehold improvements (Note 3) | $103,445 | |
| Less: accumulated amortization | (31,034) | |
| | | 72,411 |
| Equipment (Note 3) | 50,876 | |
| Less: accumulated amortization | (15,088) | |
| | | 35,788 |
| Total long-term assets | | 280,449 |
| **Total Assets** | | $   841,159 |

**Liabilities**

Current liabilities:

| | | |
|---|---|---|
| Accounts payable | | $     34,075 |
| Wages payable | | 1,750 |
| Rent payable | | 800 |
| Total liabilities | | 36,625 |

**Shareholders' equity**

| | | |
|---|---|---|
| Common shares | | 6,400,000 |
| Deficit | | (5,595,466) |
| Total shareholders' equity | | 804,534 |
| **Total Liabilities and Equities** | | $   841,159 |

*Notes:*

1. BWI owns 18% of the common shares of Ocean Growers (OG) and accounts for its investment in OG using the cost method. Sam Hickey owns the other 82% of OG's common shares. OG has incurred losses of $220,000 since BWI purchased its investment. OG's losses are due to its extensive research activities in dietary supplements designed to enhance bone density.

2. Deferred development costs relate to products in commercial production. All additional costs of development are deferred once Phase III approval is obtained. The costs are amortized straight line over 10 years.

3. The leasehold improvements were made three years ago and are being amortized over the current lease term of five years plus the time of an estimated new lease of five years (total life of 10 years). BWI has not negotiated the new lease. Equipment is amortized on a straight-line basis over the useful life of five years. On 1 October 20X0, BWI transferred to Lincoln Therapeutics, another biotechnology company, certain equipment that BWI had carried on its books for $108,000. BWI accepted other laboratory equipment in exchange. This equipment had a net book value of $125,000 on Lincoln's books. The equipment was appraised at $126,400, and BWI recorded a gain on the trade of $18,400.

## CASE 9-4

## PENGUINS IN PARADISE

"The thing you have to understand is how these stage plays work. You start out with just an idea, but generally no cash. That's where promoters like me come in. We find ways of raising the money necessary to get the play written and the actors trained. If the play is a success, we hope to recover all those costs and a whole lot more, but cash flow is the problem. Since less than half of all plays make money, you cannot get very much money from banks.

"Take my current project, Penguins in Paradise (PIP). You only have to look at the cash inflows to see how many sources I had to approach to get the cash. As you can see, most of the initial funding comes from the investors in the limited partnership. They put up their money to buy a percentage of the future profits of the play.

"The money that the investors put up is not enough to fund all the start-up costs, so you have to be creative. Take reservation fees, for example. You know how tough it is to get good seats for a really hot play. Well, PIP sold the right to buy great seats to some dedicated theatregoers this year for next year's performance. These amounts are non-refundable, and the great thing is that the buyers still have to pay full price for the tickets when they buy them.

"Consider the sale of movie rights. Lots of good plays get turned into movies. Once the stage play is a success, the movie rights are incredibly expensive. My idea was to sell the movie rights in advance. PIP got a lot less money, but at least we got it up front when we needed it.

"The other sources are much the same. We received the government grant by agreeing to have at least 50% Canadian content. We also negotiated a bank loan with an interest rate of 5% a year plus 1% of the gross revenue of the play, instead of the usual 16% annual interest a year. Even my fee for putting the deal together was taken as a percentage of the profit, so just about everybody has a strong interest in the play's performance."

### Required:

Prepare a memo addressing the major financial accounting issues to be established by PIP. Include your recommendations. Do not prepare financial statements.

(CICA, adapted)

**Summary of Cash Flows**
**For the period ended 31 December 20X4**
**($ thousands)**

Cash inflows:

| | |
|---|---:|
| Investor contributions to limited partnership | $6,000 |
| Bank loan | 2,000 |
| Sale of movie rights | 500 |
| Government grant | 50 |
| Reservation fees | 20 |
| | 8,570 |

Cash outflows:

| | |
|---|---:|
| Salaries and fees for rehearsal period | 3,500 |
| Costumes and sets | 1,000 |
| Miscellaneous costs | 1,260 |
| | 5,760 |
| Net cash inflows | $2,810 |

# ASSIGNMENTS

 **A9-1 Acquisition Cost:** Forward Company shows an account related to a machine it assembled after buying it used, at an auction, in 20X9:

Account: Machine # 20X9-231

| Item | Debit | Credit | Balance |
|---|---:|---:|---:|
| Cost of dismantling and removing old machine ($35,600 machine, fully amortized with no salvage value assumed) | $ 2,450 | | $ 2,450 |
| Cash from sale of old machine for scrap | | $300 | 2,150 |
| Auction price of new machine (expected life, eight years) | 23,700 | | 25,850 |
| GST on new machine | 1,185 | | 27,035 |
| Shipping of new machine | 670 | | 27,705 |
| Installation costs—internal labour | 5,550 | | 33,255 |
| Installation costs—external electrician | 470 | | 33,725 |
| Material and labour in test runs | 540 | | 34,265 |
| Repairs to damage done during installation | 960 | | 35,225 |
| Purchase of machine tools, expected to last three years | 1,400 | | 36,265 |
| Profit on acquisition (fair value of $ 42,000) versus cost of $36,625) | 5,375 | | 42,000 |

**Required:**
Provide a correcting entry, or entries, for the machine account.

★ **A9-2 Acquisition Cost:** The following cases are independent.

*Case A* Ming Limited bought a building for $625,300. Before using the building, the following expenditures were made:

| Repair and renovation of building | $96,000 |
|---|---|
| Construction of new driveway | 12,000 |
| Repair of existing driveways | 4,200 |
| Installation of high-speed cable | 12,000 |
| Deposits with utilities for connections | 4,000 |
| Sign for front and back of building, attached to roof | 9,800 |
| Installation of fence around property | 16,000 |

***Case B*** Romollo Company purchased a $186,000 tract of land for a factory site. Romollo razed an old building on the property and sold the materials it salvaged from the demolition. Romollo incurred additional costs and realized salvage proceeds as follows:

| Demolition of old building | $29,000 |
|---|---|
| Routine maintenance (mowing) done on purchase | 2,500 |
| Proceeds from sale of salvaged materials | 6,000 |
| Legal fees | 11,000 |
| Title guarantee insurance | 6,800 |

**Required:**

1. What balance would Ming report in the building account?
2. What balance should Romollo report in the land account?
3. If any items in the list above are excluded from the building and land accounts, indicate the appropriate classification.

---

 **A9-3 Acquisition Cost:** An examination of the property, plant, and equipment accounts of James Company, disclosed the following transactions:

a. On 1 January 20X4, a new machine was purchased having a list price of $45,000. The company did not take advantage of a 2% cash discount available upon full payment of the invoice within 30 days. Shipping cost paid by the vendor was $200. Installation cost was $600, including $200 that represented 10% of the monthly salary of the factory superintendent (installation period, two days). A wall was moved two feet at a cost of $1,100 to make room for the machine.

b. On 1 January 20X4, the company purchased an automatic counter to be attached to a machine in use, cost $700. The estimated useful life of the counter was 7 years, and the estimated life of the machine was 10 years.

c. On 1 January 20X4, the company bought plant fixtures with a list price of $4,500; paid $1,500 cash and gave a one-year, non-interest-bearing note payable for the balance. The current interest rate for this type of note was 15%.

d. During January 20X4, the first month of operations, the newly purchased machine became inoperative due to a defect in manufacture. The vendor repaired the machine at no cost to James; however, the specially trained operator was idle during the two weeks the machine was inoperative. The operator was paid regular wages ($850) during the period, although the only work performed was to observe the repair by the factory representative.

e. On 1 July 20X4, a contractor completed construction of a building for the company. The company paid the contractor by transferring $400,000 face value, 20-year, 8% James Company bonds payable. Financial consultants advised that the bonds would sell at 96 (i.e., $384,000).

f. During January 20X5, the company exchanged the electric motor on the machine in part (a) for a heavier motor and gave up the old motor and $600 cash. The market value of the new motor was $1,250. The parts list showed a $900 cost for the original motor and it had been depreciated in 20X4 (estimated life, 10 years).

**Required:**

1. Prepare the journal entries to record each of the above transactions as of the date of occurrence. Explain and justify your decisions on questionable items. James Company uses straight-line depreciation.

2. Record depreciation at the end of 20X4. None of the assets is expected to have a residual value except the fixtures (residual value is $500). Estimated useful lives: fixtures, 5 years; machinery, 10 years; and building, 40 years. Give a separate entry for each asset.

---

★ **A9-4 Expenditure Classification:** Consider each of the following items:

a. Cost of a fan belt repair on the company's truck.
b. Lawyers' fees associated with a successful patent application.
c. Lawyers' fees associated with an unsuccessful patent application.
d. Excess of the book value of an old asset over the fair market value of the new asset in a trade of assets with no commercial substance.
e. Surveyors' fees.
f. Cost to demolish an old building that is on a piece of land where a new building will be constructed.
g. Cost to bulldoze land to make it flat for a building site.
h. Cost to discover a new plastic
i. Cost to determine the properties of a new plastic
j. Cost to create a new product from a newly discovered plastic.
k. Cost of installing a new roof on the company's building.
l. Cost to add new functions to a software package unique to the company.
m. Routine maintenance of website.

**Required:**
For each of the above items, give the name of the account to which the expenditure should be charged; that is, what account should be debited? Be specific.

---

★ **A9-5 Acquisition of Land—Non-Cash Consideration:** Under the cost principle, what amount should be used to record land acquired in each of the following independent cases? Give reasons to support your answer.

a. At the middle of the current year, a cheque was given for $40,000 for land, and the buyer assumed the liability for unpaid taxes in arrears at the end of last year, $1,000, and those assessed for the current year, $900.
b. A company issued 14,000 shares of capital stock with a market value of $6 per share (based on a recent sale of 100 shares) for land. The land was recently appraised at $80,000 by independent and competent appraisers.
c. A company rejected an offer to purchase land for $8,000 cash two years ago. Instead, the company issued 1,000 shares of capital stock for the land (market value of the shares, $7.80 per share based on several recent large transactions and normal weekly share trading volume).
d. A company issued 1,000 shares of capital stock for land. The market value (shares sell daily with an average daily volume of 5,000 shares) was $60 per share at time of purchase of the land. The vendor earlier offered to sell the land for $59,000 cash. Competent appraisers valued the land at $61,000.

---

★★ **A9-6 Asset Acquisition—Non-Cash Consideration:** Machinery with a fair value of $63,000 is acquired in a non-cash exchange. Below are five independent assumptions (a) to (e) as to the consideration given in the exchange:

a. A non-interest-bearing note for $72,450 maturing in one year. Notes of similar risk required 15% interest at the date of the exchange.
b. Cash of $23,000 plus a payment of $46,000 after 12 months. The market interest rate is 15%.
c. Land with a book value of $37,000 and a market value of $64,000.
d. A similar kind of used machinery with a net book value of $36,700 and a fair value of $45,800, plus cash of $16,800. When new, the used machinery cost $56,400. There will be no change in cash flows from operating activities as the result of this exchange.

e. Inventory carried at $42,750 on the most recent balance sheet as part of a perpetual inventory carried at LCM. Cash flows are different as a result.

**Required:**
Give the journal entry required for each of the above independent assumptions.

---

★ **A9-7 Asset Acquisition:** The following three cases are unrelated:

*Case A* Brushy Machine Shop purchased the following used equipment at a special auction sale for $60,000 cash: a drill press, a lathe, and a heavy-duty air compressor. The equipment was in excellent condition except for the electric motor on the lathe, which will cost $1,200 to replace with a new motor. Brushy has determined that the selling prices for the used items in local outlets are approximately as follows: drill press, $12,600; lathe, with a good motor, $36,000 (therefore, worth $34,800 with a damaged motor); and air compressor, $21,000. The electric motor was immediately replaced.

*Case B* A large company, upon abandoning its operations at a particular site, donated a building and the land on which it was located to another company that was to hire two-thirds of the old company's workforce. The property was reliably appraised at a value of $160,000 (one-quarter related to the land). The recipient company paid transfer costs of $4,000 related to the land.

*Case C* Fairview Forestry Limited (FFL) leased a large tract of land from the provincial government for $4 million per year for six years. The present value of the lease payments is $20.4 million. FFL will log the timber resources on the land over the six-year period. Before returning the land to the government at the end of the lease, FFL is obligated to remove its entire infrastructure (e.g., roads and buildings) and reforest the land with mixed vegetation, at an estimated cost (present value) of $2.5 million.

**Required:**
Determine the cost of the assets acquired in each case. Explain your reasoning, if choices must be made.

---

★★★ **A9-8 Asset Acquisition:** At 31 December 20X4, certain accounts included in the property, plant, and equipment section of Hint Corporation's balance sheet had the following balances:

| | |
|---|---|
| Land | $ 600,000 |
| Buildings | 1,300,000 |
| Leasehold improvements | 800,000 |
| Machinery and equipment | 1,600,000 |

During 20X5, the following transactions occurred:

a. Land site number 101 was acquired for $3,000,000. Additionally, to acquire the land, Hint paid a $180,000 commission to a real estate agent. Costs of $30,000 were incurred to clear the land. During the course of clearing the land, timber, and gravel were recovered and sold for $16,000.

b. A second tract of land (site number 102) with a building was acquired for $600,000. The closing statement indicated that the land value was $400,000 and the building value was $200,000. Shortly after acquisition, the building was demolished at a cost of $40,000. A new building was constructed for $300,000 plus the following costs:

| | |
|---|---|
| Excavation fees | $12,000 |
| Architectural design fees | 16,000 |
| Building permit fee | 4,000 |

The building was completed and occupied on 30 September 20X5.

c. A third tract of land (site number 103) was acquired for $1,500,000 and was put on the market for resale.

d. Extensive work was done to a building occupied by Hint under a lease agreement that expires on 31 December 20X14. The total cost of the work was $250,000, as follows:

| Item | Cost | Useful Life (Years) |
|---|---|---|
| Painting of ceilings | $ 10,000 | 1 |
| Electrical work | 90,000 | 10 |
| Construction of extension to current working area | 150,000 | 25 |
| | $250,000 | |

The lessor paid half the costs incurred for the extension to the current working area.

e. During December 20X5, $120,000 was spent to improve leased office space.

f. A group of new machines was purchased subject to a royalty agreement, which requires payment of royalties based on units of production for the machines. The invoice price of the machines was $270,000, freight costs were $2,000, unloading costs were $3,000, and royalty payments for 20X5 were $44,000.

**Required:**

Disregard the related accumulated depreciation accounts.

1. Prepare a detailed analysis of the changes in each of the following balance sheet accounts for 20X5:
   a. Land
   b. Buildings
   c. Leasehold improvements
   d. Machinery and equipment

2. What items would appear on the cash flow statement in relation to the accounts in part (1)?

3. List the amounts in the items (a) to (f) that were not used to determine the answer to (1) above, and indicate where, or whether, these items should be included in Hint's financial statements.

(AICPA, adapted)

★ **A9-9 Donated Assets:** Markus Company received a vacant building as a donation. The building has a 25-year estimated remaining useful life ($40,000 residual value), which was recognized in the donation agreement at the time the company was guaranteed occupancy. Transfer costs of $25,000 were paid by the company. The building originally cost $700,000, 10 years earlier. The building was recently appraised at $410,000 market value by the city's tax assessor. Anticipating occupancy within the next 10 days, the company spent $84,000 for repairs and internal rearrangements, expected to have value for 8 years. There are no unresolved contingencies about the building and Markus Company's permanent occupancy.

**Required:**

1. Give all entries for Markus Company related to (a) the donation, (b) the renovation, and (c) any amortization at the end of the first year of occupancy, assuming that Markus uses straight-line amortization.

2. What would appear on the CFS in relation to the transactions recorded in requirement (1)?

3. What objections are raised concerning the accounting policy of capitalizing and depreciating a donated asset? Explain.

★ **A9-10 Lump-Sum Purchase:** Gerrard Company purchased a tract of land with an office building and equipment included. The cash purchase price was $320,000 plus $30,000 in fees connected with the purchase. The following data was collected concerning the property:

|  | Appraisal Value | Vendor's Book Value | Original Cost |
|---|---|---|---|
| Land | $ 60,000 | $ 16,000 | $ 16,000 |
| Equipment | 120,000 | 60,000 | 180,000 |
| Office building | 180,000 | 150,000 | 240,000 |

**Required:**

Give the entry to record the purchase; show computations.

---

★★ **A9-11 Capital Asset Accounting:** Moray Capital reported various transactions in 20X7:

a. Equipment with an original cost of $40,000 and accumulated depreciation of $34,000 was deemed to be unusable and was sold for $400 scrap value.

b. A new moulding system was acquired for $35,700. The invoice was marked 2/10, n/30, but Moray did not pay in time to take advantage of the 2% discount for early payment and thus paid the gross amount of $35,700. Wiring was improved to accommodate the needs of the system at a cost of $800. Related software upgrades were purchased for $2,500. Installation and testing cost $4,000.

c. Regular machine maintenance was carried out for $23,000.

d. A piece of machinery with an original cost of $77,400 and accumulated depreciation of $56,000 was traded, along with cash of $50,900, for a similar new machine with a fair market value of $62,700.

e. The building roof was replaced during the period at a cost of $22,800 to improve the insulation in the building and save on heating costs. The old roof had a cost of $13,500 and was three-quarters depreciated.

f. Two machines were acquired for a lump-sum amount of $53,800. One machine had an appraised value of $40,000; the other, $20,000.

g. A piece of land was acquired, adjacent to the company's existing manufacturing site. The land was acquired for $40,000 cash plus a zero-interest note payable in the amount of $200,000. The note is due in 10 years' time. Market interest rates are 6%.

h. Land and building were acquired from a member of the Board of Directors in exchange for 325,000 of the company's own common shares. The land was appraised at $75,000, and the building, $400,000. The facility will be used for long-term storage. The market value of common shares has been around $1.25 per share this year, with weekly highs and lows ranging from $1.80 to $0.95, respectively.

i. The company spent $430,000 in a research lab program this year. It was successful in developing three new commercial projects, which represented $157,000 of the expenditures budget. Legal fees associated with the three successful projects amount to $89,600.

j. Moray paved its factory parking lot, previously a dirt lot, at a cost of $112,100.

**Required:**

Prepare journal entries to record the transactions listed above. State any assumptions made. Use the gross method to record the note payable.

---

★★★ **A9-12 Capital Asset Transactions:** Vizard Limited began the year with modest capital asset balances; it had a $40,000 franchise fee asset, and machinery for which the company had paid $345,000 three years ago. Most capital assets are rented. Net balances are as follows:

| | |
|---|---|
| Franchise fees (cost of $40,000, less amortization of $8,000) | $ 32,000 |
| Machinery (cost of $345,000 less depreciation of $129,375) | 215,625 |

In the current year, Vizard expanded rapidly and recorded the following:

a. In January, Vizard bought the assets of a small manufacturing facility in order to achieve vertical integration. Vizard used this company's main product in its operation, and the other company was going out of business. At market values, Vizard bought accounts receivable, $45,000; prepaid expenses, $5,800; inventory of $111,400; patents worth

$55,000; machinery of $344,000; a building worth $678,000; and land worth $44,800. Vizard paid $2,200,000 for the assets; cash of $500,000 and a 10-year, 10% note payable for the balance. Ten percent represented market interest rates.

b. Vizard spent $35,000 in legal fees during an unsuccessful patent infringement case on the patent acquired in (a). Subsequently, the patent was considered worthless.

c. Vizard sold the land and building acquired in (a) for a total of $1,000,000. It accepted a $1,000,000 three-year zero-interest note receivable in full payment.

d. Vizard spent $40,000 refurbishing and repairing machinery acquired in the purchase.

e. Vizard rents its production facilities at an annual rental of $45,600. During the year, Vizard spent $11,000 painting and cleaning this space. It also spent $5,000 upgrading the wiring.

f. The company discovered that some of the equipment bought would replace, more effectively, some of its own machinery. Accordingly, Vizard disposed of its redundant assets. One machine, with an original cost of $38,000, and accumulated depreciation of $26,000, was sold for $11,500. Another, with an original cost of $25,000 and accumulated depreciation of $17,500, was traded for a new, but smaller, piece of machinery with a different function. The second piece of machinery had a fair value of $14,000. No cash changed hands in this transaction. Finally, a piece of machinery with an original cost of $17,000 and accumulated depreciation of $11,000 was exchanged, along with $500 cash, for a new machine with a similar function. The old equipment had a fair value of $8,000.

g. Vizard bought new trucks this year, for product delivery. Three vehicles, with appraised values of $15,000, $30,000, and $17,000, respectively, were purchased for $10,000 cash and a note payable that required payment of $20,000 at the end of each year for three years.

### Required:

1. Determine the balance in each capital asset account, after reflecting the transactions listed above. If expenditures are not capitalized, explain. Do not calculate the balance of the accumulated depreciation account for capital assets.

2. Calculate the gain or loss on sale or disposal of capital assets during the year. Show your calculations.

---

★ **A9-13 Self-Constructed Asset:** Amethyst Corporation needed an extension to its factory building. Amethyst obtained a construction contract bid from a major construction company for $3,200,000. However, the Amethyst general manager recommended to senior management that Amethyst construct the building itself, using the company's own workforce, as a way to keep the workforce fully employed. Amethyst approved the general manager's recommendation. Construction of the extension began on 27 July 20X3. The building will be used as additional production facilities. During 20X3, the company incurred the following costs:

| | |
|---|---:|
| Materials | $  650,000 |
| Direct labour | 1,750,000 |
| Supervision and other indirect labour | 80,000 |
| Interest on general corporate debt, allocated on basis of material costs | 10,000 |
| Overhead cost, allocated on basis of direct labour costs | 30,000 |
| Total | $2,520,000 |

At 31 December 20X3, the company's general manager estimated that the building was about 70% complete. The construction engineers estimated that it would cost an additional $1,000,000 to complete the building.

### Required:

1. Is it appropriate for Amethyst to include interest and overhead in the capitalized cost of the building extension? Discuss.

2. How should Amethyst show these costs in its 20X3 year-end financial statements?

**A9-14 Self-Constructed Asset:** Brazilia Corporation needed a warehouse and maintenance facility on its company site, which already housed three manufacturing/storage facilities and the company head office. The lowest outside bid for the facility was $3,200,000. Brazilia believed that it could successfully construct the facility, and have more control over the construction process. Accordingly, it began construction on company-owned land in 20X5. The facility was completed in 20X6. Costs related to the project have been accumulated in one account, "manufacturing facility":

| | |
|---|---|
| Materials | $1,066,200 |
| Subcontracted work (primarily electrical and plumbing) | 345,900 |
| Direct labour; plant workers assigned to construction tasks | 455,800 |
| Direct labour; construction workers hired specifically for this project | 123,600 |
| Plant foreman used for construction supervision; salary and benefits | 34,900 |
| Direct labour; plant maintenance workers assigned to construction tasks | 53,200 |
| Engineering and architectural services | 216,700 |

**ADDITIONAL INFORMATION:**

a. Overhead is assigned in the plant to cover supplies used, electricity, occupation costs, maintenance, etc. in the production environment at a rate of $0.57 for every dollar of direct plant labour. This is reasonable for the warehouse project.

b. A loan was negotiated to cover the cash flow needed for construction. Interest of $75,900 was paid on this loan. When the building was completed, a 10-year commercial mortgage was arranged on the property for $2,000,000, at an interest rate of 8%.

c. Of the $455,800 of plant workers' time assigned to construction tasks, 70% or $319,060, relates to time that would otherwise have been idle.

d. The administrative office handled the planning and paperwork related to the construction. The staff worked full time on this for approximately six months, representing salary and benefit costs of $57,000.

e. The executive team (chief executive officer and chief financial officer of the company, primarily) devoted approximately 10% of their time to this project during construction. The compensation package for these two individuals was $320,000 for this period.

**Required:**

1. Prepare a schedule showing the costs that can be capitalized for the building. If any items are not capitalized, explain why not.

2. What, if anything, would change in your answer if the outside bid on this project had been $2,400,000? Explain.

3. Under what circumstances can loan interest be capitalized as part of the cost of self-constructed assets? Explain.

 **A9-15 Self-Constructed Asset and Interest Capitalization:** Mannheim Company begins construction of a factory facility on 4 January of the current year. Mannheim uses its own employees and subcontractors to complete the facility. The following list provides information relevant to the construction. The facility is completed 27 December of the current year.

a. At the beginning of January, Mannheim obtains construction financing: a 10%, $12,000,000 loan with principal payable at the end of the year of construction provides significant financing for the project. Interest on the loan is payable semi-annually. Mannheim pays the interest and principal when due.

b. Mannheim owns the land site (cost, $4,000,000). In January, a subcontractor is employed to raze the building on the site, which was used by Mannheim for a number of years (cost, $800,000; accumulated depreciation, $600,000) for $80,000. Mannheim received $10,000 from salvaged materials.

c. Also in January, subcontractors survey, grade, and prepare the land for construction at a cost of $200,000 and excavate the foundation of the new facility for $1,000,000.

d. In January, a subcontractor poured and finished the foundation for $1,500,000. This work is financed separately through a one-year, 9% loan. Mannheim secured the financing at the beginning of January. The principal and interest were paid on 30 December.

e. The total material cost for construction, excluding other items in this list, is $8,000,000.

f. Payments to subcontractors, excluding others in this list, amount to $2,000,000.

g. Payments to Mannheim employees for work on construction are $9,000,000.

h. General overhead is assigned to all work done for customers on the basis of labour costs. If company-wide rates are used, the share of general overhead applicable to the job would be $7,000,000. The company uses a factory overhead applied account. Of the $7,000,000, $1,250,000 relates to amortization of capital assets.

i. In October, a subcontractor constructed a parking lot and fences for $300,000.

j. Incidental fees and other costs associated with facility construction were $150,000.

k. For purposes of interest capitalization, assume the company records interest to an expense and capitalizes interest once per year as an adjusting entry. Since construction costs were incurred fairly evenly over the year, the company has decided to capitalize one-half of the interest expense related to the general construction loans outstanding during the year but all of the interest on the foundation financing (see (a) and (d)).

l. The market value of the building upon completion is $25,000,000.

**Required:**

1. Provide general journal entries to account for all aspects of construction and related events. Construction costs are accumulated in Mannheim's facility under construction account. Your entries should lead to the correct total cost to record for the building. You may record the events in any order.

2. What disclosures would appear on the cash flow statement in relation to the constructed asset? Assume the company uses the indirect method to present cash flows from operations.

---

★ **A9-16 Asset Retirement Obligation:** Charlie Networks Ltd. (CNL) has a 10-year renewable lease contract with Mercator Limited (ML), the owner of a tall building in a major city. CNL is permitted to erect a transmission tower on the top of the building. CNL's contract with ML requires CNL to dismantle the tower if and when CNL discontinues its use. CNL expects to use the tower for only 10 years, due to the rapid advance in transmission technology that is likely to render the tower obsolete in 10 years. The lease payments to ML are $90,000 per year.

CNL constructed the tower at the beginning of 20X6 at a cost of $1,050,000. CNL estimates that dismantling and removal of the tower will cost $90,000, at 20X6 current prices. The risk-free interest rate is 4%; CNL's risk premium is 2%. CNL plans to use straight-line amortization; the company's policy is to take a full year's amortization in the year of acquisition but none in the year of disposal.

**Required:**

1. Prepare the journal entry to record construction of the tower and the retirement obligation.

2. Prepare the necessary adjusting entries pertaining to the tower and the retirement obligation for each of the years ending 31 December 20X6 and 20X7. Assume that there is no change in the estimated cost of the tower's removal.

---

★★ **A9-17 Asset Retirement Obligation:** At the end of 20X1, Green Collections Limited leased an abandoned mine in northern Ontario as a landfill site for non-industrial garbage. The rent is $400,000 per year, beginning in 20X2. Green has a five-year contract for garbage collection in a major city, renewable at the city's option. The lease with the mine owner requires Green to cover and plug the mine shafts used for the garbage. Green must comply with all Ontario environmental regulations. At 20X1 prices, the estimated cost of site restoration and plugging is $175,000. Whether the client city renews or not, the shaft will have to be plugged in 20X6 because it will be at capacity. Green's risk-adjusted interest rate is 8% in 20X1. Green uses straight-line amortization, which will begin in 20X2.

**Required:**

1. Prepare the journal entries, if any, to record the events in 20X1.

2. At the end of 20X2, the estimated cost to plug the shaft had increased to $215,000 due to increased Ontario environmental legislative requirements. Green's 20X2 risk-adjusted interest rate is now 7%. Prepare all journal entries in 20X2.

3. Assume there were no further estimate changes in 20X3. Provide the appropriate entries in 20X3.

 **A9-18 Asset Retirement Obligation—Remeasurement:** At the beginning of 20X1, Timber Lake Corporation (TLC) leased a tract of forest land from the provincial government for a period of four years, during which period TLC expects to harvest all of the timber. At the end of the lease (on December 20X4) or at termination of the harvest (whichever happens first), TLC is obligated to reforest the land. TLC believes that this will cost $650,000, and that it will take three years to complete logging. Reforestation is thus expected at the end of 20X3. TLC will not do any reforesting as the lease progresses, because cleared land must continue to be used for roads and other operations. TLC's risk-adjusted interest rate is 6%.

**OTHER INFORMATION:**

a. At the end of 20X1, TLC has harvested about one-third of the timber. At the end of the year, the cost of reforestation is re-estimated at $690,000. The risk-adjusted interest rate is 5%.

b. At the end of 20X2, TLC has harvested an additional 40% of the original crop. The cost of reforestation is still expected to occur at the end of 20X3, but the cost is now estimated to be $750,000. TLC's risk-adjusted interest rate is 5%.

**Required:**

Prepare the journal entries that are necessary to record the initial asset retirement obligation at the beginning of 20X1, and then adjusting entries at the end of 20X1 and 20X2.

 **A9-19 Research and Development Costs:** Airfield Answers Corporation had several expenditures in 20X5:

a. Testing new plastic prior to use in commercial production.
b. Redesign of prototype to improve performance.
c. Testing electronic instrument components during their production.
d. Study of the possible uses of a newly developed fuel.
e. Start-up activities for the production of a newly developed jet.
f. Construction of a prototype for a new jet model.
g. Design of a new, more efficient wing for an existing airplane.
h. Portion of vice-president's salary, related to the time spent managing the research lab.
i. Experimentation to establish the properties of a new plastic just discovered.
j. Current period amortization taken on the company's laboratory research facilities.
k. Salary of lab technician working on clinical trials of new drug.

**Required:**

1. Explain the accounting policies required for research and development expenditures.

2. Which of the above expenditures are considered research? Development? Neither?

 **A9-20 Research and Development Costs:** Bits Limited is involved in a scientific engineering program to develop a new-multi-hull racing sailboat, which the company hopes will become an accepted racing boat for junior sailors. This is a strong and growing market in North America, and market research indicates significant sales potential. In conjunction with this project, management has the following expenditures:

- $150,000 understanding general water flow dynamics.
- $20,000 market research with competitive sailors.
- $370,000 designing and testing certain multi-hull alternatives, of which one was chosen as the superior alternative.
- $576,000 refining and testing the chosen alternative.

**Required:**

1. Indicate how the expenditures should be accounted for.
2. How would your answer be different if sales markets were highly uncertain?

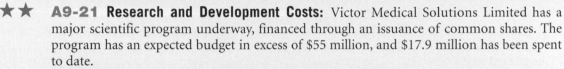

**A9-21 Research and Development Costs:** Victor Medical Solutions Limited has a major scientific program underway, financed through an issuance of common shares. The program has an expected budget in excess of $55 million, and $17.9 million has been spent to date.

The program targets technology to reduce the chronic inflammation associated with cardiovascular disease. In order to successfully market an end-product from this project, the company has to meet rigorous testing standards established by government agencies. In Phase I testing, the product must be shown to be safe in animals. In Phase II testing, the product must be shown to be safe in humans. In rigorous Phase III testing, the product must be shown to be effective in treating the condition better than available treatments on the market, or show other advantages over available treatments (e.g., fewer side effects).

As a result of the scientific program, Victor has twelve compounds in Phase I testing, three in Phase II testing, and one compound in a 2,000-individual Phase III test. All costs to date for all projects have been expensed.

**Required:**

1. Explain the required accounting treatment of research and development expenses.
2. Why are assets not established for research and many development initiatives? Evaluate GAAP requirements with reference to asset definition, matching, and conservatism.
3. Do you agree with Victor Medical Solutions's accounting policies for its scientific programs? What will be the impact on its financial statements, and how would you expect investors to react to the company's financial information?

**A9-22 Intangible Assets:** Cameras Limited is a new company whose only operation is the development of a new kind of video camera that will link to home computers and easily allow image transferring. The camera will come with a program to allow editing, so customers can edit their home movies and, for example, airbrush pictures and alter backgrounds. The camera and software are protected by several patents and copyrights, but technology in the area is moving quickly, and competition is fierce from competing products with different technology.

By the end of 20X6, a prototype existed and was being used to solicit orders. The product itself is due out in the second quarter of 20X7, in time for the Christmas season, which represents the vast majority of the annual camera-buying volume.

In 20X6, various costs were incurred: design costs ($675,800), engineering costs ($244,600), software development costs ($397,500), and market research costs ($68,900). Administration costs amounted to $670,000. Interest on bank loans was $62,500. Legal costs to register patents and copyrights amounted to $82,200. In addition, manufacturing equipment costing $450,000 was purchased and installed. It was used briefly to manufacture the prototype in the second quarter of 20X6, but is primarily idle and will continue to be idle until the first quarter of 20X7. At that time, production will begin in earnest.

**Required:**

Discuss classification of the various costs listed above. As part of your response, include a list of any additional information you would like to have.

---

 **A9-23 Software Development Costs:** GEE Software Limited is an established software development and marketing company. The following transactions were entered into in 20X5 with respect to software:

a. GEE bought the prototype of a software game from its developer, who had worked on it as a school project. GEE paid $35,000 for the prototype, and agreed to pay the creator a 15% royalty on net sales. After acquisition, costs were as follows: design and planning, $65,000; code development, $38,200; testing, $17,100; and production cost, $356,800. The company then spent $113,400 in promotion and advertising, and launched the game. GEE has spent another $21,700 on a website to support the game. So far, sales have been encouraging.

b. GEE paid $350,000 for the rights to another software game and agreed to pay the creator 10% of net revenues as a royalty. This game has been on the market for several years, and has been a modest success. GEE is in the redesign stage now, having spent $114,000 upgrading the game, and providing an expansion pack. Redesign work will be complete within the next few months. In the meantime, GEE has begun a promotion campaign, at a cost of $54,400, to boost future sales.

c. GEE has been working on a security software program, which will be useful to business websites. Costs to date, for design and planning, $88,700; code development, $156,000; and testing, $65,000. The company had a working prototype after 65% of the code development and 10% of the testing was complete. All the design and planning work preceded the prototype. Market research, part of the planning stage, indicates a strong market for this product.

**Required:**

Establish appropriate accounting treatment for each of the expenditures explained above. State any assumptions made.

---

 **A9-24 Website Development:** Worldwide Tours Corporation (WTC) established a new division in 20X8. The mandate of this new division is to establish a presence in the growing luxury eco-tourism travel business. This division will offer, through a sophisticated website, on-line quotes for travel packages to a variety of ecologically interesting locations. The website will include ratings of the various packages, including video clips of locations and interviews with local experts. WTC will underwrite various packages, and place clients with other operators, earning a commission. Initial market research indicates that there is a demand for objective information about travel opportunities, and increased purchasing over the Internet.

In 20X8, WTC incurred costs in relation to the operation:

| | |
|---|---|
| Manager salaries (half planning) | $246,000 |
| Rented space | 49,000 |
| Software purchased | 91,600 |
| Consultant's fees—graphics design | 71,800 |
| Computer equipment purchased; three-year life | 67,800 |
| Operating costs—heat, power, etc. | 45,100 |
| Travel and research costs re: travel packages | 94,800 |
| Preparation of content | 63,100 |
| Promotion of website to customers | 87,300 |

The website is just recently up and running at the end of 20X8. The winter months of 20X9 will be the first real test of the viability of the service.

**Required:**

Provide recommendations as to how to account for the expenditures listed above. Be specific.

★ **A9-25 Internally Developed Intangibles:** Baxter Limited reported the following assets at the end of 20X5:

| | |
|---|---|
| Promotion costs | $ 87,500 |
| Deferred reorganization costs | 166,000 |

These assets are being amortized over three years.

The promotion costs relate to a major advertising initiative undertaken by the company last year; the objective was improved brand recognition, which was expected to boost sales for at least three years. The deferred reorganization costs are the unamortized portion of a severance payment given to a group of workers who were dismissed after a major downsizing. Since the downsizing was expected to improve future profits, the costs were capitalized and amortized.

**Required:**

1. What are the suggested criteria that must be met in order for an internally generated intangible asset to be capitalized?
2. Do the two items above meet these criteria? Explain.

★★ **A9-26 Intangible Assets:** Transactions during 20X5, the first year of the newly organized Jenny's Discount Foods Corporation, included the following:

2 Jan.  Paid $8,000 lawyer's fees and other related costs to register the name and trademark of the company in various jurisdictions.

31 Jan.  Paid $2,000 for television commercials advertising the grand opening. This advertising increased customers' awareness of the company name and location.

1 Feb.  Paid $4,000 to an image consultant to create a logo and distinctive packaging.

1 May  Acquired a patent from an existing patent holder for $10,200. The patent will not be used in the operations of the corporation but rather will be held as a long-term investment to produce royalty revenue.

1 Oct.  Obtained a licence from the city to conduct operations in a specific location. The licence, which cost $9,000, runs for one year and is renewable.

1 Nov.  Acquired another business and paid, after analysis, $36,000 cash for its goodwill. Recorded only the goodwill.

31 Dec.  Paid $5,000 in legal fees in an unsuccessful patent defence related to the patent acquired on 1 May, which, as a result of the lawsuit, now appears to be questionable in its revenue-generating capacity.

**Required:**

Give the journal entry that Jenny should make for each of the above transactions.

★★ **A9-27 Disposal of Capital Assets—Interpretation:** Electronic Solutions Company (ESC) sells a machine on 1 June 20X5, for $208,500. ESC incurred $3,000 of removal and selling costs on disposal. The machine cost $430,000 when it was purchased on 2 January 20X2. Its estimated residual value and useful life were $60,000 and eight years, respectively. ESC uses straight-line depreciation and records annual depreciation on 31 December. ESC takes a half-year of depreciation in the year of acquisition and disposal.

**Required:**

1. Provide the journal entries needed to record the disposal. Depreciation for 20X5 has not yet been recorded.

2. How would the gain or loss in (1) be affected if the machine were scrapped (zero market value)?

3. Provide an interpretation of the gain or loss in (1) for someone with little or no background in accounting.

4. Would the gain or loss affect the cash flow statement? Explain.

★    **A9-28 Disposals:** Machinery that cost $24,000 on 1 January 20X1 was sold for $18,000 on 30 June 20X6. It was being depreciated over a 10-year life by the straight-line method, assuming its residual value would be $3,000.

A building that cost $275,000, residual value $15,000, was being depreciated over 20 years by the straight-line method. At the beginning of 20X6, when the structure was 15 years old, an additional wing was constructed at a cost of $175,000. The estimated life of the wing considered separately was 15 years, and its residual value was expected to be $5,000.

The accounting period ends 31 December.

**Required:**

1. Give all required entries to record:
   a. Sale of the equipment, including depreciation to the date of sale.
   b. The addition to the building: cash was paid.
   c. Depreciation on the building and its addition after the latter has been in use for one year.

2. Show how the building and attached wing would be reported on a balance sheet prepared immediately after entry 1(c) was recorded.

★★    **A9-29 Disposals:** VestCo recorded the following asset disposals during the year:

a. A computer system with an original cost of $35,700, 80% depreciated, was judged obsolete during the period and scrapped.

b. Automotive equipment, a large truck with an original cost of $50,800, 60% depreciated, was exchanged for a smaller truck. The smaller truck had a fair value of $25,000. The smaller truck will be used for the same general functions, but it is hoped that it will be more efficient. The larger used truck had a fair value of $23,000, and VestCo paid $2,000 in the exchange.

c. Vestco sold machinery with an original cost of $50,000 for $45,000 cash at the end of the year. It had held the machinery for three years. Originally, Vestco had planned to hold the machinery for eight years, and charged straight-line depreciation, with an estimate of a $10,000 salvage value. At the beginning of the second year, Vestco had spent $2,000 on routine maintenance of this machine, and another $7,000 to build a special base for it in the plant that improved its efficiency. The base is now worthless.

d. A trademark, with an amortized cost of $12,000, representing primarily unamortized legal fees, was sold for $86,500 cash.

e. Vestco sold a piece of land with an original cost of $180,000 during the period. It accepted 20,000 common shares of the purchasing company, $30,000 in cash, and a five-year non-interest bearing note that requires end-of-year payments of $50,000 per year for five years. The market interest rate is 7%. The purchaser's shares are widely traded in the stock market, and have had a market value of about $2 per share in the last 12 months, but have ranged from $1.10 to $5 in a volatile market. The land has been appraised a number of times over the years, with values ranging from $220,000 to $310,000.

**Required:**

1. Provide journal entries to record the disposal transactions listed above. Record the note receivable in (e) using the net method.

2. What would appear in the investing activities section of the cash flow statement as a result of each of these transactions?

★★   **A9-30 Capital Asset Exchanges:** Required: Complete the table below.

| Transaction | Value of New Asset on the Balance Sheet | Amount on the Income Statement. Indicate If a Gain or a Loss. If No Gain or Loss Is Recorded, Enter "Zero" |
| --- | --- | --- |
| FST Company exchanges a machine that cost $4,000 and has accumulated amortization of $3,560 for a similar machine. FST also receives $25 in the exchange. The fair market value of the old asset is $750. The fair market value of the new asset is $725. There is no commercial substance to the transaction. | | |
| GYT Company exchanges a machine that cost $4,000 and has accumulated amortization of $2,560 for a similar machine. GYT also receives $25 in the exchange. The fair market value of the old asset is $750. The fair market value of the new asset is $725. There is no commercial substance to the transaction. | | |
| HRT Company pays $250 and exchanges a machine that cost $2,000 and has accumulated amortization of $1,400 for a similar machine. The fair market value of the old asset is $435. The fair market value of the new asset is $680. The transaction has commercial substance. | | |
| LKC Company pays $250 and exchanges a machine that cost $3,000 and has accumulated amortization of $1,900 for a similar machine. The fair market value of the old asset is undeterminable. The fair market value of the new asset is $690. The transaction has commercial substance. | | |
| AML Company pays $500 and exchanges a machine that cost $9,000 and has accumulated amortization of $8,400 for a similar machine. The fair market value of the new asset is $1,580. The transaction has commercial substance. | | |

(Judy Cumby, adapted)

**A9-31 Capital Asset Exchanges—Four Situations:** Ricardo Heavy Hauling has some earth-moving equipment that cost $288,000; accumulated amortization is $192,000. Ricardo traded equipment with another construction company. The fair value of Ricardo's old equipment is estimated to be $150,000, and the fair value of the equipment being acquired is estimated to be $190,000. Four different possible scenarios are presented below:

a. In addition to exchanging its old equipment, Ricardo pays $24,000 cash. The characteristics of Ricardo's operating cash flow will change as a result of the exchange. The fair value of the old equipment is the more reliable estimate.

b. Assume the same facts as in (a) above, except that the exchange will not significantly alter Ricardo's cash flows.

c. The new equipment will perform essentially the same tasks as the old equipment. The estimate of the fair value of the new equipment is the more reliable of the two estimates. The exchange is a straight swap and no cash changes hands.

d. The new equipment has very different functions than the old equipment. The new equipment will permit Ricardo to attract new business that it had previously been unable to obtain. The fair value estimate of the new equipment is the more reliable of the two estimates. The exchange is a straight swap and no cash changes hands.

**Required:**
For each scenario, prepare the journal entry to record the exchange.

 **A9-32 Asset Exchange—Two Transactions:**

a. A large truck, which cost Company A $100,000 ($60,000 accumulated depreciation), has a market resale value of $70,000. The truck is traded to a dealer, plus a cash payment of $20,000, for a new truck that will perform essentially the same services as the old truck, but will look a lot nicer to the customers. The new truck has a list price of $95,000, although discounts of 3% to 4% may be negotiable.

b. Rochester Shipping Company received a new ferry that has a normal purchase price of $1.30 million. In exchange, the company gave the vendor a parcel of land and a building located on the waterfront. The market value of the land and building is $1.15 million. The land cost $300,000; the building cost $700,000 and is 30% depreciated. The vendor will use the land and building to operate a maintenance facility. The new ferry will enable Rochester Shipping to launch a new ferry service across Lake Ontario. The ferry was available because the buyer for whom it had been built went bankrupt and was unable to take delivery. The boat remained unsold for two years before Rochester was able to negotiate the exchange. Because the boat had been dormant for so long, it needed some upgrading and maintenance. Rochester agreed to pay for the necessary work, which was estimated to cost $350,000.

**Required:**
Prepare the journal entry to record each of these two independent transactions.

 **A9-33 Repairs and Other Expenditures:** Aries Corporation has various transactions in 20X6:

a. Plant maintenance was done, at a cost of $26,700.

b. The entire manufacturing facility was repainted at a cost of $34,900.

c. The roof on the manufacturing facility was replaced at a cost of $66,200. At the same time, various upgrades were done to the electrical systems at a cost of $43,800. Neither of these transactions increased the life of the manufacturing facility, although the safety of the facility was enhanced. The cost of the original roof and the replaced wiring is not known.

d. The company bought a piece of machinery at an auction at a price of $50,500. The machinery had an appraised value of $59,000, so Aries was pleased to get this bargain.

The company knew that the machine had to be painted and tuned up. Harmonized sales tax of 14% was paid on the purchase price.

e. The machine was delivered to Aries' manufacturing facility. The freight bill was $2,700.

f. The machine was painted and tuned up, at a cost of $4,100. In the process of the tune-up, it was discovered that the machine needed additional unexpected repairs that were done at a cost of $8,000.

**Required:**

Provide journal entries to record the transactions listed above. Justify your decisions. All items were acquired for cash.

---

★★ **A9-34 Replacements and Repairs:** The plant asset records of Stavros Company reflected the following at the beginning of the current year:

| | |
|---|---|
| Plant building (residual value, $60,000; estimated useful life, 20 years) | $300,000 |
| Accumulated depreciation, plant building | (180,000) |
| Machinery (residual value, $60,000; estimated useful life, 10 years) | 360,000 |
| Accumulated depreciation, machinery | (180,000) |

During the current year ending 31 December the following transactions (summarized) relating to the above accounts were completed:

1. Expenditures for non-recurring, relatively large repairs that tend to increase economic utility but not the economic lives of assets:

| | |
|---|---|
| Plant building | $90,000 |
| Machinery | 30,000 |

2. Replacement of original electrical wiring system of plant building (original cost, $36,000; 75% amortized), $58,000.

3. Additions:

| | |
|---|---|
| Plant building—added small wing to plant building to accommodate new equipment acquired; wing has useful life of 18 years and no residual value | 108,000 |
| Machinery—added special protection devices to 10 machines; devices are attached to the machines and will have to be replaced every three years (no residual value) | 20,000 |

4. Outlays for maintenance parts, labour, and so on to keep assets in normal working condition:

| | |
|---|---|
| Plant building | 31,000 |
| Machinery | 29,600 |

**Required:**

Give appropriate entries to record transactions (1) through (4). Explain the basis underlying your decisions. Indicate the amortization period, when appropriate.

---

★★★ **A9-35 Comprehensive Capital Asset Issues:** Information available for Crosby Limited in 20X4, when the market interest rate was 9%:

1. Land A was exchanged for Land B. There was no commercial substance to the transaction. Crosby estimated that Land A was worth $500,000, and Land B was worth $450,000, and so received $50,000 to complete the exchange.

2. Machine X was purchased on 1 April 20X4 for $560,000, on terms of 3/10, n/30. The potential discount was not taken. Machine A had to be repaired before use at a cost of $40,000.

3. Asset M was purchased on 1 December 20X4, for $118,000 in cash, and Crosby understands that it will cost $50,000 for site restoration costs when the asset is dismantled in eight years' time.

4. Asset S was traded for Asset T on 1 January 20X4. The trade had commercial substance and Crosby received $34,000 cash in addition to Asset T in the swap. Asset S was appraised at $90,000 prior to the sale.

5. Machine F was purchased on 1 June 20X4 and Crosby paid $67,800 in cash and signed a $200,000, five-year, no-interest note payable.

**Required:**

Complete the blanks in the table below.

| Asset | Cost | Expected residual value | Accumulated Amortization 31 December 20X3 | Gain on Exchange |
|---|---|---|---|---|
| Land A | $365,000 | n/a | n/a | ? |
| Land B | ? | n/a | n/a | n/a |
| Machine X | ? | $25,000 | 0 | n/a |
| Asset M | ? | $12,400 | 0 | n/a |
| Asset S | 135,000 | $25,700 | $78,300 | ? |
| Asset T | ? | $15,600 | 0 | n/a |
| Machine F | ? | $20,000 | 0 | n/a |

n/a = not applicable

---

★★    **A9-36 Goodwill:** On 30 June 20X5, Backlog Software Limited purchased the net assets of Sigma Software Incorporated for cash. Sigma had been operating at a loss. Sigma's balance

sheet on 30 June 20X5 was quite simple:

| | |
|---|---|
| Accounts receivable (net) | $105,000 |
| Computer equipment (net) | 235,000 |
| Total assets | $340,000 |
| | |
| Bank overdraft | $165,000 |
| Accounts payable and accrued liabilities | 205,000 |
| Common shares | 100,000 |
| Retained earnings (deficit) | (130,000) |
| Total liabilities and shareholders' equity | $340,000 |

Backlog's net assets changed by the following amounts as the result of the purchase:

| | Dr./(Cr.) |
|---|---|
| Cash | $(1,185,000) |
| Accounts receivable (net) | 105,000 |
| Computer equipment (net) | 115,000 |
| Software acquisition cost | 870,000 |
| Goodwill | 300,000 |
| Accounts payable and accrued liabilities | (205,000) |

**Required:**

1. What were the fair values of Sigma's assets and liabilities at the date of the purchase? How much did Backlog pay for Sigma's net assets?

2. Why would a purchaser record some of the purchase price as goodwill when the purchased company had been losing money?

**A9-37 Goodwill Calculation:** During 20X4, the Evergreen Corporation entered into negotiations to buy Pine Company. During December 20X4, a final cash purchase price of $267,000 was agreed on. Evergreen will acquire all assets and liabilities of Pine Company, except for the existing cash balances of Pine.

The 31 December 20X4 balance sheet prepared by Pine Company is shown below in column (a), and the revised market values added later by Evergreen Corporation are shown in column (b).

### PINE COMPANY BALANCE SHEET

| At 31 December 20X4 | (a)<br>Book Values<br>of Pine Co. | (b)<br>Market Values Developed<br>by Evergreen Corp. |
|---|---|---|
| *Assets* | | |
| Cash | $ 20,000 | not applicable |
| Accounts receivable (net) | 58,000 | $ 54,000 |
| Inventory | 160,000 | 90,000 |
| Property, plant, and equipment (net) | 309,000 | 285,000 |
| Land | 11,000 | 40,000 |
| Franchise (unamortized balance) | 19,000 | 21,000 |
| Total | $577,000 | |
| | | |
| *Liabilities and shareholders' equity* | | |
| Current liabilities | $ 37,000 | 37,000 |
| Bonds payable | 200,000 | 200,000 |
| Shareholders' equity | 340,000 | not applicable |
| Total | $577,000 | |

**Required:**

1. Compute the amount of goodwill purchased by Evergreen Corporation.

2. Give the entry for Evergreen Corporation to record the purchase of Pine Company.

★★★ **A9-38 Cash Flow Statement:** The following items have been extracted from the 20X3 financial statements of MC Limited:

*From the balance sheet*

| | 20X3 | 20X2 |
|---|---|---|
| Machinery | $172,600 | $145,600 |
| Accumulated amortization, machinery | (65,000) | (58,000) |
| Equipment | 350,000 | 124,000 |
| Accumulated amortization, equipment | (71,200) | (84,600) |
| Buildings | 276,800 | 246,000 |
| Accumulated amortization, buildings | (104,600) | (134,000) |

*From the 20X3 income statement*

| | | |
|---|---|---|
| Loss on disposal of equipment | $ 3,500 | |
| Loss on write-off of building components | 6,700 | |
| Amortization ($25,000 on machinery, $10,400<br>on equipment, and $9,600 on the building) | 45,000 | |

**ADDITIONAL INFORMATION:**

1. Equipment with a market value of $36,500 was donated by a local business to encourage manufacturing activity.

2. Equipment costing $200,000 was purchased. It was eligible for a $30,000 government grant that was credited directly to the equipment account.

3. Equipment with a cost of $58,800 and a net book value of $35,000 was sold at a loss during the year.

4. Machinery with a cost of $38,000 and a net book value of $20,000 was traded for similar equipment that had a market value of $22,000. No cash was exchanged in the transaction.

5. Buildings were renovated during the year. The old roof and electrical work, with a cost of $45,700, and accumulated depreciation of $39,000, were written off and replaced at a cost of $76,500. Further repairs of $12,500 were expensed.

6. Machinery with a fair market value of $45,000 was acquired in exchange for common shares.

7. Additional equipment was acquired for cash.

**Required:**

Prepare cash flow statement disclosures based on the above information. The company uses the indirect method to present cash flows from operations.

---

**A9-39 Government Assistance (Appendix):** On 1 July 20X4, Theriout Corporation acquired a manufacturing plant in Cape Breton for $1,750,000. The plant, employing 50 workers, began operation immediately, and is expected to be in operation for 16 years with no residual value. In connection with the purchase, the following government assistance was received:

a. Theriout received an investment tax credit of 20% of the purchase price. The company has sufficient taxable income from other sources to use the tax credit in 20X4.

b. Theriout received a loan from the provincial government to help buy the capital assets, in the amount of $1,200,000. The loan need not be repaid as long as the plant operates for at least 10 years, and employs an average of 25 people each year. Theriout is optimistic about the prospects for the plant, but is mindful of the high rate of business failure in Cape Breton.

**Required:**

1. Provide two acceptable ways to record the investment tax credit. Explain the reporting ramifications of the alternatives—that is, what is the difference between the financial statement presentations?

2. Provide the entry to record the loan. Explain your choice of entry.

3. How much net depreciation expense on the manufacturing plant would be recorded in the year ended 31 December 20X4? Provide calculations.

---

**A9-40 Government Assistance (Appendix):** The Gysbers Company Limited has embarked on a two-year pollution-control program that will require the purchase of two smokestack scrubbers costing a total of $600,000. One scrubber will be bought in 20X5, and one in 20X6. These scrubbers qualify for an investment tax credit of 20%. In addition, the federal government will lend Gysbers $100,000 for each scrubber installed. Provided that emissions are reduced 95% by the end of 20X8, the loans will be forgiven. The federal funds are received as the expenditures are made. If the emission standards are not met, the loan will have to be repaid. In 20X5, it was impossible to predict the success that the company would have with the scrubbers.

Gysbers will depreciate the devices over 20 years, straight line (no residual value), and will take a full year's depreciation in the year installed. The purchase and installation schedule is as follows:

| | | Cost |
|---|---|---|
| January 20X5 | Scrubber 1 | $300,000 |
| January 20X6 | Scrubber 2 | 300,000 |
| Total | | $600,000 |

**Required:**

1. Prepare journal entries to record the purchase of Scrubber 1 and Scrubber 2, and the receipt of the federal loans and investment tax credits. The company wishes to record the investment tax credits in a separate deferred credit account, and has enough taxable income in 20X5 and 20X6 to utilize the tax credits.

2. Prepare journal entries to record depreciation and amortization for the year ending 31 December 20X6.

3. Prepare a partial balance sheet showing the relevant information regarding the pollution control devices as at 31 December 20X6.

4. Assume that after testing in early 20X9, it is found that the emissions have been reduced only 85%. After negotiations, it was agreed that 45% of the loans will be repaid to the government in February 20X9. The balance of the loan will be forgiven. Prepare the journal entries to record the repayment and reclassification in 20X9.

## CHAPTER 10

# Amortization and Impairment

## INTRODUCTION

AOL Time Warner, the world's largest media and Internet company, recently recorded $60 billion in capital asset writedowns. The assets were written down following revision of earnings forecasts. Original forecasts had promised earnings growth of 20 to 30%; the revised figures were in the 8 to 12% range. When amortizable assets are written down, amortization in future years is decreased, enhancing future earnings. At the time of the writedown, there was speculation in the financial press that AOL's incoming CEO might prefer more conservative reporting to "promise a lot less and deliver more" in earnings.

Management chooses amortization methods. As well, management assesses the future economic benefit of capital assets and decides whether the assets should be written down as *impaired*. The primary emphasis in this chapter is on the *judgement* issues in post-acquisition capital asset accounting. Management's many estimates and choices must be viewed in the context of financial reporting objectives, as well as the more theoretical factors that influence choice.

There also are occasions when assets (and liabilities) of a company may be written *up*. Previously written-down held-for-sale assets (relating to discontinued operations) can be restored to their pre-writedown value in subsequent periods. The flexibility to write assets down and up, as long as reasonably justifiable at the time, gives managers flexibility in their quest to "manage earnings."

Finally, there are times when the assets of a company can be completely revalued, thereby establishing a new basis of accounting for those assets. Since assets may be revalued upward only in very limited circumstances, we will discuss *comprehensive revaluation* in an Appendix rather than in the main body of the chapter.

## REVIEW OF DEFINITIONS

A review of terminology is probably the best place to start. *Capital assets*, both tangible and intangible, produce revenue through use rather than through resale. They can be viewed as quantities of *economic service potential* to be consumed over time in the earning of revenues.

Accounting principles call for recognizing expense when the future economic benefit of an asset declines. As most assets are used, their future benefit declines. Amortization is an attempt to recognize the declining future benefit on a systematic and rational basis. Amortization is not intended to mimic the decline in market value of an asset—only its declining future benefit. Alternatively, amortization can be viewed as *matching* the costs of capital assets against revenue over their useful lives. The basic definitions are as follows:

- **Amortization** is the periodic allocation of the cost of any capital asset, tangible or intangible, as well as any long-term deferred charge (e.g., development costs). Amortization is a broad term that includes both depreciation and depletion. Accounting standards generally refer to "amortization" because it is the all-encompassing term.
- **Depreciation** is a term often used to mean amortization of tangible capital assets.
- **Depletion** may be used to describe amortization of the costs of acquiring and developing natural resources.
- **Residual value** is the estimated net recoverable amount from disposal or trade-in of the asset at the end of its estimated *useful* life. It is the portion of an asset's acquisition cost that is not consumed through use.
- **Salvage value** is the estimated net recoverable value of the asset at the end of its *physical* life.
- **Amortizable cost** is total capitalized asset cost *minus* estimated residual value—the total amount of amortization to be recognized over the useful life of the asset.
- **Net book value** (**carrying value**) is an asset's original cost *plus* any capitalized post-acquisition costs *minus* accumulated amortization to date.
- **Impairment** arises when the fair value of an asset is less than its carrying value.

## NATURE OF AMORTIZATION

*Amortization* is the general term that applies to the interperiod allocation of the cost of any capital asset. What is amortization *not*? There are many misconceptions:

- Accumulated amortization does not represent cash set aside for replacement of assets.
- Amortization does not imply the creation of a separate cash fund for asset replacement.
- Amortization does not measure the decline in market value during the period, and net book value does not equal market value.

In everyday conversation, people often use depreciation to describe a decline in market value—for example, "A new car will depreciate by 25% as soon as you drive it off the dealer's lot." The accounting meaning of the term "depreciate" is quite different. Generally speaking, financial statements track the cost of capital assets, not market value.

### The Conceptual Basis of Amortization

The amount of amortization recognized is not linked to the decline in an asset's utility or market value in a given period. However, the *inevitable eventual* decline in value justifies periodic recognition of amortization. The decline in utility of capital assets is caused by:

- Physical factors, mainly usage (wear and tear from operations, action of time and the elements, and deterioration and decay); and
- Obsolescence (the result of new technology).

Assets rendered obsolete are often in good condition and still capable of supplying the service originally expected of them. Technological advances may have rendered their operating costs uneconomic. Obsolescence also occurs when facility expansion renders certain

**residual value**

the estimated net recoverable amount from disposal or trade-in of an asset at the end of its estimated useful life

**salvage value**

an asset's fair value at the end of its life; often zero or scrap only

**impairment**

the loss of a portion of the asset's utility or value; a permanent reduction in value necessitating loss recognition assets unusable under new operating conditions or when demand for the product or service supplied by the asset declines.

Technological change does not automatically mean that older equipment is obsolete, however. If the older equipment meets the *present needs* of the company, obsolescence is not a factor. For example, in the computer industry, new computer chips substantially increase computer speeds and capabilities. For many companies, continual upgrades to state-of-the art hardware are not cost-effective. Older computers will still run required software and they are not obsolete. Of course, software upgrades sometimes require hardware upgrades as well, and this is the point at which obsolescence becomes a factor.

## The Requirement to Recognize Amortization Expense

Generally, capital assets must be amortized. Why?

- Amortization is an allocation of capital cost. Operations must bear this cost as a cost of assets used during the period. The general requirement for amortization is based on the declining future benefit of a long-lived asset. Recognizing this decline in the asset's future usefulness will match the costs of providing services to the revenue generated.
- Amortization is justifiable based on an *eventual* decline in market value, often caused by obsolescence.

There are three asset categories that do not have to be amortized:

**1. Land** Land is not at risk due to obsolescence nor does it suffer from wear and tear. Therefore, land is not amortized. We hope you find this intuitively appealing! Of course, if the land is a mining site, then the situation is far different and depletion would be recorded.

**2. Intangible Capital Assets with an Indefinite Life** If an asset will continue to provide service over the foreseeable future without its future benefit being reduced, it has **indefinite life**. Intangible assets with an indefinite useful life should not be amortized.

For example, a trademark can legally and effectively be protected forever. If the product associated with the trademark has indefinite sales potential, the trademark would not be amortized. At some point, the situation might change and the asset may decline in value, but the value of the trademark does not decline with use. Indeed, in an economic sense, a trademark can increase in value the more it is used as it becomes better known and trusted by customers.

"Indefinite" does not mean "infinite," however. Trademarks sometimes become outdated and must be updated or replaced. CBC and Air Canada have both updated or replaced their trademark designs in recent years. The old designs may have no more useful economic life, at which point they must be written down. Some companies amortize the costs of acquiring or designing a trademark even though the trademark has an endless legal life because the company recognizes that the trademark may lose its effectiveness over time.

Useful lives have to be reviewed regularly, and if the useful life becomes limited, amortization of these assets must commence. Intangible assets that are not amortized must be reviewed for impairment on an annual basis.

**3. Goodwill** The useful life of goodwill is assumed to be indefinite. Goodwill is not amortized, but is subject to an annual review for impairment. We will discuss the goodwill impairment test in this chapter.

## CONCEPT REVIEW

1. What are the main causes of the decline in value or usefulness of plant assets over time?

2. Why is amortization expense not necessarily an accurate measure of the decline in value of capital assets?

3. Which assets are not amortized? Why?

## ACCOUNTING POLICY CHOICE

The only general requirement for an amortization method is that it should be *rational and systematic*. The choices are:

1. *Based on equal allocation to each time period*—the straight-line (SL) method. This is used when the loss of service potential is largely a function of time, or when the utilization of the asset is expected to be fairly constant over its useful life. Straight-line also is generally used as a "default" method; if the company isn't sure what the usage pattern or future benefit decline will be, SL is the simplest method to use.

2. *Based on inputs and outputs* (variable charge).
   a. Service-hours (SH) method; or
   b. Productive output (PO), or units-of-production, method.

   These methods are used when there is a physical capacity constraint; the more intensely the asset is used, the faster its future benefit declines. It also is used when the asset's utilization is apt to vary significantly from period to period and its utilization can be measured reliably, such as for equipment used in mining operations.

3. *Accelerated methods* (decreasing charge).
   a. Declining-balance (DB) methods; or
   b. Sum-of-the-years'-digits (SYD) method.

   These are used particularly for assets that are subject to rapid obsolescence such as computer equipment and software, or for assets that will see heavy use in the earlier years and declining use as they get older.

A fourth category of amortization is *present-value methods*, the primary type of which is the sinking-fund method. These methods result in *increasing* amortization charges. This method has been used primarily in the real property development industry but has fallen out of use. We will not illustrate this method in this chapter.

For limited-life intangible assets, when the pattern of economic benefits cannot be reliably determined, a straight-line amortization method normally is used.

### Conceptual Analysis

In theory, at least, the amortization method should describe the nature and use of the asset. For example, assume that a delivery truck has an estimated useful life of five years or 300,000 kilometres. Amortization based on distance driven might yield a more accurate matching of expense and revenue than amortization based on useful life in years. Based on this reasoning, the methods based on usage appear to be the most logical, unless obsolescence is a major factor, in which case straight line is appealing.

However, GAAP allows choice with few guidelines: all methods are rational and systematic, and an evaluation of the nature of use of an asset can be subjective. Why aren't amortization methods narrowed down? The reason is that there is a lack of one "correct method," really. The amount of revenue or cash produced by the use of one specific capital asset is usually impossible to determine clearly. Revenues are not generated by assets used in isolation. Rather, they are produced by a number of assets and people working together. It is impossible to associate specific revenues (benefits) to specific assets, and thus impossible to allocate the cost of most operational assets on the basis of benefits or revenues.

As an allocation, amortization is *incorrigible*—it cannot be supported or refuted without question.[1] If you can't establish one right way, then all rational and systematic methods are

---

[1] The *incorrigibility* of accounting allocations was definitively demonstrated by Professor Arthur L. Thomas (McMaster University) in two research studies published by the American Accounting Association in the series *Studies in Accounting Research: #3: The Allocation Problem in Financial Accounting Theory* (1969), and *#9: The Allocation Problem: Part Two* (1974). The conclusions of these studies were not greeted warmly by many accountants who preferred to believe in the "truth" of their allocations, but no one has ever been able to demonstrate that allocations are not inherently arbitrary.

equally acceptable. Companies tend to let corporate reporting objectives, rather than pattern of use, dictate policy choice. This does not do wonders for comparability.

Studies of the U.S. stock market have suggested that investors are not fooled by accounting policy choices that do not have any impact on cash flows. That is, investors are smart enough to see the fundamental equivalency between two identical firms, earning identical return but reporting different incomes only because of different amortization policies, at least in the short run. However, that's just one group of users. Most Canadian companies are not traded on large, well-disciplined, stock exchanges.

### Policy Choice in Practice

*Financial Reporting in Canada 2006* reports that of 200 surveyed public companies, 105 use straight-line amortization for all of their property, plant, and equipment (PPE). Another 80 companies use straight line for some of their assets and other methods for the rest. In total, 185 or 92.5% of the companies use straight-line amortization for at least some of their PPE.

By comparison, 53 companies used units-of-production methods for some of their PPE and 37 companies used declining balance for some PPE assets. Straight line clearly is the dominant method. Simple is often best!

### Factors Influencing Choice

How do companies pick an accounting amortization policy? Here is a summary of factors considered:

- *Nature and use of asset.* To promote matching, the pattern of usage is evaluated to establish the most logical amortization pattern. The pattern of usage is a good indicator of the pattern of revenue generated.
- *Corporate reporting objectives.* On a situation-by-situation basis, it is important to analyze the various elements that drive reporting objectives. Is there a bonus based on net income? Is the entity regulated? Is it held under restrictive loan covenants governing debt-to-equity ratios, profitability, etc? These factors have a powerful impact on the accounting policies chosen.
- *Industry norms.* Comparability is an important qualitative characteristic of financial reporting. Companies' financial statements are used by investors, creditors, and others to assess their performance relative to their competition. Using the same amortization method helps. Amortization methods—such as sinking-fund amortization for rental properties and units of production for natural resources—become generally accepted within an industry.
- *Parent company preferences.* Is the company a subsidiary of another company (the parent)? If so, its financial statements will be combined, or *consolidated,* at the end of the fiscal year. These consolidated financial statements are more meaningful if all constituents follow the same accounting policies, and thus the parent company often dictates key policies to its subsidiaries. A lot of Canadian companies are wholly owned subsidiaries of foreign parents (usually American). Those subsidiaries usually do what their parents tell them, which may include accounting methods not widely used by Canadian-owned enterprises. (Of course, like all children, the subsidiaries sometimes disobey their parents.)
- *Simplified reporting.* Many smaller firms don't really care what amount of amortization is booked, but are interested in keeping their financial statements simple. Therefore, it seems logical to use an accounting policy that results in amortization that coincides with the required tax treatment (which generally is a form of declining-balance amortization, as we'll see in Appendix 1 to this chapter).
- *Accounting information system costs.* The company must keep detailed information about acquisition costs, post-acquisition costs, useful life, residual value, and accumulated amortization. Which system is the least complex?

The latitude in selection of amortization methods and the variety of estimates of useful life and residual value are at odds with the uniformity and consistency objectives of financial reporting. The large dollar amount of amortization expense reported, combined with the inherently arbitrary nature of amortization, results in a potentially difficult comparison problem for financial statement users.

## Estimates Required

Amortization methods require that the preparer make the following estimates:

1. Acquisition cost

2. Useful life

3. Residual value

**Acquisition Cost** At first glance, acquisition cost may appear to be a solid amount, not an estimate. In some cases, the cost of an asset is readily determinable. However, acquisition cost often is a bit of an approximation even for tangible capital assets because ancillary acquisition costs such as excise taxes, shipping costs, installation, and start-up training costs either are estimated or ignored. Thus, the measurement of "historical cost" is governed by various policies concerning capitalization (versus expensing), as we discussed in the previous chapter.

**Useful Life** An estimate of useful life for a tangible asset requires assumptions about potential obsolescence, severity of use, and adequate maintenance. It is especially difficult to estimate the useful life of an intangible asset. Often, the real question is how long the intangible asset will be used or can generate revenue. It's important to take a hard look at many factors:

1. The expected use of the asset;

2. The legal life of an intangible asset (see Exhibit 10-1) plus any renewal provisions;

3. The effects of economic factors, along with demand and competition;

4. Potential obsolescence;

5. The level of maintenance expenditures required (high maintenance implies an end to useful life); and

6. The expected use of another asset or process that is related to the intangible asset (for instance, a patent for a process versus the machinery that runs the process).

**Residual Value** To estimate residual value, consideration is given to the costs of dismantling, restoring, and disposing of the retired asset. Future removal and site restoration costs also reduce residual value and can be material. These include all costs to dismantle and restore a property. These costs are particularly important for natural resources. For example,

### EXHIBIT 10-1

### LEGAL LIFE OF CERTAIN INTANGIBLE ASSETS

| | |
|---|---|
| Patent | 20 years from date granted but registration period is also covered |
| Industrial design registration | Five years; renewable for a further five years |
| Trademark | 20 years; renewable for infinite successive periods |
| Franchise | Unlimited unless specified in contract with franchisor |
| Copyright | Life of the author plus 50 years |

if the estimated realizable value upon retirement of an asset is $2,500 and estimated dismantling and selling costs are $500, the net residual value is $2,000.

In practice, the residual value for a tangible asset is often assumed to be zero. This is logical when an asset will be held almost until the end of its physical life and removal cost is low.

An *intangible* asset usually has a residual value of zero. There would have to be an established market for similar intangible assets, or a specific sale agreement, to justify a residual value higher than zero.

### Amortization Period

Amortization is not recognized (that is, useful life does not begin) until the asset is in its intended condition and location and is contributing to revenue. When facilities are temporarily idle, straight line and accelerated methods continue because these methods are based on the passage of time, not use. Continued recognition of amortization reflects increasing obsolescence and reduced future economic usefulness of the asset.

When a company permanently stops using a capital asset, the asset is reclassified as **held for sale** and amortization stops. If the asset's fair value is less than its carrying value, the asset is written down to its fair value. The loss is recognized in income. We will discuss the accounting for held-for-sale capital assets in a separate section at the end of this chapter.

Assets should not be amortized below residual value under any method or system. Although declining-balance methods do not use residual value in calculating periodic amortization expense, a determination should be made at the end of each accounting period to ensure that book value is higher than residual value. Where the residual value of individual assets is relatively small, however, this test often is not performed and the assets are amortized to zero.

## CONCEPT REVIEW

1. What is the most popular method of amortization in Canada?
2. Name three factors that influence management's choice of amortization policy.
3. What estimates must be made before a capital asset can be amortized?

## AMORTIZATION METHODS

Exhibit 10-2 summarizes the amortization formulas for six common amortization methods. Each of the six amortization methods will be illustrated in the following sections, using the data shown in Exhibit 10-3. Exhibit 10-4 shows amortization schedules for the four most common methods.

### Straight-Line Method

The **straight-line (SL) method** is based on the assumption that an asset provides equivalent service, or value in use, each year of its life. The SL method relates amortization directly to the passage of time rather than to the asset's use, resulting in a constant amount of amortization recognized per time period. The formula for computing periodic SL amortization, with its application to the asset in Exhibit 10-3, is:

Yearly SL amortization

= (Acquisition cost − Residual value) ÷ Estimated useful life in years

= ($6,600 − $600) ÷ 5

= $1,200 per year

---

### EXHIBIT 10-2

## AMORTIZATION FORMULAS

**Straight line (SL):**
Annual SL amortization = (Acquisition cost − Residual value)
÷ Estimated useful life in years

**Service hours:**
Amortization rate per service hour = (Acquisition cost − Residual value)
÷ Estimated service life in hours

Annual service-hour amortization = Amortization rate per service hour
× Hours of usage

**Productive output:**
Amortization rate per unit of output = (Acquisition cost − Residual value)
÷ Estimated productive output in units

Annual productive-output amortization = Amortization rate per unit of
output × Units produced

**Declining balance (DB):**
Annual DB amortization = (Acquisition cost − Accumulated amortization)
× DB rate

**Sum of the years digits (SYD):**
Annual SYD amortization = (Acquisition cost − Residual value) × SYD Fraction

---

The SL method is logically appealing. It is especially appropriate for a tangible asset when the use of the asset is essentially the same each period, and repairs and maintenance expenditures are constant over the useful life. The method is less appropriate for assets whose decline in service potential or benefits produced relates not to the passage of time but rather to other variables, such as units produced or hours in service.

---

### EXHIBIT 10-3

## DATA USED TO ILLUSTRATE AMORTIZATION METHODS

| | |
|---|---:|
| Acquisition cost, 1 January 20X1 | $ 6,600 |
| Residual value | 600 |
| Estimated useful life: | |
|   Years | 5 |
|   Service hours | 20,000 |
|   Productive output in units | 10,000 |

| Activity | Service Hours | Units Produced |
|---|---:|---:|
| 20X1 | 3,800 | 1,800 |
| 20X2 | 4,000 | 2,000 |
| 20X3 | 4,500 | 2,400 |
| 20X4 | 4,200 | 1,800 |
| 20X5 | 3,500 | 2,000 |
| | 20,000 | 10,000 |

**EXHIBIT 10-4**

## AMORTIZATION SCHEDULES—FOUR COMMON METHODS

### Straight-Line Method

| Year | Amortization Expense | Accumulated Amortization | Cost | Net Book Value |
|---|---|---|---|---|
| 1 January 20X1 | | | $6,600 | $6,600 |
| 31 December 20X1 | $1,200 | $1,200 | 6,600 | 5,400 |
| 31 December 20X2 | 1,200 | 2,400 | 6,600 | 4,200 |
| 31 December 20X3 | 1,200 | 3,600 | 6,600 | 3,000 |
| 31 December 20X4 | 1,200 | 4,800 | 6,600 | 1,800 |
| 31 December 20X5 | 1,200 | 6,000 | 6,600 | 600 (residual) |
| Total | $6,000 | | | |

### Service-Hours Method

| Year | Service Hours | Amortization Expense | Accumulated Amortization | Cost | Net Book Value |
|---|---|---|---|---|---|
| 1 January 20X1 | | | | $6,600 | $6,600 |
| 31 December 20X1 | 3,800 | (3,800 × $.30) = $1,140 | $1,140 | 6,600 | 5,460 |
| 31 December 20X2 | 4,000 | (4,000 × $.30) = 1,200 | 2,340 | 6,600 | 4,260 |
| 31 December 20X3 | 4,500 | (4,500 × $.30) = 1,350 | 3,690 | 6,600 | 2,910 |
| 31 December 20X4 | 4,200 | (4,200 × $.30) = 1,260 | 4,950 | 6,600 | 1,650 |
| 31 December 20X5 | 3,500 | (3,500 × $.30) = 1,050 | 6,000 | 6,600 | 600 (residual) |
| Total | 20,000 | $6,000 | | | |

### Productive-Output Method

| Year | Units Produced | Amortization Expense | Accumulated Amortization | Cost | Net Book Value |
|---|---|---|---|---|---|
| 1 January 20X1 | | | | $6,600 | $6,600 |
| 31 December 20X1 | 1,800 | (1,800 × $.60) = $1,080 | $1,080 | 6,600 | 5,520 |
| 31 December 20X2 | 2,000 | (2,000 × $.60) = 1,200 | 2,280 | 6,600 | 4,320 |
| 31 December 20X3 | 2,400 | (2,400 × $.60) = 1,440 | 3,720 | 6,600 | 2,880 |
| 31 December 20X4 | 1,800 | (1,800 × $.60) = 1,080 | 4,800 | 6,600 | 1,800 |
| 31 December 20X5 | 2,000 | (2,000 × $.60) = 1,200 | 6,000 | 6,600 | 600 (residual) |
| Total | 10,000 | $6,000 | | | |

### Declining-Balance Method

| Year | Amortization Expense | Accumulated Amortization | Cost | Net Book Value |
|---|---|---|---|---|
| 1 January 20X1 | | | $6,600 | $6,600 |
| 31 December 20X1 | (40% × $6,600) = $2,640 | $2,640 | 6,600 | 3,960 |
| 31 December 20X2 | (40% × $3,960) = 1,584 | 4,224 | 6,600 | 2,376 |
| 31 December 20X3 | (40% × $2,376) = 950 | 5,174 | 6,600 | 1,426 |
| 31 December 20X4 | (40% × $1,426) = 570 | 5,744 | 6,600 | 856 |
| 31 December 20X5 | 256* | 6,000 | 6,600 | 600 (residual) |
| Total | $6,000 | | | |

*Should be 40% of $856, or $342, but limited to $256 so that net book value does not go below residual value.*

The SL method is the most popular method, by far. Ease of use partially explains the method's popularity. It is also popular because it provides a stable, smooth amortization pattern. A relatively low amount is expensed in the asset's first year, which is popular with firms that want to maximize earnings and net assets in the short run.

For intangible assets, SL amortization must be used if the pattern of economic benefits cannot be determined.

### Methods Based on Units of Service

Amortization methods that associate periodic amortization with measurable use of capital assets include the service-hours method and productive-output method (also called the units-of-production method). These methods are rational and systematic and logically match expense and revenue if the asset's utility is measurable in terms of service time or units of output.

These methods do not relate amortization to the passage of time, as the other methods do. Amortization expense under these methods is not recorded when assets are idle, and thus they are appropriate when production volumes vary greatly from period to period, provided that obsolescence is not as much of a factor in determining useful life as wear and tear. If obsolescence is an important factor, an asset's utility decreases whether used or not, and these methods will not portray this reality.

**service-hours amortization**

a method of calculating amortization expense that bases amortization expense on current service hours used as related to total service hours expected

**Service-Hours Method**   The **service-hours (SH) method** is based on the assumption that the appropriate amortization is directly related to the amount of time the asset is in use.

Amortization rate per service-hour = (Acquisition cost − Residual value)
                    ÷ Estimated service life in hours
                  = ($6,600 − $600) ÷ 20,000 = $0.30

Yearly SH amortization, 20X1     = Amortization rate per service hour
                    × Hours used
                  = $0.30 × 3,800 = $1,140

Exhibit 10-4 illustrates the service-hours method for the life of the asset.

**productive-output (PO) amortization**

a method of calculating amortization expense that bases amortization on current production output as related to expected productive output

**Productive-Output Method**   The **productive-output (PO) method** is similar except that the number of units of output is used to measure asset use. A constant amount of amortizable cost is allocated to each unit of output as a cost of production, so annual amortization amounts fluctuate with changes in the volume of output:

Amortization rate per unit of output = (Acquisition cost − Residual value)
                     ÷ Estimated productive output in units
                   = ($6,600 − $600) ÷ 10,000 = $0.60

Yearly PO amortization, 20X1     = Amortization rate per unit of output
                    × Units produced
                  = $0.60 × 1,800 = $1,080

Exhibit 10-4 illustrates the PO method over the life of this asset.

The service-hours and productive-output methods can produce different results, depending on the ratio of machine-hours to units produced. For the asset under study, 2.11 machine-hours were required to produce one unit in 20X1 (3,800 ÷ 1,800), while in 20X2 that figure was reduced to 2.00 (4,000 ÷ 2,000), indicating a greater efficiency. The SH method, therefore, yielded slightly higher amortization per unit of output in 20X1 than in 20X2. If the yield ratio is constant, the two methods would produce identical results and the firm would choose the one that is easier to implement.

The productive-output method is commonly used to measure depletion of natural resources. For example, assume that a company incurs costs of $4,000,000 to lease, explore, and develop a mine site that is expected to produce two million tonnes of coal. The land can be sold for $500,000 after mining is finished. The depletion per tonne is $1.75: ($4,000,000 − $500,000) ÷ 2,000,000. Annual depletion is based on the actual production level. For these companies, mining equipment and even buildings are often also amortized on a units-of-production basis.

**Estimates**  A significant difficulty in usage methods is an accurate estimate of total projected activity. Annual usage data is also needed to apply the method. Often, the extra cost of this data is not worth the effort. Remember, too, that if usage is relatively constant, the result will not be materially different from the straight-line method. Another problem arises when the running time of an asset varies without a corresponding effect in the output of service. For example, the increasingly heavy traffic in urban areas causes vehicles to run many more hours per week with no increase in their productive service.

## Accelerated Amortization Methods

Accelerated amortization methods recognize greater amounts of amortization early in the useful life of capital assets and lesser amounts later. Accelerated methods are based on the assumption that newer assets produce more benefits per period because they are more productive and require less maintenance and repair. Accelerated methods match more of the acquisition cost against the revenue of these earlier periods when greater benefits are obtained. A smoother pattern of total annual operating expense is often the result, because the sum of annual amortization and maintenance expense is more constant than is likely with SL amortization. The one accelerated method that is in wide use in Canada is the declining-balance method.

**declining-balance amortization**

a method of accelerated amortization in which amortization is calculated as cost less accumulated amortization multiplied by a given constant percentage until net book value declines to residual value

**Declining-Balance Method**  The **declining-balance (DB) method** is significantly different from other methods in two ways:

1. Residual value is not subtracted from cost when computing amortization. Instead, declining-balance amortization stops when the net book value of the asset is equal to residual value.

2. The amortization rate is applied to a declining (*net*) balance rather than to a constant cost.

How do companies arrive at an amortization rate? A formula exists that can be used to find the rate that will reduce the book value of the asset to its estimated salvage value at the end of its estimated useful life, but the formula is never used in practice! Instead, firms may pick a fairly arbitrary rate, based on their assessment of useful life, on industry norms, or perhaps on corporate reporting objectives.

Another approach is to use the rates established by income tax regulations for Capital Cost Allowance (CCA). CCA is mostly a declining-balance method, but uses straight line for some types of assets. CCA doesn't work exactly the same as declining-balance amortization, but, if the same rates are used (and a half-year's depreciation is charged in the year of acquisition), the tax and book amortization are often identical and future (deferred) income tax balances are minimized as a result. The CCA system is briefly described in this chapter's Appendix 1. Tax-based rates often are used by private companies for simplicity.

Another approach to determining the rate is called **double-declining balance (DDB)** amortization, which uses a rate equal to twice the straight-line rate. For example, the asset in Exhibit 10-3 has a 20% straight-line rate (the reciprocal of the years of life; 1/5 = 20%), and so the DDB rate would be 40%. This is a fairly aggressive amortization rate—40% of the capital cost would be written off in the first year. If this capital asset is a piece of machinery, its CCA rate is set (in *Class 8*) at 20%. Amortization rates, which must be disclosed, should be reviewed by financial statement users to see if they are aggressive or not.

For our example, assume that the firm has chosen a 40% DB rate.

Annual DB amortization = (Acquisition cost − Accumulated amortization)
                          × DB rate
20X1 DB amortization   = $6,600 × 40% = $2,640
20X2 DB amortization   = ($6,600 − $2,640) × 40% = $1,584

See Exhibit 10-4 for the complete set of calculations. Notice in particular the last line, where amortization expense *stops* when accumulated amortization equals the $6,000 amortizable cost, leaving the $600 residual value intact. Thus, the maximum amortization for 20X5 is $256 ($6,000 − $5,744) rather than $342 (40% of $856).

**Sum-of-the-Years'-Digits Method**  The **sum-of-the-years'-digits (SYD) method** computes annual amortization as follows:

**sum-of-the-years'-digits (SYD) amortization**

a method of accelerated amortization where amortization is calculated by multiplying the amortizable cost by a fraction whose denominator is the sum of the years' digits

Annual SYD amortization = (Acquisition cost − Residual value) × SYD Fraction

The SYD fraction is calculated with a numerator and a denominator:

- *Numerator*. The number of years remaining in the useful life at the beginning of the period. The first year for the asset in Exhibit 10-3 will have a numerator of 5; the second year, 4; the third year, 3; and so on. The numerator always declines with each year of asset use.
- *Denominator*. The name of the method tells it all: the denominator is the sum of the years' digits. For our asset, with a five-year life, this is 15, (1 + 2 + 3 + 4 + 5).

Amortization expense in 20X1 in our example:

20X1 SYD amortization = ($6,600 − $600) × (5/15) = $2,000
20X2 SYD amortization = ($6,600 − $600) × (4/15) = $1,600

Hardly any Canadian companies use this method. It's somewhat more popular in the U.S. Canadian adopters are almost always subsidiaries of U.S. parents.

## CONCEPT REVIEW

1. When is a company most likely to use a usage-based amortization method?
2. What is *double* about double-declining balance amortization?
3. Why might a company want to use an amortization method that coincides with tax-basis capital cost allowance?

## ADDITIONAL AMORTIZATION ISSUES

Additional amortization issues include a minimum amortization test, fractional-year amortization, asset retirement obligations, and amortization systems.

## Minimum Amortization Test

Capital assets are not held for sale, but sometimes their fair market values are apparent and recording amortization seems counterintuitive. For example, assume that you're in the following situation:

| | |
|---|---|
| Asset | Apartment building |
| Expected life | An additional 20 years |
| Original cost | $3,750,000 |
| Net book value | $3,150,000 |
| Salvage at the end of 20 years | nominal; structure would have to be dismantled |
| Market value of similar buildings now, excluding land value | $4,350,000 |

Market values may be responding to increased demand for rental properties or to interest rate declines. Why should any amortization be claimed on this property, whose current fair value exceeds its book value by a significant margin? Again, refer to the rationale for amortization at the beginning of the chapter; amortization is an *allocation* of capital cost, and is still appropriate in these circumstances.

However, there's another angle: what if the company announces that it plans to hold the building for only another five years, and then sell it? The amortization formula mostly start by taking cost and subtracting the residual value, the fair value on the expected sale date. Now, it's quite possible that the fair value five years hence might still be higher than the existing net book value.

Assume that several appraisals of the real estate market, and of this building in particular, conclude that the building could be sold for something in the range of $4,400,000 in five years time, excluding land value. If the company used straight-line amortization, the calculation would go as follows:

$$(\$3,150,000 - \$4,400,000) \div 5 = -\$1,250,000 \div 5 = -\$250,000$$

(Note that the calculation starts with net book value as an amortizable cost, because the company is in the process of changing the estimate of useful life; we'll take another look at accounting changes in Chapter 20.) The amortization number produced by the formula is *negative*, but negative amortization is never recorded. Capital assets are not written *up* under Canadian standards.

Can the company avoid amortization on these grounds? Remember that the company is not committed to the sale; it can easily avoid the sale when the time comes if management doesn't like market conditions, or if management really didn't really want to sell it in the first place. The accountant is relatively powerless to prevent the manipulation of "intention." Fortunately, there is a solution. In these circumstances, Canadian accounting standards provide for *minimum amortization*, which is the larger of:

1. The cost less scrap value over the life of the asset; and

2. The cost less resale value over the useful life of the asset.

Salvage value is defined as the asset's fair value *at the end of its life*; scrap value, for our building. Residual value is the asset's fair value when the company is done with it; the $4,400,000 appraisal. Assuming scrap value is negligible, this company would have to do a second calculation, under (a) ($3,150,000 − $0) ÷ 20, or $157,500. The calculation under (b) produced zero amortization, because the result was negative. The greater amount of amortization, $157,500, would have to be recorded.

This situation is not common—it's not often that a second-hand asset is worth a lot more than its net book value. But it does sometimes happen, and minimum amortization keeps companies from dodging the amortization requirements.

### Fractional-Year Amortization

The calculations illustrated in Exhibit 10-4 assume that the company takes a full year of amortization in the year that the asset was acquired. This seems logical in the specific example, because the asset was assumed to have been purchased on 1 January. However, most capital assets are not placed in service at the beginning of a reporting period, nor do disposals occur neatly at the end of a year. Firms adjust for fractional periods in two different ways. Some compute the exact amount of amortization for each fractional period, and others apply an accounting policy **convention**. A *convention* is a standardized shortcut.

**convention**

an accepted practice adopted to simplify calculations

**Exact Calculation Approach** This approach computes the "precise" amount of amortization for each fractional period. For example, assume that an asset costing $20,000 with a residual value of $2,000 and useful life of four years is placed into service on 10 April 20X1. The firm has a calendar-year reporting cycle. The asset in question is used only 265/365 of a year in 20X1. Under SL amortization, the asset's fractional service period is applied to the annual amortization amount, as illustrated:

$$\text{Amortization expense for 20X1} = (\$20,000 - \$2,000) \times (1/4) \times (265/365)$$
$$= \$3,267$$
$$\text{Amortization expense for 20X2 through 20X4} = (\$20,000 - \$2,000) \times (1/4)$$
$$= \$4,500 \text{ per year}$$
$$\text{Amortization expense for 20X5} = (\$20,000 - \$2,000) \times (1/4) \times (100/365)$$
$$= \$1,233$$

The service-hours and productive-output methods automatically adjust for fractions of a year. The number of hours used or units produced in the partial-year period is applied to the amortization rate in the normal manner.

Using declining balance, the rate for the first year is simply the assumed annual rate times the fraction of the year during which the asset was owned. For an annual amortization rate of 40%, the first year's amortization will be $40\% \times 265/365 = 29\%$. For the following years, the rate will be the normal 40% applied to the asset's net book value at the beginning of each year:

$$\text{Recognized amortization expense}$$
$$\text{20X1 amortization} = \$20,000 \times 40\% \times 265/365 = \$5,808$$
$$\text{20X2 amortization} = (\$20,000 - \$5,808) \times .40 = \$5,677, \text{ etc.}$$

The word "exact" should not be interpreted too literally. The "exact" approach usually means that amortization is calculated only to the nearest month. Seldom will a company try to figure out depreciation to the exact day—what would be the benefit? Amortization involves selecting one from among many possible policies and applying it to amounts that are estimates. There is nothing less "precise" in accounting than amortization, and therefore it makes no sense at all to try to be highly precise about a highly arbitrary number!

**Accounting Policy Convention Approach** To avoid tedious fractional-year amortization, many firms adopt a policy convention. Examples of conventions in current use are:

1. *Half-year convention.* Under this approach, a half-year's amortization is charged on all assets acquired or disposed of during the year. The implicit assumption is that assets are

acquired throughout the year and as a result are, on average, acquired in the middle of the year.

Annual depreciation expense is the depreciation rate multiplied by the simple average of the beginning and ending balances of the asset accounts. Given that amortization is an approximation at best, this assumption is as good as any. This method also has the added convenience that it coincides with the convention used for income tax purposes in the year of acquisition.

2. *Full-first-year convention.* A full year's amortization is charged to all assets that exist at the end of the year, including those acquired throughout the year. No amortization is taken on assets disposed of during the year. This is particularly popular in group depreciation methods, which generally are based on the asset account balance at the end of the year.

This method bases depreciation expense on the ending balances. It is easily calculated without reference to transactions during the period. Since there is no depreciation in the year of an asset's disposal, last-year fractional depreciation can be completely ignored.

3. *Final-year convention.* Annual amortization is determined solely on the basis of the balance in the capital asset accounts at the *beginning* of the period. Assets disposed of during a period are depreciated for a full period, and assets purchased during a period are not depreciated that period. The underlying assumption is that assets are seldom fully productive when they are first put into service.

In this method, depreciation expense is based solely on the *opening* balances in the asset accounts. This permits rapid calculation of adjusting entries at the end of the period. When pro-forma budgeted financial statements are prepared, the amount of amortization is known with assurance, thereby avoiding unexpected (and uncontrollable) increases in overhead costs charged to operating divisions or departments.

When a company has high capital expenditures and increasing asset bases, this method tends to lower the amount of depreciation taken each period, thereby enhancing net income.

When a company reports on an interim basis, such as quarterly, these conventions may be applied to the *quarter* instead of to the *year*. For example, the half-year convention becomes the *half-quarter* convention—one-half quarter's amortization is taken on all assets acquired or disposed of during the quarter.

Regardless of the convention chosen, the same policy should be used consistently. The exact approach to fractional-year amortization should be used only if the informational advantages justify the added cost.

## Group and Composite Systems of Amortization

Unique features of certain capital assets, as well as practical considerations, may cause firms to modify the application of standard amortization methods. We call these adaptations "amortization systems" because amortization is calculated on a *group* of assets rather than on individual assets, thereby dramatically reducing accounting costs. Physical control of individual assets still must be maintained, but detailed accounting records are maintained only for each group as a whole.

There are two approaches used for grouping capital assets, depending on the characteristics of the group:

**group amortization**

the amortization of a set of similar assets on average rates designed to be statistically valid for the group as a whole

1. **Group amortization** is used for homogeneous assets. For example, a company may group all of its delivery trucks together in a single account, or may account for all of its computers as a group.

**composite amortization**

the amortization of a set of related but dissimilar assets using one composite rate

2. **Composite amortization** is used for heterogeneous assets that form a working unit. For example, a pipeline pumping station functions as a single unit, but consists of a variety of different components that have different costs, useful lives, and residual values. Individual components must be replaced as they fail or wear out in order to protect the functioning of the pumping station as a whole.

Although there is a difference in the underlying rationale between group accounts and composite accounts, the calculations are identical.

*Group accounts* work on the principle of averaging. When assets are accounted for individually, the estimates of salvage value and useful life for each asset are almost certain to be incorrect. For a group of assets as a whole, however, the law of averages can be applied. As long as the estimates are correct *on average*, the amortization will be correct.

*Composite accounts* work on the principle that it is meaningless to account individually for assets that function together as a cohesive and mutually dependent group. An assembly line can function only as long as all of its component parts are functioning properly. Even at acquisition, it may be difficult to isolate the cost of each individual part of the assembly line. To amortize each part as though it were an independent asset is to ignore the economic reality of the process. Therefore, the assembly line is accounted for (and amortized) as a single unit.

An advantage of group and composite systems is that no gains or losses are recorded on the routine disposals of assets. Gains and losses on the disposal of individual assets really are the result of estimation errors in determining amortization. Group methods, in contrast, offset the gains and losses within the capital asset group account, thereby eliminating any possibility of earnings manipulation through management's adroit timing of asset disposals.

Group and composite systems are not only theoretically sound, but also much easier for accounting purposes. When a company is accounting for many similar assets (which can easily involve thousands of units for assets like desks and computers), the record keeping for individual-asset accounting is an enormous burden even in computerized systems. Group accounts do away with the need to maintain that level of detail and reflect an apt application of the cost/benefit constraint. Of course, the company must still maintain adequate *physical* control over the assets.

Although the original cost for each asset acquired is maintained, only one control account for each group of capital assets and accumulated amortization is used. Gains and losses are not recognized on disposal. Instead, the asset control account is credited for the original cost of the item, and the accumulated amortization account is debited for the difference between cash received and the original cost of the item.

For example, assume that in 20X8 a company sells a filing system that it had acquired in 20X2 for $10,000. The company received $1,200 from the sale of the asset. The asset is part of a group account that is depreciated at the rate of 10% per year, straight line. When the asset is disposed of, only two pieces of information are needed for recording the sale: (1) the original cost of the asset, and (2) the net proceeds from the sale. The sale is recorded as follows:

| | | |
|---|---|---|
| Accumulated depreciation—filing systems | 10,000 | |
|    Capital assets—filing systems | | 10,000 |
| Cash | 1,200 | |
|    Accumulated depreciation—filing systems | | 1,200 |

The full cost of the asset is removed from both the capital asset account and the accumulated depreciation account, and the disposal proceeds are credited to the accumulated depreciation account. There is no attempt to calculate the book value for the asset, nor any gain or loss.

If we collapse these two entries into a single compound entry, the entry becomes:

| | | |
|---|---|---|
| Cash | 1,200 | |
| Accumulated depreciation—filing systems | 8,800 | |
|    Capital assets—filing systems | | 10,000 |

Effectively, the entry is telling us that if the estimates of residual value and useful life were estimated correctly for this asset, its net book value would have been $1,200 at disposal. Of course we can't make such precise estimates on individual assets, but we can make very good estimates *on average* for any particular type of asset. The control account for each class of asset can be monitored over time, and the group amortization rate can be adjusted to reflect actual experience, much as we regularly adjust bad debt expense estimates on the basis of experience.

Some companies simplify this system even further by not attempting to identify the actual cost of the asset retired. Instead, a FIFO approach is often used (oldest unit is sold first, just as with inventory).

**Example** Exhibit 10-5 presents information and calculations for an example that uses composite amortization. Annual amortization expense is the product of (1) an average amortization rate and (2) the balance in the asset control account. The composite amortization rate is the percentage of total cost amortized each year.

> Annual group SL amortization ÷ Total group acquisition cost = Composite rate

Residual value is taken into account because the numerator used in determining the composite rate reflects the SL method. It also is possible to apply declining-balance amortization methods.

Calculation of annual depreciation expense in a group system involves averaging the data for the group of assets. Calculations are exactly like those for composite systems, illustrated in Exhibit 10-5. Of course, in a group system the assets are homogeneous and there will be less dispersion around the mean.

If no changes occur in the makeup of the group during the entire composite life, annual amortization does not change. When assets are added or disposed of before the end of their useful life, the original amortization rate is maintained if the changes are not significant to the overall amortizable cost and useful life composition of the group. Amortization is computed with the old rate and the new balance in the group asset control account, which reflects the addition or deletion of assets. Material changes in the makeup of composite groups may require changes in amortization rates because these assets are heterogeneous.

An additional advantage of group depreciation is that it corresponds with the way that CCA is calculated for income tax purposes, as explained in this chapter's Appendix 1.

---

### EXHIBIT 10-5

### DATA FOR COMPOSITE AMORTIZATION COMPONENTS OF OPERATING ASSEMBLY ACQUIRED EARLY 20X1

| Component | Quantity | Original Unit Cost | Residual Value | Useful Life | Annual SL Amortization |
|-----------|----------|--------------------|----------------|-------------|------------------------|
| A | 10 | $50,000 | $5,000 | 15 years | $3,000 |
| B | 4 | 20,000 | 4,000 | 10 years | 1,600 |
| C | 6 | 7,000 | 600 | 8 years | 800 |
| D | 20 | 3,000 | 0 | 3 years | 1,000 |

Total annual amortization: 10($3,000) + 4($1,600) + 6($800) + 20($1,000) = $61,200
Total asset acquisition cost: 10($50,000) + 4($20,000) + 6($7,000) + 20($3,000) = $682,000
Total amortizable cost: $682,000 − 10($5,000) − 4($4,000) − 6($600) = $612,400
Composite annual amortization rate = $61,200 ÷ $682,000 = 0.0897
Composite group useful life = $612,400 ÷ $61,200 = 10 years
Annual amortization expense = Composite rate × Acquisition cost = (.0897)($682,000) = $61,200

## Other Systems of Amortization

Unique features of certain capital assets, as well as practical considerations, may cause firms to modify the application of standard amortization methods. Two types of systems sometimes used by very large enterprises are:

1. "Inventory" appraisal systems; and

2. Retirement and replacement systems.

**Inventory Appraisal System** Although this method is called an "inventory" system, it applies to tangible capital assets, not to inventory! Under the **inventory appraisal system**, capital assets are appraised at the end of each accounting period in their present condition through application of a deterioration percentage to the cost of the assets in place or through an outside assessment of replacement cost. This system is especially suitable for firms with numerous low-cost capital assets. The word "inventory" is not used in the sense of goods available for sale, but rather in the sense of an ongoing supply of capital assets, usually of small individual value.

The decline in the total appraisal value during the period is recorded directly in the asset account as amortization expense. Cash received on disposal is recorded as a credit to amortization expense. The book value (appraisal value) of the assets at the end of the period is an estimate of current acquisition cost that takes into account current condition and usefulness.

To illustrate how this system works, assume the following information on the hand tools capital asset account of Miller Company, which began operations in 20X1:

| | |
|---|---|
| Purchases of hand tools in 20X1 | $1,900 |
| Appraisal value of tools at the end of 20X1 | $1,080 |
| Proceeds from disposal of tools in 20X1 | $    70 |

The value of tools on hand decreased $820, but the $70 received on disposal offsets that decline, resulting in $750 of net amortization expense.

Accounting cost savings are evident from the elimination of individual subsidiary accounts, with amortization recorded only for the group. Disposals do not require retrieval of accumulated amortization information, and no gain or loss is recorded when an individual asset is sold or scrapped. Furthermore, the appraisal is made for the entire group rather than for each individual asset.

Although inventory appraisal systems appear to be a departure from the historical cost principle, assets are not written up in value, and the resulting amortization expense must be consistent with results obtained with historical cost–based amortization methods. The method is open to criticism, however, because appraisals can be quite subjective.

**Retirement and Replacement Systems** **Retirement and replacement systems** are used by public utilities and railroads to reduce record-keeping costs. Such companies typically own large numbers of items dispersed over extensive geographic areas, including rolling stock, track, wire, utility poles, and telephone equipment. The bookkeeping cost to amortize these items individually is prohibitive.

Under both the retirement system and the replacement system, amortization is not recorded for individual assets, no gain or loss is recognized on disposal, and an accumulated amortization account is not used. The total original cost of acquisitions is maintained although often not on an individual asset basis. Residual value is treated as a reduction of amortization expense in the disposal period. Amortization expense under both systems is based on assets *retired* during the period.

The key difference between the two systems is the assumed cost of the retired assets, which can be substantial. *Amortization under the retirement system equals the original cost of the item retired less residual value.* If the cost of acquisition cannot be associated with specific physical units, the oldest remaining cost of the type of asset retired less residual value is used for amortization purposes. This is essentially a FIFO system.

*Amortization under the replacement system equals the cost of the most recent acquisition of the type of item retired less residual value.* This is essentially a LIFO system. The most recent acquisition is considered the replacement for the item retired.

Retirement and replacement systems can result in amortization amounts that bear no relationship to those of individually applied methods. For example, if no retirements are made, no amortization would be recorded. Furthermore, the asset balances under both systems can be distorted to the point that the balances are meaningless if there are a large number of early retirements, or a large number of delayed retirements. Only if a firm replaces assets on a regular basis will amortization results approximate those of one of the more traditional methods; neither system meets the requirement of being rational and systematic. Perhaps the most important point is that the only companies that use this approach are very, very large, with tremendous volumes in capital assets and regular replacement. This minimizes the chance that error is material.

## CONCEPT REVIEW

1. Why is it pointless to calculate and record amortization to the exact number of days that a capital asset was owned during its year of acquisition?

2. Explain the half-year convention for capital asset amortization. Why do companies use a convention like the half-year convention for amortizing capital assets?

3. Why are group and composite systems of amortization useful for large companies?

## IMPAIRMENT OF LONG-LIVED ASSETS

Long-lived assets may or may not have a determinate, finite life span. The carrying value will stay on the balance sheet for many years. However, an asset's real economic value to the enterprise may decline significantly over the years. Possible overvaluation of assets can be a major issue for long-lived assets. Therefore, one has to critically examine capital assets and goodwill periodically and ask, "Do these assets still have the ability to generate revenue commensurate with their net book value?"

It is important to understand that the question is not, "What is market value?" Market value is the value at which an asset can be sold, which implies that it is in fact available for sale. In contrast, assets that are listed as capital assets, long-term deferred charges, or goodwill are not for sale. These assets provide value to the operation through their ability to *increase net assets through profitable operation.*

An **impairment test** is the process of comparing the carrying value of an asset to its fair value *in use.* If the asset's fair value is less than its carrying value on the company's books, the asset has suffered impairment. Since we cannot report an asset at a carrying value that is higher than its value-in-use to the company, the asset's carrying value must be reduced by the amount of the impairment. The writedown is charged to expense on the income statement, never directly to retained earnings.

Impairment tests already are quite familiar to us, in the form of lower-of-cost-or-market (LCM) valuations for inventory and for other short-term assets. However, accounting standards tend to use the term "impairment" only for assets that have a long life: **long-lived assets**.

A basic assumption underlying impairment tests is that the asset is intended to be used in the company's operations and that its cost is recoverable. If the cost is completely unrecoverable through operations or sale, the asset does not meet our definition of an asset and therefore must be written off in full immediately.

Impairment tests are applied to all long-lived assets, both (1) assets with limited lives and (2) assets without limited lives, including land and some intangibles. However, the process of testing for impairment is somewhat different for the two types of assets. Therefore, we will look at impairment tests separately for each type.

Impairment losses are shown separately on the income statement. They are not reported as extraordinary items. They may well be part of a restructuring charge or discontinued operations, if circumstances warrant.

## Impairment of Long-Lived Assets with Limited Lives

**What to Test**  Broadly speaking, impairment tests are applied to:

- Tangible capital assets (property, plant, and equipment);
- Intangible assets with limited lives; and
- Long-term deferred costs.

However, the test seldom is applied to individual assets. Assets function together in a company to generate cash flows and earnings. Therefore, impairment tests normally are applied to **asset groups**—a group of assets (and directly related liabilities) for which identifiable cash flows are largely independent of the cash flows of other assets or groups of assets and liabilities. Patents, equipment, trademarks, and software all may function together as an asset group. For impairment tests, an asset group is the lowest level in a company at which it is possible to determine or identify the cash flows from a particular group of assets. Impairment is most likely to be applied to assets at an operating division level.

For example, a company may have patents on several products and processes, all of which use the same facilities for production and administrative support. If sales of one product are killed by a new product from a competitor, there has not necessarily been an impairment—the impairment test is applied to the cash flows from the assets used in production. The cash flow from the asset group is generated by all of the assets working together to produce several products.

Liabilities will be included in the group only when the sole source of cash to satisfy the liability is the asset or asset group being tested for impairment. If there are other cash sources to pay liabilities, the liabilities are not included in the group because they are general liabilities of the enterprise. Examples include mortgage debt and asset retirement obligations.

Held-for-sale assets may be subject to individual impairment tests, but even that may be rare. Most held-for-sale assets are the net assets of discontinued operations that are awaiting disposal. It is the discontinued operations as a whole that is tested for impairment, not individual assets.

**When to Test**  Sometimes asset impairment is as plain as day, such as when a building is destroyed in a fire. In such a case, the asset is written off and the insurance proceeds (if any) reduce the loss (and can even create a reported gain if the insurance proceeds are greater than the asset's net book value).

Assets should be subjected to an impairment test whenever events or changes in circumstances indicate that their carrying value may be unrecoverable. Examples of such circumstances include:

- A significant change in the business environment, such as a new product from a competitor that makes the company's product or processes obsolete;
- A history of operating and/or cash flow losses that indicate that the company isn't able to recover the cost of the asset;
- A probability of greater than 50% that the company will retire or dispose of the asset significantly earlier than planned; or
- Loss of a patent infringement lawsuit that has a significant effect on overall operations.

An asset's cost is **unrecoverable** if the sum of the *undiscounted* future cash flows from use and eventual disposal of the asset (or asset group) is less than the carrying value of the asset.

If the cost is unrecoverable by this measure, only then is the asset or asset group tested for impairment.

**How to Measure** The impairment loss is the amount by which the carrying value of an asset group exceeds its fair value. Fair value is interpreted to mean the amount that the asset group could be sold for in a fair and open transaction between willing parties, neither party being under any particular obligation to sell or buy. The difficult part is to measure fair value. One could try to piece together a fair value for the group by assembling market values for individual assets, but that would deny the synergy and productivity that is achieved when assets function together in an operating environment.

Although it makes little sense to add together the values of individual assets within a group, the group as a whole may have a measurable fair value. A group of assets can be sold to another company as an operating unit, similar to a discontinued operation. The price that a buyer would pay will be based on the *discounted* present value of the asset group's estimated future cash flows.

Take note of the difference:

- When to test for impairment is based on the relationship between the carrying value and *undiscounted* cash flows.
- The amount of impairment is determined by comparing the carrying value to the fair value as estimated on the basis of *discounted* cash flows.

Estimating future cash flows (and the probabilities attached to those cash flows) is not the job of the accountant. That is the task of management, with the assistance of professional business evaluators. But once management estimates the fair value, the accountant must assure that the impairment is properly recorded.

**Allocating the Impairment Loss** As we have just seen, impairment losses are normally applied to asset groups. But the assets usually are recorded individually on the books, not in groups. So how should the overall impairment loss be allocated to the assets?

The first rule is that *impairment losses are allocated only to the long-lived assets* of the group. If the group includes other assets, such as inventories or accounts receivable, the impairment loss is not allocated to those assets. Of course, inventories and accounts receivable are still subject to the usual LCM valuation practices.

The second rule is that the amount of an impairment should be allocated on the basis of the relative fair values of the individual long-lived assets. Suppose that Justus Limited has the following assets in its recreational products group:

| | Carrying Value (thousands) |
|---|---|
| Inventory | $   300 |
| Land | 400 |
| Building | 640 |
| Equipment | 560 |
| | $1,900 |

A change in the competitive environment suggests that the fair value of this division may be less than its carrying value. Management conducts an impairment test and finds that the undiscounted future cash flow from this group will be less than $1.9 million. An impairment test is performed, resulting in an estimated discounted present value of the future cash flows of the asset group is $1,300. The impairment loss is $600—the excess of $1,900 carrying value over $1,300 fair value.

The impairment loss must be allocated to the long-lived assets. The inventory is excluded from the allocation, but may be revalued on its own by the lower-of-cost or market rule. The

$600 impairment loss will be allocated to the other three assets in proportion to their carrying value:

| Asset | Carrying Value | Proportion | Allocation of Impairment Loss | Adjusted Carrying Value |
|---|---|---|---|---|
| Inventory | $ 300 | — | — | $ 300 |
| Land | 400 | 25% | $150 | 250 |
| Building | 640 | 40% | 240 | 400 |
| Equipment | 560 | 35% | 210 | 350 |
| | $1,900 | 100% | $600 | $1,300 |

The third rule is that an allocation of impairment loss should not reduce the carrying amount of an asset below its fair value if the fair value can be readily determined. For example, suppose that an Internet service provider (ISP) shows as an asset the historical cost for a subscriber base that it purchased from another company. An ISP subscriber list has a fairly readily determinable value. If the ISP is consistently losing money, it is probable that the company's assets are impaired. Nevertheless, that doesn't indicate that the subscriber list has no value of its own—another company may use it quite profitably. If an impairment loss is recognized, the carrying value of the subscription base should not be reduced below its fair market value. Instead, a greater portion of the impairment loss should be allocated to the other long-lived assets, such as equipment and limited-life intangibles.

In the example above, suppose that the fair value of the land is $320. Assets should not be written down below their fair value. In that case, the allocation must be (1) to reduce the land's carrying value by $80 (from $400 to $320), and then (2) to allocate the remaining $520 impairment loss to the remaining assets:

| Asset | Carrying Value | Proportion | Allocation of Impairment Loss | Adjusted Carrying Value |
|---|---|---|---|---|
| Inventory | $ 300 | — | — | $ 300 |
| Land | 400 | — | $80 | 320 |
| Building | 640 | 53% | 276 | 364 |
| Equipment | 560 | 47% | 244 | 316 |
| | $1,900 | 100% | $600 | $1,300 |

**Disclosure** Disclosure requirements for impairment losses are straightforward. The basic requirements are:

- A description of the impaired asset or asset group, and the facts and circumstances leading to the impairment;
- The amount of the impairment loss, and an indication of where it appears in the income statement if it is not presented separately on the face of the income statement; and
- The method used for determining fair value.

An example of an asset impairment charge is that of Infowave Software, Inc., a developer of mobile wireless software solutions for field service workers in the hi-tech, telecom, energy, and transportation industries. The company's disclosure notes stated:

> The Company reviewed the technology and related intangible assets acquired from Telispark and their future cash flow projections and recorded an impairment charge of $3,352,603 during the year ended December 31, 2005. The impairment

charge is equal to the amount by which the asset's carrying amount exceeded the net present value of the asset's estimated discounted future cash flows.

**Subsequent Recovery in Value** In Canada and the U.S., restoring or reversing an impairment loss has not been permitted. Once an asset has been written down, the reduced carrying value is not written back up if the recoverable amount increases.

International accounting standards, as well as the national standards in many countries, take a different approach. Those standards recommend that impairment losses be reinstated if the fair value of the asset has recovered and should be recognized in income immediately. As Canada converts to international standards, we expect the Canadian prohibition against reversing an impairment loss to disappear.

The problem with reversing an impairment loss is that this provides yet another method by which management may be tempted to "manage" or smooth earnings—take an impairment loss in a high-income year, and restore it in a low-income year. In order to guard against such manipulation, the international standard provides guidelines on how to ascertain that an impairment loss has occurred and when the value has recovered. Those safeguards will undoubtedly be integrated into Canadian standards in future years.

**Other Intangible Assets** Note that only limited-life intangible assets are tested for impairment using the process described above. For intangible assets that have an indefinite life, and for goodwill, read on!

## Impairment of Intangible Assets Not Subject to Amortization

Since goodwill and intangibles with indefinite lives are not amortized, it makes sense to examine these assets carefully for impairment. Regular impairment writedowns would have the same effect as amortization, although impairment is more likely to be infrequent. Infrequent, large write-offs will create "bumpy" earnings patterns. The prospect of using tangible asset impairment losses to "manage" earnings may be tempting to managers.

The impairment test for intangible assets that are not amortized is fairly straightforward. An asset is impaired if its fair value is less than its carrying value. The impairment loss is the difference between those two values. The loss is charged against operating income.

As with other assets, fair value is the price in a fair and open sales transaction. Fair value could be more-or-less observable, if that type of intangible asset is traded with some regularity. More often, however, there is no active market for intangible assets. This is particularly true because intangible assets, by their nature, are unique. Therefore, as with tangible capital assets, fair value is measured as the asset's probable future *undiscounted* future cash flows.

Historically, reversal of impairment losses has not been permitted in Canada. Once written down, the asset stayed written down. However, this prohibition on reversal may change in the future (except as applied to goodwill), as Canada moves to international standards.

### Goodwill Impairment

The basic requirement is that an impairment loss should be recognized when the carrying value of the goodwill (or other non-amortized intangibles) is higher than the fair value of the goodwill.

**Conditions for Impairment** As we saw in Chapter 9, goodwill is measured as a residual, as the excess of the purchase price paid for a unit over the fair value of its net assets on the acquisition date.

The key measuring unit for goodwill impairment is the *reporting unit*. Generally, a **reporting unit** is a company's operating segment that generates its own revenues and expenses and is subject to review by the chief operating decision maker as a separate earnings unit. A reporting unit also must have discrete financial information that is reported independently of the rest of the company. If revenues and expenses for the unit are not reported separately to senior internal decision makers, it is not possible to judge the unit's performance or to evaluate its possible fair value.

To establish the potential for impairment, a two-step impairment test is performed:

**Step 1.** The fair value of a unit is compared with its total net book value. As long as the fair value of *the unit* is higher than the net book value of all assets and liabilities, the impairment test stops here and no impairment loss is needed.

The relevant fair value here is the fair value of the *unit as a whole*. This fair value may be based on multiples of earnings or revenues, or on *undiscounted* cash flow projections. All these valuation models are highly sensitive to assumptions regarding sales volumes and prices. Business valuation is an art! If the fair value of the reporting unit is lower than net book value, it is necessary to go to Step 2.

**Step 2.** The goodwill calculation that was done on acquisition is repeated, using current fair values and current book values. In Step 2, the fair values used are those for each asset and liability, not for the unit as a whole. The process is identical to that illustrated in Chapter 9, and it results in a residual value assigned to goodwill. That is, goodwill is calculated as the purchase price less the current fair value of net assets acquired. If this is a lower goodwill figure than that recorded on the books, an impairment loss is recorded.

Consider the following examples:

*Example 1.* The fair value of a unit is $6,400,000. The net book value of assets less liabilities, including unamortized goodwill of $1,000,000, is $5,175,000. Fair value exceeds net book value, and the impairment test is over, with no loss recorded.

*Example 2.* The fair value of the unit is $4,300,000. The net book value of net assets is $5,175,000, including $1,000,000 of goodwill. A Step 2 valuation must be done because fair value is less than net book value.

The fair value of all assets and liabilities must be established. Some fair values will be higher than book value, and some are lower. Those with lower book value will be evaluated for a potential writedown of their own. A writedown may or may not be needed, depending on the circumstances. Capital assets subject to amortization will be written down only if the decline is permanent. Then, goodwill is recalculated.

In this example, assume that, in addition to knowing that the unit has a fair value of $4,300,000, we determine that individual assets and liabilities have a fair value of $4,100,000. Recalculated goodwill amounts to $200,000. An impairment loss of $800,000 must be recorded.

This impairment loss is *not* equal to the original differential between net book value and fair value of the unit. This original differential was $875,000 (that is, $5,175,000 − $4,300,000). The original differential can be caused by various items, not just goodwill.

There are many technical elements to this valuation and many judgemental elements as well. For instance, goodwill must be evaluated for each reporting unit. But is "a reporting unit" each division of an acquired business, or the business as a whole? What valuation model is most relevant for the unit acquired? What degree of optimism about future revenues is most appropriate? How should fair values be determined when there is no intermediate market for assets?

There are answers, or at least approaches to answers for all these questions, and more. However, the technical aspects of this impairment test are beyond the scope of this book. Our focus is on the criteria for the impairment loss, and its subsequent presentation in the financial statements.

**Timing** Goodwill must be evaluated for impairment annually. For public companies, the only exception is if there has been no real change to net assets or events and circumstances since the last valuation, and the last valuation showed a comfortable excess fair value over net book value. There has to be some margin for error. The test may be done more frequently if events take place that suggest impairment.

Private companies can opt out of annual goodwill impairment under the differential reporting provisions of the *CICA Handbook*. An impairment test will be applied only when there is some event or circumstance that suggests that the fair value may have declined significantly.

**Examples of Goodwill Impairment**    One of the interesting aspects of the goodwill impairment requirements is that the test is performed at the level of the *reporting unit*. Consider the following explanation from the financial statements of Engenuity Technologies Incorporated:

> The Company determined that at December 1, 2001, it had two reporting units, Xtend, Inc. and Loox Software S.A., and that the goodwill related to Xtend, Inc. was impaired. As a result, an amount of $1,869,000 was charged to opening deficit, in accordance with the transition provisions of the accounting standard (see Note 7). The Company performs the annual impairment test on June 30 of each year.
>
> During the third quarter of 2003, following a review by management of the Company's operations, the organizational and corporate structure was changed. The new structure operates all companies in the consolidated group as one component under a single management. Accordingly, as of April 1, 2003, the Company had one reporting unit, and goodwill is tested for impairment by comparing the carrying value of the Company to its fair value.

Did the company change its reporting structure in order to minimize the likelihood of future goodwill impairment charges? We can only guess at the company's motivation. However, having fewer reporting units will certainly reduce the amount of effort that goes into the annual impairment review.

Another example of goodwill impairment is contained in the 2003 income statement of Gemcom Software International Incorporated. Gemcom charged $31,215 against earnings as "write-off of impaired value, Peru." The disclosure note explains the impairment as follows:

> The Company completed its annual impairment test of goodwill on March 31, 2003. The goodwill allocated to the company in Peru, Gemcom Peru S.A., was determined impaired as operations in Peru have been combined with those in Chile and Brazil to form the Latin American segment. The Company in Peru is no longer being used to manage these operations and therefore the $31,215 in goodwill associated with it has been written off at year-end.

In other words, the goodwill is impaired because the company no longer uses the Peru unit to manage its Peruvian operations. The amount that was allocated to goodwill when Gemcom first purchased this subsidiary is completely written off.

**The Role of Judgement**    It would be impossible to overemphasize the role of judgement when evaluating the need for an impairment writedown. Since fair values are estimates, often based on future revenue projections, the optimism and pessimism of management will have a profound effect on the end result. There is significant temptation to take a bath in poor years, and record large writedowns. Recall the AOL Time Warner goodwill writeoff that was described in the introduction to this chapter.

## DISCLOSURE REQUIREMENTS

Not surprisingly, the requirement to disclose amortization policy is front and centre in the disclosure requirements. If you're going to let companies pick a policy, it is crucial that financial statement readers be told about the choice. Thus, companies should disclose for each major category of amortizable capital assets:

- The amortization method used, including the amortization period or rate;
- The accumulated amortization of each major category;
- The amount of amortization charged to income for the period; and
- The amount of any impairment loss or writedown during the period.

## CASH FLOW STATEMENT

Amortization expense is an add-back to the operations section of the cash flow statement, if the common indirect form of presentation is used. It's important to remember that amortization is a little different from other expenses, because amortization is a non-cash expense. Clearly, the company has to pay out cash or other resources to obtain the capital asset, but the timing of the cash paid is likely to be a lot different than the timing of the expense recognition.

Any writedowns of capital assets, including impairment of goodwill, are a non-cash charge to income. Like amortization, they are added back to net income.

## CAPITAL ASSETS HELD FOR SALE

### Definition

Eventually, a capital asset ceases to be used in a company's operations. If the asset is taken out of service only temporarily, there is no change in the accounting. Idle assets continue to be amortized. But if an asset is taken out of service permanently, one of three things will usually happen to it:

- It will be disposed of or scrapped as having no further use;
- It will be exchanged for another asset; or
- It will be put up for sale.

We already have discussed the first two options. Now we will examine the accounting when the asset is being disposed of by sale.

A long-lived asset that is taken out of service and put up for sale is classified as *held for sale*. That's a rather obvious statement, but "held for sale" has a specific meaning in accounting standards: available-for-sale financial instruments get one treatment (as you will see in the next chapter), while held-for-sale long-lived assets get a different treatment.

In order for a long-lived asset (or an asset group) to be classified as held for sale, *all* of six criteria must be me. In brief, these criteria are:

- Management must have committed to sell the asset.
- It is available for sale in its present condition.
- The company is actively seeking a buyer.
- It is being marketed at a reasonable price.
- A sale is expected to be completed within one year.
- It is unlikely that management will change its plan to sell the asset.

The point of these criteria is to reduce the possibility of income manipulation. Management may be tempted to declare assets as held for sale when there may be little probability that management will actually sell them. The temptation exists because amortization stops when assets are classified as held for sale. Without the criteria, it would be possible to classify temporarily idle assets as held for sale in slow economic times so that the amortization expense is reduced.

If an idle asset does not meet all of these six criteria, it should not be classified as held for sale—amortization will continue on the asset.

### Accounting Treatment

When an asset (or asset group) qualifies as held for sale, there are three accounting consequences:

1. Amortization ceases, as we have already pointed out.

2. The asset (or asset group) is written down to its fair value less cost to sell *if* its fair value is less than its carrying value.

3. The asset is separately classified on the balance sheet as a long-term held-for-sale asset.

Fair value is the market value for assets that have an active secondary market. If there is no active or observable market for an asset (or asset group), fair value may be measured by discounting the asset's potential future cash flows, similar to the techniques used for an asset impairment test. The estimated fair value is reduced by the estimated costs to sell the asset, such as commissions, legal fees, and closing costs.

The loss from the asset writedown should be included in net income in the period in which the asset was classified as held for sale. When the sale transaction has been completed, a gain or loss is recognized for the difference between the net sales price and the carrying value (after any writedown) of the asset.

Both the loss from a writedown and the gain/loss on the final sale are recognized in net income. If the asset is part of a discontinued operation, then gains and losses should be included in discontinued operations. Otherwise, the loss will be reported within continuing operating earnings.

If financial statements are prepared prior to completion of a sale, the carrying value of the asset is again evaluated. Any additional decline in fair value should be recognized. However, in a departure from the usual rules pertaining to written-down assets, a gain can be recognized for any subsequent increase in the fair value less cost to sell (i.e., net realizable value), but any gain is limited to the amount of loss previously recorded.

Since the asset is held for sale, it should be shown on the balance sheet at its fair value, provided that the fair value does not exceed the original carrying value. This treatment is more or less consistent with valuation of available-for-sale financial instruments, as we shall see in the next chapter. Therefore, the rule against writing impaired long-lived assets back up is relaxed if the assets are held for sale.

Assets held for sale should be presented separately on the company's balance sheet as long-term assets. They are not reclassified as current assets even though the intent is to sell them within the next year.

Additional information should be provided in a disclosure note:

- A description of the asset and the facts and circumstances leading to its disposal; and
- The amount of gain or loss, and where it is included in the income statement.

## Example

In July 20X5, Schumacher Incorporated shut down the company's Manitoba distribution centre and put the centre up for sale. The facility met all of the criteria for held-for-sale classification. The historical cost of the building was $4,300,000. At the time of abandonment, accumulated amortization was $1,850,000, resulting in a net book value of $2,450,000.

After contacting several industrial brokers, Schumacher management obtained evidence that the fair market value of the building was $2,200,000. Commission, closing costs, and transfer taxes are estimated to be 10% of the sales price. The entry to record the reclassification of the asset is:

| | | |
|---|---|---|
| Accumulated amortization—Manitoba distribution centre | 1,850,000 | |
| Long-lived assets held for sale (net of 10% costs to sell) | 1,980,000 | |
| Loss on building held for sale | 470,000 | |
| Buildings—Manitoba distribution centre | | 4,300,000 |

This entry (1) offsets the accumulated amortization against the building cost, (2) reclassifies the asset as held for sale at fair value less costs to sell, and (3) records the loss of $470,000, which will be charged against earnings.

On 31 December 20X5, Schumacher is making good progress on the sale. Indeed, due to a sharp increase in economic activity in Manitoba, the estimated market value of the building has risen sharply, to $2,600,000. At year-end, Schumacher must write the asset up to fair value, limited to the pre-abandonment carrying value of $2,450,000. At first glance, it would appear that fair value is higher than the old book value. However, the 10% selling cost must be subtracted to find the net fair value: $2,600,000 $\times$ 90% = $2,340,000. Schumacher will increase the held-for-sale asset value and decrease the previously recorded loss:

| | | |
|---|---|---|
| Long-lived assets held for sale | | |
| ($2,340,000 − $1,980,000) | 360,000 | |
| Loss on building held for sale | | 360,000 |

The 31 December 20X5 carrying value is not higher than the $2,450,000 carrying value in July 20X5, the date of abandonment.

On 17 March 20X6, Schumacher closes the sale. The final selling price is $2,650,000. The net proceeds are 90% of that amount or $2,385,000. The entry to record the sale is:

| | | |
|---|---|---|
| Cash | 2,385,000 | |
| Long-lived assets held for sale | | 2,340,000 |
| Gain on sale of building | | 45,000 |

## CONCEPT REVIEW

1. In general, when is it necessary to write down property, plant, and equipment? How can we determine the value to which it should be written down?

2. Describe the two steps followed to determine whether there has been an impairment of goodwill.

3. How do Canada's practices regarding the restoration of writedowns and the revaluation of individual assets differ from the most common international practice?

## ETHICAL ISSUES

The importance of accounting estimates has been emphasized throughout this book. Amortization requires not only a choice of method, but also estimates of useful life and residual value. A choice of method, once made, normally is not changed. The requirement that similar assets be amortized by similar methods helps to maintain consistency in measurement.

However, over the life of a capital asset, it is quite possible for a company to change any or all of the asset's (1) amortization method, (2) useful life, or (3) residual value. If a company lengthens an asset's useful life, for example, is it really because the asset will be useful longer than expected, or is it because management seeks to improve the company's apparent profitability? Auditors can scrutinize the rationale behind changes in management's estimates, but their scrutiny will have little effect unless the new estimates are quite obviously outside the feasible range.

There are two aspects that help limit the ability of management to act unethically in setting estimates relating to amortization. One is that if the company's policies and estimates get out of line with industry practice, the non-conformity will be apparent to investors and bankers, especially those who deal often with a specific industry. Non-conformity will cause statement users to suspect management's motivations and will discount the stock price or be hesitant to extend loans.

The second is that investors take changes in accounting estimates into account—efficient markets are not fooled by accounting changes in the short run. But even subtle changes can have important long-term effects on net income, and do investors really remember all of the past changes in management estimates when evaluating a company's performance?

While amortization estimates and revisions offer some scope for unethical behaviour, impairments offer a far more fertile area for bias, either intentional or unintentional. Impairment tests are based on estimates of fair values. In turn, fair value is based on estimates of *future* cash flows. By their nature, estimates of future cash flows cannot be verified. Managers may be pessimistic when they estimate future cash flows from an asset group, for example, because the company has not been successful at making its products profitable. Even when it is clear that the future cash flows of an asset group are in decline, management must estimate how quickly and how severe the decline will be.

Managers can hire professional appraisers to help estimate future cash flows and thus the fair value of assets and asset groups. Ideally, more than one appraiser is used. Professional appraisers are assumed to be essentially in agreement if their estimates of fair value are within 10% of each other. A variation of 10% in the fair value of an asset or asset group may not seem very significant. However, a relatively small variation in estimated fair value can have a major impact on the net income in the year of the writedown. The variation also affects the future earnings and EPS of the company by lowering amortization after the writedown. Furthermore, under international standards (and probably Canadian standards in the near future), management can write the asset back up again, partially or completely if the future cash flows turn out to be better than expected.

Writedowns can be a very effective tool for enabling managers to "manage" the company's reported earnings.

An additional facet relating to *goodwill* impairment tests is that the test is performed at the level of the reporting unit. By rearranging the organization's reporting lines, the need to perform impairment tests on specific operating units can be eliminated.

In summary, the practices for amortization and for impairment tests are not as objective and verifiable as they may seem at first glance. Auditors and financial statement users must be vigilant against manipulation of reported results, as must the senior accountants working with in the company itself.

## INTERNATIONAL PERSPECTIVE

The current Canadian standards on amortization and impairment were developed in conjunction with IASB's revision of the international standards. Nevertheless, there are some important differences.

### Minimum Depreciation

International standards have no provision for minimum depreciation. Scrap value is irrelevant—only residual value and estimated useful life are relevant for determining the amount of amortization. The IAS standard states quite explicitly that depreciation is zero if an asset's residual value is equal to or greater than its carrying value. Depreciation will commence only if and when the residual value drops below the asset's carrying value.

It is worth noting that while Canadian standards stick to the word *amortization* in order to include all forms, including depreciation and depletion, international standards explicitly use the word *depreciation* when referring to amortization of tangible capital assets.

## Reversal of Impairment Losses

International standards do permit the reversal of impairment losses if the fair value of an asset or asset group goes up after an impairment loss has been recorded. The carrying value of the asset or of the assets in an asset group should be increased by the amount of any subsequent increase in the fair value of an impaired asset or asset group (known as a *cash-generating unit* in international standards). The increase should be recorded as a gain on the income statement. The reversal is really a correction of accounting estimates that were made in the period of the original writedown.

Goodwill impairments should never be reversed. A subsequent increase in goodwill is viewed as internally generated goodwill, which is never recorded.

## Revaluation Accounting

Another major difference is that the IAS standard permits routine revaluation (to fair value) of property, plant, and equipment. Canadian standards, in contrast, permit revaluation only under certain rare circumstances, as we discuss in this chapter's Appendix 2. The use of historical cost is an *option* under international standards, not a *requirement*. When revaluation accounting is used, all of the items in an asset class should be revalued in order to avoid selective revaluation of only certain assets. The asset values should be kept up to date.

If assets are revalued (upward), the increase in value is credited directly to shareholders' equity as *revaluation surplus*. Subsequent depreciation is based on the revalued amount, not on historical cost. The revaluation surplus is transferred directly to retained earnings without going through the income statement. The transfer can be either:

1. When the asset is retired; or

2. Year by year, calculated as the difference between (a) depreciation based on the revalued carrying value and (b) depreciation based on historical cost.

Appendix 2 in this chapter contains an illustration of revaluation accounting.

If the revaluation is downward, the reduction in carrying value reduces any revaluation surplus relating to that asset. If the asset's carrying value is reduced to below its historical cost, the difference between the historical cost and the new lower valuation is treated as an impairment loss.

## Allocation of Impairment Loss

A final difference is in allocating an impairment loss to the assets within a cash-generating unit or group of assets. The Canadian standard requires the impairment to be allocated only to *non-current* assets. The international standard, however, requires allocation first to any goodwill that has been assigned to the unit. If goodwill does not absorb all of the impairment loss, the remaining loss is to be allocated to *all* of the other assets (including current assets). However, no asset (either current or non-current) can be written down below the higher of:

- Its net realizable value (i.e., fair value less costs to sell); or
- Its value in use (i.e., the discounted cash flow relating to that particular asset).

The international standard is silent on what to do if this restriction prevents allocation of the full amount of the impairment loss. However, the standard is implying that if the fair value of the individual assets is higher than the discounted cash flow of the unit, the fair value should be measured on an asset-by-asset basis rather than as the discounted cash flow of the unit as a whole.

International standards permit impairment losses to be reversed, *except for goodwill*. Goodwill will be on the balance sheet only if a cash-generating unit had been purchased in the past. If goodwill is impaired and written down, it is because the expected cash flow did not materialize. If the unit's earnings ability subsequently increases, the increase is assumed to have been internally generated, and therefore cannot be recognized.

## RELEVANT STANDARDS

*CICA Handbook:*
- Section 3061, Property, Plant and Equipment
- Section 3062, Goodwill and Other Intangible Assets
- Section 3063, Impairment of Long-lived Assets
- Section 3475, Disposal of Long-lived Assets and Discontinued Operations

IASB:
- *IAS* 16, Property, Plant and Equipment
- *IAS* 36, Impairment of Assets
- *IAS* 38, Intangible Assets
- *IAS* 40, Investment Property
- *IFRS* 5, Non-current Assets Held for Sale and Discontinued Operations

## SUMMARY OF KEY POINTS

1. Amortization is a rational and systematic process of allocating amortizable cost (acquisition cost less residual value) to the periods in which capital assets are used. Amortization expense for a period does not represent the change in market value of assets, nor does it necessarily equal the portion of the asset's utility consumed in the period. Amortization is justified on the basis of eventual decline in value, through physical wear and tear and obsolescence.

2. Goodwill, land, and intangible assets with an unlimited life are not amortized.

3. Several methods of amortization are rational and systematic and acceptable under GAAP: the straight-line, service-hours, productive-output, and accelerated methods. Factors affecting choice include individual corporate reporting objectives, information processing costs, a desire to minimize income tax temporary differences, industry norms, and parent company preferences.

4. Three factors contribute to the determination of periodic amortization expense: original acquisition cost and any capitalized post-acquisition costs, estimated residual value, and estimated useful life or productivity measured either in service-hours or units of output.

5. For all methods, the estimated residual value is the minimum book value. Except for the declining-balance methods, amortizable cost (cost minus residual value) is multiplied by a rate or fraction to determine periodic amortization. Declining-balance amortization is based on cost less accumulated amortization and ceases when net book value equals residual value.

6. For assets acquired during an accounting period, an accounting convention such as the half-year convention is usually used in practice.

7. Three amortization systems (composite and group, appraisal, and replacement/retirement) are alternatives to amortization methods applied individually to assets. These systems save accounting costs and are justified under cost-benefit and materiality constraints.

8. Capital assets subject to amortization must be reviewed for potential writedown on a regular basis. A loss is recognized when the sum of *undiscounted* expected future net cash inflows from use and disposal of the asset is less than carrying value. The loss equals the difference between the asset's carrying value and the asset's fair value. Fair value is based on the estimated future *discounted* cash flows.

9. Intangible assets not subject to amortization are written down to fair value if the carrying value exceeds fair value.

10. Goodwill must be evaluated annually and written down if the value is impaired. This is done in a two-step process. First, the fair value of the business unit is compared to book value. If fair value is lower, the second step is to recalculate the residual goodwill figure based on current fair value and book values for all net assets of the business unit.

11. Reversal of an impairment charge is not permitted within Canadian GAAP, but is permitted in international GAAP except for goodwill.

12. Amortization is not a cash flow; the cash flow occurred when the capital asset was acquired. Amortization and impairment writedowns are added back to net income when cash flow from operations is determined on the cash flow statement.

13. Companies should disclose the amortization method chosen for major categories of capital assets, the amortization period or rate, and the amount of amortization charged to income for the period.

14. Internationals standards differ from Canadian standards in some significant ways: (1) they require no minimum amortization test, (2) impairment losses on assets and asset groups can be reversed, and (3) historical cost accounting is not required—capital assets can be reported at appraised values instead.

## KEY TERMS

amortizable cost, 521
amortization, 521
asset group, 539
composite amortization, 534
comprehensive revaluation, 556
convention, 533
declining-balance (DB) amortization, 530
depletion, 521
depreciation, 521
double-declining balance amortization, 530
group amortization, 534
held for sale, 526
impairment, 521
impairment test, 538

indefinite life, 522
inventory appraisal system, 537
long-lived assets, 538
net book value, 521
productive output (PO) amortization, 529
reporting unit, 542
residual value, 521
retirement and replacement systems, 537
salvage value, 521
service-hours (SH) amortization, 529
straight-line (SL) amortization, 526
sum-of-the-years'-digits (SYD) amortization, 531
unrecoverable, 539

## REVIEW PROBLEM

The following cases are independent.

1. *Partial-year depreciation.* Whitney Corporation purchased equipment on 1 April 20X4 for $34,000. The equipment has a useful life of five years and a residual value of $4,000. What is depreciation for 20X4 and 20X5, using declining-balance depreciation at a 40% rate?

2. *Asset impairment.* Rancho Company purchases equipment on 1 April 20X3 for $34,000. The equipment has a useful life of five years, a residual value of $4,000, and is depreciated using the straight-line method and the half-year convention. At the end of 20X5, Rancho suspects that the original investment in the asset will not be realized; the total remaining future cash inflows expected to be generated by the equipment, including the original residual value, amounts to $10,000 (undiscounted). The equipment's fair value at 31 December 20X5 is $7,000. Determine whether the asset is impaired and, if so, the impairment loss at 31 December 20X5.

3. *Composite depreciation.* Baja Company uses the composite method of depreciation and has a composite rate of 25%. During 20X5, it sells assets with an original cost of $100,000 (residual value of $20,000) for $80,000 and acquires $60,000 worth of new assets (residual value $10,000). The original group of assets has the following characteristics:

| | |
|---|---|
| Total cost | $250,000 |
| Total residual value | 30,000 |

Assuming that the new assets conform to the group and that the company does not revise the depreciation rate, calculate depreciation expense for 20X5.

## REVIEW PROBLEM—SOLUTION

1. Depreciation for 20X4: $34,000 × 40% × 9/12 = $10,200
   Depreciation for 20X5: ($34,000   $10,200) × 40% = $9,520

2. Book value of equipment at 31 December 20X5:

| | |
|---|---|
| Cost | $34,000 |
| Accumulated depreciation, 31 December 20X5: | |
| ($34,000 − $4,000) ÷ 5 × 2.5 years | 15,000 |
| Net book value | $19,000 |

The asset is impaired because the undiscounted future cash flow of $10,000 is less than the $19,000 book value. Since depreciation is not intended to mirror the decline in fair value of a capital asset, the fact that the fair value is less than book value is not, in itself, significant. The key aspect of impairment is that the estimated future net cash flows generated by the asset are less than its book value, indicating that the unamortized cost cannot be recovered through operations.

Since the remaining cost cannot be recovered through operations, the asset must be written down to its fair value of $7,000. This is a loss of $12,000.

3. Depreciation for 20X5 = ($250,000 − $100,000 + $60,000) × 25% = $52,500

The capital asset account is adjusted for the original cost of the assets sold ($100,000) and acquired ($60,000). The proceeds from the sale ($80,000) are credited to accumulated depreciation. No gain or loss is recognized under group and composite systems.

# APPENDIX 1

## CAPITAL COST ALLOWANCE

The *Income Tax Act* does not allow the deduction of accounting amortization expense in the determination of taxable income. Instead of amortization, the taxpayer must either (1) deduct the expenditure from taxable income in the year that it is incurred or (2) use the form of amortization mandated by the *Income Tax Act*. There is not a choice between these two treatments; the tax treatment depends on the type of expenditure (that is, on the type of capital asset for accounting purposes).

Just because an expenditure (or group of expenditures) is classified as a capital asset for accounting purposes does not mean that the CRA will view it as a capital asset. Many of the costs that are capitalized for accounting purposes are viewed as expenses for tax purposes. This is particularly true of a large number of expenditures that accountants tend to capitalize as intangible assets, particularly when they are self-developed assets such as development costs.

Expenditures that are considered by the *Income Tax Act* to be capital assets are subject to amortization for tax purposes, but the amortization is completely independent of accounting amortization. Under GAAP, amortization is intended to allocate an asset's historical cost to the accounting periods in which the asset is used. In contrast, tax amortization is geared to the economic goals of the federal government, which change in response to economic conditions and the fiscal policies of Parliament. For example, the 2005 federal budget increased the CCA rate for manufacturing and processing equipment from 30% to 50% for the following seven years, in order to encourage investment.

### The Capital Cost Allowance System

Tax amortization is known as *capital cost allowance,* or *CCA*. Basically, the CCA system is a group depreciation method. CCA requires the grouping of assets into various CCA classes established by Canada Revenue Agency (CRA) regulations. An exception to the group requirement is that buildings that are held for rental (i.e., "income properties") are treated individually; each one is a separate "class."

Most classes provide a maximum rate of amortization that approximates double-declining balance amortization, although some classes use the equivalent of straight-line amortization. Classes and rates for some of the more common assets are shown in Exhibit 10A-1, with the prescribed maximum rate shown in parentheses for the declining-balance classes.

An important point is that the rates are *maximums*. A tax-paying company does not have to use the maximum rate, and in fact does not need to deduct any CCA at all if the company chooses not to do so. CCA is an optional deduction.

Why would a company not want to deduct CCA? Because it is not making any taxable income! If a company's taxable income is insufficient to absorb all of the CCA, the CCA can be "saved" to offset against future earnings. Regardless of whether or not a company takes CCA in a year, however, the CCA cannot be doubled up in future years. The maximum remains the same, but the base on which CCA is calculated is higher because the company did not take CCA in past years.

The basic rules for the capital cost allowance system can be explained (for most classes) as follows:

1. When assets are purchased, their purchase price (capital cost) is added to the balance (**unamortized capital cost**, or **UCC**) of the appropriate asset class. UCC is similar to the accounting concept of net book value—the initial capital cost minus accumulated CCA.

2. When assets are sold, either (1) the proceeds or (2) the capital cost, whichever is lower, is deducted from the balance in that asset's class.

3. Assets are considered to be purchased in the middle of the taxation year (i.e., the half-year convention).

4. The maximum CCA deductible for a particular class is the balance of unamortized capital cost (UCC), *after adjusting for the half-year rule in the year of purchase*, multiplied by the CCA rate for that class.

## EXHIBIT 10A-1

### SAMPLE CCA RATES

*Asset Classes Using Declining-Balance CCA*

| | |
|---|---|
| Class 1 (4%) | Buildings or other structures, including component parts acquired after 1987 |
| Class 8 (20%) | Tangible capital property and machinery or equipment not included in another class |
| Class 9 (25%) | Aircraft, including furniture, fittings or equipment attached, and their spare parts |
| Class 10 (30%) | Automobiles, vans, trucks, electronic data processing equipment and systems software, and timber-cutting equipment |
| Class 12 (100%) | Jigs, patterns, tools, utensils costing less than $200, linens, computer software (except systems software) |
| Class 39 (25%) | Manufacturing and processing equipment acquired after 1987 |

*Asset Classes Using Straight-Line CCA*

| | |
|---|---|
| Class 13 | Leasehold improvements (life of lease plus one renewal period; minimum five years, maximum 40 years) |
| Class 14 | Patent, franchise, concession, or licence (life of asset) with a limited life |

Exhibit 10A-2 provides an example of a calculation for CCA. Iles Machine Shop begins business in January 20X1 and purchases four lathes (class 8) for $5,000 each. A fifth lathe is purchased in 20X2 for $5,700. In 20X3, one of the original lathes is sold for $1,200 and is replaced with another lathe costing $6,500. In 20X4 one of the lathes was sold for $1,100.

When net asset additions take place, *the net addition is subject to the half-year convention* (see 20X2 and 20X3 in Exhibit 10A-2). However, when there is a net asset disposal, the entire amount is deducted prior to determining the CCA for the year (see 20X4 in Exhibit 10A-2).

## EXHIBIT 10A-2

### EXAMPLE OF CALCULATING CAPITAL COST ALLOWANCE

| | | |
|---|---:|---:|
| 20X1 UCC opening balance | | 0 |
| Additions (4 × $5,000) | | $20,000 |
| CCA for 20X1; ($20,000 × 20% × 1/2 year) | | (2,000) |
| 20X2 UCC opening balance | | $18,000 |
| Additions | | 5,700 |
| CCA for 20X2; ($18,000 × 20%) + ($5,700 × 20% × 1/2) | | (4,170) |
| 20X3 UCC opening balance | | $19,530 |
| Additions | $6,500 | |
| Proceeds on disposal | (1,200) | |
| Net additions | | 5,300 |
| CCA for 20X3; ($19,530 × 20%) + ($5,300 × 20% × 1/2) | | (4,436) |
| 20X4 UCC opening balance | | $20,394 |
| Proceeds on disposal | | (1,100) |
| CCA for 20X4; [($20,394 − $1,100) × 20%] | | (3,859) |
| 20X4 UCC closing balance | | $15,435 |

The amount deducted on an asset disposal is the lower of (1) the proceeds and (2) the asset's capital cost. Proceeds up to the original capital cost are credited to the asset pool. If the proceeds on sale are higher than the original capital cost, the excess is treated as a capital gain for tax purposes. It is possible (but unlikely) that high proceeds will drive the pool into a negative balance. The negative unamortized capital cost (UCC) is reported as taxable income. More likely, though, proceeds up to capital cost just reduce the positive balance of UCC and reduce the future CCA claimable in that class.

When *all* of the assets in a class are disposed of, any remaining balance is treated as follows:

- A positive UCC balance is deducted as a terminal loss in determining taxable income.
- A negative UCC balance is added to taxable income as *recaptured* CCA.

In effect, this treatment is similar to the gain or loss on disposal of plant assets on the assumption that either too little or too much amortization (i.e., CCA) was taken over the lives of the assets. Any proceeds received in excess of the assets' capital (original) cost are treated as a capital gain for tax purposes.

## SUMMARY OF KEY POINTS

1. Accounting amortization has no tax impact; amortization of capital assets for tax purposes is governed by the *Income Tax Act* and Regulations, and is completely independent of accounting amortization.

2. Income tax amortization is called the *capital cost allowance (CCA)* system.

3. The CCA system groups capital assets into *classes* of assets of similar types. Except for certain buildings, assets are not amortized individually.

4. The regulations specify an amortization *rate* to be used for each class of asset; the rate is a maximum—a company can claim less CCA in any year if management so chooses, without losing the maximum deduction in future years.

5. The half-year rule is applied to assets acquired during a taxation year.

6. Gains and losses are not recognized on the disposal of capital assets in a class, unless all of the assets in the class are disposed of. Proceeds on disposal of individual assets are credited to the asset class.

# APPENDIX 2

## REVALUATION OF CAPITAL ASSETS

Historical cost has long been the generally accepted basis for reporting capital assets in Canada. On rare occasions, however, a company may restate one or more of its capital assets upward, generally by using appraisal values. The general use of appraised values is permitted under international GAAP, but not under Canadian GAAP at present.

Sometimes a company will establish an entirely new basis of accountability, not only for its assets but also for its liabilities. This is known as a *comprehensive revaluation*.

### Revaluation of Individual Assets

When assets are restated on the basis of appraisal values, there is no gain recorded. Instead, the asset value is written up to the appraised value and the offsetting credit is to *accumulated other comprehensive income*. Future amortization expense on the asset is based on the new carrying value. As the asset is amortized to expense, an amount equal to the increase in amortization is transferred from accumulated other comprehensive income to the retained earnings account. When the asset has been fully amortized, the appraisal increment also will have disappeared from other comprehensive income. Alternatively, if the asset is sold, the appraisal increment is eliminated at that time.

For example, suppose that Yvan Limited has land that had been purchased for $50,000 and a building that had been purchased for $100,000 in 20X1. Yvan began depreciating the building in 20X1 on a straight-line basis over 25 years. The area in which the building is located has increased substantially in value, and in 20X6 the company decides to restate the property. Yvan obtains two independent professional appraisals but decides to use the lower of the two: $250,000 for the building and $325,000 for the land. Yvan will continue to use the original estimate of useful life for the building: 25 years from 20X1; 20 years more from 20X6. The revalued building will be depreciated at a straight-line rate of 5%.

Exhibit 10A-3 illustrates the accounting for Yvan Limited for this revaluation. Land is written up by $275,000. For the building, the undepreciated book value after four years of depreciation was $80,000. The appraisal requires an increase in the net book value of $170,000. Since a new basis of accounting is being established for the asset, the accumulated depreciation account is eliminated in the entry to record the revaluation. Subsequent depreciation is based on the fair value of the building but is partially offset by amortization of the equity account.

This treatment of asset revaluation prevents artificial income boosting that would occur if a gain was recorded. It also prevents retained earnings from being dragged down by higher depreciation on the revalued assets.

Remember that revaluations are not permitted under GAAP in Canada or the U.S. Revaluations are permissible under international accounting standards, however.

### Comprehensive Revaluation

Capital assets may be recorded at market value as part of a *financial reorganization*. In a *financial reorganization*, the standings of shareholders and unsecured (or inadequately secured) creditors are altered because the company is not able to meet its debt obligations. Financial reorganizations can be voluntary, but they also can be triggered by creditors. A financial reorganization results in a new basis of accountability for the assets, liabilities, and share equity. A key element of this procedure is that it must be *comprehensive. All assets and liabilities*, not just a selected few, must be revalued at fair market value.

**comprehensive revaluation**

restating the carrying value of a company's assets and liabilities to market value; permitted only when there has been a change in ownership of virtually all of a company's equity interests

**Comprehensive revaluation** is permitted only when one of two conditions has been satisfied and in either situation new values are reasonably determinable. Either:

1. All or virtually all of the equity interests in the enterprise have been acquired, in one or more transactions between non-related parties, by an acquirer that controls the enterprise after the transaction or transactions; or

2. The enterprise has been subject to a financial reorganization, and the same party does not control the enterprise both before and after the reorganization.

> **EXHIBIT 10A-3**
>
> ### EXAMPLE OF CAPITAL ASSET REVALUATION
>
> | | Land | Building |
> |---|---:|---:|
> | *Carrying value at date of appraisal* | | |
> | Historical cost (20X1) | $ 50,000 | $100,000 |
> | Accumulated depreciation | | |
> | ($100,000 × 4% × 5 years) | — | 20,000 |
> | Net book value at date of revaluation (20X5) | $ 50,000 | $ 80,000 |
> | Fair market value; appraisal value | $325,000 | $250,000 |
> | *Recording the appraisal* | | |
> | Capital asset—land ($325,000 − $50,000) | 275,000 | |
> | Accumulated other comprehensive income— | | |
> | appraisal increment | | 275,000 |
> | Capital asset—building ($250,000 − $100,000) | 150,000 | |
> | Accumulated depreciation | 20,000 | |
> | Accumulated other comprehensive income— | | |
> | appraisal increment | | 170,000 |
> | *Annual depreciation subsequent to the revaluation* | | |
> | Depreciation expense ($250,000 × 5%) | 12,500 | |
> | Accumulated depreciation | | 12,500 |
> | Accumulated other comprehensive income— | | |
> | appraisal increment | 8,500 | |
> | Retained earnings ($170,000 × 5%) | | 8,500 |

The crucial element in this recommendation is *that there is a change in control*. All assets and liabilities are recorded at market value to reflect this fresh start. Fair value must be determinable.

In a comprehensive revaluation, accumulated amortization accounts are eliminated, and all assets and liabilities are adjusted to appropriate fair market values. As part of the financial reorganization, equity accounts are likely shuffled around, too. For instance, the preferred shareholders might become common shareholders, or bondholders might become shareholders. Retained earnings, often a deficit, might be wiped out by reducing share capital. The gains and losses from revaluation are part of this equity reshuffling.

No gains or losses from a comprehensive revaluation are recognized on the income statement. Gains and losses should be accounted for as a capital transaction and recorded as share capital, contributed surplus, or a separately identified account within shareholders' equity. These gains and losses should *not* be included in accumulated other comprehensive income, however.

Exhibit 10A-4 shows Saskatchewan Wheat Pool's disclosure of a comprehensive revaluation.

**Circumstances Where Revaluation is Prohibited** Comprehensive revaluation is not permitted in other situations where revaluation might provide more useful or relevant information for the users of the financial statements. Those situations explicitly considered and rejected by the AcSB are when:

1. An enterprise issues shares to the public;

2. An enterprise issues debt based on asset appraisals;

3. An enterprise results from a spinoff transaction to shareholders;

4. An enterprise undergoes a change in its operations or line of business; and

5. Transactions in the equity interests occur when an enterprise is a joint venture.

## EXHIBIT 10A-4

### COMPREHENSIVE REVALUATION

### Saskatchewan Wheat Pool Inc.

The company was subject to a financial reorganization with an effective date of January 31, 2003. The company accounted for the financial reorganization by using the principles of comprehensive revaluation (fresh start accounting) as required under Canadian generally accepted accounting principles (GAAP). Fresh start accounting necessitated the revaluation of all assets and liabilities of the company at estimated fair values and the elimination of the company's deficit.

An equity value of $178.6 million was calculated in order to establish the January 31, 2003 fresh start consolidated balance sheet. The equity value reflected management's estimate, which was based on the trading value of the company's Class B shares combined with an estimate of the fair value of the non-debt component of the company's Convertible Subordinated Notes. As a result of the reorganization and the application of fresh start accounting, the share capital of the company was reduced by $435.4 million, including $88.9 million related to the elimination of the company's deficit.

*Source:* www.sedar.com, Saskatchewan Wheat Pool Inc. 2005/2006 Annual Report released on November 14, 2006.

Revaluation of all assets and liabilities *is* allowed when there has been a change of control resulting from a business combination—that is, a company has a new parent. If that parent owns more than 90% of the shares, then it is clearly the dominant shareholder. The financial statements of the subsidiary are consolidated with those of the parent under GAAP. This involves adjusting all the subsidiary's assets to market value—a tedious process in annual consolidation. To reduce bookkeeping costs, the subsidiary is permitted to record its assets and liabilities at fair value after such an acquisition. This is called *push-down accounting*, because fair market values are *pushed down* from the parent to the subsidiary. You'll encounter this in advanced accounting courses.

The common thread that you should keep in mind is that revaluation is allowed only in very limited circumstances that always involve new controlling shareholders. Also, GAAP prohibits revaluation for only a few items—all assets and liabilities must be revalued together. Finally, revaluation of specific assets may be encountered in non-GAAP situations.

## RELEVANT STANDARDS

*CICA Handbook:*
- Section 3610, Capital Transactions
- Section 3061, Property, Plant and Equipment
- Section 1625, Comprehensive Revaluation of Assets and Liabilities

IASB:
- IAS 16, Property, Plant and Equipment

## SUMMARY OF KEY POINTS

1. Upward revaluation of individual capital assets is not permitted in Canadian GAAP. Capital assets must be recorded at cost.

2. Capital assets may be written up to market value as part of a financial reorganization because a financial reorganization creates a new basis of accounting for the enterprise.

3. Financial reorganizations can either be voluntary or forced by creditors. To qualify for comprehensive revaluation in Canadian GAAP, control of the enterprise must pass from the pre-reorganization shareholders to a new shareholder group.

4. Comprehensive revaluation is also permitted for the acquired company in a business combination, provided that at least 90% of the acquired company's shares have been purchased by the parent company. This is known as *push-down accounting*.

## QUESTIONS

**Q10-1** Compare and explain the words "amortization," "depletion," and "depreciation."

**Q10-2** What effect do changes in the current market value of the asset being amortized have on amortization estimates?

**Q10-3** Explain the difference in meaning between the balances in the following two accounts: (a) allowance for amortization and (b) allowance to reduce inventory to the lower of cost or market.

**Q10-4** Why is disclosure of amortization methods and rates so important?

**Q10-5** List several factors a firm would consider in choosing an amortization method.

**Q10-6** Why might an asset with a 30-year physical life correctly be amortized over only 14 years?

**Q10-7** Why is straight-line amortization so popular in practice?

**Q10-8** What are accelerated methods of amortization. Under what circumstances would these methods generally be appropriate?

**Q10-9** Explain the minimum amortization test, and the circumstances under which it is important. Your response should include an explanation of the difference between residual value and salvage value.

**Q10-10** Explain the accounting policy alternatives that a company may use for assets acquired during the reporting year.

**Q10-11** Explain what is meant by a *system* of amortization. Under what circumstances is such a system appropriate?

**Q10-12** What is the difference between *composite* and *group* depreciation systems?

**Q10-13** Why are composite and group depreciation systems theoretically sound?

**Q10-14** What is an *impairment* in the value of property, plant, and equipment? How is it measured and reported?

**Q10-15** Assume that the fair value of a cash-generating business unit is estimated at $17,000,000, while carrying value of the net assets is $22,000,000. What is the problem? What is the next step?

**Q10-16** What estimates have to be made when recording an impairment of a capital asset?

**Q10-17** Can a writedown of goodwill of a capital asset, or of a business unit, be reversed under Canadian GAAP? How does international GAAP differ from Canadian GAAP regarding impairment loss reversals?

Q10-18  What accounting treatment is required when a company permanently stops using a capital asset?

Q10-19  What is the criterion for defining an asset group for held-for-sale accounting?

Q10-20  If a held-for-sale asset increases its value at a balance sheet date prior to its disposal, can the carrying value be written up? Explain.

Q10-21  If revaluation accounting is used under international GAAP, what entry is made when assets are revalued upward? On what basis is subsequent depreciation expense calculated?

Q10-22  What is a comprehensive revaluation? When can it be used?

## CASE 10-1

### OMEGA PROPERTIES LIMITED

Omega Properties Limited (OPL) is a public corporation that manages 63 hotels under 3 brand names in 5 countries. The main shareholder is Isadora Duncan, who owns 10% of the total outstanding shares in the form of multiple voting shares that carry 15 votes per share. All other shares carry one vote per share. Isadora Duncan is OPL's founder and chief executive officer.

Omega Properties Limited has three operating divisions, each of which is a wholly owned subsidiary of OPL:

- Omega Hotels, Ltd., which operates midrange hotels;
- Xanadu Hotels and Resorts Corporation, a group of luxury hotels; and
- Alpha Express Inc., a small chain of low-cost hotel properties.

The divisions operate largely autonomously, each setting its own operating policies that best suit conditions for its market segment. The senior executives of each division report directly to their counterparts in OPL's head office. The subsidiaries' financial results are fully consolidated with those of OPL.

It is now early December 20X7. OPL Chief Financial Officer Gary Drabinsky is considering how to reflect certain events and transactions that have occurred during the fiscal year ending 31 December 20X7. He has requested your advice as an external professional accountant, and has provided you with the information shown in Exhibit A.

### EXHIBIT A

1. Alpha Express Inc. was purchased by OPL in late 20X3 for $227 million cash. The fair value of OPL's net assets at that time was $192 million. For the first two years that OPL owned Alpha, Alpha achieved the expected profit and cash flow returns. In 20X6, however, the low-cost hotel segment suffered a downturn due to a mild recession. As well, 20X6 saw increased competition from big chains in that market, such as Holiday Inn Express. Now OPL and Alpha executives believe that Alpha will be underperforming for the foreseeable future. Indeed, it is quite possible that the OPL board of directors will decide to sell or dismantle Alpha during 20X8. As an alternative, OPL is thinking of combining Alpha with the main Omega Hotel chain, which continues to be quite profitable.

2. In early 20X7, Xanadu entered into a ten-year contract to manage a luxury hotel in Mumbai. OPL agreed to provide $63 million in loans to the hotel's owners to obtain the contract. The loans are to be used by the hotel's owners for remodelling and upgrading of facilities to meet Xanadu's standards. By the end

of 20X7, OPL had paid $54 million, of which $23 million related to obtaining the management contract and $31 million was part of the loan.

3. During the year, OPL sold a hotel in Hawaii for net proceeds of $140 million. The property had a net book value of $93 million. OPL recorded a gain of $47 million, before taxes. The sales contract stipulates that if the hotel's net operating cash flow over the next three years falls below certain benchmarks, as specified in the sales contract, OPL will be required to refund up to 20% of the sales proceeds. OPL senior management believes that it is highly unlikely that any repayment will be necessary.

4. Omega owns and manages a hotel in New Orleans. The hotel was badly damaged by a severe hurricane in late October 20X6. Just prior to the hurricane, the hotel was enjoying high occupancy and was very profitable. Its net book value was $144 million but its estimated fair value was well over $200 million. The hotel was closed immediately after the hurricane and remained closed through the remainder of 20X6 pending an opportunity for engineers and others to assess the extent of the damage. In 20X7, it became apparent that although the damage could be repaired at a tolerable cost, the future business prospects were not good due to the almost complete absence of either business or leisure travellers. Therefore, in April 20X7, the OPL Board of Directors decided to sell the property and engaged a commercial real estate broker for that purpose. The broker estimated that OPL should expect the property to sell for no more than $37 million in its present condition.

5. The Xanadu division owns no hotels. The division operates exclusively through management contracts. In many cases, the hotels are owned by an investor who also owns 22% of OPL's limited voting shares.

6. In addition to managing hotels under its own brand, OPL also earns fee revenue in both its Omega Hotels and Xanadu divisions by designing and supervising the construction and fitting out of hotels that OPL will neither own nor operate. OPL also earns commissions as a percentage of the cost of goods and materials purchased by these clients through OPL's centralized purchasing system. These fees are treated as a reduction in the cost of operating the central purchasing system.

7. Xanadu entered into a five-year contract for $20 million that permits an unrelated party to use the Xanadu brand name for a new hotel in Japan. Xanadu can cancel the contract if the hotel does not hold to Xanadu's high standards of maintenance and service; no money need be refunded if Xanadu cancels the contract. The contract is renewable by mutual consent. Xanadu has received half of the money, with the rest due in annual instalments of $2 million. The agreement also permits the hotel to use the Xanadu central reservation system at a fee that is half of the fee normally charged to non-OPL properties.

**Required:**

Prepare a report for Mr. Drabinsky in which you point out any reporting problems and recommend appropriate reporting and disclosure, based on the information that you received from him.

## CASE 10-2

### GOOD QUALITY AUTO PARTS

Good Quality Auto Parts Limited (GQAP) is a medium-sized, privately owned producer of auto parts, which are sold to car manufacturers, repair shops, and retail outlets. In March 20X0, the union negotiated a new three-year contract with the company for the 200 shop-floor employees. At the time, GQAP was in financial difficulty and management felt unable to meet the contract demands of the union. Management also believed that a strike of any length would force the company into bankruptcy.

The company proposed that, in exchange for wage concessions, the company would implement a profit-sharing plan whereby the shop-floor employees would receive 10% of the company's annual after-tax profit as a bonus in each year of the contract. Although the union generally finds this type of contract undesirable, it believed that insisting on the prevailing industry settlement would jeopardize GQAP's survival. As a result, the contract terms were accepted.

The contract specifies that no major changes in accounting policies may be made without the change being approved by GQAP's auditor. Another clause in the contract allows the union to engage a chartered accountant to examine the books of the company and meet with GQAP's management and auditor to discuss any issues. Under the terms of the contract, any controversial accounting issues are to be negotiated by the union and management to arrive at a mutual agreement. If the parties cannot agree, the positions of the parties are to be presented to an independent arbitrator for resolution.

GQAP presented to the union its annual financial statements and the unqualified audit report for the year ended 28 February 20X1, the first year during which the profit-sharing plan was in effect. The union engaged you to analyze these financial statements and determine whether there are any controversial accounting issues. As a result of your examination, you identified a number of issues that are of concern to you. You met with the controller of the company and obtained the following information:

1. GQAP wrote off $250,000 of inventory manufactured five to eight years previously. There have been no sales from this inventory in over two years. The controller explained that up until this year she had some hope that the inventory could be sold as replacement parts. However, she now believes that the parts cannot be sold.

2. The contracts GQAP has with the large auto manufacturers allow the purchaser to return items for any reason. The company has increased the allowance for returned items by 10% in the year just ended. The controller contends that, because of the weak economy and stiff competition faced by the auto manufacturers with whom GQAP does business, there will likely be a significant increase in the parts returned.

3. In April 20X0, GQAP purchased $500,000 of new manufacturing equipment. To reduce the financial strain of the acquisition, the company negotiated a six-year payment schedule. Management believed that the company would be at a serious competitive disadvantage if it did not emerge from the current downturn with updated equipment. GQAP decided to use accelerated depreciation at a rate of 40% for the new equipment. The controller argued that because of the rapid technological changes occurring in the industry, equipment purchased now is more likely to become technologically, rather than operationally, obsolete. The straight-line depreciation method applied to the existing equipment has not been changed.

4. Six years ago, GQAP purchased a small auto parts manufacturer and merged it into its own operation. At the time of acquisition, $35,000 of goodwill was recorded. It was not amortized. The company has written off the goodwill in the year just ended. The controller explained that the poor performance of the auto parts industry, and of GQAP in particular, has made the goodwill worthless.

The union has asked you to prepare a report on the position it should take on the issues identified when discussing them with management.

**Required:**

Prepare the report.                                                    (CICA, adapted)

## CASE 10-3

# PROVINCIAL HYDRO

Provincial Hydro (PH) is an electric utility that generates, supplies, and delivers electric power throughout a small Canadian province. It is incorporated as a Crown corporation and operates as a cooperative partnership with the relevant municipalities and the provincial government. It is a financially self-sustaining company without share capital, regulated by the provincial government. Its primary customers are the municipal utilities (which serve about 600,000 end users), 40 large industrial companies (direct service), and 100,000 rural retail customers. PH operates various generating stations, including both nuclear and fossil fuel–fired plants. As a result, it is very capital intensive. This, in turn, makes PH sensitive to the cost of money.

PH plays a major role in attracting industry to the province by maintaining competitive rates for electricity. It is profoundly affected by various pieces of provincial legislation.

The financial statement results are used to set utility rates, although there are specific rules about which expenses are permissible and at what time. Many accounting policies are chosen based on the rules for rate recovery. Profits of the corporation are to be applied toward the reduction of the cost of power for the municipalities with which the utility has a cooperative partnership.

Management and the municipalities are very sensitive to political pressures. PH is in the public spotlight, and financial results and policies can generate considerable publicity.

A major component of the cost of electricity is fuel cost, which includes the following components: fuel (quantity and price), interest on funds tied up in inventory, transportation, and overheads.

PH has two mothballed generating stations, which are not producing energy at present but may be used during peak demand periods when needed. The plants, all oil-fired, were mothballed as more efficient generation methods were developed.

PH has chosen to reflect the situation by accelerating the rate of depreciation to "reflect the reduced economic value" of the assets. PH has produced demand forecasts (which are regularly updated) that predict when and how much energy will have to come from the mothballed plants. Based on these probability factors, PH establishes an amortization rate, higher than the original rate, which takes the change of circumstances into account. Depreciation is charged only when the plant is used. Care is taken to avoid premature write-off while the plant may still be useful.

PH uses the CANDU reactor in its nuclear stations. This reactor has relatively low fuel cost but must use "heavy water," $H_2O_2$ (versus "light water" $H_2O$, which other reactors use). Heavy water is not consumed in the fissioning process but acts as a moderator of the process. With periodic in-station upgrading to remove impurities, heavy water has an indefinite life.

Heavy-water costs, plus interest on inventories of heavy water designated for future use, are capitalized. These capital costs are being written off over 60 years, which is the date PH estimates heavy water will be replaced by new technology. However, the last committed CANDU nuclear unit is due to be retired in 40 years. Management has indicated that nuclear units are regularly upgraded by replacing pressure tubes, which extends their useful life. In addition, the useful life of heavy water does not depend on the life of the station since it can be transferred to another station.

Inventories of fossil fuels are expensed based on an average-cost system where the average is calculated monthly on a rolling basis. Average cost was chosen as it seemed the most fair to current and future customers, and had a smoothing effect on price fluctuations. Recently, however, with significant declines in fossil fuel prices, there has been considerable public comment as electricity prices did not fall accordingly. Management is beginning to consider the alternatives and their advantages and disadvantages.

Management has reminded you that one-time writedowns are not permissible costs in utility rate-setting formulas, nor is it possible to make retroactive changes to the rate structure.

**Required:**

PH has asked you, an external adviser, to consider accounting issues raised and to provide a report incorporating your recommendations.

(ASCA, adapted)

## ASSIGNMENTS

 **A10-1 Amortization Policy:** Everett MacLaughlin, the president of MacLaughlin Enterprises, is proposing the following amortization policy for the capital assets of the company:

> Since most companies use the rates in the *Income Tax Act*, we'll do the same. Buildings will be amortized at a rate of 4%, declining balance, equipment at a rate of 20%, and automobiles and manufacturing equipment at 30%, still declining balance. Those are the tax rules! I know that the manufacturing equipment will last for at least six years, but I prefer the fast write-off to be conservative.

**Required:**

Is this amortization policy acceptable? Write a brief memo to the president explaining your position.

---

 **A10-2 Amortization Policy:** The methods of amortization demonstrated in the chapter include the following:

1. Straight line.
2. Units of production.
3. Declining balance.

**Required:**

Indicate the likely choice of amortization method expected under each of the following circumstances:

a. The firm has a lot of debt on its balance sheet and is trying to meet minimum net income levels specified in debt covenants.
b. The firm is a mining company and assets to be amortized are mine development costs.
c. The firm wants to be comparable to other firms in its industry that commonly use declining balance. However, usage patterns are level over time.
d. The firm wishes to portray stable income and expense patterns over time.
e. The firm wishes to minimize the amount of future (deferred) tax recognized in the financial statements.
f. The firm wants to minimize bookkeeping costs by keeping allocation methods simple.
g. The firm expects to use the asset heavily in initial years, and less as it grows older.
h. The firm expects to use the asset sporadically, but the asset will not wear out unless used.
i. Technological obsolescence is a significant factor in estimating the useful life of the asset.

---

 **A10-3 Amortization Computation:** Mace Company acquired equipment that cost $18,000, which will be amortized on the assumption that it will last six years and have a $1,200 residual value. Several possible methods of amortization are under consideration.

**Required:**

1. Prepare a schedule that shows annual amortization expense for the first two years, assuming the following (show computations and round to the nearest dollar):
   a. Declining-balance method, using a rate of 30%.
   b. Productive-output method. Estimated output is a total of 105,000 units, of which 12,000 will be produced the first year; 18,000 in each of the next two years; 15,000 the fourth year; and 21,000 the fifth and sixth years.
   c. Straight-line method.

2. Repeat your calculations for requirement (1), assuming a useful life of 10 years, a DB rate of 20% that reflects the longer life, but the same number of units of production. The residual value is unchanged. What conclusion can you reach by comparing the results of (1) and (2)?

3. What criteria would you consider important in selecting an amortization method?

---

★★★ **A10-4 Amortization Schedule:** Quick Producers acquired factory equipment on 1 January 20X5, costing $39,000. In view of pending technological developments, it is estimated

that the machine will have a resale value upon disposal in four years of $8,000 and that disposal costs will be $500. Quick has a fiscal year-end that ends on 31 December. Data relating to the equipment follow:

*Estimated service life:*

| | |
|---|---|
| Years | 4 |
| Service-hours | 20,000 |

*Actual operations:*

| Calendar Year | Service Hours |
|---|---|
| 20X5 | 5,700 |
| 20X6 | 5,000 |
| 20X7 | 4,800 |
| 20X8 | 4,400 |

**Required:**
Round to the nearest dollar and show computations.

1. Prepare an amortization schedule for the asset, using
   a. Straight-line amortization.
   b. Declining-balance amortization, using a 50% rate.
   c. Service-hours amortization.

2. Express straight-line amortization as a percentage of original cost.

3. Explain whether:
   a. The rate of 50% was a good choice for DB amortization, and
   b. The 20,000 estimate of total service hours was accurate.

---

★★ **A10-5 Interpreting Amortization Disclosures:** Portions of the 20X0 financial statements of William's Company, a paint manufacturer, are reproduced below ($ thousands):

*Partial Income Statement for the year ended 31 December 20X0*

| | |
|---|---|
| Net sales | $2,266,732 |
| Total expenses | 2,079,455 |
| Income before income tax | 187,277 |
| Income tax | 64,611 |
| Net income | $122,666 |

*Note 1: Significant Accounting Policies*

**Property, Plant, and Equipment.** Property, plant, and equipment are stated on the basis of cost. Amortization is provided principally by the straight-line method. The major classes of assets and ranges of amortization rates are as follows:

| | |
|---|---|
| Buildings | 2%–6% |
| Machinery | 4%–20% |
| Furniture and fixtures | 5%–20% |
| Automobiles and trucks | 10%–33% |

*Note 16: Property, Plant, and Equipment Schedules*

| Cost | Beginning | Additions | Retirements | Other | Ending |
|---|---|---|---|---|---|
| Buildings | $191,540 | $11,574 | $ (960) | ($7,185) | $194,969 |
| Machinery | 404,156 | 43,968 | (16,319) | 466 | 432,271 |

*Total accumulated amortization*

| | Beginning | Additions | Retirements | Other | Ending |
|---|---|---|---|---|---|
| Buildings | $ 62,843 | $ 7,422 | $ (769) | ($4,951) | $ 64,545 |
| Machinery | 211,662 | 37,085 | (12,302) | (845) | 235,600 |

**Required:**

1. What method of amortization is used by Williams?

2. What are the average estimated useful lives of buildings owned by Williams?

3. What percentage of the useful life of buildings remains, on average, at the end of the year?

4. What is the book value of machinery retired in the year?

5. Amortization on buildings and machinery was what percentage of (a) total expenses and (b) pretax earnings?

---

**A10-6 Analysis of Four Amortization Methods—Maximize Income:** On 1 January 20X5, Vello Company, a tool manufacturer, acquired new industrial equipment for $2 million. The new equipment had a useful life of four years, and the residual value was estimated to be $200,000. Vello estimates that the new equipment can produce 14,000 tools in its first year. Production is then estimated to decline by 1,000 units per year over the remaining useful life of the equipment.

The following amortization methods are under consideration:

a. Declining balance (50% rate);
b. Straight line;
c. Sum of the years' digits; and
d. Units of output.

**Required:**

Which amortization method would result in maximum income for financial statement reporting for the three-year period ending 31 December 20X7? Prepare a schedule showing the amount of accumulated amortization at 31 December 20X7, under each method selected. Show supporting computations in good form.

(AICPA, adapted)

---

**A10-7 Identify, Recalculate Amortization:** Beans Company purchased a special machine at a cost of $81,000 plus provincial sales tax of $6,480. The machine is expected to have a residual value of $6,000 at the end of its service life.

To assist in preparing the journal entries for amortization of this machine, your assistant prepared the following spreadsheet:

## BEANS COMPANY

| | | |
|---|---|---|
| Cost of Asset | | $87,480 |
| Asset's Residual Value | | 6,000 |
| Years of Service Life | | 4 |
| Output in units | Year 1 | 1,400 |
| | Year 2 | 1,300 |
| | Year 3 | 1,000 |
| | Year 4 | 1,100 |
| Total expected output | | 4,800 |

| | Method 1 | | Method 2 | | Method 3 | |
|---|---|---|---|---|---|---|
| Year | Amortization Expense | Accumulated Amortization | Amortization Expense | Accumulated Amortization | Amortization Expense | Accumulated Amortization |
| 1 | $21,870 | $21,870 | $27,265 | $27,265 | $21,870 | $21,870 |
| 2 | 16,403 | 38,273 | 25,318 | 52,583 | 21,870 | 43,740 |
| 3 | 12,302 | 50,575 | 19,475 | 72,058 | 21,870 | 65,610 |
| 4 | 36,905 | 87,480 | 21,422 | 93,480 | 21,870 | 87,480 |
| Total | $87,480 | | $93,480 | | $87,480 | |

The spreadsheet includes statistics relating to the machine, and calculates amortization using three different methods—productive output, straight line, and declining balance at a 50% rate. However, due to some carelessness, your assistant made at least one error in the calculations for each method.

**Required:**

1. Identify which method is the:
   a. Productive method;
   b. Straight-line method; and
   c. Declining-balance method (50% rate).
2. Describe the error(s) made in the calculations for each method.
3. Recalculate amortization expense for Year 2 under each method.

(CGA-Canada, adapted)

---

★★ **A10-8 Depreciation and Depletion—Schedule, Entries:** Gaspe Mining Corporation bought mineral-bearing land for $150,000 that engineers estimate will yield 200,000 kilograms of economically removable ore. The land will have a value of $30,000 after the ore is removed.

To work the property, Gaspe built structures and sheds on the site that cost $40,000; these will last 10 years, and because their use is confined to mining and it would be expensive to dismantle and move them, they will have no residual value. Machinery that cost $29,000 was installed at the mine, and the added cost for installation was $7,000. This machinery should last 15 years; like that of the structures, the usefulness of the machinery is confined to these mining operations. Dismantling and removal costs when the property has been fully worked will approximately equal the value of the machinery at that time; therefore, Gaspe does not plan to use the structures or the machinery after the minerals have been removed.

In the first year, Gaspe removed only 15,000 kilograms of ore; however, production was doubled in the second year. It is expected that all of the removable ore will be extracted within eight years from the start of operations.

**Required:**

Prepare a schedule showing (1) unit and total depletion and amortization and (2) net book value of the capital assets for the first and second years of operation. Use the units-of-production method of depreciation for all assets.

★★★    **A10-9 Amortization and Sale:** Gentry Hair Salons opened in April 20X4. It spent $96,000 on leasehold improvements on a property for which it signed a five-year lease on 1 April 20X4. The lease was renewable at Gentry's option for another five years. Equipment was purchased at a cost of $49,600. The equipment was expected to last for 20,000 service hours, or approximately eight years. Service hours consumed in 2,400 in 20X4, 4,900 in 20X5, and 3,700 in 20X6. Equipment will have a $2,000 residual value at the end of its 8-year useful life, but the leasehold improvements will be worthless if the leased property is vacated. Gentry has a 31 December year-end.

**Required:**

1. Calculate total amortization for 20X4, 20X5, and 20X6, assuming:
   a. Straight-line amortization for both assets. Assume Gentry claims a half-year of amortization in the year of acquisition and a half-year in the final year.
   b. Declining-balance amortization at a 40% rate for equipment and 30% for leaseholds. Assume Gentry claims a full year of amortization in the year of acquisition and none in the final year.
   c. Service-life amortization for equipment and straight-line amortization for leaseholds. For straight-line amortization, assume Gentry claims a half-year of amortization in the year of acquisition and a half-year in the final year.

2. At the end of 20X6, Gentry ceases operations. It pays a $30,000 fee to the landlord and quits the leased property, abandoning the leasehold improvements. Equipment is sold for $9,000. Provide the entry to record the payment, the write-off of the leasehold improvements, and the sale of the equipment under each of the three amortization methods in part (1).

3. Comment on the pattern of losses recorded in part (2).

★    **A10-10 Minimum Amortization Test:** AC Metals bought a piece of manufacturing equipment at the beginning of 20X5.

- The equipment had an original cost of $750,000.
- AC expects to use the equipment for 10 years, and then sell it. The equipment will likely have a five-year useful life remaining at that time.
- Expected residual value at the end of 10 years is $300,000.
- Expected salvage value at the end of 15 years is nil—scrap value only.
- AC Metals uses straight-line amortization on all manufacturing assets.

**Required:**

1. Explain the difference between the terms "residual" and "salvage values," as used above.

2. How much amortization on the equipment should AC recognize in 20X5? Explain the circumstances that cause this result.

★★    **A10-11 Cost; Minimum Amortization:** The following information relates to Jaybird Corporation's purchase of equipment on 10 April 20X7:

| | |
|---|---:|
| Invoice price | $440,000 |
| Discount for early payment (if paid by 30 April) | $ 8,800 |
| Shipping costs | $ 16,000 |
| Installation | $ 10,000 |
| Training and testing | $ 22,000 |
| Estimated physical life | 15 years |
| Estimated salvage value (removal cost) | $ (12,000) |
| Estimated useful life to Jaybird | 6 years |
| Estimated residual value | $330,000 |

The equipment was installed and tested during the week of 25 April. Training took place over the first two weeks of May. The equipment was ready for use on 17 May, and entered production on June 2. Jaybird paid the invoice price on 15 June 20X7. Jaybird management uses straight-line depreciation for the company's equipment. Jaybird's fiscal year ends on 31 December.

**Required:**

1. What is the book value of the equipment after installation?

2. Compute amortization expense for 20X7 under Canadian GAAP, using the straight-line method, under each of the following assumptions:
    a. Exact, to the closest month;
    b. Full first-year convention; and
    c. Half-year convention.

3. Calculate amortization expense for both 20X7 and 20X8 under each of the methods in requirement 2, using double-declining balance depreciation.

4. Suppose that Jaybird is reporting under international GAAP. Explain how that would change the preceding depreciation amounts, if at all. A numerical recalculation is not necessary.

★★ **A10-12 Fractional-Year Amortization:** Jackson Company's records show the following machinery acquisitions and retirements during the first two years of operations:

| | Acquisition | | Retirement | |
| Date | Cost of Machinery | Estimated Useful Life (years) | Acquisition Date | Original Cost |
|---|---|---|---|---|
| 1 January 20X5 | $50,000 | 10 | | |
| 1 April 20X5 | 40,000 | 5 | | |
| 1 December 20X6 | 20,000 | 10 | | |
| 31 December 20X6 | | | 20X5* | $7,000 |

*part of machinery acquired on 1 January 20X5

**Required:**

1. Compute amortization expense for 20X5 and for 20X6 and the balances of the machinery and related accumulated amortization accounts at the end of each year, using straight-line amortization. Machinery is depreciated according to the number of months of ownership in the year of acquisition or retirement. Assume no residual values. There are no sale proceeds upon retirement. Show computations and round to the nearest dollar. Set up separate columns in a schedule for machinery and for accumulated amortization.

2. Compute amortization expense for 20X5 and for 20X6 and the balances of the machinery and related accumulated amortization accounts at the end of each year using straight-line amortization. Machinery is depreciated for one-half year in the year of acquisition. Machinery retired is amortized for one-half year in its year of retirement. Assume no residual values. There are no sale proceeds upon retirement. Show computations and round to the nearest dollar. Set up separate columns in a schedule for machinery and for accumulated amortization.

3. Comment on the differences between requirements (1) and (2).

(AICPA, adapted)

★★★ **A10-13 Analyze Accounts, Cash Flow Statement:** Selected accounts included under property, plant, and equipment on Abel Company's balance sheet at 31 December 20X5, had the following balances (at original cost):

| | |
|---|---|
| Land | $400,000 |
| Land improvements | 135,000 |
| Accumulated amortization, land improvements | (23,143) |
| Buildings (acquired 30 October 20X0) | 900,000 |
| Accumulated amortization, building | (154,285) |
| Machinery and equipment (acquired 30 April 20X3 and 1 April 20X5) | 950,000 |
| Accumulated amortization, machinery and equipment | (463,600) |

- Building and existing land improvements amortization is based on the straight-line method over 35 years.
- Machinery and equipment amortization is based on the declining-balance method, using a rate of 20%.
- Residual values are immaterial and are not included in amortization calculations.
- The company claims a full year of amortization in the year of acquisition and none in the year of disposal.

During 20X6, the following transactions occurred:

a. A plant facility consisting of land and building was acquired from Club Company in exchange for 10,000 of Abel's common shares. On the acquisition date, Abel's shares had a closing market price of $32 per share on a national stock exchange. The plant facility was carried on Club's accounts at $95,000 for land and $130,000 for the building at the exchange date. Current appraised values for the land and building, respectively, are $120,000 and $240,000.

b. A tract of land was acquired for $230,000 as a potential future building site.

c. Machinery was purchased at a total cost of $375,000. Additional costs were incurred as follows:

| | |
|---|---|
| Freight and unloading | $ 7,500 |
| Sales taxes | 15,000 |
| Installation | 37,500 |

d. Expenditures totalling $120,000 were made for new parking lots, streets, and sidewalks at the corporation's various plant locations. These items had an estimated useful life of 15 years.

e. A machine that cost $50,000 on 1 April 20X5 was scrapped on 30 June 20X6. DB amortization, at a 20% rate, has been recorded in 20X5.

f. A machine was sold for $25,000 on 1 July 20X6. Original cost of the machine was $37,000 at 1 January 20X3, and it had been amortized from 20X3 to 20X5 using the DB method.

**Required:**

1. Prepare a detailed analysis of the changes in each balance sheet account for 20X6.

2. Show how the transactions in requirement (1) would be shown in the cash flow statement. The indirect method is used in the operating activities section.

★★ **A10-14 Comprehensive Intangibles—Accounting and Amortization:** Beta Designs Limited began operations in 20X5, and, at the end of its first year of operations, reported a balance of $1,376,950 in an account called "intangibles." Upon further investigation, it is discovered that the account had been debited throughout the year as follows:

| | | |
|---|---|---|
| 5 Jan. | Organization costs; legal fees. Economic life is indefinite. | $ 25,800 |
| 1 Feb. | Patent registration; legal fees re: patent with 20-year life to be used in research activities. | 10,750 |

| | | |
|---|---|---:|
| 1 July | Operating expenses, first six months. | 509,700 |
| 1 Aug. | Goodwill; excess of purchase price of an advertising company paid over tangible assets acquired. | 345,000 |
| 10 Nov. | Copyright acquired; remaining legal life is 29 years but economic life is 10 years. | 37,600 |
| 30 Nov. | Trademark registration; legal fees. The trademark is expected to have an indefinite economic life. | 13,400 |
| 5 Dec. | Staff training costs; staff is expected to stay with the company for an average of three years. | 45,200 |
| 31 Dec. | Research costs incurred over the year; 40% of all research costs are properly classified as development. The product developed will begin commercial production next year. | 389,500 |
| | | $1,376,950 |

**Required:**

1. Prepare a correcting entry that reallocates all amounts charged to intangibles to the appropriate accounts. State any assumptions made.

2. Calculate amortization expense on intangible assets for 20X5. Straight-line amortization, to the exact month of purchase, is used. All residual values are expected to be zero.

★ **A10-15 Inventory Appraisal System:** Mite Engineering Company acquired a large number of small tools at the beginning of operations on 1 January 20X5, for $10,000. During 20X5 and 20X6, Mite disposed of several used tools, receiving cash salvage value of $800 in 20X5 and $1,000 in 20X6. During 20X6, Mite acquired additional tools at a cost of $3,000. Inventories of tools on hand, valued at current acquisition cost adjusted for the present condition of the tools, indicated a value of $6,500 on 31 December 20X5, and $7,500 on 31 December 20X6. Mite uses the inventory appraisal system of depreciation for small tools.

**Required:**

How much amortization expense will be recognized on the small tools in 20X5 and 20X6? Show calculations.

★ **A10-16 Group Depreciation:** Witherspoon Consulting, LLP, owns 95 desktop computers. Each computer is marked with an inventory bar code so that the firm can keep physical control over the assets. For accounting purposes, the firm does not attempt to account for each computer individually. Instead, the company uses group depreciation. The firm's policy is to calculate depreciation on the ending net balance of the group account (that is, the asset account minus the accumulated depreciation), using an annual declining balance rate of 30%.

At the beginning of 20X8, the asset control account had a balance of $285,000 and accumulated depreciation of $165,000. During 20X8, the following transactions occurred:

a. On 5 March 20X8, the firm purchased 20 new desktop computers from Hewlett Packard at a total cost of $60,500.

b. On 15 March 20X8, the company's IT director removed 15 desktop computers from service and replaced them with the new computers. The retired computers had been purchased in 20X2 for an aggregate cost of $43,500. The computers were sold to a recycler for $3,000.

c. On 22 November 20X8, the firm bought another six new computers for $11,000, to provide for staff expansion.

**Required:**

Determine the amount of depreciation expense for 20X8. Show all calculations clearly.

★ **A10-17 Composite Depreciation:** WIT Company owned four machines that functioned together as a single operating system. All of the machines had been acquired as a group on 1 January 20X5:

| Machine | Original Cost | Estimated Residual Value | Estimated Life (years) |
|---------|---------------|--------------------------|------------------------|
| A | $20,000 | None | 4 |
| B | 16,000 | $2,000 | 7 |
| C | 37,500 | 1,500 | 12 |
| D | 30,000 | 4,000 | 10 |

**Required:**

1. Prepare a schedule calculating individual straight-line depreciation for each machine that shows the following: cost, residual value, depreciable cost, life in years, and annual depreciation.

2. Compute the composite depreciation rate (based on cost), composite life, and 20X5 depreciation expense if the machines are depreciated using the composite system.

★★ **A10-18 Composite Depreciation:** Capital assets acquired on 1 January 20X5 by Sculley Company are to be amortized under the composite system. Details regarding each asset are given in the schedule below.

| Component | Cost | Estimated Residual Value | Estimated Life (Years) |
|-----------|------|--------------------------|------------------------|
| A | $90,000 | $10,000 | 10 |
| B | 30,000 | 0 | 6 |
| C | 76,000 | 16,000 | 15 |
| D | 12,400 | 400 | 8 |

**Required:**

1. Calculate the composite life and annual composite amortization rate (based on cost) for the asset components listed above. Give the entry to record amortization after one full year of use. Round the amortization rate to the nearest two decimal places.

2. During 20X6, it was necessary to replace component B, which was sold for $16,000. The replacement component cost $36,000 and will have an estimated residual value of $3,000 at the end of its estimated six-year useful life. Record the disposal and substitution, which was a cash acquisition.

3. Record amortization at the end of 20X6, assuming that the company does not change the composite rate determined in requirement (1).

★★★ **A10-19 Accounting for Capital Assets:** Brannen Manufacturing Corporation was incorporated on 3 January 20X4. The corporation's financial statements for its first year's operations were not examined by a public accountant. You have been engaged to examine the financial statements for the year ended 31 December 20X5, and your examination is substantially completed. The corporation's adjusted trial balance appears as follows:

## BRANNEN MANUFACTURING CORPORATION ADJUSTED TRIAL BALANCE

| 31 December 20X5 | Debit | Credit |
|---|---|---|
| Cash | $ 11,000 | |
| Accounts receivable | 68,500 | |
| Allowance for doubtful accounts | | $ 500 |
| Inventories | 38,500 | |
| Prepaid expenses | 10,500 | |
| Machinery | 75,000 | |
| Equipment | 29,000 | |
| Accumulated amortization | | 12,100 |
| Patents | 102,000 | |
| Goodwill | 24,000 | |
| Licensing agreement 1, net | 48,750 | |
| Licensing agreement 2, net | 59,000 | |
| Accounts payable | | 152,400 |
| Unearned revenue | | 12,500 |
| Share capital | | 288,000 |
| Retained earnings deficit, opening | 17,000 | |
| Sales revenue | | 661,500 |
| Cost of goods sold | 466,000 | |
| Selling and general expenses | 173,000 | |
| Amortization expense | 0 | |
| Interest expense | 4,750 | |
| Totals | $1,127,000 | $1,127,000 |

The following information relates to accounts that may still require adjustment:

a. Patents for Brannen's manufacturing process were acquired 2 January 20X5, for $68,000. An additional $34,000 was spent in late December 20X5 to improve machinery covered by the patents and was debited to the patents account. Patents are valid for 20 years.

b. During the second week of January 20X5, an explosion caused a permanent 60% reduction in the expected revenue-producing value of licensing agreement 1. No entry was made to reflect the explosion in 20X5. The agreement is expected to have an unlimited life at this lower amount.

c. On 1 January 20X5, Brannen bought licensing agreement 2, which has a life expectancy of 10 years. The balance in the licensing agreement 2 account includes the $58,000 purchase price and $2,000 in acquisition costs, but it has been reduced by a credit of $1,000 for the advance collection of 20X6 revenue from the agreement. No amortization on agreement 2 has been recorded.

d. The balance in the goodwill account includes (1) $8,000 paid 30 April 20X5, for a software program that management believes will assist in increasing Brannen's sales over a period of three years following the disbursement, and (2) legal expenses of $16,000 incurred for Brannen's incorporation on 3 January 20X4.

e. All machinery is being amortized on a straight-line basis, assuming a 10% residual value, over its expected life of eight years. There were no acquisitions in 20X5 other than that mentioned in (a).

f. Brannen's practice is to provide a full year's amortization in the year of acquisition and no amortization in the year of disposal.

g. Equipment is amortized using the declining-balance method, at a rate of 20%, and assuming a residual value of $4,000. Of the accumulated amortization at the end of 20X4, $5,800 relates to equipment. On 1 October 20X5, a piece of equipment had been bought for $9,000, and properly debited to the equipment account.

**Required:**

1. Prepare journal entries as of 31 December 20X5, as required by the information given above, including correcting entries. State any assumptions made. Ignore income taxes.
2. What items would appear on the cash flow statement as a result of the 20X5 capital asset transactions? Assume that the indirect method is used for the operating activities section.
3. What accounting policy information does the company have to disclose? Be specific.

(AICPA, adapted)

 **A10-20 Asset Impairment—Five Situations:** Each of the following five cases is independent.

a. Marlene Incorporated produces several lines of office furniture. All of the furniture is sold through sales agents who sell the full array of lines. Each line is developed by the company internally, and the development costs are capitalized and amortized over 12 years. After several years of high revenue, one of Marlene's lines has recently suffered a significant decline. Marlene is considering shutting down production and discontinuing the line. About 40% of the development cost has not yet been amortized.
b. Antigonish Actuators Limited (AAL) has a production and sales division in northern Ontario. The divisional vice-president reports directly to the AAL CEO. AAL is decentralized, and the Northern Ontario division is one of several such divisions. The Northern Ontario division has operated at a loss for the past two years, and future prospects seem dim. The division has substantial tangible capital assets.
c. Canadian Wheels Corporation operates hardware and automotive stores throughout Canada. A few years ago, the company opened a series of stores in the northwestern U.S.. The new stores have not been doing well, and the company is thinking of selling them or shutting them down.
d. Capital Helicopter Services Corporation (CHSC) provides helicopter services for other corporations, mainly those in the resource industry that need extensive helicopter services for offshore oil and gas platforms, forestry operations, and otherwise inaccessible field operations. In addition, the company operates a separate division within Canada that manufactures airframe parts for manufacturers. This division is completely separate from the company's other operations and has a separate reporting line directly to the company's senior management. The division generates more than 10% of the company's overall revenues. However, the division has become only marginally profitable, and CHSC management has decided to sell the division and has put a plan for disposition in place.
e. Several years ago, Robertson Connectors Corporation (RCC) purchased the patents for a new type of connector. The new connector has enjoyed great success until recently. A competitor introduced a new product that is almost the same as RCC's product and that can be used interchangeably. RCC launched a patent infringement suit against the competitor, and RCC management was confident of success. In 20X4, however, the court ruled against RCC, thereby leaving the competitor free to continue its product. RCC management is considering whether to appeal the decision.

**Required:**

For each situation, explain whether an impairment test is necessary. If you need more information, explain what information you need and why you need it.

★ **A10-21 Asset Impairment:** Fellalova Corporation has recently abandoned an industrial site near the heart of a major city. The site consists of land and two adjoined buildings. The buildings have been emptied of all equipment. Following the abandonment, the company obtained a professional assessment of the value of the site. At the date of abandonment, the land is shown on Fellalova's balance sheet at its historical cost of $2,000,000. The buildings originally cost $3 million to construct, but their amortized carrying value now is $1.7 million. A professional valuation has determined that the fair value of the land is now only $200,000 in its current condition. However, the law requires Fellalova to clean the land of toxins prior to its sale or the sale of the building. Cleaning the land will cost an estimated $1,500,000. Once the land is cleaned, the fair value of the land will be $2,300,000 and the building will have a fair value of $800,000. It will take approximately eight months to clean the land. The estimated cost to sell the land and building (after cleaning the land) is $180,000 plus 5% of the sales price.

**Required:**

a. Prepare an adjusting journal entry to record the impairment.

b. What information pertaining to this abandoned site should Fellalova report in its financial statements and notes?

---

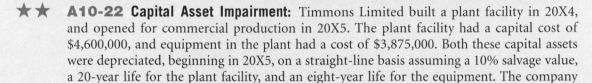

**A10-22 Capital Asset Impairment:** Timmons Limited built a plant facility in 20X4, and opened for commercial production in 20X5. The plant facility had a capital cost of $4,600,000, and equipment in the plant had a cost of $3,875,000. Both these capital assets were depreciated, beginning in 20X5, on a straight-line basis assuming a 10% salvage value, a 20-year life for the plant facility, and an eight-year life for the equipment. The company uses the half-year convention.

Late in 20X9, the market for Timmons' products declined precipitously, because of a competing product offered at a lower price. Operations in the plant were temporarily suspended while inventory was reduced, but are expected to restart on a more modest level in 20X10.

**Required:**

1. Explain the conditions that would lead to a writedown of capital assets. What factors would be examined in this case to ascertain whether a writedown was needed?

2. Calculate the net book value of the plant and equipment at the end of 20X9. Timmons charges a half-year of amortization in the year of acquisition.

3. Assume that an impairment should be recognized at the end of 20X9. Describe how the value of the capital assets, for the impairment test, would be calculated.

4. Assume that an impairment should be recognized in 20X9, and that the assets are to be written down to 60% of their net book value prior to the writedown. Provide the entry to record the writedown.

---

★ **A10-23 Asset Impairment:** Softsweat Incorporated is a software development company. It has several products on the market, including the widely used PlayMark animation  software. The cash flows from PlayMark are clearly distinguishable within Softsweat. The company has recorded development costs of $1.4 million relating to PlayMark, which is being amortized on a straight-line basis over seven years. At the end of 20X5, the carrying value was $980,000. Softsweat maintains a separate account for accumulated amortization on PlayMark.

In 20X5, a large U.S. company, Macrosoftie, released a competing product that has been hailed as a substantial improvement over PlayMark. However, the competing product requires installation of a great deal of additional Macrosoftie software to make the new product run efficiently. In addition, the high price may delay its acceptance by some users.

Because of the new competition, Softsweat management decided that an impairment test should be made. In January 20X6, as the 20X5 financial statements were being prepared, the company hired a professional business valuator. The valuator's appraisal was that the fair value of PlayMark at the end of 20X5 was $500,000.

**Required:**

1. Prepare the necessary adjusting journal entry to record the results of the impairment test.
2. Suppose that in 20X6, the Macrosoftie product was found to be unreliable, and sales of PlayMark returned to almost their 20X4 level. The fair value of PlayMark therefore was $800,000 at the end of 20X6. How (if at all) would this change be recorded in Softsweat's financial statements for 20X6?

---

★ **A10-24 Asset Group Impairment:** On 2 July 20X6, the Board of Directors of Joshi Limited approved the sale of the assets of its northern Ontario operations and began action to negotiate a sale. A sale is expected within the next year. The operation is one part of Joshi's overall operations, and therefore does not qualify as a discontinued operation. The assets were shown on Joshi's 30 June 20X6 balance sheet as follows:

|  | Book Value (thousands) |
|---|---|
| Inventory | $ 700 |
| Building | 2,000 |
| Accumulated depreciation—building | (1,100) |
| Equipment | 1,800 |
| Accumulated depreciation—equipment | (850) |
| Furniture and fixtures | 900 |
| Accumulated depreciation—furniture and fixtures | (550) |
| Total | $2,900 |

An impairment test indicated that the fair value of the northern Ontario operations as a group is $2,000. Brokerage costs will be 10% of the selling price. The fair value of the building as a separate asset is $800.

**Required:**
How will the impairment test affect the carrying value of the assets? Be specific, and show calculations.

---

★ **A10-25 Asset Group Impairment:** The abrasives group of Sarnia Chemical Products Incorporated (SCPI) has been suffering a decline in its business, due to new product introductions by competitors. At 31 December 20X5, the assets of the abrasives group are shown as follows (in millions) on the company's balance sheet:

|  | Cost | Accumulated Amortization | Net Book Value |
|---|---|---|---|
| Inventory | $ 60 | — | $ 60 |
| Equipment | 300 | $120 | 180 |
| Fixtures | 180 | 50 | 130 |
| Patent rights | 90 | 60 | 30 |
|  | $630 | $230 | $400 |

An impairment test indicates that the fair value of the abrasives group's assets is $300 million. The assets are not separable—they must be operated or sold together as a group.

**Required:**
Prepare an adjusting journal entry to record the impairment.

---

★★ **A10-26 Goodwill Impairment:** Information has been collected regarding Black Company's acquired business units:

|                          | Unit 1      | Unit 2       | Unit 3       | Unit 4      |
|--------------------------|-------------|--------------|--------------|-------------|
| *Book values, 31 December 20X5* |      |              |              |             |
| Book value, assets       |             |              |              |             |
| other than goodwill      | $3,200,000  | $17,900,000  | $20,400,000  | $3,900,000  |
| Book value, goodwill     | 500,000     | 6,000,000    | 3,000,000    | 5,600,000   |
| Book value, liabilities  | 2,100,000   | 11,700,000   | 6,900,000    | 1,700,000   |
| *Fair values, 31 December 20X5* |      |              |              |             |
| Fair value, net assets   |             |              |              |             |
| acquired                 | 2,200,000   | 7,900,000    | 13,700,000   | 2,600,000   |
| Fair value, unit as      |             |              |              |             |
| a whole                  | 3,000,000   | 16,000,000   | 14,000,000   | 6,000,000   |

**Required:**

For each unit, perform the two-step test to determine the need to record an impairment of goodwill. Calculate the impairment loss, if any.

---

★ **A10-27 Cash Flow Statement:** Idea Limited reflected the following items in the 20X5 financial statements:

*Income statement*
| | |
|---|---|
| Amortization expense, machinery | $300,000 |
| Amortization expense, patent | 60,000 |
| Loss on sale of machinery | 25,000 |
| Gain on sale of land | 30,000 |

*Balance sheet*
| | |
|---|---|
| Decrease in land account | $400,000 |
| Increase in net patent account | 65,000 |
| Decrease in net machinery account | 456,000 |

The only entry through the land account was a sale of land. The other accounts may reflect more than one transaction.

**Required:**

List the items that would appear on the cash flow statement as a result of the above items. Indicate in which section each item would appear. Assume that the indirect method is used for the operating activities section. State any assumptions that you make.

---

★★★ **A10-28 Comprehensive Capital Asset Transactions and Amortization:** MH Plumbing Incorporated (MH) is the largest plumbing contractor in Moncton. Information on selected transactions/events is given below:

a. On 15 January 20X2, MH purchased land and a warehouse building for $455,000. The land was appraised at $175,000, while the building was appraised at $375,000.
b. During January and February 20X2, MH spent $53,200 on the warehouse building, renovating it for its expected use as a storage and shipping facility.
c. MH used the warehouse building from February 20X2 until August 20X7. The building was expected to have a 20-year life and a salvage value of $11,000.
d. In late August 20X7, MH traded the warehouse and land for another facility on the other side of town. The second facility was slightly larger. MH paid $33,750 to the vendor, and $19,800 in legal fees as a result of the transaction. The new warehouse was appraised at $425,000, and the new land at $180,000. This warehouse facility was expected to have a useful life of 18 years, and a salvage value of $7,800.
e. MH used the new warehouse facility from August 20X7 until February 20X9. At that time, a fire destroyed the warehouse. MH received $356,800 from the insurance company.

f. MH called for tenders for construction of a new warehouse building in March 20X9, but the lowest bid was $788,000. The company decided to self-construct, and began in May 20X9. Monies spent were as follows:

| | |
|---|---:|
| Architect fees | $ 80,000 |
| Removing debris from building site | 13,400 |
| Material cost for construction | 245,800 |
| Labour cost for construction | 199,600 |
| Parking lot | 45,200 |
| General overhead assigned to construction | 24,800 |
| Interest on loans related to construction | 34,100 |

g. MH received a $100,000 investment tax credit in 20X9 as a result of the building activities, which reduced 20X9 taxes payable.

h. MH occupied its new warehouse in September 20X9. It was appraised at $650,000. It was expected to last for 25 years, and have a salvage value of $20,000.

**Required:**

Prepare journal entries to record all transactions listed above, including annual amortization to the end of 20X9. Record annual amortization using a declining-balance method of 10% for buildings, and 5% for parking lots. MH records a full year of amortization in the year of acquisition and no amortization in the year of disposal. Justify any decisions made with respect to accounting policy or application.

(CGA-Canada, adapted)

 **A10-29 Asset Held for Sale:** In July 20X4, the Bank of P.E.I. negotiated an outsourcing agreement with Hamlet-Packard (HP), a major computer services company. Under the agreement, HP will provide full computing services for a major segment of the bank's business, effective 16 August 20X4. As a result, the bank declared one of its own computing centres to be redundant, and asked for tender offers from other major corporations. The bank will sell the equipment only—all software will be removed prior to sale. The redundant computer installation is quite new, having been purchased by the bank only nine months previously (in November 20X3) for $2,000,000. The bank takes 7.5% declining-balance amortization per quarter, with full amortization in the quarter of acquisition.

A dealer in used computer equipment was retained on 27 July 20X4. The dealer estimates that the equipment can be sold for approximately $1,300,000. For security reasons, the bank will undertake the physical removal of the equipment. The cost of removal is estimated at $100,000. The dealer will receive a commission of 8% on the sales price.

By the end of 20X4, the dealer had received several expressions of interest from prospective buyers. As a result, the dealer revised the estimated sales price to $1,450,000. On 29 February 20X5 (after the 31 December 20X4 statements had been issued), the bank signed a sales agreement with a purchaser for $1,400,000. The Bank of P.E.I. prepares financial statements quarterly.

**Required:**

Prepare all journal entries necessary to record the above information, in accordance with Canadian GAAP.

 **A10-30 Assets Held for Sale:** On 30 September 20X7, Renége Corporation closed a "big box" retail store on the outskirts of Edmonton. The merchandise is being moved to Renége's other stores in Alberta. The interior fixtures have been sold to a disposal company for $320,000. The disposal company will dismantle and remove the fixtures.

Renége has retained a commercial real property sales agent to find a buyer for the building and land. The agent has posted an asking price of $1,900,000 for the building and land. The agent estimates that the land is worth about one-third of that amount. The agent will receive a commission of 4% when a sale closes, and transfer taxes and fees will be 3%. The agent is confident that a buyer can be found within the next 12 months. The store property is shown on Renége's books as follows, with amortization (depreciation) updated to 30 September 20X7:

|  | Land | Building | Fixtures |
|---|---|---|---|
| Cost | $400,000 | $4,800,000 | $800,000 |
| Accumulated depreciation | — | 2,560,000 | 560,000 |
|  | $400,000 | $2,240,000 | $240,000 |

In March 20X8, Renége reaches agreement with a buyer to sell the land and building for $2,000,000. The sale closes on 1 April 20X8. Renége's fiscal year ends on 31 December.

**Required:**

1. Prepare the necessary journal entries in 20X7 to record Renége's abandonment of the Edmonton store and its sale in 20X8.

2. What amounts relating to this property will appear on Renége's income statement, balance sheet, and cash flow statement on 31 December 20X7? How will each amount be classified? Renége uses the indirect method of reporting cash flows from operations.

★★ **A10-31 Asset Held for Sale:** On 17 August 20X2, the board of Hellinger Incorporated voted unanimously to sell the CEO's corporate jet. The plane had cost $20 million three years earlier and was being depreciated at 20% declining balance per year, with no amortization in the year of acquisition. At the end of 20X2, the accumulated depreciation is $7.2 million. Additional information is as follows:

- An airplane broker was retained in late August 20X2. The broker's fee is 5% of the eventual sales price.
- Due to a weak market for corporate jets, the broker estimated a potential price of $13 million, even though the plane is fairly new and is in excellent condition.
- Transportation to the eventual buyer will be the responsibility of the buyer.
- In early January 20X3, as Hellinger's 20X2 financial statements were being prepared, the broker informed the Board that the market had improved significantly; the broker now expected to be able to get about $15 million.
- The plane was sold on 17 March 20X3 for $12.4 million.

**Required:**
Prepare the appropriate journal entries to record the preceding information.

★★★ **A10-32 CCA Calculations (Appendix 1):** Dixon Company purchased several small pieces of equipment in May 20X5 for $300,000, which qualifies as a Class 8 asset for tax purposes. The equipment has a useful life of six years. Subsequent transactions were:

| | |
|---|---|
| 30 September 20X6 | Sold equipment bought in 20X5 for $20,000; proceeds, $11,200 |
| 1 February 20X7 | Sold equipment bought in 20X5 for $40,000; proceeds, $19,800 |
| 31 August 20X7 | Bought Class 8 equipment for $25,000 |
| 16 November 20X8 | Bought Class 8 equipment for $36,000 |

**Required:**
Calculate CCA and the closing UCC balance for 20X5 to 20X8.

★★ **A10-33 Asset Revaluation (Appendix 2):** Grand Corporation is a privately held corporation. The majority of the shares are held by Ed Grand, and financial statements are prepared primarily to satisfy the needs of the bankers and to keep Mr. Grand up to date on how well his company is performing. The company has a block of commercial real estate in the downtown core of a small city; this real estate was acquired in 20X1 and has appreciated significantly since then. Mr. Grand wished to reflect the current appraised value of this investment in his financial statements, as the banker continually asks for market value information when assessing loan security.

At the beginning of 20X4, the asset accounts are as follows:

| | |
|---|---|
| Land | $2,100,000 |
| Buildings, net | 810,000 |

The buildings are being amortized over 30 years, in the amount of $30,000 per year.

Appraisals indicate that land values are in the range of $5,000,000, while the buildings were worth, at the beginning of 20X4, $1,500,000. The estimate of useful life has not changed.

### Required:

1. Record the revaluation of assets as of the beginning of 20X4. Note that the accumulated amortization account for the building is eliminated when the building is revalued.

2. How much amortization would be recorded on the 20X4 income statement after the write-up in requirement (1)? Explain.

3. Are the statements reflecting the revaluation in accordance with GAAP? Explain.

4. Assume that appraisals indicated a value of $1,600,000 for land and $700,000 for the buildings. How would the picture change?

 **A10-34 Comprehensive Accounting for Capital Assets:** At the end of 20X4, Merriweather Limited had the following balances in capital asset accounts:

| | | |
|---|---|---|
| Equipment | $316,000 | |
| Accumulated depreciation, equipment | (284,000) | $ 32,000 |
| Copyright, net | | 31,000 |
| Leasehold improvements, net | | 91,800 |
| Building | 786,000 | |
| Accumulated amortization, building | (146,000) | 640,000 |
| Land | | 880,000 |

Assets are depreciated as follows:

Equipment—declining balance, 10%. Salvage value is estimated to be $32,000.

Building—declining balance, 5%. Salvage value is estimated to be $23,500.

Copyright—straight line over 20 years with no salvage value; the copyright had been held for 12 years to the end of 20X4.

Leasehold improvements—straight line over 20 years with no salvage value; the leaseholds had been held for three years to the end of 20X4.

Land—The land included mineral rights. The original price of the land was $1,200,000, of which $800,000 was appropriately assigned to mineral rights. Expected mining will last for 10 years, and the deposit was 40% exhausted at the end of 20X4. The land will be sold, likely for $500,000, net of restoration costs.

For all assets except the mineral rights, a full year of depreciation is claimed in the year of purchase, but none in the year of sale. Mineral rights are amortized as used.

*Events in 20X5:*

a. Equipment was traded in August for new equipment with a fair value of $257,800. Merriweather paid $216,000 and the old equipment. It also spent $12,300 having the new equipment transported and installed. During installation the equipment was slightly damaged, but repaired quickly at a cost of $4,900.

b. A competing product was introduced by a competitor that rendered the copyright worthless.

c. Monies were spent this year on a new product, a computer game. Costs were as follows: Designing and planning, $200,000; code development, $116,000; and testing, $45,100.

d. Another 15% of the mineral rights were mined and sold during the year.

**Required:**

1. Based on the closing balance as of 31 December 20X4, what was the original cost of the copyright and leasehold improvements? Also prove the balance in the land account.

2. Prepare the capital asset section of the balance sheet as at 31 December 20X5. Justify any accounting policy or application decisions made.

3. List the amounts and accounts that would appear on the income statement for the year ended 31 December 20X5. Include 20X5 amortization for all assets, as appropriate.

---

**A10-35 Integrative Problem, Chapters 6–10:** Hyperium Computers Limited is a small producer and marketer of software for personal computers. The company is owned by a group of about 20 shareholders, including two venture capitalists who own preferred shares that must be redeemed in 10 years' time. Bank debt, used to finance inventory and accounts receivable, allows borrowing of up to 40% of the book value of inventory and 70% of the book value of accounts receivable. The company picks many accounting policies to minimize tax payments.

Accounting policy issues facing the company this year are given below.

1. Hyperium began selling products to large discount retailers under the retailer's "house brand" for the first time in 20X5. Agreements with the retailers specify that 80% of products not sold to final customers within six months may be returned to Hyperium for a refund. Data with respect to the sales:

| | January–June | July–December |
|---|---|---|
| Sales at retail | $401,000 | $798,600 |
| Cash collected | 199,000 | 362,000 |
| Returns to date (at retail) | 76,000 | 172,500* |

*$110,000 relate to sales made in the January–June period.*

Hyperium has recorded the sales as cash has been collected. Regardless of the accounting policy chosen, taxable income must include revenue equal to cash collected.

When should revenue be recognized? Analyze the accounting policy choices and make a recommendation. Evaluate point of sale, cash collection, and the end of the return period.

2. Hyperium incurred $657,000 of costs to advertise a new software program this year. The program is expected to sell strongly in the lucrative 10-to-16-year-old age bracket over the next three years. Should the costs be deferred and amortized or immediately expensed? Provide an analysis and recommendation.

3. Hyperium incurred $340,000 of costs to revise existing software products (goods for resale) so that they utilize the more sophisticated graphics that are available on newer personal computers.

Should the costs be deferred and amortized or immediately expensed? Provide an analysis and recommendation.

4. Hyperium accrues bad debt expense in the year of sale. An aging of accounts receivable at year-end reveals the following:

| | Accounts Receivable | Percentage Expected to Be Non-Collectible |
|---|---|---|
| Current | $613,200 | 2% |
| 30–60 days | 114,900 | 20 |
| 60–90 days | 70,700 | 40 |
| Over 90 days | 54,300 | 60 |

The allowance has a debit balance of $47,900 prior to adjustment. Provide the adjusting journal entry to record bad debt expense.

5. Hyperium sold $400,000 of accounts receivable to a finance company the day before the end of the fiscal year. The finance company charged $6,960 in interest. All the receivables were expected to be collected. The cash received was debited to cash, and credited to an account called "suspense."

Provide the adjusting journal entry to correct the suspense account and record the sale. Indicate the circumstances under which the sale would be recorded as a loan.

6. Hyperium has a US$40,000 account receivable, recorded at Cdn$54,000. The year-end exchange rate is US $1 = Cdn$1.41. Hyperium has a US$98,000 account payable recorded at Cdn$132,900.

Provide adjusting journal entries.

7. Hyperium counted its finished-goods inventory and obtained a dollar value, at cost, of $4,413,000. However, it is wondering what level of inventory shrinkage has been experienced. The following data has been provided:

| | |
|---|---|
| Opening inventory, as counted, at cost | $ 4,691,400 |
| Closing inventory, as counted, at cost | 4,413,000 |
| Purchases, at invoice price | 16,924,300 |
| Sales and excise taxes | 2,030,900 |
| Freight-in | 712,800 |
| Purchase discounts and returns | 419,100 |

Gross profit margins have been stable at 32%. Net sales during the year were $28,200,000. Note that amounts appropriately exclude inventory and sales related to house brand sales described in part (1).

Provide an estimate of inventory losses due to shrinkage.

8. Hyperium acquired new computer equipment, nine months into the year, as part of a regular upgrade program to keep the company on the cutting edge of technology. These computers have an expected useful life of five years, although Hyperium has had to upgrade its computers about every two years to stay abreast of technology. Costs associated with the upgrade were:

| | |
|---|---|
| Computer invoice price | $6,450,000 |
| Sales tax | 967,500 |
| Delivery charges | 57,000 |
| Improvement to wiring necessary to connect computers to network | 116,000 |
| Training course for employees to upgrade skills | 40,900 |

The company wishes you to evaluate use of straight-line and declining-balance amortization (50%) methods. Your analysis should include calculation of amortization expense for each of the first two fiscal years. Salvage values would be 40% of cost after 24 months and 5% of cost after five years. Be sure to separately calculate the cost of the equipment, and indicate how other (non-capitalized) expenditures should be accounted for.

**Required:**

Address the accounting policy issues listed above, providing appropriate analysis and entries, as required.

## CHAPTER 11

# Investments in Debt and Equity Securities

## INTRODUCTION

The cash flow associated with an investment in the securities of another company can be straightforward. Such an investment is usually purchased for cash, produces an annual cash flow of interest or dividends that can be recorded as revenue, and is sold for cash. What can be so complicated?

Accounting for investments is affected by the fact that investments have different purposes, investment accounts can be valued in different ways, and there are alternative approaches to measurement of investment income.

For example, the cost and market value of an investment may be very different over the period during which it is held. Shaw Communications reported a $24.4 million dollar investment in Canadian Hydro Developers on its 2005 balance sheet, but disclosed that the market value of this investment was $58.9 million. If the investment can or would be sold, market value information is likely far more relevant to the financial statement user, as long as it is objectively determinable in securities markets.

However, many investments are not held for resale. Instead, long-term investments in voting shares may be used to establish an intercompany relationship through which the investor corporation can control or significantly influence the operating, investing, and financing strategies of the investee corporation. For example, Shaw Communications also reported that it had one-third interest in three specialty channel networks, for which there was an investment value of $668,000 on the balance sheet.

If the investor can control or influence the dividend policy of the investee, dividends received from the investee are not the result of an arm's-length transaction, and the amount could be manipulated. Shaw used the equity method to account for the investments in specialty channel networks, and recorded their share of losses (some $346,000 in 2005.) Market values were not reported, but since the shares were presumably not for sale, this seems appropriate.

This chapter explores the alternatives, and provides an overview of this complex area. Keep in mind, though, that many accounting programs devote an entire course to investment accounting, so this is only the tip of the proverbial iceberg!

# CLASSIFICATION OF INTERCORPORATE INVESTMENTS

## Investment Objectives

**passive investment**

an intercorporate investment in which the investor cannot significantly influence or control the operations of the investee company

Companies invest in the securities of other enterprises for a variety of reasons. The investment can be a **passive investment,** meant primarily to increase investment income, or a **strategic investment,** meant to enhance operations in some way. Reasons for investments include:

- *Investment of idle cash.* Companies often have cash on hand that is not needed at present but will be needed in the future. Rather than allow the idle cash to remain in a low-interest bank account, companies find money market investments with short terms that provide a higher return. These investments typically have low risk and are easily converted to cash.

  Some investments will generate return through interest or dividends but also be sold at a gain when market price has increased. These investments will likely be of higher risk and/or a longer term, but the intent is to sell the investment when money is needed for other activities and/or when the price is attractive.

**strategic investment**

an investment in another company for strategic purposes; usually conveys control or significant influence or is a joint venture

- *Active held-for-trading investment portfolio.* Some companies, primarily financial institutions, invest in held-for-trading investments. Securities in the portfolio are actively traded as part of the normal course of business, generally yielding a return because of price fluctuations or a dealer's margin. Such a portfolio might be used to offset, or hedge, gains or losses from other financial statement elements.

- *Long-term investments to generate earnings.* Cash on hand can be invested in less liquid securities in order to increase investment income. These investments are usually money market instruments (for example, bonds), and the intent is to keep the investment some considerable time.

- *Strategic alliances.* An investment, especially in voting shares, may establish or cement a beneficial intercompany relationship that will increase the profitability of the investing company, both directly and indirectly. Strategic decisions may be made to invest in suppliers, customers, and even competitors.

- *Legal frameworks.* Companies may choose to establish operations in one large company with numerous branches, or organize activities in a set of smaller companies, all or partially controlled by a central holding company. This may be done for tax reasons, to allow outside shareholders a small stake in particular operations, to satisfy legal requirements in particular jurisdictions, and/or to limit potential liability claims to particular portions of the enterprise.

# CLASSIFICATION OF INVESTMENTS

Many securities are **financial instruments.** A financial instrument is any contract that gives rise to both a financial asset of one party and a financial liability or equity instrument of another party. In the context of intercorporate investments, financial assets are defined as any contractual right to receive cash or another financial asset from another company. Bonds and share investment meet this definition. Classification alternatives for investments are summarized in Exhibit 11-1.

**Debt versus Equity Investments** An investment in a debt instrument of another entity can be classified as an available-for-sale, held-to-maturity, or held-for-trading investment. An investment in common shares may be an available-for-sale investment or a held-for-trading investment, or, if strategic, a control investment, a significant-influence investment, or a joint venture. It depends on intent and circumstances. These classifications are defined in the sections that follow.

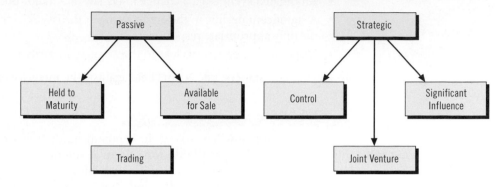

### EXHIBIT 11-1

## CLASSIFICATION OF INVESTMENTS

## Held-to-Maturity Investments

**held-to-maturity investments**

those investments that have a defined maturity date, fixed or determinable payments, and for which there is positive intent to hold to maturity

**Held-to-maturity** investments must meet three tests:

- First, rather obviously, the securities must have a maturity date. This includes bonds and other money market instruments, but excludes common shares and any other investment with an indeterminate length.
- The securities must have fixed or determinable payments: set amounts at set points in time.
- Management must have the *positive intent* to hold the investments to their maturity dates, plus the financial strength to make such a plan feasible.

For example, if a company buys a bond with a 10-year maturity date, and management plans to hold it until maturity, it is classified as a held-to-maturity security. On the other hand, if management stands ready to sell the investment if the price is appealing or if the company needs cash, then the bond is an available-for-sale investment. If management plans for the investment are *undecided*, the investment is classified as an available-for-sale investment. This is the meaning of positive intent—there must be an *active will and financial ability* to hold to maturity.

**Management Intent** Management intent can be a slippery classification tool. Management can change its intentions, or even misrepresent its intentions. This reduces the credibility of the financial statements, and future management representations.

**ETHICAL ISSUES**

Many financial statement measurements and classifications rest on the judgements and the representations of management. Auditors need to rely on management integrity, but also have to be prudent in reviewing management representations.

**Reclassification or Sale** Reclassification, or sale, of a held-to-maturity investment calls the integrity of the original classification into question. Therefore, the accounting standards require that if a held-to-maturity investment is sold or reclassified, all other investments classified as held-to-maturity are automatically reclassified as available-for-sale, and no investment is permitted to be classified as held-to-maturity in the following two fiscal years. This is a harsh consequence, indeed.

Of course, there are some exceptions to the rule—for example, the held-to-maturity category remains *open for use* if the sale involved:

- A transaction involving an insignificant amount of securities;
- An isolated event (e.g., a change in tax law or a major business combination);
- A significant decline in the credit rating of the issuer of the investment such that sale is the only appropriate response; or
- Disposal on a date very close to the original maturity date.

In these circumstances, sale is not "held against" the integrity of the initial classification.

## Available-for-Sale Investments

**available-for-sale investment**

any investment that is not classified as a control, joint venture, significant-influence, held-to-maturity, or held-for-trading investment; the catch-all category of investment

Any investment that will be sold if the company needs cash, or if the market value is appealing, is considered an **available-for-sale investment**. This category includes short-term money-market investments, such as Treasury bills, but also bonds and shares of other companies that could be sold. While the investments are held, they will generate interest or dividend income. When they are sold, they will yield a realized gain or loss on sale. Market value will fluctuate during the time that the investments are held.

This category is the catch-all. That is, investments that are not in the other categories are classified here. To understand what this involves, the other alternatives must be understood.

## Held-for-Trading Investments

**held-for-trading investment**

an investment designated by management as held for trading; part of a portfolio managed for short-term profit or acquired principally for resale

The **held-for-trading investment** category is determined primarily by management intent. That is, when the investment is bought, *the investment must be designated as a held-for-trading investment.* A held-for-trading investment is one that:

1. Management clearly states is held primarily for the purpose of resale in the near term, and/or is

2. Part of a portfolio of investments managed together for short-term profit and for which there is a pattern of short-term profit taking.

Any marketable financial instrument can be designated as a held-for-trading investment when purchased. Even if there is no set plan to sell the investment in the near future, the investment can still be a held-for-trading investment, as long as intent to trade is present.

## Controlled Investments

**controlled investment**

the investment in a controlled subsidiary; normally consolidated for financial reporting

**control**

the continuing power to determine the strategic policies of an investee without the cooperation of other shareholders

Control means that the investor can set the critical operating, investing, and financing policies of the investee without the cooperation of other voting shareholders. The result is a **controlled investment**.

Since strategic policies of the enterprise are typically established by the Board of Directors, the right to elect a majority of the Board of Directors would normally constitute **control**. Percentage share ownership is the primary input to this decision, and control should exist if an investor owns a simple majority of voting shares, or 50% plus one vote. If an investor owns more than 50% of the voting shares of another company, but *does not have* control, then the investor has to establish why it *does not* have control; if it owns 50% or less, and *has* control, the investor must establish why it *does* have control.

Many corporations are "run" by a major shareholder who owns the largest single block of shares, perhaps because other shareholders are not active, or not organized. If the block of shares owned by the major shareholder is less than 50% of the voting shares, then control does not exist *in an accounting sense.* This is because an opponent could gather enough shares (or the support of enough voting shareholders) to have 50% plus one vote, so clearly the major investor does not have legal control.

**parent company**

a corporation that controls one or more other corporations through ownership of a majority of the shares, carrying the right to elect at least a majority of the Board of Directors

**subsidiary company**

an investee company in which the investor company (the parent) controls the investee, usually by having the right to appoint a majority of the Board of Directors and/or holding in excess of 50% of the voting shares

**significant-influence investment**

an investment representing ownership interest to the extent that the investor can affect strategic operating, investing, and/or financing policies of the investee

**joint venture**

an investment resulting in a contractual arrangement whereby two or more venturers jointly control an economic activity; the joint venture is subject to joint control by the joint venturers

If the investee is controlled by the investor corporation, the investor corporation is called a **parent company** and the investee corporation is known as a **subsidiary**.

## Significant-Influence Investments

A **significant-influence investment** exists when an investor has the ability to exert influence over the strategic operating, investing, and financing policies of the investee corporation even though the investor does not control the investee. Significant influence can be exerted through several means, and not just by equity investment. Possible evidence of significant influence includes:

- Representation on the Board of Directors;
- Participation in policy-making processes;
- Material intercompany transactions;
- Interchange of managerial personnel; or
- Provision of technical information.

Normally, ownership of 20% or more of an investee corporation's shares is deemed to indicate that significant influence exists. As with control, the burden of proof shifts at this line: if an investor *has* significant influence and owns less than 20%, the investor must prove *why* it has significant influence. If the investor has more than 20% and does *not* have significant influence, the investor must prove that significant influence *is not* present.

It is important to not put *too* much weight on the percentage of share ownership, though; a great deal depends on who owns the other shares, as well as on the other (non-ownership) financial and operating relationships between the investor and the investee corporations. For example, ownership of 30% of an investee corporation may not give the investee significant influence (or any influence) if the other 70% is held by a single shareholder who will not tolerate any influence. Conversely, an ownership interest of 15% may give the investor virtually unchallenged influence if ownership of the other 85% is widely dispersed. It is the substance that matters, not the percentage ownership.

## Joint Ventures

Another type of strategic equity investment is a **joint venture**, where an economic activity is jointly controlled by two or more investors.

Joint ventures are distinct in that they are subject to *joint control*, regardless of ownership percentage. That is, the investors must unanimously agree on key operating, investing, and financing decisions before they are implemented. This feature of joint control means that majority ownership, or the right to appoint the majority of the Board of Directors, does not confer control.

Joint ventures are quite common in mining operations and in oil and gas ventures. The joint venturers all contribute something to exploration activities, and all share in any wealth generated. For example, a small mining company may have exploration rights over a property, and agree to explore the property with a larger joint venture partner. This large investor provides management, working capital, and capital assets in exchange for a certain percentage of the profits. However, key decisions over when and where to explore, or when to put the property into commercial production, etc. are subject to *common control* of both venturers.

## Change in Classification

Intent and ability to hold must be assessed at every balance sheet date. If intent changes, and the investment is still unsold, then the balance sheet classification and accounting treatment will change.

## EXHIBIT 11-3

## ACCOUNTING FOR INVESTMENTS

## SUMMARY OF ACCOUNTING METHODS

| Method | Carrying Value | Investment Income | Unrealized Holding Gains and Losses | Realized Gains and Losses |
|---|---|---|---|---|
| Cost | Cost or amortized cost | Interest or dividends; effective interest method | N/A | Included in net income |
| Fair value; unrealized G/L included in other comprehensive income | Fair value | Interest or dividends | Included in other comprehensive income; part of shareholders' equity | Cumulative amount included in net income when realized |
| Fair value; unrealized G/L included in net income | Fair value | Interest or dividends | Included in net income | Included in net income; the annual change in value |
| Equity | Cost plus unremitted earnings to date | Share of investee earnings adjusted for amortizations and intercompany profits | N/A | Included in net income; sale unlikely |
| Consolidation | Investment account replaced with financial statements elements of investee for reporting | Investment revenue represented through inclusion of investee income statement elements; adjusted for amortizations and intercompany profits | N/A | Included in net income; sale unlikely |
| Proportional consolidation | Investment account replaced with fractional financial statements elements of investee in reporting | Investment revenue represented through inclusion of *fractional* investee income statement elements; adjusted for amortizations and intercompany profits | N/A | Included in net income; sale unlikely |

- Interest or dividends declared are recorded as investment income.
- At the end of each reporting period, the investments are revalued to fair value, whether this is higher or lower than the existing balance in the investment account.
- Holding gains, defined as the difference between the existing balance in the investment account (the new fair value) and the prior investment account balance, are recorded in net income. That is, net income includes the change in value of the investment each year, whether realized through sale or unrealized because the investment is still held.

The investment is reported at fair value on the balance sheet.

**Volatility**  The difference between the two applications of the fair value method obviously relates to how the change in fair value is recorded in the financial statements. For held-for-trading investments, these changes in value, whether they are realized or unrealized, are included on the income statement. For available-for-sale investments, unrealized changes in value are collected in other comprehensive income. Only realized gains and losses are on the income statement. Realization is a traditional test for revenue recognition. For held-for-trading investments, realization is not considered necessary because of their rapid turnover.

Remember, though, that if investment prices are volatile, inclusion of holding gains introduces volatility to net income. Companies with held-for-trading portfolios have registered concern about this volatility, because they are often using their held-for-trading portfolios to hedge, or offset, fluctuations caused by similar portfolios of financial liabilities, which are carried at cost, and not adjusted to fair value. Standard setters continue to grapple with these issues.

| | |
|---|---|
| **fair value** | **Estimating Fair Value**  Since financial statements will reflect **fair value** for some investments, it stands to reason that fair value must be carefully estimated. After all, estimated fair value is not substantiated by the objective evidence of a transaction of the reporting entity. Fair value is the value of a transaction between two arm's-length parties, both of which are knowledgeable and are under no compulsion to act. |
| the value established between a willing buyer and a willing seller in a normal business transaction | |

Many equity investments have a quoted market price in an active market, which is used as fair value. These market prices reflect normal market transactions and are readily available from brokers or in the financial press. When trading is light, recent bid prices are acceptable, although light trading may indicate that estimating fair value is problematic. In addition, a recent price might not be relevant if significant events had taken place after the bid date.

What if there are no recent transactions? In these circumstances, fair value can be estimated through judicious use of valuation techniques. These valuation techniques must incorporate all factors that market participants consider when establishing prices. Fair value can be estimated through well-recognized valuation alternatives such as discounted cash flow models and option pricing models. In other cases, fair value can be inferred by referring to the current value of similar financial instruments, adjusting the market price for differences in terms and risk. Estimates are needed, and the reasonableness of any result must be carefully considered before the value can be used in the financial statements. It makes sense to disclose the method used to assess fair value, and any assumptions made.

**Fair Value not Available**  In some cases, it may not be possible to obtain fair value. In these cases, the investments must be carried at cost. This may well be the case for investments in small companies where sale of shares is rare.

### Equity Method

The **equity method** is used for significant-influence investments. Under the equity method:

**equity method of accounting for investments**

investments are initially recorded at cost, and revenue is recorded as the investor's appropriate share of earnings, increasing the investment account; dividends received reduce the investment account

- The original investment is recorded at its acquisition cost; this is initial book value.
- The investor's proportionate share of the investee's net income (subject to certain adjustments) is recognized on the investor's income statement as revenue and on the balance sheet as an increase in book value.

investment. Able includes transaction costs, if any, in acquisition cost and nets commissions on sale with proceeds received.

Notice that bond prices are quoted as percentages of the face value of the bond. A quote of 98 implies that a $30,000 face amount bond has a market price of $29,400. Able paid par, or 100, and so paid $30,000. The bond price is based on the present value of the cash flows, discounted at the market interest rate. The quoted price does not include accrued interest, which also must be paid to the seller of the bond. Able must pay four months' accrued interest, for the period 1 July to 31 October.

**Acquisition**  The entry to record the acquisition is as follows:

| | | |
|---|---:|---:|
| Investment in Charlie Corporation bonds | 30,000 | |
| Accrued interest receivable ($30,000 × 8% × 4/12) | 800 | |
| Cash | | 30,800 |

**Revenue**  When interest is received on 31 December, a portion of it represents the accrued interest recorded at the acquisition date:

| | | |
|---|---:|---:|
| Cash ($30,000 × 8% × 6/12) | 1,200 | |
| Investment income: Interest | | 400 |
| Accrued interest receivable | | 800 |

**Maturity**  When a held-to-maturity investment comes due, the investor receives the face value, plus interest, since maturity occurs on an interest date:

| | | |
|---|---:|---:|
| Cash | 31,200 | |
| Investment income: Interest | | 1,200 |
| Investment in Charlie Corporation bonds | | 30,000 |

**Sale**  In the unlikely event that the held-to-maturity security is sold before maturity, the difference between book value and the selling price (net of accrued interest), less commissions and other expenses, is recorded as a gain or loss.

Suppose that on 31 March 20X2 Able Company sells its Charlie Corporation bonds at 105 plus accrued interest, and incurs commissions and other expenses of $550. The cash generated includes the accrued interest of $600 ($30,000 × 8% × 3/12) plus the net proceeds from the bond itself, $30,950 (($30,000 × 105%), less $550 commissions.) The gain on the sale is $950, because the proceeds of $30,950 are greater than the cost of $30,000.

The entry to record the sale is as follows:

| | | |
|---|---:|---:|
| Cash | 31,550 | |
| Investment income: Interest | | 600 |
| Investment in Charlie Corporation bonds | | 30,000 |
| Gain on sale of investment | | 950 |

Gains and losses on disposal are recognized on the income statement as part of income from continuing operations.

## Amortization of Premium or Discount

What happens if debt securities are bought for an amount other than par value, for example, at 98 or 104? The investment is recorded at its cost, which is greater or less than the face

**premium**

a difference between the issuance price (or cost) and the maturity value of a debt security where the maturity value is lower

**discount**

a difference between the issuance price (or cost) and the maturity value of a debt security where the maturity value is higher

amount of the debt. Any **premium** or **discount** should be amortized in order to bring the carrying value up (or down) to par value at maturity. Otherwise, a substantial gain or loss will be recognized at maturity and interest revenue over the life of the investment is misstated.

**Issuance Price** To ascertain market value, the present value of the cash flows associated with the debt is calculated using the market interest rate as the discount rate. For example, assume that Marcus Corp. purchased Baker Company bonds when the market interest rate was 6%. The Baker bonds had a $500,000 maturity value, paid 5.5% interest semi-annually, and had a five-year life. The market value is calculated as follows:

| | |
|---|---|
| Principal $500,000 × (P/F, 3%, 10) (.74409) = | $372,045 |
| Interest $13,750 (P/A, 3%, 10) (8.53020) = | 117,290 |
| Market value (Present value) | $489,335 |

Both the principal of $500,000 and the semi-annual interest payments of $13,750 ($500,000 × 5.5% × 6/12) must be included in the present value calculation. Notice that the discount rate used is 3%. This is the 6% market rate multiplied by 6/12, as payments and compounding are semi-annual. The number of periods is 10, which is the five-year life multiplied by two payments per year. Principal is a lump sum, and the interest amount is an ordinary annuity.

The market value on this investment is $489,335, which is .97867 of face value ($489,335/$500,000). This investment would therefore be quoted at 97.867. Acquisition would be recorded as follows, assuming that this is a held-to-maturity investment:

| | | |
|---|---|---|
| Investment in debt securities: Baker bonds | 489,335 | |
| Cash | | 489,335 |

Since the bond will mature at $500,000, the $10,665 ($500,000 − $489,335) discount must be amortized to interest income over the life of the investment.

**Amortization Methods** There are two methods of amortization, the **straight-line method** and the **effective-interest method**. The straight-line method is simpler, but the effective-interest method is preferable because it provides a constant yield on the recorded value of the investment. Accounting standards state that the effective-interest method must be used. However, the difference between the two is not material if the original difference between cost and market value is small, which is often the case. For this reason, the straight-line method may be seen in practice. Both methods will be illustrated in this chapter.

**effective-interest method**

a measure of interest expense or revenue over the life of a financial instrument not issued at par; measures expense or revenue as a constant rate over the term of the financial instrument

**Example: Effective-Interest Method** Using the effective-interest amortization method, interest income is measured as a constant percentage of the bond investment. Interest income is measured using the market interest rate when the bonds were issued. The investment carrying value is multiplied by the market interest rate to obtain interest income. The difference between cash received and interest income is the premium or discount amortization. The investment value changes by the amortization, and the investment book value climbs to face value at maturity.

Effective-interest method calculations are illustrated in Exhibit 11-4. Notice that:

- The cash payment amount is constant each period, consistent with the terms of the bond. This is the stated interest rate of 2.75% each six months, or 5.5% × 6/12.
- Interest revenue is a constant percentage of the bond carrying amount. To obtain interest revenue, multiply the bond carrying value by the market interest rate. For example, the first amount is $14,680 or 3% of $489,335.

## EXHIBIT 11-4

### EFFECTIVE-INTEREST AMORTIZATION

| Period | Cash Payment | 3% Interest Revenue | Amortization | Bond Carrying Value |
|---|---|---|---|---|
| 0 | | | | $489,335 |
| 1 | $13,750 | $14,680 | $ 930 | 490,265 |
| 2 | 13,750 | 14,708 | 958 | 491,223 |
| 3 | 13,750 | 14,737 | 987 | 492,210 |
| 4 | 13,750 | 14,766 | 1,016 | 493,226 |
| 5 | 13,750 | 14,797 | 1,047 | 494,273 |
| 6 | 13,750 | 14,828 | 1,078 | 495,351 |
| 7 | 13,750 | 14,861 | 1,111 | 496,462 |
| 8 | 13,750 | 14,894 | 1,144 | 497,606 |
| 9 | 13,750 | 14,928 | 1,178 | 498,784 |
| 10 | 13,750 | 14,966* | 1,216 | 500,000 |

*$14,964 + $2 rounding error

- Amortization is the difference between the cash payment and interest revenue. On the first line, this is $930, or $14,680 less $13,750.
- The bond carrying value grows each period by the amortization amount. On the first line, this is $489,335 plus $930, to equal $490,265.
- The bond carrying value is increased to par value by the end of the 10-period amortization process.

Interest income is recorded for the first period as follows:

| | | |
|---|---|---|
| Cash | 13,750 | |
| Investment in debt securities: Baker bonds | 930 | |
| Investment income: Interest | | 14,680 |

**Example: Straight-Line Method** Using the straight-line method, interest income is measured as a constant amount each period, cash received plus a discount amortization, or less premium amortization. The investment value changes by the amortization amount, and the investment book value approaches face value at maturity.

The straight-line amortization method calculations are illustrated in Exhibit 11-5. Notice that:

- The cash payment, interest revenue, and amortization are constant each period.
- Amortization is obtained by dividing the discount of $10,665 ($500,000 − $489,335) by 10 (the number of interest payments).
- Interest revenue is the sum of cash payment plus amortization, or $13,750 plus $1,067 or $1,066.
- The bond carrying value is increased to par value by the end of the 10-period amortization process.

### EXHIBIT 11-5

## STRAIGHT-LINE AMORTIZATION

| Period | Cash Payment | Interest Revenue | Amortization | Bond Carrying Value |
|---|---|---|---|---|
| 0 | | | | $489,335 |
| 1 | $13,750 | $14,817 | $1,067* | 490,402 |
| 2 | 13,750 | 14,817 | 1,067 | 491,469 |
| 3 | 13,750 | 14,817 | 1,067 | 492,536 |
| 4 | 13,750 | 14,817 | 1,067 | 493,603 |
| 5 | 13,750 | 14,817 | 1,067 | 494,670 |
| 6 | 13,750 | 14,816 | 1,066 | 495,736 |
| 7 | 13,750 | 14,816 | 1,066 | 496,802 |
| 8 | 13,750 | 14,816 | 1,066 | 497,868 |
| 9 | 13,750 | 14,816 | 1,066 | 498,934 |
| 10 | 13,750 | 14,816 | 1,066 | 500,000 |

*$10,665/10; rounded

**Purchase at Premium**  Suppose Marcus paid more than the face of the bonds, because the market interest rate was 4% when the bonds were purchased. In this case, the market value would be:

| | |
|---|---|
| Principal $500,000 × (P/F, 2%, 10) (.82035) = | $410,175 |
| Interest $13,750 (P/A, 2%, 10) (8.98259) = | 123,511 |
| Market value (Present value) | $533,686 |

The excess paid over the face amount is a premium. At acquisition, the bonds would be recorded at $533,686, but over the period to their maturity the $33,686 premium would be amortized, reducing the carrying amount (and reducing investment income) each year. Using the effective-interest method, the amortization table would appear as in Exhibit 11-6. Only the first three interest periods have been included here; the table is constructed as for a discount situation, except that the carrying value begins at a value *higher* than face value, the interest income is cash received *less* premium amortization, and the investment carrying value is *reduced* to face value over the life of the investment.

### EXHIBIT 11-6

## EFFECTIVE-INTEREST AMORTIZATION

| Period | Cash Payment | 2% Interest Revenue | Amortization | Bond Carrying Value |
|---|---|---|---|---|
| 0 | | | | $533,686 |
| 1 | $13,750 | $10,674 | $3,076 | 530,610 |
| 2 | 13,750 | 10,612 | 3,138 | 527,472 |
| 3 | 13,750 | 10,550 | 3,200 | 524,272 |
| etc. | | | | |

The first interest payment would be recorded as follows:

| | | |
|---|---|---|
| Cash | 13,750 | |
| Investment in debt securities: Baker bonds | | 3,076 |
| Investment income: Interest | | 10,674 |

## Example: Share Investment

To illustrate the cost-basis accounting for an investment in shares, assume that on 1 November 20X1, Able Company purchases 50,000 shares of Phillips Company common shares for $20 per share. Commissions and legal fees with respect to the purchase are $50,000; Able includes these expenditures in the acquisition cost. (Alternatively, Able could follow the policy of expensing the fees.) This investment gives Able control of Phillips, and Able will consolidate at year-end. During the year, however, Able will record the investment using the cost method.

**Acquisition**  The entries to record the purchase are as follows:

| | | |
|---|---|---|
| Investment in Phillips Company common shares | 1,050,000 | |
| Cash [(50,000 shares × $20) + $50,000 fees] | | 1,050,000 |

**Revenue**  On 31 December, Phillips declares a dividend of $0.50 per share. The dividend is recorded when declared:

| | | |
|---|---|---|
| Dividends receivable (50,000 × $0.50) | 25,000 | |
| Investment income: Dividends | | 25,000 |

The dividend is paid on January 13, and the cash receipt is recorded:

| | | |
|---|---|---|
| Cash | 25,000 | |
| Dividend receivable | | 25,000 |

**Sale**  If the investment is sold, the difference between book value and the selling price, less commissions and other expenses, is recorded as a gain or loss. Assume that the shares of Phillips Company common shares were sold for $2,300,000, less $61,000 of fees and commissions.

| | | |
|---|---|---|
| Cash ($2,300,000 − $61,000) | 2,239,000 | |
| Investment in Phillips Company common shares | | 1,050,000 |
| Gain on sale of investment | | 1,189,000 |

## Impairment

The market value of a held-to-maturity debt security will fluctuate, based on market interest rates. Also, if the credit rating of the borrower changes, the market value of the investment will fluctuate, because the risk attached to future cash flow is changed. An increase in credit risk increases the risk premium appropriately included in the discount rate.

When the value of an investment falls below its acquisition cost, assets may be overstated. Conservatism might dictate loss recognition. However, since the security is not held for sale, and its maturity value is assured, market value is not a relevant measurement attribute. Therefore, the loss is not recorded.

**Impairment** is a different situation. At each year-end, investments must be reviewed to see if value is *permanently impaired*. If the value of an investment is permanently lower than

**impairment**

the portion of an asset's utility or value; a permanent reduction in value necessitating loss recognition its carrying value, the investment must be written down. The following evidence about the issuer (the investee) might suggest impairment:

1. Significant financial difficulty;

2. A breach of contract, such as failure to pay required interest or principal on outstanding debt;

3. Concessions granted because of financial difficulties;

4. Probable bankruptcy or financial reorganization;

5. Disappearance of an active market for the investment because of financial difficulties.

These situations must be evaluated to see if there is real impairment. For instance, if an active market for an investment disappears because a once-public company has gone private, but the company is still in good financial position, there is no impairment. Similarly, a downgrade in credit rating does not mean impairment unless it is accompanied by one of the above conditions.

When an impairment loss must be recorded, it is measured as the difference between the investment's carrying value and fair value. The carrying value of the investment is reduced to fair value either directly or indirectly through an allowance. Impairment losses are not reversed as long as the asset is held.

**Example** Review the facts of the Baker bond given above, originally purchased for $489,335. After three years, if the effective-interest amortization method is used, the carrying value of the bond is $495,351. Assume that the value of this investment has become impaired. Baker is in financial reorganization, and the fair value of the bond was $213,500, because interest and principal payments have been reduced significantly as part of the financial reorganization.

The impairment is recognized:

| | | |
|---|---|---|
| Impairment loss ($495,351 − $213,500) | 281,851 | |
|     Investment in debt securities: Baker bonds | | 281,851 |

Alternatively, the impairment can be recorded in a valuation allowance:

| | | |
|---|---|---|
| Impairment loss ($495,351 − $213,500) | 281,851 | |
|     Allowance for impairment loss: Baker bonds | | 281,851 |

The allowance is shown as a contra account to the investment on the balance sheet. The loss would be reported on the income statement. The investment account now has a balance of $213,500, which *cannot* be written back up to original cost if fair value subsequently recovers. Note that, for tax purposes, such losses are deductible only when realized, so the impairment loss is tax deductible only when the (reduced) payments are actually accepted.

## CONCEPT REVIEW

1. A debt security is bought for $14,700, including $700 of accrued interest, and sold for $14,900, including $900 of accrued interest. Why is there no gain or loss on sale?

2. How is the market value of a bond determined?

3. Is interest revenue on a held-to-maturity investment necessarily just the cash entitlement? Explain.

4. Suppose that the value of a company's held-to-maturity investment falls below its cost. Would the carrying value of the investment necessarily be written down? Explain.

# THE FAIR VALUE METHOD: UNREALIZED GAINS AND LOSSES RECOGNIZED IN OTHER COMPREHENSIVE INCOME

The fair value method recognizes that most financial statement users need to know the fair value of investments, making fair value more relevant than the historical cost of the investment. Therefore, at reporting dates, investments' carrying values are adjusted to fair value. Gains and losses are *excluded* from net income until the investment is sold.

**Example** As an example of the fair value method, assume that on 1 December 20X5, YZone Manufacturing Limited purchased two investments, both designated as available-for-sale investments. YZone bought 5,000 shares of Gerome Limited, a public company, for $26.75 per share plus $1,200 in broker's fees. YZone also purchased a $100,000, 9%, ten-year Provincial Hydro bond that pays interest each 31 October and 30 April, at 100 plus accrued interest. YZone includes broker's fees in the cost of the investment, and nets proceeds on sale with fees charged.

| | | |
|---|---|---|
| Investment in Provincial Hydro bonds | 100,000 | |
| Accrued interest receivable ($100,000 × 9% × 1/12) | 750 | |
| Investment in Gerome Ltd. shares | | |
| ((5,000 × $26.75) + $1,200) | 134,950 | |
| Cash ($100,750 + $134,950) | | 235,700 |

**Revenue** Dividends would be recorded if declared. Bond interest is accrued on 31 December.

| | | |
|---|---|---|
| Accrued interest receivable ($100,000 × 9% × 1/12) | 750 | |
| Investment income: Interest | | 750 |

**Fair Value Adjustment** At year-end, fair value is determined through reference to stock market quotations. The Gerome shares are trading for $24.75 and the bonds are trading at 100.5. This means that the shares must be reflected in the financial statements at $123,750 (5,000 shares at $24.75) and the bonds at $100,500. An entry is made to record changes in fair value:

| | | |
|---|---|---|
| Investment in Provincial Hydro bonds | | |
| ($100,500 − $100,000) | 500 | |
| Unrealized holding gain: Provincial Hydro Bond | | 500 |
| Unrealized holding loss: Gerome Ltd. shares | | |
| ($134,950 − $123,750) | 11,200 | |
| Investment in Gerome Ltd. shares | | 11,200 |

The 100.5 bond price is quoted exclusive of accrued interest. Notice that the unrealized loss on the Gerome Ltd. shares includes the write-off of the broker's fees.

**Reporting** Unrealized gains and losses are not recorded as income, but rather as unrealized holding gains, part of other comprehensive income in shareholders' equity. Other comprehensive income includes the *cumulative amount* of unrealized holding gains and losses to date. At this point, the balance sheet reflects a net unrealized holding loss (a debit) of $10,700:

| | |
|---|---:|
| Common shares (assumed) | $ 500,000 |
| Retained earnings (assumed) | 897,300 |
| Other comprehensive income: | |
|    Unrealized holding losses, net ($11,200 − $500) | (10,700) |
| Total shareholders' equity | $1,386,600 |

In the 20X5 income statement, YZone reports interest income of $750. The balance sheet shows $1,500 of interest receivable, but also investments at their fair value of $224,250, or $100,500 plus $123,750. The cumulative unrealized losses are disclosed as a debit balance in shareholders' equity.

**Second Year**  In 20X6, YZone has further transactions with respect to its available-for-sale investments. Interest on the Provincial Hydro bonds is paid on 30 April and 31 October.

To record receipt of interest on 30 April:

| | | |
|---|---:|---:|
| Cash ($100,000 × 9% × 6/12) | 4,500 | |
|    Investment income: Interest | | 3,000 |
|    Accrued interest receivable | | 1,500 |

To record receipt of interest on 31 October:

| | | |
|---|---:|---:|
| Cash ($100,000 × 9% × 6/12) | 4,500 | |
|    Investment income: Interest | | 4,500 |

The bond is sold on 30 November for 103 plus accrued interest. A broker's fee of $300 is charged. When an available-for-sale investment is sold, *cumulative* unrealized holding gains or losses are eliminated. This is a $500 gain in this case. The gain or loss is the difference between *original cost* and *selling price*. The recorded $2,700 gain on sale is included in net income:

| | | |
|---|---:|---:|
| Cash (($100,000 × 103%) − $300) + $750 | 103,450 | |
| Unrealized holding gain: Provincial Hydro Bond | 500 | |
|    Investment income: Interest | | 750 |
|    Investment in Provincial Hydro bonds | | 100,500 |
|    Gain on sale of investment ($102,700 − $100,000) | | 2,700 |

Gerome Ltd. paid a $0.43 per share dividend in 20X6:

| | | |
|---|---:|---:|
| Cash (5,000 × $0.43) | 2,150 | |
|    Investment revenue: Dividend revenue | | 2,150 |

The Gerome Ltd. shares are still unsold at year-end. Their quoted share price is now $31.50 or a total of $157,500. Since the shares are now recorded at $123,750, an unrealized holding gain is recorded:

| | | |
|---|---:|---:|
| Investment in Gerome Ltd. shares ($157,500 − $123,750) | 33,750 | |
| Unrealized holding gain: Gerome Ltd. shares | | 33,750 |

**Reporting** At the end of 20X6 the financial statements will reflect:
On the income statement:

| | |
|---|---:|
| Investment revenue | |
| ($3,000 + $4,500 + $750 + $2,700 + $2,150) | $13,100 |

YZone may choose to disclose the various sources on investment income together on the income statement, as illustrated, or break down the various components.

At this point, OCI has a balance of $22,550:

| | |
|---|---:|
| Opening balance (debit) | $(10,700) |
| Changes in unrealized holding gains and losses ($33,750 − $500) | 33,250 |
| Closing balance (credit) ($157,500 − $134,950) | $ 22,550 |

Other comprehensive income includes the changes in unrealized holding gains during the year. The change in unrealized amounts comes from two sources: first, the $33,750 new unrealized holding gain on Gerome Ltd. shares and, second, the $500 realization of a previously recorded unrealized gain on the Provincial Hydro bonds. The realization of a gain is a *decrease* in other comprehensive income. To prove the $22,550 unrealized gain, compare the original cost of the Gerome Ltd. shares, $134,950, and their current fair value of $157,500. The result is $22,550.

Accounts on the balance sheet are:

| | |
|---|---:|
| Available-for-sale investments, Gerome Ltd. shares | $157,500 |
| Shareholders' equity | |
|    Other comprehensive income: | |
|    Unrealized holding gains | 22,550 |

**Third Year** In 20X7, the Gerome Ltd. shares are sold for $30.50, less $1,700 in broker's fees:

| | | |
|---|---:|---:|
| Cash ((5,000 × $30.50) − $1,700) | 150,800 | |
| Unrealized holding gain: Gerome Ltd. shares | | |
|    (cumulative balance) | 22,550 | |
|      Investment in Gerome Ltd. shares | | 157,500 |
|      Gain on sale on investment ($150,800 − $134,950) | | 15,850 |

At this point, there are no unrealized amounts remaining, and all realized gains and losses have been included in net income.

## Impairment

The above example reflected an unrealized holding loss for the Gerome Ltd. shares at the end of 20X5. This loss was assumed to be the result of market fluctuations and not a *permanent impairment*. Since the shares are recorded at fair value, they are not overvalued on the balance sheet. Notice, though, that the loss is excluded from income.

If, on the other hand, the decline in market value reflected a permanent impairment, *the loss must be included in net income.* The impairment test is identical to that described under the cost method—the key element is to look for conditions that indicate a permanent decline in value.

If value of the Gerome Ltd. shares had been impaired at the end of 20X5, the entry would have been as follows:

| | | |
|---|---|---|
| Impairment loss | 11,200 | |
| Investment in Gerome Ltd. shares | | 11,200 |

When an impairment loss is recorded, any cumulative holding gains and losses in other comprehensive income are reversed out. An impairment loss cannot be later reversed, through gain recognition, until the investment is sold. In our example, the Gerome Ltd. shares recovered their value in 20X6. This could not have been recorded if the shares were written down in an impairment in 20X5. On the other hand, a recovery in value would not have occurred if the investment was truly impaired.

## Other Issues

**Basket Purchases of Securities**  A purchase of two or more classes of securities for a single lump sum is a *basket purchase*. The total purchase price must be allocated to the different types of securities. The general principles are the same as for capital assets acquired as a basket:

- When the market price of each class of security is known, the proportional method of allocation is used, wherein the total cost is allocated in proportion to the market values of the various securities in the basket.
- If the market price is known for certain acquired securities, but not known for one of the securities in the group, the incremental method can be used, wherein the purchase price is allocated first to the securities with known prices, and then the remainder of the lump-sum purchase price is attributed to the class of investment that does not have a market price. This method works only if all values are known except one.

**Investments Made in a Foreign Currency**  Often, an investor will purchase equity or debt instruments that are priced in a foreign currency. The purchase price must be converted into Canadian dollars for recording on the Canadian investor's books and reporting in the investor's financial statements. To record the purchase, the exchange rate on the date of purchase is used.

For example, assume that LeBlanc Limited purchases an available-for-sale investment, 20,000 shares of AllAm Incorporated, a U.S. corporation. The purchase price is US$65 per share, for a total of US$1,300,000. At the time of the purchase, the US dollar is worth Cdn$1.15. The purchase would be recorded in Canadian dollars as follows:

| | | |
|---|---|---|
| Investment in AllAm Inc. | 1,495,000 | |
| Cash (US$1,300,000 × Cdn$1.15) | | 1,495,000 |

This entry establishes the cost of the investment to LeBlanc, and will be the carrying value of the investment. Next year, if the market value is US$68 per share and the exchange rate is $1.14, the fair value used to calculate the change in other comprehensive income is a total of $1,550,400 (20,000 shares $\times$ $68 $\times$ $1.14). No attempt is made to segregate the foreign exchange impact.

An investment in foreign currency–denominated *bonds* must be restated on every balance sheet date to the equivalent amount in Canadian dollars, using the exchange rate at the balance sheet date (known as the spot rate). For debt instruments, treatment depends how the investment is classified:

a. For available-for-sale investments, changes in exchange rates are *part of other comprehensive income*, until sale or maturity, and

b. For held-to-maturity investments, the exchange gain or loss is reported *on the income statement.*

## THE FAIR VALUE METHOD: GAINS AND LOSSES RECOGNIZED IN NET INCOME

The fair value method, with gains and losses recognized in net income as they arise, is similar in structure to our previous example. This method is used for held-for-trading investments. The difference between the two fair value methods lies in the entries to record changes in value and the entries on sale. The other difference is that broker fees must be expensed immediately.

**Example** Return to the example of YZone Manufacturing above. YZone now has these investments in a portfolio that management has designated as a held-for-trading portfolio.

The entry to record acquisition is identical, except for the requirement to expense the commissions:

| | | |
|---|---:|---:|
| Investment in Provincial Hydro bonds | 100,000 | |
| Accrued interest receivable ($100,000 $\times$ 9% $\times$ 1/12) | 750 | |
| Investment in Gerome Ltd. shares (5,000 $\times$ $26.75) | 133,750 | |
| Commission expense | 1,200 | |
|    Cash ($100,750 + $134,950) | | 235,700 |

At the end of 20X5, YZone would record interest income and holding gains and losses *in the income statement accounts:*

| | | |
|---|---:|---:|
| Accrued interest receivable | 750 | |
|    Investment income: Interest | | 750 |
| Investment in Provincial Hydro bonds | 500 | |
|    Investment revenue; unrealized holding gain: | | |
|    Provincial Hydro Bond | | 500 |
| Investment loss; unrealized holding gain: Gerome Ltd. | | |
|    shares ($133,750 − $123,750) | 10,000 | |
|      Investment in Gerome Ltd. shares | | 10,000 |

Reporting on the income statement, assuming all amounts are shown net:

| | |
|---|---:|
| Investment income (loss) | |
| ($750 − $1,200 + $500 − $10,000) | ($9,950) |

There would be no special equity accounts recorded on the balance sheet, and the investments would be reported as before.

**Second Year** Entries in 20X6 would be identical for interest and dividends, but the sale of the Provincial Hydro bond would be recorded as follows:

| | | |
|---|---:|---:|
| Cash | 103,450 | |
| Investment income: Interest | | 750 |
| Investment in Provincial Hydro bonds | | 100,500 |
| Gain on sale of investment | | 2,200 |

A $2,700 gain was recorded in 20X6 in the available-for-sale example, versus $2,200 in this held-for-trading investment example. YZone has still earned $2,700 on the bond. In the held-for-trading investment example, $500 is included in net income in 20X5 and $2,200 in 20X6. *Timing* of gain and loss recognition has changed.

At the end of 20X6:

| | | |
|---|---:|---:|
| Investment in Gerome Ltd. shares ($157,500 − $123,750) 33,750 | | |
| Investment income: unrealized holding gain: | | |
| Gerome Ltd. shares | | 33,750 |

When the Gerome Ltd. shares are sold in 20X7:

| | | |
|---|---:|---:|
| Cash | 150,800 | |
| Loss on sale of investment | | |
| (($30.50 × 5,000) − $157,500)) | 5,000 | |
| Commissions expense | 1,700 | |
| Investment in Gerome Ltd. shares | | 157,500 |

Recognizing the gain or loss caused by the change in value (and the commissions) in net income immediately has again changed the timing, but not the amount, of the net gain. When unrealized holding gains and losses were deferred, in the prior example, a net gain of $15,850 was recognized in 20X7. When gains and losses and commissions are recognized as they occur, there is a loss of $11,200 ($10,000 + $1,200) in 20X5, a gain of $33,750 in 20X6, and a loss of $6,700 ($5,000 + 1,700) in 20X7. The total is still $15,850.

**Impairment** Since losses on declines in fair value are included in income immediately, there are no impairment rules applied to this method. Declines in market value may reverse if market value recovers.

## CONCEPT REVIEW

1. An available-for-sale investment is bought for $10,000, and has a fair value of $14,000 at the end of the first year, $16,000 at the end of the second year, and is sold for $21,000 in the third year. What amount of gain is recorded in net income in the third year?

2. Assume that the same investment is classified as a held-for-trading investment. What gain is included in income in the third year?

3. An available-for-sale investment had a carrying value of $50,000 and a fair value of $40,000. If the decline in value is considered a normal fluctuation in market value, what amount will be recorded in net income? What if the decline was considered an impairment?

## THE EQUITY METHOD

Conceptually, the equity method treats the investee company as if it were condensed into one balance sheet item and one income statement item and then merged into the investor company at the proportion owned by the investor. The equity method is sometimes called "one-line consolidation" because it results in the same effect on the investor's earnings and retained earnings as would result from consolidating the financial statements of the investor and investee companies. It does so without combining both companies' financial statements.

**Illustration** In its simplest form, the equity method requires that the investment account represent the investor's proportionate share of the acquired value of the investee and that the investment income represent the investor's proportionate share of the investee's income. Assume, for initial simplicity, that Teck Computer Company (TCC) makes an investment of $100,000 for 40% of the voting shares of RPP Software on 1 January 20X1. In 20X1, RPP has earnings of $30,000 and pays dividends totalling $10,000. If the investment is accounted for by the equity method, TCC will make the following two entries at the end of 20X1:

To record TCC's share of RPP's net income:

| | | |
|---|---|---|
| Investment in RPP Software | 12,000 | |
|     Investment income ($30,000 × 40%) | | 12,000 |

To record receipt of dividends from RPP:

| | | |
|---|---|---|
| Cash ($10,000 × 40%) | 4,000 | |
|     Investment in RPP Software | | 4,000 |

Note that dividends from the investee are not recorded as investment income. Under the equity method, the investor company records its proportionate share of the investee earnings as investment income and increases its investment account by this amount. When the investee pays dividends, its net worth is reduced, and thus the investment account of the investor is reduced. Dividends are viewed as a dis-investment, that is, a return of the investment to the investor, rather than a return *on* the investment.

Following the two entries for 20X1, the investment account for RPP will reflect the following:

| | |
|---|---|
| Investment in RPP Software, at equity | |
| Original investment | $100,000 |
| Proportionate share of earnings of investee ($30,000 × 40%) | 12,000 |
| Dividends received from investee ($10,000 × 40%) | (4,000) |
| Ending balance | $108,000 |

The difference between investee earnings and investee dividends is the amount of earnings accruing to the investor that the investee retained, or the *unremitted earnings* of the investee. Thus, the equity-based investment account is equal to the original investment plus the investor's proportionate share of the investee's unremitted earnings, or the cumulative increase in retained earnings since the investment was made. In this sense, the equity method represents an extension of accrual accounting to investments in common shares. However, the balance sheet doesn't reflect the cost of the investment any more. This $108,000 number is not fair value, either, and is hard to interpret.

**Extraordinary Items and Discontinued Operations** If the investee reports extraordinary items or discontinued operations, the investor company must report its proportionate share of these items on its income statement separately, in the same way it would if they were incurred by the investor company. However, separate disclosure is needed only if they remain material items on the income statement of the investor, which is rare.

**Necessary Adjustments** The equity method is typically more complicated than this simple example. It is usually necessary to make certain adjustments to the amount of annual income that is recorded on the investor's books. Two factors must be considered:

1. When an investor company acquires the equity securities of an investee company, it will usually pay more for the securities than their book value, because tangible assets are undervalued or intangible assets are present but not recorded. In this situation, the investor's proportionate share of the investee's net income must be adjusted to reflect *amortization of the underlying fair value of the net assets acquired, and impairment of goodwill, if any*. Therefore, it is necessary to:

    a. Measure the book value versus the fair value of net identifiable assets acquired;

    b. Compare the proportionate fair value to the price paid; and

    c. Determine the amount of goodwill, if any.

    The fair values of identifiable assets and goodwill are not explicitly recorded under the equity method, but the investor's share of income must be decreased by appropriate amortization on the fair values of amortizable assets and any writedown caused by an impairment of goodwill.

2. If the investor and the investee have transactions with each other during the year, either company, or both companies, may have *unrealized unconfirmed* profits from these transactions recorded in income. For example, assume that the investor sold inventory to the investee at a profit of $25,000. If the investee subsequently sold these goods to a third party, then the intercompany sales price is validated, or realized, in this subsequent transaction and no particular accounting concerns arise. However, if the inventory is still on the investee's balance sheet, then the profit is *unrealized* and *unconfirmed* through an independent third party. It is not acceptable to recognize an increase in net income if all that's happened is a sale to a "customer" that the vendor can significantly influence. Therefore, the equity method, properly applied, involves adjustments for unrealized, unconfirmed, intercompany profits of both companies.

## Example: Equity Method

On 2 January 20X1, Giant Company purchased 3,600 shares of the 18,000 outstanding common shares of Small Corporation for $300,000 cash. Two Giant Company senior executives were elected to the Small Corporation Board of Directors. Giant is deemed to be able to exercise significant influence over Small's operating and financial policies, so the equity method of accounting for the investment is appropriate.

**Acquisition** Giant records its investment as follows:

| | | |
|---|---|---|
| Investment in Small, at equity | 300,000 | |
| Cash | | 300,000 |

**Fair Value Increments and Goodwill** The balance sheet for Small at 2 January 20X1, and estimated market values of its assets and liabilities are as follows:

| | Book Value | Market Value | Difference |
|---|---|---|---|
| Cash and receivables | $ 500,000 | $ 500,000 | $ 0 |
| Plant and equipment, net (10-year remaining life) | 500,000 | 700,000 | 200,000 |
| Land | 150,000 | 170,000 | 20,000 |
| Total assets | $1,150,000 | $1,370,000 | |
| Less: liabilities | (150,000) | (150,000) | 0 |
| Net assets | $1,000,000 | $1,220,000 | $220,000 |

Giant bought 20% of Small's shareholders' equity, which has a book value of $200,000 ($1,000,000 × 20%); therefore, $200,000 is the proportion of Small book value purchased by Giant. Giant paid $300,000 for its 20% interest in Small. The amount above book value that Giant paid, $100,000, is called the *purchase price discrepancy*. The accounting problem is to determine why Giant paid that much, and then to account for the acquisition price accordingly.

First, each asset and liability is examined to see if book value properly states fair market value. To the extent that some assets were undervalued, the $100,000 excess is explained. Second if there is a remaining unexplained residual, it is attributed to goodwill. This is based on the assumption any excess paid is because there are unrecorded intangible assets, which promise future cash flow.

The "difference" column above shows the specific assets whose market value exceeds book value. Giant acquired a portion (20%) of each of these items, including the amount by which market value exceeds book value.

| | Book Value | Market Value | Difference | 20% of Difference |
|---|---|---|---|---|
| Plant and equipment (10-year remaining life) | $500,000 | $700,000 | $200,000 | $40,000 |
| Land | 150,000 | 170,000 | 20,000 | 4,000 |
| Totals | | | $220,000 | $44,000 |

Thus, $44,000 of the $100,000 purchase price premium over book value that Giant paid can be identified with these specific assets. The remaining difference, $56,000, cannot be specifically identified with any asset and therefore represents goodwill. Goodwill is defined as the excess of the amount invested in acquiring all or a portion of another firm over the fair value of the net identifiable assets acquired. Goodwill can also be computed as follows:

| Computation of Goodwill Purchased by Giant Company | | |
|---|---|---|
| Purchase price (of 20% interest) | | $300,000 |
| Market value of identifiable assets | $1,370,000 | |
| Less: Market value of liabilities | (150,000) | |
| Total | $1,220,000 | |
| Market value of 20% of identifiable net assets acquired: ($1,220,000 × 20%) | | (244,000) |
| Goodwill | | $ 56,000 |

Giant, then, has acquired a 20% interest in Small at a cost of $300,000, and the items acquired can be represented as follows:

| | | |
|---|---:|---:|
| 20% of the net book value of Small ($1,000,000 × .20) | | $200,000 |
| 20% of excess of market value over book value for: | | |
|   Plant and equipment (20% × $200,000) | $40,000 | |
|   Land (20% × $20,000) | 4,000 | 44,000 |
| Goodwill | | 56,000 |
| Total | | $300,000 |

**Subsequent Amortization** The equity method requires that Giant record its initial $300,000 investment in Small in one investment account, despite the fact that it has many components. No formal recognition is given to the various component parts of the investment. However, the amount of income recognized annually will be changed as a result of these components.

When Small uses or disposes of any of the above items, either in the normal course of business or by asset sales, Giant must record appropriate adjustments to its investment account through the annual entry that recognizes investment income.

For example, amortization is too low. If the plant and equipment have a remaining useful life of 10 years and Small uses straight-line amortization, Giant needs to increase the amortization expense for Small by $40,000 divided by 10 years, or $4,000 each year for the next 10 years.

Next, goodwill must be considered. Goodwill is not amortized, but must be evaluated for possible impairment. If there is an impairment, investment income must be decreased accordingly.

No annual adjustments need be made for the excess of market value over book value for the land. If Small sells the land, an adjustment would be required, showing that the cost of 20% of the land from the Giant perspective is understated by $4,000 on Small's books. Giant's proportionate share of any gain on disposal of the land would be decreased by $4,000.

**Investment Revenue** Giant's income from its investment in Small requires adjusting to reflect the above analysis. Suppose that for the fiscal year ending 31 December 20X1, Small reports the following:

| | |
|---|---:|
| Income before discontinued operations | $ 73,000 |
| Net earnings from discontinued operations | 30,000 |
| Net income | $103,000 |
| Cash dividends, paid on 31 December | $ 50,000 |

Goodwill has been evaluated for potential impairment, but no writedown is required. In 20X1, Small sold goods to Giant for $46,000 during the year, and none have been resold by Giant at year-end. The goods originally cost Small $38,000, and thus Small has recorded an $8,000 increase in income that has not been confirmed by a transaction with an outside party. Since Giant owns 20% of Small, and records only 20% of Small's income, it must eliminate 20% of the gain, or $1,600 of the $8,000 unrealized gain.

Investment income is a combination of Giant's share of a variety of items.

| | |
|---|---:|
| Small's net income before discontinued operations ($73,000 × 20%) | $14,600 |
| Additional amortization on plant and equipment fair value ($40,000 ÷ 10) | (4,000) |
| Elimination of unrealized intercompany profit in inventory ($8,000 × 20%) | (1,600) |
| Net investment income, ordinary income | $ 9,000 |
| Small's net earnings from discontinued operations ($30,000 × 20%) | $ 6,000 |

The investment revenue for 20X1, after all the adjustments, is $9,000 of ordinary income and a gain from discontinued operations of $6,000. These two items would be shown separately on Giant's income statement. This is a total of $15,000. If no adjustments had been made, Giant would have recorded a total of $20,600 of income (($73,000 + $30,000) × 20%). This result of the equity method is quite common; less income than you might expect is recorded. This happens because the investor very often pays more than book value for its interest in the investee, and resulting amortizations reduce income. Then, too, intercompany transactions are quite common, and elimination of unrealized profits will also reduce income.

**Entries**  At 31 December, Giant would make the following entries to reflect its interest in the earnings of Small:

| | | |
|---|---:|---:|
| Investment in Small, at equity | 15,000 | |
|     Investment income (as above) | | 9,000 |
|     Earnings from discontinued operations | | 6,000 |

To record the receipt of cash dividends paid by Small:

| | | |
|---|---:|---:|
| Cash ($50,000 × 20%) | 10,000 | |
|     Investment in Small, at equity | | 10,000 |

**Balance in Investment Account**  After these entries are posted, the balance in the investment in account is $305,000.

| | |
|---|---:|
| Beginning balance (acquisition price) | $300,000 |
| Proportionate share of Small's net income | 15,000 |
| Dividends received | (10,000) |
| Investment account balance, 31 December 20X1 | $305,000 |

The total investment income Giant reports from its investment in Small is $15,000. Since Giant received $10,000 of this in the form of cash dividends, the net increase of its investment is the unremitted earnings of $5,000.

## Unrealized Profit Elimination

**upstream profits**

intercompany profits on transactions between an investor company and investee where the investee records the profit

The example shown above involved an intercompany unrealized profit that had been recorded by the investee. This is called an **upstream profit**, because the transaction went from the bottom of the investment river (the investee) to the top (the investor). Since the investor picks up only its share of the investee's income, its also picks up only a partial, or 20%, elimination of the profit.

Assume instead that the transaction in the Giant example is **downstream**, a sale from the investor to the investee. Again, none of the inventory is sold at year-end. In this case, Giant has recorded, as part of gross profit, an $8,000 amount that has not been confirmed by a sale to an outside party. No adjustment is made to the investor's sales or gross profit. Instead, investment income is reduced by the *full $8,000 intercompany downstream unrealized profit.* Thus, the bottom line net income for the investor company will reflect the elimination of *all* the gross profit, but through a reduction of investment income rather than a reduction of reported gross profit.

**downstream profits**

intercompany profits on transactions between an investor company and investee where the parent records the profit

The rule is that upstream unrealized profits are fractionally eliminated (the investor's share only) but downstream unrealized profits are eliminated in their entirety, because the full amount is in the investor's accounts.

## Goodwill Impairment

The procedures for evaluating goodwill for potential impairment were explained in Chapter 10. If goodwill had to be written down, investment income is reduced by the amount of the writedown. This may well create an investment loss for the year, and the investment account on the balance sheet would be reduced as a result. This is the obvious result of a writedown: assets go down!

## Comparison to the Cost Method

An investor company may use the cost method to account for an investment during the year, and adjust from cost to equity or consolidation at year-end. Alternatively, if differential accounting is allowed, a significant-influence investment may be accounted for using the cost method instead of the equity method. If the investment in Small were accounted for using the cost method, the following entries would be made. They are compared to the equity method, side-by-side, for clarity.

| Entries | Alternative 1: Cost Method Is Appropriate | | Alternative 2: Equity Method Is Appropriate | |
|---|---|---|---|---|
| a. Entry to date of acquisition: | | | | |
| Investment in Small......................................... | 300,000 | | 300,000 | |
| Cash........................................................ | | 300,000 | | 300,000 |
| b. Entry at year-end to record net income | | | | |
| reported by Small: | No entry | | | |
| Investment in Small......................................... | | | 15,000 | |
| Investment revenue......................................... | | | | 9,000 |
| Earnings from disc. ops. ............................... | | | | 6,000 |
| c. Entry for a cash dividend: | | | | |
| Cash........................................................ | 2,000 | | | |
| Investment revenue......................................... | | 2,000 | | |
| Cash........................................................ | | | 2,000 | |
| Investment in Small......................................... | | | | 2,000 |

The two methods are significantly different in how they define investment income, whether they recognize underlying fair value and goodwill, how they deal with dividends of the investee, and the value reported on the balance sheet for the investment.

## CONCEPT REVIEW

1. Why is the equity method sometimes called one-line consolidation?

2. Explain what is meant by unrealized profits. Why should they be eliminated when the investor's financial statements are being prepared?

3. What difference is there between the amounts reported as income from equity reported investments and the dividends received from those investments?

## CONSOLIDATION

A parent company is required to consolidate its financial statements with those of its subsidiaries when general-purpose financial statements are issued. The parent company uses the cost or equity method to account for the investment during the year, but, at the end of the reporting period, must prepare consolidated financial statements for reporting to its shareholders and other financial statement users. Consolidated statements are prepared by combining the separate sets of financial statements into one, which is intended to portray the activities of the whole enterprise. This is an application of substance over form, as consolidated statements portray the economic entity that exists in substance, rather than relying on the legal form that has been used to organize the activities of an enterprise.

Consolidation is accomplished using the purchase method. That is, the parent company purchases the subsidiary, and the two companies are combined as of that date. Fair market values of the subsidiary's assets are recognized from this acquisition transaction, including goodwill. Prior results are not combined.

It is important to understand that consolidation does not happen on anyone's books; there's a spreadsheet that imports financial statements from the parent and the subsidiary. Then, certain adjustments are processed, and the consolidated financial statements are produced.

**Consolidation Process** Consolidation is mostly an additive process; the financial statements are added together, line by line. Common adjustments include:

1. The investment account must be eliminated from the parent company's financial statements, and the corresponding equity accounts must be eliminated from the subsidiary's financial statements.

2. If net assets' book values reflected on the subsidiary's books on the date of acquisition are different from their market values on that date, the difference, called a fair value increment, must be recognized in the consolidated financial statements, along with any goodwill inherent in the purchase price. This reflects the fact that the parent acquired assets, including intangible assets, at fair value.

3. If fair values (i.e., market values) were recognized, they must be amortized in subsequent years.

4. Goodwill is not amortized. Goodwill is written down if impaired. The impairment test must be done on an annual basis.

5. Any portion of the subsidiary that is consolidated but is owned by a non-controlling, or minority, subsidiary shareholder must be recognized as a separate balance sheet account. The non-controlling interest is assigned a portion of net income.

6. Intercompany receivables and payables, gains and losses, and revenues and expenses must be eliminated so that the financial statements will reflect only transactions with outsiders.

7. If there are any intercompany unrealized profits at year-end, these must be eliminated so that income is not misstated.

**Consolidated Financial Statements** Consolidation is an extremely complex area, and the purpose of this discussion is to look only at the big picture. The Appendix to this chapter contains a basic consolidation example, along with a brief explanation of the elimination entries. This example will give you a taste of the consolidation process. Consider the end result for a few minutes, even if you're not covering the Appendix material. Look at Exhibit 11A-1 now. What should you notice about these consolidated results, as shown in the final column?

- Consolidated assets are higher than just the parent's alone, and also are different than just the parent and the subsidiary added together. The subsidiary's assets are written up (or down) to reflect their fair values on the date on acquisition. Goodwill implied by the purchase price is recognized. Goodwill is shown with intangible assets.
- Assets and liabilities of the parent and the subsidiary are added together, and intercompany balances are eliminated.
- The parent's investment account and investment revenue are eliminated.
- The portion of the subsidiary that is not owned by the parent is included in consolidated totals, but the outside interests are reflected in consolidated financial statements via a balance sheet account and an income statement account that relate to the **non-controlling interests**.
- The consolidated income statement reflects higher expenses than just the two statements added together, because fair values recognized are amortized.
- The consolidated income statement reflects eliminations for intercompany unrealized profits.
- There is an allocation to the non-controlling interest that represents their share of the subsidiary's current year income.
- Dividends reported are only those dividends paid by the parent.
- Equity accounts of the subsidiary that existed on acquisition are eliminated.

**Other Adjustments** Many parent companies have more than one subsidiary, and all must be consolidated together, with all intercompany transactions eliminated. This can seem mind boggling when there are 200 subsidiaries, but it is not a big challenge for consolidation computer software as long as all of the intercompany transactions and balances are coded correctly. Data capture is the big challenge in this case.

Profit eliminations are potentially complex when the impact on future income tax is considered. Then, too, intercompany unrealized profits usually have an impact for multiple years, and appropriate entries must be made. The parent's percentage ownership in the subsidiary can change, either up or down. There are also many subtleties associated with fair value amortizations. We could go on, but we're sure you get the picture.

**Connection to the Equity Method** The calculations and adjustments that are required for the equity method are also done for consolidation. That is, the fair value of net assets acquired and goodwill are determined, and then amortized or evaluated for impairment. Intercompany unconfirmed profits are eliminated. In consolidation, however, all the different financial statement elements are recognized separately. In the equity method, the net assets are subsumed in the investment account on the balance sheet and the investment revenue line on the income statement. Overall net income and net assets will be identical, though, if the equity method is used instead of consolidation. This can help companies track key metrics during the year, prior to full consolidation. It is one of the attractions for using the equity method for recording during the year and/or for reporting in certain circumstances.

---

**non-controlling interest (minority interest)**

when a company controls a subsidiary but does not own 100% of the voting shares, it still includes 100% of the net assets and net income in the consolidated financial statements; the non-controlling interest in earnings is the portion of the subsidiary's earnings that accrue to the other, minority shareholders; the non-controlling interest in net assets—a balance sheet credit—is the portion of net assets that represent the minority shareholders' share

**Differential Accounting** Remember, though, companies that are not publicly accountable can adopt differential reporting for controlled investments and use either the cost or the equity method for accounting with unanimous shareholder approval.

**Applicable Standards** The approach to consolidation has shifted, or is shifting as you read this material. The approach to consolidation described above is the international approach, and Canadian standards will soon converge with these standards, reflecting the new Canadian position on this topic. The consolidations standards project has been a joint effort with FASB and the IASB, with the objective of making consolidation practices similar in these major constituencies.

The traditional approach in North America has been to record the *parent's* portion of fair values acquired (e.g., 80%), and the parent's goodwill, but international standards require that these amounts be recognized in their entirety (i.e., 100%) to acknowledge the fair value of the subsidiary as a *whole entity*. The non-controlling interest changes as a result of the recognition, or non-recognition, of the other 20%. Equally significant, the non-controlling interest is classified as equity using the international approach but is outside equity in the traditional North American approach. These approaches are further explored in the Appendix to this chapter.

## RECLASSIFICATION

It happens that investment intent changes, and, for instance, an available-for-sale investment may become a held-to-maturity investment, or a significant-influence investment may be reclassified as an available-for-sale investment. Standards specify that held-for-trading investments, because of the specialized nature of the portfolio category, *may not be reclassified*.

Sometimes, reclassifications are caused by the actions of others—for example, significant influence may be lost if another shareholder becomes dominant. Most often, though, management intent is the driving factor in these changes. Granted, the financial position of the investor and the investee influences management intent. It may not be possible to hold investments to maturity if the investor is in need of funds. Alternatively, the investee might be struggling, or suddenly prosperous, and this may influence intent.

If investments are reclassified, the investment is transferred to the alternate portfolio at an appropriate value. For example, if investments are transferred to the held-to-maturity or the significant-influence category, the transfer takes place at the investment's existing carrying value, and the investment is then accounted for using the cost or equity method as appropriate. If the investment becomes an available-for-sale investment, the transfer takes place at fair value and other comprehensive income is created. Future income is recognized based on the new classification rules. Refer to Exhibit 11-7 for a summary of the rules for reclassification. Note in particular that:

- If held-to-maturity investments are reclassified as available-for-sale investments, the transfer takes place at fair value and the difference between amortized cost (the carrying value) and fair value is included in other comprehensive income until realized through sale.
- If available-for-sale investments are reclassified as held-to-maturity investments, then the cumulative gain or loss in other comprehensive income is amortized to interest income over the remaining term of the investment.

Reclassifications are clearer if a formal entry is made to reclassify the investment. For example, if a held-to-maturity bond investment with a carrying value of $98,000 and a fair value of $105,000 is reclassified as an available-for-sale investment, the following entry would be made:

| | | |
|---|---|---|
| Available-for-sale investment: bonds | 105,000 | |
| Held-to-maturity investment: bonds | | 98,000 |
| Unrealized holding gain: bonds | | 7,000 |

---

EXHIBIT 11-7

## RECLASSIFICATION RULES

| Transfer From | Transfer To | Transfer Value | Prior Gains and Losses |
|---|---|---|---|
| Any appropriate category | Available-for-sale | Fair value | Holding gain or loss at date of transfer recognized in other comprehensive income until sale |
| Any appropriate category | Equity | Existing carrying value | No gain or loss recorded; any cumulative amounts in other comprehensive income remain until sale |
| Available-for-sale | Held-to-maturity | Existing carrying value | Unrealized gain or loss to date amortized to interest income |

Note: transfers to and from held-for-trading category **not permitted**

---

Remember, such a reclassification out of the held-to-maturity classification means that this classification cannot be used for two years, because management intent has proven unreliable.

## CLASSIFICATION AND DISCLOSURE REQUIREMENTS

### Current versus Long-Term Investments

Should investments be classified as current or long term in the financial statements? The answer will have a significant effect on the current liquidity picture portrayed. An investment is current if it is capable of reasonably prompt liquidation. This includes any marketable security, and any investment that matures within the next year (or operating cycle.) The security should also be held for current needs, and thus intent is an issue.

---

EXHIBIT 11-8

## DISCLOSURE EXAMPLE
## RESEARCH IN MOTION

### Extracts from Note 4 to the March 4, 2006, Financial Statements

Available-for-sale investments are recorded at fair value and comprise the following:

| As at March 4, 2006 | Amortized Cost | Unrealized Gains | Unrealized Losses | Estimated Fair Value |
|---|---|---|---|---|
| Government sponsored enterprise notes | $380,084 | $ — | $ (7,814) | $372,270 |
| Commercial paper and corporate bonds | 274,375 | 5 | (7,572) | 266,808 |
| Asset-backed securities | 139,562 | — | (2,851) | 136,711 |
| Bank certificates of deposit | 14,074 | — | (1) | 14,073 |
| | $808,095 | $ 5 | $(18,238) | $789,862 |
| Classified as current | $177,645 | $ — | $ (2,092) | $175,553 |
| Classified as non-current | 630,450 | 5 | (16,146) | 614,309 |
| Total | $808,095 | $ 5 | $(18,238) | $789,862 |

*Source:* www.sedar.com, Research in Motion Ltd., Annual Report, May 10, 2006.

Held-to-maturity investments are obviously classified as long-term investments, at least until the investment's maturity date falls within the one-year window. Available-for-sale investments may be either current or long term, depending on marketability and term.

Review RIM's investment disclosures, from the company's 2006 financial statements, and note that $175,553 (thousands, U.S. dollars) are current, while $614,309 are long term. RIM has disclosed both cost and market value, with the difference being an unrealized loss included in OCI.

## Disclosure of Financial Instruments

All held-to-maturity, available-for-sale, and held-for-trading investments are financial instruments, so disclosure must be made of:

1. The *accounting policies* used for reporting.

2. The *fair value* for each class of financial asset; this would be carrying value for available-for-sale and held-for-trading investments. The methods used to measure fair values should be disclosed.

3. The *nature and extent of risks* arising from financial instruments, including, as appropriate, credit risk, liquidity risk, and market risk.

## Disclosure Regarding Strategic Investments

Disclosures relating to strategic investments, that is, significant-influence, control, and joint venture relationships, are extensive. Disclosure is needed because:

1. By their nature, strategic investments are intended to extend the reach of the reporting enterprise and to increase the volume of non–arm's length transactions.

2. There are substantial differences between the income effects of strategic investments and their cash flow effects, as has been described in the preceding section.

The least extensive disclosure relates to controlled subsidiaries. When control exists, normal practice is to consolidate the subsidiaries and the parent, with the result that there is a single reporting entity that includes two or more separate legal entities. When the subsidiaries are consolidated, all intercompany transactions are eliminated and the several enterprises are reported as one. Little additional disclosure is required.

Some companies list their consolidated subsidiaries in their annual reports, but this is a voluntary disclosure. Most companies do not tell the readers who their subsidiaries are, perhaps because the subsidiaries are so thoroughly integrated into the parent's operations that their existence is irrelevant to most statement users.

If one company acquired another company during the accounting period—a business combination—the parent company must disclose the transaction and the amounts of the identifiable assets and liabilities that were acquired. The amount and form of consideration given for the purchase must also be disclosed, such as cash, common shares, preferred shares, long-term debt, etc. Only the amount of cash consideration is shown on the face of the cash flow statement, however.

The disclosures for investments in significantly influenced investees are quite extensive. They include disclosure of:

- The amount of investment in significantly influenced companies;
- The basis of reporting each investment (i.e., cost or equity); and
- The income from investments in significantly influenced investees, reported separately from other investment income.

In practice, compliance with these recommendations is uneven. Materiality undoubtedly plays a role, since a company may well have investments that confer significant influence but that constitute a small portion of the reporting enterprise's operations.

## CASH FLOW STATEMENT

Companies often make short-term investments in highly liquid financial instruments such as certificates of deposit, guaranteed investment certificates, or Treasury Bills. This type of investment is a temporary use of cash in order to earn a return when the company has a temporary excess of cash. In Chapter 5, we pointed out that if such financial instruments are considered to be *cash equivalents*, they are included in the definition of cash when the cash flow statement is prepared. Consequently, investments in cash equivalents do not appear in the cash flow statement, but instead are included in the cash balance.

For other investments in debt and equity securities, the cash flow impacts occur in three ways:

1. There is a cash outflow when an investment is purchased.

2. Cash payments are received by the investor (dividends or interest).

3. Cash is received when the investment is sold or is redeemed at maturity.

For most investments, the initial cash outflow is reported as an investing activity on the cash flow statement in the period that the investment is made. If securities are held for trading, they may be analogous to inventory, and related cash flows are classified as operating activities.

When the recorded values of available-for-sale investments or held-for-trading investment changes because of changes in fair value, this is a non-cash event; it does not appear on the cash flow statement. For held-for-trading investments, gains and losses on the income statement are adjusted as non-cash amounts. For available-for-sale investments, other comprehensive income is affected, but no adjustments are needed to net income on the cash flow statement.

On sale, the net cash proceeds that the company receives when it sells or redeems an investment security are reported as a positive (inflow) amount in the investing activities section of the cash flow statement. Any gain or loss on disposal must be removed from net income when computing the operating cash flow, since a gain or loss is merely the difference between the cash proceeds and the investment's carrying value at the time of the sale. Note also that premium or discount amortization in investment income on held-to-maturity investments are also non-cash items, and must be included as a reconciliation item in the operating activities section.

Reporting the periodic cash flows for dividends received on strategic investments presents a somewhat greater challenge. If the investment is being reported on the equity basis, then:

1. Cash received in dividends must be reported on the cash flow statement, as cash flow from investment revenue.

2. The investor's share of the investee's earnings must be removed from net income when calculating the operating cash flow.

If the strategic investment gives the investor control over the investee and the parent prepares consolidated statements, the cash flows between the parent and subsidiary are eliminated in consolidation and do not appear on the cash flow statement at all. A consolidated cash flow statement is prepared.

## INTERNATIONAL PERSPECTIVE

Investments that are financial instruments are classified according Section 3855 of the *CICA Handbook*, "Financial Instruments—Recognition and Measurement." This standard is effective in any fiscal year beginning after 1 October 2006—that is, in the 2007 fiscal year. However, enterprises with no public accountability (those that qualify for differential disclosure) may defer implementation. *Strategic investments* in shares are specifically excluded from the financial instruments sections of the *CICA Handbook*, but are accorded specific attention in other sections.

**Fair Value Method** IASB standards require that securities be remeasured to fair value at each balance sheet date, except for debt securities that are held-to-maturity investments and for situations where there is significant influence or control. U.S. standards require the same. As with the Canadian rules, unrealized holding gains and losses on available-for-sale investments are included in other comprehensive income until realization, while gains and losses on held-for-trading investments are included in income. Thus, the 2006 Canadian rules are a step toward international harmonization.

These rules are quite technical, though, and there are some differences between the Canadian and IASB standards. For example, international standards:

- Require reversal of impairment losses when fair value rises;
- Have a different definition of when impairment exists, and a different calculation of the extent of impairment;
- Do not allow choice of policy for transaction costs associated with held-to-maturity and available-for-sale investments; and
- Require foreign exchange gains and losses associated with available-for-sale investments be included in net income.

**Consolidation** Accounting for consolidation is an area where there have been significant differences between North American (Canadian and U.S.) and international standards. The IASB and the FASB have been working on a joint project in this area. This will culminate, late in the decade, in converged standards for consolidation practices; the converged approach is described in the chapter material. Canadian standards will fall into line. The result will be improved consistency for reporting in this global economy.

**Proportionate Consolidation** Canadian rules require use of proportional consolidation for joint ventures, while international rules also allow use of the equity method.

**Equity Method** Canadian standards for strategic investments are substantially in line with the recommendations of the IASB. The United States, however, has different classification standards. Significant influence is rigidly defined in the United States as ownership of between 20% and 50% of the outstanding equity of the investee; other factors that shape an investee's influence are ignored.

## RELEVANT STANDARDS

*CICA Handbook:*
- Section 1530, Comprehensive Income
- Section 1581, Business Combinations
- Section 1590, Subsidiaries
- Section 1600, Consolidated Financial Statements
- Section 1651, Foreign Currency Translation
- Section 3051, Long-term Investments
- Section 3055, Interests in Joint Ventures
- Section 3855, Financial Instruments—Recognition and Measurement
- Section 3861, Financial Instruments—Disclosure and Presentation
- Section 3862, Financial Instruments—Disclosures
- Section 3863, Financial Instruments—Presentation

IASB:
- *IAS* 1, Presentation of Financial Statements
- *IAS* 18, Revenue
- *IAS* 21, The Effects of Changes in Foreign Exchange Rates
- *IAS* 27, Consolidated and Separate Financial Statements
- *IAS* 28, Investments in Associates
- *IAS* 31, Interests in Joint Ventures

- *IAS* 32, Financial Instruments: Presentation
- *IAS* 36, Impairment of Assets
- *IAS* 39, Financial Instruments: Recognition and Measurement
- *IFRS* 3, Business Combinations
- *IFRS* 7, Financial Instruments: Disclosure

## SUMMARY OF KEY POINTS

1. Companies invest in the securities of other entities for a variety of reasons, including increasing return on idle funds, active trading of an investment portfolio, long-term investments for earnings generation, creating strategic alliances, and creating appropriate legal vehicles for business activities.

2. Appropriate accounting for investments is determined by the substance of the investment vehicle, and also the intent of the investor. Differential reporting can be adopted by non-public organizations in this area.

3. Investments must be classified as held-to-maturity, available-for-sale, or held-for-trading investments, or, if strategic, control investments, significant-influence investments, or joint ventures.

4. Held-to-maturity investments are accounted for using the cost method. The security is recorded at cost and interest revenue is accrued as time passes. If the investments are purchased at a premium or discount from face value, the premium or discount is amortized to income over the life of the investment.

5. Available-for-sale investments are accounted for using the fair value method, where the investment is remeasured at current fair value at each balance sheet date. Gains or losses are recognized in other comprehensive income (shareholders' equity) until the investment is sold, when the cumulative realized amount is recorded in net income.

6. Held-for-trading investments are accounted for using the fair value method, where the investment is remeasured at current fair value at each balance sheet date. Gains or losses are recognized in net income immediately.

7. Held-to-maturity and available-for-sale investments are subject to impairment tests, where a permanent decline in value is recorded as a loss, which is not reversed.

8. Certain equity instruments are classified according to the power of the investor within the corporate governance structure of the investee. If the investor controls the investee, the investment is a subsidiary, and is consolidated. If the investor has power but does not have control without the cooperation of others, there is a significant-influence investment that must be accounted for using the equity method.

9. A joint venture is accounted for using proportionate consolidation, where the parent's share of each financial statement element is added to those of the parent.

10. If a non-public organization adopts differential reporting, a significant-influence investment may be reported at cost, and controlled investments and joint ventures accounted for with cost or equity methods.

11. Investments that are acquired in a foreign currency are initially reported on the investor's books at their equivalent cost in Canadian dollars, using the exchange rate in effect at the time of the purchase. Remeasurement at the end of the year uses the current exchange rate in effect on the balance sheet date, but the treatment of the change in exchange rate depends on the nature of the investment.

12. In the equity method, the investment is first recorded at cost, but the balance of the investment account changes to reflect the investor's proportionate share of the investee's adjusted earnings, and dividends. Investment revenue includes the investor's share

of profits (or losses), less amortizations of fair values present at acquisition, goodwill writedowns, and elimination of unrealized intercompany profits.

13. Consolidation requires combining the financial statements of the parent and the subsidiary at reporting dates.

14. Under purchase accounting, the parent consolidates the fair values of identifiable assets and liabilities. Any excess of the purchase price above the fair values of the assets is recorded as goodwill.

15. When statements are consolidated, all intercompany transactions and any unrealized profits are eliminated. The portion of the subsidiary that is not owned by the parent is reflected in the consolidated statements as a non-controlling or minority interest.

16. Investments may be reclassified from one category to another. The reclassification generally takes place at the prior carrying value, and any gains and losses are subject to specific rules depending on the reclassification category.

17. Investments are classified as current assets on the balance sheet if the intention is to use the investment for current needs, and if they are capable of reasonably prompt liquidation; otherwise, they are long term.

18. Significant disclosure is needed for investments. Exact disclosures vary depending on how the investment is classified.

19. The cash flow statement reflects cash paid for investments, cash received on sale, and cash received as investment income. Non-cash gains and losses, and premium and discount amortization, are adjusted in operations when the indirect method of presentation is used.

20. IASB, Canadian, and U.S. rules for held-to-maturity, available-for-sale, and held-for-trading investments are generally harmonized but technical differences remain. Standards governing consolidations are converging as a result of a joint standards project.

## KEY TERMS

available-for-sale investment, 586
consolidation, 592
control, 586
controlled investment, 586
cost method, 588
differential reporting, 592
discount, 595
downstream profits, 611
effective-interest amortization
    method, 595
equity method, 591
fair value, 591
fair value method, 588
financial instruments, 584
held-for-trading investment, 586
held-to-maturity investments, 585

impairment, 598
joint venture, 587
non-controlling interest, 613
other comprehensive income (OCI), 588
parent company, 587
passive investment, 584
premium, 595
proportionate consolidation, 592
realized holding gain, 589
significant-influence investment, 587
straight-line amortization method, 595
strategic investment, 584
subsidiary company, 587
unrealized holding gains, 589
unremitted earnings, 592
upstream profits, 611

## REVIEW PROBLEM

On 1 January 20X5, Acme Fruit Company has the following investments:

|  | Net Carrying Value at 1 January 20X5 |
| --- | --- |
| Available-for-sale investments: | |
| Apple (2,000 common shares) | $19,000 |
| Quince (10,000 common shares) | 50,000 |
| Cherry (5,000 common shares) | 40,000 |

Other comprehensive income on the balance sheet includes a $5,000 unrealized loss with respect to the Apple shares, a $5,000 unrealized gain with respect to the Quince shares, and a $2,000 unrealized gain with respect to the Cherry shares.

The following transactions and reclassifications occur during 20X5:

a. On 1 February 20X5, Acme purchases $30,000 of face amount bonds issued by Plum Incorporated for $29,500 plus accrued interest. The bonds have a coupon rate of 8%, pay interest semi-annually on 30 June and 31 December, and mature on 31 December 20X9. The investment is classified as held to maturity. Total amortization of the discount has been calculated to be $109 in 20X5.

b. Dividends of $0.75 per share are received on the Apple common shares on 30 May.

c. Interest on the Plum bonds is received on 30 June and 31 December.

d. On 1 July, the Quince shares are sold for $58,000. The proceeds are used to buy 1,000 Banana Company shares for $40 per share.

e. On 30 November, Apple shares are sold for $21,000.

f. At 31 December, the market values of the various investments are determined to be as follows:

| | |
| --- | --- |
| i.   Cherry common | $57,500 |
| ii.  Banana common | 23,000 |
| iii. Plum bonds (excluding accrued interest) | 31,000 |

The decline in value of the Banana Company shares is deemed to be an impairment.

g. The Cherry and Banana shares are temporary investments at year-end, while the Plum bonds are long term.

### Required:

1. What amount of investment income or loss, from all sources, is shown on the income statement for 20X5?

2. Show the change in other comprehensive income for the year, and the equity balances within other comprehensive income that would be reported at the end of 20X5.

3. Show the accounts and amounts related to the investments that are reported in the assets section of the 20X5 balance sheet of Acme Fruit Company.

## REVIEW PROBLEM—SOLUTION

1. Investment income
    Plum bonds:

    | | | |
    |---|---:|---:|
    | Interest: $30,000 × 8% × 11/12 | $2,200 | |
    | Discount amortization: (given) | 109 | $ 2,309 |
    | Apple dividends: 2,000 shares × $0.75 | | 1,500 |
    | Gain on sale of Quince shares ($8,000 + $5,000) | | 13,000 |
    | Loss on sale of Apple shares ($2,000 − $5,000) | | (3,000) |
    | Impairment loss on Banana shares<br>($23,000 − $40,000) | | (17,000) |
    | Total investment income (loss) | | $ (3,191) |

2. Change in other comprehensive income, 20X5:

    | | |
    |---|---:|
    | Elimination of unrealized loss on Apple shares | $ 5,000 |
    | Elimination of unrealized gain on Quince shares | (5,000) |
    | New unrealized gain on Cherry shares | 17,500 |
    | Change in other comprehensive income in 20X5 | $17,500 |

    Other comprehensive income, balance sheet, 31 December, 20X5

    | | |
    |---|---:|
    | Unrealized gain on Cherry shares ($2,000 + $17,500)* | $19,500 |

3. Investment assets at 31 December 20X5

    | | |
    |---|---:|
    | Temporary investments ($57,500 + $23,000) | $80,500 |
    | Long-term investments ($29,500 + $109) | $29,609 |

# APPENDIX

## CONSOLIDATION ILLUSTRATION

The main body of this chapter explained the general principles underlying consolidation but did not demonstrate a consolidation because of the complexities that quickly arise. This appendix provides a simple demonstration of a consolidation following a business combination for those readers who are interested in how the numbers fit together. This material reflects the converged standards of the IASB, AcSB and FASB that are expected to be in place late in the decade. The final section of the appendix briefly addresses the issue of consolidating foreign subsidiaries.

### Basic Illustration

P Company bought 80% of the voting shares of S Company one year ago for $4,700,000. The other 20% of S Company shares are owned by a small group of S Company top management. P Company controls S Company by virtue of its voting control and must consolidate its financial statements at the end of each fiscal period. Refer to the financial statements shown in the first two columns of Exhibit 11A-1, which are at the end of the first year of ownership.

During the year, P Company used the cost method of recording the investment, and thus the investment account is still recorded at $4,700,000. P Company shows $80,000 of other income on its income statement; S Company had declared $100,000 of dividends, which were paid $80,000 to P Company and $20,000 to the other shareholders.

As of the date of acquisition, S Company had net assets (that is, assets minus liabilities) of $3,782,000 at book value. By definition, this is equal to shareholders' equity on the date of acquisition. There was $140,000 in the common shares account, and $3,642,000 in retained earnings, to equal $3,782,000. P Company would determine the fair value of net assets on this date, through appraisal and other examination. Assume that fair values were equal to book values except for capital assets with a 10-year life, which were worth $1,000,000 more than book value. There was no impairment of goodwill by the end of the first year of acquisition.

During the year, S Company had sales of $4,000,000 to P Company. All the goods had been resold to other customers, except goods for which P Company had paid $300,000, which were still in inventory. These items had cost S Company $200,000. Finally, P Company owed $175,000 to S Company at year-end.

**Goodwill**  The goodwill on acquisition is calculated as follows:

| | | |
|---|---|---|
| Implied value ($4,700,000 ÷ .80) | | $5,875,000 |
| Less: Market value acquired | | |
|   Book value | $3,782,000 | |
|   Market value increment | 1,000,000 | |
|   Total | | (4,782,000) |
| Goodwill | | $1,093,000 |

Notice that $4,700,000 was the price paid for 80% of the company and is grossed up to determine the implied price for 100% of the company.

**Elimination Entries**  Consolidation mostly involves adding together the parent and subsidiary financial statements. However, entries are needed for certain eliminations.

1. *Investment elimination entry.* This is a busy entry, as it eliminates the equity accounts of the subsidiary on the date of acquisition, eliminates the parent's investment account, sets

up the non-controlling interest on the date of acquisition, and recognizes fair value differences and goodwill inherent in the purchase price.

| | | |
|---|---:|---:|
| Common shares (S Co.) | 140,000 | |
| Retained earnings (S Co.) | 3,642,000 | |
| Capital assets (increase to fair value) | 1,000,000 | |
| Goodwill | 1,093,000 | |
|     Investment in S Co. | | 4,700,000 |
|     Non-controlling interest | | |
|         (($4,782,000 + $1,093,000) × 20%) | | 1,175,000 |

The non-controlling interest account is an equity account in the financial statements of the parent company, representing the other shareholder's equity interest in a subsidiary.

2. *Amortization entry.* Next, accounts created in the investment elimination entry must be amortized to reflect usage or sale. One year has gone by, and capital assets are amortized. A ten-year life is assumed.

| | | |
|---|---:|---:|
| Amortization expense | 100,000 | |
|     Capital assets, net ($1,000,000 ÷ 10) | | 100,000 |

If any goodwill was impaired, it would be recorded in a similar manner: an expense would be debited and goodwill credited.

3. *Dividend entry.* S Company paid dividends to its shareholders, and these are recorded in its books. Assuming that P Company uses the cost method for recording the investment, the dividend paid to the majority shareholder is recorded as dividend revenue on the parent's income statement, while the dividend paid to the non-controlling shareholders reduces their interest in remaining net assets on the subsidiary. After this elimination, the only dividends left are those paid by P Company to the shareholders of P Company.

| | | |
|---|---:|---:|
| Dividend revenue | 80,000 | |
| Non-controlling interest | 20,000 | |
|     Dividends declared | | 100,000 |

4. *Intercompany balances and transactions elimination entries.* These amounts are eliminated so that all that remains on the consolidated accounts are transactions that the consolidated entity has had with outside parties. Note that the entries do not change net income or net assets; they simply deflate offsetting components.

| | | |
|---|---:|---:|
| Sales | 4,000,000 | |
|     Cost of sales | | 4,000,000 |
| Accounts payable | 175,000 | |
|     Accounts receivable | | 175,000 |

5. *Intercompany unrealized profit eliminations.* Inventory on the books of the parent is recorded at $300,000, when it has a cost to the consolidated entity of $200,000. The $100,000 overstatement must be eliminated, and the corresponding overstatement of the subsidiary's net income must be corrected.

| Cost of sales | 100,000 | |
|---|---|---|
|    Inventory | | 100,000 |

The debit to cost of sales reduces income. This entry creates a temporary difference between accounting and taxable income, and should result in an adjustment to tax expense and the balance sheet tax future (deferred) income tax account; this tax entry has been omitted in the interests of simplicity.

6. *Non-controlling interest share of income.* The non-controlling (or minority) interest has been allocated its share of equity and subsidiary dividends, but they also have an interest in the earnings of the subsidiary for the current period ($254,000; see Exhibit 11A-1, column 2), after additional amortization ($100,000), and only if confirmed by transactions with outside parties ($100,000 intercompany profit to be eliminated). The non-controlling interest's share in confirmed subsidiary profits is allocated to them by creating an equity allocation to the non-controlling interest:

| Allocation to non-controlling interest | 10,800 | |
|---|---|---|
|    Non-controlling interest (B/S) | | |
|      (($254,000 − $100,000 − $100,000) × 20%) | | 10,800 |

All these entries are posted to the worksheet. The final step in the consolidation worksheet is to cross-add each account line, giving effect to the adjustments and eliminations above, as is illustrated in the final column of Exhibit 11A-1. The final column provides the amounts that are used to prepare the consolidated financial statements.

Be sure to remember that all of the consolidation entries are worksheet entries only. The entries listed above are not recorded on any company's books.

## Prior Standard

The above example is based on the IASB project, which will be reflected in Canadian standards toward the end of the decade. The consolidations standard that has been in effect up to that time would be different in certain ways. In particular, the non-controlling interest is treated as an "outside" interest, not an equity item, and fair value differentials and goodwill are recognized only for the portion of the subsidiary purchased by the parent. This would have the following impacts on the example given:

- Eighty percent of the fair value of capital assets would be recognized and recorded, instead of 100%. Capital assets would increase by $800,000 ($1,000,000 × 80%), not $1,000,000 in the investment elimination entry, a difference of $200,000.
- Amortization would decrease by $20,000 ($200,000 ÷ 10), reflecting amortization of the lower balance.
- Goodwill, which now represents goodwill for the whole entity, would decrease to reflect only P's 80% interest. This would be $874,400 ($1,093,000 × 80%) in the investment elimination entry.
- The initial non-controlling interest would be lower, at $756,400. (This is the non-controlling interest in the book value of the subsidiary ($3,782,000 × 20%), excluding implied goodwill and the additional fair value of assets.
- The non-controlling interest would be classified between long-term liabilities and equity, not placed in shareholders' equity.
- The annual allocation to the non-controlling interest would be $30,800, its share of net income decreased for profit eliminations but no amortization of capital assets (($254,000 − $100,000) × 20%). This would be an income statement item, rather than an equity adjustment.

## Foreign Subsidiaries

The procedure illustrated above is the same for all subsidiaries. However, an additional complication arises when the subsidiary is in a foreign country. The subsidiary's financial statements will be in a foreign currency, and must be restated to Canadian dollars before consolidation can occur. Because exchange rates change, the net asset value of the subsidiary will be different at each year-end, even if there has been no change in the assets and liabilities. Thus, a gain or loss will arise simply from the mechanics of the foreign currency translation and consolidation process.

Standard setters allow two approaches to foreign exchange translation, depending on the economic circumstances of the subsidiary. Classifying the foreign subsidiary correctly, which is a management policy choice based on the facts of the business model used by the subsidiary, is critical. The two different methods will produce potentially quite different values for net assets and net income, and usually foreign exchange gains and losses that are opposite, at least in sign. In addition, for one method, the cumulative exchange gain or loss is classified in other comprehensive income on the balance sheet, and for the other method, the exchange gain or loss is included in net income. These are not trivial differences.

---

### EXHIBIT 11A-1

## CONSOLIDATION WORKSHEET

| | P. Co. | S. Co. | Consolidation Elimination Entries | | | P. Co. + S. Co. Consolidated Results |
|---|---|---|---|---|---|---|
| Cash | $    460,000 | $    64,000 | | | | $    524,000 |
| Accounts receivable | 2,390,000 | 790,000 | (4) | 175,000 | cr. | 3,005,000 |
| Inventory | 4,910,000 | 1,700,000 | (5) | 100,000 | cr. | 6,510,000 |
| Capital assets, net | 8,224,000 | 4,622,000 | (1) | 1,000,000 | dr. | |
| | | | (2) | 100,000 | cr. | 13,746,000 |
| Investment in S. Co. | 4,700,000 | — | (1) | 4,700,000 | cr. | 0 |
| Intangible assets | 400,000 | — | (1) | 1,093,000 | dr. | 1,493,000 |
| Totals | $21,084,000 | $7,176,000 | | | | $25,278,000 |
| | | | | | | |
| Current liabilities | $ 5,320,000 | $1,100,000 | (4) | 175,000 | dr. | $ 6,245,000 |
| Long-term debt | 8,100,000 | 1,500,000 | | | | 9,600,000 |
| Future income taxes | 1,050,000 | 640,000 | | | | 1,690,000 |
| Non-controlling interest | — | — | (1) | 1,175,000 | cr. | |
| | | | (3) | 20,000 | dr. | |
| | | | (6) | 10,800 | cr. | 1,165,800 |
| Common shares | 2,600,000 | 140,000 | (1) | 140,000 | dr. | 2,600,000 |
| Retained earnings | 4,014,000 | 3,796,000 | from below | | | 3,977,200 |
| Totals | $21,084,000 | $7,176,000 | | | | $25,278,000 |
| | | | | | | |
| Sales | $16,800,000 | $9,300,000 | (4) | 4,000,000 | dr. | $22,100,000 |
| Cost of sales | 9,900,000 | 4,216,000 | (4) | 4,000,000 | cr. | |
| | | | (5) | 100,000 | dr. | 10,216,000 |
| Operating expenses | 5,650,000 | 4,590,000 | (2) | 100,000 | dr. | 10,340,000 |
| Other income | 80,000 | — | (3) | 80,000 | dr. | 0 |
| Income tax expense | 560,000 | 240,000 | | | | 800,000 |
| Net income | $    770,000 | $    254,000 | | | | $    744,000 |
| Opening retained earnings | 3,454,000 | 3,642,000 | (1) | 3,642,000 | dr. | 3,454,000 |
| Dividends | 210,000 | 100,000 | (3) | 100,000 | cr. | 210,000 |
| Non-controlling interest | — | — | (6) | 10,800 | dr. | 10,800 |
| Closing retained earnings | $ 4,014,000 | $3,796,000 | | | | $ 3,977,200 |

## SUMMARY OF KEY POINTS

1. When the subsidiary's financial statements are consolidated with those of the parent, the investment account is eliminated, and instead all the assets and liabilities of the subsidiary are included on the parent's balance sheet. Any offsetting balances between the parent and the subsidiary are eliminated against the other.

2. Goodwill is measured as the amount by which the implied fair value of the subsidiary, grossed up from the purchase price, exceeds the fair value of the subsidiary's identifiable assets at the date of acquisition.

3. Amortization of the subsidiary's assets is based on fair value. Goodwill is not amortized, but must be written down if its value is impaired.

4. The revenues and expenses of the subsidiary are included with those of the parent on the parent's consolidated income statement. Intercompany transactions are eliminated, to avoid double-counting, and any unrealized profits are eliminated.

5. If the parent does not own 100% of the subsidiary, the proportion of the subsidiary's fair value, including goodwill, that is not owned by the parent is reported by the parent on its balance sheet as a non-controlling interest, a credit in shareholders' equity.

6. The non-controlling interest's proportionate share of the subsidiary's net income is allocated to the non-controlling interest in equity, offset by the fact that all the subsidiary's revenues and expenses have been combined with the parent's.

7. The account balances of foreign subsidiaries must be translated into Canadian dollars before they can be consolidated. Exchange rate movement causes translation gains and losses. Choice of exchange rates and disposition of the exchange gain or loss are treated differently depending on how the subsidiary is classified.

## QUESTIONS

**Q11-1** Why do companies invest in the securities of other enterprises?

**Q11-2** Distinguish between debt and equity securities.

**Q11-3** How can a debt investment be classified? An equity investment? How should each category be accounted for?

**Q11-4** What criteria must be met for an investment to be classified as a held-to-maturity investment? Held-for-trading investment? Available-for-sale investment?

**Q11-5** Why are held-to-maturity investments carried at amortized cost but available-for-sale and held-for-trading investments carried at fair value?

**Q11-6** What is the difficulty encountered in relying on management intent as a classification criteria?

**Q11-7** What factors indicate that significant influence may be present between an investor and an investee? How would such an investment be reported?

**Q11-8** What factors indicate that control exists between an investor and an investee? How would such an investment be reported?

**Q11-9** It is often said that an investor with 20% of the voting shares of another company has significant influence, and an investor with 50% has control. Is this always true?

**Q11-10** What is the distinguishing feature of a joint venture? How are joint ventures accounted for?

**Q11-11** How is fair value estimated?

**Q11-12** On 1 August 20X4, Baker Company purchased $50,000 face amount of Sugar Company 6% coupon value bonds for $43,200. The market interest rate was 8% on this date. The bond pays interest semi-annually on 31 July and 31 January. At the fiscal year-end for Baker, the bonds have a market value of $45,000. Show the journal entries (a) to record the investment and (b) to record investment income and any other needed adjustments at 31 December. The investment is classified as a held-to-maturity investment and the effective-interest amortization method is used.

**Q11-13** When is it permissible to use straight-line amortization of a discount or premium on a held-to-maturity investment? Explain.

**Q11-14** Under what circumstances is it appropriate under GAAP to account for a significant-influence investment using the cost method? Explain.

**Q11-15** An investor purchased 100 shares of Zenics at $20 per share on 15 March 20X4. At the end of the 20X4 accounting period, 31 December 20X4, the stock was quoted at $19 per share. On 5 June 20X5, the investor sold the stock for $22 per share. Assuming this is an available-for-sale investment, give the journal entry to be made at each of the following dates:

- 15 March 20X4;
- 31 December 20X4; and
- 5 June 20X5.

**Q11-16** What conditions may indicate that the value of an investment has been impaired? How is an impairment accounted for if this is a held-to-maturity investment? Available-for-sale investment? Held-for-trading investment?

**Q11-17** On 31 December 20X1, ABC Company owned 10,000 shares of A Company, with a cost of $23 per share and a market value of $24 per share. The shares were purchased in 20X1. At the end of 20X2, the market value was $28 per share. The investment was sold in 20X3 at $30 per share. This is an available-for-sale investment. What would be included in other comprehensive income and net income in each of 20X1, 20X2, and 20X3?

**Q11-18** On 31 December 20X1, XYZ Company owned 10,000 shares of B Company, with a cost of $21 per share and a market value of $26 per share. The shares were purchased in 20X1. At the end of 20X2, the market value was $29 per share. The investment was sold in 20X3 at $33 per share. The investment is classified as a held-for-trading investment. What would be included in other comprehensive income and net income in each of 20X1, 20X2, and 20X3?

**Q11-19** The 31 December 20X3 balance sheet shows available-for-sale investments at $456,800, and cumulative other comprehensive income at $169,000. Interpret these two values. At what amount were the investments originally purchased?

**Q11-20** An available-for-sale investment is carried at $550,000, and there is a cumulative gain of $35,000 recorded in other comprehensive income. The investment is sold for $520,000. What gain or loss is included in net income because of the sale? What amount is included in this year's change in other comprehensive income because of the sale? Explain.

**Q11-21** On 1 July 20X2, a company bought an investment in IBM bonds for US$50,000 when the exchange rate was US$1 = Cdn$1.12. The investment is classified as available for sale. The company paid cash on the acquisition date. At 31 December, the exchange rate was US$1 = Cdn$1.08. The market value was still US$50,000. Prepare journal entries to record the purchase of bonds and any adjusting entries at year-end.

**Q11-22** Assume that Company R acquired, as a long-term investment, 30% of the outstanding voting common shares of Company S at a cash cost of $100,000. At the date of acquisition, the balance sheet of Company S showed net assets and total shareholders' equity of $250,000. The market value of the depreciable assets of Company S was $20,000 greater than their net book value at date of R's acquisition. Compute goodwill purchased, if any.

**Q11-23** Assume the same facts as in Q11-22, with the addition that net assets that were undervalued at acquisition have a remaining estimated life of 10 years (assume no residual value and straight-line depreciation). There is no goodwill impairment. How much investment revenue would Company R report using the equity method if Company S reported $80,000 of net income?

**Q11-24** Investor Limited owns 35% of Machines Limited, and has significant influence. The investment was made five years ago, when Machine's fair values equalled book values; $40,000 of goodwill was inherent in the purchase price. Goodwill is not impaired. In the current fiscal year, Machines reported $225,000 in income. This includes a $50,000 profit on inventory sold to Investor Limited, which Investor has not yet resold. How much investment revenue will Investor report using the equity method? How would your answer change if Investor had reported the sale of inventory to Machines?

**Q11-25** What accounts appear in the consolidated financial statements that are not present in either the parent's or the subsidiary's financial statements? Explain each item. What accounts always disappear from the unconsolidated financial statements?

**Q11-26** Equity income, and consolidated income, is usually lower than one would predict by simply adding the investor's income and the pro-rata share of the investee's income. Why does this happen?

**Q11-27** Under what circumstances is an investment reclassified from the held-to-maturity classification to the available-for-sale classification? What are the ramifications of the transfer? How is the transfer accounted for?

**Q11-28** Under what circumstances is an investment reclassified from an available-for-sale investment to a held-to-maturity investment? How is the cumulative other comprehensive income amount accounted for?

**Q11-29** Under what circumstances is an investment reclassified from significant influence to an available-for-sale investment? How is the transfer accounted for?

---

## CASE 11-1

### NORTHERN ENERGY LIMITED

Northern Energy Limited (NEL) is a large Canadian private company organized in three operating segments: propane operations, trucking, and mineral explorations. As a private company with no public accountability, NEL has adopted differential accounting for its investments. NEL is now considering issuing debt in a public offering, which would eliminate its ability to use differential accounting. You, a public accountant consulted on reporting issues, have been asked to prepare a report for circulation to the Board of Directors and shareholders, to help them understand the implications of this potential shift. They specifically wish to understand what financial statement elements might change with revised investment reporting.

Investments reported on the 20X6 balance sheet:

| Investment | Accounting Method | Net Book Value (in thousands) |
|---|---|---|
| Nico Investments Ltd., common shares | Cost | $416.3 |
| Canner Ltd., 5% non-voting preference shares | Cost | 174.0 |
| Later Corp., common shares | Cost | 675.3 |
| Placement Resources Corp., common shares | Cost | 455.2 |
| Trufeld Trucking Ltd., 8% bonds | Cost | 266.8 |
| Lu Trucking, common shares | Cost | 45.8 |

Additional information is contained in Exhibit 1.

**Required**

Prepare the report.

## EXHIBIT 1

### Later Corp. common shares

Later Corp. (LC) is a nationwide courier company, whose shares were acquired by NEL in 20X2. NEL purchased 57.4% of the outstanding shares from the founder of LC on his retirement; the remaining shares are owned by management and two family members of the founder. Later had real estate assets that were significantly undervalued in their financial statements, prompting NEL to pay a significant premium over book value for the company.

The LC Board of Directors consists of 14 members. NEL has the right to appoint eight directors, but to date has nominated only four individuals. The other four slots are filled by continuing members whom NEL found acceptable.

### Nico Investments Ltd.

NEL owns 80% of the common shares of this company that manufactures and distributes aluminum wheels. The remaining shares are owned by Frank Nico, the founder. Nico has had persistent challenges with its product and markets, and has achieved breakeven results at best since NEL acquired the shares in 20X0, although prospects are positive. Nico reports a deficit on its financial statements, but is solvent. Nico has never declared dividends. NEL has guaranteed loans of Nico. Nico has a nine-member Board of Directors, of which NEL appoints seven members, including the chair, who is Frank Nico. According to the terms of signed share agreements, Mr. Nico can veto certain decisions of the Board dealing with operating and financing issues.

### Trufeld Trucking Ltd., 8% bonds

These 8% bonds pay interest semi-annually and mature in 20X14. The par value is $275,000. NEL provided this debt financing to Trufeld, a long-time "friendly" competitor in NEL's trucking business. The two companies often enter joint bids for long-term hauling contracts, and take on freight for the other if overbooked. The bonds are secured against assets in Trufeld's trucking fleet. NEL has one member on the Trufeld Board of Directors as a result of the bond investment.

### Canner Ltd., 5% non-voting preference shares

NEL purchased these preferred shares in 20X4, when Canner came to NEL looking for equity financing. NEL purchases product from Canner for its propane operations. Canner is a closely held private company. Money was needed for an expansion but Canner was unwilling to agree to the terms presented by lenders. Canner is located in a small town, and many of its workers are shareholders and are related through family ties. Canner has a six-member Board of Directors, and NEL places one member on the Board. To date, this has been a positive experience for all concerned, as the Canner Board has been very receptive to the suggestions of the NEL representative; many improvements and modernization of governance and operations are being considered. Canner pays regular dividends.

### Placement Resources Corp., common shares

Placement Resources is a mineral exploration company with active exploration going on in Northern Manitoba. NEL owns 10.2% of the common shares. NEL became involved with this company in 20X5, at the suggestion of a major shareholder of NEL. This shareholder owns 14% of NEL and 44% of Placement. After appropriate investigation, NEL purchased a common share interest and has been very pleased with the results. NEL estimates that the shares owned have a current market value of at least $900, although this is an estimate because Placement is traded only over the counter. Placement has had an erratic operating history, with high net income in some years when exploration is successful and losses in other years. In good years, dividend payouts are material. NEL has two members on the 11-member Board of Directors; the NEL shareholder has four members on the Board and is highly influential.

### Lu Trucking, common shares

The common shares of Lu Trucking represent 24.3% of the voting shares and were purchased in 20X4, when NEL was considering acquiring this rival trucking company. Lu Trucking is a private company. The remaining shareholders of Lu were not enthused about a transfer of ownership. NEL originally had one member on the nine-member Board of Directors, but has ceased to appoint a representative because relations were poor. NEL has attempted to sell these shares several times to other shareholders of Lu, with little success, as they are unable to agree on a price. Lu pays regular, although modest, dividends.

## CASE 11-2

## MACKAY INDUSTRIES LIMITED

MacKay Industries Limited (MIL) is a Canadian company that manufactures leather furniture. Sales in 20X3 were $265 million, with strong exports to the United States. MIL is the leading Canadian manufacturer of leather furniture, and is ranked fourth in this category in the U.S. market. While MIL has, in the past, had manufacturing facilities in the United States, difficulties in quality control and logistics have recently convinced the owner to centralize all operations in Niagara Falls, Canada. The plant employs 250 workers.

MIL is a private company. The majority of shares are held by the president and CEO, Jeff MacKay, who inherited the business from his father. The firm was founded by Jeff MacKay's grandfather. The remainder of the shares are held by members of the MacKay family. MIL has substantial long-term bank financing in place, secured by company assets and the personal guarantees of Jeff MacKay and key family members. MacKay himself is a graduate of Harvard Business School and is well regarded in the industry. He focuses on marketing and strategy, and usually leaves operations to his production managers, all of whom receive a bonus based on overall company profits.

You, a professional accountant in public practice, review the annual financial statements of the company, prepare the tax returns, and provide advice on a wide range of issues, including financing, tax, personnel, and accounting policy.

You have been asked to look at the investment portfolio of MIL, and comment on appropriate accounting. Mr. MacKay is aware that rules have recently changed in the investments area, and he'd like a summary of how his investments should be accounted for.

Investments can be summarized as follows:

1. *Short-term investments*

   MIL has excess cash tied up in short-term investments at various times of the year. This money is often invested in treasury bills, but may also be invested in common shares of public companies, if MacKay feels there is an opportunity to earn capital appreciation.

2. *Hyperion*

   MIL bought 4,000 shares of Hyperion, an aircraft engine manufacturer, two years ago, for $43 per share. The investment is recorded at cost. Hyperion has 490,000 common shares outstanding, of which 20,000 to 40,000 change hands annually. Mr. MacKay is a personal friend of the president and CEO of this small public company. No dividends have been declared on the shares. The stock price quoted at the end of last year was $42. This year, market values have been in the $33–$35 range. Mr. MacKay has stated that he would not consider selling the investment unless market values return to $43. Mr. MacKay is confident that this will be the case sometime in the next five years.

3. *March Limited* Mr. MacKay (personally) is the sole shareholder of March Limited, which he incorporated two years ago. The Boards of Directors for March Limited and MIL are almost identical. March is engaged in researching new imitation leather fabrics, and ways of chemically treating real leather to improve its quality. Throughout the last two years, March has spent $216,000 on these activities. All this amount is financed by MIL; Mr. MacKay himself has put no money into March Limited other than a token investment to create share capital. MIL reports the $216,000 as a long-term receivable. It has no stated interest rate or term, and will be repaid only when marketable fabrics are developed by March Limited.

4. *Kusak Limited* MIL owns a $500,000, 10-year bond issued by Kusak Limited. Kusak is a public company and this bond is publicly traded. MIL bought the bond for $412,700, plus accrued interest. MIL will hold the bond until maturity, although if funds are needed for operating or capital purposes during that time, the bond would certainly be sold.

5. *DML Corporation* MIL owns 19,975 (2%) of the voting common shares of DML Corporation, a French furniture manufacturer that MacKay may use to enter the European market sometime in the future. Five years ago, MIL bought notes payable and preferred shares in the company. This year, the notes and preferred shares were exchanged for the common shares pursuant to an agreement signed when the notes and preferred shares were acquired. On the exchange date, the notes and preferred shares had a book value of $175,000, and this value was used to record the common shares. Their market value was indeterminable on that date because the securities were not recently traded. Common shares, thinly traded over the counter, have sold for $7–$9 in the last 12 months.

   MIL has one member on the 18-seat Board of Directors of DML Corporation. Mr. MacKay himself attends these meetings, and reports that he is well regarded in debate. Mr. MacKay usually takes a bilingual advisor with him, as proceedings take place in French, a language in which Mr. MacKay is not fluent. In the past year, DML reported a marginal net income; the company has never declared dividends.

**Required:**

Prepare a report summarizing investment accounting policies as they apply to MIL's investments.

---

**CASE 11-3**

## JACKSON CAPITAL INCORPORATED

Jackson Capital Incorporated (JCI) is a new private investment company that provides capital to business ventures. JCI's business mission is to support companies to allow them to compete successfully in domestic and international markets. JCI aims to increase the value of its investments, thereby creating wealth for its shareholders.

Funds to finance the investments were obtained through a private offering of share capital, conventional long-term loans payable, and a bond issue that is indexed to the TSX Composite. Annual operating expenses are expected to be $1 million before bonuses, interest, and taxes.

Over the past year, JCI has accumulated a diversified investment portfolio. Depending on the needs of the borrower, JCI provides capital in many different forms, including demand loans, short-term equity investments, fixed-term loans, and loans convertible into share capital. JCI also purchases preferred and common shares in new business ventures where JCI management anticipates a significant return. Any excess funds not committed to a particular investment are held temporarily in money market funds.

JCI has hired eight investment managers to review financing applications. These managers visit the applicants' premises to meet with management and review the operations and business plans. They then prepare a report stating their reasons for supporting or rejecting the application. JCI's senior executives review these reports at their monthly meetings and decide whether to invest and what types of investments to make.

Once the investments are made, the investment managers are expected to monitor the investments and review detailed monthly financial reports submitted by the investees. The investment managers' performance bonuses are based on the returns generated by the investments they have recommended.

It is 1 August 20X2. JCI's first fiscal year ended on 30 June 20X2. JCI's draft balance sheet and other financial information are provided in Exhibit I. An annual audit of the financial statements is required under the terms of the bond issue. Potter & Cook, Chartered Accountants, has been appointed auditor of JCI. The partner on the engagement is Richard Potter. You are the in-charge accountant on this engagement. Mr. Potter has asked you to prepare a memo discussing the significant accounting issues raised.

**Required:**
Prepare the memo requested by Mr. Potter.

## EXHIBIT 1

### JACKSON CAPITAL, INCORPORATED
### DRAFT BALANCE SHEET

**As of 30 June 20X2**

(in thousands of dollars)
*Assets*

| | |
|---|---|
| Cash and marketable securities | $ 1,670 |
| Investments (at cost) | 21,300 |
| Interest receivable | 60 |
| Furniture and fixtures (net of accumulated amortization of $2) | 50 |
| | $23,080 |
| | |
| *Liabilities* | |
| Accounts payable and accrued liabilities | $ 20 |
| Accrued interest payable | 180 |
| Loans payable | 12,000 |
| | $12,200 |
| | |
| *Shareholders' equity* | |
| Share capital | 12,000 |
| Deficit | (1,120) |
| | 10,880 |
| | $23,080 |

EXHIBIT 1    *(con't)*

## JACKSON CAPITAL INCORPORATED
## SUMMARY OF INVESTMENT PORTFOLIO

**As at 30 June 20X2**

| *Investment* | *Cost of Investment* |
|---|---|
| 15% common share interest in Fairex Resource Inc., a company listed on the TSX Venture Exchange. Management intends to monitor the performance of this mining company over the next six months to make a hold/sell decision based on reported reserves and production costs. | $5.8 million |
| 25% interest in common shares of Hellon Ltd., a private Canadian real estate company, plus 7.5% convertible debentures with a face value of $2 million, acquired at 98% of maturity value. The debentures are convertible into common shares at the option of the holder. | $6.2 million |
| 5-year loan denominated in Brazilian currency (reals) to Ipanema Ltd., a Brazilian company formed to build a power generating station. Interest at 7% per annum is due semi-annually. 75% of the loan balance is secured by the power generating station under construction. The balance is unsecured. The Brazilian currency is unstable, as is the Brazilian political situation. | $8 million |
| 50,000 stock warrants in Tornado Hydrocarbons Ltd., expiring 22 March 20X4. | |
| The underlying common shares trade publicly. | $1.3 million |

## JACKSON CAPITAL INCORPORATED
## CAPITAL STRUCTURE

**As at 30 June 20X2**

*Loans payable*
The Company has $2 million in demand loans payable with floating interest rates, and $4 million in loans due 1 September 20X6, with fixed interest rates.

In addition, the Company has long-term 5% stock indexed bonds payable. Interest at the stated rate is to be paid semi-annually, commencing 1 September 20X2. The principal repayment on 1 March 20X7 is indexed to changes in the TSX Composite as follows: the $6 million original balance of the bonds at the issue date of 1 March 20X2 is to be multiplied by the stock index at 1 March 20X7, and then divided by the stock index as at 1 March 20X2. The stock-indexed bonds are secured by the Company's investments.

*Share capital*
Issued share capital consists of
* 1 million 8% Class A (non-voting) shares redeemable at the holder's option on or after 10 August 20X6 — $7 million
* 10,000 common shares — $5 million

(CICA, adapted)

# ASSIGNMENTS

 **A11-1 Investment Classification:** Consider the following investment categories:

A. Held-to-maturity investment
B. Available-for-sale investment
C. Held-for-trading investment
D. Significant-influence investment
E. Control investment
F. Joint venture

An investor company that is a public company has the following items:

1. Sixty-day treasury bill (T-bill) to be cashed if money is needed.

2. Investment in Nortel common shares bought with idle cash in expectation that the price per share will rise.

3. Investment in Forman Company, a supplier. Forman is a supplier in some financial difficulties. The shares owned amount to 20% of the shares outstanding and allow the investor two seats on the 12-member Board of Directors. Forman will not be paying dividends in the near future. The company is currently recording losses.

4. Investment in Gotcha.com, a dot-com marketing company. The $600,000 investment gives the investor a 7.5% share of the company, and one seat on an 18-member Board. The shares are not publicly traded, but Gotcha has plans to go public. There are no buyers for these shares that could be quickly found, although Gotcha often buys back its own shares if pressured by unhappy shareholders. The investment is highly speculative. Gotcha has never paid dividends.

5. Investment of $6,000,000 in Power Corporation government-guaranteed bonds, 8%, bought at $6,135,000. The securities will be held until maturity.

6. Investment of $6,000,000 in Power Corporation government-guaranteed bonds, 8%, bought at $6,135,000. The securities will be held until the investor needs short-term cash, or until interest rates swing and increase the price of the bonds, whichever comes first.

7. Stratos preferred shares, paying a dividend of $6 per share. The shares are not intended to be sold in the near future

8. Cygnet common shares, representing 80% of outstanding voting shares. The remaining 20% are held by one other shareholder. The 80% investor receives 80% of the dividends declared, and can appoint eight of the 13-member Board of Directors, including the chair. All operating, investing, and financing decisions must be unanimously agreed to by the two shareholders.

9. Investment in bonds, held as part of a portfolio that is actively traded to match the duration of a loan portfolio held by the investor.

**Required:**
Classify the items above into one of the investment categories, as appropriate. State any assumptions made.

---

 **A11-2 Investment Classification:** For each situation below, indicate how the investment would be classified, and how it would be accounted for. Assume the investor is a public company.

1. Strip bonds (that is, those sold without interest, or "stripped" of interest) are acquired as a temporary investment. Management expects interest rates to fall and the price of the strip bonds to increase significantly over the coming year.

2. Investment in $500,000 of 10-year bonds, intended to be held to maturity. Another investment in bonds, intended to be held to maturity, was sold last year because interest rate fluctuations made the market price attractive.

3. Common shares are bought in a small, family-owned business. The investor is the only non-family shareholder. The shares constitute 20% of the voting shares and the investor has one member on an eight-member Board of Directors, all of the rest of whom are members of the family investor group. Market values for the shares are not available as they are never sold.

4. A mining property is exchanged for 60% of the voting shares in a company formed to develop the mining property. The remaining 40% of the shares are held by a large mining company that will contribute equipment and expertise to physically mine the site. All decisions regarding operations and financing must be agreed to by both shareholders.

5. Common shares are bought in a large public company, whose shares are broadly held and widely traded. The investor owns 5% of the voting shares, sits on the Board, and is the largest single shareholder. The shares will be held for a long time period, awaiting favourable market price appreciation.

6. Common shares are bought in a large public company whose shares are broadly held and widely traded. The investor owns 45% of the voting shares, puts eight people on a 20-member Board of Directors, and generally has its way in operating, investing, and financing policy of the investee.

7. Common shares are bought in a small, family-owned business. The investor is the only non-family shareholder, but sits on the family-controlled Board. The investor also allows the company to use patented production processes for a fee, a right not previously granted to any other company, and provides $5,000,000 in long-term loans to the investee.

8. To invest idle cash, common shares are bought in a large, public company, a tiny fraction of the outstanding common shares. The share price appreciated after sale, but the investor is convinced that significant additional price appreciation is probable. Therefore, the shares were not sold when cash was needed; the company borrowed from the bank instead, using the shares as collateral.

 **A11-3 Investment Classification:** Kamloop Investments (a public company) holds a number of investments in the securities of other companies as of 31 December 20X8:

1. Kamloop owns 0.2% of the common shares of Nickel Limited, a public company. Kamloop has no intent to sell the shares, which are held for long-term capital appreciation and dividend flow.

2. Kamloop owns 30% of the common shares of Computer Services Limited. The remaining shares are equally divided among three other investors. Each investor has two representatives on the eight-member Board of Directors. All strategic decisions must be unanimously agreed to by the Board members.

3. Kamloop owns 60% of the common shares of Unform Corporation. The remaining shares are held by the founder, Bill Unform. The seven-member Board of Directors consists of four members appointed by Kamloop, two appointed by Mr. Unform, and Mr. Unform himself, who is the Chair of the Board. Mr. Unform is active in company management and has personally spearheaded most recent strategic directives.

4. Kamloop holds $8,000,000 in bonds of Smith Limited. These bonds will mature in 20X10. Kamloop will sell the bonds when another attractive investment opportunity arises.

5. Kamloop holds 15% of the voting shares of Brevit Manufacturing Limited. Kamloop has two members on the 10-member Board of Directors, and has extensive intercompany transactions with Brevit.

6. Kamloop holds a $1,000,000, 10% bond that matures in 15 years time. Kamloop will keep this bond until it matures.

7. Kamloop owns 4% of the outstanding common shares of Market Research Inc., a company whose shares are thinly traded on the over-the-counter market. Kamloop would like to sell its shares, but no buyer has been found at the price that Kamloop is determined to realize.

**Required:**

How should Kamloop account for each of the above investments? Be specific, and explain your reasoning.

★ ★ ★    **A11-4 Cost Method—Debt Investment:** On 1 July 20X2, New Company purchased $600,000 of Old Corporation 5.5% bonds to be held to maturity. The bonds pay semi-annual interest each 30 June and 31 December. The market interest rate was 5% on the date of purchase. The bonds mature on 30 June 20X5.

**Required:**

1. Calculate the price paid by New Company.
2. Construct a table that shows interest revenue reported by New, and the carrying value of the investment, for each interest period to maturity. Use the effective-interest method.
3. Give entries for the first three interest periods based on your calculations in requirement 2.
4. Construct a table that shows interest revenue reported by New, and the carrying value of the investment for each interest period to maturity. Use the straight-line method.
5. Give entries for the first three interest periods based on your calculations in requirement 4.

★ ★ ★    **A11-5 Cost Method—Debt Investment:** On 1 May 20X7, Berry Limited purchased $2,000,000 of DartCo Limited 7.1% bonds to be held to maturity. The bonds pay semi-annual interest each 1 May and 1 November. The market interest rate was 8% on the date of purchase. The bonds mature on 1 November 20X11.

**Required:**

1. Calculate the price paid by Berry Limited.
2. Construct a table that shows interest revenue reported by Berry, and the carrying value of the investment, for each interest period to maturity. Use the effective-interest method.
3. Give entries for 20X7 and 20X8 for Berry Limited, including adjusting entries at the year-end, which is 31 December.
4. Assume that Berry sold the bonds on 1 February 20X9, for 99 plus accrued interest. Give the entry to record interest income to 1 February, and the entry for the sale.
5. What implications would the sale have on Berry's ability to classify other bond investments as held-to-maturity investments? Explain.

★ ★ ★    **A11-6 Cost Method—Debt Investment:** On 1 July 20X4, Wyder Door Company acquired the following bonds, which Wyder intended to hold to maturity:

| Bond | Price | Face Amount Purchased |
|---|---|---|
| Flakey Cement 10% bonds, maturity date 31 December 20X9 | 101.65 | $30,000 |
| Green Lawn 8% bonds, maturity date, 31 December 20X6 | 97.0 | 20,000 |

Both bonds pay interest annually on 31 December. Premium and discount will be amortized on a straight-line basis.

**Required:**

1. Prepare the entry to record acquisition of the investments. Accrued interest was paid on the acquisition dates, as appropriate.
2. Prepare the entries to be made at 31 December 20X4.
3. Show the items and amounts that would be reported in the 20X4 income statement and balance sheet related to these investments.
4. Prepare the entries to be made on 31 December 20X5.
5. Show the items and amounts that would be reported in the 20X5 income statement and balance sheet related to these investments.

★ **A11-7 Fair Value Method—Comprehension:** At the end of 20X9, Canfrax Corp. Limited reported available-for-sale investments on the balance sheet as follows:

| | |
|---|---:|
| Temporary investments: | |
| Star Co. common shares | $1,370,100 |
| Comet Co. common shares | 434,700 |
| Shareholders' equity; other comprehensive income: | |
| Star Co. shares, unrealized gain | $ 150,300 |
| Comet Co. shares, unrealized loss | 24,600 |

**Required:**

1. Why are the shares classified as temporary? Under what circumstances would they be classified as long term?

2. What criteria must be met for the shares to be classified as an available-for-sale investment? Could they, in other circumstances, be classified as a held-to-maturity investment? Under what circumstances would these shares be a held-for-trading investment?

3. What price would originally have been paid for the Star Co. shares? Comet Co. shares?

4. If the decline in value of the Comet Co. shares was classified as an impairment, what would change about balance sheet presentation at the end of 20X9?

5. Assume both shares are correctly classified as available-for-sale investments and the Comet Co. loss was not an impairment. If the Star Co. shares are sold for $1,500,000, and the Comet Co. shares are sold for $435,000, what gain or loss is included in net income?

 **A11-8 Fair Value Method:** On 1 November 20X8, TRF Company acquired the following available-for-sale investments:

- Lin Corporation—1,000 common shares at $30 cash per share
- Waldron Corporation—600 preferred shares at $10 cash per share

The annual reporting period ends 31 December. Quoted market prices on 31 December 20X8 were as follows:

- Lin Corporation common, $26
- Waldron Corporation preferred, $12

The following information relates to 20X9:

| | |
|---|---|
| 2 March | Received cash dividends per share as follows: Lin Corporation, $1; and Waldron Corporation, $0.50. |
| 1 October | Sold 200 shares of Waldron Corporation preferred at $12.50 per share. |
| 31 December | Market values were as follows: Lin common, $23, and Y preferred, $13. |

**Required:**

1. Give the entry for TRF Company to record the purchase of the securities.

2. Give the adjusting entry needed at the end of 20X8.

3. Give the items and amounts that would be reported on the 20X8 income statement, a calculation of the change in other comprehensive income, and asset and equity amounts on the balance sheet.

4. Give all entries required in 20X9.

5. Give the items and amounts that would be reported on the 20X9 income statement, a calculation of the change in other comprehensive income, and asset and equity amounts on the balance sheet.

6. Repeat requirement 5, assuming that the investments are held-for-trading investments.

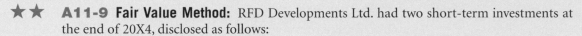

★ ★ **A11-9 Fair Value Method:** RFD Developments Ltd. had two short-term investments at the end of 20X4, disclosed as follows:

| | | |
|---|---|---|
| Moncton Ltd. | 1,000 shares | $ 45,000 |
| Chester Corp. | 6,000 shares | 132,000 |
| | | $177,000 |

At the end of 20X4, there was a cumulative unrealized loss in other comprehensive income of $3,000 related to the Moncton Ltd. shares and an unrealized gain of $24,000 related to the Chester Corp. shares.

During 20X5, RFD sold the Moncton Ltd. shares after receiving a dividend of $2.00 per share. RFD received $36,000 for the shares, less an $800 commission. RFD also received a dividend of $1 per share on the Chester Corp. shares, and then sold 2,000 shares for $24 per share, less a $500 commission. RFD also bought 500 Digby Ltd. shares for $22,000 plus a $500 commission.

At the end of the year, the market value of the Moncton Ltd. shares was $34,000, Chester Corp. shares were $28 per share, and Digby Ltd. shares had a total market value of $19,000. RFD capitalizes all commissions on share transactions as part of the cost of the shares, and reports proceeds on sale of shares net of related commission.

**Required:**

1. List the items that would appear on the 20X5 income statement with respect to the investments.
2. List the items that would appear on the 20X5 balance sheet with respect to the investments.
3. What criteria would have to be met to show these investments as short-term investments? A long-term investment?

★ ★ **A11-10 Fair Value Method:** Testco has the following securities classified as available-for-sale investments on 31 December 20X6:

- 3,000 shares of Y Co. common shares, with a fair value of $70,500 and a cumulative unrealized gain of $12,000 in other comprehensive income;
- 10,000 shares of Q Co. common stock, which have a fair value of $546,000 and a cumulative unrealized loss of $34,000 in other comprehensive income; and
- T Co. 8% bonds, $104,000 market value, purchased at par, with a $4,000 cumulative unrealized gain in other comprehensive income.

In 20X7, the following transactions occurred:

a. A dividend of $2 per share was received on the Y Co. shares.
b. 1,000 Y Co. shares were then sold for $32,000.
c. The annual interest was received on the T Co. bond ($3,500 of the amount received related to 20X6 and had been accrued at the end of 20X6 as interest receivable).
d. Testco purchased 4,000 shares of Z Co. for $53.50 per share.
e. Late in the year, the T Co. bond was sold for $102,000 plus $3,000 of accrued interest.

Market values at the end of the year: Y Co., $15 per share: T Co., $103,000: Q Co., $59 per share; and Z Co., $55 per share.

**Required:**

1. List the amounts that would appear on the income statement, and the change in other comprehensive income, in 20X7 as a result of these transactions and events.
2. List the items that would appear on the balance sheet at the end of 20X7, including both the investments and the cumulative amount of other comprehensive income.
3. Repeat requirements 1 and 2, assuming that the investments are held-for-trading investments.

★★ **A11-11 Fair Value Method:** On 31 December 20X2, Martello Company's portfolio of available-for-sale investments in equity securities was as follows (all purchased on 1 September 20X2):

| Security | Shares | Unit Cost | Unit Market |
|---|---|---|---|
| Parker Corp., common shares | 50 | $120 | $70 |
| Monty Corp., $2.40 preferred shares | 200 | 30 | 32 |
| Bekon Corp., common shares | 400 | 70 | 73 |

Transactions relating to this portfolio during 20X3 were as follows:

- 25 January—Received a dividend cheque on the Monty shares.
- 15 April—Sold 30 Parker Corporation shares at $62 per share.
- 25 July—Received a $600 dividend cheque on the Parker shares.
- 31 July—Received a $5 per share dividend on Bekon Corporation shares.
- 1 October—Sold the remaining shares of Parker Corporation at $60 per share.
- 1 December—Purchased 100 Bisset Ltd. common shares at $23 per share plus a $300 brokerage fee. The fee is part of the cost of shares.
- 5 December—Purchased 400 Sanford Corporation common shares at $15 per share.

On 31 December 20X3, the following unit market prices were available: Parker stock, $55; Bekon Corp, $61.25; Monty stock, $38; Bisset stock, $3; and Sanford stock, $16. Martello has determined that the decline in value of the Bisset shares is a permanent impairment.

**Required:**

1. Give the entries that Martello Company should make on (1) 1 September 20X2, and (2) 31 December 20X2.
2. Give the investment items and amounts that should be reported on the 20X2 income statement, the change in other comprehensive income, and balance sheet accounts.
3. Give the journal entries for 20X3 related to the investments.
4. Give the investment items and amounts that should be reported on the 20X3 income statement, the change in other comprehensive income, and balance sheet accounts.

★★ **A11-12 Fair Value Method:** During 20X2, Morran Company purchased shares in two corporations and debt securities of a third. They are classified as available-for-sale investments. Morran is a public company. Transactions in 20X2 include:

a. Purchased 3,000 of the 100,000 common shares outstanding of Front Corporation at $31 per share plus a 4% brokerage fee. The fee is part of the share cost.
b. Purchased 10,000 of 40,000 outstanding preferred shares (non-voting) of Ledrow Corporation at $78 per share plus a 3% brokerage fee. The fee is part of the share cost.
c. Purchased an additional 2,000 common shares of Front Corporation at $35 per share plus a 4% brokerage fee. The fee is part of the share cost.
d. Purchased $400,000 par value of Container Corporation, 9% bonds at 100 plus accrued interest. The purchase is made on 1 November; interest is paid semi-annually on 31 January and 31 July. The bond matures on 31 July 20X7.
e. Received $4 per share cash dividend on the Ledrow Corporation shares.
f. Interest is accrued at the end of 20X2.
g. Fair values at 31 December 20X2: Front shares, $34 per share; Ledrow, $82 per share; Container Corporation bonds, 98.

**Required:**

1. Give the entries in the accounts of Morran Company for each transaction.
2. Show how the income statement and balance sheet (including the other comprehensive income account) for Morran Company would report relevant data concerning these investments for 20X2.

3. Repeat requirements 1 and 2, assuming that the investments are held-for-trading investments. Note that all fees are expensed immediately if investments are classified as held-for-trading investments.

---

★★ **A11-13 Impairment:** Snelgrove Corporation purchased a $567,800 investment in the common shares of Wood Corporation on 15 July 20X5. Snelgrove was speculating that the value of the Wood common shares might increase dramatically when a major contract bid was accepted. Unfortunately, the bid was rejected, and Wood shares declined in value to $350,400 by the end of 20X5. Snelgrove continued to hold the investment throughout 20X6 and 20X7, waiting for positive developments that would increase share value. The aggregate market value at the end of 20X6 was $360,500 and, for 20X7, $367,100. The shares were finally sold in 20X8 for $380,900.

**Required:**

1. What criteria must be met for a decline in value of an available-for-sale investment to be considered permanent? What accounting treatment is given to an impairment?

2. When the market value of an investment, written down because of an impairment, subsequently increases, is the increase in value recorded? Explain.

3. Assume that the shares are available-for-sale investments, and the decline in value in 20X5 is considered an impairment. List the accounts and amounts that would appear on the income statement, the change in other comprehensive income, and account balances on the balance sheet for 20X5 to 20X8, inclusive.

4. Assume that the shares are held-for-trading investments, and list the accounts and amounts that would appear on the income statement and the balance sheet for 20X5 to 20X8, inclusive. Why is impairment not an issue for held-for-trading investments?

---

★★ **A11-14 Reclassification:** On 31 December 20X9, Kevens Company's investments were as follows:

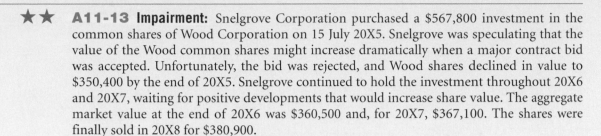

| | Carrying Value | Other Comprehensive Income (Cumulative) |
|---|---|---|
| Available-for-sale investments | | |
| Andreev Ltd., common shares | $240,000 | $89,400 gain |
| Wach Corp., $2 preferred shares | 632,000 | 10,000 gain |
| Moros Corp., 7% bonds, | | |
| $550,000 par value | 542,400 | 28,600 loss |
| Held-to-maturity investment | | |
| Verma Ltd. 9% bonds, | | |
| $700,000 par valuc | 712,000 | |
| Significant-influence investment | | |
| Boyle Commercial Ltd. | 796,000 | |

Kevens makes formal entries for reclassification.

**Required:**

1. On this date, the Verma Ltd. bonds, with a current market value of $750,000, are reclassified as available-for-sale investments. Provide the entry for the reclassification. What are the ramifications of reclassification (and subsequent sale) of a held-to-maturity investment? Explain.

2. Kevens reclassifies the Moros Corp. bonds as a held-to-maturity investment (assume that the transaction in requirement 1 has not taken place and this reclassification is permitted). Give the entry for the reclassification. What accounting treatment is required for the other comprehensive income amount recognized to date?

3. Kevens reclassifies the Boyle Commercial Ltd. shares as an available-for-sale investment. The market value of this investment is estimated to be $950,000. Record the reclassification. What accounting treatment is required for the unrealized holding gain?

★ **A11-15 Reclassification:** On 31 December 20X6, Kirwan Company's investments in equity securities were as follows:

| | Carrying Value | Other Comprehensive Income (Cumulative) |
|---|---|---|
| Available-for-sale investments | | |
| Goldhar Corp., common shares | $ 920,000 | $ 34,700 loss |
| McKinley Corp., common shares | 669,700 | 113,500 gain |
| Held-to-maturity investment | | |
| Walsh Ltd. 7% bonds, $300,000 par value | 297,000 | |
| Significant-influence investment | | |
| Orr Ltd. | 1,456,000 | |

**Required:**

1. Explain what the carrying value for each investment represents.

2. What was the original cost of each of the available-for-sale investments?

3. Kirwan reclassified the held-to-maturity investment to an available-for-sale investment on this date, when its market value was $316,000. Explain how the reclassification will be reflected in the financial statements.

4. Kirwan reclassifies the Orr common shares as an available-for-sale investment when the market value is $1,568,500. What accounting is required for this reclassification?

★ **A11-16 Basket Purchase of Securities:** On 1 December 20X9, ATY Company purchased stock in the three different companies listed below for a lump sum of $646,000, including commissions. They will be held as long-term available-for-sale investments.

- Serial Corporation, common shares, 18,000 shares.
- TY Drilling Corporation, preferred shares, 24,000 shares.
- Carbon Corporation, common shares, 30,000 shares.

At the time of purchase, the shares were quoted on the local over-the-counter stock market at the following prices per share: Serial common, $4; TY preferred, $21; and Carbon common, $3.

**Required:**

1. Give the entry to record the purchase of these investments. Record each investment in a separate account and show the cost per share.

2. How would your response to part 1 change if there was no market value available for the Carbon Corporation common shares?

★ **A11-17 Investments and Foreign Currency:** On 14 June 20X9, Rosen Limited purchased 20,000 shares of Ming Limited for US$4.30 per share, plus US$2,400 in commissions and fees. The shares were held as an available-for-sale investment. On this date, the exchange rate was US$1 = Cdn$1.17. The account was settled with the broker on 1 August 20X9, when US$1 = Cdn$1.16.

On 1 July 20X9, Rosen bought a US$500,000 five-year bond at par value, when the exchange rate was US$1 = Cdn$1.15. It paid cash on the acquisition date. There was no accrued interest. Management plans to hold this bond until maturity.

At 31 December 20X9, Ming shares had a quoted market value of US$6.08 per share, the bonds were still selling at par, and the exchange rate was US$1 = Cdn$1.12.

**Required:**

1. Provide journal entries to record the acquisition of the Ming shares on 14 June, and payment to the broker in August. Brokerage fees are part of the investment cost.

2. Provide the journal entry to record purchase of the bond on 1 July.
3. Explain the 31 December 20X9 adjustment that must be made for the shares (for market value), and for bonds, because of the exchange rate change.

 **A11-18 Equity Method:** On 1 January 20X4, JR Company purchased 400 of the 1,000 outstanding common shares of RV Corporation for $30,000. The equity method will be used to account for the investment. At that date, the balance sheet of RV showed the following book values:

| | |
|---|---|
| Assets not subject to depreciation | $40,000* |
| Assets subject to depreciation (net) | 26,000** |
| Liabilities | 6,000* |
| Common shares | 50,000 |
| Retained earnings | 10,000 |

*Book value is the same as market value.
**Market value $30,000; the assets have a 10-year remaining life (straight-line depreciation).

**Required:**
1. Give the entry by JR Company to record the acquisition.
2. Calculate goodwill purchased at acquisition.
3. Assume that at 31 December 20X4 (end of the accounting period), RV Corporation reported a net income of $10,900, and paid dividends of $5,000. Goodwill has not been impaired. Prepare the entries JR Company would record.
4. Repeat requirement 3, assuming that there was an unconfirmed profit on a sale from JR Company to RV Corporation in the amount of $2,000.

  **A11-19 Long-Term Equity Investment, Cost and Equity Methods Compared, Entries:** On 3 January 20X4, TA Company purchased 2,000 shares of the 10,000 outstanding shares of common stock of UK Corporation for $14,600 cash. TA has significant influence as a result of this acquisition. At that date, the balance sheet of UK Corporation reflected the following:

- Non-depreciable assets, $50,000 (book value is the same as market value);
- Depreciable assets (net), $30,000 (market value, $33,000);
- Total liabilities, $20,000 (book value equals market value); and
- Shareholders' equity, $60,000.

Assume a 10-year remaining life (straight-line method) for the depreciable assets. Goodwill is not been impaired over the time period in question.

**Required:**
1. Give the entries, if any are required, for TA's books for each item (a) through (d) below assuming that the cost method is appropriate.
    a. Entry at date of acquisition.
    b. Goodwill purchased—computation only.
    c. Entry on 31 December 20X4 to record $15,000 net income reported by UK.
    d. Entry on 31 March 20X5 for a cash dividend of $1 per share declared and paid by UK.
2. Repeat requirement 1 above, assuming that the equity method is appropriate.
3. Why might TA use the cost method if it has significant influence?

 **A11-20 Equity Method:** Padre Ltd. bought 40% of the outstanding common shares of Simco Ltd. in early 20X5. Padre paid a total of $21,920,000. Padre has significant influence. On this date, Simco had assets and liabilities as follows:

|  | Book Value | Market Value |
|---|---|---|
| Assets | $28,600,000 | $37,900,000 |
| Liabilities | $10,400,000 | $12,400,000 |

Most of the difference between market and book values for assets was related to an amortizable capital assets with a $12,000,000 book value and a $19,000,000 market value. This asset has a five-year remaining life. The remainder of the difference related to land. The difference between liability book values and market values related to a bond with an eight-year remaining life.

In 20X5, Simco earned $5,800,000 and declared and paid common dividends of $1,400,000. Goodwill was not impaired in 20X5.

**Required:**

1. How much is goodwill? How (and when) will goodwill affect investment income?

2. How much investment revenue will Padre report in 20X5?

3. What is the balance in the investment account on Padre's books at the end of 20X5?

---

★ **A11-21 Equity Method:** On 1 January 20X8, Father Limited purchased 40% of the common shares of Son Incorporated for $120,000. On the date of acquisition, net assets were $170,000, and shareholders' equity for Son comprised the following:

| | |
|---|---|
| Common shares | $100,000 |
| Retained earnings | 70,000 |
| Total | $170,000 |

All of Son's assets and liabilities had a fair value equal to book value, except for land, which had a fair value in excess of book value of $20,000. During 20X8, Son reported net income of $72,500 and paid dividends of $60,000. Son sold goods to Father at a gain of $5,000 late in 20X8. Father has not yet resold the goods.

**Required:**

1. What criterion must be met in order to account for this investment using the equity method?

2. Calculate the amount of goodwill purchased by Father as part of its investment in Son.

3. Prepare the journal entry under the equity method for Father to record investment income, assuming that goodwill has not been impaired.

4. Determine the balance in the Investment in Son account at the end of 20X8, using the equity method.

(CGA-Canada, adapted)

---

★★ **A11-22 Equity Investment, Entries and Reporting:** On 1 January 20X5, Redmond Company purchased 3,000 of the 15,000 outstanding common shares of Decca Computer (DC) Corporation for $80,000 cash. Redmond had significant influence as a result of the investment, and will use the equity method to account for the investment.

On 1 January 20X5, the balance sheet of DC showed the following book values (summarized):

| | |
|---|---|
| Assets not subject to depreciation | $140,000* |
| Assets subject to depreciation (net) | 100,000** |
| Liabilities | 40,000 |
| Common shares | 150,000 |
| Retained earnings | 50,000 |

*Market value, $150,000; difference relates to land held for sale, which is sold in 20X5.
**Market value, $140,000, estimated remaining life, 10 years.

Assume there is no impairment of goodwill. Additional subsequent data on DC:

| | 20X5 | 20X6 |
|---|---|---|
| Net income | $25,000 | $31,000 |
| Cash dividends declared and paid | 10,000 | 12,000 |
| Market value per share | 25 | 26 |

**Required:**

1. Provide the investor's entries or give the required information for:
   a. Entry at date of acquisition.
   b. Amount of goodwill purchased.
   c. Entries at 31 Dec. 20X5 to recognize investment revenue and dividends.
   d. Entries at 31 Dec. 20X6 to recognize investment revenue and dividends.

2. Are any entries needed to recognize a writedown to fair value at the end of 20X5 or 20X6? Explain.

3. Reconstruct the investment account, showing the opening and closing balance and all changes in the account.

4. How much investment revenue would be reported each year if the cost method was used? What would be the balance in the investment account?

★ **A11-23 Consolidation—Explanation:** In 20X1, Pepper Company bought 75% of S Company's common shares, establishing control over the Board of Directors. Pepper Company used the cost method to account for its investment in S Co. during the year, but prepared consolidated financial statements at the end of the fiscal year, which are shown in summary form:

| | P Co. | S Co. | Consolidated |
|---|---|---|---|
| Cash | $ 11,000 | $ 12,000 | $ 23,000 |
| Accounts receivable | 22,000 | 19,000 | 37,000 |
| Inventory | 14,200 | 9,200 | 22,400 |
| Capital assets | 83,000 | 64,300 | 154,000 |
| Investment in S Co. | 74,000 | — | — |
| Intangible assets | — | — | 4,967 |
| | $204,200 | $104,500 | $241,367 |
| Current liabilities | $ 30,000 | $ 9,000 | $ 35,000 |
| Long-term liabilities | 4,000 | 2,500 | 6,500 |
| Non-controlling interest | — | — | 25,942 |
| Common shares | 100,000 | 60,000 | 100,000 |
| Retained earnings | 70,200 | 33,000 | 73,925 |
| | $204,200 | $104,500 | $241,367 |
| Sales and other revenue | $ 96,000 | $ 63,000 | $146,750 |
| Cost of sales | 80,500 | 49,000 | 120,500 |
| Operating expenses | 2,500 | 4,900 | 7,533 |
| Net income | $ 13,000 | $ 9,100 | $ 18,717 |
| Opening retained earnings | 67,200 | 26,900 | 67,200 |
| Dividends | 10,000 | 3,000 | 10,000 |
| Non-controlling interest in net income | | | 1,992 |
| Closing retained earnings | $ 70,200 | $ 33,000 | $ 73,925 |

**Required:**

1. Why does the parent company use the cost method during the year?

2. Identify the accounts on the consolidated balance sheet that do not appear on either of the unconsolidated balance sheets. Explain their meaning.

3. Identify the accounts or amounts that appear on the unconsolidated financial statements that do not carry over to the consolidated statements. Explain why they have been eliminated.

4. What is the most likely reason that the unconsolidated accounts receivables and current liabilities do not add to the balance shown on the consolidated balance sheet?

 **A11-24 Reporting a Subsidiary:** Cohen Corporation, a public company, is contemplating investing in a supplier company, Abbott Metals Limited, in order to ensure a reliable source of supply. The controlling shareholder, who owns 147,000 shares, is willing to sell to Cohen for a price of $50 per share. Summarized financial statements and additional information related to Abbott, follow:

**Abbott Metals**
**Balance Sheet**

| At 30 June 20X5 | Book Value | Fair Value |
|---|---|---|
| Cash | $ 120,000 | $ 120,000 |
| Accounts receivable ($419,000 from Cohen) | 849,000 | 800,000 |
| Inventory | 1,310,000 | 1,800,000 |
| Capital assets | 1,492,000 | 700,000 |
| Mining properties | 6,701,000 | 11,400,000 |
| | $10,472,000 | $14,820,000 |
| | | |
| Accounts payable | $ 1,375,000 | $ 1,375,000 |
| Long-term debt | 4,990,000 | 5,219,000 |
| Common shares (250,000 shares) | 2,700,000 | |
| Retained earnings | 1,407,000 | |
| | $10,472,000 | |

**Required:**

Assume Cohen buys 147,000 shares of Abbott at $50 per share. Describe the resulting reporting requirements, and describe the effect on the annual financial statements of Cohen. Include a calculation of goodwill in your response.

 **A11-25 Comprehensive Investments:** Chester Corp. has the following securities in its investment portfolio on December 31, 20X8. All these securities were purchased in 20X8.

a. 3,000 shares of Y Co. common shares, which cost $58,500 and had a fair value of $61,400 at the end of 20X8 (that is, there was $2,900 in OCI).

b. 10,000 shares of Q Co. common stock, which cost $580,000 and had a fair value of $600,000 at the end of 20X8 (that is, there was $20,000 in OCI).

c. T Company 8% bonds, $100,000 par value, purchased for $103,500; amortized cost was $103,263 at the end of 20X8. The market interest rate had been 7.5% when the bond was acquired, and interest is paid annually at the end of each year.

In 20X9, the following transactions occurred:

a. A dividend of $2.00 per share was received on the Y Co. shares.

b. 1,500 Y Co. shares were then sold for $32,000.

c. The annual interest was received on the T Company bond; interest revenue is measured using the effective-interest method.

d. Purchased 4,000 share of Z Co. for $53.50 per share.

e. Sold the Q Co. shares for $570,000.

f. Market values at the end of the year: Y Co., $15 per share, Q Company, $59 per share, and Z Co., $55 per share.

**Required:**
Prepare journal entries for the 20X9 transactions and events.

---

★★★ **A11-26 Comprehensive Investments:** On 1 January 20X4, Ritchie Corp. reported the following investments:

| | |
|---|---:|
| Available-for-sale investments (at market value) | |
|    Rafuse Ltd. shares, 3,500 shares | $ 25,375 |
|    Wood Corp. shares, 6,200 shares | 316,200 |
| | |
| Held-to-maturity investments (at amortized cost) | |
|    Russell Corp. 6% bonds, maturity date 1 November | |
|      20X9, interest is paid semi-annually each 1 May | |
|      and 1 November; maturity (par) value is $500,000. | 491,250 |
|      (On 1 January 20X4, there was also $5,000 of | |
|      accrued interest receivable recorded in relation to | |
|      these bonds) | |
| | |
| Other comprehensive income | |
|    Unrealized holding loss re: Rafuse Ltd. shares | 2,625 |
|    Unrealized holding gain re: Wood Corp. shares | 63,860 |

During 20X4, Ritchie has the following transactions with respect to its investments, in chronological order.

a. Sold 1,000 Rafuse shares for $8.40 per share less a $500 brokerage fee.
b. Bought 4,000 of the 12,000 outstanding shares of Giordani Limited for $224,000. The share ownership gave Ritchie the right to appoint three members of the 11-person Giordani Board of Directors and it was felt that significant influence existed. At the time of acquisition, assets of Giordani were $600,000, liabilities were $270,000, and common equity was $330,000. It was felt that assets had fair value equal to book value except for capital assets. These had a book value of $125,000, fair value of $200,000, and eight years of life remaining. Note: provide the entry for the investment acquisition, and also calculate the goodwill inherent in the purchase price.
c. Received a $1 per share dividend on Rafuse shares and a $3 per share dividend on Wood shares.
d. Received semi-annual interest on 1 May on the Russell Corp. bond; recorded $546 of discount amortization as well.
e. Sold Russell Corp. bonds for 102 plus accrued interest on 30 June 20X4. Discount amortization of $277 was recorded prior to the sale. (Note: first record accrued interest to June 30, then record the sale)
f. Sold 4,000 Wood shares for $57 per share, less $1,700 in brokerage fees.
g. Received dividends of $2 per share on the Giordani shares. Giordani reported $435,000 of net income during the period of Ritchie's ownership.
h. At year-end, Wood shares were valued at $54 and Rafuse at $10. Giordani shares were valued at $798,000.

**Required:**

1. Provide journal entries to record these transactions and events. The company includes brokerage fees as part of the cost of the investment, and nets brokerages fees paid with proceeds on disposition.
2. What are the implications of the sale of Russell Corp. bonds?

★★ **A11-27 Comprehensive Investments:** On 1 January 20X5, Wener Corp. reported the following investments:

Available-for-sale investments (at market value)
| | |
|---|---|
| Greenidge Corp. shares, 12,400 shares | $948,600 |
| Chow Ltd. shares, 7,000 shares | 76,125 |

Held-to-maturity investments (at amortized cost)
Dooley Corp. 6.3% bonds, maturity date 30 June 20X7,
interest is paid semi-annually each 30 June and
30 December; market rate was 8% annually when
the bonds were issued; maturity (par) value is
$500,000. Effective-interest amortization is used. 481,082

Other comprehensive income
| | |
|---|---|
| Unrealized holding gain re: Greenidge Corp. shares | 62,000 |
| Unrealized holding loss re: Chow shares | 10,500 |

During 20X5, Wener has the following transactions with respect to its investments, in chronological order.

a. Sold 1,000 Chow shares for $16.20 per share.
b. Received semi-annual interest on 30 June on the Dooley Corp. bond; recorded appropriate discount amortization as well.
c. Sold 4,000 Greenidge shares for $92 per share.
d. Received dividends of $3 per share on the Chow shares and $1.50 per share on the Greenidge shares.
e. Received semi-annual interest on 30 December on the Dooley Corp. bond; recorded appropriate discount amortization as well.
f. At year-end, Greenidge shares were valued at $96 and Chow at $7.

**Required:**
Provide entries for 20X5 transactions and events.

★★★ **A11-28 Comprehensive Investments:** Reston Suppliers is a public company. It reported the following at the end of 20X5:

Available-for-sale investments
| | | |
|---|---|---|
| S Co., 20,000 shares | $448,000 | |
| R Co., $50,000 par value, 10% bond, due | | |
| 31 December 20X7 | 52,000 | $ 500,000 |

Held-to-maturity investment
T Co. bonds, $100,000 par value, 9% bond, semi-
annual interest due 30 June 20X8 (the market
interest rate was 10% on acquisition) 97,836

Significant-influence investment
V Ltd., 45,000 shares, equity method 2,578,900

Other comprehensive income
Unrealized holding gains ($2,000 related to
R Co. bonds and $13,000 related to S Co.) 15,000

The following transactions and events took place in 20X6:

a. Dividends received, S Co., $1 per share, V Ltd., $3 per share.
b. Semi-annual interest was received on both bonds on 30 June.
c. Early in July, the S Co. shares were sold for $32 per share, less $3,000 in commissions.
d. 1,000 W Ltd. shares were acquired for a total of $67,000, including $500 of commissions. This is an available-for-sale investment.

e. Reston owns 30% of the voting shares of V Ltd. V Ltd. reported earnings of $450,000 for 20X6. There was $216,000 of goodwill inherent in the original purchase price, but no other fair value allocations that require adjustment. There were no intercompany transactions requiring adjustment. A goodwill impairment of $10,800 must be recorded in 20X6.

f. The R Co. bond was sold for $51,400 plus accrued interest on 1 October 20X6.

g. X Co. shares were acquired as an available-for-sale investment, 300,000 shares for a cost of $138,000, including $3,800 of commissions.

h. Semi-annual interest was received on the T Co. bond at the end of December.

i. W Co. paid a dividend of $0.40 per share.

j. Market values on 31 December 20X6: W Ltd., $25 per share; X Co., $0.65 per share; V Ltd., $62 per share; T Co., 95. The W Ltd. decline in value is considered to be an impairment.

**Required:**

1. List the accounts and amounts that would appear on the income statement. Also calculate the change in other comprehensive income for the year ended 31 December 20X6. Broker commissions are included in original cost, and netted with the proceeds of disposition.

2. List the accounts and amounts that would appear on the balance sheet for the year ended 31 December 20X6. Available-for-sale investments are temporary investments.

 **A11-29 Comprehensive Investments:** Fetch Company, a public company, had the following transactions in securities during 20X6:

a. Purchased $700,000 par value of 6% Emera Ltd. bonds (when the market interest rate was 5%), on 1 July 20X6. The bonds will mature on 31 December 20X11, and pay interest on 1 July and 1 January. The bonds will be a held-to-maturity investment.

b. Purchased 300,000 common shares of Talcon Ltd., a publicly traded company, as an available-for-sale investment on 16 June. The price per share was $0.75, plus a $4,500 broker commission.

c. On 1 October, invested $3,000,000 in Ball Ltd., a customer that was experiencing financial difficulty but had great potential. Fetch received 25% of the common shares of Ball, and was given representation on the Board of Directors. Fetch felt that it had significant influence with Ball. On the date of acquisition, Ball had tangible assets with a book value of $14,700,000. Liabilities were $9,600,000. All book values represented fair values, except plant and equipment with a 10-year life. For plant and equipment, book value was $6,750,000 and fair values were $7,980,000. Goodwill was not impaired in 20X6.

d. Purchased $200,000 par value of 8% Ontario Electric Ltd. bonds for 100 plus accrued interest on 1 November 20X6. The bonds will mature on 31 December 20X9, and pay interest on 1 March and 1 September. The bonds are held as an available-for-sale investment.

e. Talcon Ltd. paid a cash dividend of $0.05 per share on 1 November.

f. Ball did not declare or pay any dividends in 20X6 but reported a loss, earned evenly over the year, of $475,000.

g. Interest was accrued on 31 December on bonds, and premium amortized, as appropriate.

h. Market values on 31 December: Emera bonds, 101.5; Talcon, $0.62 per share; Ball Ltd., undeterminable; Ontario Electric bonds, 98.5.

Fetch Company had the following transactions in 20X7 related to its investments:

a. Received the semi-annual interest on the Emera bonds on 1 January.

b. Received the semi-annual interest on the Ontario Electric bonds on 1 March.

c. Sold the Talcon shares for $1.20 per share, less brokerage fees of $7,900.

d. Received the semi-annual interest on the Emera bonds on 1 July. Premium amortization is also recorded.

e. Sold the Ontario Electric bonds for 99, plus accrued interest, on 1 August. There was a commission of $565 on the transaction.

f. On 1 November, purchased 16,000 shares of Vulture Corp. for $5.50 per share, plus commissions of $1,650. The shares are being held as an available-for-sale investment.

g. Ball did not declare or pay any dividends in 20X7 but reported net income, earned evenly over the year, of $79,200. Goodwill was impaired in the amount of $200,000.

h. Interest was accrued on 31 December on bonds, as appropriate. Premium amortization is also recorded.

i. Market values on 31 December: Emera bonds, 102; Talcon, $1.15 per share; Ball Ltd., undeterminable; Ontario Electric bonds, 98; Vulture Corp, $7 per share.

**Required:**

Provide entries for all transactions and adjustments related to investments. Broker commissions are included in original cost, and netted with the proceeds of disposition. Include a calculation of acquired goodwill on the acquisition of Ball.

---

★★ **A11-30 Cash Flow Statement:** For each of the following transactions, identify the item(s) that would appear on the cash flow statement. Identify the appropriate section (i.e., operating, investing, financing) and whether the item is an inflow or an outflow, or an add-back or deduction in operating activities. Assume that the indirect method of presentation is used in the operating activities section.

1. Wilcox Ltd. purchased common shares of Gentron Ltd. for $108,000, an available-for-sale investment.

2. The common shares in part 1 were revalued to $150,000 fair value at year-end, and $42,000 of other comprehensive income was recognized.

3. Wilcox reported a held-to-maturity investment of $138,000, a $150,000, 8-year bond bought at a discount in previous years. The bond pays annual interest of 7%, and $3,000 of discount amortization had been recorded in the current year.

4. Wilcox owns 460,000 shares of Salman Co., over which it has significant influence. In the current year, investment revenue of $87,000 was recorded, and cash dividends of $26,000 were received.

5. The Gentron common shares were sold for $180,000. A gain of $72,000 was recognized, and other comprehensive income was reduced by $42,000.

6. T-bills were purchased for $250,000, an available-for-sale investment that is considered a cash equivalent.

7. The T-bills in part 6 were sold for $260,000. A gain of $10,000 was recorded.

---

★★ **A11-31 Cash Flow Statement:** The following comparative data is available from the 20X4 balance sheet of Investcorp:

|  | 20X4 | 20X3 |
|---|---|---|
| Available-for-sale investments | $2,950,000 | $1,216,000 |
| Long-term investments | | |
|   Investment in Tandor Ltd., at equity | 1,071,200 | 950,000 |
|   Held-to-maturity investment in Byron | | |
|     bonds, at amortized cost | 615,000 | 609,300 |
| Shareholders' equity: | | |
|   Other comprehensive income | | |
|     Unrealized holding gains | 75,900 | 52,100 |

In 20X4, the following transactions took place, and are properly reflected in the balance sheet accounts, above.

1. Dividends of $140,000 were received from Tandor Ltd. No shares of Tandor were bought or sold during the year.

2. Available-for-sale investments, with a carrying value of $56,200 and cumulative unrealized holding gains of $21,000, were sold for $87,500.

3. Available-for-sale investments were increased to fair value at year-end.

Other "typical" transactions and entries also occurred in 20X4 that are reflected in the balance sheet accounts. (You may find it helpful to reconstruct the transactions.)

**Required:**
What items would appear on the 20X4 cash flow statement? Assume the operating section is presented using the indirect method of presentation.

★ ★ ★

**A11-32 Consolidation (Appendix):** At the beginning of the current fiscal year, Poppa Company bought 90% of the common shares of Son Limited for $7,350,000 cash. At that time, the book value of Son's assets reflected fair value except for land, which was undervalued on the books by $1,200,000. Son reported $500,000 of common stock and $5,500,000 of retained earnings on this date. Financial results at the end of the current fiscal year (in thousands):

| | Poppa | Son |
|---|---|---|
| Cash | $ 1,610 | $ 480 |
| Accounts receivable | 8,920 | 1,410 |
| Inventory | 12,100 | 1,400 |
| Capital assets | 10,520 | 1,310 |
| Investment in Son Co. | 7,350 | 0 |
| Mining properties | 0 | 6,050 |
| | $40,500 | $10,650 |
| | | |
| Current liabilities | $ 8,060 | $ 1,400 |
| Long-term debt | 20,900 | 3,102 |
| Common shares | 8,600 | 500 |
| Retained earnings | 2,940 | 5,648 |
| | $40,500 | $10,650 |
| | | |
| Sales | $49,700 | $12,900 |
| Cost of sales | 36,200 | 8,100 |
| Other expenses | 12,925 | 4,552 |
| Other revenues | 665 | 0 |
| Net income | $ 1,240 | $ 248 |
| Opening retained earnings | 2,100 | 5,500 |
| Dividends | 400 | 100 |
| Closing retained earnings | $ 2,940 | $ 5,648 |

During the year, Poppa bought $1,000,000 of goods from Son. Three-quarters had been resold at year-end. Son had recorded a $120,000 gross profit on these sales. Poppa still owed Son $800,000 at year-end. Goodwill was not impaired during the year.

**Required:**
Prepare a consolidated balance sheet, income statement, and retained earnings statement for the current fiscal year. Round calculations to the nearest thousand.

★ ★ ★ **A11-33 Consolidation (Appendix):** P Company bought 90% of the voting shares of S Company on 1 January 20X2 for $19,500,000. On that date, S Company had shareholders' equity of $15,900,000, including $6,000,000 of common shares. On that date, fair values of net assets approximated market values, except land that was undervalued on the books in the amount of $500,000, and depreciable capital assets that were undervalued by $1,400,000. Goodwill was not impaired in 20X2; amortizable capital assets are to be amortized over 14 years.

During 20X2, P Company sold goods to S Company in the amount of $600,000. All these goods were resold by S Company by the end of 20X2. S Company sold $400,000 of products to P Company; one quarter had been resold by the end of the year. S Company had recorded a $220,000 profit on the sale. P Company still owed S Company $375,000 at year-end.

Unconsolidated financial statements follow:

| Year Ended 31 December 20X2 | P Co. | S Co. |
|---|---|---|
| Cash | $    1,450,000 | $    213,000 |
| Accounts receivable | 16,300,000 | 3,415,000 |
| Inventory | 28,900,000 | 5,900,000 |
| Capital assets | 114,300,000 | 11,100,000 |
| Investment in S Co. | 19,500,000 | — |
| Intangible assets | 7,916,000 | — |
| | $188,366,000 | $20,628,000 |
| | | |
| Current liabilities | $  39,000,000 | $  2,100,000 |
| Long-term debt | 80,000,000 | 500,000 |
| Future (deferred) income tax | 10,195,000 | 1,400,000 |
| Common shares | 17,900,000 | 6,000,000 |
| Retained earnings | 41,271,000 | 10,628,000 |
| | $188,366,000 | $20,628,000 |
| | | |
| Sales | $240,350,000 | $30,600,000 |
| Cost of sales | 170,700,000 | 18,900,000 |
| Other expenses | 42,900,000 | 10,522,000 |
| Other revenue | 405,000 | — |
| Net income | $  27,155,000 | $  1,178,000 |
| Opening retained earnings | 30,316,000 | 9,900,000 |
| Dividends | 16,200,000 | 450,000 |
| Closing retained earnings | $  41,271,000 | $10,628,000 |

**Required:**

1. Prepare consolidated financial statements as of 31 December 20X2.

2. Under what circumstances would P Co. not have to consolidate its subsidiary?

3. In what way are the consolidated financial statements superior to unconsolidated statements? Why do some people believe that consolidated statements are inferior?

# Fundamentals: The Accounting Information Processing System

## ACCOUNTS, TRANSACTION RECORDING, AND FINANCIAL STATEMENTS

This appendix is a review of the mechanics of the accounting information processing system. Transactions and events are recorded in accounts, which describe specific financial statement elements. These elements are reported to investors, creditors, and other interested readers in periodic financial statements.

### Accounts

There are seven major types of accounts, grouped under two headings: **permanent accounts** or **real accounts** (assets, liabilities, and owners' equity accounts) and **temporary accounts** or **nominal accounts** (revenues, expenses, gains, and losses). Permanent accounts are also called "real accounts," and temporary accounts are also called "nominal accounts." The permanent accounts are those appearing in the balance sheet. The descriptive term "permanent" means that balances in these accounts are carried over to future accounting periods. *Temporary* accounts are closed out at the end of each fiscal year. The **accounting identity** states the relationship between the balances of the permanent accounts:

$$\text{Assets} = \text{Liabilities} + \text{Owners' Equity}$$

### Recording Transactions

To maintain the accounting entity, every transaction recorded must affect at least two accounts. This protocol, called the **double-entry system**, records the change in a resource or obligation and the reason for, or source of, the change.

Complementing the double-entry system, the **debit-credit convention** is used as a recording and balancing procedure. This convention divides accounts into two sides. In North American bookkeeping, the debit (dr.) side is always the left side, and the credit (cr.) side is always the right side.[1] These terms carry no further meaning and cannot be interpreted as "increases" or "decreases" since, depending on the account type, a debit or a credit can record an increase or decrease. This is illustrated in the T-accounts summarized in Exhibit A-1. The **T-account** is a form of account used for demonstrating transactions; its skeletal form takes the shape of the letter T. The T-account reflects the general format of general ledger accounts, as we will discuss later.

The debit-credit convention is a convenient way to check for recording errors. When the sums of debits and credits are not equal, an error is evident.

## Financial Statements

At the end of a reporting period, after all transactions and events are recorded in accounts, **financial statements** are prepared. The financial statements report account balances, changes in account balances, and aggregations of account balances, such as net income and total assets. The financial statements include the *income statement*, the *balance sheet*, and the *cash flow statement*. The income statement reports revenues, expenses, gains and losses, and thus shows net income for the year. This, in turn, changes owners' equity on the balance sheet. The balance sheet reflects the financial position of the entity and demonstrates that assets are equal to liabilities plus owners' equity. The cash flow statement reports sources and uses of cash. A retained earnings statement is also commonly reported, along with statements that describe the change in other shareholders' equity accounts, as needed. The steps leading to these financial statements are discussed in the rest of this appendix.

---

### EXHIBIT A-1

### DEBIT/CREDIT IMPACT ON T-ACCOUNTS

#### Permanent Accounts

| Assets | | = | Liabilities | | + | Owners' Equity | |
|---|---|---|---|---|---|---|---|
| Debit entries *increase* assets | Credit entries *decrease* assets | | Debit entries *decrease* liabilities | Credit entries *increase* liabilities | | Debit entries *decrease* owners' equity | Credit entries *increase* owners' equity |

#### Temporary Accounts

| Expenses | | Revenues | |
|---|---|---|---|
| Debit entries *increase* expenses | Credit entries *decrease* expenses | Debit entries *decrease* revenues | Credit entries *increase* revenues |

| Losses | | Gains | |
|---|---|---|---|
| Debit entries *increase* losses | Credit entries *decrease* losses | Debit entries *decrease* gains | Credit entries *increase* gains |

---

[1] The debit-left and credit-right is reversed in the United Kingdom, where the debits appear on the right and the credits on the left. Debit is abbreviated as "dr.," even though the letter "r" does not appear in the word because the abbreviations *dr.* and *cr.* were originally derived from the words *debtor* and *creditor*.

## THE AIS AND THE ACCOUNTING CYCLE

An **accounting information system** (AIS) is designed to record accurate financial data in a timely and chronological manner, facilitate retrieval of financial data in a form useful to management, and simplify periodic preparation of financial statements for external use. Design of the AIS, to meet the company's information requirements, depends on the firm's size, the nature of its operations, the volume of data, its organizational structure, and government regulation.

The accounting cycle, illustrated in Exhibit A-2, is a series of sequential steps leading to the financial statements. This cycle is repeated each reporting period, normally a year. Companies may combine some of these steps or change their order to suit their specific needs. Depending on the information-processing technology used, certain accounting cycle steps can be combined or in some cases omitted. Most accounting systems are computerized, in

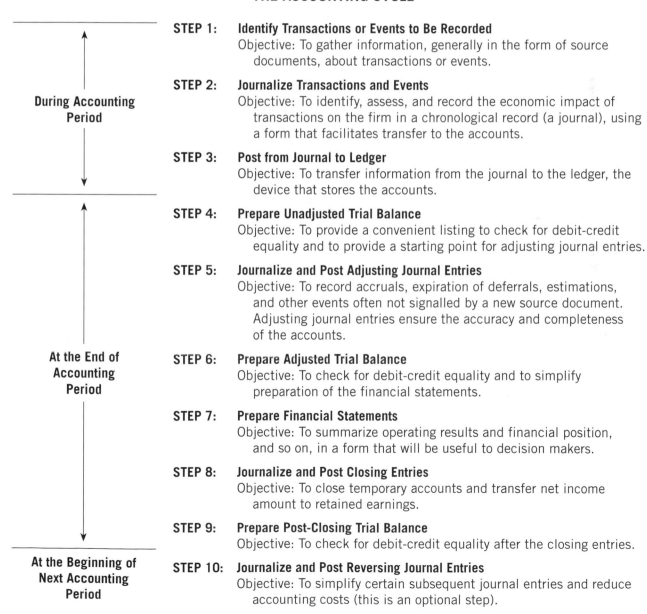

## EXHIBIT A-2

### THE ACCOUNTING CYCLE

**During Accounting Period**

**STEP 1:    Identify Transactions or Events to Be Recorded**
Objective: To gather information, generally in the form of source documents, about transactions or events.

**STEP 2:    Journalize Transactions and Events**
Objective: To identify, assess, and record the economic impact of transactions on the firm in a chronological record (a journal), using a form that facilitates transfer to the accounts.

**STEP 3:    Post from Journal to Ledger**
Objective: To transfer information from the journal to the ledger, the device that stores the accounts.

**STEP 4:    Prepare Unadjusted Trial Balance**
Objective: To provide a convenient listing to check for debit-credit equality and to provide a starting point for adjusting journal entries.

**STEP 5:    Journalize and Post Adjusting Journal Entries**
Objective: To record accruals, expiration of deferrals, estimations, and other events often not signalled by a new source document. Adjusting journal entries ensure the accuracy and completeness of the accounts.

**At the End of Accounting Period**

**STEP 6:    Prepare Adjusted Trial Balance**
Objective: To check for debit-credit equality and to simplify preparation of the financial statements.

**STEP 7:    Prepare Financial Statements**
Objective: To summarize operating results and financial position, and so on, in a form that will be useful to decision makers.

**STEP 8:    Journalize and Post Closing Entries**
Objective: To close temporary accounts and transfer net income amount to retained earnings.

**STEP 9:    Prepare Post-Closing Trial Balance**
Objective: To check for debit-credit equality after the closing entries.

**At the Beginning of Next Accounting Period**

**STEP 10:    Journalize and Post Reversing Journal Entries**
Objective: To simplify certain subsequent journal entries and reduce accounting costs (this is an optional step).

whole or in part. The fundamental nature of the process, however, is the same regardless of the technology used.

The first three steps in the accounting cycle require the most time and effort. The frequency of Step 3, posting, depends on the volume and nature of transactions, and the technology used. For example, firms with many cash transactions post to the cash account hourly or daily. Steps 4 through 9 generally occur at the end of the fiscal year. The last step, the posting of reversing entries, is optional and occurs at the beginning of the new accounting period.

## THE IMPACT OF TECHNOLOGY

Few businesses keep manual records. Computerized systems have many advantages, including speed and accuracy. The norm is to use a customized or off-the-shelf computer program that will facilitate the following steps in the accounting cycle (refer to Exhibit A-2):

- Journalizing transactions, adjustments, closing, and reversing entries;
- Posting entries;
- Preparing trial balances; and
- Preparing financial statements.

What is left for the accountant to do? First, identification and control of transactions and adjustments is crucial. The accountant manages the entire process, ensuring that information entered is accurate and complete. Second, many elements in financial reporting require the exercise of professional judgement—choice of accounting policy, composition of the notes to the financial statements, and so on. These tasks require qualified decision makers.

Regardless of how the steps in the accounting cycle are performed, they accomplish the same task—posting is posting, manual or computerized. The accountant has to understand this process to manage it.

## THE ACCOUNTING CYCLE

The annual accounting cycle includes 10 steps, explained in the following section.

### Step 1: Identify Transactions or Events to Be Recorded

The first step is the requirement to identify transactions and events that cause a change in the firm's resources or obligations, and collects relevant economic data about those transactions. Events that change a firm's resources or obligations are categorized into three types:

1. *Exchanges of resources and obligations between the reporting firm and outside parties.* These exchanges are either **reciprocal transfers** or **non-reciprocal transfers**. In a reciprocal transfer, the firm both transfers and receives resources (e.g., sale of goods for cash). In a non-reciprocal transfer, the firm either transfers *or* receives current or future resources (e.g., payment of cash dividends or receipt of a donation). All exchanges require a journal entry.

2. *Internal events within the firm that affect resources or obligations but do not involve outside parties.* Examples are recognition of amortization of capital assets and the use of inventory for production. These events also generally require a journal entry. However, other events, such as increases in the value of assets resulting from superior management and similar factors, are not recorded.

3. *External economic and environmental events beyond the control of the company.* Examples include casualty losses and changes in the market value of assets and liabilities. At the present time, accounting standards allow recording of market value changes for only a few types of assets.

**Transactions** are events requiring a journal entry. Transactions are often accompanied by a source document, generally a paper record that describes the exchange, the parties involved, the date, and the dollar amount. Examples are sales invoices, freight bills, and cash register receipts. Certain events, such as the accrual of interest, are not signalled by a separate source document. Recording these transactions requires reference to the underlying contract supporting the original exchange of resources. Source documents are essential for the initial recording of transactions in a journal and are also used for subsequent tracing and verification, for evidence in legal proceedings, and for audits of financial statements.

## Step 2: Journalize Transactions and Events

**Journals** Transactions are recorded chronologically in a **journal**—an organized medium for recording transactions in debit-credit format. A journal entry is a debit-credit description of a transaction that includes the date, the accounts and amounts involved, and a brief description. A journal entry is a temporary recording, although journals are retained as part of the audit trail; account balances are not changed until the information is transferred to the ledger accounts in Step 3.

Accounting systems usually have two types of journals: the **general journal** and **special journals**. Non-repetitive entries and entries involving infrequently used accounts are recorded in the general journal. Repetitive entries are recorded in special journals. If special journals are not used, all transactions are recorded in the general journal. Special journals are discussed later in this appendix. The general journal is used to illustrate most entries in this text.

The journal entry step is not absolutely essential; transaction data can be recorded directly into the accounts. However, the journal entry step has advantages, and it is standard practice to record all transactions first in a journal. Transaction processing is more efficient, and less costly, if transactions are grouped in a journal and processed together. By using journals, review and analysis of transactions is much simpler and the accounts consume less storage space. Also, a chronological list of transactions is provided. Transactions can be difficult to reconstruct without a journal because the debits and credits are located in different accounts. Journals are typically part of the paper trail relied on by auditors.

Some companies use computerized systems to bypass the traditional journal entry step. Retailers, for example, record relevant information about a transaction by using bar codes printed on product packages. Optical scanning equipment reads the bar code and transmits the information to a computer, which records the proper amount directly in the relevant ledger accounts. Accounting cost savings can be significant.

Exhibit A-3 illustrates an entry in a general journal. This entry records the purchase of equipment financed with cash and debt. Equipment is recorded at the value of the resources used to acquire it. The names of the accounts credited are listed below and to the right of the debited account.

**general journal**

a journal with a flexible format in which any transaction can be recorded

**special journal**

a journal with a non-flexible, predetermined format in which only specific transactions that fit the format can be recorded

---

### EXHIBIT A-3

Page J-16                                     **GENERAL JOURNAL**

| Date 20X5 | Accounts and Explanation | Posting Ref. | Amount Debit | Amount Credit |
|---|---|---|---|---|
| 2 Jan. | Equipment | 150 | 15,000 | |
| | Cash | 101 | | 5,000 |
| | Notes payable | 215 | | 10,000 |
| | Purchased equipment for use in the business. Paid $5,000 cash and gave a $10,000, one-year note with 15% interest payable at maturity. | | | |

## Step 3: Post from Journal to Ledger

Transferring transaction data from the journal to the ledger is called **posting**. Posting reclassifies the data from the journal's chronological format to an account classification format in the ledger, which is a collection of the formal accounts. Computerized systems store ledger data until it is needed for processing in another step in the accounting cycle.

**Posting** Exhibit A-4 illustrates a section of a general ledger in T-account form. This ledger depicts three general ledger accounts after posting the journal entry shown in Exhibit A-3. Posting references and page numbers are used in both the journal and the ledger to ensure that an audit trail exists—that is, to indicate where an item in the account ledger came from and to which account the item was posted. Posting references also serve to confirm that an entry was posted.

When the $5,000 cash credit from the general journal entry of Exhibit A-3 is posted to the cash ledger account, "101" is listed in the journal to indicate the account number *to which* the credit is posted. Similarly, in the cash ledger account, "J-16" indicates the journal page number *from which* this amount is posted. Cross-referencing is especially important when posting large numbers of transactions, detecting and correcting errors, and maintaining an audit trail.

---

### EXHIBIT A-4

### GENERAL LEDGER (EXCERPTS)

**Cash**                                                              Acct. 101

| 20X5 | | | 20X5 | | |
|---|---|---|---|---|---|
| 1 Jan. | Balance | 18,700 | 2 Jan. | J-16 | 5,000 |

**Equipment**                                                        Acct. 150

| 20X5 | | | | | |
|---|---|---|---|---|---|
| 1 Jan. | Balance | 62,000 | | | |
| 2 | J-16 | 15,000 | | | |

**Notes Payable**                                                    Acct. 215

| | | | 20X5 | | |
|---|---|---|---|---|---|
| | | | 2 Jan. | J-16 | 10,000 |

---

**Ledgers** Accounting systems usually have two types of ledgers: the general ledger and subsidiary ledgers. The general ledger holds all the individual accounts, grouped according to the basic elements of financial statements. Subsidiary ledgers support general ledger accounts that comprise many separate individual accounts. For example, a firm with a substantial number of customer accounts receivable will maintain one ledger account per customer, stored in an accounts receivable subsidiary ledger. The individual customer account is called the "subsidiary account." The general ledger holds only the "control account", the balance of which reflects the sum of all the individual customer account balances. Only the control accounts are used in compiling financial statements.

For example, assume that a firm's accounts receivable consists of two individual accounts with a combined balance of $6,000. The firm's general and subsidiary ledgers might show these balances:

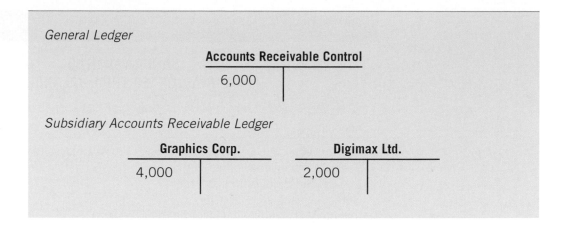

*General Ledger*

**Accounts Receivable Control**

6,000 |

*Subsidiary Accounts Receivable Ledger*

**Graphics Corp.**              **Digimax Ltd.**

4,000 |                         2,000 |

## Step 4: Prepare Unadjusted Trial Balance

An unadjusted trial balance is prepared at the end of the reporting period, after all transaction entries are recorded in the journals and posted to the ledger. The unadjusted trial balance is a list of general ledger accounts and their account balances, in the following order: assets, liabilities, owners' equity, revenues, expenses, gains, and losses. For accounts with subsidiary ledgers, only the control account balances are entered into the trial balance, after reconciliation with the subsidiary ledger.

The unadjusted trial balance is the starting point for developing adjusting entries and for the worksheet, if used. Exhibit A-5 illustrates an unadjusted trial balance for Sonora Limited, a fictitious retailing company, at the end of the fiscal year. The trial balance reflects Sonora's transaction journal entries recorded during 20X5 and is the basis for the remainder of this accounting cycle illustration.

The unadjusted trial balance is a convenient means for checking that the sum of debit account balances equals the sum of credit account balances. If the sums of debit and credit balances are not equal, the error must be found and corrected. A reexamination of source documents and postings is one way to discover the source of an error. Equality of debits and credits does not, however, imply that the accounts are error free. A completely unposted journal entry, an incorrectly classified account, and an erroneous journal entry amount are errors that do not cause inequality of total debits and credits.

As reported in Exhibit A-5, Sonora uses a **periodic inventory system**. Under this system, merchandise on hand is counted and costed at the end of each accounting period. The resulting inventory amount is used to update the inventory account balance. During the period, however, the inventory account balance remains at the 1 January amount and the cost of goods sold is not readily determinable. The unadjusted trial balance for Sonora at 31 December 20X5 reflects the 1 January 20X5 balance.

> **periodic inventory system**
>
> an inventory record-keeping system that determines the quantity of inventory on hand and related cost of goods sold only at the end of the fiscal period

In a **perpetual inventory system**, the inventory account balance is constantly updated when merchandise is purchased and sold. Thus, the inventory account balance is correctly stated at the end of the accounting period, and there will be an up-to-date cost of goods sold account before any adjustments are made. The inventory balance will be verified by a physical count.

As shown in Exhibit A-5, Sonora's retained earnings account also reflects the 1 January 20X5 balance since no transactions affected this account during 20X5. Income tax expense is not listed in the unadjusted trial balance because the corporate income tax liability for the current year is not known until pre-tax income is computed. The loss from discontinued operations also does not yet reflect any tax effect.

## Step 5: Journalize and Post Adjusting Journal Entries

Many changes in a firm's economic resources and obligations occur continuously. For example, interest accrues daily on debts, as does rent expense on an office building. Other resources and obligations, such as employee salaries, originate as service is rendered with payment to

## EXHIBIT A-5

### SONORA LIMITED
### UNADJUSTED TRIAL BALANCE

31 December 20X5

| Account | Debit | Credit |
|---|---|---|
| Cash | $ 67,300 | |
| Accounts receivable | 45,000 | |
| Allowance for doubtful accounts | | $ 1,000 |
| Notes receivable | 8,000 | |
| Inventory (1 January balance, periodic system) | 75,000 | |
| Prepaid insurance | 600 | |
| Land | 8,000 | |
| Building | 160,000 | |
| Accumulated amortization, building | | 90,000 |
| Equipment | 91,000 | |
| Accumulated amortization, equipment | | 27,000 |
| Accounts payable | | 29,000 |
| Bonds payable, 6% | | 50,000 |
| Common shares, no par, 15,000 shares | | 170,000 |
| Retained earnings (1 January balance) | | 41,500 |
| Dividends declared | 10,000 | |
| Sales revenue | | 325,200 |
| Interest revenue | | 500 |
| Rent revenue | | 1,800 |
| Purchases | 130,000 | |
| Freight on purchases | 4,000 | |
| Purchase returns | | 2,000 |
| Selling expenses* | 104,000 | |
| General and administrative expenses* | 23,600 | |
| Interest expense | 2,500 | |
| Loss on discontinued operations | 9,000 | |
| Totals | $738,000 | $738,000 |

*These broad categories of expenses are used to simplify presentation.*

follow at specified dates. The end of the accounting period generally does not coincide with the receipt or payment of cash associated with these types of resource changes.

*Accrual-basis accounting* requires the recording of these changes at the end of the accounting period so that financial statements are fairly stated. **Adjusting journal entries (AJEs)** are used to record such resource changes to ensure the accuracy of the financial statements. In all cases, AJEs are posted to the general ledger accounts.

**adjusting journal entries**

entries used to record resource changes that occur continuously and must be recorded to accurately reflect the financial results and position of an entity; also prepared for corrections

**Classification of AJEs** AJEs generally record a resource or obligation change and usually involve both a permanent and a temporary account. AJEs are recorded and dated as of the last day of the fiscal period. They are recorded in the general journal and posted to the ledger accounts. Source documents from earlier transactions are the primary information sources for AJEs. AJEs may be classified into three categories: deferrals, accruals, and other AJEs.

*Deferrals* are recorded for cash flows that occur before expense and revenue recognition. These AJEs are recorded when cash is paid for expenses that apply to more than one accounting period or when cash is received for revenue that applies to more than one accounting period. The portion of the expense or revenue that applies to future periods is deferred as a prepaid expense (asset) or unearned revenue (liability). The chart below clarifies the terminology used:

| Deferral Type | Cash Timing | Results In |
|---|---|---|
| Deferred revenue | Cash received before revenue recognition is appropriate | Deferred revenue (liability) (perhaps as unearned revenue) |
| Deferred expense | Cash paid before expense recognition is appropriate | Deferred expense (asset) (perhaps a prepaid) |

The exact AJE required for a deferral depends on the method used for first recording operational cash payments and receipts. One method, here called the **standard recording method**, records an *asset* upon payment of cash before goods or services are consumed and records a *liability* upon receipt of cash before goods or services are provided. For example, if two months' rent is prepaid on 1 July, the standard method debits prepaid rent for that amount. An adjustment later in the year recognizes rent expense and the expiration of prepaid rent.

A second method, here called the **expedient recording method**, records an *expense* upon payment of cash before goods or services are consumed and records a *revenue* upon receipt of cash before goods or services are provided. In the case of rent paid in advance, the expedient method debits rent expense for two months' rent. This method is expedient because many cash payments and receipts relate to expenses and revenues that apply only to the year in which the cash flow occurs. No AJE is required in this example because rent expense is correctly stated at year-end. If a portion of the expense or revenue applies to a future accounting period, however, an AJE is required.

*Accruals* are recorded for cash flows that occur after expense and revenue recognition. These AJEs are recorded when cash is to be paid or received in a future accounting period but all or a portion of the future cash flow applies to expenses or revenues of the current period. For example, unpaid wages accrued as wages payable at year-end represent wage costs matched against current-year revenues but not to be paid until next year. If the company is a landlord and rents space to tenants, uncollected rent accrued as rent receivable at year-end represents revenue earned in the current year but to be collected next year. In both cases, the expense or revenue is recognized before the cash flow occurs. The chart below clarifies the terminology used:

| Accrual Type | Cash Timing | Results In |
|---|---|---|
| Accrued revenue | Cash received after revenue recognition is appropriate | Accrued revenue (asset) (perhaps a receivable) |
| Accrued expense | Cash paid after expense recognition is appropriate | Accrued expense (liability) (perhaps an account payable) |

*Other types* of journal entries are often recorded at the end of the accounting period and are listed here as adjusting journal entries for completeness. These include:

- Reclassifications of permanent accounts;
- Estimation of expenses (bad debt expense, for example);
- Cost allocations (amortization, for example);
- Recognition of cost of goods sold and inventory losses; and
- Correction of errors discovered at year-end.

*Cash generally is not involved in AJEs because of the purpose of AJEs.* However, corrections of errors involving the cash account discovered at the end of the accounting period are recorded as AJEs. Also, the entry required to adjust the cash balance upon receipt of the end-of-year bank statement, which lists service charges and other items unknown until receipt, is recorded as an AJE.

In the following discussion, Sonora's 31 December 20X5 unadjusted trial balance (Exhibit A-5) and additional information are used to illustrate AJEs.

**Deferral Examples** *Deferred expenses.* Some expenses are paid in advance, and deferred until they are recognized on the income statement. For example, on 1 November 20X5, Sonora paid a six-month insurance premium of $600 in advance. On that date, the $600 payment is recorded as a debit to prepaid insurance and a credit to cash (the standard method). On the unadjusted trial balance, the full $600 payment is reflected in prepaid insurance. One third of this payment ($200) is applicable to 20X5. A $200 expense, indicating the partial expiration of the asset, must be recognized. Sonora records insurance expense and other similar expenses in the general and administrative expense account. AJE (a) adjusts prepaid insurance and recognizes the expense:

| a. 31 December 20X5 | | |
|---|---|---|
| General and administrative expenses | 200 | |
| Prepaid insurance | | 200 |

The credit to prepaid insurance records the reduction in the asset that took place during the last two months of 20X5 as insurance benefits were used up. No source document or transaction signals this entry, although the underlying insurance document was probably consulted. The remaining $400 of prepaid insurance reflects insurance coverage for the first four months of 20X6.

*Deferred revenue.* Some revenues are received in advance, and deferred until they are recognized on the income statement. For example, Sonora leased a small office in its building to a tenant on 1 January 20X5. The lease required an initial payment of $1,800 for 18 months' rent, which is recorded as a debit to cash and a credit to rent revenue (the expedient method). On 31 December 20X5, the unadjusted trial balance reports $1,800 in rent revenue, which is overstated by the $600 (one-third) relating to 20X6. AJE (b) is required to reduce the revenue recognized in 20X5 from $1,800 to $1,200 and to create a liability equal to the amount of rent relating to 20X6 ($600).

| b. 31 December 20X5 | | |
|---|---|---|
| Rent revenue | 600 | |
| Rent collected in advance (liability) | | 600 |

The result of this adjustment is a liability equal to the resources received for future services.

**Accrual Examples** *Accrued expenses.* Some expenses must be recognized on the income statement before they are paid, which results in a payable being recognized For example, Sonora has issued, at face value, $50,000 of 6% bonds paying interest yearly each 31 October. For the current accounting period, a two-month interest obligation accrues between 31 October 20X5 and 31 December 20X5. Sonora must recognize the liability and the resulting expense. The amount for the two-month period is $500 ($50,000 × 6% × 2/12). Therefore, on 31 December 20X5, both the interest expense and the associated payable are recognized in AJE (c):

| c. 31 December 20X5 | | |
| --- | --- | --- |
| Interest expense | 500 | |
| Interest payable | | 500 |

*Accrued revenue.* Some revenues must be recognized on the income statement before they are received, which results in a receivable being recognized. Sonora's unadjusted trial balance lists $8,000 in notes receivable. The interest rate on these notes is 15%, payable each 30 November. As of 31 December 20X5, the maker of the notes is obligated to Sonora for one month's interest of $100 ($8,000 × 15% × 1/12). AJE (d) records the resulting receivable and revenue:

| d. 31 December 20X5 | | |
| --- | --- | --- |
| Interest receivable | 100 | |
| Interest revenue | | 100 |

**Other Examples**  Other common adjusting journal entries are illustrated below.

*Amortization expenses.*  Property, plant, and equipment are many productive assets with a useful life exceeding one year. The cost of these assets is recognized as an expense over their period of use. *Amortization* or *depreciation* is a systematic and rational allocation of plant asset cost over a number of accounting periods. Throughout this text, the terms "depreciation" and "amortization" are used interchangeably. In practice, there is considerable diversity in the terminology used. The amount of amortization expense recognized depends on a number of factors:

- The original expenditure and subsequent capitalized expenditures;
- The asset's useful life;
- The method chosen for amortization measurement; and
- The asset's residual value.

Amortization is similar to the recognition of an expense on a deferred item such as prepaid insurance in that the cash flow occurs before the expense is recognized. The main differences are the longer life and greater uncertainty of expected benefits of capital assets. Many methods of amortization are permitted under GAAP. All entail systematic and rational allocation of the cost of a capital asset cost to accounting periods, over its useful life.

AJE (e) illustrates amortization recorded for Sonora at the end of 20X5 under the straight-line method. Sonora debits two expense accounts because the company uses the building and equipment assets both for selling and for general and administrative functions. Amortization is commonly allocated to several functions, including manufacturing operations. The adjusting entry for amortization is as follows:

| e. 31 December 20X5 | | |
| --- | --- | --- |
| Selling expense (amortization) | 8,200 | |
| General and administrative expense (amortization) | 10,800 | |
| Accumulated amortization, building | | 10,000 |
| Accumulated amortization, equipment | | 9,000 |

| Asset | Cost | Residual Value | Useful Life Years | Proportionate Use by Function | |
|---|---|---|---|---|---|
| | | | | Selling Function | G & A* Function |
| Building | $160,000 | $10,000 | 15 | 46% | 54% |
| Equipment | 91,000 | 1,000 | 10 | 40 | 60 |

Computation:

Building:

[($160,000 − $10,000)/15 yrs.]  =  $10,000  × .46 =  $4,600  × .54 =  $ 5,400

Equipment:

[($91,000 − $1,000)/10 yrs.]  =  9,000  × .40 =  3,600  × .60 =  5,400

Totals          $19,000    $8,200    $10,800

*General and administrative*

**contra account**

general ledger account that is always reported on the financial statements with its "main" account; since the two accounts will have opposite (debit versus credit) balances, the net amount will be reported

AJE (e) reduces the *net book value* of the building and equipment accounts. Accumulated amortization is a **contra account**. A contra account has the opposite balance of the related, main account. Thus, accumulated amortization is subtracted from the gross building and equipment accounts, leaving the net unamortized account balances (net book value). Sonora's balance sheet illustrates this offset.

*Bad Debt Expense* Goods and services are often sold on credit. Accounts that are never collected result in bad debt expense, which is a risk of doing business on credit terms. Firms use a bad debt estimate to reduce income and net accounts receivable in the period of sale. This practice prevents overstatement of both income and assets and is required if bad debts are probable and estimable. Recognition of bad debt expense is accomplished with an AJE that debits bad debt expense and credits the allowance for doubtful accounts, a contra account to the accounts receivable account.

Estimates of uncollectible accounts may be based on credit sales for the period or the year-end accounts receivable balance. Assume that Sonora extends credit on $120,000 of sales during 20X5. Prior experience indicates an expected 1% average bad debt rate on credit sales. Sonora treats bad debt expense as a component of selling expenses and records AJE (f):

f. 31 December 20X5

    Selling expense ($120,000 ×.01)          1,200

        Allowance for doubtful accounts                1,200

The credit is made to the allowance account, rather than to accounts receivable, because the identities of the uncollectible accounts are not yet known. In addition, the use of the contra allowance account maintains agreement between the balance in accounts receivable control and the total of account balances in the accounts receivable subsidiary ledger.

The $1,200 allowance is the portion of 20X5 credit sales not expected to be collected. Net accounts receivable, the difference between the balance in accounts receivable and the allowance account, is an estimate of the cash ultimately expected to be received from sales on account. Bad debt expense is reported in the income statement.

*Cost of Goods Sold* The methodology used to determine cost of goods sold (a retailer's largest expense) depends on whether a perpetual or a periodic inventory system is used.

*Periodic System* A periodic system does not maintain a current balance in inventory or cost of goods sold. Instead, the physical inventory count at the end of the period is used to determine the balances of these two accounts. The purchases account, rather than the inventory account, is debited for all purchases during the period. In this case, the unadjusted trial balance at the end of an accounting period reflects the beginning inventory, and cost of goods sold does not yet exist as an account. An AJE can be used to set purchases, purchases returns, and other purchase-related accounts to zero (i.e., close these accounts), to replace the beginning inventory amount with the ending inventory amount in the inventory account, and to recognize cost of goods sold for the period.

To illustrate, Sonora determines its ending inventory to be $90,000. The company uses a periodic system, computes cost of goods sold and records AJE (g) as follows:

| g. *31 December 20X5* | | |
|---|---|---|
| Inventory (ending) | 90,000 | |
| Purchase returns | 2,000 | |
| Cost of goods sold (see below) | 117,000 | |
| Inventory (beginning) | | 75,000 |
| Purchases | | 130,000 |
| Freight on purchases | | 4,000 |

| Cost of Goods Sold Computation—*31 December 20X5* | | |
|---|---|---|
| Beginning inventory | | $ 75,000 |
| Add (from the current-year accounts): | | |
| Purchases | $130,000 | |
| Freight on purchases | 4,000 | |
| Purchase returns | (2,000) | |
| Net purchases | | 132,000 |
| Total goods available for sale | | $207,000 |
| Less: Ending inventory (from physical count) | | 90,000 |
| Cost of goods sold | | $117,000 |

Two sources of information contribute to entry (g): the unadjusted trial balance, from which several account balances are taken, and the physical inventory count indicating $90,000 of inventory on hand. *Alternatively, the accounts related to cost of goods sold may be left in the adjusted trial balance, untouched, and used in detail to create the financial statements. They would then be eliminated in closing entries.* Both approaches are widely used in practice and result in the same reported income and financial position. It is really a question of which method is preferred by a particular accountant and/or computerized reporting package. The closing entry approach is illustrated below in the discussion of Step 9, closing entries.

*Perpetual System* In a perpetual system, no AJE is needed to establish cost of goods sold because cost of goods sold is recorded as each sale is made. However, an AJE might be needed to correct errors or to recognize inventory losses due to theft and economic factors.

A perpetual inventory system maintains an inventory record for each item stocked. This record contains data on each purchase and issue. An up-to-date balance is maintained in the inventory account. The cost of each item purchased is debited to the inventory account. Suppose an item that sells for $300 is carried in inventory at a cost of $180. A sale of this item requires two entries:

| Cash (or accounts receivable) | 300 | |
|---|---|---|
| Sales revenue | | 300 |
| Cost of goods sold | 180 | |
| Inventory | | 180 |

In a perpetual inventory system, the balance in the inventory account and the balance in cost of goods sold should reflect all transactions to date. A physical count is done to verify the inventory balance. If the result of the physical count is a different inventory amount than that recorded, an adjusting entry to decrease or increase inventory is recorded, with the other side of the entry changing cost of goods sold.

*Income Tax Expense* The recognition of income tax expense, an accrual item, is often the final AJE. Many firms pay estimated income taxes monthly, necessitating an AJE at the end of the accounting period to record any additional taxes due. For simplicity, assume that Sonora pays its income tax once each year after the end of the full accounting period. The amounts in square brackets indicate the account balance in the unadjusted trial balance plus or minus the effects of AJEs, denoted by letter.

Assume that Sonora faces an average income tax rate of 40%, amortization expense equals tax amortization, and the loss from discontinued operations and all other expenses are fully tax deductible. AJE (h) recognizes the resulting $20,000 ($50,000 × 40%) income tax expense:

| h. 31 December 20X5 | | |
|---|---|---|
| Income tax expense | 20,000 | |
| Income tax payable | | 20,000 |

*Calculation of Pre-tax Income*
*For the Year Ended 31 December 20X5*

| Revenues: | | |
|---|---|---|
| Sales revenue | $325,200 | |
| Interest revenue [$500 + $100 (d)] | 600 | |
| Rent revenue [$1,800 − $600 (b)] | 1,200 | $327,000 |
| | | |
| Expenses: | | |
| Cost of goods sold (g) | 117,000 | |
| Selling expenses [$104,000 + $8,200 (e) + $1,200 (f)] | 113,400 | |
| General and administrative expenses [$23,600 + $200 (a) + $10,800 (e)] | 34,600 | |
| Interest expense [$2,500 + $500 (c)] | 3,000 | |
| Discontinued operations (pre-tax) | 9,000 | 277,000 |
| Pre-tax income | | $ 50,000 |
| Income tax expense ($50,000 × .4) | | $ 20,000 |

For simplicity, the entire income tax expense is recorded in one account. Sonora's income statement (Exhibit A-7), however, separates the $3,600 income tax reduction associated with the loss from discontinued operations ($9,000 × 40%) from income tax on income before the discontinued operation. This practice is called *intraperiod tax allocation*.

## Step 6: Prepare Adjusted Trial Balance

At this point in the cycle, the transaction journal entries and the AJEs have been journalized and posted, and an adjusted trial balance is prepared. The adjusted trial balance lists all the account balances that will appear in the financial statements (with the exception of retained earnings, which does not reflect the current year's net income or dividends). The purpose of the adjusted trial balance is to calculate adjusted balances, and then confirm debit-credit equality. Exhibit A-6 presents the adjusted trial balance for Sonora.

## EXHIBIT A-6

### SONORA LIMITED
### ADJUSTED TRIAL BALANCE
### 31 DECEMBER 20X5

31 December 20X5

| Account | Debit | Credit |
|---|---|---|
| Cash | $ 67,300 | |
| Accounts receivable | 45,000 | |
| Allowances for doubtful accounts | | $  2,200 |
| Notes receivable | 8,000 | |
| Interest receivable | 100 | |
| Inventory (31 December balance) | 90,000 | |
| Prepaid insurance | 400 | |
| Land | 8,000 | |
| Building | 160,000 | |
| Accumulated amortization, building | | 100,000 |
| Equipment | 91,000 | |
| Accumulated amortization, equipment | | 36,000 |
| Accounts payable | | 29,000 |
| Interest payable | | 500 |
| Rent collected in advance | | 600 |
| Income tax payable | | 20,000 |
| Bonds payable, 6% | | 50,000 |
| Common shares, no par, 15,000 shares | | 170,000 |
| Retained earnings (1 January balance) | | 41,500 |
| Dividends declared | 10,000 | |
| Sales revenue | | 325,200 |
| Interest revenue | | 600 |
| Rent revenue | | 1,200 |
| Cost of goods sold | 117,000 | |
| Selling expenses | 113,400 | |
| General and administrative expenses | 34,600 | |
| Interest expense | 3,000 | |
| Income tax expense | 20,000 | |
| Loss on discontinued operations | 9,000 | |
| Totals | $776,800 | $776,800 |

New accounts not appearing in the unadjusted trial balance emerge from the adjustment process, while other accounts disappear. For Sonora, the new accounts are interest receivable, interest payable, rent collected in advance, income tax payable, cost of goods sold, and income tax expense. AJE (g) eliminated the following accounts: purchases, freight on purchases, and purchase returns. Accounts with zero balances have not been listed, although some prefer to include these accounts to make the trial balance complete. The financial statements now can be prepared from the adjusted trial balance.

## Step 7: Prepare Financial Statements

The financial statements are the culmination of the accounting cycle. Financial statements can be produced for a period of any duration. However, monthly, quarterly, and annual statements are the most common.

The income statement, retained earnings statement, and balance sheet are prepared directly from the adjusted trial balance. The income statement is prepared first because net income must be known before the retained earnings statement and then the balance sheet can be completed. The temporary account balances are transferred to the income statement (except for dividends), and the permanent account balances (except for retained earnings) are transferred to the balance sheet. Exhibit A-7 illustrates Sonora's 20X5 income and retained earnings statements.

Total income tax expense ($20,000) in the income statement is allocated as follows: $23,600 to income before discontinued operations and $3,600 tax savings to the loss from discontinued operations.

The retained earnings statement explains the change in retained earnings for the period. Here, it is opening retained earnings, plus net income, less dividends declared. Dividends are a distribution of capital to shareholders. They are not an expense and do not belong on the income statement.

Exhibit A-8 illustrates the 20X5 balance sheet. The ending retained earnings balance is taken from the retained earnings statement rather than from the adjusted trial balance.

## EXHIBIT A-7

### SONORA LIMITED
### INCOME STATEMENT

For the year ended 31 December 20X5

| | | |
|---|---:|---:|
| Revenues: | | |
| Sales | $325,200 | |
| Interest | 600 | |
| Rent | 1,200 | |
| Total revenues | | $327,000 |
| Expenses: | | |
| Cost of goods sold | 117,000 | |
| Selling | 113,400 | |
| General and administrative | 34,600 | |
| Interest | 3,000 | |
| Total expenses before income tax | | 268,000 |
| Income before tax and discontinued operations | | 59,000 |
| Income tax on income before discontinued operations ($59,000 × 40%) | | 23,600 |
| Income before discontinued operations | | 35,400 |
| Loss from discontinued operations | 9,000 | |
| Less tax savings ($9,000 × 40%) | 3,600 | 5,400 |
| Net income | | $ 30,000 |

### SONORA LIMITED
### RETAINED EARNINGS STATEMENT

For the year ended 31 December 20X5

| | |
|---|---:|
| Retained earnings, 1 January 20X5 | $ 41,500 |
| Net income | 30,000 |
| | $ 71,500 |
| Less: dividend declared | 10,000 |
| Retained earnings, 31 December 20X5 | $ 61,500 |

## EXHIBIT A-8

### SONORA LIMITED
### BALANCE SHEET

At 31 December 20X5

*Assets*

Current assets:

| | | |
|---|---:|---:|
| Cash | | $ 67,300 |
| Accounts receivable | $ 45,000 | |
| Allowance for doubtful accounts | (2,200) | 42,800 |
| Notes receivable | | 8,000 |
| Interest receivable | | 100 |
| Inventory | | 90,000 |
| Prepaid insurance | | 400 |
| Total current assets | | 208,600 |

Capital assets:

| | | | |
|---|---:|---:|---:|
| Land | | 8,000 | |
| Building | $160,000 | | |
| Accumulated amortization, building | (100,000) | 60,000 | |
| Equipment | 91,000 | | |
| Accumulated amortization, equipment | (36,000) | 55,000 | |
| Total capital assets | | | 123,000 |
| Total assets | | | $331,600 |

*Liabilities*

Current liabilities:

| | | |
|---|---:|---:|
| Accounts payable | | $ 29,000 |
| Interest payable | | 500 |
| Rent collected in advance | | 600 |
| Income tax payable | | 20,000 |
| Total current liabilities | | 50,100 |

Long-term liabilities:

| | | |
|---|---:|---:|
| Bonds payable, 6% | | 50,000 |
| Total liabilities | | 100,100 |

*Shareholders' Equity*

Contributed capital:

| | | |
|---|---:|---:|
| Common shares, no par, 15,000 shares issued and outstanding | $170,000 | |
| Retained earnings | 61,500 | |
| Total shareholders' equity | | 231,500 |
| Total liabilities and shareholders' equity | | $331,600 |

## Step 8: Journalize and Post Closing Entries

Closing entries:

- Reduce to zero (close) the balances of temporary accounts related to earnings measurement and dividends;
- Are recorded in the general journal at the end of the accounting period; and
- Are posted to the ledger accounts.

Because net income is measured for a specific interval of time, the balances of the income statement accounts are reduced to zero at the end of each accounting period. Otherwise, these accounts would contain data from previous periods. Permanent accounts are not closed because they carry over to the next accounting period. The retained earnings account is the only permanent account involved in the closing process.

While some accountants prefer to close temporary accounts directly to retained earnings, it is quite common to use an account called "income summary" to accumulate the balances of income statement accounts in the closing entry process. The income summary is a temporary clearing account—an account used on a short-term basis for a specific purpose. The balances in expenses and losses are reduced to zero and transferred to the income summary by crediting each of those accounts and debiting income summary for the total. Revenues and gains are debited to close them, and the income summary account is credited.

This process leaves a net balance in the income summary account equal to net income (credit balance) or net loss (debit balance) for the period. The income summary account is then closed by transferring the net income amount to retained earnings. Sonora makes three closing entries to transfer 20X5 net income to retained earnings:

---

**31 December 20X5**

1. *To close the revenue and gain accounts to the income summary*

| | | |
|---|---:|---:|
| Sales revenue | 325,200 | |
| Interest revenue | 600 | |
| Rent revenue | 1,200 | |
|    Income summary | | 327,000 |

2. *To close the expense and loss accounts to the income summary*

| | | |
|---|---:|---:|
| Income summary | 297,000 | |
|    Cost of goods sold | | 117,000 |
|    Selling expenses | | 113,400 |
|    General and administrative expenses | | 34,600 |
|    Interest expense | | 3,000 |
|    Loss from discontinued operations | | 9,000 |
|    Income tax expense | | 20,000 |

3. *To close the income summary (i.e., transfer net income to retained earnings)*

| | | |
|---|---:|---:|
| Income summary | 30,000 | |
|    Retained earnings | | 30,000 |

4. *To close dividends to retained earnings*

| | | |
|---|---:|---:|
| Retained earnings | 10,000 | |
|    Dividends declared | | 10,000 |

---

After the first two closing entries are recorded and posted, the balance in the income summary equals net income ($30,000):

| **Income Summary** | | | |
|---|---:|---|---:|
| (2) | 297,000 | (1) | 327,000 |
| | | Balance | 30,000 |

The temporary accounts now have zero balances and are ready for the next period's accounting cycle. The third entry closes the income summary account and transfers net income to retained earnings. Finally, dividends declared is closed to retained earnings. The retained earnings account in the ledger now has a balance of $61,500, per the balance sheet.

**Alternative Approach for Inventories** Inventory-related accounts can be adjusted and closed in the closing process as an alternative to the AJE approach illustrated previously in AJE (g). If the closing entry alternative is used, the following two closing entries replace AJE (g) and the first two closing entries illustrated above:

| | | | |
|---|---|---:|---:|
| 1. | Inventory (ending) | 90,000 | |
| | Sales revenue | 325,200 | |
| | Interest revenue | 600 | |
| | Rent revenue | 1,200 | |
| | Purchase returns | 2,000 | |
| |    Income summary | | 419,000 |
| | | | |
| 2. | Income summary | 389,000 | |
| | Inventory (opening) | | 75,000 |
| | Purchases | | 130,000 |
| | Freight on purchases | | 4,000 |
| | Selling expenses | | 113,400 |
| | General and administrative expenses | | 34,600 |
| | Interest expense | | 3,000 |
| | Loss from discontinued operations | | 9,000 |
| | Income tax expense | | 20,000 |

Using this approach, inventory-related accounts are included with expenses and revenues for closing entry purposes. The net impact on the income summary account and, in turn, income and retained earnings is identical under both approaches. However, this approach does not isolate cost of goods sold in a separate account.

## Step 9: Prepare Post-Closing Trial Balance

A post-closing trial balance lists only the balances of the permanent accounts after the closing process is finished. The temporary accounts have balances of zero. This step is taken to check for debit-credit equality after the closing entries are posted. Firms with a large number of accounts find this a valuable checking procedure because the chance of error increases with the number of accounts and postings. The retained earnings account is now stated at the correct ending balance and is the only permanent account with a balance different from the one shown in the adjusted trial balance. Exhibit A-9 illustrates the post-closing trial balance.

## Step 10: Journalize and Post Reversing Journal Entries

Depending on the firm's accounting system and its accounting policies, **reversing journal entries (RJEs)** may be used to simplify certain journal entries in the next accounting period. RJEs are optional entries that:

- Are dated the first day of the next accounting period;
- Relate to a specific AJE;
- Use the same accounts and amounts as an AJE but with the debits and credits reversed; and
- Are posted to the ledger.

RJEs are appropriate only for AJEs that defer the recognition of revenue or expense items originally recorded under the expedient method, or entries that accrue revenue or expense items during the current period (for example, wages expense).

EXHIBIT A-9

## SONORA LIMITED
## POST-CLOSING TRIAL BALANCE

31 December 20X5

| Account | Debit | Credit |
|---|---|---|
| Cash | $ 67,300 | |
| Accounts receivable | 45,000 | |
| Allowance for doubtful accounts | | $ 2,200 |
| Notes receivable | 8,000 | |
| Interest receivable | 100 | |
| Inventory (31 December balance) | 90,000 | |
| Prepaid insurance | 400 | |
| Land | 8,000 | |
| Building | 160,000 | |
| Accumulated amortization, building | | 100,000 |
| Equipment | 91,000 | |
| Accumulated amortization, equipment | | 36,000 |
| Accounts payable | | 29,000 |
| Interest payable | | 500 |
| Rent collected in advance | | 600 |
| Income tax payable | | 20,000 |
| Bonds payable, 6% | | 50,000 |
| Common shares, no par, 15,000 shares | | 170,000 |
| Retained earnings (31 December balance) | | 61,500 |
| Totals | $469,800 | $469,800 |

*Thus, if a deferral or accrual AJE creates or increases an asset or liability, an RJE is appropriate.* RJEs are inappropriate for AJEs that adjust assets and liabilities recorded for cash flows preceding the recognition of revenues and expenses (the standard method) and for some other AJEs, such as reclassifications, error corrections, and estimations.

In the following examples, assume a 31 December year-end.

*Deferred item* Assume that on 1 November 20X5, $300 is paid in advance for three months' rent:

| | | | | |
|---|---|---|---|---|
| *1 November 20X5—originating entry* | | | | |
| Rent expense | | | 300 | |
| Cash | | | | 300 |
| *31 December 20X5—adjusting entry* | | | | |
| Prepaid rent | | | 100 | |
| Rent expense | | | | 100 |

| | **With Reversing Entry** | **Without Reversing Entry** |
|---|---|---|
| *1 January 20X6* | | |
| *Reversing entry:* Rent expense 100 | | |
|                Prepaid rent | 100 | |
| *20X6* | | |
| *Subsequent entry:* (No entry needed) | | Rent expense 100 |
| | |         Prepaid rent 100 |

With or without an RJE, rent expense recorded in 20X6 is $100. Use of the RJE, however, saves the cost and effort of reviewing the relevant accounts and source documents to determine the subsequent year's entry. The RJE makes the necessary adjustments to the accounts while the information used in making the AJE is available.

Now consider the standard method applied to the same example.

| | | |
|---|---|---|
| *1 November 20X5—originating entry* | | |
| Prepaid rent | 300 | |
|     Cash | | 300 |
| *31 December 20X5—adjusting entry* | | |
| Rent expense | 200 | |
|     Prepaid rent | | 200 |

An RJE is not appropriate. No purpose is served by reinstating (debiting) prepaid rent $200 because that amount has expired.

*Accrued item.* Assume that the last payroll for 20X5 is on 28 December. Wages earned through 28 December are included in this payroll. The next payroll period ends 4 January 20X6, at which time $2,800 of wages will be paid. Wages earned for the three-day period ending 31 December 20X5 are $1,500, which will be paid in 20X6. The following AJE is necessary to accrue these wages:

| *31 December 20X5—adjusting entry* | | | | |
|---|---|---|---|---|
| Wages expense | | 1,500 | | |
|     Wages payable | | | | 1,500 |

| | **With Reversing Entry** | | **Without Reversing Entry** | |
|---|---|---|---|---|
| *1 January 20X6* | | | | |
| *Reversing entry:* Wages payable 1,500 | | | | |
|     Wages expense | 1,500 | | | |
| *4 January 20X6* | | | | |
| *Subsequent entry:* Wages expense 2,800 | | Wages expense 1,300 | | |
|     Cash | 2,800 | Wages payable 1,500 | | |
| | | Cash | 2,800 | |

In this example, the RJE simplifies the subsequent payroll entry, which can now be recorded in a manner identical to all other payrolls. With or without reversing entries, total 20X6 wage expense recognized through 4 January 20X6 is $1,300. RJEs often create abnormal short-term account balances. In the above 1 January 20X6 entry, the RJE creates a credit balance in wages expense. The subsequent entry changes the net balance of wages expense to a $1,300 debit.

Some of Sonora's AJEs could be reversed: entry (b) for rent expense (expedient method—deferred item); entry (c) for interest expense (accrual); entry (d) for interest revenue (accrual); and perhaps entry (h) for income tax expense (accrual).

## SUBSIDIARY LEDGERS

Companies typically maintain both *control* and *subsidiary* ledger accounts. **Subsidiary ledgers** are often kept for accounts payable and accounts receivable, although any ledger account can be supported by a subsidiary ledger if size and complexity warrant.

*The sum of all account balances in a subsidiary ledger must equal the related control account balance in the general ledger.* To ensure that the control account and its subsidiary ledger are equal, frequent reconciliations are made. All posting must be complete, both to the control account and to the subsidiary ledger, before a reconciliation can be accomplished. Postings are made *in total* to the control account and *to individual accounts* in the subsidiary ledger. These postings are described in more depth in the next section.

To illustrate a reconciliation, refer ahead to the accounts receivable subsidiary ledger in Exhibit A-14. A reconciliation for accounts receivable control and the accounts receivable subsidiary ledger based on the information in Exhibit A-14 follows:

---

### RECONCILIATION OF ACCOUNTS RECEIVABLE SUBSIDIARY LEDGER

| At 31 January 20X5 | Amount |
|---|---|
| *Subsidiary ledger balances* | |
| 112.13 Adams Co. | $  980 |
| 112.42 Miller, J. B. | 196 |
| 112.91 XY Manufacturing Co. | 1,960 |
| Total | $3,136 |
| | |
| *General ledger balance* | |
| Accounts receivable control ($5,000 + $9,360 − $11,224) | $3,136 |

---

Subsidiary ledgers contain information that helps the company operate efficiently—individual account receivable and payable balances are essential information. In smaller companies, subsidiary ledgers can be maintained through a simple filing system. For example, a copy of a sales invoice that is not paid can be kept in a special file until the money is received. At any time, the outstanding receivables are equal to the total of the invoices in the file. The same can be done with accounts payable, if all unpaid bills are kept in an accounts payable file. The point is that formal accounting systems are made necessary by size and complexity, but simple methods in simple situations can be just as effective if efficiently operated.

## SPECIAL JOURNALS

Both *general journals* and *special journals* are used in many accounting systems. Even when extensive use is made of special journals, a need exists for a general journal to record the adjusting, closing, reversing, and correcting entries and those transactions that do not apply to any of the special journals. A general journal was illustrated in Exhibit A-3.

A special journal is designed to expedite the recording of similar transactions that occur frequently. Each special journal is constructed specifically to simplify the data-processing tasks involved in journalizing and posting those types of transactions. Special journals can be custom designed to meet the particular needs of the business. Commonly used special journals include:

1. *Sales journal* for recording only sales of merchandise on credit.

2. *Purchases journal* for recording only purchases of merchandise on credit.

3. *Cash receipts journal* for recording only cash receipts, including cash sales.

4. *Cash disbursements journal* for recording only cash payments, including cash purchases.

5. *Voucher system*, designed to replace the purchases journal and cash payments journal, composed of:

   a. A *voucher register* for recording only vouchers payable. A voucher payable is prepared for each cash payment regardless of purpose.

   b. A *cheque register* for recording all cheques written in payment of approved vouchers.

The special journals illustrated in this appendix carry page numbers preceded by letters indicating the journal name. The S in the page number of Exhibit A-10 denotes the sales journal, for example.

**Sales Journal**  This special journal is designed to record sales on account, which otherwise would be recorded as follows in a general journal:

| | | |
|---|---|---|
| *2 January 20X5* | | |
| Accounts receivable ($1,000 × 98%) | 980 | |
| Sales revenue | | 980 |
| (Credit sale to Adams Company; invoice price, $1,000; terms 2/10, n/30) | | |

The sales journal can accommodate any entry that involves a debit to accounts receivable and a credit to sales. However, this is the *only* entry it can record. If the debit is to cash, or notes receivable, another journal must be used. Exhibit A-10 illustrates a typical sales journal for credit sales. The above entry is shown as the first entry in 20X5. The amount of sale is recorded only once. Each entry in the sales journal records the same information found in the traditional debit-credit format.

Terms of 2/10, n/30 means that if the account is paid within 10 days after date of sale, a 2% cash discount is granted. The cash discount encourages early payment. If the bill is not paid within the 10-day discount period, the full amount must be paid. The account is past due at the end of 30 days. Receipt of $1,000 after the 10-day discount period does not increase sales revenue but means that the seller has earned finance revenue of $20 ($1,000 − $980). Hence, it is correct to record net sales revenue of $980. However, many companies prefer to record the *gross* sale, $1,000 in this example, because it is easier to focus on the amount of the invoice. Sales discounts are then recorded when the customer pays the net amount.

The posting of amounts from the sales journal to the general and subsidiary ledgers is simplified. The two phases in posting a sales journal are the following:

1. *Daily posting.* The amount of each credit sale is posted daily to the appropriate individual account in the accounts receivable subsidiary ledger. Posting is indicated by entering the account number in the posting reference column. For example, the number 112.13 entered in the posting reference column in Exhibit A-10 is the account number assigned to Adams Company and shows that $980 is posted as a debit to Adams Company in the subsidiary ledger. The number 112 is the general number used for accounts receivable (see Exhibit A-14).

## EXHIBIT A-10

Page S-23                          **SALES JOURNAL**

| Date 20X5 | Sales Invoice No. | Accounts Receivable (name) | Terms | Post. Ref. | Receivable and Sale Amount |
|---|---|---|---|---|---|
| 2 Jan. | 93 | Adams Co. | 2/10, n/30 | 112.13 | $ 980 |
| 3 | 94 | Sayre Corp. | 2/10, n/30 | 112.80 | 490 |
| 11 | 95 | Cope & Day Co. | net | 112.27 | 5,734 |
| 27 | 96 | XY Mfg. Co. | 2/10, n/30 | 112.91 | 1,960 |
| 30 | 97 | Miller, J. B. | 2/10, n/30 | 112.42 | 196 |
| 31 | — | Total | | | $9,360 |
| 31 | — | Posting | | | (112/500) |

**2.** *Monthly posting.* At the end of each month, the receivable and sale amount column is totalled. This total is posted to two accounts in the general ledger. In Exhibit A-10, the $9,360 total is posted as a debit to account no. 112 (accounts receivable control) and as a credit to account no. 500 (sales revenue). The T-accounts shown in Exhibit A-14 illustrate how these postings are reflected in both the general ledger and the subsidiary ledger. The two ledgers show the journal page from which each amount is posted.

**Purchases Journal** This special journal is designed to accommodate frequent purchases of merchandise on account. Again, there is only one entry that can go into this journal—a debit to purchases, and a credit to accounts payable. Other entries, including purchases for cash, go elsewhere. Consider the following entry, recorded in general journal format:

| | | |
|---|---|---|
| *3 January 20X5* | | |
| Purchases ($1,000 × .99) | 990 | |
|     Accounts payable (PT Mfg. Co.) | | 990 |
| (terms 1/20, n/30) | | |

Again note the use of net recording. The invoice is recorded at its net amount, after the 1% discount. Some companies prefer to record purchase invoices gross, and record purchase discounts taken when they record payment. Notice also that the entry assumes a periodic inventory. Under a perpetual inventory system, the debit would always be to the inventory account.

This entry is recorded as the first 20X5 entry in the purchases journal illustrated in Exhibit A-11. The accounting simplifications found in the sales journal are present in the purchases journal as well. Each amount is posted daily as a credit to the account of an individual creditor in the accounts payable subsidiary ledger. At the end of the month, the total of the purchases and payable amount column ($6,760 in Exhibit A-11), is posted to the general ledger as a debit to the purchases account (no. 612) and as a credit to the accounts payable control account (no. 210).

**Cash Receipts Journal** A special cash receipts journal is used to accommodate a large volume of cash receipts transactions. This journal can accommodate any entry that involves a debit to cash. Multiple sources of cash (the credits) are accommodated by designing several credit columns for recurring credits, and a miscellaneous accounts column for infrequent credits, as shown in Exhibit A-12. Space is also provided for the names of particular accounts receivable.

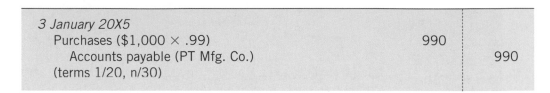

EXHIBIT A-11

Page P-6                                        **PURCHASES JOURNAL**

| Date 20X5 | Purchase Order No. | Accounts Payable (Name) | Terms | Posting Ref. | Purchases and Payable Amount |
|---|---|---|---|---|---|
| 3 Jan. | 41 | PT Mfg. Co. | 1/20, n/30 | 210.61 | $ 990 |
| 7 | 42 | Able Suppliers Ltd. | net | 210.12 | 150 |
| 31 | — | Total | — | — | 6,760 |
| 31 | — | Postings | — | — | (612/210) |

## EXHIBIT A-12

Page CR-19                          **CASH RECEIPTS JOURNAL**

| Date 20X5 | Explanation | Debit Cash | Account Title | Post. Ref. | Accounts Receivable | Sales Revenue | Misc. Accounts |
|---|---|---|---|---|---|---|---|
|  |  |  |  |  | **Credits** |  |  |
| 4 Jan. | Cash sales | $ 11,200 |  | — |  | $11,200 |  |
| 7 | On acct. | 4,490 | Sayre Corp. | 112.80 | $ 4,490 |  |  |
| 8 | Sale of land | 10,000 | Land | 123 |  |  | $ 4,000 |
|  |  |  | Gain on sale of land | 510 |  |  | 6,000 |
| 10 | On acct. | 1,000 | Adams Co. | 112.13 | 1,000 |  |  |
| 19 | Cash sales | 43,600 |  | — |  | 43,600 |  |
| 20 | On acct. | 5,734 | Cope & Day Co. | 112.27 | 5,734 |  |  |
| 31 | Totals | $116,224 |  | — | $11,224 | $71,000 | $34,000 |
| 31 | Posting | (101) |  | — | (112) | (500) | (NP)* |

*NP—not posted as one total because the individual amounts are posted as indicated in the posting reference column.*

During the month, each amount in the accounts receivable column is posted daily as a credit to an individual customer account in the accounts receivable subsidiary ledger. At the end of the month, the individual amounts in the miscellaneous account column are posted as credits to the appropriate general ledger accounts, and the totals for the cash, accounts receivable, and sales revenue columns are posted to the general ledger as indicated by the posting reference. The total of the miscellaneous accounts column is not posted because it consists of changes in different accounts. However, this column is totalled to ascertain overall debit-credit equality.

**Cash Disbursements Journal** Most companies use some form of a cash disbursements journal, which is also sometimes called a cheque register. This journal can accommodate any entry that involves a credit to cash, and has columns for the common debits and a miscellaneous debits column to make it flexible. Exhibit A-13 illustrates a typical cash disbursements journal. Journalizing and posting follow the same procedures explained for the cash receipts journal.

**The General Journal** Special journals can be used to record common entries, but there will always be entries that do not fit the format for any special journal and must be recorded in general journal format. Adjusting and reversing entries are prime examples, but unusual operating transactions will also be recorded in this format. The general journal is an essential element of accounting record keeping.

**Voucher Systems** Voucher systems are designed to enhance internal control over cash disbursements. A voucher is a document that describes a liability and lists information about the creditor, a description of the good or service received, authorizing signatures, and other details of the transaction, including invoice number, terms, amount due, and due date. In a voucher system, every transaction requiring payment by cheque begins with an invoice or other document that supplies information for completing a voucher.

**EXHIBIT A-13**

Page CD-31

## CASH DISBURSEMENTS JOURNAL

| Date 20X5 | Cheque No. | Explanation | Credit Cash | Account Name | Post. Ref. | Debits Accounts Payable | Purchases | Misc. Accounts |
|---|---|---|---|---|---|---|---|---|
| 2 Jan. | 141 | Pur. mdse. | $ 3,000 | | — | | $ 3,000 | |
| 10 | 142 | On acct. | 990 | PT Mfg. Co. | 210.61 | $ 990 | | |
| 15 | 143 | Jan. rent | 660 | Rent exp. | 1300 | | | $ 660 |
| 16 | 144 | Pur. mdse. | 1,810 | | | | 1,810 | |
| 31 | — | Totals | $98,400 | | — | $5,820 | $90,980 | $1,600 |
| 31 | — | Posting | (101) | | — | (210) | (612) | (NP) |

Together, the voucher, purchase order, receiving report, and invoice form a packet of information that must be complete before a cash disbursement can be made. All authorizations must be indicated. Verification of amounts and calculations are part of the payment authorization process. Often, several departments, including the internal audit and accounting departments, are required to authorize a large cash payment.

The completed voucher is the basis for an accounting entry in a special journal called the voucher register. The voucher register is not restricted to purchases. Before payment is made, the authorized voucher is recorded in the voucher register. Exhibit A-15 illustrates an abbreviated page from a voucher register.

A new account, vouchers payable, is used to record all routine liabilities. This new account replaces accounts payable and other payables used for routine payments. When a voucher is recorded in the voucher payable credit column, it reflects the amount of the liability. The account debited reflects the good or service received. Unlike the voucher register shown in Exhibit A-15, most voucher registers have many debit columns for speedy recording of repetitive cash payments of the same type. The total of the vouchers payable column is posted to the vouchers payable control. The cheque number and date paid do not appear in the voucher register until a cheque is issued and payment is made to the payee. Although a voucher is prepared for each item, one cheque can be issued for the payment of several vouchers to the same creditor.

Unpaid vouchers are placed into a file pending payment and are typically filed by due date. It is important that payments be initiated within cash discount periods to obtain the lowest possible price for merchandise purchases. The unpaid voucher file is the subsidiary ledger in a voucher system.

When a voucher becomes due, it is sent by the accounting department to a person authorized to issue cheques. After a review of the authorization on the voucher is made, a cheque is prepared for the correct amount. The paid voucher is sent back to the accounting department, which enters the cheque number and payment into the voucher register. Information from the voucher is also entered in the cheque register illustrated in Exhibit A-16.

The total of the amount column in the cheque register is posted to the vouchers payable control account (dr.) and to the cash account (cr.). The paid voucher is retained to substantiate cash payments and for audit trail purposes. The voucher register and cheque register replace the purchases and cash payments journals.

## GENERAL LEDGER AND SUBSIDIARY LEDGER GENERAL LEDGER (PARTIAL)

### General Ledger (Partial)

**Cash**                                                                 Acct. 101

| 20X5 | | | 20X5 | | |
|---|---|---|---|---|---|
| 1 Jan. | Balance | 18,700 | 31 Jan. | CD-31 | 98,400 |
| 31 | CR-19 | 116,224 | | | |

**Accounts Receivable Control**                                          Acct. 112

| 20X5 | | | 20X5 | | |
|---|---|---|---|---|---|
| 1 Jan. | Balance | 5,000 | 31 Jan. | CR-19 | 11,224 |
| 31 | S-23 | 9,360 | | | |

**Sales Revenue**                                                        Acct. 500

| | | | 20X5 | | |
|---|---|---|---|---|---|
| | | | 31 Jan. | S-23 | 9,360 |
| | | | 31 | CR-19 | 71,000 |

### Subsidiary Ledger for Accounts Receivable (Acct. No. 112)

| Date 20X5 | Post Ref. | Explanation | Debit | Credit | Balance |
|---|---|---|---|---|---|
| **Adams Company—Acct. No. 112.13** | | | | | |
| 1 Jan. | | Balance | | | 1,000 |
| 2 | S-23 | | 980 | | 1,980 |
| 10 | CR-19 | | | 1,000 | 980 |
| **Cope & Day Company—Acct. No. 112.27** | | | | | |
| 11 Jan. | S-23 | Balance | 5,734 | | 5,734 |
| 20 | CR-19 | | | 5,734 | 0 |
| **Miller, J. B.—Acct. No. 112.42** | | | | | |
| 30 Jan. | S-23 | Balance | 196 | | 196 |
| **Sayre Corporation—Acct. No. 112.80** | | | | | |
| 1 Jan. | | Balance | | | 4,000 |
| 3 | S-23 | | 490 | | 4,490 |
| 7 | CR-19 | | | 4,490 | 0 |
| **XY Manufacturing Company—Acct. No. 112.91** | | | | | |
| 27 Jan. | S-23 | | 1,960 | | 1,960 |

---

### EXHIBIT A-15

Page V-64

## VOUCHER REGISTER

| Date | Voucher Number | Payee | (Entered Later) Date Paid | (Entered Later) Cheque No. | Voucher Payable Credit | Account Debited (Multiple Columns) |
|------|---------------|-------|-----------|------------|------------|------------|
| 1 Jan. 20X5 | 1 | Crowell Co. | 2 Jan. 20X5 | 141 | $3,000 | Purchases |
| 3 | 2 | PT Mfg. Co. | 10 Jan. 20X5 | 142 | 990 | Purchases |
| 9 | 3 | Williams Co. | 15 Jan. 20X5 | 143 | 660 | Rent Expense |

---

## WORKSHEETS

A worksheet is a multicolumn work space that provides an organized format for performing several end-of-period accounting cycle steps and for preparing financial statements before posting AJEs. It also provides evidence, or an audit trail, of an organized and structured accounting process that can be more easily reviewed than other methods of analysis.

*Use of a worksheet is always optional.* The worksheet is not part of the basic accounting records. Worksheets assist with only a portion of the accounting cycle. Formal AJEs are recorded in the accounts in addition to those entered on the worksheet.

### Illustration of the Worksheet Approach

Exhibit A-17 illustrates the completed worksheet for Sonora Limited, the company used in this appendix to present the accounting cycle. The worksheet has a debit and a credit column for each of the following: unadjusted trial balance, AJEs, adjusted trial balance, income statement, retained earnings statement, and balance sheet. The worksheet is prepared in four steps:

**Step 1** *Enter the unadjusted trial balance in the first set of columns of the worksheet by inserting the year-end balances of all ledger accounts.*

- The inventory and retained earnings balances are the beginning-of-year balances because no transactions have affected these accounts.

**Step 2** *Enter the adjusting entries.*

- The lowercase letters refer to the same AJEs discussed in this appendix for Sonora Limited.

---

### EXHIBIT A-16

## CHEQUE REGISTER

| Date | Payee | Voucher Number | Cheque Number | Vouchers Payable Dr. and Cash Cr. |
|------|-------|---------------|---------------|-----------------|
| 2 Jan. 20X5 | Crowell Co. | 1 | 141 | $3,000 |
| 10 | PT Mfg. Co. | 2 | 142 | 990 |
| 15 | Williams Co. | 3 | 143 | 660 |

## EXHIBIT A-17

## COMPLETED WORKSHEET FOR SONORA LTD.

| Account | Unadjusted Trial Balance Debit | Unadjusted Trial Balance Credit | Adjusting Entries Debit | Adjusting Entries Credit | Adjusted Trial Balance Debit | Adjusted Trial Balance Credit | Income Statement Debit | Income Statement Credit | Retained Earnings Statement Debit | Retained Earnings Statement Credit | Balance Sheet Debit | Balance Sheet Credit |
|---|---|---|---|---|---|---|---|---|---|---|---|---|
| Cash | 67,300 | | | | 67,300 | | | | | | 67,300 | |
| Notes receivable | 8,000 | | | | 8,000 | | | | | | 8,000 | |
| Accounts receivable | 45,000 | | | | 45,000 | | | | | | 45,000 | |
| Allowance for doubtful accounts | | 1,000 | | (f) 1,200 | | 2,200 | | | | | | 2,200 |
| Interest receivable | | | (d) 100 | | 100 | | | | | | 100 | |
| Inventory (periodic) | 75,000 | | (g) 90,000 | (g) 75,000 | 90,000 | | | | | | 90,000 | |
| Prepaid insurance | 600 | | | (a) 200 | 400 | | | | | | 400 | |
| Land | 8,000 | | | | 8,000 | | | | | | 8,000 | |
| Building | 160,000 | | | | 160,000 | | | | | | 160,000 | |
| Accumulated amortization, building | | 90,000 | | (e) 10,000 | | 100,000 | | | | | | 100,000 |
| Equipment | 91,000 | | | | 91,000 | | | | | | 91,000 | |
| Accumulated amortization, equipment | | 27,000 | | (e) 9,000 | | 36,000 | | | | | | 36,000 |
| Accounts payable | | 29,000 | | | | 29,000 | | | | | | 29,000 |
| Interest payable | | | | (c) 500 | | 500 | | | | | | 500 |
| Rent collected in advance | | 500 | | (b) 600 | | 600 | | | | | | 600 |
| Bonds payable, 6% | | 50,000 | | | | 50,000 | | | | | | 50,000 |
| Common shares, no par, 15,000 shares | | 170,000 | | | | 170,000 | | | | | | 170,000 |
| Retained earnings | | 41,500 | | | | 41,500 | | | | 41,500 | | |
| Dividends declared | 10,000 | | | | 10,000 | | | | 10,000 | | | |
| Sales revenue | | 325,200 | | | | 325,200 | | 325,200 | | | | |
| Rent revenue | | 1,800 | (b) 600 | | | 1,200 | | 1,200 | | | | |
| Purchases | 130,000 | | | (g) 130,000 | | | | | | | | |
| Freight on purchases | 4,000 | | | (g) 4,000 | | | | | | | | |
| Purchase returns | | 2,000 | (g) 2,000 | | | | | | | | | |
| Cost of goods sold | | | (g) 117,000 | | 117,000 | | 117,000 | | | | | |
| Selling expenses | 104,000 | | (e) 8,200 (f) 1,200 | | 113,400 | | 113,400 | | | | | |
| General and administrative expenses | 23,600 | | (a) 200 (e) 10,800 | | 34,600 | | 34,600 | | | | | |
| Interest expense | 2,500 | | (c) 500 | | 3,000 | | 3,000 | | | | | |
| Loss on discontinued operations | 9,000 | | | | 9,000 | | 9,000 | | | | | |
| Totals | 738,000 | 738,000 | 230,600 | 230,600 | 756,800 | 756,800 | 277,000 | 327,000 | | | | |
| Income tax expense | | | (h) 20,000 | | 20,000 | | 20,000 | | | | | |
| Income tax payable | | | | (h) 20,000 | | 20,000 | | | | | | 20,000 |
| | | | 20,000 | 20,000 | 776,800 | 776,800 | 297,000 | 327,000 | | | | |
| Net income to retained earnings | | | | | | | 30,000 | | | 30,000 | | |
| Retained earnings to balance sheet | | | | | | | | | 61,500 | | | 61,500 |
| Totals | | | | | | | | | 71,500 | 71,500 | 469,800 | 469,800 |

- The worksheet AJEs are facilitating entries only and are not formally recorded in the general journal at this point. If a new account is created by an AJE, it is inserted in its normal position or at the bottom of the worksheet.
- Determine income tax expense and payable. (Sonora's tax computation was illustrated earlier.) Enter the accounts and the amounts in the AJE columns. Income tax expense (entry (h)) is positioned below the totals of the AJE columns because this reflects its sequence in the adjustment process.

**Step 3** *Cross-add.*

- Enter the adjusted trial balance by adding or subtracting across the unadjusted trial balance sheet columns and AJE columns, for each account. For example, the adjusted balance of the allowance for doubtful accounts is the sum of its unadjusted balance ($1,000) and the $1,200 increase from AJE (f).
- The inventory account now displays ending inventory, purchases and related accounts have zero balances, and cost of goods sold has a positive balance to show the activity for the year.
- Confirm the debit-credit equality of all totals.

**Step 4** *Extend the adjusted trial balance amounts to the financial statements; complete the worksheet.*

- Each account in the adjusted trial balance is extended to one of the three sets of remaining debit-credit columns. Temporary accounts are sorted to the income statement columns (revenues to the credit column, expenses to the debit column). Permanent accounts are sorted to the balance sheet columns except for the beginning balance in retained earnings, which is extended to the retained earnings columns. Dividends go in the retained earnings columns.
- Total the income statement columns before income tax expense. Pre-tax income is the difference between the debit and credit column totals. A net credit represents income; a net debit represents a loss. For Sonora, pre-tax income is $50,000 ($327,000 − $277,000). Next, determine net income after taxes by extending the income tax expense amount ($20,000) into the debit column and again totalling the columns. Net income is the difference between the columns, equalling $30,000 for Sonora ($327,000 − $297,000).
- Next, add a line description (net income to retained earnings) and enter the $30,000 net income amount as a balancing value in the income statement columns: positive net income is a debit balancing value; negative income is a credit. Then complete this entry by recording $30,000 in the credit column under the retained earnings columns. (Positive net income is a credit entry, and negative income is a debit entry.)
- Total the retained earnings columns and enter a balancing amount (the ending retained earnings balance) in the appropriate column to achieve debit-credit equality. For Sonora, the balancing amount is a $61,500 debit. Add a line description (retained earnings to balance sheet) and enter the balancing amount into the appropriate balance sheet column.
- Total the balance sheet columns and confirm debit-credit equality.

The worksheet is now complete, and the financial statements are prepared directly from the last three sets of worksheet columns. The formal AJEs are then journalized and posted.

**Combined Version** To save space, the retained earnings and balance sheet columns can be combined. If this is done, the opening retained earnings account and dividends are entered in the balance sheet columns and net income is included at the bottom of the balance sheet columns to balance the worksheet.

## SUMMARY OF KEY POINTS

1. The AIS provides information for daily management information needs and for preparation of financial statements.

2. There are seven basic types of accounts. The balance sheet discloses the balances of the permanent accounts, which include assets, liabilities, and owners' equity accounts. The income statement discloses the pre-closing balances of most temporary accounts, which include revenues, gains, expenses, and losses.

3. Transactions are recorded in a double-entry system, where each transactions changes two or more accounts. Debits to assets, expenses, and losses increase those accounts. Credits to liabilities, owners' equity, revenues, and gains increase those accounts.

4. There are 10 steps in the accounting cycle that culminate in the financial statements. Refer to Exhibit A-2.

5. AJEs are required under accrual accounting to complete the measurement and recording of changes in resources and obligations.

6. RJEs are optional entries, dated at the beginning of the accounting period, that reverse certain AJEs from the previous period and are used to facilitate subsequent journal entries.

7. Subsidiary ledgers are used to maintain records on the component elements of ledger control accounts.

8. Special journals are used to record repetitive entries, such as sales, purchases, cash receipts, and cash disbursements. A general journal is used to record entries that do not fit into special journals. A voucher register may replace a purchases journal.

9. A worksheet may be used to organize the adjustment and financial statement preparation phases of the accounting cycle.

## KEY TERMS

accounting identity, 653
accounting information system (AIS), 655
adjusting journal entries (AJEs), 660
contra account, 664
debit-credit convention, 653
double-entry system, 653
expedient recording method, 661
financial statement, 654
general journal, 657
general ledger, 658
journal, 657
nominal accounts, 653
non-reciprocal transfer, 656

periodic inventory system, 659
permanent accounts, 653
perpetual inventory system, 659
posting, 658
real accounts, 653
reciprocal transfer, 656
reversing journal entries, 671
special journal, 657
standard recording method, 661
subsidiary ledger, 673
T-account, 654
temporary accounts, 653
transactions, 656

## REVIEW PROBLEM

Bucknell Company developed its unadjusted trial balance dated 31 December 20X5, which appears below. Bucknell uses the expedient recording method whenever possible, adjusts its accounts once per year, records all appropriate RJEs, and adjusts its periodic inventory-related accounts in an AJE. Ignore income taxes.

### BUCKNELL COMPANY
### UNADJUSTED TRIAL BALANCE

| 31 December 20X5 | Debit | Credit |
|---|---:|---:|
| Cash | $ 40,000 | |
| Accounts receivable | 60,000 | |
| Allowance for doubtful accounts | | $ 6,000 |
| Inventory | 90,000 | |
| Equipment | 780,000 | |
| Accumulated amortization | | 100,000 |
| Land | 150,000 | |
| Accounts payable | | 22,000 |
| Notes payable, 8%, due 1 April 20X10 | | 200,000 |
| Common shares, no-par, 60,000 shares | | 400,000 |
| Retained earnings | | 50,000 |
| Sales revenue (all on account) | | 900,000 |
| Subscription revenue | | 24,000 |
| Purchases | 250,000 | |
| Rent expense | 60,000 | |
| Interest expense | 12,000 | |
| Selling expense | 40,000 | |
| Insurance expense | 30,000 | |
| Wages expense | 110,000 | |
| General and administrative expense | 80,000 | |
| Totals | $1,702,000 | $1,702,000 |

*Additional information:*

a. Ending inventory by physical count is $70,000.

b. The equipment has a total estimated useful life of 14 years and an estimated residual value of $80,000. Bucknell uses straight-line amortization and treats amortization expense as a general and administrative expense.

c. Bad debt expense for 20X5 is estimated to be 1% of sales.

d. The note payable requires interest to be paid semi-annually, every 1 October and 1 April.

e. $5,000 of wages were earned in December but not recorded or paid.

f. The rent expense represents a payment made on 2 January 20X5, for two years' rent (20X5 and 20X6).

g. The insurance expense represents payment made for a one-year policy, paid 30 June 20X5. Coverage began on that date.

h. The subscription revenue represents cash received from several university libraries for an 18-month subscription to a journal published by Bucknell. The subscription period began 1 July 20X5.

**Required:**

1. Record the required AJEs.

2. Prepare the adjusted trial balance.

3. Prepare the income statement and a balance sheet for 20X5.

4. Prepare closing entries.

5. Prepare RJEs.

# REVIEW PROBLEM—SOLUTION

*Requirement 1*

a. Inventory (ending) ......................................... 70,000

   Cost of goods sold ......................................... 270,000

      Purchases ......................................... 250,000

      Inventory (beginning) ......................................... 90,000

b. General and administrative expense

   ($780,000 − $80,000)/14 ......................................... 50,000

      Accumulated amortization ......................................... 50,000

c. Bad debt expense (.01 × $900,000) ......................................... 9,000

      Allowance for doubtful accounts ......................................... 9,000

d. Interest expense ($200,000 × .08 × 3/12). ......................................... 4,000

      Interest payable ......................................... 4,000

e. Wages expense ......................................... 5,000

      Wages payable ......................................... 5,000

f. Prepaid rent ($60,000 × 1/2) ......................................... 30,000

      Rent expense ......................................... 30,000

g. Prepaid insurance ($30,000 × 6/12) ......................................... 15,000

      Insurance expense ......................................... 15,000

h. Subscription revenue ($24,000 × 12/18) ......................................... 16,000

      Unearned subscriptions ......................................... 16,000

*Requirement 2*

## BUCKNELL COMPANY
## ADJUSTED TRIAL BALANCE

| 31 December 20X5 | Debit | Credit |
|---|---|---|
| Cash | $ 40,000 | |
| Accounts receivable | 60,000 | |
| Allowance for doubtful accounts | | $ 15,000 |
| Prepaid rent | 30,000 | |
| Prepaid insurance | 15,000 | |
| Inventory | 70,000 | |
| Equipment | 780,000 | |
| Accumulated amortization | | 150,000 |
| Land | 150,000 | |
| Accounts payable | | 22,000 |
| Interest payable | | 4,000 |
| Wages payable | | 5,000 |
| Unearned subscriptions | | 16,000 |
| Notes payable, 8%, due 1 April 20X10 | | 200,000 |
| Common shares, no-par, 60,000 shares | | 400,000 |
| Retained earnings | | 50,000 |
| Sales revenue | | 900,000 |
| Subscription revenue | | 8,000 |
| Cost of goods sold | 270,000 | |
| Rent expense | 30,000 | |
| Interest expense | 16,000 | |
| Selling expense | 40,000 | |
| Insurance expense | 15,000 | |
| Wages expense | 115,000 | |
| Bad debt expense | 9,000 | |
| General and administrative expense | 130,000 | |
| Totals | $1,770,000 | $1,770,000 |

*Requirement 3*

## BUCKNELL COMPANY
## INCOME STATEMENT

For the year ended 31 December 20X5

| | | |
|---|---:|---:|
| Revenues: | | |
| Sales revenue | $900,000 | |
| Subscription revenue | 8,000 | |
| Total revenue | | $908,000 |
| | | |
| Expenses: | | |
| Cost of goods sold | 270,000 | |
| Rent expense | 30,000 | |
| Interest expense | 16,000 | |
| Selling expense | 40,000 | |
| Insurance expense | 15,000 | |
| Wages expense | 115,000 | |
| Bad debt expense | 9,000 | |
| General and administrative expense | 130,000 | |
| Total expenses | | 625,000 |
| Net income | | $283,000 |

## BUCKNELL COMPANY
## BALANCE SHEET

31 December 20X5

| | | | |
|---|---:|---:|---:|
| *Assets* | | | |
| Current assets | | | |
| Cash | | $ 40,000 | |
| Accounts receivable | $ 60,000 | | |
| Allowance for doubtful accounts | (15,000) | 45,000 | |
| Inventory | | 70,000 | |
| Prepaid rent | | 30,000 | |
| Prepaid insurance | | 15,000 | |
| Non-current assets | | | $200,000 |
| Equipment | 780,000 | | |
| Accumulated amortization | (150,000) | 630,000 | |
| Land | | 150,000 | 780,000 |
| Total assets | | | $980,000 |
| | | | |
| *Liabilities* | | | |
| Current liabilities | | | |
| Accounts payable | | $ 22,000 | |
| Interest payable | | 4,000 | |
| Wages payable | | 5,000 | |
| Unearned subscriptions | | 16,000 | $ 47,000 |
| Non-current liabilities | | | |
| Notes payable, 8%, due 1 April 20X10 | | | 200,000 |
| Total liabilities | | | $247,000 |
| Shareholders' Equity | | | |
| Common shares, no-par, | | | |
| 60,000 shares outstanding | | 400,000 | |
| Retained earnings | | 333,000* | |
| Total owners' equity | | | 733,000 |
| Total liabilities and owners' equity | | | $980,000 |

*$50,000 + $283,000

*Requirement 4*

| | | |
|---|---:|---:|
| Sales revenue | 900,000 | |
| Subscription revenue | 8,000 | |
|    Income summary | | 908,000 |
| Income summary | 625,000 | |
|    Cost of goods sold | | 270,000 |
|    Rent expense | | 30,000 |
|    Interest expense | | 16,000 |
|    Selling expense | | 40,000 |
|    Insurance expense | | 15,000 |
|    Wages expense | | 115,000 |
|    Bad-debt expense | | 9,000 |
|    General and administrative expense | | 130,000 |
| Income summary | 283,000 | |
|    Retained earnings | | 283,000 |

*Requirement 5*

| | | |
|---|---:|---:|
| Interest payable | 4,000 | |
|    Interest expense | | 4,000 |
| Wages payable | 5,000 | |
|    Wages expense | | 5,000 |
| Rent expense | 30,000 | |
|    Prepaid rent | | 30,000 |
| Insurance expense | 15,000 | |
|    Prepaid insurance | | 15,000 |
| Unearned subscriptions | 16,000 | |
|    Subscription revenue | | 16,000 |

# ASSIGNMENTS

★ **A-1 Journalize Transactions:** Rivers Company, which uses a perpetual inventory system, recorded the following transactions in the month of August:

a. Bought merchandise on credit, $395,600.
b. Borrowed an additional $150,000 from the bank.
c. Sold merchandise on account, $184,800. These goods had a cost of $110,900.
d. Cash sales, $414,900. These goods had a cost of $248,200.
e. Paid $92,800 for operating expenses.
f. Collected $146,800 from customers on account.
g. Bought automotive equipment, $46,200; paid $8,000 in cash and borrowed the rest.
h. Paid for $272,800 of the goods bought on credit in (a), plus $23,600 from last month's outstanding bills.
i. Paid dividends to common shareholders, $9,000.
j. Paid wages of $44,200.
k. Paid $8,900 in interest to the bank.

**Required:**

1. Journalize each of the above transactions in general journal form.
2. Indicate in which special journal each transaction would normally be recorded, assuming that a company keeps purchases (inventory purchases), sales, cash receipts, cash disbursements,

and general journals. For this company, the cash receipts and sales journals are designed to allow recording of cost of goods sold for the perpetual inventory system.

★★ **A-2 Journalize Transactions and Adjustments; Valuation:** Zfind Corporation reports the following in the month of April:

a. Issued 17,000 no-par common shares for cash, $68,000.

b. Issued 15,000 no-par common shares for a piece of used equipment with an appraised value of $52,000. The equipment had an original cost of $76,000 to the seller three years ago. The net book value (cost less accumulated depreciation) on the books of the seller was $42,900 on the date of sale.

c. Bought land with an appraised value of $70,000. An 8%, three-year note payable was issued in the amount of $50,000, and $20,000 was paid in cash.

d. Bought office supplies on account, $1,200. A balance sheet account is debited.

e. Hired three employees at the beginning of the month. All employees are paid on a monthly basis. Monthly salaries for the three will amount to $8,000. (Two will be paid $3,000 per month each, and one will be paid $2,000 per month.)

f. Three months' rent is paid in advance. The lease calls for $1,000 of rent per month. A balance sheet account is debited.

g. Goods for resale in the amount of $120,000 are bought. Twenty percent of the price is paid in cash, and the rest is on account. These goods are priced to sell at $266,000.

h. Received an order from a customer for goods worth $50,000. The goods will be shipped in the next week (see (j)).

i. Miscellaneous operating expenses are paid in the amount of $14,400, cash.

j. Goods are delivered to customers and they are billed, on account, $245,000. The order, in (h) above, is included in this total. The goods delivered to the customers cost $110,000. There are still goods that cost $10,000, with a retail value of $21,000, in inventory.

k. One month has gone by, and monthly rent expense is recorded.

l. Employee salaries for one month are paid.

m. The Board of Directors declares, but does not pay, a dividend in the amount of $13,600.

n. Office supplies on hand at year-end, per physical count, $400.

o. Goods purchased on account in (g) above are paid for in full.

p. Eighty percent of the accounts receivable from customers, as recorded in (j) above, are received.

**Required:**

1. Journalize the transactions and events listed above. If no journal entry is needed, write "no entry." Zfind uses a perpetual inventory system. If there is a choice of value to use, justify your choice.

2. Which entries recorded are transactions, and which are adjustments? Explain.

★★ **A-3 Journalize and Post; Unadjusted Trial Balance:** The following selected transactions were completed during 20X5 by Marlon Corporation, a retailer of Scandinavian furniture:

a. Issued 60,000 shares of its own no-par common shares for $16.50 per share and received cash in full.

b. Borrowed $600,000 cash on a 9%, one-year note, interest payable at maturity on 30 April 20X6.

c. Purchased equipment for use in operating the business at a net cash cost of $588,000; paid in full.

d. Purchased merchandise for resale at a cash cost of $560,000; paid cash. Assume a periodic inventory system; therefore, debit purchases.

e. Purchased merchandise for resale on credit terms 2/10, n/60. The merchandise will cost $19,600 if paid within 10 days; after 10 days, the payment will be $20,000. The company plans to take the discount; therefore, this purchase is recorded net of discount.

f. Sold merchandise for $180,000; collected $110,000 cash, and the balance is due in one month.

g. Paid $120,000 cash for operating expenses.

h. Paid three-quarters of the balance for the merchandise purchased in (e) within five days; the balance remains unpaid and the discount has been lost.

i. Collected 50% of the balance due on the sale in (f); the remaining balance is uncollected.

j. Paid cash for an insurance premium, $3,600; the premium is for two years' coverage (debit prepaid insurance).

k. Purchased a tract of land for a future building for company operations, $196,000 cash.

l. Paid damages to a customer who was injured on the company premises, $80,000 cash.

**Required:**

1. Enter transactions in a general journal; use J1 for the first journal page number. Use the letter of the transaction in place of the date.

2. Set up appropriate T-accounts and post the journal entries. Use posting reference numbers in your posting. Assign each T-account an appropriate title, and number each account in balance sheet order followed by the income statement accounts; start with Cash, No. 101.

3. Prepare an unadjusted trial balance.

---

★ **A-4 Trial Balance Errors:** The trial balance for Nguyen Repairs Limited as at 31 July 20X8 does not balance because of a number of errors. These errors include copying errors, posting errors, and so on, as described below.

## NGUYEN REPAIRS LTD.

### Trial Balance as of 31 July 20X8

| | Debit | Credit |
|---|---|---|
| Cash | $ 5,800 | |
| Accounts receivable | 12,376 | |
| Supplies | 3,520 | |
| Prepaid insurance | 896 | |
| Equipment | 27,720 | |
| Notes payable | | $ 6,000 |
| Accounts payable | | 2,280 |
| Common shares | | 10,200 |
| Retained earnings | | 3,600 |
| Dividends | 800 | |
| Sales | | 59,060 |
| Wages expense | 18,600 | |
| Rent expense | 4,400 | |
| Advertising expense | 324 | |
| Utilities expense | 980 | |
| Totals | $75,416 | $81,140 |

Errors noted:

a. As the result of a copying error when listing the trial balance, the balance of cash was overstated by $400.

b. A cash receipt of $1,280 was posted as a debit to cash $1,820.

c. A credit of $360 to accounts receivable was not posted.

d. A return of $840 of defective supplies was erroneously posted as a $480 credit to supplies.

e. An insurance policy, acquired at year-end for the next fiscal year, with a cost of $4,400 was posted as a credit to prepaid insurance.

f. The balance of notes payable was understated by $800.

g. A debit of $1,040 in accounts payable was overlooked when determining the balance of the account.

h. A debit of $800 for a dividend was posted as a credit to the common share account.

i. The balance of $1,324 in advertising expense was entered as $324 in the trial balance.

j. Miscellaneous expense, with a balance of $1,250, was omitted from the trial balance.

k. A credit to sales of $2,753 was posted as a debit.

**Required:**

Prepare a corrected trial balance.

---

 **A-5 Adjusting Entries:** Rivers Corporation manufactures zippers in Quebec. It adjusts and closes its accounts each 31 December. The following situations require adjusting entries at the current year-end:

a. Machine A is to be depreciated for the full year. It cost $90,000, and the estimated useful life is five years, with an estimated residual value of $10,000. Use straight-line depreciation.

b. Credit sales for the current year amounted to $160,000. The estimated bad debt loss rate on credit sales is 0.5%.

c. Property taxes for the current year have not been recorded or paid. A statement for the calendar year was received near the end of December for $4,000; if paid after 1 February in the next year, a 10% penalty is assessed.

d. Office supplies that cost $800 were purchased during the year and debited to office supplies inventory. The inventories of these supplies on hand were $200 at the end of the prior year and $300 at the end of the current year.

e. Rivers rented an office in its building to a tenant for one year, starting on 1 September. Rent for one year amounting to $6,000 was collected at that date. The total amount collected was credited to rent revenue.

f. Rivers recorded a note receivable from a customer dated 1 November of the current year. It is a $12,000, 10% note, due in one year. At the maturity date, Rivers will collect the amount of the note plus interest for one year.

**Required:**

Prepare adjusting entries in the general journal for each situation. If no entry is required for an item, explain why.

---

 **A-6 Adjusting Entries:** The following items are independent. Assume that the original transactions have been recorded correctly, or as described.

a. Prepaid insurance had a debit balance of $18,200 at the beginning of January. This represents the remaining 14 months in an insurance policy that was purchased in a prior year. On 1 April of the current year, a 30-month policy was bought for $50,400, which was debited to prepaid insurance. There were no other entries to the prepaid insurance account during the year. On 1 November, an 18-month policy was bought for $9,360. This policy was debited to insurance expense.

b. Certain invoices had not been recorded at 31 December: a $7,400 bill for power, a $920 phone bill, and a repair bill for $1,350. All these bills are due in January.

c. Salaries payable has a balance of $3,700, unadjusted from the last year-end. There are 14 employees. They were paid up to Friday, 27 December. There were two additional working days prior to the year-end. Three employees earn $600 per (five-day) week each, three earn $500 per week, and eight earn $400 per week.

d. There are two notes payable outstanding. The first is an $890,000, 4% note, issued on 1 September. No interest has been paid to date. The second is a $700,000, 3.5% note issued on 1 April. Six months' interest was paid on 1 October. The notes payable themselves were properly recorded on issuance but interest must be accrued to 31 December, the year-end.

e. There is an unearned revenue account with a balance of $160,000. This includes a $10,000 security deposit from a tenant. This deposit will be returned when the tenant eventually vacates. The remaining $150,000 is six months' rent received, on a lease beginning 1 December, on commercial property.

f. Supplies inventory had a balance of $23,600 at the end of last year. During the year, $69,800 of supplies were purchased, and were debited directly to supplies expense. At year-end, an inventory count was conducted, and the balance was ascertained to be $24,750.

g. Advertising expense of $94,800 includes a $6,300 payment for an advertisement that will run in January of next year.

**Required:**

1. Prepare adjusting journal entries to reflect the facts above.

2. Prepare reversing entries for adjusting journal entries that must be reversed.

---

★ **A-7 Adjusting Entries:** Watkins Company, an accounting firm, adjusts and closes its accounts each 31 December.

1. On 1 June, the company collected cash, $12,600, which was for rent collected in advance from a tenant for the next 12 months. Give the adjusting journal entry assuming the following at the time of the collection:

   *Case A* $12,600 was credited to rent revenue.

   *Case B* $12,600 was credited to rent collected in advance.

2. On 31 December 20X5, the maintenance supplies inventory account showed a balance on hand amounting to $4,200. During 20X6, purchases of maintenance supplies amounted to $9,000. An inventory of maintenance supplies on hand at 31 December 20X6 reflected unused supplies amounting to $3,600. Give the adjusting journal entry that should be made on 31 December 20X6, under the following conditions:

   *Case A* Purchases were debited to the maintenance supplies inventory account.

   *Case B* Purchases were debited to maintenance supplies expense.

3. On 31 December 20X5, the prepaid insurance account showed a debit balance of $5,700, which was for coverage for the three months, January to March. On 1 April 20X6, the company obtained another policy covering a two-year period from that date. The two-year premium, amounting to $50,400, was paid on 1 April. Give the adjusting journal entry that should be made on 31 December 20X6.

   *Case A* $50,400 was debited to prepaid insurance.

   *Case B* $50,400 was debited to insurance expense.

**Required:**

Provide adjusting journal entries.

---

★★ **A-8 Adjusting Entries:** Quando Company adjusts and closes its books each 31 December. It is now 31 December 20X5, and the adjusting entries are to be made. You are requested to prepare, in general journal format, the adjusting entry that should be made for each of the following items:

a. The company rented a warehouse on 1 June 20X5, for one year. It had to pay the full amount of rent one year in advance on 1 June, amounting to $10,800, which was debited to rent expense.

b. The company received from a customer a 6% note with a face amount of $40,000, in exchange for products purchased. The note was dated 1 September 20X5; the principal plus the interest is payable one year later. Notes receivable was debited, and sales revenue was credited on the date of sale, 1 September 20X5.

c. Credit sales for the year amounted to $1,280,000. The estimated loss rate on bad debts is one-quarter of 1%.

d. Unpaid and unrecorded wages incurred at 31 December amounted to $8,400.

e. The company paid a two-year insurance premium in advance on 1 November 20X5, amounting to $38,400, which was debited to prepaid insurance.

f. Machine A, which cost $300,000, is to be depreciated for the full year. The estimated useful life is 10 years, and the residual value, $4,000. Use straight-line depreciation.

g. On 31 December 20X5, the property tax bill was received in the amount of $30,000. This amount applied only to 20X5 and had not been previously recorded or paid. The taxes are due, and will be paid, on 15 January 20X6.

h. On 1 April 20X5, the company signed a $240,000, 6% note payable. On that date, cash was debited and notes payable credited for $240,000. The note is payable on 31 March 20X6, for the face amount plus interest for one year.

i. The company was granted a patent on 1 January 20X5, at a legal cost of $47,600. On that date, the patent account was debited and cash credited for $47,600. The patent has an estimated useful life of 17 years, but will be used for 10 years. There will be no residual value.

j. Pre-tax income has been computed to be $320,000 after all the above adjustments. Assume an average income tax rate of 40%.

---

★★  **A-9 Adjusting Entries:** The following situations are unrelated:

a. On 1 January, ABC Corporation had a supplies inventory of $13,500. During the year, supplies of $65,700 were bought and recorded in temporary accounts. At the end of the year, inventory of $27,600 was on hand.

b. On 10 December, ABC Corporation received a deposit of $90,000 on a consulting project that was just beginning. This was accounted for as revenue. By the end of the year, the $150,000 job was 40% complete.

c. During the year, ABC Corporation sold 10,000 units of a product that was subject to a warranty. Past history indicates that 3% of units sold require repairs at an average cost of $120 per unit. The sales have been recorded; costs incurred for the warranty to date, totalling $26,100, were debited to warranty liability when paid. No warranty expense has been recognized.

d. The company uses the percentage-of-sales method to calculate bad debt expense: 1% of credit sales of $18,750,000 is expected to be uncollectible.

e. In 20X3, a machine was purchased for $522,000. It had a useful life of 12 years and a $72,000 residual value. A full year's depreciation was charged in 20X3 and 20X4. In 20X5, the accountant discovered that she had forgotten to deduct the salvage value when calculating (straight-line) depreciation for these two years. Prepare a journal entry to correct the error (to retained earnings) and record 20X5 depreciation. Ignore income tax.

f. ABC Corporation wrote off a $48,000 bad debt. The allowance method is used.

g. ABC Corporation buys one-year insurance policies each 1 November. The year ends on 31 December. On 1 January 20X5, there was a balance of $28,320 in the prepaid insurance account; a cheque for $38,130 was issued on 1 November 20X5, for new one-year policies and debited to the prepaid insurance account.

**Required:**
Prepare adjusting journal entries.

---

  **A-10 Adjusting Entries:** The following transactions and events for Stellar Manufacturing Corporation are under consideration for adjusting entries at 31 December 20X5 (the end of the accounting period):

a. Machine A used in the factory cost $450,000; it was purchased on 1 July 20X2. It has an estimated useful life of 12 years and a residual value of $30,000. Straight-line depreciation is used.

b. Sales for 20X5 amounted to $4,000,000, including $600,000 in credit sales. It is estimated, based on the experience of the company, that bad debt losses will be one quarter of 1% of credit sales.

c. At the beginning of 20X5, office supplies inventory amounted to $600. During 20X5, office supplies amounting to $8,800 were purchased; this amount was debited to office supplies expense. An inventory of office supplies at the end of 20X5 showed $400 on the shelves. The 1 January balance of $600 is still reflected in the office supplies inventory account.

d. On 1 July 20X5, the company paid a three-year insurance premium amounting to $2,160; this amount was debited to prepaid insurance.

e. On 1 October 20X5, the company paid rent on some leased office space. The payment of $7,200 cash was for the following six months. At the time of payment, rent expense was debited for the $7,200.

f. On 1 August 20X5, the company borrowed $120,000 from the Royal Bank. The loan was for 12 months at 9% interest payable at maturity date. The loan was properly recorded on 1 August.

g. Finished goods inventory on 1 January 20X5 was $200,000, and on 31 December 20X5 it was $260,000. These amounts are reflected in the perpetual inventory system. The ledger indicates that the cost of goods sold is $2,400,000.

h. The company owned some property (land) that was rented to B. R. Speir on 1 April 20X5, for 12 months for $8,400. On 1 April, the entire annual rental of $8,400 was credited to rent collected in advance, and cash was debited.

i. On 31 December 20X5, wages earned by employees but not yet paid (or recorded in the accounts) amounted to $18,000. Disregard payroll taxes.

j. On 1 September 20X5, the company loaned $60,000 to an outside party. The loan was at 10% per annum and was due in six months; interest is payable at maturity. Cash was credited for $60,000 and notes receivable debited on 1 September for the same amount.

k. On 1 January 20X5, factory supplies on hand amounted to $200. During 20X5, factory supplies that cost $4,000 were purchased and debited to factory supplies inventory. At the end of 20X5, a physical inventory count revealed that factory supplies on hand amounted to $800.

l. The company purchased a gravel pit on 1 January 20X3, at a cost of $60,000; it was estimated that approximately 60,000 tonnes of gravel could be removed prior to exhaustion. It was also estimated that the company would take five years to mine this natural resource. Tonnes of gravel removed and sold were 20X3, 3,000; 20X4, 7,000; and 20X5, 5,000. Hint: Deplete on an output basis; no residual value. Only 20X5 depletion should be recorded.

m. At the end of 20X5, it was found that postage stamps that cost $120 were on hand (in a "postage" box in the office). When the stamps were purchased, miscellaneous expense had been debited and cash credited.

n. At the end of 20X5, property taxes for 20X5 amounting to $59,000 were assessed on property owned by the company. The taxes are due no later than 1 February 20X6. The taxes have not been recorded on the books because payment has not been made.

o. The company borrowed $120,000 from the bank on 1 December 20X5. The loan is due in 60 days' time, along with interest at 9.5% per annum. On 1 December 20X5, cash was debited and loans payable credited for $120,000.

p. On 1 July 20X5, the company paid the city a $1,000 licence fee for the next 12 months. On that date, cash was credited and licence expense debited for $1,000.

q. On 1 March 20X5, the company made a loan to the company president and received a $30,000 note receivable. The loan was due in one year and called for 6% annual interest payable at maturity date.

r. The company owns three cars used by the executives. A six-month maintenance contract on them was signed on 1 October 20X5, whereby a local garage agreed to do "all the required maintenance." The payment was made for the following six months in advance. On 1 October 20X5, cash was credited and maintenance expense was debited for $9,600.

**Required:**
Give the adjusting entry (or entries) that should be made on 31 December 20X5, for each item. If an adjusting entry is not required, explain why. Assume all amounts are material.

**A-11 Adjusting Entries:** Selected account balances, taken from the ledger of Electronics Services Corporation as of 31 December 20X4, appear below in alphabetical order:

| | |
|---|---:|
| Accounts payable | $ 75,200 |
| Accounts receivable | 18,200 |
| Allowance for doubtful accounts | 650 |
| Cash | 51,300 |
| Dividends | 8,600 |
| Interest expense | 1,080 |
| Interest revenue | 2,100 |
| Note payable | 24,000 |
| Note receivable | 12,000 |
| Purchases | 492,000 |
| Purchase returns | 16,200 |
| Sales | 850,000 |
| Sales furniture | 44,400 |
| Sales salaries | 46,510 |
| Store supplies inventory | 4,100 |
| Tax expense (property) | 4,200 |
| Unearned revenue | 12,000 |

**Required:**

Record adjusting entries, as needed, for the following facts and events:

1. The note payable had an interest rate of 8% and was borrowed on 1 February 20X4. No interest was paid in 20X4.

2. There was $610 of outstanding accrued interest on the note receivable at 31 December 20X4.

3. Four percent of the outstanding accounts receivable are expected to prove uncollectible. The allowance for doubtful accounts is now in a credit balance but must be increased to the required 4% of accounts receivable.

4. Unearned revenue represented an advance payment from a customer; 75% was still unearned at year-end.

5. Closing merchandise inventory was $122,000. There was no opening inventory. Prepare an adjusting journal entry to record the change in the inventory account and cost of goods sold.

6. Depreciation of sales furniture is to be recorded straight line over eight years. The furniture will have no salvage value.

7. Unpaid and unrecorded advertising bills at 31 December 20X4 totalled $2,390.

8. Property taxes paid (the tax expense of $4,200, above) in 20X4 were paid on 1 July 20X4 and were related to the period 1 April 20X4 to 31 March 20X5.

9. Store supplies inventory at 31 December 20X4 was $780.

 **A-12 Entries and Financial Statements:** Set forth below is the adjusted trial balance of the Whitehead Company as of 31 October 20X5:

| Account | Debit | Credit |
|---|---:|---:|
| Cash | $ 8,400 | |
| Accounts receivable | 45,000 | |
| Merchandise inventory | 150,000 | |
| Prepaid rent | 9,000 | |
| Equipment | 25,200 | |
| Accumulated amortization | | $ 3,600 |
| Accounts payable | | 60,000 |
| Note payable | | 30,000 |
| Accrued interest payable | | 750 |
| Capital stock | | 75,000 |
| Retained earnings | | 68,250 |
| | $237,600 | $237,600 |

The following information describes all of Whitehead's November transactions and provides all the data required for month-end adjustments:

- Whitehead had cash sales of $75,300.
- Whitehead had sales on account of $60,000.
- Whitehead collected $51,000 in cash from its customers on account.
- Whitehead acquired $90,000 of merchandise on account.
- The cost of merchandise sold during November was $75,000.
- Whitehead paid its suppliers $57,000 (cash) on account.
- Whitehead spent $6,000 for November's advertising.
- During November, Whitehead paid $16,500 in cash for wages.
- Miscellaneous expenses of $15,000 were paid in cash.
- $3,000 of wages earned by Whitehead's employees in November had not yet been paid.
- Whitehead had earlier paid its rent in advance to 31 December 20X5.
- The store equipment had been purchased by Whitehead for $25,200 on 1 November 20X4. This equipment is expected to last seven years and to have no salvage or residual value at that time.
- The note payable was dated 1 June 20X5 and the principal is due in two equal instalments on 1 June 20X6 and 20X7. Interest on the note is also to be paid on 1 June 20X6 and 20X7. The note bears an interest rate of 6% per year.

### Required:

1. Journalize November transactions and adjusting journal entries. Include an adjusting journal entry for cost of goods sold.
2. Prepare an income statement and balance sheet for the month of November.

---

★★ **A-13 Adjustments and Financial Statements:** Dan Richards incorporated an appliance repair shop on 1 January 20X2, and has been quite pleased with the results of his first year. His cash receipts and disbursements:

| Inflows: | |
| --- | --- |
| Repair revenue received | $49,000 |
| Rent revenue received | 6,000 |
| Cash refunds from suppliers, for returned parts | 1,200 |
| Cash originally invested by Dan | 3,000 |
| Bank loan | 18,000 |
| | $77,200 |

| Outflows: | |
| --- | --- |
| Wages paid | 18,000 |
| Dividends paid | 3,400 |
| Parts and supplies paid for | 9,000 |
| Insurance premiums paid | 2,000 |
| Rent paid | 12,500 |
| Equipment purchased | 9,500 |
| Other operating expenses paid | 2,000 |
| | $56,400 |

*Notes:*

- Equipment has a 10-year life and a $500 salvage value, and is to be depreciated using the declining-balance method, using a rate of 20%.
- Parts still on hand amount to $2,760.
- The insurance premium was paid on August 1 for an eight-month policy.
- Rental revenue is from a tenant who rents excess space. She paid 12 months rent on April 1 when she moved in.

- Dan owes his workers another $1,200 in wages, and customers owe him $7,560 for repair work done.
- Dan owes his suppliers $1,490 for parts.
- The bank loan was taken out on 1 March and has an interest rate of 12%.
- Bad debts are likely 4% of repair revenue.
- Rent paid was for the 12-month calendar year of 20X2. Dan must also pay 1% of repair revenue to his landlord but has not done this yet.
- For simplicity, assume that there are no income taxes.

**Required:**

1. Prepare an income statement for Dan for the year ended 31 December 20X2. Show all calculations.
2. Prepare a balance sheet as of 31 December 20X2.

 **A-14 Adjustments and Balance Sheet:** On 31 December 20X4, the Hearth & Stove Corp. is preparing financial statements. The following unadjusted trial balance has been prepared:

## HEARTH & STOVE CORP.

### Trial Balance

| | Debit | Credit |
|---|---|---|
| Accounts payable | | $ 44,300 |
| Accounts receivable | $ 211,090 | |
| Advertising expense | 12,800 | |
| Accumulated depreciation—office equipment | | 39,800 |
| Allowance for doubtful accounts | | 4,500 |
| Cash | 16,800 | |
| Cost of goods sold | 660,000 | |
| Common shares | | 45,000 |
| Dividends declared | 10,400 | |
| Insurance expense | 1,800 | |
| Interest expense | 2,640 | |
| Interest revenue | | 840 |
| Inventory | 50,000 | |
| Land | 145,000 | |
| Long-term investments | 312,600 | |
| Mortgage payable | | 297,000 |
| Notes payable—short term | | 10,800 |
| Office equipment | 72,000 | |
| Office expense | 13,100 | |
| Prepaid insurance | 0 | |
| Retained earnings, opening | | 45,820 |
| Revenue received in advance | | 34,800 |
| Sales | | 1,222,000 |
| Supplies inventory | 400 | |
| Supplies expense | 4,200 | |
| Miscellaneous expense | 15,430 | |
| Rent expense | 72,000 | |
| Wages expense | 144,600 | |
| | $1,744,860 | $1,744,860 |

The following facts are also available at the end of 20X4:

a. The inventory on hand is $46,700 according to the physical count.
b. The allowance for doubtful accounts should have a balance of $5,600.
c. The office equipment is depreciated at a rate of 8% per year (straight line).
d. There are supplies of $1,200 on hand.
e. On March 31 of this year, the company bought a $1,800 insurance policy with a 12-month term.
f. Customers have not yet been billed for products delivered on the last day of the year. The products have a retail value of $54,000. The cost of goods sold for this transaction was properly recorded.
g. Income tax is estimated to be 40% of all income before income tax. No income tax has been recorded or paid.

### Required:

1. Prepare adjusting journal entries to reflect the information in parts (a) to (g), above.

2. Prepare a retained earning statement in good form that reflects the trial balance above and your journal entries.

3. Prepare a classified balance sheet in good form that reflects the trial balance above and your journal entries.

 **A-15 Adjustments and Financial Statements:** Toronado Ltd. reported the following items in its unadjusted trial balance as of 31 December, 20X4, for the 20X4 fiscal year. This trial balance is listed in alphabetical order. Note that this is a *partial* trial balance and does not include all accounts. Accounts have normal (debit or credit) balances.

| | |
|---|---:|
| Administration expense | $ 235,700 |
| Accounts payable | 76,800 |
| Accounts receivable | 99,800 |
| Allowance for doubtful accounts (credit) | 2,000 |
| Cash dividends declared | 31,000 |
| Freight-out (delivery to customers) | 26,900 |
| Gain on sale of automobile | 1,400 |
| Insurance expense | 38,400 |
| Interest expense | 27,100 |
| Loans receivable, 8% | 75,000 |
| Merchandise inventory, 1 January | 89,400 |
| Notes payable, 6% | 500,000 |
| Purchases | 560,300 |
| Salaries and employee benefits | 120,900 |
| Sales returns and allowances | 42,100 |
| Sales revenues | 1,876,000 |
| Selling expense | 34,000 |
| Supplies expense | 45,900 |
| Supplies inventory | 600 |
| Retained earnings, 1 January | 568,300 |
| Unearned revenue | 32,000 |
| Utilities expense | 65,400 |

*Other information:*

• The tax rate is 30%, but no tax has yet been recorded.

• Closing merchandise inventory is $76,500. Closing supplies inventory is $1,300.

• The insurance expense represents a payment made on 1 May for a 24-month fire insurance policy.

- Customers owe $53,000 for goods delivered on 31 December; this amount has not yet been recorded.
- All sales are on account, except those that are prepaid.
- Unearned revenue represents all customer deposits received during the year. Of this amount, 60% is still unearned at the end of the year.
- Bad debt expense is to be recognized as 1% of total sales.
- Interest on the note payable was last paid and recorded on 31 October.
- The company owes $3,200 in utilities.
- Interest on the loan receivable has not been paid or recorded all year.

**Required:**

1. Prepare journal entries to reflect the required adjustments. Round adjustments to the nearest $100, if necessary.
2. Prepare an income statement based on the adjusted balances.
3. Prepare a retained earnings statement based on the adjusted balances.

---

★ **A-16 Prepare a Balance Sheet:** Your assistant has prepared the following *partial* adjusted trial balance data for the Lopez Supply Corporation as of 31 December 20X8. The accounts are arranged in alphabetical order; unfortunately, the debit and credit balances have been listed in the same column. Some income statement accounts may be missing.

| | |
|---|---|
| Accounts payable | $ 72,000 |
| Accounts receivable | 134,400 |
| Accumulated depreciation—buildings | 39,600 |
| Accumulated depreciation—equipment | 20,000 |
| Advertising expense | 9,600 |
| Bonds payable | 80,000 |
| Buildings | 144,000 |
| Capital stock | 432,000 |
| Cash | 48,000 |
| Depreciation expense—buildings | 16,000 |
| Depreciation expense—equipment | 4,000 |
| Dividends declared | 28,800 |
| Dividends payable | 4,000 |
| Equipment | 108,560 |
| Expired insurance | 2,880 |
| Interest earned | 1,320 |
| Interest receivable | 600 |
| Inventory (merchandise) (closing balance) | 121,200 |
| Land | 139,200 |
| Long-term investments | 109,200 |
| Mortgage payable | 96,000 |
| Notes payable—short term | 30,000 |
| Office expenses | 32,160 |
| Premium on bonds payable | 4,000 |
| Prepaid insurance | 1,000 |
| Property tax expense | 15,960 |
| Retained earnings—31 December 20X7 | 19,680 |
| Sales | 492,000 |
| Supplies on hand | 1,600 |
| Unearned revenue | 2,400 |

**Required:**

Prepare the 31 December 20X8 balance sheet. For the closing retained earnings, use the value that will make the balance sheet balance.

★★  **A-17 Prepare Financial Statements:** The following trial balance for Falcon Corporation is in alphabetical order.

| 31 December 20X7 | Debit | Credit |
|---|---|---|
| Accounts payable | | 235,900 |
| Accounts receivable | 344,000 | |
| Accumulated amortization, building | | 200,700 |
| Allowance for doubtful accounts | | 46,200 |
| Bank loans payable, short-term | | 460,000 |
| Building | 456,000 | |
| Cash | 26,500 | |
| Common shares | | 170,000 |
| Cost of goods sold | 933,100 | |
| Dividends | 24,000 | |
| Income tax expense | 116,000 | |
| Interest expense | 52,100 | |
| Inventory, 31 December 20X7 | 291,700 | |
| Land | 36,000 | |
| Long-term bond payable | | 120,000 |
| Long-term investments | 230,000 | |
| Notes receivable (short-term) | 100,000 | |
| Office supplies | 3,600 | |
| Operating expenses | 458,000 | |
| Operating expenses payable | | 48,900 |
| Prepaid insurance | 1,500 | |
| Rent revenue | | 24,700 |
| Retained earnings (1 January 20X7) | | 44,300 |
| Sales | | 1,822,200 |
| Selling expenses | 107,800 | |
| Unearned revenue | | 4,000 |
| Wages payable | | 3,400 |
| | $3,180,300 | $3,180,300 |

**Required:**

1. Prepare an income statement from the information given.
2. Prepare a balance sheet and a statement of retained earnings.

★★  **A-18 Entries and Worksheet:** Pinehill Ltd. is a retail operation that uses a perpetual inventory system. The unadjusted trial balance for the year ended 31 December 20X8 follows.

### PINEHILL LTD.

### Unadjusted Trial Balance

| | | |
|---|---|---|
| Cash | $ 50,000 | |
| Accounts receivable | 150,000 | |
| Allowance for doubtful accounts | | $ 12,000 |
| Merchandise inventory | 305,000 | |
| Store equipment | 160,000 | |
| Accumulated amortization, store equipment | | 20,000 |
| Accounts payable | | 200,000 |
| Loan payable—long term | | 134,000 |
| Common shares | | 120,000 |
| Retained earnings | | 66,000 |
| Sales revenue | | 1,560,000 |
| Sales returns and allowances | 35,000 | |
| Cost of goods sold | 987,000 | |
| Selling expenses | 345,000 | |
| Administrative expenses | 80,000 | |
| | $2,112,000 | $2,112,000 |

*Additional information:*

- The allowance for doubtful accounts should have a balance of $15,000. This is a selling expense.
- The company uses a perpetual inventory system, but the closing inventory is verified by physical count. This count showed that the correct balance for closing inventory is $289,000.
- No amortization has been recorded for 20X8. The store equipment is being amortized using the straight-line method over an estimated useful life of eight years with no residual value. This is a selling expense.
- The long-term loan was a two-year loan from a local bank. The interest rate is 6%, payable at the end of each 12-month period. The money was borrowed on May 1, 20X8. This is an administrative expense.
- The income tax rate is 40%; no tax has yet been paid or recorded.

**Required:**

1. Prepare adjusting entries for the year ended 31 December 20X8.
2. Complete the year-end worksheet. Combine the balance sheet and retained earnings columns.

 **A-19 Entries and Worksheet:** The following information pertains to the first year of operations for Carmen Corp.

## CARMEN CORP.

### Unadjusted trial balance

| 31 December 20X6 | Debit | Credit |
|---|---|---|
| Cash | $ 5,100 | |
| Accounts receivable | 11,700 | |
| Office equipment | 6,900 | |
| Computer equipment | 5,400 | |
| Accounts payable | | 7,550 |
| Loan payable—long term | | 30,000 |
| Common shares | | 70 |
| Sales revenue | | 36,300 |
| Rent expense | 12,000 | |
| Supplies inventory | 18,100 | |
| Interest expense | 2,100 | |
| Insurance expense | 1,320 | |
| Miscellaneous expense | 11,300 | |
| | $73,920 | $73,920 |

*Additional information:*

a. On 1 July, the company signed a five-year lease for office space in a new industrial park. The company moved immediately. Rent is $1,500 per month and two month's rent was paid as a deposit.
b. On 15 June, the company borrowed $30,000 from the bank. Interest at 14% is payable at the middle of every month. Payments have been made to date.
c. Leasehold improvements were made to the rented premises. Total cost for such things as partitions, painting, and wiring was $8,000 and was charged to miscellaneous expense.
d. Used computer equipment was purchased at an auction for $5,400. It was worth $9,000.
e. There was one job completed at year-end but not billed in the amount of $10,000.

f. Bad debts relating to the year-end accounts receivable are expected to be $350.

g. Year-end accounting fees are estimated to be $1,800.

h. On 1 October the company bought a used car for $7,600. Although the vehicle was to be used primarily on company business, the owner/manager used personal funds to pay for it. Consequently no entry was made in the books of the company. The company will repay the owner/manager when there is enough money.

i. The following amortization policies are to be used; a full year of amortization is charged in the first year of ownership. There are no residual values.

> Office and computer equipment: 5 years straight-line
> Vehicles: 8 years straight-line
> Leasehold improvements: 5 years straight-line

j. Supplies inventory was $3,000 at the year-end count.

k. The effective tax rate for the company is 25%.

### Required:

1. Prepare the adjusting journal entries required at year-end.

2. Complete the year-end worksheet. Combine the retained earnings and balance sheet columns.

---

★★★ **A-20 The Accounting Cycle:** At 31 December 20X5, the post-closing trial balance of Fox Ltd., a retailer of health food supplements, reflects the following:

| Acct. No. | Account | Debit | Credit |
|---|---|---|---|
| 101 | Cash | $ 81,000 | |
| 102 | Accounts receivable | 63,000 | |
| 103 | Allowance for doubtful accounts | | $ 3,000 |
| 104 | Inventory (perpetual inventory system) | 105,000 | |
| 105 | Prepaid insurance (20 months remaining at 1 January) | 2,700 | |
| 200 | Equipment (20-year estimated life, no residual value) | 150,000 | |
| 201 | Accumulated depreciation, equipment | | 67,500 |
| 300 | Accounts payable | | 22,500 |
| 301 | Wages payable | | |
| 302 | Income taxes payable (for 20X5) | | 12,000 |
| 400 | Common shares, no-par, 100,000 shares | | 240,000 |
| 401 | Retained earnings | | 56,700 |
| 500 | Sales revenue | | |
| 600 | Cost of goods sold | | |
| 601 | Operating expenses | | |
| 602 | Income tax expense | | |
| 700 | Income summary | | |
| | | $401,700 | $401,700 |

The following transactions occurred during 20X6 in the order given (use the letter at the left in place of date):

a. Sales revenue of $90,000, of which $30,000 was on credit; cost of goods sold, provided by perpetual inventory record, $58,500. (Note: When the perpetual system is used, make two entries to record a sale: *first*, debit cash or accounts receivable and credit sales revenue; *second*, debit cost of goods sold and credit inventory.)

b. Collected $51,000 on accounts receivable.

c. Paid income taxes payable (20X5), $12,000.

d. Purchased merchandise, $120,000, of which $24,000 was on credit.

e. Paid accounts payable, $18,000.

f. Sales revenue of $216,000 (in cash); cost of goods sold, $140,400.

g. Paid operating expenses, $57,000.

h. Issued 1,000 common shares for $3,000 cash.

i. Purchased merchandise, $300,000, of which $81,000 was on credit.

j. Sales revenue of $294,000, of which $90,000 was on credit; cost of goods sold, $191,100.

k. Collected cash on accounts receivable, $78,000.

l. Paid accounts payable, $84,000.

m. Paid various operating expenses in cash, $54,000.

### Required:

1. Journalize each of the transactions listed above for 20X6; use only a general journal.

2. Set up T-accounts in the general ledger for each of the accounts listed in the above trial balance and enter the account number and 31 December 20X5 balance.

3. Post the journal entries; use posting reference numbers.

4. Prepare an unadjusted trial balance.

5. Journalize the adjusting entries and post them to the ledger. Assume a bad debt rate of 0.5% of credit sales for the period at 31 December 20X6; accrued wages were $900. The average income tax rate was 40%. Record straight-line depreciation and insurance expense. Debit expenses to the operating expense account. (Check your work: Income tax expense is $35,352.)

6. Prepare an adjusted trial balance.

7. Prepare the income statement and balance sheet.

8. Journalize and post the closing entries.

9. Prepare a post-closing trial balance.

---

 **A-21 The Accounting Cycle:** The post-closing trial balance of Gensing Enterprises, a farming operation, at 31 December 20X6, reflects the following:

| Acct. No. | Account | Debit | Credit |
|---|---|---|---|
| 101 | Cash | $  42,000 | |
| 102 | Accounts receivable | 35,800 | |
| 103 | Allowance for doubtful accounts | | $    2,000 |
| 104 | Inventory, 31 December 20X6 | 46,000 | |
| 105 | Fertilizer and supplies inventory | 6,700 | |
| 106 | Prepaid insurance (expires at the end of November 20X7) | 9,000 | |
| 200 | Equipment | 344,800 | |
| 201 | Accumulated amortization, equipment | | 124,600 |
| 202 | Land | 682,000 | |
| 300 | Accounts payable | | 67,500 |
| 301 | Unearned revenue | | 32,000 |
| 302 | Notes payable | | 75,000 |
| 400 | Common shares | | 400,000 |
| 401 | Retained earnings | | 465,200 |
| 500 | Sales revenue | | |
| 600 | Cost of goods sold | | |
| 601 | Operating expenses | | |
| 700 | Income summary | | |
| | | $1,166,300 | $1,166,300 |

Various transactions occurred in 20X7:

a. Sales amounted to $767,000. Cash sales were 25% of the total, and the rest was on account.
b. At the beginning of the year, there was unearned revenue. This revenue was earned in 20X7, in addition to the sales transactions in (a).
c. Operating expenses of $67,200 were paid in cash.
d. Fertilizer and other supplies were bought for $46,900, on credit.
e. Harvesting costs of $244,200 were paid. Harvesting costs of the crop are debited to inventory.
f. The cost of all goods sold for the period was $281,400. This should be recorded as a journal entry that increases cost of goods sold and reduces the inventory account.
g. The opening accounts receivable were collected in the amount of $31,000. No accounts were written off. Seventy percent of the current year sales on account were also collected.
h. The opening balance of accounts payable was paid in full.
i. Ninety percent of the fertilizer and other supplies, bought on credit, were paid for.
j. Paid dividends of $22,000.
k. A $10,800, 12-month insurance policy was paid on 1 December. The amount was debited to prepaid insurance.
l. A contract was signed with a customer for a certain quantity of next year's crop. The customer paid the full $50,000 price in cash in advance.
m. The note payable was partially repaid at the end of November, in the amount of $50,000. Interest of $5,500 was also paid on the entire note, all pertaining to 20X7. The remaining $25,000 balance of the note payable has an interest rate of 12% per annum. Interest must be accrued for the month of December 20X7 in requirement 5. The $25,000 balance is long term.

### Required:

1. Journalize the transactions for 20X7. Use only a general journal. Debit all operating expenses to a general "operating expense" account, for simplicity. Add other accounts if needed. Interest expense is recorded in a separate account.
2. Set up T-accounts in the general ledger for each of the accounts listed in the above trial balance and enter the account number and the 31 December balance.
3. Post the journal entries; use posting reference numbers. Assign account numbers as needed.
4. Prepare an unadjusted trial balance.
5. Journalize and post the following adjusting journal entries:
   a. Depreciation for the year, $45,000.
   b. Bad debts are expected to be 2% of credit sales.
   c. Inventory of fertilizer and other supplies was $7,600 at year-end.
   d. Interest expense was accrued for December 20X7.
   e. Prepaid insurance expired.
   f. Wages earned but unpaid at year-end, $5,000.
   Debit expenses other than interest to operating expenses, and payables to accounts payable, for simplicity.
6. Prepare an adjusted trial balance.
7. Prepare the income statement and balance sheet. The remaining note payable is long term.
8. Journalize and post the closing entries.
9. Prepare a post-closing trial balance.
10. For which adjusting journal entries in requirement 5 above would reversing entries be appropriate? Explain.

★★★  **A-22 Worksheet, Adjusting and Closing Entries, Statements:** Darma Corporation is currently completing the end-of-the-period accounting process. At 31 December 20X5, the following unadjusted trial balance was developed from the general ledger:

| Account | Debit | Credit |
|---|---|---|
| Cash | $ 120,520 | |
| Accounts receivable | 76,000 | |
| Allowance for doubtful accounts | | $ 4,000 |
| Interest receivable | 0 | |
| Inventory (perpetual inventory system) | 210,000 | |
| Sales supplies inventory | 1,800 | |
| Long-term note receivable, 14% | 24,000 | |
| Equipment | 360,000 | |
| Accumulated depreciation, equipment | | 128,000 |
| Patent (net) | 16,800 | |
| Accounts payable | | 46,000 |
| Interest payable | | 0 |
| Income tax payable | | 0 |
| Property tax payable | | 0 |
| Rent collected in advance | | |
| Mortgage payable, 12% | | 120,000 |
| Common shares, no-par, 10,000 shares | | 230,000 |
| Retained earnings | | 64,880 |
| Sales revenue | | 1,400,000 |
| Investment revenue | | 2,240 |
| Rent revenue | | 6,000 |
| Cost of goods sold | 760,000 | |
| Selling expenses | 328,800 | |
| General and administrative expenses | 110,000 | |
| Interest expense | 13,200 | |
| Discontinued operations gain (pre-tax) | | 20,000 |
| | $2,021,120 | $2,021,120 |

*Additional data for adjustments and other purposes:*

a. Estimated bad debt loss rate is 0.25% of credit sales. Credit sales for the year amounted to $400,000; classify as a selling expense.

b. Interest on the long-term note receivable was last collected and recorded on 31 August 20X5.

c. Estimated useful life of the equipment is 10 years; residual value, $40,000. Allocate 10% of depreciation expense to general and administrative expense and the balance to selling expense to reflect proportionate use. Use straight-line depreciation.

d. Estimated remaining economic life of the patent is 14 years (from 1 January 20X5) with no residual value. Use straight-line amortization and classify as selling expense (used in sales promotion).

e. Interest on the mortgage payable was last paid and recorded on 30 November 20X5.

f. On 1 June 20X5, the company rented office space to a tenant for one year and collected $6,000 rent in advance for the year; the entire amount was credited to rent revenue on this date.

g. On 31 December 20X5, the company received a statement for calendar-year 20X5 property taxes amounting to $2,600. The payment is due 15 February 20X6. Classify the adjustment as a selling expense.

h. Sales supplies on hand at 31 December 20X5 amounted to $600; classify as a selling expense.

i. Assume an average 40% corporate income tax rate on all items including the discontinued operations gain. (Check your work: Total income tax expense is $70,264.)

**Required:**

1. Enter the above unadjusted trial balance on a worksheet.
2. Complete the worksheet.

3. Prepare the income statement and balance sheet.

4. Journalize the closing entries.

---

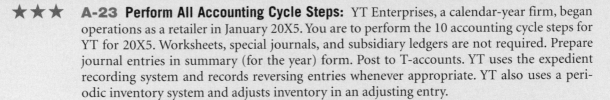 **A-23 Perform All Accounting Cycle Steps:** YT Enterprises, a calendar-year firm, began operations as a retailer in January 20X5. You are to perform the 10 accounting cycle steps for YT for 20X5. Worksheets, special journals, and subsidiary ledgers are not required. Prepare journal entries in summary (for the year) form. Post to T-accounts. YT uses the expedient recording system and records reversing entries whenever appropriate. YT also uses a periodic inventory system and adjusts inventory in an adjusting entry.

Information about transactions in 20X5:

1. Investors contributed $400,000 in exchange for 10,000 shares of no-par common shares. On the advice of its underwriter, YT offered the shares at $40 per share.

2. YT obtained a 12%, $200,000 bank loan on 1 February. This loan is evidenced by a signed promissory note calling for interest payments every 1 February. The note is due in full on 31 January 20X9.

3. A rental contract for production and office facilities was signed 1 February, which required $8,000 immediate payment covering the first month's rent and a $4,000 deposit refundable in three years or upon termination of the contract, whichever occurs first. Monthly rent is $4,000. As an added incentive to pay rent in advance, YT accepted an offer to maintain rent at $4,000 per month for the first three years if YT paid the 2nd through the 13th (March 20X5 through February 20X6) months' rent immediately. In all, YT paid $56,000 for rent on 1 February. YT intends to occupy the facilities for at least three years.

4. Equipment costing $220,000 was purchased for cash in early February. It has an estimated residual value of $20,000 and a five-year useful life. YT uses the straight-line method of depreciation and treats depreciation as a separate-period expense. A full year of depreciation is recorded in the year of acquisition.

5. YT recognized various cash operating expenses for the year, including the following:

| | |
|---|---|
| Wages | $160,000 |
| Utilities | 60,000 |
| Selling | 50,000 |
| General and administrative | 125,000 |

6. Total merchandise purchases for the year amounted to $2,775,000. Ending inventory amounted to $300,000 at cost. YT uses a periodic inventory system.

7. Total payables relating to merchandise purchases and other operating expenses are $70,000 at year-end.

8. All sales are made on credit and totalled $3,500,000 in 20X5; $2,850,000 was collected on account during the year. YT estimates that 0.5% of total sales will be uncollectible and has written off $7,000 of accounts.

9. YT declared a cash dividend of $84,000, payable in January 20X6.

10. Income tax expense is $260,000. All taxes for a fiscal year are payable in April of the following year.

---

★★ **A-24 Special Journals:** THJ Limited incurred the following transactions in October 20X5:

**Oct.**

4 Board of Directors declared a $160,000 dividend. The dividend was both recorded and paid on this date.

5 Purchased goods for resale on credit, $58,200.

5 Purchased goods for resale with cash, $12,350.

6 Borrowed $50,000 from the bank, and signed a 60-day, 8% note payable.

8   Bought office supplies on credit, $1,250.
9   Bought machinery, and issued a 120-day, 12% note payable for the full amount of $32,200.
9   Sold goods to customers on account, $35,600.
9   Sold goods to customers for cash, $68,400.
14  Paid for the goods bought on credit on 5 October.
16  Bought goods from a supplier on credit, $31,100.
17  Sold goods to customer on account, $100,700.
22  Paid wages and salaries, $33,700.
23  Paid electricity bill, $1,600.
25  Received payment from customers for 80% of 9 October sale.
27  Returned goods to supplier from order of 16 October and got a credit note of $3,600.
27  Repaid note payable of $50,000, borrowed and properly recorded in August, plus $1,000 interest.
30  Paid net amount due to supplier for goods purchased on 16 October.
30  Received goods back from customer of 17 October and issued a credit note for $5,200.
31  Recorded amortization expense on plant machinery of $7,400 for the month of October.

### Required:

1. Draft special journals for cash receipts, cash disbursements, sales, and purchases. Also open a general journal.
2. Record the transactions in the appropriate journal. Leave the column blank if details (name or account number, for example) are not available. There are no discounts offered to or by THJ Limited, so all sales and purchases are recorded gross.

---

★ **A-25 Special Journals:** Next to each transaction place the letter of the journal in which that transaction would be recorded. Assume that the company uses special journals whenever appropriate.

### TRANSACTIONS:

1. Borrow money from the bank.
2. Collect cash on account.
3. Purchase merchandise on account.
4. Record adjusting entries.
5. Pay dividends.
6. Receive cash for cash sales.
7. Pay employee wages.
8. Record a completed but unpaid voucher.
9. Correct an erroneous journal entry.
10. Sell merchandise on credit.
11. Pay accounts payable.
12. Pay interest on bank loan.
13. Pay the voucher in (8).
14. Pay income tax instalment.

### JOURNALS:

A. General journal
B. Sales journal
C. Purchases journal
D. Cash receipts journal
E. Cash disbursements journal
F. Voucher register
G. Cheque register (for use with voucher register)

★★   **A-26 Special Journals:** Marigold Corporation had transactions in June 20X5 as follows:

**June**

1   Received merchandise and an invoice dated 31 May, terms n/60, from Hollingsworth Company, $47,800.

2   Purchased office equipment on account from Dunlap Company, invoice dated 2 June, terms n/10 EOM, $14,625.

3   Sold merchandise on account to Tamara Smith, Invoice No. 902, $22,300. (Terms of all credit sales are 2/10, n/30.)

8   Issued cheque No. 548 to *The Monthly News* for advertising, $275.

10   Issued cheque No. 549 to Hollingsworth Company in payment of its 31 May invoice, previously recorded.

11   Sold unneeded office supplies at cost for cash, $940.

16   Sold merchandise on account to Mary Cortez, invoice No. 903, $9,735.

18   Received payment from Tamara Smith for the sale of 3 June.

20   Received merchandise and an invoice dated 18 June, terms n/60, from Riteway Company, $17,500.

21   Issued a credit memorandum to Mary Cortez for defective merchandise sold on 16 June and returned for credit, $1,835.

24   Received a $1,700 credit memorandum from Riteway Company for defective merchandise received on 20 June and returned for credit.

25   Purchased on account from The Store Depot, merchandise, $22,390, invoice dated 25 June, terms n/10 EOM.

26   Received payment from Mary Cortez for the 16 June sale. She paid the net amount due within the discount period, and deducted 2% from the amount owing.

28   Issued cheque No. 550 to Riteway Company in payment of its 18 June invoice, less the purchase return.

30   Cash sales for the month ended 30 June were $31,230.

**Required:**

1. Draft special journals for cash receipts, cash disbursements, sales, and purchases. The company also maintains a general journal.

2. Record the transactions in the appropriate journal. Leave columns blank if details (account numbers, for example) are not available. Sales are recorded at the gross amount.

★★   **A-27 Special Journals:** Morra Limited incurred the following transactions in September 20X5:

**Sept.**

1   Invested $10,000 in the corporation.

2   Purchased $6,000 of automotive equipment for cash.

2   Purchased office equipment by issuing a note payable, $4,760.

5   Purchased inventory priced at $10,320 on account, terms 1/15, n/30.

10   Sold merchandise for $6,210 to a customer on account, terms 2/10, n/30.

12   Received a credit memo from the supplier re: the inventory acquired on 5 September, $1,320 gross ($1,306.80 net).

12   Borrowed $10,000 from the bank at an interest rate of 12%.

13   Paid the supplier for the net purchase of 5 September.

22   Received payment from the customer re: sale on 10 September. This cheque was issued within the discount period.

25   Paid salaries of $1,200.

29   Cash sales for the month of September amounted to $47,250.

**Required:**

1. Draft special journals for cash receipts, cash disbursements, sales, and purchases. The company also maintains a general journal.

2. Record the transactions in the appropriate journal. Leave columns blank if details (account numbers, for example) are not available. Purchases and sales are recorded at the net amount.

 **A-28 Transactions and Financial Statements:** Multimedia Incorporated, a producer of graphics and artwork for movie theatres and other media distributors, provided the following information for 20X5:

*Selected Accounts from the Balance Sheet, as of 1 January 20X5*

| | |
|---|---:|
| Accounts receivable | $ 10,000 |
| Prepaid insurance | 20,000 |
| Supplies | 5,000 |
| Equipment (net) | 80,000 |
| Accounts payable (suppliers) | 40,000* |
| Unearned rent | 13,000 |
| Wages payable | 7,000 |
| Common shares | 27,000 |
| Retained earnings | 50,000 |

*The 31 December 20X5 balance is $50,000.

*Income Statement, year ended 31 December 20X5*

| | |
|---|---:|
| Sales | $200,000 |
| Insurance expense | (15,000) |
| Amortization expense | (10,000) |
| Supplies expense | (30,000) |
| Wages expense | (60,000) |
| Rent revenue | 12,000 |
| Net income | $ 97,000 |

*Cash Flow Statement, year ended 31 December 20X5*
Operating activities:

| | |
|---|---:|
| Collections from customers | $ 90,000 |
| Insurance payments | (25,000) |
| Payments to suppliers | (45,000) |
| Payments to employees | (52,000) |
| Rental receipts | 19,000 |
| Net operating cash flow | $ (13,000) |
| Cash balance, 1 January 20X5 | 22,000 |
| Cash balance, 31 December 20X5* | $ 9,000 |

*No investing or financing cash flows.

**Required:**
Prepare the 31 December 20X5 balance sheet for Multimedia.

**A-29 Transactions and Financial Statements:** During the first week of January 20X8, Gary Benneford began an office design business, Efficient Interiors Limited. He kept no formal accounting records; however, his record of cash receipts and disbursements was accurate. The business was an instant success. In fact, it was so successful that he required additional financing to keep up. He approached his bank for a $10,000 loan and was "put on hold" until he brought a balance sheet and an income statement prepared on an accrual basis.

Knowing very little about accounting, he engages you to prepare statements requested by the bank. He supplies you with the following information:

|  | Receipts | Disbursements |
|---|---|---|
| Investment | $ 90,000 | |
| Equipment | | $ 55,200 |
| Supplies | | 36,600 |
| Rent payments | | 28,800 |
| Insurance premium | | 5,400 |
| Advertising—all ads complete | | 10,800 |
| Wages of assistant | | 55,200 |
| Telephone | | 2,940 |
| Payments to Gary Benneford | | 57,000 |
| Design revenue received | 184,500 | |
| Cash balance | | 22,560 |
| | $274,500 | $274,500 |

*Additional information:*

- The equipment has an estimated 10-year life and $1,200 salvage value.
- Supplies on hand 31 December 20X8 were $5,300.
- Rent payments included $2,250 per month rental and $1,800 deposit refundable at termination of the two-year lease.
- Insurance premium was for a two-year policy that expires on 31 December 20X9.
- Wages earned in the last week of December 20X8 to be paid in January 20X9 amounted to $1,600.
- Design revenue earned but not yet collected amounted to $11,400.
- The organization is set up as a company; the $57,000 withdrawn by Gary is $54,000 salary and $3,000 dividends.

**Required:**

Prepare the financial statements as requested.

(CGA-Canada, adapted)

---

 **A-30 Transactions and Financial Statements:** Shirt Shack is a retail store operating in a downtown shopping mall. On 1 January 20X8, it reported the following:

### SHIRT SHACK
### BALANCE SHEET

As of 1 January 20X8

| | |
|---|---|
| Cash | $ 4,000 |
| Accounts receivable (net of allowance of $2,000) | 28,000 |
| Prepaid rent (rental deposit) | 1,000 |
| Inventory | 36,000 |
| Leasehold improvements (net) | 16,000 |
| Total assets | $85,000 |
| | |
| Accounts payable | $32,000 |
| Accrued wages payable | 3,500 |
| Accrued interest payable | 200 |
| Accrued rent payable | 0 |
| Notes payable, 10% | 14,800 |
| Common shares | 10,000 |
| Retained earnings | 24,500 |
| Total liabilities plus equity | $85,000 |

During 20X8, the company reported the following:

a. Cash paid to employees (salaries and commissions), $67,000. Cash paid to suppliers, $90,000.
b. Cash collected from customers, $220,000.
c. On 31 December 20X8, a physical inventory count revealed that inventory was $42,000.
d. At 31 December 20X8, customers owed Shirt Shack $35,000, and the company owed its suppliers $14,000. Of the accounts receivable, aging analysis indicated that $4,000 was expected to be uncollectible. No accounts were written off in 20X8.
e. Cash paid to landlord, $12,000 ($1,000 per month for 12 months). Shirt Shack is required to pay monthly rent and, at year-end, make an additional payment to bring the total rent expense up to 10% of sales. This payment will be made in January 20X9.
f. Cash paid for miscellaneous operating expenses, $6,000.
g. Cash paid in dividends, $14,500; in interest, $1,680. No interest is owing at 31 December 20X8.
h. Shirt Shack owed employees $500 in wages and $1,000 in commissions at year-end.
i. The leasehold improvements were acquired on 1 January 20X7. They had an expected life of 10 years and were installed in leased premises that had a five-year lease on 1 January 20X7.

### Required:

1. Prepare journal entries for all transactions and needed adjustments.
2. Prepare an income statement for the year ended 31 December 20X8. Ignore income tax. Show all calculations.

## TABLE I-1: Present value of 1: (P/F, *i*, *n*)

$$P/F = \frac{1}{(1+i)^n}$$

| n | 2% | 2.5% | 3% | 4% | 5% | 6% | 7% | 8% | 9% | 10% | 11% | 12% | 14% | 15% |
|---|---|---|---|---|---|---|---|---|---|---|---|---|---|---|
| 1 | 0.98039 | 0.97561 | 0.97087 | 0.96154 | 0.95238 | 0.94340 | 0.93458 | 0.92593 | 0.91743 | 0.90909 | 0.90090 | 0.89286 | 0.87719 | 0.86957 |
| 2 | 0.96117 | 0.95181 | 0.94260 | 0.92456 | 0.90703 | 0.89000 | 0.87344 | 0.85734 | 0.84168 | 0.82645 | 0.81162 | 0.79719 | 0.76947 | 0.75614 |
| 3 | 0.94232 | 0.92860 | 0.91514 | 0.88900 | 0.86384 | 0.83962 | 0.81630 | 0.79383 | 0.77218 | 0.75131 | 0.73119 | 0.71178 | 0.67497 | 0.65752 |
| 4 | 0.92385 | 0.90595 | 0.88849 | 0.85480 | 0.82270 | 0.79209 | 0.76290 | 0.73503 | 0.70843 | 0.68301 | 0.65873 | 0.63552 | 0.59208 | 0.57175 |
| 5 | 0.90573 | 0.88385 | 0.86261 | 0.82193 | 0.78353 | 0.74726 | 0.71299 | 0.68058 | 0.64993 | 0.62092 | 0.59345 | 0.56743 | 0.51937 | 0.49718 |
| 6 | 0.88797 | 0.86230 | 0.83748 | 0.79031 | 0.74622 | 0.70496 | 0.66634 | 0.63017 | 0.59627 | 0.56447 | 0.53464 | 0.50663 | 0.45559 | 0.43233 |
| 7 | 0.87056 | 0.84127 | 0.81309 | 0.75992 | 0.71068 | 0.66506 | 0.62275 | 0.58349 | 0.54703 | 0.51316 | 0.48166 | 0.45235 | 0.39964 | 0.37594 |
| 8 | 0.85349 | 0.82075 | 0.78941 | 0.73069 | 0.67684 | 0.62741 | 0.58201 | 0.54027 | 0.50187 | 0.46651 | 0.43393 | 0.40388 | 0.35056 | 0.32690 |
| 9 | 0.83676 | 0.80073 | 0.76642 | 0.70259 | 0.64461 | 0.59190 | 0.54393 | 0.50025 | 0.46043 | 0.42410 | 0.39092 | 0.36061 | 0.30751 | 0.28426 |
| 10 | 0.82035 | 0.78120 | 0.74409 | 0.67556 | 0.61391 | 0.55839 | 0.50835 | 0.46319 | 0.42241 | 0.38554 | 0.35218 | 0.32197 | 0.26974 | 0.24718 |
| 11 | 0.80426 | 0.76214 | 0.72242 | 0.64958 | 0.58468 | 0.52679 | 0.47509 | 0.42888 | 0.38753 | 0.35049 | 0.31728 | 0.28748 | 0.23662 | 0.21494 |
| 12 | 0.78849 | 0.74356 | 0.70138 | 0.62460 | 0.55684 | 0.49697 | 0.44401 | 0.39711 | 0.35553 | 0.31863 | 0.28584 | 0.25668 | 0.20756 | 0.18691 |
| 13 | 0.77303 | 0.72542 | 0.68095 | 0.60057 | 0.53032 | 0.46884 | 0.41496 | 0.36770 | 0.32618 | 0.28966 | 0.25751 | 0.22917 | 0.18207 | 0.16253 |
| 14 | 0.75788 | 0.70773 | 0.66112 | 0.57748 | 0.50507 | 0.44230 | 0.38782 | 0.34046 | 0.29925 | 0.26333 | 0.23199 | 0.20462 | 0.15971 | 0.14133 |
| 15 | 0.74301 | 0.69047 | 0.64186 | 0.55526 | 0.48102 | 0.41727 | 0.36245 | 0.31524 | 0.27454 | 0.23939 | 0.20900 | 0.18270 | 0.14010 | 0.12289 |
| 16 | 0.72845 | 0.67362 | 0.62317 | 0.53391 | 0.45811 | 0.39365 | 0.33873 | 0.29189 | 0.25187 | 0.21763 | 0.18829 | 0.16312 | 0.12289 | 0.10686 |
| 17 | 0.71416 | 0.65720 | 0.60502 | 0.51337 | 0.43630 | 0.37136 | 0.31657 | 0.27027 | 0.23107 | 0.19784 | 0.16963 | 0.14564 | 0.10780 | 0.09293 |
| 18 | 0.70016 | 0.64117 | 0.58739 | 0.49363 | 0.41552 | 0.35034 | 0.29586 | 0.25025 | 0.21199 | 0.17986 | 0.15282 | 0.13004 | 0.09456 | 0.08081 |
| 19 | 0.68643 | 0.62553 | 0.57029 | 0.47464 | 0.39573 | 0.33051 | 0.27651 | 0.23171 | 0.19449 | 0.16351 | 0.13768 | 0.11611 | 0.08295 | 0.07027 |
| 20 | 0.67297 | 0.61027 | 0.55368 | 0.45639 | 0.37689 | 0.31180 | 0.25842 | 0.21455 | 0.17843 | 0.14864 | 0.12403 | 0.10367 | 0.07276 | 0.06110 |
| 21 | 0.65978 | 0.59539 | 0.53755 | 0.43883 | 0.35894 | 0.29416 | 0.24151 | 0.19866 | 0.16370 | 0.13513 | 0.11174 | 0.09256 | 0.06383 | 0.05313 |
| 22 | 0.64684 | 0.58086 | 0.52189 | 0.42196 | 0.34185 | 0.27751 | 0.22571 | 0.18394 | 0.15018 | 0.12285 | 0.10067 | 0.08264 | 0.05599 | 0.04620 |
| 23 | 0.63416 | 0.56670 | 0.50669 | 0.40573 | 0.32557 | 0.26180 | 0.21095 | 0.17032 | 0.13778 | 0.11168 | 0.09069 | 0.07379 | 0.04911 | 0.04017 |
| 24 | 0.62172 | 0.55288 | 0.49193 | 0.39012 | 0.31007 | 0.24698 | 0.19715 | 0.15770 | 0.12640 | 0.10153 | 0.08170 | 0.06588 | 0.04308 | 0.03493 |
| 25 | 0.60953 | 0.53939 | 0.47761 | 0.37512 | 0.29530 | 0.23300 | 0.18425 | 0.14602 | 0.11597 | 0.09230 | 0.07361 | 0.05882 | 0.03779 | 0.03038 |
| 26 | 0.59758 | 0.52623 | 0.46369 | 0.36069 | 0.28124 | 0.21981 | 0.17220 | 0.13520 | 0.10639 | 0.08391 | 0.06631 | 0.05252 | 0.03315 | 0.02642 |
| 27 | 0.58586 | 0.51340 | 0.45019 | 0.34682 | 0.26785 | 0.20737 | 0.16093 | 0.12519 | 0.09761 | 0.07628 | 0.05974 | 0.04689 | 0.02908 | 0.02297 |
| 28 | 0.57437 | 0.50088 | 0.43708 | 0.33348 | 0.25509 | 0.19563 | 0.15040 | 0.11591 | 0.08955 | 0.06934 | 0.05382 | 0.04187 | 0.02551 | 0.01997 |
| 29 | 0.56311 | 0.48866 | 0.42435 | 0.32065 | 0.24295 | 0.18456 | 0.14056 | 0.10733 | 0.08215 | 0.06304 | 0.04849 | 0.03738 | 0.02237 | 0.01737 |
| 30 | 0.55207 | 0.47674 | 0.41199 | 0.30832 | 0.23138 | 0.17411 | 0.13137 | 0.09938 | 0.07537 | 0.05731 | 0.04368 | 0.03338 | 0.01963 | 0.01510 |
| 31 | 0.54125 | 0.46511 | 0.39999 | 0.29646 | 0.22036 | 0.16425 | 0.12277 | 0.09202 | 0.06915 | 0.05210 | 0.03935 | 0.02980 | 0.01722 | 0.01313 |
| 32 | 0.53063 | 0.45377 | 0.38834 | 0.28506 | 0.20987 | 0.15496 | 0.11474 | 0.08520 | 0.06344 | 0.04736 | 0.03545 | 0.02661 | 0.01510 | 0.01142 |
| 33 | 0.52023 | 0.44270 | 0.37703 | 0.27409 | 0.19987 | 0.14619 | 0.10723 | 0.07889 | 0.05820 | 0.04306 | 0.03194 | 0.02376 | 0.01325 | 0.00993 |
| 34 | 0.51003 | 0.43191 | 0.36604 | 0.26355 | 0.19035 | 0.13791 | 0.10022 | 0.07305 | 0.05339 | 0.03914 | 0.02878 | 0.02121 | 0.01162 | 0.00864 |
| 35 | 0.50003 | 0.42137 | 0.35538 | 0.25342 | 0.18129 | 0.13011 | 0.09366 | 0.06763 | 0.04899 | 0.03558 | 0.02592 | 0.01894 | 0.01019 | 0.00751 |
| 36 | 0.49022 | 0.41109 | 0.34503 | 0.24367 | 0.17266 | 0.12274 | 0.08754 | 0.06262 | 0.04494 | 0.03235 | 0.02335 | 0.01691 | 0.00894 | 0.00653 |
| 37 | 0.48061 | 0.40107 | 0.33498 | 0.23430 | 0.16444 | 0.11579 | 0.08181 | 0.05799 | 0.04123 | 0.02941 | 0.02104 | 0.01510 | 0.00784 | 0.00568 |
| 38 | 0.47119 | 0.39128 | 0.32523 | 0.22529 | 0.15661 | 0.10924 | 0.07646 | 0.05369 | 0.03783 | 0.02673 | 0.01896 | 0.01348 | 0.00688 | 0.00494 |
| 39 | 0.46195 | 0.38174 | 0.31575 | 0.21662 | 0.14915 | 0.10306 | 0.07146 | 0.04971 | 0.03470 | 0.02430 | 0.01708 | 0.01204 | 0.00604 | 0.00429 |
| 40 | 0.45289 | 0.37243 | 0.30656 | 0.20829 | 0.14205 | 0.09722 | 0.06678 | 0.04603 | 0.03184 | 0.02209 | 0.01538 | 0.01075 | 0.00529 | 0.00373 |
| 45 | 0.41020 | 0.32917 | 0.26444 | 0.17120 | 0.11130 | 0.07265 | 0.04761 | 0.03133 | 0.02069 | 0.01372 | 0.00913 | 0.00610 | 0.00275 | 0.00186 |
| 50 | 0.37153 | 0.29094 | 0.22811 | 0.14071 | 0.08720 | 0.05429 | 0.03395 | 0.02132 | 0.01345 | 0.00852 | 0.00542 | 0.00346 | 0.00143 | 0.00092 |

## TABLE I-2: Present value of an ordinary annuity of $n$ payments of 1: $(P/A, i, n)$

$$P/A = \frac{1 - \dfrac{1}{(1+i)^n}}{i}$$

| n | 2% | 2.5% | 3% | 4% | 5% | 6% | 7% | 8% | 9% | 10% | 11% | 12% | 14% | 15% |
|---|---|---|---|---|---|---|---|---|---|---|---|---|---|---|
| 1 | 0.98039 | 0.97561 | 0.97087 | 0.96154 | 0.95238 | 0.94340 | 0.93458 | 0.92593 | 0.91743 | 0.90909 | 0.90090 | 0.89286 | 0.87719 | 0.86957 |
| 2 | 1.94156 | 1.92742 | 1.91347 | 1.88609 | 1.85941 | 1.83339 | 1.80802 | 1.78326 | 1.75911 | 1.73554 | 1.71252 | 1.69005 | 1.64666 | 1.62571 |
| 3 | 2.88388 | 2.85602 | 2.82861 | 2.77509 | 2.72325 | 2.67301 | 2.62432 | 2.57710 | 2.53129 | 2.48685 | 2.44371 | 2.40183 | 2.32163 | 2.28323 |
| 4 | 3.80773 | 3.76197 | 3.71710 | 3.62990 | 3.54595 | 3.46511 | 3.38721 | 3.31213 | 3.23972 | 3.16987 | 3.10245 | 3.03735 | 2.91371 | 2.85498 |
| 5 | 4.71346 | 4.64583 | 4.57971 | 4.45182 | 4.32948 | 4.21236 | 4.10020 | 3.99271 | 3.88965 | 3.79079 | 3.69590 | 3.60478 | 3.43308 | 3.35216 |
| 6 | 5.60143 | 5.50813 | 5.41719 | 5.24214 | 5.07569 | 4.91732 | 4.76654 | 4.62288 | 4.48592 | 4.35526 | 4.23054 | 4.11141 | 3.88867 | 3.78448 |
| 7 | 6.47199 | 6.34939 | 6.23028 | 6.00205 | 5.78637 | 5.58238 | 5.38929 | 5.20637 | 5.03295 | 4.86842 | 4.71220 | 4.56376 | 4.28830 | 4.16042 |
| 8 | 7.32548 | 7.17014 | 7.01969 | 6.73274 | 6.46321 | 6.20979 | 5.97130 | 5.74664 | 5.53482 | 5.33493 | 5.14612 | 4.96764 | 4.63886 | 4.48732 |
| 9 | 8.16224 | 7.97087 | 7.78611 | 7.43533 | 7.10782 | 6.80169 | 6.51523 | 6.24689 | 5.99525 | 5.75902 | 5.53705 | 5.32825 | 4.94637 | 4.77158 |
| 10 | 8.98259 | 8.75206 | 8.53020 | 8.11090 | 7.72173 | 7.36009 | 7.02358 | 6.71008 | 6.41766 | 6.14457 | 5.88923 | 5.65022 | 5.21612 | 5.01877 |
| 11 | 9.78685 | 9.51421 | 9.25262 | 8.76048 | 8.30641 | 7.88687 | 7.49867 | 7.13896 | 6.80519 | 6.49506 | 6.20652 | 5.93770 | 5.45273 | 5.23371 |
| 12 | 10.57534 | 10.25776 | 9.95400 | 9.38507 | 8.86325 | 8.38384 | 7.94269 | 7.53608 | 7.16073 | 6.81369 | 6.49236 | 6.19437 | 5.66029 | 5.42062 |
| 13 | 11.34837 | 10.98318 | 10.63496 | 9.98565 | 9.39357 | 8.85268 | 8.35765 | 7.90378 | 7.48690 | 7.10336 | 6.74987 | 6.42355 | 5.84236 | 5.58315 |
| 14 | 12.10625 | 11.69091 | 11.29607 | 10.56312 | 9.89864 | 9.29498 | 8.74547 | 8.24424 | 7.78615 | 7.36669 | 6.98187 | 6.62817 | 6.00207 | 5.72448 |
| 15 | 12.84926 | 12.38138 | 11.93794 | 11.11839 | 10.37966 | 9.71225 | 9.10791 | 8.55948 | 8.06069 | 7.60608 | 7.19087 | 6.81086 | 6.14217 | 5.84737 |
| 16 | 13.57771 | 13.05500 | 12.56110 | 11.65230 | 10.83777 | 10.10590 | 9.44665 | 8.85137 | 8.31256 | 7.82371 | 7.37916 | 6.97399 | 6.26506 | 5.95423 |
| 17 | 14.29187 | 13.71220 | 13.16612 | 12.16567 | 11.27407 | 10.47726 | 9.76322 | 9.12164 | 8.54363 | 8.02155 | 7.54879 | 7.11963 | 6.37286 | 6.04716 |
| 18 | 14.99203 | 14.35336 | 13.75351 | 12.65930 | 11.68959 | 10.82760 | 10.05909 | 9.37189 | 8.75563 | 8.20141 | 7.70162 | 7.24967 | 6.46742 | 6.12797 |
| 19 | 15.67846 | 14.97889 | 14.32380 | 13.13394 | 12.08532 | 11.15812 | 10.33560 | 9.60360 | 8.95011 | 8.36492 | 7.83929 | 7.36578 | 6.55037 | 6.19823 |
| 20 | 16.35143 | 15.58916 | 14.87747 | 13.59033 | 12.46221 | 11.46992 | 10.59401 | 9.81815 | 9.12855 | 8.51356 | 7.96333 | 7.46944 | 6.62313 | 6.25933 |
| 21 | 17.01121 | 16.18455 | 15.41502 | 14.02916 | 12.82115 | 11.76408 | 10.83553 | 10.01680 | 9.29224 | 8.64869 | 8.07507 | 7.56200 | 6.68696 | 6.31246 |
| 22 | 17.65805 | 16.76541 | 15.93692 | 14.45112 | 13.16300 | 12.04158 | 11.06124 | 10.20074 | 9.44243 | 8.77154 | 8.17574 | 7.64465 | 6.74294 | 6.35866 |
| 23 | 18.29220 | 17.33211 | 16.44361 | 14.85684 | 13.48857 | 12.30338 | 11.27219 | 10.37106 | 9.58021 | 8.88322 | 8.26643 | 7.71843 | 6.79206 | 6.39884 |
| 24 | 18.91393 | 17.88499 | 16.93554 | 15.24696 | 13.79864 | 12.55036 | 11.46933 | 10.52876 | 9.70661 | 8.98474 | 8.34814 | 7.78432 | 6.83514 | 6.43377 |
| 25 | 19.52346 | 18.42438 | 17.41315 | 15.62208 | 14.09394 | 12.78336 | 11.65358 | 10.67478 | 9.82258 | 9.07704 | 8.42174 | 7.84314 | 6.87293 | 6.46415 |
| 26 | 20.12104 | 18.95061 | 17.87684 | 15.98277 | 14.37519 | 13.00317 | 11.82578 | 10.80998 | 9.92897 | 9.16095 | 8.48806 | 7.89566 | 6.90608 | 6.49056 |
| 27 | 20.70690 | 19.46401 | 18.32703 | 16.32959 | 14.64303 | 13.21053 | 11.98671 | 10.93516 | 10.02658 | 9.23722 | 8.54780 | 7.94255 | 6.93515 | 6.51353 |
| 28 | 21.28127 | 19.96489 | 18.76411 | 16.66306 | 14.89813 | 13.40616 | 12.13711 | 11.05108 | 10.11613 | 9.30657 | 8.60162 | 7.98442 | 6.96066 | 6.53351 |
| 29 | 21.84438 | 20.45355 | 19.18845 | 16.98371 | 15.14107 | 13.59072 | 12.27767 | 11.15841 | 10.19828 | 9.36961 | 8.65011 | 8.02181 | 6.98304 | 6.55088 |
| 30 | 22.39646 | 20.93029 | 19.60044 | 17.29203 | 15.37245 | 13.76483 | 12.40904 | 11.25778 | 10.27365 | 9.42691 | 8.69379 | 8.05518 | 7.00266 | 6.56598 |
| 31 | 22.93770 | 21.39541 | 20.00043 | 17.58849 | 15.59281 | 13.92909 | 12.53181 | 11.34980 | 10.34280 | 9.47901 | 8.73315 | 8.08499 | 7.01988 | 6.57911 |
| 32 | 23.46833 | 21.84918 | 20.38877 | 17.87355 | 15.80268 | 14.08404 | 12.64656 | 11.43500 | 10.40624 | 9.52638 | 8.76860 | 8.11159 | 7.03498 | 6.59053 |
| 33 | 23.98856 | 22.29188 | 20.76579 | 18.14765 | 16.00255 | 14.23023 | 12.75379 | 11.51389 | 10.46444 | 9.56943 | 8.80054 | 8.13535 | 7.04823 | 6.60046 |
| 34 | 24.49859 | 22.72379 | 21.13184 | 18.41120 | 16.19290 | 14.36814 | 12.85401 | 11.58693 | 10.51784 | 9.60857 | 8.82932 | 8.15656 | 7.05985 | 6.60910 |
| 35 | 24.99862 | 23.14516 | 21.48722 | 18.66461 | 16.37419 | 14.49825 | 12.94767 | 11.65457 | 10.56682 | 9.64416 | 8.85524 | 8.17550 | 7.07005 | 6.61661 |
| 36 | 25.48884 | 23.55625 | 21.83225 | 18.90828 | 16.54685 | 14.62099 | 13.03521 | 11.71719 | 10.61176 | 9.67651 | 8.87859 | 8.19241 | 7.07899 | 6.62314 |
| 37 | 25.96945 | 23.95732 | 22.16724 | 19.14258 | 16.71129 | 14.73678 | 13.11702 | 11.77518 | 10.65299 | 9.70592 | 8.89963 | 8.20751 | 7.08683 | 6.62881 |
| 38 | 26.44064 | 24.34860 | 22.49246 | 19.36786 | 16.86789 | 14.84602 | 13.19347 | 11.82887 | 10.69082 | 9.73265 | 8.91859 | 8.22099 | 7.09371 | 6.63375 |
| 39 | 26.90259 | 24.73034 | 22.80822 | 19.58448 | 17.01704 | 14.94907 | 13.26493 | 11.87858 | 10.72552 | 9.75696 | 8.93567 | 8.23303 | 7.09975 | 6.63805 |
| 40 | 27.35548 | 25.10278 | 23.11477 | 19.79277 | 17.15909 | 15.04630 | 13.33171 | 11.92461 | 10.75736 | 9.77905 | 8.95105 | 8.24378 | 7.10504 | 6.64178 |
| 45 | 29.49016 | 26.83302 | 24.51871 | 20.72004 | 17.77407 | 15.45583 | 13.60552 | 12.10840 | 10.88120 | 9.86281 | 9.00791 | 8.28252 | 7.12322 | 6.65429 |
| 50 | 31.42361 | 28.36231 | 25.72976 | 21.48218 | 18.25593 | 15.76186 | 13.80075 | 12.23348 | 10.96168 | 9.91481 | 9.04165 | 8.30450 | 7.13266 | 6.66051 |

**TABLE I-3:** Present value of an annuity due of $n$ payments of 1: $(P/AD, i, n)$

$$P/AD = \left[ \frac{1 - \dfrac{1}{(1+i)^n}}{i} \right] \times (1+i)$$

| n | 2% | 2.5% | 3% | 4% | 5% | 6% | 7% | 8% | 9% | 10% | 11% | 12% | 14% | 15% |
|---|---|---|---|---|---|---|---|---|---|---|---|---|---|---|
| 1 | 1.00000 | 1.00000 | 1.00000 | 1.00000 | 1.00000 | 1.00000 | 1.00000 | 1.00000 | 1.00000 | 1.00000 | 1.00000 | 1.00000 | 1.00000 | 1.00000 |
| 2 | 1.98039 | 1.97561 | 1.97087 | 1.96154 | 1.95238 | 1.94340 | 1.93458 | 1.92593 | 1.91743 | 1.90909 | 1.90090 | 1.89286 | 1.87719 | 1.86957 |
| 3 | 2.94156 | 2.92742 | 2.91347 | 2.88609 | 2.85941 | 2.83339 | 2.80802 | 2.78326 | 2.75911 | 2.73554 | 2.71252 | 2.69005 | 2.64666 | 2.62571 |
| 4 | 3.88388 | 3.85602 | 3.82861 | 3.77509 | 3.72325 | 3.67301 | 3.62432 | 3.57710 | 3.53129 | 3.48685 | 3.44371 | 3.40183 | 3.32163 | 3.28323 |
| 5 | 4.80773 | 4.76197 | 4.71710 | 4.62990 | 4.54595 | 4.46511 | 4.38721 | 4.31213 | 4.23972 | 4.16987 | 4.10245 | 4.03735 | 3.91371 | 3.85498 |
| 6 | 5.71346 | 5.64583 | 5.57971 | 5.45182 | 5.32948 | 5.21236 | 5.10020 | 4.99271 | 4.88965 | 4.79079 | 4.69590 | 4.60478 | 4.43308 | 4.35216 |
| 7 | 6.60143 | 6.50813 | 6.41719 | 6.24214 | 6.07569 | 5.91732 | 5.76654 | 5.62288 | 5.48592 | 5.35526 | 5.23054 | 5.11141 | 4.88867 | 4.78448 |
| 8 | 7.47199 | 7.34939 | 7.23028 | 7.00205 | 6.78637 | 6.58238 | 6.38929 | 6.20637 | 6.03295 | 5.86842 | 5.71220 | 5.56376 | 5.28830 | 5.16042 |
| 9 | 8.32548 | 8.17014 | 8.01969 | 7.73274 | 7.46321 | 7.20979 | 6.97130 | 6.74664 | 6.53482 | 6.33493 | 6.14612 | 5.96764 | 5.63886 | 5.48732 |
| 10 | 9.16224 | 8.97087 | 8.78611 | 8.43533 | 8.10782 | 7.80169 | 7.51523 | 7.24689 | 6.99525 | 6.75902 | 6.53705 | 6.32825 | 5.94637 | 5.77158 |
| 11 | 9.98259 | 9.75206 | 9.53020 | 9.11090 | 8.72173 | 8.36009 | 8.02358 | 7.71008 | 7.41766 | 7.14457 | 6.88923 | 6.65022 | 6.21612 | 6.01877 |
| 12 | 10.78685 | 10.51421 | 10.25262 | 9.76048 | 9.30641 | 8.88687 | 8.49867 | 8.13896 | 7.80519 | 7.49506 | 7.20652 | 6.93770 | 6.45273 | 6.23371 |
| 13 | 11.57534 | 11.25776 | 10.95400 | 10.38507 | 9.86325 | 9.38384 | 8.94269 | 8.53608 | 8.16073 | 7.81369 | 7.49236 | 7.19437 | 6.66029 | 6.42062 |
| 14 | 12.34837 | 11.98318 | 11.63496 | 10.98565 | 10.39357 | 9.85268 | 9.35765 | 8.90378 | 8.48690 | 8.10336 | 7.74987 | 7.42355 | 6.84236 | 6.58315 |
| 15 | 13.10625 | 12.69091 | 12.29607 | 11.56312 | 10.89864 | 10.29498 | 9.74547 | 9.24424 | 8.78615 | 8.36669 | 7.98187 | 7.62817 | 7.00207 | 6.72448 |
| 16 | 13.84926 | 13.38138 | 12.93794 | 12.11839 | 11.37966 | 10.71225 | 10.10791 | 9.55948 | 9.06069 | 8.60608 | 8.19087 | 7.81086 | 7.14217 | 6.84737 |
| 17 | 14.57771 | 14.05500 | 13.56110 | 12.65230 | 11.83777 | 11.10590 | 10.44665 | 9.85137 | 9.31256 | 8.82371 | 8.37916 | 7.97399 | 7.26506 | 6.95423 |
| 18 | 15.29187 | 14.71220 | 14.16612 | 13.16567 | 12.27407 | 11.47726 | 10.76322 | 10.12164 | 9.54363 | 9.02155 | 8.54879 | 8.11963 | 7.37286 | 7.04716 |
| 19 | 15.99203 | 15.35336 | 14.75351 | 13.65930 | 12.68959 | 11.82760 | 11.05909 | 10.37189 | 9.75563 | 9.20141 | 8.70162 | 8.24967 | 7.46742 | 7.12797 |
| 20 | 16.67846 | 15.97889 | 15.32380 | 14.13394 | 13.08532 | 12.15812 | 11.33560 | 10.60360 | 9.95011 | 9.36492 | 8.83929 | 8.36578 | 7.55037 | 7.19823 |
| 21 | 17.35143 | 16.58916 | 15.87747 | 14.59033 | 13.46221 | 12.46992 | 11.59401 | 10.81815 | 10.12855 | 9.51356 | 8.96333 | 8.46944 | 7.62313 | 7.25933 |
| 22 | 18.01121 | 17.18455 | 16.41502 | 15.02916 | 13.82115 | 12.76408 | 11.83553 | 11.01680 | 10.29224 | 9.64869 | 9.07507 | 8.56200 | 7.68696 | 7.31246 |
| 23 | 18.65805 | 17.76541 | 16.93692 | 15.45112 | 14.16300 | 13.04158 | 12.06124 | 11.20074 | 10.44243 | 9.77154 | 9.17574 | 8.64465 | 7.74294 | 7.35866 |
| 24 | 19.29220 | 18.33211 | 17.44361 | 15.85684 | 14.48857 | 13.30338 | 12.27219 | 11.37106 | 10.58021 | 9.88322 | 9.26643 | 8.71843 | 7.79206 | 7.39884 |
| 25 | 19.91393 | 18.88499 | 17.93554 | 16.24696 | 14.79864 | 13.55036 | 12.46933 | 11.52876 | 10.70661 | 9.98474 | 9.34814 | 8.78432 | 7.83514 | 7.43377 |
| 26 | 20.52346 | 19.42438 | 18.41315 | 16.62208 | 15.09394 | 13.78336 | 12.65358 | 11.67478 | 10.82258 | 10.07704 | 9.42174 | 8.84314 | 7.87293 | 7.46415 |
| 27 | 21.12104 | 19.95061 | 18.87684 | 16.98277 | 15.37519 | 14.00317 | 12.82578 | 11.80998 | 10.92897 | 10.16095 | 9.48806 | 8.89566 | 7.90608 | 7.49056 |
| 28 | 21.70690 | 20.46401 | 19.32703 | 17.32959 | 15.64303 | 14.21053 | 12.98671 | 11.93516 | 11.02658 | 10.23722 | 9.54780 | 8.94255 | 7.93515 | 7.51353 |
| 29 | 22.28127 | 20.96489 | 19.76411 | 17.66306 | 15.89813 | 14.40616 | 13.13711 | 12.05108 | 11.11613 | 10.30657 | 9.60162 | 8.98442 | 7.96066 | 7.53351 |
| 30 | 22.84438 | 21.45355 | 20.18845 | 17.98371 | 16.14107 | 14.59072 | 13.27767 | 12.15841 | 11.19828 | 10.36961 | 9.65011 | 9.02181 | 7.98304 | 7.55088 |
| 31 | 23.39646 | 21.93029 | 20.60044 | 18.29203 | 16.37245 | 14.76483 | 13.40904 | 12.25778 | 11.27365 | 10.42691 | 9.69379 | 9.05518 | 8.00266 | 7.56598 |
| 32 | 23.93770 | 22.39541 | 21.00043 | 18.58849 | 16.59281 | 14.92909 | 13.53181 | 12.34980 | 11.34280 | 10.47901 | 9.73315 | 9.08499 | 8.01988 | 7.57911 |
| 33 | 24.46833 | 22.84918 | 21.38877 | 18.87355 | 16.80268 | 15.08404 | 13.64656 | 12.43500 | 11.40624 | 10.52638 | 9.76860 | 9.11159 | 8.03498 | 7.59053 |
| 34 | 24.98856 | 23.29188 | 21.76579 | 19.14765 | 17.00255 | 15.23023 | 13.75379 | 12.51389 | 11.46444 | 10.56943 | 9.80054 | 9.13535 | 8.04823 | 7.60046 |
| 35 | 25.49859 | 23.72379 | 22.13184 | 19.41120 | 17.19290 | 15.36814 | 13.85401 | 12.58693 | 11.51784 | 10.60857 | 9.82932 | 9.15656 | 8.05985 | 7.60910 |
| 36 | 25.99862 | 24.14516 | 22.48722 | 19.66461 | 17.37419 | 15.49825 | 13.94767 | 12.65457 | 11.56682 | 10.64416 | 9.85524 | 9.17550 | 8.07005 | 7.61661 |
| 37 | 26.48884 | 24.55625 | 22.83225 | 19.90828 | 17.54685 | 15.62099 | 14.03521 | 12.71719 | 11.61176 | 10.67651 | 9.87859 | 9.19241 | 8.07899 | 7.62314 |
| 38 | 26.96945 | 24.95732 | 23.16724 | 20.14258 | 17.71129 | 15.73678 | 14.11702 | 12.77518 | 11.65299 | 10.70592 | 9.89963 | 9.20751 | 8.08683 | 7.62881 |
| 39 | 27.44064 | 25.34860 | 23.49246 | 20.36786 | 17.86789 | 15.84602 | 14.19347 | 12.82887 | 11.69082 | 10.73265 | 9.91859 | 9.22099 | 8.09371 | 7.63375 |
| 40 | 27.90259 | 25.73034 | 23.80822 | 20.58448 | 18.01704 | 15.94907 | 14.26493 | 12.87858 | 11.72552 | 10.75696 | 9.93567 | 9.23303 | 8.09975 | 7.63805 |
| 45 | 30.07996 | 27.50385 | 25.25427 | 21.54884 | 18.66277 | 16.38318 | 14.55791 | 13.07707 | 11.86051 | 10.84909 | 9.99878 | 9.27642 | 8.12047 | 7.65244 |
| 50 | 32.05208 | 29.07137 | 26.50166 | 22.34147 | 19.16872 | 16.70757 | 14.76680 | 13.21216 | 11.94823 | 10.90630 | 10.03624 | 9.30104 | 8.13123 | 7.65959 |

# Index